Biographical Dictionary
of the
History of Technology

Biographical Dictionary
of the
History of Technology

Edited by

Lance Day and Ian McNeil

London and New York

First published in 1996
by Routledge
11 New Fetter Lane, London EC4P 4EE
29 West 35th Street, New York, NY 10001

© 1996 Routledge

Printed in England by Clays Ltd, St Ives plc
Typeset in Galliard by Routledge
Printed on acid-free paper

British Library Cataloguing in Publication Data
A catalogue record for this book is available from the British Library

Library of Congress Cataloging-in-Publication Data
A catalog record for this book is available on request

ISBN 0–415–06042–7

CONTENTS

EDITORIAL TEAM

General Editors
Lance Day and Ian McNeil

Consultant Advisors

R. Angus Buchanan
Emeritus Professor of Technology, University of Bath

Robert B. Gaither
Emeritus Professor of Mechanical Engineering, University of Florida

Carl-Goren Nilson
Emeritus Professor of Mechanical Engineering, University of Luleå

The Contributors

J.K. Almond (JKA) *metallurgy*

K.A. Barlow (KAB) *internal combustion engines*

John A. Barnes (JB) *steam and internal combustion engines*

Brian Bowers (BB) *electricity*

John H. Boyes (JHB) *canals*

George Brock-Nannestad (GB-N) *recording*

R. Angus Buchanan (AB) *public utilities*

Brian Coe (BC) *photography and film*

Alan S. Darling (ASD) *metallurgy*

Joan Day (JD) *metallurgy*

Lance Day (LRD) *chemical and allied industries, printing and other subjects*

Ken Freeman (KF) *electronics*

Michael Gilkes (MG) *medical technology*

Richard L. Hills (RLH) *textiles, steam engines*

Werner Kroker (WK) *mining technology*

Ian McNeil (IMcN) *road transport, space technology and other subjects*

J. Kenneth Major (KM) *architecture*

Charles Messenger (CM) *weapons & armour*

Jovana Muir (JM) *Chinese technologists*

Herbert Ohlman (HO) *broadcasting*

Andrew Patterson (AP) *agricultural technology*

P.J.G. Ransom (PJGR) *railways and locomotives*

Ray T. Smith (RTS) *mechanical engineering*

J. Donald Storer (JDS) *aerospace*

Denys Vaughan (DV) *horology*

Fred M. Walker (FMW) *ports and shipping*

John Ward (JW) *photography and film*

Gordon Woodward (GW) *electricity*

Doreen Yarwood (DY) *domestic appliances and interiors*

PREFACE

In 1990 Routledge published *An Encyclopaedia of the History of Technology*, edited by my good friend and fellow editor of the present work, Ian McNeil. The *Encyclopaedia* told the story of the inventiveness of human beings in applying their knowledge of the physical world to rendering their material circumstances less inconvenient and uncomfortable. Throughout the thousand and more pages of the *Encyclopaedia*, hundreds of characters flitted in and out, making tantalizingly brief appearances, before receding into the shadows. It is the aim of this biographical dictionary to bring these characters into the light of day, so we can see the background that produced them, the development of their inventions or discoveries and their significance in the area of technology concerned. We have selected almost 1,300 names of those whom we judge to have made a significant contribution, in one way or another, to the advance of technology.

The selection of these names was perhaps the most difficult part of the whole work. Technology has such wide ramifications, with vague boundaries with arts and crafts and, most difficult, with science. We have therefore encountered difficulties in selection which the compiler of a national biography, for example, does not have to cope with. We have tried not to duplicate the several biographical dictionaries of scientists, ranging from the handy works of reference to the magnificent series of volumes of the *Dictionary of Scientific Biography*. Nevertheless, many scientists have applied their discoveries to solving practical problems and thus also been 'technologists', or their discoveries have been so intimately bound up with a technological advance that it would seem too rigid to exclude them. Other names have been excluded for a variety of reasons. We would like to have included the inventors of the wheel, the smelting furnace or the glass blowing iron, but their names are lost in the mists of antiquity. At the other end of the time scale, it is not easy to identify discoverers, because many technical achievements this century have been by teams of workers at the behest of large companies. Sometimes a leading name can be identified; his or her co-worker will then be mentioned in the entry for the main contributor rather than duplicate much of the information in an entry for the co-worker. Indeed, many names of those who have made some contribution to a great advance but who do not rate an entry of their own are similarly 'mentioned in dispatches': they can all be traced by consulting the name index at the end of the book. Again, a number of inventors have achieved useful inventions, yet otherwise have left few traces. Sometimes we have decided that the importance of their contribution did not justify their inclusion; sometimes we felt the inventions were so useful that their authors merited an entry, however scrappy the information on them might be. The line we had to draw was often very fine.

We took as a starting point for the selection of names the name index to the *Encyclopaedia*, on the rude assumption that the authors of the chapters in that work would have mentioned any names worth mentioning. Some names, which had been given merely a passing reference, such as Queen Victoria and King Solomon, were quickly deleted. We then divided the names into their respective subject areas and submitted them to whichever of our twenty six authors was expert in that subject. Here we should like to pay tribute to the technical and historical expertise and literary skill of the authors who have contributed to this work, as also to their patience, co-operation and determination. Their first task was to scan the list of names in their field and suggest additions or deletions. Their advice was much valued but we must make clear that the final responsibility for the content of this work is our own.

The content of these lists of names remained fluid until the end, for further names were thrown up by consulting the indexes of other works in technology, further reading and discussion, or even a chance news item on television or in the press, or out of the blue.

During the course of the work, we stepped back from the selection of names, to gain a general impression of it. It was clear that very nearly all the names fell, or fall – some living persons are included – within the category 'male, white, European' (including North American). There are, of course, rather sound historical reasons for what John Roberts has termed 'the Triumph of the West' in his recent book and television series. The scientific revolution of the seventeenth century was a European phenomenon, stemming from the intellectual developments of medieval Catholic Europe, with contributing influences from the Ancient and Oriental worlds. Again, the mass application of knowledge of the physical world in industrial-scale exploitation of natural and human resources, which we have come to call the 'Industrial Revolution', was likewise a European achievement. So it is unavoidable that this incredible concentration of technological activity should be reflected in the content of this work.

Nevertheless we have been keenly aware that skills and inventiveness are to be found in all cultures and all ages, and we have tried to incorporate those who are known by name to have made notable inventions or other technological advances. This has not been easy: we do not know who achieved that extraordinary piece of ironwork known as the Delhi Pillar, but we do know who in China has been credited with the invention of paper. We have received help and advice from a number of consultants in this and in other matters, recorded in the list of consultants and on the acknowledgements page, but it is perhaps right here to mention the outstanding help given by the Needham Research Institute, founded in Cambridge by the late Joseph Needham, without whom we could not have done anything like justice to the remarkable technological achievements of the Chinese.

Turning to a completely different culture, we noticed the efforts of the African-Americans:

many inventors have struggled against crippling handicaps of rejection and poverty but few have had to contend with such adversity as the African-Americans of the last century, yet even while labouring under the yoke of slavery, they showed remarkable inventiveness and made useful contributions to humanity's technological achievements. It is gratifying to be able to include here 'the Real McCoy'.

Another aspect of the content has also been touched on: our consultants and our sources have suggested the names of many outstanding women scientists including a number of Nobel Prize winners. But we came to the conclusion that nearly all of them belonged rightly to the dictionaries of scientists, where many of their names are to be found, rather than the present work. Our attention has also been drawn to the recent book by Autumn Stanley, *Mothers and Daughters of Invention*, which surveys women's contribution to technology. Here, although we found much of interest, we did not feel that many reached the tip of the great iceberg of the world's inventive achievements, which is all we have had the space to describe in this volume.

Finally we, together with the contributing authors, would like to acknowledge gratefully the help that has been given to us by many people and institutions. Individuals who have helped with particular entries are recorded on a separate page. Here we should like to express our gratitude to those who have helped in a general way. First we thank the publishers Routledge for launching this project and seeing it through with enthusiastic support, especially Mark Barragry, Senior Academic Reference Editor, Alex Clark and Colville Wemyss, Development Editors, and Kerry Munro, Copy Editor. Then, many libraries have been consulted but above all this country's principal, national library for the history of science and technology, the Science Museum Library, and we thank Ian Carter, Readers Services Librarian, and all his colleagues who have unfailingly rendered efficient and friendly help. Lastly, we thank our wives (one each), Mary and Cis, without whose forbearance and encouragement we might have started the course but would hardly have stayed it to the end.

LRD
November 1995

Acknowledgements

The Editors would like to express their thanks to the following people and organizations for their help in the preparation of this book; names of those whose help is acknowledged are given below in alphabetical order, followed by a note of the entries with which they helped and, in parentheses, the initials of the authors of those entries.

Sadao Aoki, Seimelkai Foundation: *Inoue Masaru* (PJGR)

John Bagley: *entries relating to aeronautics* (JDS)

F. Boyle, Royal Society of Chemistry Library: *Crawford, John William Croom* (LRD)

Judit Brody: *women technologists*

Dr J.A. Brongers: *Vermuyden, Sir Cornelius* (KM/LRD)

Denise Carter, ICI Chemicals & Polymers Library: *Gibson, R.O.* (LRD)

Dave Fairhurst: *England, George* (PJGR)

Professor Ahmad Y. al-Hassan, Department of Middle Eastern Studies, University of Toronto: *Islamic technologists*

David Gestetner (grandson): *Gestetner, David* (LRD)

Christine Heap, National Railway Museum: *Chapelon, André; England, George; Forrester, George; Stephenson, Robert* (PJGR)

The late Professor Alexander Kholodilin, University of Ocean Technology, St Petersburg: *Krylov, Alexei Nicolaevitch; Peter the Great; Popoff, Andrei Alexandrovitch; Yourkevitch, Vladimir Ivanovitch* (FMW)

Professor James Lovelock: *Lovelock, James Ephraim* (LRD)

Mr Philip Monro, Hampshire Advisory Technical Services Ltd: *Monro, Philip Peter* (LRD)

Dr Alex Moulton: *Moulton, Alexander* (IMcN)

The Needham Research Institute, Cambridge, and the late Dr Joseph Needham: *entries relating to the Chinese* (LRD)

The Printing History Library, St Bride's, London: *several entries relating to printing technology* (LRD)

Dr J.S. Reid, University of Aberdeen: *Davidson, Robert* (PJGR)

K.C. Rudd, Brunel University: *Inoue Masaru* (PJGR)

Michael Seymour, Honorary Curator of Archives, Festiniog Railway Company: *Fairlie, Robert Francis; Spooner, Charles Easton* (PJGR)

Roar Stenersen, Norwegian State Railways Museum: *Pihl, Carl Abraham* (PJGR)

Ms D.G. Stobbs, Archive Consultant, Information Management & Storage, St Helens: *Pilkington, Sir Lionel Alexander Bethune* (LRD)

I.F. Wayman, Parker Pens: *Parker, George Salford* (LRD)

Ian Whitehead, Tyne & Wear Museum Service: *Thompson, Benjamin* (PJGR)

HOW TO USE THE DICTIONARY

In using this dictionary, the following notes will be useful. Cross reference entries are made from alternative forms of a name. If there is no entry for a desired name, the name index should be consulted, to direct the reader to the entry or entries where that name is mentioned. There is also an index to subjects and an index of inventions and discoveries, referring the reader to entries where these matters are mentioned.

Each entry has the same structure: after the name of the individual, his or her dates and places of birth and death are given, so far as these can be ascertained. Then follows the subject's nationality and a brief statement of his or her principal achievements. The nationality is normally that of the present description of the country of origin: thus Nikola Tesla is not given as 'Austrian' or 'Yugoslavian' but as 'Serbian'. Citizens of the United States of America are given as 'American'. British subjects are generally referred to as English, Scottish or Welsh, unless it is difficult to assign one of these to an individual. For emigrants, the countries of origin and adoption are normally given, as for example 'German/American'.

Then follows a brief biography of the subject, the main part of the entry. The aim is to sketch the subject's background and to describe his or her significance in the history of technology: how he or she came to make his or her discovery or invention and what its consequences were. For scientists, the emphasis is on their technological contributions rather than their scientific discoveries. Names printed in bold type in the text indicate other entries where relevant information can be found.

At the end of the entry, we give principal honours and distinctions, bibliography, that is, the subject's principal writings and publications (in chronological order), and 'further reading', giving a select few references to literature where further information can be found (in order of importance). The entry concludes with the initials of the author, whose identity can be traced by consulting the list of contributors which precedes the editors' preface.

BIOGRAPHICAL DICTIONARY
OF THE
HISTORY OF TECHNOLOGY

A

Abel, Sir Frederick August

b. 17 July 1827 Woolwich, London, England
d. 6 September 1902 Westminster, London, England

English chemist, co-inventor of cordite and explosives expert.

His family came from Germany and he was the son of a music master. He first became interested in science at the age of 14, when visiting his mineralogist uncle in Hamburg, and studied chemistry at the Royal Polytechnic Institution in London. In 1845 he became one of the twenty-six founding students, under A.W. von **Hofmann**, of the Royal College of Chemistry. Such was his aptitude for the subject that within two years he became von Hofmann's assistant and demonstrator. In 1851 Abel was appointed Lecturer in Chemistry, succeeding Michael Faraday, at the Royal Military Academy, Woolwich, and it was while there that he wrote his *Handbook of Chemistry*, which was co-authored by his assistant, Charles Bloxam.

Abel's four years at the Royal Military Academy served to foster his interest in explosives, but it was during his thirty-four years, beginning in 1854, as Ordnance Chemist at the Royal Arsenal and at Woolwich that he consolidated and developed his reputation as one of the international leaders in his field. In 1860 he was elected a Fellow of the Royal Society, but it was his studies during the 1870s into the chemical changes that occur during explosions, and which were the subject of numerous papers, that formed the backbone of his work. It was he who established the means of storing gun-cotton without the danger of spontaneous explosion, but he also developed devices (the Abel Open Test and Close Test) for measuring the flashpoint of petroleum. He also became interested in metal alloys, carrying out much useful work on their composition. A further avenue of research occurred in 1881 when he was appointed a member of the Royal Commission set up to investigate safety in mines after the explosion that year in the Seal-

ham Colliery. His resultant study on dangerous dusts did much to further understanding on the use of explosives underground and to improve the safety record of the coal-mining industry. The achievement for which he is most remembered, however, came in 1889, when, in conjunction with Sir James **Dewar**, he invented cordite. This stable explosive, made of wood fibre, nitric acid and glycerine, had the vital advantage of being a 'smokeless powder', which meant that, unlike the traditional ammunition propellant, gunpowder ('black powder'), the firer's position was not given away when the weapon was discharged. Although much of the preliminary work had been done by the Frenchman Paul Vieille, it was Abel who perfected it, with the result that cordite quickly became the British Army's standard explosive.

Abel married, and was widowed, twice. He had no children, but died heaped in both scientific honours and those from a grateful country.

Principal Honours and Distinctions
Grand Commander of the Royal Victorian Order 1901. Knight Commander of the Most Honourable Order of the Bath 1891 (Commander 1877). Knighted 1883. Created Baronet 1893. FRS 1860. President, Chemical Society 1875–7. President, Institute of Chemistry 1881–2. President, Institute of Electrical Engineers 1883. President, Iron and Steel Institute 1891. Chairman, Society of Arts 1883–4. Telford Medal 1878, Royal Society Royal Medal 1887, Albert Medal (Society of Arts) 1891, Bessemer Gold Medal 1897. Hon. DCL (Oxon.) 1883, Hon. DSc (Cantab.) 1888.

Bibliography
1854, with C. L. Bloxam, *Handbook of Chemistry: Theoretical, Practical and Technical*, London: John Churchill; 2nd edn 1858.
Besides writing numerous scientific papers, he also contributed several articles to *The Encyclopaedia Britannica*, 1875–89, 9th edn.

Further Reading
Dictionary of National Biography, 1912, Vol. 1, Suppl. 2, London: Smith, Elder.

CM

Abel, John Jacob

b. 19 May 1857 near Cleveland, Ohio, USA
d. 26 May 1938 Baltimore, Maryland, USA

American pharmacologist and physiologist, proponent of the 'artificial kidney' and the isolator of pure insulin.

Born of German immigrant farming stock, his early scientific education at the University of Michigan, where he graduated PhB in 1883, suffered from a financially dictated interregnum of three years. In 1884 he moved to Leipzig and worked under **Ludwig**, moving to Strasbourg where he obtained his MD in 1888. In 1891 he was able to return to the University of Michigan as Lecturer in Materia Medica and Therapeutics, and in 1893 he was offered the first Chair of Pharmacology at Johns Hopkins University, a position he occupied until 1932. He was a pioneer in emphasizing the importance of chemistry, in its widest sense, in medicine and physiology. In his view, 'the investigator must associate himself with those who have laboured in fields where molecules and atoms rather than multi-cellular tissues or even unicellular organisms are the units of study'.

Soon after coming to Baltimore he commenced work on extracts from the adrenal medulla and in 1899 published his work on epinephrine. In later years he developed an 'artificial kidney' which could be used to remove diffusible substances from the blood. In 1913 he was able to demonstrate the existence of free amino-acids in the blood and his investigations in this field foreshadowed not only the developments of blood and plasma transfusion but also the possibility of the management of renal failure.

From 1917 to 1924 he moved to a study of the hormone content of pituitary extracts, but in 1924 he suddenly transferred his attention to the study of insulin. In 1925 he announced the discovery of pure crystalline hormone. This work at first failed to gain full acceptance, but as late as 1955 the full elucidation of the protein structure of insulin proved the final culmination of his studies.

Abel's dedication to laboratory research and his disdain for matters of administration may explain the relative paucity of worldy honours awarded to such an outstanding figure.

Principal Honours and Distinctions
FRS.

Bibliography
1913, 'On the removal of diffusible substances from the circulating blood by means of dialysis', *Transactions of the Association of American Physiologists*.

Further Reading
1939, *Obituary Notices, Fellows of the Royal Society*, London: Royal Society.
1946, *Biographical Memoir: John Jacob Abel. 1857–1938*, Washington, DC: National Academy of Sciences.

MG

Abney, William de Wiveleslie

b. 24 July 1843 England
d. 2 December 1920 England

English photographic scientist, inventor and author.

Abney began his career as an officer in the Army and was an instructor in chemistry in the Royal Engineers at Chatham, where he made substantial use of photography as a working tool. He retired from the Army in 1877 and joined the Science and Art Department at South Kensington. It was at Abney's suggestion that a collection of photographic equipment and processes was established in the South Kensington Museum (later to become the Science Museum Photography Collection).

Abney undertook significant researches into the nature of gelatine silver halide emulsions at a time when they were being widely adopted by photographers. Perhaps his most important practical innovations were the introduction of hydroquinone as a developing agent in 1880 and silver gelatine citrochloride emulsions for printing-out paper (POP) in 1882. However, Abney was at the forefront of many aspects of photographic research during a period of great innovation and change in photography. He devised new techniques of photomechanical printing and conducted significant researches in the fields of photochemistry and spectral analysis. Abney published throughout his career for both the specialist scientist and the more general photographic practitioner.

Principal Honours and Distinctions
KCB 1900. FRS 1877. Served at different times as President of the Royal Astronomical, Royal Photographic and Physical Societies. Chairman, Royal Society of Arts.

Further Reading
Obituary, 1921, *Proceedings of the Royal Society* (Series A) 99.
J.M. Eder, 1945, *History of Photography*, trans. E. Epstein, New York.

JW

Abt, Roman
b. 17 July 1850 Bünzen, Switzerland
d. 1 May 1933 Lucerne, Switzerland

Swiss locomotive engineer, inventor of the Abt rack rail system.

Abt trained under N. **Riggenbach** and worked for his short-lived International Company for Mountain Railways during the 1870s, and subsequently invented the Abt rack system as an improvement on Riggenbach's ladder rack, in which the rungs gave trouble by working loose. Abt's rack system, in what became its usual form, comprises two machined racks side by side with their teeth staggered so that a tooth in one rack is opposite a recess in the other, and at least one tooth is always engaged with a locomotive's driving pinions. This system was first used in 1884 on the mixed rack-and-adhesion Harz Railway in Germany, and then largely superseded Riggenbach's system for new rack railways built worldwide to an eventual total of seventy-two, including the Snowdon Mountain Railway in the UK that was built in the 1890s. In many cases Abt himself designed locomotives and rolling stock, and supervised their construction.

Bibliography
1877–8, Abstract in *Minutes of Proceedings of the Institution of Civil Engineers*, Vol. 52 (part II) (abstract of a paper given by Abt in which he described eight Riggenbach system railways then operating; his own system was patented in 1882).

Further Reading
J. Marshall, 1978, *A Biographical Dictionary of Railway Engineers*, Newton Abbot: David & Charles.
O.J. Morris, 1951, *Snowdon Mountain Railway*, Ian Allan.

PJGR

Achard, Franz
b. 1753 Germany
d. 1821 Germany

German scientist of French descent who built the world's first factory to extract sugar from beet.

The descendant of a French refugee, Achard began the systematic study of beet on his estate at Caulsdorf in 1786. The work had been stimulated by the discovery in 1747 of the presence of sugar in fodder beet. This research had been carried out by Andreas Marggraf, under whom Franz Achard trained. After a fire destroyed his laboratories Achard established himself on the domain of Französisch in Buchholtz near Berlin.

After thirteen years of study he felt sufficiently confident to apply for an interview with Frederick William III, King of Prussia, which took place on 11 January 1799. Achard presented the King with a loaf of sugar made from raw beet by his Sugar Boiling House method. He requested a ten-year monopoly on his idea, as well as the grant of land on which to carry out his work. The King was sufficiently impressed to establish a committee to supervise further trials, and asked Achard to make a public statement on his work. The King ordered a factory to be built at his own expense, and paid Achard a salary to manage it. In 1801 he was granted the domain of Cunern in Silesia; he built his first sugar factory there and began production in 1802. Unfortunately Achard's business skills were negligible, and he was bankrupt within the year. In 1810 the State relieved him of his debt and gave him a pension, and in 1812 the first sugar factory was turned into a school of sugar technology.

Bibliography
Achard's public response to the King's request was his paper *Abhandlungen über die Kultur der Runkelrube*.

Further Reading
Noel Deerr, 1950, *The History of Sugar*, Vol. II,

London (deals with the development of sugar extraction from beet, and therefore the story of both Marggraf and Achard).

AP

Ackermann, Rudolph
b. 20 April 1764 Stolberg, Saxony
d. 30 March 1834 Finchley, London, England

German-born fine-art publisher and bookseller, noted for his arrangement of the steering of the front wheels of horse-drawn carriages, which is still used in automobiles today.

Ackermann's father was a coachbuilder and harness-maker who in 1775 moved to Schneeberg. Rudolph was educated there and later entered his father's workshop for a short time. He visited Dresden, among other towns in Germany, and was resident in Paris for a short time, but eventually settled in London. For the first ten years of his life there he was employed in making designs for many of the leading coachbuilders. His steering-gear consisted of an arrangement of the track arms on the stub axles and their connection by the track rod in such a way that the inner wheel moved through a greater angle than the outer one, so giving approximately true rolling of the wheels in cornering. A necessary condition for this is that, in the plan view, the point of intersection of the axes of all the wheels must be at a point which always lies on the projection of the rear axle. In addition, the front wheels are inclined to bring the line of contact of the front wheels under the line of the pivots, about which they turn when cornering. This mechanism was not entirely new, having been proposed for windmill carriages in 1714 by Du Quet, but it was brought into prominence by Ackermann and so has come to bear his name.

In 1801 he patented a method of rendering paper, cloth and other materials waterproof and set up a factory in Chelsea for that purpose. He was one of the first private persons to light his business premises with gas. He also devoted some time to a patent for movable carriage axles between 1818 and 1820. In 1805 he was put in charge of the preparation of the funeral car for Lord Nelson.

Most of his life and endeavours were devoted to fine-art printing and publishing. He was responsible for the introduction into England of lithography as a fine art: it had first been introduced as a mechanical process in 1801, but was mainly used for copying until Ackermann took it up in 1817, setting up a press and engaging the services of a number of prominent artists, including W.H. Pyne, W. Combe, Pugin and Thomas Rowlandson. In 1819 he published an English translation of J.A. Senefelder's *A Complete Course of Lithography*, illustrated with lithographic plates from his press. He was much involved in charitable works for widows, children and wounded soldiers after the war of 1814. In 1830 he suffered 'an attack of paralysis' which left him unable to continue in business. He died four years later and was buried at St Clement Danes.

Bibliography
His fine-art publications are numerous and well known, and include the following:
The Microcosm of London
University of Oxford
University of Cambridge
The Thames
The Rhine
English Lakes

Further Reading
Aubrey F. Burstall, 'A history of mechanical engineering', *Dictionary of National Biography*.

IMcN

Acres, Birt
b. 23 July 1854 Virginia, USA
d. 1918

American photographer, inventor and pioneer cinematographer.

Born of English parents and educated in Paris, Acres travelled to England in the 1880s. He worked for the photographic manufacturing firm Elliott & Co. in Barnet, near London, and became the Manager. He became well known through his frequent lectures, demonstrations and articles in the photographic press. The appearance of the Edison kinetoscope in 1893 seems to have aroused his interest in the recording and reproduction of movement.

At the beginning of 1895 he took his idea for a camera to Robert **Paul**, an instrument maker, and they collaborated on the building of a working camera, which Acres used to record the Oxford and Cambridge Boat Race on 30 March

1895. He filmed the Derby at Epsom on 29 May and the opening of the Kiel Canal in June, as well as ten other subjects for the kinetoscope, which were sold by Paul. Acres's association with Paul ended in July 1895. Acres had patented the camera design, the Kinetic Lantern, on 27 May 1895 and then went on to design a projector with which he gave the first successful presentation of projected motion pictures to take place in Britain, at the Royal Photographic Society's meeting on 14 January 1896. At the end of the month Acres formed his own business, the Northern Photographic Company, to supply film stock, process and print exposed film, and to make finished film productions.

His first shows to the public, using the renamed Kineopticon projector, started in Piccadilly Circus on 21 March 1896. He later toured the country with his show. He was honoured with a Royal Command Performance at Marlborough House on 21 July 1896 before members of the royal family. Although he made a number of films for his own use, they and his equipment were used only for his own demonstrations. His last contribution to cinematography was the design and patenting in 1898 of the first low-cost system for amateur use, the Birtac, which was first shown on 25 January 1899 and marketed in May of that year. It used half-width film, 17.5 mm wide, and the apparatus served as camera, printer and projector.

Principal Honours and Distinctions
Fellow of the Royal Photographic Society 1895.

Bibliography
27 May 1895 (the Kinetic Lantern).
9 June 1898 (the Birtac).

Further Reading
J. Barnes, 1976, *The Beginnings of the Cinema in England*, London.
B. Coe, 1980, *The History of Movie Photography*, London.

BC

Adam, Robert
b. 3 July 1728 Kirkcaldy, Scotland
d. 3 March 1792 London, England

Scottish architect, active mostly in England, who led the neo-classical movement between 1760 and 1790.

Robert Adam was a man of outstanding talent, immense energy dedicated to his profession, and of great originality, who utilized all sources of classical art from ancient Greece and Rome as well as from the Renaissance and Baroque eras in Italy. He was also a very practical exponent of neo-classicism and believed in using the latest techniques to produce fine craftsmanship.

Of particular interest to him was stucco, the material needed for elegant, finely crafted ceiling and wall designs. Stucco, though the Italian word for plaster, refers architecturally to a specific form of the material. Known as *Stucco duro* (hard plaster), its use and composition dates from the days of ancient Rome. Giovanni da Udine, a pupil of Raphael, having discovered some fine *stucco antico* in the ruins of the Palace of Titus in Rome, carried out extensive research during the Italian Renaissance in order to discover its precise composition; it was a mixture of powdered crystalline limestone (travertine), river sand, water and powdered white marble. The marble produced an exceptionally hard stucco when set, thereby differentiating it from plasterwork, and was a material fine enough to make delicate relief and statuary work possible.

In the 1770s Robert Adam's ceiling and wall designs were characterized by low-relief, delicate, classical forms. He and his brothers, who formed the firm of Adam Brothers, were interested in a stucco which would be especially fine grained and hard setting. A number of new products then appearing on the market were easier to handle than earlier ones. These included a stucco by Mr David Wark, patented in 1765, and another by a Swiss clergyman called Liardet in 1773; the Adam firm purchased both patents and obtained an Act of Parliament authorizing them to be the sole vendors and makers of this stucco, which they called 'Adam's new invented patent stucco'. More new versions appeared, among which was one by a Mr Johnson, who claimed it to be an improvement. The Adam Brothers, having paid a high price for their rights, took him to court. The case was decided in 1778 by Lord Mansfield, a fellow Scot and a patron (at Kenwood), who, unsurprisingly, gave judgement in favour of the Adams.

Principal Honours and Distinctions
Member of the Society of Arts 1758. FRS 1761.
Architect to the King's Works 1761.

Bibliography
1764, *Ruins of the Palace of the Emperor Diocletian at Spalatro.*
1773, *Works in Architecture of Robert and James Adam.*

Further Reading
A.T. Bolton, 1922, *The Architecture of Robert and James Adam, 1758–1794*, 2 vols, Country Life.
J. Fleming, 1962, *Robert Adam and his Circle*, Murray.
J. Lees-Milne, 1947, *The Age of Adam*, Batsford.
J. Rykwert and A. Rykwert, 1985, *The Brothers Adam*, Collins.
D. Yarwood, 1970, *Robert Adam*, Dent.

DY

Adams, William Bridges

b. 1797 Madeley, Staffordshire, England
d. 23 July 1872 Broadstairs, Kent, England

English inventor, particularly of road and rail vehicles and their equipment.

Ill health forced Adams to live abroad when he was a young man and when he returned to England in the early 1830s he became a partner in his father's firm of coachbuilders. Coaches during that period were steered by a centrally pivoted front axle, which meant that the front wheels had to swing beneath the body and were therefore made smaller than the rear wheels. Adams considered this design defective and invented equirotal coaches, built by his firm, in which the front and rear wheels were of equal diameter and the coach body was articulated midway along its length so that the front part pivoted. He also applied himself to improving vehicles for railways, which were developing rapidly then.

In 1843 he opened his own engineering works, Fairfield Works in north London (he was not related to his contemporary William Adams, who was appointed Locomotive Superintendent to the North London Railway in 1854). In 1847 he and James Samuel, Engineer to the Eastern Counties Railway, built for that line a small steam inspection car, the Express, which was light enough to be lifted off the track. The following year Adams built a broad-gauge steam railcar, the Fairfield, for the Bristol & Exeter Railway at the insistance of the line's Engineer, C.H. Gregory: self-propelled and passenger-carrying, this was the first railcar. Adams developed the concept further into a light locomotive that could haul two or three separate carriages, and light locomotives built both by his own firm and by other noted builders came into vogue for a decade or more.

In 1847 Adams also built eight-wheeled coaches for the Eastern Counties Railway that were larger and more spacious than most others of the day: each in effect comprised two four-wheeled coaches articulated together, with wheels that were allowed limited side-play. He also realized the necessity for improvements to railway track, the weakest point of which was the joints between the rails, whose adjoining ends were normally held in common chairs. Adams invented the fishplated joint, first used by the Eastern Counties Railway in 1849 and subsequently used almost universally.

Adams was a prolific inventor. Most important of his later inventions was the radial axle, which was first applied to the leading and trailing wheels of a 2–4–2 tank engine, the *White Raven*, built in 1863; Adams's radial axle was the forerunner of all later radial axles. However, the sprung tyres with which *White Raven* was also fitted (an elastic steel hoop was interposed between wheel centre and tyre) were not perpetuated. His inventiveness was not restricted to engineering: in matters of dress, his adoption, perhaps invention, of the turn-down collar at a time when men conventionally wore stand-up collars had lasting effect.

Bibliography
Adams took out some thirty five British patents, including one for the fishplate in 1847. He wrote copiously, as journalist and author: his most important book was *English Pleasure Carriages* (1837), a detailed description of coachbuilding, together with ideas for railway vehicles and track. The 1971 reprint (Bath: Adams & Dart) has a biographical introduction by Jack Simmons.

Further Reading
C. Hamilton Ellis, 1958, *Twenty Locomotive Men*, Shepperton: Ian Allan, Ch. 1.

See also **England, George**.

PJGR

Adamson, Daniel
b. 1818 Shildon, Co. Durham, England
d. January 1890 Didsbury, Manchester, England

English mechanical engineer, pioneer in the use of steel for boilers, which enabled higher pressures to be introduced; pioneer in the use of triple- and quadruple-expansion mill engines.

Adamson was apprenticed between 1835 and 1841 to Timothy Hackworth, then Locomotive Superintendent on the Stockton & Darlington Railway. After this he was appointed Draughtsman, then Superintendent Engineer, at that railway's locomotive works until in 1847 he became Manager of Shildon Works. In 1850 he resigned and moved to act as General Manager of Heaton Foundry, Stockport. In the following year he commenced business on his own at Newton Moor Iron Works near Manchester, where he built up his business as an iron-founder and boilermaker. By 1872 this works had become too small and he moved to a 4 acre (1.6 hectare) site at Hyde Junction, Dukinfield. There he employed 600 men making steel boilers, heavy machinery including mill engines fitted with the American Wheelock valve gear, hydraulic plant and general millwrighting.

His success was based on his early recognition of the importance of using high-pressure steam and steel instead of wrought iron. In 1852 he patented his type of flanged seam for the firetubes of Lancashire boilers, which prevented these tubes cracking through expansion. In 1862 he patented the fabrication of boilers by drilling rivet holes instead of punching them and also by drilling the holes through two plates held together in their assembly positions. He had started to use steel for some boilers he made for railway locomotives in 1857, and in 1860, only four years after **Bessemer**'s patent, he built six mill engine boilers from steel for Platt Bros, Oldham. He solved the problems of using this new material, and by his death had made *c.*2,800 steel boilers with pressures up to 250 psi (17.6 kg/cm^2).

He was a pioneer in the general introduction of steel and in 1863–4 was a partner in establishing the Yorkshire Iron and Steel Works at Penistone. This was the first works to depend entirely upon Bessemer steel for engineering purposes and was later sold at a large profit to Charles Cammell & Co., Sheffield. When he started this works, he also patented improvements both to the Bessemer converters and to the engines which provided their blast. In 1870 he helped to turn Lincolnshire into an important ironmaking area by erecting the North Lincolnshire Ironworks. He was also a shareholder in ironworks in South Wales and Cumberland.

He contributed to the development of the stationary steam engine, for as early as 1855 he built one to run with a pressure of 150 psi (10.5 kg/cm^2) that worked quite satisfactorily. He reheated the steam between the cylinders of compound engines and then in 1861–2 patented a triple-expansion engine, followed in 1873 by a quadruple-expansion one to further economize steam. In 1858 he developed improved machinery for testing tensile strength and compressive resistance of materials, and in the same year patents for hydraulic lifting jacks and riveting machines were obtained.

He was a founding member of the Iron and Steel Institute and became its President in 1888 when it visited Manchester. The previous year he had been President of the Institution of Civil Engineers when he was presented with the Bessemer Gold Medal. He was a constant contributor at the meetings of these associations as well as those of the Institution of Mechanical Engineers. He did not live to see the opening of one of his final achievements, the Manchester Ship Canal. He was the one man who, by his indomitable energy and skill at public speaking, roused the enthusiasm of the people in Manchester for this project and he made it a really practical proposition in the face of strong opposition.

Principal Honours and Distinctions
President, Institution of Civil Engineers 1887. President, Iron and Steel Institute 1888. Institution of Civil Engineers Bessemer Gold Medal 1887.

Further Reading
Obituary, *Engineer* 69: 56.
Obituary, *Engineering* 49:66–8.
Obituary, *Proceedings of the Institution of Civil Engineers* 100: 374–8.
H.W. Dickinson, 1938, *A Short History of the Steam Engine*, Cambridge University Press (provides an illustration of Adamson's flanged seam for boilers).
R.L. Hills, 1989, *Power from Steam. A History of*

the Stationary Steam Engine, Cambridge University Press (covers the development of the triple-expansion engine).

RLH

Ader, Clément
b. 2 April 1841 Muret, France
d. 3 May 1925 Toulouse, France

French engineer who made a short 'hop' in a powered aeroplane in 1890.

Ader was a distinguished engineer and versatile inventor who was involved with electrical developments, including the telephone and air-cushion vehicles. In the field of aeronautics he became the centre of a long-lasting controversy: did he, or did he not, fly before the **Wright** brothers' flight of 1903?

In 1882 Ader started work on his first aeroplane, the *Eole* (god of the winds), which was bat-like in appearance and powered by a very well-designed lightweight steam engine developing about 15 kW (20 hp). On 9 October 1890 the *Eole* was ready, and with Ader as pilot it increased speed over a level surface and lifted off the ground. It was airborne for about 5 seconds and covered some 50 m (164 ft), reaching a height of 20 cm (8 in.). Whether such a short hop constituted a flight has caused much discussion and argument over the years. An even greater controversy followed Ader's claim in 1906 that his third aeroplane (*Avion III*) had made a flight of 300 m (328 yd) in 1897. He repeated this claim in his book written in 1907, and many historians accepted his account of the 'flight'. C.H. Gibbs-Smith, an eminent aviation historian, investigated the Ader controversy and in his book published in 1966 came to the conclusion that the *Avion III* did not fly at all. *Avion III* was donated to the Museum of the Conservatoire des Arts et Métiers in Paris, and still survives. From 1906 onwards Ader concentrated his inventive efforts elsewhere, but he did mount a successful campaign to persuade the French War Ministry to create an air force.

Principal Honours and Distinctions
In 1990 the French Government accepted him as the 'Father of Aviation who gave wings to the world'.

Bibliography
1890, patent no. 205,155 (included a description of the *Eole*).
1907, *La Première étape de l'aviation militaire en France*, Paris (the most significant of his published books and articles).

Further Reading
C.H. Gibbs-Smith, 1968, *Clément Ader: His Flight Claims and His Place in History*, London.
The centenary of Ader's 1890 flight resulted in several French publications, including:
C. Carlier, 1990, *L'Affaire Clément Ader: la vérité rétablie*, Paris;
Pierre Lissarrague, 1990, *Clément Ader: inventeur d'avions*, Toulouse.

JDS

Af Chapman, Frederik Henrik
See **Chapman, Frederik Henrik af.**

Agricola, Georgius (Georg Bauer)
b. 24 March 1494 Glauchau, Saxony
d. 21 November 1555 Chemnitz, Germany

German metallurgist, who wrote the book De Re Metallica under the latinized version of his name.

Agricola was a physician, scientist and metallurgist of note and it was this which led to the publication of *De Re Metallica*. He studied at Leipzig University and between 1518 and 1522 he was a school teacher in Zwickau. Eventually he settled as a physician in Chemnitz. Later he continued his medical practice at Joachimstal in the Erzgebirge. This town was newly built to serve the mining community in what was at the time the most important ore-mining field in both Germany and Europe.

As a physician in the sixteenth century he would naturally have been concerned with the development of medicines, which would have led him to research the medical properties of ores and base metals. He studied the mineralogy of his area, and the mines, and the miners who were working there. He wrote several books in Latin on geology and mineralogy. His important work during that period was a glossary of mineralogical and mining terms in both Latin and German. It is, however, *De Re Metallica* for which he is best known. This large volume contains twelve books which deal with mining and metallurgy, including an account of glassmaking. Whilst one can understand the text of this book very easily, the quality of the illustrative woodcuts should not be neglected. These illustrations detail the mines, furnaces, forges and the plant associated with them, unfortunately the name of the artist is unknown. The importance of the work lies in the fact that it is an assemblage of information on all the methods and practices current at that time. The book was clearly intended as a textbook of mining and mineralogy and as such it would have been brought to England by German engineers when they were employed by the Mines Royal in the Keswick area in the late sixteenth century. In addition to his studies in preparation for De Re Metallica, Agricola was an 'adventurer' holding shares in the Gottesgab mine in the Erzegebirge.

Principal Honours and Distinctions

Bibliography
1556, *De Re Metallica*, Basel; 1912, trans. H. Hoover and L.H. Hoover, London.

KM

Albert, Prince Consort
b. 26 August 1819 The Rosenau, near Coburg, Germany
d. 14 December 1861 Windsor Castle, England

German/British polymath and Prince Consort to Queen Victoria.

Albert received a sound education in the arts and sciences, carefully designed to fit him for a role as consort to the future Queen Victoria. After their marriage in 1840, Albert threw himself into the task of establishing his position as, eventually, Prince Consort and uncrowned king of England. By his undoubted intellectual gifts, unrelenting hard work and moral rectitude, Albert moulded the British constitutional monarchy into the form it retains to this day. The purchase in 1845 of the Osborne estate in the Isle of Wight provided not only the growing royal family with a comfortable retreat from London and public life, but Albert with full scope for his abilities as architect and planner. With Thomas **Cubitt**, the eminent engineer and contractor, Albert erected at Osborne one of the most remarkable

buildings of the nineteenth century. He went on to design the house and estate at Balmoral in Scotland, another notable creation.

Albert applied his abilities as architect and planner in the promotion of such public works as the London sewer system and, in practical form, the design of cottages for workers, such as those in south London, as well as those on the royal estates. Albert's other main contribution to technology was as educationist in a broad sense. In 1847, he was elected Chancellor of Cambridge University. He was appalled at the low standards and narrow curriculum prevailing there and at Oxford. He was no mere figurehead, but took a close and active interest in the University's affairs. With his powerful influence behind them, the reforming fellows were able to force measures to raise standards and widen the curriculum to take account, in particular, of the rapid progress in the natural sciences. Albert was instrumental in ending the lethargy of centuries and laying the foundations of the modern British university system.

In 1847 the Prince became Secretary of the Royal Society of Arts. With Henry Cole, the noted administrator who shared Albert's concern for the arts, he promoted a series of exhibitions under the auspices of the Society. From these grew the idea of a great exhibition of the products of the decorative and industrial arts. It was Albert who decided that its scope should be international. As Chairman of the organizing committee, by sheer hard work he drove the project through to a triumphant conclusion. The success of the Exhibition earned it a handsome profit for which Albert had found a use even before it closed. The proceeds went towards the purchase of a site in South Kensington, for which he drew up a grand scheme for a complex of museums and colleges for the education of the people in the sciences and the arts. This largely came to fruition and South Kensington today is a fitting memorial to the Prince Consort's wisdom and concern for the public good.

Further Reading
Sir Theodore Martin, 1875–80, *The Life of His Royal Highness, the Prince Consort*, 5 vols, London; German edn 1876; French edn 1883 (the classic life of the Prince).
R.R. James, 1983, *Albert, Prince Consort: A*

Biography, London: Hamish Hamilton (the standard modern biography).

L.R. Day, 1989, 'Resources for the study of the history of technology in the Science Museum Library', IATUL Quarterly 3: 122–39 (provides a short account of the rise of South Kensington and its institutions).

LRD

Albert, Wilhelm August Julius

b. 24 January 1787 Hannover, Germany
d. 4 July 1846 Clausthal, Harz, Germany

German mining official, successful applier of wire cable.

After studying law at the University of Göttingen, Albert turned to the mining industry and in 1806 started his career in mining administration in the Harz district, where he became Chief Inspector of mines thirty years later. His influence on the organization of the mining industry was considerable and he contributed valuable ideas for the development of mining technology. For example, he initiated experiments with **Reichenbach**'s water-column pump in Harz when it had been working successfully in the transportation of brine in Bavaria, and he encouraged **Dörell** to work on his miner's elevator.

The increasing depths of shafts in the Harz district brought problems with hoisting as the ropes became too heavy and tended to break. At the beginning of the nineteenth century, iron link chains replaced the hempen ropes which were expensive and wore out too quickly, especially in the wet conditions in the shafts. After he had experimented for six years using counterbalancing iron link chains, which broke too easily, in 1834 he conceived the idea of producing stranded cables from iron wires. Their breaking strength and flexibility depended greatly on the softness of the iron and the way of laying the strands. Albert produced the cable by attaching the wires to strings which he turned evenly; this method became known as 'Albert lay'. He was not the first to conceive the idea of metal cables: there exists evidence for such cables as far back as Pompeii; **Leonardo da Vinci** made sketches of cables made from brass wires; and in 1780 the French engineer Reignier applied iron cables for lightning conductors. The idea also developed in various other mining areas, but Albert cables were the first to gain rapidly direct common usage worldwide.

Bibliography
1835, 'Die Anfertigung von Treibseilen aus geflochtenem Eisendraht', *Karstens Archiv* 8: 418–28.

Further reading
K. Karmarsch, 'W.A.J. Albert', *Allgemeine deutsche Biographie* 1: 212–3.
W. Bornhardt, 1934, *W.A.J. Albert und die Erfindung der Eisendrahtseile*, Berlin (a detailed description of his inventions, based on source material).
C. Bartels, 1992, *Vom frühneuzeitlichen Montangewerbe zur Bergbauindustrie*, Bochum: Deutsches Bergbau-Museum (evaluates his achievements within the framework of technological development in the Harz mining industry).

WK

Albone, Daniel

b. *c.*1860 Biggleswade, Bedfordshire, England
d. 1906 England

English engineer who developed and manufactured the first commercially successful lightweight tractor.

The son of a market gardener, Albone's interest lay in mechanics, and by 1880 he had established his own business as a cycle maker and repairer. His inventive mind led to a number of patents relating to bicycle design, but his commercial success was particularly assisted by his achievements in cycle racing. From this early start he diversified his business, designing and supplying, amongst other things, axle bearings for the Great Northern Railway, and also building motor cycles and several cars. It is possible that he began working on tractors as early as 1896. Certainly by 1902 he had built his first prototype, to the three-wheeled design that was to remain in later production models. Weighing only 30 cwt, yet capable of pulling two binders or a two-furrow plough, Albone's Ivel tractor was ahead of anything in its time, and its power-to-weight ratio was to be unrivalled for almost a decade. Albone's commercial success was not entirely due to the mechanical tractor's superiority, but owed a considerable amount to his ability as a showman and demonstrator. He held two working demonstrations a month in the village of Biggleswade in Bedfordshire, where the tractors were made. The tractor was named after the river Ivel, which flowed through the village. The Ivel tractor gained twenty-six gold and silver medals at agricultural shows between 1902 and 1906, and was a significant contributor to Britain's position as the world's largest exporter of tractors between 1904 and 1914. Albone tried other forms of his tractor to increase its sales. He built a fire engine, and also an armoured vehicle, but failed to impress the War Office with its potential.

Albone died at the age of 46. His tractor continued in production but remained essentially unimproved, and the company finally lost its sales to other designs, particularly those of American origin.

Further Reading
Detailed contemporary accounts of tractor development occur in the British periodical *Implement and Machinery Review*. Accounts of the Ivel appear in 'The Trials of Agricultural Motors', *Journal of the Royal Agricultural Society of England* (1910), pp. 179–99. A series of general histories by Michael Williams have been published by Blandfords, of which *Classic Farm Tractors* (1984) includes an entry on the Ivel.

AP

Alden, George I.
b. 22 April 1843 Templeton, Massachusetts, USA
d. 13 September 1926 Princeton, Massachusetts, USA

American mechanical engineer and professor of engineering.

From 1868 to 1896 George Alden was head of the steam and mechanical engineering departments at the Worcester Polytechnic Institute, Worcester, Massachusetts. He made a donation in 1910 to establish a hydraulic laboratory at the Institute, and later a further donation for an extension of the laboratory which was completed in 1925. He was Chairman of the Board of Norton (Abrasives) Company and made a significant contribution to the theory of grinding in his paper in 1914 to the American Society of Mechanical Engineers. He was a member of that society from 1880, the year of its foundation, and took an active part in its proceedings.

Principal Honours and Distinctions
Vice-President, American Society of Mechanical Engineers 1891–3.

Bibliography
1914, 'Operation of grinding wheels in machine grinding', *Transactions of the American Society of Mechanical Engineers* 36: 451–60.

Further Reading
For a description of the Alden Hydraulic Laboratory, see *Mechanical Engineering*, June 1926: 634–5.

RTS

Alexanderson, Ernst Frederik Werner
b. 25 January 1878 Uppsala, Sweden
d. ? May 1975 Schenectady, New York, USA

Swedish-American electrical engineer and prolific radio and television inventor responsible for developing a high-frequency alternator for generating radio waves.

After education in Sweden at the High School and University of Lund and the Royal Institution of Technology in Stockholm, Alexanderson took a postgraduate course at the Berlin-Charlottenburg Engineering College. In 1901 he began work for the Swedish C & C Electric Company, joining the General Electric Company, Schenectady, New York, the following year. There, in 1906, together with **Fessenden**, he developed a series of high-power, high-frequency alternators, which had a dramatic effect on radio communications and resulted in the first real radio broadcast. His early interest in television led to working demonstrations in his own home in 1925 and at the General Electric laboratories in 1927, and to the first public demonstration of large-screen (7 ft (2.13 m) diagonal) projection TV in 1930. Another invention of significance was the 'amplidyne', a sensitive manufacturing-control system subsequently used during the Second World War for controlling anti-aircraft guns. He also contributed to developments in electric propulsion and radio aerials.

He retired from General Electric in 1948, but continued television research as a consultant for the Radio Corporation of America (RCA), filing his 321st patent in 1955.

Principal Honours and Distinctions
Institution of Radio Engineers Medal of Honour 1919. President, IERE 1921. Edison Medal 1944.

Bibliography
Publications relating to his work in the early days of radio include:
'Magnetic properties of iron at frequencies up to 200,000 cycles', *Transactions of the American Institute of Electrical Engineers* (1911) 30: 2,443.
'Transatlantic radio communication', *Transactions of the American Institute of Electrical Engineers* (1919) 38: 1,269.
The amplidyne is described in E. Alexanderson, M. Edwards and K. Boura, 1940, 'Dynamo-electric amplifier for power control', *Transactions of the American Institution of Electrical Engineers* 59: 937.

Further Reading
E. Hawkes, 1927, *Pioneers of Wireless*, Methuen (provides an account of Alexanderson's work on radio).
J.H. Udelson, 1982, *The Great Television Race: A History of the American Television Industry 1925–1941*, University of Alabama Press (provides further details of his contribution to the development of television).

KF

Alexandria, Ctesibius of
See **Ctesibius of Alexandria**.

Alexandria, Hero of
See **Hero of Alexandria**.

al-Jazari, Ibn al-Razzaz
fl. *c*.1200 Arabia

Arab mechanician who constructed a series of ingenious water clocks with automata.

Al-Jazari entered the service of the Artuqid Kings of Diyar Bakir *c*.1180. In 1206 the then King, Nasir al-Din, instructed him to write a book describing the things he had constructed, among which were six water clocks. The timekeeping mechanism of these clocks was not innovative and was derived from earlier Hellenistic examples. Unlike Chinese and Hellenistic water clocks, al-Jazari's clocks had no astronomical in-

dications and were intended to display the time, in temporal or unequal hours, both audibly and visually in an arresting and entertaining manner. The timekeeping was controlled by the flow of water from a vessel which contained a float to operate the clock mechanism. An ingenious device was used to ensure that the flow of water was constant during the day and could be set to a different constant flow during the night, to allow for the variation in the length of the temporal hours. Al-Jazari's clocks have not survived, but models have been constructed from the description and illustrations in the manuscripts.

Bibliography
1206, *The Book of Knowledge of Ingenious Mechanical Devices* (an annotated translation by D.R. Hill was published in Dordrecht in 1974).

Further Reading
D.R. Hill, 1979, *The Country Life International Dictionary of Clocks*, ed. Alan Smith, London, pp. 130, 135 (a very brief but more accessible account).
— 1981, *Arabic Water-Clocks*, Aleppo.

DV

Allen, Horatio
b. 10 May 1802 Schenectady, New York, USA
d. 1 January 1890 South Orange, New Jersey, USA

American engineer, pioneer of steam locomotives.

Allen was the Resident Engineer for construction of the Delaware & Hudson Canal and in 1828 was instructed by J.B. **Jervis** to visit England to purchase locomotives for the canal's rail extension. He drove the locomotive *Stourbridge Lion*, built by J.U. **Rastrick**, on its first trial on 9 August 1829, but weak track prevented its regular use.

Allen was present at the Rainhill Trials on the Liverpool & Manchester Railway in October 1829. So was E.L. Miller, one of the promoters of the South Carolina Canal & Rail Road Company, to which Allen was appointed Chief Engineer that autumn. Allen was influential in introducing locomotives to this railway, and the West Point Foundry built a locomotive for it to his design; it was the first locomotive built in the USA for sale. This locomotive, which bore some resemblance to *Novelty*, built for Rainhill by John Braithwaite and John **Ericsson**, was named *Best Friend of Charleston*. On Christmas Day 1830 it hauled the first scheduled steam train to run in America, carrying 141 passengers.

In 1832 the West Point Foundry built four double-ended, articulated 2–2–0+0–2–2 locomotives to Horatio Allen's design for the South Carolina railroad. From each end of a central firebox extended two boiler barrels side by side with common smokeboxes and chimneys; wheels were mounted on swivelling sub-frames, one at each end, beneath these boilers. Allen's principal object was to produce a powerful locomotive with a light axle loading.

Allen subsequently became a partner in Stillman, Allen & Co. of New York, builders of marine engines, and in 1843 was President of the Erie Railroad.

Further Reading

J. Marshall, 1978, *A Biographical Dictionary of Railway Engineers*, Newton Abbot: David & Charles.

Dictionary of American Biography.

R.E. Carlson, 1969, *The Liverpool & Manchester Railway Project 1821–1831*, Newton Abbot: David & Charles.

J.F. Stover, 1961, *American Railroads*, Chicago: University of Chicago Press.

J.H. White Jr, 1994, 'Old debts and new visions', in *Common Roots – Separate Branches*, London: Science Museum, 79–82.

PJGR

Allen, John F.

b. 1829 England
d. 2 October 1900 New York (?), USA

English inventor of the Allen valve used on his pioneering high-speed engines.

Allen was taken to the United States from England when he was 12 years old. He became an engineer on the *Curlew*, a freight boat running between New York and Providence. A defect which caused the engine to race in rough weather led Allen to invent a new valve gear, but he found it could not be fitted to the **Corliss** engine. In 1856 he patented an improved form of valve and operating gear to reduce back-pressure in the cylinder, which was in fact the reverse of what happened in his later engines. In 1860

he repaired the engines of a New York felt-hat manufacturer, Henry Burr, and that winter he was introduced to Charles **Porter**. Porter realized the potential of Allen's valves for his idea of a high-speed engine, and the Porter–Allen engine became the pioneer of high-speed designs.

Porter persuaded Allen to patent his new valves and two patents were obtained in 1862. These valves could be driven positively and yet the travel of the inlet could be varied to give the maximum expansion at different cut-offs. Also, the valves allowed an exceptionally good flow of steam. While Porter went to England and tried to interest manufacturers there, Allen remained in America and continued work on the engine. Within a few years he invented an inclined water-tube boiler, but he seemed incapable of furthering his inventions once they had been placed on the market. Although he mortgaged his own house in order to help finance the factory for building the steam engine, in the early 1870s he left Porter and built a workshop of his own at Mott Haven. There he invented important systems for riveting by pneumatic machines through both percussion and pressure which led into the production of air compressors and riveting machines.

Further Reading

Obituaries appeared in engineering journals at the time of his death.

Dictionary of American Biography, 1928, Vol. I, New York: C. Scribner's Sons.

C.T. Porter, 1908, *Engineering Reminiscences*, New York: J. Wiley & Sons, reprint 1985, Bradley, Ill.: Lindsay Publications (provides details of Allen's valve design).

R.L. Hills, 1989, *Power from Steam. A History of the Stationary Steam Engine*, Cambridge University Press (covers the development of the Porter–Allen engine).

RLH

Alleyne, Sir John Gay Newton

b. 8 September 1820 Barbados
d. 20 February 1912 Falmouth, Cornwall, England

English iron and steel manufacturer, inventor of the reversing rolling mill.

Alleyne was the heir to a baronetcy created in 1769, which he succeeded to on the death of his father in 1870. He was educated at Harrow and at Bonn University, and from 1843 to 1851 he was Warden at Dulwich College, to the founder of which the family claimed to be related.

Alleyne's business career began with a short spell in the sugar industry at Barbados, but he returned to England to enter Butterley Iron Works Company, where he remained for many years. He was at first concerned with the production of rolled-iron girders for floors, especially for fireproof flooring, and deck beams for iron ships. The demand for large sections exceeded the capacity of the small mills then in use at Butterley, so Alleyne introduced the welding of T-sections to form the required H-sections.

In 1861 Alleyne patented a mechanical traverser for moving ingots in front of and behind a rolling mill, enabling one person to manipulate large pieces. In 1870 he introduced his major innovation, the two-high reversing mill, which enabled the metal to be passed back and forth between the rolls until it assumed the required size and shape. The mill had two steam engines, which supplied the motion in opposite directions. These two inventions produced considerable economies in time and effort in handling the metal and enabled much heavier pieces to be processed.

During Alleyne's regime, the Butterley Company secured some notable contracts, such as the roof of St Pancras Station, London, in 1868, with the then-unparalleled span of 240 ft (73 m). The manufacture and erection of this awe-inspiring structure was a tribute to Alleyne's abilities. In 1872 he masterminded the design and construction of the large railway bridge over the Old Maas at Dordrecht, Holland. Alleyne also devised a method of determining small quantities of phosphorus in iron and steel by means of the spectroscope. In his spare time he was a skilled astronomical observer and metalworker in his private workshop.

Bibliography
1875, 'The estimation of small quantities of phosphorus in iron and steel by spectrum analysis', *Journal of the Iron and Steel Institute*: 62.

Further Reading
Obituary, 1912, *Journal of the Iron and Steel Institute*: 406–8.

LRD

Ampère, André-Marie
b. 22 Jan 1775 Lyon, France
d. 10 June 1836 Marseille, France

French physicist and mathematician who established laws and principles relating magnetism and electricity to each other.

Ampère was reputed to have mastered all the then-known mathematics by the age of 12. He became Professor of Physics and Chemistry at Bourg in 1801 and a professor of mathematics at the Ecole Polytechnique in Paris in 1809. Observing a demonstration in 1820 of Oersted's discovery that a magnetic needle was deflected when placed near a current-carrying wire, Ampère was inspired to investigate the subject of electricity, of which he had no previous experience. Within a week he had prepared the first of several important communications on his discoveries to the Academy of Sciences in Paris. Included was a new hypothesis formed on the basis of his experiments on the relation between electricity and magnetism. He investigated the forces exerted on each other by current-carrying conductors and the properties of a solenoid. His mathematical theory describing these phenomena provided the foundations for the development of electro-dynamics and his classic work *Théorie mathématique des phénomènes électro-dynamiques* was published in 1827.

The name 'ampere' was adopted to replace the name 'weber' as a unit of current after Helmholtz proposed such a change in 1881.

Principal Honours and Distinctions
FRS 1827

Bibliography
1827, *Théorie mathématique des phénomènes électro-dynamiques*, Paris; repub. 1958, Paris (his chief published work).

Further reading
P. Lenard, 1933, *Great Men of Science*, London, pp. 223–30 (provides a short account).
C.C. Gillispie (ed.), 1970, *Dictionary of Scientific Biography*, Vol. 1, New York, pp. 139–46.
GW

Anderson, John
b. 1726 Roseneath, Dumbartonshire, Scotland
d. 13 January 1796

Scottish natural philosopher.

Born in Roseneath manse, son of the minister, he was educated after his father's death by an aunt, a Mrs Turner, to whom he later paid back the cost, and was later an officer in the corps that was raised to resist the rebellion of 1745. He studied at Glasgow, where in 1756 he became Professor of Oriental Languages and, in 1760, Professor of Natural Philosophy; he is notable for allowing artisans to attend his lectures in their working clothes. He planned the fortifications set up to defend Greenock in 1759, and was sympathetic with the French Revolution. He invented a cannon in which the recoil was counteracted by the condensation of air in the carriage. After unsuccessfully trying to interest the Government in this gun, he went to Paris in 1791 and offered it to the National Convention. While there he invented a means of smuggling French newspapers into Germany by the use of small balloons. He lost in a lawsuit with the other professors. In 1786 he published *Institutes of Physics*, which ran to five editions in ten years, and in 1800 he wrote on Roman antiquities. Upon his death he left all his library and apparatus to an educational institute, which was named after him but has now become the University of Strathclyde, Glasgow.

Bibliography
1786, *Institutes of Physics.*

Further Reading
Glasgow Mechanics' Magazine.

IMcN

Anschütz, Ottomar
b. 1846 Lissa, Prussia (now Leszno, Poland)
d. 1907

German photographer, chronophotographer and inventor.

The son of a commercial photographer, Anschütz entered the business in 1868 and developed an interest in the process of instantaneous photography. The process was very difficult with the contemporary wet-plate process, but with the introduction of the much faster dry plates in the late 1870s he was able to make progress. Anschütz designed a focal plane shutter capable of operating at speeds up to 1/1000 of a second in 1883, and patented his design in 1888. it involved a vertically moving fabric roller-blind that worked at a fixed tension but had a slit the width of which could be adjusted to alter the exposure time. This design was adopted by C.P. Goerz, who from 1890 manufactures a number of cameras that incorporated it.

Anschütz's action pictures of flying birds and animals attracted the attention of the Prussian authorities, and in 1886 the Chamber of Deputies authorized financial support for him to continue his work, which had started at the Hanover Military Institute in October 1885. Inspired by the work of Eadweard **Muybridge** in America, Anschütz had set up rows of cameras whose focal-plane shutters were released in sequence by electromagnets, taking twenty-four pictures in about three-quarters of a second. He made a large number of studies of the actions of people, animals and birds, and at the Krupp artillery range at Meppen, near Essen, he recorded shells in flight. His pictures were reproduced, and favourably commented upon, in scientific and photographic journals.

To bring the pictures to the public, in 1887 he created the Electro-Tachyscope. The sequence negatives were printed as 90 x 120 mm transparencies and fixed around the circumference of a large steel disc. This was rotated in front of a spirally wound Geissler tube, which produced a momentary brilliant flash of light when a high voltage from an induction coil was applied to it, triggered by contacts on the steel disc. The flash duration, about 1/1000 of a second, was so short that it 'froze' each picture as it passed the tube. The pictures succeeded each other at intervals of about 1/30 of a second, and the observer saw an apparently continuously lit moving picture. The Electro-Tachyscope was shown publicly in Berlin at the Kulturministerium from 19 to 21 March 1887; subsequently **Siemens** & **Halske** manufactured 100 machines, which were shown throughout Europe and America in the early 1890s. From 1891 his pictures were available for the home in the form of the Tachyscope viewer, which used the principle of the zoetrope: sequence photographs were printed on long strips of thin card, perforated with narrow slots between the pictures. Placed around the circumference of a shallow cylinder and rotated, the pictures could be seen in life-like movement when viewed through the slots.

In November 1894 Anschütz displayed a projector using two picture discs with twelve images each, which through a form of Maltese cross movement were rotated intermittently and alternately while a rotating shutter allowed each picture to blend with the next so that no flicker occurred. The first public shows, given in Berlin, were on a screen 6 x 8 m (20 x26 ft) in size. From 22 February 1895 they were shown regularly to audiences of 300 in a building on the Leipzigstrasse; they were the first projected motion pictures seen in Germany.

Further Reading
J. Deslandes, 1966, *Histoire comparée du cinéma*, Vol. I, Paris.
B. Coe, 1992, *Muybridge and the Chronophotographers*, London.

BC

Anthelm, Ludwig
fl. 1897, Germany

German who used carbon tetrachloride as a dry-cleaning agent.

Until the mid-nineteenth century, washing with soap and water was the only way to clean clothes. Around 1850 a kind of turpentine, camphene, began to be used (see J.B. **Jolly-Bellin**), but this necessitated taking the garments apart and re-sewing together after they had been cleaned. When benzene was introduced in 1866 by Pullars of Perth, Scotland, garments no longer needed to be taken apart. In 1897 Ludwig Anthelm of Leipzig started to use carbon tetrachloride (tetrachloromethane); however this was found to corrode the equipment and was dangerous to breathe, and it was replaced in Britain with trichlorethylene in 1918.

Further Reading
I. McNeil (ed.), 1990, *An Encyclopaedia of the History of Technology*, London: Routledge, p. 854 (an account of the introduction of dry-cleaning).

RLH

Anthemios of Tralles
fl. sixth century AD Tralles, Lydia, Asia Minor

Greek architect, geometer, mathematician and physicist.

Tralles was a wealthy city in ancient Greece. Ruins of the city are situated on a plateau above the present-day Turkish city of Aydin, in Asia Minor, which is near to Ephesus. In 334 BC Tralles was used as a base by Alexander the Great and later it was occupied by the Romans. After the collapse of the western half of the Roman Empire in the fifth century AD Tralles remained a part of the Byzantine Empire until its destruction in 1282.

Anthemios was one of the great sons of Tralles and was probably educated in Alexandria. He is especially famed as architect (with Isodorus of Miletos) of the great Church of Santa Sophia in Istanbul. This vast building, later a Turkish mosque and now a museum, was built for the Emperor Justinian between 532 and 537 AD. It was an early and, certainly for many centuries, the largest example of pendentive construction to support a dome. This form, using the spherical triangles of the pendentives, enabled a circular-based dome to be supported safely upon piers that stood on a square plan below. It gradually replaced the earlier squinch type of structure, though both forms of design stem from Middle Eastern origins. At Santa Sophia the dome rises to 180 ft (55 m) above floor level and has a diameter of over 100 ft (30 m). Together with Isodorus, Anthemios also worked upon the Church of the Holy Apostles in Istanbul.

Further Reading
G.L. Huxley, 1959, *Anthemius of Tralles: A Study in Later Greek Geometry*, Cambridge, Mass.: Harvard University Press.
Procopius, 1913, *De Aedificiis, On the Buildings Constructed by the Emperor Justinian*, Leipzig.
Richard Krautheimer, 1965, *Early Christian and Byzantine Architcture*, Penguin.

DY

Apollonius of Perga
b. c.240 BC Perga, Pamphylia, Greece
d. 190 BC

Greek mathematician, geometer and astronomer.

Ruins of the ancient Greek city of Perga lie near to the Turkish town of Murtana, just inland from Antalya on the southern coast of Asia Minor. Apollonius, while quite young, went to Alexandria to study under the successors to Euclid. He also worked in Ephesus and Pergamum. He later carried out original studies into the geometrical proportions of conic sections, producing his famous work *Conics* and naming the ellipse, the parabola and the hyperbola. *Conics*, which appeared soon after 200 BC, consisted of eight treatises and earned him the name 'the great geometer', given to him by his contemporaries. Seven of the eight treatises have survived, four in the original Greek and three in Arabic translation; a Latin translation was edited by Halley in 1710. Apollonius also published works on the cylindrical helix and theories of the epicycles and eccentrics, with reference to the motion of the planets.

Further Reading
G.J. Toomer, *Apollonius: Conics*, Berlin: Springer Verlag.

DY

Appert, Nicolas
b. 1749 Châlons-sur-Marne, France
d. 1841

French confectioner who invented canning as a method of food preservation.

As the son of an inn keeper, Nicolas Appert would have learned about pickling and brewing, but he chose to become a chef and confectioner, establishing himself in the rue des Lombards in Paris in 1780. He prospered there until about 1795, and in that year he began experimenting in ways to preserve foodstuffs, succeeding with soups, vegetables, juices, dairy products, jellies, jams and syrups. His method was to place food in glass jars, seal the jars with cork and sealing wax, then sterilize them by immersion in boiling water for a predetermined time.

In 1810 the French Government offered a 12,000 franc award to anyone succeeding in preserving high-quality foodstuffs for its army and navy. Appert won the award and in 1812 used the money to open the world's first food-bottling factory, La Maison Appert, in the town of Massey, near Paris. He established agents in all the major sea ports, recognizing the marine market as his most likely customer, and supplied products to Napoleon's troops in the field. By 1820 Appert's method was in use all over the United States, in spite of the simultaneous development of other containers of tin or other metals by an English merchant, Peter **Durand**, and the pro-

duction of canned food products by the Bermondsey firm of Donkin & Hall, London. The latter had opened the first canning factory in England in 1811.

Initially Appert used glass jars and bottles, but in 1822 he changed to tin-plated metal cans. To heat the cans he used an autoclave, which heated the water to a temperature higher than its boiling point. A hammer and chisel were needed to open cans until the invention of a can opener by an Englishman named Yates in 1855. Despite Appert's successes, he received little financial reward and died in poverty; he was buried in a common grave.

Bibliography
1810, *L'Art de conserver pendant plusieurs années toutes les sustenances animales et végétales* (the Société d'Encouragement pour l'Industrie Nationale produced a report in its annual bulletin in 1809).

Further Reading
English historians have tended to concentrate on Bryan Donkin, who established tin cans as the primary container for long-term food preservation.
J. Potin, 1891, *Biographie de Nicolas Appert*.
1960, *Canning and Packing* 2–5.

AP

Appleby, John F.
b. 1840 New York, USA
d. ? USA

American inventor of the knotting mechanism used on early binders and still found on modern baling machines.

As a young man John Appleby worked as a labourer for a farmer near Whitewater in Wisconsin. He was 18 when the farmer bought a new reaping machine. Appleby believed that the concept had not been progressed far enough and that the machine should be able to bind sheaths as well as to cut the corn. It is claimed that while watching a dog playing with a skipping rope he noticed a particular knot created as the dog removed its head from the loop that had passed over it, and recognized the potential of the way in which this knot had been formed. From a piece of apple wood he carved a device that would produce the knot he had seen. A local schoolteacher backed Appleby's idea with a $50 loan, but the American Civil War and service in the Union Army prevented any further development until 1869 when he took out a patent on a wire-tying binder. A number of the devices were made for him by a company in Beloit. Trials of wire binders held in 1873 highlighted the danger of small pieces of wire caught up in the hay leading to livestock losses. Appleby looked again at the possibility of twine. In 1875 he successfully operated a machine and the following season four were in operation. A number of other developments, not least Behel's 'bill hook' knotting device, were also to have an influence in the final development of Appleby's twine-tying binder. As so often happens, it was the vision of the entrepreneur which ultimately led to the success of Appleby's device. In 1877 Appleby persuaded William **Deering** to produce and market his binder, and 3,000 twine binders, together with the twine produced for them, were put on the market in 1880, with immediate success. Over the next dozen years all harvesting-machine manufacturers adopted the idea, under licence to Appleby.

Further Reading
G. Quick and W. Buchele, 1978, *The Grain Harvesters*, American Society of Agricultural Engineers (provides an account of the development of harvesting machinery and the various tying devices developed for them).
1927, 'Twine knotter history', *Wisconsin Magazine of History* (a more specific account).

AP

Applegath, Augustus
fl. 1816–58 London, England

English printer and manufacturer of printing machinery.

After **Koenig** and Bauer had introduced the machine printing-press and returned to Germany, it fell to Applegath and his mechanic brother-in-law Edward Cooper to effect improvements. In particular, Applegath succeeded Koenig and Bauer as machine specialist to *The Times* newspaper, then in the vanguard of printing technology.

Applegath and Cooper first came into prominence when the Bank of England began to seek ways of reducing the number of forged banknotes. In 1816 Cooper patented a device for printing banknotes from curved stereotypes fixed to a cylinder. These were inked and printed by the rotary method. Although Applegath and Cooper were granted money to develop their invention, the Bank did not pursue it. The idea of rotary printing was interesting, but it was not followed up, possibly due to lack of demand.

Applegath and Cooper were then engaged by John Walter of *The Times* to remedy defects in Koenig and Bauer's presses; in 1818 Cooper patented an improved method of inking the forme and Applegath also took out patents for improvements. In 1821 Applegath had enough experience of these presses to set up as a manufacturer of printing machinery in premises in Duke Street, Blackfriars, in London. Increases in the size and circulation of *The Times* led Walter to ask Applegath to build a faster press. In 1827 he produced a machine with the capacity of four presses, his steam-driven four-feeder press. Its flat form carrying the type passed under four impression cylinders in a row. It could make 4,200 impressions an hour and sufficed to print *The Times* for twenty years, until it was superseded by the rotary press devised by **Hoe**. By 1826, however, Applegath was in financial difficulties; he sold his Duke Street workshop to William Clowes, a book printer. In the following year he gave up being a full-time manufacturer of printing machinery and turned to silk printing. In 1830 he patented a machine for printing rolls of calico and silk from bent intaglio plates.

In 1848 Applegath was persuaded by *The Times* to return to newspaper printing. He tackled rotary printing without the benefit of curved printing plates and roll paper feed, and he devised a large 'type revolving' machine which set the pattern for newspaper printing-presses for some twenty years.

Further Reading
J. Moran, 1973, *Printing Presses*, London: Faber & Faber.

LRD

Appleton, Sir Edward Victor
b. 6 September 1892 Bradford, England
d. 21 April 1965 Edinburgh, Scotland

English physicist awarded the Nobel Prize for Physics for his discovery of the ionospheric layer, named after him, which is an efficient reflector of short radio waves, thereby making possible long-distance radio communication.

After early ambitions to become a professional cricketer, Appleton went to St John's College, Cambridge, where he studied under J.J. Thompson and Ernest Rutherford. His academic career interrupted by the First World War, he served as a captain in the Royal Engineers, carrying out investigations into the propagation and fading of radio signals. After the war he joined the Cavendish Laboratory, Cambridge, as a demonstrator in 1920, and in 1924 he moved to King's College, London, as Wheatstone Professor of Physics.

In the following decade he contributed to developments in valve oscillators (in particular, the 'squegging' oscillator, which formed the basis of the first hard-valve time-base) and gained international recognition for research into electromagnetic-wave propagation. His most important contribution was to confirm the existence of a conducting ionospheric layer in the upper atmosphere capable of reflecting radio waves, which had been predicted almost simultaneously by **Heaviside** and **Kennelly** in 1902. This he did by persuading the BBC in 1924 to vary the frequency of their Bournemouth transmitter, and he then measured the signal received at Cambridge. By comparing the direct and reflected rays and the daily variation he was able to deduce that the Kennelly–Heaviside (the so-called E-layer) was at a height of about 60 miles (97 km) above the earth and that there was a further layer (the Appleton or F-layer) at about 150 miles (240 km), the latter being an efficient reflector of the shorter radio waves that penetrated the lower layers. During the period 1927–32 and aided by Hartree, he established a magneto-ionic theory to explain the existence of the ionosphere. He was instrumental in obtaining agreement for international co-operation for ionospheric and other measurements in the form of the Second Polar Year (1932–3) and, much later, the International Geophysical Year (1957–8). For all this work, which made it possible to forecast the optimum frequencies for long-distance short-wave communication as a function of the location of transmitter and receiver and of the time of day and year, in 1947 he was awarded the Nobel Prize for Physics.

He returned to Cambridge as Jacksonian Professor of Natural Philosophy in 1939, and with M.F. Barnett he investigated the possible use of radio waves for radio-location of aircraft. In 1939 he became Secretary of the Government Department of Scientific and Industrial Research, a post he held for ten years. During the Second World War he contributed to the development of both radar and the atomic bomb, and subsequently served on government committees concerned with the use of atomic energy (which led to the establishment of Harwell) and with scientific staff.

Principal Honours and Distinctions
Knighted (KCB 1941, GBE 1946). Nobel Prize for Physics 1947. FRS 1927. Vice-President, American Institute of Electrical Engineers 1932. Royal Society Hughes Medal 1933. Institute of Electrical Engineers Faraday Medal 1946. Vice-Chancellor, Edinburgh University 1947. Institution of Civil Engineers Ewing Medal 1949. Royal Medallist 1950. Institute of Electrical and Electronics Engineers Medal of Honour 1962. President, British Association 1953. President, Radio Industry Council 1955–7. Légion d'honneur. LLD University of St Andrews 1947.

Bibliography
1925, joint paper with Barnett, *Nature* 115: 333 (reports Appleton's studies of the ionosphere).
1928, 'Some notes of wireless methods of investigating the electrical structure of the upper atmosphere', *Proceedings of the Physical Society* 41 (Part III): 43.
1932, *Thermionic Vacuum Tubes and Their Applications* (his work on valves).
1947, 'The investigation and forecasting of ionospheric conditions', *Journal of the Institution of Electrical Engineers* 94, Part IIIA: 186 (a review of British work on the exploration of the ionosphere).
with J.F. Herd & R.A. Watson-Watt, British patent no. 235,254 (squegging oscillator).

Further Reading
Who Was Who, 1961–70 1972, VI, London: A. & C. Black (for fuller details of honours).
R. Clark, 1971, *Sir Edward Appleton*, Pergamon (biography).
J. Jewkes, D. Sawers & R. Stillerman, 1958, *The Sources of Invention*.

KF

Archer, Frederick Scott

b. 1813 Bishops Stortford, Hertfordshire, England
d. May 1857 London, England

English photographer, inventor of the wet-collodion process, the dominant photographic process between 1851 and c.1880.

Apprenticed to a silversmith in London, Archer's interest in coin design and sculpture led to his taking up photography in 1847. Archer began experiments to improve **Talbot**'s calotype process and by 1848 he was investigating the properties of a newly discovered material, collodion, a solution of gun-cotton in ether. In 1851 Archer published details of a process using collodion on glass plates as a carrier for silver salts. The process combined the virtues of both the calotype and the daguerreotype processes, then widely practised, and soon displaced them from favour. Collodion plates were only sensitive when moist and it was therefore essential to use them immediately after they had been prepared. Popularly known as 'wet plate' photography, it became the dominant photographic process for thirty years.

Archer introduced other minor photographic innovations and in 1855 patented a collodion stripping film. He had not patented the wet-plate process, however, and made no financial gain from his photographic work. He died in poverty in 1857, a matter of some embarrassment to his contemporaries. A subscription fund was raised, to which the Government was subsequently persuaded to add an annual pension.

Bibliography
1851, *Chemist* (March) (announced Archer's process).

Further Reading
J. Werge, 1890, *The Evolution of Photography*.
H. Gernsheim and A. Gernsheim, 1969, *The History of Photography*, rev. edn, London.

JW

Archimedes of Syracuse

b. 287 BC
d. 212 BC

Greek engineer who made the first measurement of specific gravity.

He studied in Alexandria, after which he returned to Syracuse where he spent most of the rest of his life. He made many mathematical discoveries, including the most accurate calculation of *pi* made up to that time. In engineering he was the founder of the science of hydrostatics. He is well known for the discovery of 'Archimedes' Law', that a body wholly or partly immersed in a fluid loses weight equal to the weight of the fluid displaced. He thus made the first measurement of specific gravity.

Archimedes also proved the law of the lever and developed the theory of mechanical advantage, boasting to his cousin Hieron, 'Give me a place to stand on and with a lever I will move the whole world.' To prove his point, he launched one of the biggest ships built up to that date. During his time in Egypt, he devised the 'Archimedean Screw', still used today in Middle Eastern countries for pumping water. He also built an astronomical instrument to demonstrate the movements of the heavenly bodies, a form of orrery.

He was General of Ordnance to Heiron, and when the Romans besieged Syracuse, a legionary came across Archimedes drawing geometrical diagrams in the sand. Archimedes immediately told him to 'Keep off' and the soldier killed him. He also experimented with burning glasses and mirrors for setting fire to wooden ships.

Further Reading
L. Sprague de Camp, 1963, *Ancient Engineers*, Souvenir Press.
E.J. Dijksterhuis, 1956, *Archimedes*, Copenhagen: Munksgaard.

IMcN

Arezzo, Guido d'
See **Guido d'Arezzo**.

Argand, François-Pierre Amis
b. 5 July 1750 Geneva, Switzerland
d. October 1803 London, England

Swiss inventor of the Argand lamp.

Son of a clockmaker, he studied physics and chemistry under H.-D. de Saussure (1740–99). In 1775 he moved to Paris, where he taught chemistry and presented a paper on electrical phenomena to the Académie Royale des Sciences. He assisted the **Montgolfier** brothers in their Paris balloon ascents.

From 1780 Argand spent some time in Montpellier, where he conceived the idea of the lamp that was to make him famous. It was an oil lamp with gravity oil feed, in which the flame was enlarged by burning it in a current of air induced by two concentric iron tubes. It produced ten times the illumination of the simple oil lamp. From the autumn of 1783 to summer 1785, Argand travelled to London and Birmingham to promote the manufacture and sale of his lamp. Upon his return to Paris, he found that his design had been plagiarized; with others, Argand sought to establish his priority, and Paul Abeille published a tract, *Découverte des lampes à courant d'air et à cylindre* (1785). As a result, the Académie granted Argand a licence to manufacture the lamp. However, during the Revolution, Argand's factories were destroyed and his licence annulled. He withdrew to Versoix, near Geneva. In 1793, the English persuaded him to take refuge in England and tried, apparently without success, to obtain recompense for his losses.

Argand is also remembered for his work on distillation and on the water distributor or hydraulic ram, which was conceived with Joseph Montgolfier in 1797 and recognized by the grant of a patent in the same year.

Further Reading

M. Schroder, 1969, *The Argand Burner: Its Origin and Development in France and England, 1781–1800*, Odense University Press.

LRD

Arkwright, Sir Richard

b. 23 December 1732 Preston, England
d. 3 August 1792 Cromford, England

English inventor of a machine for spinning cotton.

Arkwright was the youngest of thirteen children and was apprenticed to a barber; when he was about 18, he followed this trade in Bolton. In 1755 he married Patients Holt, who bore him a son before she died, and he remarried in 1761, to Margaret Biggins. He prospered until he took a public house as well as his barber shop and began to lose money. After this failure, he travelled around buying women's hair for wigs.

In the late 1760s he began spinning experiments at Preston. It is not clear how much Arkwright copied earlier inventions or was helped by Thomas **Highs** and John **Kay** but in 1768 he left Preston for Nottingham, where, with John **Smalley** and David **Thornley** as partners, he took out his first patent. They set up a mill worked by a horse where machine-spun yarn was produced successfully. The essential part of this process lay in drawing out the cotton by rollers before it was twisted by a flyer and wound onto the bobbin. The partners' resources were not sufficient for developing their patent so Arkwright found new partners in Samuel **Need** and Jedediah **Strutt**, hosiers of Nottingham and Derby. Much experiment was necessary before they produced satisfactory yarn, and in 1771 a water-driven mill was built at Cromford, where the spinning process was perfected (hence the name 'waterframe was given to his spinning machine); some of this first yarn was used in the hosiery trade. Sales of all-cotton cloth were initially limited because of the high tax on calicoes, but the tax was lowered in 1774 by Act of Parliament, marking the beginning of the phenomenal growth of the cotton industry. In the evidence for this Act, Arkwright claimed that he had spent £12,000 on his machine. Once Arkwright had solved the problem of mechanical spinning, a bottleneck in the preliminary stages would have formed but for another patent taken out in 1775. This covered all preparatory processing, including some ideas not invented by Arkwright, with the result that it was disputed in 1783 and finally annulled in 1785. It contained the 'crank and comb' for removing the cotton web off carding engines which was developed at Cromford and solved the difficulty in carding. By this patent, Arkwright had mechanized all the preparatory and spinning processes, and he began to establish water-powered cotton mills even as far away as Scotland. His success encouraged many others to copy him, so he had great difficulty in enforcing his patent.

Need died in 1781 and the partnership with Strutt ended soon after. Arkwright became very rich and financed other spinning ventures beyond his immediate control, such as that with Samuel Oldknow. It was estimated that 30,000 people were employed in 1785 in establishments using Arkwright's patents. In 1786 he received a knighthood for delivering an address of thanks when an attempt to assassinate George III failed, and the following year he became High Sheriff of Derbyshire. He purchased the manor of Cromford, where he died in 1792.

Principal Honours and Distinctions
Knighted 1786.

Bibliography
1769, British patent no. 931.
1775, British patent no. 1,111.

Further Reading
R.S. Fitton, 1989, *The Arkwrights, Spinners of Fortune*, Manchester (a thorough scholarly work which is likely to remain unchallenged for many years).
R.L. Hills, 1973, *Richard Arkwright and Cotton Spinning*, London (written for use in schools and concentrates on Arkwright's technical achievements).
R.S. Fitton and A.P. Wadsworth, 1958, *The Strutts and the Arkwrights*, Manchester (concentrates on the work of Arkwright and Strutt).
A.P. Wadsworth and J. de L. Mann, 1931, *The Cotton Trade and Industrial Lancashire*, Manchester (covers the period leading up to the Industrial Revolution).
F. Nasmith, 1932, 'Richard Arkwright', *Transactions of the Newcomen Society* 13 (looks at the actual spinning invention).
R.L. Hills, 1970, *Power in the Industrial Revolution*, Manchester (discusses the technical problems of Arkwright's invention).

RLH

Armstrong, Edwin Howard

b. 18 December 1890 New York City, New York, USA
d. 31 January 1954 New York City, New York, USA

American engineer who invented the regenerative and superheterodyne amplifiers and frequency modulation, all major contributions to radio communication and broadcasting.

Interested from childhood in anything mechanical, as a teenager Armstrong constructed a variety of wireless equipment in the attic of his parents' home, including spark-gap transmitters and receivers with iron-filing 'coherer' detectors capable of producing weak Morse-code signals. In 1912, while still a student of engineering at Columbia University, he applied positive, i.e. regenerative, feedback to a Lee **De Forest** triode amplifier to just below the point of oscillation and obtained a gain of some 1,000 times, giving a receiver sensitivity very much greater than hitherto possible. Furthermore, by allowing the circuit to go into full oscillation he found he could generate stable continuous-waves, making possible the first reliable CW radio transmitter. Sadly, his claim to priority with this invention, for which he filed US patents in 1913, the year he graduated from Columbia, led to many years of litigation with De Forest, to whom the US Supreme Court finally, but unjustly, awarded the patent in 1934. The engineering world clearly did not agree with this decision, for the Institution of Radio Engineers did not revoke its previous award of a gold medal and he subsequently received the highest US scientific award, the Franklin Medal, for this discovery.

During the First World War, after some time as an instructor at Columbia University, he joined the US Signal Corps laboratories in Paris, where in 1918 he invented the superheterodyne, a major contribution to radio-receiver design and for which he filed a patent in 1920. The principle of this circuit, which underlies virtually all modern radio, TV and radar reception, is that by using a local oscillator to convert, or 'heterodyne', a wanted signal to a lower, fixed, 'intermediate' frequency it is possible to obtain high amplification and selectivity without the need to 'track' the tuning of numerous variable circuits.

Returning to Columbia after the war and eventually becoming Professor of Electrical Engineering, he made a fortune from the sale of his patent rights and used part of his wealth to fund his own research into further problems in radio communication, particularly that of receiver noise. In 1933 he filed four patents covering the use of wide-band frequency modulation (FM) to achieve low-noise, high-fidelity sound broadcasting, but unable to interest RCA he eventually built a complete broadcast transmitter at his own expense in 1939 to prove the advantages of his system. Unfortunately, there followed another long battle to protect and exploit his patents, and exhausted and virtually ruined he took his own life in 1954, just as the use of FM became an established technique.

Principal Honours and Distinctions
Institution of Radio Engineers Medal of Honour

1917. Franklin Medal 1937. IERE Edison Medal 1942. American Medal for Merit 1947.

Bibliography

1922, 'Some recent developments in regenerative circuits', *Proceedings of the Institute of Radio Engineers* 10: 244.
1924, 'The superheterodyne. Its origin, developments and some recent improvements', *Proceedings of the Institute of Radio Engineers* 12: 549.
1936, 'A method of reducing disturbances in radio signalling by a system of frequency modulation', *Proceedings of the Institute of Radio Engineers* 24: 689.

Further Reading

L. Lessing, 1956, *Man of High-Fidelity: Edwin Howard Armstrong*, pbk 1969 (the only definitive biography).
W.R. Maclaurin and R.J. Harman, 1949, *Invention & Innovation in the Radio Industry*.
J.R. Whitehead, 1950, *Super-regenerative Receivers*.
A.N. Goldsmith, 1948, *Frequency Modulation* (for the background to the development of frequency modulation, in the form of a large collection of papers and an extensive bibliography).

KF

Armstrong, Sir William George, Baron Armstrong of Cragside

b. 26 November 1810 Shieldfield, Newcastle upon Tyne, England
d. 27 December 1900 Cragside, Northumbria, England

English inventor, engineer and entrepreneur in hydraulic engineering, shipbuilding and the production of artillery.

The only son of a corn merchant, Alderman William Armstrong, he was educated at private schools in Newcastle and at Bishop Auckland Grammar School. He then became an articled clerk in the office of Armorer Donkin, a solicitor and a friend of his father. During a fishing trip he saw a water-wheel driven by an open stream to work a marble-cutting machine. He felt that its efficiency would be improved by introducing the water to the wheel in a pipe. He developed an interest in hydraulics and in electricity, and be-

came a popular lecturer on these subjects. From 1838 he became friendly with Henry Watson of the High Bridge Works, Newcastle, and for six years he visited the Works almost daily, studying turret clocks, telescopes, papermaking machinery, surveying instruments and other equipment being produced. There he had built his first hydraulic machine, which generated 5 hp when run off the Newcastle town water-mains. He then designed and made a working model of a hydraulic crane, but it created little interest. In 1845, after he had served this rather unconventional apprenticeship at High Bridge Works, he was appointed Secretary of the newly formed Whittle Dene Water Company. The same year he proposed to the town council of Newcastle the conversion of one of the quayside cranes to his hydraulic operation which, if successful, should also be applied to a further four cranes. This was done by the Newcastle Cranage Company at High Bridge Works. In 1847 he gave up law and formed W.G. Armstrong & Co. to manufacture hydraulic machinery in a works at Elswick. Orders for cranes, hoists, dock gates and bridges were obtained from mines, docks and railways.

Early in the Crimean War, the War Office asked him to design and make submarine mines to blow up ships that were sunk by the Russians to block the entrance to Sevastopol harbour. The mines were never used, but this set him thinking about military affairs and brought him many useful contacts at the War Office. Learning that two eighteen-pounder British guns had silenced a whole Russian battery but were too heavy to move over rough ground, he carried out a thorough investigation and proposed light field guns with rifled barrels to fire elongated lead projectiles rather than cast-iron balls. He delivered his first gun in 1855; it was built of a steel core and wound-iron wire jacket. The barrel was multigrooved and the gun weighed a quarter of a ton and could fire a 3 lb (1.4 kg) projectile. This was considered too light and was sent back to the factory to be rebored to take a 5 lb (2.3 kg) shot. The gun was a complete success and Armstrong was then asked to design and produce an equally successful eighteen-pounder. In 1859 he was appointed Engineer of Rifled Ordnance and was knighted. However, there was considerable opposition from the notably conservative officers of the Army who resented the intrusion of this civilian engineer in their affairs. In 1862, contracts with the Elswick Ordnance Company were terminated, and the Government rejected breechloading and went back to muzzle-loading. Armstrong resigned and concentrated on foreign sales, which were successful worldwide.

The search for a suitable proving ground for a 12-ton gun led to an interest in shipbuilding at Elswick from 1868. This necessitated the replacement of an earlier stone bridge with the hydraulically operated Tyne Swing Bridge, which weighed some 1450 tons and allowed a clear passage for shipping. Hydraulic equipment on warships became more complex and increasing quantities of it were made at the Elswick works, which also flourished with the reintroduction of the breech-loader in 1878. In 1884 an openhearth acid steelworks was added to the Elswick facilities. In 1897 the firm merged with Sir Joseph Whitworth & Co. to become Sir W.G. Armstrong Whitworth & Co. After Armstrong's death a further merger with Vickers Ltd formed Vickers Armstrong Ltd.

In 1879 Armstrong took a great interest in Joseph **Swan**'s invention of the incandescent electric light-bulb. He was one of those who formed the Swan Electric Light Company, opening a factory at South Benwell to make the bulbs. At Cragside, his mansion at Rothbury, he installed a water turbine and generator, making it one of the first houses in England to be lit by electricity.

Armstrong was a noted philanthropist, building houses for his workforce, and endowing schools, hospitals and parks. His last act of charity was to purchase Bamburgh Castle, Northumbria, in 1894, intending to turn it into a hospital or a convalescent home, but he did not live long enough to complete the work.

Principal Honours and Distinctions
Knighted 1859. FRS 1846. President, Institution of Mechanical Engineers; Institution of Civil Engineers; British Association for the Advancement of Science 1863. Baron Armstrong of Cragside 1887.

Further Reading
E.R. Jones, 1886, *Heroes of Industry*, London: Low.
D.J. Scott, 1962, *A History of Vickers*, London: Weidenfeld & Nicolson.

IMcN

Arnold, Aza

b. 4 October 1788 Smithfield, Pawtucket, Rhode Island, USA
d. 1865 Washington, DC, USA

American textile machinist who applied the differential motion to roving frames, solving the problem of winding on the delicate cotton rovings.

He was the son of Benjamin and Isabel Arnold, but his mother died when he was 2 years old and after his father's second marriage he was largely left to look after himself. After attending the village school he learnt the trade of a carpenter, and following this he became a machinist. He entered the employment of Samuel **Slater**, but left after a few years to engage in the unsuccessful manufacture of woollen blankets. He became involved in an engineering shop, where he devised a machine for taking wool off a carding machine and making it into endless slivers or rovings for spinning. He then became associated with a cotton-spinning mill, which led to his most important invention.

The carded cotton sliver had to be reduced in thickness before it could be spun on the final machines such as the mule or the waterframe. The roving, as the mass of cotton fibres was called at this stage, was thin and very delicate because it could not be twisted to give strength, as this would not allow it to be drawn out again during the next stage. In order to wind the roving on to bobbins, the speed of the bobbin had to be just right but the diameter of the bobbin increased as it was filled. Obtaining the correct reduction in speed as the circumference increased was partially solved by the use of double-coned pulleys, but the driving belt was liable to slip owing to the power that had to be transmitted.

The final solution to the problem came with the introduction of the differential drive with bevel gears or a sun-and-planet motion. Arnold had invented this compound motion in 1818 but did not think of applying it to the roving frame until 1820. It combined the direct-gearing drive from the main shaft of the machine with that from the cone-drum drive so that the latter only provided the difference between flyer and bobbin speeds, which meant that most of the transmission power was taken away from the belt. The patent for this invention was issued to Arnold on 23 January 1823 and was soon copied in Britain by Henry **Houldsworth**, although J. Green of Mansfield may have originated it independently in the same year. Arnold's patent was widely infringed in America and he sued the Proprietors of the Locks and Canals, machine makers for the Lowell manufacturers, for $30,000, eventually receiving $3,500 compensation. Arnold had his own machine shop but he gave it up in 1838 and moved the Philadelphia, where he operated the Mulhausen Print Works. Around 1850 he went to Washington, DC, and became a patent attorney, remaining as such until his death. On 24 June 1856 he was granted patent for a self-setting and self-raking saw for sawing machines.

Bibliography
28 June 1856, US patent no. 15,163 (self-setting and self-raking saw for sawing machines).

Further Reading
Dictionary of American Biography, Vol. 1.
W. English, 1969, *The Textile Industry*, London (a description of the principles of the differential gear applied to the roving frame).
D.J. Jeremy, 1981, *Transatlantic Industrial Revolution. The Diffusion of Textile Technologies Between Britain and America, 1790–1830*, Oxford (a discussion of the introduction and spread of Arnold's gear).

RLH

Arnold, John
b. 1735/6 Bodmin (?), Cornwall, England
d. 25 August 1799 Eltham, London, England

English clock, watch, and chronometer maker who invented the isochronous helical balance spring and an improved form of detached detent escapement.

John Arnold was apprenticed to his father, a watchmaker, and then worked as an itinerant journeyman in the Low Countries and, later, in England. He settled in London in 1762 and rapidly established his reputation at Court by presenting George III with a miniature repeating watch mounted in a ring. He later abandoned the security of the Court for a more precarious living developing his chronometers, with some financial assistance from the Board of Longitude. Symbolically, in 1771 he moved from the vicinity of the Court at St James's to John Adam Street, which was close to the premises of the Royal So-

ciety for the Encouragement of Arts, Manufactures & Commerce.

By the time Arnold became interested in chronometry, **Harrison** had already demonstrated that longitude could be determined by means of a timekeeper, and the need was for a simpler instrument that could be sold at an affordable price for universal use at sea. **Le Roy** had shown that it was possible to dispense with a remontoire by using a detached escapement with an isochronous balance; Arnold was obviously thinking along the same lines, although he may not have been aware of Le Roy's work. By 1772 Arnold had developed his detached escapement, a pivoted detent which was quite different from that used on the European continent, and three years later he took out a patent for a compensation balance and a helical balance spring (Arnold used the spring in torsion and not in tension as Harrison had done). His compensation balance was similar in principle to that described by Le Roy and used riveted bimetallic strips to alter the radius of gyration of the balance by moving small weights radially. Although the helical balance spring was not completely isochronous it was a great improvement on the spiral spring, and in a later patent (1782) he showed how it could be made more truly isochronous by shaping the ends. In this form it was used universally in marine chronometers.

Although Arnold's chronometers performed well, their long-term stability was less satisfactory because of the deterioration of the oil on the pivot of the detent. In his patent of 1782 he eliminated this defect by replacing the pivot with a spring, producing the spring detent escapement. This was also done independently at about the same time by Berthoud and Earnshaw, although Earnshaw claimed vehemently that Arnold had plagiarized his work. Ironically it was Earnshaw's design that was finally adopted, although he had merely replaced Arnold's pivoted detent with a spring, while Arnold had completely redesigned the escapement. Earnshaw also improved the compensation balance by fusing the steel to the brass to form the bimetallic element, and it was in this form that it began to be used universally for chronometers and high-grade watches.

As a result of the efforts of Arnold and Earnshaw, the marine chronometer emerged in what was essentially its final form by the end of the eighteenth century. The standardization of the design in England enabled it to be produced economically; whereas Larcum Kendall was paid £500 to copy Harrison's fourth timekeeper, Arnold was able to sell his chronometers for less than one-fifth of that amount. This combination of price and quality led to Britain's domination of the chronometer market during the nineteenth century.

Bibliography
30 December 1775, 'Timekeepers', British patent no. 1,113.
2 May 1782, 'A new escapement, and also a balance to compensate the effects arising from heat and cold in pocket chronometers, and for incurving the ends of the helical spring . . .', British patent no. 1,382.

Further Reading
R.T. Gould, 1923, *The Marine Chronometer: Its History and Development*, London; reprinted 1960, Holland Press (provides an overview).
V. Mercer, 1972, *John Arnold & Son Chronometer Makers 1726–1843*, London.

See also **Phillips, Edouard**.

DV

Arsonval, Jacques Arsène d'
b. 8 June 1851 Borie, France
d. 31 December 1940 Borie, France

French physician and physicist noted for his invention of the reflecting galvanometer and for contributions to electrotherapy.

After studies at colleges in Limoges and later in Paris, Arsonval became a doctor of medicine in 1877. In 1882 the Collège de France established a laboratory of biophysics with Arsonval as Director, and he was Professor from 1894.

His most outstanding scientific contributions were in the field of biological applications of electricity. His interest in muscle currents led to a series of inventions to assist in research, including the moving-coil galvanometer. In 1881 he made a significant improvement to the galvanometer by reversing the magnetic elements. It had been usual to suspend a compass needle in the centre of a large, stationary coil, but Arsonval's invention was to suspend a small, light coil between the poles of a powerful fixed magnet. This simple arrangement was independent of the earth's magnetic field and insensitive to vibration. A great increase in sensitivity was achieved by attaching a mirror to the coil in order to reflect a spot of light. For bacterial-research purposes he designed the first constant-temperature incubator controlled by electricity. His experiments on the effects of high-frequency, low-voltage alternating currents on animals led to the first high-frequency heat-therapy unit being established in 1892, and later to methods of physiotherapy becoming a professional discipline.

Principal Honours and Distinctions
Académie des Sciences, Prix Montyon 1882. Chevalier de la Légion d'honneur 1884. Grand Cross 1931.

Bibliography
1882, *Comptes rendus de l'Académie des Sciences* 94: 1347–50 (describes the galvanometer).
1903, *Traité de physique biologique*, 2 vols, Paris (an account of his technological work).

Further Reading
C.C. Gillispie (ed.), 1970, *Dictionary of Scientific Biography*, Vol. 1, New York, pp. 302–5.
D.O. Woodbury, 1949, *A Measure for Greatness*, New York.

GW

Arup, Sir Ove
b. 16 April 1895 Newcastle upon Tyne, England
d. 5 February 1988 Highgate, London, England

English consultant engineer.

Of Scandinavian parentage, Arup attended school in Germany and Denmark before taking his degree in mathematics and philosophy at Copenhagen University in 1914. He then graduated as a civil engineer from the Royal Technical College in the same city, specializing in the theory of structures.

Arup retained close ties with Europe for some time, working in Hamburg as a designer for the Danish civil engineering firm of Christiani & Nielsen. Then, in the 1930s, he began what was to be a long career in England as an engineering consultant to a number of architects who were beginning to build with modern materials (particularly concrete) and methods of construction. He became consultant to the famous firm of Tecton (under the direction of Berthold **Lubetkin**) and was closely associated with the leading projects of that firm at the time, notably the High-point flats at Highgate, the Finsbury Health Centre and the award-winning Penguin Pool at the Regent's Park Zoological Gardens, all in London.

In 1945 Arup founded his own firm, Ove Arup & Partners, working entirely as a consultant to architects, particularly on structural schemes, and in 1963 he set up a partnership of architects and engineers, Arup Associates. The many and varied projects with which he was concerned included Coventry Cathedral and the University of Sussex with Sir Basil Spence, the Sydney Opera House with Joern Utzon and St Catherine's College, Oxford, with Arne Jacobsen.

Principal Honours and Distinctions
CBE 1953. Commander of the Order of Danneborg, awarded by King Frederik of Denmark, 1975. Honorary Doctorate Tekniske Hojskole, Lyngby, Denmark 1954. Honorary DSc Durham University 1967, University of East Anglia 1968, Heriot-Watt University 1976. RIBA Gold Medal 1966. Institution of Structural Engineers Gold Medal 1973. Fellow of the American Concrete Institution 1975.

Further Reading
J.M. Richards, 1953, *An Introduction to Modern Architecture*, London: Penguin.
H. Russell-Hitchcock, 1982, *Architecture, Nineteenth and Twentieth Centuries*, London: Pelican.
C. Jencks, 1980, *Late-Modern Architecture*, London: Academy Editions.

DY

Ashley, Howard Matravers
b. 1841
d. 1914 England

English inventor of the semi-automatic bottle-making machine.

Ashley, manager of an iron foundry at Ferry-bridge, Yorkshire, began trying to construct a bottle-making machine in the 1880s. In 1886 he obtained a patent for a two-stage machine. This proved to be impracticable, but improvements were described in further patents in 1887 and 1889, leading to a three-stage process, embodying the basic elements of a machine to make narrow-necked glass bottles. The Ashley (Machine-Made) Bottle Company was set up to exploit the invention, but had failed by 1894 due to poor management, although it had claimed to make bottles in a tenth of the time taken to make them by hand. Ashley had shown the way, however, and his machines were still producing good bottles in 1918. The process was a stage along the way to complete mechanization brought about by M.J. **Owens**'s machine.

Bibliography
Ashley took out nine British patents during 1886–90, including:
2 July 1886, British patent no. 8,677 (two-stage bottle-making machine).

Further Reading
R.E. Moody, 1985, 'A century of mechanical bottle making', *Glass Technology* 26 (2): 109 ff.

LRD

Aspdin, Joseph
b. 1778 Leeds, England
d. 20 March 1855 Wakefield (?), England

English pioneer in the development of the cement industry.

Joseph Aspdin was the eldest of the six children of Thomas Aspdin, a bricklayer. He became interested in making advanced cements for rendering brickwork and, on 21 October 1824, patented a calcined mixture of limestone, clay and water that he called Portland Cement because he thought it resembled Portland Stone in colour.

Aspdin established his first cement works at Kirkgate in Wakefield in 1825: this was demolished in 1838 due to railway development, and a new works was established in the town in 1843. A year later Joseph Aspdin retired and handed the business over to his elder son James. Meanwhile, William, a younger son of Joseph, had also entered the business of manufacturing cement. Born in Leeds on 23 September 1815, he joined his father's firm at the age of 14, but left in 1841 to set up his own firm at Rotherhithe,

London. There he manufactured an improved cement that was better and stronger than **Parker's** Roman Cement, probably because it contained a higher proportion of clinkered material. Further improvements were made during the following years and new factories were established, first at Northfleet in Kent and later at Gateshead on the south bank of the River Tyne (1853). It is interesting that Sir Marc **Brunel** later preferred to use William Aspdin's cement in the Thames railway tunnel construction because of its greater strength (see **Frost**). William Aspdin died at Itzehoe in Germany in 1864.

Further Reading
A.J. Francis, 1977, *The Cement Industry 1796–1914: A History*, David & Charles.

DY

Aspinall, Sir John Audley Frederick
b. 25 August 1851 Liverpool, England
d. 19 January 1937 Woking, England

English mechanical engineer, pioneer of the automatic vacuum brake for railway trains and of railway electrification.

Aspinall's father was a QC, Recorder of Liverpool, and Aspinall himself became a pupil at Crewe Works of the London & North Western Railway, eventually under F.W. **Webb**. In 1875 he was appointed Manager of the works at Inchicore, Great Southern & Western Railway, Ireland. While he was there, some of the trains were equipped, on trial, with continuous brakes of the non-automatic vacuum type. Aspinall modified these to make them automatic, i.e. if the train divided, brakes throughout both parts would be applied automatically. Aspinall vacuum brakes were subsequently adopted by the important Great Northern, Lancashire & Yorkshire, and London & North Western Railways.

In 1883, aged only 32, Aspinall was appointed Locomotive Superintendent of the Great Southern & Western Railway, but in 1886 he moved in the same capacity to the Lancashire & Yorkshire Railway, where his first task was to fit out the new works at Horwich. The first locomotive was completed there in 1889, to his design. In 1899 he introduced a 4–4–2, the largest express locomotive in Britain at the time, some of which were fitted with smokebox superheaters to Aspinall's design.

Unusually for an engineer, in 1892 Aspinall was appointed General Manager of the Lancashire & Yorkshire Railway. He electrified the Liverpool–Southport line in 1904 at 600 volts DC with a third rail; this was an early example of main-line electrification, for it extended beyond the Liverpool suburban area. He also experimented with 3,500 volt DC overhead electrification of the Bury–Holcombe Brook branch in 1913, but converted this to 1,200 volts DC third rail to conform with the Manchester–Bury line when this was electrified in 1915. In 1918 he was made a director of the Lancashire & Yorkshire Railway.

Principal Honours and Distinctions
Knighted 1917. President, Institution of Mechanical Engineers 1909. President, Institution of Civil Engineers 1918.

Further Reading
H.A.V. Bulleid, 1967, *The Aspinall Era*, Shepperton: Ian Allan (provides a good account of Aspinall and his life's work).
C. Hamilton Ellis, 1958, *Twenty Locomotive Men*, Shepperton: Ian Allan , Ch. 19 (a good brief account).

See also **Gresley, Sir Herbert Nigel**; **Schmidt, Wilhelm**; **Westinghouse, George**.

PJGR

Atwood, George
b. 1746 England
d. July 1807 London, England

English mathematician, author of a theory on ship stability.

Atwood was educated at Westminster School and entered Trinity College, Cambridge, in 1765 with a scholarship. He graduated with high honours (third wrangler) in 1796, and went on to become a fellow and tutor of his college. In 1776 he was elected Fellow of the Royal Society. Eight years later, William Pitt the Younger (1759–1806) appointed him a senior officer of the Customs, this being a means of reimbursing him for the arduous and continuing task of calculating the national revenue. As a lecturer he was greatly renowned and his abilities as a calculator and as a musician were of a high order.

In the late 1790s Atwood presented a paper to

the Royal Society that showed a means of obtaining the righting lever on a ship inclined from the vertical; this was a major step forward in the study of ship stability. Among his other inventions was a machine to exhibit the accelerative force of gravity.

Principal Honours and Distinctions
FRS 1776.

Further Reading
A.M. Robb, 1952, *Theory of Naval Architecture*, London: Charles Griffin (for a succinct description of the various factors in ship stability, and the importance of Atwood's contribution).

FMW

Aubert, Jean
b. 7 February 1894 Paris, France
25 November 1984 Paris, France

French civil engineer.

Aubert was educated at the Lycée Louis-le-Grand in Paris, and entered the Ecole Polytechnique in 1913. His studies were interrupted by the First World War, when he served as an artillery officer, being wounded twice and awarded the Croix de Guerre in 1916. He returned to the Ecole Polytechnique in 1919, and from 1920 to 1922 he attended the Ecole Nationale des Ponts et Chaussées; he graduated as Bachelor of Law from the University of Paris.

In 1922 he began his long career, devoted principally to river and canal works. He was engineer in charge of the navigation works in Paris until 1932; he was then appointed Professor in the Chair of Internal Navigation at the Ecole des Ponts et Chaussées, a post he held until his retirement in 1961. From 1933 to 1945 he was general manager and later chairman of the Compagnie Nationale du Rhône; from 1945 to 1953, chairman of the electricity board of the Société Nationale des Chemins de Fer français; and from 1949 to 1967, chairman of the Rhine Navigation Company. Following his retirement, he was chairman of the Société des Constructions des Batignolles, and from 1966 consulting engineer and honorary chairman of SPIE Batignolles; he was also chairman of several other companies.

In 1919 he published *La Probabilité dans les tires de guerre*, for which he was awarded the

Pierson-Perrim prize by the Académie des Sciences in 1922. During his career he wrote numerous articles and papers on technical and economic subjects, his last, entitled 'Philosophie de la pente d'eau', appearing in the journal *Travaux* in 1984 when he was ninety years old.

Aubert's principal works included the construction of the Pont Edouard-Herriort on the Rhône at Lyon; the design and construction of the Génissiat and Lonzères-Mondragon dams on the Rhône; and the conception and design of the Denouval dam on the Seine near Andresy, completed in 1980. He was awarded the Caméré prize in 1934 by the Académie des Sciences for a new type of movable dam. Overseas governments and the United Nations consulted him on river navigation *inter alia* in Brazil, on the Mahanadi river in India, on the Konkomé river in Guinea, on the Vistula river in Poland, on the Paraguay river in South America and others.

In 1961 he published his revolutionary ideas on the *pente d'eau*, or 'water slope', which was designed to eliminate delays and loss of water in transferring barges from one level to another, without the use of locks. This design consisted of a sloping flume or channel through which a wedge of water, in which the barge was floating, was pushed by a powered unit. A prototype at Montech on the Canal Latéral at La Garonne, bypassing five locks, was opened in 1973. A second was opened in 1984 on the Canal du Midi at Fonserannes, near Béziers.

Principal Honours and Distinctions
Croix de Guerre 1916. Académie des Sciences: Prix Pierson-Perrim 1922, Prix Caméré 1934. Ingénieur Général des Ponts et Chaussées 1951. Commandeur de la Légion d'honneur 1960.

Further Reading
David Tew, 1984, *Canal Inclines and Lifts*, Gloucester: Alan Sutton.

JHB

Auenbrugger, Leopold Elder von
b. 19 November 1722 Graz, Austria
d. 18 May 1809 Vienna, Austria

Austrian physician and the first to describe percussion as an aid to diagnosis of diseases of the chest.

The son of an innkeeper, Auenbrugger had

originally learned to use percussion to ascertain the level of wine in casks. When later he became Physician to the Military Hospital of Vienna, he developed the technique, stating in the monograph that he published on the subject, 'I here present the reader with a new sign which I have discovered for detecting disease of the chest. It consists in percussion of the human thorax whereby . . . an opinion is formed of the internal state of that cavity'. The monograph attracted little attention until some twenty years later. Jean Corvisart, personal physician to Napoleon, translated it into French in 1808, giving full credit to its original author. Auenbrugger also had some musical expertise, and with Salieri composed an opera for Maria Theresa.

Principal Honours and Distinctions
Ennobled 1784.

Bibliography
1761, *Inventum novum ex percussione thoracis humani ut signo abstrusos interni pectoris morbos detegendi*, Vienna.

Further Reading
J. Forbes (trans.), 1936, 'On percussion of the chest; a translation of Auenbrugger's original treatise, *Bulletin of the History of Medicine*.
Z. Cope, 1957, *Sidelights on the History of Medicine*, London.

MG

Austin, Herbert, Baron Austin

b. 8 November 1866 Little Missenden, Buckinghamshire, England
d. 23 May 1941 Lickey Grange, near Bromsgrove, Herefordshire, England

English manufacturer of cars.

The son of Stephen (or Steven) Austin, a farmer of Wentworth, Yorkshire, he was educated at Rotherham Grammar School and then went to Australia with an uncle in 1884. There he became apprenticed as an engineer at the Langlands Foundry in Melbourne. He moved to the Wolseley Sheep Shearing Company, and soon after became its Manager; in 1893 he returned to England, where he became Production Manager to the English branch of the same company in Birmingham. The difficulties of travel in Australia gave him an idea of the advantages of motor-driven vehicles, and in 1895 he produced the first Wolseley car. In 1901 he was appointed to the Wolseley board, and from 1911 he was Chairman.

His first car was a three-wheeler. An improved model was soon available, and in 1901 the Wolseley company took over the machine tool and motor side of Vickers Sons and Maxim and traded under the name of the Wolseley Tool and Motor Car Company. Herbert Austin was the General Manager. In 1905 he decided to start his own company and formed the Austin Motor Company Ltd, with works at Longbridge, near Birmingham. With a workforce of 270, the firm produced 120 cars in 1906; by 1914 a staff of 2,000 were producing 1,000 cars a year. The First World War saw production facilities turned over to the production of aeroplanes, guns and ammunition.

Peacetime brought a return to car manufacture, and 1922 saw the introduction of the 7 hp 'Baby Austin', a car for the masses. Many other models followed. By 1937 the original Longbridge factory had grown to 220 acres, and the staff had increased to over 16,000, while the number of cars produced had grown to 78,000 per year.

Herbert Austin was a philanthropist who endowed many hospitals and not a few universities; he was created a Baron in 1936.

Principal Honours and Distinctions
Baron 1936.

Further Reading
1941, *Austin Magazine* (June).

IMcN

Austin, John

fl. 1789 Scotland

Scottish contributor to the early development of the power loom.

On 6 April 1789 John Austin wrote to James **Watt**, seeking advice about patenting 'a weaving loom I have invented to go by the hand, horse, water or any other constant power, to comb, brush, or dress the yarn at the same time as it is weaving & by which one man will do the work of three and make superior work to what can be done by the common loom' (Boulton & Watt Collection, Birmingham, James Watt Papers,

JW/22). Watt replied that 'there is a Clergyman by the name of Cartwright at Doncaster who has a patent for a similar contrivance' (Boulton & Watt Collection, Birmingham, Letter Book 1, 15 April 1789). Watt pointed out that there was a large manufactory running at Doncaster and something of the same kind at Manchester with working power looms. Presumably, this reply deterred Austin from taking out a patent. However, some members of the Glasgow Chamber of Commerce continued developing the loom, and in 1798 one that was tried at the spinning mill of J. Monteith, of Pollokshaws, near Glasgow, answered the purpose so well that a building was erected and thirty of the looms were installed. Later, in 1800, this number was increased to 200, all of which were driven by a steam engine, and it was stated that one weaver and a boy could tend from three to five of these looms.

Austin's loom was worked by eccentrics, or cams. There was one cam on each side with 'a sudden beak or projection' that drove the levers connected to the picking pegs, while other cams worked the heddles and drove the reed. The loom was also fitted with a weft stop motion and could produce more cloth than a hand loom, and worked at about sixty picks per minute. The pivoting of the slay at the bottom allowed the loom to be much more compact than previous ones.

Further Reading
A. Rees, 1819, *The Cyclopaedia: or Universal Dictionary of Arts, Sciences and Literature*, London.
R. Guest, 1823, *A Compendius History of the Cotton Manufacture*, Manchester.
A.P. Usher, 1958, *A History of Mechanical Inventions*.
W. English, 1969, *The Textile Industry*, London.
R.L. Hills, 1970, *Power in the Industrial Revolution*, Manchester.

See also **Cartwright, Revd Edmund.**

RLH

Ayre, Sir Amos Lowrey

b. 23 July 1885 South Shields, England
d. 13 January 1952 London, England

English shipbuilder and pioneer of the inter-war 'economy' freighters; Chairman of the Shipbuilding Conference.

Amos Ayre grew up on the Tyne with the stimulus of shipbuilding and seafaring around him. After an apprenticeship as a ship draughtsman and distinction in his studies, he held responsible posts in the shipyards of Belfast and later Dublin. His first dramatic move came in 1909 when he accepted the post of Manager of the new Employment Exchange at Govan, then just outside Glasgow. During the First World War he was in charge of fleet coaling operations on the River Forth, and later was promoted Admiralty District Director for shipyard labour in Scotland.

Before the conclusion of hostilities, with his brother Wilfrid (later Sir Wilfrid Ayre) he founded the Burntisland Shipbuilding Company in Fife. Setting up on a green field site allowed the brothers to show innovation in design, production and marketing. Such was their success that the new yard was busy throughout the Depression, building standard ships which incorporated low operating costs with simplicity of construction.

Through public service culminating in the 1929 Safety of Life at Sea Conference, Amos Ayre became recognized not only as an eminent naval architect, but also as a skilled negotiator. In 1936 he was invited to become Chairman of the Shipbuilding Conference and thereby virtual leader of the industry. As war approached he planned with meticulous care the rearrangement of national shipbuilding capacity, enabling Britain to produce standard hulls ranging from the legendary TID tugs to the standard freighters built in Sunderland or Port Glasgow. In 1939 he became Director of Merchant Shipbuilding, a position he held until 1944, when with typical foresight he asked to be released to plan for shipbuilding's return to normality.

Principal Honours and Distinctions
Knighted 1937. KBE 1943. Officer of the Order of Orange-Nassau.

Bibliography
1919, 'The theory and design of British shipbuilding', *The Syren and Shipping*, London.

Further Reading
Wilfrid Ayre, 1968, *A Shipbuilders Yesterdays*, Fife (published privately).
James Reid, 1964, *James Lithgow, Master of Work*, London.
Maurice E. Denny, 1955, 'The man and his work' (First Amos Ayre Lecture), *Transactions of the Institution of Naval Architects* vol. 97.

FMW

Ayrton, William Edward

b. 14 September 1847 London, England
d. 8 November 1908 London, England

English physicist, inventor and pioneer in technical education.

After graduating from University College, London, Ayrton became for a short time a pupil of Sir William **Thomson** in Glasgow. For five years he was employed in the Indian Telegraph Service, eventually as Superintendent, where he assisted in revolutionizing the system, devising methods of fault detection and elimination. In 1873 he was invited by the Japanese Government to assist as Professor of Physics and Telegraphy in founding the Imperial College of Engineering in Tokyo. There he created a teaching laboratory that served as a model for those he was later to organize in England and which were copied elsewhere. It was in Tokyo that his joint researches with Professor John **Perry** began, an association that continued after their return to England. In 1879 he became Professor of Technical Physics at the City and Guilds Institute in Finsbury, London, and later was appointed Professor of Physics at the Central Institution in South Kensington.

The inventions of Ayrton and Perry included an electric tricycle in 1882, the first practicable portable ammeter and other electrical measuring instruments. By 1890, when the research partnership ended, they had published nearly seventy papers in their joint names, the emphasis being on a mathematical treatment of subjects including electric motor design, construction of electrical measuring instruments, thermodynamics and the economical use of electric conductors. Ayrton was then employed as a consulting engineer by government departments and acted as an expert witness in many important patent cases.

Principal Honours and Distinctions
FRS 1881. President, Physical Society 1890–2. President, Institution of Electrical Engineers 1892. Royal Society Royal Medal 1901.

Bibliography
28 April 1883, British patent no. 2,156 (Ayrton and Perry's ammeter and voltmeter).
1887, *Practical Electricity*, London (based on his early laboratory courses; 7 edns followed during his lifetime).
1892, 'Electrotechnics', *Journal of the Institution of Electrical Engineers* 21, 5–36 (for a survey of technical education).

Further Reading
D.W. Jordan, 1985, 'The cry for useless knowledge: education for a new Victorian technology', *Proceedings of the Institution of Electrical Engineers*, 132 (Part A): 587–601.
G. Gooday, 1991, *History of Technology*, 13: 73–111 (for an account of Ayrton and the teaching laboratory).

GW

B

Babbage, Charles

b. 26 December 1791 Walworth, Surrey, England
d. 18 October 1871 London, England

English mathematician who invented the forerunner of the modern computer.

Charles Babbage was the son of a banker, Benjamin Babbage, and was a sickly child who had a rather haphazard education at private schools near Exeter and later at Enfield. Even as a child, he was inordinately fond of algebra, which he taught himself. He was conversant with several advanced mathematical texts, so by the time he entered Trinity College, Cambridge, in 1811, he was ahead of his tutors. In his third year he moved to Peterhouse, whence he graduated in 1814, taking his MA in 1817. He first contributed to the *Philosophical Transactions of the Royal Society* in 1815, and was elected a fellow of that body in 1816. He was one of the founders of the Astronomical Society in 1820 and served in high office in it.

While he was still at Cambridge, in 1812, he had the first idea of calculating numerical tables by machinery. This was his first difference engine, which worked on the principle of repeatedly adding a common difference. He built a small model of an engine working on this principle between 1820 and 1822, and in July of the latter year he read an enthusiastically received note about it to the Astronomical Society. The following year he was awarded the Society's first gold medal. He submitted details of his invention to Sir Humphry **Davy**, President of the Royal Society; the Society reported favourably and the Government became interested, and following a meeting with the Chancellor of the Exchequer Babbage was awarded a grant of £1,500. Work proceeded and was carried on for four years under the direction of Joseph **Clement**.

In 1827 Babbage went abroad for a year on medical advice. There he studied foreign workshops and factories, and in 1832 he published his observations in *On the Economy of Machinery and Manufactures*. While abroad, he received the news that he had been appointed Lucasian Professor of Mathematics at Cambridge University. He held the Chair until 1839, although he neither resided in College nor gave any lectures. For this he was paid between £80 and £90 a year!

Differences arose between Babbage and Clement. Manufacture was moved from Clement's works in Lambeth, London, to new, fireproof buildings specially erected by the Government near Babbage's house in Dorset Square, London. Clement made a large claim for compensation and, when it was refused, withdrew his workers as well as all the special tools he had made up for the job. No work was possible for the next fifteen months, during which Babbage conceived the idea of his 'analytical engine'. He approached the Government with this, but it was not until eight years later, in 1842, that he received the reply that the expense was considered too great for further backing and that the Government was abandoning the project. This was in spite of the demonstration and perfectly satisfactory operation of a small section of the analytical engine at the International Exhibition of 1862. It is said that the demands made on manufacture in the production of his engines had an appreciable influence in improving the standard of machine tools, whilst similar benefits accrued from his development of a system of notation for the movements of machine elements. His opposition to street organ-grinders was a notable eccentricity; he estimated that a quarter of his mental effort was wasted by the effect of noise on his concentration.

Principal Honours and Distinctions
FRS 1816. Astronomical Society Gold Medal 1823.

Bibliography
Babbage wrote eighty works, including:
1864, *Passages from the Life of a Philosopher*.
1832, *On the Economy of Manufacture and Machinery*.
July 1822, Letter to Sir Humphry Davy, PRS, on the Application of Machinery to the purpose

of calculating and printing Mathematical Tables.

Further Reading
1961, *Charles Babbage and His Calculating Engines: Selected Writings by Charles Babbage and Others*, eds Philip and Emily Morrison, New York: Dover Publications.

IMcN

Bachelier, Nicolas

b. 1485
d. prior to December 1557 Toulouse, France

French surveyor, architect and mason.

Between 1515 and 1522 Francis I of France became ruler of part of Italy, including Milan. He discussed with Leonardo da Vinci the possibility of providing canals in France similar to those constructed or under construction in Italy. One idea was to provide a link between the Garonne at Toulouse and the Aude at Carcassonne. In 1539 Bachelier and his colleague Arnaud Casanove, who described themselves as 'expert levellers', proposed a survey of the Toulouse to Carcassonne route and also suggested that barges could either float down the Garonne to Bordeaux or could travel along a canal dug parallel to the river. Francis I authorized them to do the work and approved the plans, which comprised a lock-free canal of variable depth, when they had completed them. However, their plans were hopelessly inaccurate, and nothing was done. In 1598 Henri IV re-examined the plans, but it was left to Pierre Paul **Riquet** in 1662 to reassess the concept of a Biscay-to-Mediterranean waterway.

Further Reading
H. Graillet, 1914, *Nicolas Bachelier, imagier et maçon de Toulouse.*
B. Lavigne, 1879, *Etude biographique sur Nicolas Bachelier.*

JHB

Bacon, Francis Thomas

b. 21 December 1904 Billericay, England
d. 24 May 1992 Little Shelford, Cambridge, England

English mechanical engineer, a pioneer in the modern phase of fuel-cell development.

After receiving his education at Eton and Trinity College, Cambridge, Bacon served with C.A. **Parsons** at Newcastle upon Tyne from 1925 to 1940. From 1946 to 1956 he carried out research on Hydrox fuel cells at Cambridge University and was a consultant on fuel-cell design to a number of organizations throughout the rest of his life.

Sir William **Grove** was the first to observe that when oxygen and hydrogen were supplied to platinum electrodes immersed in sulphuric acid a current was produced in an external circuit, but he did not envisage this as a practical source of electrical energy. In the 1930s Bacon started work to develop a hydrogen–oxygen fuel cell that operated at moderate temperatures and pressures using an alkaline electrolyte. In 1940 he was appointed to a post at King's College, London, and there, with the support of the Admiralty, he started full-time experimental work on fuel cells. His brief was to produce a power source for the propulsion of submarines. The following year he was posted as a temporary experimental officer to the Anti-Submarine Experimental Establishment at Fairlie, Ayrshire, and he remained there until the end of the Second World War.

In 1946 he joined the Department of Chemical Engineering at Cambridge, receiving a small amount of money from the Electrical Research Association. Backing came six years later from the National Research and Development Corporation (NRDC), the development of the fuel cell being transferred to Marshalls of Cambridge, where Bacon was appointed Consultant.

By 1959, after almost twenty years of individual effort, he was able to demonstrate a 6 kW (8 hp) power unit capable of driving a small truck. Bacon appreciated that when substantial power was required over long periods the hydrogen–oxygen fuel cell associated with high-pressure gas storage would be more compact than conventional secondary batteries.

The development of the fuel-cell system pioneered by Bacon was stimulated by a particular need for a compact, lightweight source of power in the United States space programme. Electrochemical generators using hydrogen–oxygen cells were chosen to provide the main supplies on the Apollo spacecraft for landing on the surface of the moon in 1969. An added advantage of the cells was that they simultaneously provided water. NRDC was largely responsible for the formation of Energy Conversion Ltd, a company that was set up to exploit Bacon's patents and to manufacture fuel cells, and which was supported by British Ropes Ltd, British Petroleum and Guest, Keen & Nettlefold Ltd at Basingstoke. Bacon was their full-time consultant. In 1971 Energy Conversion's operation was moved to the UK Atomic Energy Research Establishment at Harwell, as Fuel Cells Ltd. Bacon remained with them until he retired in 1973.

Principal Honours and Distinctions
OBE 1967. FRS 1972. Royal Society S.G. Brown Medal 1965. Royal Aeronautical Society British Silver Medal 1969.

Bibliography
27 February 1952, British patent no. 667,298 (hydrogen–oxygen fuel cell).
1963, contribution in W. Mitchell (ed.), *Fuel Cells*, New York, pp. 130–92.
1965, contribution in B.S. Baker (ed.), *Hydrocarbon Fuel Cell Technology*, New York, pp. 1–7.

Further Reading
Obituary, 1992, *Daily Telegraph* (8 June).
A. McDougal, 1976, *Fuel Cells*, London (makes an acknowledgement of Bacon's contribution to the design and application of fuel cells).
D.P. Gregory, 1972, *Fuel Cells*, London (a concise introduction to fuel-cell technology).

GW

Baekeland, Leo Hendrik
b. 14 November 1863 Saint-Martens-Latern, Belgium
d. 23 February 1944 Beacon, New York, USA

Belgian/American inventor of the Velox photographic process and the synthetic plastic Bakelite.

The son of an illiterate shoemaker, Baekeland was first apprenticed in that trade, but was encouraged by his mother to study, with spectacular results. He won a scholarship to Gand University and graduated in chemistry. Before he was 21 he had achieved his doctorate, and soon afterwards he obtained professorships at Bruges and then at Gand. Baekeland seemed set for a distinguished academic career, but he turned towards the industrial applications of chemistry, es-

pecially in photography.

Baekeland travelled to New York to further this interest, but his first inventions met with little success so he decided to concentrate on one that seemed to have distinct commercial possibilities. This was a photographic paper that could be developed in artificial light; he called this 'gas light' paper Velox, using the less sensitive silver chloride as a light-sensitive agent. It proved to have good properties and was easy to use, at a time of photography's rising popularity. By 1896 the process began to be profitable, and three years later Baekeland disposed of his plant to Eastman Kodak for a handsome sum, said to be $3–4 million. That enabled him to retire from business and set up a laboratory at Yonkers to pursue his own research, including on synthetic resins. Several chemists had earlier obtained resinous products from the reaction between phenol and formaldehyde but had ignored them. By 1907 Baekeland had achieved sufficient control over the reaction to obtain a good thermosetting resin which he called 'Bakelite'. It showed good electrical insulation and resistance to chemicals, and was unchanged by heat. It could be moulded while plastic and would then set hard on heating, with its only drawback being its brittleness. Bakelite was an immediate success in the electrical industry and Baekeland set up the General Bakelite Company in 1910 to manufacture and market the product. The firm grew steadily, becoming the Bakelite Corporation in 1924, with Baekeland still as active President.

Principal Honours and Distinctions
President, Electrochemical Society 1909. President, American Chemical Society 1924. Elected to the National Academy of Sciences 1936.

Further Reading
J. Gillis, 1965, *Leo Baekeland*, Brussels.
A.R. Matthis, 1948, *Leo H. Baekeland, Professeur, Docteur ès Sciences, chimiste, inventeur et grand industriel*, Brussels.
J.K. Mumford, 1924, *The Story of Bakelite*.
C.F. Kettering, 1947, memoir on Baekeland, *Biographical Memoirs of the National Academy of Sciences* 24 (includes a list of his honours and publications).

LRD

Bailey, Sir Donald Coleman

b. 15 September 1901 Rotherham, Yorkshire, England
d. 5 May 1985 Bournemouth, Dorset, England

English engineer, designer of the Bailey bridge.

Bailey was educated at the Leys School, Cambridge, before going to Sheffield University where he studied for a degree in engineering. He joined the Civil Service in 1928 and was posted to the staff of the Experimental Bridging Establishment of the Ministry of Supply at Christchurch, Hampshire. There he continued his boyhood hobby of making model bridges of wood and string. He evolved a design for a prefabricated metal bridge assembled from welded panels linked by pinned joints; this became known as the Bailey bridge. Its design was accepted by the War Office in 1941 and from then on it was used throughout the subsequent conflict of the Second World War. It was a great improvement on its predecessor, the Inglis bridge, designed by a Cambridge University professor of engineering, Charles Inglis, with tubular members that were 10 or 12 ft (3.66 m) long; this bridge was notoriously difficult to construct, particularly in adverse weather conditions, whereas the Bailey bridge's panels and joints were far more manageable and easy to assemble. The simple and standardized component parts of the Bailey bridge made it highly adaptable: it could be strengthened by increasing the number of truss girders, and wide rivers could be crossed by a series of Bailey bridges connected by pontoons. Field Marshal Montgomery is recorded as saying that 'without the Bailey bridge we should not have won the war'.

Principal Honours and Distinctions
Knighted 1946.

Further Reading
Obituary, 1985, *The Guardian* 6 May.

IMcN

Bain, Alexander

b. October 1810 Watten, Scotland
d. 2 January 1877 Kirkintilloch, Scotland

Scottish inventor and entrepreneur who laid the foundations of electrical horology and designed an electromagnetic means of transmitting images (facsimile).

Alexander Bain was born into a crofting family in a remote part of Scotland. He was apprenticed to a watchmaker in Wick and during that time he was strongly influenced by a lecture on 'Heat, sound and electricity' that he heard in nearby Thurso. This lecture induced him to take up a position in Clerkenwell in London, working as a journeyman clockmaker, where he was able to further his knowledge of electricity by attending lectures at the Adelaide Gallery and the Polytechnic Institution. His thoughts naturally turned to the application of electricity to clockmaking, and despite a bitter dispute with Charles **Wheatstone** over priority he was granted the first British patent for an electric clock. This patent, taken out on 11 January 1841, described a mechanism for an electric clock, in which an oscillating component of the clock operated a mechanical switch that initiated an electromagnetic pulse to maintain the regular, periodic motion. This principle was used in his master clock, produced in 1845. On 12 December of the same year, he patented a means of using electricity to control the operation of steam railway engines via a steam-valve. His earliest patent was particularly far-sighted and anticipated most of the developments in electrical horology that occurred during the nineteenth century. He proposed the use of electricity not only to drive clocks but also to distribute time over a distance by correcting the hands of mechanical clocks, synchronizing pendulums and using slave dials (here he was anticipated by Steinheil). However, he was less successful in putting these ideas into practice, and his electric clocks proved to be unreliable. Early electric clocks had two weaknesses: the battery; and the switching mechanism that fed the current to the electromagnets. Bain's earth battery, patented in 1843, overcame the first defect by providing a reasonably constant current to drive his clocks, but unlike **Hipp** he failed to produce a reliable switch.

The application of Bain's numerous patents for electric telegraphy was more successful, and he derived most of his income from these. They included a patent of 12 December 1843 for a form of fax machine, a chemical telegraph that could be used for the transmission of text and of images (facsimile). At the receiver, signals were passed through a moving band of paper impregnated with a solution of ammonium nitrate and potassium ferrocyanide. For text, **Morse** code signals were used, and because the system could respond to signals faster than those generated by hand, perforated paper tape was used to transmit the messages; in a trial between Paris and Lille, 282 words were transmitted in less than one minute. In 1865 the Abbé Caselli, a French engineer, introduced a commercial fax service between Paris and Lyons, based on Bain's device. Bain also used the idea of perforated tape to operate musical wind instruments automatically. Bain squandered a great deal of money on litigation, initially with Wheatstone and then with Morse in the USA. Although his inventions were acknowledged, Bain appears to have received no honours, but when towards the end of his life he fell upon hard times, influential persons in 1873 secured for him a Civil List Pension of £80 per annum and the Royal Society gave him £150.

Bibliography
1841, British patent no. 8,783; 1843, British patent no. 9,745; 1845, British patent no. 10,838; 1847, British patent no. 11,584; 1852, British patent no. 14,146 (all for electric clocks).
1852, *A Short History of the Electric Clocks with Explanation of Their Principles and Mechanism and Instruction for Their Management and Regulation*, London; reprinted 1973, introd. W. Hackmann, London: Turner & Devereux (as the title implies, this pamphlet was probably intended for the purchasers of his clocks).

Further Reading
The best account of Bain's life and work is in papers by C.A. Aked in *Antiquarian Horology*: 'Electricity, magnetism and clocks' (1971) 7: 398–415; 'Alexander Bain, the father of electrical horology' (1974) 9: 51–63; 'An early electric turret clock' (1975) 7: 428–42. These papers were reprinted together (1976) in *A Conspectus of Electrical Timekeeping*, Monograph No. 12, Antiquarian Horological Society: Tilehurst.
J. Finlaison, 1834, *An Account of Some Remarkable Applications of the Electric Fluid to the Useful Arts by Alexander Bain*, London (a contemporary account between Wheatstone and Bain over the invention of the electric clock).
J. Munro, 1891, *Heroes of the Telegraph*, Religious Tract Society.
J. Malster & M.J. Bowden, 1976, 'Facsimile. A Review', *Radio & Electronic Engineer* 46: 55.
D.J. Weaver, 1982, *Electrical Clocks and Watches*, Newnes.
T. Hunkin, 1993, 'Just give me the fax', *New Scientist* (13 February): 33–7 (provides details of Bain's and later fax devices).

See also **Bakewell, Frederick C.**

DV/KF

Baird, John Logie

b. 13 August 1888 Helensburgh, Dumbarton, Scotland
d. 14 June 1946 Bexhill-on-Sea, Sussex, England

Scottish inventor of mechanically-based television.

Baird attended Larchfield Academy, then the Royal Technical College and Glasgow University. However, before he could complete his electrical-engineering degree, the First World War began, although poor health kept him out of the armed services.

Employed as an engineer at the Clyde Valley Electrical Company, he lost his position when his diamond-making experiment caused a power failure in Glasgow. He then went to London, where he lived with his sister and tried manufacturing household products of his own design. To recover from poor health, he then went to Hastings and, using scrap materials, began experiments with imaging systems. In 1924 he transmitted outline images over wires, and by 1925 he was able to transmit recognizable human faces. In 1926 he was able to transmit moving images at a resolution of thirty lines per image and a frequency of ten images per second over an infrared link. Also that year, he started the world's first television station, which he named 2TV. In 1927 he transmitted moving images from London to Glasgow, and later that year to a passenger liner. In 1928 he demonstrated colour television.

In 1936, when the BBC wanted to begin television service, Baird's system lost out in a competition with Marconi Electric and Musical Industries (EMI). In 1946 Baird reported that he had successfully completed research on a stereo television system.

Further Reading
R. Tiltman, 1933, *Baird of Television*, London: Seeley Service; repub. 1974, New York: Arno Press.
J. Rowland, 1967, *The Television Man: The Story of John Logie Baird*, New York: Roy Publishers.
F. Macgregor, 1984, *Famous Scots*, Gordon Wright (contains a short biography on Baird).
HO

Bakewell, Frederick C.
fl. 1850s

British inventor of the 'copying telegraph', the basis of facsimile transmission.

Although little appears to be known about his life, Bakewell deserves a place in this dictionary for a single invention that was to have a significant impact upon communication. The invention of photography early in the nineteenth century soon led to a desire to transmit images over a distance. Although telegraphy was still very much in its infancy, Bakewell realized that the key to a viable system of facsimile, as it came to be known, was to dissect the image to be transmitted sequentially by scanning it in a series of parallel lines with some sort of sensor and to synchronously reconstruct it at the receiving end – a process that anticipated the way in which modern television works. To this end the line image was drawn with varnish on a sheet of tin foil, which was then wrapped around a cylinder. As the cylinder was rotated, presumably by some kind of regulated clockwork mechanism similar to that used later in the early phonographs of **Edison**, an electrical contact driven by a screw thread caused the image to be scanned along a spiral path, giving a series of on–off signals. At the receiving end, instead of the tin foil, a sheet of paper wetted with a suitable chemical was darkened by the current pulses as they arrived.

A practicable system did not become possible until a dry form of receiving-paper that was insensitive to light became available in the 1930s; once established, however, the technique remained the basis of commercial machines into the 1980s.

Bibliography
1853, *Electric Science*.
1857, *A Manual of Electricity*.

Further Reading
J. Malster & M.J. Bowden, 1976, 'Facsimile. A Review', *Radio & Electronic Engineer* 46: 55.

See also **Bain, Alexander**.

KF

Bakewell, Robert
b. 23 May 1725 Loughborough, England
d. 1 October 1795 Loughborough, England

English livestock breeder who pioneered the practice of progeny testing for selecting breeding stock; he is particularly associated with the development of the Improved Leicester breed of sheep.

Robert Bakewell was the son of the tenant farming the 500-acre (200 hectare) Dishley Grange Farm, near Loughborough, where he was born. The family was sufficiently wealthy to allow Robert to travel, which he began to do at an early age, exploring the farming methods of the West Country, Norfolk, Ireland and Holland. On taking over the farm he continued the development of the irrigation scheme begun by his father. Arthur **Young** visited the farm during his tour of east England in 1771. At that time it consisted of 440 acres (178 hectares), 110 acres (45 hectares) of which were arable, and carried a stock of 60 horses, 400 sheep and 150 other assorted beasts. Of the arable land, 30 acres (12 hectares) were under root crops, mainly turnips.

Bakewell was not the first to pioneer selective breeding, but he was the first successfully to apply selection to both the efficiency with which an animal utilized its food, and its physical appearance. He always had a clear idea of the animal he wanted, travelled extensively to collect a range of animals possessing the characteristics he sought, and then bred from these towards his goal. He was aware of the dangers of inbreeding, but would often use it to gain the qualities he wanted. His early experiments were with Longhorn cattle, which he developed as a meat rather than a draught animal, but his most famous achievement was the development of the Improved Leicester breed of sheep. He set out to produce an animal that would put on the most meat in the least time and with the least feeding. As his base he chose the Old Leicester, but there is still doubt as to which other breeds he may have introduced to produce the desired results.

The Improved Leicester was smaller than its ancestor, with poorer wool quality but with greatly improved meat-production capacity.

Bakewell let out his sires to other farms and was therefore able to study their development under differing conditions. However, he made stringent rules for those who hired these animals, requiring the exclusive use of his rams on the farms concerned and requiring particular dietary conditions to be met. To achieve this control he established the Dishley Society in 1783. Although his policies led to accusations of closed access to his stock, they enabled him to keep a close control of all offspring. He thereby pioneered the process now recognized as 'progeny testing'.

Bakewell's fame and that of his farm spread throughout the country and overseas. He engaged in an extensive correspondence and acted as host to all of influence in British and overseas agriculture, but it would appear that he was an over-generous host, since he is known to have been in financial difficulties in about 1789. He was saved from bankruptcy by a public subscription raised to allow him to continue with his breeding experiments; this experience may well have been the reason why he was such a staunch advocate of State funding of agricultural research.

Further Reading

William Houseman, 1894, biography, *Journal of the Royal Agricultural Society*: 1–31.

H.C. Parsons, 1957, *Robert Bakewell* (contains a more detailed account).

R. Trow Smith, 1957, *A History of British Livestock Husbandry to 1700*, London: Routledge & Kegan Paul.

—— *A History of British Livestock Husbandry 1700 to 1900* (places Bakewell within the context of overall developments).

M.L. Ryder, 1983, *Sheep and Man*, Duckworth (a scientifically detailed account which deals with Bakewell within the context of its particular subject).

AP

Baldwin, Matthias William

b. 10 November 1795 Elizabethtown, New Jersey, USA
d. 7 September 1866 Philadelphia, Pennsylvania, USA

American builder of steam locomotives, founder of Baldwin Locomotive Works.

After apprenticeship as a jeweller, Baldwin set up a machinery manufacturing business, and built stationary steam engines and, in 1832, his first locomotive, *Old Ironsides*, for the then-new Philadelphia, Germantown & Norristown Railroad. *Old Ironsides* achieved only 1 mph (1.6 km/h) on trial, but after experimentation reached 28 mph (45 km/h). Over the next ten years Baldwin built many stationary engines and ten more locomotives, and subsequently built locomotives exclusively.

He steadily introduced detail improvements in locomotive design; standardized components by means of templates and gauges from 1838 onwards; introduced the cylinder cast integrally with half of the smokebox saddle in 1858; and in 1862 imported steel tyres, which had first been manufactured in Germany by **Krupp** of Essen in 1851, and began the practice in the USA of shrinking them on to locomotive wheels. At the time of Matthias Baldwin's death, the Baldwin Locomotive Works had built some 1,500 locomotives: it went on to become the largest locomotive building firm to develop from a single foundation, and by the time it built its last steam locomotive, in 1955, had produced about 75,000 in total.

Further Reading

J.H. White Jr, 1979, *A History of the American Locomotive – Its Development 1830–1880*, New York: Dover Publications Inc.

J. Marshall, 1978, *A Biographical Dictionary of Railway Engineers*, Newton Abbot: David & Charles.

Dictionary of American Biography.

PJGR

Banu Musa ibn Shakir

fl. *c*.850

Arab astronomers and engineers.

The Banu were the three sons of Musa ibn Shakir. His origins were unpromising, for he was a robber, but the caliph al-Ma'mun, a great patron of science and learning, took the sons into his academy and had them educated. The eldest and most prominent, Muhammed, took up the study of geometry, logic and astronomy, while another, al-Hasan, also studied geometry. The third, Ahmad, turned to mechanics. Together, the Banu established a group for the translation of texts from antiquity, especially Greece, on science and mechanics. They were responsible for compiling the *Kitab al-Hiyal* (*Book of Ingenious Devices*), the first of two major works on mechanics that appeared in the medieval Islamic world. The authors drew freely from earlier Greek writers, particularly **Hero** and Philon. The work is a technical manual for making devices such as lamps, pipes in spring wells and drinking vessels, most depending on differences in air pressure generated by the movement of liquids. These principles were applied to make a self-filling oil lamp. The work also demonstrated the lifting of heavy weights by means of pulleys. In another work, the *Qarastun* (*Book of the Balance*), the Banu showed how different weights could be balanced by varying the distance from the fulcrum.

Further Reading
Dictionary of Scientific Biography.

LRD

Barber, John
baptized 22 October 1734 Greasley, Nottinghamshire, England
d. 6 November 1801 Attleborough, Nuneaton, England

English inventor of the gas turbine and jet propulsion.

He was the son of Francis Barber, coalmaster of Greasley, and Elizabeth Fletcher. In his will of 1765, his uncle, John Fletcher, left the bulk of his property, including collieries and Stainsby House, Horsley Woodhouse, Derbyshire, to John Barber. Another uncle, Robert, bequeathed him property in the next village, Smalley. It is clear that at this time John Barber was a man of considerable means. On a tablet erected by John in 1767, he acknowledges his debt to his uncle John in the words 'in remembrance of the man who trained him up from a youth'. At this time John Barber was living at Stainsby House and had already been granted his first patent, in 1766. The contents of this patent, which included a reversible water turbine, and his subsequent patents, suggest that he was very familiar with mining equipment, including the **Newcomen** engine. It comes as rather a surprise that

*c.*1784 he became bankrupt and had to leave Stainsby House, evidently moving to Attleborough. In a strange twist, a descendent of Mr Sitwell, the new owner, bought the prototype Akroyd **Stuart** oil engine from the Doncaster Show in 1891.

The second and fifth (final) patents, in 1773 and 1792, were concerned with smelting and the third, in 1776, featured a boiler-mounted impulse steam turbine. The fourth and most important patent, in 1791, describes and engine that could be applied to the 'grinding of corn, flints, etc.', 'rolling, slitting, forging or battering iron and other metals', 'turning of mills for spinning', 'turning up coals and other minerals from mines', and 'stamping of ores, raising water'. Further, and importantly, the directing of the fluid stream into smelting furnaces or at the stern of ships to propel them is mentioned. The engine described comprised two retorts for heating coal or oil to produce an inflammable gas, one to operate while the other was cleansed and recharged. The resultant gas, together with the right amount of air, passed to a beam-operated pump and a water-cooled combustion chamber, and then to a water-cooled nozzle to an impulse gas turbine, which drove the pumps and provided the output. A clear description of the thermodynamic sequence known as the Joule Cycle (Brayton in the USA) is thus given. Further, the method of gas production predates **Murdoch**'s lighting of the Soho foundry by gas.

It seems unlikely that John Barber was able to get his engine to work; indeed, it was well over a hundred years before a continuous combustion chamber was achieved. However, the details of the specification, for example the use of cooling water jackets and injection, suggest that considerable experimentation had taken place.

To be active in the taking out of patents over a period of 26 years is remarkable; that the best came after bankruptcy is more so. There is nothing to suggest that the cost of his experiments was the cause of his financial troubles.

Further Reading
A.K. Bruce, 1944, 'John Barber and the gas turbine', *Engineer* 29 December: 506–8; 8 March (1946): 216, 217.
C. Lyle Cummins, 1976, *Internal Fire*, Carnot Press.

JB

Barclay, Robert

b. *c.*1833
d. November 1876

English inventor of the offset method in printing.

Barclay, a member of the celebrated banking family, ran a printing business in the City of London in partnership with John Doyle Fry, of the (also famous) chocolate-making family. In 1875 Barclay took out two patents, the first bearing Fry's name as well, for printing on to tinplate by way of the offset principle. He recognized that transferring or 'offsetting' the print on to an impression cylinder of a yielding material would give the best results. The cylinder would be covered with glazed or varnished cardboard, rather than the rubber that was later to be used.

Barclay disposed of his patents to Bryant and May, the match manufacturers, for printing decorative metal matchbox covers. It was recognized that the method had applications in other industries, and eventually the principle was applied in the currently most widely used method of printing, offset lithography.

Further Reading
Journal of Printing History 8 (1972): 60; 9 (1973): 4 (brief details of Barclay's life).

LRD

Bardeen, John

b. 23 May 1908 Madison, Wisconsin, USA
d. 30 January 1991 Boston, Massachusetts, USA

American physicist, the first to win the Nobel Prize for Physics twice.

Born the son of a professor of anatomy, he studied electrical engineering at the University of Wisconsin. He then worked for three years as a geophysicist at the Gulf Research Laboratories before taking a PhD in mathematical physics at Princeton, where he was a graduate student. For some time he held appointments at the University of Minnesota and at Harvard, and during the Second World War he joined the US Naval Ordnance Laboratory. In 1945 he joined the Bell Telephone Laboratories to head a new department to work on solid-state devices. While there, he and W.H. **Brattain** in 1948 published a paper that introduced the transistor. For this he, Brattain and **Shockley** won the Nobel Prize for Phys-

ics in 1956. In 1951 he moved to the University of Illinois as Professor of Physics and Electrical Engineering. There he worked on superconductivity, a phenomenon described in 1911 by Kamerling-Onnes. Bardeen worked with L.N. Cooper and J.A. Schrieffer, and in 1972 they were awarded the Nobel Prize for Physics for the 'BCS Theory', which suggested that, under certain circumstances at very low temperatures, electrons can form bound pairs.

Principal Honours and Distinctions
Nobel Prize for Physics (jointly with Brattain and Shockley) 1956, (jointly with Cooper and Schrieffer) 1972.

Further Reading
A. Isaacs and E. Martin (eds), 1985, *Longmans Dictionary of 20th Century Biography.*

IMcN

Barlow, Edward

baptized 15 December 1636 near Warrington, Cheshire, England
d. 1716

English priest and mechanician who invented rack striking, repeating mechanisms for clocks and watches and, with others, patented a horizontal escapement for watches.

Barlow was the son of Edward Booth, but he adopted the surname of his godfather, the Benedictine monk Ambrose Barlow, as a condition of his will. In 1659 he entered the English College at Lisbon, and after being ordained a priest he was sent to the English mission. There he resided at Parkhall in Lancashire, the seat of Mr Houghton, with whom he later collaborated on the horizontal escapement.

At a time when it was difficult to produce a light to examine the dial of a clock or watch at night, a mechanism that would indicate the hours and subdivisions of the hour audibly and at will was highly desirable. The count wheel, which had been used from the earliest times to control the striking of a clock, was unsuitable for this purpose as it struck the hours in sequence. If the mechanism was set off manually to determine the time, the strike would no longer correspond with the indications on the dial. In 1675 Barlow invented rack striking, where the hour struck was determined solely by the position of the hour hand. With this mechanism it was therefore possible to repeat the hour at will, without upsetting the sequence of striking. In 1687 Barlow tried to patent a method of repeating for watches, but it was rejected by James II in favour of a system produced by the watchmaker Daniel Quare and which was simpler to operate. He was successful in obtaining a patent for a horizontal escapement for watches in 1695, in collaboration with William Houghton and Thomas **Tompion**. Although this escapement was little used, it can be regarded as the forerunner of the cylinder escapement that George **Graham** introduced *c*.1725.

Bibliography
1695 (with William Houghton and Thomas Tompion), British patent no. 344 (a horizontal escapement).

Further Reading
Dictionary of National Biography, 1885, Vol. 1, Oxford, S.V. Barlow.
Britten's Old Clocks & Watches and Their Makers, 1982, rev. Cecil Clutton, 9th edn, London, pp. 148, 310, 313 (provides a technical description of rack striking, repeating work and the horizontal escapement).

DV

Barlow, Peter
b. 13 October 1776 Norwich, England
d. 1 March 1862 Kent, England

English mathematician, physicist and optician.

Barlow had little formal academic education, but by his own efforts rectified this deficiency. His contributions to various periodicals ensured that he became recognized as a man of considerable scientific understanding. In 1801, through competitive examination, he became Assistant Mathematics Master at the Royal Military Academy, Woolwich, and some years later was promoted to Professor. He resigned from this post in 1847, but retained full salary in recognition of his many public services.

He is remembered for several notable achievements, and for some experiments designed to overcome problems such as the deviation of compasses in iron ships. Here, he proposed the use of small iron plates designed to overcome other attractions: these were used by both the British and Russian navies. Optical experiments commenced around 1827 and in later years he carried out tests to optimize the size and shape of many parts used in the railways that were spreading throughout Britain and elsewhere at that time.

In 1814 he published mathematical tables of squares, cubes, square roots, cube roots and reciprocals of all integers from 1 to 10,000. This volume was of great value in ship design and other engineering processes where heavy numerical effort is required; it was reprinted many times, the last being in 1965 when it had been all but superseded by the calculator and the computer. In the preface to the original edition, Barlow wrote, 'the only motive which prompted me to engage in this unprofitable task was the utility that I conceived might result from my labour ... if I have succeeded in facilitating abstruse arithmetical calculations, then I have obtained the object in view.'

Principal Honours and Distinctions
FRS 1823; Copley Medal (for discoveries in magnetism) 1825. Honorary Member, Institution of Civil Engineers 1820.

Bibliography
1811, *An Elementary Investigation of the Theory of Numbers*.
1814, *Barlow's Tables* (these have continued to be published until recently, one edition being in 1965 (London: Spon); later editions have taken the integers up to 12,500).
1817, *Essay on the Strength of Timber and Other Materials*.

Further Reading
Dictionary of National Biography.

FMW

Barnaby, Kenneth C.
b. *c*.1887 England
d. 22 March 1968 England

English naval architect and technical author.

Kenneth Barnaby was an eminent naval architect, as were his father and grandfather before him: his grandfather was Sir Nathaniel Barnaby KCB, Director of Naval Construction, and his father was Sydney W. Barnaby, naval architect of John I. Thornycroft & Co., Shipbuilders, Southampton.

At one time all three were members of the Institution of Naval Architects, the first time that this had ever occurred with three members from one family.

Kenneth Barnaby served his apprenticeship at the Thornycroft shipyard in Southampton and later graduated in engineering from the Central Technical College, South Kensington, London. He worked for some years at Le Havre and at John Brown's shipyard at Clydebank before rejoining his old firm in 1916 as Assistant to the Shipyard Manager. In 1919 he went to Rio de Janeiro as a chief ship draughtsman, and finally he returned to Thornycroft, in 1924 he succeeded his father as Naval Architect, and remained in that post until his retirement in 1955, having been appointed a director in 1950.

Barnaby had a wide knowledge and understanding of ships and ship design and during the Second World War he was responsible for much of the development work for landing craft, as well as for many other specialist ships built at the Southampton yard. His experience as a deep-sea yachtsman assisted him. He wrote several important books; however, none can compare with the *Centenary Volume* of the Royal Institution of Naval Architects. In this work, which is used and read widely to this day by naval architects worldwide, he reviewed every paper presented and almost every verbal contribution made to the *Transactions* during its one hundred years.

Principal Honours and Distinctions
OBE 1945. Associate of the City and Guilds Institute. Royal Institution of Naval Architects Froude Gold Medal 1962. Honorary Vice-President, Royal Institution of Naval Architects 1960–8.

Bibliography
c.1900, *Marine Propellers*, London.
1949, *Basic Naval Architecture*, London.
1960, *The Institution of Naval Architects 1860–1960*, London.
1964, *100 Years of Specialised Shipbuilding and Engineering*, London.
1968, *Some Ship Disasters and their Causes*, London.

FMW

Barnack, Oskar
b. 1879 Berlin, Germany
d. January 1936 Wetzlar, Germany

German camera designer who conceived the first Leica camera and many subsequent models.

Oskar Barnack was an optical engineer, introspective and in poor health, when in 1910 he was invited through the good offices of his friend the mechanical engineer Emil Mechau, who worked for Ernst Leitz, to join the company at Wetzlar to work on research into microscope design. He was engaged after a week's trial, and on 2 January 1911 he was put in charge of microscope research. He was an enthusiastic photographer, but excursions with his large and heavy plate camera equipment taxed his strength. In 1912, Mechau was working on a revolutionary film projector design and needed film to test it. Barnack suggested that it was not necessary to buy an expensive commercial machine – why not make one? Leitz agreed, and Barnack constructed a 35 mm movie camera, which he used to cover events in and around Wetzlar.

The exposure problems he encountered with the variable sensitivity of the cine film led him to consider the design of a still camera in which short lengths of film could be tested before shooting – a kind of exposure-meter camera. Dissatisfied with the poor picture quality of his first model, which took the standard cine frame of 18 x 24 mm, he built a new model in which the frame size was doubled to 36 x 24 mm. It used a simple focal-plane shutter adjustable to 1/500 of a second, and a **Zeiss** Milar lens of 42 mm focal length. This is what is now known as the UR-Leica. Using his new camera, 1/250 of the weight of his plate equipment, Barnack made many photographs around Wetzlar, giving postcard-sized prints of good quality.

Ernst Leitz Junior was lent the camera for his trip in June 1914 to America, where he was urged to put it into production. Visiting George **Eastman** in Rochester, Leitz passed on Barnack's requests for film of finer grain and better quality. The First World War put an end to the chances of developing the design at that time. As Germany emerged from the postwar chaos, Leitz Junior, then in charge of the firm, took Barnack off microscope work to design prototypes for a commercial model. Leitz's Chief Optician, Max Berek, designed a new lens, the f3.5 Elmax, for the new camera. They settled on the name Leica, and the first production models went on show at the Leipzig Spring Fair in 1925. By the end of the year, 1,000 cameras had been shipped, despite costing about two months' good wages.

The Leica camera established 35 mm still photography as a practical proposition, and film manufacturers began to create the special fine-grain films that Barnack had longed for. He continued to improve the design, and a succession of new Leica models appeared with new features, such as interchangeable lenses, coupled range-finders, 250 exposures. By the time of his sudden death in 1936, Barnack's life's work had forever transformed the nature of photography.

Further Reading
J. Borgé and G. Borgé, 1977, *Prestige de la photographie.*

BC

Barnett, James Rennie

b. 6 September 1864 Johnstone, Renfrewshire, Scotland
d. 13 January 1965 Glasgow, Scotland

Scottish naval architect described as one of the 'Fathers of the Modern Lifeboat Fleet'.

Barnett studied naval architecture at the University of Glasgow and served an apprenticeship under the yacht designer George L. **Watson**. This was unusual as most undergraduates tended, then as now, to spend their initial years in the various departments of a shipyard, with concentration on the work of the drawing office. In 1904 Barnett succeeded Watson as Principal of the firm, and was simultaneously appointed Consulting Naval Architect to the Royal National Lifeboat Institution (RNLI), a post he held until his retirement in 1947. During this period many changes in lifeboat design brought increasing efficiency, better ranges of stability and improvements in operational safety. The RNLI recognized the great service of Barnett and his predecessor by naming two lifeboat types after them: the *Watson* and the *Barnett*.

Principal Honours and Distinctions
OBE 1918. Royal National Lifeboat Institution Gold Medal.

Bibliography
Barnett was a member of both the Institution of Naval Architects and the Institution of Engineers and Shipbuilders in Scotland. Between 1900 and 1931 he presented a total of six papers to these institutions, on steam yachts, sailing yachts, motor yachts and on lifeboat design.

FMW

Barry, Sir Charles

b. 23 May 1795 Westminster, London, England
d. 12 May 1860 Clapham, London, England

English architect who was a leader in the field between the years 1830 and 1860.

Barry was typical of the outstanding architects of this time. His work was eclectic, and he suited the style – whether Gothic or classical – to the commission and utilized the then-traditional materials and methods of construction. He is best known as architect of the new Palace of Westminster; he won the competition to rebuild it after the disastrous fire of the old palace in 1834. Bearing this in mind in the rebuilding, Barry utilized that characteristic nineteenth-century material, iron for joists and roofing plates.

Principal Honours and Distinctions
Knighted 1852. Member of the Royal Academy; the Royal Society; the Academies of St Luke, Rome; St Petersburg (and others); and the American Institute of Architects. RIBA Gold Medal 1850.

Further Reading
Marcus Whiffen, *The Architecture of Sir Charles Barry in Manchester and Neighbourhood*, Royal Manchester Institution.
H. M. Port (ed.), 1976, *The Houses of Parliament*, Yale University Press.
H.M. Colvin (ed.), *The History of the King's Works*, Vol. 6, HMSO.

DY

Barsanti, Eugenio

b. 1821 Italy
d. 1864 Liège, Belgium

Italian co-inventor of the internal combustion engine; lecturer in mechanics and hydraulics.

A trained scientist and engineer, Barsanti became acquainted with a distinguished engineer, Felice **Matteucci**, in 1851. Their combined talents enabled them to produce a number of so-called free-piston atmospheric engines from 1854 onwards. Using a principle demonstrated by the Swiss engineer Isaac de Rivaz in 1827, the troublesome explosive shocks encountered by other pioneers were avoided. A piston attached to a long toothed rack was propelled from beneath by the expansion of burning gas and allowed unrestricted movement. A resulting partial vacuum enabled atmospheric pressure to return the piston and produce the working stroke. Electric ignition was a feature of all the Italian engines.

With many successful applications, a company was formed in 1860. A 20 hp (15 kW) engine stimulated much interest. Attempts by John Cockerill of Belgium to mass-produce small power units of up to 4 hp (3 kW) came to an abrupt end; during the negotiations Barsanti contracted typhoid fever and later died. The project was abandoned, but the working principle of the Italian engine was used successfully in the Otto–Langen engine of 1867.

Bibliography
13 May 1854, British Provisional Patent no. 1,072 (the Barsanti and Matteucci engine).
12 June 1857, British patent no. 1,655 (contained many notable improvements to the design).

Further Reading
The Engineer (1858) 5: 73–4 (for an account of the Italian engine).
Vincenzo Vannacci, 1955, *L'invenzione del motore a scoppio realizzota dai toscani Barsanti e Matteucci 1854–1954*, Florence.

See also **Langen, Eugen**; **Otto, Niklaus August**.

KAB

Bateman, John Frederic La Trobe

b. 30 May 1810 Lower Wyke, near Halifax, Yorkshire, England
d. 10 June 1889 Moor Park, Farnham, Surrey, England

English civil engineer whose principal works were concerned with reservoirs, water-supply schemes and pipelines.

Bateman's maternal grandfather was a Moravian missionary, and from the age of 7 he was educated at the Moravian schools at Fairfield and Ockbrook. At the age of 15 he was apprenticed to a 'civil engineer, land surveyor and agent' in Oldham. After this apprenticeship, Bateman commenced his own practice in 1833. One of his early schemes and reports was in regard to the flooding of the river Medlock in the Manchester area. He came to the attention of William **Fairbairn**, the engine builder and millwright of Canal Street, Ancoats, Manchester. Fairbairn used Bateman as his site surveyor and as such he prepared much of the groundwork for the Bann reservoirs in Northern Ireland. Whilst the reports on the proposals were in the name of Fairbairn, Bateman was, in fact, appointed by the company as their engineer for the execution of the works. One scheme of Bateman's which was carried forward was the Kendal Reservoirs. The Act for these was signed in 1845 and was implemented not for the purpose of water supply but for the conservation of water to supply power to the many mills which stood on the river Kent between Kentmere and Morecambe Bay. The Kentmere Head dam is the only one of the five proposed for the scheme to survive, although not all the others were built as they would have retained only small volumes of water.

Perhaps the greatest monument to the work of J.F. La Trobe Bateman is Manchester's water supply; he was consulted about this in 1844, and construction began four years later. He first built reservoirs in the Longdendale valley, which has a very complicated geological stratification. Bateman favoured earth embankment dams and gravity feed rather than pumping; the five reservoirs in the valley that impound the river Etherow were complex, cored earth dams. However, when completed they were greatly at risk from landslips and ground movement. Later dams were inserted by Bateman to prevent water loss should the older dams fail. The scheme was not completed until 1877, by which time Manchester's population had exceeded the capacity of the original scheme; Thirlmere in Cumbria was chosen by Manchester Corporation as the site of the first of the Lake District water-supply schemes. Bateman, as Consulting Engineer, designed the great stone-faced dam at the west end of the lake, the 'gothic' straining well in the middle of the east shore of the lake, and the 100-mile (160 km) pipeline to Manchester. The Act for the Thirlmere reservoir was signed in 1879 and, whilst Bateman continued as Consulting Engineer, the work was supervised by G.H. Hill and was completed in 1894.

Bateman was also consulted by the authorities in Glasgow, with the result that he constructed an impressive water-supply scheme derived from Loch Katrine during the years 1856–60. It was claimed that the scheme bore comparison with 'the most extensive aqueducts in the world, not excluding those of ancient Rome'. Bateman went on to superintend the waterworks of many cities, mainly in the north of England but also in Dublin and Belfast. In 1865 he published a pamphlet, *On the Supply of Water to London from the Sources of the River Severn*, based on a survey funded from his own pocket; a Royal Commission examined various schemes but favoured Bateman's.

Bateman was also responsible for harbour and dock works, notably on the rivers Clyde and Shannon, and also for a number of important water-supply works on the Continent of Europe and beyond. Dams and the associated reservoirs were the principal work of J.F. La Trobe Bateman; he completed forty-three such schemes during his professional career. He also prepared many studies of water-supply schemes, and appeared as professional witness before the appropriate Parliamentary Committees.

Principal Honours and Distinctions
FRS 1860. President, Institution of Civil Engineers 1878, 1879.

Bibliography
Among his publications *History and Description of the Manchester Waterworks*, (1884, London), and *The Present State of Our Knowledge on the Supply of Water to Towns*, (1855, London: British Association for the Advancement of Science) are notable.

Further Reading
Obituary, 1889, *Minutes of the Proceedings of the Institution of Civil Engineers* 97: 392–8.
Obituary, 1889, *Proceedings of the Royal Society*

46: xlii–xlviii.
G.M. Binnie, 1981, *Early Victorian Water Engineers*, London.
P.N. Wilson, 1973, 'Kendal reservoirs', *Transactions of the Cumberland and Westmorland Antiquarian and Archaeological Society* 73.

KM/LRD

Baudot, Jean-Maurice-Emile
b. 11 September 1845 Magneux, France
d. 28 March 1903 Sceaux, France

French engineer who developed the multiplexed telegraph and devised a 5-bit code for data communication and control.

Baudot had no formal education beyond his local primary school and began his working life as a farmer, as was his father. However, in September 1869 he joined the French telegraph service and was soon sent on a course on the recently developed Hughes printing telegraph. After service in the Franco-Prussian war as a lieutenant with the military telegraph, he returned to his civilian duties in Paris in 1872. He was there encouraged to develop (in his own time!) a multiple Hughes system for time-multiplexing of several telegraph messages. By using synchronized clockwork-driven rotating switches at the transmitter and receiver he was able to transmit five messages simultaneously; the system was officially adopted by the French Post & Telegraph Administration five years later. In 1874 he patented the idea of a 5-bit (i.e. 32-permutation) code, with equal on and off intervals, for telegraph transmission of the Roman alphabet and punctuation signs and for control of the typewriter-like teleprinter used to display the message. This code, known as the Baudot code, was found to be more economical than the existing **Morse** code and was widely adopted for national and international telegraphy in the twentieth century. In the 1970s it was superseded by 7- and 8-bit codes.

Further development of his ideas on multiplexing led in 1894 to methods suitable for high-speed telegraphy. To commemorate his contribution to efficient telegraphy, the unit of signalling speed (i.e. the number of elements transmitted per second) is known as the baud.

Bibliography
17 June 1874, 'Système de télégraphie rapide' (Baudot's first patent).

Further Reading

1965, *From Semaphore to Satellite*, Geneva: International Telecommunications Union.

P. Lajarrige, 1982, 'Chroniques téléphoniques et télégraphiques', *Collection historique des télécommunications*.

KF

Bauer, Georg

See **Agricola, Georgius**.

Bauer, H.

fl. *c*.1885

German (?) inventor of a press-stud fastener.

Fastenings are an essential component of the majority of garments. Great advances were made in Germany with press studs in the late nineteenth century after the original invention by Louis **Hannart** in 1863. In 1885, Bauer patented a spring and stud fastener.

Further Reading

I. McNeil (ed.), 1990, *An Encyclopaedia of the History of Technology*, London: Routledge, pp. 852–3 (provides an account of the development of fastenings).

RLH

Baumann, Karl

b. 18 April 1884 Switzerland
d. 14 July 1971 Ilkley, Yorkshire

Swiss/British mechanical engineer, designer and developer of steam and gas turbine plant.

After leaving school in 1902, he went to the Ecole Polytechnique, Zurich, leaving in 1906 with an engineering diploma. He then spent a year with Professor A. Stodola, working on steam engines, turbines and internal combustion engines. He also conducted research in the strength of materials. After this, he spent two years as Research and Design Engineer at the Nuremberg works of Maschinenfabrik Augsburg–Nürnberg. He came to England in 1909 to join the British Westinghouse Co. Ltd in Manchester, and by 1912 was Chief Engineer of the Engine Department of that firm. The firm later became the Metropolitan-Vickers Electrical Co. Ltd (MV), and Baumann rose from Chief Mechanical Engineer through to, by 1929, Special Director and Member of the Executive Management Board; he remained a director until his retirement in 1949.

For much of his career, Baumann was in the forefront of power station steam-cycle development, pioneering increased turbine entry pressures and temperatures, in 1916 introducing multi-stage regenerative feed-water heating and the Baumann turbine multi-exhaust. His 105 MW set for Battersea 'A' station (1933) was for many years the largest single-axis unit in Europe. From 1938 on, he and his team were responsible for the first axial-flow aircraft propulsion gas turbines to fly in England, and jet engines in the 1990s owe much to the 'Beryl' and 'Sapphire' engines produced by MV. In particular, the design of the compressor for the Sapphire engine later became the basis for Rolls-Royce units, after an exchange of information between that company and Armstrong-Siddeley, who had previously taken over the aircraft engine work of MV. Further, the Beryl engine formed the basis of 'Gatric', the first marine gas turbine propulsion engine.

Baumann was elected to full membership for the Institution of Mechanical Engineers in 1929 and a year later was awarded the Thomas Hawksley Gold Medal by that body, followed by their James Clayton Prize in 1948: in the same year he became the thirty-fifth Thomas Hawksley lecturer. Many of his ideas and introductions have stood the test of time, being based on his deep and wide understanding of fundamentals.

JB

Baxter, George

b. 31 July 1804 Lewes, Sussex, England
d. 11 January 1867 Sydenham, London, England

English pioneer in colour printing.

The son of a printer, Baxter was apprenticed to a wood engraver and there began his search for improved methods of making coloured prints, hitherto the perquisite of the rich, in order to bring them within reach of a wider public. After marriage to the daughter of Robert Harrild, founder of the printing firm of Harrild & Co., he set up house in London, where he continued his experiments on colour while maintaining the run-of-the-mill work that kept the family.

The nineteenth century saw a tremendous advance in methods of printing pictures, produced as separate prints or as book illustrations. For the first three decades colour was supplied by hand, but from the 1830s attempts were made to print in colour, using a separate plate for each one. Coloured prints were produced by chromolithography and relief printing on a small scale. Prints were first made with the latter method on a commercial scale by Baxter with a process that he patented in 1835. He generally used a key plate that was engraved, aquatinted or lithographed; the colours were then printed separately from wood or metal blocks. Baxter was a skilful printer and his work reached a high standard. An early example is the frontispiece to Robert Mudie's *Summer* (1837). In 1849 he began licensing his patent to other printers, and after the Great Exhibition of 1851 colour relief printing came into its own. Of the plethora of illustrated literature that appeared then, Baxter's *Gems of the Great Exhibition* was one of the most widely circulated souvenirs of the event.

Baxter remained an active printer through the 1850s, but increasing competition from the German coloured lithographic process undermined his business and in 1860 he gave up the unequal struggle. In May of that year, all his oil pictures, engravings and blocks went up for auction, some 3,000 lots altogether. Baxter retired to Sydenham, then a country place, making occasional visits to London until injuries sustained in a mishap while he was ascending a London omnibus led to his death. Above all, he helped to initiate the change from the black and white world of pre-Victorian literature to the riotously colourful world of today.

Further Reading
C.T. Courtney Lewis, 1908, *George Baxter, the Picture Printer*, London: Sampson Lowe, Marsden (the classic account).
M.E. Mitzmann, 1978, *George Baxter and the Baxter Prints*, Newton Abbot: David & Charles.

LRD

Bayard, Hippolyte
b. 1801 Breteuil-sur-Noye, France
d. 1887

French photographer, inventor of an early direct positive paper process.

Educated as a notary's clerk, Bayard began his working life in Paris in the Ministry of Finance. His interest in art led him to investigations into the chemical action of light, and he began his experiments in 1837. In May 1839 Bayard described an original photographic process which produced direct positive images on paper. It was devised independently of **Talbot** and before details of **Daguerre**'s process had been published. During the same period, similar techniques were announced by other investigators and Bayard became involved in a series of priority disputes. Bayard's photographs were well received when first exhibited, and examples survive to the present day. Because the process required long exposure times it was rarely practised, but Bayard is generally credited with being an independent inventor of photography.

Bibliography
1840, *Comptes rendus* (24 February): 337 (the first published details of Bayard's process).

Further Reading
H. Gernsheim and A. Gernsheim, 1969, *The History of Photography*, rev. edn, London.

JW

Beau de Rochas, Alphonse Eugène
b. 1815 France
d. 1893 France

French railway engineer, patentee of a four-stroke cycle engine.

Renowned more for his ideas on technical matters than his practical deeds, Beau de Rochas was a prolific thinker. Within a few years he proposed a rail tunnel beneath the English Channel, a submarine telegraph, a new kind of drive for canal boats, the use of steel for high-pressure boilers and a method of improving the adhesion of locomotive wheels travelling the Alps.

The most notable of Beau de Rochas's ideas occurred in 1862 when he was employed as Ingenieur Attaché to the Central de Chemins. With remarkable foresight, he expressed the theoretical considerations for the cycle of operations for the now widely used four-stroke cycle engine. A French patent of 1862 lapsed with a failure to pay the annuity and thus the proposals for a new motive power lapsed into obscurity. Resurrected some twenty years later, the Beau de Rochas tract figures prominently in patent litigation cases. In

1885, a German court upheld a submission by a German patent lawyer that **Otto's** four-stroke engine of 1876 infringed the Beau de Rochas patent. It remains a mystery why Beau de Rochas never emerged at any time to defend his claims. In France he is regarded as the inventor of the four-stroke cycle engine.

Principal Honours and Distinctions
Société d'Encouragement pour l'Industrie Nationale, prize of 3000 francs, 1891.

Bibliography
1885, *The Engineer* 60: 441 (an English translation of the Beau de Rochas tract).

Further Reading
1938, *Bulletin de la Société d'Encouragement pour l'Industrie Nationale* 137: 209–39.
1962, *Document pour l'histoire des techniques* Cahier no. 2: pp. 3–42.
B. Donkin, 1900, *The Gas, Oil and Air Engine*, London: p. 467.

See also **Langen, Eugen**.

KAB

Beaumont, Huntingdon

b. *c.*1560 Coleorton (?), Leicestershire, England
d. 1624 Nottingham, England

English speculator in coal-mining, constructor of the first surface railway in Britain.

Huntingdon Beaumont was a younger son of a landed family whose estates included coal-mines at Coleorton and Bedworth. From these, no doubt, originated his great expertise in coal-mining and mine management. His subsequent story is a complex one of speculation in coal mines: agreements, partnerships, and debts, and, in trying to extricate himself from the last, attempts to improve profitability, and ever-greater enterprises. He leased mines in 1601 at Wollaton, near Nottingham, and in 1603 at Strelley, which adjoins Wollaton but is further from Nottingham, where lay the market for coal. To reduce the transport cost of Strelley coal, Beaumont laid a wooden wagonway for two miles or so to Wollaton Lane End, the point at which the coal was customarily sold. In earlier times wooden railways had probably been used in mines, following

practice on the European continent, but Beaumont's was the first on the surface in Britain. The market for coal in Nottingham being limited, Beaumont, with partners, attempted to send coal to London by water, but the difficult navigation of the Trent at this period made the venture uneconomic. With a view still to supplying London, *c.*1605 they took leases of mines near Blyth, north of Newcastle upon Tyne. Here too Beaumont built wagonways, to convey coal to the coast, but despite considerable expenditure the mines could not be made economic and Beaumont returned to Strelley. Although he worked the mine night and day, he was unable to meet the demands of his creditors, who eventually had him imprisoned for debt. He died in gaol.

Further Reading
R.S. Smith, 1957, 'Huntingdon Beaumont. Adventurer in coal mines', *Renaissance & Modern Studies* 1; Smith, 1960, 'England's first rails: a reconsideration', *Renaissance & Modern Studies* 4, University of Nottingham (both are well-researched papers discussing Beaumont and his wagonways).

PJGR

Beckett, Sir Edmund

See **Grimthorpe (of Grimthorpe), Edmund Beckett, Baron**.

Bedson, George

b. 3 November 1820 Sutton Coldfield, Warwickshire, England
d. 12 December 1884 Manchester (?), England

English metallurgist, inventor of the continuous rolling mill.

He acquired a considerable knowledge of wire-making in his father's works before he took a position in 1839 at the works of James Edleston at Warrington. From there, in 1851, he went to Manchester as Manager of Richard Johnson & Sons' wire mill, where he remained for the rest of his life. It was there that he initiated several important improvements in the manufacture of wire. These included a system of circulating puddling furnace water bottoms and sides, and a galvanizing process. His most important innovation, however, was the continuous mill for producing iron rod for wiredrawing. Previously the red-hot iron billets had to be handled

49

repeatedly through a stand or set of rolls to reduce the billet to the required shape, with time and heat being lost at each handling. In Bedson's continuous mill, the billet entered the first of a succession of stands placed as closely to each other as possible and emerged from the final one as rod suitable for wiredrawing, without any intermediate handling. A second novel feature was that alternate rolls were arranged vertically to save turning the piece manually through a right angle. That improved the quality as well as the speed of production. Bedson's first continuous mill was erected in Manchester in 1862 and had sixteen stands in tandem. A mill on this principle had been patented the previous year by Charles While of Pontypridd, South Wales, but it was Bedson who made it work and brought it into use commercially. A difficult problem to overcome was that as the piece being rolled lengthened, its speed increased, so that each pair of rolls had to increase correspondingly. The only source of power was a steam engine working a single drive shaft, but Bedson achieved the greater speeds by using successively larger gearwheels at each stand.

Bedson's first mill was highly successful, and a second one was erected at the Manchester works; however, its application was limited to the production of small bars, rods and sections. Nevertheless, Bedson's mill established an important principle of rolling-mill design that was to have wider applications in later years.

Further Reading

Obituary, 1884, *Journal of the Iron and Steel Institute* 27: 539–40.

W.K.V. Gale, 1969, *Iron and Steel*, London: Longmans, pp. 81–2.

LRD

Behr, Fritz Bernhard

b. 9 October 1842 Berlin, Germany
d. 25 February 1927

German (naturalized British in 1876)
engineer, promoter of the Lartigue monorail
system.

Behr trained as an engineer in Britain and had several railway engineering appointments before becoming associated with C.F.M.-T. **Lartigue** in promoting the Lartigue monorail system in the British Isles. In Lartigue's system, a single rail was supported on trestles; vehicles ran on the rail, their bodies suspended pannier-fashion, stabilized by horizontal rollers running against light guide rails fixed to the sides of the trestles. Behr became Managing Director of the Listowel & Ballybunion Railway Company, which in 1888 opened its Lartigue system line between those two places in the south-west of Ireland. Three locomotives designed by J.T.A. **Mallet** were built for the line by Hunslet Engine Company, each with two horizontal boilers, one either side of the track. Coaches and wagons likewise were in two parts. Technically the railway was successful, but lack of traffic caused the company to go bankrupt in 1897: the railway continued to operate until 1924.

Meanwhile Behr had been thinking in terms far more ambitious than a country branch line. Railway speeds of 150 mph (240 km/h) or more then lay far in the future: engineers were uncertain whether normal railway vehicles would even be stable at such speeds. Behr was convinced that a high-speed electric vehicle on a substantial Lartigue monorail track would be stable. In 1897 he demonstrated such a vehicle on a 3 mile (4.8 km) test track at the Brussels International Exhibition. By keeping the weight of the motors low, he was able to place the seats above rail level. Although the generating station provided by the Exhibition authorities never operated at full power, speeds over 75 mph (120 km/h) were achieved.

Behr then promoted the Manchester–Liverpool Express Railway, on which monorail trains of this type running at speeds up to 110 mph (177 km/h) were to link the two cities in twenty minutes. Despite strong opposition from established railway companies, an Act of Parliament authorizing it was made in 1901. The Act also contained provision for the Board of Trade to require experiments to prove the system's safety. In practice this meant that seven miles of line, and a complete generating station to enable trains to travel at full speed, must be built before it was known whether the Board would give its approval for the railway or not. Such a condition was too severe for the scheme to attract investors and it remained stillborn.

Further Reading

H. Fayle, 1946, *The Narrow Gauge Railways of Ireland*, Greenlake Publications, Part 2, ch. 2 (describes the Listowel & Ballybunion Railway and Behr's work there).

D.G. Tucker, 1984, 'F.B. Behr's development of

the Lartigue monorail', *Transactions of the Newcomen Society* 55 (covers mainly the high-speed lines).

See also **Brennan, Louis**.

PJGR

Behrens, Peter
b. 14 April 1868 Hamburg, Germany
d. 27 February 1940 Berlin, Germany

German pioneer of modern architecture, developer of the combined use of steel, glass and concrete in industrial work.

During the 1890s Behrens, as an artist, was a member of the German branch of *Sezessionismus* and then moved towards *Jugendstil* (Art Nouveau) types of design in different media. His interest in architecture was aroused during the first years of the twentieth century, and a turning-point in his career was his appointment in 1907 as Artistic Supervisor and Consultant to AEG, the great Berlin electrical firm. His Turbine Factory (1909) in the city was a breakthrough in design and is still standing: in steel and glass, with visible girder construction, this is a truly functional modern building far ahead of its time. In 1910 two more of Behrens's factories were completed in Berlin, followed in 1913 by the great AEG plant at Riga, Latvia.

After the First World War Behrens was in great demand for industrial construction. He designed office schemes such as those at the Mannesmann Steel Works in Düsseldorf (1911–12; now destroyed) and, in a departure from his earlier work, was responsible for a more Expressionist form of design, mainly in brick, in his extensive complex for I.G. Farben at Höchst (1920–4).

In the years before the First World War, some of those who were later amongst the most famous names in modern architecture were among his pupils: **Gropius**, **Mies van der Rohe** and Le Corbusier (Charles-Edouard **Jeanneret**).

Further Reading
T. Buddenseig, 1979, *Industrielkultur: Peter Behrens und die AEG 1907–14*, Berlin: Mann.
W. Weber (ed.), 1966, *Peter Behrens (1868–1940)*, Kaiserslautern, Germany: Pfalzgalerie.

DY

Belidor, Bernard Forest de
b. 1698 Catalonia, Spain
d. 8 September 1761 Paris, France

French engineer and founder of the science of modern ballistics.

Belidor was the son of a French army officer, who died when he was six months old, and was thereafter brought up by a brother officer. He soon demonstrated a scientific bent, and gravitated to Paris, where he became involved in the determination of the Paris meridian. He was then appointed Professor at the artillery school at La Fère, where he began to pursue the science of ballistics in earnest. He was able to disprove the popular theory that range was directly proportional to the powder charge, and also argued that the explosive power of a charge was greatest at the end of the explosion; he advocated spherical chambers in order to take advantage of this. His ideas made him unpopular with the 'establishment', especially the Master of the King's artillery, and he was forced to leave France for a time, becoming a consultant to authorities in Bohemia and Bavaria. However, he was reinstated, and in 1758 he was appointed Royal Inspector of Artillery, a post that he held until his death.

Belidor also made a name for himself in hydraulics and influenced design in this field for more than a century after his death. In addition, he was the first to make practical application of integral calculus.

Bibliography
Belidor was the author of several books, of which the most significant were:
1739, *La Science des ingénieurs*, Paris (reprinted several times, the last edition being as late as 1830).
1731, *Le Bombardier françois*, Paris: L'Imprimerie royale.
1737, *Architecture hydraulique*, 2 vols, Paris.

Further Reading
R.S. Kirby and P.G. Laurson, 1932, *The Early History of Modern Civil Engineering*, New Haven: Yale University Press (describes his work in the field of hydraulics).
D. Chandler, 1976, *The Art of Warfare in the Age of Marlborough*, London: Batsford (mentions the ballistics aspect).

CM

Bell, Alexander Graham

b. 3 March 1847 Edinburgh, Scotland
d. 3 August 1922 Beinn Bhreagh, Baddeck,
Cape Breton Island, Nova Scotia, Canada

Scottish/American inventor of the telephone.

Bell's grandfather was a professor of elocution in London and his father an authority on the physiology of the voice and on elocution; Bell was to follow in their footsteps. He was educated in Edinburgh, leaving school at 13. In 1863 he went to Elgin, Morayshire, as a pupil teacher in elocution, with a year's break to study at Edinburgh University; it was in 1865, while still in Elgin, that he first conceived the idea of the electrical transmission of speech. He went as a master to Somersetshire College, Bath (now in Avon), and in 1867 he moved to London to assist his father, who had taken up the grandfather's work in elocution. In the same year, he matriculated at London University, studying anatomy and physiology, and also began teaching the deaf. He continued to pursue the studies that were to lead to the invention of the telephone. At this time he read Helmholtz's *The Sensations of Tone*, an important work on the theory of sound that was to exert a considerable influence on him.

In 1870 he accompanied his parents when they emigrated to Canada. His work for the deaf gained fame in both Canada and the USA, and in 1873 he was apponted professor of vocal physiology and the mechanics of speech at Boston University, Massachusetts. There, he continued to work on his theory that sound wave vibrations could be converted into a fluctuating electric current, be sent along a wire and then be converted back into sound waves by means of a receiver. He approached the problem from the background of the theory of sound and voice production rather than from that of electrical science, and by 1875 he had succeeded in constructing a rough model. On 7 March 1876 Bell spoke the famous command to his assistant, 'Mr Watson, come here, I want you': this was the first time a human voice had been transmitted along a wire. Only three days earlier, Bell's first patent for the telephone had been granted. Almost simultaneously, but quite independently, Elisha **Gray** had achieved a similar result. After a period of litigation, the US Supreme Court awarded Bell priority, although Gray's device was technically superior.

In 1877, three years after becoming a naturalized US citizen, Bell married the deaf daughter of his first backer. In August of that year, they travelled to Europe to combine a honeymoon with promotion of the telephone. Bell's patent was possibly the most valuable ever issued, for it gave birth to what later became the world's largest private service organization, the Bell Telephone Company.

Bell had other scientific and technological interests: he made improvements in telegraphy and in **Edison**'s gramophone, and he also developed a keen interest in aeronautics, working on **Curtiss**'s flying machine. Bell founded the celebrated periodical *Science*.

Principal Honours and Distinctions
Legion of Honour; Hughes Medal, Royal Society, 1913.

Further Reading
Obituary, 7 August 1922, *The Times*.
Dictionary of American Biography.
R. Burlingame, 1964, *Out of Silence into Sound*, London: Macmillan.

LRD

Bell, Henry

b. 1767 Torphichen Mill, near Linlithgow, Scotland
d. 1830 Helensburgh, Scotland

Scottish projector of the first steamboat service in Europe.

The son of Patrick Bell, a millwright, Henry had two sisters and an elder brother and was educated at the village school. When he was 9 years old Henry was sent to lodge in Falkirk with an uncle and aunt of his mother's so that he could attend the school there. At the age of 12 he left school and agreed to become a mason with a relative. In 1783, after only three years, he was bound apprentice to his Uncle Henry, a millwright at Jay Mill. He stayed there for a further three years and then, in 1786, joined the firm of Shaw & Hart, shipbuilders of Borrowstoneness. These were to be the builders of William **Symington**'s hull for the *Charlotte Dundas*. He also spent twelve months with Mr James Inglis, an engineer of Bellshill, Lanarkshire, and then went to London to gain experience, working for the famous John **Rennie** for some eighteen months. By 1790 he was back in Glasgow, and a year later he took a partner, James Paterson, into his new business of builder and contractor, based in the Trongate. He later referred to himself as 'architect', and his partnership with Paterson lasted seven years. He is said to have invented a discharging machine for calico printing, as well as a steam dredger for clearing the River Clyde.

The Baths Hotel was opened in Helensburgh in 1808, with the hotel-keeper, who was also the first provost of the town, being none other than Henry Bell. It has been suggested that Bell was also the builder of the hotel and this seems very likely. Bell installed a steam engine for pumping sea water out of the Clyde and into the baths, and at first ran a coach service to bring customers from Glasgow three days a week. The driver was his brother Tom. The coach was replaced by the *Comet* steamboat in 1812.

While Henry was busy with his provost's duties and making arrangements for the building of his steamboat, his wife Margaret, née Young, whom he married in March 1794, occupied herself with the management of the Baths Hotel. Bell did not himself manufacture, but supervised the work of experts: John and Charles Wood of Port Glasgow, builders of the 43 ft 6 in. (13.25 m)-long hull of the *Comet*; David Napier of Howard Street Foundry for the boiler and other castings; and John Robertson of Dempster Street, who had previously supplied a small engine for pumping water to the baths at the hotel in Helensburgh, for the 3 hp engine. The first trials of the finished ship were held on 24 July 1812, when she was launched from Wood's yard. A regular service was advertised in the Glasgow Chronicle on 5 August and was the first in Europe, preceded only by that of Robert Fulton in the USA. The *Comet* continued to run until 1820, when it was wrecked.

Bell received little reward for his promotion of steam navigation, merely small pensions from the Clyde trustees and others. He was buried at the parish church of Rhu.

Further Reading
Edward Morris, 1844, *Life of Henry Bell*.
Henry Bell, 1813, *Applying Steam Engines to Vessels*.

IMcN

Bell, Imrie
b. 1836 Edinburgh, Scotland
d. 21 November 1906 Croydon, Surrey, England

Scottish civil engineer who built singular and pioneering structures.

Following education at the Royal High School of Edinburgh, Bell served an apprenticeship with a Mr Bertram, engineer and shipwright of Leith, before continuing as a regular pupil with Bell and Miller, the well-known civil engineers of Glasgow. A short period at Pelton Colliery in County Durham followed, and then at the early age of 20 Bell was appointed Resident Engineer on the construction of the Meadowside Graving Dock in Glasgow.

The Meadowside Dry Dock was opened on 28 January 1858 and was a remarkable act of faith by the proprietors Messrs Tod and McGregor, one of the earliest companies in iron shipbuilding in the British Isles. It was the first dry dock in the City of Glasgow and used the mouth of the river Kelvin for canting ships; at the time the dimensions of 144 x 19 x 5.5 m depth were regarded as quite daring. This dock was to remain in regular operation for nearly 105 years and is testimony to the skills of Imrie Bell and his colleagues.

In the following years he worked for the East India Railway Company, where he was in charge of the southern half of the Jumna Railway Bridge at Allahabad, before going on to other exciting civil engineering contracts in India. On his return home, Bell became Engineer to Leith Docks, and three years later he became Executive Engineer to the States of Jersey, where he constructed St Helier's Harbour and the lighthouse at La Corbiere – the first in Britain to be built with Portland cement. In 1878 he rejoined his old firm of Bell and Miller, and ultimately worked from their Westminster office. One of his last jobs in Scotland was supervising the building of the Great Western Road Bridge in Glasgow, one of the beautiful bridges in the West End of the city.

Bell retired from business in 1898 and lived in Surrey for the rest of his life.

Bibliography
1879–80, 'On the St Helier's Harbour works', *Transactions of the Institution of Engineers and Shipbuilders in Scotland* 23.

Further Reading
Fred M. Walker, 1984, *Song of the Clyde*, Cambridge: PSL.

FMW

Bell, Sir Isaac Lowthian

b. 15 February 1816 Newcastle upon Tyne, England
d. 20 December 1904 Rounton Grange, Northallerton, Yorkshire, England

English ironworks proprietor, chemical manufacturer and railway director, widely renowned for his scientific pronouncements.

Following an extensive education, in 1835 Bell entered the Tyneside chemical and iron business where his father was a partner; for about five years from 1845 he controlled the ironworks. In 1844, he and his two brothers leased an iron blast-furnace at Wylam on Tyne. In 1850, with partners, he started chemical works at Washington, near Gateshead. A few years later, with his two brothers, he set up the Clarence Ironworks on Teesside. In the 1880s, salt extraction and soda-making were added there; at that time the Bell Brothers' enterprises, including collieries, employed 6,000 people.

Lowthian Bell was a pioneer in applying thermochemistry to blast-furnace working. Besides his commercial interests, scientific experimentation and international travel, he found time to take a leading part in the promotion of British technical organizations; upon his death he left evidence of a prodigious level of personal activity.

Principal Honours and Distinctions
Created baronet 1885. FRS 1875. Légion d'honneur 1878. MP, Hartlepool, 1875–80. President: British Iron Trade Association; Iron and Steel Institute; Institution of Mechanical Engineers; North of England Institute of Mining and Mechanical Engineers; Institution of Mining Engineers; Society of the Chemical Industry. Iron and Steel Institute Bessemer Gold Medal 1874 (the first recipient). Society of Arts Albert Medal 1895.

Bibliography
The first of several books, Bell's *Chemical Phenomena of Iron Smelting* . . . (1872), was soon translated into German, French and Swedish.

He was the author of more than forty technical articles.

Further Reading
1900–1910, *Dictionary of National Biography*.
C. Wilson, 1984, article in *Dictionary of Business Biography*, Vol. I, ed.J. Jeremy, Butterworth (a more discursive account).
D. Burn, 1940, *The Economic History of Steelmaking, 1867–1939: A Study in Competition*, Cambridge (2nd edn 1961).

JKA

Bell, Revd Patrick

b. 1799 Auchterhouse, Scotland
d. 22 April 1869 Carmyllie, Scotland

Scottish inventor of the first successful reaping machine.

The son of a Forfarshire tenant farmer, Patrick Bell obtained an MA from the University of St Andrews. His early association with farming kindled an interest in engineering and mechanics and he was to maintain a workshop not only on his father's farm, but also, in later life, at the parsonage at Carmyllie.

He was still studying divinity when he invented his reaping machine. Using garden shears as the basis of his design, he built a model in 1827 and a full-scale prototype the following year. Not wishing the machine to be seen during his early experiments, he and his brother planted a sheaf of oats in soil laid out in a shed, and first tried the machine on this. It cut well enough but left the straw in a mess behind it. A canvas belt system was devised and another secret trial in the barn was followed by a night excursion into a field, where corn was successfully harvested.

Two machines were at work during 1828, apparently achieving a harvest rate of one acre per hour. In 1832 there were ten machines at work, and at least another four had been sent to the United States by this time. Despite their success Bell did not patent his design, feeling that the idea should be given free to the world. In later years he was to regret the decision, feeling that the many badly-made imitations resulted in its poor reputation and prevented its adoption.

Bell's calling took precedence over his inventive interests and after qualifying he went to Canada in 1833, spending four years in Fergus, Ontario. He later returned to Scotland and became the minister at Carmyllie, with a living of £150 per annum.

Principal Honours and Distinctions

Late in the day he was honoured for his part in the development of the reaping machine. He received an honorary degree from the University of St Andrews and in 1868 a testimonial and £1,000 raised by public subscription by the Highland and Agricultural Society of Scotland.

Bibliography

1854, *Journal of Agriculture* (perhaps stung by other claims, Bell wrote his own account).

Further Reading

G. Quick and W. Buchele, 1978, *The Grain Harvesters*, American Society of Agricultural Engineers (gives an account of the development of harvesting machinery).

L.J. Jones, 1979, *History of Technology*, pp. 101–48 (gives a critical assessment of the various claims regarding the originality of the invention).

J. Hendrick, 1928, *Transactions of the Highland and Agricultural Society of Scotland*, pp. 51–69 (provides a celebration of Bell's achievement on its centenary).

AP

Bell, Thomas
fl. 1770–1785 Scotland

Scottish inventor of a calico printing machine with the design engraved on rollers.

In November 1770, John Mackenzie, owner of a bleaching mill, took his millwright Thomas Bell to Glasgow to consult with James **Watt** about problems they were having with the calico printing machine invented by Bell some years previously. Bell rolled sheets of copper one eighth of an inch (3 mm) thick into cyliders, and filled them with cement which was held in place by cast iron ends. After being turned true and polished, the cylinders were engraved; they cost about £10 each. The printing machines were driven by a water-wheel, but Bell and Mackenzie appeared to have had problems with the doctor blades which scraped off excess colour, and this may have been why they visited Watt.

They had, presumably, solved the technical problems when Bell took out a patent in 1783

which describes him as 'the Elder', but there are no further details about the man himself. The machine is described as having six printing rollers arranged around the top of the circumference of a large central bowl. In later machines, the printing rollers were placed all round a smaller cylinder. All of the printing rollers, each printing a different colour, were driven by gearing to keep them in register. The patent includes steel doctor blades which would have scraped excess colour off the printing rollers. Another patent, taken out in 1784, shows a smaller three-colour machine. The printing rollers had an iron core covered with copper, which could be taken off at pleasure so that fresh patterns could be cut as desired. Bell's machine was used at Masney, near Preston, England, by Messrs Livesey, Hargreaves, Hall & Co in 1786. Although copper cylinders were difficult to make and engrave, and the soldered seams often burst, these machines were able to increase the output of the cheaper types of printed cloth.

Bibliography

1783, patent no. 1,378 (calico printing machine with engraved copper rollers).

1784, patent no. 1,443 (three-colour calico printing machine).

Further Reading

W.E.A. Axon, 1886, *Annals of Manchester*, Manchester (provides an account of the invention).

R.L. Hills, 1970, *Power in the Industrial Revolution*, Manchester (provides a brief description of the development of calico printing).

RLH

Belling, Charles Reginald
b. 11 May 1884 Bodmin, Cornwall, England
d. 8 February 1965 while on a cruise

English electrical engineer best known as the pioneer of the wire-wound clay-former heating element which made possible the efficient domestic electric fire.

Belling was educated at Burts Grammar School in Lostwithiel, Cornwall, and at Crossley Schools in Halifax, Yorkshire. In 1903 he was apprenticed to Crompton & Co. at Chelmsford in Essex, the firm that in 1894 offered for sale the earliest electric heaters. These electric radiant panels were intended as heating radiators or cooking hotplates, but were not very successful because, being cast-iron panels into which heating wires had been embedded in enamel, they tended to fracture due to the different rates of thermal expansion of the iron and the enamel. Other designs of electric heaters followed, notably the introduction of large, sausage-shaped carbon filament bulbs fitted into a fire frame and backed by reflectors. This was the idea of H. Dowsing, a collaborator of **Crompton**, in 1904.

After qualifying in 1906, Belling left Crompton & Co. and went to work for Ediswan at Ponders End in Hertfordshire. He left in 1912 to set up his own business, which he began in a small shed in Enfield. With a small staff and capital of £450, he took out his first patent for his wire-wound-former electric fire in the same year. The resistance wire, made from nickel–chrome alloy such as that patented in 1906 by A.L. Marsh, was coiled round a clay former. Six such bars were attached to a cast-iron frame with heating control knobs, and the device was marketed as the Standard Belling Fire. Advertised in 1912, the fire was an immediate success and was followed by many other variations. Improvements to the first model included wire safety guards, enamel finishes and a frame ornamented with copper and brass.

Belling turned his attention to hotplates, cookers, immersion heaters, electric irons, water urns and kettles, producing the Modernette Cooker (1919), the multi-parabola fire bar (1921), the plate and dish warmer (1924), the storage heater (1926) and the famous Baby Belling cookers, the first of which appeared in 1929. By 1955 business had developed so well that Belling opened another factory at Burnley, Lancashire. He partly underwrote, for the amount of £1 million, a proposed scientific technical college for the electrical industry at Enfield.

Further Reading
1985, *Dictionary of Business Biography*, Butterworth.
G. Jukes, 1963, *The Story of Belling*, Belling and Co. Ltd (produced by the company in its Golden Jubilee year).

DY

Bennett, Charles Harper
b. 1840 Clapham, London, England
d. 1927 Sydney, Australia

English inventor of the 'ripening' technique for increasing the sensitivity of gelatine silver halide emulsions.

The son of a hatter, Bennett studied medicine and was interested in mechanical devices, chemistry and later photography. An interior view shown at a South London Photographic Society meeting in March 1878 prompted requests for details of Bennett's procedure, and these were published almost immediately. It involved heating gelatine silver bromide for extremely long periods with an excess of silver bromide. The resulting emulsion had greatly enhanced sensitivity. This 'ripening' process proved to be a major advance in the development of modern photographic emulsions. It was not patented and was soon widely adopted. Bennett's process became a key factor in the establishment of a new industry, the mass production of gelatine dry plates.

Bibliography
1878, *British Journal of Photography* (29 March): 146; and 21 March 1879: 71 (first published details of Bennett's process).

Further Reading
H. Gernsheim and A. Gernsheim, 1969, *The History of Photography*, rev. edn, London.

JW

Bentham, Sir Samuel
b. 11 January 1757 England
d. 31 May 1831 London, England

English naval architect and engineer.

He was the son of Jeremiah Bentham, a lawyer. His mother died when he was an infant and his early education was at Westminster. At the age of 14 he was apprenticed to a master shipwright at Woolwich and later at Chatham Dockyard, where he made some small improvements in the fittings of ships. In 1778 he completed his apprenticeship and sailed on the *Bienfaisant* on a summer cruise of the Channel Fleet where he suggested and supervised several improvements to the steering gear and gun fittings.

Unable to find suitable employment at home, he sailed for Russia to study naval architecture and shipbuilding, arriving at St Petersburg in 1780, whence he travelled throughout Russia as far as the frontier of China, examining mines and methods of working metals. He settled in Kritchev in 1782 and there established a small shipyard with a motley work-force. In 1784 he was appointed to command a battalion. He set up a yard on the 'Panopticon' principle, with all workshops radiating from his own central office. He increased the armament of his ships greatly by strengthening the hulls and fitting guns without recoil, which resulted in a great victory over the Turks at Liman in 1788. For this he was awarded the Cross of St George and promoted to Brigadier-General. Soon after, he was appointed to a command in Siberia, where he was responsible for opening up the resources of the country greatly by developing river navigation.

In 1791 he returned to England, where he was at first involved in the development of the Panopticon for his brother as well as with several other patents. In 1795 he was asked to look into the mechanization of the naval dockyards, and for the next eighteen years he was involved in improving methods of naval construction and machinery. He was responsible for the invention of the steam dredger, the caisson method of enclosing the entrances to docks, and the development of non-recoil cannonades of large calibre.

His intervention in the maladministration of the naval dockyards resulted in an enquiry that brought about the clearing-away of much corruption, making him very unpopular. As a result he was sent to St Petersburg to arrange for the building of a number of ships for the British navy, in which the Russians had no intention of co-operating. On his return to England after two years he was told that his office of Inspector-General of Navy Works had been abolished and he was appointed to the Navy Board; he had several disagreements with John **Rennie** and in 1812 was told that this office, too, had been abolished. He went to live in France, where he stayed for thirteen years, returning in 1827 to arrange for the publication of some of his papers.

There is some doubt about his use of his title: there is no record of his having received a knighthood in England, but it was assumed that he was authorized to use the title, granted to him in Russia, after his presentation to the Tsar in 1809.

Further Reading
Mary Sophia Bentham, *Life of Brigadier-General Sir Samuel Bentham, K.S.G., Formerly Inspector of Naval Works* (written by his wife, who died before completing it; completed by their daughter).

IMcN

Bentley, John Francis
b. 30 January 1839 Doncaster, Yorkshire, England
d. 2 March 1902 Clapham, London, England

English architect who specialized chiefly in ecclesiastical building, especially Roman Catholic churches.

Bentley's work was of high quality, particularly with regard to the decorative materials and finish. Notable among his churches was the Church of the Holy Rood (begun in 1887) at Watford, which is in Gothic Revival style, with fine decorative materials.

Bentley's *chef-d'oeuvre* is the Roman Catholic Cathedral of Westminster in London: begun in 1895, the shell was completed in 1903. He based the banded pattern of the exterior upon the Italian medieval cathedrals of Siena and Orvieto, but at Westminster the banding is in red brick and white stone instead of marble. The cathedral interior is Byzantine in style, with pendentive construction. Built of load-bearing brick, with the saucer domes inside being made of concrete strengthened with brick inserts, there is no steel reinforcement: in choosing this type of structural material, Bentley was more closely following ancient Roman technology than modern use of concrete. The intention was to have all surfaces clad in mosaic of marble, but sadly only a portion of this has yet been achieved.

Principal Honours and Distinctions
Bentley was nominated in 1902 to receive the RIBA Gold Medal but died before the presentation ceremony.

Further Reading
W. de l'Hopital, 1919, *Westminster Cathedral and its Architect*, Hutchinson.

DY

Benton, Linn Boyd
b. 13 May 1844 Little Falls, New York, USA
d. 15 July 1932 Plainfield, New Jersey, USA

American typefounder, cutter and designer, inventor of the automatic punch-cutting machine.

Benton spent his childhood in Milwaukee and La Crosse, where he early showed a talent for mechanical invention. His father was a lawyer with an interest in newspapers and who acquired the Milwaukee *Daily News*. Benton became familiar with typesetting equipment in his father's newspaper office. He learned the printer's trade at another newspaper office, at La Crosse, and later worked as bookkeeper at a type foundry in Milwaukee. When that failed in 1873, Benton acquired the plant, and when he was joined by R.V. Waldo the firm became Benton, Waldo & Co. Benton began learning and improving type-cutting practice. He first devised unit-width or 'self-spacing' type which became popular with compositors, saving, it was reckoned, 20 per cent of their time. Meanwhile, Benton worked on a punch-cutting machine to speed up the process of cutting letters in the steel punches from which matrices or moulds were formed to enable type to be cast from molten metal. His first mechanical punch-cutter worked successfully in 1884. The third machine, patented in 1885, was the model that revolutionized the typefounding operation. So far, punch-cutting had been done by hand, a rare and expensive skill that was insufficient to meet the demands of the new typesetting machines, the monotype of **Lanston** and the linotype of **Merganthaler**. These were threatened with failure until Benton saved the day with his automatic punch-cutter. Mechanizing punch-cutting and the forming of matrices made possible the typesetting revolution brought about by mono- and linotype.

In 1892 Benton's firm merged with others to form the American Type Founders Company. Benton's equipment was moved to New York and he with it, to become a board member and Chief Technical Advisor. In 1894 he became Manager of the company's new plant for type manufacture in Jersey City. Benton steadily improved both machinery and processes, for which he was granted twenty patents. With his son Morris Fuller, he was also notable and prolific in the field of type design. Benton remained in active association with his company until just two weeks before his death.

Further Reading
Obituary, 1932, *Inland Printer* (August): 53–4.
P. Cost, 1985, 'The contributions of Lyn [sic] Boyd Benton and Morris Fuller Benton to the technology of typesetting and the art of typeface design', unpublished MSc thesis, Rochester Institute of Technology (the most thorough treatment).
H.L. Bullen, 1922, *Inland Printer* (October) (describes Benton's life and work).

LRD

Benz, Karl

b. 25 November 1844 Pfaffenrot, Black Forest, Germany
d. 4 April 1929 Ladenburg, near Mannheim, Germany

German inventor of one of the first motor cars.

The son of a railway mechanic, it is said that as a child one of his hobbies was the repair of Black Forest clocks. He trained as a mechanical engineer at the Karlsruhe Lyzeum and Polytechnikum under Ferdinand Redtenbacher (d. 1863), who pointed out to him the need for a more portable power source than the steam engine. He went to Maschinenbau Gesellschaft Karlsruhe for workshop experience and then joined Schweizer & Cie, Mannheim, for two years. In 1868 he went to the Benkiser Brothers at Pforzheim. In 1871 he set up a small machine-tool works at Mannheim, but in 1877, in financial difficulties, he turned to the idea of an entirely new product based on the internal-combustion engine. At this time, N.A. **Otto** held the patent for the four-stroke internal-combustion engine, so Benz had to put his hopes on a two-stroke design. He avoided the trouble with Dugald **Clerk**'s engine and designed one in which the fuel would not ignite in the pump and in which the cylinder was swept with fresh air between each two firing strokes. His first car had a sparking plug and coil ignition. By 1879 he had developed the engine to a stage where it would run satisfactorily with little attention. On 31 December 1879, with his wife Bertha working the treadle of her sewing machine to charge the batteries, he demonstrated his engine in street trials in Mannheim. In the summer of 1888, unknown to her husband, Bertha drove one of his cars the 80 km (50 miles) to Pforzheim and back with her two sons, aged 13 and 15. She and the elder boy pushed the car up hills while the younger one steered. They bought petrol from an apothecary in Wiesloch and had a brake block repaired in Bauschlott by the village cobbler. Karl Benz's comments on her return from this venture are not recorded!

Financial problems prevented immediate commercial production of the automobile, but in 1882 Benz set up the Gasmotorenfabrik Mannheim. After trouble with some of his partners, he left in 1883 and formed a new company, Benz & Cie, Rheinische Gasmotorenfabrik. Otto's patent was revoked in 1886 and in that year Benz patented a motor car with a gas engine drive. He manufactured a 0.8 hp car, the engine running at 250 rpm with a horizontal flywheel, exhibited at the Paris Fair in 1889. He was not successful in finding anyone in France who would undertake manufacture. This first car was a three-wheeler, and soon after he produced a four-wheeled car, but he quarrelled with his co-directors, and although he left the board in 1902 he rejoined it soon after.

Further Reading

St J. Nixon, 1936, *The Invention of the Automobile*.

E. Diesel *et al.*, 1960, *From Engines to Autos*.

E. Johnson, 1986, *The Dawn of Motoring*.

IMcN

Berezin, Evelyn
b. 1925 New York, USA

American pioneer in computer technology.

Born into a poor family in the Bronx, New York City, Berezin first majored in business studies but transferred her interest to physics. She graduated in 1946 and then, with the aid of an Atomic Energy Commission fellowship, she obtained her PhD in cosmic ray physics at New York University. When the fellowship expired, opportunities in the developing field of electronic data processing seemed more promising than thise in physics. Berezin entered the firm of Electronic Computer Corporation in 1951 and was asked to 'build a computer', although few at that time had actually seen one; the result was the Elecom 200. In 1953, for Underwood Corporation, she designed the first office computer, although it was never marketed, as Underwood sold out to Olivetti.

Berezin's next position was as head of logic design for Teleregister Corporation in the late 1950s. Here, she led a team specializing in the design of on-line systems. Her most notable achievement was the design of a nationwide on-line computer reservation system for United Airlines, the first system of this kind and the precursor of similar on-line systems. It was installed in the early 1960s and was the first large non-military on-line interactive system.

In the 1960s Berezin moved to the Digitronics Corporation as manager of logic design. her work here resulted in the first high-speed commercial digital communications terminal. Also in the 1960s, her involvement in Data Secretary, a challenger to the IBM editing typewriter, makes it possible to regard her as one of the pioneers of word processing. In 1976 Berezin transferred from the electronic data and computing field to that of financial management.

Further Reading

A. Stanley, 1993, *Mothers and Daughters of Invention*, Meruchen, NJ: Scarecrow Press, 651–3.

LRD

Berger, Hans
b. 21 May 1873 Neuses bei Coburg, Germany
d. 1 June 1941 Jena, Germany

German psychiatrist and neurophysiologist, discoverer of the human electroencephalogram (EEG).

Berger studied medicine at the University of Jena from 1892. In 1897 he became Assistant to the psychiatric clinic, in 1912 he became Chief Doctor and then Director and Professor of Psychiatry, remaining in this post until his retirement in 1938.

The central theme of his research work was the correlation between the objective activity of the brain and subjective psychic phenomena. His early attempts involving the blood flow and temperature of the brain yielded no positive results, and it was not until 1929 that he had developed methods of recording the fluctuations of electric potential arising from brain activity. This electroencephalogram (EEG) proved to be of immediate value in the diagnosis and treatment of brain disease, but it did not prove to be an indicator of a connection between brain and psychic energy.

Although Berger continued to study the EEG intensively, the technique did not gain widespread recognition until its development by Adrian and Matthews from 1934 onwards.

Bibliography
Various papers, including 'Über das Elektrenkephalogramm des Menschens', Archiv für Psychiatrie, 1929–38.

Further Reading
Adrian and Matthews, 1934, 'The Berger Rhythm', *Brain*.

MG

Bergius, Friedrich Carl Rudolf
b. 11 October 1884 Goldschmieden, near Breslau, Germany
d. 31 March Buenos Aires, Argentina

German chemist who invented the coal-liquefaction process

After studying chemistry in Breslau and Leipzig and assisting *inter alia* at the institute of Fritz Haber in Karlsruhe on the catalysis of ammonia under high pressure, in 1909 he went to Hannover to pursue his idea of turning coal into liquid hydrocarbon under high hydrogen pressure (200 atm) and high temperatures (470° C). As experiments with high pressure in chemical processes were still in their initial stages and the Technical University could not support him sufficiently, he set up a private laboratory to develop the methods and to construct the equipment himself. Four years later, in 1913, his process for producing liquid or organic compounds from coal was patented.

The economic aspects of this process were apparent as the demand for fuels and lubricants increased more rapidly than the production of oil, and Bergius's process became even more important after the outbreak of the First World War. The Th. Goldschmidt company of Essen contracted him and tried large-scale production near Mannheim in 1914, but production failed because of the lack of capital and experience to operate with high pressure on an industrial level. Both capital and experience were provided jointly by the BASF company, which produced ammonia at Merseburg, and IG Farben, which took over the Bergius process in 1925, the same year that the synthesis of hydrocarbon had been developed by Fischer-Tropsch. Two years later, at the Leuna works, almost 100,000 tonnes of oil were produced from coal; during the following years, several more hydrogenation plants were to follow, especially in the eastern parts of Germany as well as in the Ruhr area, while the government guaranteed the costs. The Bergius process was extremely important for the supply of fuels to Germany during the Second World War, with the monthly production rate in 1943–4 being more than 700,000 tonnes. However, the plants were mostly destroyed at the end of the war and were later dismantled.

As a consequence of this success Bergius, who had gained an international reputation, went abroad to work as a consultant to several foreign governments. Experiments aiming to reduce the costs of production are still continued in some countries. By 1925, after he had solved all the principles of his process, he had turned to the production of dextrose by hydrolyzing wood with highly concentrated hydrochloric acid.

Principal Honours and Distinctions
Nobel Prize 1931. Honorary doctorates, Heidelberg, Harvard and Hannover.

Bibliography
1907, '*Über absolute Schwefelsäure als Lösungsmittel*', unpublished thesis, Weida.
1913, *Die Anwendung hoher Drucke bei chemischen Vorgängen und eine Nachbildung des Entstehungsprozesses der Steinkohle*, Halle.
1913, DRP no. 301, 231 (coal-liquefaction process).
1925, 'Verflüssigung der Kohle', *Zeitschrift des Vereins Deutscher Ingenieure*, 69: 1313–20, 1359–62.
1933, 'Chemische Reaktionen unter hohem Druck', *Les Prix Nobel en 1931*, Stockholm, pp. 1–37.

Further Reading
Deutsches Bergbau-Museum, 1985, *Friedrich Bergius und die Kohleverflüssigung. Stationen einer Entwicklung*, Bochum (gives a comprehensive and illustrated description of the man and the technology).
H. Beck, 1982, *Friedrich Bergius, ein Erfinderschicksal*, Munich: Deutsches Museum (a detailed biographical description).
W. Birkendfeld, 1964, *Der synthetische Treibstoff*

1933–1945. Ein Beitrag zur nationalsozialistischen Wirtschafts- und Rüstungspolitik, Göttingen, Berlin and Frankfurt (describes the economic value of synthetic fuels for the Third Reich).

WK

Berliner, Emile
b. 20 May 1851 Hannover, Germany
d. 3 August 1929 Montreal, Canada

German (naturalized American) inventor, developer of the disc record and lateral mechanical replay.

After arriving in the USA in 1870 and becoming an American citizen, Berliner worked as a dry-goods clerk in Washington, DC, and for a period studied electricity at Cooper Union for the Advancement of Science and Art, New York. He invented an improved microphone and set up his own experimental laboratory in Washington, DC. He developed a microphone for telephone use and sold the rights to the Bell Telephone Company. Subsequently he was put in charge of their laboratory, remaining in that position for eight years. In 1881 Berliner, with his brothers Joseph and Jacob, founded the J. Berliner Telephonfabrik in Hanover, the first factory in Europe specializing in telephone equipment.

Inspired by the development work performed by T.A. **Edison** and in the **Volta** Laboratory (see C.S. **Tainter**), he analysed the existing processes for recording and reproducing sound and in 1887 developed a process for transferring lateral undulations scratched in soot into an etched groove that would make a needle and diaphragm vibrate. Using what may be regarded as a combination of the Phonautograph of Léon **Scott de Martinville** and the photo-engraving suggested by Charles **Cros**, in May 1887 he thus demonstrated the practicability of the laterally recorded groove. He termed the apparatus 'Gramophone'. In November 1887 he applied the principle to a glass disc and obtained an inwardly spiralling, modulated groove in copper and zinc. In March 1888 he took the radical step of scratching the lateral vibrations directly onto a rotating zinc disc, the surface of which was protected, and the subsequent etching created the groove. Using well-known principles of printing-plate manufacture, he developed processes for duplication by making a negative mould from which positive copies could be pressed in a thermoplastic compound. Toy gramophones were manufactured in Germany from 1889 and from 1892–3 Berliner manufactured both records and gramophones in the USA. The gramophones were hand-cranked at first, but from 1896 were based on a new design by E.R. **Johnson**. In 1897–8 Berliner spread his activities to England and Germany, setting up a European pressing plant in the telephone factory in Hanover, and in 1899 a Canadian company was formed. Various court cases over patents removed Berliner from direct running of the reconstructed companies, but he retained a major economic interest in E.R. Johnson's Victor Talking Machine Company. In later years Berliner became interested in aeronautics, in particular the autogiro principle. Applied acoustics was a continued interest, and a tile for controlling the acoustics of large halls was successfully developed in the 1920s.

Bibliography
16 May 1888, *Journal of the Franklin Institute* 125 (6) (Lecture of 16 May 1888) (Berliner's early appreciation of his own work).
1914, *Three Addresses*, privately printed (a history of sound recording).
US patent no. 372,786 (basic photo-engraving principle).
US patent no. 382,790 (scratching and etching).
US patent no. 534,543 (hand-cranked gramophone).

Further Reading
R. Gelatt, 1977, *The Fabulous Phonograph*, London: Cassell (a well-researched history of reproducible sound which places Berliner's contribution in its correct perspective).
J.R. Smart, 1985, 'Emile Berliner and nineteenth-century disc recordings', in *Wonderful Inventions*, ed. Iris Newson, Washington, DC: Library of Congress, pp. 346–59 (provides a reliable account).
O. Read and W.L. Welch, 1959, *From Tin Foil to Stereo*, Indianapolis: Howard W. Sams, pp. 119–35 (provides a vivid account, albeit with less precision).

GB-N

Berry, George
b. Missouri, USA
fl. 1880s

*American farmer who developed the first
steam-powered, self-propelled combine harvester.*

Born in Missouri, George Berry moved to a
4,000 acre (1,600 hectare) farm at Lindsay in
California, and between 1881 and 1886 built
himself a steam-driven combine harvester. Berry's machine was the first self-propelled harvester
and the first to use straw as a fuel. A single boiler
powered two engines: a 26 hp (19 kW) Mitchell
Fisher engine provided the forward drive, whilst
a 6 hp (4 kW) **Westinghouse** engine drove the
threshing mechanism. Cleaned straw was passed
by conveyor back to the firebox, where it provided the main fuel. The original machine had a
22 ft cut, but a later machine extended this to 40
ft and harvested 50 acres a day, although on one
occasion it achieved the distinction of being the
first harvester to cut over 100 acres in one day.
The traction engine used for motive power was
removable and was used after harvest for ploughing. It was the first engine to be capable of forward and reverse motion.

In later life Berry moved into politics, becoming a member of the California Senate for Inyo
and Tulare in the 1890s.

Further Reading
G. Quick and W. Buchele, 1978, *The Grain
Harvesters*, American Society of Agricultural
Engineers (gives an account of combine-har-
vester development).

AP

Berry, Henry
b. 1720 Parr (?), near St Helens, Lancashire,
England
d. 30 July 1812 Liverpool, England

*English canal and dock engineer who was
responsible for the first true canal, as distinct
from a canalized river, in England.*

Little is known of Berry's early life, but it is certain that he knew the district around St Helens
intimately, which was of assistance to him in his
later canal works. He became Clerk and Assistant
to Thomas **Steers** and proved his natural engineering ability in helping Steers in both the construction of the Newry navigation in Ireland and
his supervision of the construction of Salthouse
Dock in Liverpool. On Steers's death in 1750
Berry was appointed, at the age of 30, Dock En-

gineer for Liverpool Docks, and completed the
Salthouse Dock three years later. In 1755 he was
allowed by the Liverpool Authority – presumably
because his full-time service was not required at
the docks at that time – to survey and construct
the Sankey Brook Navigation (otherwise known
as the St Helens Canal), which was completed in
1757. Berry was instructed to make the brook
navigable, but with the secret consent and con-
nivance of one of the proprietors he built a lateral
canal, the work commencing on 5 September
1755. This was the first dead-water canal in the
country, as distinct from an improved river navigation, and preceded **Brindley**'s Bridgewater
Canal by some five or six years. On the canal he
also constructed at Blackbrook the first pair of
staircase locks to be built in England.

Berry later advised on improvements to the
Weaver Navigation, and his design for the new
locks was accepted. He also carried out in 1769
a survey for a Leeds and Liverpool Canal, but this
was not proceeded with and it was left to others
to construct this canal. He advised turnpike trustees on bridge construction, but his main work
was in Liverpool dock construction and between
1767 and 1771 he built the George's Dock. His
final dock work was King's Dock, which was opened on 3 October 1788; he resigned at the age
of 68 when the dock was completed. He lived for
another 24 years, during which he was described
in the local directories as 'gentleman' instead of
'engineer' or 'surveyor' as he had been previously.

Further Reading
S.A. Harris, 1937, 'Liverpool's second dock en-
gineer', *Transactions of the Historic Society of
Lancashire and Cheshire* 89.

JHB

Berthollet, Claude-Louis
b. 9 November 1748 Talloise, near Lake Annecy, France
d. 6 November 1822 Arceuil, France

*French chemist who made important innovations
in textile chemistry.*

Berthollet qualified as a medical doctor and pursued chemical researches, notably into 'muriatic
acid' (chlorine), then recently discovered by
Scheele. He was one of the first chemists to embrace the new system of chemistry advanced by

Lavoisier. Berthollet held several official appointments, among them inspector of dye works (from 1784) and Director of the Manufacture Nationale des Gobelins. These appointments enabled him to continue his researches and embark on a series of publications on the practical applications of chlorine, prussic acid (hydrocyanic acid) and ammonia. He clearly demonstrated the benefits of the French practice of appointing scientists to the state manufactories.

There were two practical results of Berthollet's studies of chlorine. First, he produced a powerful explosive by substituting potassium chlorate, formed by the action of chlorine on potash, in place of nitre (potassium nitrate) in gunpowder. Then, mainly from humanitarian motives, he followed up Scheele's observation of the bleaching properties of chlorine water, in order to release for cultivation the considerable areas of land that had hitherto been required by the old bleaching process. The chlorine method greatly speeded up bleaching; this was a vital factor in the revolution in the textile industries.

After a visit to Egypt in 1799, Berthollet carried out many experiments on dyeing, seeking to place this ancient craft onto a scientific basis. His work is summed up in his *Eléments de l'art de la teinture*, Paris, 1791.

Bibliography

1791, *Eléments de l'art de la teinture*, Paris (covers his work on dyeing).

Berthollet published two books of importance in the early history of physical chemistry:

1801, *Recherches sur les lois de l'affinité*, Paris.

1803, *Essai de statique chimique*, Paris.

His scientific papers appeared mainly in *Mémores de l'Académie Royal des Sciences* and *Annales de Chimie*.

Further Reading

E.F. Jomard, 1844, *Notice sur la vie et les ouvrages de Claude-Louis Berthollet*, Annecy.

E. Farber, 1961, *Great Chemists*, New York: Interscience, pp. 32–4 (includes a short biographical account).

LRD

Bessemer, Sir Henry

b. 19 January 1813 Charlton (near Hitchin), Hertfordshire, England
d. 15 January 1898 Denmark Hill, London, England

English inventor of the Bessemer steelmaking process.

The most valuable part of Bessemer's education took place in the workshop of his inventor father. At the age of only 17 he went to London to seek his fortune and set himself up in the trade of casting art works in white metal. He went on to the embossing of metals and other materials and this led to his first major invention, whereby a date was incorporated in the die for embossing seals, thus preventing the wholesale forgeries that had previously been committed. For this, a grateful Government promised Bessemer a paid position, a promise that was never kept; recognition came only in 1879 with a belated knighthood. Bessemer turned to other inventions, mainly in metalworking, including a process for making bronze powder and gold paint. After he had overcome technical problems, the process became highly profitable, earning him a considerable income during the forty years it was in use.

The Crimean War presented inventors such as Bessemer with a challenge when weaknesses in the iron used to make the cannon became apparent. In 1856, at his Baxter House premises in St Pancras, London, he tried fusing cast iron with steel. Noticing the effect of an air current on the molten mixture, he constructed a reaction vessel or converter in which air was blown through molten cast iron. There was a vigorous reaction which nearly burned the house down, and Bessemer found the iron to be almost completely decarburized, without the slag threads always present in wrought iron. Bessemer had in fact invented not only a new process but a new material, mild steel. His paper 'On the manufacture of malleable iron and steel without fuel' at the British Association meeting in Cheltenham later that year created a stir. Bessemer was courted by ironmasters to license the process. However, success was short-lived, for they found that phosphorus in the original iron ore passed into the metal and rendered it useless. By chance, Bessemer had used in his trials pig-iron, derived from haematite, a phosphorus-free ore. Bessemer tried hard to overcome the problem, but lacking chemical knowledge he resigned himself to limiting his process to this kind of pig-iron. This limitation was removed in 1879 by Sidney Gilchrist **Thomas**, who substituted a chemically basic lining in the converter in place of the acid lining used by Bessemer. This reacted with the phosphorus to form a substance that could be tapped off with the slag, leaving the steel free from this harmful element. Even so, the new material had begun to be applied in engineering, especially for railways. The open-hearth process developed by **Siemens** and the **Martin** brothers complemented rather than competed with Bessemer steel. The widespread use of the two processes had a revolutionary effect on mechanical and structural engineering and earned Bessemer around £1 million in royalties before the patents expired.

Principal Honours and Distinctions
Knighted 1879. FRS 1879. Royal Society of Arts Albert Gold Medal 1872.

Bibliography
1905, *Sir Henry Bessemer FRS: An Autobiography*, London.

LRD

Bettini, Gianni
b. 1860 Novara, Italy
d. 27 February 1938 San Remo, Italy

Italian developer of equipment for recording, duplicating and reproducing phonograph cylinders.

He was a nobleman and an Italian cavalry lieutenant and went to the USA, where he married Daisy Abbott (of Stamford, Connecticut). From 1888 he made amateur recordings of a wide circle of artistic acquaintances and improved the recording diaphragm attachment by the development of a 'spider' (a mechanical link that attacks the diaphragm in several points on its surface, rather than in the centre only). From 1892, through the Bettini Phonograph Laboratories, he published recordings of operatic artists and selections, and this led to the development of improved duplicating techniques by the so-called pantographic method. In 1901 he sold his US company and moved to Paris, although he continued to publish both cylinders and discs. In 1908 Bettini made a venture into cinematography, without success.

Bibliography
US patent no. 409,003 (the 'spider' device).
US patent no. 488,381 (duplication).

Further Reading
O. Read and W.L. Welch, 1959, *From Tin Foil to Stereo*, Indianapolis: Howard W. Sams, pp. 69–78.

GB-N

Bevan, Edward John
b. 11 December 1856 Birkenhead, England
d. 17 October 1921 London, England

English co-inventor of the 'viscose rayon' process for making artificial silk.

Bevan began his working life as a chemist in a soap works at Runcorn, but later studied chemistry at Owens College, Manchester. It was there that he met and formed a friendship with C.F. **Cross**, with whom he started to work on cellulose. Bevan moved to a paper mill in Scotland but then went south to London, where he and Cross set up a partnership in 1885 as consulting and analytical chemists. Their work was mainly concerned with the industrial utilization of cellulose, and with the problems of the paper and jute industries. Their joint publication, *A Text-book of Paper-making*, which first appeared in 1888 and went into several editions, became the standard reference and textbook on the subject. The book has a long introductory chapter on cellulose.

In 1892 Cross, Bevan and Clayton Beadle discovered viscose, or sodium cellulose xanthate, and took out the patent which was to be the foundation of the 'viscose rayon' industry. They had their own laboratory at Station Avenue, Kew Gardens, where they carried out much work that eventually resulted in viscose: cellulose, usually in the form of wood pulp, was treated first with caustic soda and then with carbon disulphide to form the xanthate, which was then dissolved in a solution of dilute caustic soda to produce a viscous liquid. After being aged, the viscose was extruded through fine holes in a spinneret and coagulated in a dilute acid to regenerate the cellulose as spinnable fibres. At first there was no suggestion of spinning it into fibre, but the hope was to use it for filaments in incandescent electric light bulbs. The sheen on the fibres suggested their possible use in textiles and the term 'artificial silk' was later introduced. Cross and Bevan also discovered the acetate 'Celanese', which was cellulose triacetate dissolved in acetone and spun in air, but both inventions needed much development before they could be produced commercially.

In 1892 Bevan turned from cellulose to food

and drugs and left the partnership to become Public Analyst to Middlesex County Council, a post he held until his death, although in 1895 he and Cross published their important work *Cellulose*. He was prominent in the affairs of the Society of Public Analysts and became one of its officials.

Bibliography
1888, with C.F. Cross, *A Text-book of Paper-making.*
1892, with C.F. Cross and C. Beadle, British patent no. 8,700 (viscose).
1895, with C.F. Cross, *Cellulose.*

Further Reading
Obituary, 1921, *Journal of the Chemical Society.*
Obituary, 1921, *Journal of the Society of Chemical Industry.*
Edwin J. Beer, 1962–3, 'The birth of viscose rayon', *Transactions of the Newcomen Society* 35 (an account of the problems of developing viscose rayon; Beer worked under Cross in the Kew laboratories).

RLH

Bewick, Thomas

b. August 1753 Cherryburn House, Ovingham, Northumberland, England
d. 8 November 1828 Gateshead, England

English perfecter of wood-engraving.

The son of a farmer, Bewick was educated locally, but his progress was unremarkable save for demonstrating an intense love of nature and of drawing. In 1767 he was apprenticed to Ralph Beilby, an engraver in Newcastle. Wood-engraving at that time was at a low ebb, restricted largely to crude decorative devices, and Hogarth, commenting on a recent book on the art, doubted whether it would ever recover. Beilby's business was of a miscellaneous character, but Bewick's interest in wood-engraving was noticed and encouraged: Beilby submitted several of his engravings to the Royal Society of Arts, which awarded a premium of £80 for them. His apprenticeship ended in 1774 and he went to London, where he readily found employment with several printers. The call of the north was too strong, however, and two years later he returned to Newcastle, entering into partnership with Beilby. With the publication of *Select Fables* in

1784, Bewick really showed both his expertise in the art of wood-engraving as a medium for book illustration and his talents as an artist. His engravings for the *History of British Birds* mark the high point of his achievement. The second volume of this work appeared in 1804, the year in which his partnership with Beilby was dissolved.

The essential feature of Bewick's wood-engravings involved cutting across the grain of the wood instead of along it, as in the old woodcut technique. The wood surface thus obtained offered a much more sensitive medium for engraving than before. It paved the way for the flowering of engraving on wood, and then on steel, for the production of illustrated material for an ever wider public through the Victorian age.

Bibliography
1864, *Memoir of Thomas Bewick* (autobiography, completed by his daughter).
1784, *Select Fables.*

Further Reading
M. Weekley, 1963, *Thomas Bewick*, Oxford: Oxford University Press.

LRD

Beyer, Charles Frederick

b. 14 May 1813 Plauen, Saxony, Germany
d. 2 June 1876 Llantysilio, Denbighshire, Wales

German (naturalized British in 1852) engineer, founder of locomotive builders Beyer, Peacock & Co.

Beyer came from a family of poor weavers, but showed talent as an artist and draftsman and was educated at Dresden Polytechnic School. He was sent to England in 1834 to report on improvements in cotton spinning machinery and settled in Manchester, working for the machinery manufacturers Sharp Roberts & Co., initially as a draftsman. When the firm started to build locomotives he moved to this side of the business. The Institution of Mechanical Engineers was founded at his house in 1847. In 1853 Beyer entered into a partnership with Richard Peacock, Locomotive Engineer to the Manchester, Sheffield & Lincolnshire Railway, and Henry Robertson to establish Beyer, Peacock & Co. The company soon established a reputation for soundly designed, elegant locomotives: it exported worldwide, and survived until the 1960s.

Further Reading
Obituary, 1877, *Minutes of Proceedings of the Institution of Civil Engineers* 47.
R.L. Hills, 1967–8 'Some contributions to locomotive development by Beyer, Peacock & Co.', *Transactions of the Newcomen Society* 40 (a good description of Beyer, Peacock & Co's locomotive work).

See also **Garratt, Herbert William**.

PJGR

Bickford, William
b. 1774 Devonshire, England
d. 1834 Tuckingmill, Cornwall, England

English leather merchant, inventor of the safety fuse.

Having tried in vain to make his living as a currier in Truro, Cornwall, he set up as a leather merchant in Tuckingmill and became aware of the high casualty rates suffered by local tin-miners in shot-firing accidents. He therefore started attempts to discover a safe means of igniting charges, and came up with a form of safety fuse that made the operation of blasting much less hazardous. It was patented in 1831 and consisted of a cable of jute and string containing a thin core of powder; it provided a dependable means for conveying the flame to the charge so that the danger of hang fires was almost eliminated. Its accurate and consistent timing allowed the firing of several holes at a time without the fusing of the last being destroyed by the blast from the first. By 1840, a gutta-percha fuse had been developed which could be used in wet conditions and was an improvement until the use of dynamite for shot-firing.

Accounts of the invention, after it had been described in the *Report from the Select Committee on Accidents in Mines* (1835, London) were widespread in various foreign mining journals, and in the 1840s factories were set up in different mining areas on the European continent, in America and in Australia. Bickford himself founded a firm at Tuckingmill in the year that he came up with his invention which was later controlled by his descendants until it finally merged with Imperial Chemical Industries (ICI) after the

First World War.

Further Reading
F. Heise, 1904, *Sprengstoffe und Zündung der Sprengschüsse*, Berlin (provides a detailed description of the development).
W.J. Reader, 1970, *Imperial Chemical Industries. A History*, Vol. I, London: Oxford University Press (throws light on the tight international connections of Bickford's firm with Nobel industries).

WK

Bigelow, Erastus Brigham
b. 2 April 1814 West Boyleston, Massachusetts, USA
d. 6 December 1879 USA

American inventor of power looms for making lace and many types of carpets.

Bigelow was born in West Boyleston, Massachusetts, where his father struggled as a farmer, wheelwright, and chairmaker. Before he was 20, Bigelow had many different jobs, among them farm labourer, clerk, violin player and cotton-mill employee. In 1830, he went to Leicester Academy, Massachusetts, but he could not afford to go on to Harvard. He sought work in Boston, New York and elsewhere, making various inventions.

The most important of his early inventions was the power loom of 1837 for making coach lace. This loom contained all the essential features of his carpet looms, which he developed and patented two years later. He formed the Clinton Company for manufacturing carpets at Leicester, Massachusetts, but the factory became so large that its name was adopted for the town. The next twenty years saw various mechanical discoveries, while his range of looms was extended to cover Brussels, Wilton, tapestry and velvet carpets. Bigelow has been justly described as the originator of every fundamental device in these machines, which were amongst the largest textile machines of their time. The automatic insertion and withdrawal of strong wires with looped ends was the means employed to raise the looped pile of the Brussels carpets, while thinner wires with a knife blade at the end raised and then severed the loops to create the rich Wilton pile. At the Great Exhibition in 1851, it was declared that his looms made better carpets than any from hand looms. He also developed other looms for special materials.

He became a noted American economist, writing two books about tariff problems, advocating that the United States should not abandon its protectionist policies. In 1860 he was narrowly defeated in a Congress election. The following year he was a member of the committee that established the Massachusetts Institute of Technology.

Further Reading
National Cyclopedia of American Biography III (the standard account of his life).
F.H. Sawyer, 1927, *Clinton Item* (provides a broad background to his life).
C. Singer (ed.), 1958, *A History of Technology*, Vol. V, Oxford: Clarendon Press (describes Bigelow's inventions).

RLH

Biles, Sir John Harvard
b. 1854 Portsmouth, England
d. 27 October 1933 Scotland (?)

English naval architect, academic and successful consultant in the years when British shipbuilding was at its peak.

At the conclusion of his apprenticeship at the Royal Dockyard, Portsmouth, Biles entered the Royal School of Naval Architecture, South Kensington, London; as it was absorbed by the Royal Naval College, he graduated from Greenwich to the Naval Construction Branch, first at Pembroke and later at the Admiralty. From the outset of his professional career it was apparent that he had the intellectual qualities that would enable him to oversee the greatest changes in ship design of all time. He was one of the earliest proponents of the revolutionary work of the hydrodynamicist William **Froude**.

In 1880 Biles turned to the merchant sector, taking the post of Naval Architect to J. & G. Thomson (later John Brown & Co.). Using Froude's Law of Comparisons he was able to design the record-breaking *City of Paris* of 1887, the ship that started the fabled succession of fast and safe Clydebank-built North Atlantic liners. For a short spell, before returning to Scotland, Biles worked in Southampton. In 1891 Biles accepted the Chair of Naval Architecture at the University of Glasgow. Working from the

campus at Gilmorehill, he was to make the University (the oldest school of engineering in the English-speaking world) renowned in naval architecture. His workload was legendary, but despite this he was admired as an excellent lecturer with cheerful ways which inspired devotion to the Department and the University. During the thirty years of his incumbency of the Chair, he served on most of the important government and international shipping committees, including those that recommended the design of HMS *Dreadnought*, the ordering of the Cunarders *Lusitania* and *Mauretania* and the lifesaving improvements following the *Titanic* disaster. An enquiry into the strength of destroyer hulls followed the loss of HMS *Cobra* and *Viper*, and he published the report on advanced experimental work carried out on HMS *Wolf* by his undergraduates.

In 1906 he became Consultant Naval Architect to the India Office, having already set up his own consultancy organization, which exists today as Sir J.H. Biles and Partners. His writing was prolific, with over twenty-five papers to professional institutions, sundry articles and a two-volume textbook.

Principal Honours and Distinctions
Knighted 1913. Knight Commander of the Indian Empire 1922. Master of the Worshipful Company of Shipwrights 1904.

Bibliography
1905, 'The strength of ships with special reference to experiments and calculations made upon HMS *Wolf*', *Transactions of the Institution of Naval Architects*.
1911, *The Design and Construction of Ships*, London: Griffin.

Further Reading
C.A. Oakley, 1973, *History of a Faculty*, Glasgow University.

FMW

Bilgram, Hugo
b. 13 January 1847 Memmingen, Bavaria, Germany
d. 27 August 1932 Moylan, Pennsylvania, USA

German (naturalized American) mechanical engineer, inventor of bevel-gear generator and economist.

Hugo Bilgram studied mechanical engineering at the Augsburg Maschinenbau Schule and graduated in 1865. He worked as a machinist and draughtsman for several firms in Germany before going to the United States in 1869.

In America he first worked for L.B. Flanders Company and Southwark Foundry & Machine Company in Philadelphia, designing instruments and machines. In the 1870s he also assisted in an evening class in drawing at The Franklin Institute. He devised the Bilgram Valve Diagram for analysing the action of steam engine slide valves and he developed a method of drawing accurate outlines of gear teeth. This led him to design a machine for cutting the teeth of gear wheels, particularly bevel wheels, which he patented in 1884. He was in charge of the American branch of Brehmer Brothers Company from 1879 and in 1884 became the sole owner of the company, which was later incorporated as the Bilgram Machine Works. He was responsible for several other inventions and developments in gear manufacture.

Bilgram was a member of the Franklin Institute, the American Academy of Political and Social Science, the Philadelphia Technische Verein and the Philadelphia Engineer's Club, and was elected a member of the American Society of Mechanical Engineers in 1885. He was also an amateur botanist, keenly interested in microscopic work.

Principal Honours and Distinctions
Franklin Institute Elliott Cresson Gold Medal. City of Philadelphia John Scott Medal.

Bibliography
Hugo Bilgram was granted several patents and was the author of:
1877, *Slide Valve Gears*.
1889, *Involuntary Idleness*.
1914, *The Cause of Business Depression*.
1928, *The Remedy for Overproduction and Unemployment*.

Further Reading
Robert S. Woodbury, 1958, *History of the Gear-cutting Machine*, Cambridge, Mass. (describes Bilgram's bevel-gear generating machine).

RTS

Birdseye, Clarence
b. 9 December 1886 Brooklyn, New York, USA
d. 7 October 1956 USA

American inventor of the fast-freezing method of food preservation.

Clarence Birdseye went to high school at Montclair in New Jersey, and from there to Amherst College between 1906 and 1910. He became a field naturalist on the US Department of Agriculture's survey of 1910 to 1912, and during the following five years worked as a fur trader. He was the Purchasing Agent for the US Navy Corps between 1917 and 1919, and acted as Assistant to the President of the US Fisherman's Association between 1920 and 1922.

Birdseye was a keen fisherman, and during his time in Labrador learnt how to fast-freeze his catch in the wind. He formed the Birdseye Seafood Company in 1923 and pioneered the development of quick-freezing methods for the preservation of dressed seafood. His first company went bankrupt, but he quickly formed the General Seafoods Corporation. He filed his first patent in 1924 for the plate freezer, and in the late 1920s developed the double belt freezer. In 1929 Birdseye's company was bought out for $22 million, Birdseye himself receiving $1 million. He was an active member of the American Fisherman's Society, the American Society of Refrigeration Engineers, the American Society of Mechanical Engineers, the American Society of Mammalogists and the Institute of Food Technologists.

Principal Honours and Distinctions
Nutrition Foundation Stephen M. Babcock Award 1949.

Further Reading
W.H. Clark and J. Moynahan, *Famous Leaders of Industry* (gives a brief account of Birdseye's life).
1982, *Frozen Food Age* (August) (an account of the development of the industry he created).

AP

Biringuccio, Vanoccio Vincenzio Agustino Luca

b. 1480 Siena, Italy
d. 1537 Rome, Italy

Italian author of the celebrated 'Pirotechnia' on mining and metallurgy.

Biringuccio spent much of his life in the service of, or under the patronage of, the Petruccis, one of the leading families of Siena. In his youth, he was able to travel widely in Italy and Germany, observing mining and metallurgical processes at first hand. For example, his visit to the brass-works in Milan was to be the source of the detailed description in *Pirotechnia*, published after his death. He held various appointments in charge of mines or other concerns, such as the Siena mint, under the patronage of the Petruccis. During two periods of exile, while the Petrucci fortunes were in eclipse, he engaged in military activities such as the casting of cannon. That included the great culverin of Florence cast in 1529, also described in the *Pirotechnia*. In December 1534 Pope Paul III offered him the post of Director of the papal foundry and munitions. He did not take up the post until 1536, but he died the following year.

Pirotechnia, which made Biringuccio famous, was published in Venice in 1540, three years after his death. The word 'pirotechnia' had a wider meaning than that of fireworks, extending to the action of fire on various substances and including distillation and the preparation of acids. While owing something to earlier written sources, the book is substantially based on a lifetime of practical experience of mining and metalworking, including smelting, casting and alloying, and evidence in the book suggests that it was written between 1530 and 1535. Curzio Navo brought out the second and third editions in 1550 and 1559, as well as a Latin edition. A fourth edition was also printed in 1559. The appearance of four editions in such a short time testifies to the popularity and usefulness of the work.

Bibliography
1942, *Pirotechnia, Translated from the Italian with an Introduction and Notes*, ed. Cyril S. Smith and Martha T. Gnudi, New York: American Institute of Mining and Metallurgical Engineers (the best account of Biringuccio's life, with bibliographical details of the various editions of the *Pirotechnia*, is in the preface).

LRD

Biro, Laszlo Joszef (Ladislao José)

b. 29 September 1899 Budapest, Hungary
d. 24 October 1985 Buenos Aires, Argentina

Hungarian inventor of the ballpoint pen.

Details of Biro's early life are obscure, but by 1939 he had been active as a painter, a member of the Hungarian Academy of Sciences and an inventor, patenting over thirty minor inventions. During the 1930s he edited a cultural magazine and noticed in the printing shop the advantages of quick-drying ink. He began experimenting with crude ballpoint pens. The idea was not new, for an American, John Loud, had patented a cumbersome form of pen for marking rough surfaces in 1888; it had failed commercially. Biro and his brother Georg patented a ballpoint pen in 1938, although they had not yet perfected a suitable ink or a reservoir to hold it.

In 1940 Biro fled the Nazi occupation of Hungary and settled in Argentina. Two years later, he had developed his pen to the point where he could seek backers for a company to exploit it commercially. His principal backer appears to have been an English accountant, Henry George Martin. In 1944 Martin offered the invention to the US Army Air Force and the British Royal Air Force to overcome the problems aircrews were experiencing at high altitudes with leaking fountain pens. Some 10,000 ballpoints were made for the RAF. Licences were granted in the USA for the manufacture of the 'biro', and in 1944 the Miles–Martin Pen Company was formed in Britain and began making them on a large scale at a factory near Reading, Berkshire; by 1951 its workforce had grown to over 1,000. Other companies followed suit; by varying details of the pen, they avoided infringing the original patents. One such entrepreneur, Miles Reynolds, was the first to put the pen on sale to the public in New York; it is reputed that 10,000 were sold on the first day.

Biro had little taste for commercial exploitation, and by 1947 he had withdrawn from the Argentine company, mainly to resume his painting, in the surrealist style. Examples of his work are exhibited in the Fine Arts Museum in Budapest. He created an instrument that had a greater impact on written communication than any other single invention.

Further Reading
'Nachruf: Ladislao José Biro (1899–1985)', *Historische Burowelt* (1988) 21: 5–8 (with English summary).
J. Jewkes, *The Sources of Invention*, pp. 234–5.
LRD

Bi Sheng (Pi Sheng)

b. *c*.990 China
d. *c*.1051 China

Chinese inventor of movable type for printing.

Bi Sheng was a commoner, 'a man of unofficial position'. The only record of his invention is **Shen Gua**'s writings, the *Meng Qi Bi Tan* (*c*.1088), which give a clear and complete description of the making of type, typesetting, printing and distribution of the type after printing. Each character was cut in a piece of clay and then baked hard. The type was placed in an iron frame or forme set on an iron plate coated with a sticky resin, wax and paper ash. Printing a few copies was laborious, but for 100 or 1,000 copies the process was relatively quick. Each character had several types, and the commoner ones had as many as twenty or more. No further information about the type has survived, nor has any book produced in this way. Bi Sheng died soon after his invention was made, and so he was probably unable to pass the details on to an apprentice or follower.

Further Reading
Joseph Needham, 1985, *Science and Civilisation in China*, Vol. V(1) Cambridge: Cambridge University Press, vols V (1), pp. 201–3; V (3), p. 187.
LRD

Bissell, George Henry

b. 8 November 1821 Hanover, New Hampshire, USA
d. 19 November 1884 New York, USA

American promoter of the petroleum industry.

Bissell first pursued a career in education, as Professor of Languages at the University of Norwich, Vermont, and then as Superintendent of Schools in New Orleans. After dabbling in journalism, he turned to law and was admitted to the Bar in New York City in 1853. The following year he was deeply impressed by the picture of a derrick on the label on a bottle of brine from Samuel M. Kier's brine well. Bissell saw in it a new possibility of producing petroleum and, with Jonathan G. Elveleth, formed the world's first oil company, the Pennsylvania Rock Oil Company, on 30 December 1854. The Company obtained a sample of oil at Hibbard Farm, Titusville, Pennsylvania, and sent it for examination to Benjamin Silliman Jr, Professor of Chemistry at Yale University. He reported on 16 April 1855 that by simple means nearly all the oil could be converted into useful substances. Bissell acted on this and began drilling near Oil Creek, Pennsylvania. On 27 August 1859 his contractor struck oil at 60 ft (18 m). This date is usually taken as the starting point of the modern oil industry, even though oil had been obtained two years earlier in Europe by drilling near Hannover and at Ploesti in Romania. Bissell returned to New York in 1863 and spent the rest of his life promoting enterprises connected with the oil industry.

Further Reading
Obituary, 1884, *New York Herald*, 20 November.
W.B. Kaempffert, 1924, *A Popular History of American Inventions*, New York.
I.M. Tarbell, 1904, *History of the Standard Oil Company*, New York.
LRD

Black, Harold Stephen

b. 14 April 1898 Leominster, Massachusetts, USA
d. 11 December 1983 Summit, New Jersey, USA

American electrical engineer who discovered that the application of negative feedback to amplifiers improved their stability and reduced distortion.

Black graduated from Worcester Polytechnic Institute, Massachusetts, in 1921 and joined the Western Electric Company laboratories (later the Bell Telephone Laboratories) in New York City. There he worked on a variety of electronic-communication problems. His major contribution was the discovery in 1927 that the application of negative feedback to an amplifier, whereby a fraction of the output signal is fed back to the input in the opposite phase, not only increases the stability of the amplifier but also has the effect of reducing the magnitude of any distortion introduced by it. This discovery has found wide application in the design of audio hi-fi amplifiers and various control systems, and has also given valuable insight into the way in which many animal control functions operate.

During the Second World War he developed a form of pulse code modulation (PCM) to provide a practicable, secure telephony system for the US Army Signal Corps. From 1963–6, after his retirement from the Bell Labs, he was Principal Research Scientist with General Precision Inc., Little Falls, New Jersey, following which he became an independent consultant in communications. At the time of his death he held over 300 patents.

Principal Honours and Distinctions
Institute of Electronic and Radio Engineers Lamme Medal 1957.

Bibliography
1934, 'Stabilised feedback amplifiers', *Electrical Engineering* 53:114 (describes the principles of negative feedback).
21 December 1937, US patent no. 2,106,671 (for his negative feedback discovery.
1947, with J.O. Edson, 'Pulse code modulation', *Transactions of the American Institute of Electrical Engineers* 66: 895.
1946, 'A multichannel microwave radio relay system', *Transactions of the American Institute of Electrical Engineers* 65: 798.
1953, *Modulation Theory*, New York: D. van Nostrand.
1988, *Laboratory Management: Principles & Practice*, New York: Van Nostrand Rheinhold.

Further Reading
For early biographical details see 'Harold S. Black, 1957 Lamme Medalist', *Electrical Engineering* (1958) 77: 720; 'H.S. Black', *Institute of Electrical and Electronics Engineers Spectrum* (1977) 54.

See also **Bode, Hendrik Wade**; **Nyquist, Harry**.

KF

Blackett, William Cuthbert
b. 18 November 1859 Durham, England
d. 13 June 1935 Durham, England

English mine manager, expert in preventing mine explosions and inventor of a coal-face conveyor.

After leaving Durham college of Physical Science and having been apprenticed in different mines, he received the certificate for colliery managers and subsequently, in 1887, was appointed Manager of all the mines of Charlaw and Sacriston collieries in Durham. He remained in this position for the rest of his working life.

Frequent explosions in mines led him to investigate the causes. He was among the first to recognize the role contributed by coal-dust on mine roads, pioneered the use of inert rock- or stone-dust to render the coal-dust harmless and was the originator of many technical terms on the subject. He contributed many papers on explosion and was appointed a member of many advisory committees on prevention measures. A liquid-air rescue apparatus, designed by him and patented in 1910, was installed in various parts of the country.

Blackett also developed various new devices in mining machinery. He patented a wire-rope socket which made use of a metal wedge; invented a rotary tippler driven by frictional contact instead of gearing and which stopped automatically; and he designed a revolving cylindrical coal-washer, which also gained interest among German mining engineers. His most important invention, the first successful coal-face conveyor, was patented in 1902. It was driven by compressed air and consisted of a trough running along the length of the face through which ran an endless scraper chain. Thus fillers cast the coal into the trough, and the scraper chain drew it to the main gate to be loaded into trams.

Principal Honours and Distinctions
Knight of Grace of the Order of St John of Jerusalem. OBE. Honorary MSc University of Durham; Honorary LLD University of Birmingham. Honorary Member, Institution of Mining and Metallurgy. Honorary Member, American Institute of Mining and Metallurgical Engineers. Royal Humane Society Medal.

Further Reading
Transactions of the Institution of Mining Engin-
eers (1934–5) 89: 339–41.
Mining Association of Great Britain (ed.), 1924,
Historical Review of Coal Mining, London
(describes early mechanical devices for the extraction of coal).

WK

Blanchard, Helen Augusta
b. 25 October 1840 Portland, Maine, USA
d. 1922 USA

American inventor who made improvements in
the sewing machine.

Blanchard was the daughter of a wealthy ship
owner. She was said to have had inventive talents
but seems to have had no technical training. She
patented nothing until she was over 30, although
that may have been due to shortage of funds.
Inheriting the family wealth after the death of her
father brought her talents out into the open. She
moved to Boston, Massachusetts, and made and
patented a number of mechanical devices to improve the sewing machine: these included the
'over seaming' machine, a crochet attachment
and methods of making knitwear. In 1881, with
an unmarried sister, she founded the Blanchard
Overseam Machine Company to exploit her sewing machine inventions. Her company seems to
have prospered, for in 1891 she was said to own
'great estates', a factory and many patent rights,
the returns from which made her a wealthy
woman. Patents for sewing machine improvements and attachments continued to flow until
1915. She suffered a stroke in 1916, and died six
years later; no will was ever probated, so the fate
of her wealth can only be surmised.

Further Reading
A. Stanley, 1993, *Mothers and Daughters of In-*
vention, Meruchen, NJ: Scarecrow Press, pp.
518–21.

LRD

Blanquart-Evrard, Louis-Désiré
b. 2 August 1802 Lille, France
d. 28 April 1872 Lille, France

French photographer, photographic innovator
and entrepreneur.

After beginning his working life in a tobacco

company, Blanquart-Evrard became Laboratory
Assistant to a chemist. He also became interested
in painting on ivory and porcelain, foreshadow-
ing a life-long interest in science and art. Following his marriage to the daughter of a textile
merchant, Blanquart-Evrard became a partner in
the family business in Lyon. During the 1840s he
became interested in **Talbot**'s calotype process
and found that by applying gallic acid alone, as a
developing agent after exposure, the exposure
time could be shorter and the resulting image
clearer. Blanquart-Evrard recognized that his
process was well suited to producing positive
prints in large numbers. During 1851 and 1852,
in association with an artist friend, he became
involved in producing quantities of prints for
book illustrations. In 1849 he had announced a
glass negative process similar to that devised two
years earlier by **Niepce de St Victor**. The
carrying agent for silver salts was albumen, and
more far-reaching was his albumen-coated printing-out paper announced in 1850. Albumen
printing paper was widely adopted and the vast
majority of photographs made in the nineteenth
century were printed in this form. In 1870 Blanquart-Evrard began an association with the pioneer colour photographer **Ducos du Hauron**
with a view to opening a three-colour printing
establishment. Unfortunately plans were delayed
by the Franco-Prussian War, and Blanquart-Evrard died in 1872 before the project could be
brought to fruition.

Bibliography
1851, *Traité de photographie sur papier*, Paris
(provides details of his improvements to Talbot's process).

Further Reading
J.M. Eder, 1945, *History of Photography*, trans. E.
Epstein, New York.

JW

Blenkinsop, John
b. 1783 near Newcastle upon Tyne, England
d. 22 January 1831 Leeds, England

English coal-mine manager who made the first
successful commercial use of steam locomotives.

In 1808 Blenkinsop became agent to J.C. Brandling, MP, owner of Middleton Colliery, from
which coal was carried to Leeds over the Middle-

ton Waggonway. This had been built by Brandling's ancestor Charles Brandling, who in 1758 obtained an Act of Parliament to establish agreements with owners of land over which the wagonway was to pass. That was the first railway Act of Parliament.

By 1808 horse haulage was becoming uneconomic because the price of fodder had increased due to the Napoleonic wars. Brandling probably saw the locomotive *Catch-Me-Who-Can* demonstrated by Richard **Trevithick**. In 1811 Blenkinsop patented drive by cog-wheel and rack rail, the power to be provided preferably by a steam engine. His object was to produce a locomotive able to haul a substantial load, while remaining light enough to minimize damage to rails made from cast iron which, though brittle, was at that date the strongest material from which rails could be made. The wagonway, formerly of wood, was relaid with iron-edge rails; along one side rails cast with rack teeth were laid beside the running surface. Locomotives incorporating Blenkinsop's cog-wheel drive were designed by Matthew **Murray** and built by Fenton Murray & Wood. The design was developed from Trevithick's to include two cylinders, for easier starting and smoother running. The first locomotive was given its first public trial on 24 June 1812, when it successfully hauled eight wagons of coal, on to which fifty spectators climbed. Locomotives of this type entered regular service later in the summer and proved able to haul loads of 110 tons; Trevithick's locomotive of 1804 had managed 25 tons.

Blenkinsop-type locomotives were introduced elsewhere in Britain and in Europe, and those upon the Kenton & Coxlodge Wagonway, near Newcastle upon Tyne, were observed by George **Stephenson**. The Middleton locomotives remained at work until 1835.

Bibliography

10 April, 1811, 'Certain Mechanical Means by which the Conveyance of Coals, Minerals and Other Articles is Facilitated . . . .', British patent no. 3,431.

Further Reading

J. Bushell, 1975, *The World's Oldest Railway*, Sheffield: Turntable (describes Blenkinsop's work).

E.K. Scott (ed.), 1928, *Matthew Murray, Pioneer*

Engineer, Leeds.

C. von Oeynhausen and H. von Dechen, 1971, *Railways in England 1826 and 1827*, Cambridge: W. Heffer & Sons

PJGR

Blériot, Louis

b. 1 July 1872 Cambrai, France
d. 2 August 1936 Paris, France

French aircraft manufacturer and pilot who in 1909 made the first flight across the English Channel in an aeroplane.

Having made a fortune with his patented automobile lamp, Blériot started experimenting with model aircraft in about 1900. He tried a flapping-wing layout which, surprisingly, did fly, but a full-size version was a failure. Blériot tried out a wide variety of designs: a biplane float-glider built with Gabriel **Voisin**; a powered float-plane with ellipsoidal biplane wings; a canard (tail-first) monoplane; a tandem monoplane; and in 1907 a monoplane of conventional layout. This last was not an immediate success, but it led to the *Type XI* in which Blériot made history by flying from France to England on 25 July 1909.

Without a doubt, Blériot was an accomplished pilot and a successful manufacturer of aircraft, but he sometimes employed others as designers (a fact not made known at the time). It is now accepted that much of the credit for the design of the *Type XI* should go to Raymond **Saulnier**, who later made his name with the Morane-Saulnier Company.

Blériot-Aéronautique became one of the leading manufacturers of aircraft and by the outbreak of war in 1914 some eight hundred aircraft had been produced. By 1918, aircraft were being built at the rate of eighteen per day. The Blériot company continued to produce aircraft until it was nationalized in 1937.

Principal Honours and Distinctions

Commandeur de la Légion d'honneur. *Daily Mail* £1,000 prize for the first cross-Channel aeroplane flight.

Further Reading

C.H. Gibbs-Smith, 1965, *The Invention of the Aeroplane 1799–1909*, London (contains a list of all Blériot's early aircraft).

J. Stroud, 1966, *European Transport Aircraft*

since 1910, London (for information about Blériot's later aircraft).

For information relating to the cross-Channel flight, see:

C. Fontaine, 1913, *Comment Blériot a traversé la Manche*, Paris.

T.D. Crouch, 1982, *Blériot XI, the Story of a Classic Aircraft*, Washington, DC: National Air & Space Museum.

JDS

Blickensderfer, George Canfield
b. 1850 Erie, Pennsylvania, USA
d. 14 August 1917

American maker of the first successful portable typewriter and the first electric typewriter.

Blickensderfer was educated at the academy in Erie and at Allegheny College. He seems to have followed a business career, and in the course of his travels he became aware of the need for a simple, durable, but portable typewriter. He was in business in Stanford, Connecticut, where he developed but did not patent a number of typewriters, including a machine in which a type wheel could print short words such as 'an' and 'as' by depressing a single key. In 1889 he set up the Blickensderfer Manufacturing Company to perfect and mass-produce the machine he had in mind. He needed two years to test and perfect the model, and in 1891 work started on the factory that was to manufacture it. On the verge of mass-production in 1893, he produced a few machines for the Chicago World Exhibition in that year. Their success was sensational, and the 'Blickensderfer' received the highest accolades from the judges, who hailed it as 'extraordinary progress in the art of typewriting'. The 'Blickensderfer' appeared with successive modifications in the following years: they were durable, lightweight machines, with interchangeable type wheels, and were the first widely-used readily-portable typewriters.

Around 1902 Blickensderfer produced the first electric typewriter. A few electric machines were produced and some were sent to Europe, including England, but they are now very rare. One Blick Electric has been preserved in the Beeching Typewriter Collection in Bournemouth, England.

Further Reading

M.H. Adler, 1973, *The Writing Machine*, London: Allen & Unwin.

Historische Burowelt 10 (July 1985): 11 (provides brief biographical details in German with an English summary).

LRD

Blith, Walter
b. Seventeenth century Warwickshire, England
d. Seventeenth century England

English farmer and agricultural writer

Blith was the son of a cereal and dairy farmer from the Forest of Arden. He wrote a treatise on farming which was of contemporary value in its description of drainage and water meadows, both subjects of particular relevance in the mid-seventeenth century. The book, *The English Improver*, contains illustrations of agricultural equipment which have become an almost obligatory inclusion in any book on agricultural history. His understanding of the plough is apparent from the text and illustrations, and his was an important step in the understanding of the scientific principles to be applied to its later design. The introduction to the book is addressed to both Houses of Parliament, and is very much an attempt to highlight and seek solutions to the problems of the agriculture of the day. In it he advocates the passing of legislation to improve agricultural practice, whether this be for the destruction of moles or for the compulsory planting of trees to replace those felled.

Blith himself became a captain in the Roundhead Army during the English Civil War, and even added a dedication to Cromwell in the introduction to his second book, *The English Improver Improved*, published in 1652. This book contains additional information on both practice and crops, an expansion in knowledge which presumably owes something to Blith's employment as a surveyor of Crown lands between 1649 and 1650. He himself bought and farmed such land in Northamptonshire. His advice on the choice of land for particular crops and the implements of best use for that land expressed ideas in advance of their times, and it was to be almost a century before his writings were taken up and developed.

Bibliography

1649, *The English Improver; or, A New Survey of Husbandry Discovering to the Kingdom That Some Land, Both Arable and Pasture May be Advance Double or Treble, and Some Five or Tenfold.*
1652, *The English Improver Improved.*

Further Reading

J. Thirsk (ed.), 1985, *The Agrarian History of England and Wales*, Vol. II (deals with Blith and the agriculture of his time).

AP

Bloch, Jacob
fl. 1888

European inventor of a machine for cutting layers of cloth.

In mass production of garments, layers of cloth are laid out on top of each other and multiples of each different part are cut out at the same time. The first portable cutting machine was invented by Joseph Bloch in 1888. It was operated from a DC electricity supply and had a circular knife, which was difficult to use when cutting round curves. Therefore the cloth had to be raised on curves so that it would reach the furthest part of the circular blade. In the same year in the USA, G.P. Eastman produced a vertically reciprocating cutting machine with a straight blade.

Further Reading

C. Singer (ed.), 1978, *A History of Technology*, Vol. VI, Oxford: Clarendon Press (describes Bloch's invention).
I. McNeil (ed.), 1990, *An Encyclopaedia of the History of Technology*, London: Routledge, pp. 850–2 (provides a brief description of the making-up trade).
D. Sinclair, 'The current climate for research and development in the European clothing industry with particular reference to single ply cutting', unpublished MSc thesis, Salford University (discusses developments in garment production).

RLH

Bloch, Marcel
See **Dassault, Marcel**.

Blumlein, Alan Dower
b. 29 June 1903 Hampstead, London, England
d. 7 June 1942

English electronics engineer, developer of telephone equipment, highly linear electromechanical recording and reproduction equipment, stereo techniques, video and radar technology.

He was a very bright scholar and received a BSc in electrical technology from City and Guilds College in 1923. He joined International Western Electric (later to become Standard Telephone and Cables) in 1924 after a period as an instructor/demonstrator at City and Guilds. He was instrumental in the design of telephone measuring equipment and in international committee work for standards for long-distance telephony.

From 1929 Blumlein was employed by the Columbia Graphophone Company to develop an electric recording cutterhead that would be independent of Western Electric's patents for the system developed by **Maxfield** and Harrison. He attacked the problems in a most systematic fashion, and within a year he had developed a moving-coil cutterhead that was much more linear than the iron-cored systems known at the time. Eventually Blumlein designed a complete line of recording equipment, from microphone and through-power amplifiers. The design was used by Columbia; after the merger with the Gramophone Company in 1931 to form Electrical and Musical Industries Ltd (later known as EMI) it became the company standard, certainly for coarse-groove records, until *c.*1950.

Blumlein became interested in stereophony (binaural sound), and developed and demonstrated a complete line of equipment, from correctly placed microphones via two-channel records and stereo pick-ups to correctly placed loudspeakers. The advent of silent surfaces of vinyl records made this approach commercial from the late 1950s. His approach was independent and quite different from that of A.C. **Keller**.

His extreme facility for creating innovative solutions to electronic problems was used in EMI's development from 1934 to 1938 of the electronic television system, which became the BBC standard of 405 lines after the Second World War, when television broadcasting again became possible. Independent of official requirements, EMI developed a 60 MHz radar system and Blumlein was involved in the development of a centimetric radar and display system. It was during testing of this aircraft mounted equipment that he was killed in a crash.

Bibliography
Blumlein was inventor or co-inventor of well over 120 patents, a complete list of which is to be found in Burns (1992; see below). The major sound-recording achievements are documented by British patent nos. 350,954, 350,998, 363,627 (highly linear cutterhead, 1930) and 394,325 (reads like a textbook on stereo technology, 1931).

Further Reading
The definitive biography of Blumlein has not yet been written; the material seems to have been collected, but is not yet available. However, R.W. Burns, 1992, 'A.D. Blumlein, engineer extraordinary', *Engineering Science and Education Journal* (February): 19–33 is a thorough account. Also B.J. Benzimra, 1967, 'A.D. Blumlein: an electronics genius', *Electronics & Power* (June): 218–24 provides an interesting summary.

GB-N

Bode, Hendrik Wade
b. 24 December 1905 Madison, Wisconsin, USA
d. 21 June 1982 Cambridge, Massachusetts, USA

American engineer who developed an extensive theoretical understanding of the behaviour of electronic circuits.

Bode received his bachelor's and master's degrees from Ohio State University in 1924 and 1926, respectively, and his PhD from Columbia University, New York, in 1935. In 1926 he joined the Bell Telephone Laboratories, where he made many theoretical contributions to the understanding of the behaviour of electronic circuits and, in particular, in conjunction with Harry **Nyquist**, of the conditions under which amplifier circuits become unstable.

During the Second World War he worked on the design of gun control systems and afterwards was a member of a team that worked with **Dou-**glas Aircraft to develop the Nike anti-aircraft missile. A member of the Bell Laboratories Mathematical Research Group from 1929, he became its Director in 1952, and then Director of Physical Sciences. Finally he became Vice-President of the Laboratories, with responsibility for systems engineering, and a director of Bellcomm, a Bell company involved in the Moon-landing programme. When he retired from Bell in 1967, he became Professor of Systems Engineering at Harvard University.

Principal Honours and Distinctions
Presidential Certificate of Merit 1946. Institute of Electrical and Electronics Engineers Edison Medal 1969.

Bibliography
1940, 'Relation between attenuation and phase in feedback amplifier design', *Bell System Technical Journal* 19: 421.
1945, *Network Analysis and Feedback Amplifier Design*, New York: Van Nostrand.
1950, with C.E. Shannon, 'A simplified derivation of linear least squares smoothing and prediction theory', *Proceedings of the Institute of Radio Engineers* 38: 417.
1961, 'Feedback. The history of an idea', *Proceedings of the Symposium on Active Networks and Feedback Systems*, Brooklyn Polytechnic.
1971, *Synergy: Technical Integration and Technical Innovation in the Bell System Bell Laboratories*, Bell Telephone Laboratories (provides background on his activities at Bell).

Further Reading
P.C. Mahon, 1975, *Mission Communications*, Bell Telephone Laboratories.

See also **Black, Harold Stephen**; **Shannon, Claude Elwood**.

KF

Bodmer, Johann Georg
b. 9 December 1786 Zurich, Switzerland
d. 30 May 1864 Zurich, Switzerland

Swiss mechanical engineer and inventor.

John George Bodmer (as he was known in England) showed signs of great inventive ability even as a child. Soon after completing his apprenticeship to a local millwright, he set up his own workshop at Zussnacht. One of his first inventions, in 1805, was a shell which exploded on impact. Soon after this he went into partnership with Baron d'Eichthal to establish a cotton mill at St Blaise in the Black Forest. Bodmer designed the water-wheels and all the machinery. A few years later they established a factory for firearms and Bodmer designed special machine tools and developed a system of interchangeable manufacture comparable with American developments at that time. More inventions followed, including a detachable bayonet for breech-loading rifles and a rifled, breech-loading cannon for 12 lb (5.4 kg) shells.

Bodmer was appointed by the Grand Duke of Baden to the posts of Director General of the Government Iron Works and Inspector of Artillery. He left St Blaise in 1816 and entered completely into the service of the Grand Duke, but before taking up his duties he visited Britain for the first time and made an intensive five-month tour of textile mills, iron works, workshops and similar establishments.

In 1821 he returned to Switzerland and was engaged in setting up cotton mills and other engineering works. In 1824 he went back to England, where he obtained a patent for his improvements in cotton machinery and set up a mill near Bolton incorporating his ideas. His health failing, he was obliged to return to Switzerland in 1828, but he was soon busy with engineering works there and in France. In 1833 he went to England again, first to Bolton and four years later to Manchester in partnership with H.H. Birley. In the next ten years he patented many more inventions in the fields of textile machinery, steam engines and machine tools. These included a balanced steam engine, a mechanical stoker, steam engine valve gear, gear-cutting machines and a circular planer or vertical lathe, anticipating machines of this type later developed in America by E.P. **Bullard**. The metric system was used in his workshops and in gearing calculations he introduced the concept of diametral pitch, which then became known as 'Manchester Pitch'. The balanced engine was built in stationary form and in two locomotives, but although their running was remarkably smooth the additional complication prevented their wider use.

After the death of H.H. Birley in 1846, Bodmer removed to London until 1848, when he went to Austria. About 1860 he returned to his native town of Zurich. He remained actively en-

gaged in all kinds of inventions up to the end of his life. He obtained fourteen British patents, each of which describes many inventions; two of these patents were extended beyond the normal duration of fourteen years. Two others were obtained on his behalf, one by his brother James in 1813 for his cannon and one relating to railways by Charles Fox in 1847. Many of his inventions had little direct influence but anticipated much later developments. His ideas were sound and some of his engines and machine tools were in use for over sixty years. He was elected a Member of the Institution of Civil Engineers in 1835.

Bibliography
1845, 'The advantages of working stationary and marine engines with high-pressure steam, expansively and at great velocities; and of the compensating, or double crank system', *Minutes of the Proceedings of the Institution of Civil Engineers* 4: 372–99.
1846, 'On the combustion of fuel in furnaces and steam-boilers, with a description of Bodmer's fire-grate', *Minutes of the Proceedings of the Institution of Civil Engineers* 5: 362–8.

Further Reading
Obituary, 1868–9, *Minutes of the Proceedings of the Institution of Civil Engineers* 28: 573–608.
H.W. Dickinson, 1929–30, 'Diary of John George Bodmer, 1816–17', *Transactions of the Newcomen Society* 10: 102–14.
D. Brownlie, 1925–6, John George Bodmer, his life and work, particularly in relation to the evolution of mechanical stoking', *Transactions of the Newcomen Society* 6: 86–110.
W.O. Henderson (ed.), 1968, *Industrial Britain Under the Regency: The Diaries of Escher, Bodmer, May and de Gallois 1814–1818*, London: Frank Cass (a more complete account of his visit to Britain).

RTS

Boeing, William Edward
b. 1 October 1881 Detroit, Michigan, USA
d. 28 September 1956 USA

American aircraft designer, creator of one of the most successful aircraft manufacturing companies in the world.

In 1915 William E. Boeing and his friend Commander Conrad Westervelt decided that they could improve on the aeroplanes then being produced in the United States. Boeing was a prominent Seattle businessman with interests in land and timber, while Westervelt was an officer in the US Navy. They bought a Martin *Model T* floatplane in order to gain some experience and then produced their own design, the *B & W*, which first flew in June 1916. Westervelt was transferred to the East, leaving Boeing to continue the production of the *B & W* floatplanes, for which purpose he set up the Pacific Aero Products Company. On 26 April 1917 this became the Boeing Airplane Company, which prospered following the US involvement in the First World War.

In March 1919 Boeing and Edward Hubbard inaugurated the world's first international airmail service between Seattle and Vancouver, British Columbia, Canada. The Boeing Company then had to face the slump in aircraft manufacturing after the war: they survived, and by 1922 they had started producing a successful series of fighters while continuing to develop their flying-boat and floatplane designs. Boeing set up the Boeing Air Transport Corporation to tender for lucrative airmail contracts and then produced aircraft which could out-perform those of his rivals. The company went from strength to strength and by the end of the 1920s a huge conglomerate had been built up: the United Aircraft and Transport Corporation. They produced an advanced high-speed monoplane mailplane, the model 200 *Monomail* in 1930, which saw the birth of a new era of Boeing designs.

The Wall Street crash of 1929 and legislation in 1934, which banned any company from both building aeroplanes and running an airline, were setbacks which the Boeing Airplane Company overcame, moving ahead to become world leaders. William E. Boeing decided that it was time he retired, but he returned to work during the Second World War.

Principal Honours and Distinctions
Guggenheim Medal 1934.

Further Reading
C. Chant, 1982, *Boeing: The World's Greatest Planemakers*, Hadley Wood, England (describes William E. Boeing's part in the founding and building up of the Boeing Company).
P.M. Bowers, 1990, *Boeing Aircraft since 1916*,

3rd edn, London (covers Boeing's aircraft).
Boeing Company, 1977, *Pedigree of Champions: Boeing since 1916*, Seattle.

JDS

Bogardus, James
b. 14 March 1800 Catskill, New York, USA
d. 13 April 1874 New York, New York, USA

American constructor of the first buildings composed entirely of cast iron, and inventor of engraving and die-sinking machinery.

James Bogardus was neither architect nor engineer but he manufactured iron grinding machinery and was known especially for inventing his engraving and die-sinking machinery. He completed his first iron-fronted building in 1848, the five-storeyed chemist shop of John Milhau at 183 Broadway in New York City, but the building for which he is best known was the slightly later example (begun in 1848) that was created as a factory for his own use. This four-storeyed structure was in Center Street, New York City, and its exterior consisted entirely of cast-iron piers and lintels. He went on to build other iron structures around the middle of the century, and these early examples were both functional and attractive, with their simple classical columns and plain architraves contrasting with the heavier and richer ornamentation of such buildings in the second half of the century.

Further Reading
H. Russell-Hitchcock, 1958, *Architecture: Nineteenth and Twentieth Centuries*, Penguin, Pelican History of Art series (section on 'Building with Iron and Glass').
D. Yarwood, 1985, *Encyclopaedia of Architecture*, Batsford (section on 'Ironwork').

DY

Bollée, Ernest-Sylvain
b. 19 July 1814 Clefmont (Haute-Marne), France
d. 11 September 1891 Le Mans, France

French inventor of the rotor–stator wind engine and founder of the Bollée manufacturing industry.

Ernest-Sylvain Bollée was the founder of an extensive dynasty of bellfounders based in Le Mans and in Orléans. He and his three sons, Amédée

(1844–1917), Ernest-Sylvain *fils* (1846–1917) and Auguste (1847–?), were involved in work and patents on steam- and petrol-driven cars, on wind engines and on hydraulic rams. The presence of the Bollées' car industry in Le Mans was a factor in the establishment of the car races that are held there.

In 1868 Ernest-Sylvain Bollée *père* took out a patent for a wind engine, which at that time was well established in America and in England. In both these countries, variable-shuttered as well as fixed-blade wind engines were in production and patented, but the Ernest-Sylvain Bollée patent was for a type of wind engine that had not been seen before and is more akin to the water-driven turbine of the Jonval type, with its basic principle being parallel to the 'rotor' and 'stator'. The wind drives through a fixed ring of blades on to a rotating ring that has a slightly greater number of blades. The blades of the fixed ring are curved in the opposite direction to those on the rotating blades and thus the air is directed onto the latter, causing it to rotate at a considerable speed: this is the 'rotor'. For greater efficiency a cuff of sheet iron can be attached to the 'stator', giving a funnel effect and driving more air at the 'rotor'. The head of this wind engine is turned to the wind by means of a wind-driven vane mounted in front of the blades. The wind vane adjusts the wind angle to enable the wind engine to run at a constant speed.

The fact that this wind engine was invented by the owner of a brass foundry, with all the gear trains between the wind vane and the head of the tower being of the highest-quality brass and, therefore, small in scale, lay behind its success. Also, it was of prefabricated construction, so that fixed lengths of cast-iron pillar were delivered, complete with twelve treads of cast-iron staircase fixed to the outside and wrought-iron stays. The drive from the wind engine was taken down the inside of the pillar to pumps at ground level.

Whilst the wind engines were being built for wealthy owners or communes, the work of the foundry continued. The three sons joined the family firm as partners and produced several steam-driven vehicles. These vehicles were the work of Amédée *père* and were *l'Obéissante* (1873); the *Autobus* (1880–3), of which some were built in Berlin under licence; the tram *Bollée–Dalifol* (1876); and the private car *La Mancelle* (1878). Another important line, in parallel with the pumping mechanism required for the wind engines, was the development of hydraulic rams, following the **Montgolfier** patent. In accordance with French practice, the firm was split three ways when Ernest-Sylvain Bollée *père* died. Amédée *père* inherited the car side of the business, but it is due to Amédée *fils* (1867–1926) that the principal developments in car manufacture came into being. He developed the petrol-driven car after the impetus given by his grandfather, his father and his uncle Ernest-Sylvain *fils*. In 1887 he designed a four-stroke single-cylinder engine, although he also used engines designed by others such as Peugeot. He produced two luxurious saloon cars before putting *Torpilleur* on the road in 1898; this car competed in the Tour de France in 1899. Whilst designing other cars, Amédée's son Léon (1870–1913) developed the *Voiturette*, in 1896, and then began general manufacture of small cars on factory lines. The firm ceased work after a merger with the English firm of **Morris** in 1926. Auguste inherited the *Eolienne* or wind-engine side of the business; however, attracted to the artistic life, he sold out to Ernest Lebert in 1898 and settled in the Paris of the Impressionists. Lebert developed the wind-engine business and retained the basic 'stator–rotor' form with a conventional lattice tower. He remained in Le Mans, carrying on the business of the manufacture of wind engines, pumps and hydraulic machinery, describing himself as a 'Civil Engineer'.

The hydraulic-ram business fell to Ernest-Sylvain *fils* and continued to thrive from a solid base of design and production. The foundry in Le Mans is still there but, more importantly, the bell foundry of Dominique Bollée in Saint-Jean-de-Braye in Orléans is still at work casting bells in the old way.

Further Reading
André Gaucheron and J. Kenneth Major, 1985, *The Eolienne Bollée*, The International Molinological Society.
Cénomane (Le Mans), 11, 12 and 13 (1983 and 1984).

KM

Bond, George Meade
b. 17 July 1852 Newburyport, Massachusetts, USA
d. 6 January 1935 Hartford, Connecticut, USA

American mechanical engineer and metrologist, co-developer of the Rogers–Bond Comparator.

After leaving school at the age of 17, George Bond taught in local schools for a few years before starting an apprenticeship in a machine shop in Grand Rapids, Michigan. He then worked as a machinist with Phoenix Furniture Company in that city until his savings permitted him to enter the Stevens Institute of Technology at Hoboken, New Jersey, in 1876. He graduated with the degree of Mechanical Engineer in 1880. In his final year he assisted William A. Rogers, Professor of Astronomy at Harvard College Observatory, Cambridge, Massachusetts, in the design of a comparator for checking standards of length. In 1880 he joined the Pratt & Whitney Company, Hartford, Connecticut, and was Manager of the Standards and Gauge Department from then until 1902. During this period he developed cylindrical, calliper, snap, limit, thread and other gauges. He also designed the Bond Standard Measuring Machine. Bond was elected a member of the American Society of Mechanical Engineers in 1881 and of the American Society of Civil Engineers in 1887, and served on many of their committees relating to standards and units of measurement.

Principal Honours and Distinctions
Vice-President, American Society of Mechanical Engineers 1908–10. Honorary degrees of DEng, Stevens Institute of Technology 1921, and MSc, Trinity College, Hartford, 1927.

Bibliography
1881, 'Standard measurements', *Transactions of the American Society of Mechanical Engineers* 2: 81.
1882, 'A standard gauge system', *Transactions of the American Society of Mechanical Engineers* 3: 122.
1886, 'Standard pipe and pipe threads', *Transactions of the American Society of Mechanical Engineers* 7: 311.
1887, *Standards of Length and Their Practical Application*, Hartford.

Further Reading
'Report of the Committee on Standards and Gauges', 1883, *Transactions of the American Society of Mechanical Engineers* 4: 21–9 (describes the Rogers–Bond Comparator).

See also **Pratt, Francis Ashbury**; **Whitney, Amos**.

RTS

Boole, George
b. 2 November 1815 Lincoln, England
d. 8 December 1864 Ballintemple, Coounty Cork, Ireland

English mathematician whose development of symbolic logic laid the foundations for the operating principles of modern computers.

Boole was the son of a tradesman, from whom he learned the principles of mathematics and optical-component manufacturing. From the early age of 16 he taught in a number of schools in West Yorkshire, and when only 20 he opened his own school in Lincoln. There, at the Mechanical Institute, he avidly read mathematical journals and the works of great mathematicians such as Lagrange, Laplace and Newton and began to tackle a variety of algebraic problems. This led to the publication of a constant stream of original papers in the newly launched *Cambridge Mathematical Journal* on topics in the fields of algebra and calculus, for which in 1844 he received the Royal Society Medal.

In 1847 he wrote *The Mathematical Analysis of Logic*, which applied algebraic symbolism to logical forms, whereby the presence or absence of properties could be represented by binary states and combined, just like normal algebraic equations, to derive logical statements about a series of operations. This laid the foundations for the binary logic used in modern computers, which, being based on binary on–off devices, greatly depend on the use of such operations as 'and', 'nand' ('not and'), 'or' and 'nor' ('not or'), etc. Although he lacked any formal degree, this revolutionary work led to his appointment in 1849 to the Chair of Mathematics at Queen's College, Cork, where he continued his work on logic and also produce treatises on differential equations and the calculus of finite differences.

Principal Honours and Distinctions
Royal Society Medal 1844. FRS 1857.

Bibliography
Boole's major contributions to logic available in

republished form include *George Boole: Investigation of the Laws of Thought*, Dover Publications; *George Boole: Laws of Thought*, Open Court, and *George Boole: Studies in Logic & Probability*, Open Court.

1872, *A Treatise on Differential Equations.*

Further Reading

W. Kneale, 1948, 'Boole and the revival of logic', *Mind* 57: 149.

G.C. Smith (ed.), 1982, *George Boole & Augustus de Morgan. Correspondence 1842–1864*, Oxford University Press.

——, 1985, *George Boole: His Life and Work*, McHale.

E.T. Bell, 1937, *Men of Mathematics*, London: Victor Gollancz.

KF

Boot, Henry Albert Howard

b. 29 July 1917 Birmingham, England
d. 8 February 1983 Cambridge, England

*English physicist who, with John **Randall**, invented the cavity magnetron used in radar systems.*

After secondary education at King Edward School, Birmingham, Boot studied physics at Birmingham University, obtaining his BSc in 1938 and PhD in 1941. With the outbreak of the Second World War, he became involved with Randall and others in the development of a source of microwave power suitable for use in radar transmitters. Following unsuccessful attempts to use klystrons, they turned to investigation of the magnetron, and by adding cavity resonators they obtained useful power on 21 February 1940 at a wavelength of 9.8 cm. By May a cavity magnetron radar system had been constructed at TRE, Swanage, and in September submarine periscopes were detected at a range of 7 miles (11 km).

In 1943 the physics department at Birmingham resumed its research in atomic physics and Boot moved to BTH at Rugby to continue development of magnetrons, but in 1945 he returned to Birmingham as Nuffield Research Fellow and helped construct the cyclotron there. Three years later he took up a post as a Principal Scientific Officer (PSO) at the Services Electronic Research Laboratories at Baldock, Hertfordshire, becoming a Senior PSO in 1954. He

remained there until his retirement in 1977, variously carrying out research on microwaves, magnetrons, plasma physics and lasers.

Principal Honours and Distinctions
Royal Society of Arts Thomas Gray Memorial Prize 1943. Royal Commission Inventors Award 1946. Franklin Institute John Price Wetherill Medal 1958. City of Pennsylvania John Scott Award 1959. (All jointly with Randall.)

Bibliography
1976, with J.T. Randall, 'Historical notes on the cavity magnetron', *Transactions of the Institute of Electrical and Electronics Engineers* ED–23: 724 (provides an account of their development of the cavity magnetron).

Further Reading
E.H. Dix and W.H. Aldous, 1966, *Microwave Valves.*

KF

Booth, Henry

b. 4 April 1789 Liverpool, England
d. 28 March 1869 Liverpool, England

English railway administrator and inventor.

Booth followed his father as a Liverpool corn merchant but had great mechanical aptitude. In 1824 he joined the committee for the proposed Liverpool & Manchester Railway (L & MR) and after the company obtained its Act of Parliament in 1826 he was appointed Treasurer.

In 1829 the L & MR announced a prize competition, the Rainhill Trials, for an improved steam locomotive: Booth, realizing that the power of a locomotive depended largely upon its capacity to raise steam, had the idea that this could be maximized by passing burning gases from the fire through the boiler in many small tubes to increase the heating surface, rather than in one large one, as was then the practice. He was apparently unaware of work on this type of boiler even then being done by Marc **Seguin**, and the 1791 American patent by John **Stevens**. Booth discussed his idea with George **Stephenson**, and a boiler of this type was incorporated into the locomotive *Rocket*, which was built by Robert **Stephenson** and entered in the Trials by Booth and the two Stephensons in partnership. The boiler enabled

Rocket to do all that was required in the trials, and far more: it became the prototype for all subsequent conventional locomotive boilers.

After the L & MR opened in 1830, Booth as Treasurer became in effect the general superintendent and was later General Manager. He invented screw couplings for use with sprung buffers. When the L & MR was absorbed by the Grand Junction Railway in 1845 he became Secretary of the latter, and when, later the same year, that in turn amalgamated with the London & Birmingham Railway (L & BR) to form the London & North Western Railway (L & NWR), he became joint Secretary with Richard Creed from the L & BR.

Earlier, completion in 1838 of the railway from London to Liverpool had brought problems with regard to local times. Towns then kept their own time according to their longitude: Birmingham time, for instance, was 7¼ minutes later than London time. This caused difficulties in railway operation, so Booth prepared a petition to Parliament on behalf of the L & MR that London time should be used throughout the country, and in 1847 the L & NWR, with other principal railways and the Post Office, adopted Greenwich time. It was only in 1880, however, that the arrangement was made law by Act of Parliament.

Bibliography

1835, British patent no. 6,814 (grease lubricants for axleboxes).

1836, British patent no. 6,989 (screw couplings).

Booth also wrote several pamphlets on railways, uniformity of time, and political matters.

Further Reading

H. Booth, 1980, *Henry Booth*, Ilfracombe: Arthur H. Stockwell (a good full-length biography, the author being the great-great-nephew of his subject; with bibliography).

R.E. Carlson, 1969, *The Liverpool & Manchester Railway Project 1821–1831*, Newton Abbot: David & Charles.

PJGR

Booth, Hubert Cecil

b. 1871 Gloucester, England
d. 1955

English mechanical, civil and construction engineer best remembered as the inventor of the vacuum cleaner.

As an engineer Booth contributed to the design of engines for Royal Navy battleships, designed and supervised the erection of a number of great wheels (in Blackpool, Vienna and Paris) and later designed factories and bridges.

In 1900 he attended a demonstration, at St Pancras Station in London, of a new form of railway carriage cleaner that was supposed to blow the dirt into a container. It was not a very successful experiment and Booth, having considered the problem carefully, decided that sucking might be better than blowing. He tried out his idea by placing a piece of damp cloth over an upholstered armchair. When he sucked air by mouth through his cloth the dirt upon it was tangible proof of his theory.

Various attempts were being made at this time, especially in America, to find a successful cleaner of carpets and upholstery. Booth produced the first truly satisfactory machine, which he patented in 1901, and coined the term 'vacuum cleaner'. He formed the Vacuum Cleaner Co. (later to become Goblin BVC Ltd) and began to manufacture his machines. For some years the company provided a cleaning service to town houses, using a large and costly vacuum cleaner (the first model cost £350). Painted scarlet, it measured 54 x 10 x 42 in. (137 x 25 x 110 cm) and was powered by a petrol-driven 5 hp piston engine. It was transported through the streets on a horse-driven van and was handled by a team of operators who parked outside the house to be cleaned. With the aid of several hundred feet of flexible hose extending from the cleaner through the windows into all the rooms, the machine sucked the dirt of decades from the carpets; at the first cleaning the weight of many such carpets was reduced by 50 per cent as the dirt was sucked away.

Many attempts were made in Europe and America to produce a smaller and less expensive machine. Booth himself designed the chief British model in 1906, the Trolley-Vac, which was wheeled around the house on a trolley. Still elaborate, expensive and heavy, this machine could, however, be operated inside a room and was powered from an electric light fitting. It consisted of a sophisticated electric motor and a belt-driven rotary vacuum pump. Various hoses and fitments made possible the cleaning of many different surfaces and the dust was trapped in a cloth filter within a small metal canister. It was a superb vacuum cleaner but cost 35 guineas and weighed a hundredweight (50 kg), so it was difficult to take upstairs.

Various alternative machines that were cheaper and lighter were devised, but none was truly efficient until a prototype that married a small electric motor to the machine was produced in 1907 in America.

Further Reading
The Story of the World's First Vacuum Cleaner, Leatherhead: BSR (Housewares) Ltd.

See also **Hoover, William Henry**.

DY

Born, Ignaz Edler von
b. 26 December 1742 Karlsburg, Transylvania (now Alba Iulia, Romania)
d. 24 July 1791 Vienna, Austria

Austrian metallurgical and mining expert, inventor of the modern amalgamation process.

At the University of Prague he studied law, but thereafter turned to mineralogy, physics and different aspects of mining. In 1769–70 he worked with the mining administration in Schemnitz (now Banská Stiavnica, Slovakia) and Prague and later continued travelling to many parts of Europe, with special interests in the mining districts. In 1776, he was charged to enlarge and systematically to reshape the natural-history collection in Vienna. Three years later he was appointed *Wirklicher Hofrat* at the mining and monetary administration of the Austrian court.

Born, who had been at a Jesuit college in his youth, was an active freemason in Vienna and exercised remarkable social communication. The intensity of his academic exchange was outstanding, and he was a member of more than a dozen learned societies throughout Europe. When with the construction of a new metallurgic plant at Joachimsthal (now Jáchymov, Czech Republic) the methods of extracting silver and gold from ores by the means of quicksilver demanded acute consideration, it was this form of scientific intercourse that induced him in 1786 to invite many of his colleagues from several countries to meet in Schemnitz in order to discuss his ideas. Since the beginnings of the 1780s Born had developed the amalgamation process as had first been applied in Mexico in 1557, by mixing the roasted and chlorinated ores with water, ingredients of iron and quicksilver in drums and having the quicksilver refined from the amalgam in the next step. The meeting led to the founding of the *Societät der Bergbaukunde*, the first internationally structured society of scientists in the world. He died as the result of severe injuries suffered in an accident while he was studying fire-setting in a Slovakian mine in 1770.

Bibliography
1772–5, *Lithophylacium Borniarum seu Index fossilium*, 2 vols, Prague.
1774 (ed.), *Briefe an J.J. Ferber über mineralogische Gegenstände*, Frankfurt and Leipzig.
1775–84, *Abhandlungen einer Privatgesellschaft in Böhmen, zur Aufnahme der Mathematik, der vaterländischen Geschichte und der Naturgeschichte*, 6 vols, Prague.
1786, *Über das Anquicken der gold- und silberhaltigen Erze, Rohsteine, Schwarzkupfer und Hüttenspeise*, Vienna.
1789–90, co-edited with F.W.H. von Trebra, *Bergbaukunde*, 2 vols, Leipzig.

Further Reading
C. von Wurzbach, 1857, *Biographisches Lexikon des Kaiserthums Österreich*, Vol. II, pp. 71–4.
L. Molnár and A Weiß, 1986, *Ignaz Edler von Born und die Societät der Bergbaukunde 1786*, Vienna: Bundesministerium für Handel, Gewerbe und Industrie (provides a very detailed description of his life, the amalgamation process and the society of 1786).
G.B. Fettweis, and G. Hamann (eds), 1989, *Über Ignaz von Born und die Societät der Bergbaukunde*, Vienna: Verlag der Österreichischen Akademie der Wissenschaft (provides a very detailed description).

WK

Borsig, Johann Carl Friedrich August

b. 25 June 1804 Breslau, Germany (now Wroclaw, Poland)
d. 7 July 1854 Berlin, Germany

German pioneer manufacturer of locomotives and rails.

Borsig established a small works at Berlin in 1837 that ten years later had expanded sufficiently to employ 1,200 people. In that year it produced sixty-seven locomotives. Borsig copied the long-boiler type then popular in Britain and which had been exported to Germany by British manufacturers: it became the standard goods engine in Germany for many years, and the name Borsig became one of the famous names of locomotive building. In 1847 Borsig established an ironworks near Berlin that from 1851 started to produce good-quality rails; German railways previously had to import these from Britain.

Further Reading
J. Marshall, 1978, *A Biographical Dictionary of Railway Engineers*, Newton Abbot: David & Charles.

PJGR

Bosch, Carl

b. 27 August 1874 Cologne, Germany
d. 26 April 1940 Heidelberg, Germany

German industrial chemist who developed the industrial synthesis of ammonia.

Bosch spent a year as a metalworker before studying chemistry at Leipzig University, obtaining his doctorate in 1898. The following year, he entered Badische Soda-, Anilin Fabrik (BASF), the leading German manufacturer of dyestuffs. Between 1902 and 1907 he spent much time investigating processes for nitrogen fixation. In 1908 Fritz **Haber** told BASF of his laboratory-scale synthesis of ammonia from its constituent elements, and in the following year Bosch was assigned to developing it to the industrial scale. Leading a large team of chemists and engineers, Bosch designed the massive pressure converter and other features of the process and was the first to use the water gas shift reaction to produce the large quantities of hydrogen that were required. By 1913 Bosch had completed the largest chemical engineering plant at BASF's works at Oppau,

and soon it was producing 36,000 tons of ammonium sulphate a year. Bosch enlarged the Oppau plant and went on to construct a larger plant at Leuna.

In 1914 Bosch was appointed a Director of BASF. At the end of the First World War he became Technical Adviser to the German delegation at the peace conference. During the 1920s BASF returned to its position of pre-eminence in high-pressure technology, thanks largely to Bosch's leadership. Although increasingly absorbed in administrative matters, Bosch was able to support the synthesis of methane and the hydrogenation of coal tar and lignite to make petrol. In 1925 BASF merged with other companies to form the giant IG Farbenindustrie AG, of which Bosch became Chairman of the Managing Board. His achievements received international recognition in 1931 when he was awarded, with F. **Bergius**, the Nobel Prize in Chemistry for high-pressure synthesis.

Bibliography
1932, *Über die Entwicklung der chemischen Hochdruckindustrie bei der Aufbau der neuen Ammoniakindustrie.*

Further Reading
K. Holdermann, 1953, *Carl Bosch, Leben und Werk.*
See also biographical memoir in *Chemische Berichte* 190 (1957), pp. xix–xxxix.

LRD

Bosch, Robert August

b. 23 September 1861 Albeck, near Ulm, Germany
d. 9 March 1942 Stuttgart, Germany

German engineer, industrialist and pioneer of internal combustion engine electrical systems.

Robert was the eighth of twelve children of the landlord of a hotel in the village of Albeck. He wanted to be a botanist and zoologist, but at the age of 18 he was apprenticed as a precision mechanic. He travelled widely in the south of Germany, which is unusual for an apprenticeship. In 1884, he went to the USA, where he found employment with Thomas A. **Edison** and his colleague, the German electrical engineer Siegmund **Bergmann**. During this period he became interested and involved in the rights of workers.

In 1886 he set up his own workshop in Stuttgart, having spent a short time with **Siemens** in England. He built up a sound reputation for quality, but the firm outgrew its capital and in 1892 he had to sack nearly all his employees. Fortunately, among the few that he was able to retain were Arnold Zähringer, who later became Manager, and an apprentice, Gottlieb Harold. These two, under Bosch, were responsible for the development of the low-tension (1897) and the high-tension (1902) magneto. They also developed the Bosch sparking plug, again in 1902. The distributor for multi-cylinder engines followed in 1910. These developments, with a strong automotive bias, were stimulated by Bosch's association with Frederick **Simms**, an Englishman domiciled in Hamburg, who had become a director of **Daimler** in Canstatt and had secured the UK patent rights of the Daimler engine. Simms went on to invent, in about 1898, a means of varying ignition timing with low-tension magnetos.

It must be emphasized, as pointed out above, that the invention of neither type of magneto was due to Bosch. Nikolaus **Otto** introduced a crude low-tension magneto in 1884, but it was not patented in Germany, while the high-tension magneto was invented by Paul Winand, a nephew of Otto's partner Eugen **Langen**, in 1887, this patent being allowed to lapse in 1890.

Bosch's social views were advanced for his time. He introduced an eight-hour day in 1906 and advocated industrial arbitration and free trade, and in 1932 he wrote a book on the prevention of world economic crises, *Die Verhütung künftiger Krisen in der Weltwirtschaft*. Other industrialists called him the 'Red Bosch' because of his short hours and high wages; he is reputed to have replied, 'I do not pay good wages because I have a lot of money, I have a lot of money because I pay good wages.' The firm exists to this day as the giant multi-national company Robert Bosch GmbH, with headquarters still in Stuttgart.

Further Reading

T. Heuss, 1994, Robert Bosch: His Life and Achievements (trans. S. Gillespie and J. Kapczynski), New York: Henry Holt & Co.

JB

Bothe, Walter Wilhelm Georg Franz

b. 8 January 1891 Oranienburg, Berlin, Germany
d. 8 February 1957 Heidelberg, Germany

German nuclear scientist.

Bothe studied under Max Planck at the University of Berlin, gaining his doctorate in 1914. After military service during the First World War, he resumed his investigations into nuclear physics and achieved a breakthrough in 1929 when he developed a method of studying cosmic radiation by placing one Geiger counter on top of another. From this he evolved the means of high-speed counting known as 'coincidence counting'. The following year, in conjunction with Hans Becker, Bothe made a further stride forward when they identified a very penetrative neutral particle by bombarding beryllium with alpha particles; this was a significant advance towards creating nuclear energy in that the neutral particle was what Chadwick later identified as the neutron.

In 1934 Bothe's achievements were recognized by his appointment as Director of the Max Planck Institute for Medical Research, although this was after Planck himself had been deposed because of his Jewish sympathies. Bothe did, however, become primarily involved in Germany's pursuit of the atomic bomb and in 1944 constructed Germany's first cyclotron for accelerating nuclear particles. By that time Germany was faced with military defeat and Bothe was not able to develop his ideas further. Even so, for his work in the field of cosmic radiation Bothe shared the 1954 Nobel Prize for Physics with the naturalized Briton (formerly German) Max Born, whose subject was statistical mechanics.

Principal Honours and Distinctions
Co-winner of the Nobel Prize for Physics 1954.

CM

Böttger, Johann Friedrich

b. 4 February 1682 Scheiz, Germany
d. 13 March 1719 Dresden, Germany

German inventor of Meissen porcelain.

After the early death of his father, Böttger spent his childhood in Magdeburg, where he received instruction in mathematics, fortification and pyrotechnics. He spent twelve years with the apothecary F. Zorn in Berlin, where there was a flourishing colony of alchemists. Böttger became an adept himself and claimed to have achieved transmutations into gold by 1701.

In March 1702 Böttger moved near to Dresden, in the service of August II, Elector of Saxony and King of Poland. While there, he made friends with E.W. von Tschirnhaus (1651–1708), scientist and possessor of glass- and ironworks. It was this association that led eventually to the founding of the celebrated Meissen porcelain factory. By 1708, Böttger had succeeded in making fine red stoneware by adding a flux, alabaster or marble, to infusible Saxony clay. By varying his raw materials, and in particular in using white china clay from the Erzgebirge, he obtained the first European true, hard, white porcelain, which had eluded European workers for centuries. At the same time he improved the furnace to achieve a temperature of around 1,350°C. To exploit his discovery, the Meissen factory was set up in 1710 and its products began to be marketed in 1713. Böttger managed the factory until his death in 1719, although throughout the period of experimentation and exploitation he had worked in conditions of great secrecy, in a vain attempt to preserve the secret of the process.

Further Reading
C.A. Engelhardt, 1837, *J.F. Böttger: Erfinder des sachsischen Porzellan*, Leipzig; reprinted 1982, Verlag Weidlich (the classic biography).
K. Hoffman, 1985, *Johann Friedrich Böttger: von Alchemistengold zum weissen Porzellan*, Berlin: Verlag Neues Leben.

LRD

Bouch, Sir Thomas

b. 22 February 1822 Thursby, Cumberland, England
d. 1880 Moffat

English designer of the ill-fated Tay railway bridge.

The third son of a merchant sea captain, he was at first educated in the village school. At the age of 17 he was working under a Mr Larmer, a civil engineer, constructing the Lancaster and Carlisle railway. He later moved to be a resident engineer on the Stockton & Darlington Railway, and from 1849 was Engineer and Manager of the Edinburgh & Northern Railway. In this last position he became aware of the great inconvenience caused to traffic by the broad estuaries of the Tay and the Forth on the eastern side of Scotland. The railway later became the Edinburgh, Perth & Dundee, and was then absorbed into the North British in 1854 when Bouch produced his first plans for a bridge across the Tay at an estimated cost of £200,000. A bill was passed for the building of the bridge in 1870. Prior to this, Bouch had built many bridges up to the Redheugh Viaduct, at Newcastle upon Tyne, which had two spans of 240 ft (73 m) and two of 260 ft (79 m). He had also set up in business on his own. He is said to have designed nearly 300 miles (480 km) of railway in the north, as well as a 'floating railway' of steam ferries to carry trains across the Forth and the Tay. The Tay bridge, however, was his favourite project; he had hawked it for some twenty years before getting the go-ahead, and the foundation stone of the bridge was laid on 22 July 1871. The total length of the bridge was nearly two miles (3.2 km), while the shore-to-shore distance over the river was just over one mile (1.6 km). It consisted of eighty-five spans, thirteen of which, i.e. 'the high girders', were some 245 ft (75 m) long and 100 ft (30 m) above water level to allow for shipping access to Perth, and was a structure of lattice girders on brick and masonry piers topped with ironwork. The first crossing of the bridge was made on 26 September 1877, and the official opening was on 31 May 1878. On Sunday 28 December 1879, at about 7.20 pm, in a wind of probably 90 mph (145 km/h), the thirteen 'high girders' were blown into the river below, drowning the seventy-five passengers and crew aboard the 5.20 train from Burntisland. A Court of Enquiry was held and revealed design faults in that the effect of wind pressure had not been adequately taken into account, faults in manufacture in the plugging of flaws in the castings, and inadequate inspection and maintenance; all of these faults were attributed to Bouch, who had been knighted for the building of the bridge. He died at his house in Moffat four months after the enquiry.

Principal Honours and Distinctions
Knighted. Cross of St George.

Further Reading
John Prebble, 1956, *The High Girders*.

IMcN

Bouchon, Basile

fl. *c.*1725 Lyon, France

French pioneer in automatic pattern selection for weaving.

In the earliest draw looms, the pattern to be woven was selected by means of loops of string that were loosely tied round the appropriate leashes, which had to be lifted to make that pick of the pattern by raising the appropriate warp threads. In Isfahan, Persia, looms were seen in the 1970s where a boy sat in the top of the loom. Before the weaver could weave the next pick, the boy selected the appropriate loop of string, pulled out those leashes which were tied in it and lifted them up by means of a forked stick. The weaver below him held up these leashes by a pair of wooden sticks and sent the shuttle through that shed while the boy was sorting out the next loop of string with its leashes. When the pick had been completed, the first loop was dropped further down the leashes and, presumably, when the whole sequence of that pattern was finished, all the loops had be pushed up the leashes to the top of the loom again.

Models in the Conservatoire National des Arts et Métiers, Paris, show that in 1725 Bouchon, a worker in Lyon, dispensed with the loops of string and selected the appropriate leashes by employing a band of pierced paper pressed against a row of horizontal wires by the drawboy using a hand-bar so as to push forward those which happened to lie opposite the blank spaces. These connected with loops at the lower extremity of vertical wires linked to the leashes at the top of the loom. The vertical wires could be pulled down by a comb-like rack beside the drawboy at the side of the loom in order to pull up the appropriate leashes to make the next shed. Bouchon seems to have had only one row of needles or wires, which must have limited the width of the patterns. This is an early form of mechanical memory, used in computers much later. The apparatus was improved subsequently by **Falcon** and **Jacquard**.

Further Reading
A. Barlow, 1878, *The History and Principles of Weaving by Hand and by Power*, London (a brief description of Bouchon's apparatus).
M. Daumas (ed.), 1968, *Histoire générale des techniques* Vol III: *L'Expansion du machinisme*, Paris (a description of this apparatus, with a diagram).
Conservatoire National des Arts et Métiers, 1942, *Catalogue du musée, section T, industries textiles, teintures et apprêts*, Paris (another brief description; a model can be seen in this museum).
C. Singer, (ed.), 1957, *A History of Technology*, Vol. III, Oxford: Clarendon Press (provides an illustration of Bouchon's apparatus).

RLH

Boulle, André-Charles

b. 11 November 1642 Paris, France
d. 29 February 1732 Paris, France

French cabinet-maker noted for his elaborate designs and high-quality technique in marquetry using brass and tortoiseshell.

As with the Renaissance artists and architects of fifteenth- and sixteenth-century Italy, Boulle worked as a young man in varied media, as a painter, engraver and metalworker an in mosaic techniques. It was in the 1660s that he turned more specifically to furniture and in the following decade, under the patronage of Louis XIV, that he became a leading *ébéniste* or cabinet-maker, In 1672 the King's Controller-General, Jean-Baptiste Colbert, recommended Boulle as an outstanding cabinet-maker and he was appointed *ébéniste du roi*. From then he spent the rest of his life working in the royal palaces, notably the Louvre and Versailles, and also carried out commissions for the French aristocracy and from abroad, particularly Spain and Germany.

Before the advent of Boulle, the quality furniture made for the French court and aristocracy had come from foreign craftsmen, particularly Domenico Cucci of Italy and Pierre Colle of the Low Countries. Boulle made his name as their equal in his development of new forms of furniture such as his bureaux and commodes, the immense variety of his designs and their architectural quality, the beauty of his sculptural, gilded mounts, and the development of his elaborate marquetry. He was a leading exponent of the contemporary styles, which meant the elaborately rich baroque forms in the time of Louis XIV and the more delicate rococo elegance in that of Louis XV. The technique to which Boulle gave his name (sometimes referred to in its German spelling of *Bühl*) incorporated a rich variety of veneering materials into his designs: in particular, he used tortoiseshell and brass with ebony. Even greater richness was created with the introduction of an engraved design upon the brass surfaces. Further delicate elaboration derived from the use of paired panels of decoration to be used in reverse form in one piece, or two matching pieces, of furniture. In one panel, designated as *première partie*, the marquetry took the form of brass upon tortoiseshell, while in the other (*contre-partie*) the tortoiseshell was set into the brass background.

Further Reading

J. Fleming and H. Honour, 1977, *The Penguin Dictionary of Decorative Arts*: Allen Lane, pp. 107–9.

1982, *The History of Furniture*: Orbis (contains many references to Boulle).

DY

Boulsover, Thomas

b. 1704
d. 1788

English cutler, metalworker and inventor of Sheffield plate.

Boulsover, originally a small-scale manufacturer of cutlery, is believed to have specialized in making knife-handle components. About 1742 he found that a thin sheet of silver could be fused to copper sheet by rolling or beating to flatten it. Thus he developed the plating of silver, later called Sheffield plate.

The method when perfected consisted of copper sheet overlaid by thin sheet silver being annealed by red heat. Protected by iron sheeting, the copper and silver were rolled together, becoming fused to a single plate capable of undergoing further manufacturing processes. Later developments included methods of edging the fused sheets and the placing of silver sheet on both lower and upper surfaces of copper, to produce high-quality silver plate, in much demand by the latter part of the century. Boulsover himself is said to have produced only small articles such as buttons and snuff

boxes from this material, which by 1758 was being exploited more commercially by Joseph Hancock in Sheffield making candlesticks, hot-water pots and coffee pots. Matthew **Boulton** introduced its manufacture in very high-quality products during the 1760s to Birmingham, where the technique was widely adopted later. By the 1770s Boulsover was engaged in rolling his plated copper for industry elsewhere, also trading in iron and purchasing blister steel which he converted by the Huntsman process to crucible steel. Blister steel was converted on his behalf to shear steel by forging. He is thought to have also been responsible for improving this product further, introducing 'double-shear steel', by repeating the forging and faggoting of shear steel bars. Thomas Boulsover had become a Sheffield entrepreneur, well known for his numerous skills with metals.

Further Reading

H.W. Dickinson, 1937, *Matthew Boulton*, Cambridge: Cambridge University Press (describes Boulsover's innovation and further development of Sheffield plate).

J. Holland, 1834, *Manufactures in Metal* III, 354–8.

For activities in steel see:

K.C. Barraclough, 1991, 'Steel in the Industrial Revolution', in J. Day and R.F. Tylecote (eds), *The Industrial Revolution in Metals*, The Institute of Metals.

JD

Bourn, Daniel

fl. 1744 Lancashire, England

English inventor of a machine with cylinders for carding cotton.

Daniel Bourn may well have been a native of Lancashire. He set up a fourth Paul–Wyatt cotton-spinning mill at Leominster, Herefordshire, possibly in 1744, although the earliest mention of it is in 1748. His only known partner in this mill was Henry Morris, a yarn dealer who in 1743 had bought a grant of spindles from **Paul** at the low rate of 30 shillings or 40 shillings per spindle when the current price was £3 or £4. When Bourn patented his carding engine in 1748, he asked **Wyatt** for a grant of spindles, to which Wyatt agreed because £100 was offered immediately. The mill, which was probably the only one outside the control of Paul and his backers, was destroyed by fire in 1754 and was not rebuilt, although Bourn and his partners had considerable hopes for it. Bourn was said to have lost over £1,600 in the venture.

Daniel Bourn described himself as a wool and cotton dealer of Leominster in his patent of 1748 for his carding engine. The significance of this invention is the use of rotating cylinders covered with wire clothing. The patent drawing shows four cylinders, one following the other to tease out the wool, but Bourn was unable to discover a satisfactory method of removing the fibres from the last cylinder. It is possible that Robert Peel in Lancashire obtained one of these engines through Morris, and that James **Hargreaves** tried to improve it; if so, then some of the early carding engines in the cotton industry were derived from Bourn's.

Bibliography
1748, British patent no. 628 (carding engine).

Further Reading
A.P. Wadsworth and J. de Lacy Mann, 1931, *The Cotton Trade and Industrial Lancashire 1600–1780*, Manchester (the most significant reference to Bourn).
R.L. Hills, 1970, *Power in the Industrial Revolution*, Manchester (provides an examination of the carding patent).
R.S. Fitton, 1989, *The Arkwrights, Spinners of Fortune*, Manchester (mentions Bourn in his survey of the textile scene before Arkwright).
R. Jenkins, 1936–7, 'Industries of Herefordshire in Bygone Times', *Transactions of the Newcomen Society* 17 (includes a reference to Bourn's mill).
C. Singer (ed.), 1957, *A History of Technology*, Vol. III, Oxford: Clarendon Press; ibid., 1958, Vol, IV (brief mentions of Bourn's work).

RLH

Bourseul, Charles
b. 1829 France
d. 1912

French engineer who in 1854 predicted the possibility of speech transmission.

Surprisingly, Bourseul's idea envisaged a digital rather than analogue method, with sound being transmitted by means of a moving diaphragm making and breaking contact with a second electrode.

See also **Bell, Alexander Graham.**

KF

Bousquet, Gaston du
b. 20 August 1839 Paris, France
d. 24 March 1910 Paris, France

French locomotive engineer noted for the successful development of compound locomotives.

Bousquet spent his entire working life with the Northern Railway of France, reaching the position of Chief Engineer of Rolling Stock and Motive Power in 1890. In 1886 he was associated with Alfred de Glehn, technical head of locomotive builder Société Alsacienne de Constructions Mécaniques, in the building of a four-cylinder, four-crank, compound 2–2–2–0 partly derived from the work of F.W. **Webb**. In continuing association with de Glehn, Bousquet then designed a four-cylinder, compound 4–4–0 with the low-pressure cylinders beneath the smokebox and the high-pressure ones outside the frames; the first was completed in 1891. The details were well designed and the locomotive was the forerunner of a highly successful series. It was developed into 4–6–0, 4–4–2 and 4–6–2 types, and examples were used in quantity by all the principal French railways and by some in Germany, while G.J. **Churchward** brought three of the 4–4–2s to the Great Western Railway in England for comparison with his own locomotives. In 1905 Bousquet introduced an articulated 0–6–2+2–6–0 compound tank locomotive for freight trains: the two driving bogies supported a frame carrying boiler, tanks, etc. At the time of his death he was working on compound 4–6–4 locomotives.

Further Reading
J.T. van Riemsdijk, 1970, 'The compound locomotive (Part 1)', *Transactions of the Newcomen Society* 43; 1972, Part 2, *Transactions of the Newcomen Society* 44 (fully describes Bousquet's locomotives).

See also **Mallet, Jules Théodore Anatole.**

PJGR

Boutheroue, Guillaume

b. Loire Valley (?), France
d. 1648

French canal entrepreneur.

Nothing is known of Boutheroue's early life, but he later became Controller of the salt store at Sully-sur-Loire and in 1623 he was the Poor Rate and Tax Collector at Beaugency. Ten years later he was described as 'King's Counsellor'. In 1638, jointly with his brother-in-law Jacques Guyon, he obtained letters patent from Louis XIII authorizing them to complete the Canal de Briare, which was commenced by **Cosnier** to connect the Loire and the Seine but was abandoned on the death of Henri IV. In anticipation of their proposed work they were granted full proprietary rights in the canal, subject to holding the canal in fief from the king, and were ennobled. In order to raise the necessary funds they were allowed to bring in others as shareholders; a partnership was formed and included Boutheroue's brother François. After many difficulties largely stirred up by the riparian owners, the 37-mile (60 km) canal was completed and opened to navigation in 1642. Another brother, Hector, also worked on the canal and later, in 1655, directed the navigation works on the Lot.

JHB

Bouton, Georges Thadé

b. 22 November 1847 Paris, France
d. November 1938

French pioneer in automobile manufacture.

Bouton was the son of a painter and learned mechanics at Honfleur and Paris. In 1870 he was fighting in Les Mobiles de Calvados, and in 1881, having finished his training, he joined his brother-in-law, Trepardoux, to open a workshop in rue de la Chapelle for the construction of steam engines for scientific toys. The comte de Dion discovered the workshop and became associated with it in 1882. They also built steam-boilers for automobiles. In 1883 they built their first quadricycle, and in 1887 their first steam tricycle. These were followed in 1892 and 1893 by a car and a steam tractor. After the appearance of the petrol engine they put in hand a star-shaped four-cylinder engine of this type, but it was not until 1895 and 1898 that the first de Dion–Bouton single-cylinder tricycle and their

petrol bicycle, respectively, came out. From 1899 the manufacture of de Dion–Bouton was concentrated on the *voiturette*. Georges Bouton was responsible for the manufacture of all these machines and took part in the first motor races.

Further Reading
1933, *Dictionnaire de biographie française.*

IMcN

Bovie, William

b. 11 September 1882 Augusta, Michigan, USA
d. 1 January 1958 Fairfield, Maine, USA

American biophysicist and inventor of the electrosurgical (electrocoagulating) knife.

Of farming stock, Bovie entered the University of Michigan in 1904 but did not obtain his degree until 1908. During this time he taught geology and biology at Antioch and attended the University of Missouri. In 1910 he moved to Harvard and engaged in plant growth research using an instrument invented by him, the auxometer. In 1914 he gained his PhD in connection with studies on the effects of ultraviolet light on protoplasm. He was Director of the Cancer Commission laboratory and in 1916 investigated the effects of heat and radiation on living tissues and assisted in the development of radium applicators.

Bovie's invention, in 1926, of the electrosurgical knife, which permitted the performance of bloodless surgery, came to the attention of **Cushing**, who was able in 1927 to report on its use in 547 neurosurgical operations. In 1927 Bovie was appointed Professor and Chairman of the Department of Biophysics at Northwestern University, Illinois, and in 1929 he moved to Maine to set up his own private laboratory.

Principal Honours and Distinctions
City of Philadelphia John Scott Medal 1928.

Bibliography
H.W. Cushing, 1928, 'Electrosurgery as an aid to the removal of intracranial tumours', *Surg. Obstet. Gynec.*
Kelly and Ward, 1932, *Electrosurgery*, Philadelphia.

Further Reading
1979, 'W.T. Bovie: The man and the machine', *Ann. Plast. Surg.*

MG

Bowser, Sylvanus F.
fl. 1880s

American mechanic and inventor of the first fuel-dispensing pump.

Bowser lived and worked in Fort Wayne, Texas. In 1885 he was approached by a local store-keeper, Jake Gumper, who had been receiving complaints from some of his customers. Gumper's store stocked both kerosene (lamp oil) and butter, and the two were stored alongside each other; the kerosene cask leaked and tainted the butter. Gumper consulted Bowser, but neither of them considered the obvious idea of moving the two containers further apart; instead, working in an adjacent barn, Bowser set about devising a means of dispensing kerosene in given quantities.

He delivered his invention to Gumper on 5 September 1885. It was a circular tank with a cylinder soldered inside and an outlet pipe attached to the top. A hand-operated piston controlled two marble valves and wooden plungers which were fitted inside the cylinder. When the wooden handle was raised, a gallon of kerosene flowed from the tank into the cylinder, and when the handle was lowered the liquid was discharged.

He formed S.F. Bowser & Co. of Fort Wayne to exploit his invention, and twenty years later the company was producing pumps for motor spirit. In 1925 the Bowser Red Sentry, which registered quantity on a clock dial, was introduced. The first automatic 'Bowser' in Britain was put into operation in a Manchester garage in 1921.

Further Reading
P. Robertson, 1974, *The Shell Book of Firsts*, London: Ebury Press & Michael Joseph.

IMcN

Boxer, Major-General Edward Mourrier
b. February 1822
d. 11 January 1897 Isle of Wight, England

English Ammunition designer and inventor of the brass, fully obturating cartridge case.

Commissioned into the Royal Artillery in 1839, Boxer's flair for the technical aspects of gunnery led to his appointment, at the early age of 33, as Superintendent of the Laboratory at the Royal Arsenal, Woolwich. He was able to devote his attention to the design of more effective shells, cartridges and fuses, with his greatest achievement being the invention, in 1866, of the Boxer cartridge, which had a case made of brass and a percussion cap set into the base. The real significance of the cartridge was that for the first time the chamber could be fully sealed, by way of the propellant gases expanding the case against the chamber wall, with the result that effective weapon range and accuracy could be dramatically increased. His achievement was recognized when Parliament voted a special financial grant, and the Boxer cartridge is still in wide use today. Boxer was promoted Colonel in 1868 and retired the following year as an honorary Major-General.

Principal Honours and Distinctions
FRS 1858.

Bibliography
1855, *Treatise on Artillery. Prepared for the Use of the Practical Class, Royal Military Academy*, London: Eyre & Spottiswode.
1858, *Diagrams to Illustrate the Service and Management of Heavy Ordnance Referred to in Treatise on Artillery*, London: Eyre & Spottiswode.

CM

Bramah, Joseph
b. 2 April 1749 Stainborough, Yorkshire, England
d. 9 December 1814 Pimlico, London, England

English inventor of the second patented water-closet, the beer-engine, the Bramah lock and, most important, the hydraulic press.

Bramah was the son of a tenant farmer and was educated at the village school before being apprenticed to a local carpenter, Thomas Allot. He walked to London c.1773 and found work with a Mr Allen that included the repair of some of the comparatively rare water-closets of the period. He invented and patented one of his own, which was followed by a water cock in 1783. His next invention, a greatly improved lock, involved the devising of a number of special machine tools, for it was one of the first devices involving interchangeable components in its manufacture. In this he had the help of Henry **Maudslay,** then a young and unknown engineer, who became Bramah's foreman before setting up business on his own. In 1784 he moved his premises from Denmark Street, St Giles, to 124 Piccadilly, which was later used as a showroom when he set up a factory in Pimlico. He invented an engine for putting out fires in 1785 and 1793, in effect a reciprocating rotary-vane pump. He undertook the refurbishment and modernization of Norwich waterworks *c.*1793, but fell out with Robert **Mylne**, who was acting as Consultant to the Norwich Corporation and had produced a remarkably vague specification. This was Bramah's only venture into the field of civil engineering.

In 1797 he acted as an expert witness for Hornblower & Maberley in the patent infringement case brought against them by Boulton and Watt. Having been cut short by the judge, he published his proposed evidence in 'Letter to the Rt Hon. Sir James Eyre, Lord Chief Justice of the Common Pleas . . . etc'. In 1795 he was granted his most important patent, based on **Pascal**'s Hydrostatic Paradox, for the hydraulic press which also incorporated the concept of hydraulics for the transmission of both power and motion and was the foundation of the whole subsequent hydraulic industry. There is no truth in the oft-repeated assertion originating from Samuel Smiles's *Industrial Biography* (1863) that the hydraulic press could not be made to work until Henry Maudslay invented the self-sealing neck leather. Bramah used a single-acting upstroking ram, sealed only at its base with a U-leather. There was no need for a neck leather.

He also used the concept of the weight-loaded, in this case as a public-house beer-engine. He devised machinery for carbonating soda water. The first banknote-numbering machine was of his design and was bought by the Bank of England. His development of a machine to cut twelve nibs from one goose quill started a patent specification which ended with the invention of the fountain pen, patented in 1809. His coach brakes were an innovation that was followed by

a form of hydropneumatic carriage suspension that was somewhat in advance of its time, as was his patent of 1812. This foresaw the introduction of hydraulic power mains in major cities and included the telescopic ram and the air-loaded accumulator.

In all Joseph Bramah was granted eighteen patents. On 22 March 1813 he demonstrated a hydraulic machine for pulling up trees by the roots in Hyde Park before a large crowd headed by the Duke of York. Using the same machine in Alice Holt Forest in Hampshire to fell timber for ships for the Navy, he caught a chill and died soon after at his home in Pimlico.

Bibliography
1778, British patent no. 1177 (water-closet).
1784, British patent no. 1430 (Bramah Lock).
1795, British patent no. 2045 (hydraulic press).
1809, British patent no. 3260 (fountain pen).
1812, British patent no. 3611.

Further Reading
I. McNeil, 1968, *Joseph Bramah, a Century of Invention.*
S. Smiles, 1863, *Industrial Biography.*
H.W. Dickinson, 1942, 'Joseph Bramah and his inventions', *Transactions of the Newcomen Society* 22: 169–86.

IMcN

Branca, Giovanni de
b. 1571 Italy
d. 1640 Italy

Italian architect who proposed what has been suggested as an early turbine, using a jet of steam to turn a wheel.

Branca practised architecture at Loretto. In 1629 he published *Le Machine: volume nuovo et di molto artificio*, in which he described various mechanisms. One was the application of rolls for working copper, lead or the precious metals gold and silver. The rolls were powered by a form of smokejack with the gases from the fire passing up a long tube forming a chimney which, through gearing, turned the rolls. Another device used a jet of steam from a boiler issuing from a mouthpiece shaped like the head of a person to impinge upon blades around the circumference of a horizontal wheel, connected through triple reduction gearing to drop stamps, for pounding drugs.

This was a form of impulse turbine and has been claimed as the first machine worked by steam to do a particular operation since Heron's temple doors.

Further Reading
H.W. Dickinson, 1938, *A Short History of the Steam Engine*, Cambridge University Press (includes a description and picture of the turbine).
C. Singer (ed.), 1957, *A History of Technology*, Vols III and IV, Oxford University Press (provides notes on Branca).

RLH

Brandt, Alfred
b. 3 September 1846 Hamburg, Germany
d. 29 November 1899 Brig, Switzerland

German mechanical engineer, developer of a hydraulic rock drill.

The son of a Hamburg merchant, he studied mechanical engineering at the Polytechnikum in Zurich and was engaged in constructing a railway line in Hungary and Austria before he returned to Switzerland. At Airolo, where the Gotthard tunnel was to commence, he designed a hydraulic rock drill; the pneumatic ones, similar to the **Ingersoll** type, did not satisfy him. His drill consisted of two parts instead of three: the hydraulic motor and the installation for drilling. At the Sulzer company of Winterthur his first design, a percussion drill, in 1876, was developed into a rotary drill which worked with greatest success in the construction of various railway tunnels and also helped to reduce costs in the mining industry.

His Hamburg-based firm Brandt & Brandau consequently was soon engaged in many tunnelling and mining projects throughout Germany, as well as abroad. During the years 1883 and 1895 Brandt spent time in exploration in Spain and reopening the lead-mines in Posada. His most ambitious task was to co-operate in drafting the Simplon tunnel, the construction of which relied greatly on his knowledge and expertise. The works began several years behind schedule, in 1898, and consequently he was unable to see its completion.

Bibliography
1877, 'Beschreibung und Abbildung der Brandtschen Bohrmaschine', *Eisenbahn* 7 (13).

Further Reading
C. Matschoss, 1925, *Männer der Technik*, Berlin.
G.E. Lucas, 1926, *Der Tunnel. Anlage und Bau*, Vol. 2, Berlin, pp. 49–55 (deals with his achievements in the construction of tunnels).

WK

Branly, Edouard Eugène
b. 23 October 1844 Amiens, France
d. 24 March 1940 Paris, France

French electrical engineer, who c.1890 invented the coherer for detecting radio waves.

Branly received his education at the Lycée de Saint Quentin in the Département de l'Aisne and at the Henri IV College of Paris University, where he became a Fellow of the University, graduating as a Doctor of Physics in 1873. That year he was appointed a professor at the College of Bourges and Director of Physics Instruction at the Sorbonne. Three years later he moved to the Free School in Paris as Professor of Advanced Studies. In addition to these responsibilities, he qualified as an MD in 1882 and practised medicine from 1896 to 1916. Whilst carrying out experiments with Hertzian (radio) waves in 1890, Branly discovered that a tube of iron filings connected to a source of direct voltage only became conductive when the radio waves were present. This early form of rectifier, which he called a coherer and which needed regular tapping to maintain its response, was used to operate a relay when the waves were turned on and off by **Morse** signals, thus providing the first practical radio communication.

Principal Honours and Distinctions
Papal Order of Commander of St George 1899. Légion d'honneur, Chevalier 1900, Commandeur 1925. Osiris Prize (jointly with Marie Curie) 1903. Argenteuil Prize and Associate of the Royal Belgian Academy 1910. Member of the Academy of Science 1911. State Funeral at Notre Dame Cathedral.

Bibliography
Amongst his publications in *Comptes rendus* were 'Conductivity of mediocre conductors', 'Conductivity of gases', 'Telegraphic conduction

without wires' and 'Conductivity of imperfect conductors realised at a distance by wireless by spark discharge of a capacitor'.

Further Reading
E. Hawkes, 1927, *Pioneers of Wireless*, London: Methuen.
E. Larien, 1971, *A History of Invention*, London: Victor Gollancz.
V.J. Phillips: 1980, *Early Radio Wave Detectors*, London: Peter Peregrinus.

See also **Hertz, Heinrich Rudolph**; **Marconi, Marchese Guglielmo**.

KF

Brassey, Thomas
b. 7 November 1805 Buerton, Cheshire, England
d. 8 December 1870 St Leonards-on-Sea, East Sussex, England

English railway construction contractor.

Brassey was initially a surveyor and road builder; his first railway contract was for ten miles (16 km) of the Grand Junction Railway in 1835, for which the engineer was Joseph **Locke**, with whom Brassey became closely associated. Gaining a justified reputation for integrity, Brassey built much of the London & Southampton, Chester & Crewe, and Sheffield Ashton-under-Lyne & Manchester Railways, the Le Havre & Rouen Railway and many others: by the late 1840s he was employing some 75,000 workers on his contracts. Subsequently, as sole contractor or with partners, Brassey built railways in many European countries, and in Canada, India, Australia and other countries. Between 1848 and 1861 he constructed 2,374 miles (3,820 km) of railway.

Principal Honours and Distinctions
Croix de la Légion d'honneur (France). Order of the Iron Crown (Austria).

Further Reading
Obituary, 1872, *Minutes of Proceedings of the Institution of Civil Engineers* 33.
Arthur Helps, 1872, *Life and Labours of Mr Brassey*, reissued 1969, Augustus Kelley (this is the noted biography).

PJGR

Brattain, Walter Houser
b. 10 February 1902 Amoy, China (now Hsiamen)
d. 13 October 1987 Seattle, Washington, USA

American physicist and co-inventor of the transistor.

Born of American parents in China, he was brought up on a cattle-ranch and graduated from Whitman College, Walla Walla, Washington, in 1924. He then went to the University of Minnesota, where he obtained a PhD in 1929. The same year he joined the staff of Bell Telephone Laboratories as a research physicist and there, during the First World War, he worked on the magnetic detection of submarines. For his work on the invention and development of the transistor, he was awarded the 1956 Nobel Prize for Physics jointly with John **Bardeen** and William **Shockley**. He retired in 1967. His interests have been concentrated on the properties of semiconductors such as germanium and silicon.

Principal Honours and Distinctions
Nobel Prize for Physics (jointly with Bardeen and Shockley) 1956.

Further Reading
A. Isaacs and E. Martin (eds), 1985, *Longmans Dictionary of 20th Century Biography*.

IMcN

Braun, Karl Ferdinand
b. 6 June 1850 Fulda, Hesse, Germany
d. 20 April 1918 New York City, New York, USA

*German physicist who shared with **Marconi** the 1909 Nobel Prize for Physics for developments in wireless telegraphy; inventor of the cathode ray oscilloscope.*

After obtaining degrees from the universities of Marburg and Berlin (PhD) and spending a short time as Headmaster of the Thomas School in Berlin, Braun successively held professorships in theoretical physics at the universities of Marburg (1876), Strasbourg (1880) and Karlsruhe (1883) before becoming Professor of Experimental Physics at Tübingen in 1885 and Director and Professor of Physics at Strasbourg in 1895.

During this time he devised experimental

apparatus to determine the dielectric constant of rock salt and developed the Braun high-tension electrometer. He also discovered that certain mineral sulphide crystals would only conduct electricity in one direction, a rectification effect that made it possible to detect and demodulate radio signals in a more reliable manner than was possible with the coherer. Primarily, however, he was concerned with improving Marconi's radio transmitter to increase its broadcasting range. By using a transmitter circuit comprising a capacitor and a spark-gap, coupled to an aerial without a spark-gap, he was able to obtain much greater oscillatory currents in the latter, and by tuning the transmitter so that the oscillations occupied only a narrow frequency band he reduced the interference with other transmitters. Other achievements include the development of a directional aerial and the first practical wavemeter, and the measurement in Strasbourg of the strength of radio waves received from the **Eiffel** Tower transmitter in Paris. For all this work he subsequently shared with Marconi the 1909 Nobel Prize for Physics.

Around 1895 he carried out experiments using a torsion balance in order to measure the universal gravitational constant, **g**, but the work for which he is probably best known is the addition of deflecting plates and a fluorescent screen to the **Crooke's** tube in 1897 in order to study the characteristics of high-frequency currents. The oscilloscope, as it was called, was not only the basis of a now widely used and highly versatile test instrument but was the forerunner of the cathode ray tube, or CRT, used for the display of radar and television images.

At the beginning of the First World War, while in New York to testify in a patent suit, he was trapped by the entry of the USA into the war and remained in Brooklyn with his son until his death.

Principal Honours and Distinctions
Nobel Prize for Physics (jointly with Marconi) 1909.

Bibliography
1874, 'Assymetrical conduction of certain metal sulphides', *Pogg. Annal.* 153: 556 (provides an account of the discovery of the crystal rectifier).
1897, 'On a method for the demonstration and study of currents varying with time', *Wiedemann's Annalen* 60: 552 (his description of the cathode ray oscilloscope as a measuring tool).

Further Reading
K. Schlesinger & E.G. Ramberg, 1962, 'Beamdeflection and photo-devices', *Proceedings of the Institute of Radio Engineers* 50, 991.

KF

Braun, Wernher Manfred von
b. 23 March 1912 Wirsitz, Germany
d. 16 June 1977 Alexandria, Virginia, USA

German pioneer in rocket development.

Von Braun's mother was an amateur astronomer who introduced him to the futuristic books of Jules Verne and H.G. Wells and gave him an astronomical telescope. He was a rather slack and undisciplined schoolboy until he came across Herman **Oberth**'s book *By Rocket to Interplanetary Space*. He discovered that he required a good deal of mathematics to follow this exhilarating subject and immediately became an enthusiastic student.

The Head of the Ballistics and Armaments branch of the German Army, Professor Karl Becker, had asked the engineer Walter Dornberger to develop a solid-fuel rocket system for short-range attack, and one using liquid-fuel rockets to carry bigger loads of explosives beyond the range of any known gun. Von Braun joined the Verein für Raumschiffsfahrt (the German Space Society) as a young man and soon became a leading member. He was asked by Rudolf Nebel, VfR's chief, to persuade the army of the value of rockets as weapons. Von Braun wisely avoided all mention of the possibility of space flight and some financial backing was assured. Dornberger in 1932 built a small test stand for liquid-fuel rockets and von Braun built a small rocket to test it; the success of this trial won over Dornberger to space rocketry.

Initially research was carried out at Kummersdorf, a suburb of Berlin, but it was decided that this was not a suitable site. Von Braun recalled holidays as a boy at a resort on the Baltic, Peenemünde, which was ideally suited to rocket testing. Work started there but was not completed until August 1939, when the group of eighty engineers and scientists moved in. A great fillip to rocket research was received when Hitler was shown a film and was persuaded of the efficacy of rockets as weapons of war. A factory was set up in excavated tunnels at Mittelwerk in the Harz mountains. Around 6,000 'vengeance' weapons were built, some 3,000 of which were fired on targets in Britain and 2,000 of which were still in storage at the end of the Second World War.

Peenemünde was taken by the Russians on 5 May 1945, but by then von Braun was lodging with many of his colleagues at an inn, Haus Ingeburg, near Oberjoch. They gave themselves up to the Americans, and von Braun presented a 'prospectus' to the Americans, pointing out how useful the German rocket team could be. In 'Operation Paperclip' some 100 of the team were moved to the United States, together with tons of drawings and a number of rocket missiles. Von Braun worked from 1946 at the White Sands Proving Ground, New Mexico, and in 1950 moved to Redstone Arsenal, Huntsville, Alabama. In 1953 he produced the Redstone missile, in effect a V2 adapted to carry a nuclear warhead a distance of 320 km (199 miles). The National Aeronautics and Space Administration (NASA) was formed in 1958 and recruited von Braun and his team. He was responsible for the design of the Redstone launch vehicles which launched the first US satellite, Explorer 1, in 1958, and the Mercury capsules of the US manned spaceflight programme which carried Alan Shepard briefly into space in 1961 and John Glenn into earth orbit in 1962. He was also responsible for the Saturn series of large, staged launch vehicles, which culminated in the Saturn V rocket which launched the Apollo missions taking US astronauts for the first human landing on the moon in 1969. Von Braun announced his resignation from NASA in 1972 and died five years later.

Bibliography
1981, with F.L. Ordway, *History of Rocketry and Space Travel*.

Further Reading
P. Marsh, 1985, *The Space Business*, Penguin.
J. Trux, 1985, *The Space Race*, New English Library.
T. Osman, 1983, *Space History*, Michael Joseph.

IMcN

Brayton, George Bailey
b. 1839 Rhode Island, USA
d. 1892 Leeds, England

American engineer, inventor of gas and oil engines.

During the thirty years prior to his death, Brayton devoted considerable effort to the development of internal-combustion engines. He designed the first commercial gas engine of American origin in 1872. An oil-burning engine was produced in 1875. An aptitude for mechanical innovation became apparent whilst he was employed at the Exeter Machine Works, New Hampshire, where he developed a successful steam generator for use in domestic and industrial heating systems. Brayton engines were distinguished by the method of combustion. A pressurized air–fuel mixture from a reservoir was ignited as it entered the working cylinder – a precursor of the constant-pressure cycle. A further feature of these early engines was a rocking beam. There exist accounts of Brayton engines fitted into river craft, and of one in a carriage which operated for a few months in 1872–3. However, the appearance of the four-stroke **Otto** engine in 1876, together with technical problems associated with backfiring into the fuel reservoir, prevented large-scale acceptance of the Brayton engine. Although Thompson Sterne & Co. of Glasgow became licensees, the engine failed to gain usage in Britain. A working model of Brayton's gas engine is exhibited in the Museum of History and Technology in Washington, DC.

Bibliography
1872, US patent no. 125,166 (Brayton gas engine).
July 1890, British patent no. 11,062 (oil engine; under patent agent W.R. Lake).

Further Reading
D. Clerk, 1895, *The Gas and Oil Engine*, 6th edn, London, pp. 152–62 (includes a description and report of tests carried out on a Brayton engine).

KAB

Brearley, Harry
b. 18 February 1871 Sheffield, England
d. 14 July 1948 Torquay, Devon, England

English inventor of stainless steel.

Brearley was born in poor circumstances. He received little formal education and was nurtured rather in and around the works of Thomas Firth & Sons, where his father worked in the crucible steel-melting shop. One of his first jobs was to help in their chemical laboratory where the chief chemist, James Taylor, encouraged him and helped him fit himself for a career as a steelworks chemist.

In 1901 Brearley left Firth's to set up a laboratory at Kayser Ellison & Co., but he returned to Firth's in 1904, when he was appointed Chief Chemist at their Riga works, and Works Manager the following year. In 1907 he returned to Sheffield to design and equip a research laboratory to serve both Firth's and John Brown & Co. It was during his time as head of this laboratory that he made his celebrated discovery. In 1913, while seeking improved steels for rifle barrels, he used one containing 12.68 per cent chromium and 0.24 per cent carbon, in the hope that it would resist fouling and erosion. He tried to etch a specimen for microscopic examination but failed, from which he concluded that it would resist corrosion by, for example, the acids encountered in foods and cooking. The first knives made of this new steel were unsatisfactory and the 1914–18 war interrupted further research. But eventually the problems were overcome and Brearley's discovery led to a range of stainless steels with various compositions for domestic, medical and industrial uses, including the well-known '18–8' steel, with 18 per cent chromium and 8 per cent nickel.

In 1915 Brearley left the laboratory to become Works Manager, then Technical Director, at Brown Bayley's steelworks until his retirement in 1925.

Principal Honours and Distinctions
Iron and Steel Institute Bessemer Gold Medal 1920.

Bibliography
Brearley wrote several books, including:
1915 (?), with F. Ibbotson, *The Analysis of Steelworks Materials*, London.
The Heat Treatment of Tool Steels.
Ingots and Ingot Moulds.
Later books include autobiographical details:

1946, *Talks on Steelmaking*, American Society for Metals.
1941, *Knotted String: Autobiography of a Steelmaker*, London: Longmans, Green.

Further Reading
Obituary, 1948, *Journal of the Iron and Steel Institute*: 428–9.

LRD

Breguet, Abraham-Louis
baptized 10 January 1747 Neuchâtel, Switzerland
d. 17 September 1823 Paris, France

Swiss clock- and watchmaker who made many important contributions to horology.

When Breguet was 11 years old his father died and his mother married a Swiss watchmaker who had Paris connections. His stepfather introduced him to horology and this led to an apprenticeship in Paris, during which he also attended evening classes in mathematics at the Collège Mazarin. In 1775 he married and set up a workshop in Paris, initially in collaboration with Xavier Gide. There he established a reputation among the aristocracy for elegant and innovative timepieces which included a *perpétuelle*, or self-winding watch, which he developed from the ideas of Perrelet. He also enjoyed the patronage of Marie Antoinette and Louis XVI. During the French Revolution his life was in danger and in 1793 he fled to Neuchâtel. The two years he spent there comprised what was intellectually one of his most productive periods and provided many of the ideas that he was able to exploit after he had returned to Paris in 1795. By the time of his death he had become the most prestigious watchmaker in Europe: he supplied timepieces to Napoleon and, after the fall of the Empire, to Louis XVIII, as well as to most of the crowned heads of Europe.

Breguet divided his contributions to horology into three categories: improvements in appearance and functionality; improvements in durability; and improvements in timekeeping. His *pendule sympathique* was in the first category and consisted of a clock which during the night set a watch to time, regulated it and wound it. His *parachute*, a spring-loaded bearing, made a significant contribution to the durability of a watch by preventing damage to its movement if it was dropped. Among the many improvements that Breguet made to timekeeping, two important ones were the introduction of the overcoil balance spring and the tourbillon. By bending the outside end of the balance spring over the top of the coils Breguet was able to make the oscillations of the balance isochronous, thus achieving for the flat spring what **Arnold** had already accomplished for the cylindrical balance spring. The timekeeping of a balance is also dependent on its position, and the tourbillon was an attempt to average-out positional errors by placing the balance wheel and the escapement in a cage that rotated once every minute. This principle was revived in a simplified form in the *karussel* at the end of the nineteenth century.

Principal Honours and Distinctions
Horloger de la marine 1815. Chevalier de la Légion d'honneur 1815.

Bibliography
Breguet gathered information for a treatise on horology that was never published but which was later plagiarized by Louis Moinet in his *Traité d'horlogerie, 1848*.

Further Reading
G. Daniels, 1974, *The Art of Breguet*, London (an account of his life with a good technical assessment of his work).

DV

Breguet, Louis
b. 2 January 1880 Paris, France
d. 4 May 1955 Paris, France

French aviation pioneer who built a helicopter in 1907 and designed many successful aircraft.

The Breguet family had been manufacturing fine clocks since before the French Revolution, but Louis Breguet and his brother Jacques used their mechanical skills to produce a helicopter, or 'gyroplane' as they named it. It was a complex machine with four biplane rotors (i.e. thirty-two lifting surfaces). Louis Breguet had carried out many tests to determine the most suitable rotor design. The Breguet brothers were assisted by Professor Charles Richet and the Breguet–Richet *No. 1* was tested in September 1907 when it succeeded in lifting itself, and its pilot, to a height of 1.5 metres. Unfortunately, the gyroplane was rather unstable and four helpers had to steady it; consequently, the flight did not qualify as a 'free' flight. This was achieved two months later, also in France, by Paul Cornu who made a 20-second free flight.

Louis Breguet turned his attention to aeroplane design and produced a tractor biplane when most other biplanes followed the **Wright** brothers' layout with a forward elevator and pusher propeller. The Breguet *I* made quite an impression at the 1909 Reims meeting, but the Breguet *IV* created a world record the following year by carrying six people. During the First World War the Breguet *Type 14* bomber was widely used by French and American squadrons. Between the First and Second World Wars a wide variety of designs were produced, including flying boats and another helicopter, the Breguet–Dorand *Gyroplane* which flew for over one hour in 1936. The Breguet company survived World War II and in the late 1940s developed a successful four-engined airliner/transport, the *Deux-Ponts*, which had a bulbous double-deck fuselage.

Breguet was an innovative designer, although his designs were functional rather than elegant. He was an early advocate of metal construction and developed an oleo- (oil-spring) undercarriage leg.

Bibliography
1925, *Le Vol à voile dynamique des oiseaux. Analyse des effets des pulsations du vent sur la résultante aérodynamique moyenne d'un planeur*, Paris.

Further Reading
P. Faure, 1938, *Louis Breguet*, Paris (biography).
C.H. Gibbs-Smith, 1965, *The Invention of the Aeroplane 1799–1909*, London (provides a careful analysis of Breguet's early aircraft).

JDS

Brennan, Louis
b. 28 January 1852 Castlebar, Ireland
d. 17 January 1932 Montreux, Switzerland

Irish inventor of the Brennan dirigible torpedo, and of a gyroscopically balanced monorail system.

The Brennan family, including Louis, emigrated to Australia in 1861. He was an inventive genius from childhood, and while at Melbourne invented his torpedo. Within it were two drums, each with several miles of steel wire coiled upon it and mounted on one of two concentric propeller shafts. The propellers revolved in opposite directions. Wires were led out of the torpedo to winding drums on land, driven by high-speed steam engines: the faster the drums on shore were driven, the quicker the wires were withdrawn from the drums within the torpedo and the quicker the propellers turned. A steering device was operated by altering the speeds of the wires relative to one another. As finally developed, Brennan torpedoes were accurate over a range of 1½ miles (2.4 km), in contrast to contemporary self-propelled torpedoes, which were unreliable at ranges over 400 yards (366 m).

Brennan moved to England in 1880 and sold the rights to his torpedo to the British Government for a total of £110,000, probably the highest payment ever made by it to an individual inventor. Brennan torpedoes became part of the defences of many vital naval ports, but never saw active service: improvement of other means of defence meant they were withdrawn in 1906. By then Brennan was deeply involved in the development of his monorail. The need for a simple and cheap form of railway had been apparent to him when in Australia and he considered it could be met by a ground-level monorail upon which vehicles would be balanced by gyroscopes. After overcoming many manufacturing difficulties, he demonstrated first a one-eighth scale version and then a full-size, electrically driven vehicle, which ran on its single rail throughout the summer of 1910 in London, carrying up to fifty passengers at a time. Development had been supported financially by, successively, the War Office, the India Office and the Government of the Indian state of Jammu and Kashmir, which had no rail access; despite all this, however, no further financial support, government or commercial, was forthcoming.

Brennan made many other inventions, worked on the early development of helicopters and in 1929 built a gyroscopically balanced, two-wheeled motor car which, however, never went into production.

Principal Honours and Distinctions
Companion of the Bath 1892.

Bibliography
1878, British patent no. 3359 (torpedo)
1903, British patent no. 27212 (stability mechanisms).

Further Reading
R.E. Wilkes, 1973, *Louis Brennan CB*, 2 parts, Gillingham (Kent) Public Library.
J.R. Day and B.G. Wilson, 1957, *Unusual Railways*, London: F. Muller.

See also **Behr, Fritz Bernhard**; **Lartigue, Charles François Marie-Thérèse**; **Palmer, Henry Robinson** (monorails); **Whitehead, Robert** (torpedoes).

PJGR

Breuer, Marcel Lajos
b. 22 May 1902 Pécs, Hungary
d. 1 July 1981 New York (?), USA

Hungarian member of the European Bauhaus generation in the 1920s, who went on to become a leader in the modern school of architectural and furniture design in Europe and the United States.

Breuer began his student days following an art course in Vienna, but joined the Bauhaus at Weimar, where he later graduated, in 1920. When **Gropius** re-established the school in purpose-built structures at Dessau, Breuer became a member of the teaching staff in charge of the carpentry and furniture workshops. Much of his time there was spent in design and research into new materials being applied to furniture and interior decoration. The essence of his contribution was to relate the design of furniture to industrial production; in this field he developed the tubular-steel structure, especially in chair design, and experimented with aluminium as a furniture material as well as pieces of furniture made up from modular units. His furniture style was characterized by an elegance of line and a careful avoidance of superfluous detail. By 1926 he had furnished the Bauhaus with such furniture in chromium-plated steel, and two years later had developed a cantilevered chair.

Breuer left the Bauhaus in 1928 and set up an architectural practice in Berlin. In the early 1930s he also spent some time in Switzerland. Notable from these years was his Harnischmacher Haus in Wiesbaden and his apartment buildings in the Dolderthal area of Zurich. His architectural work was at first influenced by constructivism, and then by that of Le Corbusier (see Charles-Edouard **Jeanneret**). In 1935 he moved to England, where in partnership with F.R.S. Yorke he built some houses and continued to practise furniture design. The Isokon Furniture Co. commissioned him to develop ideas that took advantage of the new bending and moulding processes in laminated wood, one result being his much-copied reclining chair.

In 1937, like so many of the European architectural refugees from Nazism, he found himself under-occupied due to the reluctance of English clients to embrace the modern architectural movement. He went to the United States at Gropius's invitation to join him as a professor at Harvard. Breuer and Gropius were influential in training a new generation of American architects, and in particular they built a number of houses. This partnership ended in 1941 and Breuer set up practice in New York. His style of work from this time on was still modern, but became more varied. In housing, he adapted his style to American needs and used local materials in a functional manner. In the Whitney Museum (1966) he worked in a sculptural, granite-clad style. Often he utilized a bold reinforced-concrete form, as in his collaboration with Pier Luigi **Nervi** and Bernard Zehrfuss in the Paris UNESCO Building (1953–8) and the US Embassy in the Hague (1954–8). He displayed his masterly handling of poured concrete used in a strikingly expressionistic, sculptural manner in his St John's Abbey (1953–61) in Collegeville, Minnesota, and in 1973 his Church of St Francis de Sale in Michigan won him the top award of the American Institute of Architects.

Principal Honours and Distinctions
American Institute of Architects Medal of Honour 1964, Gold Medal 1968. Jefferson Foundation Medal 1968.

Bibliography
1955, *Sun and Shadow, the Philosophy of an Architect*, New York: Dodd-Read (autobiography).

Further Reading
C. Jones (ed.), 1963, *Marcel Breuer: Buildings and Projects 1921–1961*, New York: Praeger.
T. Papachristou (ed.), 1970, *Marcel Breuer: New*

Buildings and Projects 1960–1970, New York: Praeger.

DY

Brewster, Sir David

b. 11 December 1781 Jedburgh, Roxburghshire, Scotland
d. 10 February 1868 Allerly, Scotland

Scottish scientist and popularizer of science, inventor of the kaleidoscope and lenticular stereoscope.

Originally destined to follow his father into the Church, Brewster studied divinity at Edinburgh University, where he met many distinguished men of science. He began to take a special interest in optics, and eventually abandoned the clerical profession. In 1813 he presented his first paper to the Royal Society on the properties of light, and within months invented the principle of the kaleidoscope. In 1844 Brewster described a binocular form of **Wheatstone**'s reflecting stereoscope where the mirrors were replaced with lenses or prisms. The idea aroused little interest at the time, but in 1850 a model taken to Paris was brought to the notice of L.J. **Duboscq**, who immediately began to manufacture Brewster's stereoscope on a large scale; shown at the Great Exhibition of 1851, it attracted the attention of Queen Victoria. Stereoscopic photography rapidly became one of the fashionable preoccupations of the day and did much to popularize photography. Although originally marketed as a scientific toy and drawing-room pastime, stereoscopy later found scientific application in such fields as microscopy, photogrammetry and radiography. Brewster was a prolific scientific author throughout his life. His income was derived mainly from his writing and he was one of the nineteenth century's most distinguished popularizers of science.

Principal Honours and Distinctions
Knighted 1832. FRS 1815.

Further Reading
Dictionary of National Biography, 1973, Vol. II, Oxford, pp. 1,207–11.
A.D. Morrison-Low and J.R.R. Christie (eds), 1984, *Martyr of Science*, Edinburgh (proceedings of a Bicentenary Symposium).

JW

Bridgewater, 3rd Duke of

See **Egerton, Francis**.

Briggs, Henry

b. February 1561 Warley Wood, Yorkshire, England
d. 26 January 1630 Oxford, England

English mathematician who invented common, or Briggsian, logarithms and whose writings led to their general acceptance throughout Europe.

After education at Warley Grammar School, Briggs entered St John's College, Cambridge, in 1577 and became a fellow in 1588. Having been Reader of the Linacre Lecture in 1592, he was appointed to the new Chair in Geometry at Gresham House (subsequently Gresham College), London, in 1596. Shortly after, he concluded that the logarithms developed by John **Napier** would be much more useful if they were calculated to the decimal base 10, rather than to the base *e* (the 'natural' number 2.71828 . . .), a suggestion with which Napier concurred. Until the advent of modern computing these decimal logarithms were invaluable for the accurate calculations involved in surveying, navigation and astronomy. In 1619 he accepted the Savilian Chair in Geometry at Oxford University, having two years previously published the base 10 logarithms of 1,000 numbers. The year 1624 saw the completion of his monumental *Arithmetica Logarithmica*, which contained fourteen-figure logarithms of 30,000 numbers, together with their trigonometric sines to fifteen decimal places and their tangents and secants to ten places!

Bibliography
1617, *Logarithmorum Chilias Primi* (the first published reference to base 10 logarithms).
1622, *A Treatise of the North West Passage to the South Sea: Through the Continent of Virginia and by Fretum Hudson.*
1633, *Arithmetica Logarithmica*, Gouda, the Netherlands; pub. in 1633 as *Trigonmetria Britannica*, London.

Further Reading
E.T. Bell, 1937, *Men of Mathematics*, London: Victor Gollancz.

See also **Burgi, Jost**.

KF

Bright, Sir Charles Tilston

b. 8 June 1832 Wanstead, Essex, England
d. 3 May 1888 Abbey Wood, London, England

English telegraph engineer responsible for laying the first transatlantic cable.

At the age of 15 years Bright left the London Merchant Taylors' School to join the two-year-old Electric Telegraph Company. By 1851 he was in charge of the Birmingham telegraph station. After a short time as Assistant Engineer with the newly formed British Telegraph Company, he joined his brother (who was Manager) as Engineer-in-Chief of the English and Irish Magnetic Telegraph Company in Liverpool, for which he laid thousands of miles of underground cable and developed a number of innovations in telegraphy including a resistance box for locating cable faults and a two-tone bell system for signalling. In 1853 he was responsible for the first successful underwater cable between Scotland and Ireland. Three years later, with the American financier Cyrus **Field** and John Brett, he founded and was Engineer-in-Chief of the Atlantic Telegraph Company, which aimed at laying a cable between Ireland and Newfoundland. After several unsuccessful attempts this was finally completed on 5 August 1858, Bright was knighted a month later, but the cable then failed! In 1860 Bright resigned from the Magnetic Telegraph Company to set up an independent consultancy with another engineer, Joseph Latimer Clark, with whom he invented an improved bituminous cable insulation. Two years later he supervised construction of a telegraph cable to India, and in 1865 a further attempt to lay an Atlantic cable using **Brunel**'s new ship, the *Great Eastern*. This cable broke during laying, but in 1866 a new cable was at last successfully laid and the 1865 cable recovered and repaired. The year 1878 saw extension of the Atlantic cable system to the West Indies and the invention with his brother of a system of neighbourhood fire alarms and even an automatic fire alarm.

In 1861 Bright presented a paper to the British Association for the Advancement of Science on the need for electrical standards, leading to the creation of an organization that still exists in the 1990s. From 1865 until 1868 he was Liberal MP for Greenwich, and he later assisted with preparations for the 1881 Paris Exhibition.

Principal Honours and Distinctions
Knighted 1858. Légion d'honneur. First President, Société Internationale des Electriciens. President, Society of Telegraph Engineers & Electricians (later the Institution of Electrical Engineers) 1887.

Bibliography
1852, British patent (resistance box).
1855, British patent no. 2,103 (two-tone bell system).
1878, British patent no. 3,801 (area fire alarms).
1878, British patent no. 596 (automatic fire alarm).
'The physical & electrical effects of pressure & temperature on submarine cable cores', *Journal of the Institution of Electrical Engineers* XVII (describes some of his investigations of cable characteristics).

Further Reading
C. Bright, 1898, *Submarine Cables, Their History, Construction & Working.*
—— 1910, *The Life Story of Sir Charles Tilston Bright*, London: Constable & Co.

KF

Brindley, James
b. 1716 Tunstead, Derbyshire, England
d. 27 September 1772 Turnhurst, Staffordshire, England

English canal engineer.

Born in a remote area and with no material advantages, Brindley followed casual rural labouring occupations until 1733, when he became apprenticed to Abraham Bennett of Macclesfield, a wheelwright and millwright. Though lacking basic education in reading and writing, he demonstrated his ability, partly through his photographic memory, to solve practical problems. This established his reputation, and after Bennett's death in 1742 he set up his own business at Leek as a millwright. His skill led to an invitation to solve the problem of mine drainage at Wet Earth Colliery, Clifton, near Manchester. He tunnelled 600 ft (183 m) through rock to provide a leat for driving a water-powered pump.

Following work done on a pump on Earl Gower's estate at Trentham, Brindley's name was suggested as the engineer for the proposed canal for which the Duke of Bridgewater (Francis **Egerton**) had obtained an Act in 1759. The Earl and the Duke were brothers-in-law, and the agents for the two estates were, in turn, the **Gilbert** brothers. The canal, later known as the Bridgewater Canal, was to be constructed to carry coal from the Duke's mines at Worsley into Manchester. Brindley advised on the details of its construction and recommended that it be carried across the river Irwell at Barton by means of an aqueduct. His proposals were accepted, and under his supervision the canal was constructed on a single level and opened in 1761. Brindley had also surveyed for Earl Gower a canal from the Potteries to Liverpool to carry pottery for export, and the signal success of the Bridgewater Canal ensured that the Trent and Mersey Canal would also be built. These undertakings were the start of Brindley's career as a canal engineer, and it was largely from his concepts that the canal system of the Midlands developed, following the natural contours rather than making cuttings and constructing large embankments. His canals are thus winding navigations unlike the later straight waterways, which were much easier to traverse. He also adopted the 7 ft (2.13 m) wide lock as a ruling dimension for all engineering features. For cheapness, he formed his canal tunnels without a towpath, which led to the notorious practice of legging the boats through the tunnels.

Brindley surveyed a large number of projects and such was his reputation that virtually every proposal was submitted to him for his opinion. Included among these projects were the Staffordshire and Worcestershire, the Rochdale, the Birmingham network, the Droitwich, the Coventry and the Oxford canals. Although he was nominally in charge of each contract, much of the work was carried out by his assistants while he rushed from one undertaking to another to ensure that his orders were being carried out. He was nearly 50 when he married Anne Henshall, whose brother was also a canal engineer. His fees and salaries had made him very wealthy. He died in 1772 from a chill sustained when carrying out a survey of the Caldon Canal.

Further Reading
A.G. Banks and R.B. Schofield, 1968, *Brindley at Wet Earth Colliery: An Engineering Study,*

Newton Abbot: David & Charles.

S.E. Buckley, 1948, *James Brindley*, London: Harrap.

JHB

Brinell, Johann August

b. 1849 Småland, Sweden
d. 17 November 1925 Stockholm, Sweden

Swedish metallurgist, inventor of the well-known method of hardness measurement which uses a steel-ball indenter.

Brinell graduated as an engineer from Borås Technical School, and his interest in metallurgy began to develop in 1875 when he became an engineer at the ironworks of Lesjöfors and came under the influence of Gustaf Ekman. In 1882 he was appointed Chief Engineer at the Fagersta Ironworks, where he became one of Sweden's leading experts in the manufacture and heat treatment of tool steels.

His reputation in this field was established in 1885 when he published a paper on the structural changes which occurred in steels when they were heated and cooled, and he was among the first to recognize and define the critical points of steel and their importance in heat treatment. Some of these preliminary findings were first exhibited at Stockholm in 1897. His exhibit at the World Exhibition at Paris in 1900 was far more detailed and there he displayed for the first time his method of hardness determination using a steel-ball indenter. For these contributions he was awarded the French Grand Prix and also the Polhem Prize of the Swedish Technical Society.

He was later concerned with evaluating and developing the iron-ore deposits of north Sweden and was one of the pioneers of the electric blast-furnace. In 1903 he became Chief Engineer of the Jernkontoret and remained there until 1914. In this capacity and as Editor of the *Jernkontorets Annaler* he made significant contributions to Swedish metallurgy. His pioneer work on abrasion resistance, undertaken long before the term tribology had been invented, gained him the Rinman Medal, awarded by the Jernkontoret in 1920.

Principal Honours and Distinctions

Member of the Swedish Academy of Science 1902. Dr Honoris Causa, University of Upsala 1907. French Grand Prix, Paris World Exhibition 1900; Swedish Technical Society Polhem Prize 1900; Iron and Steel Institute Bessemer Medal 1907; Jernkontorets Rinman Medal 1920.

Further Reading

Axel Wahlberg, 1901, *Journal of the Iron and Steel Institute* 59: 243 (the first English-language description of the Brinell Hardness Test).

Machinery's Encyclopedia, 1917, Vol. III, New York: Industrial Press, pp. 527–40 (a very readable account of the Brinell test in relation to the other hardness tests available at the beginning of the twentieth century).

Hardness Test Research Committee, 1916, Bibliography on hardness testing, *Proceedings of the Institution of Mechanical Engineers*.

ASD

Brodrick, Cuthbert

b. 1822 Hull, Yorkshire, England
d. 2 March 1905 Jersey, C.I.

English architect whose best-known buildings – Leeds Town Hall (1853–8) and the Grand Hotel in Scarborough (1863–7) – were of powerful baroque design.

Like a number of his contemporaries, Brodrick experimented with ferrovitreous construction, which by the second half of the nineteenth century was the favoured method of handling immense roofing spans of structures such as railway stations, shopping arcades and large exhibition and functional halls in England and America. The pattern for this had been set in 1851 with Sir Joseph **Paxton**'s Crystal Palace in Hyde Park, London.

Brodrick's ferrovitreous venture was the Leeds Corn Exchange (1861–3). This is an oval building with its exterior severely rusticated in fifteenth-century Florentine-palace manner, but inside is a two-storeyed ring of offices, bounded by ironwork galleries surrounding a large, central area roofed by an iron and glass roof. This listed building was recently in poor condition but has now been rescued and restored for use as a shopping centre; however, the local traders still retain their right, according to the bye-laws, to trade there, and once a week a section of the hall is cleared so that corn trading can take place.

Further Reading
D. Lindstrom, 1967, *Architecture of Cuthbert Brodrick*, Country Life.
—— 1978, *West Yorkshire: Architects and Architecture*, Lund Humphries.

DY

Brotan, Johann

b. 24 June 1843 Kattau, Bohemia (now in the Czech Republic)
d. 20 November 1923 Vienna, Austria

Czech engineer, pioneer of the watertube firebox for steam locomotive boilers.

Brotan, who was Chief Engineer of the main workshops of the Royal Austrian State Railways at Gmund, found that locomotive inner fireboxes of the usual type were both expensive, because the copper from which they were made had to be imported, and short-lived, because of corrosion resulting from the use of coal with high sulphur content. He designed a firebox of which the side and rear walls comprised rows of vertical watertubes, expanded at their lower ends into a tubular foundation ring and at the top into a longitudinal water/steam drum. This projected forward above the boiler barrel (which was of the usual firetube type, though of small diameter), to which it was connected. Copper plates were eliminated, as were firebox stays.

The first boiler to incorporate a Brotan firebox was built at Gmund under the inventor's supervision and replaced the earlier boiler of a 0–6–0 in 1901. The increased radiantly heated surface was found to produce a boiler with very good steaming qualities, while the working pressure too could be increased, with consequent fuel economies. Further locomotives in Austria and, experimentally, elsewhere were equipped with Brotan boilers.

Disadvantages of the boiler were the necessity of keeping the tubes clear of scale, and a degree of structural weakness. The Swiss engineer E. Deffner improved the latter aspect by eliminating the forward extension of the water/steam drum, replacing it with a large-diameter boiler barrel with the rear section of tapered wagon-top type so that the front of the water/steam drum could be joined directly to the rear tubeplate. The first locomotives to be fitted with this Brotan–Deffner boiler were two 4–6–0s for the Swiss Federal Railways in 1908 and showed very favourable results. However, steam locomotive development ceased in Switzerland a few years later in favour of electrification, but boilers of the Brotan–Deffner type and further developments of it were used in many other European countries, notably Hungary, where more than 1,000 were built. They were also used experimentally in the USA: for instance, Samuel **Vauclain**, as President of Baldwin Locomotive Works, sent his senior design engineer to study Hungarian experience and then had a high-powered 4–8–0 built with a watertube firebox. On stationary test this produced the very high figure of 4,515 ihp (3,370 kW), but further development work was frustrated by the trade depression commencing in 1929. In France, Gaston du **Bousquet** had obtained good results from experimental installations of Brotan–Deffner-type boilers, and incorporated one into one of his high-powered 4–6–4s of 1910. Experiments were terminated suddenly by his death, followed by the First World War, but thirty-five years later André **Chapelon** proposed using a watertube firebox to obtain the high pressure needed for a triple-expansion, high-powered, steam locomotive, development of which was overtaken by electrification.

Further Reading
G. Szontagh, 1991, 'Brotan and Brotan–Deffner type fireboxes and boilers applied to steam locomotives', *Transactions of the Newcomen Society* 62 (an authoritative account of Brotan boilers).

PJGR

Brown, Andrew

b. October 1825 Glasgow, Scotland
d. 6 May 1907 Renfrew, Scotland

Scottish engineer and specialist shipbuilder, dredge-plant authority and supplier.

Brown commenced his apprenticeship on the River Clyde in the late 1830s, working for some of the most famous marine engineering companies and ultimately with the Caledonian Railway Company. In 1850 he joined the shipyard of A. & J. Inglis Ltd of Partick as Engineering Manager; during his ten years there he pioneered the fitting of link-motion valve gear to marine engines. Other interesting engines were built, all ahead of their time, including a three-cylinder direct-acting steam engine.

His real life's work commenced in 1860 when he entered into partnership with the Renfrew shipbuilder William Simons. Within one year he had designed the fast Clyde steamer *Rothesay Castle*, a ship less than 200 ft (61 m) long, yet which steamed at *c*.20 knots and subsequently became a notable American Civil War blockade runner. At this time the company also built the world's first sailing ship with wire-rope rigging. Within a few years of joining the shipyard on the Cart (a tributary of the Clyde), he had designed the first self-propelled hopper barges built in the United Kingdom. He then went on to design, patent and supervise the building of hopper dredges, bucket ladder dredges and sand dredges, which by the end of the century had capacity of 10,000 tons per hour. In 1895 they built an enclosed hopper-type ship which was the prototype of all subsequent sewage-dumping vessels. Typical of his inventions was the double-ended screw-elevating deck ferry, a ship of particular value in areas where there is high tidal range. Examples of this design are still to be found in many seaports of the world. Brown ultimately became Chairman of Simons shipyard, and in his later years took an active part in civic affairs, serving for fifteen years as Provost of Renfrew. His influence in establishing Renfrew as one of the world's centres of excellence in dredge design and building was considerable, and he was instrumental in bringing several hundred ship contracts of a specialist nature to the River Clyde.

Principal Honours and Distinctions

Vice-President, Institution of Engineers and Shipbuilders in Scotland.

Bibliography

A Century of Shipbuilding 1810 to 1910, Renfrew: Wm Simons.

Further Reading

F.M. Walker, 1984, *Song of the Clyde. A History of Clyde Shipbuilding*, Cambridge.

FMW

Brown, Charles Eugene Lancelot

b. 17 June 1863 Winterthur, Switzerland
d. 2 May 1924 Montagnola, Italy

English engineer who developed polyphase electrical generation and transmission plant.

After attending the Technical College in Winterthur, Brown served with Emile Burgin in Basle before entering the Oerlikon engineering works near Zurich. Two years later he became Director of the electrical department of Oerlikon and from that time was involved in the development of electrical equipment for the generation and distribution of power. The Lauffen–Frankfurt 110-mile (177 km) transmission line of 1891 demonstrated the commercial feasibility of transmitting electrical power over great distances with three-phase alternating current. For this he designed a generator and early examples of oil-cooled transformers, and the scheme gave an impetus to the development of electric-power transmission throughout Europe. In 1891, in association with Walter Boveri, Brown founded the works of Brown Boveri & Co. at Baden, Switzerland, and until his retirement in 1911 he devoted his energies to the design of polyphase alternating-current machinery. Important installations included the Frankfurt electricity works (1894), the Paderno–Milan transmission line, and the Lugano tramway of 1894, the first system in Europe to use three-phase traction motors. This tramway was followed by many other polyphase and mountain railways. The acquisition by Brown Boveri & Co. in 1900 of the manufacturing rights of the Parsons steam turbine directed Brown's attention to problems associated with high-speed machines. Recognizing the high centrifugal stress involved, he began to employ solid cylindrical generator rotors with slots for the excitation winding, a method that has come to be universally adopted in large alternators.

Bibliography

3 December 1901, British patent no. 24,632 (slotted rotor for alternators).

Further Reading

Obituary, 1924, *The Engineer* 137: 543.
Ake T. Vrenthem, 1980, *Jonas Wenstrom and the Three Phase System*, Stockholm, pp. 26–8 (obituary).
75 Years of Brown Boveri, 1966, Baden, Switzerland (for a company history).

GW

Brown, Joseph Rogers

b. 26 January 1810 Warren, Rhode Island, USA
d. 23 July 1876 Isles of Shoals, New Hampshire, USA

American machine-tool builder and co-founder of Brown & Sharpe.

Joseph Rogers Brown was the eldest son of David Brown, who was modestly established as a maker of and dealer in clocks and watches. Joseph assisted his father during school vacations and at the age of 17 left to obtain training as a machinist. In 1829 he joined his father in the manufacture of tower clocks at Pawtucket, Rhode Island, and two years later went into business for himself in Pawtucket making lathes and small tools. In 1833 he rejoined his father in Providence, Rhode Island, as a partner in the manufacture of clocks, watches and surveying and mathematical instruments. David Brown retired in 1841.

J.R. Brown invented and built in 1850 a linear dividing engine which was the first automatic machine for graduating rules in the United States. In 1851 he brought out the vernier calliper, the first application of a vernier scale in a workshop measuring tool. Lucian Sharpe was taken into partnership in 1853 and the firm became J.R. Brown & Sharpe; in 1868 the firm was incorporated as the Brown & Sharpe Manufacturing Company.

In 1855 Brown invented a precision gear-cutting machine to make clock gears. The firm obtained in 1861 a contract to make Wilcox & Gibbs sewing machines and gave up the manufacture of clocks. At about this time F.W. **Howe** of the Providence Tool Company arranged for Brown & Sharpe to make a turret lathe required for the manufacture of muskets. This was basically Howe's design, but Brown added a few features, and it was the first machine tool built for sale by the Brown & Sharpe Company. It was followed in 1862 by the universal milling machine invented by Brown initially for making twist drills. Particularly for cutting gear teeth, Brown invented in 1864 a formed milling cutter which could be sharpened without changing its profile. In 1867 the need for an instrument for checking the thickness of sheet material became apparent, and in August of that year J.R. Brown and L. Sharpe visited the Paris Exhibition and saw a micrometer calliper invented by Jean Laurent Palmer in 1848. They recognized its possibilities and with a few developments marketed it as a convenient, hand-held measuring instrument. Grinding lathes were made by Brown & Sharpe in the early 1860s, and from 1868 a universal grinding machine was developed, with the first one being completed in 1876. The patent for this machine was granted after Brown's sudden death while on holiday.

Further Reading

J.W. Roe, 1916, *English and American Tool Builders*, New Haven: Yale University Press; repub. 1926, New York and 1987, Bradley, Ill.: Lindsay Publications Inc. (further details of Brown & Sharpe Company and their products).
R.S. Woodbury, 1958, *History of the Gear-Cutting Machine*, Cambridge, Mass.: MIT Press
——, 1959, *History of the Grinding Machine*, Cambridge, Mass.: MIT Press.
——, 1960, *History of the Milling Machine*, Cambridge, Mass.: MIT Press.

RTS

Brown, Samuel

b. unknown
d. 1849 England

English cooper, inventor of a gas vacuum engine.

Between the years 1823 and 1833, Brown achieved a number of a firsts as a pioneer of internal-combustion engines. In 1824 he built a full-scale working model of a pumping engine; in 1826, a vehicle fitted with a gas vacuum engine ascended Shooters Hill in Kent; and in 1827 he conducted trials of a motor-driven boat on the Thames that were witnessed by Lords of the Admiralty. The principle of Brown's engine had been demonstrated by **Cecil** in 1820. A burning gas flame was extinguished within a closed cylinder, creating a partial vacuum; atmospheric pressure was then utilized to produce the working stroke. By 1832 a number of Brown's engines in use for pumping water were reported, the most notable being at Croydon Canal. However, high fuel consumption and running costs prevented a wide acceptance of Brown's engines, and a company formed in 1825 was dissolved only two years later. Brown continued alone with his work until his death.

Bibliography

1823, British patent no. 4,874 (gas vacuum engine).

1826, British patent no. 5,350 (improved gas vacuum engine).

1846, British patent no. 11,076, 'Improvements in Gas Engines and in Propelling Carriages and Vessels' (no specification was enrolled).

Further Reading

Various discussions of Brown's engines can be found in *Mechanics Magazine* (1824) 2: 360, 385; (1825) 3: 6; (1825) 4: 19, 309; (1826) 5: 145; (1826) 6: 79; (1827) 7: 82–134; (1832) 17: 273.

The Engineer 182: 214.

A.K. Bruce, *Samuel Brown and the Gas Engine*.

Dugald Clerk, 1895, *The Gas and Oil Engine*, 6th edn, London, pp. 2–3.

KAB

Bruce, David

b. *c.*1801 USA
d. 13 September 1892 USA

American inventor of the first successful typecaster.

He was the son of David Bruce, typefounder, who introduced stereotyping into the USA. As a boy, he was employed on various tasks about the typefoundry and printing works of D. & G. Bruce until 1819, when he was apprenticed to William Fry of Philadelphia, at that time the most eminent printer in America. However, he ran away from Fry and returned to his father, from whom he continued to learn the typefounder's trade. Around 1828 he moved to Albany, where he took charge of a typefoundry. Two years later he was back in New York and joined the firm of George Bruce & Co. In 1834 he moved to New Jersey, where he set about producing the improved form of typecasting machine for which he is chiefly known. Having achieved success, he set up in business again in New York and remained there until his retirement some twenty-five years before his death. Bruce in fact invented the first effective typecasting machine in New York in 1838 and patented it the same year. His machine incorporated a force pump to drive the molten metal from the pot into the mould. The machine, operated by a wheel turned by hand, could produce forty sorts of various sizes per minute.

The machine speeded up the production of type: between 3,000 and 7,000 pieces of type could be cast by hand, whereas these figures were raised to between 12,000 and 20,000 by the casting machine. The Bruce caster was not introduced into Britain until 1853. It was later supplanted by improved machines, notably that invented by **Wicks**.

Bibliography

1887, letter, *Inland Printer* (September) (provides some biographical details).

Further Reading

Obituary, 1892, *Inland Printer* (November): 150.

James Moran, 1965, *The Composition of Reading Matter*, London: Wace (provides some details of the Bruce machine).

LRD

Brunel, Isambard Kingdom

b. 9 April 1806 Portsea, Hampshire, England
d. 15 September 1859 18 Duke Street, St James's, London, England

English civil and mechanical engineer.

The son of Marc Isambard **Brunel** and Sophia Kingdom, he was educated at a private boarding-school in Hove. At the age of 14 he went to the College of Caen and then to the Lycée Henri-Quatre in Paris, after which he was apprenticed to Louis Breguet. In 1822 he returned from France and started working in his father's office, while spending much of his time at the works of Maudslay, Sons & Field.

From 1825 to 1828 he worked under his father on the construction of the latter's Thames Tunnel, occupying the position of Engineer-in-Charge, exhibiting great courage and presence of mind in the emergencies which occurred not infrequently. These culminated in January 1828 in the flooding of the tunnel and work was suspended for seven years. For the next five years the young engineer made abortive attempts to find a suitable outlet for his talents, but to little avail. Eventually, in 1831, his design for a suspension bridge over the River Avon at Clifton Gorge was accepted and he was appointed Engineer. (The bridge was eventually finished five years after Brunel's death, as a memorial to him, the delay being due to inadequate financing.) He next planned and supervised improvements to the Bristol docks. In March 1833 he was appointed Engineer of the Bristol Railway, later called the Great Western Railway. He immediately started to survey the route between London and Bristol that was completed by late August that year. On 5 July 1836 he married Mary Horsley and settled into 18 Duke Street, Westminster, London, where he also had his office. Work on the Bristol Railway started in 1836. The foundation stone of the Clifton Suspension Bridge was laid the same year. Whereas George **Stephenson** had based his standard railway gauge as 4 ft 8½ in (1.44 m), that or a similar gauge being usual for colliery wagonways in the Newcastle area, Brunel adopted the broader gauge of 7 ft (2.13 m). The first stretch of the line, from Paddington to Maidenhead, was opened to traffic on 4 June 1838, and the whole line from London to Bristol was opened in June 1841. The continuation of the line through to Exeter was completed and opened on 1 May 1844. The normal time for the 194-mile (312 km) run from Paddington to Exeter was 5 hours, at an average speed of 38.8 mph (62.4 km/h) including stops. The Great Western line included the Box Tunnel, the longest tunnel to that date at nearly two miles (3.2 km).

Brunel was the engineer of most of the railways in the West Country, in South Wales and much of Southern Ireland. As railway networks developed, the frequent break of gauge became more of a problem and on 9 July 1845 a Royal Commission was appointed to look into it. In spite of comparative tests, run between Paddington–Didcot and Darlington–York, which showed in favour of Brunel's arrangement, the enquiry ruled in favour of the narrow gauge, 274 miles (441 km) of the former having been built against 1,901 miles (3,059 km) of the latter to that date. The Gauge Act of 1846 forbade the building of any further railways in Britain to any gauge other than 4 ft 8½ in (1.44 m).

The existence of long and severe gradients on the South Devon Railway led to Brunel's adoption of the atmospheric railway developed by Samuel **Clegg** and later by the **Samuda** brothers. In this a pipe of 9 in. (23 cm) or more in diameter was laid between the rails, along the top of which ran a continuous hinged flap of leather backed with iron. At intervals of about 3 miles (4.8 km) were pumping stations to exhaust the pipe. Much trouble was experienced with the flap valve and its lubrication – freezing of the leather in winter, the lubricant being sucked into the pipe or eaten by rats at other times – and the experiment was abandoned at considerable cost.

Brunel is to be remembered for his two great West Country tubular bridges, the Chepstow and the Tamar Bridge at Saltash, with the latter opened in May 1859, having two main spans of 465 ft (142 m) and a central pier extending 80 ft (24 m) below high water mark and allowing 100 ft (30 m) of headroom above the same. His timber viaducts throughout Devon and Cornwall became a feature of the landscape. The line was extended ultimately to Penzance.

As early as 1835 Brunel had the idea of extending the line westwards across the Atlantic from Bristol to New York by means of a steamship. In 1836 building commenced and the hull left Bristol in July 1837 for fitting out at Wapping. On 31 March 1838 the ship left again for Bristol but the boiler lagging caught fire and Brunel was injured in the subsequent confusion. On 8 April the ship set sail for New York (under steam), its rival, the 703-ton *Sirius*, having left four days earlier. The 1,340-ton *Great Western* arrived only a few hours after the *Sirius*. The hull was of wood, and was copper-sheathed. In 1838 Brunel planned a larger ship, some 3,000 tons, the *Great Britain*, which was to have an iron hull.

The *Great Britain* was screwdriven and was launched on 19 July 1843, 289 ft (88 m) long by 51 ft (15.5 m) at its widest. The ship's first voyage, from Liverpool to New York, began on 26 August 1845. In 1846 it ran aground in Dundrum Bay, County Down, and was later sold for use on the Australian run, on which it sailed no fewer than thirty-two times in twenty-three years, also serving as a troop-ship in the Crimean War. During this war, Brunel designed a 1,000-bed hospital which was shipped out to Renkioi ready for assembly and complete with shower-baths and vapour-baths with printed instructions on how to use them, beds and bedding and water closets with a supply of toilet paper!

Brunel's last, largest and most extravagantly conceived ship was the *Great Leviathan*, eventually named *The Great Eastern*, which had a double-skinned iron hull, together with both paddles and screw propeller. Brunel designed the ship to carry sufficient coal for the round trip to

Australia without refuelling, thus saving the need for and the cost of bunkering, as there were then few bunkering ports throughout the world. The ship's construction was started by John Scott Russell in his yard at Millwall on the Thames, but the building was completed by Brunel due to Russell's bankruptcy in 1856. The hull of the huge vessel was laid down so as to be launched sideways into the river and then to be floated on the tide. Brunel's plan for hydraulic launching gear had been turned down by the directors on the grounds of cost, an economy that proved false in the event. The sideways launch with over 4,000 tons of hydraulic power together with steam winches and floating tugs on the river took over two months, from 3 November 1857 until 13 January 1858. The ship was 680 ft (207 m) long, 83 ft (25 m) beam and 58 ft (18 m) deep; the screw was 24 ft (7.3 m) in diameter and paddles 60 ft (18.3 m) in diameter. Its displacement was 32,000 tons (32,500 tonnes).

The strain of overwork and the huge responsibilities that lay on Brunel began to tell. He was diagnosed as suffering from Bright's disease, or nephritis, and spent the winter travelling in the Mediterranean and Egypt, returning to England in May 1859. On 5 September he suffered a stroke which left him partially paralysed, and he died ten days later at his Duke Street home.

Further Reading
L.T.C. Rolt, 1957, *Isambard Kingdom Brunel*, London: Longmans Green.
J. Dugan, 1953, *The Great Iron Ship*, Hamish Hamilton.

IMcN

Brunel, Sir Marc Isambard

b. 26 April 1769 Hacqueville, Normandy, France
d. 12 December 1849 London, England

French (naturalized American) engineer of the first Thames Tunnel.

His mother died when he was 7 years old, a year later he went to college in Gisors and later to the Seminary of Sainte-Nicaise at Rouen. From 1786 to 1792 he followed a career in the French navy as a junior officer. In Rouen he met Sophie Kingdom, daughter of a British Navy contractor, whom he was later to marry. In July 1793 Marc sailed for America from Le Havre. He was to remain there for six years, and became an American citizen, occupying himself as a land surveyor and as an architect. He became Chief Engineer to the City of New York. At General Hamilton's dinner table he learned that the British Navy used over 100,000 ship's blocks every year; this started him thinking how the manufacture of blocks could be mechanized. He roughed out a set of machines to do the job, resigned his post as Chief Engineer and sailed for England in February 1799.

In London he was shortly introduced to Henry **Maudslay**, to whom he showed the drawings of his proposed machines and with whom he placed an order for their manufacture. The first machines were completed by mid-1803. Altogether Maudslay produced twenty-one machines for preparing the shells, sixteen for preparing the sheaves and eight other machines.

In February 1809 he saw troops at Portsmouth returning from Corunna, the victors, with their lacerated feet bound in rags. He resolved to mechanize the production of boots for the Army and, within a few months, had twenty-four disabled soldiers working the machinery he had invented and installed near his Battersea sawmill. The plant could produce 400 pairs of boots and shoes a day, selling at between 9s. 6d. and 20s. a pair.

One day in 1817 at Chatham dockyard he observed a piece of scrap keel timber, showing the ravages wrought by the shipworm, *Teredo navalis*, which, with its proboscis protected by two jagged concave triangular shells, consumes, digests and finally excretes the ship's timbers as it gnaws its way through them. The excreted material provided material for lining the walls of the tunnel the worm had drilled. Brunel decided to imitate the action of the shipworm on a large scale: the Thames Tunnel was to occupy Marc Brunel for most of the remainder of his life. Boring started in March 1825 and was completed by March 1843. The project lay dormant for long periods, but eventually the 1,200 ft (366 m)-long tunnel was completed. Marc Isambard Brunel died at the age of 80 and was buried at Kensal Green cemetery.

Principal Honours and Distinctions
FRS 1814. Vice-President, Royal Society 1832.

Further Reading
P. Clements, 1970, *Marc Isambard Brunel*, London: Longmans Green.

IMcN

Brunelleschi, Filippo

b. 1377 Florence, Italy
d. 15 April 1446 Florence, Italy

Italian artist, craftsman and architect who introduced the Italian Renaissance style of classical architecture in the fifteenth century.

Brunelleschi was a true 'Renaissance Man' in that he excelled in several disciplines, as did most artists of the Italian Renaissance of the fifteenth and sixteenth centuries. He was a goldsmith and sculptor; fifteenth-century writers acknowledge him as the first to study and demonstrate the principles of perspective, and he clearly possessed a deep mathematical understanding of the principles of architectural structure.

Brunelleschi's Foundling Hospital in Florence, begun in 1419, is accepted as the first Renaissance building, one whose architectural style is based upon a blend of the classical principles and decoration of Ancient Rome and those of the Tuscan Romanesque. Brunelleschi went on to design a number of important Renaissance structures in Florence, such as the basilicas of San Lorenzo and Santo Spirito, the Pazzi Chapel at Santa Croce, and the unfinished church of Santa Maria degli Angeli.

However, the artistic and technical feat for which Brunelleschi is most famed is the completion of Florence Cathedral by constructing a dome above the octagonal drum which had been completed in 1412. The building of this dome presented what appeared to be at the time insuperable problems, which had caused previous cathedral architects to shy away from tackling it. The drum was nearly 140 ft (43 m) in diameter and its base was 180 ft (55 m) above floor level: no wooden centering was possible because no trees long enough to span the gap could be found, and even if they had been available, the weight of such a massive framework would have broken centering beneath. In addition, the drum had no external abutment, so the weight of the dome must exert excessive lateral thrust. Aesthetically, the ideal Renaissance dome, like the Roman dome before it (for example, the Pantheon) was a hemisphere, but in the case of the Florence Cathedral such a structure would have been unsafe, so Brunelleschi created a pointed dome that would create less thrust laterally. He constructed eight major ribs of stone and, between them, sixteen minor ones, using a light infilling. He constructed a double-shell dome, which was the first of this type but is a design that has been followed by nearly all major architects since this date (for example Michelangelo's Saint Peter's in Rome, and Wren's Saint Paul's in London). Further strength is given by a herringbone pattern of masonry and brick infilling, and by tension chains of massive blocks, fastened with iron and with iron chains above, girding the dome at three levels. A large lantern finally stops the 50 ft (15.25 m) diameter eye at the point of the dome. Construction of the Florence Cathedral dome was begun on 7 August 1420 and was completed to the base of the lantern sixteen years later. It survives as the peak of Brunelleschi's Renaissance achievement.

Further Reading
Peter Murray, 1963, *The Architecture of the Italian Renaissance*, Batsford, Ch. 2.
Howard Saalman, 1980, *Filippo Brunelleschi: The Cupola of Santa Maria del Fiore*, Zwemmer.
Piero Sanpaolesi, 1977, *La Cupola di Santa Maria del Fiore: Il Progetto: La Costruzione*, Florence: Edam.
Eugenio Battisti, 1981, *Brunelleschi: The Complete Work*, Thames and Hudson.

DY

Brunschwig, Hieronymus

b. *c.*1440 Strasbourg, Alsace
d. 1512/13 Strasbourg, Alsace

German surgeon and chemist.

Brunschwig was a widely read and highly respected surgeon of the city of Strasbourg. He was a writer of two works, one on surgery and the other, of greater importance, on chemical distillation. In this he was the inheritor of a tradition of the practice of distillation going back to the first centuries AD. The most familiar chemical tradition in the Middle Ages was that of alchemy, devoted to the attempt to make gold. The appearance of a number of printed books of a severely practical nature after 1500, however, testifies to the existence of a practical tradition that had flourished alongside alchemy. Brunschwig's first essay in this field was printed in 1500 and dealt with the preparation of 'simples', or remedies with a single active constituent. In 1507 he brought out a work on the distilling of 'composites', remedies with two or more active constituents. In these works Brunschwig sought to present a comprehensive account of the various kinds of apparatus available and the methods of preparing medicines, together with an account of the diseases it was hoped to cure with them. It was one of the earliest printed books on a chemical subject and the earliest to include illustrations of chemical apparatus. The works were widely used and did much to turn chemistry away from its preoccupation with gold-making, towards the making of substances useful in medicine.

Further Reading
The best account of Brunschwig's life and work is the introduction to *Book of Distillation by Hieronymus Bruunschwig*, 1971, introd. Harold J. Abrahams, New York, Johnson Reprint (the best account of Brunschwig's life and work).

LRD

Brush, Charles Francis
b. 17 March 1849 Euclid, Michigan, USA
d. 15 June 1929 Cleveland, Ohio, USA

American engineer, inventor of a multiple electric arc lighting system and founder of the Brush Electric Company.

Brush graduated from the University of Michigan in 1869 and worked for several years as a chemist. Believing that electric arc lighting would be commercially successful if the equipment could be improved, he completed his first dynamo in 1875 and a simplified arc lamp. His original system operated a maximum of four lights, each on a separate circuit, from one dynamo. Brush envisaged a wider market for his product and by 1879 had available on arc lighting system principally intended for street and other outdoor illumination. He designed a dynamo that generated a high voltage and which, with a carbon-pile regulator, provided an almost constant current permitting the use of up to forty lamps on one circuit. He also improved arc lamps by incorporating a slipping-clutch regulating mechanism and automatic means of bringing

into use a second set of carbons, thereby doubling the period between replacements.

Brush's multiple electric arc lighting system was first demonstrated in Cleveland and by 1880 had been adopted in a number of American cities, including New York, Boston and Philadelphia. It was also employed in many European towns until incandescent lamps, for which the Brush dynamo was unsuitable, came into use. To market his apparatus, Brush promoted local lighting companies and thereby secured local capital.

Principal Honours and Distinctions
Chevalier de la Légion d'honneur 1881. American Academy of Arts and Sciences Rumford Medal 1899. American Institute of Electrical Engineers Edison Medal 1913.

Bibliography
18 May 1878, British patent no. 2,003 (Brush dynamo).
11 March 1879, British patent no. 947 (arc lamp).
26 February 1880, British patent no. 849 (current regulator).

Further Reading
J.W. Urquhart, 1891, *Electric Light,* London (for a detailed description of the Brush system).
H.C. Passer, 1953, *The Electrical Manufacturers: 1875–1900*, Cambridge, Mass., pp. 14–21 (for the origins of the Brush Company).
S. Steward, 1980, in *Electrical Review*, 206: 34–5 (a short account).

See also **Hammond, Robert.**

GW

Buckle, William
b. 29 July 1794 Alnwick, Northumberland, England
d. 30 September 1863 London, England

English mechanical engineer who introduced the first large screw-cutting lathe to Boulton, Watt & Co.

William Buckle was the son of Thomas Buckle (1759–1849), a millwright who later assisted the 9th Earl of Dundonald (1749–1831) in his various inventions, principally machines for the manufacture of rope. Soon after the birth of

William, the family moved from Alnwick to Hull, Yorkshire, where he received his education. The family again moved *c.*1808 to London, and William was apprenticed to Messrs Woolf & Edwards, mill-wrights and engineers of Lambeth. During his apprenticeship he attended evening classes at a mechanical drawing school in Finsbury, which was then the only place of its kind in London.

After completing his apprenticeship, he was sent by Messrs Humphrys to Memel in Prussia to establish steamboats on the rivers and lakes there under the patronage of the Prince of Hardenburg. After about four years he returned to Britain and was employed by Boulton, Watt & Co. to install the engines in the first steam mail packet for the service between Dublin and Holyhead. He was responsible for the engines of the steamship *Lightning* when it was used on the visit of George IV to Ireland.

About 1824 Buckle was engaged by **Boulton, Watt** & Co. as Manager of the Soho Foundry, where he is credited with introducing the first large screw-cutting lathe. At Soho about 700 or 800 men were employed on a wide variety of engineering manufacture, including coining machinery for mints in many parts of the world, with some in 1826 for the Mint at the Soho Manufactory. In 1851, following the recommendations of a Royal Commission, the Royal Mint in London was reorganized and Buckle was asked to take the post of Assistant Coiner, the senior executive officer under the Deputy Master. This he accepted, retaining the post until the end of his life.

At Soho, Buckle helped to establish a literary and scientific institution to provide evening classes for the apprentices and took part in the teaching. He was an original member of the Institution of Mechanical Engineers, which was founded in Birmingham in January 1847, and a member of their Council from then until 1855. He contributed a number of papers in the early years, including a memoir of William **Murdock** whom he had known at Soho; he resigned from the Institution in 1856 after his move to London. He was an honorary member of the London Association of Foreman Engineers.

Bibliography
1850, 'Inventions and life of William Murdock', *Proceedings of the Institution of Mechanical Engineers* 2 (October): 16–26.

RTS

Buckminster Fuller, Richard
See **Fuller, Richard Buckminster**.

Budding, Edwin Beard
b. *c.*1796 Bisley (?), Gloucestershire, England
d. 1846 Dursley, Gloucestershire, England

English inventor of the lawn mower.

Budding was an engineer who described himself as a mechanic on his first patent papers and as a manager in later applications.

A rotary machine had been developed at Brimscombe Mill in Stroud for cutting the pile on certain clothes and Budding saw the potential of this principle for a machine for cutting grass on lawns. It is not clear whether Budding worked for the Lewis family, who owned the mill, or whether he saw the machines during their manufacture at the Phoenix Foundry. At the age of 35 Budding entered into partnership with John Ferrabee, who had taken out a lease on Thrupp Mill. They reached an agreement in which Ferrabee would pay to obtain letter patent on the mower and would cover all the development costs, after which they would have an equal share in the profits. The agreement also allowed Ferrabee to license the manufacture of the machine and in 1832 he negotiated with the agricultural manufacturer Ransomes, allowing them to manufacture the mower.

Budding invented a screw-shifting spanner at a time when he might have been working as a mechanic at Thrupp Mill. He later rented a workshop in which he produced Pepperbox pistols. In the late 1830s he moved to Dursley, where he became Manager for Mr G. Lister, who made clothing machinery. Together they patented an improved method of making cylinders for carding engines, but Budding required police protection from those who saw their jobs threatened by the device. He made no fortune from his inventions and died at the age of 50.

Further Reading
H.A. Randall, 1965–6 'Some mid-Gloucestershire engineers and inventors', *Transactions of the Newcomen Society* 38: 89–96 (looks at the careers of both Budding and Ferrabee).

AP

Buddle, John

b. 15 November 1773 Kyloe, Northumberland, England
d. 10 October 1843 Wallsend, Northumberland, England

English colliery inspector, manager and agent.

Buddle was educated by his father, a former
schoolteacher who was from 1781 the first inspector and manager of the new Wallsend colliery. When his father died in 1806, John Buddle
assumed full responsibility at the Wallsend colliery, and he remained as inspector and manager
there until 1819, when he was appointed as colliery agent to the third Marquis of Londonderry.
In this position, besides managing colliery business, he acted as an entrepreneur, gaining political influence and organizing colliery owners into
fixing prices; Buddle and Londonderry were also
responsible for the building of Seaham harbour.
Buddle became known as the 'King of the Coal
Trade', gaining influence throughout the important Northumberland and Durham coalfield.

Buddle's principal contribution to mining
technology was with regard to the improvement
of both safety standards and productivity. In
1807 he introduced a steam-driven air pump
which extracted air from the top of the upcast
shaft. Two years later, he drew up plans which
divided the coalface into compartments; this enabled nearly the whole seam to be exploited. The
system of compound ventilation greatly reduced
the danger of explosions: the incoming air was
divided into two currents, and since each current
passed through only half the underground area,
the air was less heavily contaminated with gas.

In 1813 Buddle presented an important paper
on his method for mine ventilation to the
Sunderland Society for Preventing Accidents in
Coal-mines, which had been established in that
year following a major colliery explosion. He emphasized the need for satisfactory underground
lighting, which influenced the development of
safety-lamps, and assisted actively in the experiments with Humphrey **Davy**'s lamp which he
was one of the first mine managers to introduce.
Another mine accident, a sudden flood,
prompted him to maintain a systematic record of
mine-workings which ultimately resulted in the
establishment of the Mining Record Office.

Bibliography
1838, *Transactions of the Natural History Society
of Northumberland* 11, pp. 309–36 (Buddle's
paper on keeping records of underground
workings).

Further Reading
R.L. Galloway, 1882, *A History of Coalmining
in Great Britain*, London (deals extensively
with Buddle's underground devices).
R.W. Sturgess, 1975, *Aristocrat in Business: The
Third Marquis of Londonderry as Coalowner
and Portbuilder*, Durham: Durham County
Local History Society (concentrates on Bud-
dle's work after 1819).
C.E. Hiskey, 1978, *John Buddle 1773–1843,
Agent and Entrepreneur in the Northeast Coal
Trade*, unpublished MLitt thesis, Durham
University (a very detailed study).

WK

Bullard, Edward Payson

b. 18 April 1841 Uxbridge, Massachusetts,
USA
d. 22 December 1906 Bridgeport, Connecticut, USA

*American mechanical engineer and
machine-tool manufacturer who designed
machines for boring.*

Edward Payson Bullard served his apprenticeship
at the Whitin Machine Works, Whitinsville, Massachusetts, and worked at the Colt Armory in
Hartford, Connecticut, until 1863; he then entered the employ of Pratt & Whitney, also in
Hartford. He later formed a partnership with
J.H. Prest and William Parsons manufacturing
millwork and tools, the firm being known as Bullard & Prest. In 1866 Bullard organized the
Norwalk Iron Works Company of Norwalk,
Connecticut, but afterwards withdrew and continued the business in Hartford. In 1868 the firm
of Bullard & Prest was dissolved and Bullard became Superintendent of a large machine shop in
Athens, Georgia. He later organized the machine tool department of Post & Co. at Cincinnati, and in 1872 he was made General
Superintendent of the Gill Car Works at Columbus, Ohio. In 1875 he established a machinery business in Beekman Street, New York,
under the name of Allis, Bullard & Co. Mr Allis
withdrew in 1877, and the Bullard Machine

Company was organized.

In 1880 Bullard secured entire control of the business and also became owner of the Bridgeport Machine Tool Works, Bridgeport, Connecticut. In 1883 he designed his first vertical boring and turning mill with a single head and belt feed and a 37 in. (94 cm) capacity; this was the first small boring machine designed to do the accurate work previously done on the face plate of a lathe. In 1889 Bullard gave up his New York interests and concentrated his entire attention on manufacturing at Bridgeport, the business being incorporated in 1894 as the Bullard Machine Tool Company. The company specialized in the construction of boring machines, the design being developed so that it became essentially a vertical turret lathe. After Bullard's death, his son Edward Payson Bullard II (b. 10 July 1872 Columbus, Ohio, USA; d. 26 June 1953 Fairfield, Connecticut, USA) continued as head of the company and further developed the boring machine into a vertical multi-spindle automatic lathe which he called the 'Mult-au-matic' lathe. Both father and son were members of the American Society of Mechanical Engineers.

Further Reading
J.W. Roe, 1916, *English and American Tool Builders*, New Haven: Yale University Press; repub. 1926, New York and 1987, Bradley, Ill.: Lindsay Publications Inc. (describes Bullard's machines).

RTS

Bulleid, Oliver Vaughan Snell

b. 19 September 1882 Invercargill, New Zealand
d. 25 April 1970 Malta

New Zealand (naturalized British) locomotive engineer noted for original experimental work in the 1940s and 1950s.

Bulleid's father died in 1889 and mother and son returned to the UK from New Zealand; Bulleid himself became a premium apprentice under H.A. **Ivatt** at Doncaster Works, Great Northern Railway (GNR). After working in France and for the Board of Trade, Bulleid returned to the GNR in 1912 as Personal Assistant to Chief Mechanical Engineer H.N. **Gresley**. After a break for war service, he returned as Assistant to Gresley on the latter's appointment as Chief Mechanical Engin-

eer of the London & North Eastern Railway in 1923. He was closely associated with Gresley during the late 1920s and early 1930s.

In 1937 Bulleid was appointed Chief Mechanical Engineer of the Southern Railway (SR). Concentration of resources on electrification had left the Southern short of up-to-date steam locomotives, which Bulleid proceeded to provide. His first design, the 'Merchant Navy' class 4–6–2, appeared in 1941 with chain-driven valve gear enclosed in an oil-bath, and other novel features. A powerful 'austerity' 0–6–0 appeared in 1942, shorn of all inessentials to meet wartime conditions, and a mixed-traffic 4–6–2 in 1945. All were largely successful.

Under Bulleid's supervision, three large, mixed-traffic, electric locomotives were built for the Southern's 660 volt DC system and incorporated flywheel-driven generators to overcome the problem of interruptions in the live rail. Three main-line diesel–electric locomotives were completed after nationalization of the SR in 1948. All were carried on bogies, as was Bulleid's last steam locomotive design for the SR, the 'Leader' class 0–6–6–0 originally intended to meet a requirement for a large, passenger tank locomotive. The first was completed after nationalization of the SR, but the project never went beyond trials. Marginally more successful was a double-deck, electric, suburban, multiple-unit train completed in 1949, with alternate high and low compartments to increase train capacity but not length. The main disadvantage was the slow entry and exit by passengers, and the type was not perpetuated, although the prototype train ran in service until 1971.

In 1951 Bulleid moved to Coras Iompair Éireann, the Irish national transport undertaking, as Chief Mechanical Engineer. There he initiated a large-scale plan for dieselization of the railway system in 1953, the first such plan in the British Isles. Simultaneously he developed, with limited success, a steam locomotive intended to burn peat briquettes: to burn peat, the only native fuel, had been a long-unfulfilled ambition of railway engineers in Ireland. Bulleid retired in 1958.

Bibliography
Bulleid took out six patents between 1941 and 1956, covering *inter alia* valve gear, boilers, brake apparatus and wagon underframes.

Further Reading
H.A.V. Bulleid, 1977, *Bulleid of the Southern*, Shepperton: Ian Allan (a good biography written by the subject's son).
C. Fryer, 1990, *Experiments with Steam*, Wellingborough: Patrick Stephens (provides details of the austerity 0–6–0, the 'Leader' locomotive and the peat-burning locomotive: see Chs 19, 20 and 21 respectively).

PJGR

Bunch, Cordia C.

b. 30 April 1885 Tama, Iowa, USA
d. 1942 St Louis, Missouri, USA

American otolaryngological psychiatrist, principal exponent and developer of the techniques of audiometry.

Bunch graduated as a teacher in Iowa at Tama College in 1902 and held posts as a teacher and the school head until 1914. He was engaged in various posts as a psychologist and otolaryngologist from 1917 to 1925, obtaining his PhD in 1920, and was involved in otolaryngological research at Johns Hopkins University from 1927 to 1930. He was appointed Professor of Applied Physiology of Otolaryngology at Washington University, St Louis, in 1930, and became engaged in the development and applications of pure tone audiometry.

Bibliography
1943, *Clinical Audiometry.*

Further Reading
Hester & Stevens, 1984, 'Audiometers', *Audiology.*

MG

Bunning, James Bunstone

b. 1802 London, England
d. 1863 London (?), England

English surveyor responsible for some impressive structures in London.

For the last twenty years of his life Bunning served as architect to the Corporation of London. During this time he was especially noted for three large buildings: Holloway Prison (1849–52), built in stone in a bold, castellated style; Caledonian Market (1855); and, most important and original, the Coal Exchange (1847–9).

Bunning's larger replacement for an earlier building in Lower Thames Street was a ferrovitreous triumph. The exterior was of fashionable Italianate design, but inside it contained an elegant 60 ft (18 m) diameter rotunda of cast iron intended for the meeting of merchants. Galleries made entirely of iron and supported on brackets encircled the walls at three levels, and above was a glazed dome of ground plate glass rising to over 74 ft (22.5 m) from ground level, supported by thirty-two iron ribs. For decoration there were twenty-four painted panels depicting plants and fossils found in coal seams, and eight smaller compartments showing coal implements. The demolition of this outstanding structure in 1962 so that the road could be widened, served as a trigger to public concern over the then-increasing rate of demolition of notable nineteenth-century structures. During excavation for this building, a structure which cost £40,000, a Roman hypocaust system was found beneath and preserved.

Further Reading
G. Godwin, 1850, 'Buildings and Monuments: Modern and Medieval', *The Builder.*

DY

Bunsen, Robert Wilhelm

b. 31 March 1811 Göttingen, Germany
d. 16 August 1899 Heidelberg, Germany

German chemist, pioneer of chemical spectroscopy.

Bunsen's father was Librarian and Professor of Linguistics at Göttingen University and Bunsen himself studied chemistry there. Obtaining his doctorate at the age of only 19, he travelled widely, meeting some of the leading chemists of the day and visiting many engineering works. On his return he held various academic posts, finally as Professor of Chemistry at Heidelberg in 1852, a post he held until his retirement in 1889.

During 1837–41 Bunsen studied a series of compounds shown to contain the cacodyl $(CH_3)_2As-$ group or radical. The elucidation of the structure of these compounds gave support to the radical theory in organic chemistry and earned him fame, but it also cost him the sight of an eye and other ill effects resulting from these dangerous and evil-smelling substances. With the chemist Gustav Robert Kirchhoff (1824–87), Bunsen pioneered the use of spectroscopy in chemical analysis from 1859, and with its aid he discovered the elements caesium and rubidium. He developed the Bunsen cell, a zinc–carbon primary cell, with which he isolated a number of alkali and other metals by electrode-position from solution or electrolysis of fused chlorides.

Bunsen's main work was in chemical analysis, in the course of which he devised some important laboratory equipment, such as a filter pump. The celebrated Bunsen gas burner was probably devised by his technician Peter Desdega. During 1838–44 Bunsen applied his methods of gas analysis to the study of the gases produced by blast furnaces for the production of cast iron. He demonstrated that no less than 80 per cent of the heat was lost during smelting, and that valuable gaseous by-products, such as ammonia, were also lost. Lyon Playfair in England was working along similar lines, and in 1848 the two men issued a paper, 'On the gases evolved from iron furnaces', to draw attention to these drawbacks.

Bibliography

1904, Bunsen's collected papers were published in 3 vols, Leipzig.

Further Reading

G. Lockemann, 1949, *Robert Wilhelm Bunsen: Lebensbild eines deutschen Forschers*, Stuttgart.
T. Curtin, 1961, biog. account, in E. Farber (ed.), *Great Chemists*, New York, pp. 575–81.
Henry E. Roscoe, 1900, 'Bunsen memorial lecture, 29th March 1900', *Journal of the Chemical Society* 77: 511–54.

LRD

Burgi, Jost

b. 28 February 1552 Lichtensteig, Switzerland
d. 31 January 1632 Kassel, Germany

Swiss clockmaker and mathematician who invented the remontoire and the cross-beat escapement, also responsible for the use of exponential notation and the calculation of tables of anti-logarithms.

Burgi entered the service of Duke William IV of Hesse in 1579 as Court Clockmaker, although he also assisted William with his astronomical observations. In 1584 he invented the cross-beat escapement which increased the accuracy of spring-driven clocks by two orders of magnitude.

During the last years of the century he also worked on the development of geometrical and astronomical instruments for the Royal Observatory at Kassel.

On the death of Duke Wilhelm in 1603, and with news of his skills having reached the Holy Roman Emperor Rudolph II, in 1604 he went to Prague to become Imperial Watchmaker and to assist in the creation of a centre of scientific activity, subsequently becoming Assistant to the German astronomer, Johannes Kepler. No doubt this association led to an interest in mathematics and he made significant contributions to the concept of decimal fractions and the use of exponential notation, i.e. the use of a raised number to indicate powers of another number. It is likely that he was developing the idea of logarithms at the same time (or possibly even before) **Napier**, for in 1620 he made his greatest contribution to mathematics, science and, eventually, engineering, namely the publication of tables of anti-logarithms.

At Prague he continued the series of accurate clocks and instruments for astronomical measurements that he had begun to produce at Kassel. At that period clocks were very poor timekeepers since the controller, the *foliot* or balance, had no natural period of oscillation and was consequently dependent on the driving force. Although the force of the driving weight was constant, irregularities occurred during the transmission of the power through the train as a result of the poor shape and quality of the gearing. Burgi attempted to overcome this directly by superb craftsmanship and indirectly by using a remontoire. This device was wound at regular intervals by the main driving force and fed the power directly to the escape wheel, which impulsed the *foliot*. He also introduced the cross-beat escapement (a variation on the verge), which consisted of two coupled *foliots* that swung in opposition to each other. According to contemporary evidence his clocks produced a remarkable improvement in timekeeping, being accurate to within a minute a day. This improvement was probably a result of the use of a remontoire and the high quality of the workmanship rather than a result of the cross-beat escapement, which did not have a natural period of oscillation.

Burgi or Prague clocks, as they were known, were produced by very few other makers and were supplanted shortly afterwards by the intro-

duction of the pendulum clock. Burgi also produced superb clockwork-driven celestial globes.

Principal Honours and Distinctions
Ennobled 1611.

Bibliography
Burgi only published one book, and that was
concerned with mathematics.

Further Reading
L. von Mackensen, 1979, *Die erste Sternwarte
Europas mit ihren Instrumenten and Uhren –
400 Jahre Jost Burgi in Kassel*, Munich.
K. Maurice and O. Mayr (eds), 1980, *The Clock-
work Universe*, Washington, DC, pp. 87–102.
H.A. Lloyd, 1958, *Some Outstanding Clocks Over
700 Years, 1250–1950*, London.
E.T. Bell, 1937, *Men of Mathematics*, London:
Victor Gollancz.

See also **Briggs, Henry**.

KF/DV

Burks, Arthur Walter
b. 13 October 1915 Duluth, Minnesota, USA

*American engineer involved in the development
of the ENIAC and Whirlwind computers.*

After obtaining his AB degree from De Pere
University, Wisconsin (1937), and his AM and
PhD from the University of Michigan (1938 and
1941, respectively), Burks carried out research at
the Moore School of Engineering, University of
Pennsylvania, during the Second World War,
and at the same time taught philosophy in another department. There, with Herman **Goldstine**, he was involved in the construction of
ENIAC (the Electronic Numerical Integrator
and Computer).

In 1946 he took a post as Assistant Professor
of Engineering at Michigan University, and subsequently became Associate Professor (1948)
and Full Professor (1954). Between 1946 and
1948 he was also associated with the computer
activities of John von Neumann at the Institute
of Advanced Studies, Princeton, and was involved in the development of the Whirlwind I
computer (the first stored-program computer)
by Jay **Forrester** at the Massachusetts Institute
of Technology. From 1948 until 1954 he was a
consultant for the Burroughs Corporation and

also contributed to the Oak Ridge computer
ORACLE. He was Chairman of the Michigan
University Department of Communications
Science in 1967–71 and at various times was Vi-
siting Professor at Harvard University and the
universities of Illinois and Stanford. In 1975 he
became Editor of the *Journal of Computer and
System Sciences*.

Bibliography
1946, 'Super electronic computing machine',
Electronics Industry 62.
1947, 'Electronic computing circuits of the
ENIAC', *Proceedings of the Institute of Radio
Engineers* 35: 756.
1980, 'From ENIAC to the stored program
computer. Two revolutions in computing', in
N. Metropolis, J. Howlett & G.-C. Rota (eds),
A History of Computing in the 20th Century,
London: Academic Press.

Further Reading
J.W. Corlada, 1987, *Historical Dictionary of
Data Processing* (provides further details of
Burk's career).

KF

Burrell, William
b. *c.*1570 England
d. 1630 near Huntingdon, England

*English shipbuilder and Chief Shipwright to the
East India Company.*

Born into comfortable circumstances, Burrell
chose ship construction as his career. Ability
aided by financial influence helped professional
advancement, and by his early thirties he possessed a shipyard at Ratcliffe on the River
Thames. Ship design was then unscientific,
shrouded in mystique, and it required patience
and perseverance to penetrate the conventions of
the craft.

From the 1600s Burrell had been investing in
the East India Company. In 1607 the Company
decided to build ships in their own right, and
Burrell was appointed as the first Master Shipwright, a post he held for nearly twenty years.
The first ship, *Trade's Increase*, of 1,000-tons
burthen, was the largest ship built in England
until the eighteenth century, but following a
mishap at launch and the ship's subsequent loss
on its maiden voyage, the Company reassessed its

policy and built smaller ships. Burrell's foresight can be gauged by his involvement in two private commercial undertakings in Ireland; one to create oak forests for shipbuilding, and the other to set up a small ironworks. In 1618 a Royal Commission was appointed to enquire into the poor condition of the Navy, and with the help of Burrell it was ruled that the main problems were neglect and corruption. With his name being known and his good record of production, the Royal Navy ordered no fewer than ten warships from Burrell in the four-year period from 1619 to 1623. With experience in the military and commercial sectors, Burrell can be regarded as an all-round and expert shipbuilder of the Stuart period. He used intuition at a time when there were no scientific rules and little reliable empiric guidance on ship design.

Principal Honours and Distinctions
First Warden of the Shipwrights' Company after its new Charter of 1612.

Further Reading
A.P. McGowan, 1978, 'William Burrell (*c.*1570–1630). A forgotten Stuart shipwright', *Ingrid and other Studies* (National Maritime Museum Monograph No. 36).
W. Abell, 1948, *The Shipwright's Trade*, Cambridge.

FMW

Burroughs, Michael
b. mid-twentieth century

English inventor who developed a new design of racing bicycle.

His father was a pattern-maker who worked for a time at the **de Havilland** aircraft factory at Hatfield, Hertfordshire; later he worked in an aeroplane-model shop before turning his attentions to boats and cars. Mike Burroughs left school at the age of 15 to become a self-taught engineer and inventor, regarding himself as an eccentric. Among other things, he invented a machine for packaging coins.

In the 1970s he began to take an interest in bicycles, and he subjected the design and materials of existing machines of conventional design to searching reappraisal. As a result, Burroughs 'reinvented' the bicycle, producing an entirely new concept. His father carved the shape of the single-piece frame in wood, from which a carbon-fibre cast was made. The machine proved to be very fast, but neither the sporting nor the industrial world showed much interest in it. Then in 1991 Rudi Terman, of the motor manufacturers Lotus, saw it and was impressed by its potential; he agreed to develop the machine further, but kept the details secret.

The invention was released to an unsuspecting public at the Barcelona Olympic Games of 1992, ridden by Chris Boardman, who won the pursuit gold medal for Great Britain, a triumph for both rider and inventor. In subsequent months, Boardman went on to break several world records on the Lotus bicycle, including on 23 July 1993 the one-hour record with a distance of 52.27 km (32.48 miles).

Further Reading
C. Boardman and P. Liggett, 1994, *The Fastest Man on Two Wheels: In Pursuit of Chris Boardman*, London: Boxtree (looks at the revolutionary Lotus racing cycle designed by Burroughs).

IMcN

Bury, Edward
b. 22 October 1794 Salford, Lancashire, England
d. 25 November 1858 Scarborough, Yorkshire, England

English steam locomotive designer and builder.

Bury was the earliest engineer to build locomotives distinctively different from those developed by Robert **Stephenson** yet successful in main-line passenger service. A Liverpool sawmill owner, he set up as a locomotive manufacturer while the Liverpool & Manchester Railway was under construction and, after experiments, completed the four-wheeled locomotive *Liverpool* in 1831. It included features that were to be typical of his designs: a firebox in the form of a vertical cylinder with a dome-shaped top and the front flattened to receive the tubes, and inside frames built up from wrought-iron bars. In 1838 Bury was appointed to supply and maintain the locomotives for the London & Birmingham Railway (L & BR), then under construction by Robert Stephenson, on the grounds that the latter should not also provide its locomotives. For several years the L & BR used Bury locomotives exclusively, and they were also used on several other early main lines. Following export to the USA, their bar frames became an enduring feature of locomotive design in that country. Bury claimed, with justification, that his locomotives were economical in maintenance and fuel: the shape of the firebox promoted rapid circulation of water. His locomotives were well built, but some of their features precluded enlargement of the design to produce more powerful locomotives and within a few years they were outclassed.

Principal Honours and Distinctions
FRS 1844.

Bibliography
1840, 'On the locomotive engines of the London and Birmingham Railway', *Transactions of the Institution of Civil Engineers* 3 (4) (provides details of his locomotives and the thinking behind them).

Further Reading
C.F. Dendy Marshall, 1953, *A History of Railway Locomotives Down to the End of the Year 1831*, London: The Locomotive Publishing Co. (describes Bury's early work).
P.J.G. Ransom, 1990, *The Victorian Railway and How It Evolved*, London: Heinemann, pp. 167–8 and 174–6.

PJGR

Butler, Edward
b. 1863
d. 1940

English motoring pioneer, designer of a motor tricycle.

In 1884 Butler patented a design for a motor tricycle that was shown that year at the Stanley Cycle Show and in the following year at the Inventions Exhibition. In 1887 he patented his 'Petrol-tricycle', which was built the following year. The cycle was steered through its two front wheels, while it was driven through its single rear wheel. The motor, which was directly connected to the rear wheel hub by means of overhung cranks, consisted of a pair of water-cooled 2¼ in. (57 mm) bore cylinders with an 8 in. (203 mm) stroke working on the **Clerk** two-stroke cycle. Ignition was by electric spark produced by

a wiper breaking contact with the piston, adopted from Butler's own design of electrostatic ignition machine; this was later replaced by a Ruhmkorff coil and a battery. There was insufficient power with direct drive and the low engine speed of *c*.100 rpm, producing a road speed of approximately 12 mph (19 km/h), so Butler redesigned the engine with a 6¾ in. (171 mm) stroke and a four-stroke cycle with an epicyclic reduction gear drive of 4:1 and later 6:1 ratio which could run at 600 rpm. The combination of restrictive speed-limit laws and shortsightedness of his backers prevented development, despite successful road demonstrations. Interest was non-existent by 1895, and the following year this first English internal combustion engined motorcycle was broken up for the scrap value of some 163 lb (74 kg) of copper and brass contained in its structure.

Further Reading
C.F. Caunter, 1982, *Motor Cycles*, 3rd edn, London: HMSO/Science Museum.

IMcN

By, Lieutenant-Colonel John
b. 7 (?) August 1779 Lambeth, London, England
d. 1 February 1836 Frant, Sussex, England

English Engineer-in-Charge of the construction of the Rideau Canal, linking the St Lawrence and Ottawa Rivers in Canada.

Admitted in 1797 as a Gentleman Cadet in the Royal Military Academy at Woolwich, By was commissioned on 1 August 1799 as a second lieutenant in the Royal Artillery, but was soon transferred to the Royal Engineers. Posted to Plymouth upon the development of the fortifications, he was further posted to Canada, arriving there in August 1802.

In 1803 By was engaged in canal work, assisting Captain Bruyères in the construction of a short canal (1,500 ft (460 m) long) at the Cascades on the Grand, now the Ottawa, River. In 1805 he was back at the Cascades repairing ice damage caused during the previous winter. He was promoted Captain in 1809. Meanwhile he worked on the fortifications of Quebec and in 1806–7 he built a scale model of the Citadel, which is now in the National War Museum of

Canada. He returned to England in 1810 and served in Portugal in 1811. Back in England at the end of the year, he was appointed Royal Engineer Officer in charge at the Waltham Abbey Gunpowder Works on 1 January 1812 and later planned the new Small Arms Factory at Enfield; both works were on the navigable River Lee.

In the post-Napoleonic period Major By, as he then was, retired on half-pay but was promoted to Lieutenant-Colonel on 2 December 1824. Eighteen months later, in March 1826, he returned to Canada on active duty to build the Rideau Canal. This was John By's greatest work. It was conceived after the American war of 1812–14 as a connection for vessels to reach Kingston and the Great Lakes from Montreal while avoiding possible attack from the United States forces. Ships would pass up the Ottawa River using the already-constructed locks and bypass channels and then travel via a new canal cut through virgin forest southwards to the St Lawrence at Kingston. By based his operational headquarters at the Ottawa River end of the new works and in a forest clearing he established a small settlement. Because of the regard in which By was held, this settlement became known as Bytown. In 1855, long after By's death, the settlement was designated by Queen Victoria as capital of United Canada (which was to become a self-governing Dominion in 1867) and renamed Ottawa; as a result of the presence of the national government, the growth of the town accelerated greatly.

Between 1826–7 and 1832 the Rideau Canal was constructed. It included the massive engineering works of Jones Falls Dam (62 ft 6 in. (19 m) high) and 47 locks. By exercised an almost paternal care over those employed under his direction. The canal was completed in June 1832 at a cost of £800,000. By was summoned back to London to face virulent and unjust criticism from the Treasury. He was honoured in Canada but vilified by the British Government.

Further Reading
R.F. Leggett, 1982, *John By*, Historical Society of Canada.
— 1976, *Canals of Canada*, Newton Abbot: David & Charles.
— 1972, *Rideau Waterway*, Toronto: University of Toronto Press.
Bernard Pothier, 1978, 'The Quebec Model',

Canadian War Museum Paper 9, Ottawa: National Museums of Canada.

JHB

Byron, Ada Augusta, Countess of Lovelace
b. 12 December 1815 Piccadilly Terrace, London, England
d. 23 November 1852 East Horsley, Surrey, England

English mathematician, active in the early development of the calculating machine.

Educated by a number of governesses in a number of houses from Yorkshire to Ealing, she was the daughter of a hypochondriac mother and her absent, separated, husband, the poet George Gordon, Lord Byron. As a child a mysterious and undiagnosed illness deprived her 'of the use of her limbs' and she was 'obliged to use crutches'. The complaint was probably psychosomatic as it cleared up when she was 17 and was about to attend her first court ball. On 8 July 1835 she was married to William King, 1st Earl of Lovelace. She later bore two sons and a daughter. She was an avid student of science and in particular mathematics, in the course of which Charles **Babbage** encouraged her. In 1840 Babbage was invited to Turin to present a paper on his analytical engine. In the audience was a young Italian military engineer, L.F. Menabrea, who was later to become a general in Garibaldi's army. The paper was written in French and published in 1842 in the Bibliothèque Universelle de Genève. This text was translated into English and published with extensive annotations by the Countess of Lovelace, appearing in *Taylor's Scientific Memoirs*. The Countess thoroughly understood and appreciated Babbage's machine and the clarity of her description was so great that it is undoubtedly the best contemporary account of the engine: even Babbage recognized the Countess's description as superior to his own. Ada often visited Babbage in his workshop and listened to his explanations of the structure and use of his engines. She shared with her husband a love of horse-racing and, with Babbage, tried to develop a system for backing horses. Babbage and the Earl apparently stopped their efforts in time, but the Countess lost so heavily that she had to pawn all her family jewels. Her losses at the 1851 Derby alone amounted to £3,200, while borrowing a further £1,800 from her husband. This situation involved her in being blackmailed. She became an opium addict due to persistent pain from gastritis, intermittent anorexia and paroxysmal tachycardia. Charles Babbage was always a great comfort to her, not only for their shared mathematical interests but also as a friend helping in all manner of small services such as taking her dead parrot to the taxidermist. She died after a protracted illness, thought to be cancer, at East Horsley Towers.

Further Reading

D. Langley Moore, 1977, *Ada, Countess of Lovelace: Byron's Legitimate Daughter*, John Murray.

P. Morrison and E. Morrison, 1961, *Charles Babbage and His Calculating Engine*, Dover Publications.

IMcN

C

Cady, Walter Guyton

b. 10 December 1874 Providence, Rhode Island, USA
d. 9 December 1974 Providence, Rhode Island, USA

American physicist renowned for his pioneering work on piezo-electricity.

After obtaining BSc and MSc degrees in physics at Brown University in 1896 and 1897, respectively, Cady went to Berlin, obtaining his PhD in 1900. Returning to the USA he initially worked for the US Coast and Geodetic Survey, but in 1902 he took up a post at the Wesleyan University, Connecticut, remaining as Professor of Physics from 1907 until his retirement in 1946. During the First World War he became interested in piezo-electricity as a result of attending a meeting on techniques for detecting submarines, and after the war he continued to work on the use of piezo-electricity as a transducer for generating sonar beams. In the process he discovered that piezo-electric materials, such as quartz, exhibited high-stability electrical resonance, and in 1921 he produced the first working piezo-electric resonator. This idea was subsequently taken up by George Washington **Pierce** and others, resulting in very stable oscillators and narrow-band filters that are widely used in the 1990s in radio communications, electronic clocks and watches.

Internationally known for his work, Cady retired from his professorship in 1946, but he continued to work for the US Navy. From 1951 to 1955 he was a consultant and research associate at the California Institute of Technology, after which he returned to Providence to continue research at Brown, filing his last patent (one of over fifty) at the age of 93 years.

Principal Honours and Distinctions
President, Institute of Radio Engineers 1932. London Physical Society Duddell Medal. Institute of Electrical and Electronics Engineers Morris N. Liebmann Memorial Prize 1928.

Bibliography
28 January 1920, US patent no. 1,450,246 (piezo-electric resonator).
1921, 'The piezo-electric resonator', *Physical Review* 17: 531.
1946, *Piezoelectricity*, New York: McGraw Hill (his classic work).

Further Reading
B. Jaffe, W.R. Cooke & H. Jaffe, 1971, *Piezoelectric Ceramics*.

KF

Cai Lun (Tsai Lun)

b. *c.*57 AD China
d. *c.*121 AD China

Chinese Director of Imperial Workshops who is usually credited with the invention of paper.

He was a confidential secretary to the Emperor. He became Director of the Imperial Workshops and he is said to have invented, or sponsored the invention of, paper around the year 105 AD. Recent studies, however, suggest that paper was already known in China two centuries earlier. The method of making it has hardly varied in principle since that time. The raw materials, then usually old fishing nets and clothing rags, were boiled with water, to which alkali in the form of wood ash was sometimes added. The resulting pulp was then beaten in a stone mortar with a stone or a wooden mallet. The pulp was then mixed and stirred with a large amount of water, and a sieve or mould (formed on a wooden frame carrying a mat of thin reeds sewn together) was dipped into it and was shaken to help the fibres in the layer of pulp to interlock and thus form a sheet of paper. The rest of the process consisted, then as now, of getting rid of the water: the sheets of paper were dried and bleached by leaving them to lie in the sun.

Some of China's many inventions were achieved independently in Western Europe, but it seems that Europe's knowledge of papermaking stems from the Chinese. It was not until the eighth century that it passed into the Islamic world and so, first by contact with the Moors in Spain in the twelfth century, into Western Europe.

Cai Lun was later made a marquis. Further promotion followed when he was regarded as the god of papermaking.

Further Reading
J. Needham, 1985, *Science and Civilisation in China*, Cambridge: Cambridge University Press, Vol. V (1): *Clerks and Craftsmen in China and the West*, 1970.

LRD

Caird, Sir James
b. 2 January 1864 Glasgow, Scotland
d. 27 September 1954 Wimbledon, London, England

Scottish shipowner and shipbuilder.

James Caird was educated at Glasgow Academy. While the connections are difficult to unravel, it is clear he was related to the Cairds of Greenock, whose shipyard on the Clyde built countless liners for the P & O Company, and to the Caird family who were munificent benefactors of Dundee and the Church of Scotland.

In 1878 Caird joined a firm of East India Merchants in Glasgow, but later went to London. In 1890 he entered the service of Turnbull, Martin & Co., managers of the Scottish Shire Line of Steamers; he quickly rose to become Manager, and by 1903 he was the sole partner and owner. In this role his business skill became apparent, as he pioneered (along with the Houlder and Federal Lines) refrigerated shipping connections between the United Kingdom and Australia and New Zealand. In 1917 he sold his shipping interests to Messrs Cayzer Irvine, managers of the Clan Line.

During the First World War, Caird set up a new shipyard on the River Wye at Chepstow in Wales. Registered in April 1916, the Standard Shipbuilding and Engineering Company took over an existing shipbuilder in an area not threatened by enemy attacks. The purpose of the yard was rapid building of standardized merchant ships during a period when heavy losses were being sustained because of German U-boat attacks. Caird was appointed Chairman, a post he held until the yard came under full government control later in the war. The shipyard did not meet the high expectations of the time, but it did pioneer standard shipbuilding which was later successful in the USA, the UK and Japan.

Caird's greatest work may have been the service he gave to the councils which helped form the National Maritime Museum at Greenwich. He used all his endeavours to ensure the successful launch of the world's greatest maritime museum; he persuaded friends to donate, the Government to transfer artefacts and records, and he gave of his wealth to purchase works of art for the nation. Prior to his death he endowed the Museum with £1.25 million, a massive sum for the 1930s, and this (the Caird Fund) is administered to this day by the Trustees of Greenwich.

Principal Honours and Distinctions
Baronet 1928 (with the title Sir James Caird of Glenfarquhar).

Further Reading
Frank C. Bowen, 1950, 'The Chepstow Yards and a costly venture in government shipbuilding', *Shipbuilding and Shipping Record* (14 December).

FMW

Camm, Sir Sydney
b. 5 August 1893 Windsor, Berkshire, England
d. 12 March 1966 Richmond, Surrey, England

English military aircraft designer.

He was the eldest of twelve children and his father was a journeyman carpenter, in whose footsteps Camm followed as an apprentice woodworker. He developed an early interest in aircraft, becoming a keen model maker in his early teens and taking a major role in founding a local society to this end, and in 1912 he designed and built a glider able to carry people. During the First World War he worked as a draughtsman for the aircraft firm Martinsyde, but became increasingly involved in design matters as the war progressed. In 1923 Camm was recruited by **Sopwith** to join his Hawker Engineering Company as Senior Draughtsman, but within two years had risen to be Chief Designer. His first important contribution was to develop a method of producing metal aircraft, using welded steel tubes, and in 1926 he designed his first significant aircraft, the Hawker Horsley torpedo-bomber, which briefly held the world long-distance record before it was snatched by Charles Lindbergh in his epic New York–Paris flight in 1927. His Hawker Hart light bomber followed in 1928, after which came his Hawker Fury fighter.

By the mid-1930s Camm's reputation as a designer was such that he was able to wield significant influence on the Air Ministry when Royal Air Force (RAF) aircraft specifications were being drawn up. His outstanding contribution came, however, with the unveiling of his Hawker Hurricane in 1935. This single-seater fighter was to prove one of the backbones of the RAF during 1939–45, but during the war he also designed two other excellent fighters: the Tempest and the Typhoon. After the Second World War Camm turned to jet aircraft, producing in 1951 the Hawker Hunter fighter/ground-attack aircraft, which saw lengthy service in the RAF and many other air forces. His most revolutionary contribution was the design of the Harrier jump-jet, beginning with the P.1127 prototype in 1961, followed by the Kestrel three years later. These were private ventures, but eventually the Government saw the enormous merit in the vertical take-off and landing concept, and the Harrier came to fruition in 1967. Sadly Camm, who was on the Board of Sopwith Hawker Siddeley Group, died before the aircraft came into service. He is permanently commemorated in the Camm Memorial Hall at the RAF Museum, Hendon, London.

Principal Honours and Distinctions
CBE 1941. Knighted 1953. Associate Fellow of the Royal Aeronautical Society 1918, Fellow 1932, President 1954–5, Gold Medal 1958. Daniel Guggenheim Medal (USA) 1965.

Further Reading
Alan Bramson, 1990, *Pure Luck: The Authorized Biography of Sir Thomas Sopwith, 1888–1989*, Wellingborough: Patrick Stephens (provides information about Camm and his association with Sopwith).
Dictionary of National Biography, 1961–70.

CM

Campbell-Swinton, Alan Archibald
b. 18 October 1863 Kimmerghame, Berwickshire, Scotland
d. 19 February 1930 London, England

Scottish electrical engineer who correctly predicted the development of electronic television.

After a time at Cargilfield Trinity School, Campbell-Swinton went to Fettes College in Edinburgh from 1878 to 1881 and then spent a year abroad in France. From 1882 until 1887 he was employed at Sir W.G. Armstrong's works in Elswick, Newcastle, following which he set up his own electrical contracting business in London. This he gave up in 1904 to become a consultant. Subsequently he was an engineer with many industrial companies, including the W.T. Henley Telegraph Works Company, Parson Marine Steam Turbine Company and Crompton Parkinson Ltd, of which he became a director. During this time he was involved in electrical and scientific research, being particularly associated with the development of the Parson turbine.

In 1903 he tried to realize distant electric vision by using a **Braun** oscilloscope tube for the image display, a second tube being modified to form a synchronously scanned camera, by replacing the fluorescent display screen with a photoconductive target. Although this first attempt at what was, in fact, a vidicon camera proved unsuccessful, he was clearly on the right lines and in 1908 he wrote a letter to *Nature* with a fairly accurate description of the principles of an all-electronic television system using magnetically deflected cathode ray tubes at the camera and receiver, with the camera target consisting of a mosaic of photoconductive elements that were scanned and discharged line by line by an electron beam. He expanded on his ideas in a lecture to the Roentgen Society, London, in 1911, but it was over twenty years before the required technology had advanced sufficiently for **Shoenberg**'s team at EMI to produce a working system.

Principal Honours and Distinctions
FRS (Member of Council 1927 and 1929). Freeman of the City of London. Liveryman of Goldsmiths' Company. First President, Wireless Society 1920–1. Vice-President, Royal Society of Arts, and Chairman of Council 1917–19, 1920–2. Chairman, British Scientific Research Association. Vice-President, British Photographic Research Association. Member of the Broadcasting Board 1924. Vice-President, Roentgen Society 1911–12. Vice-President, Institution of

Electrical Engineers 1921–5. President, Radio Society of Great Britain 1913–21. Manager, Royal Institution 1912–15.

Bibliography
1908, *Nature* 78: 151; 1912, *Journal of the Roentgen Society* 8: 1 (both describe his original ideas for electronic television).
1924, 'The possibilities of television', *Wireless World* 14: 51 (gives a detailed description of his proposals, including the use of a three-stage valve video amplifier).
1926, *Nature* 118: 590 (describes his early experiments of 1903).

Further Reading
The Proceedings of the International Conference on the History of Television. From Early Days to the Present, November 1986, Institution of Electrical Engineers Publication No. 271 (a report of some of the early developments in television).
A.A. Campbell-Swinton FRS 1863–1930, Royal Television Society Monograph, 1982, London (a biography).

See also **Baird, John Logie.**

KF

Cane, Peter du
See **Du Cane, Peter.**

Cannon, Walter Bradford
b. 19 October 1871 Prairie du Chien, Wisconsin, USA
d. 1 October 1945 Franklin, New Hampshire, USA

American physiologist, pioneer of radiodiagnostic imaging with the use of radio-opaque media.

Cannon graduated with an arts degree from Harvard University in 1896. He then became a medical student and carried out an investigation into stomach movements using the technique of radio-opaque meals, initially in a cat. He qualified in medicine from Harvard in 1900 and was soon appointed Assistant Professor of Physiology. In 1906 he succeeded to the Chair of Physiology, which he held for thirty-six years.

Apart from his early work, Cannon's demonstration of the humoral transmission of the nerve impulse was fundamental, as were his investigations, including researches on himself and his colleagues, into the relationship between emotion and the sympathetic-adrenal system.

During the First World War he served with both the British and American armies and was decorated.

Principal Honours and Distinctions
DSM (USA). CB (UK). Foreign member, Royal Society, 1939. Linacre Lecturer, Cambridge, 1930. Royal College of Physicians Baly Medal 1931.

Bibliography
1898, 'The movements of the stomach studied by means of the Roentgen rays', *Amer. J. Physiol.*
1915, 1920, *Bodily Changes in Pain, Fear, Hunger and Rage.*

Further Reading
W.B. Cannon, 1945, *The Way of an Investigator.*

MG

Caproni, Giovanni Battista (Gianni), Conte di Taliedo
b. 3 June 1886 Massone, Italy
d. 29 October 1957 Rome, Italy

Italian aircraft designer and manufacturer, well known for his early large-aircraft designs.

Gianni Caproni studied civil and electrical engineering in Munich and Liège before moving on to Paris, where he developed an interest in aeronautics. He built his first aircraft in 1910, a biplane with a tricycle undercarriage (which has been claimed as the world's first tricycle undercarriage). Caproni and his brother, Dr Fred Caproni, set up a factory at Malpensa in northern Italy and produced a series of monoplanes and biplanes. In 1913 Caproni astounded the aviation world with his *Ca 30* three-engined biplane bomber. There followed many variations, of which the most significant were the *Ca 32* of 1915, the first large bomber to enter service in significant numbers, and the *Ca 42* triplane of 1917 with a wing span of almost 30 metres.

After the First World War, Caproni designed an even larger aircraft with three pairs of triplane wings (i.e. nine wings each of 30 metres span) and eight engines. This *Ca 60* flying boat was designed to carry 100 passengers. In 1921 it made one short flight lightly loaded; however, with a load of sandbags representing sixty passengers, it crashed soon after take-off. The project was abandoned but Caproni's company prospered and expanded to become one of the largest groups of companies in Italy. In the 1930s Caproni aircraft twice broke the world altitude record. Several Caproni types were in service when Italy entered the Second World War, and an unusual research aircraft was under development. The Caproni-Campini *No. 1* (*CC 2*) was a jet, but it did not have a gas-turbine engine. Dr Campini's engine used a piston engine to drive a compressor which forced air out through a nozzle, and by burning fuel in this airstream a jet was produced. It flew with limited success in August 1940, amid much publicity: the first German jet (1939) and the first British jet (1941) were both flown in secret. Caproni retained many of his early aircraft for his private museum, including some salvaged parts from his monstrous flying boat.

Principal Honours and Distinctions
Created Conte di Taliedo 1940.

Further Reading
Dizionario biografico degli Italiani, 1976, Vol. XIX.
The Caproni Museum has published two books on the Caproni aeroplanes: *Gli Aeroplani Caproni – 1909–1935* and *Gli Aeroplani Caproni dal 1935 in poi*. See also *Jane's Fighting Aircraft of World War 1*; 1919, republished 1990.

See also: **Heinkel, Ernst**; **Ohain, Hans von**; **Whittle, Sir Frank**.

JDS

Caprotti, Arturo

b. 22 March 1881 Cremona, Italy
d. 9 February 1938 Milan, Italy

Italian engineer, inventor of Caprotti poppet valve gear for steam locomotives.

Caprotti graduated as a mechanical engineer at Turin Royal Polytechnic College and spent some years in the motor car industry. After researching the application of poppet valves to railway locomotives, he invented his rotary cam valve gear for poppet valves in 1915. Compared with usual

slide and piston valves and valve gears, it offered independent timing of inlet and exhaust valves and a saving in weight. Valve gear to Caprotti's design was first fitted in 1920 to a 2–6–0 locomotive of the Italian State Railways, and was subsequently widely used there and elsewhere. Caprotti valve gear was first applied in Britain in 1926 to a Claughton class 4–6–0 of the London, Midland & Scottish Railway, resulting in substantial fuel savings compared with a similar locomotive fitted with **Walschaert**'s valve gear and piston valves. Others of the class were then fitted similarly. Caprotti valve gear never came into general use in Britain and its final application was in 1954 to British Railways class 8 4–6–2 no. 71000; this was intended as the prototype of a class of standard locomotives for express trains, but the class was never built, because diesel and electric locomotives took their place. Some components survived scrapping, and a reconstruction of the locomotive is in working order.

Further Reading
John Marshall, 1978, *A Biographical Dictionary of Railway Engineers*, Newton Abbot: David & Charles.
P. Ransome-Wallis (ed.), 1959, *The Concise Encyclopaedia of World Railway Locomotives*, London: Hutchinson (contains a note about Caprotti (p. 497) and a description of the valve gear (p. 301).

PJGR

Carbutt, John

b. 1832 Sheffield, England
d. 1905 Philadelphia, Pennsylvania, USA

Anglo-American photographer and photographic manufacturer.

Carbutt emigrated in 1853 from England to the United States, where he remained for the rest of his life. He began working as a photographer in Chicago, where he soon earned a considerable reputation and became the official photographer for the Canadian Pacific Railway. In 1870 he purchased the American rights of **Woodbury**'s photomechanical printing process and established a business to produce Woodburytypes in Philadelphia. In 1879 Carbutt set up the first successful gelatine halide dry-plate factory in America. A year later he was elected first President of the Photographers' Association of

America. He began experimenting with flexible film supports in 1884 and was the first to produce satisfactory flat films on celluloid commercially. The first kinetoscope film strips used by Thomas **Edison** were supplied by Carbutt. Carbutt's celluloid films were exported to Europe, where nothing comparable was available at the time. He was also a pioneer manufacturer of orthochromatic plates, X-ray plates and photographic colour filters.

Further Reading
Obituary, 1905, *Journal of the Franklin Institute*: 461–3.
L.W. Shipley, 1965, *Photography's Great Inventors*, Philadelphia.
G. Hendricks, 1961, *The Edison Motion Picture Myth* (makes reference to aspects of Carbutt's work on celluloid).

JW

Cardew, Philip
b. 24 September 1851 Leatherhead, Surrey, England
d. 17 May 1910 Godalming, Surrey, England

English electrical engineer and inventor, adviser to the Board of Trade.

After education at the Royal Military Academy in Woolwich, Cardew was placed in charge of Bermudan military telegraphs in 1876. In 1889 he was appointed the first Electrical Adviser to the Board of Trade, where he formulated valuable regulations for the safety and control of public electricity supplies. In 1883 Cardew invented the thermogalvanometer, a hot-wire measuring instrument, that became widely used as a voltmeter but was obsolete by 1907. The device depended for its action on the heating and subsequent elongation of a platinum wire and could be used on alternating currents of high frequency. Retiring from the Board of Trade in 1899, Cardew joined a partnership of consulting engineers with Sir William **Preece** and his son. Taking a particular interest in railway electrification, he became a director of the London Brighton & South Coast Railway.

Principal Honours and Distinctions
Inventions Exhibition Gold Medal 1885.

Bibliography
1881, *Journal of the Society of Telegraph Engineers* 10: 111–14 (describes the application of electricity to railways).
5 February 1883, British patent no. 623 (Cardew's hot-wire instrument).
1898, *Journal of the Institution of Electrical Engineers* 19: 425–47 (his account of Board of Trade legislation).

Further Reading
J.T. Stock and D. Vaughan, 1983, *The Development of Instruments to Measure Electric Current*, London: Science Museum (for instrument origins).
Dictionary of National Biography, 1912, Vol. I, Suppl. 2, pp. 313–14.

GW

Carlson, Chester Floyd
b. 8 July 1906 Seattle, Washington, USA
d. 19 September 1968 New York, USA

American inventor of xerography

Carlson studied physics at the California Institute of Technology and in 1930 he took a research position at Bell Telephone Laboratories, but soon transferred to their patent department. To equip himself in this field, Carlson studied law, and in 1934 he became a patent attorney at P.R. Mallory & Co., makers of electrical apparatus. He was struck by the difficulty in obtaining copies of documents and drawings; indeed, while still at school, he had encountered printing problems in trying to produce a newsletter for amateur chemists. He began experimenting with various light-sensitive substances, and by 1937 he had conceived the basic principles of xerography ('dry writing'), using the property of certain substances of losing an electrostatic charge when light impinges on them. His work for Mallory brought him into contact with the Battelle Memorial Institute, the world's largest non-profit research organization; their subsidiary, set up to develop promising ideas, took up Carlson's invention. Carlson received his first US patent for the process in 1940, with two more in 1942, and he assigned to Battelle exclusive patent rights in return for a share of any future proceeds. It was at Battelle that selenium was substituted as the light-sensitive material.

In 1946 the Haloid Company of Rochester,

manufacturers of photographic materials and photocopying equipment, heard of the Xerox copier and, seeing it as a possible addition to their products, took out a licence to develop it commercially. The first Xerox Copier was tested during 1949 and put on the market the following year. The process soon began to displace older methods, such as Photostat, but its full impact on the public came in 1959 with the advent of the Xerox 914 Copier. It is fair to apply the overworked word 'revolution' to the change in copying methods initiated by Carlson. He became a multimillionaire from his royalties and stock holding, and in his last years he was able to indulge in philanthropic activities.

Further Reading
Obituary, 1968, *New York Times*, 20 September.
R.M. Schaffert, 1954, 'Developments in xerography', *Penrose Annual*.
J. Jewkes, 1969, *The Sources of Invention*, 2nd edn, London: Macmillan, pp. 405–8.

LRD

Carnegie, Andrew

b. 25 November 1835 Dunfermline, Fife, Scotland
d. 11 August 1919 Lenox, Massachusetts, USA

Scottish industrialist and philanthropist.

Andrew Carnegie was a highly successful entrepreneur and steel industrialist rather than an engineer, but he made a significant contribution to engineering both through his work in industry and through his philanthropic and educational activities. His parents emigrated to the United States in 1848 and the family settled in Pennsylvania. Beginning as a telegraph boy in Pittsburgh in 1850, the young Carnegie rose through successful enterprises in railways, bridges, locomotives and rolling stock, pursuing a process of 'vertical integration' in the iron and steel industry which led to him becoming the leading American ironmaster by 1881. His interests in the Carnegie Steel Company were incorporated in the United States Steel Corporation in 1901, when Carnegie retired from business and devoted himself to philanthropy. He was particularly involved in benefactions to provide public libraries in the United States, Great Britain and other English-speaking countries. Remembering his ancestry, he was especially generous toward

Scottish universities, as a result of which he was elected Rector of the University of St Andrews, Scotland's oldest university, by its students. Other large endowments were made for funds in recognition of heroic deeds, and he financed the building of the Temple of Peace at The Hague.

Bibliography
1889, *The Gospel of Wealth* (sets out his views on the responsible use of riches).

Further Reading
J.F. Wall, 1989, *Andrew Carnegie*, Pittsburgh: University of Pittsburgh Press.

AB

Carnot, Nicolas Léonard Sadi

b. 1 June 1796 Paris, France
d. 24 August 1831 Paris, France

French laid the foundations for modern thermodynamics through his book Réflexions sur la puissance motrice du feu when he stated that the efficiency of an engine depended on the working substance and the temperature drop between the incoming and outgoing steam.

Sadi was the eldest son of Lazare Carnot, who was prominent as one of Napoleon's military and civil advisers. Sadi was born in the Palais du Petit Luxembourg and grew up during the Napoleonic wars. He was tutored by his father until in 1812, at the minimum age of 16, he entered the Ecole Polytechnique to study stress analysis, mechanics, descriptive geometry and chemistry. He organized the students to fight against the allies at Vincennes in 1814. He left the Polytechnique that October and went to the Ecole du Génie at Metz as a student second lieutenant. While there, he wrote several scientific papers, but on the Restoration in 1815 he was regarded with suspicion because of the support his father had given Napoleon. In 1816, on completion of his studies, Sadi became a second lieutenant in the Metz engineering regiment and spent his time in garrison duty, drawing up plans of fortifications. He seized the chance to escape from this dull routine in 1819 through an appointment to the army general staff corps in Paris, where he took leave of absence on half pay and began further courses of study at the Sorbonne, Collège de France, Ecole des Mines and the Conservatoire des Arts et Métiers. He was interested in industrial development, political economy, tax reform and the fine arts.

It was not until 1821 that he began to concentrate on the steam-engine, and he soon proposed his early form of the Carnot cycle. He sought to find a general solution to cover all types of steam-engine, and reduced their operation to three basic stages: an isothermal expansion as the steam entered the cylinder; an adiabatic expansion; and an isothermal compression in the condenser. In 1824 he published his *Réflexions sur la puissance motrice du feu*, which was well received at the time but quickly forgotten. In it he accepted the caloric theory of heat but pointed out the impossibility of perpetual motion. His main contribution to a correct understanding of a heat engine, however, lay in his suggestion that power can be produced only where there exists a temperature difference due 'not to an actual consumption of caloric but to its transportation from a warm body to a cold body'. He used the analogy of a water-wheel with the water falling around its circumference. He proposed the true Carnot cycle with the addition of a final adiabatic compression in which motive power was consumed to heat the gas to its original incoming temperature and so closed the cycle. He realized the importance of beginning with the temperature of the fire and not the steam in the boiler. These ideas were not taken up in the study of thermodynamics until after Sadi's death when B.P.E. Clapeyron discovered his book in 1834.

In 1824 Sadi was recalled to military service as a staff captain, but he resigned in 1828 to devote his time to physics and economics. He continued his work on steam-engines and began to develop a kinetic theory of heat. In 1831 he was investigating the physical properties of gases and vapours, especially the relationship between temperature and pressure. In June 1832 he contracted scarlet fever, which was followed by 'brain fever'. He made a partial recovery, but that August he fell victim to a cholera epidemic to which he quickly succumbed.

Bibliography
1824, *Réflexions sur la puissance motrice du feu*; pub. 1960, trans. R.H. Thurston, New York: Dover Publications; pub. 1978, trans. Robert Fox, Paris (full biographical accounts are provided in the introductions of the translated editions).

Further Reading
Dictionary of Scientific Biography, 1971, Vol. III, New York: C. Scribner's Sons.
T.I. Williams (ed.), 1969, *A Biographical Dictionary of Scientists*, London: A. & C. Black.
Chambers Concise Dictionary of Scientists, 1989, Cambridge.
D.S.L. Cardwell, 1971, *From Watt to Clausius. The Rise of Thermodynamics in the Early Industrial Age*, London: Heinemann (discusses Carnot's theories of heat).

RLH

Caro, Heinrich
b. 13 February 1834 Poznan, Poland
d. 11 October 1911 Dresden, Germany

German dyestuffs chemist.

Caro received vocational training as a dyer at the Gewerbeinstitut in Berlin from 1852, at the same time attending chemistry lectures at the university there. In 1855 he was hired as a colourist by a firm of calico printers in Mulheim an der Ruhr, where he was able to demonstrate the value of scientific training in solving practical problems. Two years later, the year after **Perkin**'s discovery of aniline dyes, he was sent to England in order to learn the latest dyeing techniques. He took up a post an analytical chemist with the chemical firm Roberts, Dale & Co. in Manchester; after finding a better way of synthesizing Perkin's mauve, he became a partner in the business. Caro was able to enlarge both his engineering experience and his chemical knowledge there, particularly by studying **Hofmann**'s researches on the aniline dyes. He made several discoveries, including induline, Bismark brown and Martius yellow.

Like other German chemists, however, he found greater opportunities opening up in Germany, and in 1866 he returned to take up a post in **Bunsen**'s laboratory in Heidelberg. In 1868 Caro obtained the important directorship of Badische Anilin-Soda-Fabrik (BASF), the first true industrial research organization and leading centre of dyestuffs research. A steady stream of commercial successes followed. In 1869, after Graebe and Liebermann had showed him their laboratory synthesis of the red dye alizarin, Caro went on to develop a cheaper and commercially viable method. During the 1870s he collaborated with Adolf von Baeyer to make methylene blue and related dyes, and then went on to the azo dyes. His work on indigo was important, but was not crowned with commercial success; that came in 1897 when his successor at BASF discovered a suitable process for producing indigo on a commercial scale. Caro had resigned his post in 1889, by which time he had made notable contributions to German supremacy in the fast-developing dyestuffs industry.

Further Reading
A. Bernthsen, 1912, obituary, *Berichte der Deutschen Chemischen Gesellschaft*, 45; 1,987–2,042 (a substantial obituary).

LRD

Carothers, Wallace Hume
b. 27 April 1896 Burlington, Iowa, USA
d. 29 April 1937 Philadelphia, Pennsylvania, USA

American chemist, inventor of nylon.

After graduating in chemistry, Carothers embarked on academic research at several universities, finally at Harvard University. His earliest published papers, from 1923, heralded the brilliance and originality of his later work. In 1928, Du Pont de Nemours persuaded him to forsake the academic world to lead their new organic-chemistry group in a programme of fundamental research at their central laboratories at Wilmington, Delaware. The next nine years were extraordinarily productive, yielding important contributions to theoretical organic chemistry and the foundation of two branches of chemical industry, namely the production of synthetic rubber and of wholly synthetic fibres.

Carothers began work on high molecular weight substances yielding fibres and introduced polymerization by condensation: polymerization by addition was already known. He developed a clear understanding of the relation between the repeating structural units in a large molecule and its physical chemical properties. In 1931, Carothers found that chloroprene could be polymerized much faster than isoprene, the monomer in natural rubber. This process yielded polychloroprene or neoprene, a synthetic rubber with improved properties. Manufacture began the following year, and the material has continued to be used for speciality rubbers.

There followed many publications announcing new condensations polymers. On 2 January 1935, he obtained a patent for the formation of new polyamides, including one from adipic acid and hexamethylenediamene. After four years of development work, which cost Du Pont some $27 million, this new polyamide, or nylon, reached the stage of commercial production, beginning on 23 October 1938. Nylon stockings appeared the following year and 64 million were sold during the first twelve months. However, Carothers saw none of this spectacular success: he had died by his own hand in 1937, after a long history of gradually intensifying depression.

Principal Honours and Distinctions
Elected to the National Academy of Science 1936 (he was the first industrial organic chemist to be so honoured).

Bibliography
H.M. Whitby and G.S. Whitby, 1940, *Collected Papers of Wallace H. Carothers on Polymerisation*, New York.

Further Reading
R. Adams, 1939, memoir, *Biographical Memoirs of the National Academy of Sciences* 20: 293–309 (includes a complete list of Carothers's sixty-two scientific papers and most of his sixty-nine US patents).

LRD

Carrel, Alexis
b. 28 June 1873 Lyon, France
d. 5 November 1944 Paris, France

French surgeon and experimental biologist, pioneer of blood-vessel repair techniques and 'in vitro' tissue culture.

He entered the university of Lyon as a medical student in 1890, but although attached to the Chasseurs Alpins as a surgeon, and to the department of anatomy, he did not qualify as a doctor until 1900. Soon after, he developed an interest in the repair of blood vessels and reported his first successes in 1902.

In consequence of local political difficulties he left for Paris, and after a further year, in 1904, he became Assistant in Physiology at the University of Chicago. His further development of vascular surgical advances led to organ transplants in animals. By 1908 he had moved to *in vitro* cultivation of heart tissue from a chick embryo (a culture of which, in the care of an assistant, outlived him).

He returned to service in the French Army in 1914 and was associated with **Dakin** in developing the irrigation treatment of infected wounds. In 1930 he initiated a programme aimed at the cultivation of whole organs, and with the assistance of a pump developed by Charles Lindbergh he succeeded in maintaining thyroid gland and kidney tissue for some weeks. Something of a mystic, Carrel returned to France in 1939 to head his Institute for the Study of Human Problems.

Principal Honours and Distinctions
Nobel Prize for Medicine or Physiology 1912.

Bibliography
1911, 'The surgery of blood vessels', *Johns Hopkins Bulletin*.
1911, 'Rejuvenation of cultures of tissues', *Journal of the American Medical Association*.
1938, *The Culture of Organs*, New York.
1938, *Man the Unknown*, New York.

Further Reading
R. Soupault, 1952, *Alexis Carrel. 1873–1944*, Paris (contains full bibliography of papers).
MG

Carroll, Thomas

b. 1888 Melbourne, Victoria, Australia
d. 22 February 1968 Australia

Australian engineer responsible for many innovations in combine-harvester design, and in particular associated with the Massey Harris No. 20 used in the 'Harvest Brigade' during the Second World War.

Carroll worked first with the Buckeye Harvester Co., then with J.J. Mitchell & Co. In 1911 he was hired by the Argentinian distributor for Massey Harris to help in the introduction of their new horse-drawn reaper–thresher. Carroll recommended modifications to suit Argentinian conditions, and these resulted in the production of a new model. In 1917 he joined the Toronto staff of Massey Harris as a product design leader, the *No. 5* reaper–thresher being the first designed under him. Many significant new developments can be attributed to Carroll: welded sections, roller chains, oil-bath gears, antifriction ball bearings and the detachable cutting table allowing easy transfer of combines between fields were all innovations of which he was the source.

In the 1930s he became Chief Engineer with responsibility for the design of a self-propelled harvester. The *20 SP* was tested in Argentina only eight months after design work had begun, and it was to this machine that the name 'combine harvester' was applied for the first time. Improvements to this original design produced a lighter 12 ft (3.65 m) cut machine which came off the production line in 1941. Three years later 500 of these machines were transported to the southern United States, and then gradually harvested their way northwards as the corn ripened. It has been estimated that the famous 'Harvest Brigade' harvested over 1 million acres, putting 25 million bushels into store, with a saving in excess of 300,000 labour hours and half a million gallons of fuel.

Carroll retired from Massey Ferguson in 1961.

Principal Honours and Distinctions
American Society of Agricultural Engineers C.H. McCormick Gold Medal 1958.

Bibliography
1948, 'Basic requirements in the design and development of the self propelled combine' *Agricultural Engineer.* 29 (3), 101–5.

Further Reading
G. Quick and W. Buchele, 1978, *The Grain Harvesters*, American Society of Agricultural Engineers (provides a detailed account of the development of the combine harvester).
K.M. Coppick, 1972, gave an account of the wartime effort, which he mistakenly called 'Massey Ferguson Harvest Brigade', presented to the *Canadian Society for Agricultural Engineers*, Paper 72–313.

AP

Cartwright, Revd Edmund

b. 24 April 1743 Marnham, Nottingham, England
d. 30 October 1823 Hastings, Sussex, England

English inventor of the power loom, a combing machine and machines for making ropes, bread and bricks as well as agricultural improvements.

Edmund Cartwright, the fourth son of William

Cartwright, was educated at Wakefield Grammar School, and went to University College, Oxford, at the age of 14. By special act of convocation in 1764, he was elected Fellow of Magdalen College. He married Alice Whitaker in 1772 and soon after was given the ecclesiastical living of Brampton in Derbyshire. In 1779 he was presented with the living of Goadby, Marwood, Leicestershire, where he wrote poems, reviewed new works, and began agricultural experiments. A visit to Matlock in the summer of 1784 introduced him to the inventions of Richard **Arkwright** and he asked why weaving could not be mechanized in a similar manner to spinning. This began a remarkable career of inventions.

Cartwright returned home and built a loom which required two strong men to operate it. This was the first attempt in England to develop a power loom. It had a vertical warp, the reed fell with the weight of at least half a hundredweight and, to quote Cartwright's own words, 'the springs which threw the shuttle were strong enough to throw a Congreive [sic] rocket' (Strickland 1971:8 – for background to the 'rocket' comparison, see **Congreve, Sir William**). Nevertheless, it had the same three basics of weaving that still remain today in modern power looms: shedding or dividing the warp; picking or projecting the shuttle with the weft; and beating that pick of weft into place with a reed. This loom he proudly patented in 1785, and then he went to look at hand looms and was surprised to see how simply they operated. Further improvements to his own loom, covered by two more patents in 1786 and 1787, produced a machine with the more conventional horizontal layout that showed promise; however, the Manchester merchants whom he visited were not interested. He patented more improvements in 1788 as a result of the experience gained in 1786 through establishing a factory at Doncaster with power looms worked by a bull that were the ancestors of modern ones. Twenty-four looms driven by steam-power were installed in Manchester in 1791, but the mill was burned down and no one repeated the experiment. The Doncaster mill was sold in 1793, Cartwright having lost £30,000. However, in 1809 Parliament voted him £10,000 because his looms were then coming into general use.

In 1789 he began working on a wool-combing machine which he patented in 1790, with further improvements in 1792. This seems to have been the earliest instance of mechanized combing. It used a circular revolving comb from which the long fibres or 'top' were carried off into a can, and a smaller cylinder-comb for teasing out short fibres or 'noils', which were taken off by hand. Its output equalled that of twenty hand combers, but it was only relatively successful. It was employed in various Leicestershire and Yorkshire mills, but infringements were frequent and costly to resist. The patent was prolonged for fourteen years after 1801, but even then Cartwright did not make any profit. His 1792 patent also included a machine to make ropes with the outstanding and basic invention of the 'cordelier' which he communicated to his friends, including Robert **Fulton**, but again it brought little financial benefit. As a result of these problems and the lack of remuneration for his inventions, Cartwright moved to London in 1796 and for a time lived in a house built with geometrical bricks of his own design.

Other inventions followed fast, including a tread-wheel for cranes, metallic packing for pistons in steam-engines, and bread-making and brick-making machines, to mention but a few. He had already returned to agricultural improvements and he put forward suggestions in 1793 for a reaping machine. In 1801 he received a prize from the Board of Agriculture for an essay on husbandry, which was followed in 1803 by a silver medal for the invention of a three-furrow plough and in 1805 by a gold medal for his essay on manures. From 1801 to 1807 he ran an experimental farm on the Duke of Bedford's estates at Woburn.

From 1786 until his death he was a prebendary of Lincoln. In about 1810 he bought a small farm at Hollanden near Sevenoaks, Kent, where he continued his inventions, both agricultural and general. Inventing to the last, he died at Hastings and was buried in Battle church.

Principal Honours and Distinctions
Board of Agriculture Prize 1801 (for an essay on agriculture). Society of Arts, Silver Medal 1803 (for his three-furrow plough); Gold Medal 1805 (for an essay on agricultural improvements).

Bibliography
1785, British patent no. 1,270 (power loom).
1786, British patent no. 1,565 (improved power

loom).

1787, British patent no. 1,616 (improved power loom).

1788, British patent no. 1,676 (improved power loom).

1790, British patent no. 1,747 (wool-combing machine).

1790, British patent no. 1,787 (wool-combing machine).

1792, British patent no. 1,876 (improved wool-combing machine and rope-making machine with cordelier).

Further Reading

M. Strickland, 1843, *A Memoir of the Life, Writings and Mechanical Inventions of Edmund Cartwright, D.D., F.R.S.*, London (remains the fullest biography of Cartwright).

Dictionary of National Biography (a good summary of Cartwright's life).

For discussions of Cartwright's weaving inventions, see:

A. Barlow, 1878, *The History and Principles of Weaving by Hand and by Power*, London; R.L. Hills, 1970, *Power in the Industrial Revolution*, Manchester.

F. Nasmith, 1925–6, 'Fathers of machine cotton manufacture', *Transactions of the Newcomen Society* 6.

H.W. Dickinson, 1942–3, 'A condensed history of rope-making', *Transactions of the Newcomen Society* 23.

W. English, 1969, *The Textile Industry*, London (covers both his power loom and his wool-combing machine).

RLH

Carver, George Washington
b. 1861 USA
d. 1943 USA

African-American agriculturalist.

In 1896 Carver was invited by Booker T. Washington, noted for his efforts to improve the education of African American craftspeople after the Civil War, to join the teaching staff at the Tuskegee Institute, Alabama. Carver became renowned for his innovative work in developing agricultural products, particularly from the peanut, sweet potato and cowpea. He was one of the first agriculturalists of that time to promote the use of organic fertilizers, and he was noted for his

work in the hybridization of local plants. In spite of these achievements, his immediate impact on the African American farming community lay in promoting agricultural education and extension work. In 1897 Carver was appointed the first director of the Tuskegee agricultural experiment station. Here, he developed teaching techniques in agricultural education, such as issuing a series of clearly-written information bulletins. He also devised the first mobile school in the American South, which consisted of a farm wagon equipped with educational material and travelled from farm to farm, demonstrating the latest agricultural techniques.

Carver was granted only three patents: one in 1923 for a cosmetic and two, in 1925 and 1927, for processes for making pigments.

Further Reading

P.P. James, 1989, *The Real McCoy: African American Invention and Innovation 1619–1930*, Washington, DC: Smithsonian Institution Press, 69–70.

LRD

Casablancas, Fernando
fl. 1912 Spain

Spanish inventor of the first of the high-draft cotton-spinning systems.

In 1912, Casablancas took out three patents in Britain. The first of these was for putting false twist into textile fibres during the drawing part of spinning. In his next we can find the origins of his interest in his high-draft system, for it contains intermediate sectors or rollers between the usual drawing rollers. It was not until the third patent that there appeared the basis of the modern system with endless inextensible strips of material passing round the rollers to help support the fibres. His first system was for spinning fibres of medium length, giving a much greater draft. This consisted of two aprons around the middle pair of drafting rollers which reached almost to the front ones. The aprons lightly pressed the fibres together in the drafting zone and yet allowed the more-quickly rotating front rollers to pull fibres out of the aprons quite easily. This enabled slivers or rovings to be reduced in thickness more quickly and evenly. In 1913, a further patent showed a development of the apron system where guides made the aprons move in an

'S' pattern. Then in 1914 a patent illustrated something similar to the modern layout, while two further patents in the following year contained slightly different layouts. His system was soon applied to both ring frames and the mule, and while it was first applied to cotton, it soon spread to worsted. High-draft spinning was also envisaged by Casablancas and he took out a further patent in 1920 to obtain drafts in a ratio of several hundreds. His principles are used today on some of the most recent open-end spinning frames.

Bibliography
1912, British patent no. 11,376 (textile fibres with false twist).
1912, British patent no. 11,783.
1912, British patent no. 12,477.
1913, British patent no. 11,613.
1914, British patent no. 19,372
1915, British patent no. 3,366.
1915, British patent no. 14,228.

Further Reading
C. Singer (ed.), 1978, *A History of Technology*, Vol. 6, Oxford: Clarendon Press (mentions his spinning methods).

RLH

Case, Jerome Increase
b. 1819 Williamstown, Oswego County, New York, USA
d. 1891 USA

American manufacturer and founder of the Case company of agricultural engineers.

J.I. Case was the son of a farmer and began his working life operating the family's Groundhog threshing machine. He moved into contract threshing, and used the money he earned to pay his way through a business academy. He became the agent for the Groundhog thresher in his area and at the age of 23 decided to move west, taking six machines with him. He sold five of these to obtain working capital, and in 1842 moved from Williamstown, New York, to Rochester, Wisconsin, where he established his manufacturing company. He produced the first combined thresher–winnower in the US in 1843. Two years later he moved to Racine, on the shores of Lake Michigan in the same state. Within four years the Case company became Racine's biggest company

and largest employer, a position it was to retain into the twentieth century. As early as 1860 Case was shipping threshing machines around the Horn to California.

Apart from having practical expertise Case was also a skilled demonstrator, and it was this combination which resulted in the sure growth of his company. In 1869 he produced his first portable steam engine and in 1876 his first traction engine. By the mid 1870s he was selling a significant proportion of the machines in use in America. By 1878 Case threshing machines had penetrated the European market, and in 1885 sales to South America began. Case also became the world's largest manufacturer of steam engines.

J.I. Case himself, whilst still actively involved with the company, also became involved in politics. He was Mayor of Racine for three terms and State Senator for two. He was also President of the Manufacturers' National Bank of Racine and Founder of the First National Bank of Burlington. He founded the Wisconsin Academy of Science, Arts and Letters and was President of the Racine County Agricultural Society. He had time for sport and was owner of the world's all-time champion trotter-pacer.

Continued expansion of the company after J.I. Case's death led eventually to its acquisition by Tenneco in 1967, and in 1985 the company took over International Harvester. As Case I.H. it continues to produce a full range of agricultural, earth-moving and heavy-transport equipment.

Further Reading
Despite the size and importance of the company he created, very little has been written about Case. On particular anniversaries the company has produced celebratory publications, and surprisingly these still seem to be the main source of information about him.
R.B. Gray, 1975, *The Agricultural Tractor 1855–1950*, American Society of Agricultural Engineers (traces the history of power on the farm, in which Case and his machines played such an important role).

AP

Castner, Hamilton Young
b. 11 September 1858 Brooklyn, New York, USA
d. 11 October 1899 Saranoe Lake, New York, USA

American chemist, inventor of the electrolytic production of sodium.

Around 1850, the exciting new metal aluminium began to be produced by the process developed by Sainte-Claire **Deville**. However, it remained expensive on account of the high cost of one of the raw materials, sodium. It was another thirty years before Castner became the first to work successfully the process for producing sodium, which consisted of heating sodium hydroxide with charcoal at a high temperature. Unable to interest American backers in the process, Castner took it to England and set up a plant at Oldbury, near Birmingham. At the moment he achieved commercial success, however, the demand for cheap sodium plummeted as a result of the development of the electrolytic process for producing aluminium. He therefore sought other uses for cheap sodium, first converting it to sodium peroxide, a bleaching agent much used in the straw-hat industry. Much more importantly, Castner persuaded the gold industry to use sodium instead of potassium cyanide in the refining of gold. With the 'gold rush', he established a large market in Australia, the USA, South Africa and elsewhere, but the problem was to meet the demand, so Castner turned to the electrolytic method. At first progress was slow because of the impure nature of the sodium hydroxide, so he used a mercury cathode, with which the released sodium formed an amalgam. It then reacted with water in a separate compartment in the cell to form sodium hydroxide of a purity hitherto unknown in the alkali industry; chlorine was a valuable by-product.

In 1894 Castner began to seek international patents for the cell, but found he had been anticipated in Germany by **Kellner**, an Austrian chemist. Preferring negotiation to legal confrontation, Castner exchanged patents and processes with Kellner, although the latter's had been less successful. The cell became known as the Castner–Kellner cell, but the process needed cheap electricity and salt, neither of which was available near Oldbury, so he set up the Castner–Kellner Alkali Company works at Runcorn in Cheshire; at the same time, a pilot plant was set up in the USA at Saltville, Virginia, with a larger plant being established at Niagara Falls.

Further Reading
A. Fleck, 1947, 'The life and work of Hamilton Young Castner' (Castner Memorial Lecture), *Chemistry and Industry* 44: 515–; *Fifty Years of Progress: The Story of the Castner–Kellner Company*, 1947.
T.K. Derry and T.I. Williams, 1960, *A Short History of Technology*, Oxford: Oxford University Press, pp. 549–50 (provides a summary of his work).

LRD

Caxton, William
b. *c.*1422 Kent, England
d. 1491 Westminster, England

English printer who produced the first book to be printed in English.

According to his own account, Caxton was born in Kent and received a schooling before entering the Mercers' Company, one of the most influential of the London guilds and engaged in the wholesale export trade in woollen goods and other wares, principally with the Low Countries. Around 1445, Caxton moved to Bruges, where he engaged in trade with such success that in 1462 he was appointed Governor of the English Nation in Bruges. He was entrusted with diplomatic missions, and his dealings with the court of Burgundy brought him into contact with the Duchess, Margaret of York, sister of the English King Edward IV. Caxton embarked on the production of fine manuscripts, making his own translations from the French for the Duchess and other noble patrons with a taste for this kind of literature. This trend became more marked after 1470–1 when Caxton lost his post in Bruges, probably due to the temporary overthrow of King Edward. Perhaps to satisfy an increasing demand for his texts, Caxton travelled to Cologne in 1471 to learn the art of printing. He set up a printing business in Bruges, in partnership with the copyist and bookseller Colard Mansion. There, late in 1474 or early the following year, Caxton produced the first book to be printed in English, and the first by an English printer, *The Recuyell of the Histories of Troy*, which he had translated from the French.

In 1476 Caxton returned to England and set up his printing and publishing business 'at the sign of the Red Pale' within the precincts of Westminster Abbey. This was more conveniently placed than the City of London for the likely customers among the court and Members of Parliament for the courtly romances and devotional works he aimed to produce. Other printers followed but survived only a few years, whereas Caxton remained successful for fifteen years and then bequeathed a flourishing concern to his assistant Wynkyn de Worde. During that time, 107 printed works, including seventy-four books, issued from Caxton's press. Of these, some twenty were his own translations. As printer and publisher, he did much to promote English literature, above all by producing the first editions of the literary masterpieces of the Middle Ages, such as the works of Chaucer, Gower and Lydgate and Malory's *Morte d'Arthur*. Among the various dialects of spoken English in use at the time, Caxton adopted the language of London and the court and so did much to fix a permanent standard for written English.

Further Reading

W. Blades, 1877, *The Biography and Typography of William Caxton, England's First Printer*, London; reprinted 1971 (the classic life of Caxton, superseded in detail by modern scholarship but still indispensable).

G.D. Painter, 1976, *William Caxton: A Quincentenary Biography of England's First Printer*, London: Chatto & Windus (the most thorough recent biography, describing every known Caxton document and edition, with corrected and new interpretations based on the latest scholarship).

N.F. Blake, 1969, *Caxton and His World*, London (a reliable account, set against the background of English late-medieval life).

See also **Gutenberg, Johann**.

LRD

Cayley, Sir George

b. 27 December 1773 Scarborough, England
d. 15 December 1857 Brompton Hall, Yorkshire, England

English pioneer who laid down the basic principles of the aeroplane in 1799 and built a manned glider in 1853.

Cayley was born into a well-to-do Yorkshire family living at Brompton Hall. He was encouraged to study mathematics, navigation and mechanics, particularly by his mother. In 1792 he succeeded to the baronetcy and took over the daunting task of revitalizing the run-down family estate.

The first aeronautical device made by Cayley was a copy of the toy helicopter invented by the Frenchmen Launoy and Bienvenu in 1784. Cayley's version, made in 1796, convinced him that a machine could 'rise in the air by mechanical means', as he later wrote. He studied the aerodynamics of flight and broke away from the unsuccessful ornithopters of his predecessors. In 1799 he scratched two sketches on a silver disc: one side of the disc showed the aerodynamic force on a wing resolved into lift and drag, and on the other side he illustrated his idea for a fixed-wing aeroplane; this disc is preserved in the Science Museum in London. In 1804 he tested a small wing on the end of a whirling arm to measure its lifting power. This led to the world's first model glider, which consisted of a simple kite (the wing) mounted on a pole with an adjustable cruciform tail. A full-size glider followed in 1809 and this flew successfully unmanned. By 1809 Cayley had also investigated the lifting properties of cambered wings and produced a low-drag aerofoil section. His aim was to produce a powered aeroplane, but no suitable engines were available. Steam-engines were too heavy, but he experimented with a gunpowder motor and invented the hot-air engine in 1807. He published details of some of his aeronautical researches in 1809–10 and in 1816 he wrote a paper on airships. Then for a period of some twenty-five years he was so busy with other activities that he largely neglected his aeronautical researches. It was not until 1843, at the age of 70, that he really had time to pursue his quest for flight. The *Mechanics' Magazine* of 8 April 1843 published drawings of 'Sir George Cayley's Aerial Carriage', which consisted of a helicopter design with four circular lifting rotors – which could be adjusted to become wings – and two pusher propellers. In 1849 he built a full-size triplane glider which lifted a boy off the ground for a brief hop. Then in 1852 he proposed a monoplane glider which could be launched from a balloon. Late in 1853 Cayley built his 'new flyer', another monoplane glider, which carried his coachman as a reluctant passenger across a dale at Brompton.

Cayley became involved in public affairs and was MP for Scarborough in 1832. He also took a leading part in local scientific activities and was co-founder of the British Association for the Advancement of Science in 1831 and of the Regent Street Polytechnic Institution in 1838.

Bibliography
Cayley wrote a number of articles and papers, the most significant being 'On aerial navigation', *Nicholson's Journal of Natural Philosophy* (November 1809 – March 1810) (published in three numbers); and two further papers with the same title in *Philosophical Magazine* (1816 and 1817) (both describe semi-rigid airships).

Further Reading
L. Pritchard, 1961, *Sir George Cayley*, London (the standard work on the life of Cayley).
C.H. Gibbs-Smith, 1962, *Sir George Cayley's Aeronautics 1796–1855*, London (covers his aeronautical achievements in more detail).
—— 1974, 'Sir George Cayley, father of aerial navigation (1773–1857)', *Aeronautical Journal* (Royal Aeronautical Society) (April) (an updating paper).

JDS

Cecil, Revd William
b. 1792 England
d. 1882 England

English inventor of a gas vacuum engine.

Admitted to Magdalene College, Cambridge, in 1810, Cecil was elected a Fellow in 1814. The son of an Anglican priest, he was himself ordained in 1820; he devoted his life to the Church of England, but he also showed a commendable aptitude for technical matters. His paper on a means of motive power, presented to the Cambridge Philosophical Society in 1820, created immense interest. A working model of his engine, using hydrogen as fuel, was demonstrated during the presentation. The operating principle required that a vacuum be produced in a closed cylinder by quenching a burning flame, the pressure difference between the vacuum and atmosphere then being used to produce the working stroke. Cecil's engine was never manufactured in any number, but the working principle was adapted by other pioneers, namely Samuel **Brown**, in 1824, and, more successfully, **Otto–Langen** in 1867.

Bibliography
1820, 'On the application of hydrogen gas to produce a moving power in machinery', *Transactions of the Cambridge Philosophical Society* 1(2): 217–39.

Further Reading
John Venn, *Alumni Cantabrienses* Part II (1752–1900): p. 567.

KAB

Cerletti, Ugo
b. 26 September 1877 Treviso, Italy
d. 25 July 1963 Rome, Italy

Italian psychiatrist who was the originator, with L. Bini, of electroconvulsive therapy for severe psychiatric disorders.

Cerletti qualified in medicine at the University of Turin in 1901. Following some years as an assistant in the psychiatric clinic, during which he demonstrated the presence of spirochaetes in the brain of syphilitics, he was appointed in 1919 Director of the Istituto Neurologica A. Varga in Milan. In 1924 he moved to the University of Bari, and then in 1928 to the faculty of medicine in Genoa.

In 1935 he assumed the directorship of the clinic for mental and nervous diseases in the University of Rome, and it was there, following the precedent of the treatment of mania, depression and schizophrenia by insulin or cardiazol shock, that Cerletti and Bini, who assisted with the apparatus, administered electroconvulsive therapy (ECT) to their first patient in April 1935. The results appeared to be at least comparable with the other agents, and although the rationale of the treatment has never been fully clarified it gained a wide degree of acceptance for many years, even up to the 1990s.

Principal Honours and Distinctions
President, Italian Psychiatric Society 1946–59. Honorary degrees Sao Paolo, Rio de Janeiro and Montréal. Gold Medal of Public Health 1953.

Bibliography
1940, 'L'Elletroshock', *Riv.spir. et freniatra* 64 (monograph).
1938, 'L'Elletroshock', *Arch. Gen. Neurolk Psychat. Psiconal* 19.

MG

Chain, Ernst Boris

b. 19 June 1906 Berlin, Germany
d. 12 August 1979 Ireland

Anglo-German biochemist and physiologist,
co-worker with **Florey** *in the isolation of*
sufficient supplies of the antibiotic penicillin for
clinical use during wartime.

Chain graduated in Berlin at the Charite Hospital in 1930. A refugee from political persecution, in 1933 he went to the School of Biochemistry in Cambridge, and in 1935 moved to the School of Pathology at Oxford. He became a British subject in 1939. His interests had involved the study of enzymes and the isolation of physiologically active substances from natural sources. In 1938 he drew Florey's attention to Fleming's note of 1929 reporting the bacterial growth inhibiting qualities of *Penicillium* mould. Using makeshift equipment and with little initial support, they isolated small quantities of penicillin, which they were then able to use clinically with dramatic effect.

Chain had always hoped for adequate resources to develop penicillin and other antibiotics in Britain. This was not forthcoming, however, and in 1948 a research chair and institute was created for him in Rome, at the International Research Centre for Chemical Microbiology. In 1961 he returned to London to the Chair of Biochemistry at Imperial College. There, with the help of a large donation from the Wolfson Foundation, an appropriate building with facilities for the large-scale development and production of biochemical substances was finally made available. His co-equal part in the development of penicillin was recognized by the sharing of the Nobel Prize for Medicine between Florey, Fleming and himself, and he received numerous honours and honorary degrees from a large number of governments and international institutions.

Principal Honours and Distinctions
Knighted 1944. Nobel Prize for Medicine (jointly with H.W. Florey and A. Fleming) 1945. Fellow of the Royal Society 1949. Ehrlich Prize 1954.

Bibliography
1941, 'Penicillin as a chemotherapeutic agent', *Lancet* (with Florey).
1941, 'Further observations on penicillin', *Lancet*.
1949, *Antibiotics*, Oxford, (with Florey *et al.*)

MG

Chamberlen (the Elder), Peter

b. *c.*1601 London, England
d. 22 December 1683 Woodham Mortimer, Essex, England

English obstetrician who was a member of a
family of obstetricians of the same name who
made use of a secret design of obstetric forceps
(probably designed by him).

Of Huguenot stock, his ancestor William having probably come to England in 1569, he was admitted to Cambridge University in 1615 at the age of 14. He graduated Doctor of Medicine in Padua in 1619, having also spent some time at Heidelberg. In 1628 he was elected a Fellow of the College of Physicians, though with some reservations on account of his dress and conduct; these appear to have had some foundation for he was dismissed from the fellowship for repeated contumacy in 1659. Nonetheless, he was appointed Physician in Ordinary to Charles I in 1660. There are grounds for suspecting that in later years he developed some signs of insanity.

Chamberlen was engaged extensively in the practice of midwifery, and his reputation and that of the other members of the family, several of whom were also called Peter, was enhanced by their possession of their own pattern of obstetric forceps, hitherto unknown and kept carefully guarded as a family secret. The original instruments were discovered hidden at the family home in Essex in 1815 and have been preserved by the Royal Society of Medicine. Chamberlen appears to have threatened the physicians' obstetric monopoly by attempting to organize midwives into a corporate company, to be headed by himself, a move which was successfully opposed by the College of Physicians.

Principal Honours and Distinctions
Physician in Ordinary to King Charles I, King Charles II, King James II, Queen Mary and Queen Anne.

Bibliography
1662, *The Accomplished Midwife. The Sober Mans Vindication, discovering the true cause and manner how Dr. Chamberlen came to be reported mad*, London.

Further Reading
Mariceau, 1668, *Des Malades des femmes grosses et accouchées*, Paris.
J.H. Aveling, 1883, *The Chamberlens and the Midwifery Forceps*, London.

MG

Champion, Nehemiah
b. 1678 probably Bristol, England
d. 9 September 1747 probably Bristol, England

English merchant and brass manufacturer of Bristol.

Several members of Champion's Quaker family were actively engaged as merchants in Bristol during the late seventeenth and the eighteenth centuries. Port records show Nehemiah in receipt of Cornish copper ore at Bristol's Crews Hole smelting works by 1706, in association with the newly formed brassworks of the city. He later became a leading partner, managing the company some time after Abraham **Darby** left the Bristol works to pursue his interest at Coalbrookdale. Champion, probably in company with his father, became the largest customer for Darby's Coalbrookdale products and also acted as Agent, at least briefly, for Thomas **Newcomen**.

A patent in 1723 related to two separate innovations introduced by the brass company. The first improved the output of brass by granulating the copper constituent and increasing its surface area. A greater proportion of zinc vapour could permeate the granules compared with the previous practice, resulting in the technique being adopted generally in the cementation process used at the time. The latter part of the same patent introduced a new type of coal-fired furnace which facilitated annealing in bulk so replacing the individual processing of pieces. The principle of batch annealing was generally adopted, although the type of furnace was later improved. A further patent, in 1739, in the name of Nehemiah, concerned overshot water-wheels possibly intended for use in conjunction with the Newcomen atmospheric pumping engine employed for recycling water by his son William.

Champion's two sons, John and William, and their two sons, both named John, were all concerned with production of non-ferrous metals and responsible for patented innovations. Nehemiah, shortly before his death, is believed to have partnered William at the Warmley works to exploit his son's new patent for producing metallic zinc.

Bibliography
1723, British patent no. 454 (granulated copper technique and coal-fired furnace).
1739, British patent no. 567 (overshot water-wheels).

Further Reading
A. Raistrick, 1950, *Quakers in Science and Industry*, London: Bannisdale Press (for the Champion family generally).
J. Day, 1973, *Bristol Brass, a History of the Industry*, Newton Abbot: David & Charles (for the industrial activities of Nehemiah).

JD

Champion, William
b. 1710 Bristol, England
d. 1789 England

English metallurgist, the first to produce metallic zinc in England on an industrial scale.

William, the youngest of the three sons of Nehemiah **Champion**, stemmed from a West Country Quaker family long associated with the metal trades. His grandfather, also called Nehemiah, had been one of Abraham **Darby**'s close Quaker friends when the brassworks at Baptist Mills was being established in 1702 and 1703. Nehemiah II took over the management of these works soon after Darby went to Coalbrookdale, and in 1719, as one of a group of Bristol copper smelters, he negotiated an agreement with Lord Falmouth to develop copper mines in the Redruth area in Cornwall. In 1723 he was granted a patent for a cementation brass-making process using finely granulated copper rather than the broken fragments of massive copper hitherto employed.

In 1730 he returned to Bristol after a tour of European metallurgical centres, and he began to develop an industrial process for the manufacture of pure zinc ingots in England. Metallic zinc or spelter was then imported at great expense from the Far East, largely for the manufacture of copper alloys of golden colour used for cheap jewellery. The process William developed, after six years of experimentation, reduced zinc oxide with charcoal at temperatures well above the boiling point of zinc. The zinc vapour obtained was condensed rapidly to prevent reoxidation and finally collected under water. This process, patented in 1738, was operated in secret until 1766 when Watson described it in his *Chemical Essays*. After encountering much opposition from the Bristol merchants and zinc importers, William decided to establish his own integrated brassworks at Warmley, five meals east of Bristol. The Warmley plant began to produce in 1748 and expanded rapidly. By 1767, when Warmley employed about 2,000 men, women and children, more capital was needed, requiring a Royal Charter of Incorporation. A consortium of Champion's competitors opposed this and secured its refusal. After this defeat William lost the confidence of his fellow directors, who dismissed him. He was declared bankrupt in 1769 and his works were sold to the British Brass Company, which never operated Warmley at full capacity, although it produced zinc on that site until 1784.

Bibliography
1723, British patent no. 454 (cementation brass-making process).
1738, British patent no. 564 (zinc ingot production process).
1767, British patent no. 867 (brass manufacture wing zinc blende).

Further Reading
J. Day, 1973, *Bristol Brass: The History of the Industry*, Newton Abbot: David & Charles.
A. Raistrick, 1970, *Dynasty of Ironfounders: The Darbys and Coalbrookdale*, Newton Abbot: David & Charles.
J.R. Harris, 1964, *The Copper King*, Liverpool University Press.

ASD

Chang Ssu Hsun
See **Zhang Sixun**.

Chanute, Octave Alexandre
b. 18 February 1832 Paris, France
d. 24 November 1910 Chicago, USA

American engineer, developer of successful hang-gliders in the 1890s and disseminator of aeronautical information.

Chanute was born in Paris, but from the age of 6 he lived in the United States, where he became a prominent railway engineer. He developed an interest in aviation relatively late in life, and in fact built his first glider at the age of 64. Before that, he had collected all the information he could find on aviation, especially on the work of Otto **Lilienthal** in Germany. In 1894 he published an account of these researches in a classic work, *Progress in Flying Machines*.

By 1896 Chanute was ready to carry out practical experiments of his own and designed a series of hang-gliders. He started with a Lilienthal-type monoplane and progressed to his very successful biplane glider. He used a bridge-truss method of cross-bracing to give his wings the required strength, a system used by many of his successors, including the **Wright** brothers. Chanute's gliders were flown on the shore of Lake Michigan by his two young assistants A.M. Herring and W. Avery. The biplane glider made some seven hundred flights without mishap, covering up to 100 m (110 yds). In 1898 Herring fitted an engine into a modified glider and claimed to have made two short hops.

In 1900 the Wright brothers made contact with Chanute and sought his advice, which he readily gave, indeed, he became one of their most trusted advisors. In 1903 Chanute travelled to Paris and gave an illustrated lecture describing his own and the Wrights' gliding successes, generating much interest amongst European aviators.

Principal Honours and Distinctions
Royal Aeronautical Society Gold Medal 1910.

Bibliography
1894, *Progress in Flying Machines*, New York (Chanute's classic work).

Further Reading
C.H. Gibbs-Smith, 1986, *Aviation*, London.
— 1965, *The Invention of the Aeroplane 1799–1909*, London (both describe Chanute's place in the history of aviation).
T.D. Crouch, *A Dream of Wings, Americans and the Airplane 1875–1905* (includes several chapters on Chanute and a comprehensive bibliography).
Chanute is also mentioned in most of the biographies of the Wright brothers.

JDS

Chapelon, André

b. 26 October 1892 Saint-Paul-en-Cornillon,
Loire, France
d. 29 June 1978 Paris, France

*French locomotive engineer who developed
high-performance steam locomotives.*

Chapelon's technical education at the Ecole
Centrale des Arts et Manufactures, Paris, was interrupted by extended military service during the
First World War. From experience of observing
artillery from the basket of a captive balloon, he
developed a method of artillery fire control
which was more accurate than that in use and
which was adopted by the French army.

In 1925 he joined the motive-power and roll-
ing-stock department of the Paris–Orléans Railway under Chief Mechanical Engineer Maurice
Lacoin and was given the task of improving the
performance of its main-line 4–6–2 locomotives,
most of them compounds. He had already made
an intensive study of steam locomotive design
and in 1926 introduced his Kylchap exhaust system, based in part on the earlier work of the
Finnish engineer Kyläla. Chapelon improved the
entrainment of the hot gases in the smokebox by
the exhaust steam and so minimized back pressure in the cylinders, increasing the power of a
locomotive substantially. He also greatly increased the cross-sectional area of steam passages, used poppet valves instead of piston valves
and increased superheating of steam. PO (Paris–
Orléans) 4–6–2s rebuilt on these principles from
1929 onwards proved able to haul 800-ton
trains, in place of the previous 500-ton trains,
and to do so to accelerated schedules with reduced coal consumption. Commencing in 1932,
some were converted, at the time of rebuilding,
into 4–8–0s to increase adhesive weight for hauling heavy trains over the steeply graded Paris–
Toulouse line.

Chapelon's principles were quickly adopted
on other French railways and elsewhere. H.N.
Gresley was particularly influenced by them.
After formation of the French National Railways
(SNCF) in 1938, Chapelon produced in 1941 a
prototype rebuilt PO 2–10–0 freight locomotive
as a six-cylinder compound, with four low-pressure cylinders to maximize expansive use of steam
and with all cylinders steam-jacketed to minimize heat loss by condensation and radiation.
War conditions delayed extended testing until

1948–52. Meanwhile Chapelon had, by rebuilding, produced in 1946 a high-powered, three-cylinder, compound 4–8–4 intended as a stage in
development of a proposed range of powerful
and thermally efficient steam locomotives for the
postwar SNCF: a high-speed 4–6–4 in this range
was to run at sustained speeds of 125 mph (200
km/h). However, plans for improved steam locomotives were then overtaken in France by electrification and dieselization, though the
performance of the 4–8–4, which produced
4,000 hp (3,000 kW) at the drawbar for the first
time in Europe, prompted modification of electric locomotives, already on order, to increase
their power.

Chapelon retired from the SNCF in 1953, but
continued to act as a consultant. His principles
were incorporated into steam locomotives built
in France for export to South America, and even
after the energy crisis of 1973 he was consulted
on projects to build improved, high-powered
steam locomotives for countries with reserves of
cheap coal. The eventual fall in oil prices brought
these to an end.

Bibliography

1938, *La Locomotive à vapeur*, Paris: J.B. Bailière
(a comprehensive summary of contemporary
knowledge of every function of the locomotive).

Further Reading

H.C.B. Rogers, 1972, *Chapelon, Genius of
French Steam*, Shepperton: Ian Allan.
1986, 'André Chapelon, locomotive engineer: a
survey of his work', *Transactions of the Newcomen Society* 58 (a symposium on Chapelon's
work).
Obituary, 1978, *Railway Engineer* (Septem-
ber/October) (makes reference to the technical significance of Chapelon's work).

PJGR

Chapman, Frederik Henrik af

b. 9 September 1721 Gothenburg, Sweden
d. 19 August 1808 Karlskrona, Sweden

*Swedish naval architect and shipbuilder; one of
the foremost ship designers of all time.*

Chapman was born on the west coast of Sweden
and was the son of a British naval officer serving
in the Swedish Navy. In 1738 he followed in his

father's footsteps by joining the naval dockyards as a shipbuilding apprentice. Subsequent experience was gained in other shipyards and by two years (1741–3) in London. His assiduous note taking and study of British shipbuilding were noticed and he was offered appointments in England, but these were refused and he returned to Sweden in 1744 and for a while operated as a ship repairer in partnership with a man called Bagge. In 1749 he started out on his own. He began with a period of study in Stockholm and in London, where he worked for a while under Thomas Simpson, and then went on to France and the Netherlands. During his time in England he learned the art of copper etching, a skill that later stood him in good stead. After some years he was appointed Deputy Master Shipwright to the Swedish Navy, and in 1760 he became Master Shipwright at Sveaborg (now Suomenlinna), the fortress island of Helsinki. There Chapman excelled by designing the coastal defence or skerry fleet that to this day is accepted as beautiful and fit for purpose. He understood the limitations of ship design and throughout his life strove to improve shipbuilding by using the advances in mathematics and science that were then being made. His contribution to the rationalization of thought in ship theory cannot be overemphasized.

In 1764 he became Chief Shipbuilder to the Swedish Navy, with particular responsibility for Karlskrona and for Stockholm. He assisted in the new rules for the classification of warships and later introduced standardization to the naval dockyards. He continued to rise in rank and reputation until his retirement in 1793, but to the end his judgement was sought on many matters concerning not only ship design but also the administration of the then powerful Swedish Navy.

His most important bequest to his profession is the great book *Architectura Navalis Mercatoria*, first published in 1768. Later editions were larger and contained additional material. This volume remains one of the most significant works on shipbuilding.

Principal Honours and Distinctions
Knighted 1772. Rear Admiral 1783, Vice-Admiral 1791.

Bibliography
1768, *Architectura Navalis Mercatoria*; 1975, pub. in English, trans. Adlard Coles.
1775, *Tractat om Skepps-Buggeriet*.

Further Reading
D.G. Harris, 1989, *F.H. Chapman, the First Naval Architect and His Work*, London: Conway (an excellent biography).

FMW

Chappe, Claude
b. 25 December 1763 Brulon, France
d. 23 January 1805 Paris, France

French engineer who invented the semaphore visual telegraph.

Chappe began his studies at the Collège de Joyeuse, Rouen, and completed them at La Flèche. He was educated for the church with the intention of becoming an Abbé Commendataire, but this title did not in fact require him to perform any religious duties. He became interested in natural science and amongst other activities he carried out experiments with electrically charged soap bubbles.

When the *bénéfice* was suppressed in 1781 he returned home and began to devise a system of telegraphic communication. With the help of his three brothers, particularly Abraham, and using an old idea, in 1790 he made a visual telegraph with suspended pendulums to relay coded messages over a distance of half a kilometre. Despite public suspicion and opposition, he presented the idea to the Assemblée Nationale on 22 May 1792. No doubt due to the influence of his brother, Ignace, a member of the Assemblée Nationale, the idea was favourably received, and on 1 April 1793 it was referred to the National Convention as being of military importance. As a result, Chappe was given the title of Telegraphy Engineer and commissioned to construct a semaphore (Gk. bearing a sign) link between Paris and Lille, a distance of some 240 km (150 miles), using twenty-two towers. Each station contained two telescopes for observing the adjacent towers, and each semaphore consisted of a central beam supporting two arms, whose positions gave nearly two hundred possible arrangements. Hence, by using a code book as a form of look-up table, Chappe was able to devise a code of over 8,000 words. The success of the system for communication during subsequent military conflicts resulted in him being commissioned to extend it with further links, a work that was continued by his brothers after his suicide during a period of illness and depression. Providing as it did an effective message speed of several thousand kilometres per hour, the system remained in use until the mid-nineteenth century, by which time the electric telegraph had become well established.

Further Reading

R. Appleyard, 1930, *Pioneers of Electrical Communication*.

International Telecommunications Union, 1965, *From Semaphore to Satellite*, Geneva.

See also **Morse, Samuel Finley Breeze**.

KF

Charles, Jacques Alexandre César

b. 12 November 1746 Beaugency, France
d. 7 April 1823 Paris, France

French physicist who developed the first hydrogen balloon, in 1783.

In 1783, following the early experiments with small hot-air balloons by the **Montgolfier** brothers, there was a growing interest in the prospect of a balloon flight with people on board. The Paris Académie des Sciences encouraged one of their physicists, Charles, to carry out experiments and produce a balloon. Charles enlisted the assistance of two brothers, Anne-Jean and Marie-Noël Robert, who were practical craftsmen with experience of coating silk fabric with rubber to make it impermeable to gases. Charles decided to use the recently discovered lighter-than-air gas, hydrogen, for his experiments rather than hot air. After making several unmanned balloons, he had a manned balloon ready for testing on 1 December 1783. Despite the fact that a Montgolfier balloon had already flown with two passengers, there was enormous public interest in the flight: one estimate suggested that 400,000 people turned out to watch. Charles and Marie-Noël Robert ascended from the gardens of the Tuileries and landed after two hours, having covered 45 km (28 miles). Technically the 'Charlière' was far superior to the 'Montgolfière' and was therefore used by most subsequent balloonists until the introduction of

the modern hot-air balloon by the American Paul E. **Yost** in the 1960s. Following **Meusnier**'s proposals for a dirigible (steerable) balloon, put forward during 1783–5, Charles and the Robert brothers built an elongated balloon incorporating Meusnier's *ballonnet* principle. It had a rudder but the method of propulsion, by opening and closing parasols used as paddles, was totally ineffective.

Principal Honours and Distinctions
Member of the Académie des Sciences 1795.

Further Reading
L.T.C. Rolt, 1966, *The Aeronauts*, London.
C. Dollfus, 1961, *Balloons*, trans. C. Mason, London.
J.B.F. Fourier, 1825, *Notice*.

JDS

Charnley, John

b. 29 August 1911 Bury, Lancashire, England
d. 5 August 1982 Lancashire, England

English orthopedic surgeon, pioneer of ultra-clean-air operating-theatre environments and of total hip-joint replacement.

During his medical training at Manchester he qualified for the Fellowship of the Royal College of Surgeons and obtained his FRCS in 1936, within a year of becoming medically qualified. Following military service as an orthopaedic specialist, he was appointed a consultant at the Manchester Royal Infirmary in 1947.

Charnley investigated the problems of joint lubrication using polytetrafluoroethylene (PTFE) and a series of 300 initially successful cases laid the foundation for further developments, involving total hip-joint replacement, when in 1962 high-density polythene became available as a suitable inert material. The need for a totally sterile operating environment in which to carry out such procedures led him to develop ultra-clean-air operating-theatre modules which proved to have wide application in relation to other surgical disciplines and to the problems of hospital building. To further these principles he resigned from the Royal Infirmary and was the guiding spirit in the establishment of the centre for hip surgery at Wrightington Hospital in Lancashire, which gained wide international recognition.

Bibliography
1961, 'Arthroplasty of the hip', *Lancet*.
1974, *Wound Infection after Hip Replacement
Performed in a Clean-Air Operating Room*,
Wrightington.
1970, *Acrylic Cement in Orthopaedic Surgery*,
Baltimore.

MG

Charpy, Augustin Georges Albert
b. 1 September 1865 Ouillins, Rhône, France
d. 25 November 1945 Paris, France

*French metallurgist, originator of the Charpy
pendulum impact method of testing metals.*

After graduating in chemistry from the Ecole
Polytechnique in 1887, Charpy continued to
work there on the physical chemistry of solutions
for his doctorate. He joined the Laboratoire
d'Artillerie de la Marine in 1892 and began to
study the structure and mechanical properties of
various steels in relation to their previous heat
treatment. His first memoir, on the mechanical
properties of steels quenched from various temperatures, was published in 1892 on the advice
of Henri **Le Chatelier**. He joined the Compagnie de Chatillon Commentry Fourchamboult et
Decazeville at their steelworks in Imphy in 1898,
shortly after the discovery of Invar by G.E. **Guillaume**. Most of the alloys required for this investigation had been prepared at Imphy, and their
laboratories were therefore well equipped with
sensitive and refined dilatometric facilities.
Charpy and his colleague L. Grenet utilized this
technique in many of their earlier investigations,
which were largely concerned with the transformation points of steel. He began to study the
magnetic characteristics of silicon steels in 1902,
shortly after their use as transformer laminations
had first been proposed by **Hadfield** and his colleagues in 1900. Charpy was the first to show
that the magnetic hysteresis of these alloys decreased rapidly as their grain size increased.

The first details of Charpy's pendulum impact
testing machine were published in 1901, about
two years before **Izod** read his paper to the British Association. As with Izod's machine, the energy of fracture was measured by the retardation
of the pendulum. Charpy's test pieces, however,
unlike those of Izod, were in the form of centrally
notched beams, freely supported at each end
against rigid anvils. This arrangement, it was believed, transmitted less energy to the frame of the
machine and allowed the energy of fracture to be
more accurately measured. In practice, however,
the blow of the pendulum in the Charpy test caused
visible distortion in the specimen as a whole. Both
tests were still widely used in the 1990s.

In 1920 Charpy left Imphy to become Director-
General of the Compagnie des Aciéries de la
Marine et Homecourt. After his election to the
Académie des Sciences in 1918, he came to be associated with Floris Osmond and Henri Le Chatelier as one of the founders of the 'French School of
Physical Metallurgy'. Around the turn of the century he had contributed much to the development
of the metallurgical microscope and had helped to
introduce the Chatelier thermocouple into the laboratory and to industry. He also popularized the
use of platinum-wound resistance furnaces for laboratory purposes. After 1920 his industrial responsibilities increased greatly, although he
continued to devote much of his time to teaching
at the Ecole Supérieure des Mines in Paris, and at
the Ecole Polytechnique. His first book, *Leçons de
Chimie* (1892, Paris), was written at the beginning
of his career, in association with H. Gautier. His
last, *Notions élémentaires de sidérurgie* (1946,
Paris), with P. Pingault as co-author, was published
posthumously.

Bibliography
Charpy published important metallurgical papers
in *Comptes rendus ... Académie des Sciences,
Paris*.

Further Reading
R. Barthélemy, 1947, 'Notice sur la vie et
l'oeuvre de Georges Charpy', *Notices et dis-
cours, Académie des Sciences, Paris* (June).
M. Caullery, 1945, 'Annonce du décès de M.G.
Charpy' *Comptes rendus Académie des Sciences,
Paris* 221: 677.
P.G. Bastien, 1963, 'Microscopic metallurgy in
France prior to 1920', Sorby Centennial Sym-
posium on the History of Metallurgy, *AIME
Metallurgical Society Conference* Vol.27, pp.
171–88.

ASD

Chatelier, Henri Louis le
See **Le Chatelier, Henri Louis**.

Chaudron, Joseph
b. 29 November 1822 Gosselies, Belgium
d. 16 January 1905 Auderghem, Belgium

Belgian mining engineer, pioneer in boring shafts.

In 1842, as a graduate of the Ecole des Mines in Liège, he became a member of the Belgian Corps Royal des Mines, which he left ten years later as Chief Engineer. By that time he had become decisively influential in the Société Anglo-Belge des Mines du Rhin, founded in 1848. After it became the Gelsenkirchen-based Bergwerkgesellschaft Dahlbusch in 1873, he became President of its Board of Directors and remained in this position until his death. Thanks to his outstanding technical and financial abilities, the company developed into one of the largest in the Ruhr coal district.

When K.G. **Kind** practised his shaft-boring for the company in the early 1850s but did not overcome the difficulty of making the bottom of the bore-hole watertight, Chaudron joined forces with him to solve the problem and constructed a rotary heading which was made watertight with a box stuffed with moss; rings of iron tubing were placed on this as the sinking progressed, effectively blocking off the aquiferous strata as a result of the hydrostatic pressure which helped support the weight of the tubing until it was secured permanently. The Kind–Chaudron system of boring shafts in the full section marked an important advance upon existing methods, and was completely applied for the first time at a coalmine near Mons, Belgium, in 1854–6. In Brussels Chaudron and Kind founded the Société de Fonçage par le Procédé Kind et Chaudron in 1854, and Chaudron was granted a patent the next year. Foreign patents followed and the Kind–Chaudron system was the one most frequently applied in the latter part of the nineteenth century. Altogether, under Chaudron's control, there were more than eighty shafts sunk in wet strata in Germany, Belgium, France and England.

Bibliography
1853–4, 'Notice sur le procédé inventé par l'ingénieur Kind, pour l'établissement des puits de mines', *Annales des travaux publics de Belgique* 12: 327–38.
1862, 'Über die nach dem Kindschen Erdbohrverfahren in Belgien ausgeführten Schachtbohrarbeiten', *Berg- und Hüttenmännische Zeitschrift* 21: 402–7, 419–21, 444–7.
1867, 'Notice sur les travaux exécutés en France, en Belgique et en Westphalie de 1862–1867', *Annales des travaux publics de Belgique* 25: 136–45.
1872, 'Remplacement d'un cuvelage en bois par un cuvelage en fonte', *Annales des travaux publics de Belgique* 30: 77–91.

Further Reading
D. Hoffmann, 1962, *Acht Jahrzehnte Gefrierverfahren nach Pötsch*, Essen, pp. 12–18 (evaluates the Kind–Chaudron system as a new era).
W. Kesten, 1952, *Geschichte der Bergwerksgesellschaft Dahlbusch*, Essen (gives a delineation of the mining company's flourishing as well as the technical measures under his influence).
T. Tecklenburg, 1914, *Handbuch der Tiefbohrkunde*, 2nd edn, Vol VI, Berlin, pp. 39–58 (provides a detailed description of Chaudron's tubing).

WK

Chevalier, Charles-Louis
b. 18 April 1804 France
d. 21 November 1859 Paris, France

French instrument maker and optician.

The son of a distinguished Parisian instrument maker, Charles Chevalier supplied equipment to all the major photographic pioneers of the period. He sold a camera obscura to **Niepce de St Victor** as early as 1826 and was largely responsible for bringing Niepce de St Victor and **Daguerre** together. Chevalier was one of the first opticians to design lenses specifically for photographic use; the first photographic camera to be offered for sale to the public, the Giroux daguerreotype camera of 1839, was in fact fitted with a Chevalier achromatic lens. Chevalier also supplied lenses, equipment and examples of daguerreotypes to **Talbot** in England. In 1841 Chevalier was awarded first prize in a competition for the improvement of photographic lenses, sponsored by the Société d'Encouragement of Paris. Contemporary opinion, however, favoured the runner-up, the Petzval Portrait lens by **Voigtländer** of Vienna, and Chevalier subsequently became embroiled in an acrimonious dispute which did him little credit. It did not stop him designing lenses, and he went on to become an extremely successful supplier of quality daguerreotype equipment. He was a founder member of the Société Héliographique in 1851.

Further Reading

Pavillon de Photographie du Parc Naturel Régional de Brotonne, 1974, *Charles-Louis Chevalier* (an authoritative account of Chevalier's life and work).

H. Gernsheim and A. Gernsheim, 1969, *The History of Photography*, rev. edn, London.

JW

Chevenard, Pierre Antoine Jean Sylvestre

b. 31 December 1888 Thizy, Rhône, France
d. 15 August 1960 Fontenoy-aux-Roses, France

French metallurgist, inventor of the alloys Elinvar and Platinite and of the method of strengthening nickel–chromium alloys by a precipitate of Ni_3Al which provided the basis of all later super-alloy development.

Soon after graduating from the Ecole des Mines at St-Etienne in 1910, Chevenard joined the Société de Commentry Fourchambault et Decazeville at their steelworks at Imphy, where he remained for the whole of his career. Imphy had for some years specialized in the production of nickel steels. From this venture emerged the first austenitic nickel–chromium steel, containing 6 per cent chromium and 22–4 per cent nickel and produced commercially in 1895. Most of the alloys required by **Guillaume** in his search for the low-expansion alloy Invar were made at Imphy. At the Imphy Research Laboratory, established in 1911, Chevenard conducted research into the development of specialized nickel-based alloys. His first success followed from an observation that some of the ferro-nickels were free from the low-temperature brittleness exhibited by conventional steels. To satisfy the technical requirements of Georges Claude, the French cryogenic pioneer, Chevenard was then able in 1912 to develop an alloy containing 55–60 per cent nickel, 1–3 per cent manganese and 0.2–0.4 per cent carbon. This was ductile down to -190°C, at which temperature carbon steel was very brittle.

By 1916 Elinvar, a nickel–iron–chromium alloy with an elastic modulus that did not vary appreciably with changes in ambient temperature, had been identified. This found extensive use in horology and instrument manufacture, and even for the production of high-quality tuning forks. Another very popular alloy was Platinite, which had the same coefficient of thermal expansion as platinum and soda glass. It was used in considerable quantities by incandescent-lamp manufacturers for lead-in wires. Other materials developed by Chevenard at this stage to satisfy the requirements of the electrical industry included resistance alloys, base-metal thermocouple combinations, magnetically soft high-permeability alloys, and nickel–aluminium permanent magnet steels of very high coercivity which greatly improved the power and reliability of car magnetos. Thermostatic bimetals of all varieties soon became an important branch of manufacture at Imphy.

During the remainder of his career at Imphy, Chevenard brilliantly elaborated the work on nickel–chromium–tungsten alloys to make stronger pressure vessels for the Haber and other chemical processes. Another famous alloy that he developed, ATV, contained 35 per cent nickel and 11 per cent chromium and was free from the problem of stress-induced cracking in steam that had hitherto inhibited the development of high-power steam turbines. Between 1912 and 1917, Chevenard recognized the harmful effects of traces of carbon on this type of alloy, and in the immediate postwar years he found efficient methods of scavenging the residual carbon by controlled additions of reactive metals. This led to the development of a range of stabilized austenitic stainless steels which were free from the problems of intercrystalline corrosion and weld decay that then caused so much difficulty to the manufacturers of chemical plant.

Chevenard soon concluded that only the nickel–chromium system could provide a satisfactory basis for the subsequent development of high-temperature alloys. The first published reference to the strengthening of such materials by additions of aluminium and/or titanium occurs in his UK patent of 1929. This strengthening approach was adopted in the later wartime development in Britain of the Nimonic series of alloys, all of which depended for their high-temperature strength upon the precipitated compound Ni₃Al.

In 1936 he was studying the effect of what is now known as 'thermal fatigue', which contributes to the eventual failure of both gas and steam turbines. He then published details of equipment for assessing the susceptibility of nickel–chromium alloys to this type of breakdown by a process of repeated quenching. Around this time he began to make systematic use of the thermo-gravimetric balance for high-temperature oxidation studies.

Principal Honours and Distinctions
President, Société de Physique. Commandeur de la Légion d'honneur.

Bibliography
1929, *Analyse dilatométrique des matériaux*, with a preface be C.E. Guillaume, Paris: Dunod (still regarded as the definitive work on this subject).
The *Dictionary of Scientific Biography* lists around thirty of his more important publications between 1914 and 1943.

Further Reading
'Chevenard, a great French metallurgist', 1960, *Acier Fins* (Spec.) 36: 92–100.
L. Valluz, 1961, 'Notice sur les travaux de Pierre Chevenard, 1888–1960', Paris: Institut de France, Académie des Sciences.

ASD

Chevreul, Michel Eugène
b. 31 August 1786 Angers, France
d. 9 April 1889 Paris, France

French chemist who made significant research contributions to scientific knowledge in the field of colour contrast and standardization and demonstrated the chemical nature of fats.

Between 1811 and 1823, Chevreul's work on the fundamental basis of fats led to a great improvement in both the quality of wax candles and in the fats used in the manufacture of soap, and this had considerable advantageous implications for domestic life. The publication of his researches provided the first specific account of the nature of the fats used in the manufacture of soap. His work also led to the development and manufacture of the stearine candle. Stearine was

first described by Chevreul in 1814 and was produced by heating glycerine with stearic acid. As early as 1825 M. Gay Lussac obtained a patent in England for making candles from a similar substance. The stearine candle was much more satisfactory than earlier products; it was firmer and gave a brighter light without any accompanying odour. Chevreul became Director of Dyeing in 1824 at the Royal Manufactory of Gobelins, the French national tapestry firm. While there, he carried out research into 1,442 different shades of colour. From 1830 he occupied the Chair of Chemistry at the Muséum d'Histoire Naturelle in Paris.

Further Reading
G. Bouchard, 1932, *Chevreul* (biography).
Albert da Costa, 1962, *Michel Eugène Chevreul: Pioneer of Organic Chemistry*, Wisconsin: Dept of History, University of Wisconsin.

DY

Chia Ssu-Hsieh
See **Jia Sixie**.

Chiao Wei-Yo
See **Qiao Weiyu**.

Chippendale, Thomas
baptized 5 June 1718 Otley, Yorkshire, England
d. 13 November 1779 London, England

English cabinet-maker who published the first comprehensive book of furniture.

Thomas Chippendale was the son of a carpenter. The business that he set up in London was so well established by 1753 that he was able to move to larger premises – a workshop, timberyard and shop – in the furniture-making centre of London, at 60–62 St Martin's Lane. In 1754 he published his folio work *The Gentleman and Cabinet-Maker's Director*, which contained illustrations of every conceivable type of furniture. No previously published book was as comprehensive. The *Director*, as it came to be called, made Chippendale famous and he became the best known of all such English craftsmen and designers. Further editions of the book followed in 1755 and 1762.

Stylistically most of the furniture designs in the *Director* followed the contemporary rococo fashion, but a number followed other popular themes such as the so-called 'literary Gothic' and chinoiserie. Indeed, the Chinese versions became so well known that such furniture became known as 'Chinese Chippendale'. Chippendale's later work was more neo-classical, much of it produced at the request of Robert **Adam** for the many great houses whose interiors he was re-designing in the 1760s and 1770s.

From a technical viewpoint, Chippendale's furniture was made from a variety of woods and incorporated diverse decoration. Mahogany was the fashionable wood of the age, particularly during the middle years of the eighteenth century, and lent itself especially to the fine and elaborate carving that characterized Chippendale's intricate chair and settee backs. By the later 1760s other woods were also often in use, sometimes gilded and turned, sometimes inlaid with materials such as ivory or ceramic plaques and fine ormolu mounts. Later still, painted designs were applied to panel surfaces. Alternatively, a delicate form of marquetry had been fashionably revived.

Further Reading
C. Gilbert, 1972, *The Life and Work of Thomas Chippendale*: Studio Vista.
1986, *Dictionary of English Furniture-Makers*, The Furniture History Society and W.F. Maney.

DY

Chrétien, Henri Jacques
b. 1879 Paris, France
d. 7 February 1956 Washington, USA

French astrophysicist, inventor of the anamorphoser, which became the basis of the Cinemascope motion picture system.

Chrétien studied science, and after obtaining his bachelors degree he started his working life at Meudon Observatory. He married in 1910, the same year as he was appointed Head of Astrophysics at Nice. In 1917 he helped to found the Institut d'Optique in Paris. Chrétien became Professor of astrophysics at the Sorbonne and in 1927, as part of his work on optical systems, demonstrated the use of an anamorphic lens for wide-screen motion pictures. Although the system was demonstrated in Washington as early as 1928 and again at the Paris International Exposition of 1937, it was not until 1952 that Twentieth-Century Fox were able to complete purchase of the patents which became the basis of their Cinemascope system. Cinemascope was one of the most successful technical innovations introduced by film studios in the early 1950s as part of their attempts to combat competition from television. The first Cinemascope epic, *The Robe*, shown in 1953, was an outstanding commercial success, and a series of similarly spectacular productions followed.

Further Reading
Obituary, 1956, *Journal of the Society of Motion Picture and Television Engineers* 65: 110.
R. Kingslake, 1989, *A History of the Photographic Lens*, Boston (biographical information and technical details of the anamorphic lens).

JW

Chubb, Charles
b. 1779 Fordingbridge, Hampshire, England
d. 16 May 1845 Islington, London, England.

English locksmith.

Both Charles Chubb and his younger brother Jeremiah served as apprentices to a blacksmith. The brothers were in business together in Daniel Street, Portsea, Hampshire, from 1804 until 1820, when Charles moved to London to establish the firm of Chubb & Son. In 1818, Jeremiah Chubb had patented a detector lock; this invention proved to be the foundation of the later success of the firm of Chubb & Son. Charles Chubb made improvements on this lock, for which he took out patents in 1824, 1828 and 1833. He also took out several patents for fireproof and burglarproof safes.

In the Portsea factory, at first there were only two or three employees engaged in lockmaking, but when Charles Chubb moved to London another twelve were taken on and thus things remained until 1830, when a factory was opened in Wolverhampton with up to two hundred employees. The manufacture of fireproof and burglarproof safes was carried out at a separate factory in London, which had up to one hundred and fifty employees. The two factories supplied nearly 1,500,000 patent locks and about 30,000 safes and strongrooms, costing between £8 and £5,000, the latter being the largest-ever safe supplied to a bank at that time.

See also: **Chubb, John.**

IMcN

Chubb, John

b. 1816 Portsea, Hampshire, England
d. 30 October 1872 Brixton Rise, London, England.

English locksmith.

He succeeded his father, who had founded the family firm of Chubb & Son, and patented many improvements to locks, safes, strong rooms and the like. He was elected a member of the Institution of Civil Engineers in 1845, where he delivered an important paper on locks and keys which included a list of all British patents in the field up to the date of the paper as well as of all communications on the same subject to the Royal Society of Arts; for this he was awarded the Telford Medal.

John Chubb was followed into the family business by his three sons, John C. Chubb, George H. Chubb (who was created Lord Hayter of Chislehurst in 1928) and Henry W. Chubb.

Principal Honours and Distinctions
Institution of Civil Engineers Telford Medal 1845.

See also: **Chubb, Charles**.

IMcN

Churchward, George Jackson

b. 31 January 1857 Stoke Gabriel, Devon, England
d. 19 December 1933 Swindon, Wiltshire, England

English mechanical engineer who developed for the Great Western Railway a range of steam locomotives of the most advanced design of its time.

Churchward was articled to the Locomotive Superintendent of the South Devon Railway in 1873, and when the South Devon was absorbed by the Great Western Railway in 1876 he moved to the latter's Swindon works. There he rose by successive promotions to become Works Manager in 1896, and in 1897 Chief Assistant to William Dean, who was Locomotive Carriage and Wagon Superintendent, in which capacity Churchward was allowed extensive freedom of action. Churchward eventually succeeded Dean in 1902: his title changed to Chief Mechanical Engineer in 1916.

In locomotive design, Churchward adopted the flat-topped firebox invented by A.J. Belpaire of the Belgian State Railways and added a tapered barrel to improve circulation of water between the barrel and the firebox legs. He designed valves with a longer stroke and a greater lap than usual, to achieve full opening to exhaust. Passenger-train weights had been increasing rapidly, and Churchward produced his first 4–6–0 express locomotive in 1902. However, he was still developing the details – he had a flair for selecting good engineering practices – and to aid his development work Churchward installed at Swindon in 1904 a stationary testing plant for locomotives. This was the first of its kind in Britain and was based on the work of Professor W.F.M. Goss, who had installed the first such plant at Purdue University, USA, in 1891. For comparison with his own locomotives Churchward obtained from France three 4–4–2 compound locomotives of the type developed by A. de Glehn and G. du **Bousquet**. He decided against compounding, but he did perpetuate many of the details of the French locomotives, notably the divided drive between the first and second pairs of driving wheels, when he introduced his four-cylinder 4–6–0 (the Star class) in 1907. He built a lone 4–6–2, the *Great Bear*, in 1908: the wheel arrangement enabled it to have a wide firebox, but the type was not perpetuated because Welsh coal suited narrow grates and 4–6–0 locomotives were adequate for the traffic. After Churchward retired in 1921 his successor, C.B. Collett, was to enlarge the Star class into the Castle class and then the King class, both 4–6–0s, which lasted almost as long as steam locomotives survived in service. In Churchward's time, however, the Great Western Railway was the first in Britain to adopt six-coupled locomotives on a large scale for passenger trains in place of four-coupled locomotives. The 4–6–0 classes, however, were but the most celebrated of a whole range of standard locomotives of advanced design for all types of traffic and shared between them many standardized components, particularly boilers, cylinders and valve gear.

Further Reading
H.C.B. Rogers, 1975, *G.J. Churchward. A Locomotive Biography*, London: George Allen & Unwin (a full-length account of Churchward and his locomotives, and their influence on

subsequent locomotive development).

C. Hamilton Ellis, 1958, *Twenty Locomotive Men*, Shepperton: Ian Allan, Ch. 20 (a good brief account).

Sir William Stanier, 1955, 'George Jackson Churchward', *Transactions of the Newcomen Society* 30 (a unique insight into Churchward and his work, from the informed viewpoint of his former subordinate who had risen to become Chief Mechanical Engineer of the London, Midland & Scottish Railway).

See also **Gresley, Sir Herbert Nigel**; **Stanier, Sir William Arthur**.

PJGR

Cierva, Juan de la
b. 21 September 1895 Murcia, Spain
d. 9 December 1936 Croydon, England

Spanish engineer who played a major part in developing the autogiro in the 1920s and 1930s.

At the age of 17, Cierva and some of his friends built a successful two-seater biplane, the *BCD-1* (*C* for Cierva). By 1919 he had designed a large three-engined biplane bomber, the *C 3*, which unfortunately crashed when its wing stalled (list its lift) during a slow-speed turn. Cierva turned all his energies to designing a flying machine which could not stall: his answer was the autogiro. Although an autogiro looks like a helicopter, its rotor blades are not driven by an engine, but free-wheel like a windmill. Forward speed is provided by a conventional engine and propeller, and even if this engine fails, the autogiro's rotors continue to free-wheel and it descends safely. Cierva patented his autogiro design in 1920, but it took him three years to put theory into practice. By 1925, after further improvements, he had produced a practical rotary-winged flying machine. He moved to England and in 1926 established the Cierva Autogiro Company Ltd. The Air Ministry showed great interest and a year later the British company Avro was commissioned to manufacture the *C 6A* Autogiro under licence. Probably the most significant of Cierva's autogiros was the *C 30A*, or Avro *Rota*, which served in the Royal Air Force from 1935 until 1945. Several other manufacturers in France, Germany, Japan and the USA built Cierva autogiros under licence, but only in small numbers and they never really rivalled

fixed-wing aircraft. The death of Cierva in an airliner crash in 1936, together with the emergence of successful helicopters, all but extinguished interest in the autogiro.

Principal Honours and Distinctions
Daniel Guggenheim Medal. Royal Aeronautical Society Silver Medal, Gold Medal (posthumously) 1937.

Bibliography
1931, *Wings of To-morrow: The Story of the Autogiro*, New York (an early account of his work).
He read a paper on his latest achievements at the Royal Aeronautical Society on 15 March 1935.

Further Reading
P.W. Brooks, 1988, *Cierva Autogiros: The Development of Rotary Wing Flight*, Washington, DC (contains a full account of Cierva's work).
Jose Warleta. 1977, *Autogiro: Juan de la Cierva y su obra*, Madrid (a detailed account of his work in Spain).
Oliver Stewart, 1966, *Aviation: The Creative Ideas*, London (contains a chapter on Cierva).

JDS

Clark, Edward
fl. 1850s New York State, USA

American co-developer of mass-production techniques at the Singer sewing machine factory.

Born in upstate New York, where his father was a small manufacturer, Edward Clark attended college at Williams and graduated in 1831. He became a lawyer in New York City and from then on lived either in the city or on his rural estate near Cooperstown in upstate New York. After a series of share manipulations, Clark acquired a one-third interest in Isaac M. **Singer**'s company. They soon bought out one of Singer's earlier partners, G.B. Zeiber, and in 1851, under the name of I.M. Singer & Co., they set up a permanent sewing machine business with headquarters in New York.

The success of their firm initially rested on marketing. Clark introduced door-to-door salespeople and hire-purchase for their sewing machines in 1856 ($50 cash down, or $100 with a cash payment of $5 and $3 a month thereafter).

He also trained women to demonstrate to potential customers the capabilities of the Singer sewing machine. At first their sewing machines continued to be made in the traditional way, with the parts fitted together by skilled workers through hand filing and shaping so that the parts would fit only onto one machine. This resembled European practice rather than the American system of manufacture that had been pioneered in the armouries in that country. In 1856 Singer brought out their first machine intended exclusively for home use, and at the same time manufacturing capacity was improved. Through increased sales, a new factory was built in 1858–9 on Mott Street, New York, but it soon became inadequate to meet demand.

In 1863 the Singer company was incorporated as the Singer Manufacturing Co. and began to modernize its production methods with special jigs and fixtures to help ensure uniformity. More and more specialized machinery was built for making the parts. By 1880 the factory, then at Elizabethport, New Jersey, was jammed with automatic and semi-automatic machine tools. In 1882 the factory was producing sewing machines with fully interchangeable parts that did not require hand fitting in assembly. Production rose from 810 machines in 1853 to half a million in 1880. A new family model was introduced in 1881. Clark had succeeded Singer, who died in 1875, as President of the company, but he retired in 1882 after he had seen through the change to mass production.

Further Reading
National Cyclopaedia of American Biography.
D.A. Hounshell, 1984, *From the American System to Mass Production, 1800–1932. The Development of Manufacturing Technology in the United States*, Baltimore (a thorough account of Clark's role in the development of Singer's factories).
F.B. Jewell, 1975, *Veteran Sewing Machines. A Collector's Guide*, Newton Abbot.

RLH

Clark, Edwin

b. 7 January 1814 Marlow, Buckinghamshire, England
d. 22 October 1894 Marlow, Buckinghamshire, England

English civil engineer.

After a basic education in mathematics, latin, French and geometry, Clark was articled to a solicitor, but he left after two years because he did not like the work. He had no permanent training otherwise, and for four years he led an idle life, becoming self-taught in the subjects that interested him. He eventually became a teacher at his old school before entering Cambridge, although he returned home after two years without taking a degree. He then toured the European continent extensively, supporting himself as best he could. He returned to England in 1839 and obtained further teaching posts. With the railway boom in progress he decided to become a surveyor and did some work on a proposed line between Oxford and Brighton.

After being promised an interview with Robert **Stephenson**, he managed to see him in March 1846. Stephenson took a liking to Clark and asked him to investigate the strains on the Britannia Bridge tubes under various given conditions. This work so gained Stephenson's full approval that, after being entrusted with experiments and designs, Clark was appointed Resident Engineer for the Britannia Bridge across the Menai Straits. He not only completed the bridge, which was opened on 19 October 1850, but also wrote the history of its construction. After the completion of the bridge – and again without any professional experience – he was appointed Engineer-in-Chief to the Electric and International Telegraph Company. He was consulted by Captain Mark Huish of the London & North Western Railway on a telegraphic system for the railway, and in 1853 he introduced the Block Telegraph System.

Clark was engaged on the Crystal Palace and was responsible for many railway bridges in Britain and abroad. He was Engineer and part constructor of the harbour at Callao, Peru, and also of harbour works at Colón, Panama. On canal works he was contractor for the marine canal, the Morskoy Canal, in 1875 between Kronstadt and St Petersburg. His great work on canals, however, was the concept with Edward Leader **Williams** of the hydraulically operated barge lift at Anderton, Cheshire, linking the Weaver Navigation to the Trent & Mersey Canal, whose water levels have a vertical separation of 50 ft (15 m). This was opened on 26 July 1875. The structure so impressed the French engineers who were faced with a bottleneck of five locks on the Neuf-fossée Canal south of Saint-Omer that they commissioned Clark to design a lift there. This was completed in 1878 and survives as a historic monument. The design was also adopted for four lifts on the Canal du Centre at La Louvière in Belgium, but these were not completed until after Clark's death.

JHB

Clarke, Arthur Charles
b. 16 December 1917 Minehead, Somerset, England

English writer of science fiction who correctly predicted the use of geo-stationary earth satellites for worldwide communications.

Whilst still at Huish's Grammar School, Taunton, Clarke became interested in both space science and science fiction. Unable to afford a scientific education at the time (he later obtained a BSc at King's College, London), he pursued both interests in his spare time while working in the Government Exchequer and Audit Department between 1936 and 1941. He was a founder member of the British Interplanetary Society, subsequently serving as its Chairman in 1946–7 and 1950–3. From 1941 to 1945 he served in the Royal Air Force, becoming a technical officer in the first GCA (Ground Controlled Approach) radar unit. There he began to produce the first of many science-fiction stories. In 1949–50 he was an assistant editor of *Science Abstracts* at the Institution of Electrical Engineers.

As a result of his two interests, he realized during the Second World War that an artificial earth satellite in an equatorial orbital with a radius of 35,000 km (22,000 miles) would appear to be stationary, and that three such geo-stationary, or synchronous, satellites could be used for worldwide broadcast or communications. He described these ideas in a paper published in *Wireless World* in 1945. Initially there was little response, but within a few years the idea was taken up by the US National Aeronautics and Space Administration and in 1965 the first synchronous satellite, *Early Bird*, was launched into orbit.

In the 1950s he moved to Ceylon (now Sri Lanka) to pursue an interest in underwater exploration, but he continued to write science fic-

tion, being known in particular for his contribution to the making of the classic Stanley Kubrick science-fiction film *2001: A Space Odyssey*, based on his book of the same title.

Principal Honours and Distinctions
Clarke received many honours for both his scientific and science-fiction writings. For his satellite communication ideas his awards include the Franklin Institute Gold Medal 1963 and Honorary Fellowship of the American Institute of Aeronautics and Astronautics 1976. For his science-fiction writing he received the UNESCO Kalinga Prize (1961) and many others. In 1979 he became Chancellor of Moratuwa University in Sri Lanka and in 1980 Vikran Scrabhai Professor at the Physical Research Laboratory of the University of Ahmedabad.

Bibliography
1945, 'Extra-terrestrial relays: can rocket stations give world wide coverage?', *Wireless World* L1: 305 (puts forward his ideas for geo-stationary communication satellites).
1946, 'Astronomical radar: some future possibilities', *Wireless World* 52: 321.
1948, 'Electronics and space flight', *Journal of the British Interplanetary Society* 7: 49.
Other publications, mainly science-fiction novels, include: 1955, *Earthlight*; 1956, *The Coast of Coral*; 1958, *Voice Across the Sea*; 1961, *Fall of Moondust*; 1965, *Voices from the Sky*; 1977, *The View from Serendip*; 1979, *Fountain of Paradise*; 1984, *Ascent to Orbit: A Scientific Autobiography*; and 1984, *2010: Odyssey Two* (a sequel to *2001: A Space Odyssey* that was also made into a film).

Further Reading
1986, *Encyclopaedia Britannica*.
1991, *Who's Who*, London: A. & C. Black.

See also **Pierce, John Robinson**.

KF

Claudet, Antoine François Jean
b. 12 August 1797 France
d. 27 December 1867 London, England

French pioneer photographer and photographic inventor in England.

He began his working life in banking but soon

went into glassmaking and in 1829 he moved to London to open a glass warehouse. On hearing of the first practicable photographic processes in 1834, Claudet visited Paris, where he received instruction in the daguerreotype process from the inventor **Daguerre**, and purchased a licence to operate in England. On returning to London he began to sell daguerreotype views of Paris and Rome, but was soon taking and selling his own views of London. At this time exposures could take as long as thirty minutes and portraiture from life was impracticable. Claudet was fascinated by the possibilities of the daguerreotype and embarked on experiments to improve the process. In 1841 he published details of an accelerated process and took out a patent proposing the use of flat painted backgrounds and a red light in dark-rooms. In June of that year Claudet opened the second daguerreotype portrait studio in London, just three months after his rival, Richard Beard. He took stereoscopic photographs for **Wheatstone** as early as 1842, although it was not until the 1850s that stereoscopy became a major interest. He suggested and patented several improvements to viewers derived from **Brewster**'s pattern.

Claudet was also one of the first photographers to practise professionally **Talbot**'s calotype process. He became a personal friend of Talbot, one of the few from whom the inventor was prepared to accept advice. Claudet died suddenly in London following an accident that occurred when he was alighting from an omnibus. A memoir produced shortly after his death lists over forty scientific papers relating to his researches into photography.

Principal Honours and Distinctions
FRS 1853.

Further Reading
'The late M. Claudet', 1868, *Photographic News* 12: 3 (obituary).
'A. Claudet, FRS, a memoir', 1968, (reprinted from *The Scientific Review*), London: British Association (a fulsome but valuable Victorian view of Claudet).
H. Gernsheim and A. Gernsheim, 1969, *The History of Photography*, rev. edn, London (a comprehensive account of Claudet's daguerreotype work).
H.J.P. Arnold, 1977, *William Henry Fox Talbot*,

London (provides details of Claudet's relationship with Talbot).

JW

Clegg, Samuel
b. 2 March 1781 Manchester, England
d. 8 January 1861 Haverstock Hill, Hampstead, London, England

English inventor and gas engineer.

Clegg received scientific instruction from John Dalton, the founder of the atomic theory, and was apprenticed to **Boulton** & **Watt**. While at their Soho factory in Birmingham, he assisted William **Murdock** with his experiments on coal gas. He left the firm in 1804 and set up as a gas engineer on his own account. He designed and installed gas plant and lighting in a number of factories, including Henry Lodge's cotton mill at Sowerby Bridge and in 1811 the Jesuit College at Stoneyhurst in Lancashire, the first non-industrial establishment to be equipped with gas lighting.

Clegg moved to London in 1813 and successfully installed gas lighting at the premises of Rudolf **Ackermann** in the Strand. His success in the manufacture of gas had earned him the Royal Society of Arts Silver Medal in 1808 for furthering 'the art of gas production', and in 1813 it brought him the appointment of Chief Engineer to the first gas company, the Chartered Gas, Light & Coke Company. He left in 1817, but remained in demand to set up gas works and advise on the formation of gas companies. Throughout this time there flowed from Clegg a series of inventions of fundamental importance in the gas industry. While at Lodge's mill he had begun purifying gas by adding lime to the gas holder, and at Stoneyhurst this had become a separate lime purifier. In 1815, and again in 1818, Clegg patented the wet-meter which proved to be the basis for future devices for measuring gas. He invented the gas governor and, favouring the horizontal retort, developed the form which was to become standard for the next forty years. But after all this, Clegg joined a concern in Liverpool which failed, taking all his possessions with it. He made a fresh start in Lisbon, where he undertook various engineering works for the Portuguese government. He returned to England to find railway construction gathering pace, but he again backed a loser by engaging in the ill-fated atmospheric-railway project. He was finally discouraged from taking part in further enterprises, but he received a government appointment as Surveying Officer to conduct enquiries in connection with the various Bills on gas that were presented to Parliament. Clegg also contributed to his son's massive treatise on the manufacture of coal gas.

Principal Honours and Distinctions
Royal Society of Arts Silver Medal 1808.

Further Reading
Minutes of Proceedings of the Institution of Civil Engineers (1862) 21: 552–4.
S. Everard, 1949, *The History of the Gas Light and Coke Company*, London: Ernest Benn.

LRD

Clement (Clemmet), Joseph
bapt. 13 June 1779 Great Asby, Westmoreland, England
d. 28 February 1844 London, England

English machine tool builder and inventor.

Although known as Clement in his professional life, his baptism at Asby and his death were registered under the name of Joseph Clemmet. He worked as a slater until the age of 23, but his interest in mechanics led him to spend much of his spare time in the local blacksmith's shop. By studying books on mechanics borrowed from his cousin, a watchmaker, he taught himself and with the aid of the village blacksmith made his own lathe. By 1805 he was able to give up the slating trade and find employment as a mechanic in a small factory at Kirkby Stephen. From there he moved to Carlisle for two years, and then to Glasgow where, while working as a turner, he took lessons in drawing; he had a natural talent and soon became an expert draughtsman. From about 1809 he was employed by Leys, Mason & Co. of Aberdeen designing and making power looms. For this work he built a screw-cutting lathe and continued his self-education. At the end of 1813, having saved about £100, he made his way to London, where he soon found employment as a mechanic and draughtsman. Within a few months he was engaged by Joseph **Bramah**, and after a trial period a formal agreement dated 1 April 1814 was made by which Clement was to be Chief Draughtsman and Superintendent of Bramah's Pimlico works for five years. However, Bramah died in December 1814 and after his sons took over the business it was agreed that Clement should leave before the expiry of the five-year period. He soon found employment as Chief Draughtsman with Henry Maudslay & Co. By 1817 Clement had saved about £500, which enabled him to establish his own business at Prospect Place, Newington Butts, as a mechanical draughtsman and manufacturer of high-class machinery. For this purpose he built lathes for his own use and invented various improvements in their detailed design. In 1827 he designed and built a facing lathe which incorporated an ingenious system of infinitely variable belt gearing. He had also built his own planing machine by 1820 and another, much larger one in 1825. In 1828 Clement began making fluted taps and dies and standardized the screw threads, thus anticipating on a small scale the national standards later established by Sir Joseph **Whitworth**. Because of his reputation for first-class workmanship, Clement was in the 1820s engaged by Charles **Babbage** to carry out the construction of his first Difference Engine.

Principal Honours and Distinctions
Society of Arts Gold Medal 1818 (for straight-line mechanism), 1827 (for facing lathe); Silver Medal 1828 (for lathe-driving device).

Bibliography
Examples of Clement's draughtsmanship can be found in the *Transactions of the Society of Arts* 33 (1817), 36 (1818), 43 (1925), 46 (1828) and 48 (1829).

Further Reading
S. Smiles, 1863, *Industrial Biography*, London, reprinted 1967, Newton Abbot (virtually the only source of biographical information on Clement).
L.T.C. Rolt, 1965, *Tools for the Job*, London (repub. 1986); W. Steeds, 1969, *A History of Machine Tools 1700–1910*, Oxford (both contain descriptions of his machine tools).

RTS

Clerk, Sir Dugald
b. 31 March 1854 Glasgow, Scotland
d. 12 November 1932 Ewhurst, Surrey, England

Scottish mechanical engineer, inventor of the two-stroke internal combustion engine.

Clerk began his engineering training at about the age of 15 in the drawing office of H.O. Robinson & Company, Glasgow, and in his father's works. Meanwhile, he studied at the West of Scotland Technical College and then, from 1871 to 1876, at Anderson's College, Glasgow, and at the Yorkshire College of Science, Leeds. Here he worked under and then became assistant to the distinguished chemist T.E. Thorpe, who set him to work on the fractional distillation of petroleum, which was to be useful to him in his later work. At that time he had intended to become a chemical engineer, but seeing a **Lenoir** gas engine at work, after his return to Glasgow, turned his main interest to gas and other internal combustion engines. He pursued his investigations first at Thomson, Sterne & Company (1877–85) and then at Tangyes of Birmingham (1886–88. In 1888 he began a lifelong partnership in Marks and Clerk, consulting engineers and patent agents, in London.

Beginning his work on gas engines in 1876, he achieved two patents in the two following years. In 1878 he made his principal invention, patented in 1881, of an engine working on the two-stroke cycle, in which the piston is powered during each revolution of the crankshaft, instead of alternate revolutions as in the **Otto** four-stroke cycle. In this engine, Clerk introduced supercharging, or increasing the pressure of the air intake. Many engines of the Clerk type were made but their popularity waned after the patent for the Otto engine expired in 1890. Interest was later revived, particularly for application to large gas engines, but Clerk's engine eventually came into its own where simple, low-power motors are needed, such as in motor cycles or motor mowers.

Clerk's work on the theory and design of gas engines bore fruit in the book *The Gas Engine* (1886), republished with an extended text in 1909 as *The Gas, Petrol and Oil Engine*; these and a number of papers in scientific journals won him international renown. During and after the First World War, Clerk widened the scope of his interests and served, often as chairman, on many bodies in the field of science and industry.

Principal Honours and Distinctions
Knighted 1917; FRS 1908; Royal Society Royal Medal 1924; Royal Society of Arts Alber Medal 1922.

Further Reading
Obituary Notices of Fellows of the Royal Society, no. 2, 1933.

LRD

Clerke, Sir Clement
d. 1693

English entrepreneur responsible, with others, for attempts to introduce coal-fired smelting of lead and, later, of copper.

Clerke, from Launde Abbey in Leicestershire, was involved in early experiments to smelt lead using coal fuel, which was believed to have been located on the Leicestershire–Derbyshire border. Concurrently, Lord Grandison was financing experiments at Bristol for similar purposes, causing the downfall of an earlier unsuccessful patented method before securing his own patent in 1678. In that same year Clerke took over management of the Bristol works, claiming the ability to secure financial return from Grandison's methods. Financial success proved elusive, although the technical problems of adapting the reverberatory furnace to coal fuel appear to have been solved when Clerke was found to have established another lead works nearby on his own account. He was forced to cease work on lead in 1684 in respect of Grandison's patent rights. Clerke then turned to investigations into the coal-fired smelting of other metals and started to smelt copper in coal-fired reverberatory furnaces. By 1688–9 small supplied of merchantable copper were offered for sale in London in order to pay his workers, possibly because of further financial troubles. The practical success of his smelting innovation is widely acknowledged to have been the responsibility of John **Coster** and, to a smaller extent, Gabriel Wayne, both of whom left Clerke and set up separate works elsewhere. Clerke's son Talbot took over administration of his father's works, which declined still further and closed *c*.1693, at about the time of Sir Clement's death. Both Coster and Wayne continued to develop smelting techniques, establishing a new British industry in the smelting of copper with coal.

Clinton, De Witt

Principal Honours and Distinctions
Created baronet 1661.

Further Reading
Rhys Jenkins, 1934, 'The reverberatory furnace with coal fuel', *Transactions of the Newcomen Society* 34: 67–81.
—— 1943–4, 'Copper smelting in England: Revival at the end of the seventeenth century', *Transactions of the Newcomen Society* 24: 78–80.
J. Morton, 1985, *The Rise of the Modern Copper and Brass Industry: 1690 to 1750*, unpublished PhD thesis, University of Birmingham, 87–106.

JD

Clinton, De Witt

b. 2 March 1769 Little Britain, Orange County, New York, USA
d. 11 February 1828 Albany, New York, USA

American statesman and entrepreneur.

After gaining his degree at Columbia College, Clinton studied law and then entered politics. After a defeat in 1795 he studied natural science, until in 1798 he was elected to the State Senate. In 1802 he was elected to the US Senate, but he resigned in 1803 to become Mayor of New York City; he occupied this post, apart from two short breaks, until 1815, when he was removed from office. He was very concerned for the welfare of ordinary people and introduced many improvements. From 1815 Clinton devoted himself to what was to become the Erie Canal. He had already been appointed one of the canal commissioners in 1810 and had himself surveyed a possible route to Lake Erie that would be a safer passage from New York to the Great Lakes in the event of war with Great Britain. The war of 1812, in fact, interfered with the project, but in 1816 Clinton realized that the time was propitious. He arranged meetings, and on 17 April 1816 the legislature adopted his idea and a new survey for a link between the Hudson and Lake Erie was undertaken. In March 1817 he became Governor of New York State and vigorously pursued the canal scheme both in writing and by personal supervision of the works. Party politics removed him from his post as Canal Commissioner on 12 April 1824, but in November he was re-elected as Governor. He held this position when the Erie

Canal (362 miles or 583 km long) and the Champlain Canal (71 miles or 114 km) were opened in 1825. In his character he was overbearing, but he was administratively competent.

Further Reading
J. Renwick, 1840, *Life of De Witt Clinton*, New York.

JHB

Clymer, George E.

b. 1754 Bucks County, Pennsylvania, USA
d. 27 August 1834 London, England

American inventor of the Columbian printing press.

Clymer was born on his father's farm, of a family that emigrated from Switzerland in the early eighteenth century. He attended local schools, helping out on the farm in his spare time, and he showed a particular talent for maintaining farm machinery. At the age of 16 he learned the trade of carpenter and joiner, which he followed in the same district for over twenty-five years. During that time, he showed his talent for mechanical invention in many ways, including the invention of a plough specially adapted to the local soils. Around 1800, he moved to Philadelphia, where his interest was aroused by the erection of the first bridge over the Schuylkill River. He devised a pump to remove water from the cofferdams at a rate of 500 gallons per day, superior to any other pumps then in use. He obtained a US patent for this in 1801, and a British one soon after.

Clymer then turned his attention to the improvement of the printing press. For three and a half centuries after its invention, the old wooden-framed press had remained virtually unchanged except in detail. The first real change came in 1800 with the introduction of the iron press by Earl **Stanhope**. Modified versions were developed by other inventors, notably George Clymer, who after more than ten years' effort achieved his *Columbian* press. With its new system of levers, it enabled perfect impressions to be obtained with far less effort by the pressman. The *Columbian* was also notable for its distinctive cast-iron ornamentation, including a Hermes on each pillar and alligators and other reptiles on the levers. Most spectacular, it was surmounted by an American spread eagle, usually covered in gilt, which also served as a counterweight to raise the platen. The earliest known *Columbian*, surviving only in an illustration, bears the inscription *Columbian Press/No.25/invented by George Clymer/Anno Domini 1813/Made in Philadelphia 1816*. Few American printers could afford the US$400 selling price, so in 1817 Clymer went to England, where it was taken up enthusiastically. He obtained a British patent for it the same year, and by the following March it was being manufactured by the engineering firm R.W. Cope, although Clymer was probably making it on his own account soon afterwards. The *Columbian* was widely used for many years and continued to be made even into the twentieth century. The King of the Netherlands awarded Clymer a gold medal for his invention and the Tsar of Russia gave him a present for installing the press in Russia. Doubtless for business reasons, Clymer spent most of his remaining years in England and Europe.

Further Reading
J. Moran, 1973, *Printing Presses*, London: Faber & Faber.
— 1969, contributed a thorough survey of the press in *J. Printing Hist. Soc.*, no. 3.

LRD

Coade, Eleanor

b. 24 June 1733 Exeter, Devon, England
d. 18 November 1821 Camberwell, London, England

English proprietor of the Coade Factory, making artificial stone.

Born Elinor Coade, she never married but adopted, as was customary in business in the eighteenth century, the courtesy title of Mrs. Following the bankruptcy and death of her father, George Coade, in Exeter, Eleanor and her mother (also called Eleanor) moved to London and founded the works at Lambeth, South London, in 1769 that later became famous as the Coade factory. The factory was located at King's Arms Stairs, Narrow Wall. During the eighteenth century, several attempts had been made in other businesses to manufacture a durable, malleable artificial stone that would be acceptable to architects for decorative use. These substances were not very successful, but Coade stone was different. Although stories are legion about the secret formula supposedly used in this artifi-

cial stone, modern methods have established the exact formula.

Coade stone was a stoneware ceramic material fired in a kiln. The body was remarkable in that it shrank only 8 per cent in drying and firing: this was achieved by using a combination of china clay, sand, crushed glass and grog (i.e. crushed and ground, previously fired stoneware). The Coade formula thus included a considerable proportion of material that, having been fired once already, was unshrinkable. Mrs Coade's name for the firm, Coade's Lithodipyra Terra-Cotta or Artificial Stone Manufactory (where 'Lithodipyra' is a term derived from three Greek words meaning 'stone', 'twice' and 'fire'), made reference to the custom of including such material (such as in Josiah **Wedgwood**'s basalt and jasper ware). The especially low rate of shrinkage rendered the material ideal for making extra-life-size statuary, and large architectural, decorative features to be incorporated into stone buildings.

Coade stone was widely used for such purposes by leading architects in Britain and Ireland from the 1770s until the 1830s, including Robert **Adam**, Sir Charles **Barry**, Sir William Chambers, Sir John **Soane**, John **Nash** and James Wyatt. Some architects introduced the material abroad, as far as, for example, Charles Bulfinch's United States Bank in Boston, Massachusetts, and Charles Cameron's redecoration for the Empress Catherine of the great palace Tsarkoe Selo (now Pushkin), near St Petersburg. The material so resembles stone that it is often mistaken for it, but it is so hard and resistant to weather that it retains sharpness of detail much longer than the natural substance. The many famous British buildings where Coade stone was used include the Royal Hospital, Chelsea, Carlton House and the Sir John Soane Museum (all of which are located in London), St George's Chapel at Windsor, Alnwick Castle in Northumberland, and Culzean Castle in Ayrshire, Scotland.

Apart from the qualities of the material, the Coade firm established a high reputation for the equally fine quality of its classical statuary. Mrs Coade employed excellent craftsmen such as the sculptor John Bacon (1740–99), whose work was mass-produced by the use of moulds. One famous example which was widely reproduced was the female caryatid from the south porch of the Erechtheion on the acropolis of Athens. A drawing of this had appeared in the second edition of Stuart and Revett's *Antiquities of Athens* in 1789, and many copies were made from the original Coade model; Soane used them more than once, for example on the Bank of England and his own houses in London.

Eleanor Coade was a remarkable woman, and was important and influential on the neo-classical scene. She had close and amicable relations with leading architects of the day, notably Robert Adam and James Wyatt. The Coade factory was enlarged and altered over the years, but the site was finally cleared during 1949–50 in preparation for the establishment of the 1951 Festival of Britain.

Further Reading
A. Kelly, 1990, *Mrs Coade's Stone*, pub. in conjunction with the Georgian Group (an interesting, carefully written history; includes a detailed appendix on architects who used Coade stone and buildings where surviving work may be seen).

DY

Cobbett, William
b. 9 March 1762 Farnham, Surrey, England
d. 17 June 1835 Guildford, Surrey, England

English political writer and activist; writer on rural affairs, with a particular concern for the conditions of the agricultural worker; a keen experimental farmer who claimed responsibility for the import of Indian maize to Britain.

The son of a smallholder farmer and self-taught surveyor, William Cobbett was brought up to farm work from an early age. In 1783 he took employment as an attorney's clerk in London, but not finding this to his liking he travelled to Chatham with the intention of joining the Navy. A mistake in 'taking the King's shilling' found him in an infantry regiment. After a year's training he was sent out to Nova Scotia and quickly gained the rank of sergeant major. On leaving the Army he brought corruption charges against three officers in his regiment, but did not press with the prosecution. England was not to his taste, and he returned to North America with his wife.

In America Cobbett taught English to the growing French community displaced by the French Revolution. He found American criticism of Britain ill-balanced and in 1796 began to publish a daily newspaper under the title *Porcupine's Gazetteer*, in which he wrote editorials in defence of Britain. His writings won him little support from the Americans. However, on returning to London in 1800 he was offered, but turned down, the management of a Government newspaper. Instead he began to produce a daily paper called the *Porcupine*, which was superseded in 1802 by *Cobbett's Political Register*; this publication continued on a weekly basis until after his death. In 1803 he also began the Parliamentary Debates, which later merged into Hansard, the official report of parliamentary proceedings.

In 1805 Cobbett took a house and 300-acre (120-hectare) farm in Hampshire, from which he continued to write, but at the same time followed the pursuits he most enjoyed. In 1809 his criticism of the punishment given to mutineers in the militia at Ely resulted in his own imprisonment. On his release in 1812 he decided that the only way to remain an independent publisher was to move back to the USA. He bought a farm at Hampstead, Long Island, New York, and published *A Year's Residence in America*, which contains, amongst other things, an interesting account of a farmer's year.

Returning to Britain in the easier political climate of the 1820s, Cobbett bought a small seed farm in Kensington, then outside London. From there he made a number of journeys around the country, publishing accounts of them in his famous *Rural Rides*. His experiments and advice on the sowing and cultivation of crops, particularly turnips and swedes, and on forestry, were an important mechanism for the spread of ideas within the UK. He also claimed that he was the first to introduce the acacia and Indian maize to Britain. Much of his writing expresses a concern for the rural poor and he was firmly convinced that only parliamentary reform would achieve the changes needed. His political work and writing led to his election as Member of Parliament for Oldham in the 1835 election, which followed the Reform Act of 1832. However, by this time his energy was failing rapidly and he died peacefully at Normandy Farm, near Guildford, at the age of 73.

Bibliography
Cobbett's *Observations on Priestley's Emigration*, published in 1794, was the first of his

pro-British tracts written in America. On the basis of his stay in that country he wrote *A Year's Residence in America*. His books on agricultural practice included *Woodlands* (1825) and *Treatise on Cobbett's Corn* (1828). Dealing with more social problems he wrote an *English Grammar for the use of Apprentices, Plough Boys, Soldiers and Sailors* in 1818, and *Cottage Economy* in 1821.

Further Reading

Albert Pell, 1902, article in *Journal of the Royal Agricultural Society of England* 63: 1–26 (describes the life and writings of William Cobbett).

James Sambrook, 1973, *William Cobbett*, London: Routledge (a more detailed study).

AP

Cobham, Sir Alan John

b. 6 May 1894 London, England
d. 21 October 1973 British Virgin Islands

English pilot who pioneered worldwide air routes and developed an in-flight refuelling system which is in use today.

Alan Cobham was a man of many parts. He started as a veterinary assistant in France during the First World War, but transferred to the Royal Flying Corps in 1917. After the war he continued flying, by giving joy-rides and doing aerial photography work. In 1921 he joined the De Havilland Aircraft Company (see **de Havilland, Geoffrey**) as a test and charter pilot; he was also successful in a number of air races. During the 1920s Cobham made many notable flights to distant parts of the British Empire, pioneering possible routes for airline operations. During the early 1930s Sir Alan (he was knighted in 1926) devoted his attention to generating a public interest in aviation and to campaigning for more airfields. Cobham's Flying Circus toured the country giving flying displays and joy-rides, which for thousands of people was their first experience of flying.

In 1933 Cobham planned a non-stop flight to India by refuelling his aircraft while flying: this was not a new idea but the process was still experimental. The flight was unsuccessful due to a fault in his aircraft, unrelated to the in-flight refuelling system. The following year Flight Refuelling Ltd was founded, and by 1939 two

Short flying boats were operating the first in-flight-refuelled service across the Atlantic. In-flight refuelling was not required during the early years of the Second World War, so Cobham turned to other projects such as thermal de-icing of wings, and a scheme which was not carried out, for delivering fighters to the Middle East by towing them behind *Wellington* bombers.

After the Second World War the fortunes of Flight Refuelling Ltd were at a low ebb, especially when British South American Airways abandoned the idea of using in-flight refuelling. Then an American contract and the use of their tanker aircraft to ferry oil during the Berlin Airlift saved the day. In 1949 Cobham's chief designer, Peter Macgregor, came up with an idea for refuelling fighters using a probe and drogue system. A large tanker aircraft trailed a hose with a conical drogue at the free end. The fighter pilot manoeuvred the probe, fitted to his aircraft, so that it locked into the drogue, enabling fuel to be transferred. Since the 1950s this system has become the effective world standard.

Principal Honours and Distinctions

Knighted 1926. Air Force Cross 1926.

Bibliography

1978, *A Time to Fly*, ed. C. Derrick, London; pub. in paperback 1986 (Cobham's memoirs).

Cobham produced films of some of his flights and published *Skyways*, 1925, London; *My Flight to the Cape and Back*, 1926, London; *Australia and Back*, 1926, London; *Twenty Thousand Miles in a Flying Boat*, 1930, London.

Further Reading

Peter G. Proctor, 1975, 'The life and work of Sir Alan Cobham', *Aerospace (RAeS)* (March).

JDS

Cochran, Josephine C.

b. *c.*1842 Ohio, USA
d. after November 1908 USA

American inventor of the dishwashing machine.

Amidst the growing cohorts of American inventors who began to deluge the patent office with their inventions from around the middle of the nineteenth century are at least 30 women who received patents for dishwashers. Of these, it seems that Josephine C. Cochran can be credited with the invention of the first commercially available dishwasher. She developed her machine over a period of ten years, achieving patents in 1886 and 1888, with a third in 1894 for a 'dishcleaner'. She completed the work in 1889, only after the death of her husband, who had kept her too short of funds to perfect her invention. Cochran exhibited her dishwasher at the Columbian Exposition in Chicago in 1892. There was a smaller, 'family'-size machine for domestic use and a larger model, steam-driven, for major hotels and restaurants; this latter model was used by many such establishments in Chicago. It was said that the large machine could scald, rinse and dry up to 240 plates of various shapes and sizes in two minutes. Her invention had won her sufficient fame to earn her a place in a list, published in 1886, of prominent American women inventors.

Little is known of Cochran's personal details, save that she was married to a circuit clerk ten years her senior, by whom she had a daughter. She was still active in November 1908, for she exhibited again at the Martha Washington Hotel Suffrage Bazaar in New York City.

Further Reading
A. Stanley, 1993, *Mothers and Daughters of Invention*, Meruchen, NJ: Scarecrow Press, pp. 438–9.

LRD

Cockerell, Christopher Sydney
b. 4 June 1910 Cambridge, England

British designer and engineer who invented the hovercraft.

He was educated at Gresham's School in Holt and at Peterhouse College, Cambridge, where he graduated in engineering in 1931; he was made an Honorary Fellow in 1974. Cockerell entered the engineering firm of W.H. Allen & Sons of Bedford as a pupil in 1931, and two years later he returned to Cambridge to engage in radio research for a further two years. In 1935 he joined **Marconi** Wireless Telegraph Company, working on very high frequency (VHF) transmitters and direction finders. During the Second World War he worked on airborne navigation and communication equipment, and later he worked on radar. During this period he filed thirty six patents in the fields of radio and navigational systems.

In 1950 Cockerell left Marconi to set up his own boat-hire business on the Norfolk Broads. He began to consider how to increase the speed of boats by means of air lubrication. Since the 1870s engineers had at times sought to reduce the drag on a boat by means of a thin layer of air between hull and water. After his first experiments, Cockerell concluded that a significant reduction in drag could only be achieved with a thick cushion of air. After experimenting with several ways of applying the air-cushion principle, the first true hovercraft 'took off' in 1955. It was a model in balsa wood, 2 ft 6 in. (762 mm) long and weighing $4\frac{1}{2}$ oz. (27.6 g); it was powered by a model-aircraft petrol engine and could travel over land or water at 13 mph (20.8 km/h). Cockerell filed his first hovercraft patent on 12 December 1955. The following year he founded Hovercraft Ltd and began the search for a manufacturer. The government was impressed with the invention's military possibilities and placed it on the secret list. The secret leaked out, however, and the project was declassified. In 1958 the National Research and Development Corporation decided to give its backing, and the following year Saunders Roe Ltd with experience of making flying boats, produced the epoch-making *SR N1*, a hovercraft with an air cushion produced by air jets directed downwards and inwards arranged round the periphery of the craft. It made a successful crossing of the English Channel, with the inventor on board.

Meanwhile Cockerell had modified the hovercraft so that the air cushion was enclosed within flexible skirts. In this form it was taken up by manufacturers throughout the world and found wide application as a passenger-carrying vehicle, for military transport and in scientific exploration and survey work. The hover principle found other uses, such as for air-beds to relieve severely burned patients and for hover mowers.

The development of the hovercraft has occupied Cockerell since then and he has been actively involved in the several companies set up to exploit the invention, including Hovercraft Development Ltd and British Hovercraft Corporation. In the 1970s and 1980s he took up the idea of the generation of electricity by wavepower; he was Founder of Wavepower Ltd, of which he was Chairman from 1974 to 1982.

Principal Honours and Distinctions
Knighted 1969. CBE 1955. FRS 1967.

LRD

Cockerill, William

b. 1759 Lancashire, England
d. 1832 near Aix-la-Chapelle, France (now Aachen, Germany)

English (naturalized Belgian c.1810) engineer, inventor and an important figure in the European textile machinery industry.

William Cockerill began his career in Lancashire by making 'roving billies' and flying shuttles. He was reputed to have an extraordinary mechanical genius and it is said that he could make models of almost any machine. He followed in the footsteps of many other enterprising British engineers when in 1794 he went to St Petersburg in Russia, having been recommended as a skilful artisan to the Empress Catherine II. After her death two years later, her successor Paul sent Cockerill to prison because he failed to finish a model within a certain time. Cockerill, however, escaped to Sweden where he was commissioned to construct the locks on a public canal. He attempted to introduce textile machinery of his own invention but was unsuccessful and so in 1799 he removed to Verviers, Belgium, where he established himself as a manufacturer of textile machinery. In 1802 he was joined by James Holden, who before long set up his own machine-building business. In 1807 Cockerill moved to Liège where, with his three sons (William Jnr, Charles James and John), he set up factories for the construction of carding machines, spinning frames and looms for the woollen industry. He secured for Verviers supremacy in the woollen trade and introduced at Liège an industry of which England had so far possessed the monopoly. His products were noted for their fine craftsmanship, and in the heyday of the Napoleonic regime about half of his output was sold in France. In 1813 he imported a model of a Watt steam-engine from England and so added another range of products to his firm. Cockerill became a naturalized Belgian subject *c.*1810, and a few years later he retired from the business in favour of his two younger sons, Charles James and John (b. 30 April 1790 Haslingden, Lancashire, England; d. 19 June 1840 Warsaw, Poland), but in 1830 at Andenne he converted a vast factory formerly used for calico printing into a paper mill. Little is known of his eldest son William, but the other two sons expanded the enterprise, setting up a woollen factory at Berlin after 1815 and establishing at Seraing-on-the-Meuse in 1817 blast furnaces, an iron foundry and a machine workshop which became the largest on the European continent. William Cockerill senior died in 1832 at the Château du Behrensberg, the residence of his son Charles James, near Aix-la-Chapelle.

Further Reading
W.O. Henderson, 1961, *The Industrial Revolution on the Continent*, Manchester (a good account of the spread of the Industrial Revolution in Germany, France and Russia).

RTS/RLH

Codd, Hiram

fl. 1850–1900 London, England

English inventor of a mineral-water bottle stopper.

Hiram Codd of Camberwell patented the celebrated Codd mineral-water bottle in 1875. The bottle had a glass marble stopper that was kept pressed against a rubber ring in the neck of the bottle by the internal pressure of the mineral water. Pressure was released by forcing the stopper down. It was most popular in Britain during the period 1890 to 1914, but it was still in use in the 1930s and remained in use in the Far East into the 1990s.

Further Reading
R.W. Douglas and S. Franks, 1972, *A History of Glassmaking*, Henley-on-Thames: G.T. Foulis.

LRD

Cody, 'Colonel' Samuel Franklin

b. probably 6 March 1861 Texas, USA
d. 7 August 1913 Farnborough, England

American (naturalized British) aviation pioneer who made the first sustained aeroplane flight in Britain.

'Colonel' Cody was one of the most colourful and controversial characters in aviation history. He dressed as a cowboy, frequently rode a horse, and appeared on the music-hall stage as a sharpshooter.

Cody lived in England from 1896 and became a British subject in 1909. He wrote a melodrama, *The Klondyke Nugget*, which was first performed in 1898, with Cody as the villain and his wife as the heroine. It was a great success and Cody made enough money to indulge in his hobby of flying large kites. Several man-lifting kites were being developed in the mid-1890s, primarily for military observation purposes. Captain B.S.F. Baden-Powell built multiple hexagonal kites in England, while Lawrence Hargrave, in Australia, developed a very successful boxkite. Cody's man-lifting kites were so good that the British Government engaged him to supply kites, and act as an instructor with the Royal Engineers at the Balloon Factory, Farnborough. Cody's kites were rather like a box-kite with wings and, indeed, some were virtually tethered gliders. In 1905 a Royal Engineer reached a record height of 2,600 ft (790 m) in one of Cody's kites. While at Farnborough, Cody assisted with the construction of the experimental airship 'British Army Dirigible No. 1', later known as *Nulli Secundus*. Cody was on board for the first flight in 1907. In the same year, Cody fitted an engine to one of his kites and it flew with no one on board; he also built a free-flying glider version. He went on to build a powered aeroplane with an Antoinette engine and on 16 October 1908 made a flight of 1,390 ft (424 m) at Farnborough; this was the first real flight in Britain. During the following years, Cody's large 'Flying Cathedral' became a popular sight at aviation meetings, and in 1911 his 'Cathedral' was the only British aeroplane to complete the course in the Circuit of Britain Contest. In 1912 Cody won the first British Military Aeroplane competition (a similar aeroplane is preserved by the Science Museum, London). Unfortunately, Cody and a passenger were killed when his latest aeroplane crashed at Farnborough in 1913; because Cody was such a popular figure at Farnborough, the tree to which he sometimes tethered his aeroplane was preserved as a memorial. Later, there was a great controversy over who the first person to make an aeroplane flight in Britain was, as A.V. **Roe**, Horatio **Phillips** and Cody had all made hops before October 1908; most historians, however, now accept that it was Cody. Cody's title of 'Colonel' was unofficial, although it was used by King George V on one of several visits to see Cody's work.

Bibliography
Cody gave a lecture to the (Royal) Aeronautical Society which was published in their *Aeronautical Journal*, London, January 1909.

Further Reading
P.B. Walker, 1971, *Early Aviation at Farnborough*, 2 vols, London (an authoritative source).
A. Gould Lee, 1965, *The Flying Cathedral*, London (biography).
G.A. Broomfield, 1953, *Pioneer of the Air*, Aldershot (a less-reliable biography).

JDS

Coffey, Aeneas

b. 1779/80 England
d. 26 November 1852 Bromley, England

English inventor of the Coffey still for fractional distillation.

As Surveyor and Inspector General of Excise in Ireland, Coffey was responsible for the suppression of the illicit distilling of alcohol. In 1818 he published a pamphlet refuting charges of oppression and brutality brought against him by Irish revenue officers. He seems to have hunted with the hounds, for as a distiller himself in Dublin, he patented in 1831 the improved form of still that bears his name. The still was quickly adopted by the whisky industry as it accomplished in a single operation what had previously required several stages using the old pot stills. It is still used in the making of potable spirits, and consists of two adjacent columns, an analyser and a rectifier. Steam is passed through the liquor in the analyser, which removes the volatile fraction, and is then fractionally condensed in the rectifier column; almost pure alcohol could be produced by this means.

Further Reading
E.J. Rothery, 1968, *Annals of Science* 24: 53.

LRD

Coignet, François

b. 1814
d. 1888

French pioneer in the development of the structural use of iron reinforcement of concrete.

As early as 1847, Coignet built some houses of

poured (unreinforced) concrete, but in 1852, in a house at 72 rue Charles Michel, in St Denis, he first employed his own system of what he called *béton armé*, meaning reinforced concrete. Coignet exhibited his technique of reinforcement using iron bars at the Paris Exposition of 1855 and was quoted as forecasting that cement, concrete and iron were destined to replace stone. A year later he patented a method of reinforcing concrete with iron *tirants*, a reference to the metal ropes or bars being under tension, and in 1861 he published a treatise on concrete. Coignet is credited with building several examples of concrete shell casing to iron structures in conjunction with different architects – e.g., the Church of Le Vésinet (1863, Seine et Oise).

Further Reading
Nikolaus Pevsner, 1984, *Pioneers of Modern Design*, Penguin.

DY

Colpitts, Edwin Henry
b. 9 January 1872 Pointe de Bute, Canada
d. 6 March 1949 Orange, New Jersey, USA

Canadian physicist and electrical engineer responsible for important developments in electronic-circuit technology.

Colpitts obtained Bachelor's degrees at Mount Allison University, Sackville, New Brunswick, and Harvard in 1894 and 1896, respectively, followed by a Master's degree at Harvard in 1897. After two years as assistant to the professor of physics there, he joined the American Bell Telephone Company. When the Bell Company was reorganized in 1907, he moved to the Western Electric branch of the company in New York as Head of the Physical Laboratories. In 1911 he became a director of the Research Laboratories, and in 1917 he became Assistant Chief Engineer of the company. During this time he invented both the push–pull amplifier and the Colpitts oscillator, both major developments in communications. In 1917, during the First World War, he spent some time in France helping to set up the US Signal Corps Research Laboratories. Afterwards he continued to do much, both technically and as a manager, to place telephone communications on a firm scientific basis, retiring as Vice-President of the Bell Telephone Laboratories in 1937. With the outbreak of the Second World War in 1941 he was recalled from retirement and appointed Director of the Engineering Foundation to work on submarine warfare techniques, particularly echo-ranging.

Principal Honours and Distinctions
Order of the Rising Sun, Japan, 1938. US Medal of Merit 1948.

Bibliography
1919, with E.B. Craft, 'Radio telephony', *Proceedings of the American Institution of Electrical Engineers* 38: 337.
1921, with O.B. Blackwell, 'Carrier current telephony and telegraphy', *American Institute of Electrical Engineers Transactions* 40: 205.
11 September 1915, US reissue patent no. 15,538 (control device for radio signalling).
28 August 1922, US patent no. 1,479,638 (multiple signal reception).

Further Reading
M.D. Fagen, 1975, *A History of Engineering & Science in the Bell System, Vol. 1*, Bell Laboratories.

See also **Hartley, Ralph V.L.**

KF

Colt, Samuel
b. 19 July 1814 Hartford, Connecticut, USA
d. 10 January 1862 Hartford, Connecticut, USA

American inventor of the revolver.

The son of a textile manufacturer, as a youth Colt displayed an interest in chemistry, largely through bleaching and dyeing processes used in his father's business, and lectured to lay audiences on it. In 1832 he took ship as a deckhand on a voyage to India; the concept of the revolver is supposed to have come to him from watching the ship's wheel. Upon his return to the USA he described the idea to the US Patent Office, but did not register it until four years later, having taken out patents in Britain and France during a visit to Europe in 1835. He formed a company to manufacture his invention, but it failed in 1842. Even so, note had been taken of his weapon, and in 1846, upon the outbreak of the war with Mexico, the US Government placed an order for his revolver that was executed by the Eli

Whitney arms factory in his native Hartford. Thereafter Colt set up another company, this time successfully. He also took an interest in other fields, experimenting with a submarine battery and electrically detonated mines, and opened a submarine telegraph between New York and Coney Island in 1843.

CM

Columella, Lucius Iunius Moderatus
b. first century AD Gades (now Cádiz), Spain
d. first century AD Tarentum (now Taranto), Italy

Spanish writer on agricultural practice during the Roman era.

Columella was a native of Gades, a Roman *municipium* in southern Spain. The only knowledge of him is through his writings, in which he makes reference to his uncle, but not to his parents. His uncle was an expert farmer of the region, and it would appear that Columella spent much of his youth with him. As an adult he moved near to Rome, and spent the rest of his life in that region, owning at least three farms in Latium, and a fourth probably near the Etruscan town of Caere. There is evidence that he visited Syria in Cilicia, where it is possible that he was doing military service. His fame lies in the twelve books of the *Res Rustica*, which provide the most detailed extant discussion of Roman agricultural practice, and a single volume on trees. Each volume of *Res Rustica* was addressed and sent to Publius Silvinius as it was completed. The single volume *De Arboribus*, dealing with trees, vines and olives, was addressed to Epruis Marcellus. Columella was quoted by Seneca (4 BC–65 AD) and Pliny the elder (23–79 AD).

Bibliography
1941, *Res Rustica*, Vols I–IV, trans. H. Boyd; Vols V–XII, trans. E.S. Forster and E.H. Heffner, Heinemann, Loeb Classical Library series (Vol. I has a biog. introd. with full bibliographical details).

AP

Congreve, Sir William
b. 20 May 1772 London, England
d. 16 May 1828 Toulouse, France

English developer of military rockets.

He was the eldest son of Lieutenant-General Sir William Congreve, Colonel Commandant of the Royal Artillery, Superintendent of Military Machines and Superintendent Comptroller of the Royal Laboratory at Woolwich, and the daughter of a naval officer. Congreve passed through the Naval Academy at Woolwich and in 1791 was attached to the Royal Laboratory (formerly known as the Woolwich Arsenal), of which his father was then in command. In the 1790s, an Indian prince, Hyder Ali, had had some success against British troops with solid-fuelled rockets, and young Congreve set himself to develop the idea. By about 1806 he had made some 13,000 rockets, each with a range of about 2 km (1¼ miles). The War Office approved their use, and they were first tested in action at sea during the sieges of Boulogne and Copenhagen in 1806 and 1807 respectively. Congreve was commissioned to raise two companies of rocket artillery; in 1813 he commanded one of his rocket companies at the Battle of Leipzig, where although the rockets did little damage to the enemy, the noise and glare of the explosions had a considerable effect in frightening the French and caused great confusion; for this, the Tsar of Russia awarded Congreve a knighthood. The rockets were similarly effective in other battles, including the British attack on Fort McHenry, near Baltimore, in 1814; it is said that this was the inspiration for the lines 'the rocket's red glare, the bombs bursting in air' in Francis Scott Key's poem *The Star Spangled Banner*, which became the United States' national anthem.

Congreve's father died in 1814, and he succeeded him in the baronetcy and as Comptroller of the Royal Laboratory and Superintendent of Military Machines, holding this post until his death. For the last ten years of his life he was Member of Parliament for Plymouth, having previously represented Gatton when elected for that constituency in 1812.

Principal Honours and Distinctions
FRS 1812.

Further Reading
F.H. Winter, 1990, *The First Golden Age of Rocketry: Congreve and Hale Rockets of the Nine-*

teenth Century, Washington, DC: Smithsonian Institution Press.

IMcN

Cooke, William Fothergill
b. 1806 Ealing, London, England
d. 25 June 1879 Farnham, Surrey, England

English physicist, pioneer of electric telegraphy.

The son of a surgeon who became Professor of Anatomy at Durham University, Cooke received a conventional classical education, with no science, in Durham and at Edinburgh University. He joined the East India Company's army in Madras, but resigned because of ill health in 1833. While convalescent, Cooke travelled in Europe and began making wax models of anatomical sections, possibly as teaching aids for his father. In Germany he saw an experimental electric-telegraph demonstration, and was so impressed with the idea of instantaneous long-distance communication that he dropped the modelling and decided to devote all his energies to developing a practical electric telegraph. His own instruments were not successful: they worked across a room, but not over a mile of wire. His search for scientific advice led him to Charles **Wheatstone**, who was working on a similar project, and together they obtained a patent for the first practical electric telegraph. Cooke's business drive and Wheatstone's scientific abilities should have made a perfect partnership, but the two men quarrelled and separated. Cooke's energy and enthusiasm got the telegraph established, first on the newly developing railways, then independently. Sadly, the fortune he made from the telegraph was lost in other ventures, and he died a poor man.

Further Reading
G. Hubbard, 1965, *Cooke and Wheatstone and the Invention of the Electric Telegraph,* London, Routledge & Kegan Paul (provides a short account of Cooke's life; there is no full biography).

BB

Cookworthy, William
b. 1705 Kingsbridge, Devon, England
d. 16 October 1780 Plymouth, England

English pioneer of porcelain manufacture in England.

The family fortunes having been extinguished by the South Sea Bubble of 1720, Cookworthy and his brother had to fend for themselves. They set up, and succeeded, in the pharmacy trade. At the age of 31, however, William left the business, and after a period of probation he became a minister in the Society of Friends. In a letter of 5 May 1745, Cookworthy mentions some samples of kaolin and china or growan stone that had been brought to him from Virginia. He found similar materials at Treginning Hill in Cornwall, and between 1755 and 1758 he found sufficiently pure china clay and china stone to make a pure white porcelain. Cookworthy took out a patent for his discovery in 1768 which covered the manufacture of porcelain from moonstone or growan and growan clay, with a glaze made from china stone to which lime and fern ash or magnesia alba (basic carbonate of magnesium) were added. Cookworthy's experiments had been carried out on the property of Lord Camelford, who later assisted him, in the company of other Quakers, in setting up a works at Coxside, Plymouth, to manufacture the ware; the works employed between fifty and sixty people. In the absence of coal, Cookworthy resorted to wood as fuel, but this was scarce, so in 1770 he transferred his operation to Castle Green, Bristol. However, he had no greater success there, and in 1773 he sold the entire interest in porcelain manufacture to Richard Champion (1743–91), although Cookworthy and his heirs were to receive royalties for ninety-nine years. Champion, who had been working with Cookworthy since 1764 and was active in Bristol city affairs, continued the firm as Richard Champion & Co., but when in 1775 Champion tried to renew Cookworthy's patent, **Wedgwood** and other Staffordshire potters challenged him. After litigation, the use of kaolin and china stone was thrown open to general use. The Staffordshire potters made good use of this newfound freedom and Champion was forced to sell the patent to them and dispose of his factory the following year. The potters of Staffordshire said of Cookworthy, 'the greatest service ever conferred by one person on the pottery manufacturers is that of making them acquainted with china clay'.

Further Reading
W. Harrison, 1854, *Memoir of William Cook-worthy by His Grandson*, London.
F.S. Mackenna, 1946, *Cookworthy's Plymouth and Bristol Porcelain*, Leigh on Sea: Lewis.
A.D. Selleck, 1978, *Cookworthy 1705–80 and his Circle*, privately published.

LRD

Coolidge, William David

b. 23 October 1873 Hudson, Massachusetts, USA
d. 3 February 1975 New York, USA

American physicist and metallurgist who invented a method of producing ductile tungsten wire for electric lamps.

Coolidge obtained his BS from the Massachusetts Institute of Technology (MIT) in 1896, and his PhD (physics) from the University of Leipzig in 1899. He was appointed Assistant Professor of Physics at MIT in 1904, and in 1905 he joined the staff of the General Electric Company's research laboratory at Schenectady. In 1905 Schenectady was trying to make tungsten-filament lamps to counter the competition of the tantalum-filament lamps then being produced by their German rival Siemens. The first tungsten lamps made by Just and Hanaman in Vienna in 1904 had been too fragile for general use. Coolidge and his life-long collaborator, Colin G. Fink, succeeded in 1910 by hot-working directly dense sintered tungsten compacts into wire. This success was the result of a flash of insight by Coolidge, who first perceived that fully recrystallized tungsten wire was always brittle and that only partially work-hardened wire retained a measure of ductility. This grasped, a process was developed which induced ductility into the wire by hot-working at temperatures below those required for full recrystallization, so that an elongated fibrous grain structure was progressively developed. Sintered tungsten ingots were swaged to bar at temperatures around 1,500°C and at the end of the process ductile tungsten filament wire was drawn through diamond dies around 550°C. This process allowed General Electric to dominate the world lamp market. Tungsten lamps consumed only one-third the energy of carbon lamps, and for the first time the cost of electric lighting was reduced to that of gas. Between 1911 and 1914, manufacturing licences for the General Electric patents had been granted for most of the developed work. The validity of the General Electric monopoly was bitterly contested, though in all the litigation that followed, Coolidge's fibering principle was upheld. Commercial arrangements between General Electric and European producers such as Siemens led to the name 'Osram' being commonly applied to any lamp with a drawn tungsten filament. In 1910 Coolidge patented the use of thoria as a particular additive that greatly improved the high-temperature strength of tungsten filaments. From this development sprang the technique of 'dispersion strengthening', still being widely used in the development of high-temperature alloys in the 1990s. In 1913 Coolidge introduced the first controllable hot-cathode X-ray tube, which had a tungsten target and operated *in vacuo* rather than in a gaseous atmosphere. With this equipment, medical radiography could for the first time be safely practised on a routine basis. During the First World War, Coolidge developed portable X-ray units for use in field hospitals, and between the First and Second World Wars he introduced between 1 and 2 million X-ray machines for cancer treatment and for industrial radiography. He became Director of the Schenectady laboratory in 1932, and from 1940 until 1944 he was Vice-President and Director of Research. After retirement he was retained as an X-ray consultant, and in this capacity he attended the Bikini atom bomb trials in 1946. Throughout the Second World War he was a member of the National Defence Research Committee.

Bibliography
1965, 'The development of ductile tungsten', Sorby Centennial Symposium on the History of Metallurgy, *AIME Metallurgy Society Conference*, Vol. 27, ed. Cyril Stanley Smith, Gordon and Breach, pp. 443–9.

Further Reading
D.J. Jones and A. Prince, 1985, 'Tungsten and high density alloys', *Journal of the Historical Metallurgy Society* 19 (1): 72–84.

ASD

Cooper, Peter

b. 12 February 1791 New York, USA
d. 4 April 1883 New York, USA

American entrepreneur and steam locomotive pioneer.

Cooper had minimal formal education, but following a childhood spent helping his small-businessman father, he had by his early twenties become a prosperous glue maker. In 1828, with partners, he set up an ironworks at Baltimore. The Baltimore & Ohio Railroad, intended for horse haulage, was under construction and, to confound those sceptical of the powers of steam, Cooper built a steam locomotive, with vertical boiler and single vertical cylinder, that was so small that it was called *Tom Thumb*. Nevertheless, when on test in 1830, it proved a match for horse power and became one of the first locomotives to run on an American railway. Cooper did not, however, personally take this line of development further; rather, he built up a vast industrial empire and later in life became a noted philanthropist.

Further Reading
J.F. Stover, 1961, *American Railroads*, Chicago: University of Chicago Press.
Dictionary of American Biography.

See also: **Allen, Horatio**; **Stevens, John**; **Winans, Ross**.

PJGR

Corbusier, Le
See **Jeanneret, Charles-Edouard**.

Corliss, George Henry
b. 2 June 1817 Easton, Washington City, New York, USA
d. 21 February 1888 USA

American inventor of a cut-off mechanism linked to the governor which revolutionized the operation of steam engines.

Corliss's father was a physician and surgeon. The son was educated at Greenwich, New York, but while he showed an aptitude for mathematics and mechanics he first of all became a storekeeper and then clerk, bookkeeper, salesperson and official measurer and inspector of the cloth produced at W. Mowbray & Son. He went to the Castleton Academy, Vermont, for three years and at the age of 21 returned to a store of his own in Greenwich. Complaints about stitching

in the boots he sold led him to patent a sewing machine. He approached Fairbanks, Bancroft & Co., Providence, Rhode Island, machine and steam engine builders, about producing his machine, but they agreed to take him on as a draughtsman providing he abandoned it. Corliss moved to Providence with his family and soon revolutionized the design and construction of steam engines. Although he started working out ideas for his engine in 1846 and completed one in 1848 for the Providence Dyeing, Bleaching and Calendering Company, it was not until March 1849 that he obtained a patent. By that time he had joined John Barstow and E.J. Nightingale to form a new company, Corliss Nightingale & Co., to build his design of steam-engines. He used paired valves, two inlet and two exhaust, placed on opposite sides of the cylinder, which gave good thermal properties in the flow of steam. His wrist-plate operating mechanism gave quick opening and his trip mechanism allowed the governor to regulate the closure of the inlet valve, giving maximum expansion for any load. It has been claimed that Corliss should rank equally with James Watt in the development of the steam-engine. The new company bought land in Providence for a factory which was completed in 1856 when the Corliss Engine Company was incorporated. Corliss directed the business activities as well as technical improvements. He took out further patents modifying his valve gear in 1851, 1852, 1859, 1867, 1875, 1880. The business grew until well over 1,000 workers were employed. The cylindrical oscillating valve normally associated with the Corliss engine did not make its appearance until 1850 and was included in the 1859 patent. The impressive beam engine designed for the 1876 Centennial Exhibition by E. **Reynolds** was the product of Corliss's works. Corliss also patented gear-cutting machines, boilers, condensing apparatus and a pumping engine for waterworks. While having little interest in politics, he represented North Providence in the General Assembly of Rhode Island between 1868 and 1870.

Further Reading
Many obituaries appeared in engineering journals at the time of his death.
Dictionary of American Biography, 1930, Vol. IV, New York: C. Scribner's Sons.
R.L. Hills, 1989, *Power from Steam. A History of*

the Stationary Steam Engine, Cambridge University Press (explains Corliss's development of his valve gear).

J.L. Wood, 1980–1, 'The introduction of the Corliss engine to Britain', *Transactions of the Newcomen Society* 52 (provides an account of the introduction of his valve gear to Britain).

W.H. Uhland, 1879, *Corliss Engines and Allied Steam-motors*, London: E. & F.N. Spon.

RLH

Cort, Henry

b. 1740 Lancaster, England
d. 1800 Hampstead, near London, England

English ironmaster, inventor of the puddling process and grooved rollers for forming iron into bars.

His father was a mason and brickmaker but, anxious to improve himself, Cort set up in London in 1765 as a navy agent, said to have been a profitable business. He recognized that, at that time, the conversion of pig iron to malleable or wrought iron, which was needed in increasing quantities as developments in industry and mechanical engineering gathered pace, presented a bottleneck in the ironmaking process. The finery hearth was still in use, slow and inefficient and requiring the scarce charcoal as fuel. To tackle this problem, Cort gave up his business and acquired a furnace and slitting mill at Fontley, near Fareham in Hampshire. In 1784 he patented his puddling process, by which molten pig iron on the bed of a reverberatory furnace was stirred with an iron bar and, by the action of the flame and the oxygen in the air, the carbon in the pig iron was oxidized, leaving nearly pure iron, which could be forged to remove slag. In this type of furnace, the fuel and the molten iron were separated, so that the cheaper coal could be used as fuel. It was the stirring action with the iron bar that gave the name 'puddling' to the process. Others had realized the problem and reached a similar solution, notably the brothers Thomas and George Cranage, but only Cort succeeded in developing a commercially viable process. The laborious hammering of the ball of iron thus produced was much reduced by an invention of the previous year, 1783. This too was patented. The iron was passed between grooved rollers to form it into bars. Cort entered into an agreement with Samuel Jellico to set up an iron-works at Gosport to exploit his inventions. Samuel's father Adam, Deputy Paymaster of the Navy, advanced capital for this venture, Cort having expended much of his own resources in the experimental work that preceded his inventions. However, it transpired that Jellico senior had, unknown to Cort, used public money to advance the capital; the Admiralty acted to recover the money and Cort lost heavily, including the benefits from his patents. Rival ironmasters were quick to pillage the patents. In 1790, and again the following year, Cort offered unsuccessfully to work for the military. Finally, in 1794, at the instigation of the Prime Minister, William Pitt the Younger, Cort was paid a pension of £200 per year in recognition of the value of his improvements in the technology of ironmaking, although this was reduced by deductions to £160. After his death, the pension to his widow was halved, while some of his children received a pittance. Without the advances made by Cort, however, the iron trade could not have met the rapidly increasing demand for iron during the industrial revolution.

Bibliography

1787, *A Brief State of Facts Relative to the New Method of Making Bar Iron with Raw Pit Coal and Grooved Rollers* (held in the Science Museum Library archive collection).

Further Reading

H.W. Dickinson, 1941, 'Henry Cort's bicentary', *Transactions of the Newcomen Society* 21: 31–47 (there are further references to grooved rollers and the puddling process in Vol. 49 of the same periodical (1978), on pp. 153–8).

R.A. Mott, 1983, *Henry Cort, the Great Finery Creator of Puddled Iron*, Sheffield: Historical Metallurgy Society.

LRD

Cosnier, Hugues

b. Angers (?) or Tours (?), France
d. between July 1629 and March 1630

French engineer.

Cosnier was probably an Angevin as he had property in Tours although he lived in Paris; his father was *valet de chambre* to King Henri IV. Although he qualified as an engineer, he was primarily a man of ideas. On 23 December 1603 he obtained a grant to establish silkworm breeding, or sericulture, in Poitou by introducing 100,000 mulberry plants, together with 200 oz (5.7 kg) of mulberry seed. He had 2,000 instruction leaflets on silkworm breeding printed, but his project collapsed when the Poitevins refused to co-operate. Cosnier then distributed the plants and seeds to other parts of France. The same year he approached Henri IV with the proposal to build a canal from the Loire to the Seine, partly via the Loing, from Briare to Montargis. On the king's acceptance of his proposal, Cosnier on 11 March 1604 undertook to complete the canal, which necessitated crossing the ridge between the two rivers, over a three-year period for 505,000 livres. The Canal de Briare, as it became known, with thirty-six locks including the flight of seven at Rogny, was almost complete in 1610; however, the death of Henri IV led to its abandonment. Cosnier offered to complete it at his own expense, but his offer was refused. Instead, his accounts were examined and it was found that he had already exceeded his authorized credits by 35,000 livres. In settlement, after some quibbling, he was awarded the two seigneuries of Trousse near Briare. Cosnier then suggested encircling the Paris suburbs with a canal which would not only be navigable but would also provide a water supply for fountains and drains. His proposal was accepted in 1618, but the works were never started. In the 1620s the marquis d'Effiet proposed the completion of the Canal de Briare and Cosnier was invited to resume work. Before anything more could be done Cosnier died, some time between July 1629 and March 1630, and the work was again abandoned. The canal was ultimately completed by **Boutheroue** in 1642, but the seven locks at Rogny remain a dramatic monument to Cosnier's ability.

Further Reading

P. Pinsseau, 1943, *Le Canal Henri IV ou Canal de Briare*, Paris.

G. Fagniez, 1897, *L'Economie sociale de la France sous Henri IV*, Paris.

JHB

Coster, John

b. *c.*1647 Gloucestershire, England
d. 13 October 1718 Bristol, England

English innovator in the mining, smelting and working of copper.

John Coster, son of an iron-forge manager in the Forest of Dean, by the age of 38 was at Bristol, where he was 'chief agent and sharer therein' in the new lead-smelting methods using coal fuel. In 1685 the work, under Sir Clement **Clerke**, was abandoned because of patent rights claimed by Lord Grandison, who financed of earlier attempts. Clerke's business turned to the coal-fired smelting of copper under Coster, later acknowledged as responsible for the subsequent success through using an improved reverberatory furnace which separated coal fume from the ores being smelted. The new technique, applicable also to lead and tin smelting, revitalized copper production and provided a basis for new British industry in both copper and brass manufacture during the following century. Coster went on to manage a copper-smelting works, and by the 1690s was supplying Esher copper- and brass-works in Surrey from his Redbrook, Gloucestershire, works on the River Wye. In the next decade he extended his activities to Cornish copper mining, buying ore and organizing ore sales, and supplying the four major copper and brass companies which by then had become established. He also made copper goods in additional water-powered rolling and hammer mills acquired in the Bristol area. Coster was ably assisted by three sons; of these, John and Robert were mainly active in Cornwall. In 1714 the younger John, with his father, patented an 'engine for drawing water out of deep mines'. The eldest son, Thomas, was more involved at Redbrook, in South Wales and the Bristol area. A few years after the death of his father, Thomas became partner in the brass company of Bristol and sold them the Redbrook site. He became Member of Parliament for Bristol and, by then the only surviving son, planned a large new smelting works at White Rock, Swansea, South Wales, before his death in 1734. Partners outside the family continued the business under a new name.

Bibliography

1714, British patent 397, with John Coster Jr.

Further Reading

Rhys Jenkins, 1942, 'Copper works at Redbrook and Bristol', *Transactions of the Bristol and*

Gloucestershire Archaeological Society 63.

Joan Day, 1974–6, 'The Costers: copper smelters and manufacturers', *Transactions of the Newcomen Society* 47: 47–58.

JD

Cotchett, Thomas
fl. 1700s

English engineer who set up the first water-powered textile mill in Britain at Derby.

At the beginning of the eighteenth century, silk weaving was one of the most prosperous trades in Britain, but it depended upon raw silk worked up on hand twisting or throwing machines. In 1702 Thomas Cotchett set up a mill for twisting silk by water-power at the northern end of an island in the river Derwent at Derby; this would probably have been to produce organzine, the hard twisted thread used for the warp when weaving silk fabrics. Such mills had been established in Italy beginning with the earliest in Bologna in 1272, but it would appear that Cotchett used Dutch silk-throwing machinery that was driven by a water wheel that was 13½ ft (4.1 m) in diameter and built by the local engineer, George **Sorocold**. The enterprise soon failed, but it was quickly revived and extended by Thomas and John **Lombe** with machinery based on that being used successfully in Italy.

Further Reading

D.M. Smith, 1965, *Industrial Archaeology of the East Midlands*, Newton Abbot (provides an account of Cotchett's mill).

W.H. Chaloner, 1963, 'Sir Thomas Lombe (1685–1739) and the British silk industry', *History Today* (Nov.).

R.L. Hills, 1970, *Power in the Industrial Revolution*, Manchester (a brief coverage of the development of early silk throwing mills).

D. Kuhn, 1988, *Science and Civilisation in China*, Vol. V: *Chemistry and Chemical Technology, Part 9, Textile Technology: spinning and reeling*, Cambridge (covers the diffusion of the techniques of the mechanization of the silk-throwing industry from China to the West).

RLH

Cotton, William
b. 1819 Seagrave, Leicestershire, England
d. after 1878

English inventor of a power-driven flat-bed knitting machine.

Cotton was originally employed in Loughborough and became one of the first specialized hosiery-machine builders. After the introduction of the latch needle by Matthew **Townsend** in 1856, knitting frames developed rapidly. The circular frame was easier to work automatically, but attempts to apply power to the flat frame, which could produce fully fashioned work, culminated in 1863 with William Cotton's machine. In that year he invented a machine that could make a dozen or more stockings or hose simultaneously and knit fashioned garments of all kinds. The difficulty was to reduce automatically the number of stitches in the courses where the hose or garment narrowed to give it shape. Cotton had early opportunities to apply himself to the improvement of hosiery machines while employed in the patent shop of Cartwright & Warner of Loughborough, where some of the first rotaries were made. He remained with the firm for twenty years, during which time sixty or seventy of these machines were turned out. Cotton then established a factory for the manufacture of warp fabrics, and it was here that he began to work on his ideas. He had no knowledge of the principles of engineering or drawing, so his method of making sketches and then getting his ideas roughed out involved much useless labour. After twelve years, in 1863, a patent was issued for the machine that became the basis of the Cotton's Patent type. This was a flat frame driven by rotary mechanism and remarkable for its adaptability. At first he built his machine upright, like a cottage piano, but after much thought and experimentation he conceived the idea of turning the upper part down flat so that the needles were in a vertical position instead of being horizontal, and the work was carried off horizontally instead of vertically. His first machine produced four identical pieces simultaneously, but this number was soon increased. Cotton was induced by the success of his invention to begin machine building as a separate business and thus established one of the first of a class of engineering firms that sprung up as an adjunct to the new hosiery manufacture. He employed only a dozen men and turned out six machines in the first year, entering into an agreement with Hine & Mundella for their exclusive use. This was later extended to the firm of I. & R. Morley. In 1878, Cotton began to build on his own account, and the business steadily increased until it employed some 200 workers and had an output of 100 machines a year.

Bibliography

1863, British patent no. 1,901 (flat-frame knitting machine).

Further Reading

F.A. Wells, 1935, *The British Hosiery and Knitwear Industry: Its History and Organisation*, London (based on an article in the *Knitters' Circular* (Feb. 1898).

A brief account of the background to Cotton's invention can be found in T.K. Derry and T.I. Williams, 1960, *A Short History of Technology from the Earliest Times to AD 1900*, Oxford; C. Singer (ed.), 1958, *A History of Technology*, Vol. V, Oxford: Clarendon Press.

F. Moy Thomas, 1900, *I. & R. Morley. A Record of a Hundred Years*, London (mentions cotton's first machines).

RLH

Cousteau, Jacques-Yves

b. 11 June 1910 Saint-André-de-Cubzac, France

French marine explorer who invented the aqualung.

He was the son of a country lawyer who became legal advisor and travelling companion to certain rich Americans. At an early age Cousteau acquired a love of travel, of the sea and of cinematography: he made his first film at the age of 13. After an interrupted education he nevertheless passed the difficult entrance examination to the Ecole Navale in Brest, but his naval career was cut short in 1936 by injuries received in a serious motor accident. For his long recuperation he was drafted to Toulon. There he met Philippe Tailliez, a fellow naval officer, and Frédéric Dumas, a champion spearfisher, with whom he formed a long association and began to develop his underwater swimming and photography. He apparently took little part in the Second World War, but under cover he applied his photographic skills to espionage, for which he was awarded the Légion d'honneur after the war.

Cousteau sought greater freedom of movement underwater and, with Emile Gagnan, who worked in the laboratory of Air Liquide, he began experimenting to improve portable underwater breathing apparatus. As a result, in 1943 they invented the aqualung. Its simple design and robust construction provided a reliable and low-cost unit and revolutionized scientific and recreational diving. Gagnan shunned publicity, but Cousteau revelled in the new freedom to explore and photograph underwater and exploited the publicity potential to the full.

The Undersea Research Group was set up by the French Navy in 1944 and, based in Toulon, it provided Cousteau with the Opportunity to develop underwater exploration and filming techniques and equipment. Its first aims were minesweeping and exploration, but in 1948 Cousteau pioneered an extension to marine archaeology. In 1950 he raised the funds to acquire a surplus US-built minesweeper, which he fitted out to further his quest for exploration and adventure and named *Calypso*. Cousteau also sought and achieved public acclaim with the publication in 1953 of *The Silent World*, an account of his submarine observations, illustrated by his own brilliant photography. The book was an immediate success and was translated into twenty-two languages. In 1955 *Calypso* sailed through the Red Sea and the western Indian Ocean, and the outcome was a film bearing the same title as the book: it won an Oscar and the Palme d'Or at the Cannes film festival. This was his favoured medium for the expression of his ideas and observations, and a stream of films on the same theme kept his name before the public.

Cousteau's fame earned him appointment by Prince Rainier as Director of the Oceanographic Institute in Monaco in 1957, a post he held until 1988. With its museum and research centre, it offered Cousteau a useful base for his worldwide activities.

In the 1980s Cousteau turned again to technological development. Like others before him, he was concerned to reduce ships' fuel consumption by harnessing wind power. True to form, he raised grants from various sources to fund research and enlisted technical help, namely Lucien Malavard, Professor of Aerodynamics at the Sorbonne. Malavard designed a 44 ft (13.4 m) high non-rotating cylinder, which was fitted onto a catamaran hull, christened *Moulin à vent*. It was intended that its maiden Atlantic crossing in 1983 should herald a new age in ship propulsion, with large royalties to Cousteau. Unfortunately the vessel was damaged in a storm and limped to the USA under diesel power. A more robust vessel, the *Alcyone*, was fitted with two 'Turbosails' in 1985 and proved successful, with a 40 per cent reduction in fuel consumption. However, oil prices fell, removing the incentive to fit the new device; the lucrative sales did not materialize and *Alcyone* remained the only vessel with Turbosails, sharing with *Calypso* Cousteau's voyages of adventure and exploration. In September 1995, Cousteau was among the critics of the decision by the French President Jacques Chirac to resume testing of nuclear explosive devices under the Mururoa atoll in the South Pacific.

Principal Honours and Distinctions
Légion d'honneur. Croix de Guerre with Palm. Officier du Mérite Maritime and numerous scientific and artistic awards listed in such directories as *Who's Who*.

Bibliography
1953, *The Silent World*.
1972, *The Ocean World of Jacques Cousteau*, 21 vols.
He produced many other titles which are listed with his films in *Who's Who*.

Further Reading
R. Munson, 1991, *Cousteau, the Captain and His World*, London: Robert Hale (published in the USA 1989).

LRD

Cowper, Edward Alfred
b. 10 December 1819 London, England
d. 9 May 1893 Weybridge, Surrey, England

English inventor of the hot-blast stove used in ironmaking.

Cowper was apprenticed in 1834 to John Braithwaite of London and in 1846 obtained employment at the engineers Fox & Henderson in Birmingham. In 1851 he was engaged in the contract drawings for the Crystal Palace housing the Great Exhibition, and in the same year he set up in London as a consulting engineer. Cowper designed the 211 ft (64.3 m) span roof of Birmingham railway station, the first large-span station roof to be constructed. Cowper had an inventive turn of mind. While still an apprentice, he devised the well-known railway fog-signal and, at Fox & Henderson, he invented an improved method of casting railway chairs. Other inventions included a compound steam-engine with receiver, patented in 1857; a bicycle wheel with steel spokes and rubber tyre (1868); and an electric writing telegraph (1879). Cowper's most important invention by far was the hot-blast stove, the first application of C.W. **Siemens**'s regenerative principle to ironmaking, patented in 1857. Waste gases from the blast furnace were burnt in an iron chamber lined with a honeycomb of firebricks. When they were hot, the gas was directed to a second similar chamber while the incoming air blast for the blast furnace was heated by passing it through the first chamber. The stoves alternatively received and gave up heat and the heated blast, introduced by J.B. **Neilson**, led to considerable fuel economies in blast-furnace operation; the system is still in use. Cowper played an active part in the engineering institutions of his time, becoming President of the Institution of Mechanical Engineers in 1880-1. He was commissioned by the Science and Art Department to catalogue the collections of machinery and inventions at the South Kensington Museum, whose science collections now form the Science Museum, London.

Principal Honours and Distinctions
President, Institution of Mechanical Engineers 1880-1.

Further Reading
Obituary, 1893, *Journal of the Iron and Steel Institute*: 172–3, London.
W.K.V. Gale, 1969, *Iron and Steel*, London: Longmans, pp. 42, 75 (describes his hot-blast stoves).

LRD

Cowper-Coles, Sherard Osborn
b. 8 October 1866 East Harting, Sussex, England
d. 9 September 1936

English inventor of the sherardizing process for metal protection.

He was the son of Captain Cowper-Coles, Royal Navy, the inventor of the swivelling turret for naval guns. He inherited his father's inventive talents and investigated a variety of inventions in his workshop at his home at Sunbury-on-Thames, assisted by a number of scientific workers. He had been educated by governesses, but he lacked a sound scientific background. His inventions, rarely systematically pursued, ranged from electrolytic processes for making copper sheets and parabolic reflectors to a process for inlaying and decorating metallic surfaces. Overall, however, he is best known for the invention of 'sherardizing', the process for producing a rustproof coating of zinc on small metallic articles. The discovery came by chance, when he was annealing iron and steel packed in zinc dust to exclude air. The metal was found to be coated with a thin layer of zinc with some surface penetration. The first patent for the process was obtained in 1900, and later the American rights were sold, with a company being formed in 1908 to control them. A small plant was set up in Chelsea, London, to develop the process to the point where it could be carried out on a commercial scale in a plant in Willesden. Sherardizing has not been a general protective finish, but is restricted to articles such as nuts and bolts which are then painted or finished. The process was still in use in 1977, operated by the Zinc Alloy Company (London) Ltd.

Further Reading
C.A. Smith, 1978, 'Sherard Cowper-Coles: a review of the inception of sherardizing', *Transactions of the Newcomen Society* 49: 1–4.

LRD

Cælius, Per Anton

b. 2 November 1854 Stockholm, Sweden
d. 7 August 1905 Stockholm, Sweden

Swedish mining engineer, inventor of the core drilling technique for prospecting purposes.

Having completed his studies at the Technological Institute in Stockholm and the Mining School at Falun, Cælius was awarded a grant by the Swedish Jernkontoret and in 1879 he travelled to Germany, France and Belgium in order to study technological aspects of the mining, iron and steel industries. In the same year he went to the United States, where he worked with an iron works in Colorado and a mining company in Nevada. In 1884, having returned to Sweden, he obtained an appointment in the Norberg mines; two years later, he took up employment at the Ängelsberg oilmill.

His mining experience had shown him the demand for a reliable, handy and cheap method of drilling, particularly for prospecting purposes. He had become acquainted with modern drilling methods in America, possibly including Albert Fauck's drilling jar. In 1886, Cælius designed his first small-diameter drill, which was assembled in one unit. Its rotating boring rod, smooth on the outside, was fixed inside a hollow mandrel which could be turned in any direction. This first drill was hand-driven, but the hydraulic version of it became the prototype for all near-surface prospecting drills in use worldwide in the late twentieth century.

Between 1890 and 1900 Cælius was managing director of the Morgårdshammar mechanical workshops, where he was able to continue the development of his drilling apparatus. He successfully applied diesel engines in the 1890s, and in 1895 he added diamond crowns to the drill. The commercial exploitation of the invention was carried out by Svenska Diamantbergborrings AB, of which Cælius was a director from its establishment in 1886.

Further Reading
G. Glockemeier, 1913, *Diamantbohrungen für Schürf- und Aufschlußarbeiten über und unter Tage*, Berlin (examines the technological aspects of Cælius's drilling method).
A. Nachmanson and K. Sundberg, 1936, *Svenska Diamantbergborrings Aktiebolaget 1886–1936*, Uppsala (outlines extensively the merits of Cælius's invention).

See also **Fauvelle, Pierre-Pascal**.

WK

Crampton, Thomas Russell

b. 6 August 1816 Broadstairs, Kent, England
d. 19 April 1888 London, England

English engineer, pioneer of submarine electric telegraphy and inventor of the Crampton locomotive.

After private education and an engineering apprenticeship, Crampton worked under Marc **Brunel**, Daniel **Gooch** and the Rennie brothers before setting up as a civil engineer in 1848. His developing ideas on locomotive design were expressed through a series of five patents taken out between 1842 and 1849, each making a multiplicity of claims. The most typical feature of the Crampton locomotive, however, was a single pair of driving wheels set to the rear of the firebox. This meant they could be of large diameter, while the centre of gravity of the locomotive remained low, for the boiler barrel, though large, had only small carrying-wheels beneath it. The cylinders were approximately midway along the boiler and were outside the frames, as was the valve gear. The result was a steady-riding locomotive which neither pitched about a central driving axle nor hunted from side to side, as did other contemporary locomotives, and its working parts were unusually accessible for maintenance. However, adhesive weight was limited and the long wheelbase tended to damage track. Locomotives of this type were soon superseded on British railways, although they lasted much longer in Germany and France. Locomotives built to the later patents incorporated a long, coupled wheelbase with drive through an intermediate crankshaft, but they mostly had only short lives. In 1851 Crampton, with associates, laid the first successful submarine electric telegraph cable. The previous year the brothers Jacob and John Brett had laid a cable, comprising a copper wire insulated with gutta-percha, beneath the English Channel from Dover to Cap Gris Nez: signals were passed but within a few hours the cable failed. Crampton joined the Bretts' company, put up half the capital needed for another attempt, and designed a much stronger cable. Four gutta-percha-insulated copper wires were twisted together, surrounded by tarred hemp and armoured by galvanized iron wires; this cable was successful.

Crampton was also active in railway civil engineering and in water and gas engineering, and *c.*1882 he invented a hydraulic tunnel-boring machine intended for a Channel tunnel.

Principal Honours and Distinctions

Vice-President, Institution of Mechanical Engineers. Officier de la Légion d'Honneur (France).

Bibliography

1842, British patent no. 9,261.
1845, British patent no. 10,854.
1846, British patent no. 11,349.
1847, British patent no. 11,760.
1849, British patent no. 12,627.
1885, British patent no. 14,021.

Further Reading

M. Sharman, 1933, *The Crampton Locomotive*, Swindon: M. Sharman; P.C. Dewhurst, 1956–7, 'The Crampton locomotive', Parts I and II, *Transactions of the Newcomen Society* 30: 99 (the most important recent publications on Crampton's locomotives).
C. Hamilton Ellis, 1958, *Twenty Locomotive Men*, Shepperton: Ian Allen.
J. Kieve, 1973, *The Electric Telegraph*, Newton Abbot: David & Charles, 102–4.
R.B. Matkin, 1979, 'Thomas Crampton: Man of Kent', *Industrial Past* 6 (2).

PJGR

Craufurd, Henry William
fl. 1830s

English patentee of the process of coating iron with zinc (galvanized iron).

Although described as Commander of the Royal Navy, other personal details of Craufurd appear to be little known. His process for coating sheet iron with a protective layer of zinc, conveyed as a communication from abroad, was granted a patent in 1837. The details closely resembled, indeed are believed to have been based upon, those developed and patented in France in 1836 by Sorel, who had worked in collaboration with Ledru. There had been French interest in substituting zinc for tin as a coating for iron from 1742 with work by **Malouin**. Zinc-coated iron saucepans were produced in Rouen in the 1780s, but the work was later abandoned. Craufurd's patent directed that iron objects should be dipped into molten zinc, protected from volatilization by a layer of sal ammoniac (ammonium chloride, NH_4Cl which also served as a flux. The quite misleading term 'galvanizing' had already been introduced by Sorel for his process. Later its protective properties were discovered to depend for effectiveness on the formation of a thin layer of zinc–iron alloy between the iron sheet and its zinc coating. Craufurd's patent was infringed in England soon after being granted, and was followed by several improvements, particularly those of Edmund Morewood, collaborating with George Rogers in five patents, of which four referred to methods of corrugation. The resulting production of zinc-coated iron implements, together with corrugated iron sheeting quickly adopted for building purposes, developed into an important industry of the West Midlands, Bristol, London and other parts of Britain.

Bibliography
1837, British patent no. 7,355 (coating sheet iron with zinc).

Further Reading
H.W. Dickinson, 1943–4, 'A study of galvanised and corrugated sheet metal', *Transactions of the Newcomen Society* 24: 27–36 (the best and most concise account).

JD

Crawford, John William Croom
b. 13 January 1891
d. 5 May 1987

English chemist who pioneered the manufacture of Perspex.

In 1934, by a brilliant piece of research at Imperial Chemical Industries at Ardeer, Crawford devised the synthetic method of making the monomer from which Perspex is derived, based on acetone, methanol, cyanamide and sulphuric acid. This was the basis of the commercial production of Perspex and is still in use. Crawford left ICI to work for a time at University College, Dublin, and returned to England in 1964.

Further Reading
C.E.D. Miles, 1955, *A History of Research in the Nobel Division of ICI*, ICI, p. 132.

LRD

Crompton, Rookes Evelyn Bell
b. 31 May 1845 near Thirsk, Yorkshire, England
d. 15 February 1940 Azerley Chase, Ripon, Yorkshire, England

English electrical and transport engineer.

Crompton was the youngest son of a widely travelled diplomat who had retired to the country and become a Whig MP after the Reform Act of 1832. During the Crimean War Crompton's father was in Gibraltar as a commander in the militia. Young Crompton enrolled as a cadet and sailed to Sebastopol, visiting an older brother, and, although only 11 years old, he qualified for the Crimean Medal. Returning to England, he was sent to Harrow, where he showed an aptitude for engineering. In the holidays he made a steam road engine on his father's estate. On leaving school he was commissioned into the Rifle Brigade and spent four years in India, where he worked on a system of steam road haulage to replace bullock trains. Leaving the Army in 1875, Crompton bought a share in an agricultural and general engineering business in Chelmsford, intending to develop his interests in transport. He became involved in the newly developing technology of electric arc lighting and began importing electric lighting equipment made by Gramme in Paris. Crompton soon decided that he could manufacture better equipment himself, and the Chemlsford business was transformed into Crompton & Co., electrical engineers. After lighting a number of markets and railway stations, Crompton won contracts for lighting the new Law Courts in London, in 1882, and the Ring Theatre in Vienna in 1883. Crompton's interests then broadened to include domestic electrical appliances, especially heating and cooking apparatus, which provided a daytime load when lighting was not required. In 1899 he went to South Africa with the Electrical Engineers Volunteer Corps, providing telegraphs and searchlights in the Boer War. He was appointed Engineer to the new Road Board in 1910, and during the First World War worked for the Government on engineering problems associated with munitions and tanks. He believed strongly in the value of engineering standards, and in 1906 became the first Secretary of the International Electrotechnical Commission.

Bibliography
1928, *Reminiscences*.

Further Reading
B. Bowers, 1969, *R.E.B. Crompton. Pioneer Electrical Engineer*, London: Science Museum.

BB

Crompton, Samuel

b. 3 December 1753 Firwood, near Bolton,
Lancashire, England
d. 26 June 1827 Bolton, Lancashire, England

English inventor of the spinning mule.

Samuel Crompton was the son of a tenant farmer, George, who became the caretaker of the old house Hall-i-th-Wood, near Bolton, where he died in 1759. As a boy, Samuel helped his widowed mother in various tasks at home, including weaving. He liked music and made his own violin, with which he later was to earn some money to pay for tools for building his spinning mule. He was set to work at spinning and so in 1769 became familiar with the spinning jenny designed by James **Hargreaves**; he soon noticed the poor quality of the yarn produced and its tendency to break. Crompton became so exasperated with the jenny that in 1772 he decided to improve it. After seven years' work, in 1779 he produced his famous spinning 'mule'. He built the first one entirely by himself, principally from wood. He adapted rollers similar to those already patented by **Arkwright** for drawing out the cotton rovings, but it seems that he did not know of Arkwright's invention. The rollers were placed at the back of the mule and paid out the fibres to the spindles, which were mounted on a moving carriage that was drawn away from the rollers as the yarn was paid out. The spindles were rotated to put in twist. At the end of the draw, or shortly before, the rollers were stopped but the spindles continued to rotate. This not only twisted the yarn further, but slightly stretched it and so helped to even out any irregularities; it was this feature that gave the mule yarn extra quality. Then, after the spindles had been turned backwards to unwind the yarn from their tips, they were rotated in the spinning direction again and the yarn was wound on as the carriage was pushed up to the rollers.

The mule was a very versatile machine, making it possible to spin almost every type of yarn. In fact, Samuel Crompton was soon producing yarn of a much finer quality than had ever been spun in Bolton, and people attempted to break into Hall-i-th-Wood to see how he produced it. Crompton did not patent his invention, perhaps because it consisted basically of the essential features of the earlier machines of Hargreaves and Arkwright, or perhaps through lack of funds.

Under promise of a generous subscription, he disclosed his invention to the spinning industry, but was shabbily treated because most of the promised money was never paid. Crompton's first mule had forty-eight spindles, but it did not long remain in its original form for many people started to make improvements to it. The mule soon became more popular than Arkwright's waterframe because it could spin such fine yarn, which enabled weavers to produce the best muslin cloth, rivalling that woven in India and leading to an enormous expansion in the British cotton-textile industry. Crompton eventually saved enough capital to set up as a manufacturer himself and around 1784 he experimented with an improved carding engine, although he was not successful. In 1800, local manufacturers raised a sum of £500 for him, and eventually in 1812 he received a government grant of £5,000, but this was trifling in relation to the immense financial benefits his invention had conferred on the industry, to say nothing of his expenses. When Crompton was seeking evidence in 1811 to support his claim for financial assistance, he found that there were 4,209,570 mule spindles compared with 155,880 jenny and 310,516 waterframe spindles. He later set up as a bleacher and again as a cotton manufacturer, but only the gift of a small annuity by his friends saved him from dying in total poverty.

Further Reading

H.C. Cameron, 1951, *Samuel Crompton, Inventor of the Spinning Mule*, London (a rather discursive biography).
Dobson & Barlow Ltd, 1927, *Samuel Crompton, the Inventor of the Spinning Mule*, Bolton.
G.J. French, 1859, *The Life and Times of Samuel Crompton, Inventor of the Spinning Machine Called the Mule*, London.
The invention of the mule is fully described in H. Catling, 1970, *The Spinning Mule*, Newton Abbot; W. English, 1969, *The Textile Industry*, London; R.L. Hills, 1970, *Power in the Industrial Revolution*, Manchester.
C. Singer (ed.), 1958, *A History of Technology*, Vol. IV, Oxford: Clarendon Press (provides a brief account).

RLH

Crompton, Thomas Bonsor

b. 1791/2
d. 1858

English papermaker and inventor of a drying machine.

The papermaking machine developed by the **Fourdrinier** brothers in 1807 produced a reel of paper which was cut into sheets, which were then hung up to dry in a loft. The paper often became badly cockled as a result, and ways were sought to improve the drying part of the process. Drying cylinders were introduced, but the first real benefit came from the use of dry felt in Crompton's drying machine. Various materials could be used, but Crompton found that felt made from linen wrap and a woollen weft was best. In 1820 he took out a patent for steam-heated drying cylinders, and in the following year a patent for a cutter to cut the paper reel into sheets. With Crompton's improvements, the papermaking machine assumed its modern form in essentials. In 1839 Crompton installed centrifugal air fans for reciprocating suction pumps in the suction boxes to extract water from the paper on the continuous wire mould. Crompton owned and operated a successful paper mill at Farnworth in Lancashire, supplying the principal merchants and newspaper publishers in London. He was also a cotton manufacturer and, for a time, owned the *Morning Post* and other newspapers. By the time he died in 1858 he had amassed a considerable fortune.

Further Reading
R.H. Clapperton, 1967, *The Paper-making Machine*, London: Pergamon Press.

LRD

Crookes, Sir William

b. 17 June 1832 London, England
d. 4 April 1919 London, England

English chemist and physicist who carried out studies of electrical discharges and cathode rays in rarefied gases, leading to the development of the cathode ray tube; discoverer of the element thallium and the principle of the Crookes radiometer.

Crookes entered the Royal College of Chemistry at the age of 15, and from 1850 to 1854 held the appointment of Assistant at the college. In 1854

he became Superintendent of the Meteorological Department at the Radcliffe Observatory in Oxford. He moved to a post at the College of Science in Chester the following year. Soon after this he inherited a large fortune and set up his own private laboratory in London. There he studied the nature of electrical discharges in gases at low pressure and discovered the dark space (later named after him) that surrounds the negative electrode, or cathode. He also established that the rays produced in the process (subsequently shown by J.J. Thompson to be a stream of electrons) not only travelled in straight lines, but were also capable of producing heat and/or light upon impact with suitable anode materials. Using a variety of new methods to investigate these 'cathode' rays, he applied them to the spectral analysis of compounds of selenium and, as a result, in 1861 he discovered the element thallium, finally establishing its atomic weight in 1873. Following his discovery of thallium, he became involved in two main lines of research: the properties of rarified gases, and the investigation of the elements of the 'rare earths'. It was also during these experiments that he discovered the principle of the Crookes radiometer, a device in which light is converted into rotational motion and which used to be found frequently in the shop windows of English opticians. Also among the fruits of this work were the Crookes tubes and the development of spectacle lenses with differential ranges of radiational absorption. In the 1870s he became interested in spiritualism and acquired a reputation for his studies of psychic phenomena, but at the turn of the century he returned to traditional scientific investigations. In 1892 he wrote about the possibility of wireless telegraphy. His work in the field of radioactivity led to the invention of the spinthariscope, an early type of detector of alpha particles. In 1900 he undertook investigations into uranium which led to the study of scintillation, an important tool in the study of radioactivity.

While the theoretical basis of his work has not stood the test of time, his material discoveries, observations and investigations of new facts formed a basis on which others such as J.J. Thomson were to develop subatomic theory. His later involvement in the investigation of spiritualism led to much criticism, but could be justified on the basis of a belief in the duty to investigate all phenomena.

Principal Honours and Distinctions
Knighted 1897. Order of Merit 1910. FRS 1863. President, Royal Society 1913–15. Honorary LLD Birmingham. Honorary DSc Oxon, Cambridge, Sheffield, Durham, Ireland and Cape of Good Hope.

Bibliography
1874, *On Attraction and Repulsion Resulting from Radiation.*
1874, 'Researches in the phenomenon of spiritualism', *Society of Metaphysics;* reprinted in facsimile, 1986.
For many years he was also Proprietor and Editor of *Chemical News.*

Further Reading
E.E. Fournier D'Albe, 1923, *Life of Sir William Crookes.*
Who Was Who II, 1916–28, London: A. & C. Black.
T.I. Williams, 1969, *A Biographical Dictionary of Scientists.*

See also **Braun, Karl Ferdinand**.

KF/MG

Cros, Charles
b. 1842 France
d. 1888

French doctor, painter and man of letters who pioneered research into colour photography.

A man of considerable intellect, Cros occupied himself with studies of topics as diverse as Sanskrit and the synthesis of precious stones. He was in particular interested in the possibility of colour photography, and deposited an account of his theories in a sealed envelope with the Académie des Sciences on 2 December 1867, with instructions that it should be opened in 1876. Learning of a forthcoming presentation on colour photography by **Ducos du Hauron** at the Société Française de Photographie, he arranged for the contents of his communication to be published on 25 February 1869 in *Les Mondes*. At the Société's meeting on 7 May 1869, Cros's letter was read and samples of colour photography from Ducos du Hauron were shown. Both had arrived at similar conclusions: that colour photography was possible with the analysis of colours using negatives exposed through red, green and blue

filters, as demonstrated by Clerk Maxwell in 1861. These records could be reproduced by combining positive images produced in blue-green, magenta and yellow pigments or dyes. Cros and Ducos du Hauron had discovered the principle of subtractive colour photography, which is used in the late twentieth century. In 1878 Cros designed the Chromometre, a device for measuring colours by mixing red, green and blue light, and described the device in a paper to the Société Française de Photographie on 10 January 1879. With suitable modification, the device could be used as a viewer for colour photographs, combining red, green and blue positives. In 1880 he patented the principle of imbibition printing, in which dye taken up by a gelatine relief image could be transferred to another support. This principle, which he called *hydrotypie*, readily made possible the production of three-colour subtractive photographic prints.

Further Reading
J.S. Friedman, 1944, *History of Colour Photography*, Boston.
Gert Koshofer, 1981, *Farbefotografie*, Vol. I, Munich.

BC

Cros, Hortensius Emile Charles
b. 1 October 1842 Fabrezan (Aude), France
d. 9 August 1888 Paris, France

French inventor of chromolithography and the principles of reproducible sound recording.

He received no formal education, but was brought up by his father, a distinguished teacher and philosopher. He dabbled in diverse subjects (modern and ancient languages, mathematics, drawing) in 1856–60 when he became an instructor at the institute of the Deaf-Mute at Paris. He became a prolific inventor and poet and took part in artistic life in Paris. In the 1867 Exposition Universelle in Paris, Cros contributed a facsimile telegraph; he deposited with the Académie des Sciences a sealed text on photography which was not opened until 1876. In the meantime he published a small text on a general solution of the problem of colour photography which appeared almost simultaneously with a similar publication by Louis **Ducos du Hauron** and which gave rise to bitter discussions over priority. He deposited a sealed paper on 18 April

1877 concerning his concept of apparatus for recording and reproduction of sound which he called the *paléophone*. When it was opened on 3 December 1877 it was not known that T.A. **Edison** was already active in this field: Cros is considered the conceptual founder of reproducible sound, whereas Edison was the first 'to reduce to practice', which is one of the US criteria for patentability.

Bibliography
French patent no. 124,213 (filed 1 May and 2 August 1878).

Further Reading
Louis Forestier, 1969, *Charles Cros: L'Homme et l'oeuvre*, Paris: Seghers.

GB-N

Crosby, Caresse
b. 1892
d. 1970

American promoter, and possibly inventor, of the brassiere.

Caresse Crosby, born Mary Phelps Jacob, was a New York socialite. She became a debutante and is reputed to have invented the brassiere. In fact, a soft-topped corset had been patented by a London foundation-garment maker, Kate Morgan, in 1903, and a separate brassiere had been advertised in the magazine *Vogue* in America in 1909. However, it was Mrs Crosby and her personal maid who popularized the idea in 1913. Together they assembled two handkerchiefs and a sufficient length of pink ribbon into a garment of sufficient structural strength and flexibility for the average woman. Mrs Crosby adopted the name Caresse to please her second husband, the millionaire poet Harry Crosby (1898–1929).

Further Reading
1982, *Inventions that Changed the World*, Readers Digest.

IMcN

Cross, Charles Frederick
b. 11 December 1855 Brentwood, Middlesex, England
d. 15 April 1935 Hove, England

English chemist who contributed to the development of viscose rayon from cellulose.

Cross was educated at the universities of London, Zurich and Manchester. It was at Owens College, Manchester, that Cross first met E.J. **Bevan** and where these two first worked together on the nature of cellulose. After gaining some industrial experience, Cross joined Bevan to set up a partnership in London as analytical and consulting chemists, specializing in the chemistry and technology of cellulose and lignin. They were at the Jodrell laboratory, Kew Gardens, for a time and then set up their own laboratory at Station Avenue, Kew Gardens. In 1888, the first edition of their joint publication *A Textbook of Paper-making*, appeared. It went into several editions and became the standard reference and textbook on the subject. The long introductory chapter is a discourse on cellulose.

In 1892, Cross, Bevan and Clayton Beadle took out their historic patent on the solution and regeneration of cellulose. The modern artificial-fibre industry stems from this patent. They made their discovery at New Court, Carey Street, London: wood-pulp (or another cheap form of cellulose) was dissolved in a mixture of carbon disulphide and aqueous alkali to produce sodium xanthate. After maturing, it was squirted through fine holes into dilute acid, which set the liquid to give spinnable fibres of 'viscose'. However, it was many years before the process became a commercial operation, partly because the use of a natural raw material such as wood involved variations in chemical content and each batch might react differently. At first it was thought that viscose might be suitable for incandescent lamp filaments, and C.H. Stearn, a collaborator with Cross, continued to investigate this possibility, but the sheen on the fibres suggested that viscose might be made into artificial silk. The original Viscose Spinning Syndicate was formed in 1894 and a place was rented at Erith in Kent. However, it was not until some skeins of artificial silk (a term to which Cross himself objected) were displayed in Paris that textile manufacturers began to take an interest in it. It was then that Courtaulds decided to investigate this new fibre, although it was not until 1904 that they bought the English patents and developed the first artificial silk that was later called 'rayon'. Cross was also concerned with the development of viscose films and of cellulose acetate, which became a rival to rayon in the form of 'Celanese'. He retained his interest in the paper industry and in publishing, in 1895 again collaborating with Bevan and publishing a book on *Cellulose* and other technical articles. He was a cultured man and a good musician. He was elected a Fellow of the Royal Society in 1917.

Principal Honours and Distinctions
FRS 1917.

Bibliography
1888, with E.J. Bevan, *A Text-book of Paper-making*.
1892, British patent no. 8,700 (cellulose).

Further Reading
Obituary Notices of the Royal Society, 1935, London.
Obituary, 1935, *Journal of the Chemical Society* 1,337.
Chambers Concise Dictionary of Scientists, 1989, Cambridge.
Edwin J. Beer, 1962–3, 'The birth of viscose rayon, *Transactions of the Newcomen Society* 35 (an account of the problems of developing viscose rayon; Beer worked under Cross in the Kew laboratories).
C. Singer (ed.), 1978, *A History of Technology*, Vol. VI, Oxford: Clarendon Press.

RLH

Crossley, Sir Francis
b. 26 October 1817 Halifax, England
d. 5 January 1872 Belle Vue, Halifax, England

English developer of a power loom for weaving carpets.

Francis Crossley was the youngest of three brothers employed in their father's carpet-weaving business in Halifax and who took over the running of the company on their father's death in 1837. Francis seems to have been the one with technical ability, for it was he who saw the possibilities of weaving by power. Growth of the company was rapid through his policy of acquiring patents and then improving them, and it was soon at the forefront of the carpet-manufacturing trade. He had taken out rights on the patents of John Hill of Manchester, but his experiments with Hill's looms for weaving carpets were not successful.

In the spring of 1850 Francis asked a textile inventor, George Collier of Barnsley, to develop a power loom for carpet manufacture. Collier produced a model that was a distinct advance on earlier looms, and Francis engaged him to perfect a power loom for weaving tapestry and Brussels carpets. After a great deal of money had been expended, a patent was taken out in 1850 in the name of his brother, Joseph **Crossley**, for a loom that could weave velvet as well as carpets and included some of the ideas of the American E.B. **Bigelow**. This new loom proved to be a great advance on all the earlier ones, and thus brought the Crossleys a great fortune from both sales of patent rights and the production of carpets from their mills, which were soon enlarged.

According to the *Dictionary of National Biography*, Francis Crossley was Mayor of Halifax in 1849 and 1850, but Hogg gives this position to his elder brother John. In 1852 Francis was returned to Parliament as the Liberal member for Halifax, and in 1859 he became the member for the West Riding. Among his benefactions, in 1855 he gave to the town of Halifax a twelve-acre park that cost £41,300; a statue of him was erected there. In the same year he endowed twenty-one almshouses. In 1863 a baronetcy was conferred upon him in recognition of his commercial and public services, which he continued to perform until his death. In 1870 he gave the London Missionary Society £20,000, their largest single donation up to that time, and another £10,000 to the Congregational Pastor's Retiring Fund. He became ill when on a journey to the Holy Land in 1869, but although he made a partial recovery he grew worse again towards the end of 1871 and died early in the following year. He left £800,000 in his will.

Principal Honours and Distinctions
Baronet 1863.

Further Reading
Obituary, 1872, *The Times* 6 January.
Dictionary of National Biography.
J. Hogg (ed.), n.d., *Fortunes Made in Business*, London (provides an account of Crossley's career).

RLH

Crossley, Joseph

b. Halifax (?), England
d. September 1868 Halifax (?), England

*English patentee of successful power-driven
carpet looms.*

Joseph Crossley was the second son of John, the
founder of a carpet-weaving firm in Halifax. He
did not figure much in public life for he was essentially a business man. It was under his direct
superintendence that most of the extensions at
Dean Clough Mill, Halifax, were built, and to a
very great degree the successful working of the
vast establishment that these mills became,
covering fifteen acres, was due to him. In 1864
the firm became a limited-liability company,
worth over a million pounds *c.*1880.

The company's vital patents for the power-
driven carpet looms were taken out in his name.
The first, in 1850 in the names of Joseph Crossley,
George Collier and James Hudson, was for weaving carpets in a manner similar to the way velvet was
woven, with the pile warp threads passing over
wires. After a couple of picks of weft, a wire was
inserted from the side over the main warp threads
but under the pile warp threads. These were lowered and another couple of weft shoots bound in
the pile warp. The pile was cut with a knife running
along a slot in the top of the wire, and then the wire
was removed. There was a further patent in 1851,
in the name of Joseph Crossley alone, for improvements in the manufacture of Brussels and cut-pile
carpets. An interesting part of this patent was the
use of a partly coloured warp to make patterns in
the carpets. These vital patents gave the Crossley
brothers their dominance in carpet weaving; production on their power looms was six times quicker
than by hand. Like his brothers, one of whom was
Francis **Crossley**, he was a great benefactor to
charities. The brothers built the Crossley Orphan
Home at a cost of £50,000 and endowed it with
about £3,000 a year.

Bibliography
1850, British patent no. 13,267 (power-driven
carpet loom).
1851, British patent no. 13,474 (improvements
in manufacture of Brussels and cut-pile carpets).

Further Reading
J. Hogg (ed.), *Fortunes Made in Business,*

London (contains an account of the firm of
John Crossley & Sons).

RLH

Cruickshank, William

d. 1810/11 Scotland

*Scottish chemist and surgeon, inventor of a
trough battery developed from Volta's pile.*

Cruickshank graduated MA from King's College, Aberdeen, in 1765, and later gained a Diploma of the Royal College of Surgeons. When
chemistry was introduced in 1788 into the
course at the Royal Military Academy in Woolwich, Cruickshank became a member of staff,
serving as Assistant to Dr A. Crawford, the Lecturer in Chemistry. Upon Crawford's death in
1796 Cruickshank succeeded him as Lecturer
and held the post until his retirement due to ill
health in 1804. He also held the senior posts of
Chemist to the Ordnance at Woolwich and Surgeon to the Ordnance Medical Department. He
should not be confused with William Cumberland Cruickshank (1745–1800), who was also a
surgeon and Fellow of the Royal Society. In
1801, shortly after **Volta**'s announcement of his
pile, Cruickshank built a voltaic pile to facilitate
his experiments in electrochemistry. The pile had
zinc and silver plates about $1\frac{1}{2}$ in^2 (10 cm^2)
with interposed papers moistened with am-
monium chloride. Dissatisfied with this arrangement, Cruickshank devised a horizontal trough
battery in which a wooden box was divided into
cells, each holding a pair of zinc and silver or zinc
and copper plates. Charged with a dilute solution
of ammonium chloride, the battery, which was
typically of sixty cells, was found to be more convenient to use than a pile and it, or a derivative,
was generally adopted for electrochemical experiments including tose of Humphrey **Davy**
during the early years of the nineteenth century.

Principal Honours and Distinctions
FRS 1802.

Bibliography
1801, article in *Nicholsons Journal* 4: 187–91
(describes Cruickshank's original pile).
1801, article in *Nicholsons Journal* 4: 245–64
(describes his trough battery).

Further Reading
B. Bowers, 1982, *A History of Electric Light and Power*, London (a short account).
A. Coutts, 1959, 'William Cruickshank', *Annals of Science* 15: 121–33

GW

Ctesibius (Ktesibios) of Alexandria
fl. *c.*270 BC Alexandria

Alexandrian mechanician and inventor.

Ctesibius made a number of inventions of great importance, which he described in his book *Pneumatics,* now lost. The Roman engineer and architect **Vitruvius** quoted extracts from Ctesibius' work in his *De Architectura* and tells us that Ctesibius was the son of a barber and that he arranged an adjustable mirror controlled by a lead counterweight descending in a cylinder. He noticed that the weight compressed the air, which could be released with a loud noise. That led him to realize that the air was a body or substance: by means of a cylinder and plunger, he went on to invent an air pump with valves. This he connected to the keyboard and rows of pipes of an organ. He also invented a force pump for water.

Ctesibius also improved the *clepsydra* or water clock, which measured time by the fall of water level in a vessel as the water escaped through a hole in the bottom. The rate of flow varied as the level dropped, so Ctesibius interposed a cistern with an overflow pipe, enabling the water level to be maintained; there was thus a constant flow into a cylinder and the passage of time was indicated by a float with a pointer. He fitted a rack to the float which turned a toothed wheel, to activate bells, singing birds or other 'toys'. This is probably the first known use of toothed gearing.

Ctesibius is credited with some other inventions of a military nature, such as a catapult, but it was his pumps that established a tradition in antiquity for mechanical invention using the pressure of the air and other fluids, stretching through Philo of Byzantium (*c.*150 BC) and **Hero** of Alexandria (*c.* 62 AD) and on through Islam into medieval Western Europe.

Further Reading
A.G. Drachmann, 1948, *Ktesibios, Philon and Heron: A Study in Ancient Pneumatics,* Copen-hagen: Munksgaard (*Acta Hist. Sci. Nat. Med.* 4).

LRD

Cubitt, Thomas
b. 25 February 1788 Buxton, Norfolk, England
d. 20 December 1855 Dorking, Surrey, England

English master builder and founder of the first building firm of modern type.

He started his working life as a carpenter at a time when work in different trades such as bricklaying, masonry, carpentry and plumbing was subcontracted. The system had worked well enough until about 1800, but when large-scale development was required, as in the nineteenth century, it showed itself to be inefficient and slow. To avoid long delays in building, Cubitt bought land and established workshops, founding a firm that employed all the craftsmen necessary to the building trade on a permanent-wage basis. To keep his firm financially solvent he had to provide continuous work for his staff, which he achieved by large-scale, speculative building even while maintaining high architectural standards.

Cubitt performed a major service to London, with many of his houses, squares and terraces still surviving as sound and elegant as they were over 150 years ago in the large estates he laid out. His most ambitious enterprise was Belgravia, where he built 200 imposing houses for the aristocracy upon an area of previously swampy land that he leased from Lord Grosvenor. His houses expose as inferior much of the later phases of development which surround them. All his life Cubitt used his influence to combat the abuses of architecture, building and living standards to which speculative building is heir. He was especially interested in drainage, smoke control and London's sewage arrangement, and constantly worked to improve these. He supplied first-class amenities in the way of land drainage, sewage disposal, street lighting and roads, and his own houses were soundly built, pleasant to live in and created to last.

Further Reading
Hermione Hobhouse, 1971, *Thomas Cubitt: Master Builder*, Macmillan.
Henry Russell-Hitchcock, 1976, *Early Victorian Architecture*, 2 vols, New York: Da Capo.

DY

Cubitt, William

b. 1785 Dilham, Norfolk, England
d. 13 October 1861 Clapham Common, Surrey, England

English civil engineer and contractor.

The son of a miller, he received a rudimentary education in the village school. At an early age he was helping his father in the mill, and in 1800 he was apprenticed to a cabinet maker. After four years he returned to work with his father, but, preferring to leave the parental home, he not long afterwards joined a firm of agricultural-machinery makers in Swanton in Norfolk. There he acquired a reputation for making accurate patterns for the iron caster and demonstrated a talent for mechanical invention, patenting a self-regulating windmill sail in 1807. He then set up on his own as a millwright, but he found he could better himself by joining the engineering works of Ransomes of Ipswich in 1812. He was soon appointed their Chief Engineer, and after nine years he became a partner in the firm until he moved to London in 1826. Around 1818 he invented the treadmill, with the aim of putting prisoners to useful work in grinding corn and other applications. It was rapidly adopted by the principal prisons, more as a means of punishment than an instrument of useful work.

From 1814 Cubitt had been gaining experience in civil engineering, and upon his removal to London his career in this field began to take off. He was engaged on many canal-building projects, including the Oxford and Liverpool Junction canals. He accomplished some notable dock works, such as the Bute docks at Cardiff, the Middlesborough docks and the coal drops on the river Tees. He improved navigation on the river Severn and compiled valuable reports on a number of other leading rivers.

The railway construction boom of the 1840s provided him with fresh opportunities. He engineered the South Eastern Railway (SER) with its daringly constructed line below the cliffs between Folkestone and Dover; the railway was completed in 1843, using massive charges of explosive to blast a way through the cliffs. Cubitt was Consulting Engineer to the Great Northern Railway and tried, with less than his usual success, to get the atmospheric system to work on the Croydon Railway.

When the SER began a steamer service between Folkestone and Boulogne, Cubitt was engaged to improve the port facilities there and went on to act as Consulting Engineer to the Boulogne and Amiens Railway. Other commissions on the European continent included surveying the line between Paris and Lyons, advising the Hanoverian government on the harbour and docks at Hamburg and directing the water-supply works for Berlin.

Cubitt was actively involved in the erection of the Crystal Palace for the Great Exhibition of 1851; in recognition of this work Queen Victoria knighted him at Windsor Castle on 23 December 1851.

Cubitt's son Joseph (1811–72) was also a notable civil engineer, with many railway and harbour works to his credit.

Principal Honours and Distinctions

Knighted 1851. FRS 1830. President, Institution of Civil Engineers 1850 and 1851.

Further Reading

Obituary, 1862, *Minutes of the Proceedings of the Institution of Civil Engineers* 21: 552–8.

LRD

Cugnot, Nicolas Joseph

b. 26 February 1725 Void, Meuse, France
d. 2 October 1804 Paris, France

French military engineer.

Cugnot studied military engineering in Germany and returned to Paris by 1769, having left the service of Austria, where he taught military engineering. It was while serving in the army of Les Pays Bas that he invented a 'fusil' or carbine, which was adopted by the Archduke Charles and put into service in the Uhlan regiments.

In 1769 he invented a *fardier à feu*, also called a *cabriolet*, a steam-driven, heavy three-wheeled vehicle. This tractor, designed to pull artillery pieces, was driven through its single front wheel by two single-acting cylinders which rotated the wheel through ratchets. The ratchet pawls were carried on levers pivoted on the wheel axis, coupled to the piston rods by connecting rods. Links from pivots half-way along the levers connected upwards to a rocking cross-beam fixed on the end of the steam cock so as to pass steam alternately from the undersized boiler to the two cylinders. The tractor had to be stopped whenever it needed stoking, and its maximum speed was 4 mph (6.4 km/h). The difficulty of controlling it led to its early demolition of a wall, after which it was locked away and eventually preserved in the Conservatoire des Arts et Métiers in Paris. This was, in fact, Cugnot's second vehicle: the first model was presented to the duc de Choiseul et Guiberuval, who asked for a more robust and powerful machine which was built at the Arsenal at the expense of the state and tested in 1771. Cugnot was granted a pension of 600 livres. After the revolution he tried in vain in 1798 and 1801 to interest Bonaparte in this invention.

Bibliography
Cugnot published a number of military textbooks, including:
1766, *Eléments de l'art militaire*.
1769, *Fortification et campagne théorie et practice*.
1778, *Theory of Fortification*.

Further Reading
D.J.H. Day, 1980, *Engines*.
A.F. Burstall, 1963, *A History of Mechanical Engineering*.
1933, *Dictionnaire de biographie française*.

IMcN

Curr, John
b. 1756 Kyo, near Lanchester, or in Greenside, near Ryton-on-Tyne, Durham, England
d. 27 January 1823 Sheffield, England

English coal-mine manager and engineer, inventor of flanged, cast-iron plate rails.

The son of a 'coal viewer', Curr was brought up in the West Durham colliery district. In 1777 he went to the Duke of Norfolk's collieries at Sheffield, where in 1880 he was appointed Superintendent. There coal was conveyed underground in baskets on sledges: Curr replaced the wicker sledges with wheeled corves, i.e. small four-wheeled wooden wagons, running on 'rail-roads' with cast-iron rails and hauled from the coal-face to the shaft bottom by horses. The rails employed hitherto had usually consisted of plates of iron, the flange being on the wheels of the wagon. Curr's new design involved flanges on the rails which guided the vehicles, the wheels of which were unflanged and could run on any hard

surface. He appears to have left no precise record of the date that he did this, and surviving records have been interpreted as implying various dates between 1776 and 1787. In 1787 John **Buddle** paid tribute to the efficiency of the rails of Curr's type, which were first used for surface transport by Joseph Butler in 1788 at his iron furnace at Wingerworth near Chesterfield: their use was then promoted widely by Benjamin **Outram**, and they were adopted in many other English mines. They proved serviceable until the advent of locomotives demanded different rails.

In 1788 Curr also developed a system for drawing a full corve up a mine shaft while lowering an empty one, with guides to separate them. At the surface the corves were automatically emptied by tipplers. Four years later he was awarded a patent for using double ropes for lifting heavier loads. As the weight of the rope itself became a considerable problem with the increasing depth of the shafts, Curr invented the flat hemp rope, patented in 1798, which consisted of several small round ropes stitched together and lapped upon itself in winding. It acted as a counterbalance and led to a reduction in the time and cost of hoisting: at the beginning of a run the loaded rope began to coil upon a small diameter, gradually increasing, while the unloaded rope began to coil off a large diameter, gradually decreasing.

Curr's book *The Coal Viewer* (1797) is the earliest-known engineering work on railway track and it also contains the most elaborate description of a **Newcomen** pumping engine, at the highest state of its development. He became an acknowledged expert on construction of Newcomen-type atmospheric engines, and in 1792 he established a foundry to make parts for railways and engines.

Because of the poor financial results of the Duke of Norfolk's collieries at the end of the century, Curr was dismissed in 1801 despite numerous inventions and improvements which he had introduced. After his dismissal, six more of his patents were concerned with rope-making: the one he gained in 1813 referred to the application of flat ropes to horse-gins and perpendicular drum-shafts of steam engines. Curr also introduced the use of inclined planes, where a descending train of full corves pulled up an empty one, and he was one of the pioneers employing fixed steam engines for hauling. He may have resided in France for some time before his death.

Bibliography
1788, British patent no. 1,660 (guides in mine shafts).
1789, *An Account of an Improved Method of Drawing Coals and Extracting Ores, etc., from Mines*, Newcastle upon Tyne.
1797, *The Coal Viewer and Engine Builder's Practical Companion*; reprinted with five plates and an introduction by Charles E. Lee, 1970, London: Frank Cass, and New York: Augustus M. Kelley.
1798, British patent no. 2,270 (flat hemp ropes).

Further Reading
F. Bland, 1930–1, 'John Curr, originator of iron tram roads', *Transactions of the Newcomen Society* 11: 121–30.
R.A. Mott, 1969, 'Tramroads of the eighteenth century and their originator: John Curr', *Transactions of the Newcomen Society* 42: 1–23 (includes corrections to Fred Bland's earlier paper).
Charles E. Lee, 1970, introduction to John Curr, *The Coal Viewer and Engine Builder's Practical Companion*, London: Frank Cass, pp. 1–4; orig. pub. 1797, Sheffield (contains the most comprehensive biographical information).
R. Galloway, 1898, *Annals of Coalmining*, Vol. I, London; reprinted 1971, London (provides a detailed account of Curr's technological alterations).

WK/PJGR

Curtiss, Glenn Hammond

b. 21 May 1878 Hammondsport, New York, USA
d. 23 July 1930 Buffalo, New York, USA

American designer of aeroplanes, especially seaplanes.

Curtiss started his career in the bicycle business, then became a designer of motor-cycle engines, and in 1904 he designed and built an airship engine. The success of his engine led to him joining the Aerial Experimental Association (AEA), founded by the inventor Alexander Graham **Bell**. Working with the AEA, Curtiss built several engines and designed a biplane, *June Bug*, in which he won a prize for the first recorded flight of over 1 km (1,100 yd) in the USA. In 1909 Curtiss joined forces with Augustus M. Herring, who had earlier flown Octave **Chanute**'s gliders, to form the Herring–Curtiss Company. Their *Gold Bug* was a success and led to the *Golden Flyer*, in which Glenn Curtiss won the Gordon Bennett Cup at Rheims in France with a speed of 75.7 km/h (47 mph). At this time the **Wright** brothers accused Curtiss and the new Curtiss Aeroplane Company of infringing their patent rights, and a bitter lawsuit ensued. The acrimony subsided during the First World War and in 1929 the two companies merged to form the Curtiss–Wright Corporation.

Curtiss had started experimenting with water-based aircraft in 1908, but it was not until 1911 that he managed to produce a successful float-plane. He then co-operated with the US Navy in developing catapults to launch aircraft from ships at sea. During the First World War, Curtiss produced the *JN-4 Jenny* trainer, which became probably his best-known design. This sturdy bi-plane continued in service long after the war and was extensively used by 'barnstorming' pilots at air shows and for early mail flights. In 1919 a Navy–Curtiss *NC-4* flying boat achieved the first flight across the Atlantic, having made the crossing in stages, refuelling en route. Curtiss himself, however, had little interest in aviation in his later years and turned his attention to real-estate development in Florida.

Principal Honours and Distinctions
Robert J. Collier Trophy 1911, 1912. US Aero Club Gold Medal 1911, 1912. Smithsonian Institution Langley Gold Medal 1913.

Further Reading
L.S. Casey, 1981, *Curtiss: The Hammondsport Era 1907–1915*, New York.
C.R. Roseberry, 1972, *Glenn Curtiss, Pioneer of Flight*, New York.
R. Taylor and Walter S. Taylor, 1968, *Over Land and Sea*, New York (biography).
Alden Heath, 1942, *Glenn Curtiss: Pioneer of Naval Aviation*, New York.

JDS

Cushing, Harvey Williams

b. 8 April 1869 Cleveland, Ohio, USA
d. 7 October 1939 New Haven, Connecticut, USA

American neurosurgeon and innovator of antihaemorrhagic techniques including the use of electrocoagulation.

Cushing graduated in medicine from Harvard University in 1895, having already acquired an arts degree at Yale (1891). He held posts in Boston and at Johns Hopkins Hospital, Baltimore, from 1897 until 1890, and then travelled abroad. After studying in Germany and England he returned to Baltimore to become Assistant Professor of Surgery in 1903 working under W.S. **Halsted**, a post he held until 1912. In 1905 he started specializing in neurosurgery, undertaking much experimental work and developing new instruments and techniques, such as spinal anaesthesia and in particular the electrosurgical methods pioneered by W.T. **Bovie**.

Returning to Harvard as Professor of Surgery, he established a renowned school of neurosurgery. He retired from Harvard in 1932, becoming Stirling Professor of Neurosurgery until 1937 and then Director of Studies in the History of Medicine at Yale.

His researches in neurophysiology were extensive and the eponymous pituitary syndrome is only one of a large number of discoveries in the field. He was awarded numerous honours, both American and international. He was a noted bibliophile, particularly of medical books and manuscripts, and his own extensive collection was bequeathed to Yale, becoming an important part of the Historical Medical Library.

Bibliography
1928, 'Electrosurgery as an aid to the removal of intracranial tumours', *Surg. Gynec. Obstet.*
1912, *The Pituitary Body and its Disorders.*
1928, *Tumours Arising from the Blood-vessels of the Brain.*
1925, *Life of Sir William Osler.*

Further Reading
J.F. Fulton, 1946, *Harvey Cushing: A Biography.*
MG

D

Daft, Leo

b. 13 November 1843 Birmingham, England
d. 28 March 1922

*English electrical engineer, pioneer of
electric-power generation and electric railways
in the USA.*

Leo Daft, son of a British civil engineer, studied electricity and emigrated to the USA in 1866. After various occupations including running a photographic studio, he joined in 1879 the New York Electric Light Company, which was soon merged into the Daft Electric Company. This company developed electrically powered machinery and built electric-power plants. In 1883 Daft built an electric locomotive called Ampere for the Saratoga & Mount McGregor Railroad. This is said to have been the first electric main-line locomotive for standard gauge. It collected current from a central rail, had an output of 12 hp (9 kW) and hauled 10 tons at speeds up to 9 mph (14.5 km/h). Two years later Daft made a much improved locomotive for the New York Elevated Railway, the Benjamin Franklin, which drew current at 250 volts from a central rail and had two 48 in.(122 cm)-diameter driving wheels and two 33 in.(84 cm)-diameter trailing wheels. Re-equipped in 1888 with four driving wheels and a 125 hp (93 kW) motor, this could haul an eight-car train at 10 mph (16 km/h). Meanwhile, in 1884, Daft's company had manufactured all the electrical apparatus for the Massachusetts Electric Power Company, the first instance of a complete central station to generate and distribute electricity for power on a commercial scale. In 1885 it electrified a branch of the Baltimore Union Passenger Railway, the first electrically operated railway in the USA. Subsequently Daft invented a process for vulcanizing rubber onto metal that came into general use. He never became an American citizen.

Further Reading
Dictionary of American Biography.
F.J.G. Haut, 1969, *The History of the Electric Locomotive*, London: George Allen & Unwin.

See also **Siemens, Dr Ernst Werner von**.

PJGR

Dagron, Prudent René-Patrice

b. 1819 Beaumont, France
d. June 1900 Paris, France

*French photographer who specialized in
microphotography.*

Dagron studied chemistry, but little else is known of his early career. He was the proprietor of a Paris shop selling stationery and office equipment in 1860, when he proposed making microscopic photographs mounted in jewellery. Dagron went on to produce examples using equipment constructed by the optician Debozcq. In 1864 Dagron became one of the celebrities of the day when he recorded 450 portraits on a single photograph that measured 1 mm^3. The image was viewed by means of a tiny magnifying lens popularly known as a 'Stanhope' after its supposed inventor, the English Lord Charles Stanhope. The great demand for Stanhoped jewellery soon allowed Dagron to build a factory for its manufacture. Dagron's main claim to fame rests on his work during the Franco-Prussian War. At the siege of Paris, Dagron was ballooned out of the city to organize a carrier-pigeon communication service. Thousands of microphotographed dispatches could be carried by a single pigeon, and Dagron set up a regular service between Paris and Tours. In Paris the messages from the outside world were enlarged and projected onto a white wall and transcribed by a team of clerks. After the war, Dagron dabbled in aerial photography from balloons, but his interest in microphotography continued until his death in 1900.

Further Reading
G. Tissandier, 1874, *Les Merveilles de la*

photographie, Paris (a contemporary account of Dagron's work during the siege of Paris).

H. Gernsheim and A. Gernsheim, 1969, *The History of Photography*, rev. edn, London.

JW

Daguerre, Louis Jacques Mandé

b. 18 November 1787 Carmeilles-en-Parisis, France
d. 10 July 1851 Petit-Bry-sur-Marne, France

French inventor of the first practicable photographic process.

The son of a minor official in a magistrate's court, Daguerre showed an early aptitude for drawing. He was first apprenticed to an architect, but in 1804 he moved to Paris to learn the art of stage design. He was particularly interested in perspective and lighting, and later showed great ingenuity in lighting stage sets. Fascinated by a popular form of entertainment of the period, the panorama, he went on to create a variant of it called the diorama. It is assumed that he used a camera obscura for perspective drawings and, by purchasing it from the optician **Chevalier**, he made contact with Joseph Nicéphore **Niepce**. In 1829 Niepce and Daguerre entered into a formal partnership to perfect Niepce's heliographic process, but the partnership was dissolved when Niepce died in 1833, when only limited progress had been made. Daguerre continued experimenting alone, however, using iodine and silver plates; by 1837 he had discovered that images formed in the camera obscura could be developed by mercury vapour and fixed with a hot salt solution. After unsuccessfully attempting to sell his process, Daguerre approached F.J.D. Arago, of the Académie des Sciences, who announced the discovery in 1839. Details of Daguerre's work were not published until August of that year when the process was presented free to the world, except England. With considerable business acumen, Daguerre had quietly patented the process through an agent, Miles Berry, in London a few days earlier. He also granted a monopoly to make and sell his camera to a Monsieur Giroux, a stationer by trade who happened to be a relation of Daguerre's wife. The daguerreotype process caused a sensation when announced. Daguerre was granted a pension by a grateful government and honours were showered upon him all over the world. It was a direct

positive process on silvered copper plates and, in fact, proved to be a technological dead end. The future was to lie with negative–positive photography devised by Daguerre's British contemporary, W.H.F. **Talbot**, although Daguerre's was the first practicable photographic process to be announced. It captured the public's imagination and in an improved form was to dominate professional photographic practice for more than a decade.

Principal Honours and Distinctions

Officier de la Légion d'honneur 1839. Honorary FRS 1839. Honorary Fellow of the National Academy of Design, New York, 1839. Honorary Fellow of the Vienna Academy 1843. Pour le Mérite, bestowed by Frederick William IV of Prussia, 1843.

Bibliography

14 August 1839, British patent no. 8,194 (daguerrotype photographic process).

The announcement and details of Daguerre's invention were published in both serious and popular English journals. See, for example, 1839 publications of *Athenaeum*, *Literary Gazette*, *Magazine of Science* and *Mechanics Magazine*.

Further Reading

H. Gernsheim and A. Gernsheim, 1956, *L.J.M. Daguerre* (the standard account of Daguerre's work).

— 1969, *The History of Photography*, rev. edn, London (a very full account).

J.M. Eder, 1945, *History of Photography*, trans. E. Epstean, New York (a very full account).

JW

Daimler, Gottlieb

b. 17 March 1834 Schorndorff, near Stuttgart, Germany
d. 6 March 1900 Cannstatt, near Stuttgart, Germany

German engineer, pioneer automobile maker.

The son of a baker, his youthful interest in technical affairs led to his being apprenticed to a gunsmith with whom he produced his apprenticeship piece: a double-barrelled pistol with a rifled barrel and 'nicely chased scrollwork', for which he received high praise. He remained there until

1852 before going to technical school in Stuttgart from 1853 to 1857. He then went to a steam-engineering company in Strasbourg to gain practical experience. He completed his formal education at Stuttgart Polytechnik, and in 1861 he left to tour France and England. There he worked in the engine-shop of Smith, Peacock & Tanner and then with Roberts & Co., textile machinery manufacturers of Manchester. He later moved to Coventry to work at Whitworths, and it was in that city that he was later involved with the Daimler Motor Company, who had been granted a licence by his company in Germany. In 1867 he was working at Bruderhaus Engineering Works at Reutlingen and in 1869 went to Maschinenbau Gesellschaft Karlsruhe where he became Manager and later a director. Early in the 1870s, N.A. **Otto** had reorganized his company into Gasmotorenfabrik Deutz and he appointed Gottlieb Daimler as Factory Manager and Wilhelm **Maybach** as Chief Designer. Together they developed the Otto engine to its limit, with Otto's co-operation. Daimler and Maybach had met previously when both were working at Bruderhaus. In 1875 Daimler left Deutz, taking Maybach with him to set up a factory in Stuttgart to manufacture light, high-speed internal-combustion engines. Their first patent was granted in 1883. This was for an engine fuelled by petrol and with hot tube ignition which continued to be used until Robert **Bosch**'s low-voltage ignition became available in 1897. Two years later he produced his first vehicle, a motor cycle with outriggers. They showed a motor car at the Paris exhibition in 1889, but French manufacturers were slow to come forward and no French company could be found to undertake manufacture. Eventually Panhard and Levassor established the Daimler engine in France. Daimler Motoren GmbH was started in 1895, but soon after Daimler and Maybach parted, having provided an engine for a boat on the River Neckar in 1887 and that for the Wolfert airship in 1888. Daimler was in sole charge of the company from 1895, but his health began to decline in 1899 and he died in 1900.

Further Reading
E. Johnson, 1986, *The Dawn of Motoring*.
P. Siebetz, 1942, *Gottlieb Daimler*.

IMcN

Dakin, Henry Drysdale
b. 12 March 1880 Hampstead, England
d. 10 February 1952 Scarborough-on-Hudson, New York, USA

English biochemist, advocate and exponent of the treatment of wounds with antiseptic fluid, Dakin's solution (Eusol).

The youngest of a family of eight of moderate means, Dakin received his early education in Leeds experiencing strict scientific training as a public analyst. He regarded this as having been of the utmost value to him in his lifelong commitment to the emerging discipline of biochemistry.

He was one of the earliest to specialize in the significance of optical activity in organic chemistry, and obtained his BSc from Manchester in 1901. Following this, he worked at the Lister (Jenner) Institute of Preventive Medicine and at Heidelberg. He then received an invitation to join Christian Herter in a private research laboratory that had been established in New York. There, for the rest of his life, he continued his studies into a wide variety of biochemical topics. Christian Herter died in 1910, and six years later his widow and Dakin were married.

Unable to serve in the First World War, he made a major contribution, in collaboration with **Carrel**, with the technique for the antiseptic irrigation of wounds with a buffered hypochlorite solution (Eusol), a therapy which in the 1990s is still an accepted approach to the treatment of infected wounds. The original trials were carried out on the liner *Aquitania*, then serving as a hospital ship in the Dardanelles.

Principal Honours and Distinctions
Fellow of the Royal Society 1917. Davy Medal 1941. Honorary doctorates, Yale, Leeds and Heidelberg Universities.

Bibliography
1915, 'On the use of certain antiseptic substances in the treatment of infected wounds', *British Medical Journal*.
1915, with A. Carrel, 'Traitement abortif de l'infection des plaies', *Bulletin of the Academy of Medicine*.

MG

Dale, David

b. 6 January 1739 Stewarton, Ayrshire, Scotland
d. 17 March 1806 Glasgow, Scotland

Scottish developer of a large textile business in and around Glasgow, including the cotton-spinning mills at New Lanark.

David Dale, the son of a grocer, began his working life by herding cattle. His connection with the textile industry started when he was apprenticed to a Paisley weaver. After this he travelled the country buying home-spun linen yarns, which he sold in Glasgow. At about the age of 24 he settled in Glasgow as Clerk to a silk merchant. He then started a business importing fine yarns from France and Holland for weaving good-quality cloths such as cambrics. Dale was to become one of the pre-eminent yarn dealers in Scotland. In 1778 he acquired the first cotton-spinning mill built in Scotland by an English company at Rothesay on the Isle of Bute. In 1784 he met Richard **Arkwright**, who was touring Scotland, and together they visited the Falls of the Clyde near the town of Lanark. Arkwright immediately recognized the potential of the site for driving water-powered mills. Dale acquired part of the area from Lord Braxfield and in 1785 began to build his first mill there in partnership with Arkwright. The association with Arkwright soon ceased, however, and by *c.*1795 Dale had erected four mills. Because the location of the mills was remote, he built houses for the workers and then employed pauper children brought from the slums of Edinburgh and Glasgow; at one time there were over 400 of them. Dale's attitude to his workers was benevolent and humane. He tried to provide reasonable working conditions and the mills were well designed with a large workshop in which machinery was constructed. Dale was also a partner in mills at Catrine, Newton Stewart, Spinningdale in Sutherlandshire and some others. In 1785 he established the first Turkey red dye works in Scotland and was in partnership with George Macintosh, the father of Charles **Macintosh**. Dale manufactured cloth in Glasgow and from 1783 was Agent for the Royal Bank of Scotland, a lucrative position. In 1799 he was persuaded by Robert **Owen** to sell the New Lanark mills for £60,000 to a Manchester partnership which made Owen the Manager. Owen had married Dale's daughter, Anne Caroline, in 1799. Possibly due in part to poor health, Dale retired in 1800 to Rosebank near Glasgow, having made a large fortune. In 1770 he had withdrawn from the established Church of Scotland and founded a new one called the 'Old Independents'. He visited the various branches of this Church, as well as convicts in Bridewell prison, to preach. He was also a great benefactor to the poor in Glasgow. He had a taste for music and sang old Scottish songs with great gusto.

Further Reading
Dictionary of National Biography.
R. Owen, 1857, *The Life of Robert Owen, written by himself*, London (mentions Dale).
Through his association with New Lanark and Robert Owen, details about Dale may be found in J. Butt (ed.), 1971, *Robert Owen, Prince of Cotton Spinners*, Newton Abbot; S. Pollard and J. Salt (eds), 1971, *Robert Owen, Prophet of the Poor: essays in honour of the two-hundredth anniversary of his birth*, London.

RLH

Dalen, Nils Gustav

b. 30 November 1869 Stenstorp, Sweden
d. 9 December 1937 Stockholm, Sweden

Swedish physicist and engineer who was awarded the Nobel Prize for his 'sun valve'.

Nils Gustav Dalen is probably best known as the inventor of the solid-fuel Aga Cooker. He was confined at home for some time in the 1920s, having been blinded as the result of an accident, and found the time to consider the need for an efficient, clean, attractive-looking cooker that would be economical in fuel consumption. The resultant cooking range of 1924 was based on sound scientific principles, was simple to manage and needed a minimum of attention.

The first Aga contained a cast-iron firebox enclosed in an insulated jacket of kieselguhr. The firebox was connected to cast-iron hotplates and ovens, all designed so that the heat was conducted to the various parts at precisely the correct temperatures for all types of cooking: simmering, boiling, roasting, baking and grilling. The hotplate heat was maintained at the desired temperature by way of insulated hinged covers that were lifted only when the hotplate was in use. The Aga was made in Sweden and was introduced into Britain in 1929. It was noted for being costly to purchase but inexpensive to run as no energy was wasted.

Dalen is also known for his invention of the 'sun valve', a device which, as required, automatically lighted or extinguished light beacons and buoys; this invention brought him the Nobel Prize for Physics in 1912.

DY

Dallmeyer, John Henry

b. 6 September 1830 Loxten, Westphalia, Germany
d. 30 December 1883 at sea off New Zealand

German/English manufacturing optician and lens designer.

Son-in-law of the great optician Andrew **Ross**, for whom he worked, Dallmeyer founded his own business in 1860, in which year he introduced his triple achromat lens, which combined the features of a flat field, high definition, a wide angle of view and straight marginal lines, eliminating both the barrel distortion given by the single achromat and the pincushion distortion of the orthochromatic lens. In 1866 he patented the Rectilinear lens, a double achromat pattern which remained in use for over half a century. His portrait lenses, based on the **Petzval** pattern, were widely used throughout the nineteenth century in studios around the world. Ill health forced Dallmeyer's retirement from business in 1882.

BC

Dallmeyer, Thomas Rudolphus

b. May 1859
d. 25 December 1906

English camera-lens designer.

The second son of J.H. **Dallmeyer**, after graduating at King's College he joined his father's factory, learning lens grinding and optical brass-work manufacture. When his father retired because of ill health in 1882, he took over the business, in which he remained active until his death. He made many improvements in lens design, chiefly in his introduction of the first practical telephoto lens in 1891, for which he received the Progress Medal of the Royal Photographic Society in 1896. He also developed a number of variable focal length lenses, including

the soft-focus Bergheim Portrait lens of 1896.

BC

Dallos, Joseph

b. 1906 Budapest, Hungary
d. 27 June 1979 London, England

Hungarian ophthalmologist and contact-lens specialist who pioneered the technique of individually fitted moulded-glass contact lenses.

Dallos graduated from the University of Budapest in 1929 and almost at once specialized in contact-lens work and was appointed Assistant Professor. At that time the fitting of lenses was and had been, since their inception *c*.1885, a matter of trial and error. He developed a method of taking a moulding of the surface of the eye and then producing a blown-glass lens to this shape. His work was based on a concept of corneal physiology and the need to maintain its normal respiration and metabolism.

In 1937 he was invited to England to set up a centre in London making these innovations available. During the Second World War he worked in collaboration with the services and their special needs, and at its conclusion was invited to work at Moorfields Eye Hospital and later at the Western Opthalmic Hospital. Although plastic materials have now superseded Dallos's technology, the fundamental basis of his work remains relevant.

Bibliography
1933, 'Über Haftgläser und Kontaktschalen', *Klin. med. Augenheilk.*
1937, 'The individual fitting of contact lenses', *Trans. Ophth. Soc. UK.*
1930–37, Papers in the *Klinische Monatsblätter für Augenheilkunde.*

Further Reading
S. Duke-Elder, 1970, *System of Ophthalmology*, Vol. 5, London.

MG

Dancer, John Benjamin

b. 1812 England
d. 1887 England

English instrument maker and photographer, pioneer of microphotography.

The son of a scientific instrument maker, Dancer

was educated privately in Liverpool, where from 1817 his father practised his trade. John Benjamin became a skilled instrument maker in his own right, assisting in the family business until his father's death in 1835. He set up on his own in Liverpool in 1840 and in Manchester in 1841. In the course of his career Dancer made instruments for several of the leading scientists of the day, his clients including **Brewster**, Dalton and Joule.

Dancer became interested in photography as soon as the new art was announced in 1839 and practised the processes of both **Talbot** and **Daguerre**. It was later claimed that as early as 1839 he used an achromatic lens combination to produce a minute image on a daguerreotype plate, arguably the world's first microphotograph and the precursor of modern microfilm. It was not until the introduction of **Archer**'s wet-collodion process in 1851 that Dancer was able to perfect the technique however. He went on to market a long series of microphotographs which proved extremely popular with both the public and contemporary photographers. It was examples of Dancer's microphotographs that prompted the French photographer **Dagron** to begin his work in the same field. In 1853 Dancer constructed a binocular stereoscopic camera, the first practicable instrument of its type. In an improved form it was patented and marketed in 1856.

Dancer also made important contributions to the magic lantern. He was the first to suggest the use of limelight as an illuminant, pioneered the use of photographic lantern slides and devised an ingenious means of switching gas from one lantern illuminant to another to produce what were known as dissolving views. He was a resourceful innovator in other fields of instrumentation and suggested several other minor improvements to scientific apparatus before his working life was sadly terminated by the loss of his sight.

Further Reading

Anon., 1973, 'John Benjamin Dancer, originator of microphotography', *British Journal of Photography* (16 February): 139–41.

H. Gernsheim and A. Gernsheim, 1969, *The History of Photography*, rev. edn, London.

JW

Daniell, John Frederick
b. 12 March 1790 London, England
d. 13 March 1845 London, England

English chemist, inventor of the Daniell primary electric cell.

With an early bias towards science, Daniell's interest in chemistry was formed when he joined a relative's sugar-refining business. He formed a lifelong friendship with W.T. Brande, Professor of Chemistry at the Royal Institution, and together they revived the journal of the Royal Institution, to which Daniell submitted many of his early papers on chemical subjects. He made many contributions to the science of meteorology and in 1820 invented a hydrometer, which became widely used and gave precision to the measurement of atmospheric moisture. As one of the originators of the Society for Promoting Useful Knowledge, Daniell edited several of its early publications. His work on crystallization established his reputation as a chemist and in 1831 he was appointed the first Professor of Chemistry at King's College, London, where he was largely responsible for establishing its department of applied science. He was also involved in the Chemical Society of London and served as its Vice-President. At King's College he began the research into current electricity with which his name is particularly associated. His investigations into the zinc–copper cell revealed that the rapid decline in power was due to hydrogen gas being liberated at the positive electrode. Daniell's cell, invented in 1836, employed a zinc electrode in dilute sulphuric acid and a copper electrode in a solution of copper sulphate, the electrodes being separated by a porous membrane, typically an unglazed earthenware pot. He was awarded the Copley Medal of the Royal Society for his invention which avoided the 'polarization' of the simple cell and provided a further source of current for electrical research and for commercial applications such as electroplating. Although the high internal resistance of the Daniell cell limited the current and the potential was only 1.1 volts, the voltage was so unchanging that it was used as a reference standard until the 1870s, when J. Lattimer Clark devised an even more stable cell.

Principal Honours and Distinctions
FRS 1814. Royal Society Rumford Medal 1832, Copley Medal 1837, Royal Medal 1842.

Bibliography

1836, 'On voltaic combinations', *Phil. Transactions of the Royal Society* 126: 107–24, 125–9 (the first report of his experiments).

Listings of his scientific papers can be found in *Catalogue of Scientific Papers*, 1868, Vol. II, London: Royal Society.

Further Reading

Obituary, 1845, *Proceedings of the Royal Society*, 5: 577–80.

J.R. Partington, 1964, *History of Chemistry*, Vol. IV, London (describes the Daniell cell and his electrical researches).

B. Bowers, 1982, *History of Electric Light and Power*, London.

GW

Darby, Abraham

b. 1678 near Dudley, Worcestershire, England
d. 5 May 1717 Madely Court, Coalbrookdale, Shropshire, England

English ironmaster, inventor of the coke smelting of iron ore.

Darby's father, John, was a farmer who also worked a small forge to produce nails and other ironware needed on the farm. He was brought up in the Society of Friends, or Quakers, and this community remained important throughout his personal and working life. Darby was apprenticed to Jonathan Freeth, a malt-mill maker in Birmingham, and on completion of his apprenticeship in 1699 he took up the trade himself in Bristol. Probably in 1704, he visited Holland to study the casting of brass pots and returned to Bristol with some Dutch workers, setting up a brassworks at Baptist Mills in partnership with others. He tried substituting cast iron for brass in his castings, without success at first, but in 1707 he was granted a patent, 'A new way of casting iron pots and other pot-bellied ware in sand without loam or clay'. However, his business associates were unwilling to risk further funds in the experiments, so he withdrew his share of the capital and moved to Coalbrookdale in Shropshire. There, iron ore, coal, water-power and transport lay close at hand. He took a lease on an old furnace and began experimenting. The shortage and expense of charcoal, and his knowledge of the use of coke in malting, may well have led him to try using coke to smelt iron ore. The furnace was brought into blast in 1709 and records show that in the same year it was regularly producing iron, using coke instead of charcoal. The process seems to have been operating successfully by 1711 in the production of cast-iron pots and kettles, with some pig-iron destined for Bristol. Darby prospered at Coalbrookdale, employing coke smelting with consistent success, and he sought to extend his activities in the neighbourhood and in other parts of the country. However, ill health prevented him from pursuing these ventures with his previous energy. Coke smelting spread slowly in England and the continent of Europe, but without Darby's technological breakthrough the ever-increasing demand for iron for structures and machines during the Industrial Revolution simply could not have been met; it was thus an essential component of the technological progress that was to come.

Darby's eldest son, Abraham II (1711–63), entered the Coalbrookdale Company partnership in 1734 and largely assumed control of the technical side of managing the furnaces and foundry. He made a number of improvements, notably the installation of a steam engine in 1742 to pump water to an upper level in order to achieve a steady source of water-power to operate the bellows supplying the blast furnaces. When he built the Ketley and Horsehay furnaces in 1755 and 1756, these too were provided with steam engines. Abraham II's son, Abraham III (1750–89), in turn, took over the management of the Coalbrookdale works in 1768 and devoted himself to improving and extending the business. His most notable achievement was the design and construction of the famous Iron Bridge over the river Severn, the world's first iron bridge. The bridge members were cast at Coalbrookdale and the structure was erected during 1779, with a span of 100 ft (30 m) and height above the river of 40 ft (12 m). The bridge still stands, and remains a tribute to the skill and judgement of Darby and his workers.

Further Reading

A. Raistrick, 1989, *Dynasty of Iron Founders*, 2nd edn, Ironbridge Gorge Museum Trust (the best source for the lives of the Darbys and the work of the company).

H.R. Schubert, 1957, *History of the British Iron and Steel Industry AD 430 to AD 1775*, London: Routledge & Kegan Paul.

LRD

Dassault (Bloch), Marcel

b. 22 January 1892 Paris, France
d. 18 April 1986 Paris, France

*French aircraft designer and manufacturer, best
known for his jet fighters the Mystère and Mirage.*

During the First World War, Marcel Bloch (he
later changed his name to Dassault) worked on
French military aircraft and developed a very successful propeller. With his associate, Henri Potez,
he set up a company to produce their *Eclair*
wooden propeller in a furniture workshop in
Paris. In 1917 they produced a two-seater aircraft which was ordered but then cancelled when
the war ended. Potez continued to built aircraft
under his own name, but Bloch turned to
property speculation, at which he was very successful. In 1930 Bloch returned to the aviation
business with an unsuccessful bomber followed
by several moderately effective airliners, including the Bloch *220* of 1935, which was similar to
the *DC-3*. He was involved in the design of a
four-engined airliner, the SNCASE *Languedoc*,
which flew in September 1939. During the Second World War, Bloch and his brothers became
important figures in the French Resistance
Movement. Marcel Bloch was eventually captured but survived; however, one of his brothers
was executed, and after the war Bloch changed
his name to Dassault, which had been his brother's code name in the Resistance. During the
1950s, Avions Marcel Dassault rapidly grew to
become Europe's foremost producer of jet
fighters. The *Ouragon* was followed by the *Mystère*, *Etendard* and then the outstanding *Mirage*
series. The basic delta-winged *Mirage III*, with a
speed of Mach 2, was soon serving in twenty
countries around the world. From this evolved a
variable geometry version, a vertical-take-off aircraft, an enlarged light bomber capable of
carrying a nuclear bomb, and a swept-wing version for the 1970s. Dassault also produced a successful series of jet airliners starting with the *Fan
Jet Falcon* of 1963. When the Dassault and **Breguet** companies merged in 1971, Marcel Dassault was still a force to be reckoned with.

Principal Honours and Distinctions
Guggenheim Medal. Deputy, Assemblée nationale 1951–5 and 1958–86.

Bibliography
1971, *Le Talisman*, Paris: Editions J'ai lu (autobiography).

Further Reading
1976, 'The Mirage Maker', *Sunday Times Magazine* (1 June).
Jane's All the World's Aircraft, London: Jane's
(details of Bloch and Dassault aircraft can be
found in various years' editions).

JDS

Davenport, Thomas

b. 9 July 1802 Williamstown, Vermont, USA
d. 6 July 1851 Salisbury, Vermont, USA

*American craftsman and inventor who
constructed the first rotating electrical machines
in the United States.*

When he was 14 years old Davenport was apprenticed to a blacksmith for seven years. At the
close of his apprenticeship in 1823 he opened a
blacksmith's shop in Brandon, Vermont. He
began experimenting with electromagnets after
observing one in use at the Penfield Iron Works
at Crown Point, New York, in 1831. He saw the
device as a possible source of power and by July
1834 had constructed his first electric motor.
Having totally abandoned his regular business,
Davenport built and exhibited a number of miniature machines; he utilized an electric motor to
propel a model car around a circular track in
1836, and this became the first recorded instance
of an electric railway. An application for a patent
and a model were destroyed in a fire at the
United States Patent Office in December 1836,
but a second application was made and Davenport received a patent the following year for *Improvements in Propelling Machinery by Magnetism
and Electromagnetism*. A British patent was also
obtained. A workshop and laboratory were established in New York, but Davenport had little financial backing for his experiments. He built a
total of over one hundred motors but was defeated by the inability to obtain an inexpensive
source of power. Using an electric motor of his
own design to operate a printing press in 1840,
he undertook the publication of a journal, *The
Electromagnet and Mechanics' Intelligencer*. This
was the first American periodical on electricity,
but it was discontinued after a few issues. In failing health he retired to Vermont where in the last

year of his life he continued experiments in electromagnetism.

Bibliography

1837, US patent no. 132, 'Improvements in Propelling Machinery by Magnetism and Electromagnetism'.
6 June 1837 British patent no. 7,386.

Further Reading

F.L. Pope, 1891, 'Inventors of the electric motor with special reference to the work of Thomas Davenport', *Electrical Engineer*, 11: 1–5, 33–9, 65–71, 93–8, 125–30 (the most comprehensive account).
Annals of Electricity (1838) 2: 257–64 (provides a description of Davenport's motor).
W.J. King, 1962, *The Development of Electrical Technology in the 19th Century*, Washington, DC: Smithsonian Institution, Paper 28, pp. 263–4 (a short account).

GW

Davidson, Robert

b. 18 April 1804 Aberdeen, Scotland
d. 16 November 1894 Aberdeen, Scotland

Scottish chemist, pioneer of electric power and builder of the first electric railway locomotives.

Davidson, son of an Aberdeen merchant, attended Marischal College, Aberdeen, between 1819 and 1822: his studies included mathematics, mechanics and chemistry. He subsequently joined his father's grocery business, which from time to time received enquiries for yeast: to meet these, Davidson began to manufacture yeast for sale and from that start built up a successful chemical manufacturing business with the emphasis on yeast and dyes. About 1837 he started to experiment first with electric batteries and then with motors. He invented a form of electromagnetic engine in which soft iron bars arranged on the periphery of a wooden cylinder, parallel to its axis, around which the cylinder could rotate, were attracted by fixed electromagnets. These were energized in turn by current controlled by a simple commutating device. Electric current was produced by his batteries. His activities were brought to the attention of Michael **Faraday** and to the scientific world in general by a letter from Professor Forbes of King's College, Aberdeen. Davidson

declined to patent his inventions, believing that all should be able freely to draw advantage from them, and in order to afford an opportunity for all interested parties to inspect them an exhibition was held at 36 Union Street, Aberdeen, in October 1840 to demonstrate his 'apparatus actuated by electro-magnetic power'. It included: a model locomotive carriage, large enough to carry two people, that ran on a railway; a turning lathe with tools for visitors to use; and a small printing machine. In the spring of 1842 he put on a similar exhibition in Edinburgh, this time including a sawmill. Davidson sought support from railway companies for further experiments and the construction of an electromagnetic locomotive; the Edinburgh exhibition successfully attracted the attention of the proprietors of the Edinburgh & Glasgow Railway (E & GR), whose line had been opened in February 1842. Davidson built a full-size locomotive incorporating his principle, apparently at the expense of the railway company. The locomotive weighed 7 tons: each of its two axles carried a cylinder upon which were fastened three iron bars, and four electromagnets were arranged in pairs on each side of the cylinders. The motors he used were reluctance motors, the power source being zinc–iron batteries. It was named *Galvani* and was demonstrated on the E & GR that autumn, when it achieved a speed of 4 mph (6.4 km/h) while hauling a load of 6 tons over a distance of 1½ miles (2.4 km); it was the first electric locomotive. Nevertheless, further support from the railway company was not forthcoming, although to some railway workers the locomotive seems to have appeared promising enough: they destroyed it in Luddite reaction. Davidson staged a further exhibition in London in 1843 without result and then, the cost of battery chemicals being high, ceased further experiments of this type. He survived long enough to see the electric railway become truly practicable in the 1880s.

Bibliography

1840, letter, *Mechanics Magazine*, 33: 53–5 (comparing his machine with that of William Hannis Taylor (2 November 1839, British patent no. 8,255)).

Further Reading
1891, *Electrical World*, 17: 454.
J.H.R. Body, 1935, 'A note on electro-magnetic engines', *Transactions of the Newcomen Society* 14: 104 (describes Davidson's locomotive).
F.J.G. Haut, 1956, 'The early history of the electric locomotive', *Transactions of the New-comen Society* 27 (describes Davidson's locomotive).
A.F. Anderson, 1974, 'Unusual electric machines', *Electronics & Power* 14 (November) (biographical information).
— 1975, 'Robert Davidson. Father of the electric locomotive', *Proceedings of the Meeting on the History of Electrical Engineering*, Institution of Electrical Engineers, 8/1–8/17 (the most comprehensive account of Davidson's work).
A.C. Davidson, 1976, 'Ingenious Aberdonian', *Scots Magazine* (January) (details of his life).
PJGR/GW

Daviel, Jacques

b. 11 August 1696 La Barre, Normandy, France
d. 30 September 1762 Geneva, Switzerland

French ophthalmic surgeon who originated the technique of the removal of the cataractous lens of the eye.

Apprenticed in surgery to his uncle in Rouen, he became a student surgeon in the French Army in 1713. In 1719 he was honoured for his work during an outbreak of plague in Marseille, and in 1723 he was appointed Surgeon to the Hôtel-Dieu. In 1746 he moved to Paris, and in 1749 he became Surgeon-Oculist to Louis XV. Although he had, like many others, performed couchings (intra-ocular displacement of the lens) for the treatment of cataracts, his dissection of cadavers at Marseille led him to attempt the actual removal from the eye of the opaque lens. He performed the first such operation on a monk of Provence on 8 April 1745, and by 1753 he was able to report 115 cases with 100 successes. The difficulties of the technique precluded its immediate adoption, and couching remained the standard treatment for much of the century.

Principal Honours and Distinctions
Cross of the Knights of Saint Roch. Corresponding member of the Royal Academy of Surgery.

Bibliography
1748, 'Lettre sur les maladies des yeux', *Mercure de France*.
1753, 'Sur une nouvelle méthode de guérir la cataracte par l'extraction du crystallin', *Mem. Acad. roy. chir. Paris*.

Further Reading
S. Duke-Elder, 1969, *System of Ophthalmology*, Vol. 11, London.
MG

Davis, Robert Henry

b. 6 June 1870 London, England
d. 29 March 1965 Epsom, Surrey, England

English inventor of breathing, diving and escape apparatus.

Davis was the son of a detective with the City of London police. At the age of 11 he entered the employment of Siebe, Gorman & Co., manufacturers of diving and other safety equipment since 1819, at their Lambeth works. By good fortune, his neat handwriting attracted the notice of Mr Gorman and he was transferred to work in the office. He studied hard after working hours and rose steadily in the firm. In his twenties he was promoted to Assistant Manager, then General Manager, Managing Director and finally Governing Director. He retired in 1960, having been made Life President the previous year, and continued to attend the office regularly until May 1964.

Davis's entire career was devoted to research and development in the firm's special field. In 1906 he perfected the first practicable oxygen-breathing apparatus for use in mine rescue; it was widely adopted and with modifications was still in use in the 1990s. With Professor Leonard Hill he designed a deep-sea diving-bell incorporating a decompression chamber. He also invented an oxygen-breathing apparatus and heated apparel for airmen flying at high altitudes.

Immediately after the first German gas attacks on the Western Front in April 1915, Davis devised a respirator, known as the stocking skene or veil mask. He quickly organized the mass manufacture of this device, roping in members of his family and placing the work in the homes of Lambeth: within 48 hours the first consignment was being sent off to France.

He was a member of the Admiralty Deep Sea

Diving Committee, which in 1933 completed tables for the safe ascent of divers with oxygen from a depth of 300 ft (91 m). They were compiled by Davis in conjunction with Professors J.B.S. Haldane and Leonard Hill and Captain G.C. Damant, the Royal Navy's leading diving expert. With revisions these tables have been used by the Navy ever since. Davis's best-known invention was first used in 1929: the Davis Submarine Escape Apparatus. It became standard equipment on submarines until it was replaced by the Built-In Breathing System, which the firm began manufacturing in 1951.

The firm's works were bombed during the Second World War and were re-established at Chessington, Surrey. The extensive research facilities there were placed at the disposal of the Royal Navy and the Admiralty Experimental Diving Unit. Davis worked with Haldane and Hill on problems of the underwater physiology of working divers. A number of inventions issued from Chessington, such as the human torpedo, midget submarine and human minesweeper. In the early 1950s the firm helped to pioneer the use of underwater television to investigate the sinking of the submarine *Affray* and the crashed *Comet* jet airliners.

Principal Honours and Distinctions
Knighted 1932.

Bibliography
Davis was the author of several manuals on diving including *Deep Sea Diving and Submarine Operations* and *Breathing in Irrespirable Atmospheres*. He also wrote *Resuscitation: A Brief Personal History of Siebe, Gorman & Co. 1819–1957*.

Further Reading
Obituary, 1965, *The Times,* 31 March, p. 16.

LRD

Davy, Sir Humphry

b. 17 December 1778 Penzance, Cornwall, England
d. 29 May 1829 Geneva, Switzerland

English chemist, discoverer of the alkali and alkaline earth metals and the halogens, inventor of the miner's safety lamp.

Educated at the Latin School at Penzance and from 1792 at Truro Grammar School, Davy was apprenticed to a surgeon in Penzance. In 1797 he began to teach himself chemistry by reading, among other works, **Lavoisier**'s elementary treatise on chemistry. In 1798 Dr Thomas Beddoes of Bristol engaged him as assistant in setting up his Pneumatic Institution to pioneer the medical application of the newly discovered gases, especially oxygen.

In 1799 he discovered the anaesthetic properties of nitrous oxide, discovered not long before by the chemist Joseph Priestley. He also noted its intoxicating qualities, on account of which it was dubbed 'laughing-gas'. Two years later Count Rumford, founder of the Royal Institution in 1800, appointed Davy Assistant Lecturer, and the following year Professor. His lecturing ability soon began to attract large audiences, making science both popular and fashionable.

Davy was stimulated by **Volta**'s invention of the voltaic pile, or electric battery, to construct one for himself in 1800. That enabled him to embark on the researches into electrochemistry by which is chiefly known. In 1807 he tried decomposing caustic soda and caustic potash, hitherto regarded as elements, by electrolysis and obtained the metals sodium and potassium. He went on to discover the metals barium, strontium, calcium and magnesium by the same means. Next, he turned his attention to chlorine, which was then regarded as an oxide in accordance with Lavoisier's theory that oxygen was the essential component of acids; Davy failed to decompose it, however, even with the aid of electricity and concluded that it was an element, thus disproving Lavoisier's view of the nature of acids. In 1812 Davy published his *Elements of Chemical Philosophy*, in which he presented his chemical ideas without, however, committing himself to the atomic theory, recently advanced by John Dalton.

In 1813 Davy engaged **Faraday** as Assistant, perhaps his greatest service to science. In April 1815 Davy was asked to assist in the development of a miner's lamp which could be safely used in a firedamp (methane) laden atmosphere. The 'Davy lamp', which emerged in January 1816, had its flame completely surrounded by a fine wire mesh; George **Stephenson**'s lamp, based on a similar principle, had been introduced into the Northumberland pits several months earlier, and a bitter controversy as to priority of invention ensued, but it was Davy who was awarded the prize for inventing a successful safety lamp.

In 1824 Davy was the first to suggest the possibility of conferring cathodic protection to the copper bottoms of naval vessels by the use of sacrificial electrodes. Zinc and iron were found to be equally effective in inhibiting corrosion, although the scheme was later abandoned when it was found that ships protected in this way were rapidly fouled by weeds and barnacles.

Principal Honours and Distinctions
Knighted 1812. FRS 1803; President, Royal Society 1820. Royal Society Copley Medal 1805.

Bibliography
1812, *Elements of Chemical Philosophy*.
1839–40, *The Collected Works of Sir Humphry Davy*, 9 vols, ed. John Davy, London.

Further Reading
J. Davy, 1836, *Memoirs of the Life of Sir Humphry Davy*, London (a classic biography).
J.A. Paris, 1831, *The Life of Sir Humphry Davy*, London (a classic biography).
H. Hartley, 1967, *Humphry Davy*, London (a more recent biography).
J.Z. Fullmer, 1969, Cambridge, Mass. (a bibliography of Davy's works).

ASD

Dawson, William
b. mid-eighteenth century
d. *c.*1805 London, England

English inventor of the notched wheel for making patterns on early warp knitting machines.

William Dawson, a Leicester framework knitter, made an important addition to William **Lee**'s knitting machine with his invention of the notched wheel in 1791. Lee's machine could make only plain knitting; to be able to knit patterns, there had to be some means of mechanically selecting and operating, independently of all the others, any individual thread, needle, lever or bar at work in the machine. This was partly achieved when Dawson devised a wheel that was irregularly notched on its edge and which, when rotated, pushed sprung bars, which in turn operated on the needles or other parts of the recently invented warp knitting machines. He seems to

have first applied the idea for the knitting of military sashes, but then found it could be adapted to plait stay laces with great rapidity. With the financial assistance of two Leicester manufacturers and with his own good mechanical ability, Dawson found a way of cutting his wheels. However, the two financiers withdrew their support because he did not finish the design on time, although he was able to find a friend in a Nottingham architect, Mr Gregory, who helped him to obtain the patent. A number of his machines were set up in Nottingham but, like many other geniuses, he squandered his money away. When the patent expired, he asked Lord Chancellor Eldon to have it renewed: he moved his workshop to London, where Eldon inspected his machine, but the patent was not extended and in consequence Dawson committed suicide.

Bibliography
1791, British patent no. 1,820 (notched wheel for knitting machine).

Further Reading
W. Felkin, 1867, *History of Machine-Wrought Hosiery and Lace Manufacture* (covers Dawson's invention).
W. English, 1969, *The Textile Industry*, London (provides an outline history of the development of knitting machines).

RLH

Deacon, Henry
b. 30 July 1822 London, England
d. 23 July 1876 Widnes, Cheshire, England

English industrial chemist.

Deacon was apprenticed at the age of 14 to the London engineering firm of Galloway & Sons. **Faraday** was a friend of the family and gave Deacon tuition, allowing him to use the laboratories at the Royal Institution. When the firm failed in 1839, Deacon transferred his indentures to Nasmyth & Gaskell on the Bridgewater Canal at Patricroft. **Nasmyth** was then beginning work on his steam hammer and it is said that Deacon made the first model of it, for patent purposes. Around 1848, Deacon joined Pilkington's, the glassmakers at St Helens, where he learned the alkali industry, which was then growing up in that district on account of the close proximity of the necessary raw materials, coal, lime and salt.

Wishing to start out on his own, he worked as Manager at the chemical works of a John Hutchinson. This was followed by a partnership with William Pilkington, a former employer, who was later replaced by Holbrook Gaskell, another former employer. Deacon's main activity was the manufacture of soda by the **Leblanc** process. He sought improvement by substituting the ammonia-soda process, but this failed and did not succeed until it was perfected by **Solvay**. Deacon did, however, with his Chief Chemist F. Hurter, introduce improvements in the Leblanc process during the period 1866–70. Hydrochloric acid, which had previously been a waste product and a nuisance, was oxidized catalytically to chlorine; this could be converted with lime to bleaching powder, which was in heavy demand by the textile industry. The process was patented in 1870.

Further Reading
D.W.F. Hardie, 1950, *A History of the Chemical Industry in Widnes*, London.
J. Fenwick Allen, 1907, *Some Founders of the Chemical Industry*, London.

LRD

Deane, Sir Anthony
b. 1638 Harwich (?), England
d. 1721 England

English master shipwright, one of the most influential of seventeenth-century England.

It is believed that Deane was born in Harwich, the son of a master mariner. When 22 years of age, having been trained by Christopher **Pett**, he was appointed Assistant Master Shipwright at Woolwich Naval Dockyard, indicating an ability as a shipbuilder and also that he had influence behind him. Despite abruptness and a tendency to annoy his seniors, he was acknowledged by no less a man than Pepys (1633–1703) for his skill as a ship designer and -builder, and he was one of the few who could accurately estimate displacements and drafts of ships under construction. While only 26 years old, he was promoted to Master Shipwright of the Naval Base at Harwich and commenced a notable career. When the yard was closed four years later (on the cessation of the threat from the Dutch), Deane was transferred to the key position of Master Shipwright at Portsmouth and given the opportunity to construct large men-of-war. In 1671 he built his first

three-decker and was experimenting with underwater hull sheathing and other matters. In 1672 he became a member of the Navy Board, and from then on promotion was spectacular, with almost full responsibility given him for decisions on ship procurement for the Navy. Owing to political changes he was out of office for some years and endured a short period in prison, but on his release he continued to work as a private shipbuilder. He returned to the King's service for a few years before the 'Glorious Revolution' of 1688; thereafter little is known of his life, beyond that he died in 1721.

Deane's monument to posterity is his *Doctrine of Naval Architecture*, published in 1670. It is one of the few books on ship design of the period and gives a clear insight into the rather pedantic procedures used in those less than scientific times. Deane became Mayor of Harwich and subsequently Member of Parliament. It is believed that he was **Peter the Great**'s tutor on shipbuilding during his visit to the Thames in 1698.

Principal Honours and Distinctions
Knighted 1673.

Bibliography
1670, *Doctrine of Naval Architecture*; repub. 1981, with additional commentaries by Brian Lavery, as *Deane's Doctrine of Naval Architecture 1670*, London: Conway Maritime.

Further Reading
Westcott Abell, 1948, *The Shipwright's Trade*, Cambridge: Cambridge University Press.

FMW

Deas, James
b. 30 October 1827 Edinburgh, Scotland
d. *c.*1900 Glasgow, Scotland

Scottish civil engineer responsible for the River Clyde in the period of expansion around the end of the nineteenth century.

On completing his schooling, Deas spent some years in a locomotive manufacturing shop in Edinburgh and then in a civil engineer's office. He selected the railway for his career, and moved upwards through the professional ranks, working for different companies until 1864 when he became Engineer-in-Chief of the Edinburgh &

Glasgow Railway. This later became the North British Railway and after some years, in 1869, Deas moved to the Clyde Navigation Trust as their Engineer. For thirty years he controlled the development of this great river, and with imaginative vision and determined hard work he saw a trebling in revenue, length of quayage and water area under the Trust's jurisdiction. His office worked on a wide range of problems, including civil engineering, maintenance of harbour craft and the drafting of reports for the many Parliamentary Acts required for the extension of Glasgow Harbour. To understand the immensity of the task, one must appreciate that the River Clyde then had sixty-five shipyards and could handle the largest ships afloat. This had come through the canalization of the old meandering and shallow stream and the difficult removal of the river bed's rock barriers.

Bibliography
1876, *The River Clyde*, Glasgow.

Further Reading
John F. Riddell, 1979, *Clyde Navigation, A History of the Development and Deepening of the River Clyde*, Edinburgh: John Donald.

FMW

Deere, John
b. 7 February 1804 Rutland, Vermont, USA
d. 17 May 1886 USA

American inventor and manufacturer of agricultural equipment.

John Deere was the son of a tailor, and first worked as a tanner before becoming apprenticed to a blacksmith. He married Demarius Lamb in 1827, but it appears that competition for blacksmiths was fierce, and the Deere family moved frequently. Two attempts to establish forges ended in fires, and changing partnerships and arguments over debts were to be a feature of Deere's working life. In 1836 John Deere moved west on his own, in an attempt to establish himself. He settled in Grand Detour, Illinois. In this new frontier a blacksmith's skills were sought after, and the blacksmith, with no ready supply of raw materials, had to be able to operate both a furnace for melting metal and a forge for working it. Deere was sufficiently successful for his family to be able to join him. A chance visit to a

sawmill and the acquisition of a broken saw blade led to the making of a plough that was to establish John Deere in manufacturing. There were two distinctive features associated with the plough: the soil in the area failed to stick to the steel blade, with obvious benefits to the draught of the implement; and second, the shape of the working mouldboard was square. The reputation that developed with his first three ploughs established that Deere had made the transition from blacksmith to manufacturer. Over the next decade he had a number of partnerships and eventually set up a factory in Moline, Illinois, in 1848. The following year he sold 2,136 ploughs, and by early 1850 he was producing 350 ploughs per month. Deere was devastated by the loss of his eldest son in the year that the company moved to Moline. However, his second son, Charles, joined him in 1851 and was to be a major influence on the way in which the company developed over the next half-century. The company branched out into the production of cultivators, harrows, drills and wagons. John Deere himself played an active part in the company, but also played an increasing role in public life, with a particular interest in education. The company was incorporated in 1868.

Further Reading
The following both provide biographical details of John Deere, but are mainly concerned with the company and the equipment it produced:
W.G. Broehl, 1984, *John Deere's Company: A History of Deere and Company and its Times*, American Society of Agricultural Engineers.
D. Macmillan, 1988, *John Deere Tractors and Equipment*, American Society of Agricultural Engineers.

AP

Deering, William
b. 1826 USA
d. 1913 USA

American entrepreneur who invested in the developing agricultural machinery manufacturing industry and became one of the founders of the International Harvester Company.

Deering began work in his father's woollen mill and, with this business experience, developed Deering, Milliken & Co., a wholesale dry goods business. Deering invested $40,000 in the Marsh reaper business in 1870, and became a partner in 1872. In 1880 he gained full control of the company and took up residence in Chicago, where he set up a factory. In 1878 he saw the **Appleby** binders, and in November of that year he negotiated a licence agreement for their manufacture. Deering was aware that with only two twine manufacturers operating in the US, the high price of twine was discouraging sales of binders. He therefore entered into an agreement with Edwin H. Fitler of Philadelphia for the production of very large quantities of twine, and in so doing dramatically reduced its price. In 1880 Deering released onto the market 3,000 binders and ten cartloads of twine that he had manufactured secretly. By 1890 **McCormick** and Deering were market leaders; Deering anticipated McCormick in a number of technical areas and also diversified his business into ore, timber, and a rolling and casting mill. After several false starts, a merger between the two companies took place on 12 August 1902 to form the International Harvester Company, with Deering as chairman of the voting trust which was established to control it. The company expanded into Canada in 1903 and into Europe in 1905. It began its first experiments with tractors in that same year and produced the first production models in 1906. The company went into truck production in 1907.

Further Reading
C.H. Wendell, 1981, *150 Years of International Harvester*, Crestlink Publishing (though more concerned with the machinery produced by International Harvester, this gives an account of its originating companies, and the personalities behind them).
H.N. Casson, 1908, *The Romance of the Reaper*, Doubleday Page (deals with McCormick, Deering and the formation of International Harvester).

AP

De Forest, Lee
b. 26 August 1873 Council Bluffs, Iowa, USA
d. 30 June 1961 Hollywood, California, USA

American electrical engineer and inventor principally known for his invention of the Audion, or triode, vacuum tube; also a pioneer of sound in the cinema.

De Forest was born into the family of a Congregational minister that moved to Alabama in 1879 when the father became President of a college for African-Americans; this was a position that led to the family's social ostracism by the white community. By the time he was 13 years old, De Forest was already a keen mechanical inventor, and in 1893, rejecting his father's plan for him to become a clergyman, he entered the Sheffield Scientific School of Yale University. Following his first degree, he went on to study the propagation of electromagnetic waves, gaining a PhD in physics in 1899 for his thesis on the 'Reflection of Hertzian Waves from the Ends of Parallel Wires', probably the first US thesis in the field of radio.

He then joined the Western Electric Company in Chicago where he helped develop the infant technology of wireless, working his way up from a modest post in the production area to a position in the experimental laboratory. There, working alone after normal working hours, he developed a detector of electromagnetic waves based on an electrolytic device similar to that already invented by **Fleming** in England. Recognizing his talents, a number of financial backers enabled him to set up his own business in 1902 under the name of De Forest Wireless Telegraphy Company; he was soon demonstrating wireless telegraphy to interested parties and entering into competition with the American **Marconi** Company.

Despite the failure of this company because of fraud by his partners, he continued his experiments; in 1907, by adding a third electrode, a wire mesh, between the anode and cathode of the thermionic diode invented by Fleming in 1904, he was able to produce the amplifying device now known as the triode valve and achieve a sensitivity of radio-signal reception much greater than possible with the passive carborundum and electrolytic detectors hitherto available. Patented under the name *Audion*, this new vacuum device was soon successfully used for experimental broadcasts of music and speech in New York and Paris. The invention of the *Audion* has been described as the beginning of the electronic era.

Although much development work was required before its full potential was realized, the *Audion* opened the way to progress in all areas of sound transmission, recording and reproduction. The patent was challenged by Fleming and it was not until 1943 that De Forest's claim was finally recognized.

Overcoming the near failure of his new company, the De Forest Radio Telephone Company, as well as unsuccessful charges of fraudulent promotion of the *Audion*, he continued to exploit the potential of his invention. By 1912 he had used transformer-coupling of several *Audion* stages to achieve high gain at radio frequencies, making long-distance communication a practical proposition, and had applied positive feedback from the *Audion* output anode to its input grid to realize a stable transmitter oscillator and modulator. These successes led to prolonged patent litigation with Edwin **Armstrong** and others, and he eventually sold the manufacturing rights, in retrospect often for a pittance.

During the early 1920s De Forest began a fruitful association with T.W. Case, who for around ten years had been working to perfect a moving-picture sound system. De Forest claimed to have had an interest in sound films as early as 1900, and Case now began to supply him with photoelectric cells and primitive sound cameras. He eventually devised a variable-density sound-on-film system utilizing a glow-discharge modulator, the *Photion*. By 1926 De Forest's *Phonofilm* had been successfully demonstrated in over fifty theatres and this system became the basis of *Movietone*. Though his ideas were on the right lines, the technology was insufficiently developed and it was left to others to produce a system acceptable to the film industry. However, De Forest had played a key role in transforming the nature of the film industry; within a space of five years the production of silent films had all but ceased.

In the following decade De Forest applied the *Audion* to the development of medical diathermy. Finally, after spending most of his working life as an independent inventor and entrepreneur, he worked for a time during the Second World War at the Bell Telephone Laboratories on military applications of electronics.

Principal Honours and Distinctions

Institute of Electronic and Radio Engineers Medal of Honour 1922. President, Institute of Electronic and Radio Engineers 1930. Institute of Electrical and Electronics Engineers Edison Medal 1946.

Bibliography

1904, 'Electrolytic detectors', *Electrician* 54: 94 (describes the electrolytic detector).

1907, US patent no. 841,387 (the *Audion*).

1950, *Father of Radio*, Chicago: WIlcox & Follett (autobiography).

De Forest gave his own account of the development of his sound-on-film system in a series of articles:

1923, 'The Phonofilm', *Transactions of the Society of Motion Picture Engineers* 16 (May): 61–75;

1924, 'Phonofilm progress', *Transactions of the Society of Motion Picture Engineers* 20: 17–19;

1927, 'Recent developments in the Phonofilm', *Transactions of the Society of Motion Picture Engineers* 27: 64–76;

1941, 'Pioneering in talking pictures', *Journal of the Society of Motion Picture Engineers* 36 (January): 41–9.

Further Reading

G. Carneal, 1930, *A Conqueror of Space* (biography).

I. Levine, 1964, *Electronics Pioneer, Lee De Forest* (biography).

E.I. Sponable, 1947, 'Historical development of sound films', *Journal of the Society of Motion Picture Engineers* 48 (April): 275–303 (an authoritative account of De Forest's sound-film work, by Case's assistant).

W.R. McLaurin, 1949, *Invention and Innovation in the Radio Industry*.

C.F. Booth, 1955, 'Fleming and De Forest. An appreciation', in *Thermionic Valves 1904–1954*, IEE.

V.J. Phillips, 1980, *Early Radio Detectors*, London: Peter Peregrinus.

KF/JW

de Havilland, Sir Geoffrey

b. 27 July 1882 High Wycombe, Buckinghamshire, England
d. 21 May 1965 Stanmore, Middlesex, England

English designer of some eighty aircraft from 1909 onwards.

Geoffrey de Havilland started experimenting with aircraft and engines of his own design in 1908. In the following year, with the help of his friend Frank Hearle, he built and flew his first aircraft; it crashed on its first flight. The second aircraft used the same engine and made its first flight on 10 September 1910, and enabled de Havilland to teach himself to fly. From 1910 to 1914 he was employed at Farnborough, where in 1912 the Royal Aircraft Factory was established. As Chief Designer and Chief Test Pilot he was responsible for the *BE 2*, which was the first British military aircraft to land in France in 1914.

In May 1914 de Havilland went to work for George Holt Thomas, whose Aircraft Manufacturing Company Ltd (Airco) of Hendon was expanding to design and build aircraft of its own design. However, because de Havilland was a member of the Royal Flying Corps Reserve, he had to report for duty when war broke out in August. His value as a designer was recognized and he was transferred back to Airco, where he designed eight aircraft in four years. Of these, the *DH 2*, *DH 4*, *DH 5*, *DH 6* and *DH 9* were produced in large numbers, and a modified *DH 4A* operated the first British cross-Channel air service in 1919.

On 25 September 1920 de Havilland founded his own company, the De Havilland Aircraft Company Ltd, at Stag Lane near Edgware, London. During the 1920s and 1930s de Havilland concentrated on civil aircraft and produced the very successful *Moth* series of small biplanes and monoplanes, as well as the *Dragon*, *Dragon Rapide*, *Albatross* and *Flamingo* airliners. In 1930 a new site was acquired at Hatfield, Hertfordshire, and by 1934 a modern factory with a large airfield had been established. His *Comet* racer won the England–Australia air race in 1934 using de Havilland engines. By this time the company had established very successful engine and propeller divisions. The *Comet* used a wooden stressed-skin construction which de Havilland developed and used for one of the outstanding aircraft of the Second World War: the *Mosquito*. The de Havilland Engine Company started work on jet engines in 1941 and their *Goblin* engine powered the *Vampire* jet fighter first flown by Geoffrey de Havilland Jr in 1943.

Unfortunately, Geoffrey Jr and his brother John were both killed in flying accidents. The *Comet* jet airliner first flew in 1949 and the *Trident* in 1962, although by 1959 the De Havilland Company had been absorbed into Hawker Siddeley Aviation.

Principal Honours and Distinctions
Knight Bachelor 1944. Order of Merit 1962. CBE 1934. Air Force Cross 1919. (A full list is contained in R.M. Clarkson's paper (see below)).

Bibliography
1961, *Sky Fever*, London; repub. 1979, Shrewsbury (autobiography).

Further Reading
R.M. Clarkson, 1967, 'Geoffrey de Havilland 1882–1965', *Journal of the Royal Aeronautical Society* (February) (a concise account of de Havilland, his achievements and honours).
C.M. Sharp, 1960, *D.H. – An Outline of de Havilland History*, London (mostly a history of the company).
A.J. Jackson, 1962, *De Havilland Aircraft since 1915*, London.

JDS

Della Porta, Giambattista
See **Porta, Giambattista della**.

Delvigne, Captain Henri-Gustave
b. 1799 Hamburg, Germany
d. 18 October 1876 Toulon, France

French soldier and firearms designer.

He joined the French army after the restoration of the monarchy in 1815 and rose to the rank of Captain in the Royal Guard. His main interest was in developing a more effective rifle, and in 1826 he produced a model in which the chamber was narrower than the bore. By tapping the musket ball with the ramrod, the ball could be made to fit into the grooves of the rifling, thus ensuring greater accuracy and increased effective range over previous models. The French army adopted Delvigne's rifle and used it with some success in Algeria in the 1830s. In the meantime Delvigne tried to go a stage further by designing a cylindro-conical bullet with a hollow base, which would enable it to expand into the grooves when fired, but his concept did not come to total fruition and was left to Minié to develop some twenty years later. Even so, in 1842 Delvigne completed the design of a chambered breech rifle, which was also adopted by the French army.

CM

Demenÿ, Georges
b. 1850 Douai, France
d. 1917

French chronophotographer.

As a young man Georges Demenÿ was a pioneer of physical education in France, and this led him to contact the physiologist Professor **Marey** in 1880. Marey had made a special study of animal movement, and Demenÿ hoped to work with him on research into physiological problems related to gymnastics. He joined Marey the following year, and when in 1882 the Physiological Station was set up near Paris to develop sequence photography for the study of movement. Demenÿ was made Head of the laboratory. He worked with the multiple-image fixed-plate cameras, and was chiefly responsible for the analysis of the records, having considerable mathematical and graphical ability. He also appeared as the subject in a number of the sequences. When in 1888 Marey began the development of a film camera, Demenÿ was involved in its design and operation. He became interested in the possibility of using animated sequence photographs as an aid to teaching of the deaf. He made close-up records of himself speaking short phrases, '*Je vous aime*' and '*Vive la France*' for example, which were published in such journals as *Paris Photographe* and *La Nature* in 1891 and 1892. To present these in motion, he devised the Phonoscope, which he patented on 3 March 1892. The series of photographs were mounted around the circumference of a disc and viewed through a counter-rotating slotted disc. The moving images could be viewed directly, or projected onto a screen. *La Nature* reported tests he had made in which deaf lip readers could interpret accurately what was being said. On 20 December 1892 Demenÿ formed a company, Société Générale du Phonoscope, to exploit his invention, hoping that 'speaking portraits' might replace family-album pictures. This commercial activity led to a rift between Marey and Demenÿ in July 1893. Deprived of access to the film cameras, Demenÿ developed designs of his own, patenting new camera models in France on 10 October 1893 and 27 July 1894. The design covered by the latter had been included in English and German patents filed in December 1893, and was to be of some significance in the early development of cinematography. It was for an intermittent movement of the film, which used an eccentrically mounted blade or roller that, as it rotated, bore on the film, pulling down the length of one frame. As the blade moved away, the film loop so formed was taken up by the rotation of the take-up reel. This 'beater' movement was employed extensively in the early years of cinematography, being effective yet inexpensive. It was first employed in the *Chronophotographe* apparatus marketed by Gaumont, to whom Demenÿ had licensed the patent rights, from the autumn of 1896. Demenÿ's work provided a link between the scientific purposes of sequence photography – chronophotography – and the introduction of commercial cinematography.

Further Reading
J. Deslandes, 1966, *Histoire comparée du cinéma*, Vol. I , Paris.
B. Coe, 1992, *Muybridge and the Chronophotographers*, London.

BC

Denison, Edmund Beckett
See **Grimthorpe (of Grimthorpe), Edmund Beckett, Baron**.

Denny, William
b. 25 May 1847 Dumbarton, Scotland
d. 17 March 1887 Buenos Aires, Argentina

Scottish naval architect and partner in the leading British scientific shipbuilding company.

From 1844 until 1962, the Clyde shipyard of William Denny and Brothers, Dumbarton, produced over 1,500 ships, trained innumerable students of all nationalities in shipbuilding and marine engineering, and for the seventy-plus years of their existence were accepted worldwide as the leaders in the application of science to ship design and construction. Until the closure of the yard members of the Denny family were among the partners and later directors of the firm: they included men as distinguished as Dr Peter Denny

(1821(?)–95), Sir Archibald Denny (1860–1936) and Sir Maurice Denny (1886–1955), the main collaborator in the design of the Denny–Brown ship stabilizer.

One of the most influential of this shipbuilding family was William Denny, now referred to as William 3! His early education was at Dumbarton, then on Jersey and finally at the Royal High School, Edinburgh, before he commenced an apprenticeship at his father's shipyard. From the outset he not only showed great aptitude for learning and hard work but also displayed an ability to create good relationships with all he came into contact with. At the early age of 21 he was admitted a partner of the shipbuilding business of William Denny and Brothers, and some years later also of the associated engineering firm of Denny & Co. His deep-felt interest in what is now known as industrial relations led him in 1871 to set up a piecework system of payment in the shipyard. In this he was helped by the Yard Manager, Richard Ramage, who later was to found the Leith shipyard, which produced the world's most elegant steam yachts. This research was published later as a pamphlet called *The Worth of Wages*, an unusual and forward-looking action for the 1860s, when Denny maintained that an absentee employer should earn as much contempt and disapproval as an absentee landlord! In 1880 he initiated an awards scheme for all company employees, with grants and awards for inventions and production improvements. William Denny was not slow to impose new methods and to research naval architecture, a special interest being progressive ship trials with a view to predicting effective horsepower. In time this led to his proposal to the partners to build a ship model testing tank beside the Dumbarton shipyard; this scheme was completed in 1883 and was to the third in the world (after the Admiralty tank at Torquay, managed by William **Froude** and the Royal Netherlands Navy facility at Amsterdam, under B.J. **Tideman**. In 1876 the Denny Shipyard started work with mild-quality shipbuilding steel on hulls for the Irrawaddy Flotilla Company, and in 1879 the world's first two ships of any size using this weight-saving material were produced: they were the *Rotomahana* for the Union Steamship Company of New Zealand and the *Buenos Ayrean* for the Allan Line of Glasgow. On the naval-architecture side he was involved in Denny's proposals for standard cross

curves of stability for all ships, which had far-reaching effects and are now accepted worldwide. He served on the committee working on improvements to the Load Line regulations and many other similar public bodies. After a severe bout of typhoid and an almost unacceptable burden of work, he left the United Kingdom for South America in June 1886 to attend to business with La Platense Flotilla Company, an associate company of William Denny and Brothers. In March the following year, while in Buenos Aires, he died by his own hand, a death that caused great and genuine sadness in the West of Scotland and elsewhere.

Principal Honours and Distinctions

President, Institution of Engineers and Shipbuilders in Scotland 1886. FRS Edinburgh 1879.

Bibliography

William Denny presented many papers to various bodies, the most important being to the Institution of Naval Architects and to the Institution of Engineers and Shipbuilders in Scotland. The subjects include: trials results, the relation of ship speed to power, Lloyd's Numerals, tonnage measurement, layout of shipyards, steel in shipbuilding, cross curves of stability, etc.

Further Reading

A.B. Bruce, 1889, *The Life of William Denny, Shipbuilder*, London: Hodder & Stoughton.

Denny Dumbarton 1844–1932 (a souvenir hardback produced for private circulation by the shipyard).

Fred M. Walker, 1984, *Song of the Clyde. A History of Clyde Shipbuilding*, Cambridge: PSL.

FMW

Deringer, Henry

b. 26 October 1786 Easton, Pennsylvania, USA
d. 1868

American gunsmith and inventor of the derringer [sic] pistol.

Deringer was the son of a gunsmith and was apprenticed at an early age to a firearms manufacturer in Richmond, Virginia. In 1806 he set up his own small-arms plant in Philadelphia, his contracts coming from the US Government. He concentrated primarily on long-barrelled, percussion-cap pistols designed to fit in the belt, but from 1825 devoted his main attention to the design and production of single-shot pistols small enough to fit in the pocket. These became very popular during the 1840s and several manufacturers took up the concept. It was after John Wilkes Booth used one to assassinate President Lincoln in 1865 that they became known by the generic term 'derringer' as a result of a journalist's misspelling.

CM

Deverill, Hooton
fl. *c.*1835 England

English patentee of the first successful adaptation of the Jacquard machine for patterned lacemaking.

After John **Levers** had brought out his lacemaking machine in 1813, other lacemakers proceeded to elaborate their machinery so as to imitate the more complicated forms of handwork. One of these was Samuel Draper of Nottingham, who took out one patent in 1835 for the use of a **Jacquard** mechanism on a lacemaking machine, followed by another in 1837. However, material made on his machine cost more than the handmade article, so the experiment was abandoned after three years. Then, in Nottingham in 1841, Hooton Deverill patented the first truly successful application of the Jacquard to lacemaking. The Jacquard needles caused the warp threads to be pushed sideways to form the holes in the lace while the bobbins were moved around them to bind them together. This made it possible to reproduce most of the traditional patterns of handmade lace in both narrow and wide pieces. Lace made on these machines became cheap enough for most people to be able to hang it in their windows as curtains, or to use it for trimming clothing. However, it raised in a most serious form the problem of patent rights between the two patentees, Deverill and Draper, threatening much litigation. Deverill's patent was bought by Richard Birkin, who with his partner Biddle relinquished the patent rights. The lacemaking trade on these machines was thus thrown open to the public and a new development of the trade took place. Levers lace is still made in the way described here.

Bibliography
1841, British patent no. 8,955 (adaptation of Jacquard machine for patterned lacemaking).

Further Reading
W. Felkin, 1867, *History of Machine-Wrought Hosiery and Lace Manufacture* (provides an account of Deverill's patent).
C. Singer (ed.), 1958, *A History of Technology*, Vol. V, Oxford: Clarendon Press (a modern account).
T.K. Derry and T. I. Williams, 1960, *A Short History of Technology from the Earliest Times to AD 1900*, Oxford.

RLH

Deville, Henri Etienne Sainte-Claire
b. 11 March 1818 St Thomas, Virgin Islands
d. 1 July 1881 Boulogne-sur-Seine, France

French chemist and metallurgist, pioneer in the large-scale production of aluminium and other light metals.

Deville was the son of a prosperous shipowner with diplomatic duties in the Virgin Islands. With his elder brother Charles, who later became a distinguished physicist, he was sent to Paris to be educated. He took his degree in medicine in 1843, but before that he had shown an interest in chemistry, due particularly to the lectures of Thenard. Two years later, with Thenard's influence, he was appointed Professor of Chemistry at Besançon. In 1851 he was able to return to Paris as Professor at the Ecole Normale Supérieure. He remained there for the rest of his working life, greatly improving the standard of teaching, and his laboratory became one of the great research centres of Europe. His first chemical work had been in organic chemistry, but he then turned to inorganic chemistry, specifically to improve methods of producing the new and little-known metal aluminium. Essentially, the process consisted of forming sodium aluminium trichloride and reducing it with sodium to metallic aluminium. He obtained sodium in sufficient quantity by reducing sodium carbonate with carbon. In 1855 he exhibited specimens of the metal at the Paris Exhibition, and the same year Napoleon III asked to see them, with a view to using it for breastplates for the Army and for spoons and forks for State banquets. With the resulting government support, he set up a pilot plant at Jarvel to develop the process, and then set up a small company, the Société d'Aluminium at Nanterre. This raised the output of this attractive and useful metal, so it could be used more widely than for the jewellery to which it had hitherto been restricted. Large-scale applications, however, had to await the electrolytic process that began to supersede Deville's in the 1890s. Deville extended his sodium reduction method to produce silicon, boron and the light metals magnesium and titanium. His investigations into the metallurgy of platinum revolutionized the industry and led in 1872 to his being asked to make the platinum–iridium (90–10) alloy for the standard kilogram and metre. Deville later carried out important work in high-temperature chemistry. He grieved much at the death of his brother Charles in 1876, and his retirement was forced by declining health in 1880; he did not survive for long.

Bibliography

Deville published influential books on aluminium and platinum; these and all his publications are listed in the bibliography in the standard biography by J. Gray, 1889, *Henri Sainte-Claire Deville: sa vie et ses travaux*, Paris.

Further Reading

M. Daumas, 1949, 'Henri Sainte-Claire Deville et les débuts de l'industrie de l'aluminium', *Rev.Hist.Sci* 2: 352–7.

J.C. Chaston, 1981, 'Henri Sainte-Claire Deville: his outstanding contributions to the chemistry of the platinum metals', *Platinum Metals Review* 25: 121–8.

LRD

Dickinson, John

b. 29 March 1782
d. 11 January 1869 London, England

English papermaker and inventor of a papermaking machine.

After education at a private school, Dickinson was apprenticed to a London stationer. In 1806 he started in business as a stationer, in partnership with George Longman; they transferred to 65 Old Bailey, where the firm remained until their premises were destroyed during the Second World War. In order to secure the supply of paper and be less dependent on the papermakers, Dickinson turned to making paper on his own account. In 1809 he acquired Apsley Mill, near Hemel Hempstead on the river Gade in Hertfordshire. There, he produced a new kind of paper for cannon cartridges which, unlike the paper then in use, did not smoulder, thus reducing the risk of undesired explosions. The new paper proved very useful during the Napoleonic War.

Dickinson developed a continuous papermaking machine about the same time as the **Fourdrinier** brothers, but his worked on a different principle. Instead of a continuous flat wire screen, Dickinson used a wire-covered cylinder which dipped into the dilute pulp as it revolved. A felt-covered roller removed the layer of wet pulp, which was then subjected to drying, as in the Fourdrinier machine. The latter was first in use at Frogmore, just upstream from Apsley Mill on the river Gade. Dickinson patented his machine in 1809 and claimed that it was superior for some kinds of paper. In fact, both types of machine have survived, in much enlarged and modified form: the Fourdrinier for general papermaking, the Dickinson cylinder for the making of board. In 1810 Dickinson acquired the nearby Nash Mill, and over the years he extended the scope of his papermaking business, introducing many technical improvements. Among his inventions was a machine to paste together continuous webs of paper to form cardboard. Another, patented in 1829, was a process for incorporating threads of cotton, flax or silk into the body of the paper to make forgery more difficult. He became increasingly prosperous, overcoming labour disputes with unemployed hand-papermakers and lawsuits against a canal company which threatened the water supply to his mills. Dickinson was the first to use percolation gauges to predict river flow, and his work on water supply brought him election to a Fellowship of the Royal Society in 1845.

Principal Honours and Distinctions

FRS 1845.

Further Reading

R.H. Clapperton, 1967, *The Paper-making Machine*, Oxford: Pergamon Press, pp. 331–5 (provides a biography and full details of Dickinson's inventions).

LRD

Dickson, J.T.
b. *c*.1920 Scotland

*Scottish co-inventor of the polyester fibre,
Terylene.*

The introduction of one type of artificial fibre
encouraged chemists to look for more. J.T. Dickson and J.R. **Whinfield** discovered one such
fibre in 1941 when they derived polyester from
terephthalic acid and ethylene glycol. Dickson, a
21-year-old Edinburgh graduate, was working
under Whinfield at the Calico Printers' Association research laboratory at Broad Oak Print
Works in Accrington. He was put onto fibre research: probably in April, but certainly by 5 July
1941, a murky-looking resin had been synthesized, out of which Dickson successfully drew
a filament, which was named 'Terylene' by its
discoverers. Owing to restrictions imposed in
Britain during the Second World War, this fibre
was developed initially by the DuPont Company
in the USA, where it was marketed under the
name 'Dacron'. When Imperial Chemical Industries (ICI) were able to manufacture it in Britain,
it acquired the brand name 'Terylene' and became very popular. Under the microscope, Terylene appears identical to nylon: longitudinally,
it is completely devoid of any structure and the
filaments appear as glass rods with a perfectly circular cross-section. The uses of Terylene are
similar to those of nylon, but it has two advantages. First, it can be heat-set by exposing the fabric to a temperature about 30°C higher than is
likely to be encountered in everyday use, and
therefore can be the basis for 'easy-care' clothing
such as drip-dry shirts. It can be blended with
other fibres such as wool, and when pressed at a
high temperature the creases are remarkably durable. It is also remarkably resistant to chemicals,
which makes it particularly suitable for industrial
purposes under conditions where other textile
materials would be degraded rapidly. Dickson
later worked for ICI.

Further Reading
For accounts of the discovery of Terylene, see:
J.R. Whinfield, 1953, *Textile Research Journal*
 (May).
R. Collins, 1991, 'Terylene', *Historian* 30
 (Spring).
Accounts of the introduction of synthetic fibres
are covered in:
D.S. Lyle, 1982, *Modern Textiles*, New York.
S.R. Cockett, *An Introduction to Man-Made
 Fibres.*
G.R. Wray, *Modern Yarn Production.*

RLH

Dickson, William Kennedy Laurie
b. August 1860 Brittany, France
d. 28 September 1935 Twickenham, England

Scottish inventor and photographer.

Dickson was born in France of English and Scottish parents. As a young man of almost 19 years,
he wrote in 1879 to Thomas **Edison** in America,
asking for a job. Edison replied that he was not
taking on new staff at that time, but Dickson,
with his mother and sisters, decided to emigrate
anyway. In 1883 he contacted Edison again, and
was given a job at the Goerk Street laboratory of
the Edison Electric Works in New York. He soon
assumed a position of responsibility as Superintendent, working on the development of electric
light and power systems, and also carried out
most of the photography Edison required. In
1888 he moved to the Edison West Orange laboratory, becoming Head of the ore-milling department. When Edison, inspired by
Muybridge's sequence photographs of humans
and animals in motion, decided to develop a motion picture apparatus, he gave the task to Dickson, whose considerable skills in mechanics,
photography and electrical work made him the
obvious choice. The first experiments, in 1888,
were on a cylinder machine like the phonograph,
in which the sequence pictures were to be taken
in a spiral. This soon proved to be impractical,
and work was delayed for a time while Dickson
developed a new ore-milling machine. Little progress with the movie project was made until
George **Eastman**'s introduction in July 1889 of
celluloid roll film, which was thin, tough, transparent and very flexible. Dickson returned to his
experiments in the spring of 1891 and soon had
working models of a film camera and viewer, the
latter being demonstrated at the West Orange
laboratory on 20 May 1891. By the early summer
of 1892 the project had advanced sufficiently for
commercial exploitation to begin. The Kinetograph camera used perforated 35 mm film (essentially the same as that still in use in the late
twentieth century), and the kinetoscope, a peep-

show viewer, took fifty feet of film running in an endless loop. Full-scale manufacture of the viewers started in 1893, and they were demonstrated on a number of occasions during that year. On 14 April 1894 the first kinetoscope parlour, with ten viewers, was opened to the public in New York. By the end of that year, the kinetoscope was seen by the public all over America and in Europe. Dickson had created the first commercially successful cinematograph system. Dickson left Edison's employment on 2 April 1895, and for a time worked with Woodville Latham on the development of his Panoptikon projector, a projection version of the kinetoscope. In December 1895 he joined with Herman Casler, Henry N. Marvin and Elias Koopman to form the American Mutoscope Company. Casler had designed the Mutoscope, an animated-picture viewer in which the sequences of pictures were printed on cards fixed radially to a drum and were flipped past the eye as the drum rotated. Dickson designed the Biograph wide-film camera to produce the picture sequences, and also a projector to show the films directly onto a screen. The large-format images gave pictures of high quality for the period; the Biograph went on public show in America in September 1896, and subsequently throughout the world, operating until around 1905. In May 1897 Dickson returned to England and set up as a producer of Biograph films, recording, among other subjects, Queen Victoria's Diamond Jubilee celebrations in 1897, Pope Leo XIII in 1898, and scenes of the Boer War in 1899 and 1900. Many of the Biograph subjects were printed as reels for the Mutoscope to produce the 'what the butler saw' machines which were a feature of fairgrounds and seaside arcades until modern times. Dickson's contact with the Biograph Company, and with it his involvement in cinematography, ceased in 1911.

Further Reading
Gordon Hendricks, 1961, *The Edison Motion Picture Myth.*
—— 1966, *The Kinetoscope.*
—— 1964, *The Beginnings of the Biograph.*

BC

Diderot, Denis
b. 1713 Lagnes, Champagne, France
d. 1784 Paris, France

French editor of the thirty-five-volume Encyclopédie.

In spite of a Jesuit education, Diderot became a teacher and scholar instead of a lawyer or doctor. He then proceeded to write prolifically, though many of his works ran contrary to government opinion and dictate. In 1727 Ephraim Chambers published the *Chambers Encyclopaedia* and a Parisian publisher persuaded Diderot and D'Alembert to translate it. The authors quickly moved away from the translation and undertook the great *Encyclopédie*. Political and philosophical militancy prevented its publication many times and caused the collaboration to fail in 1758. The first volume, written by many authors and edited by Diderot, appeared in 1751, and the last, the thirty-fifth, in 1776. The *Encyclopédie* is valued because of the accuracy with which the objects are described and illustrated in the folio volumes.

Bibliography
1751–76, *Encyclopédie, ou dictionnaire raisonné des sciences, des arts et des métiers* (ed.).

KM

Diesel, Rudolph Christian Karl
b. 1858 Paris, France
d. 1913 at sea, in the English Channel

German inventor of the Diesel or Compression Ignition engine.

A German born in Paris, he was educated in Augsburg and later in Munich, where he graduated first in his class. There he took some courses under Professor Karl von Linde, pioneer of mechanical refrigeration and an authority on thermodynamics, who pointed out the low efficiency of the steam engine. He went to work for the Linde Ice Machine Company as an engineer and later as Manager; there he conceived a new basic cycle and worked out its thermodynamics, which he published in 1893 as 'The theory and construction of a rational heat motor'. Compressing air adiabatically to one-sixteenth of its volume caused the temperature to rise to $1,000°F$ ($540°C$). Injected fuel would then ignite automatically without any electrical system. He obtained permission to use the laboratories of the Augsburg–Nuremburg Engine Works to build a single-cylinder prototype. On test it blew up, nearly killing Diesel. He proved his principle, however, and obtained financial support from the firm of Alfred **Krupp**. The design was refined until successful and in 1898 an engine was put on display in Munich with the result that many business people invested in Diesel and his engine and its worldwide production. Diesel made over a million dollars out of the invention. The heart of the engine is the fuel-injection pump, which operates at a pressure of $c.500$ psi (35 kg/cm^2). The first English patent for the engine was in 1892. The firms in Augsburg sent him abroad to sell his engine; he persuaded the French to adopt it for submarines, Germany having refused this. Diesel died in 1913 in mysterious circumstances, vanishing from the Harwich–Antwerp ferry.

Further Reading

E. Diesel, 1937, *Diesel, der Mensch, das Werk, das Schicksal*, Hamburg.

J.S. Crowther, 1959, *Six Great Engineers*, London.

John F. Sandfort, 1964, *Heat Engines*.

IMcN

Diggle, Squire
fl. *c.*1845 England

English inventor of a mechanized drop box for shuttles on power looms.

Robert **Kay** improved his father John's flying shuttle by inventing the drop box, in which up to four shuttles could be stored one below the other. The weaver's left hand controlled levers and catches to raise or lower the drop box in order to bring the appropriate shuttle into line with the shuttle race on the slay. The shuttle could then be driven across the loom, leaving its particular type or colour of weft. On the earliest power looms of Edmund **Cartwright** in 1785, and for many years later, it was possible to use only one shuttle. In 1845 Squire Diggle of Bury, Lancashire, took out a patent for mechanizing the drop box so that different types or colours of weft could be woven without the weaver attending to the shuttles. He used an endless chain on which plates of different heights could be fixed to raise the boxes to the required height; later this would be operated by either the dobby or **Jacquard** pattern-selecting mechanisms. He took out further patents for improvements to looms. One, in 1854, was for taking up the cloth

with a positive motion. Two more, in 1858, improved his drop box mechanism: the first was for actually operating the drop box, while the second was for tappet chains which operated the timing for raising the boxes.

Bibliography

1845, British patent no. 10,462 (mechanized drop box).

1854, British patent no. 1,100 (positive uptake of cloth)

1858, British patent no. 2,297 (improved drop-box operation).

1858, British patent no. 2,704 (tappet chains).

Further Reading

A. Barlow, 1878, *The History and Principles of Weaving by Hand and by Power*, London (provides drawings of Diggle's invention).

C. Singer (ed.), 1958, *A History of Technology*, Vol. IV, Oxford: Clarendon Press.

See also **Kay, John**.

RLH

Ding Huan (Ting Huan)
fl. *c.*100 AD China

Chinese inventor of various devices.

Ding Huan invented a form of suspension rediscovered by the French Renaissance mathematician Jerome Cardan, although a reference in the 'Ode to beautiful women' (*c.*740) indicates that the device was probably in existence earlier (see vol. IV.2, p. 233 in the reference given below). Ding Huan also invented the zoetrope lamp (*c.*180), which had a thin canopy bearing vanes at the top that were caused to rotate by an ascending current of warm air from the lamp. The canopy bore images which, if the canopy were rotated fast enough, gave the impression of movement, as in early forerunners of the cinematograph. In the *Xi Jing Za Ji* (Miscellaneous Records of the Western Capital), it is recorded that Ding Huan devised an air-conditioning fan that consisted of a set of seven fans, each 10 ft (3 m) in diameter, connected so that they could be worked together by one person. The device could cool a hall so that 'people would even begin to shiver'.

Further Reading
J. Needham, 1972–4, *Science and Civilisation in China*, Cambridge: Cambridge University Press, vols IV.1, pp. 123, 125; IV.2, pp. 150–1, 233, 236; V.2, p. 133.

LRD

Doane, Thomas

b. 20 September 1821 Orleans, Massachusetts, USA
d. 22 October 1897 West Townsend, Massachusetts, USA

American mechanical engineer.

The son of a lawyer, he entered an academy in Cape Cod and, at the age of 19, the English Academy at Andover, Massachusetts, for five terms. He was then in the employ of Samuel L. Fenton of Charlestown, Massachusetts. He served a three-year apprenticeship, then went to the Windsor White River Division of the Vermont Central Railroad. He was Resident Engineer of the Cheshire Railroad at Walpote, New Hampshire, from 1847 to 1849, and then worked in independent practice as a civil engineer and surveyor until his death. He was involved with nearly all the railroads running out of Boston, especially the Boston & Maine. In April 1863 he was appointed Chief Engineer of the Hoosac Tunnel, which was already being built. He introduced new engineering methods, relocated the line of the tunnel and achieved great accuracy in the meeting of the borings. He was largely responsible for the development in the USA of the advanced system of tunnelling with machinery and explosives, and pioneered the use of compressed air in the USA. In 1869 he was Chief Engineer of the Burlington & Missouri River Railroad in Nebraska, laying down some 240 miles (386 km) of track in four years. During this period he became interested in the building of a Congregational College at Crete, Nebraska, for which he gave the land and which was named after him. In 1873 he returned to Charlestown and was again appointed Chief Engineer of the Hoosac Tunnel. At the final opening of the tunnel on 9 February 1875 he drove the first engine through. He remained in charge of construction for a further two years.

Principal Honours and Distinctions
President, School of Civil Engineers.

Further Reading
Duncan Malone (ed.), 1932–3, *Dictionary of American Biography*, New York: Charles Scribner.

IMcN

Dockwra, William

d. 1716

English merchant; manufacturer of copper, brass, wire and pins.

William Dockwra established a penny postal system in London in 1683. He was appointed Comptroller of the Penny Post in 1697, but following enquiries into his activities he was dismissed on charges of maladministration. In the early 1690s he was heading a partnership with premises at Esher, formerly the brassworks of Jacob **Momma**. Brass was made there and both brass and copper sheet was manufactured by water-powered rolling mills, at a time when such techniques were new to England. Wire was drawn and used for pinmaking on the premises, making this the first comprehensive works of its kind. Dockwra was involved in a further partnership based at Redbrook on the Wye in Gloucestershire, where copper was smelted by John **Coster** using new coal-fired reverberatory furnaces. It was from there that the Esher works received its copper for brassmaking and other manufacturing processes. Following his dismissal as Comptroller of the Penny Post, Dockwra's fortunes declined. By the early years of the eighteenth century he had withdrawn from his involvement in manufacturing, no longer being included in either of his former partnerships, although their work continued.

Further Reading
J. Day, 1973, *Bristol Brass: A History of the Industry* (puts Dockwra's manufacturing activities in context).
J. Houghton, 1697, *Husbandry and Trade Improv'd* (a contemporary account of Dockwra's industrial activities).

JD

Dolby, Ray M.

b. 1933 Portland, Oregon, USA

American electronics engineer who developed professional systems for noise reduction.

He was employed by Ampex Corporation from 1949 to 1957 and received a BSc in electrical engineering from Stanford University in 1957. He studied in England and received a PhD in physics from Cambridge University in 1961. He was a United Nations adviser in India 1963–5 and established the Dolby Laboratories in London in 1965. The Dolby Laboratories continuously developed systems for background-noise reduction, and in 1966 introduced Dolby A for professional tape and film formats. In 1968 Dolby B was developed and quickly found its use in the Philips Compact Cassette, which had become the new consumer medium for music. In 1981 Dolby C was an improvement designed for the consumer market, but it also was used in professional video equipment. In 1986 Dolby SR was introduced for professional sound recording. It is a common feature that the equipment has to be in a good state of calibration in order to obtain the advantages of these compander systems.

Principal Honours and Distinctions
OBE 1986.

GB-N

Domagk, Gerhard Johannes Paul
b. 30 October 1895 Lagow, Brandenburg, Germany
d. 24 April 1964 Burgberg, Germany

German physician, biochemist and pharmacologist, pioneer of antibacterial chemotherapy.

Domagk's studies in medicine were interrupted by the outbreak of the First World War and his service in the Army, delaying his qualification at Kiel until 1921. For a short while he worked at the University of Greifswald, but in 1925 he was appointed Reader in Pathology at the University of Münster, where he remained as Extraordinary Professor of General Pathology and Pathological Anatomy (1928) and Professor (1958).

In 1924 he published a paper on the role of the reticulo-endothelial system against infection. This led to his appointment as Director of Research by IG Farbenindustrie in their laboratory for experimental pathology and bacteriology. The planned programme of research into potential antibacterial chemotherapeutic drugs led, via the discovery of the dye *Prontosil rubrum* by his colleagues, to his reporting in 1936 the clinical antistreptococcal effects of the sulphonamide drugs. These results were confirmed in other countries, but owing to problems with the Nazi authorities he was unable to receive until 1947 the Nobel Prize that he was awarded in 1939.

Domagk turned his interest to the chemotherapy of tuberculosis, and in 1946 he was able to report the therapeutic activity of the thiosemicarbazones, which, although too toxic for general use, in their turn led to the discovery of the potent and effective isoniazid. In his later years he moved into the field of cancer chemotherapy, but interestingly he wrote, 'One should not have too great expectations of the future of cytostatic agents.' His only daughter was one of the first patients to have a severe streptococcal infection successfully treated with *Prontosil rubrum*.

Principal Honours and Distinctions
Nobel Prize for Medicine 1939. Foreign Member of the Royal Society. Paul Ehrlich Gold Medal.

Bibliography
1935, 'Ein Beitrag zur Chemotherapie der bakteriellen Infektionen', *Deutsche med. Woch.*
1924, *Virchows Archiv für Path. Anat. und Physiol. u.f. klin. Med.* 253: 294–638.

Further Reading
1964, *Biographical Memoirs of the Royal Society: Gerhard Domagk*, London.

MG

Donald, Ian
b. 27 December 1910 Paisley, Scotland
d. 19 June 1987 Paglesham, Essex, England

Scottish obstetrician and gynaecologist, pioneer of the diagnostic use of ultrasound in medicine.

After he received his initial education in Scotland, Donald's family moved to South Africa, where he obtained a BA degree in Cape Town in 1930. After the death of his parents he returned to England, graduating in medicine in 1937. He served in the RAF from 1942 to 1946 and was awarded the MBE for bravery in rescuing aircrews. In 1954, following a fruitful period as Reader and Lecturer at St Thomas's Hospital and the Hammersmith Hospital, he was appointed Regius Professor of Midwifery in Glasgow. It was while at St Thomas's and

Hammersmith that he evolved a demand-response respirator for infants. With the assistance of Tom Brown, an engineer, and the company Kelvin Hughes – which had earlier produced ultrasound equipment for detecting flaws in metal castings – he was able to originate, develop and improve the diagnostic use of ultrasound in obstetrics and gynaecology. The use of this technique rapidly spread into other disciplines. Donald was fortunate in that the procedure proved to have no untoward influence on pregnancy; at the time, little was known of possible side effects.

He was the proponent of other advances in the speciality, including laparoscopy, breast-feeding and the preservation of the membranes during labour. An ardent anti-abortionist, his authoritarian Scottish approach made Glasgow a world centre, with himself as a renowned and loved teacher. Despite undergoing three major cardiac interventions, his longevity did not surprise those who knew of his immense vitality.

Principal Honours and Distinctions
CBE 1973. Honorary DSc, London and Glasgow Universities. Royal College of Obstetricians and Gynaecologists Eardley Holland Gold Medal. Royal College of Surgeons Victor Bonney Prize. Royal Society of Medicine Blair Bell Gold Medal.

Bibliography
1958, 'Investigation of abdominal masses by pulsed ultrasound', *Lancet* (with Brown and MacVicar).
Numerous other papers in learned journals.

Further Reading
Obituary, 1987, *Lancet* (18 July).

MG

Dondi, Giovanni
b. 1318 Chioggia, Italy
d. 22 June 1389 Milan, Italy

Italian physician and astronomer who produced an elaborate astronomical clock.

Giovanni was the son of Jacopo de'Dondi dall'-Orologio, a physician who designed a public clock that was installed in Padua in 1344. The careers of both father and son followed similar paths, for Giovanni became Physician to Emperor Charles IV and designed a complicated astronomical clock (astrarium) for which he became famous. Around 1350 he was appointed Professor of Astronomy at the University of Padua. Dondi completed his astrarium in 1381, having worked on it for sixteen years. Unlike the clock of **Richard of Wallingford**, it used the common form of verge escapement and had no facility for sounding the hours on a bell. It did, however, indicate time on a 24-hour dial and had calendars for both the fixed and movable feasts of the Church. Its principal function was to show the motions of the planets on the Ptolemaic theory, i.e. the Sun, Moon, Mercury, Venus, Mars, Jupiter and Saturn. Like the Wallingford clock, it also indicated the position of the nodes, or points where the orbits of the Sun and Moon intersected, so that eclipses could be predicted. The astrarium was acquired by the Duke of Milan and its history can be traced to *c.*1530, when it was in disrepair. It is now known only from copies of Dondi's manuscript 'Tractus astarii'. Several modern reconstructions have been made based upon the details in the various manuscripts.

Bibliography
1987, *Astrarium Johannis de Dondis; fac-simile du manuscript de Padoue et traduction française par Emmanuel Poulle*, Padua/Paris. For an English translation of *Astrarium*, see G.H. Baillie, H.A. Lloyd and F.A.B. Ward, 1974, *The Planetarium of Giovanni de Dondi*, London; however, this translation is less satisfactory as it is a composite of two manuscripts, with illustrations from a third.

Further Reading
S. Bedini and F. Maddison, 1966, 'Mechanical universe. The astrarium of Giovanni de'Dondi' *Transactions of the American Philosophical Society* 56: 1–69 (for the history of the clock).
H.A. Lloyd, 1958, *Some Outstanding Clocks Over 700 Years, 1250–1950*, London, pp. 9–24 (for its construction).

DV

Donisthorpe, George Edmond
fl. *c.*1842 England

English inventor of a wool-combing machine.

Edmund **Cartwright**'s combing machine needed a great deal of improvement before it could be used to tackle the finer qualities of wool. Various people carried out experiments over the next thirty years, including G.E. Donisthorpe of Leicester. Together with Henry Rawson, Donisthorpe obtained his first patent for improvements to wool combing in 1835, but his important ones were obtained in 1842 and 1843. These attracted the attention of S.C. **Lister**, who had become interested in developing a machine to comb wool after seeing the grim working conditions of the hand-combers supplying his mill at Manningham. Lister was quick to perceive that Donisthorpe's invention carried sufficient promise to replace the hand-comber, so in 1842 he made Donisthorpe an offer, which was accepted, of £2,000 for half the patent rights. In the following year Lister purchased the other half of the patent for £10,000, whereby Donisthorpe ceased to have any pecuniary interest in it. Lister took Donisthorpe into partnership and they worked together over the ensuing years with patience and diligence until they eventually succeeded in bringing out a combing machine that was generally acceptable. They were combing fine botany wool for the first time by machine in 1843. Further patents were taken out in their joint names in 1849 and 1850: these included the 'nip' mechanism, the priority of which was disputed by **Heilmann**. Donisthorpe also took out patents for wool combing with John Whitehead in 1849 and John Crofts in 1853.

Bibliography
1835, British patent no. 6,808 (improvements to wool combing).
1842, British patent no. 9,404.
1843, British patent no. 9,966.
1843, British patent no. 9,780.
1849, with S.C. Lister, British patent no. 12,712.
1849, with S.C. Lister, British patent no. 13,009.
1849, with S.C. Lister, British patent no. 13,532.
1849, with John Whitehead, British patent no. 12,603.
1853, with John Crofts, British patent no. 216.

Further Reading
J. Hogg (ed.), *c.*1888, *Fortunes Made in Business*, London (provides an account of the associ-
ation between Donisthorpe and Lister).
W. English, 1969, *The Textile Industry*, London (explains the technical details of combing machines).
C. Singer (ed.), 1958, *A History of Technology*, Vol. IV, Oxford: Clarendon Press (includes a good section on combing machines).

RLH

Donkin, Bryan I

b. 22 March 1768 Sandoe, Northumberland, England
d. 27 February 1855 London, England

English mechanical engineer and inventor.

It was intended that Bryan Donkin should follow his father's profession of surveyor and land agent, so he spent a year or so in that occupation before he was apprenticed to John Hall, millwright of Dartford, Kent. Donkin remained with the firm after completing his apprenticeship, and when the **Fourdrinier** brothers in 1802 introduced from France an invention for making paper in continuous lengths they turned to John Hall for help in developing the machine: Donkin was chosen to undertake the work. In 1803 the Fourdriniers established their own works in Bermondsey, with Bryan Donkin in charge. By 1808 Donkin had acquired the works, but he continued to manufacture paper-making machines, paying a royalty to the patentees. He also undertook other engineering work including water-wheels for driving paper and other mills. He was also involved in the development of printing machinery and the preservation of food in airtight containers. Some of these improvements were patented, and he also obtained patents relating to gearing, steel pens, paper-making and railway wheels. Other inventions of Bryan Donkin that were not patented concerned revolution counters and improvements in accurate screw threads for use in graduating mathematical scales. Donkin was elected a member of the Society of Arts in 1803 and was later Chairman of the Society's Committee of Mechanics and a Vice-President of the society. He was also a member of the Royal Astronomical Society. In 1818 a group of eight young men founded the Institution of Civil Engineers; two of them were apprentices of Bryan Donkin and he encouraged their enterprise. After a change in the rules permitted the election of members over the age of 35, he himself became a member in 1821. He served on the Council and became a Vice-President, but he resigned from the Institution in 1848.

Principal Honours and Distinctions
FRS 1838. Vice-President, Institution of Civil Engineers 1826–32, 1835–45. Member, Smeatonian Society of Civil Engineers 1835; President 1843. Society of Arts Gold Medal 1810, 1819.

Further Reading
S.B. Donkin, 1949–51, 'Bryan Donkin, FRS, MICE 1768–1855', *Transactions of the Newcomen Society* 27: 85–95.

RTS

Donkin, Bryan II
b. 29 April 1809 London, England
d. 4 December 1893 Blackheath, Kent, England

English mechanical engineer.

Bryan Donkin was the fifth son of Bryan **Donkin** I (1768–1855) and was educated at schools in Bromley (Kent), London, Paris and Nantes. He was an apprentice in his father's Bermondsey works and soon became an active and valuable assistant in the design and construction of papermaking, printing, pumping and other machinery. In 1829 he was sent to France to superintend the construction of paper mills and other machinery at Nantes. He later became a partner in the firm which in 1858 received an order to construct and set up a large paper mill at St Petersburg. This work took him to Russia several times before its completion in 1862. He obtained several patents relating to paper-making and steam engines. He was elected an associate of the Institution of Civil Engineers in 1835 and a member in 1840.

Principal Honours and Distinctions
Member, Smeatonian Society of Civil Engineers 1859; President 1872.

RTS

Donkin, Bryan III
b. 29 August 1835 London, England
d. 4 March 1902 Brussels, Belgium

English mechanical engineer.

Bryan Donkin was the eldest son of John Donkin

(1802–54) and grandson of Bryan **Donkin** I (1768–1855). He was educated at University College, London, and at the Ecole Centrale des Arts et Métiers in Paris, and then served an apprenticeship in the firm established by his grandfather. He assisted his uncle, Bryan **Donkin** II (1809–93), in setting up paper mills at St Petersburg. He became a partner in the Donkin firm in 1868 and Chairman in 1889, and retained this position after the amalgamation with Clench & Co. of Chesterfield in 1900. Bryan Donkin was one of the first engineers to carry out scientific tests on steam engines and boilers, the results of his experiments being reported in many papers to the engineering institutions. In the 1890s his interests extended to the internal-combustion engine and he translated Rudolf Diesel's book *Theory and Construction of a Rational Heat Motor*. He was a frequent contributor to the weekly journal *The Engineer*. He was a member of the Institution of Civil Engineers and of the Institution of Mechanical Engineers, as well as of many other societies, including the Royal Institution, the American Society of Mechanical Engineers, the Société Industrielle de Mulhouse and the Verein Deutscher Ingenieure. In his experimental work he often collaborated with others, notably Professor A.B.W. Kennedy (1847–1928), with whom he was also associated in the consulting engineering firm of Kennedy & Donkin.

Principal Honours and Distinctions
Vice-President, Institution of Mechanical Engineers 1901. Institution of Civil Engineers, Telford premiums 1889, 1891; Watt Medal 1894; Manby premium 1896.

Bibliography
1894, *Gas, Oil and Air Engines*, London.
1896, with A.B.W. Kennedy, *Experiments on Steam Boilers*, London.
1898, *Heat Efficiency of Steam Boilers*, London.

RTS

Donkin, Bryan IV
b. 29 April 1903 London, England
d. 17 October 1964 Albury, Surrey, England

English electrical engineer.

Bryan Donkin IV was the son of S.B. Donkin (1871–1952) and the great-great-grandson of

Bryan **Donkin** I (1768–1855). He was educated at Gresham's School in Holt, and at Pembroke College, Cambridge. He served a three-year apprenticeship with the English Electric Company Ltd, followed by a special one-year course with the General Electric Company of America. He became a partner in the consulting firm of Kennedy & Donkin in 1933 (see **Donkin, Bryan III**) and was associated with the construction of 132 kV and 275 kV overhead-transmission lines in Britain and with many electricity generating schemes. He was responsible for the design of the Pimlico district heating scheme, and was a member of the Institution of Civil Engineers, the Institution of Electrical Engineers and the American Institute of Electrical Engineers.

Principal Honours and Distinctions
President, Association of Supervising Electrical Engineers 1954–6. President, Engineer's Guild 1954–6. President, Junior Institution of Engineers 1956–7. Vice-President, Institution of Electrical Engineers 1960–4.

RTS

Dony, Jean-Jacques Daniel
b. 24 February 1759 Liège, Belgium
d. 6 November 1819 Liège, Belgium

Belgian inventor of the horizontal retort process of zinc manufacture.

Dony trained initially for the Church, and it is not known how he became interested in the production of zinc. Liège, however, was close to extensive deposits of the zinc ore calamine, and brass had been made since Roman times in the region between Liège and Aix-la-Chapelle (now Aachen). William **Champion**'s technique of brass manufacture was known there and was considered to be too complicated and expensive for the routine manufacture of brass. Dony may have learned about earlier processes of manufacturing zinc on the European continent from his friend Professor Villette of Liège University, and about English methods from Henri Delloye, a friend of both Villette and Dony and who visited Birmingham and Bristol on their behalf to study zinc smelting processes and brass manufacture at first hand. By 21 March 1805 Dony had succeeded in extracting zinc from calamine and casting it in ingots. On the basis of this success he applied to

the French Republican administration for assistance and in 1806 was assigned by Napoleon the sole mining rights to the calamine deposits of the Vieille Montagne, or Altenberg, near Moresnet, five miles (8 km) from Aachen. With these rights went the obligation of developing an industrially viable method of zinc refining. In 1807 he constructed a small factory at Isle and there, after much effort, he perfected his celebrated horizontal retort process, the 'Liège Method'. After July 1809 zinc was being produced in abundance, and in January 1810 Dony was granted an Imperial Patent giving him a monopoly of zinc manufacture for fifteen years. He erected a rolling mill at Saint-Léonard and attempted to persuade the Minister of Marine to use zinc sheets rather than copper for the protection of ships. Between 1809 and 1810 Dony reduced the price of zinc in Liège from 8.60 to 2.60 francs per kilo. However, after 1813 he began to encounter financial problems and in 1818 he surrendered his commercial interests to his partner Dominique Mosselman (d. 1837). The horizontal retort process soon rendered obsolete that of William Champion, and variants of the Liège Method were rapidly evolved in Germany, Britain and the USA.

Further Reading
A. Dony, 1941, *A Propos de l'industrie belge du zinc au début du XIXe siècle*, Brussels.
L. Boscheron, 'The zinc industry of the Liège District', *Journal of the Institution of Metals* 36 (2): 21–6.
H. Delloye, 1810, *Recherches sur la calamine, le zinc et les emplois*, Liège: Dauvrain.
1836, *Bibliographie Liégeoise*.

ASD

Dore (Dorr), Samuel Griswold
b. USA
d. 1794 England

American inventor of the first rotary shearing machine.

To give a smooth surface to cloth such as the old English broadcloth, the nap was raised and then sheared off. Hand-operated shears of enormous size cut the fibres standing proud of the surface while the cloth was laid over a curved table top. Great skill was required to achieve a smooth finish. Various attempts, such as that in 1784 by

James Harmer, a clergyman of Sheffield, were made to mechanize the process by placing several pairs of shears in a frame and operating them by cranks, but these were not successful. The first version of a rotary machine was made by Samuel Griswold Dore (sometimes spelt Dorr), an American from Albany, New York. His first frame, patented in 1792 in America, consisted of a wheel of twelve 'spring knives' that were fixed like spokes and set at an angle of about 45° to the horizontal. Under this wheel, and on the same axle, rode a second one, carrying four 'tangent knives' that lay almost flat upon the cloth. As the two wheels rotated above the cloth's surface, they acted in 'the manner of shears'. The principle used in Dore's machine is certainly different from that in the later, successful machine of John **Lewis**. The machine was thought to be too complicated and expensive for American woollen manufacturers and was much better suited to circumstances in the English industry, Dore therefore moved to England. However, in his British patent in 1793, he introduced a different design, which was more like that on which both Lewis's machine and the lawnmower were based, with knives set across the periphery of a hollow cylinder or barrel. Little more was heard of his machine in Britain, possibly because of Dore's death, which is mentioned in his patent of 1794, although it was used in America and France. Dore's son and others improved the machine in America and brought new specifications to England in 1811, when several patents were taken out.

Bibliography

1792, US patent (rotary shearing machine).
1793, British patent no. 1,945 (rotary shearing machine).
1794, British patent no. 1,985.

Further Reading

D.J. Jeremy, 1981, *Transatlantic Industrial Revolution. The Diffusion of Textile Technologies Between Britain and America, 1790–1830s*, Oxford (examines Dore's inventions and their transfer to Britain).
Mention of Dore can be found in:
J. de L. Mann, 1971, *The Cloth Industry in the West of England from 1660 to 1880*, Oxford;
K.G. Ponting, 1971, *The Woollen Industry of South-West England*, Bath.
C. Singer (ed.), 1958, *A History of Technology*, Vol. IV, Oxford: Clarendon Press (discusses Dore's inventions).

RLH

Dörell, Georg Ludwig Wilhelm

b. 17 December 1793 Clausthal, Harz, Germany
d. 30 October 1854 Zellerfeld, Harz, Germany

German mining engineer who introduced the miner's elevator into the Harz Mountains.

After studying at the Freiberg Mining Academy he returned to his home region to serve in the mining administration, first at Clausthal. In 1848 he became an inspector of mines in Zellerfeld. He had become aware that in the early nineteenth century, when 500 m (1,640 ft) shafts were no longer unusual, devices other than ladders were needed for access to mines. Dörell found out that miners, in terms of physical strength, had to consume almost one-third more of their energy to climb up the shaft than they had to spend at work during the shift in the mine. Accordingly, in 1833 he constructed the miner's elevator. Two timbered bars, similar to those used for pumps, were installed in the shaft and were driven by water-wheel and moved in opposite directions. They were placed at such a distance from each other that the miners could easily step from one to the other in order to go up or down the shaft as desired.

Dörell's elevators worked with great success and their use soon became widespread among Central European mining districts. Their use is particularly associated with Cornish tin-mines, where several such elevators operated over considerable distances.

Bibliography

1837, 'Über die seit dem Jahre 1833 beim Oberharzischen Bergbau angewendeten Fahrmaschinen', *Die Bergwerks-Verwaltung des Hannoverschen Ober-Harzes in den Jahren 1831–1836*, ed. W.A.J. Albert, Berlin, pp. 199–214.

Further Reading

C. Bartels, 1992, *Vom frühneuzeitlichen Montangewerbe zur Bergbauindustrie. Erzbergbau im Oberharz 1635–1880*, Bochum: Deutsches Bergbau-Museum, esp. pp. 382–411 (elaborates upon the context of contemporary technological innovations in Harz ore mining).

WK

Dorr, Samuel Griswold
See **Dore, Samuel Griswold**.

Douglas, Donald Wills
b. 6 April 1892 Brooklyn, New York, USA
d. 1 February 1981 Palm Springs, California, USA

American aircraft designer best known for his outstanding airliner, the DC-3.

In 1912 Donald Douglas went to the Massachusetts Institute of Technology to study aeronautical engineering. After graduating in this relatively new subject he joined the Glenn L. Martin Company as Chief Engineer. In 1920 he founded the Davis–Douglas Company in California to build an aircraft capable of flying across America nonstop: unfortunately, the *Cloudster* failed to achieve its target. Douglas reorganized the company in 1921 as the Douglas Company (later it became the Douglas Aircraft Company). In 1924 a team of US Army personnel made the first round-the-world flight in specially designed Douglas *World Cruisers*, a feat which boosted Douglas's reputation considerably. This reputation was further enhanced by his airliner, designed in 1935, that revolutionized air travel: the Douglas *Commercial 3*, or *DC-3*, of which some 13,000 were built. A series of piston-engined airliners followed, culminating in the *DC-7*. Meanwhile, in the military field, Douglas aircraft played a major part in the Second World War. In the jet age Douglas continued to produce a wide range of successful civil and military aircraft, and the company also moved into the rocket and guided missile business. In 1966 Donald W. Douglas was still Chairman of the company, with Donald W. Douglas Jr as President. In 1967 the company merged with the McDonnell Aircraft Company to become the giant McDonnell Douglas Corporation.

Principal Honours and Distinctions
American Institute of Aeronautics and Astronautics; Daniel Guggenheim Medal 1939.

Bibliography
1935, 'The development and reliability of the modern multi-engined airliner', *Journal of the Royal Aeronautical Society*, London (lecture).

Further Reading
B. Yenne, 1985, *McDonnell Douglas: A Tale of Two Giants*, London (pays some attention to both Douglas and McDonnell, but also covers the history of the companies and the aircraft they produced).
René J. Francillon, 1979, *McDonnell Douglas Aircraft since 1920*, London; 1988, 2nd edn (a comprehensive history of the company's aircraft).

JDS

Dow, Herbert Henry
b. 26 February 1866 Belleville, Ontario, Canada
d. 15 October 1930 Rochester, Minnesota, USA

American industrial chemist, pioneer manufacturer of magnesium alloys.

Of New England ancestry, his family returned there soon after his birth and later moved to Cleveland, Ohio. In 1884, Dow entered the Case School of Applied Science, graduating in science four years later. His thesis dealt partly with the brines of Ohio, and he was persuaded to present a paper on brine to the meeting of the American Association for he Advancement of Science being held in Cleveland the same year. That entailed visits to collect samples of brines from various localities, and led to the observation that their composition varied, one having a higher lithium content while another was richer in bromine. This study of brines proved to be the basis for his career in industrial chemistry. In 1888 Dow was appointed Professor of Chemistry at the Homeopathic Hospital College in Cleveland, but he continued to work on brine, obtaining a patent in the same year for extracting bromine by blowing air through slightly electrolysed brine. He set up a small company to exploit the process, but it failed; the process was taken up and successfully worked by the Midland Chemical Company in Midland, Michigan. The electrolysis required a direct-current generator which, when it was installed in 1892, was probably the first of its kind in America. Dow next set up a company to produce chlorine by the electrolysis of brine. It moved to Midland in 1896, and the Dow Central Company purchased the

Midland Chemical Company in 1900. Its main concern was the manufacture of bleaching powder, but the company continued to grow, based on Dow's steady development of chemical compounds that could be derived from brines. His search for further applications of chlorine led to the making of insecticides and an interest in horticulture. Meanwhile, his experience at the Homeopathic Hospital doubtless fired an interest in pharmaceuticals. One of the substances found in brine was magnesium chloride, and by 1918 magnesium metal was being produced on a small scale by electrolysis. An intensive study of its alloys followed, leading to the large-scale production of these important light-metal alloys, under the name of Dowmetals. Two other 'firsts' achieved by the company were the synthetic indigo process and the production of the element iodine in the USA. The Dow company became one of the leading chemical manufacturers in the USA, and at the same time Dow played an active part in public life, serving on many public and education boards.

Principal Honours and Distinctions
Society of Chemical Industry Perkin Medal 1930.

Bibliography
Dow was granted 65 patents for a wide range of chemical processes.

Further Reading
Obituary, 1930, *Ind. Eng. Chem.* (October).
'The Dow Chemical Company', 1925, *Ind. Eng. Chem.* (September)

LRD

Downing, Samuel
b. 19 July 1811 Bagenalstown, Co. Carlow, Ireland
d. 21 April 1882

Irish engineer and teacher.

Samuel Downing had a formative influence on the development of engineering education in Ireland. He was educated at Kilkenny College and Trinity College, Dublin, where he took a BA in 1834. He subsequently attended courses in natural philosophy at Edinburgh, before taking up work as a railway and bridge engineer. Amongst structures on which he worked were

the timber viaduct connecting Portland Island to the mainland in Dorset, England, and the curved viaduct at Coed-re-Coed on the Taff Vale Railway, Wales. In 1847 he was persuaded to return to Trinity College, Dublin, as Assistant to Sir John **MacNeill**, who had been appointed Professor of Engineering in the School of Engineering on its establishment in 1842. MacNeill always found it difficult to give up time on his engineering practice to spend on his teaching duties, so the addition of Downing to the staff gave a great impetus to the effectiveness of the School. When MacNeill retired from the Chair in 1852, Downing was his obvious successor and held the post until his death. For thirty years Downing devoted his engineering expertise and the energy of his warm personality to the School of Engineering and its students, of whom almost four hundred passed through the School in the years when he was responsible for it.

Principal Honours and Distinctions
Associate Member, Institution of Civil Engineers 1852.

Bibliography
Elements of Practical Hydraulics
Elements of Practical Construction

Further Reading
Proceedings of the Institution of Civil Engineers 72: 310–11.

AB

Drais, Baron von
See **Sauerbrun, Charles de, Baron von Drais**.

Drake, Edwin Laurentine
b. 29 March 1819 Greenville, New York, USA
d. 8 November 1880 Bethlehem, Pennsylvania, USA

American pioneer oil driller.

He worked on his father's farm, was a clerk in a hotel and a store, and then became an express agent at a railway company in Springfield, Massachusetts, *c.*1845. After he had been working as a railway conductor in New Haven, Connecticut, for eight years, he resigned because of ill health. Owning some stocks in a Pennsylvania rock-oil company, which gathered oil from ground-level seepages mainly for medicinal use, he was engaged by this company and moved to Titusville, Pennsylvania, at the age of almost 40. After studying salt-well drilling by cable tool, which was still percussive, he became enthusiastic about the idea of using the same method to drill for oil, especially after researches in chemistry had revealed this new sort of fossil energy some years before.

As a manager of the Seneca Oil Company, which referred to him as 'Colonel' in letters of introduction simply to impress people with such titles, Drake began drilling in 1858, almost at the same time as pole-tool drilling for oil was started in Germany. His main contribution to the technology was the use of an iron pipe driven through the quicksand and the bedrock to prevent the bore-hole from filling. After nineteen months he struck oil at a depth of 21 m (69 ft) in August 1859. This was the first time that petroleum was struck at its source and the first proof of the presence of oil reservoirs within the earth's surface. Drake inaugurated the search for and the exploitation of the deep oil resources of the world and he initiated the science of petroleum engineering which became established at the beginning of the twentieth century.

Drake failed to patent his drilling method; he was content being an oil commission merchant and Justice of the Peace in Titusville, which like other places in Pennsylvania became a boom town. Four years later he went to New York, where he lost all his money in oil speculations. He became very ill again and lived in poverty in Vermont and New Jersey until 1873, when he moved to Bethlehem, Pennsylvania, where he was pensioned by the state of Pennsylvania. The city of Titusville erected a monument to him and founded the Drake Museum.

Further Reading
Dictionary of American Biography, Vol. III, pp. 427–8.
Ida M. Tarbell, 1904, 'The birth of industry', *History of the Standard Oil Company*, Vol. I, New York (gives a lively description of the booming years in Pennsylvania caused by Drake's successful drilling).
H.F. Williamson and A.R. Daum, 1959, *The American Petroleum Industry. The Age of Illumination*, Evanston, Ill.

WK

Drinker, Cecil Kent
b. 17 March 1887 Philadelphia, Pennsylvania, USA
d. 14 April 1956 Falmouth, Massachusetts, USA

American physiologist, co-inventor of the Drinker respirator (iron lung).

Drinker attended the University of Pennsylvania and graduated MD in 1913. After clinical experience in Boston and, in 1915–16, at Johns Hopkins, he joined the Department of Physiology at Harvard and was appointed Professor in 1924. Apart from continuing his activities in applied physiology, he was also head of the Department of Public Health. As well as investigating poisoning from radium, manganese and carbon monoxide, he was also engaged in a study of the lymphatics and respiration. During the Second World War his earlier work on the iron lung, which he had developed in 1927 with his brother Philip (1894–1972), was deployed in the study and improvement of high-altitude oxygen masks and decompression equipment for service use. He continued an association with the Naval Medical College until 1954, but retired from Harvard in 1948.

Bibliography
1929, 'The use of a new apparatus for the prolonged administration of artificial respiration', *American Medical Association* (with P. McKhann).
1954, *The Clinical Physiology of the Lungs.*
1945, *Pulmonary Edema and Inflammation.*

Further Reading
C. Drinker Bowen, 1970, *Family Portrait.*

MG

Drummond, Thomas
b. 10 October 1797 Edinburgh, Scotland
d. 15 April 1840 Dublin, Ireland

Scottish inventor of limelight.

Drummond entered Woolwich Arsenal as a cadet in 1813 and the Royal Engineers two years later. In 1820 he joined Colonel Colby at work on the ordnance survey, meanwhile continuing his studies in mathematics and chemistry under Brand and **Faraday** at the Royal Institution. His two chief inventions, limelight, or Drummond light, and the heliostatia, were aimed to facilitate the work of the survey by day and night. The light had a sensational effect on the scientific world; Sir John Herschel has left a vivid account of demonstrations of various lights far surpassed in brilliance by limelight. Limelight was brought into use in the autumn of 1825 during the survey of Ireland. In 1829 Drummond began adapting it for use in lighthouses. It was effective, but expensive to operate, and Drummond was seeking ways of making it cheaper when, after a meeting with Brougham in 1831, he gave up the work and turned to politics and administration. From 1835, he was in all but name governor of Ireland, spending himself in the service of his adopted country until overwork brought about his early death in 1840.

LRD

Du Cane, Peter
b. England
d. 31 October 1984

English engineer, one of the foremost designers of small high-speed ships.

Peter Du Cane was appointed a midshipman in the Royal Navy in 1913, having commenced as a cadet at the tender age of 13. At the end of the First World War he transferred to the engineering branch and was posted ultimately to the Yangtze River gunboat fleet. In 1928 he resigned, trained as a pilot and then joined the shipbuilders Vosper Ltd of Portsmouth. For thirty-five years he held the posts of Managing Director and Chief Designer, developing the company's expertise in high-speed, small warships, pleasure craft and record breakers. During the Second World War the company designed and built many motor torpedo-boats, air–sea rescue craft and similar ships. Du Cane served for some months in the Navy, but at the request of the Government he returned to his post in the shipyard. The most glamorous products of the yard were the record breakers *Bluebird II*, with which Malcolm Campbell took the world water speed record in 1939, and the later *Crusader*, in which John Cobb lost his life. Despite this blow the company went from strength to strength, producing the epic Brave class fast patrol craft for the Royal Navy, which led to export orders. In 1966 the yard merged with John I. Thornycroft Ltd. Commander Du

Cane retired seven years later.

Principal Honours and Distinctions
Commander of the Royal Navy. CBE 1965.

Bibliography
1951, *High Speed Small Craft*, London: Temple Press.

Further Reading
C. Dawson, 1972, *A Quest for Speed at Sea*, London: Hutchinson.

FMW

Ducos du Hauron, Arthur-Louis
b. 1837 Langon, Bordeaux, France
d. 19 August 1920 Agen, France

French scientist and pioneer of colour photography.

The son of a tax collector, Ducos du Hauron began researches into colour photography soon after the publication of Clerk Maxwell's experiment in 1861. In a communication sent in 1862 for presentation at the Académie des Sciences, but which was never read, he outlined a number of methods for photography of colours. Subsequently, in his book *Les Couleurs en photographie*, published in 1869, he outlined most of the principles of additive and subtractive colour photography that were later actually used. He covered additive processes, developed from Clerk Maxwell's demonstrations, and subtractive processes which could yield prints. At the time, the photographic materials available prevented the processes from being employed effectively. The design of his Chromoscope, in which transparent reflectors could be used to superimpose three additive images, was sound, however, and formed the basis of a number of later devices. He also proposed an additive system based on the use of a screen of fine red, yellow and blue lines, through which the photograph was taken and viewed. The lines blended additively when seen from a certain distance. Many years later, in 1907, Ducos du Hauron was to use this principle in an early commercial screen-plate process, *Omnicolore*. With his brother Alcide, he published a further work in 1878, *Photographie des Couleurs*, which described some more-practical subtractive processes. A few prints made at this time still survive and they are remarkably good for the period.

In a French patent of 1895 he described yet another method for colour photography. His '*polyfolium chromodialytique*' involved a multiple-layer package of separate red-, green- and blue-sensitive materials and filters, which with a single exposure would analyse the scene in terms of the three primary colours. The individual layers would be separated for subsequent processing and printing. In a refined form, this is the principle behind modern colour films. In 1891 he patented and demonstrated the anaglyph method of stereoscopy, using superimposed red and green left and right eye images viewed through green and red filters. Ducos du Hauron's remarkable achievement was to propose theories of virtually all the basic methods of colour photography at a time when photographic materials were not adequate for the purpose of proving them correct. For his work on colour photography he was awarded the Progress Medal of the Royal Photographic Society in 1900, but despite his major contributions to colour photography he remained in poverty for much of his later life.

Further Reading
B. Coe, 1978, *Colour Photography: The First Hundred Years*, London.
J.S. Friedman, 1944, *History of Colour Photography*, Boston.
E.J. Wall, 1925, *The History of Three-Colour Photography*, Boston.

See also **Cros, Charles**.

BC

Duddell, William du Bois
b. 1872 Kensington, London, England
d. 4 November 1917 London, England

English engineer, inventor of the first practical oscillograph.

After an education at the College of Stanislas, Cannes, Duddell served an apprenticeship with Davy Paxman of Colchester. Studying under **Ayrton** and Mather at the Central Technical College in South Kensington, he found the facilities for experimental work of exceptional value to him and remained there for some years. In 1897 Duddell produced a galvanometer which was sufficiently responsive to display an alternating-current wave-form. This instrument,

with a coil carrying a mirror in the air gap of a powerful electromagnet, had a small periodic time. An oscillating mirror driven by a synchronous motor spread out the deflection on a time-scale. This development became the first commercial oscillograph and brought Duddell into prominence as a first-rate designer of special instruments. The Duddell oscillograph remained in use until after the Second World War, examples being used for recording short-circuit tests on high-power switchgear and other rapidly varying or transient phenomena. His next important work was to collaborate with Professor Marchant at Liverpool University to investigate the characteristics of the electric arc. This led to the suggestion that, coupled to a resonant circuit, the electric arc could form a generator of high-frequency currents. This arrangement was later developed by **Poulson** for wireless telegraphy. Duddell spent the last years of his life on government research as a member of the Admiralty Board of Inventions and Research and also of the Inventions Board of the Ministry of Munitions.

Principal Honours and Distinctions
CBE 1916. FRS 1907. Royal Society Hughes Medal 1912. President, Institution of Electrical Engineers 1912 and 1913.

Bibliography
1897, *Electrician*, 39: 636–8 (describes his oscillograph).
5 March 1898, British patent no. 5,449 (the oscillograph).
1899, with E.W. Marchant, 'Experiments on alternate current arcs by aid of oscillograph', *Journal of the Institution of Electrical Engineers* 28: 1–107.

Further Reading
V.J. Phillips, 1987, *Waveforms*, Bristol (a comprehensive account).
1945, '50 years of scientific instrument manufacture', *Engineering*, 159: 461.

GW

Dudley, Dud
b. 1599
d. 25 October 1684 Worcester, England

English ironmaster who drew attention to the need to change from charcoal to coal as a fuel for iron smelting.

Dudley was the fourth natural son of Edward Sutton, fifth Baron Dudley. In 1619 he was summoned from Balliol College, Oxford, to superintend his father's ironworks at Pensnet in Worcestershire. There had long been concern at the destruction of the forests in order to make charcoal for the smelting of iron ore, and unsuccessful attempts had been made to substitute coal as a fuel. Finding that charcoal was in short supply and coal plentiful near Pensnet, Dudley was stimulated by these attempts to try the process for himself. He claimed to have made good, marketable iron and in 1621 his father obtained a patent from the King to protect his process for thirty-one years. After a serious flood, Dudley moved to Staffordshire and continued his efforts there. In 1639 he was granted a further patent for making iron with coal. Although he probably made some samples of good iron, more by luck than judgement, it is hardly possible that he achieved consistent success. He blamed this on the machinations of other ironmasters. The day that King Charles II landed in England to assume his throne, Dudley petitioned him to renew his patents, but he was refused and he ceased to promote his invention. In 1665, however, he published his celebrated book *Metallum Martis, Iron Made with Pit-Coale, Sea-Coale . . . .* In this he described his efforts in general terms, but neither there nor in his patents does he give any technical details of his methods. He implied the use of slack or small coal from the Staffordshire Thick or Ten Yard coal, but this has a sulphur content that would have rendered the iron unusable; in addition, this coal would not have been suitable for converting to coke in order to remove the sulphur. Nevertheless, Dudley recognized the need to change from charcoal to coal as a fuel for iron smelting and drew attention to it, even though he himself achieved little success.

Further Reading

H.R. Schubert, 1957, *History of the British Iron and Steel Industry AD 430 to AD 1775*, London: Routledge & Kegan Paul.
W.K.V. Gale, 1967, *The British Iron and Steel Industry: A Technical History*, London (provides brief details of Dudley's life in relation to the history of ironmaking).

LRD

Dumont, Alberto Santos

See **Santos-Dumont, Alberto**.

Dunlop, John Boyd

b. 5 February 1840 Dreghorn, Ayrshire, Scotland
d. 23 October 1921 Ballsbridge, Dublin, Ireland

Scottish inventor and pioneer of the pneumatic tyre.

Reared in an agricultural community, Dunlop became a qualified veterinary surgeon and practised successfully in Edinburgh and then in Belfast when he moved there in 1867. In October 1887, Dunlop's 9-year-old son complained of the rough ride he experienced with his tricycle over the cobbled streets of Belfast. Dunlop devised and fitted rubber air tubes, held on to a wooden ring by tacking a linen covering which he fixed around the wheels of the tricycle. A marked improvement in riding quality was noted. After further development, a new tricycle was ordered, with the new air-tube wheels. This was so successful that Dunlop applied for a patent on 23 July 1889, granted on 7 December. With tyres made in Edinburgh to his specification, bicycles were manufactured by Edlin & Co. of Belfast and put on sale complete with pneumatic tyres. The successful performance of a racing bicycle thus equipped inspired an unsuccessful competitor, William Harvey de Cros, who had used a solid-tyred machine, to take an interest in Dunlop's invention. With Dunlop, he refloated a company in Dublin, the Pneumatic Tyre & Booth's Cycle Agency. Dunlop made over his patents, for the tyre, valves, rims and fixing methods, to Du Cros and took shares in the company. Although he was involved in it for many years, it was Du Cros who steered the company through several struggles to success.

The pneumatic tyre revolutionized cycling and made possible the success of the motor vehicle, although Dunlop did not profit greatly from his invention. After the sale of the company in 1896, to E.T. Hooley for $3 million, he took no further part in the development of the pneumatic tyre. The company went on to become the great Dunlop Rubber Company.

Further Reading
J. McClintock, 1923, *History of the Pneumatic Tyre*, Belfast (written by Dunlop's daughter, who based the book on her father's reminiscences).
LRD

Dunne, John William

b. 2 December 1875 Co. Kildare, Ireland
d. 24 August 1949 Oxfordshire, England

Irish inventor who pioneered tailless aircraft designed to be inherently stable.

After serving in the British Army during the Boer War. Dunne returned home convinced that aeroplanes would be more suitable than balloons for reconnaissance work. He built models to test his ideas for a tailless design based on the winged seed of a Javanese climbing plant. In 1906 Dunne joined the staff of the Balloon Factory at Farnborough, where the Superintendent, Colonel J.E. Capper, was also interested in manned kites and aeroplanes. Since 1904 the colourful American 'Colonel' S.F. Cody had been experimenting at Farnborough with manned kites, and in 1908 his 'British Army Dirigible No. 1' made the first powered flight in Britain. Dunne's first swept-wing tailless glider was ready to fly in the spring of 1907, but it was deemed to be a military secret and flying it at Farnborough would be too public. Dunne, Colonel Capper and a team of army engineers took the glider to a remote site at Blair Atholl in Scotland for its test flights. It was not a great success, although it attracted snoopers, with the result that it was camouflaged. Powered versions made short hops in 1908, but then the War Office withdrew its support. Dunne and his associates set up a syndicate to continue the development of a new tailless aeroplane, the D 5; this was built by Short Brothers (see Short, Hugh Oswald) and flew successfully in 1910. It had combined elevators and ailerons on the wing tips (or elevons as they are now called when fitted to modern delta-winged aircraft). In 1913 an improved version of the D 5 was demonstrated in France, where the pilot left his cockpit and walked along the wing in flight. Dunne had proved his point and designed a stable aircraft, but his health was suffering and he retired. During the First World War, however, it was soon learned that military aircraft needed to be manoeuvrable rather than stable.

Bibliography
1913, 'The theory of the Dunne aeroplane', *Jour-*

nal of the Royal Aeronautical Society (April).
After he left aviation, Dunne became well known for his writings on the nature of the universe and the interpretation of dreams. His best known-work was *An Experiment With Time* (1927; and reprints).

Further Reading
P.B. Walker, 1971, *Early Aviation at Farnborough*, Vol. I, London; 1974, Vol. II (provides a detailed account of Dunne's early work; Vol. II is the more relevant).
P. Lewis, 1962, *British Aircraft 1809–1914*, London (for details of Dunne's aircraft).
JDS

Dunwoody, General Henry H.C.

fl. *c*.1906 USA

American soldier and engineer noted for his discovery of the carborundum radio-signal detector.

An associate of Lee **De Forest**, Henry Dunwoody discovered in 1906 that the newly invented material silicon carbide (SiC) could be used as a solid-state detector of radio waves. His invention was patented in the UK on 23 March 1906.

Bibliography
23 March 1906, British patent no. 5,332 (use of silicon carbide as a solid-state detector of radio waves).

Further Reading
G.G. Blake, 1926, *History of Telegraphy and Telephony*, London: Radio Press.

See also **Branly, Edouard Eugène**.

KF

Durand, Peter

fl. early 1800s England

English merchant who initiated the process of canning food.

Durand sold his idea to Bryan **Donkin** I and John Hall, who opened the first canned food factory in 1811.

See also **Appert, Nicolas**.

IMcN

Duryea, Charles Edgar

b. 15 December 1861 Cawton, Ohio, USA
d. 28 September 1938 Philadelphia, Pennsylvania, USA

American inventor and pioneer car maker.

He began his career in the bicycle trade, in which he invented a number of devices. He launched his own business in Peoria, Illinois, and later moved to Springfield, Massachusetts. In 1891 he had designed a motor-driven carriage and a gas engine and, with his brother, J. Frank Duryea, he built the first successful American car, which was demonstrated in Springfield in September, 1893. An improved version, largely designed by Frank Duryea, won several races both at home and abroad in 1895–6. The Duryea Motor Wagon Company made the first sale of an American-made automobile in 1896. Charles later organized the Duryea Power Company, manufacturing a three-cylinder car until 1914, the brothers parting company in 1898. Frank developed the Stevens–Duryea between 1903 and 1914.

Further Reading
Dictionary of American Biography, Vol. XI (Suppl. 2), New York: Charles Scribner.

IMcN

Du Shi (Tu Shih)

fl. 25/57 AD China

Chinese official of high rank and patron of engineers.

He was Prefect of Nanyang, a region that had long been noted as a centre for metallurgical operations. He devised or at least sponsored the construction of water-powered blowing engines (hydraulic reciprocators or *shui pai*) for blast furnaces and forges in ironworks for making agricultural implements. This invention is significant because it incorporated all the components needed to convert rotary motion to reciprocating motion. The only watermills previously known in China were those recorded by Huan Tan in the first century BC.

Further Reading
Joseph Needham, *Science and Civilisation in China*, Cambridge: Cambridge University Press, 1965, Vol. IV.2, pp. 31, 32, 85, 370,

377; *Clerks and Craftsmen in China and the West*, 1970, pp. 119, 177, 186–7, 189.

LRD

Du Yu (Tu Yu)

b. 222 China
d. 284 China

Chinese general and engineer.

Du Yu was one of the generals who reduced the San Guo state of Wu for the Chin in 280. He is credited with the diffusion of the water-powered trip hammer and the multiple-geared watermill for the grinding of cereals. A battery of trip hammers was developed, operated by several shafts working off one large water-wheel. He was responsible for the construction of the Heyang pontoon bridges over the Yellow River northeast of Leyang in 274 and also devised new designs for water-powered blowing engines, against the advice of the imperial advisors but with the emperor's encouragement.

Further Reading
Joseph Needham, *Science and Civilisation in China*, Cambridge: Cambridge University Press, 1959–1965, Vols III, p. 601; IV.1, p. 35, IV.2, pp. 30, 86, 195, 393, 394, 396; IV.3, pp. 160–1.

LRD

Dyer, Henry

b. 1848 Scotland
d. 4 September 1918

Scottish engineer and educator.

Henry Dyer was educated at Anderson's College and Glasgow University. He was apprenticed to the Glasgow marine engineer Alexander **Kirk**, and in 1870 he became an early holder of a Whitworth Scholarship. He was recruited at the age of 24 to establish the Tokyo Engineers' College in 1873. He had been recommended to Matheson, the Scottish businessman who was acting for the Japanese government, by W.J.M. **Rankine** of Glasgow University, who regarded Dyer as one of his most outstanding students. Dyer secured the services of a team of able young British engineers and scientists to staff the college, which opened in 1873 with 56 students and became the Imperial College of Engineering. Together they gave the first generation of Japanese engineers a firm grounding in engineering theory and practice. Dyer served as Principal and Professor of Civil and Mechanical Engineering. He left Tokyo in 1882 and returned to Britain. The remainder of his career was rather an anticlimax, although he became an active supporter of the technical education movement and was involved in the development of the Glasgow and West of Scotland Technical College, of which he was a Life Governor.

Further Reading
Who was Who, 1916–28.
W.H. Brock, 1981, 'The Japanese connexion', *BJHS* 14: 227–43.

AB

Dyer, John
fl. *c.*1833 England

English inventor of an improved milling machine for woollen cloth.

After being woven, woollen cloth needed to be cleaned and compacted to thicken it and take out the signs of weaving. The traditional way of doing this was to place the length of cloth in fulling stocks, where hammers pounded it in a solution of fuller's earth, but in 1833 John Dyer, a Trowbridge engineer, took out a patent for the first alternative way with real possibilities. He sold the patent the following year but must have reserved the right to make his machine himself, incorporating various additions and improvements into it, because many of the machines used in Trowbridge after 1850 came from him. Milling machines were often used in conjunction with fulling stocks. The cloth was made up into a continuous length and milled by rollers forcing it through a hole or spout, from where it dropped into the fulling liquid to be soaked before being pulled out and pushed through the hole again. Dyer had three pairs of rollers, with one pair set at right angles to the others so that the cloth was squeezed in two directions. These machines do not seem to have come into general use until the 1850s. His machine closely resembled those still in use.

Bibliography
1833, British patent no. 6,460 (milling machine).

Further Reading
J. de L. Mann, 1971, *The Cloth Industry in the West of England from 1660 to 1880*, Oxford (provides a brief account of the introduction of the milling machine).
K.G. Ponting, 1971, *The Woollen Industry of South-West England*, Bath (a general account of the textile industry in the West Country).

RLH

Dyer, Joseph Chessborough
b. 15 November 1780 Stonnington Point, Connecticut, USA
d. 2 May 1871 Manchester, England

American inventor of a popular type of roving frame for cotton manufacture.

As a youth, Dyer constructed an unsinkable lifeboat but did not immediately pursue his mechanical bent, for at 16 he entered the counting-house of a French refugee named Nancrède and succeeded to part of the business. He first went to England in 1801 and finally settled in 1811 when he married Ellen Jones (d. 1842) of Gower Street, London. Dyer was already linked with American inventors and brought to England **Perkins**'s plan for steel engraving in 1809, shearing and nail-making machines in 1811, and also received plans and specifications for **Fulton**'s steamboats. He seems to have acted as a sort of British patent agent for American inventors, and in 1811 took out a patent for carding engines and a card clothing machine. In 1813 there was a patent for spinning long-fibred substances such as hemp, flax or grasses, and in 1825 there was a further patent for card making machinery. Joshua **Field**, on his tour through Britain in 1821, saw a wire drawing machine and a leather splitting machine at Dyer's works as well as the card-making machines. At first Dyer lived in Camden Town, London, but he had a card clothing business in Birmingham. He moved to Manchester *c.*1816, where he developed an extensive engineering works under the name 'Joseph C. Dyer, patent card manufacturers, 8 Stanley Street, Dale Street'. In 1832 he founded another works at Gamaches, Somme, France, but this enterprise was closed in 1848 with heavy losses through the mismanagement of an agent. In 1825 Dyer improved on Danforth's roving frame and started to manufacture it. While it was still a comparatively crude machine when compared with later versions, it had the merit of turning out a large quantity of work and was very popular, realizing a large sum of money. He patented the machine that year and must have continued his interest in these machines as further patents followed in 1830 and 1835. In 1821 Dyer had been involved in the foundation of the *Manchester Guardian* (now *The Guardian*) and he was linked with the construction of the Liverpool & Manchester Railway. He was not so successful with the ill-fated Bank of Manchester, of which he was a director and in which he lost £98,000. Dyer played an active role in the community and presented many papers to the Manchester Literary and Philosophical Society. He helped to establish the Royal Institution in London and the Mechanics Institution in Manchester. In 1830 he was a member of the delegation to Paris to take contributions from the town of Manchester for the relief of those wounded in the July revolution and to congratulate Louis-Philippe on his accession. He called for the reform of Parliament and helped to form the Anti-Corn Law League. He hated slavery and wrote several articles on the subject, both prior to and during the American Civil War.

Bibliography
1811, British patent no. 3,498 (carding engines and card clothing machine).
1813, British patent no. 3,743 (spinning long-fibred substances).
1825, British patent no. 5,309 (card making machinery).
1825, British patent no. 5,217 (roving frame).
1830, British patent no. 5,909 (roving frame).
1835, British patent no. 6,863 (roving frame).

Further Reading
Dictionary of National Biography.
J.W. Hall, 1932–3, 'Joshua Field's diary of a tour in 1821 through the Midlands', *Transactions of the Newcomen Society* 6.
Evan Leigh, 1875, *The Science of Modern Cotton Spinning*, Vol. II, Manchester (provides an account of Dyer's roving frame).
D.J. Jeremy, 1981, *Transatlantic Industrial Revolution: The Diffusion of Textile Technologies Between Britain and America, 1790–1830s*, Oxford (describes Dyer's links with America).

See also **Arnold, Aza**.

RLH

E

Eads, James Buchanan

b. 23 May 1820 Lawrenceburg, Indiana, USA
d. 8 March 1887 Nassau, Bahamas

American bridge-builder and hydraulic engineer.

The son of an immigrant merchant, he was educated at the local school, leaving at the age of 13 to take on various jobs, eventually becoming a purser on a Mississippi steamboat. He was struck by the number of wrecks lying in the river; he devised a diving bell and, at the age of 22, set up in business as a salvage engineer. So successful was he at this venture that he was able to retire in three years' time and set up the first glassworks west of the Ohio River. This, however, was a failure and in 1848 he returned to the business of salvage on the Ohio River. He was so successful that he was able to retire permanently in 1857. From the start of the American Civil War in 1861 he recommended to President Lincoln that he should obtain a fleet of armour-plated, steam-powered gunboats to operate on the western rivers. He built seven of these himself, later building or converting a further eighteen. After the end of the war he obtained the contract to design and build a bridge over the Mississippi at St Louis. In this he made use of his considerable knowledge of the river-bed currents. He built a bridge with a 500 ft (150 m) centre span and a clearance of 50 ft (15 m) that was completed in 1874. The three spans are, respectively, 502 ft, 520 ft and 502 ft (153 m, 158 m and 153 m), each being spanned by an arch. The Mississippi river is subject to great changes, both seasonal and irregular, with a range of over 41 ft (12.5 m) between low and high water and a velocity varying from 4 ft (1.2 m) to 12½ ft (3.8 m) per second. The Eads Bridge was completed in 1874 and in the following year Eads was commissioned to open one of the mouths of the Mississippi, for which he constructed a number of jetty traps. He was involved later in attempts to construct a ship railway across the isthmus of Panama. He had been suffering from indifferent health for some years, and this effort was too much for him. He died on 8 March 1887. He was the first American to be awarded the Royal Society of Arts' Albert Medal.

Principal Honours and Distinctions
Royal Society of Arts Albert Medal.

Further Reading
D.B. Steinman and S.R. Watson, 1941, *Bridges and their Builders*, New York: Dover Publications.
T.I. Williams, *Biographical Dictionary of Science*.
IMcN

Eastman, George

b. 12 July 1854 Waterville, New York, USA
d. 14 March 1932 Rochester, New York, USA

American industrialist and pioneer of popular photography.

The young Eastman was a clerk-bookkeeper in the Rochester Savings Bank when in 1877 he took up photography. Taking lessons in the wet-plate process, he became an enthusiastic amateur photographer. However, the cumbersome equipment and noxious chemicals used in the process proved an obstacle, as he said, 'It seemed to be that one ought to be able to carry less than a pack-horse load.' Then he came across an account of the new gelatine dry-plate process in the *British Journal of Photography* of March 1878. He experimented in coating glass plates with the new emulsions, and was soon so successful that he decided to go into commercial manufacture. He devised a machine to simplify the coating of the plates, and travelled to England in July 1879 to patent it. In April 1880 he prepared to begin manufacture in a rented building in Rochester, and contacted the leading American photographic supply house, E. & H.T. Anthony, offering them an option as agents. A local whip manufacturer, Henry A. Strong, invested $1,000 in the enterprise and the Eastman Dry Plate Company was formed on 1 January 1881. Still working at the Savings Bank, he ran the business in his spare time, and demand grew for the quality product he was producing. The fledgling company survived a near disaster in 1882 when the quality of the emulsions dropped alarmingly. Eastman later discovered this was due to impurities in the gelatine used, and this led him to test all raw materials rigorously for quality. In 1884 the company became a corporation, the Eastman Dry Plate & Film Company, and a new product was announced. Mindful of his desire to simplify photography, Eastman, with a camera maker, William H. Walker, designed a roll-holder in which the heavy glass plates were replaced by a roll of emulsion-coated paper. The holders were made in sizes suitable for most plate cameras. Eastman designed and patented a coating machine for the large-scale production of the paper film, bringing costs down dramatically. the roll-holders were acclaimed by photographers worldwide, and prizes and medals were awarded, but Eastman was still not satisfied. The next step was to incorporate the roll-holder in a smaller, hand-held camera. His first successful design was launched in June 1888: the Kodak camera. A small box camera, it held enough paper film for 100 circular exposures, and was bought ready-loaded. After the film had been exposed, the camera was returned to Eastman's factory, where the film was removed, processed and printed, and the camera reloaded. This developing and printing service was the most revolutionary part of his invention, since at that time photographers were expected to process their own photographs, which required access to a darkroom and appropriate chemicals. The Kodak camera put photography into the hands of the countless thousands who wanted photographs without complications. Eastman's marketing slogan neatly summed up the advantage: 'You Press the Button, We Do the Rest.'

The Kodak camera was the last product in the design of which Eastman was personally involved. His company was growing rapidly, and he recruited the most talented scientists and technicians available. New products emerged regularly – notably the first commercially produced celluloid roll film for the Kodak cameras in July 1889; this material made possible the introduction of cinematography a few years later. Eastman's philosophy of simplifying photography and reducing its costs continued to influence products: for example, the introduction

of the one dollar, or five shilling, Brownie camera in 1900, which put photography in the hands of almost everyone. Over the years the Eastman Kodak Company, as it now was, grew into a giant multinational corporation with manufacturing and marketing organizations throughout the world. Eastman continued to guide the company; he pursued an enlightened policy of employee welfare and profit sharing decades before this was common in industry. He made massive donations to many concerns, notably the Massachusetts Institute of Technology, and supported schemes for the education of black people, dental welfare, calendar reform, music and many other causes. he withdrew from the day-to-day control of the company in 1925, and at last had time for recreation. On 14 March 1932, suffering from a painful terminal cancer and after tidying up his affairs, he shot himself through the heart, leaving a note: 'To my friends: My work is done. Why wait?' Although Eastman's technical innovations were made mostly at the beginning of his career, the organization which he founded and guided in its formative years was responsible for many of the major advances in photography over the years.

Further Reading

C. Ackerman, 1929, *George Eastman*, Cambridge, Mass.

B. Coe, 1973, *George Eastman and the Early Photographers*, London.

BC

Ebener, Erasmus
b. 21 December 1511 Nuremberg, Germany
d. 24 November 1577 Helmstedt, Germany

German mining entrepreneur who introduced a new method of brassmaking.

A descendant of Nuremberg nobility, Ebener became recognized as a statesman in his native city and was employed also by foreign dignitaries. His appointment as Privy Councillor to the Dukes of Brunswick involved him in mining and metallurgical affairs at the great Rammelsberg mixed-ore mine at Goslar in the Harz mountains. About 1550, at Rammelsberg, Ebener is believed to have made brass by incorporating accretions of zinc formed in crevices of local lead-smelting furnaces. This small-scale production of impure zinc, formerly discarded as waste, could be used to replace calamine, the carbonate ore of zinc, which by tradition had been combined with copper in European brassmaking. **Ercker**, writing in 1574, mentions the accretions at Goslar obtained by removing furnace sections to make this material available for brass. The true nature of the zinc ore, calamine, and zinc metal compared with these accretions was determined only much later, but variation in quality with respect to impurities made the material most suitable for cast brassware rather than beaten goods. As quantities were small and much valued, distribution from Goslar was limited, not normally reaching Britain, where production of brasses continued to rely on calamine or expensive zinc imports from the East. Rammelsberg profited from the waste material accumulating over the years and its use at Bundheim brassworks east of Goslar. Ebener partnered Duke Henry the Younger of Brunswick in financing a new drainage adit at Rammelsberg, and was later granted several iron mines and smelting works. From 1556 he was granted rights to market calamine from the Lower Harz and copper sulphate from Rammelsberg. Ebener later had an important role at the court of Duke Julius, son of Henry, advising him on the founding of Helmstedt University.

Bibliography
1572, 'Sundry expositions on mines, metals and other useful things found in the Harz and especially at the Rammelsberg', reproduced and annotated by F.J.F. Meyer and J.F.L. Hausmann, 1805 Hercynian Archive.

Further Reading
Beckmann, 1846, *History of Inventions*, Vol. II, trans. William Johnston, London (the most concise account).
W. Bornhardt, 1989, 'The History of Rammelsberg Mine', trans. T.A. Morrison, *The Mining Journal* (has additional brief references to Ebener in the context of Rammelsberg).

JD

Eccles, William Henry
b. 23 August 1875 Ulverston, Cumbria, England
d. 27 April 1966 Oxford, England

English physicist who made important contributions to the development of radio communications.

After early education at home and at private school, Eccles won a scholarship to the Royal College of Science (now Imperial College), London, where he gained a First Class BSc in physics in 1898. He then worked as a demonstrator at the college and studied coherers, for which he obtained a DSc in 1901. Increasingly interested in electrical engineering, he joined the Marconi Company in 1899 to work on oscillators at the Poole experimental radio station, but in 1904 he returned to academic life as Professor of Mathematics and Physics and Department Head at South West Polytechnic, Chelsea. There he discovered ways of using the negative resistance of galena-crystal detectors to generate oscillations and gave a mathematical description of the operation of the triode valve. In 1910 he became Reader in Engineering at University College, London, where he published a paper explaining the reflection of radio waves by the ionosphere and designed a 60 MHz short-wave transmitter. From 1916 to 1926 he was Professor of Applied Physics and Electrical Engineering at the Finsbury City & Guilds College and a private consulting engineer. During the First World War he was a military scientific adviser and Secretary to the Joint Board of Scientific Societies. After the war he made many contributions to electronic-circuit development, many of them (including the Eccles–Jordan 'flip-flop' patented in 1918 and used in binary counters) in conjunction with F.W. Jordan, about whom little seems to be known. Illness forced Eccles's premature academic retirement in 1926, but he remained active as a consultant for many years.

Principal Honours and Distinctions
FRS 1921. President, Institution of Electrical Engineers, 1926–7. President, Physical Society 1929. President, Radio Society of Great Britain.

Bibliography
1912, 'On the diurnal variation of the electric waves occurring in nature and on the propagation of electric waves round the bend of the earth', *Proceedings of the Royal Society* 87: 79.
1919, with F.W. Jordan, 'Method of using two

triode valves in parallel for generating oscillations', *Electrician* 299: 3.
1915, *Handbook of Wireless Telegraphy*.
1921, *Continuous Wave Wireless Telegraphy*.

Further Reading
1971, 'William Henry Eccles, 1875–1966', *Biographical Memoirs of the Royal Society*, London, 17.

See also: **Heaviside, Oliver**; **Kenelly, Arthur Edwin**.

KF

Edison, Thomas Alva
b. 11 February 1847 Milan, Ohio, USA
d. 18 October 1931 Glenmont

American inventor and pioneer electrical developer.

He was the son of Samuel Edison, who was in the timber business. His schooling was delayed due to scarlet fever until 1855, when he was 8½ years old, but he was an avid reader. By the age of 14 he had a job as a newsboy on the railway from Port Huron to Detroit, a distance of sixty-three miles (101 km). He worked a fourteen-hour day with a stopover of five hours, which he spent in the Detroit Free Library. He also sold sweets on the train and, later, fruit and vegetables, and was soon making a profit of $20 a week. He then started two stores in Port Huron and used a spare freight car as a laboratory. He added a hand-printing press to produce 400 copies weekly of *The Grand Trunk Herald*, most of which he compiled and edited himself. He set himself to learn telegraphy from the station agent at Mount Clements, whose son he had saved from being run over by a freight car.

At the age of 16 he became a telegraphist at Port Huron. In 1863 he became railway telegraphist at the busy Stratford Junction of the Grand Trunk Railroad, arranging a clock with a notched wheel to give the hourly signal which was to prove that he was awake and at his post! He left hurriedly after failing to hold a train which was nearly involved in a head-on collision. He usually worked the night shift, allowing himself time for experiments during the day. His first invention was an arrangement of two Morse registers so that a high-speed input could be decoded at a slower speed. Moving from place to place he held many positions as a telegraphist. In Boston he invented an automatic vote recorder for Congress and patented it, but the idea was rejected. This was the first of a total of 1180 patents that he was to take out during his lifetime. After six years he resigned from the Western Union Company to devote all his time to invention, his next idea being an improved ticker-tape machine for stockbrokers. He developed a duplex telegraphy system, but this was turned down by the Western Union Company. He then moved to New York.

Edison found accommodation in the battery room of Law's Gold Reporting Company, sleeping in the cellar, and there his repair of a broken transmitter marked him as someone of special talents. His superior soon resigned, and he was promoted with a salary of $300 a month. Western Union paid him $40,000 for the sole rights on future improvements on the duplex telegraph, and he moved to Ward Street, Newark, New Jersey, where he employed a gathering of specialist engineers. Within a year, he married one of his employees, Mary Stilwell, when she was only 16: a daughter, Marion, was born in 1872, and two sons, Thomas and William, in 1876 and 1879, respectively.

He continued to work on the automatic telegraph, a device to send out messages faster than they could be tapped out by hand: that is, over fifty words per minute or so. An earlier machine by Alexander **Bain** worked at up to 400 words per minute, but was not good over long distances. Edison agreed to work on improving this feature of Bain's machine for the Automatic Telegraph Company (ATC) for $40,000. He improved it to a working speed of 500 words per minute and ran a test between Washington and New York. Hoping to sell their equipment to the Post Office in Britain, ATC sent Edison to England in 1873 to negotiate. A 500-word message was to be sent from Liverpool to London every half-hour for six hours, followed by tests on 2,200 miles (3,540 km) of cable at Greenwich. Only confused results were obtained due to induction in the cable, which lay coiled in a water tank. Edison returned to New York, where he worked on his quadruplex telegraph system, tests of which proved a success between New York and Albany in December 1874. Unfortunately, simultaneous negotiation with Western Union and ATC resulted in a lawsuit.

Alexander Graham **Bell** was granted a patent for a telephone in March 1876 while Edison was still working on the same idea. His improvements allowed the device to operate over a distance of hundreds of miles instead of only a few miles. Tests were carried out over the 106 miles (170 km) between New York and Philadelphia. Edison applied for a patent on the carbon-button transmitter in April 1877, Western Union agreeing to pay him $6,000 a year for the seventeen-year duration of the patent. In these years he was also working on the development of the electric lamp and on a duplicating machine which would make up to 3,000 copies from a stencil. In 1876–7 he moved from Newark to Menlo Park, twenty-four miles (39 km) from New York on the Pennsylvania Railway, near Elizabeth. He had bought a house there around which he built the premises that would become his 'inventions factory'. It was there that he began the use of his 200-page pocket notebooks, each of which lasted him about two weeks, so prolific were his ideas. When he died he left 3,400 of them filled with notes and sketches.

Late in 1877 he applied for a patent for a phonograph which was granted on 19 February 1878, and by the end of the year he had formed a company to manufacture this totally new product. At the time, Edison saw the device primarily as a business aid rather than for entertainment, rather as a dictating machine. In August 1878 he was granted a British patent. In July 1878 he tried to measure the heat from the solar corona at a solar eclipse viewed from Rawlins, Wyoming, but his 'tasimeter' was too sensitive.

Probably his greatest achievement was 'The Subdivision of the Electric Light' or the 'glow bulb'. He tried many materials for the filament before settling on carbon. He gave a demonstration of electric light by lighting up Menlo Park and inviting the public. Edison was, of course, faced with the problem of inventing and producing all the ancillaries which go to make up the electrical system of generation and distribution – meters, fuses, insulation, switches, cabling – even generators had to be designed and built; everything was new. He started a number of manufacturing companies to produce the various components needed.

In 1881 he built the world's largest generator, which weighed 27 tons, to light 1,200 lamps at the Paris Exhibition. It was later moved to England to be used in the world's first central power station with steam engine drive at Holborn Viaduct, London. In September 1882 he started up his Pearl Street Generating Station in New York, which led to a worldwide increase in the application of electric power, particularly for lighting. At the same time as these developments, he built a 1,300 yd (1,190 m) electric railway at Menlo Park.

On 9 August 1884 his wife died of typhoid. Using his telegraphic skills, he proposed to 19-year-old Mina Miller in Morse code while in the company of others on a train. He married her in February 1885 before buying a new house and estate at West Orange, New Jersey, building a new laboratory not far away in the Orange Valley.

Edison used direct current which was limited to around 250 volts. Alternating current was largely developed by George **Westinghouse** and Nicola **Tesla**, using transformers to step up the current to a higher voltage for long-distance transmission. The use of AC gradually overtook the Edison DC system.

In autumn 1888 he patented a form of cine-photography, the kinetoscope, obtaining film-stock from George **Eastman**. In 1893 he set up the first film studio, which was pivoted so as to catch the sun, with a hinged roof which could be raised. In 1894 kinetoscope parlours with 'peep shows' were starting up in cities all over America. Competition came from the Latham Brothers with a screen-projection machine, which Edison answered with his 'Vitascope', shown in New York in 1896. This showed pictures with accompanying sound, but there was some difficulty with synchronization. Edison also experimented with captions at this early date.

In 1880 he filed a patent for a magnetic ore separator, the first of nearly sixty. He bought up deposits of low-grade iron ore which had been developed in the north of New Jersey. The process was a commercial success until the discovery of iron-rich ore in Minnesota rendered it uneconomic and uncompetitive. In 1898 cement rock was discovered in New Village, west of West Orange. Edison bought the land and started cement manufacture, using kilns twice the normal length and using half as much fuel to heat them as the normal type of kiln. In 1893 he met Henry **Ford**, who was building his second car, at an Edison convention. This started him on the development of a battery for an electric car on which he made over 9,000 experiments. In 1903 he sold his patent for wireless telegraphy 'for a song' to Guglielmo **Marconi**.

In 1910 Edison designed a prefabricated concrete house. In December 1914 fire destroyed three-quarters of the West Orange plant, but it was at once rebuilt, and with the threat of war Edison started to set up his own plants for making all the chemicals that he had previously been buying from Europe, such as carbolic acid, phenol, benzol, aniline dyes, etc. He was appointed President of the Navy Consulting Board, for whom, he said, he made some forty-five inventions, 'but they were pigeonholed, every one of them'. Thus did Edison find that the Navy did not take kindly to civilian interference.

In 1927 he started the Edison Botanic Research Company, founded with similar investment from Ford and Firestone with the object of finding a substitute for overseas-produced rubber. In the first year he tested no fewer than 3,327 possible plants, in the second year, over 1,400, eventually developing a variety of Golden Rod which grew to 14 ft (4.3 m) in height. However, all this effort and money was wasted, due to the discovery of synthetic rubber.

In October 1929 he was present at Henry Ford's opening of his Dearborn Museum to celebrate the fiftieth anniversary of the incandescent lamp, including a replica of the Menlo Park laboratory. He was awarded the Congressional Gold Medal and was elected to the American Academy of Sciences. He died in 1931 at his home, Glenmont; throughout the USA, lights were dimmed temporarily on the day of his funeral.

Principal Honours and Distinctions
Member of the American Academy of Sciences. Congressional Gold Medal.

Further Reading
M. Josephson, 1951, *Edison*, Eyre & Spottiswode.
R.W. Clark, 1977, *Edison, the Man who Made the Future*, Macdonald & Jane.

IMcN

Edwards, Humphrey
fl. *c.*1808–25 London (?), England
d. after 1825 France (?)

English co-developer of Woolf's compound steam engine.

When Arthur Woolf left the Griffin Brewery, London, in October 1808, he formed a partnership with Humphrey Edwards, described as a millwright at Mill Street, Lambeth, where they started an engine works to build Woolf's type of compound engine. A number of small engines were constructed and other ordinary engines modified with the addition of a high-pressure cylinder. Improvements were made in each succeeding engine, and by 1811 a standard form had been evolved. During this experimental period, engines were made with cylinders side by side as well as the more usual layout with one behind the other. The valve gear and other details were also improved. Steam pressure may have been around 40 psi (2.8 kg/cm^2). In an advertisement of February 1811, the partners claimed that their engines had been brought to such a state of perfection that they consumed only half the quantity of coal required for engines on the plan of Messrs Boulton & Watt. Woolf visited Cornwall, where he realized that more potential for his engines lay there than in London; in May 1811 the partnership was dissolved, with Woolf returning to his home county. Edwards struggled on alone in London for a while, but when he saw a more promising future for the engine in France he moved to Paris. On 25 May 1815 he obtained a French patent, a *Brevet d'importation*, for ten years. A report in 1817 shows that during the previous two years he had imported into France fifteen engines of different sizes which were at work in eight places in various parts of the country. He licensed a mining company in the north of France to make twenty-five engines for winding coal. In France there was always much more interest in rotative engines than pumping ones. Edwards may have formed a partnership with Goupil & Cie, Dampierre, to build engines, but this is uncertain. He became a member of the firm Scipion, Perrier, Edwards & Chappert, which took over the Chaillot Foundry of the Perrier Frères in Paris, and it seems that Edwards continued to build steam engines there for the rest of his life. In 1824 it was claimed that he had made about 100 engines in England and another 200 in France, but this is probably an exaggeration.

The Woolf engine acquired its popularity in

France because its compound design was more economical than the single-cylinder type. To enable it to be operated safely, Edwards first modified Woolf's cast-iron boiler in 1815 by placing two small drums over the fire, and then in 1825 replaced the cast iron with wrought iron. The modified boiler was eventually brought back to England in the 1850s as the 'French' or 'elephant' boiler.

Further Reading
Most details about Edwards are to be found in the biographies of his partner, Arthur Woolf. For example, see T.R. Harris, 1966, *Arthur Woolf, 1766–1837, The Cornish Engineer*, Truro: D. Bradford Barton; Rhys Jenkins, 1932–3, 'A Cornish Engineer, Arthur Woolf, 1766–1837', *Transactions of the Newcomen Society* 13. These use information from the originally unpublished part of J. Farey, 1971, *A Treatise on the Steam Engine*, Vol. II, Newton Abbot: David & Charles.

RLH

Egerton, Francis, 3rd Duke of Bridgewater
b. 21 May 1736
d. 9 March 1803 London, England

English entrepreneur, described as the 'father of British inland navigation'.

Francis Egerton was the younger of the two surviving sons of Scroop, 1st Duke of Bridgewater, and on the death of his brother, the 2nd Duke, he succeeded to the title in 1748. Until that time he had received little or no education as his mother considered him to be of feeble intellect. His guardians, the Duke of Bedford and Lord Trentham, decided he should be given an opportunity and sent him to Eton in 1749. He remained there for three years and then went on the 'grand tour' of Europe. During this period he saw the Canal du Midi, though whether this was the spark that ignited his interest in canals is hard to say. On his return to England he indulged in the social round in London and raced at Newmarket. After two unsuccessful attempts at marriage he retired to Lancashire to further his mining interests at Worsley, where the construction of a canal to Manchester was already being considered. In fact, the Act for the Bridgewater Canal had been passed at the time he left Lon-

don. John **Gilbert**, his land agent at Worsley, encouraged the Duke to pursue the canal project, which had received parliamentary approval in March 1759. **Brindley** had been recommended on account of his work at Trentham, the estate of the Duke's brother-in-law, and Brindley was consulted and subsequently appointed Engineer; the canal opened on 17 July 1761. This was immediately followed by an extension project from Longford Brook to Runcorn to improve communications between Manchester and Liverpool; this was completed on 31 December 1772, after Brindley's death. The Duke also invested heavily in the Trent & Mersey Canal, but his interests were confined to his mines and the completed canals for the rest of his life.

It is said that he lacked a sense of humour and even refused to read books. He was untidy in his dress and habits yet he was devoted to the Worsley undertakings. When travelling to Worsley he would have his coach placed on a barge so that he could inspect the canal during the journey. He amassed a great fortune from his various activities, but when he died, instead of leaving his beloved canal to the beneficiaries under his will, he created a trust to ensure that the canal would endure; the trust did not expire until 1903. The Duke is commemorated by a large Corinthian pillar, which is now in the care of the National Trust, in the grounds of his mansion at Ashridge, Hertfordshire.

Further Reading
H. Malet, 1961, *The Canal Duke*, Dawlish: David & Charles.

JHB

Ehrlich, Paul
b. 14 March 1854 Strehlen, Silesia, Germany
d. 20 August 1915 Homburg, Saarland, Germany

German medical scientist who laid the foundations of intra-vital staining in histology, and of chemotherapy.

After studying medicine at a number of schools in Germany, Ehrlich graduated from Leipzig in 1878. After some years at the Charite in Berlin, an attack of tuberculosis compelled a three-year sojourn in Egypt for treatment. Upon his return in 1890, he was invited by **Koch** to work at the new Institute for Infectious Diseases. There he commenced his work on immunity, having already, while a student, discovered the mast cells in the blood (1877) and then developed the techniques of differential staining which identified the other white cells of the blood. In 1882 he established the diazo reaction in the urine of typhoid patients, and in the same year he identified the acid-fast staining reactions of the tubercle bacillus. He then moved to the study of immunity in infectious disease, which led him to the search for synthetic chemical substances which would act on the causative organism without harming the patient's tissue. The outcome of his specific investigation of syphilis was the discovery of the first two specific chemotherapeutic agents: salvarsan (being the 606th compound to be tested); and the later, but less toxic, neosalvarsan (the 909th). In 1896 he became Director of the State Institute for Serum Research, and in 1906 Director of the new Royal Institute for Experimental Therapy at Frankfurt-am-Main. He received numerous awards and honours from governments and learned societies.

Principal Honours and Distinctions
Nobel Prize for Medicine or Physiology (jointly with E. Metchnikov) 1908.

Bibliography
1879, 'Beiträge für Kentnis der granulierten Bindegewabszellen und der Eosinophilen Leucocythen' *Arch. Anat. Physiol. Abt.*
1914, *Paul Ehrlich: eine Darstellung seines wissenschaftlichen Wirkens, Festschrift zum 60. Geburtstage des Forschers.*

Further Reading
M. Marquardt, 1924, *Paul Ehrlich als Mensch und Arbeiter.*

MG

Eiffel, Alexandre Gustave
b. 15 December 1832 Dijon, France
d. 27 December 1923 Paris, France

French engineer, best known for the famous tower in Paris that bears his name.

During his long life Eiffel, together with a number of architects, was responsible for the design and construction of a wide variety of bridges, viaducts, harbour installations, exhibition halls, galleries and department stores; he set up his own

firm in 1867 to handle such construction. Of particular note were his great arched bridges, such as the 530 ft (162 m) span arch over the River Douro at Oporto in Portugal (1877–9) and the 550 ft (168 m) span of the Pont de Garabit over the Truyère in France (1880–4). He was responsible in 1884 for the protective ironwork for the Statue of Liberty in New York and, a year later, for the great dome over the Nice Observatory. In 1876 he had collaborated with Boileau to build the Bon Marché department store in Paris. The predominant material for all these structures was iron, and, in some cases glass was important. The famous Eiffel Tower in Paris is entirely of wrought iron, and the legs are supported on masonry piers that are each set into concrete beneath the ground. The idea of the tower was first conceived in 1884 by Maurice Koechlin and Emile Nougier, and Eiffel won a competition for the commission to built the structure. His imaginative and practical scheme was for a strong lightweight construction 984 ft (300 m) high, with its 12,000 sections to be prefabricated and riveted together largely before erection; the open, perforated design reduced the problems of wind resistance. The tower was constructed on schedule by 1889 to commemorate the centenary of the outbreak of the French Revolution and was the tallest structure in the world until the erection of the Empire State Building in New York in 1930–2.

Further Reading
J. Harriss, 1975, *The Tallest Tower: Eiffel and the Belle Epoque*, Boston: Houghton Mifflin.
F. Poncetton, 1939, *Eiffel: Le Magicien du Fer*, Paris: Tournelle.

DY

Einthoven, Willem
b. 21 May 1860 Semarang, Java
d. 28 September 1927 Leiden, the Netherlands

Dutch physiologist, inventor of the string galvanometer and discoverer of the electrocardiogram (ECG).

As a medical student in Utrecht from 1879 Einthoven published an account of pronation and supination of the arm (following his own injury) as well as a paper on stereoscopy through colour differentiation. Soon after graduating in July 1885, he was appointed Professor of Physiology at Leiden.

In 1895, while involved in the study of the electric action potentials of the heart, he developed the sensitive string galvanometer, and in 1896 he was able to register the electrocardiograms of animals and humans, relating them to the heart sounds. Developing this work, he not only established the detailed geometry of the leads for these recordings, but was able to build up an insight into their variations in different forms of heart disease. In 1924 he further investigated the action currents of the sympathetic nervous system.

Principal Honours and Distinctions
Nobel Prize for Medicine or Physiology 1924.

Bibliography
1895, 'Über die form des menschlichen Elektrocardiogramms', *Pflügers Archiv*.

Further Reading
A. de Waart, 1957, *Einthoven*, Haarlem (complete list of works).

MG

Eisler, Paul
b. 1907 Vienna, Austria

Austrian engineer responsible for the invention of the printed circuit.

At the age of 23, Eisler obtained a Diploma in Engineering from the Technical University of Vienna. Because of the growing Nazi influence in Austria, he then accepted a post with the His Master's Voice (HMV) agents in Belgrade, where he worked on the problems of radio reception and sound transmission in railway trains. However, he soon returned to Vienna to found a weekly radio journal and file patents on graphical sound recording (for which he received a doctorate) and on a system of stereoscopic television based on lenticular vertical scanning.

In 1936 he moved to England and sold the TV patent to **Marconi** for £250. Unable to find a job, he carried out experiments in his rooms in a Hampstead boarding-house; after making circuits using strip wires mounted on bakelite sheet, he filed his first printed-circuit patent that year. He then tried to find ways of printing the circuits, but without success. Obtaining a post with Odeon Theatres, he invented a sound-level control for films and devised a mirror-drum con-

tinuous-film projector. but with the outbreak of war in 1939, when the company was evacuated, he chose to stay in London and was interned for a while. Released in 1941, he began work with Henderson and Spalding, a firm of lithographic printers, to whom he unwittingly assigned all future patents for the paltry sum of £1. In due course he perfected a means of printing conducting circuits and on 3 February 1943 he filed three patents covering the process. The British Ministry of Defence rejected the idea, considering it of no use for military equipment, but after he had demonstrated the technique to American visitors it was enthusiastically taken up in the US for making proximity fuses, of which many millions were produced and used for the war effort. Subsequently the US Government ruled that all airborne electronic circuits should be printed.

In the late 1940s the Instrument Department of Henderson and Spalding was split off as Technograph Printed Circuits Ltd, with Eisler as Technical Director. In 1949 he filed a further patent covering a multilayer system; this was licensed to Pye and the Telegraph Condenser Company. A further refinement, patented in the 1950s, the use of the technique for telephone exchange equipment, but this was subsequently widely infringed and although he negotiated licences in the USA he found it difficult to license his ideas in Europe. In the UK he obtained finance from the National Research and Development Corporation, but they interfered and refused money for further development, and he eventually resigned from Technograph. Faced with litigation in the USA and open infringement in the UK, he found it difficult to establish his claims, but their validity was finally agreed by the Court of Appeal (1969) and the House of Lords (1971).

As a freelance inventor he filed many other printed-circuit patents, including foil heating films and batteries. When his Patent Agents proved unwilling to fund the cost of filing and prosecuting Complete Specifications he set up his own company, Eisler Consultants Ltd, to promote food and space heating, including the use of heated cans and wallpaper! As Foil Heating Ltd he went into the production of heating films, the process subsequently being licensed to Thermal Technology Inc. in California.

Bibliography

1953, 'Printed circuits: some general principles and applications of the foil technique', *Journal of the British Institution of Radio Engineers* 13: 523.

1959, *The Technology of Printed Circuits: The Foil Technique in Electronic Production.*

1984–5, 'Reflections of my life as an inventor', *Circuit World* 11: 1–3 (a personal account of the development of the printed circuit).

1989, *My Life with the Printed Circuit*, Bethlehem, Pennsylvania: Lehigh University Press.

KF

Elder, John

b. 9 March 1824 Glasgow, Scotland
d. 17 September 1869 London, England

Scottish engineer who introduced the compound steam engine to ships and established an important shipbuilding company in Glasgow.

John was the third son of David Elder. The father came from a family of millwrights and moved to Glasgow where he worked for the well-known shipbuilding firm of Napier's and was involved with improving marine engines. John was educated at Glasgow High School and then for a while at the Department of Civil Engineering at Glasgow University, where he showed great aptitude for mathematics and drawing. He spent five years as an apprentice under Robert **Napier** followed by two short periods of activity as a pattern-maker first and then a draughtsman in England. He returned to Scotland in 1849 to become Chief Draughtsman to Napier, but in 1852 he left to become a partner with the Glasgow general engineering company of Randolph Elliott & Co. Shortly after his induction (at the age of 28), the engineering firm was renamed Randolph Elder & Co.; in 1868, when the partnership expired, it became known as John Elder & Co. From the outset Elder, with his partner, Charles Randolph, approached mechanical (especially heat) engineering in a rigorous manner. Their knowledge and understanding of entropy ensured that engine design was not a hit-and-miss affair, but one governed by recognition of the importance of the new kinetic theory of heat and with it a proper understanding of thermodynamic principles, and by systematic development. In this Elder was joined by W.J.M. **Rankine**, Professor of Civil Engineering and

Mechanics at Glasgow University, who helped him develop the compound marine engine. Elder and Randolph built up a series of patents, which guaranteed their company's commercial success and enabled them for a while to be the sole suppliers of compound steam reciprocating machinery. Their first such engine at sea was fitted in 1854 on the SS *Brandon* for the Limerick Steamship Company; the ship showed an improved performance by using a third less coal, which he was able to reduce still further on later designs.

Elder developed steam jacketing and recognized that, with higher pressures, triple-expansion types would be even more economical. In 1862 he patented a design of quadruple-expansion engine with reheat between cylinders and advocated the importance of balancing reciprocating parts. The effect of his improvements was to greatly reduce fuel consumption so that long sea voyages became an economic reality.

His yard soon reached dimensions then unequalled on the Clyde where he employed over 4,000 workers; Elder also was always interested in the social welfare of his labour force. In 1860 the engine shops were moved to the Govan Old Shipyard, and again in 1864 to the Fairfield Shipyard, about 1 mile (1.6 km) west on the south bank of the Clyde. At Fairfield, shipbuilding was commenced, and with the patents for compounding secure, much business was placed for many years by shipowners serving long-distance trades such as South America; the Pacific Steam Navigation Company took up his ideas for their ships. In later years the yard became known as the Fairfield Shipbuilding and Engineering Company Ltd, but it remains today as one of Britain's most efficient shipyards and is known now as Kvaerner Govan Ltd.

In 1869, at the age of only 45, John Elder was unanimously elected President of the Institution of Engineers and Shipbuilders in Scotland; however, before taking office and giving his eagerly awaited presidential address, he died in London from liver disease. A large multitude attended his funeral and all the engineering shops were silent as his body, which had been brought back from London to Glasgow, was carried to its resting place. In 1857 Elder had married Isabella Ure, and on his death he left her a considerable fortune, which she used generously for Govan, for Glasgow and especially the University. In 1883 she endowed the world's first Chair of Naval Architecture at the University of Glasgow, an act which was reciprocated in 1901 when the University awarded her an LLD on the occasion of its 450th anniversary.

Principal Honours and Distinctions
President, Institution of Engineers and Shipbuilders in Scotland 1869.

Further Reading
Obituary, 1869, *Engineer* 28.
1889, *The Dictionary of National Biography*, London: Smith Elder & Co.
W.J. Macquorn Rankine, 1871, 'Sketch of the life of John Elder' *Transactions of the Institution of Engineers and Shipbuilders in Scotland*.
Maclehose, 1886, *Memoirs and Portraits of a Hundred Glasgow Men*.
The Fairfield Shipbuilding and Engineering Works, 1909, London: Offices of Engineering.
F.M. Walker, 1984, *Song of the Clyde, A History of Clyde Shipbuilding*, Cambridge: PSL.
R.L. Hills, 1989, *Power from Steam. A History of the Stationary Steam Engine*, Cambridge: Cambridge University Press (covers Elder's contribution to the development of steam engines).

RLH/FMW

Elgar, Francis
b. April 1845 Portsmouth, England
d. 16 January 1909 Monte Carlo, Monaco

English naval architect and shipbuilder.

Elgar enjoyed a fascinating professional life, during which he achieved distinction in the military, merchant, academic and political aspects of his profession. At the age of 14 he was apprenticed as a shipwright to the Royal Dockyard at Portsmouth but when he was in his late teens he was selected as one of the Admiralty students to further his education at the Royal School of Naval Architecture at South Kensington, London. On completion of the course he was appointed to Birkenhead, where the ill-fated HMS *Captain* was being built, and then to Portsmouth Dockyard. In 1870 the *Captain* was lost at sea and Francis Elgar was called on to prepare much of the evidence for the Court Martial. This began his life-long interest in ship stability and in ways of presenting this information in an easily under-

stood form to ship operators.

In 1883 he accepted the John **Elder** Chair of Naval Architecture at Glasgow University, an appointment which formalized the already well-established teaching of this branch of engineering at Glasgow. However, after only three years he returned to public service in the newly created post of Director of Royal Dockyards, a post that he held for a mere six years but which brought about great advances in the speed of warship construction, with associated reductions in cost. In 1892 he was made Naval Architect and Director of the Fairfield Shipbuilding Company in Glasgow, remaining there until he retired in 1907. The following year he accepted the post of Chairman of the Birkenhead shipyard of Cammell Laird & Co.; this was a recent amalgamation of two companies, and he retained this position until his death. Throughout his life, Elgar acted on many consultative bodies and committees, including the 1884 Ship Load Line Enquiry. His work enabled him to keep abreast of all current thinking in ship design and construction.

Principal Honours and Distinctions
FRS. FRSE. Chevalier de la Légion d'honneur.

Bibliography
Elgar produced some remarkable papers, which were published by the Institutions of Naval Architects, Civil Engineers and Engineers and Shipbuilders in Scotland as well as by the Royal Society. He published several books on shipbuilding.

FMW

Elkington, George Richard
b. 17 October 1801 Birmingham England
d. 22 September 1865 Pool Park, Denbighshire, England

English pioneer in electroplating.

He was apprenticed to his uncles, makers of metalware, in 1815 and showed such aptitude for business that he was taken into partnership. On their deaths, Elkington assumed sole ownership of the business. In conjunction with his cousin Henry (1810–52), by unrelenting enterprise, he established an industry for electroplating and electrogilding. Up until c.1840, silver-plated goods were produced by rolling or soldering thin sheets of silver to a base metal, such as copper.

Back in 1801, the English chemist William **Wollaston** had deposited one metal upon another by means of an electric current generated from a voltaic pile or battery. In the 1830s, certain inventors, such as **Bessemer** used this result to produce plated articles and these efforts in turn induced the Elkingtons to apply the method in their trade. In 1836 and 1837 they took out patents for 'mercurial gilding', and one patent of 1838 refers to a separate electric current. In 1840 they bought from John Wright, a Birmingham surgeon, his discovery of what proved to be the best electroplating solution: namely, solutions of cyanides of gold and silver in potassium cyanide. They also purchased rights to use the electric machine invented by J.S. **Woolrich**. Armed with these techniques, the Elkingtons produced in their large new works in Newhall Street a wide range of gold- and silver-plated decorative and artistic ware. Henry was particularly active on the artistic side of the business, as was their employee Alexander **Parkes**. For some twenty-five years, Britain enjoyed a virtual monopoly of this kind of ware, due largely to the enterprise of the Elkingtons, although by the end of the century rising tariffs had closed many foreign markets and the lead had passed to Germany. George spent all his working life in Birmingham, taking some part in the public life of the city. He was a governor of King Edward's Grammar School and a borough magistrate. He was also a caring employer, setting up houses and schools for his workers.

Bibliography
1864, *Journal of the Royal Society for Arts* (29 January).

LRD

Ellehammer, Jacob Christian Hansen

b. 14 June 1871 South Zealand, Denmark
d. b. 20 May 1946 Copenhagen, Denmark

Danish inventor who took out some four hundred patents for his inventions, including aircraft.

Flying kites as a boy aroused Ellehammer's interest in aeronautics, and he developed a kite that could lift him off the ground. After completing an apprenticeship, he started his own manufacturing business, whose products included motor cycles. He experimented with model aircraft as a

sideline and used his motor-cycle experience to build an aero engine during 1903–4. It had three cylinders radiating from the crankshaft, making it, in all probability, the world's first air-cooled radial engine. Ellehammer built his first full-size aircraft in 1905 and tested it in January 1906. It ran round a circular track, was tethered to a central mast and was unmanned. A more powerful engine was needed, and by September Ellehammer had improved his engine so that it was capable of lifting him for a tethered flight. In 1907 Ellehammer produced a new five-cylinder radial engine and installed it in the first manned triplane, which made a number of free-flight hops. Various wing designs were tested and during 1908–9 Ellehammer developed yet another radial engine, which had six cylinders arranged in two rows of three. Ellehammer's engines had a very good power-to-weight ratio, but his aircraft designs lacked an understanding of control; consequently, he never progressed beyond short hops in a straight line. In 1912 he built a helicopter with contra-rotating rotors that was a limited success. Ellehammer turned his attention to his other interests, but if he had concentrated on his excellent engines he might have become a major aero engine manufacturer.

Bibliography
1931, *Jeg fløj* [I Flew], Copenhagen (Ellehammer's memoirs).

Further Reading
C.H. Gibbs-Smith, 1965, *The Invention of the Aeroplane 1799–1909*, London (contains concise information on Ellehammer's aircraft and their performance).
J.H. Parkin, 1964, *Bell and Baldwin*, Toronto (provides more detailed descriptions).

JDS

Ellet, Charles

b. 1 January 1810 Penn's Manor, Pennsylvania, USA
d. 21 June 1862 Cairo, Illinois, USA

American engineer who built the world's first long-span wire-cable bridge.

Ellet worked for three years as a surveyor and assistant engineer and then studied at the Ecole Polytechnique in Paris. He travelled widely in Europe and returned to the USA in 1832. In

1842 he completed the first wire suspension bridge in the USA at Fairmont, Pennsylvania, and in 1846–9 redesigned and built the world's first long-span wire-cable bridge over the Ohio River at Wheeling. It had a central span of 308 m (1,010 ft). It failed in 1854 due to aerodynamic instability. He invented naval rams and in the American Civil War he equipped nine Mississippi river boats as rams; they defeated a fleet of Confederate rams. He died in battle.

Further Reading
The Macmillan Dictionary of Biography, 1981.

IMcN

Ellington, Edward Bayzard
b. 2 August 1845 London, England
d. 10 November 1914 London, England

English hydraulic engineer who developed a direct-acting hydraulic lift.

Ellington was educated at Denmark Hill Grammar School, London, after which he became articled to John Penn of Greenwich. He stayed there until 1868, working latterly in the drawing office after a period of erecting plant and attending trials on board ship. For some twelve months he superintended the erection of Glengall Wharf, Old Kent Road, and the machinery used therein.

In 1869 he went into partnership with Bryan Johnson of Chester, the company being known as Johnson & Ellington, manufacturing mining and milling machinery. Under Ellington's influence, the firm specialized in the manufacture of hydraulic machinery. In 1874 the company acquired the right to manufacture the Brotherhood three-cylinder hydraulic engine; the company became the Hydraulic Engineering Company Ltd of Chester. Ellington developed a direct-acting hydraulic lift with a special balance arrangement that was smooth-acting and economical in water. He described the lift in a paper that was read to the Institution of Mechanical Engineers (IMechE) in 1882.

Soon after Ellington joined the Chester firm, an Act of Parliament was passed, mainly due to his efforts, for the distribution of water under high pressure for the working of passenger and goods lifts and other hydraulic machinery in large towns. In 1872 he initiated the first hydraulic mains company at Hull, thus proving the practicability of the system of a high-pressure water-mains supply. Ellington remained as engineer to the Hull company until he was appointed a director in 1875. He was general manager and engineer of the General Hydraulic Power Company, which operated in London and had subsidiaries in Liverpool (opened in 1889), Manchester (1894) and Glasgow (1895). He maintained an interest in all these companies, as general manager and engineer, until his death.

In 1895 he read another paper, 'On hydraulic power in towns', to the Institution of Mechanical Engineers. In 1911 he became President of the IMechE; his Presidential Address was on the education of young engineers. In 1913 he delivered the Thomas Hawksley Lecture on 'Water as a mechanical agent'. He was Chairman of the Building Committee during the extension of the Institution's headquarters. Ellington was also a Member of Council of the Institution of Civil Engineers, a member of the Société des Ingénieurs Civils de France and a Governor of Imperial College of Science and Technology.

Principal Honours and Distinctions
Member of the Institution of Mechanical Engineers 1875; Member of Council 1898–1903; President 1911–12.

IMcN

Engerth, Wilhelm
b. 26 May 1814 Pless, Prussian Silesia (now Poland)
d. 4 September 1884 Baden, Austria

German engineer, designer of the Engerth articulated locomotive.

Engerth was Chairman of the judges for the Semmering Locomotive Trials, held in 1851 to find locomotives suitable for working the sharply curved and steeply graded section of the Vienna–Trieste railway that was being built over the Semmering Pass, the first of the transalpine main lines. When none of the four locomotives entered proved suitable, Engerth designed his own. Six coupled wheels were at the fore part of the locomotive, with the connecting rods driving the rear pair: at the back of the locomotive the frames of the tender were extended forward on either side of the firebox, the front wheels of the tender were ahead of it, and the two parts were connected by a spherical pivot ahead of these. Part of the locomotive's weight was carried by the tender portion, and the two pairs of tender wheels were coupled by rods and powered by a geared drive from the axle of the rear driving-wheels. The powered drive to the tender wheels proved a failure, but the remaining characteristics of the locomotive, namely short rigid wheelbase, large firebox, flexibility and good tracking on curves (as drawbar pull was close behind the driving axle), were sufficient for the type to be a success. It was used on many railways in Europe and examples in modified form were built in Spain as recently as 1956. Engerth became General Manager of the Austro-Hungarian State Railway Company and designed successful flood-prevention works on the Danube at Vienna.

Principal Honours and Distinctions
Knighted as Ritter von Engerth 1861. Ennobled as Freiherr (Baron) von Engerth 1875.

Further Reading
D.R. Carling, 1985, 'Engerth and similar locomotives', *Transactions of the Newcomen Society* 57 (a good description).
J.B. Snell, 1964, *Early Railways*, London: Weidenfeld & Nicolson, pp. 68–73 (for Semmering Trials).

PJGR

England, George
b. 1811 or 1812 Newcastle upon Tyne, England
d. 4 March 1878 Cannes, France

English locomotive builder who built the first locomotives for the narrow-gauge Festiniog Railway.

England trained with John Penn & Sons, marine engine and boilermakers, and set up his own business at Hatcham Iron Works, South London, in about 1840. This was initially a general engineering business and made traversing screw jacks, which England had patented, but by 1850 it was building locomotives. One of these, *Little England*, a 2–2–2T light locomotive owing much to the ideas of W. Bridges **Adams**, was exhibited at the Great Exhibition of 1851, and England then prospered, supplying many railways at home and abroad with small locomotives. In 1863 he built two exceptionally small 0–4–0 tank locomotives for the Festiniog Railway,

which enabled the latter's Manager and Engineer C.E. **Spooner** to introduce steam traction on this line with its gauge of just under 2 ft (60 cm). England's works had a reputation for good workmanship, suggesting he inspired loyalty among his employees, yet he also displayed increasingly tyrannical behaviour towards them: the culmination was a disastrous strike in 1865 that resulted in the loss of a substantial order from the South Eastern Railway. From 1866 George England became associated with development of locomotives to the patent of Robert **Fairlie**, but in 1869 he retired due to ill health and leased his works to a partnership of his son (also called George England), Robert Fairlie and J.S. Fraser under the title of the Fairlie Engine & Steam Carriage Company. However, George England junior died within a few months, locomotive production ceased in 1870 and the works was sold off two years later.

Bibliography
1839, British patent no. 8,058 (traversing screw jack).

Further Reading
Aspects of England's life and work are described in:
C.H. Dickson, 1961, 'Locomotive builders of the past', *Stephenson Locomotive Society Journal*, p. 138.
A.R. Bennett, 1907, 'Locomotive building in London', *Railway Magazine*, p. 382.
R. Weaver, 1983, 'English Ponies', *Festiniog Railway Magazine* (spring): 18.

PJGR

England, William
b. early 19th century
d. 1896 London, England

English photographer, inventor of an early focal-plane shutter.

England began his distinguished photographic career taking daguerreotype portraits in London in the 1840s. In 1854 he joined the London Stereoscopic Company and became its chief photographer, taking thousands of stereoscopic views all over the world. In 1859 he travelled to America to take views of the Niagara Falls. On returning to Britain he became a freelance photographer, adding to his considerable reputation with a long series of stereoscopic alpine views. He also became interested in panoramic photography and, later, photolithography. England's most important technical innovation was a drop shutter with a horizontal slit sited immediately in front of the plate. Proposed in 1861, this was a crude device, but is usually recognized as the precursor of the modern focal-plane shutter.

Further Reading

Michael Aver, 1985, *Photographers Encyclopedia International*, Vol. I (A–K), Hermance, Switzerland.

H. Gernsheim and A. Gernsheim, 1969, *The History of Photography*, rev. edn, London.

JW

Ercker, Lazarus
b. *c.*1530 Annaberg, Saxony, Germany
d. 1594 Prague, Bohemia

German chemist and metallurgist.

Educated at Wittenberg University during 1547–8, Ercker obtained in 1554, through one of his wife's relatives, the post of Assayer from the Elector Augustus at Dresden. From then on he took a succession of posts in mining and metallurgy. In 1555 he was Chief Consultant and Supervisor of all matters relating to mines, but for some unknown reason was demoted to Warden of the Mint at Annaberg. In 1558 he travelled to the Tyrol to study the mines in that region, and in the same year Prince Henry of Brunswick appointed him Warden, then Master, of the Mint at Goslar. Ercker later moved to Prague where, through another of his wife's relatives, he was appointed Control Tester at Kutna Hora. It was there that he wrote his best-known book, *Die Beschreibung allfürnemisten mineralischen Ertz*, which drew him to the attention of the Emperor Maximilian, who made him Courier for Mining and a clerk of the Supreme Court of Bohemia. The next Emperor, Rudolf II, a noted patron of science and alchemy, promoted Ercker to Chief Inspector of Mines and ennobled him in 1586 with the title 'von Schreckenfels'. His second wife managed the mint at Kutna Hora and his two sons became assayers. These appointments gained him much experience of the extraction and refining of metals. This first bore fruit in a book on assaying, *Probierbüchlein*, printed in 1556, followed by one on minting, *Münzbuch*, in 1563. His main work,

Die Beschreibung, was a systematic review of the methods of obtaining, refining and testing the alloys and minerals of gold, silver, copper, antimony, mercury and lead. The preparation of acids, salts and other compounds is also covered, and his apparatus is fully described and illustrated. Although Ercker used **Agricola**'s *De re metallica* as a model, his own work was securely based on his practical experience. *Die Beschreibung* was the first manual of analytical and metallurgical chemistry and influenced later writers such as **Glauber** on assaying. After the first edition in Prague came four further editions in Frankfurt-am-Main.

Bibliography

Die Beschreibung allfürnemisten mineralischen Ertz, Prague.
1556, *Probierbuchlein*.
1563, *Munzbuch*.

Further Reading

P.R. Beierlein, 1955, *Lazarus Ercker, Bergmann, Hüttenmann und Münzmeister im 16. Jahrhundert*, Berlin (the best biography, although the chemical details are incomplete).

J.R. Partington, 1961, *History of Chemistry*, London, Vol. II, pp. 104–7.

E.V. Armstrong and H. Lukens, 1939, 'Lazarus Ercker and his *Probierbuch*', *J. Chem. Ed.* 16: 553–62.

LRD

Ericsson, John
b. 31 July 1803 Farnebo, Sweden
d. 8 March 1899 New York, USA

Swedish (naturalized American 1848) engineer and inventor.

The son of a mine owner and inspector, Ericsson's first education was private and haphazard. War with Russia disrupted the mines and the father secured a position on the Gotha Canal, then under construction. He enrolled John, then aged 13, and another son as cadets in a corps of military engineers engaged on the canal. There John was given a sound education and training in the physical sciences and engineering. At the age of 17 he decided to enlist in the Army, and on receiving a commission he was drafted to cartographic survey duties. After some years he decided that a career outside the Army offered him the best opportunities, and in 1826 he moved to London to pursue a career of mechanical invention.

Ericsson first developed a heat (external combustion) engine, which proved unsuccessful. Three years later he designed and constructed the steam locomotive *Novelty*, which he entered in the Rainhill locomotive trials on the new Liverpool & Manchester Railway. The engine began by performing promisingly, but it later broke down and failed to complete the test runs. Later he devised a self-regulating lead (1835) and then, more important and successful, he invented the screw propeller, patented in 1835 and installed in his first screw-propelled ship of 1839. This work was carried out independently of Sir Francis Pettit **Smith**, who contemporaneously developed a four-bladed propeller that was adopted by the British Admiralty. Ericsson saw that with screw propulsion the engine could be below the waterline, a distinct advantage in warships. He crossed the Atlantic to interest the American government in his ideas and became a naturalized citizen in 1848. He pioneered the gun turret for mounting heavy guns on board ship. Ericsson came into his own during the American Civil War, with the construction of the epoch-making warship *Monitor*, a screw-propelled ironclad with gun turret. This vessel demonstrated its powers in a signal victory at Hampton Roads on 9 March 1862.

Ericsson continued to design warships and torpedoes, pointing out to President Lincoln that success in war would now depend on technological rather than numerical superiority. Meanwhile he continued to pursue his interest in heat engines, and from 1870 to 1888 he spent much of his time and resources in pursuing research into alternative energy sources, such as solar power, gravitation and tidal forces.

Further Reading
W.C. Church, 1891, *Life of John Ericsson*, 2 vols, London.

LRD

Essen, Louis
b. 6 September 1908 Nottingham, England

English physicist who produced the first practical caesium atomic clock, which was later used to define the second.

Louis Essen joined the National Physical Laboratory (NPL) at Teddington in 1927 after graduating from London University. He spent his whole working life at the NPL and retired in 1972; his research there was recognized by the award of a DSc in 1948. At NPL he joined a team working on the development of frequency standards using quartz crystals and he designed a very successful quartz oscillator, which became known as the 'Essen ring'. He was also involved with radio frequency oscillators. His expertise in these fields was to play a crucial role in the development of the caesium clock. The idea of an atomic clock had been proposed by I.I. Rabbi in 1945, and an instrument was constructed shortly afterwards at the National Bureau of Standards in the USA. However, this device never realized the full potential of the concept, and after seeing it on a visit to the USA Essen was convinced that a more successful instrument could be built at Teddington. Assisted by J.V.L. Parry, he commenced work in the spring of 1953 and by June 1955 the clock was working reliably, with an accuracy that was equivalent to one second in three hundred years. This was significantly more accurate than the astronomical observations that were used at that time to determine the second: in 1967 the second was redefined in terms of the value for the frequency of vibration of caesium atoms that had been obtained with this clock.

Principal Honours and Distinctions
FRS 1960. Clockmakers' Company Tompion Gold Medal 1957. Physical Society C.V. Boys Prize 1957. USSR Academy of Science Popov Gold Medal 1959.

Bibliography
1957, with J.V.L. Parry, 'The caesium resonator as a standard of frequency and time', *Philosophical Transactions of the Royal Society* (Series A) 25: 45–69 (the first comprehensive description of the caesium clock).

Further Reading
P. Forman, 1985, 'Atomichron: the atomic clock from concept to commercial product', *Proceedings of the IEEE* 75: 1,181–204 (an authoritative critical review of the development of the atomic clock).
N. Cossons (ed.), 1992, *The Making of the Modern World*, London: Science Museum, pp. 190–1 (contains a short account).

See also **Marrison, Warren Alvin**.

DV

Evans, Oliver

b. 13 September 1755 Newport, Delaware,
USA
d. 15 April 1819 New York, USA

*American millwright and inventor of the first
automatic corn mill.*

He was the fifth child of Charles and Ann Stal-
crop Evans, and by the age of 15 he had four
sisters and seven brothers. Nothing is known of
his schooling, but at the age of 17 he was apprenticed to a Newport wheelwright and wagon-
maker. At 19 he was enrolled in a Delaware
Militia Company in the Revolutionary War but
did not see active service. About this time he invented a machine for bending and cutting off the
wires in textile carding combs. In July 1782, with
his younger brother, Joseph, he moved to Tuc-
kahoe on the eastern shore of the Delaware
River, where he had the basic idea of the automatic flour mill. In July 1782, with his elder
brothers John and Theophilus, he bought part of
his father's Newport farm, on Red Clay Creek,
and planned to build a mill there. In 1793 he
married Sarah Tomlinson, daughter of a Delaware farmer, and joined his brothers at Red Clay
Creek. He worked there for some seven years on
his automatic mill, from about 1783 to 1790.

His system for the automatic flour mill consisted of bucket elevators to raise the grain, a
horizontal screw conveyor, other conveying devices and a 'hopper boy' to cool and dry the meal
before gathering it into a hopper feeding the
bolting cylinder. Together these components
formed the automatic process, from incoming
wheat to outgoing flour packed in barrels. At
that time the idea of such automation had not
been applied to any manufacturing process in
America. The mill opened, on a non-automatic
cycle, in 1785. In January 1786 Evans applied to
the Delaware legislature for a twenty-five-year
patent, which was granted on 30 January 1787
although there was much opposition from the
Quaker millers of Wilmington and elsewhere. He
also applied for patents in Pennsylvania, Maryland and New Hampshire. In May 1789 he went
to see the mill of the four Ellicot brothers, near
Baltimore, where he was impressed by the design
of a horizontal screw conveyor by Jonathan Ellicot and exchanged the rights to his own elevator
for those of this machine. After six years' work on
his automatic mill, it was completed in 1790. In

the autumn of that year a miller in Brandywine
ordered a set of Evans's machinery, which set the
trend toward its general adoption. A model of it
was shown in the Market Street shop window of
Robert Leslie, a watch- and clockmaker in Philadelphia, who also took it to England but was
unsuccessful in selling the idea there.

In 1790 the Federal Plant Laws were passed;
Evans's patent was the third to come within the
new legislation. A detailed description with a
plate was published in a Philadelphia newspaper
in January 1791, the first of a proposed series,
but the paper closed and the series came to nothing. His brother Joseph went on a series of sales
trips, with the result that some machinery of
Evans's design was adopted. By 1792 over one
hundred mills had been equipped with Evans's
machinery, the millers paying a royalty of $40 for
each pair of millstones in use. The series of articles that had been cut short formed the basis of
Evans's *The Young Millwright and Miller's
Guide*, published first in 1795 after Evans had
moved to Philadelphia to set up a store selling
milling supplies; it was 440 pages long and ran to
fifteen editions between 1795 and 1860.

Evans was fairly successful as a merchant. He
patented a method of making millstones as well
as a means of packing flour in barrels, the latter
having a disc pressed down by a toggle-joint arrangement. In 1801 he started to build a steam
carriage. He rejected the idea of a steam wheel
and of a low-pressure or atmospheric engine. By
1803 his first engine was running at his store,
driving a screw-mill working on plaster of Paris
for making millstones. The engine had a 6 in. (15
cm) diameter cylinder with a stroke of 18 in. (45
cm) and also drove twelve saws mounted in a
frame and cutting marble slabs at a rate of 100 ft
(30 m) in twelve hours. He was granted a patent
in the spring of 1804. He became involved in a
number of lawsuits following the extension of his
patent, particularly as he increased the licence
fee, sometimes as much as sixfold. The case of
Evans v. Samuel Robinson, which Evans won,
became famous and was one of these. *Patent
Right Oppression Exposed, or Knavery Detected*, a
200-page book with poems and prose included,
was published soon after this case and was probably written by Oliver Evans. The steam engine
patent was also extended for a further seven
years, but in this case the licence fee was to remain at a fixed level. Evans anticipated **Edison** in

his proposal for an 'Experimental Company' or 'Mechanical Bureau' with a capital of thirty shares of $100 each. It came to nothing, however, as there were no takers. His first wife, Sarah, died in 1816 and he remarried, to Hetty Ward, the daughter of a New York innkeeper. He was buried in the Bowery, on Lower Manhattan; the church was sold in 1854 and again in 1890, and when no relative claimed his body he was reburied in an unmarked grave in Trinity Cemetery, 57th Street, Broadway.

Further Reading
E.S. Ferguson, 1980, *Oliver Evans: Inventive Genius of the American Industrial Revolution*, Hagley Museum.
G. Bathe and D. Bathe, 1935, *Oliver Evans: Chronicle of Early American Engineering*, Philadelphia, Pa.

IMcN

Ewart, Peter

b. 14 May 1767 Traquair, near Peebles, Scotland
d. September 1842 London, England

Scottish pioneer in the mechanization of the textile industry.

Peter Ewart, the youngest of six sons, was born at Traquair manse, where his father was a clergyman in the Church of Scotland. He was educated at the Free School, Dumfries, and in 1782 spent a year at Edinburgh University. He followed this with an apprenticeship under John **Rennie** at Musselburgh before moving south in 1785 to help Rennie erect the Albion corn mill in London. This brought him into contact with **Boulton** & **Watt**, and in 1788 he went to Birmingham to erect a waterwheel and other machinery in the Soho Manufactory. In 1789 he was sent to Manchester to install a steam engine for Peter Drinkwater and thus his long connection with the city began. In 1790 Ewart took up residence in Manchester as Boulton & Watt's representative. Amongst other engines, he installed one for Samuel Oldknow at Stockport. In 1792 he became a partner with Oldknow in his cotton-spinning business, but because of financial difficulties he moved back to Birmingham in 1795 to help erect the machines in the new Soho Foundry. He was soon back in Manchester in partnership with Samuel Greg at Quarry Bank Mill, Styal, where he was responsible for developing the water power,

installing a steam engine, and being concerned with the spinning machinery and, later, gas lighting at Greg's other mills.

In 1798, Ewart devised an automatic expansion-gear for steam engines, but steam pressures at the time were too low for such a device to be effective. His grasp of the theory of steam power is shown by his paper to the Manchester Literary and Philosophical Society in 1808, *On the Measure of Moving Force*. In 1813 he patented a power loom to be worked by the pressure of steam or compressed air. In 1824 Charles **Babbage** consulted him about automatic looms. His interest in textiles continued until at least 1833, when he obtained a patent for a self-acting spinning mule, which was, however, outclassed by the more successful one invented by Richard Roberts. Ewart gave much help and advice to others. The development of the machine tools at Boulton & Watt's Soho Foundry has been mentioned already. He also helped James Watt with his machine for copying sculptures. While he continued to run his own textile mill, Ewart was also in partnership with Charles **Macintosh**, the pioneer of rubber-coated cloth. He was involved with William **Fairbairn** concerning steam engines for the boats that Fairbairn was building in Manchester, and it was through Ewart that Eaton Hodgkinson was introduced to Fairbairn and so made the tests and calculations for the tubes for the Britannia Railway Bridge across the Menai Straits. Ewart was involved with the launching of the Liverpool & Manchester Railway as he was a director of the Manchester Chamber of Commerce at the time.

In 1835 he uprooted himself from Manchester and became the first Chief Engineer for the Royal Navy, assuming responsibility for the steamboats, which by 1837 numbered 227 in service. He set up repair facilities and planned workshops for overhauling engines at Woolwich Dockyard, the first establishment of its type. It was here that he was killed in an accident when a chain broke while he was supervising the lifting of a large boiler. Engineering was Ewart's life, and it is possible to give only a brief account of his varied interests and connections here.

Further Reading
Obituary, 1843, 'Institution of Civil Engineers', Annual General Meeting, January.
Obituary, 1843, *Manchester Literary and Philosophical Society Memoirs* (NS) 7.
R.L. Hills, 1987–8, 'Peter Ewart, 1767–1843',

Manchester Literary and Philosophical Society Memoirs 127.

M.B. Rose, 1986, *The Gregs of Quarry Bank Mill. The Rise and Decline of a Family Firm, 1750–1914*, Cambridge (covers Ewart's involvement with Samuel Greg).

R.L. Hills, 1970, *Power in the Industrial Revolution*, Manchester; R.L. Hills, 1989, *Power from Steam*, Cambridge (both look at Ewart's involvement with textiles and steam engines).

RLH

Ewing, Sir James Alfred

b. 27 March 1855 Dundee, Scotland
d. 1935

Scottish engineer and educator.

Sir Alfred Ewing was one of the leading engineering academics of his generation. He was the son of a minister in the Free Church of Scotland, and was educated at Dundee High School and Edinburgh University, where he studied engineering under Professor Fleeming Jenkin. On Jenkin's nomination, Ewing was recruited as Professor of Mechanical Engineering at the University of Tokyo, where he spent five years from 1878 to 1883. While in Tokyo, he devised an instrument for measuring and recording earthquakes. Ewing returned to his home town of Dundee in 1883, as the first Professor of Engineering at the University College recently established there. After seven years building up the department in Dundee, he moved to Cambridge where he succeeded James **Stuart** as Professor of Mechanism and Applied Mechanics. In thirteen creative years at Cambridge, he established the Engineering Tripos (1892) and founded the first engineering laboratories at the University (1894). From 1903 to 1917 Ewing served the Admiralty as Director of Naval Education, in which role he took a leading part in the revolution in British naval traditions which equipped the Royal Navy to fight the First World War. In that war, Ewing made an important contribution to the intelligence operation of deciphering enemy wireless messages. In 1916 he returned to Edinburgh as Principal and Vice-Chancellor, and following the war he presided over a period of rapid expansion at the University. He retired in 1929.

Principal Honours and Distinctions
FRS 1887. KCB 1911. President, British Association for the Advancement of Science 1932.

Bibliography
He wrote extensively on technical subjects, and his works included *Thermodynamics for Engineers* (1920). His many essays and papers on more general subjects are elegantly and attractively written.

Further Reading
Dictionary of National Biography Supplement.
A.W. Ewing, 1939, *Life of Sir Alfred Ewing* (biography by his son).

AB

F

Fabre, Henri

b. 29 November 1882 Marseilles, France
d. June 1984 France

French engineer, designer of the first seaplane, in which he made the first flight from water.

After obtaining a degree in engineering, Fabre specialized in hydrodynamics. Around 1904 he developed an interest in flying and followed the progress of early French aviators such as Archdeacon, **Voisin** and **Blériot** who were experimenting with float-gliders. Fabre carried out many experiments during the following years, including airflow tests on various surfaces and hydrodynamic tests on different designs for floats. He also built a propeller-driven motor car to develop the most efficient design for a propeller. In 1909 he built his first 'hydro-aeroplane', but it failed to fly. By March 1910 he built a new float plane which was very different from contemporary French aeroplanes. It was a tail-first (canard) monoplane and had unusual Warren girder spars exposed to the airstream. The engine was a conventional *Gnome* rotary mounted at the rear of the machine. On 28 March 1910 Fabre, who had no previous experience of flying, decided he was ready to test his hydro-aeroplane. First he made several straight runs to test the planing properties of his three floats, then he made several short hops. In the afternoon Fabre took off from the harbour at La Mède near Marseille before official witnesses: he was able to claim the first flight by a powered seaplane. His hydro-aeroplane is preserved in the Musée de l'Air et de l'Espace in Paris.

Despite several accidents, Fabre continued to improve his design and in October of 1910 Glenn **Curtiss**, the American designer, visited Fabre to compare notes. A year later Curtiss built the first of his many successful seaplanes. Fabre did not continue as an aircraft designer, but he went on to design and manufacture floats for other people.

Bibliography
1980, *J'ai vu naître l'aviation*, Grenoble (autobiography).

JDS

Fabricius (of Aquapendente), Hieronymus

b. 20 May 1537 Aquapendente, central Italy
d. 21 May 1619 Padua, Italy

Italian physician and anatomist, teacher of William Harvey, first known exponent of tracheotomy.

Of well-to-do origins, Fabricius studied at the University of Padua and obtained his doctorate in medicine and philosophy *c.*1559. He succeeded his master Fallopius in the Chair of Surgery at Padua in 1565 and was created Professor Supraordinarius for life *c.*1600. His discoveries and researches embraced a wide range of subjects, from the course and valves of blood-vessels to the embryology of the chick. He also covered a great variety of surgical innovations. His description of the technique of tracheotomy is clearly based on practical experience and sets out the contraindications as well as the practical requirements. He also wrote extensively on the senses, the mechanics of body movement, the mechanism of respiration and the language of animals.

Principal Honours and Distinctions
Knighthood of St Mark of Venice.

Bibliography
1617, *Opera chirurgica in duas partes divisa*, Padua.
1621, *The Formation of the Egg and of the Chick*, Padua.

Further Reading
Zimmerman and Veith, 1961, *Great Ideas in the History of Surgery*, Baltimore.

MG

Fairbairn, Sir Peter

b. September 1799 Kelso, Roxburghshire, Scotland
d. 4 January 1861 Leeds, Yorkshire, England

British inventor of the revolving tube between drafting rollers to give false twist.

Born of Scottish parents, Fairbairn was apprenticed at the age of 14 to John Casson, a millwright and engineer at the Percy Main Colliery, Newcastle upon Tyne, and remained there until 1821 when he went to work for his brother William in Manchester. After going to various other places, including Messrs Rennie in London and on the European continent, he eventually moved in 1829 to Leeds where Marshall helped him set up the Wellington Foundry and so laid the foundations for the colossal establishment which was to employ over one thousand workers. To begin with he devoted his attention to improving wool-weaving machinery, substituting iron for wood in the construction of the textile machines. He also worked on machinery for flax, incorporating many of Philippe de **Girard**'s ideas. He assisted Henry **Houldsworth** in the application of the differential to roving frames, and it was to these machines that he added his own inventions. The longer fibres of wool and flax need to have some form of support and control between the rollers when they are being drawn out, and inserting a little twist helps. However, if the roving is too tightly twisted before passing through the first pair of rollers, it cannot be drawn out, while if there is insufficient twist, the fibres do not receive enough support in the drafting zone. One solution is to twist the fibres together while they are actually in the drafting zone between the rollers. In 1834, Fairbairn patented an arrangement consisting of a revolving tube placed between the drawing rollers. The tube inserted a 'middle' or 'false' twist in the material. As stated in the specification, it was 'a well-known contrivance . . . for twisting and untwisting any roving passing through it'. It had been used earlier in 1822 by J. **Goulding** of the USA and a similar idea had been developed by C. Danforth in America and patented in Britain in 1825 by J.C. **Dyer**. Fairbairn's machine, however, was said to make a very superior article. He was also involved with waste-silk spinning and rope-yarn machinery.

Fairbairn later began constructing machine tools, and at the beginning of the Crimean War was asked by the Government to make special tools for the manufacture of armaments. He supplied some of these, such as cannon rifling machines, to the arsenals at Woolwich and Enfield.

He then made a considerable number of tools for the manufacture of the **Armstrong** gun. He was involved in the life of his adopted city and was elected to Leeds town council in 1832 for ten years. He was elected an alderman in 1854 and was Mayor of Leeds from 1857 to 1859, when he was knighted by Queen Victoria at the opening of the new town hall. He was twice married, first to Margaret Kennedy and then to Rachel Anne Brindling.

Principal Honours and Distinctions
Knighted 1858.

Bibliography
1834, British patent no. 6,741 (revolving tube between drafting rollers to give false twist).

Further Reading
Dictionary of National Biography.
Obituary, 1861, *Engineer* 11.
W. English, 1969, *The Textile Industry*, London (provides a brief account of Fairbairn's revolving tube).
C. Singer (ed.), 1958, *A History of Technology*, Vols IV and V, Oxford: Clarendon Press (provides details of Fairbairn's silk-dressing machine and a picture of a large planing machine built by him).

RLH

Fairbairn, William
b. 19 February 1789 Kelso, Roxburghshire, Scotland
d. 18 August 1874 Farnham, Surrey, England

Scottish engineer and shipbuilder, pioneer in the use of iron in structures.

Born in modest circumstances, Fairbairn nevertheless enjoyed a broad and liberal education until around the age of 14. Thereafter he served an apprenticeship as a millwright in a Northumberland colliery. This seven-year period marked him out as a man of determination and intellectual ability; he planned his life around the practical work of pit-machinery maintenance and devoted his limited free time to the study of mathematics, science and history as well as 'Church, Milton and Recreation'. Like many before and countless thousands after, he worked in London for some difficult and profitless years, and then moved to Manchester, the city he was to regard as home for the rest of his life. In 1816 he was married. Along with a workmate, James Lillie, he set up a general engineering business, which steadily enlarged and ultimately involved both shipbuilding and boiler-making. The partnership was dissolved in 1832 and Fairbairn continued on his own. Consultancy work commissioned by the Forth and Clyde Canal led to the construction of iron steamships by Fairbairn for the canal; one of these, the PS *Manchester* was lost in the Irish Sea (through the little-understood phenomenon of compass deviation) on her delivery voyage from Manchester to the Clyde. This brought Fairbairn to the forefront of research in this field and confirmed him as a shipbuilder in the novel construction of iron vessels. In 1835 he operated the Millwall Shipyard on the Isle of Dogs on the Thames; this is regarded as one of the first two shipyards dedicated to iron production from the outset (the other being Tod and MacGregor of Glasgow). Losses at the London yard forced Fairbairn to sell off, and the yard passed into the hands of John Scott **Russell**, who built the I.K. **Brunel**-designed *Great Eastern* on the site. However, his business in Manchester went from strength to strength: he produced an improved Cornish boiler with two firetubes, known as the Lancashire boiler; he invented a riveting machine; and designed the beautiful swan-necked box-structured crane that is known as the Fairbairn crane to this day.

Throughout his life he advocated the widest use of iron; he served on the Admiralty Committee of 1861 investigating the use of this material in the Royal Navy. In his later years he travelled widely in Europe as an engineering consultant and published many papers on engineering. His contribution to worldwide engineering was recognized during his lifetime by the conferment of a baronetcy by Queen Victoria.

Principal Honours and Distinctions
Created Baronet 1869. FRS 1850. Elected to the Academy of Science of France 1852. President, Institution of Mechnical Engineers 1854. Royal Society Gold Medal 1860. President, British Association 1861.

Bibliography
Fairbairn wrote many papers on a wide range of engineering subjects from water-wheels to iron metallurgy and from railway brakes to the strength of iron ships. In 1856 he contributed the article on iron to the 8th edition of *Encyclopaedia Britannica*.

Further Reading
W. Pole (ed.), 1877, *The Life of Sir William Fairbairn Bart*, London: Longmans Green; reprinted 1970, David and Charles Reprints (written in part by Fairbairn, but completed and edited by Pole).

FMW

Fairlie, Robert Francis
b. March 1831 Scotland
d. 31 July 1885 Clapham, London, England

British engineer, designer of the double-bogie locomotive, advocate of narrow-gauge railways.

Fairlie worked on railways in Ireland and India, and established himself as a consulting engineer in London by the early 1860s. In 1864 he patented his design of locomotive: it was to be carried on two bogies and had a double boiler, the barrels extending in each direction from a central firebox. From smokeboxes at the outer ends, return tubes led to a single central chimney. At that time in British practice, locomotives of ever-increasing size were being carried on longer and longer rigid wheelbases, but often only one or two of their three or four pairs of wheels were powered. Bogies were little used and then only for carrying-wheels rather than driving-wheels: since their pivots were given no sideplay, they were of little value. Fairlie's design offered a powerful locomotive with a wheelbase which though long would be flexible; it would ride well and have all wheels driven and available for adhesion.

The first five double Fairlie locomotives were built by James Cross & Co. of St Helens during 1865–7. None was particularly successful: the single central chimney of the original design had been replaced by two chimneys, one at each end of the locomotive, but the single central firebox was retained, so that exhaust up one chimney tended to draw cold air down the other. In 1870 the next double Fairlie, *Little Wonder*, was built for the Festiniog Railway, on which C.E. **Spooner** was pioneering steam trains of very narrow gauge. The order had gone to George **England**, but the locomotive was completed by his successor in business, the Fairlie Engine & Steam Carriage Company, in which Fairlie and George England's son were the principal partners. *Little Wonder* was given two inner fireboxes separated by a water space and proved outstandingly successful. The spectacle of this locomotive hauling immensely long trains up grade, through the Festiniog Railway's sinuous curves, was demonstrated before engineers from many parts of the world and had lasting effect. Fairlie himself became a great protagonist of narrow-gauge railways and influenced their construction in many countries.

Towards the end of the 1860s, Fairlie was designing steam carriages or, as they would now be called, railcars, but only one was built before the death of George England Jr precipitated closure of the works in 1870. Fairlie's business became a design agency and his patent locomotives were built in large numbers under licence by many noted locomotive builders, for narrow, standard and broad gauges. Few operated in Britain, but many did in other lands; they were particularly successful in Mexico and Russia.

Many Fairlie locomotives were fitted with the radial valve gear invented by Egide **Walschaert**; Fairlie's role in the universal adoption of this valve gear was instrumental, for he introduced it to Britain in 1877 and fitted it to locomotives for New Zealand, whence it eventually spread worldwide. Earlier, in 1869, the Great Southern & Western Railway of Ireland had built in its works the first 'single Fairlie', a 0–4–4 tank engine carried on two bogies but with only one of them powered. This type, too, became popular during the last part of the nineteenth century. In the USA it was built in quantity by William Mason of Mason Machine Works, Taunton, Massachusetts, in preference to the double-ended type.

Double Fairlies may still be seen in operation on the Festiniog Railway; some of Fairlie's ideas were far ahead of their time, and modern diesel and electric locomotives are of the powered-bogie, double-ended type.

Bibliography

1864, British patent no. 1,210 (Fairlie's master patent).
1864, *Locomotive Engines, What They Are and What They Ought to Be*, London; reprinted 1969, Portmadoc: Festiniog Railway Co.

(promoting his ideas for locomotives).
1865, British patent no. 3,185 (single Fairlie).
1867, British patent no. 3,221 (combined locomotive/carriage).
1868, 'Railways and their Management', *Journal of the Society of Arts*: 328.
1871, 'On the Gauge for Railways of the Future', abstract in *Report of the Fortieth Meeting of the British Association in 1870*: 215.
1872, British patent no. 2,387 (taper boiler).
1872, *Railways or No Railways. 'Narrow Gauge, Economy with Efficiency; or Broad Gauge, Costliness with Extravagance'*, London: Effingham Wilson; repr. 1990s Canton, Ohio: Railhead Publications (promoting the cause for narrow-gauge railways).

Further Reading

Fairlie and his patent locomotives are well described in:
P.C. Dewhurst, 1962, 'The Fairlie locomotive', Part 1, *Transactions of the Newcomen Society* 34; 1966, Part 2, *Transactions* 39.
R.A.S. Abbott, 1970, *The Fairlie Locomotive*, Newton Abbot: David & Charles.

PJGR

Falcon

fl. *c*.1728 France

French improver of the pattern-selection apparatus of Bouchon for weaving.

In 1728, Falcon used punched cards, one for each pick, to replace the roll of pierced paper that **Bouchon** had used for storing the pattern to be woven. The selection of the leashes was the same as the method used by Bouchon. The appropriate card was pressed against a set of horizontal needles at the side of the loom by the drawboy, who then lifted those leashes that had been selected ready for the weaver to send the shuttle across for that pick. The cards could be sewn up into an endless loop so the pattern could be repeated time after time. This apparatus could select a greater width of pattern than Bouchon's because the cards were pressed against the needles by a square block of wood known as the prism or cylinder. This meant that rows of needles could be mounted below each other, allowing for many more to be fitted into the space. Vaucanson tried to make alterations to this apparatus, but the Falcon method remained in use until 1817 at Lyon and formed the basis for the later improvements by **Jacquard**.

Further Reading
M. Daumas (ed.), 1968, *Histoire générale des techniques*, Vol. III, *L'Expansion du machinisme*, Paris.
Conservatoire National des Arts et Métiers, 1942, *Catalogue du musée, section T, industries textiles, teintures et apprêtes*, Paris (includes a picture of a model of Falcon's apparatus in the museum).

RLH

Faraday, Michael

b. 22 September 1791 Newington, Surrey, England
d. 25 August 1867 London, England

English physicist, discoverer of the principles of the electric motor and dynamo.

Faraday's father was a blacksmith recently moved south from Westmorland. The young Faraday's formal education was limited to attendance at 'a Common Day School', and then he worked as an errand boy for George Riebau, a bookseller and bookbinder in London's West End. Riebau subsequently took him as an apprentice bookbinder, and Faraday seized every opportunity to read the books that came his way, especially scientific works.

A customer in the shop gave Faraday tickets to hear Sir Humphry **Davy** lecturing at the Royal Institution. He made notes of the lectures, bound them and sent them to Davy, asking for scientific employment. When a vacancy arose for a laboratory assistant at the Royal Institution, Davy remembered Faraday, who he took as his assistant on an 18-month tour of France, Italy and Switzerland (despite the fact that Britain and France were at war!). The tour, and especially Davy's constant company and readiness to explain matters, was a scientific education for Faraday, who returned to the Royal Institution as a competent chemist in his own right. Faraday was interested in electricity, which was then viewed as a branch of chemistry. After Oersted's announcement in 1820 that an electric current could affect a magnet, Faraday devised an arrangement in 1821 for producing *continuous* motion from an electric current and a magnet. This was the basis of the electric motor. Ten years later, after much thought and experiment,

he achieved the converse of Oersted's effect, the production of an electric current from a magnet. This was magneto-electric induction, the basis of the electric generator.

Electrical engineers usually regard Faraday as the 'father' of their profession, but Faraday himself was not primarily interested in the practical applications of his discoveries. His driving motivation was to understand the forces of nature, such as electricity and magnetism, and the relationship between them. Faraday delighted in telling others about science, and studied what made a good scientific lecturer. At the Royal Institution he introduced the Friday Evening Discourses and also the Christmas Lectures for Young People, now televised in the UK every Christmas.

Bibliography
1991, *Curiosity Perfectly Satisfyed. Faraday's Travels in Europe 1813–1815*, ed. B. Bowers and L. Symons, Peter Peregrinus (Faraday's diary of his travels with Humphry Davy).

Further Reading
L. Pearce Williams, 1965, *Michael Faraday. A Biography*, London: Chapman & Hall; 1987, New York: Da Capo Press (the most comprehensive of the many biographies of Faraday and accounts of his work).
For recent short accounts of his life see:
B. Bowers, 1991, *Michael Faraday and the Modern World*, EPA Press.
G. Cantor, D. Gooding and F. James, 1991, *Faraday*, Macmillan.
J. Meurig Thomas, 1991, *Michael Faraday and the Royal Institution*, Adam Hilger.

BB

Farman, Henri

b. 26 May 1874 Paris, France
d. 17 July 1958 Paris, France

*French aeroplane designer who modified **Voisin** biplanes and later, with his brother Maurice (b. 21 March 1877 Paris, France; d. 26 February 1964 Paris, France), created a major aircraft-manufacturing company.*

The parents of Henri and Maurice Farman were British subjects living in Paris, but their sons lived all their lives in France and became French citizens. As young men, both became involved in cycle and automobile racing. Henri (or Henry – he used both versions) turned his attention to aviation in 1907 when he bought a biplane from Gabriel Voisin. Within a short time he had established himself as one of the leading pilots in Europe, with many record-breaking flights to his credit. Farman modified the Voisin with his own improvements, including ailerons, and then in 1909 he designed the first Farman biplane. This became the most popular biplane in Europe from the autumn of 1909 until well into 1911 and is one of the classic aeroplanes of history. Meanwhile, Maurice Farman had also begun to design and build biplanes; his first design of 1909 was not a great success but from it evolved two robust biplanes nicknamed the 'Longhorn' and the 'Shorthorn', so called because of their undercarriage skids. In 1912 the brothers joined forces and set up a very large factory at Billancourt. The 'Longhorn' and 'Shorthorn' became the standard training aircraft in France and Britain during the early years of the First World War. The Farman brothers went on to produce a number of other wartime designs, including a large bomber. After the war the Farmans produced a series of large airliners which played a key role in establishing France as a major airline operator. Most famous of these was the *Goliath*, a twin-engined biplane capable of carrying up to twelve passengers. This was produced from 1918 to 1929 and was used by many airlines, including the Farman Line. The brothers retired when their company was nationalized in 1937.

Bibliography
1910, *The Aviator's Companion*, London (with his brother Dick Farman).

Further Reading
M. Farman, 1901, *3,000 kilomètres en ballon*, Paris (an account of several balloon flights from 1894 to 1900).
J. Liron, 1984, *Les Avions Farman*, Paris (provides comprehensive descriptions of all Farman aircraft).
Jane's Fighting Aircraft of World War I, 1990, London (reprint) (gives details of all early Farman aircraft).
J. Stroud, 1966, *European Aircraft since 1910*, London (provides details about Farman airliners).

JDS

Farnsworth, Philo Taylor

b. 19 August 1906 Beaver, Utah, USA
d. 11 March 1971 Salt Lake City, Utah, USA

American engineer and independent inventor who was a pioneer in the development of television.

Whilst still in high school, Farnsworth became interested in the possibility of television and conceived many of the basic features of a practicable system of TV broadcast and reception. Following two years of study at the Brigham Young University in Provo, Utah, in 1926 he cofounded the Crocker Research Laboratories in San Francisco, subsequently Farnsworth Television Inc. (1929) and Farnsworth Radio & Television Corporation, Fort Wayne, Indiana (1938). There he began a lifetime of research, primarily in the field of television. In 1927, with the backing of the Radio Corporation of America (RCA) and the collaboration of Vladimir **Zworykin**, he demonstrated the first all-electronic television system, based on his early ideas for an image dissector tube, the first electronic equivalent of the **Nipkow** disc. With this rudimentary sixty-line system he was able to transmit a recognizable dollar sign and file the first of many TV patents. From then on he contributed to a variety of developments in the fields of vacuum tubes, radar and atomic-power generation, with patents on cathode ray tubes, amplifying and pick-up tubes, electron multipliers and photoelectric materials.

Principal Honours and Distinctions
Institute of Radio Engineers Morris Leibmann Memorial Prize 1941.

Bibliography
1930, British patent nos. 368,309 and 368,721 (for his image dissector).
1934, 'Television by electron image scanning', *Journal of the Franklin Institute* 218: 411 (describes the complete image-dissector system).

Further Reading
J.H. Udelson, 1982, *The Great Television Race: A History of the American Television Industry 1925–1941*, University of Alabama Press.
O.E. Dunlop Jr, 1944, *Radio's 100 Men of Science*.
G.R.M. Garratt & A.H. Mumford, 1952, 'The

history of television', *Proceedings of the Institution of Electrical Engineers IIIA Television* 99.

See also: **Baird, John Logie**; **Jenkins, Charles Francis**.

KF

Fauchard, Pierre

b. 1678 Brittany, France
d. 27 March 1761 Paris, France

French surgeon and dentist, pioneer of dental fillings.

With John **Hunter**, Fauchard was the pioneer of rational dentistry. His treatise published in 1728 stated, 'The most celebrated surgeons having abandoned this branch of surgery, . . . their negligence gave rise to a class of persons who, without theoretic knowledge or experience . . . practised it at hazard, having neither principles or system.' He described how to fill a dental cavity using either tin, lead or gold and proposed porcelain as an improvement on bone or ivory for artificial teeth. This latter proposal is thought to have been suggested by René-Antoine Ferchault de Réaumur (1683–1757) who was connected with the porcelain factory at Sèvres.

Bibliography
1728, *Le Chirurgien dentiste, ou traité des dents,* Paris.

Further Reading
R.F.C. Minn, 1941, *Pierre Fauchard – Surgeon Dentist.*

MG

Faure, Camille Alphonse

b. 21 May 1840 Vizille, France
d. September 1898

French chemist, inventor of an improved method of preparing the plates for Planté lead–acid secondary cells.

After technical training at the Ecole des Arts et Métiers at Aix, Faure was employed superintending the erection of factories in France and England. These included the Cotton Powder Company plant in Faversham for the manufacture of the explosive Tonite invented by Faure. He also invented distress signals used by the merchant navy. It was between 1878 and 1880 that he performed his most important work, the improvement of the Planté cell. Faure's invention of coating the lead plates with a paste of lead oxide substantially reduced the time taken to form the plates. Their construction was subsequently further improved by **Swan** and others. These developments appeared at a particularly opportune time because lead–acid secondary cells found immediate application in telegraphy and later in electric lighting and traction systems, where their use resulted in reduced costs of providing supplies during peak-load periods. In his later years Faure's attention was directed to other electrochemical problems, including the manufacture of aluminium.

Bibliography
1881, 'Sur la pile secondaire de M C. Faure', *Comptes rendus* 92: 951–3 (announcing his cell).
11 January 1881, British patent no. 129 (Faure's improvement of the Planté cell).

Further Reading
Electrician (1882) 7: 122–3 (describes the Faure cell).
G. Wood Vinal, 1955, *Storage Batteries*, 4th edn, London (describes later developments).

GW

Fauvelle, Pierre-Pascal

b. 4 June 1797 Rethel, Ardennes, France
d. 19 December 1867 Perpignan, France

French inventor of hydraulic boring.

While attending the drilling of artesian wells in southern France in 1833, Fauvelle noticed that the debris from the borehole was carried out by the ascending water. This observation caused him to conceive the idea that the boring process need not necessarily be interrupted in order to clear the hole with an auger. It took him eleven years to develop his idea and to find financial backing to carry out his project in practice. In 1844, within a period of fifty-four days, he secretly bored an artesian well 219 m (718 ft) deep in Perpignan. One year later he secured his invention with a patent in France, and with another the following year in Spain.

Fauvelle's process involved water being forced by a pressure pump through hollow rods to the bottom of the drill, whence it ascended through the annular space between the rod and the wall of the borehole, thus flushing the mud up to the surface. This method was similar to that of Robert Beart who had secured a patent in Britain but had not put it into practice. Although Fauvelle was not primarily concerned with the rotating action of the drill, his hydraulic boring method and its subsequent developments by his stepson, Alphonse de Basterot, formed an important step towards modern rotary drilling, which began with the work of Anthony F. **Lucas** near Beaumont, Texas, at the turn of the twentieth century. In the 1870s Albert Fauck, who also contributed important developments to the structure of boring rigs, had combined Fauvelle's hydraulic system with core-boring in the United States.

Bibliography
1846, 'Sur un nouveau système de forage', *Comptes rendus de l'Académie des sciences*, pp. 438–40; also printed in 1847 in *Le Technologiste* 8, pp. 87–8.

Further Reading
A. Birembeaut, 1968, 'Pierre-Pascal Fauvelle', *Dictionnaire de biographie française*, vol. 13, pp. 808–10; also in *L'Indépendant*, Perpignan, 5–10 February (biography).
A. de Basterot, 1868, *Puits artésiens, sondages de mines, sondages d'études, système Fauvelle et de Basterot*, Brussels (a detailed description of Fauvelle's methods and de Basterot's developments).

See also **Crælius, Per Anton**.

WK

Ferguson, Harry
b. 4 November 1884 County Down, Ireland
d. 25 October 1960 England

Irish engineer who developed a tractor hydraulic system for cultivation equipment, and thereby revolutionized tractor design.

Ferguson's father was a small farmer who expected his son to help on the farm from an early age. As a result he received little formal education, and on leaving school joined his brother in a backstreet workshop in Belfast repairing motor bikes. By the age of 19 he had built his own bike and began hill-climbing competitions and

racing. His successes in these ventures gained useful publicity for the workshop. In 1907 he built his own car and entered it into competitions, and in 1909 became the first person in Britain to build and fly a machine that was heavier than air.

On the outbreak of the First World War he was appointed by the Irish Department of Agriculture to supervise the operation and maintenance of all farm tractors. His experiences convinced him that even the Ford tractor and the implements available for it were inadequate for the task, and he began to experiment with his own plough designs. The formation of the Ferguson–Sherman Corporation resulted in the production of thousands of the ploughs he had designed for the Ford tractor, but in 1928 Ford discontinued production of tractors, and Ferguson returned to Ireland. He immediately began to design his own tractor. Six years of development led to the building of a prototype that weighed only 16 cwt (813 kg). In 1936 David Brown of Huddersfield, Yorkshire, began production of these tractors for Ferguson, but the partnership was not wholly successful and was dissolved after three years. In 1939 Ferguson and Ford reached their famous 'Handshake agreement', in which no formal contract was signed, and the mass production of the Ford Ferguson system tractors began that year. During the next nine years 300,000 tractors and a million implements were produced under this agreement. However, on the death of Henry Ford the company began production, under his son, of their own tractor. Ferguson returned to the UK and negotiated a deal with the Standard Motor Company of Coventry for the production of his tractor. At the same time he took legal action against Ford, which resulted in that company being forced to stop production and to pay damages amounting to US$9.5 million.

Aware that his equipment would only operate when set up properly, Ferguson established a training school at Stoneleigh in Warwickshire which was to be a model for other manufacturers. In 1953, by amicable agreement, Ferguson amalgamated with the Massey Harris Company to form Massey Ferguson, and in so doing added harvesting machinery to the range of equipment produced. A year later he disposed of his shares in the new company and turned his attention again to the motor car. Although a number of experimental cars were produced, there were no long-lasting developments from this venture other than a four-wheel-drive system based on hydraulics; this was used by a number of manufacturers on occasional models. Ferguson's death heralded the end of these developments.

Principal Honours and Distinctions
Honorary DSc Queen's University, Belfast, 1948.

Further Reading
C. Murray, 1972, *Harry Ferguson, Inventor and Pioneer*. John Murray.

AP

Ferguson, Peter Jack
b. 21 July 1840 Partick, near Glasgow, Scotland
d. 17 March 1911 Greenock, Scotland

Scottish marine engineer, pioneer of multiple-expansion steam reciprocating machinery.

Ferguson was educated at the High School of Glasgow before going on to serve his apprenticeship in the engineering department of Thomas Wingate's shipyard. This yard, situated at Whiteinch, then just outside the Glasgow boundary, built interesting and innovative craft and had a tradition of supplying marine engines that were at the leading edge of technology. On his appointment as Manager, Ferguson designed several new types of engines, and in 1872 he was responsible for the construction of what is claimed to be the world's first triple-expansion engine, predating the machinery on SS *Propontis* by two years and **Napier**'s masterpiece, the SS *Aberdeen*, by nine years. In 1885, along with others, he founded the shipyard of Fleming and Ferguson, of Paisley, which in the subsequent eighty-five years was to build nearly seven hundred ships. From the outset they built advanced steam reciprocating machinery as well as dredging and other types of plant. The new shipyard was to benefit from Ferguson's experience and from the inspiration he had gained in Wingate's, where experimentation was the norm.

Further Reading
F.M. Walker, 1984, *Song of the Clyde. A History of Clyde Shipbuiding*, Cambridge: PSL.

FMW

Fermi, Enrico
b. 29 September 1901 Rome, Italy
d. 28 November 1954 Chicago, USA

Italian nuclear physicist.

Fermi was one of the most versatile of twentieth-century physicists, one of the few to excel in both theory and experiment. His greatest theoretical achievements lay in the field of statistics and his theory of beta decay. His statistics, parallel to but independent of Dirac, were the key to the modern theory of metals and the statistical models of the atomic nucleus. On the experimental side, his most notable discoveries were artificial radioactivity produced by neutron bombardment and the realization of a controlled nuclear chain reaction, in the world's first nuclear reactor.

Fermi received a conventional education with a chemical bias, but reached proficiency in mathematics and physics largely through his own reading. He studied at Pisa University, where he taught himself modern physics and then travelled to extend his knowledge, spending time with Max Born at Göttingen. On his return to Italy, he secured posts in Florence and, in 1927, in Rome, where he obtained the first Italian Chair in Theoretical Physics, a subject in which Italy had so far lagged behind. He helped to bring about a rebirth of physics in Italy and devoted himself to the application of statistics to his model of the atom. For this work, Fermi was awarded the Nobel Prize in Physics in 1938, but in December of that year, finding the Fascist regime uncongenial, he transferred to the USA and Columbia University. The news that nuclear fission had been achieved broke shortly before the Second World War erupted and it stimulated Fermi to consider this a way of generating secondary nuclear emission and the initiation of chain reactions. His experiments in this direction led first to the discovery of slow neutrons.

Fermi's work assumed a more practical aspect when he was invited to join the Manhattan Project for the construction of the first atomic bomb. His small-scale work at Columbia became large-scale at Chicago University. This culminated on 2 December 1942 when the first controlled nuclear reaction took place at Stagg Field, Chicago, an historic event indeed. Later, Fermi spent most of the period from September 1944 to early 1945 at Los Alamos, New Mexico, taking part in the preparations for the first test explosion of the atomic bomb on 16 July 1945. President Truman invited Fermi to serve on his Committee to advise him on the use of the bomb. Then Chicago University established an Institute for Nuclear Studies and offered Fermi a professorship, which he took up early in 1946, spending the rest of his relatively short life there.

Principal Honours and Distinctions
Nobel Prize for Physics 1938.

Bibliography
1962–5, *Collected Papers*, ed. E. Segrè *et al.*, 2 vols, Chicago (includes a biographical introduction and bibliography).

Further Reading
L. Fermi, 1954, *Atoms in the Family*, Chicago (a personal account by his wife).
E. Segrè, 1970, *Enrico Fermi, Physicist*, Chicago (deals with the more scientific aspects of his life).

LRD

Ferranti, Sebastian Ziani de
b. 9 April 1864 Liverpool, England
d. 13 January 1930 Zurich, Switzerland

English manufacturing engineer and inventor, a pioneer and early advocate of high-voltage alternating-current electric-power systems.

Ferranti, who had taken an interest in electrical and mechanical devices from an early age, was educated at St Augustine's College in Ramsgate and for a short time attended evening classes at University College, London. Rather than pursue an academic career, Ferranti, who had intense practical interests, found employment in 1881 with the Siemens Company (see Werner von **Siemens**) in their experimental department. There he had the opportunity to superintend the installation of electric-lighting plants in various parts of the country. Becoming acquainted with Alfred Thomson, an engineer, Ferranti entered into a short-lived partnership with him to manufacture the Ferranti alternator. This generator, with a unique zig-zag armature, had an efficiency

exceeding that of all its rivals. Finding that Sir William **Thomson** had invented a similar machine, Ferranti formed a company with him to combine the inventions and produce the Ferranti–Thomson machine. For this the Hammond Electric Light and Power Company obtained the sole selling rights.

In 1885 the Grosvenor Gallery Electricity Supply Corporation was having serious problems with its Gaulard and Gibbs series distribution system. Ferranti, when consulted, reviewed the design and recommended transformers connected across constant-potential mains. In the following year, at the age of 22, he was appointed Engineer to the company and introduced the pattern of electricity supply that was eventually adopted universally. Ambitious plans by Ferranti for London envisaged the location of a generating station of unprecedented size at Deptford, about eight miles (13 km) from the city, a departure from the previous practice of placing stations within the area to be supplied. For this venture the London Electricity Supply Corporation was formed. Ferranti's bold decision to bring the supply from Deptford at the hitherto unheard-of pressure of 10,000 volts required him to design suitable cables, transformers and generators. Ferranti planned generators with 10,000 hp (7,460 kW) engines, but these were abandoned at an advanced stage of construction. Financial difficulties were caused in part when a Board of Trade enquiry in 1889 reduced the area that the company was able to supply. In spite of this adverse situation the enterprise continued on a reduced scale. Leaving the London Electricity Supply Corporation in 1892, Ferranti again started his own business, manufacturing electrical plant. He conceived the use of wax-impregnated paper-insulated cables for high voltages, which formed a landmark in the history of cable development. This method of flexible-cable manufacture was used almost exclusively until synthetic materials became available. In 1892 Ferranti obtained a patent which set out the advantages to be gained by adopting sector-shaped conductors in multi-core cables. This was to be fundamental to the future design and development of such cables.

A total of 176 patents were taken out by S.Z. de Ferranti. His varied and numerous inventions included a successful mercury-motor energy meter and improvements to textile-yarn production. A transmission-line phenomenon where the open-circuit voltage at the receiving end of a long line is greater than the sending voltage was named the Ferranti Effect after him.

Principal Honours and Distinctions
FRS 1927. President, Institution of Electrical Engineers 1910 and 1911. Institution of Electrical Engineers Faraday Medal 1924.

Bibliography
18 July 1882, British patent no. 3,419 (Ferranti's first alternator).
13 December 1892, British patent no. 22,923 (shaped conductors of multi-core cables).
1929, 'Electricity in the service of man', *Journal of the Institution of Electrical Engineers* 67: 125–30.

Further Reading
G.Z. de Ferranti and R. Ince, 1934, *The Life and Letters of Sebastian Ziani de Ferranti*, London.
A. Ridding, 1964, *S.Z. de Ferranti. Pioneer of Electric Power*, London: Science Museum and HMSO (a concise biography).
R.H. Parsons, 1939, *Early Days of the Power Station Industry*, Cambridge, pp. 21–41.
GW

Fessenden, Reginald Aubrey
b. 6 October 1866 East Bolton, Quebec, Canada
d. 22 July 1932 Bermuda

Canadian radio pioneer who made the first known broadcast of speech and music.

After initial education at Trinity College School, Port Hope, Ontario, Fessenden studied at Bishops University, Lennoxville, Quebec. When he graduated in 1885, he became Principal of the Whitney Institute in Bermuda, but he left the following year to go to New York in pursuit of his scientific interests. There he met **Edison** and eventually became Chief Chemist at the latter's Laboratory in Orange, New Jersey. In 1890 he moved to the Westinghouse Electric and Manufacturing Company, and two years later he returned to an academic career as Professor of Electrical Engineering, initially at Purdue University, Lafayette, Indiana, and then at the Western University of Pennsylvania, where he worked on wireless communication. From 1900

to 1902 he carried out experiments in wireless telegraphy at the US Weather Bureau, filing several patents relating to wire and liquid thermal detectors, or barretters. Following this he set up the National Electric Signalling Company; under his direction, **Alexanderson** and other engineers at the General Electric Company developed a high-frequency alternator that enabled him to build the first radiotelephony transmitter at Brant Rock, Massachusetts. This made its initial broadcast of speech and music on 24 December 1906, received by ship's wireless operators several hundred miles away. Soon after this the transmitter was successfully used for two-way wireless telegraphy communication with Scotland. Following this landmark event, Fessenden produced numerous inventions, including a radio compass, an acoustic depth-finder and several submarine signalling devices, a turboelectric drive for battleships and, notably, in 1912 the heterodyne principle used in radio receivers to convert signals to a lower (intermediate) frequency.

Principal Honours and Distinctions
Institute of Electrical and Electronics Engineers Medal of Honour 1921.

Bibliography
US patents relating to barretters include nos. 706,740, 706,742 and 706,744 (wire, 1902) and 731,029 (liquid, 1903). His invention of the heterodyne was filed as US patent no. 1,050,441 (1913).

Further Reading
Helen M. Fessenden, 1940, *Fessenden. Builder of Tomorrow*.
E. Hawkes, 1927, *Pioneers of Wireless*, London: Methuen.
O.E. Dunlop, 1944, *Radio's 100 Men of Science*.
KF

Field, Cyrus West
b. 30 November 1819 Stockbridge, Massachusetts, USA
d. 12 July 1892 New York City, New York, USA

American financier and entrepreneur noted for his successful promotion of the first transatlantic telegraph cable.

At the age of 15 Field left home to seek his fortune in New York, starting work on Broadway as an errand boy for $1 per week. Returning to Massachusetts, in 1838 he became an assistant to his brother Matthew, a papermaker, leaving to set up his own business two years later. By the age of 21 he was also a partner in a New York firm of paper wholesalers, but this firm collapsed because of large debts. Out of the wreckage he set up Cyrus W. Field & Co., and by 1852 he had paid off all the debts. With $250,000 in the bank he therefore retired and travelled in South America. Returning to the USA, he then became involved with the construction of a telegraph line in Newfoundland by an English engineer, F.N. Osborne. Although the company collapsed, he had been fired by the dream of a transatlantic cable and in 1854 was one of the founders of the New York, Newfoundland and London Telegraph Company. He began to promote surveys and hold discussions with British telegraph pioneers and with Isambard Brunel, who was then building the Great Eastern steamship. In 1856 he helped to set up the Atlantic Telegraph Company in Britain and, as a result of his efforts and those of the British physicist and inventor Sir William Thomson (Lord Kelvin), work began in 1857 on the laying of the first transatlantic cable from Newfoundland to Ireland. After many tribulations the cable was completed on 5 August 1857, but it failed after barely a month. Following several unsuccessful attempts to repair and replace it, the cable was finally completed on 27 July 1866. Building upon his success, Field expanded his business interests. In 1877 he bought a controlling interest in and was President of the New York Elevated Railroad Company. He also helped develop the Wabash Railroad and became owner of the New York Mail and Express newspaper; however, he subsequently suffered large financial losses.

Principal Honours and Distinctions
Congressional Gold Medal.

Further Reading
A.C. Clarke, 1958, *Voice Across the Sea*, London: Frederick Muller (describes the development of the transatlantic telegraph).
H.M. Field, 1893, *Story of the Atlantic Telegraph* (also describes the transatlantic telegraph development).
L.J. Judson (ed.), 1893, *Cyrus W. Field: His Life and Work* (a complete biography).

KF

Field, Joshua
b. 1786 Hackney, London, England
d. 11 August 1863 Balham Hill, Surrey, England

English mechanical engineer, co-founder of the Institution of Civil Engineers.

Joshua Field was educated at a boarding school in Essex until the age of 16, when he obtained employment at the Royal Dockyards at Portsmouth under the Chief Mechanical Superintendent, Simon Goodrich (1773–1847), and later in the drawing office at the Admiralty in Whitehall. At this time, machinery for the manufacture of ships' blocks was being made for the Admiralty by Henry **Maudslay**, who was in need of a competent draughtsman, and Goodrich recommended Joshua Field. This was the beginning of Field's long association with Maudslay; he later became a partner in the firm which was for many years known as Maudslay, Sons & Field. They undertook a variety of mechanical engineering work but were renowned for marine steam engines, with Field being responsible for much of the design work in the early years. Joshua Field was the eldest of the eight young men who in 1818 founded the Institution of Civil Engineers; he was the first Chairman of the Institution and later became a vice-president. He was the only one of the founders to be elected President and was the first mechanical engineer to hold that office. James **Nasmyth** in his autobiography relates that Joshua Field kept a methodical account of his technical discussions in a series of note books which were later indexed. Some of these diaries have survived, and extracts from the notes he made on a tour of the industrial areas of the Midlands and the North West in 1821 have been published.

Principal Honours and Distinctions
FRS 1836. President, Institution of Civil Engineers 1848–9. Member, Smeatonian Society of Civil Engineers 1835; President 1848.

Bibliography
1925–6, 'Joshua Field's diary of a tour in 1821 through the Midlands', introd. and notes J.W. Hall,

Transactions of the Newcomen Society 6: 1–41.
1932–3, 'Joshua Field's diary of a tour in 1821 through the provinces', introd. and notes E.C. Smith, *Transactions of the Newcomen Society* 13: 15–50.

RTS

Fife, William

b. 15 June 1857 Fairlie, Scotland
d. 11 August 1944 Fairlie, Scotland

Scottish naval architect and designer of sailing yachts of legendary beauty and performance.

Following his education at Brisbane Academy in Largs, William Fife (the third generation of the name) became apprenticed at the age of 14 to the already famous yacht-building yard owned by his family at Fairlie in Ayrshire. On completion of his apprenticeship, he joined the Paisley shipbuilders John Fullerton & Co. to gain experience in iron shipbuilding before going on as Manager to the Marquis of Ailsa's Culzean Steam Launch and Yacht Works. Initially the works was sited below the famous castle at Culzean, but some years later it moved a few miles along the Ayrshire Coast to Maidens. The Culzean Company was wound up in 1887 and Fife then returned to the family yard, where he remained for the rest of his working life. Many outstanding yachts were the product of his hours on the drawing board, including auxiliary sailing cruisers, motor yachts and well-known racing craft. The most outstanding designs were for two of Sir Thomas Lipton's challengers for the America's Cup: *Shamrock I* and *Shamrock III*. The latter yacht was tested at the Ship Model Experiment Tank owned by Denny of Dumbarton before being built at their Leven Shipyard in 1903. *Shamrock III* may have been one of the earliest America's Cup yachts to have been designed with a high level of scientific input. The hull construction was unusual for the early years of the twentieth century, being of alloy steel with decks of aluminium.

William Fife was decorated for his service to shipbuilding during the First World War. With the onset of the Great Depression the shipyard's output slowed, and in the 1930s it was sold to other interests; this was the end of the 120-year Fife dynasty.

Principal Honours and Distinctions
OBE *c.*1919.

FMW

Finsen, Neils Ryberg

b. 15 December 1860 Thorshavn, Faeroe Islands
d. 24 September 1904 Copenhagen, Denmark

Icelandic physician, investigator and pioneer of actinotherapy.

Following his early education in Reykjavik, Finsen moved to Copenhagen and obtained his medical degree in 1891. Appointed as a demonstrator in anatomy at the University of Copenhagen, he soon abandoned a career in academic medicine, preferring the sunlit environment of outdoor life. He was soon studying the nature of light-induced inflammation and proceeded to identify the radiation in the blue-violet and ultraviolet (actinic) parts of the solar spectrum as being particularly responsible. By 1893 he had discovered the beneficial effect of red light on the lesions of smallpox and in 1894 he put forward his conclusion that light possessed a direct therapeutic quality. In 1895 he amplified this work with the treatment of *lupus vulgaris* (tuberculosis of the skin) using a carbon-arc source suitably filtered to expose the tissues to high concentrations of ultraviolet rays. Extensions of this form of therapy were applied in a number of other conditions until superseded by the development of serology, chemotherapy and antibiotic drugs.

In his final years, afflicted with a cardiac condition possibly related to the endemic hydatid disease of Iceland, he carried out an important self-study on salt and water metabolism, laying the foundations for the therapeutic concept of low fluid and low salt intake therapy.

Principal Honours and Distinctions
Nobel Prize for Medicine or Physiology 1903 (the first such award).

Bibliography
1894, 'Les rayons chimiques et la variole', *La Semaine médicale*.
1895, 'The red light treatment of smallpox', *British Medical Journal*.

Further Reading
P. de Kruif, 1932, *Men Against Death*, New York.

MG

Fischer, E.
fl. 1930s Switzerland

Swiss engineer who invented the Eidophor large-screen television projector.

Fischer was a professor of engineering at the Swiss Federal Institute of Technology in the late 1930s. Interested in the emerging technology for television, he was of the opinion that the growth of television would take place through the development and use of large-screen cinema-type displays serving large audiences. He therefore carried out research into suitable techniques. Realizing the brightness limitations of projection systems based on the optical magnification of the image produced by a conventional cathode ray tube, he used the deflected electron-beam, not to excite a phosphor screen, but to deposit a variable charge on the surface of a film or oil. By means of a Schlieren slit system, the consequent deformations of the surface were used to spatially modulate the light from an electric arc or a discharge tube, giving a large, high-brightness image. Although the idea, first put forward in 1939, was not taken up for cinema television, the subsequent requirement of the US National Aeronautics and Space Administration in the 1960s for large colour displays in its Command and Control Centres led to the successful development of the idea by Gretag AG, a subsidiary of Ciba-Geigy: separate units were used for the red, green and blue images. In the 1990s, colour Eidophor projectors were used for large conference meetings and pop concerts.

Bibliography
1946, 'Views on the suitability of a cathode ray tube with a fluorescent screen for projection in cinemas', *Bulletin of the Association of Swiss Electricians* 39: 468 (describes the concept of the Eidophor).

Further Reading
E.H. Baumann, 1953, 'The Fischer large screen projection system', *Journal of Society of Motion Picture and Television Engineers* 60: 344.
A. Robertson, 1976, 'Projection television. A review of current practice in large-screen projectors', *Wireless World* 47.

KF

Fizeau, Armand Hippolyte Louis
b. 23 September 1819 Paris, France
d. 18 September 1896 Nanteuil-le-Haudouin, France

French physicist who introduced early improvements to the daguerreotype process.

Fizeau's interest in photography was comparatively brief, but during this period he was at the forefront of French attempts to explore and exploit the potential of the recently announced daguerreotype process (see **Daguerre**). Fizeau is best remembered for his introduction in August 1840 of the practice of gold-toning daguerreotypes. This improvement not only helped protect the delicate surface of the plate from abrasion and tarnishing, but also enhanced the quality of the image. The technique was not patented and was immediately adopted by all daguerreotypists. Between 1839 and 1841, in association with Alfred Donné, Fizeau conducted experiments with the aim of converting daguerreotypes into printing plates. Prints from two of his plates were published in 1842, but the technique was never widely practised. In association with J.B. Léon Foucault, Fizeau discovered the reciprocity failure of daguerreotypes, and the same partnership produced what were probably the first daguerreotypes of the sun. Fizeau is best known in physics for making the first accurate determination of the speed of light, in 1849.

Further Reading
W.H. Thornthwaite, 1843, *Photographic Manipulation*, London (provides details of Fizeau's gold-toning process).
H. Gernsheim and A. Gernsheim, 1969, *The History of Photography*, rev. edn, London (a more general account of Fizeau's contributions to photography).

JW

Flechsig, W.
fl. *c*.1938 Germany

German engineer notable for early patents that foreshadowed the development of the shadowmask colour cathode ray tube.

In 1938, whilst working for a German electrical company, Flechsig filed a patent in which he described the use of an array of stretched parallel wires to control the landing of either one or three electron beams on separate red, green and blue phosphor stripes within a single cathode ray tube. Whilst the single-beam arrangement required subsidiary deflection to alternate the beam landing angle, the three-beam version effectively used the wires to 'mask' the landing of the electron beams so that each one only illuminated the relevant colour phosphor stripes. Although not developed at the time, the concept anticipated the subsequent invention of the shadowmask tube by RCA in the early 1950s and, even more closely, the development of the Sony Trinitron some years later.

Bibliography
1938, German patent no. 736,575.
1941, French patent no. 866,065.

Further Reading
E.W. Herold, 1976, 'A history of colour television displays', *Proceedings of the Institute of Electrical and Electronics Engineers* 64: 1,331.
K.G. Freeman, 'The history of colour CRTs. A personal view', *International Conference on the History of Television*, Institution of Electrical Engineers Publication no. 271, p. 38.

See also: **Baird, John Logie**; **Goldmark, Peter Carl**.

KF

Flettner, Anton
b. 1 November 1885 Eddersheim-am-Main, Germany
d. 29 December 1961 New York, USA

German engineer and inventor who produced a practical helicopter for the German navy in 1940.

Anton Flettner was an engineer with a great interest in hydraulics and aerodynamics. At the beginning of the First World War Flettner was recruited by **Zeppelin** to investigate the possibility of radio-controlled airships as guided missiles. In 1915 he constructed a small radio-controlled tank equipped to cut barbed-wire defences; the military experts rejected it, but he was engaged to investigate radio-controlled pilotless aircraft and he invented a servo-control device to assist their control systems. These servo-controls, or trim tabs, were used on large German bombers towards the end of the war. In 1924 he invented a sailing ship powered by rotating cylinders, but although one of these crossed the Atlantic they were never a commercial success. He also invented a windmill and a marine rudder. In the late 1920s Flettner turned his attention to rotating-wing aircraft, and in 1931 he built a helicopter with small engines mounted on the rotor blades. Progress was slow and it was abandoned after being damaged during testing in 1934. An autogiro followed in 1936, but it caught fire on a test flight and was destroyed. Undeterred, Flettner continued his development work on helicopters and in 1937 produced the *Fl 185*, which had a single rotor to provide lift and two propellers on outriggers to combat the torque and provide forward thrust. This arrangement was not a great success, so he turned to twin contra-rotating rotors, as used by his rival **Focke**, but broke new ground by using intermeshing rotors to make a more compact machine. The *Fl 265* with its 'egg-beater' rotors was ordered by the German navy in 1938 and flew the following year. After exhaustive testing, Flettner improved his design and produced the two-seater *Fl 282 Kolibri*, which flew in 1940 and became the only helicopter to be used operationally during the Second World War.

After the war, Flettner moved to the United States where his intermeshing-rotor idea was developed by the Kaman Aircraft Corporation.

Bibliography
1926, *Mein Weg zum Rotor*, Leipzig; also published as *The Story of the Rotor*, New York (describes his early work with rotors – i.e. cylinders).

Further Reading
W. Gunston and J. Batchelor, 1977, *Helicopters 1900–1960*, London.
R.N. Liptrot, 1948, *Rotating Wing Activities in Germany during the Period 1939–45*, London.
K. von Gersdorff and K. Knobling, 1982, *Hubschrauber und Tragschrauber*, Munich (a more recent publication, in German).

JDS

Florey, Howard Walter
b. 24 September 1898 Adelaide, Australia
d. 21 February 1968 Oxford, England

Australian pathologist who contributed to the research and technology resulting in the practical clinical availability of penicillin.

After graduating MB and BS from Adelaide University in 1921, he went to Oxford University, England, as a Rhodes Scholar in 1922. Following a period at Cambridge and as a Rockefeller Fellow in the USA, he returned to Cambridge as Lecturer in Pathology. He was appointed to the Chair of Pathology at Sheffield at the age of 33, and to the Sir William Dunne Chair of Pathology at Oxford in 1935.

Although historically his name is inseparable from that of penicillin, his experimental interests and achievements covered practically the whole range of general pathology. He was a determined advocate of the benefits to research of maintaining close contact between different disciplines. He was an early believer in the need to study functional changes in cells as much as the morphological changes that these brought about.

With E. **Chain**, Florey perceived the potential of Fleming's 1929 note on the bacteria-inhibiting qualities of *Penicillium* mould. His forthright and dynamic character played a vital part in developing what was perceived to be not just a scientific and medical discovery of unparalleled importance, but a matter of the greatest significance in a war of survival. Between them, Florey and Chain were able to establish the technique of antibiotic isolation and made their findings available to those implementing large-scale fermentation production processes in the USA.

Despite being domiciled in England, he played an active role in Australian medical and educational affairs and was installed as Chancellor of the Australian National University in 1966.

Principal Honours and Distinctions
Life peer 1965. Order of Merit 1965. Knighted 1944. FRS 1941. President, Royal Society 1960–5. Nobel Prize for Medicine or Physiology (jointly with E.B. Chain and A. Fleming) 1945. Copley Medal 1957. Commander, Légion d'honneur 1946. British Medical Association Gold Medal 1964.

Bibliography
1940, 'Penicillin as a chemotherapeutic agent', *Lancet* (with Chain).
1949, *Antibiotics,* Oxford (with Chain *et al.*).

1962, *General Pathology,* Oxford.

MG

Floyer, Sir John
b. 3 March 1649 Hints, Warwickshire, England
d. 1734 Lichfield, Staffordshire, England

English physician, pioneer in the measurement of pulse and respiration rate.

The younger son of a landed Midlands family, Floyer embarked on medical studies at Oxford at the age of 15 and graduated in 1674. He returned to Lichfield where he resided and practised, as well as being acquainted with the family of Samuel Johnson, for the remainder of a long life. Described by a later biographer as 'fantastic, whimsical, pretentious, research-minded and nebulous', he none the less, as his various medical writings testify, became a pioneer in several fields of medical endeavour. It seems likely that he was well aware of the teachings of **Sanctorius** in relation to measurement in medicine and he probably had a copy of Sanctorius's weighing-machine made and put to use in Lichfield.

He also embarked on extensive studies relating to pulse, respiration rate, temperature, barometric readings and even latitude. Initially he used the minute hand of a pendulum clock or a navigational minute glass. He then commissioned from Samuel Watson, a London watch- and clockmaker, a physicians' pulse watch incorporating a second-hand and a stop mechanism. In 1707 and 1710 he published a massive work, dedicated to Queen Anne, that emphasized the value of the accurate measurement of pulse rates in health and disease.

His other interests included studies of blood pressure, asthma, and the medical value of cold bathing. It is of interest that it was at his suggestion that the young Samuel Johnson was taken to London to receive the Royal Touch, from Queen Anne, for scrofula.

Principal Honours and Distinctions
Knighted 1686.

Bibliography
1707–10, *The Physicians Pulse Watch,* 2 vols, London.

Further Reading
D.D. Gibb, 1969, 'Sir John Floyer, M.D. (1649–1734), *British Medical Journal*.

MG

Flügge-Lotz, Irmgard
b. 1903 Germany
d. 1974 USA

German/American aeronautical engineer, specializing in flight control.

Both her father, a mathematician, and her mother encouraged Flügge-Lotz in her desire, unusual for a woman at that time, for a technical education. Her interest in aeronautics was awakened when she was a child, by seeing zeppelins (see **Zeppelin, Ferdinand, Count von**) being tested. In 1923 she entered the Technische Hochschule in Hannover to study engineering, specializing in aeronautics; she was often the only woman in the class. She obtained her doctorate in 1929 and began working in aeronautics. Two years later she derived the Lotz Method for calculating the distribution in aircraft wings of different shapes, which became widely used. Later, Flügge-Lotz took up an interest in automatic flight control of aircraft, notably of the discontinuous or 'on-off' type. These were simple in design, inexpensive to manufacture and reliable in operation. By 1928 she had risen to the position of head of the Department of Theoretical Aerodynamics at Göttingen University, but she and her husband, Wilhelm Flügge, an engineering academic known for his anti-Nazi views, felt themselves increasingly discriminated against by the Hitler regime. In 1948 they emigrated to the USA, where Flügge was soon offered a professorship in engineering, while his wife had at first to make do with a lectureship. But her distinguished work eventually earned her appointment as the first woman full professor in the Engineering Department at Stanford University.

She later extended her work on automatic flight control to the guidance of rockets and missiles, earning herself the description 'a female Werner von **Braun**'.

Principal Honours and Distinctions
Society of Women Engineers Achievement Award 1970. Fellow, Institution of Aeronautics and Astronautics.

Bibliography
Flügge-Lotz was the author of two books on automatic control and over fifty scientific papers.

Further Reading
A. Stanley, 1993, *Mothers and Daughters of Invention*, Meruchen, NJ: Scarecrow Press, pp. 899–901.

LRD

Focke, E.H. Heinrich
b. October 1890 Bremen, Germany
d. February 1979 Bremen, Germany

German aircraft designer who was responsible for the first practical helicopter, in 1936.

Between 1911 and 1914 Heinrich Focke and Georg Wulf built a monoplane and some years later, in 1924, they founded the Focke–Wulf company. They designed and built a variety of civil and military aircraft including the *F 19 Ente*, a tail-first design of 1927. This canard layout was thought to be safer than conventional designs but, unfortunately, it crashed, killing Wulf. Around 1930 Focke became interested in rotary-wing aircraft, and in 1931 he set up a company with Gerd Achgelis to conduct research in this field. The Focke–Wulf company took out a licence to build **Cierva** autogiros. Focke designed an improved autogiro, the *Fw 186*, which flew in 1938; it was entered for a military competition, but it was beaten by a fixed-wing aircraft, the Fieseler *Storch*. In May 1935 Focke resigned from Focke–Wulf to concentrate on helicopter development with the Focke–Achgelis company. His first design was the *Fa 61* helicopter, which utilized the fuselage and engine of a conventional aeroplane but instead of wings had two out-riggers, each carrying a rotor. The engine drove these rotors in opposite directions to counteract the adverse torque effect (with a single rotor the fuselage tends to rotate in the opposite direction to the rotor). Following its first flight on 26 June 1936, the *Fa 61* went on to break several world records. However, it attracted more public attention when it was flown inside the huge Deutschlandhalle in Berlin by the famous female test pilot Hanna Reitsch in February 1938. Focke continued to develop his helicopter projects for the Focke–Achgelis company and produced the *Fa 223 Drache* in 1940.

This used twin contra-rotating rotors, like the *Fa 61*, but could carry six people. Its production was hampered by allied bombing of the factory. During the Second World War Focke–Achgelis also produced a rotor kite which could be towed behind a U-boat to provide a flying 'crow's nest', as well as designs for an advanced convertiplane (part aeroplane, part helicopter). After the war, Focke worked in France, the Netherlands and Brazil, then in 1954 he became Professor of Aeroplane and Helicopter Design at the University of Stuttgart.

Principal Honours and Distinctions
Wissenschaftliche, Gesellschaft für Luftfahrt Lilienthal Medal, Prandtl-Ring.

Bibliography
1965, 'German thinking on rotary-wing development', *Journal of the Royal Aeronautical Society*, (May).

Further Reading
W. Gunston and J. Batchelor, 1977, *Helicopters 1900–1960*, London.
J.R. Smith, 1973, *Focke–Wulf: An Aircraft Album*, London (primarily a picture book).
R.N. Liptrot, 1948, *Rotating Wing Activities in Germany during the Period 1939–45*, London.
K. von Gersdorff and K. Knobling, 1982, *Hubschrauber und Tragschrauber*, Munich (a more recent publication, in German).

JDS

Fokker, Anthony Herman Gerard

b. 6 April 1890 Kediri, Java, Dutch East Indies (now Indonesia)
d. 23 December 1939 New York, USA

Dutch designer of German fighter aircraft during the First World War and of many successful airliners during the 1920s and 1930s.

Anthony Fokker was born in Java, where his Dutch father had a coffee plantation. The family returned to the Netherlands and, after schooling, young Anthony went to Germany to study aeronautics. With the aid of a friend he built his first aeroplane, the *Spin*, in 1910: this was a monoplane capable of short hops. By 1911 Fokker had improved the *Spin* and gained a pilot's licence. In 1912 he set up a company called Fokker Aeroplanbau at Johannistal, outside Berlin, and a series of monoplanes followed.

When war broke out in 1914 Fokker offered his designs to both sides, and the Germans accepted them. His *E I* monoplane of 1915 caused a sensation with its manoeuvrability and forward-firing machine gun. Fokker and his collaborators improved on the French deflector system introduced by Raymond **Saulnier** by fitting an interrupter gear which synchronized the machine gun to fire between the blades of the rotating propeller. The Fokker *Dr I* triplane and *D VII* biplane were also outstanding German fighters of the First World War. Fokker's designs were often the work of an employee who received little credit: nevertheless, Fokker was a gifted pilot and a great organizer. After the war, Fokker moved back to the Netherlands and set up the Fokker Aircraft Works in Amsterdam. In 1922, however, he emigrated to the USA and established the Atlantic Aircraft Corporation in New Jersey. His first significant success there came the following year when one of his *T-2* monoplanes became the first aircraft to fly non-stop across the USA, from New York to San Diego. He developed a series of civil aircraft using the well-proven method of construction he used for his fighters: fuselages made from steel tubes and thick, robust wooden wings. Of these, probably the most famous was the *F VII/3m*, a high-wing monoplane with three engines and capable of carrying about ten passengers. From 1925 the *F VII/3m* airliner was used worldwide and made many record-breaking flights, such as Lieutenant-Commander Richard Byrd's first flight over the North Pole in 1926 and Charles Kingsford-Smith's first transpacific flight in 1928. By this time Fokker had lost interest in military aircraft and had begun to see flight as a means of speeding up global communications and bringing people together. His last years were spent in realizing this dream, and this was reflected in his concentration on the design and production of passenger aircraft.

Principal Honours and Distinctions
Royal Netherlands Aeronautical Society Gold Medal 1932.

Bibliography
1931, *The Flying Dutchman: The Life of Anthony Fokker*, London: Routledge & Sons (an interesting, if rather biased, autobiography).

Further Reading

A.R. Weyl, 1965, *Fokker: The Creative Years*, London; reprinted 1988 (a very detailed account of Fokker's early work).

Thijs Postma, 1979, *Fokker: Aircraft Builders to the World*, Holland; 1980, English edn, London (a well-illustrated history of Fokker and the company).

Henri Hegener, 1961, *Fokker: The Man and His Aircraft*, Letchworth, Herts.

JDS/CM

Ford, Henry

b. 30 July 1863 Dearborn, Michigan, USA
d. 7 April 1947 Dearborn, Michigan, USA

American pioneer motor-car maker and developer of mass-production methods.

He was the son of an Irish immigrant farmer, William Ford, and the oldest son to survive of Mary Litogot; his mother died in 1876 with the birth of her sixth child. He went to the village school, and at the age of 16 he was apprenticed to Flower brothers' machine shop and then at the Drydock & Engineering Works in Detroit. In 1882 he left to return to the family farm and spent some time working with a 1½ hp steam engine doing odd jobs for the farming community at $3 per day. He was then employed as a demonstrator for **Westinghouse** steam engines. He met Clara Jane Bryant at New Year 1885 and they were married on 11 April 1888. Their only child, Edsel Bryant Ford, was born on 6 November 1893.

At that time Henry worked on steam engine repairs for the **Edison** Illuminating Company, where he became Chief Engineer. He became one of a group working to develop a 'horseless carriage' in 1896 and in June completed his first vehicle, a 'quadricycle' with a two-cylinder engine. It was built in a brick shed, which had to be partially demolished to get the carriage out.

Ford became involved in motor racing, at which he was more successful than he was in starting a car-manufacturing company. Several early ventures failed, until the Ford Motor Company of 1903. By October 1908 they had started with production of the Model T. The first, of which over 15 million were built up to the end of its production in May 1927, came out with bought-out steel stampings and a planetary gear-box, and had a one-piece four-cylinder block with a bolt-on head. This was one of the most successful models built by Ford or any other motor manufacturer in the life of the motor car.

Interchangeability of components was an important element in Ford's philosophy. Ford was a pioneer in the use of vanadium steel for engine components. He adopted the principles of Frederick **Taylor**, the pioneer of time-and-motion study, and installed the world's first moving assembly line for the production of magnetos, started in 1913. He installed blast furnaces at the factory to make his own steel, and he also promoted research and the cultivation of the soya bean, from which a plastic was derived.

In October 1913 he introduced the 'Five Dollar Day', almost doubling the normal rate of pay. This was a profit-sharing scheme for his employees and contained an element of a reward for good behaviour. About this time he initiated work on an agricultural tractor, the 'Fordson' made by a separate company, the directors of which were Henry and his son Edsel.

In 1915 he chartered the *Oscar II*, a 'peace ship', and with fifty-five delegates sailed for Europe a week before Christmas, docking at Oslo. Their objective was to appeal to all European Heads of State to stop the war. He had hoped to persuade manufacturers to replace armaments with tractors in their production programmes. In the event, Ford took to his bed in the hotel with a chill, stayed there for five days and then sailed for New York and home. He did, however, continue to finance the peace activists who remained in Europe. Back in America, he stood for election to the US Senate but was defeated. He was probably the father of John Dahlinger, illegitimate son of Evangeline Dahlinger, a stenographer employed by the firm and on whom he lavished gifts of cars, clothes and properties. He became the owner of a weekly newspaper, the *Dearborn Independent*, which became the medium for the expression of many of his more unorthodox ideas. He was involved in a lawsuit with the *Chicago Tribune* in 1919, during which he was cross-examined on his knowledge of American history: he is reputed to have said 'History is bunk'. What he actually said was, 'History is bunk as it is taught in schools', a very different comment. The lawyers who thus made a fool of him would have been surprised if they could have foreseen the force and energy that their actions were to release. For years Ford employed a team of specialists to scour America and Europe for furniture, artefacts and relics of all kinds, illustrating various aspects of history. Starting with the Wayside Inn from South Sudbury, Massachusetts, buildings were bought, dismantled and moved, to be reconstructed in Greenfield Village, near Dearborn. The courthouse where Abraham Lincoln had practised law and the Ohio bicycle shop where the **Wright** brothers built their first primitive aeroplane were added to the farmhouse where the proprietor, Henry Ford, had been born. Replicas were made of Independence Hall, Congress Hall and the old City Hall in Philadelphia, and even a reconstruction of Edison's Menlo Park laboratory was installed. The Henry Ford museum was officially opened on 21 October 1929, on the fiftieth anniversary of Edison's invention of the incandescent bulb, but it continued to be a primary preoccupation of the great American car maker until his death.

Henry Ford was also responsible for a number of aeronautical developments at the Ford Airport at Dearborn. He introduced the first use of radio to guide a commercial aircraft, the first regular airmail service in the United States. He also manufactured the country's first all-metal multi-engined plane, the Ford Tri-Motor.

Edsel became President of the Ford Motor Company on his father's resignation from that position on 30 December 1918. Following the end of production in May 1927 of the Model T, the replacement Model A was not in production for another six months. During this period Henry Ford, though officially retired from the presidency of the company, repeatedly interfered and countermanded the orders of his son, ostensibly the man in charge. Edsel, who died of stomach cancer at his home at Grosse Point, Detroit, on 26 May 1943, was the father of Henry Ford II. Henry Ford died at his home, 'Fair Lane', four years after his son's death.

Bibliography
1922, with S. Crowther, *My Life and Work*, London: Heinemann.

Further Reading
R. Lacey, 1986, *Ford, the Men and the Machine*, London: Heinemann.
W.C. Richards, 1948, *The Last Billionaire, Henry Ford*, New York: Charles Scribner.

IMcN

Forest, Lee de
See **De Forest, Lee**.

Forlanini, Carlo
b. 11 June 1847 Milan, Italy
d. 26 May 1918 Nervi, Italy

Italian physician who originated the technique of therapeutic pneumothorax.

After a medical education at Turin, where he qualified in 1870, he held assistant posts before becoming chief of the medical clinic by 1880. He later moved to Pavia as Professor of Medicine and soon became engaged in the development of his procedure for inducing artificial pneumothorax in the treatment of tuberculosis.

He treated his first case using this technique in 1882, and by 1894 he was able to report a series of forty-five cases in which a cure had been facilitated. The treatment soon gained wide acceptance and remained an important element of the anti-tubercular armamentarium until the development of chemotherapeutic drugs effective for this purpose.

Bibliography
1882, 'Contribuzione della terapia chirurgica della tisi. Ablazione der pulmone? Pneumothorace artificiale', *Gazy. Osp. Clin.*
1894, 'Primo caso did tisi pulmonale arangata curato feliciamente col pneumothorace artificiale', *Gazy. med. di Torino.*

Further Reading
Riviere, 1917, *The Pneumothorax Treatment of Pulmonary Tuberculosis*, London.

MG

Forrester, George
b. 1780/1 Scotland
d. after 1841

Scottish locomotive builder and technical innovator.

George Forrester & Co. built locomotives at the Vauxhall Foundry, Liverpool, between 1834 and c.1847. The first locomotives built by them, in 1834, were three for the Dublin & Kingstown Railway and one for the Liverpool & Manchester Railway; they were the first locomotives to have outside horizontal cylinders and the first to have four fixed eccentrics to operate the valves, in place of two loose eccentrics. Two locomotives built by Forrester in 1835 for the Dublin & Kingstown Railway were the first tank locomotives to run regularly on a public railway, and two more supplied in 1836 to the London & Greenwich Railway were the first such locomotives in England. Little appears to be known about Forrester himself. In the 1841 census his profession is shown as 'civil engineer, residence 1 Lord Nelson Street'. Directories for Liverpool, contemporary with Forrester & Co.'s locomotive building period, describe the firm variously as engineers, iron founders and boilermakers, located at (successively) 234, 224 and 40 Vauxhall Road. Works Manager until 1840 was Alexander Allan, who subsequently used the experience he had gained with Forrester in the design of his 'Crewe Type' outside-cylinder locomotive, which became widely used.

Further Reading

E.L. Ahrons, 1927, *The British Steam Railway Locomotive 1825–1925*, The Locomotive Publishing Co., pp. 29, 43, 50 and 83.

J. Lowe, 1975, *British Steam Locomotive Builders*, Cambridge: Goose & Son.

R.H.G. Thomas, 1986, *London's First Railway: The London & Greenwich*, B.T. Batsford, p. 176.

PJGR

Forrester, Jay Wright

b. 14 July 1918 Anselmo, Nebraska, USA

American electrical engineer and management expert who invented the magnetic-core random access memory used in most early digital computers.

Born on a cattle ranch, Forrester obtained a BSc in electrical engineering at the University of Nebraska in 1939 and his MSc at the Massachusetts Institute of Technology (MIT) in Cambridge, Massachusetts, where he remained to teach and carry out research. Becoming interested in computing, he established the Digital Computer Laboratory at MIT in 1945 and became involved in the construction of Whirlwind I, an early general-purpose computer completed in March 1951 and used for flight-simulation by the US Army Air Force. Finding the linear memories then available for storing data a major limiting factor in the speed at which computers were able

to operate, he developed a three-dimensional store based on the binary switching of the state of small magnetic cores that could be addressed and switched by a matrix of wires carrying pulses of current. The machine used parallel synchronous fixed-point computing, with fifteen binary digits and a plus sign, i.e. 16 bits in all, and contained 5,000 vacuum tubes, eleven semiconductors and a 2 MHz clock for the arithmetic logic unit. It occupied a two-storey building and consumed 150 kW of electricity. From his experience with the development and use of computers, he came to realize their great potential for the simulation and modelling of real situations and hence for the solution of a variety of management problems, using data communications and the technique now known as interactive graphics. His later career was therefore in this field, first at the MIT Lincoln Laboratory in Lexington, Massachusetts (1951) and subsequently (from 1956) as Professor at the Sloan School of Management at the Massachusetts Institute of Technology.

Principal Honours and Distinctions

National Academy of Engineering 1967. George Washington University Inventor of the Year 1968. Danish Academy of Science Valdemar Poulsen Gold Medal 1969. Systems, Man and Cybernetics Society Award for Outstanding Accomplishments 1972. Computer Society Pioneer Award 1972. Institution of Electrical Engineers Medal of Honour 1972. National Inventors Hall of Fame 1979. Magnetics Society Information Storage Award 1988. Honorary DEng Nebraska 1954, Newark College of Engineering 1971, Notre Dame University 1974. Honorary DSc Boston 1969, Union College 1973. Honorary DPolSci Mannheim University, Germany. Honorary DHumLett, State University of New York 1988.

Bibliography

1951, 'Data storage in three dimensions using magnetic cores', *Journal of Applied Physics* 20: 44 (his first description of the core store).

Publications on management include: 1961, *Industrial Dynamics*, Cambridge, Mass.: MIT Press; 1968, *Principles of Systems*; 1971, *Urban Dynamics*; 1980, with A.A. Legasto & J.M. Lyneis, *System Dynamics*, North Holland. 1975, *Collected Papers*, Cambridge, Mass.: MIT.

Further Reading
K.C. Redmond & T.M. Smith, *Project Whirl-wind, the History of a Pioneer Computer* (provides details of the Whirlwind computer).
H.H. Goldstine, 1993, *The Computer from Pascal to von Neumann*, Princeton University Press (for more general background to the development of computers).
Serrell et al., 1962, 'Evolution of computing machines', *Proceedings of the Institute of Radio Engineers* 1,047.
M.R. Williams, 1975, *History of Computing Technology*, London: Prentice-Hall.

See also: **Burks, Arthur Walter**; **Goldstine, Herman H.**; **Wilkes, Maurice Vincent**; **Williams, Sir Frederic Calland**.

KF

Forsmann, Werner Theodor Otto
b. 29 August 1904 Berlin, Germany
d. 1 June 1979 Schofheim, Germany

German cardiologist and surgeon, pioneer of cardiac catheterization in humans.

Forsmann studied medicine at the University of Berlin, graduating in 1929. He later became chief of the surgical clinic in Dresden-Friedrichstadt, and in 1958 he became head of the surgical division of the Evangelical Hospital in Düsseldorf.

Intravascular catheterization had been undertaken in research with animals by Marey in 1861, and had been used in 1912 by Unger *et al.* in the treatment of puerperal sepsis. In 1929 Forsmann inserted a catheter into his own cubital vein and up into the heart, monitoring its position with X-rays. Continuing experiments demonstrated that it was possible to undertake radiographic studies of the heart using contrast media. Despite the outstanding potential of the technique, its immediate adoption was held to present unacceptable dangers; it was not until developments in anaesthesia and antibiotics that the technique achieved its present position as a routine investigation permitting the widespread practice of angiocardiography. Deterred by criticism, Forsmann turned his energies to urology, gaining much distinction in this field.

Principal Honours and Distinctions
Nobel Prize for Medicine or Physiology (jointly with A.F. Cournand and D.W. Richards) 1956.

Bibliography
1929, 'Die Sonderung des rechten Herzens', *Klin. Woch.*

Further Reading
J.A. Meyer, 1990, 'Werner Forsmann and the catheterisation of the heart', *Ann. Thorac. Surg.*

MG

Forsyth, Alexander John
b. 28 December 1769 Belhevie, Aberdeenshire, Scotland
d. 11 June 1843 Belhevie, Aberdeenshire, Scotland

Scottish cleric and ammunition designer.

The son of a Scottish Presbyterian minister, Forsyth also took Holy Orders and took over his father's parish on his death. During his spare time he experimented with explosives and in 1805 he succeeded in developing mercury fulminate as a percussion cap for use in small-arms ammunition, thus paving the way for the eventual design of the self-contained metallic cartridge and contact fuse. This he did by rolling the compound into small pellets, which he placed in a nipple at the breech end of the barrel, where they could be detonated by the falling hammer of the gun. In spring 1806 he went to London, and so impressed was the Master-General of the Ordnance by Forsyth's concept that he gave him facilities in the Tower of London in order to allow him to perfect it. Unfortunately, the Master-General of the Ordnance was replaced shortly afterwards and his successor abruptly stopped the project. Forsyth returned to Scotland and his parish, and it was only after much persuasion by his friends that he eventually petitioned Parliament for recognition of his invention. He was ultimately awarded a small state pension, but died before he received any of it.

CM

Fourdrinier, Henry
b. 11 February 1766 London, England
d. 3 September 1854 Mavesyn Ridware, near Rugeley, Staffordshire, England

English pioneer of the papermaking machine.

Fourdrinier's father was a paper manufacturer and stationer of London, from a family of French Protestant origin. Henry took up the same trade and, with his brother Sealy (d. 1847), devoted many years to developing the papermaking machine. Their first patent was taken out in 1801, but success was still far off. A machine for making paper had been invented a few years previously by Nicolas **Robert** at the Didot's mill at Essonnes, south of Paris. Robert quarrelled with the Didots, who then contacted their brother-in-law in England, John Gamble, in an attempt to raise capital for a larger machine. Gamble and the Fourdriniers called in the engineer Bryan **Donkin**, and between them they patented a much improved machine in 1807. In the new machine, the paper pulp flowed on to a moving continuous woven wire screen and was then squeezed between rollers to remove much of the water. The paper thus formed was transferred to a felt blanket and passed through a second press to remove more water, before being wound while still wet on to a drum. For the first time, a continuous sheet of paper could be made. Other inventors soon made further improvements: in 1817 John **Dickinson** obtained a patent for sizing baths to improve the surface of the paper; while in 1820 Thomas **Crompton** patented a steam-heated drum round which the paper was passed to speed up the drying process. The development cost of £60,000 bankrupted the brothers. Although Parliament extended the patent for fourteen years, and the machine was widely adopted, they never reaped much profit from it. Tsar Alexander of Russia became interested in the papermaking machine while on a visit to England in 1814 and promised Henry Fourdrinier £700 per year for ten years for superintending the erection of two machines in Russia; Henry carried out the work, but he received no payment. At the age of 72 he travelled to St Petersburg to seek recompense from the Tsar's successor Nicholas I, but to no avail. Eventually, on a motion in the House of Commons, the British Government awarded Fourdrinier a payment of £7,000. The paper trade, sensing the inadequacy of this sum, augmented it with a further sum which they subscribed so that an annuity could be purchased for Henry, then the only surviving brother, and his two daughters, to enable them to live in modest comfort. From its invention in ancient China (see **Cai Lun**), its appearance in the Middle Ages in Europe and through the first three and a half centuries of printing, every sheet of paper had to made by hand. The daily output of a hand-made paper mill was only 60–100 lb (27–45 kg), whereas the new machine increased that tenfold. Even higher speeds were achieved, with corresponding reductions in cost; the old mills could not possibly have kept pace with the new mechanical printing presses. The Fourdrinier machine was thus an essential element in the technological developments that brought about the revolution in the production of reading matter of all kinds during the nineteenth century. The high-speed, giant papermaking machines of the late twentieth century work on the same principle as the Fourdrinier of 1807.

Further Reading
R.H. Clapperton, 1967, *The Paper-making Machine*, Oxford: Pergamon Press.
D. Hunter, 1947, *Papermaking. The History and Technique of an Ancient Craft*, London.

LRD

Fowler, John
b. 11 July 1826 Melksham, Wiltshire, England
d. 4 December 1864 Ackworth, Yorkshire, England

English engineer and inventor who developed a steam-powered system of mole land drainage, and a two-engined system of land cultivation, founding the Steam Plough Works in Leeds.

The son of a Quaker merchant, John Fowler entered the business of a county corn merchant on leaving school, but he found this dull and left as soon as he came of age, joining the Middlesbrough company of Gilkes, Wilson & Hopkins, railway locomotive manufacturers. In 1849, at the age of 23, Fowler visited Ireland and was so distressed by the state of Irish agriculture that he determined to develop a system to deal with the drainage of land. He designed an implement which he patented in 1850 after a period of experimentation. It was able to lay wooden pipes to a depth of two feet, and was awarded the Silver Medal at the 1850 Royal Agriculture Show. By 1854, using a steam engine made by Clayton & Shuttleworth, he had applied steam power to his invention and gained another award that year at the Royal Show. The following year he turned his attention to steam ploughing. He first developed a single-engined system that used a double windlass with which to haul a plough backwards and forwards across fields. In 1856 he patented his balance plough, and the following year he read a paper to the Institution of Mechanical Engineers at their Birmingham premises, describing the system. In 1858 he won the Royal Agricultural Society award with a plough built for him by Ransomes. Fowler founded the Steam Plough Works in Leeds and in 1862 production began in partnership with William Watson Hewitson. Within two years they were producing the first of a series of engines which were to make the name Fowler known worldwide. John Fowler saw little of his success because he died in 1864 at his Yorkshire home as a result of tetanus contracted after a riding accident.

Further Reading
M. Lane, 1980, *The Story of the Steam Plough Works*, Northgate Publishing (provides biographical details of John Fowler, but is mostly concerned with the company that he founded).

AP

Fox, Sir Charles
b. 11 March 1810 Derby, England
d. 14 June 1874 Blackheath, London, England

English railway engineer, builder of Crystal Palace, London.

Fox was a pupil of John **Ericsson**, helped to build the locomotive *Novelty*, and drove it at the Rainhill Trials in 1829. He became a driver on the Liverpool & Manchester Railway and then a pupil of Robert **Stephenson**, who appointed him an assistant engineer for construction of the southern part of the London & Birmingham Railway, opened in 1837. He was probably responsible for the design of the early bow-string girder bridge which carried the railway over the Regent's Canal. He also invented turnouts with switch blades, i.e. 'points'. With Robert Stephenson he designed the light iron train sheds at Euston Station, a type of roof that was subsequently much used elsewhere. He then became a partner in Fox, Henderson & Co., railway contractors and manufacturers of railway equipment and bridges. The firm built the Crystal Palace in London for the Great Exhibition of 1851: Fox did much of the detail design work personally and

was subsequently knighted. It also built many station roofs, including that at Paddington. From 1857 Fox was in practice in London as a consulting engineer in partnership with his sons, Charles Douglas Fox and Francis Fox. Sir Charles Fox became an advocate of light and narrow-gauge railways, although he was opposed to break-of-gauge unless it was unavoidable. He was joint Engineer for the Indian Tramway Company, building the first narrow-gauge (3 ft 6 in. or 107 cm) railway in India, opened in 1865, and his firm was Consulting Engineer for the first railways in Queensland, Australia, built to the same gauge at the same period on recommendation of Government Engineer A.C. Fitzgibbon.

Principal Honours and Distinctions
Knighted 1851.

Further Reading
Obituary, 1875, *Minutes of Proceedings of the Institution of Civil Engineers* 39: 264.
F. Fox, 1904, *River, Road, and Rail*, John Murray, Ch. 1 (personal reminiscences by his son).
L.T.C. Rolt, 1970, *Victorian Engineering*, London: Allen Lane.

PJGR

Fox, James
b. *c.*1760
d. 1835 Derby, England

English machine-tool builder.

Very little is known about the life of James Fox, but according to Samuel Smiles (1863) he was as a young man a butler in the service of the Reverend Thomas Gisborne of Foxhall Lodge, Staffordshire. His mechanical abilities were evident from his spare-time activities in the handling of tools and so impressed his employer that he supplied the capital to enable Fox to set up a business in Derby for the manufacture of machinery for the textile and lacemaking industries. To construct this machinery, Fox had to build his own machine tools and later, in the early nineteenth century, made them for sale, some being exported to France, Germany and Poland. He was renowned for his lathes, some of which were quite large; one built in 1830 has been preserved and is 22 ft (6.7 m) long with a swing of 27 in. (69 cm). He was responsible for many improvements in the design of the lathe and he also built some of the earliest planing machines (the first, it has been claimed, as early as 1814) and a gear-cutting machine, although this was apparently for cutting wooden patterns for cast gears. The business was continued by his sons Joseph and James (who died in 1859 aged 69) and into the 1860s by the sons of Joseph.

Further Reading
S. Smiles, 1863, *Industrial Biography*, London, reprinted 1967, Newton Abbot (makes brief mention of Fox).
Letters relating to the invention of the planing machine can be found in *Engineer* 14 (1862): 189, 204, 219, 246 and 247.
His lathes are described in:
R.S. Woodbury, 1961, *History of the Lathe to 1850*, Cleveland, Ohio;
L.T.C. Rolt, 1965, *Tools for the Job*, London; repub. 1986;
W. Steeds, 1969, *A History of Machine Tools 1700–1910*, Oxford.

RTS

Fox, Samson

b. 11 July 1838 Bowling, near Bradford, Yorkshire, England
d. 24 October 1903 Walsall, Staffordshire, England

English engineer who invented the corrugated boiler furnace.

He was the son of a cloth mill worker in Leeds and at the age of 10 he joined his father at the mill. Showing a mechanical inclination, he was apprenticed to a firm of machine-tool makers, Smith, Beacock and Tannett. There he rose to become Foreman and Traveller, and designed and patented tools for cutting bevelled gears. With his brother and one Refitt, he set up the Silver Cross engineering works for making special machine tools. In 1874 he founded the Leeds Forge Company, acting as Managing Director until 1896 and then as Chairman until shortly before his death.

It was in 1877 that he patented his most important invention, the corrugated furnace for steam-boilers. These furnaces could withstand much higher pressures than the conventional form, and higher working pressures in marine boilers enabled triple-expansion en-gines to be installed, greatly improving the performance of steamships, and the outcome was the great ocean-going liners of the twentieth century. The first vessel to be equipped with the corrugated furnace was the *Pretoria* of 1878. At first the furnaces were made by hammering iron plates using swage blocks under a steam hammer. A plant for rolling corrugated plates was set up at Essen in Germany, and Fox installed a similar mill at his works in Leeds in 1882.

In 1886 Fox installed a Siemens steelmaking plant and he was notable in the movement for replacing wrought iron with steel. He took out several patents for making pressed-steel underframes for railway wagons. The business prospered and Fox opened a works near Chicago in the USA, where in addition to wagon underframes he manufactured the first American pressed-steel carriages. He later added a works at Pittsburgh.

Fox was the first in England to use water gas for his metallurgical operations and for lighting, with a saving in cost as it was cheaper than coal gas. He was also a pioneer in the acetylene industry, producing in 1894 the first calcium carbide, from which the gas is made.

Fox took an active part in public life in and around Leeds, being thrice elected Mayor of Harrogate. As a music lover, he was a benefactor of musicians, contributing no less than £45,000 towards the cost of building the Royal College of Music in London, opened in 1894. In 1897 he sued for libel the author Jerome K. Jerome and the publishers of the *Today* magazine for accusing him of misusing his great generosity to the College to give a misleading impression of his commercial methods and prosperity. He won the case but was not awarded costs.

Principal Honours and Distinctions
Royal Society of Arts James Watt Silver Medal and Howard Gold Medal. Légion d'honneur 1889.

Bibliography
1877, British Patent nos. 1097 and 2530 (the corrugated furnace or 'flue', as it was often called).

Further Reading
Obituary, 1903, *Proceedings of the Institution of*

Mechanical Engineers: 919–21.

Obituary, 1903, *Proceedings of the Institution of Civil Engineers* (the fullest of the many obituary notices).

G.A. Newby, 1993, 'Behind the fire doors: Fox's corrugated furnace 1877 and the high pressure steamship', *Transactions of the Newcomen Society* 64.

LRD

Fox, Samuel

b. 1815 Bradfield, near Sheffield, England
d. February 1887 Sheffield, England

English inventor of the curved steel umbrella frame.

Samuel Fox was the son of a weaver's shuttle maker in the hamlet of Bradwell (probably Bradfield, near Sheffield) in the remote hills. He went to Sheffield and served an apprenticeship in the steel trade. Afterwards, he worked with great energy and industry until he acquired sufficient capital to start in business on his own account at Stocksbridge, near Sheffield. It was there that he invented what became known as 'Fox's Paragon Frame' for umbrellas. Whalebone or solid steel had previously been used for umbrella ribs, but whalebone was unreliable and steel was heavy. Fox realized that if he grooved the ribs he could make them both lighter and more elastic. In his first patent, taken out in 1852, he described making the ribs and stretchers of parasols and umbrellas from a narrow strip of steel plate partially bent into a trough-like form. He took out five more patents. The first, in 1853, was for strengthening the joints. His next two, in 1856 and 1857, were more concerned with preparing the steel for making the ribs. Another patent in 1857 was basically for improving the formation of the bit at the end of the rib where it was fixed to the stretcher and where the end of the rib has to be formed into a boss: this was so it could have a pin fixed through it to act as a pivot when the umbrella has to be opened or folded and yet support the rib and stretcher. The final patent, in 1865, reverted once more to improving the manufacture of the ribs. He made a fortune before other manufacturers knew what he was doing. Fox established a works at Lille when he found that the French import duties and other fiscal arrangements hindered exporting umbrellas and successful trading there, and was thereby able to develop a large and lucrative business.

Bibliography

1852, British patent no. 14,055 (curved steel ribs and stretchers for umbrellas).

1853, British patent no. 739 (strengthened umbrella joints).

1856, British patent no. 2,741 (ribs and stretchers for umbrellas).

1857, British patent no. 1,450 (steel wire for umbrellas).

1857, British patent no. 1,857 (forming the bit attached to the ribs).

1865, British patent no. 2,348 (improvements in making the ribs).

Further Reading

Obituary, 1887, *Engineer* 63.
Obituary, 1887, *Iron* 29.

RLH

Fox, Uffa

b. 15 January 1898 Cowes, Isle of Wight, England
d. 27 October 1972 Isle of Wight (?), England

English yacht designer.

Coming from a family that had originated in East Anglia, his first name was that of an early British king and was to typify his unusual and refreshing zest for life. Fox commenced his professional career as an apprentice with the flying boat and high-speed craft builders Messrs S.E. Saunders, and shortly after the outbreak of the First World War he was conscripted into the Royal Naval Air Service. In 1920 he made his first transatlantic crossing under sail, a much greater adventure then than now, and returned to the United Kingdom as deck-hand on a ship bound for Liverpool. He was to make the crossing under sail twice more. Shortly after his marriage in 1925, he purchased the old Floating Bridge at Cowes and converted it to living accommodation, workshops and drawing offices. By the 1930s his life's work was in full swing, with designs coming off his drawing board for some of the most outstanding mass-produced craft ever built, as well as for some remarkable one-off yachts. His experimentation with every kind of sailing craft, and even with the Eskimo kayak, gave him the knowledge and experience that made his name known worldwide. During the Second World War he designed and produced the world's first airborne parachuted lifeboat. Despite what could be described as a robust lifestyle, coupled with interests in music, art and horseriding, Fox continued to produce great designs and in the late 1940s he introduced the *Firefly*, followed by the beautiful Flying Fifteen class of racing keel boats. One of his most unusual vessels was *Britannia*, the 24 ft (7.3 m) waterline craft that John Fairfax was to row across the Atlantic. Later came *Britannia II*, which Fairfax took across the Pacific!

Principal Honours and Distinctions
CBE 1959. Royal Designer to Industry (RDI).

Bibliography
Fox produced a series of yachting books, most first published in the late 1930s, and some more lighthearted volumes of reminiscences in the 1960s. Some of the best-known titles are: *Sail and Power, Racing and Cruising Design, Uffa Fox's Second Book* and *The Crest of the Wave*.

Further Reading
J. Dixon, 1978, *Uffa Fox. A Personal Biography*, Brighton: Angus & Robertson.

FMW

Fox Talbot, William Henry
See **Talbot, William Henry Fox**.

Foyn, Svend
b. 1809 Tønsberg, Norway
d. after 1873

Norwegian founder of the modern whaling industry; sea captain and sealer.

Svend Foyn's background typified the best of the Norwegian merchant marine: good seamanship, deep religious faith and an investigative and adventurous approach to life based on sound commercial judgement. After the period of training normal to his time, Foyn became a shipmaster and then followed the sealer's trade. By the early 1860s he had amassed a considerable sum of money and began to look around for an area of further conquest. He built whale catchers and operated them with scientific care, and by 1862 his work was recognized in Norway, Scotland and some other countries as personifying the whaling industry. Foyn's inventive approach to this new trade ensured that innovative ideas were accepted and that his inventions – such as the

rubber accumulator, the recoil absorber and the harpoon braking system – became an accepted part of the whaler's trade. It is said that his first harpoon gun, invented in 1864, weighed 1 ton. Foyn designed a special whaling winch in 1873 that was protected by patent, the same year that the Norwegian Government granted him a ten-year monopoly on his system for catching whales.

Further Reading
J.H. Harland, 1992, *Catchers and Corvettes, the Steam Whalecatcher in Peace and War 1860–1960*, Rotherfield, East Sussex: Jean Boudriot.
P. Budker, 1958, *Whales and Whaling*, London: Harrap.

FMW

Franklin, Benjamin
b. 17 January 1706 Boston, Massachusetts, USA
d. 17 April 1790 Philadelphia, Pennsylvania, USA

American diplomat, statesman, scientist and inventor of bifocal spectacle lenses.

Described as a versatile genius, although less fairly also as an amateur dabbler, Franklin was of immediate English ancestry from Northamptonshire. During a long and prolific life, his innovations included the Franklin stove, arrangements for house ventilation and aeronautical and electrical experimentation. He was awarded the Copley Medal of the Royal Society in 1753 for his discoveries in relation to lighting conductors.

His principal contribution to medicine was the invention of bifocal lenses constructed by the cementing of glass wafers to existing spectacle lenses. The date of this invention is uncertain, but was probably *c*.1774. A letter he wrote to a friend in 1775 refers to Peter Dollond, of the London optical firm, who has sometimes been thought to have contemporaneously developed some form of bifocal lens. Franklin's invention of the lens was prompted by his own visual difficulties.

Principal Honours and Distinctions
Royal Medical Society of Paris 1777. Medical Society of London 1787. Royal Society Copley Medal 1753.

Bibliography
1888, *The Life of Benjamin Franklin, Written by Himself*, Philadelphia.

Further Reading
C. van Dorek, 1938, *Benjamin Franklin*.
H. Barty-King, 1986, *Eyes Right*, London.

MG

Freyssinet, Eugène

b. 13 July 1879 Objat, Corrèze, France
d. 8 June 1962 Saint-Martin Vésubié, France

French civil engineer who is generally recognized as the originator of pre-stressed reinforced concrete.

Eugène Freyssinet was an army engineer during the First World War who pioneered pre-stressed reinforced concrete and experimented with building concrete bridges. After 1918 he formed his own company to develop his ideas. He investigated the possibilities of very high-strength concrete, and in so doing studied shrinkage and creep. He combined high-quality concrete with highly stressed, stretched steel to give top quality results. His work in 1926 on Plougastel Bridge, at that time the longest reinforced concrete bridge, is a notable example of his use of this technique. In 1916 Freyssinet had built his famous airship hangars at Orly, which were destroyed in the Second World War; the hangars were roofed in parabolic sections to a height of about 200 ft. In 1934 he succeeded in saving the Ocean Terminal at Le Havre from sinking into the mud and being covered by the sea by using his pre-stressing techniques. By 1938 he had developed a superior method of pre-stressing with steel which led to widespread adoption of his methods.

Further Reading
C.C. Stanley, 1979, *Highlights in the History of Concrete*, Cement and Concrete Association.
1977, *Who's Who in Architecture*, Weidenfeld and Nicolson.

DY

Frost, James

b. late 18th century Finchley (?), London, England
d. mid-19th century probably New York, USA

English contributor to investigations into the making of hydraulic cements in the early nineteenth century.

As early as 1807 Frost, who was originally a builder and bricklayer in Finchley in north London, was manufacturing Roman Cement, patented by James **Parker** in 1796, in the Harwich area and a similar cement further south, at Sheerness. In the early 1820s Frost visited Louis J. Vicat (1796–1861) in France. Vicat was a French engineer who began in 1812 a detailed investigation into the properties of various limestones found in France. He later published his conclusions, which were that the best hydraulic lime was that produced from limestone containing clay incorporating silica and alumina. He experimented with adding different clays in varying proportions to slaked lime and calcined the mixture. Benefiting from Vicat's research, Frost obtained a patent in 1822 for what he called British Cement. This patent specified an artificial cement made from limestone and silica, and he calcined chalk with the clay to produce a quick-setting product. This was made at Swanscombe near Northfleet on the south bank of the River Thames. In 1833 the Swanscombe manufactory was purchased by Francis & White for £3,500 and Frost emigrated to America, setting up practice as a civil engineer in New York. The cement was utilized by Sir Marc **Brunel** in 1835 in his construction of the Thames Tunnel, and at the same time it was used in building the first all-concrete house at Swanscombe for Mr White.

Further Reading
A.J. Francis, 1977, *The Cement Industry 1796–1914: A History*, David & Charles.
C.C. Stanley, 1979, *Highlights in the History of Concrete*, Cement and Concrete Association.

DY

Froude, William

b. 1810 Dartington, Devon, England
d. 4 May 1879 Simonstown, South Africa

English naval architect; pioneer of experimental ship-model research.

Froude was educated at a preparatory school at Buckfastleigh, and then at Westminster School, London, before entering Oriel College, Oxford, to read mathematics and classics. Between 1836 and 1838 he served as a pupil civil engineer, and then he joined the staff of Isambard Kingdom **Brunel** on various railway engineering projects in southern England, including the South Devon Atmospheric Railway. He retired from professional work in 1846 and lived with his invalid father at Dartington Parsonage. The next twenty years, while apparently unproductive, were important to Froude as he concentrated his mind on difficult mathematical and scientific problems. Froude married in 1839 and had five children, one of whom, Robert Edmund Froude (1846–1924), was to succeed him in later years in his research work for the Admiralty. Following the death of his father, Froude moved to Paignton, and there commenced his studies on the resistance of solid bodies moving through fluids. Initially these were with hulls towed through a house roof storage tank by wires taken over a pulley and attached to falling weights, but the work became more sophisticated and was conducted on ponds and the open water of a creek near Dartmouth. Froude published work on the rolling of ships in the second volume of the *Transactions* of the then new Institution of Naval Architects and through this became acquainted with Sir Edward Reed. This led in 1870 to the Admiralty's offer of £2,000 towards the cost of an experimental tank for ship models at Torquay. The tank was completed in 1872 and tests were carried out on the model of HMS *Greyhound* following full-scale towing trials which had commenced on the actual ship the previous year. From this Froude enunciated his Law of Comparisons, which defines the rules concerning the relationship of the power required to move geometrically similar floating bodies across fluids. It enabled naval architects to predict, from a study of a much less expensive and smaller model, the resistance to motion and the power required to move a full-size ship. The work in the tank led Froude to design a model-cutting machine, dynamometers and machinery for the accurate ruling of graph paper. Froude's work, and later that of his son, was prodigious and covered many fields of ship design, including powering, propulsion, rolling, steering and stability. In only six years he had stamped his academic authority on the new science of hydrodynamics, served on many national committees and corresponded with fellow researchers throughout the world. His health suffered and he sailed for South Africa

to recuperate, but he contracted dysentery and died at Simonstown. He will be remembered for all time as one of the greatest 'fathers' of naval architecture.

Principal Honours and Distinctions
FRS. Honorary LLD Glasgow University.

Bibliography
1955, *The Papers of William Froude*, London: Institution of Naval Architects (the Institution also published a memoir by Sir Westcott Abell and an evaluation of his work by Dr R.W.L. Gawn of the Royal Corps of Naval Constructors; this volume reprints all Froude's papers from the Institution of Naval Architects and other sources as diverse as the British Association, the Royal Society of Edinburgh and the Institution of Civil Engineers.

Further Reading
A.T. Crichton, 1990, 'William and Robert Edmund Froude and the evolution of the ship model experimental tank', *Transactions of the Newcomen Society* 61: 33–49.

FMW

Fuller, Richard Buckminster
b. 12 July 1895 Milton, Massachusetts, USA
d. 1 July 1983 Los Angeles, California, USA

American engineer, designer and inventor noted particularly for his creation of the geodesic dome.

After naval service during the First World War, Fuller worked for some time in the building industry with his father, who was an architect. In 1927 he became interested in trying to solve social problems by providing good, low-cost housing for an expanding population. Utilizing modern techniques applicable in other industries, such as the design of aircraft and ships, he produced his 'Dymaxion House', which was transportable and cheap. This was followed in 1946 by his aluminium, stressed-skin, prefabricated house. The geodesic dome is the structural concept for which Fuller is particularly known. It was patented in 1954 and 300,000 were built over a thirty-year period. He had envisaged the dome being utilized on smaller or larger, simple or complex patterns for a wide variety of needs such as enclosing a covered area for a house, a botanical garden, an exhibition pavilion, a factory, a weather station or, indeed, an entire city. A famous example that he designed was that for the US pavilion at Expo '67 in Montreal. A geodesic dome is generally spherical in form, the chief structural elements of which are interconnected in a geodesic pattern, i.e. one in which the lines connecting two points are the shortest possible. The structure is composed of slender, lightweight struts (usually of aluminium) arranged in geometrical patterns, with the metal skeleton covered by a light, plastic material. Inside the dome, all the space is usable and the climate is controllable. Fuller wrote and lectured widely on his patented invention, explaining the importance of structural research particularly in relation to world needs.

Bibliography
1975, *Synergetics: Exploration on the Geometry of Thinking*, Macmillan.
1973, with R.W. Marks, *The Dymaxion World of Buckminster Fuller*, New York: Reprint Anchor.

Further Reading
M. Pawley, 1990, *Buckminster Fuller*, Trefoil Books.

DY

Fulton, Robert

b. 14 November 1765 Lancaster, Pennsylvania, USA
d. 24 February 1815 New York, USA

American pioneer of steamships and of North American steam navigation.

The early life of Fulton is documented sparsely; however, it is clear that he was brought up in poor circumstances along with three sisters and one brother by a widowed mother. The War of Independence was raging around them for some years, but despite this it is believed that he spent some time learning the jeweller's trade in Philadelphia and had by then made a name for himself as a miniaturist. Throughout his life he remained skilled with his hands and well able to record technical detail on paper. He witnessed many of the early trials of American steamboats and saw the work of William Henry and John Fitch, and in 1787 he set off for the first time to Europe. For some years he examined steamships in Paris and without doubt saw the *Charlotte Dundas* on the Forth and Clyde Canal near Glasgow. In 1803 he built a steamship that ran on the Seine at 4½ mph (7.25 km/h), and when it was lost, another to replace it. All his designs were based on principles that had been tried and proved elsewhere, and in this respect he was more of a developer than an inventor. After some time experimenting with submersibles and torpedoes for the British and French governments, in 1806 he returned to the United States. In 1807 he took delivery of the 100 ton displacement paddle steamer *Clermont* from the yard of Charles Browne of East River, New York. In August of that year it started the passenger services on the Hudson River and this can be claimed as the commencement of world passenger steam navigation. Again the ship was traditional in shape and the machinery was supplied by Messrs Boulton and Watt. This was followed by other ships, including *Car of Neptune*, *Paragon* and the world's first steam warship, *Demolgos*, launched in New York in October 1814 and designed by Fulton for coastal defence and the breaking of the British blockade. His last and finest boat was named *Chancellor Livingston* after his friend and patron Robert Livingston (1746–1813); the timber hull was launched in 1816, some months after Fulton's death.

Further Reading
H.P. Spratt, 1958, *The Birth of the Steamboat*, London: Griffin.
J.T. Flexner, 1978, *Steamboats Come True*, Boston: Little, Brown.
'Robert Fulton and the centenary of steam navigation', *Engineer* (16 August 1907).

FMW

G

Gabor, Dennis (Dénes)

b. 5 June 1900 Budapest, Hungary
d. 9 February 1979 London, England

Hungarian (naturalized British) physicist, inventor of holography.

Gabor became interested in physics at an early age. Called up for military service in 1918, he was soon released when the First World War came to an end. He then began a mechanical engineering course at the Budapest Technical University, but a further order to register for military service prompted him to flee in 1920 to Germany, where he completed his studies at Berlin Technical University. He was awarded a Diploma in Engineering in 1924 and a Doctorate in Electrical Engineering in 1927. He then went on to work in the physics laboratory of **Siemens & Halske**. He returned to Hungary in 1933 and developed a new kind of fluorescent lamp called the plasma lamp. Failing to find a market for this device, Gabor made the decision to abandon his homeland and emigrate to England. There he joined British Thompson–Houston (BTH) in 1934 and married a colleague from the company in 1936. Gabor was also unsuccessful in his attempts to develop the plasma lamp in England, and by 1937 he had begun to work in the field of electron optics. His work was interrupted by the outbreak of war in 1939, although as he was not yet a British subject he was barred from making any significant contribution to the British war effort. It was only when the war was near its end that he was able to return to electron optics and begin the work that led to the invention of holography. The theory was developed during 1947 and 1948; Gabor went on to demonstrate that the theories worked, although it was not until the invention of the laser in 1960 that the full potential of his invention could be appreciated. He coined the term 'hologram' from the Greek *holos*, meaning complete, and *gram*, meaning written. The three-dimensional images have since found many applications in various fields, including map making, medical imaging, computing, information technology, art and advertising. Gabor left BTH to become an associate professor at the Imperial College of Science and Technology in 1949, a position he held until his retirement in 1967. In 1971 he was awarded the Nobel Prize for Physics for his work on holography.

Principal Honours and Distinctions
Royal Society Rumford Medal 1968. Franklin Institute Michelson Medal 1968. CBE 1970. Nobel Prize for Physics 1971.

Bibliography
1948, 'A new microscopic principle', *Nature* 161: 777 (Gabor's earliest publication on holography).
1949, 'Microscopy by reconstructed wavefronts', *Proceedings of the Royal Society* A197: 454–87.
1951, 'Microscopy by reconstructed wavefronts II', *Proc. Phys. Soc. B*, 64: 449–69.
1966, 'Holography or the "Whole Picture"', *New Scientist* 29: 74–8 (an interesting account written after laser beams were used to produce optical holograms).

Further Reading
T.E. Allibone, 1980, contribution to *Biographical Memoirs of Fellows of the Royal Society* 26: 107–47 (a full account of Gabor's life and work).

JW

Gaius Plinius Secundus
See **Pliny the Elder**.

Galilei, Galileo

b. 15 February 1564 Pisa, Italy
d. 8 January 1642 Arcetri, near Florence, Italy

Italian mathematician, astronomer and physicist who established the principle of the pendulum and was first to exploit the telescope.

Galileo began studying medicine at the University of Pisa but soon turned to his real interests, mathematics, mechanics and astronomy. He became Professor of Mathematics at Pisa at the age of 25 and three years later moved to Padua. In 1610 he transferred to Florence. While still a student he discovered the isochronous property of the pendulum, probably by timing with his pulse the swings of a hanging lamp during a religious ceremony in Pisa Cathedral. He later designed a pendulum-controlled clock, but it was not constructed until after his death, and then not successfully; the first successful pendulum clock was made by the Dutch scientist Christiaan **Huygens** in 1656. Around 1590 Galileo established the laws of motion of falling bodies, by timing rolling balls down inclined planes and not, as was once widely believed, by dropping different weights from the Leaning Tower of Pisa. These and other observations received definitive treatment in his *Discorsi e dimostrazioni matematiche intorno a due nuove scienzi attenenti alla meccanica* (Dialogues Concerning Two New Sciences . . .) which was completed in 1634 and first printed in 1638. This work also included Galileo's proof that the path of a projectile was a parabola and, most importantly, the development of the concept of inertia.

In astronomy Galileo adopted the Copernican heliocentric theory of the universe while still in his twenties, but he lacked the evidence to promote it publicly. That evidence came with the invention of the telescope by the Dutch brothers **Lippershey**. Galileo heard of its invention in 1609 and had his own instrument constructed, with a convex object lens and concave eyepiece, a form which came to be known as the Galilean telescope. Galileo was the first to exploit the telescope successfully with a series of striking astronomical discoveries. He was also the first to publish the results of observations with the telescope, in his *Sidereus nuncius* (Starry Messenger) of 1610. All the discoveries told against the traditional view of the universe inherited from the ancient Greeks, and one in particular, that of the four satellites in orbit around Jupiter, supported the Copernican theory in that it showed that there could be another centre of motion in the universe besides the Earth: if Jupiter, why not the Sun? Galileo now felt confident enough to advocate the theory, but the advance of new ideas was opposed, not for the first or last time, by established opinion, personified in Galileo's time by the ecclesiastical authorities in Rome. Eventually he was forced to renounce the Copernican the-

ory, at least in public, and turn to less contentious subjects such as the 'two new sciences' of his last and most important work.

Bibliography

1610, *Sidereus nuncius* (Starry Messenger); translation by A. Van Helden, 1989, *Sidereus Nuncius, or the Sidereal Messenger*, Chicago: University of Chicago Press.

1623, *Il Saggiatore* (The Assayer).

1632, *Dialogo sopre i due massimi sistemi del mondo, tolemaico e copernicano* (Dialogue Concerning the Two Chief World Systems, Ptolemaic and Copernican); translation, 1967, Berkeley: University of California Press.

1638, *Discorsi e dimostrazioni matematiche intorno a due nuove scienzi attenenti alla meccanica* (Dialogues Concerning Two New Sciences . . .); translation, 1991, Buffalo, New York: Prometheus Books (reprint).

Further Reading

G. de Santillana, 1955, *The Crime of Galileo*, Chicago: University of Chicago Press; also 1958, London: Heinemann.

H. Stillman Drake, 1980, *Galileo*, Oxford: Oxford Paperbacks.

M. Sharratt, 1994, *Galileo: Decisive Innovator*, Oxford: Blackwell.

J. Reston, 1994, *Galileo: A Life*, New York: HarperCollins; also 1994, London: Cassell.

A. Fantoli, 1994, *Galileo: For Copernicanism and for the Church*, trans. G.V. Coyne, South Bend, Indiana: University of Notre Dame Press.

LRD

Gamond, Aimé Thomé de

b. 1807
d. 1876

French civil engineer and early advocate of the Channel Tunnel.

He became interested in the possibility of a tunnel or a bridge link between England and France in 1833 when he did his own geological survey of a route between Calais and Dover, and in 1834 he proposed an immersed tube tunnel. However, at the Great Exhibition of 1855 he promoted a scheme incorporating an artificial stone isthmus with movable bridges, which was estimated to cost £33,600,000, but this idea was eventually abandoned. He reverted to the idea of a tunnel and did further survey in 1855, with 180 lb (80 kg) of flint for ballast, ten inflated pig bladders to bring him to the surface and pieces of buttered lint plastered over his ears to protect them against the water pressure. He touched bottom between 99 and 108 ft (30 and 33 m). In 1856 Napoleon III granted him an audience and promised a scientific commission to evaluate his scheme, which it eventually approved. In 1858 he went to London and got the backing of Robert **Stephenson**, Isambard K. **Brunel** and Joseph **Locke**. He also obtained an interview with Prince **Albert**. In 1858, after an assassination attempt on Napoleon III, relations between France and England cooled off and Thomé de Gamond's plans were halted. He revived them in 1867, but others were by now also putting forward schemes. He had worked on the scheme for thirty-five years and expended a small fortune. In 1875 *The Times* reported that he was 'living in humble circumstances, his daughter supporting him by giving lessons on the piano'. He died the following year.

Further Reading
T. Whiteside, 1962, *The Tunnel under the Channel.*

IMcN

Garforth, William Edward

b. 1845 Dukinfield, Cheshire, England
d. 1 October 1921 Pontefract, Yorkshire, England

English colliery manager, pioneer in machine-holing and the safety of mines.

After **Menzies** conceived his idea of breaking off coal with machines in 1761, many inventors subsequently followed his proposals through into the practice of underground working. More than one century later, Garforth became one of the principal pioneers of machine-holing combined with the longwall method of working in order to reduce production costs and increase the yield of coal. Having been appointed agent to Pope & Pearson's Collieries, West Yorkshire, in 1879, of which company he later became Managing Director and Chairman, he gathered a great deal of experience with different methods of cutting coal. The first disc machine was exhibited in London as early as 1851, and ten years later a pick machine was invented. In 1893 he intro-

duced an improved type of deep undercutting machine, his 'diamond' disc coal-cutter, driven by compressed air, which also became popular on the European continent.

Besides the considerable economic advantages it created, the use of machinery for mining coal increased the safety of working in hard and thin seams. The improvement of safety in mining technology was always his primary concern, and as a result of his inventions and his many publications he became the leading figure in the British coal mining industry at the beginning of the twentieth century; safety lamps still carry his name. In 1885 he invented a firedamp detector, and following a severe explosion in 1886 he concentrated on coal-dust experiments. From the information he obtained of the effect of stone-dust on a coal-dust explosion he proposed the stone-dust remedy to prevent explosions of coal-dust. As a result of discussions which lasted for decades and after he had been entrusted with the job of conducting the British coal-dust experiments, in 1921 an Act made it compulsory in all mines which were not naturally wet throughout to treat all roads with incombustible dust so as to ensure that the dust always consisted of a mixture containing not more than 50 per cent combustible matter. In 1901 Garforth erected a surface gallery which represented the damaged roadways of a mine and could be filled with noxious fumes to test self-contained breathing apparata. This gallery formed the model from which all the rescue-stations existing nowadays have been developed.

Principal Honours and Distinctions
Knighted 1914. LLD Universities of Birmingham and Leeds 1912. President, Midland Institute 1892–4. President, The Institution of Mining Engineers 1911–14. President, Mining Association of Great Britain 1907–8. Chairman, Standing Committee on Mining, Advisory Council for Scientific and Industrial Research. Fellow of the Geological Society of London. North of England Institute of Mining and Mechanical Engineers Greenwell Silver Medal 1907. Royal Society of Arts Fothergill Gold Medal 1910. Medal of the Institution of Mining Engineers 1914.

Bibliography
1901–2, 'The application of coal-cutting

machines to deep mining', *Transactions of the Federated Institute of Mining Engineers* 23: 312–45.

1905–6, 'A new apparatus for rescue-work in mines', *Transactions of the Institution of Mining Engineers* 31: 625–57.

1902, 'British Coal-dust Experiments'. Paper communicated to the International Congress on Mining, Metallurgy, Applied Mechanics and Practical Geology, Düsseldorf.

Further Reading
Garforth's name is frequently mentioned in connection with coal-holing, but his outstanding achievements in improving safety in mines are only described in W.D. Lloyd, 1921, 'Memoir', *Transactions of the Institution of Mining Engineers* 62: 203–5.

WK

Garnier, Tony
b. 13 August 1869 Lyon, France
d. 19 January 1948 Bedoule, France

French architect and urban planner, a pioneer of the concept of segregation of pedestrian and wheeled traffic and of the use of concrete in building construction.

Garnier spent almost all his life in Lyon, apart from the years that he passed in Rome as a result of winning the Prix de Rome in 1889. While there, he evolved his concept of the *cité industrielle*, plans of which he exhibited and published early in the twentieth century. This was an idealized town, powered electrically, with its industrial areas separated from leisure ones. Garnier envisaged flat-roofed buildings supported on *pilotis*, with glass cladding, a steel structure, and extensive use of concrete. He proposed that each family should occupy its own house in a garden-city concept. In 1905 Garnier became city architect to Lyon, where he was able to carry out some of his ideas of the *cité industrielle*. He used concrete widely in such schemes as the municipal stadium, the Abattoirs de la Mouche and various housing schemes.

Principal Honours and Distinctions
Conseil Supérieur de l'Orde des Architectes. Honorary Degree Princeton University, USA.

Bibliography
1932, *Une Cité industrielle*, Paris: Vincent.
1920, *Les Grands travaux de la ville de Lyon*, Paris: Massin.

Further Reading
C. Pawlowski, 1967, *Tony Garnier et les débuts de l'urbanisme functionnel en France*, Paris: Centre de la Recherche d'Urbanisme.
M. Rovigalti, 1985, *Tony Garnier: Architettura per la città industriale*, Rome: Officini Edizioni.

DY

Garratt, Herbert William
b. 8 June 1864 London, England
d. 25 September 1913 Richmond, Surrey, England

English engineer, inventor of the Beyer–Garratt articulated locomotive.

After apprenticeship at the North London Railway's locomotive works, Garratt had a varied career which included responsibility for the locomotive departments of several British-owned railways overseas. This gave him an insight into the problems of such lines: locomotives, which were often inadequate, had to be operated over lines with weak bridges, sharp curves and steep gradients. To overcome these problems, he designed an articulated locomotive in which the boiler, mounted on a girder frame, was suspended between two power bogies. This enabled a wide firebox and large-diameter boiler barrel to be combined with large driving-wheels and good visibility. Coal and water containers were mounted directly upon the bogies to keep them steady. The locomotive was inherently stable on curves because the central line of the boiler between its pivots lay within the curve of the centre line of the track. Garratt applied for a patent for his locomotive in 1907 and manufacture was taken up by Beyer, Peacock & Co. under licence: the type became known as the Beyer–Garratt. The earliest Beyer–Garratt locomotives were small, but subsequent examples were larger. Sadly, only twenty-six locomotives of the type had been built or were under construction when Garratt died in 1913. Subsequent classes came to include some of the largest and most powerful steam locomotives: they were widely used and particularly successful in Central and Southern

Africa, where examples continue to give good service in the 1990s.

Bibliography
H.W. Garratt took out nine British patents, of which the most important is: 1907, British patent no. 17,165, 'Improvements in and Relating to Locomotive Engines'.

Further Reading
R.L. Hills, 1979–80, 'The origins of the Garratt locomotive', *Transactions of the Newcomen Society* 51: 175 (a good description of Garratt's career and the construction of the earliest Beyer–Garratt locomotives).
A.E. Durrant, 1981, *Garratt Locomotives of the World*, Newton Abbot: David & Charles.
L. Wiener, 1930, *Articulated Locomotives*, London: Constable & Co.

See also **Beyer, Charles Frederick**.

PJGR

Gartside

fl. 1760s England

English manufacturer who set up what was probably the first power-driven weaving shed.

A loom on which more than one ribbon could be woven at once may have been invented by Anton **Möller** at Danzig in 1586. It arrived in England from the Low Countries and was being used in London by 1616 and in Lancashire by 1680. Means were being devised in Switzerland *c.*1730 for driving these looms by power, but this was prohibited because it was feared that these looms would deprive other weavers of work. In England, a patent was taken out by John **Kay** of Bury and John Stell of Keighley in 1745 for improvements to these looms and it is probably that Gartside received permission to use this invention. In Manchester, Gartside set up a mill with swivel looms driven by a water-wheel; this was probably prior to 1758, because a man was brought up at the Lancaster Assizes in March of that year for threatening to burn down 'the Engine House of Mr. Gartside in Manchester, Merchant'. He set up his factory near Garrett Hall on the south side of Manchester and it may still have been running in 1764. However, the enterprise failed because it was necessary for each loom to be attended by one person in order to prevent any mishap occurring, and therefore it was more economic to use hand-frames, which the operatives could control more easily.

Further Reading
J. Aikin, 1795, *A Description of the Country from Thirty to Forty Miles Round Manchester*, London (provides the best account of Gartside's factory).
Both R.L. Hills, 1970, *Power in the Industrial Revolution*, Manchester; and A.P. Wadsworth and J. de L. Mann, 1931, *The Cotton Trade and Industrial Lancashire*, Manchester, make use of Aikin's material as they describe the development of weaving.
A. Barlow, 1878, *The History and Principles of Weaving by Hand and by Power*, London (covers the development of narrow fabric weaving).

RLH

Gascoigne, William

b. 1612 (?) near Leeds, Yorkshire, England
d. 2 July 1644 Marston Moor, Yorkshire, England

English astronomer and inventor of the micrometer.

As the son of a country gentleman, William Gascoigne would have had opportunities to receive reasonable schooling, but there is no record of how or where he was educated. However, by the late 1630s he had acquired a considerable knowledge of astronomy and was in correspondence with other scholars. About 1638 he invented an instrument to measure small angles in a telescope, consisting of two parallel wires in the eye piece moved by a calibrated screw. His invention remained unknown until it was reinvented thirty years later. He is said to have left the manuscript of a treatise on optics, but this did not survive. He was killed fighting for the royalist side at the battle of Marston Moor.

Further Reading
C.C. Gillespie (ed.), 1970–6, *Dictionary of Scientific Biography*, New York, s.v. Gascoigne; Towneley.
A.F. Burstall, 1963, *A History of Mechanical Engineering*, London, p. 159 (includes a drawing of Gascoigne's micrometer).

RTS

Gaskill, Harvey Freeman

b. 19 January 1845 Royalton, New York, USA
d. 1 April 1889 Lockport, New York, USA

American mechanical engineer, inventor of the water-pumping engine with flywheel and reciprocating pumps.

Gaskill's father was a farmer near New York, where the son attended the local schools until he was 16 years old. At the age of 13 he already showed his mechanical aptitude by inventing a revolving hayrake, which was not exploited because the family had no money. His parents moved to Lockport, New York, where Harvey became a student at Lockport Union School and then the Poughkeepsie Commercial College, from which he graduated in 1866. After a period in his uncle's law office, he entered the firm of Penfield, Martin & Gaskill to manufacture a patent clock. Then he was involved in a planing mill and a sash-and-blind manufactory. He devised a clothes spinner and a horse hayrake, but he did not manufacture them. In 1873 he became a draughtsman in the Holly Manufacturing Company in Lockport, which made pumping machinery for waterworks. He was promoted first to Engineer and then to Superintendent of the company in 1877. In 1885 he became a member of the Board of Directors and Vice-President. But for his untimely death, he might have become President. He was also a director of several other manufacturing concerns, public utilities and banks. In 1882 he produced a pump driven by a Woolf compound engine, which was the first time that rotary power with a crank and flywheel had been applied in waterworks. His design was more compact, more economical and lower in cost than previous types and gave the Holly Company a considerable advantage for a time over their main rivals, the Worthington Pump & Machinery Company. These steam pumps became very popular in the United States and the type was also adopted in Britain.

Further Reading
As well as obituaries appearing in many American engineering journals on Gaskill's death, there is an entry in the *Dictionary of American Biography*, 1931, Vol. VII, New York, C. Scribner's Sons.

RLH

Gatling, Dr Richard Jordan

b. 12 September 1818 Winston, North Carolina, USA
d. 26 February 1903 New York, USA

American weapons designer and metallurgist.

Gatling first became interested in inventing when helping his father develop more-efficient agricultural machines, and as early as 1839 he developed a screw propeller for ships. Shortly after this he was struck down by smallpox, and it was this that caused him, when he recovered, to study medicine; he did this at the Ohio Medical College, graduating in 1850. The outbreak of the American Civil War in 1861 triggered an immediate interest in weaponry and he set about designing a rapid-fire weapon, which would both bear his name and be one of the forerunners of the machine gun: he completed his design of the Gatling Gun in 1862. His concept of using several barrels was not unique, with other inventors such as the Belgian Fafschamps and the Frenchman Reffye also employing it. However, Gatling's gun was superior to the others in the soundness of its engineering. The rounds were fed through a hopper on top of the gun into the chambers of each barrel, and the barrels themselves were fixed in a cluster. An endless screw operated by a hand crank controlled the operation, opening the breech of each barrel in turn, enabling the round to drop into the chamber through a series of grooves, and then closing the breech and releasing the striker. In the face of fierce competition, the Gatling was adopted by the US Army in 1866, and many other armies followed suit. Although a version powered by an electric motor was introduced in 1893, the Gatling was gradually superseded by the fully automatic machine gun, first developed by **Maxim**. Even so, such was the excellence of the Gatling's mechanics that the concept was readopted by the Americans in the late 1950s and employed in such systems as the Vulcan air-defence gun and the airborne Minigun. Gatling's inventions did not end with his gun. In 1886 he developed a new steel and aluminium alloy and also experimented with the production of cast-steel cannon.

CM

Ged, William

b. 1690 Edinburgh, Scotland
d. 19 October 1749 Edinburgh, Scotland

Scottish inventor of stereotyping.

While in business as a goldsmith and jeweller, he came across the earliest known attempt to make stereotypes, that by Van der Meys of Leiden in the sixteenth century. He soldered types to the bases of a bed of type, but the process proved too expensive to be adopted. Ged took out a patent of privilege in 1725 to develop Mey's method, agreeing with a printer that if they could make casts of made-up pages of type they 'would make a fortune'. After many experiments to find a suitable metal, he arrived at an alloy similar to type metal. However, Ged's efforts to promote his stereotypes were blocked by the indifference of the printers and the opposition of the compositors. He tried his luck in London but failed again for much the same reason as in Edinburgh. Thither he returned, but he died in poverty.

Further Reading
J. Nichols, 1781, *Biographical Memoir of William Ged* (the 1819 edition includes 'Supplementary narrative of William Ged and his inventions, written by his daughter').

LRD

Gensfleisch zum Gutenberg, Johann
See **Gutenberg, Johann Gensfleisch zum**.

Gesner, Abraham
b. 1797 England
d. 1864

English pioneer in the extraction of paraffin.

Gesner qualified as a physician in London in 1827 and developed an interest in geology. Possibly through his friendship with Admiral Thomas Cochrane, later tenth Earl of Dundonald, he began experimenting with asphalt rock from Trinidad; he obtained several patents for the processes he employed to extract an oil from the rock. In 1853 the Asphalt Mining and Kerosene Company was founded to work his patents, which described how to purify the liquid produced by the dry distillation of asphalt, by mixing the liquid first with 5–10 per cent by volume of sulphuric acid to remove tars, and then with freshly calcined lime to remove water. It was then redistilled to produce an inflammable oil. Gesner called it kerosene, from the Greek *keros*, meaning 'wax'; in Britain it came to be known as paraffin.

The new oil sold well, especially when accompanied by a cheap lamp with a flat wick and glass chimney. By 1856 Gesner considered his product could replace whale oil as a fuel for lamps; success was short-lived, however, for the oil was overtaken three years later by the drilling of the first American petroleum wells.

LRD

Gestetner, David
b. March 1854 Csorna, Hungary
d. 8 March 1939 Nice, France

Hungarian/British pioneer of stencil duplicating.

For the first twenty-five years of his life, Gestetner was a rolling stone and accordingly gathered no moss. Leaving school in 1867, he began working for an uncle in Sopron, making sausages. Four years later he apprenticed himself to another uncle, a stockbroker, in Vienna. The financial crisis of 1873 prompted a move to a restaurant, also in the family, but tiring of a menial existence, he emigrated to the USA, travelling steerage. He began to earn a living by selling Japanese kites: these were made of strong Japanese paper coated with lacquer, and he noted their long fibres and great strength, an observation that was later to prove useful when he was searching for a suitable medium for stencil duplicating. However, he did not prosper in the USA and he returned to Europe, first to Vienna and finally to London in 1879. He took a job with Fairholme & Co., stationers in Shoe Lane, off Holborn; at last Gestetner found an outlet for his inventive genius and he began his life's work in developing stencil duplicating. His first patent was in 1879 for an application of the hectograph, an early method of duplicating documents. In 1881, he patented the toothed-wheel pen, or Cyclostyle, which made good ink-passing perforations in the stencil paper, with which he was able to pioneer the first practicable form of stencil duplicating. He then adopted a better stencil tissue of Japanese paper coated with wax, and later an improved form of pen. This assured the success of Gestetner's form of stencil duplicating and it became established practice in offices in the late 1880s. Gestetner began to manufacture the apparatus in premises in Sun Street, at first under the name of Fairholme, since they had defrayed the patent expenses and otherwise supported him financially, in return for which Gestetner assigned them his patent rights. In 1882 he patented the wheel pen in the USA and appointed an agent to sell the equipment there. In 1884 he moved to larger premises, and three years later to still larger premises. The introduction of the typewriter prompted modifications that enabled stencil duplicating to become both the standard means of printing short runs of copy and an essential piece of equipment in offices. Before the First World War, Gestetner's products were being sold around the world; in fact he created one of the first truly international distribution networks. He finally moved to a large factory to the north-east of London: when his company went public in 1929, it had a share capital of nearly £750,000. It was only with the development of electrostatic photocopying and small office offset litho machines that stencil duplicating began to decline in the 1960s. The firm David Gestetner had founded adapted to the new conditions and prospers still, under the direction of his grandson and namesake.

Further Reading
W.B. Proudfoot, 1972, *The Origin of Stencil Duplicating*, London: Hutchinson (gives a good account of the method and the development of the Gestetner process, together with some details of his life).
H.V. Culpan, 1951, 'The House of Gestetner', in *Gestetner 70th Anniversary Celebration Brochure*, London: Gestetner.

LRD

Gibbon, John Heysham
b. 29 September 1903 Philadelphia, Pennsylvania, USA
d. 5 February 1973 Philadelphia, Pennsylvania, USA

American cardiothoracic surgeon, pioneer of the heart–lung apparatus and artificial ventilation in thoracic surgery.

Gibbon studied medicine at Jefferson Medical College, Philadelphia, and qualified MD in 1929. He held research fellowships at Harvard from 1930 to 1936 and then moved to similar posts and an assistant professorship at the University of Pennsylvania. After a period involving service with the Army, he was appointed Professor of Surgery and Director of Surgical Research at Jefferson in 1946. His research, assisted by his wife, was particularly directed towards the construction of an artificial mechanical heart and lung apparatus which would maintain circulation and respiration during the course of chest surgery involving heart and lungs. The resulting developments have been fundamental to the expansion of cardiac and coronary surgery.

Principal Honours and Distinctions
City of Philadelphia John Scott Medal 1953. American Heart Association 1965.

Bibliography
1939, 'An oxygenator with a large surface volume ratio', *J. Lab. Clin. Med.*
1954, 'Application of a mechanical heart and lung apparatus to cardiac surgery', *Minn. Med.*
1962 (ed.), *Surgery of the Chest.*
1970, 'The development of the heart-lung apparatus', *Rev. Surg.*

MG

Gibbons, John
fl. 1800–50 Staffordshire, England

English ironmaster who introduced the round hearth in the blast furnace.

Gibbons was an ironmaster in the Black Country, South Staffordshire, in charge of six blast furnaces owned by the family business. Until Gibbons's innovation in 1832, small changes in the form of the furnace had at times been made, but no one had seriously questioned the square shape of the hearth. Gibbons noticed that a new furnace often worked poorly by improved as time went on. When it was 'blown out', i.e. taken out of commission, he found that the corners of the hearth had been rounded off and the sides gouged out, so that it was roughly circular in shape. Gibbons wisely decided to build a blast furnace with a round hearth alongside an existing one with a traditionally shaped hearth and work them in exactly the same conditions. The old furnace produced 75 tons of iron in a week, about normal for the time, while the new one produced 100 tons. Further improvements followed and in 1838 a fellow ironmaster in the same district, T. Oakes, considerably enlarged the furnace, its height attaining no less than 60 ft (18 m). As a result, output soared to over 200 tons a week. Most other ironmasters adopted the new form with enthusiasm and it proved to be the basis for the modern blast furnace. Gibbons made another interesting innovation: he began charging his furnace with the 'rubbish', slag or cinder, from earlier ironmaking operations. It contained a significant amount of iron and was cheaper to obtain than iron ore, as it was just lying around in heaps. Some ironmasters scorned to use other people's throw-outs, but Gibbons sensibly saw it as a cheap source of iron; it was a useful source for some years during the nineteenth century but its use died out when the heaps were used up. Gibbons published an account of his improvements in ironmaking in a pamphlet entitled *Practical Remarks on the Construction of the Staffordshire Blast Furnace*.

Bibliography

1839, *Practical Remarks on the Construction of the Staffordshire Blast Furnace*, Birmingham; reprinted 1844.

Further Reading

J. Percy, 1864, *Metallurgy. Iron and Steel*, London, p. 476.
W.K.V. Gale, 1969, *Iron and Steel*, London: Longmans, pp. 44–6.

LRD

Gibson, R.O.
fl. 1920s–30s

English chemist who, with E.O. Fawcett, discovered polythene.

Dr Gibson's work towards the discovery of polythene had its origin in a visit in 1925 to Dr A. Michels of Amsterdam University; the latter had made major advances in techniques for studying chemical reactions at very high pressures. After working with Michels for a time, in 1926 Gibson joined Brunner Mond, one of the companies that went on to form the chemical giant Imperial Chemical Industries (ICI). The company supported research into fundamental chemical research that had no immediate commercial application, including the field being cultivated by Michels and Gibson. In 1933 Gibson was joined by another ICI chemist, E.O. Fawcett, who had worked with W.H. **Carothers** in the USA on polymer chemistry. They were asked to study the effects of high pressure on various reaction systems, including a mixture of benzalde-

hyde and ethylene. Gibson's notebook for 27 March that year records that after a loss of pressure during which the benzaldehyde was blown out of the reaction tube, a waxy solid was observed in the tube. This is generally recognized as the first recorded observation of polythene. By the following June they had shown that the white, waxy solid was a fairly high molecular weight polymer of ethylene formed at a temperature of 443°K and a pressure of 2,000 bar. However, only small amounts of the material were produced and its significance was not immediately recognized. It was not until two years later that W.P. Perrin and others, also ICI chemists, restarted work on the polymer. They showed that it could be moulded, drawn into threads and cast into tough films. It was a good electrical insulator and almost inert chemically. A British patent for producing polythene was taken out in 1936, and after further development work a production plant began operating in September 1939, just as the Second World War was breaking out. Polythene had arrived in time to make a major contribution to the war effort, for it had the insulating properties required for newly developing work on radar. When peacetime uses became possible, polythene production surged ahead and became the major industry it is today, with a myriad uses in industry and in everyday life.

Bibliography

1964, *The Discovery of Polythene*, Royal Institute of Chemistry Lecture Series 1, London.

LRD

Giffard, Baptiste Henry Jacques (Henri)
b. 8 February 1825 Paris, France
d. 14 April 1882 Paris, France

French pioneer of airships and balloons, inventor of an injector for steam-boiler feedwater.

Giffard entered the works of the Western Railway of France at the age of 16 but became absorbed by the problem of steam-powered aerial navigation. He proposed a steam-powered helicopter in 1847, but he then turned his attention to an airship. He designed a lightweight coke-burning, single-cylinder steam engine and boiler which produced just over 3 hp (2.2 kW) and mounted it below a cigar-shaped gas bag 44 m

(144 ft) in length. A triangular rudder was fitted at the rear to control the direction of flight. On 24 September 1852 Giffard took off from Paris and, at a steady 8 km/h (5 mph), he travelled 28 km (17 miles) to Trappes. This can be claimed to be the first steerable lighter-than-air craft, but with a top speed of only 8 km/h (5 mph) even a modest headwind would have reduced the forward speed to nil (or even negative). Giffard built a second airship, which crashed in 1855, slightly injuring Giffard and his companion; a third airship was planned with a very large gas bag in order to lift the inherently heavy steam engine and boiler, but this was never built. His airships were inflated by coal gas and refusal by the gas company to provide further supplies brought these promising experiments to a premature end.

As a draughtsman Giffard had the opportunity to travel on locomotives and he observed the inadequacies of the feed pumps then used to supply boiler feedwater. To overcome these problems he invented the injector with its series of three cones: in the first cone (convergent), steam at or below boiler pressure becomes a high-velocity jet; in the second (also convergent), it combines with feedwater to condense and impart high velocity to it; and in the third (divergent), that velocity is converted into pressure sufficient to overcome the pressure of steam in the boiler. The injector, patented by Giffard, was quickly adopted by railways everywhere, and the royalties provided him with funds to finance further experiments in aviation. These took the form of tethered hydrogen-inflated balloons of successively larger size. At the Paris Exposition of 1878 one of these balloons carried fifty-two passengers on each tethered 'flight'. The height of the balloon was controlled by a cable attached to a huge steam-powered winch, and by the end of the fair 1,033 ascents had been made and 35,000 passengers had seen Paris from the air. This, and similar balloons, greatly widened the public's interest in aeronautics. Sadly, after becoming blind, Giffard committed suicide; however, he died a rich man and bequeathed large sums of money to the State for humanitarian an scientific purposes.

Principal Honours and Distinctions
Croix de la Légion d'honneur 1863.

Bibliography
1860, *Notice théorique et pratique sur l'injecteur automoteur.*
1870, *Description du premier aérostat à vapeur.*

Further Reading
Dictionnaire de biographie française.
Gaston Tissandier, 1872, *Les Ballons dirigeables*, Paris.
—— 1878, *Le Grand ballon captif à vapeur de M. Henri Giffard*, Paris.
W. de Fonvielle, 1882, *Les Ballons dirigeables à vapeur de H. Giffard*, Paris.
Giffard is covered in most books on balloons or airships, e.g.:
Basil Clarke, 1961, *The History of Airships*, London.
L.T.C. Rolt, 1966, *The Aeronauts*, London.
Ian McNeill (ed.), 1990, *An Encyclopaedia of the History of Technology*, London: Routledge, pp. 575 and 614.
J.T. Hodgson and C.S. Lake, 1954, *Locomotive Management*, Tothill Press, p. 100.

PJGR/JDS

Gilbert, Cass

b. 24 November 1859 Zanesville, Ohio, USA
d. 17 May 1934 Brockenhurst, Hampshire, England

American architect who designed a variety of high-quality, large-scale public buildings in eclectic mode.

Gilbert travelled widely in Europe before returning to the USA to join the well-known firm of McKim, Mead & White, for whom he designed the Minnesota State Capitol at Saint Paul (1896–1903). This building, like the majority of Gilbert's work, was in classical form, the great dome modelled on that of Saint Peter's Basilica in Rome. Other designs, on similar classical themes, included his large US Customs House in New York (1907). The structure for which Gilbert is best known, however, was an adaptation of French Gothic style to a sixty-storeyed skyscraper. This was the Woolworth Building, an office tower of romantic silhouette in downtown New York (1913). In contra-distinction to the high-rise designs of Louis **Sullivan**, who broke new ground in relating the design of the building to the verticality of the structure, Gilbert continued the skyscraper pattern of earlier years by clothing the steel structure in eclectic manner unrelated to the form beneath. The result, if backward-looking, is an elegant, attractive and familiar part of the New York skyline.

Further Reading
W.H. Jordy, 1976, *American Buildings and their Architects*, Vol. 3, Garden City, New York: Anchor.
W. Weisman, 1970, *The Rise of American Architecture*, New York: Praeger.

DY

Gilbert, John
b. 1724 Cotton Hall, Cotton, Staffordshire, England
d. 3 August 1795 Worsley, Lancashire, England

English land agent, mining engineer and canal entrepreneur.

Younger son of a gentleman farmer, Gilbert was apprenticed to Matthew Boulton, a buckle maker of Birmingham and father of the Matthew **Boulton** who was associated with James **Watt**. He also gained mining experience. Through the influence of his older brother, Thomas **Gilbert**, he became Land Agent to the Duke of Bridgewater (Francis **Egerton**) for the Worsley estate. He proposed extensions to the underground waterway system and also made a preliminary survey for a canal from Worsley to Salford, a project which **Brindley** joined as Assistant Engineer. Gilbert was therefore the prime mover in the construction of the Bridgewater Canal, which received its Act in 1759. He then collected evidence for the second Act to permit construction of the aqueduct across the Irwell at Barton. He was involved in a consortium with his brother Thomas and Earl Gower to develop the Earl's East Shropshire mines and to build the Shrewsbury and the Shropshire Coal Canals. He also excavated the Speedwell Mine at Castleton in Derbyshire between 1774 and 1781 and constructed the underground canal to serve the workings. With his brother, he was involved in the promotion of the Trent & Mersey Canal and was a shareholder in the undertaking. Among his other entrepreneurial activities, he entered the canal-carrying business. His last work was beginning the underground inclined planes at Worsley, but these were not completed until after his death. His important place in the historical development of the inland navigational system in England has been very much overlooked.

Further Reading
P. Lead, 1990, *Agents of Revolution: John and Thomas Gilbert – Entrepreneurs*, Keele University Centre for Local History.

JHB

Gilbert, Joseph Henry
b. 1 August 1817 Hull, England
d. 23 December 1901 England

English chemist who co-established the reputation of Rothampsted Experimental Station as at the forefront of agricultural research.

Joseph Gilbert was the son of a congregational minister. His schooling was interrupted by the loss of an eye as the result of a shooting accident, but despite this setback he entered Glasgow University to study analytical chemistry, and then went to University College, London, where he was a fellow student of John Bennet **Lawes**. During his studies he visited Giessen, Germany, and worked in the laboratory of Justus von **Liebig**. In 1843, at the age of 26, he was hired as an assistant by Lawes, who was 29 at that time; an unbroken friendship and collaboration existed between the two until Lawes died in 1900. They began a series of experiments on grain production and grew plots under different applications of nitrogen, with control plots that received none at all. Much of the work at Rothampsted was on the nitrogen requirements of plants and how this element became available to them. The grain grown in these experiments was analyzed to determine whether nitrogen input affected grain quality. Gilbert was a methodical worker who by the time of his death had collected together some 50,000 carefully stored and recorded samples.

Principal Honours and Distinctions
Knighted 1893. FRS 1860. Fellow of the Chemistry Society 1841, President 1882–3. President, Chemical Section of the British Association 1880. Sibthorpian Professor of Rural Economy, Oxford University, 1884. Honorary Professor of the Royal Agricultural College, Cirencester. Honorary member of the Royal Agricultural Society of England 1883. Royal Society Royal

Medal 1867 (jointly with Lawes). Society of Arts Albert Gold Medal 1894 (jointly with Lawes). Liebig Foundation of the Royal Bavarian Academy of Science Silver Medal 1893 (jointly with Lawes).

AP

Gilbert, Thomas
b. 1720 Cotton Hall, Cotton, Staffordshire, England
d. 18 December 1798

English politician, mine and canal entrepreneur.

He was the older brother of John **Gilbert** and, trained as a lawyer, he became Land Agent to Earl Gower and Legal Adviser to the Duke of Bridgewater (Francis **Egerton**). **Brindley** had carried out work for Gilbert on the Gower estates and the standard of work impressed him. In 1759 he recommended Brindley to his brother at Worsley as a competent engineer who would be valuable in the construction of the new canal. Gilbert became Member of Parliament for Newcastle under Lyme in 1763 and was thus able to sponsor the Trent and Mersey Bill when it came before Parliament. He joined the committee of the Trent and Mersey, representing the interests of both Earl Gower and himself. He was also involved with the East Shropshire mines and canals with his brother. He continued as a Member of Parliament (until 1768 for Newcastle and afterwards for Lichfield) until December 1794.

Further Reading
P. Lead, 1990, *Agents of Revolution: John and Thomas Gilbert – Entrepreneurs*, Keele University Centre for Local History.

JHB

Giles, Francis
b. 1787 England
d. 4 March 1847 England

English civil engineer engaged in canal, harbour and railway construction.

Trained as a surveyor in John **Rennie**'s organization, Giles carried out surveys on behalf of Rennie before setting up in practice on his own. His earliest survey seems to have been on the line of the proposed Weald of Kent Canal in 1809. Then in 1811 he surveyed the proposed London & Cambridge Canal linking Bishops Stortford

on the Stort with Cambridge and with a branch to Shefford on the Ivel. In the same year he surveyed the line of the Wey & Arun Junction Canal, and in 1816, in the same area, the Portsmouth & Arundel Canal. In 1819 he carried out what is regarded as his first independent commission – the extension of the River Ivel Navigation from Biggleswade to Shefford. At this time he was helping John Rennie on the Aire & Calder Navigation and continued there after Rennie's death in 1821. In 1825 he was engaged on plans for a London to Portsmouth Ship Canal and also on a suggested link between the Basingstoke and Kennet & Avon Canals. Later, on behalf of Sir George Duckett, he was Engineer to the Hertford Union Canal, which was completed in 1830, and linked the Regent's Canal to the Lee Navigation. In 1833 he completed the extension of the Sankey Brook Navigation from Fiddler's Ferry to the Mersey at Widnes. One of his last canal works was a survey of the River Lee in 1844. Apart from his canal work, he was appointed Engineer to the Newcastle & Carlisle Railway in 1829 and designed, among other works, the fine viaducts at Wetheral and Corby. He was also, for a very short time, Engineer to the London & Southampton Railway. Among other commissions, he was involved in harbour surveys and works at Dover, Rye, Holyhead, Dundee, Bridport and Dun Laoghaire (Kingstown). He was elected a member of the Institution of Civil Engineers in 1842 and succeeded **Telford** on the Exchequer Bill Loans Board.

Further Reading
1848, *Memoir* 17, London: Institution of Civil Engineers, 9.

JHB

Gillette, King Camp
b. 5 January 1855 Fond du Lac, Wisconsin, USA
d. 9 July 1932 Los Angeles, California, USA

American inventor and manufacturer, inventor of the safety razor.

Gillette's formal education in Chicago was brought to an end when a disastrous fire destroyed all his father's possessions. Forced to fend for himself, he worked first in the hardware trade in Chicago and New York, then as a travelling salesman. Gillette inherited the family talent for invention, but found that his successful inventions barely paid for those that failed. He was advised by a previous employer, William Painter (inventor of the Crown Cork), to look around for something that could be used widely and then thrown away. In 1895 he succeeded in following that advice of inventing something which people could use and then throw away, so that they would keep coming back for more. An idea came to him while he was honing an old-fashioned razor one morning; he was struck by the fact that only a short piece of the whole length of a cutthroat razor is actually used for shaving, as well as by the potentially dangerous nature of the implement. He 'rushed out to purchase some pieces of brass, some steel ribbon used for clock springs, a small hand vise and some files'. He thought of using a thin steel blade sharpened on each side, placed between two plates and held firmly together by a handle. Though coming from a family of inventors, Gillette had no formal technical education and was entirely ignorant of metallurgy. For six years he sought a way of making a cheap blade from sheet steel that could be hardened, tempered and sharpened to a keen edge.

Gillette eventually found financial supporters: Henry Sachs, a Boston lamp manufacturer; his brother-in-law Jacob Heilbron; and William Nickerson, who had a considerable talent for invention. By skilled trial and error rather than expert metallurgical knowledge, Nickerson devised ways of forming and sharpening the blades, and it was these that brought commercial success. In 1901, the American Safety Razor Company, later to be renamed the Gillette Safety Razor Company, was set up. When it started production in 1903 the company was badly in debt, and managed to sell only fifty-one razors and 168 blades; but by the end of the following year, 90,000 razors and 12.4 million blades had been sold. A sound invention coupled with shrewd promotion ensured further success, and eight plants manufacturing safety razors were established in various parts of the world. Gillette's business experiences led him into the realms of social theory about the way society should be organized. He formulated his views in a series of books published over the years 1894 to 1910. He believed that competition led to a waste of up to 90 per cent of human effort and that want and crime would be eliminated by substituting a giant trust to plan production centrally. Unfortunately, the public in America, or anywhere else for that matter, were not ready for this form of Utopia; no omniscient planners were available, and human wants and needs were too various to be supplied by a single agency. Even so, some of his ideas have found favour: air conditioning and government provision of work for the unemployed. Gillette made a fortune from his invention and retired from active participation in the business in 1913, although he remained President until 1931 and Director until his death.

Bibliography
'Origin of the Gillette razor', *Gillette Blade* (February/March).

Further Reading
Obituary, 1932, *New York Times* (11 July).
J. Jewkes, D. Sawers and R. Stillerman, 1958, *The Sources of Invention*, London: Macmillan.

LRD/IMcN

Gillott, Joseph
b. 1799 Sheffield, Yorkshire
d. 1877

English maker of steel pens.

The name Joseph Gillott became synonymous with pen making at a time when the basic equipment for writing was undergoing a change. The quill pen had served writers for centuries, but attempts had been made since the seventeenth century to improve on it. The first major technical development was the steel nib, which began to be made *c.*1829. The steel nib was still little known in Birmingham in 1839, but ten years later it was in common use. Its stiffness was at first a drawback, but Gillott was among the first to improve its flexibility by introducing three slots, which later became standard practice. Mechanical methods of manufacture made the pen cheaper and improved its quality. In 1840 Gillott issued a 'precept' informing the public that he was pen maker to the Queen and that he had been manufacturing pens for twenty years at his Victoria Works in Birmingham. He announced the successful reception by the public of his new patent pen. There were also special 'warranted school' pens designed for the various grades of writing taught in schools. Finally, he warned against inferior imitations and recommended the public to buy only those pens stamped with his name.

Further Reading
J.T. Bunce and S. Timmins, *c.*1880, *Joseph Gillott 1799–1877: A Sketch of His Life.*
H. Bore, 1890, *The Story of the Invention of the Steel Pen*, London.
J. Whalley, 1975, *Writing Implements and Accessories*, Newton Abbot: David & Charles.

LRD

Gilpin, Thomas

b. 18 March 1728 Chester County, Pennsylvania, USA
d. 30 April 1778 Winchester, Virginia, USA

American manufacturer.

Thomas Gilpin belonged to a wealthy Quaker family descended from Joseph Gilpin, who had emigrated from England in 1696. He received little formal education and was mainly self-educated in mathematics, surveying and science, in which subjects he was particularly interested. With estates in Delaware and Maryland, he was involved in farming and manufacturing. He moved to Philadelphia in 1769, which further extended his activities. With his fortune he was able to indulge his interest in science, and he was one of the original members of the American Philosophical Society in 1769. He wrote papers on the wheat fly, the seventeen-year locust and the migration of herrings. It was through this Society that he became friendly with Benjamin **Franklin**, to whom he wrote on 10 October 1769 setting out his proposals for and advocacy of a canal linking the Elk River on Chesapeake Bay with the Delaware River and Bay, thereby cutting off a long haul of several hundred miles for vessels around Cape Charles with a dangerous passage unto the Atlantic Ocean. Gilpin also invented a hydraulic pump that delighted Franklin very much. Gilpin had visited England in 1768 during the formation of his ideas for the Chesapeake & Delaware Canal, and probably visited the Bridgewater Canal while there. Despite his pressing advocacy the canal had to wait until after his death, but later his son Joshua, a director from 1803 to 1824, saw the canal through many difficulties although he had resigned before the official opening in 1829. At the outbreak of the American War of Independence, in 1777, Gilpin, together with other Quakers, was arrested in Philadelphia owing to suspicions of his loyalty on the grounds that as a Quaker he refused to sign the Oath of Allegiance. He was later exiled to Winchester, Virginia, where he died in April 1778.

Further Reading
1925, 'Memoir of Thomas Gilpin', *Pennsylvania Magazine of History and Biography.*
R.D. Gray, 1967, *The National Waterway: A History of the Chesapeake and Delaware Canal, 1769–1985*, Urbana: Illinois University Press.

JHB

Girard, Philippe de

b. 1775 France
d. 1845

French developer of a successful flax-heckling machine for the preparation of fibres for power-spinning.

Early drawing and spinning processes failed to give linen yarn the requisite fineness and homogeneity. In 1810 Napoleon offered a prize of a million francs for a successful flax-spinning machine as part of his policy of stimulating the French textile industries. Spurred on by this offer, Girard suggested three improvements. He was too late to win the prize, but his ideas were patented in England in 1814, although not under his own name. He proposed that the fibres should be soaked in a very hot alkaline solution both before drawing and immediately before they went to the spindles. The actual drawing was to be done by passing the dried material through combs or gills that moved alternately; gill drawing was taken up in England in 1816. His method of wet spinning was never a commercial success, but his processes were adopted in part and developed in Britain and spread to Austria, Poland and France, for his ideas were essentially good and produced a superior product. The successful power-spinning of linen thread from flax depended primarily upon the initial processes of heckling and drawing. The heckling of the bundles or stricks of flax, so as to separate the long fibres of 'line' from the shorter ones of 'tow', was extremely difficult to mechanize, for each strick had to be combed on both sides in turn and then in the reverse direction. It was to this problem that Girard next turned his attention, inventing a successful machine in 1832 that subsequently was improved in England. The strick was placed between two vertical sheets of combs that moved opposite to each other, depositing the tow upon a revolving cylinder covered with a brush at the bottom of the machine, while the holder from which the strick was suspended moved up and down so as to help the teeth to penetrate deeper into the flax. The tow was removed from the cylinder at the bottom of the machine and taken away to be spun like cotton. The long line fibres were removed from the top of the machine and required further processing if the yarn was to be uniform.

When N.L. Sadi **Carnot**'s book *Réflexions sur la puissance motrice du feu*, was published in 1824, Girard made a favourable report on it.

Further Reading
M. Daumas (ed.), 1968, *Histoire générale des techniques*, Vol. III: *L'Expansion du Machinisme*, Paris.
C. Singer (ed.), 1958, *A History of Technology*, Vol. IV, Oxford: Clarendon Press.
T.K. Derry and T.I. Williams, 1960, *A Short History of Technology from the Earliest Times to AD 1900*, Oxford.
W.A. McCutcheon, 1966–7, 'Water power in the North of Ireland', *Transactions of the Newcomen Society* 39 (discusses the spinning of flax and mentions Girard).

RLH

Glauber, Johann Rudolf

b. 1604 Karlstadt, Germany
d. March 1670 Amsterdam, Holland

German chemist and metallurgist.

The son of a barber, Glauber took up the study of alchemy and travelled widely in search of its secrets. Around 1639, the political uncertainties of the Thirty Years War persuaded him to leave Germany for a more settled life in Amsterdam. While there, he carried out most of the practical work for which he is famous, including his distillation furnace, which made it possible to reach higher temperatures and to heat substances in a variety of conditions. To earn a living he set up in the wine trade, but he continued his alchemical pursuits, under cover on account of the unpopularity of the would-be gold makers. After the end of the war, he returned to Germany, but

in 1655 personal disputes and religious friction drove him back to Amsterdam. He set about constructing the largest and most elaborate chemical laboratory in Europe.

Glauber's best-known writing, the *Furni novi philosophici* (1646–9) gives the clearest idea of his practical methods and was influential on some of the leading chemists of the time and later. His name survives today in Glauber's salt for hydrated sodium sulphate. Glauber described several methods for preparing the mineral acids, materials of great importance to the chemist, and obtained the concentrated acids by using his distilling furnace. He tried distilling any substance he could lay hands on, and in the course of this work became probably the first chemist to distil coal and, using hydrochloric acid, obtain benzene and phenol. Glauber was the best practical chemist of the age and the first industrial chemist.

Bibliography
1646–9, *Furni novi philosophici*

Further Reading
K.F. Gugel, 1955, *Johann Rudolf Glauber (1604–1670), Leben und Werke*, Würzburg (the fullest account of his life; with a bibliography).
P. Walden, 1929, 'Glauber', in *Das Buch der grossen Chemiker*, ed. G. Bugge, Berlin, pp. 151–72 (the best account of Glauber's practical methods).
E. Farber, 1961, *Great Chemists*, New York, pp. 115–31 (an abridged translation of ibid.).

LRD

Glenck, Karl Christian Friedrich

b. 13 April 1779 Schwäbisch Hall, Germany
d. 21 November 1845 Gotha, Germany

German salt-mining expert who introduced large-scale salt explorations.

Having studied law at the University of Erlangen, he became Confidential Secretary to the Prince of Hohenlohe-Ingelfingen, in whose territory his father had been in charge of a saltworks. When this small country fell to Württemberg in 1806, Glenck continued his mineralogical and geological studies in order to develop methods of finding deposits of salt. He was the first to carry out systematic large-scale salt explorations in Germany, mostly in southern and central parts, and achieved remarkable results that far exceeded former non-systematic findings. He worked either on behalf of governments or companies or at his own risk, and in the early 1820s he settled in Gotha to live in the centre of the regions of greatest interest to him.

His career began in 1819 with the discovery of the deposits of Ludwigshall near Wimpfen, Neckar, and prospecting salt near Basel in 1836 was his greatest success: Schweizerhall, opened one year later, made Switzerland self-sufficient in salt production. For fifteen years he had invested large sums into this project, which became the fifth salt-works to come into existence due to his drilling. Glenck worked with stir rods and he developed several new technical devices, such as casing the bore holes with iron pipes instead of wood (1830), and using wooden instead of iron rods to reduce the weight (1834). A flexible connection between rod and drill was to be introduced later by Karl von **Oeynhausen**. One of Glenck's most important followers in the field of deep-drilling was K.G. **Kind**.

Further Reading

W. Carlé, 1969, 'Die Salinistenfamilie Glenck', *Lebensbilder aus Schwaben und Franken* 11: 118–49 (with substantial biographical information).

D. Hoffmann, 1959, *150 Jahre Tiefbohrungen in Deutschland*, Vienna and Hamburg, (provides an evaluation of his technological developments).

WK

Goddard, Dr Robert Hutchings

b. 5 October 1882 Worcester, Massachusetts, USA
d. 10 August 1945 Baltimore, Maryland, USA

American inventor, developer of rocket propulsion.

At the age of seventeen Goddard climbed a tree and, seeing the view from above, he became determined to make some device with which to ascend towards the planets. In an autobiography, published in 1959 in the journal *Astronautics*, he stated, 'I was a different boy when I descended the ladder. Life now had a purpose for me.'

His first idea was to launch a projectile by cen-

trifugal force, but in 1909 he started to design a rocket that was to be multi-stage and fuelled by liquid oxygen and hydrogen. Not long before the First World War he produced a report, 'A method of reaching extreme altitudes', which was for the Smithsonian Institution and was published in book form in 1919. During the war he worked on solid-fuelled rockets as weapons. His book contained notes on the amount of fuel required to raise 1 lb (454 g) of payload to an infinite altitude. He incurred ridicule as 'the moon man' when he proposed the use of flash powder to indicate successful arrival on the moon. In 1923 he severed his connections with military work and returned to the University of Massachusetts. On 16 March 1926 he launched the world's first liquid-fuelled rocket from his aunt's farm in Auburn, Massachusetts; powered by gasoline and liquid oxygen, it flew to a height of 12 m (40 ft) and travelled 54 m (177 ft) in 2.4 seconds.

In November 1929 he met the aviator Charles Lindbergh, who persuaded both the Guggenheim Foundation and the Carnegie Institute to support Goddard's experiments financially. He moved to the more suitable location of the Mescalere Ranch, near Roswell, New Mexico, where he worked until 1941. His liquid-fuelled rockets reached speeds of 1,100 km/h (700 mph) and heights of 2,500 m (8,000 ft). He investigated the use of the gyroscope to steady his rockets and the assembly of power units in clusters to increase the total thrust. In 1941 he moved to the naval establishment at Annapolis, Maryland, working on liquid-fuelled rockets to assist the take-off of aircraft from carriers. He worked for the US Government on this and the development of military rockets until his death from throat cancer in 1945. In all, he was granted 214 patents, roughly three per year of his life.

In 1960 the US Government admitted infringement of Goddard's patents during the rocket programme of the 1950s and awarded his widow a payment of $1,000,000, while the National Aeronautics and Space Administration (NASA) honoured him by naming the Goddard Spaceflight Center near Washington, DC, after him. The Goddard Memorial Library at Clark University, in his home town of Worcester, Massachusetts, was also named in his honour.

Further Reading
A. Osman, 1983, *Space History*, London: Michael Joseph.
P. Marsh, 1985, *The Space Business*, Harmondsworth: Penguin.
K.C. Farley, 1991, *Robert H. Goddard*, Englewood Cliffs, NJ: Silver Burdett Press.
T. Streissguth, 1994, *Rocket Man: The Story of Robert Goddard*, Minneapolis: Carolrhoda Books.

IMcN

Godowsky, Leopold Jr

b. 27 May 1900 Chicago, Illinois, USA
d. 1983

American musician and photographic experimenter whose researches, with those of his colleague Mannes, led to the introduction of the first commercial tripack colour film, Kodachrome.

Both from distinguished musical families, Godowsky and Leopold Damrosch Mannes met at Riverdale School in New York in 1916, and shared an interest in photography. They began experiments in methods of additive colour photography, gaining a patent for a three-colour projector. Godowsky went to the University of California to study chemistry, physics and mathematics, while working as a professional violinist; Mannes, a pianist, went to Harvard to study music and physics. They kept in touch, and after graduating they joined up in New York, working as musicians and experimenting in colour photography in their spare time.

Initially working in kitchens and bathrooms, they succeeded in creating a two-layer colour photographic plate, with emulsions separately sensitized to parts of the spectrum, and patented the process. This achievement was all the greater since they were unable to make the emulsions themselves and had to resort to buying commercial photographic plates so that they could scrape off the emulsions, remelt them and coat their experimental materials. In 1922 their work came to the attention of C.E.K. Mees, the leading photographic scientist and Director of the Eastman Kodak Research Laboratory in Rochester, New York. Mees arranged for plates to be coated to their specifications. With a grant from Kuhn, Loeb & Co. they were able to rent laboratory space. Learning of Rudolf Fischer's early work

on dye couplers, they worked to develop a new process incorporating them. Mees saw that their work, however promising, would not develop in an amateur laboratory, and in 1930 he invited them to join the Kodak Research Laboratory, where they arrived on 15 June 1931. Their new colleagues worked on ways of coating multi-layer film, while Mannes and Godowsky worked out a method of separately processing the individual layers in the exposed film. The result was Kodachrome film, the first of the modern integral tripack films, launched on 15 April 1935.

They remained with Eastman Kodak until December 1939; their work contributed to the later appearance of Ektachrome colour-reversal film and the Kodacolor and Eastman Color negative–positive colour processes. Mannes became the Director of his father's Music Academy in New York, remaining as such until his death in 1964. Godowsky returned to Westport, Connecticut, and continued to study mathematics at Columbia University. He carried out photographic research in his private laboratory up until the time of his death in 1983.

Further Reading
C.E.K. Mees, 1961, *From Dry Plates to Ektachrome Film*, New York.

BC

Goldberger, Joseph

b. 16 July 1874 Giralt, Hungary
d. 17 January 1929 Washington, DC, USA

American physician, virologist and epidemiologist, pioneer of egg viral culture and of the social approach to the aetiology of disease.

Of immigrant stock, Goldberger entered the College of New York in 1890 as an engineering student. In 1892 he transferred to medicine, and in 1895 he qualified at Bellevue Hospital. Following an internship and unhappy experience of private medical practice in Pennsylvania, he qualified for the US Public Health Service in 1899, remaining there until his death.

By 1910 he had been involved in field investigations of yellow fever, dengue and typhus. It was during this time that, with J.F. Anderson, he developed the egg culture techniques which enabled the demonstration of the filter-passing measles virus. The work with which he was most identified, however, was in connection with pellagra, at that time thought to be of microbial or protozoal origin. Using epidemiological techniques, he was able to demonstrate that it was in fact a nutritional deficiency disease, inducing the disease in prison volunteers on an abundant but protein-deficient diet.

Bibliography
1910, with J. Anderson, *Experimental Measles in the Monkey*, Public Health Report RG90, US Public Health Service, National Archives.

Further Reading
R.P. Parsons, 1943, *Trail to Light. A Biography of Joseph Goldberger*, New York.

MG

Goldmark, Peter Carl

b. 2 December 1906 Budapest, Hungary
d. 7 December 1977 Westchester Co., New York, USA

Austro-Hungarian engineer who developed the first commercial colour television system and the long-playing record.

After education in Hungary and a period as an assistant at the Technische Hochschule, Berlin, Goldmark moved to England, where he joined Pye of Cambridge and worked on an experimental thirty-line television system using a cathode ray tube (CRT) for the display. In 1936 he moved to the USA to work at Columbia Broadcasting Laboratories. There, with monochrome television based on the CRT virtually a practical proposition, he devoted his efforts to finding a way of producing colour TV images: in 1940 he gave his first demonstration of a working system. There then followed a series of experimental field-sequential colour TV systems based on segmented red, green and blue colour wheels and drums, where the problem was to find an acceptable compromise between bandwidth, resolution, colour flicker and colour-image breakup. Eventually he arrived at a system using a colour wheel in combination with a CRT containing a panchromatic phosphor screen, with a scanned raster of 405 lines and a primary colour rate of 144 fields per second. Despite the fact that the receivers were bulky, gave relatively poor, dim pictures and used standards totally incompatible with the existing 525-line, sixty fields per second interlaced monochrome (black and white) sys-

tem, in 1950 the Federal Communications Commission (FCC), anxious to encourage postwar revival of the industry, authorized the system for public broadcasting. Within eighteen months, however, bowing to pressure from the remainder of the industry, which had formed its own National Television Systems Committee (NTSC) to develop a much more satisfactory, fully compatible system based on the RCA three-gun shadowmask CRT, the FCC withdrew its approval.

While all this was going on, Goldmark had also been working on ideas for overcoming the poor reproduction, noise quality, short playing-time (about four minutes) and limited robustness and life of the long-established 78 rpm 12 in. (30 cm) diameter shellac gramophone record. The recent availability of a new, more robust, plastic material, vinyl, which had a lower surface noise, enabled him in 1948 to reduce the groove width some three times to 0.003 in. (0.0762 mm), use a more lightly loaded synthetic sapphire stylus and crystal transducer with improved performance, and reduce the turntable speed to $33\frac{1}{3}$ rpm, to give thirty minutes of high-quality music per side. This successful development soon led to the availability of stereophonic recordings, based on the ideas of Alan **Blumlein** at EMI in the 1930s.

In 1950 Goldmark became a vice-president of CBS, but he still found time to develop a scan conversion system for relaying television pictures to Earth from the *Lunar Orbiter* spacecraft. He also almost brought to the market a domestic electronic video recorder (EVR) system based on the thermal distortion of plastic film by separate luminance and coded colour signals, but this was overtaken by the video cassette recorder (VCR) system, which uses magnetic tape.

Principal Honours and Distinctions
Institute of Electrical and Electronics Engineers Morris N. Liebmann Award 1945. Institute of Electrical and Electronics Engineers Vladimir K. Zworykin Award 1961.

Bibliography
1951, with J.W. Christensen and J.J. Reeves, 'Colour television. USA Standard', *Proceedings of the Institute of Radio Engineers* 39: 1,288 (describes the development and standards for the short-lived field-sequential colour TV standard).

1949, with R. Snepvangers and W.S. Bachman, 'The Columbia long-playing microgroove recording system', *Proceedings of the Institute of Radio Engineers* 37: 923 (outlines the invention of the long-playing record).

Further Reading
E.W. Herold, 1976, 'A history of colour television displays', *Proceedings of the Institute of Electrical and Electronics Engineers* 64: 1,331.

See also **Baird, John Logie**.

KF

Goldstine, Herman H.
b. 13 September 1913 USA

American mathematician largely responsible for the development of ENIAC, an early electronic computer.

Goldstine studied mathematics at the University of Chicago, Illinois, gaining his PhD in 1936. After teaching mathematics there, he moved to a similar position at the University of Michigan in 1939, becoming an assistant professor. After the USA entered the Second World War, in 1942 he joined the army as a lieutenant in the Ballistic Missile Research Laboratory at the Aberdeen Proving Ground in Maryland. He was then assigned to the Moore School of Engineering at the University of Pennsylvania, where he was involved with Arthur **Burks** in building the valve-based Electronic Numerical Integrator and Computer (ENIAC) to compute ballistic tables. The machine was completed in 1946, but prior to this Goldstine had met John von Neumann of the Institute for Advanced Studies (IAS) at Princeton, New Jersey, and active collaboration between them had already begun. After the war he joined von Neumann as Assistant Director of the Computer Project at the Institute of Advanced Studies, Princeton, becoming its Director in 1954. There he developed the idea of computer-flow diagrams and, with von Neumann, built the first computer to use a magnetic drum for data storage. In 1958 he joined IBM as Director of the Mathematical Sciences Department, becoming Director of Development at the IBM Data Processing Headquarters in 1965. Two years later he became a Research Consultant, and in 1969 he became an IBM Research Fellow.

Principal Honours and Distinctions
Goldstine's many awards include three honorary degrees for his contributions to the development of computers.

Bibliography
1946, with A. Goldstine, 'The Electronic Numerical Integrator and Computer (ENIAC)', *Mathematical Tables and Other Aids to Computation* 2: 97 (describes the work on ENIAC).
1946, with A.W. Burks and J. von Neumann, 'Preliminary discussions of the logical design of an electronic computing instrument', *Princeton Institute for Advanced Studies*.
1972, *The Computer from Pascal to von Neumann*, Princeton University Press.
1977, 'A brief history of the computer', *Proceedings of the American Physical Society* 121: 339.

Further Reading
M. Campbell-Kelly & M.R. Williams (eds), 1985, *The Moore School Lectures (1946)*, Charles Babbage Institute Report Series for the History of Computing, Vol. 9.
M.R. Williams, 1985, *History of Computing Technology*, London: Prentice-Hall.

KF

Gongshu Pan (Kungshu Phan)
b. *c.*470 BC China
d. *c.*380 BC China

Chinese inventor of rampart-scaling ladders and flying automata.

Some traditions give Gongshu Pan's birth date as *c.*570 BC. Much of what is said of him is legendary, but this must derive from a hard core of fact. He was a noted artisan and engineer to the state of Lu. The invention of rampart-scaling ladders (used in siege operations) and of flying automata is attributed to him. He also devised a hook fender to grapple ships in combat. Yun Shi is traditionally regarded as Gongshu's wife and is credited with the invention of the collapsible umbrella. Gongshu is also credited with the invention of the kite (see vols. IV.1, p. 143, IV.3, p. 576 in the reference below).

Further Reading
J. Needham, *Science and Civilisation in China*, Cambridge: Cambridge University Press,

1965, 1971, vols. IV.2, pp. 43, 44, 96, 189, 192, 313, 573ff., 577; IV.3, pp. 681–2.

LRD

Gonin, Jules

b. 10 August 1870 Vaud, Switzerland
d. 11 June 1935 Lausanne, Switzerland

Swiss ophthalmic surgeon, originator of the therapy of retinal detachment with cautery.

After graduating form the University of Berne in 1894, Gonin was appointed Assistant to Marc Dufour, Professor of Ophthalmology at the Hôpital de l'Asile des Aveugles, Lausanne. At the International Congress of Ophthalmology at Lucerne in 1904, the general opinion was expressed that the condition of retinal detachment was untreatable. Gonin spent the following decade studying the condition, and by 1920 he was able to inform the French Ophthalmological Society that he had been able to cure a number of cases by the use of localized cautery. In the same year Gonin succeeded to the chair in Lausanne, which became a centre for the treatment of retinal detachment; despite initial scepticism, by 1929 a convincing series of cases led to international acceptance and the further development of the technique with the use of diathermy. On his death he left a substantial bequest to the blind of Lausanne whom he had not been able to cure. The Gonin Medal is awarded quadrennially to the outstanding international figure in ophthalmology.

Principal Honours and Distinctions
Marcel Benoist Prize 1928. Mackenzie Medal 1933. Von Graefe Medal 1936.

Bibliography
1918, *The Anatomical Causes of Detachment of the Retina.*
1929, 'Detachment of the retina', *Proceedings of the International Congress of Ophthalmology, Amsterdam.*

Further Reading
S. Duke-Elder, 1960–70, *System of Ophthalmology*, London.

MG

Gooch, Sir Daniel

b. 24 August 1816 Bedlington, Northumberland, England
d. 15 October 1889 Clewer Park, Berkshire, England

English engineer, first locomotive superintendent of the Great Western Railway and pioneer of transatlantic electric telegraphy.

Gooch gained experience as a pupil with several successive engineering firms, including Vulcan Foundry and Robert **Stephenson** & Co. In 1837 he was engaged by I.K. **Brunel**, who was then building the Great Western Railway (GWR) to the broad gauge of 7 ft ¼ in. (2.14 m), to take charge of the railway's locomotive department. He was just 21 years old. The initial locomotive stock comprised several locomotives built to such extreme specifications laid down by Brunel that they were virtually unworkable, and two 2-2-2 locomotives, *North Star* and *Morning Star*, which had been built by Robert Stephenson & Co. but left on the builder's hands. These latter were reliable and were perpetuated. An enlarged version, the 'Fire Fly' class, was designed by Gooch and built in quantity: Gooch was an early proponent of standardization. His highly successful 4-2-2 *Iron Duke* of 1847 became the prototype of GWR express locomotives for the next forty-five years, until the railway's last broad-gauge sections were narrowed. Meanwhile Gooch had been largely responsible for establishing Swindon Works, opened in 1843. In 1862 he designed 2-4-0 condensing tank locomotives to work the first urban underground railway, the Metropolitan Railway in London. Gooch retired in 1864 but was then instrumental in arranging for Brunel's immense steamship *Great Eastern* to be used to lay the first transatlantic electric telegraph cable: he was on board when the cable was successfully laid in 1866. He had been elected Member of Parliament for Cricklade (which constituency included Swindon) in 1865, and the same year he had accepted an invitation to become Chairman of the Great Western Railway Company, which was in financial difficulties; he rescued it from near bankruptcy and remained Chairman until shortly before his death. The greatest engineering work undertaken during his chairmanship was the boring of the Severn Tunnel.

Principal Honours and Distinctions
Knighted 1866 (on completion of transatlantic telegraph).

Bibliography
1972, *Sir Daniel Gooch, Memoirs and Diary*, ed. R.B. Wilson, with introd. and notes, Newton Abbot: David & Charles.

Further Reading
A. Platt, 1987, *The Life and Times of Daniel Gooch*, Gloucester: Alan Sutton (puts Gooch's career into context).
C. Hamilton Ellis, 1958, *Twenty Locomotive Men*, Ian Allan (contains a good short biography).
J. Kieve, 1973, *The Electric Telegraph*, Newton Abbot: David & Charles, pp. 112–5.

PJGR

Goodyear, Charles

b. 29 December 1800 New Haven, Connecticut, USA
d. 1 July 1860 New York, USA

American inventor of the vulcanization of rubber.

Goodyear entered his father's country hardware business before setting up his own concern in Philadelphia. While visiting New York, he noticed in the window of the Roxburgh India Rubber Company a rubber life-preserver. Goodyear offered to improve its inflating valve, but the manager, impressed with Goodyear's inventiveness, persuaded him to tackle a more urgent problem, that of seeking a means of preventing rubber from becoming tacky and from melting or decomposing when heated. Goodyear tried treatments with one substance after another, without success. In 1838 he started using Nathaniel M. Hayward's process of spreading sulphur on rubber. He accidentally dropped a mass of rubber and sulphur on to a hot stove and noted that the mixture did not melt: Goodyear had discovered the vulcanization of rubber. More experiments were needed to establish the correct proportions for a uniform mix, and eventually he was granted his celebrated patent no. 3633 of 15 June 1844. Goodyear's researches had been conducted against a background of crippling financial difficulties and he was forced to dispose of licences to vulcanize rubber at less than their real value, in order to pay off his most pressing debts.

Goodyear travelled to Europe in 1851 to extend his patents. To promote his process, he designed a spectacular exhibit for London, consisting of furniture, floor covering, jewellery and other items made of rubber. A similar exhibit in Paris in 1855 won him the Grande Médaille d'honneur and the Croix de la Légion d'honneur from Napoleon III. Patents were granted to him in all countries except England. The improved properties of vulcanized rubber and its stability over a much wider range of temperatures greatly increased its applications; output rose from a meagre 31.5 tonnes a year in 1827 to over 28,000 tonnes by 1900. Even so, Goodyear profited little from his invention, and he bequeathed to his family debts amounting to over $200,000.

Principal Honours and Distinctions
Grande Médaille d'honneur 1855. Croix de la Légion d'honneur 1855.

Bibliography
15 June 1844, US patent no. 3633 (vulcanization of rubber).
1853, *Gum Elastic and Its Varieties* (includes some biographical material).

Further Reading
B.K. Pierce, 1866, *Trials of an Inventor: Life and Discoveries of Charles Goodyear*.
H. Allen, 1989, *Charles Goodyear: An Intimate Biographical Sketch*, Akron, Ohio: Goodyear Tire & Rubber Company.

LRD

Gordon, Lewis Dunbar Brodie

b. 6 March 1815 Edinburgh, Scotland
d. 1876

Scottish civil engineer.

Lewis Gordon attended the High School in Edinburgh and Edinburgh University. He was unusual amongst British engineers of his generation in also spending some time at foreign educational establishments, including the School of Mines at Freiberg in Saxony and the Ecole Polytechnique in Paris. He served under Marc **Brunel** in the final stages of the construction of the Thames Tunnel, from 1837 to 1840. After this, he set up a civil engineering partnership with

Lawrence Hill in Glasgow in 1840 and was then appointed as the first holder of the Regius Chair of Civil Engineering and Mechanics at Glasgow University, 1841–55. He seems to have been frustrated by the lack of facilities at Glasgow, and handed over to his deputy, W.J.M. **Rankine** in 1855, in order to concentrate on his growing private practice which he had been building up during his professorship at the university. His practice was involved in designing iron bridges and introducing wire rope into Britain; he also became involved with submarine cables and telegraphy. With Charles **Liddell**, he was the engineer for several railways in England and Wales, including the Crumlin Viaduct on the Newport, Abergavenny and Hereford Railway.

Further Reading
Although he was frequently referred to in accounts of the period, there appears to be no good biographical work on Gordon. However, see Buchanan, 1989, *The Engineers.*

AB

Gorton, Richard
fl. 1790s England

English patentee of a power loom for weaving narrow fabrics.

In May 1791, Richard Gorton took out a patent for a new type of power-driven loom for narrow fabrics to 'work one or several pieces at the same time, either by hand, lath, steam engine, or by water-machinery'. The sley with the reed was worked by a crank, and the picker by a lever and cam. The shuttle-box had springs to retain the shuttle, and the warp was kept tight by weights. A stop, which was usually pushed out of the way by the shuttle entering the box, prevented the sley or lath 'driving the shuttle against the piece' when the shuttle stuck in the middle. One particularly interesting feature was the sizing of the warp threads by means of brushes and a roller that turned in a square trough filled with size. This pre-dates **Radcliffe**'s sizing machine, which is always considered the first, by a number of years. The mill in which these machines worked was at Cuckney, near Mansfield, England. In 1788 Thomas Gorton had installed one of the earliest **Boulton** & **Watt** rotative steam engines there.

Bibliography
May 1791, British patent no. 1,804 (power loom for weaving narrow fabrics).

Further Reading
R.L. Hills, 1970, *Power in the Industrial Revolution*, Manchester (provides an account of Gorton's patent).
S.D. Chapman, 1967, *The Early Factory Masters*, Newton Abbot (makes a brief mention of this invention).

RLH

Gossage, William
b. 1799 Burgh-in-the-Marsh, Lincolnshire, England
d. 9 April 1877 Bowdon, Cheshire, England

English industrial chemist, inventor of the absorption tower.

At the age of 12 he was working for his father, who was a chemist and druggist. When he was old enough, he started in the same trade on his own account at Leamington, but soon turned to the making of salt and alkali at a works in Stoke Prior, Worcestershire. In 1850 he moved to Widnes, Lancashire, and established a plant for the manufacture of alkali and soap. Gossage's soap became famous, and some 200,000 tons of it were sold during the period 1862 to 1887. Gossage made important improvements to the **Leblanc** process. Hitherto, the large quantities of hydrogen chloride discharged into the atmosphere had been a considerable nuisance and a cause of much litigation from aggrieved parties. Gossage introduced the absorption tower, in which the ascending hydrogen chloride was absorbed by a descending stream of water. An outcome of this improvement was the Alkali Act of 1863, which required manufacturers to absorb up to 95 per cent of the offending gas. Gossage later took out many other industrial chemical patents, and for a time he was engaged in copper smelting with works in both Widnes and Neath, South Wales.

Further Reading
J. Fenwick Allen, 1907, *Some Founders of the Chemical Industry*, London.
D.W.F. Hardie, 1950, *A History of the Chemical Industry in Widnes*, London.

LRD

Goucher, John

b. *c.*1831 Woodsetts, Yorkshire, England
d. unknown

English engineer and inventor of the rubbing bars used on threshing machines and combine harvesters.

John Goucher was the son of a Yorkshire farmer who began his employed life as a carpenter. In 1851, at the age of 20, he was living on the farm of his father and employing four labourers. He developed and patented a means of wrapping wire around the individual bars of a threshing machine drum in such a way that grooves were formed in them. These grooves allowed the threshed grain to pass through without being crushed or otherwise damaged.

Bibliography
Other patents credited to him range from devices for the propelling of ships in 1854, beaters for threshing machines in 1848, 1856, and again in 1861, stacking corn and other crops in the same year, improvements to steam boilers in 1863, for preserving life in water in 1867, threshing machines in 1873 and 1874, steam engines in 1884, and threshing machines in 1885.

AP

Goulding, John

b. 1791 Massachusetts, USA
d. 1877

American inventor of an early form of condenser carding machine.

The condenser method of spinning was developed chiefly by manufacturers and machine makers in eastern Massachusetts between 1824 and 1826. John Goulding, a machinist from Dedham in Massachusetts, combined the ring doffer, patented by Ezekiel Hale in 1825, and the revolving twist tube, patented by George Danforth in 1824; with the addition of twisting keys in the tubes, the carded woollen sliver could be divided and then completely and continuously twisted. He divided the carded web longitudinally with the ring doffer and twisted these strips to consolidate them into slubbings. The dividing was carried out by covering the periphery of the doffer cylinder with separate rings of card clothing and spacing these rings apart by rings of leather, so that instead of width-way detached strips leaving the card, the strips were continuous and did not require piecing. The strips were passed through rotating tubes and wound on bobbins, and although the twist was false it sufficed to compress the fibres together ready for spinning. Goulding patented his invention in both Britain and the USA in 1826, but while his condensers were very successful and within twenty years had been adopted by a high proportion of woollen mills in America, they were not adopted in Britain until much later. Goulding also worked on other improvements to woollen machinery: he developed friction drums, on which the spools of roving from the condenser cards were placed to help transform the woollen jenny into the woollen mule or jack.

Bibliography
1826, British patent no. 5,355 (condenser carding machine).

Further Reading
D.J. Jeremy, 1981, *Transatlantic Industrial Revolution. The Diffusion of Textile Technologies Between Britain and America, 1790–1830s,* Oxford (provides a good explanation of the development of the condenser card).
W. English, 1969, *The Textile Industry,* London (a brief account).
C. Singer (ed.), 1958, *A History of Technology,* Vol. IV, Oxford: Clarendon Press (a brief account).

RLH

Graham, George

b. *c.*1674 Cumberland, England
d. 16 November 1751 London, England

English watch- and clockmaker who invented the cylinder escapement for watches, the first successful dead-beat escapement for clocks and the mercury compensation pendulum.

Graham's father died soon after his birth, so he was raised by his brother. In 1688 he was apprenticed to the London clockmaker Henry Aske, and in 1695 he gained his freedom. He was employed as a journeyman by **Tompion** in 1696 and later married his niece. In 1711 he formed a partnership with Tompion and effectively ran the business in Tompion's declining years; he took over the business after Tompion died in 1713. In addition to his horological interests he also made scientific instruments, specializing in those for astronomical use. As a person, he was well respected and appears to have lived up to the epithet 'Honest George Graham'. He befriended John **Harrison** when he first went to London and lent him money to further his researches at a time when they might have conflicted with his own interests.

The two common forms of escapement in use in Graham's time, the anchor escapement for clocks and the verge escapement for watches, shared the same weakness: they interfered severely with the free oscillation of the pendulum and the balance, and thus adversely affected the timekeeping. Tompion's two frictional rest escapements, the dead-beat for clocks and the horizontal for watches, had provided a partial solution by eliminating recoil (the momentary reversal of the motion of the timepiece), but they had not been successful in practice. Around 1720 Graham produced his own much improved version of the dead-beat escapement which became a standard feature of regulator clocks, at least in Britain, until its supremacy was challenged at the end of the nineteenth century by the superior accuracy of the **Riefler** clock. Another feature of the regulator clock owed to Graham was the mercury compensation pendulum, which he invented in 1722 and published four years later. The bob of this pendulum contained mercury, the surface of which rose or fell with changes in temperature, compensating for the concomitant variation in the length of the pendulum rod. Graham devised his mercury pendulum after he had failed to achieve compensation by means of the difference in expansion between various metals. He then turned his attention to improving Tompion's horizontal escapement, and by 1725 the cylinder escapement existed in what was virtually its final form. From the following year he fitted this escapement to all his watches, and it was also used extensively by London makers for their precision watches. It proved to be somewhat lacking in durability, but this problem was overcome later in the century by using a ruby cylinder, notably by Abraham Louis **Breguet**. It was revived, in a cheaper form, by the Swiss and the French in the nineteenth century and was produced in vast quantities.

Principal Honours and Distinctions
FRS 1720. Master of the Clockmakers' Company 1722.

Bibliography
Graham contributed many papers to the *Philosophical Transactions of the Royal Society*, in particular 'A contrivance to avoid the irregularities in a clock's motion occasion'd by the action of heat and cold upon the rod of the pendulum' (1726) 34: 40–4.

Further Reading
Britten's Watch & Clock Maker's Handbook Dictionary and Guide, 1978, rev. Richard Good, 16th edn, London, pp. 81, 84, 232 (for a technical description of the dead-beat and cylinder escapements and the mercury compensation pendulum).
A.J. Turner, 1972, 'The introduction of the dead-beat escapement: a new document', *Antiquarian Horology* 8: 71.
E.A. Battison, 1972, biography, *Biographical Dictionary of Science*, ed. C.C. Gillespie, Vol. V, New York, 490–2 (contains a résumé of Graham's non-horological activities).

See also **Barlow, Edward**; **Guillaume, Charles-Edouard**.

DV

Gramme, Zénobe Théophile

b. 4 April 1826 Jehay-Bodignée, Belgium
d. 20 January 1901 Bois de Colombes, Paris, France

Belgian engineer whose improvements to the dynamo produced a machine ready for successful commercial exploitation.

Gramme trained as a carpenter and showed an early talent for working with machinery. Moving to Paris he found employment in the Alliance factory as a model maker. With a growing interest in electricity he left to become an instrument maker with Heinrich Daniel Rühmkorff. In 1870 he patented the uniformly wound ring-armature dynamo with which his name is associated. Together with Hippolyte Fontaine, in 1871 Gramme opened a factory to manufacture his dynamos. They rapidly became a commercial success for both arc lighting and electrochemical purposes, international publicity being achieved at exhibitions in Vienna, Paris and Philadelphia. It was the realization that a Gramme machine was capable of running as a motor, i.e. the reversibility of function, that illustrated the entire concept of power transmission by electricity. This was first publicly demonstrated in 1873. In 1874 Gramme reduced the size and increased the efficiency of his generators by relying completely on the principle of self-excitation. It was the first practical machine in which were combined the features of continuity of commutation, self-excitation, good lamination of the armature core and a reasonably good magnetic circuit. This dynamo, together with the self-regulating arc lamps then available, made possible the innumerable electric-lighting schemes that followed. These were of the greatest importance in demonstrating that electric lighting was a practical and economic means of illumination. Gramme also designed an alternator to operate **Jablochkoff** candles. For some years he took an active part in the operations of the Société Gramme and also experimented in his own workshop without collaboration, but made no further contribution to electrical technology.

Principal Honours and Distinctions
Knight Commander, Order of Leopold of Belgium 1897. Chevalier de la Légion d'honneur. Chevalier, Order of the Iron Crown, Austria.

Bibliography
9 June 1870, British patent no. 1,668 (the ring armature machine).
1871, *Comptes rendus* 73: 175–8 (Gramme's first description of his invention).

Further Reading
W.J. King, 1962, *The Development of Electrical Technology in the 19th Century*, Washington, DC: Smithsonian Institution, Paper 30, pp. 377–90 (an extensive account of Gramme's machines).
S.P. Thompson, 1901, obituary, *Electrician* 66: 509–10.
C.C. Gillispie (ed.), 1972, *Dictionary of Scientific Biography*, Vol. V, New York, p. 496.

GW

Grant, George Barnard

b. 21 December 1849 Farmingdale, Gardiner, Maine, USA
d. 16 August 1917 Pasadena, California, USA

American mechanical engineer and inventor of Grant's Difference Engine.

George B. Grant was descended from families who came from Britain in the seventeenth century and was educated at the Bridgton (Maine) Academy, the Chandler Scientific School of Dartmouth College and the Lawrence Scientific School of Harvard College, where he graduated with the degree of BS in 1873. As an undergraduate he became interested in calculating machines, and his paper 'On a new difference engine' was published in the *American Journal of Science* in August 1871. He also took out his first patents relating to calculating machines in 1872 and 1873. A machine of his design known as 'Grant's Difference Engine' was exhibited at the Centennial Exposition in Philadelphia in 1876. Similar machines were also manufactured for sale; being sturdy and reliable, they did much to break down the prejudice against the use of calculating machines in business. Grant's work on calculating machines led to a requirement for accurate gears, so he established a machine shop for gear cutting at Charlestown, Massachusetts. He later moved the business to Boston and incorporated it under the name of Grant's Gear Works Inc., and continued to control it until his death. He also established two other gear-cutting shops, the Philadelphia Gear Works Inc., which he disposed of in 1911, and the Cleveland Gear Works Inc., which he also disposed of after a few years. Grant's commercial success was in connection with gear cutting and in this field he obtained several patents and contributed articles to the *American Machinist*. However, he continued to take an interest in calculating machines and in his later years carried out experimental work on their development.

Bibliography
1871, 'On a new difference engine', *American Journal of Science* (August).
1885, *Chart and Tables for Bevel Gears*.
1885, *A Handbook on the Teeth of Gear Wheels*, Boston, Mass.
1891, *Odontics, or the Theory and Practice of the Teeth of Gears*, Lexington, Mass.

Further Reading
R.S. Woodbury, 1958, *History of the Gear-cutting Machine*, Cambridge, Mass. (describes his gear-cutting machine).

RTS

Gray, Elisha

b. 2 August 1835 Barnesville, Ohio, USA
d. 21 January 1901 Newtonville, Massachusetts, USA

American inventor who was only just beaten by Alexander Graham Bell in the race for the first telephone patent.

Initially apprenticed to a carpenter, Gray soon showed an interest in chemistry, but he eventually studied electrical engineering at Oberlin College, Oberlin, Ohio, in the late 1850s. In 1869 he founded the Western Electric Manufacturing Company, where he devised an electric-needle annunciator for use in hotels and lifts and carried out experimental work aimed at the development of a means of distant-speech communication. After successful realization of a liquid-based microphone and public demonstrations of a receiver using a metal diaphragm, on 14 February 1876 he deposited a caveat of intention to file a patent claim within three months for the invention of the telephone, only to learn that Alexander Graham Bell had filed a full patent claim only three hours earlier on the same day. Following litigation, the patent was eventually awarded to Bell. In 1880 Gray was appointed Professor of Dynamic Electricity at Oberlin College, but he appears to have retained his business interests since in 1891 he was both a member of the firm of Gray and Barton and electrician to his old firm, Western Electric. Subsequently, in 1895, he invented the TelAutograph, a form of remote-writing telegraph, or facsimile, capable of operating over short distances. The system used a transmitter in which the x and y movements of a writing stylus were coupled to a pair of variable resistors. In turn, these were connected by two telegraph wires to a pair of receiving coils, which were used to control the position of a pen on a sheet of paper, thus replicating the movement of the original stylus.

Bibliography
1878, *Experimental Research in Electro-Harmonic Telegraph and Telephony, 1867–76*.

Further Reading
J. Munro, 1891, *Heroes of the Telegraph*.
D.A. Hounshill, 1975, 'Elisha Gray and the telephone. On the disadvantage of being an expert', *Technology and Culture* 16: 133.
—— 1976, 'Bell and Gray. Contrast in style, politics and etiquette', *Proceedings of the Institute of Electrical and Electronics Engineers* 64: 1,305.
International Telecommunications Union, 1965, *From Semaphore to Satellite*, Geneva.

KF

Gray, Gustave le

See **Le Gray, Gustave**.

Greathead, James Henry

b. 6 August 1844 Grahamstown, Cape Colony (now South Africa)
d. 21 October 1896 Streatham, London, England

British civil engineer, inventor of the Greathead tunnelling shield.

Greathead came to England in 1859 to complete his education. In 1864 he began a three-year pupillage with the civil engineer Peter W. Barlow, after which he was engaged as an assistant engineer on the extension of the Midland Railway from Bedford to London. In 1869 he was entrusted with the construction of the Tower Subway under the River Thames; this was carried out using a cylindrical wrought-iron shield which was forced forward by six large screws as material was excavated in front of it. This work was completed the same year. In 1870 he set himself up as a consulting engineer, and from 1873 he was Resident Engineer on the Hammersmith and Richmond extensions of the Metropolitan District Railway. He assisted in the preparation of several other railway projects including the Regent's Canal Railway in 1880, the Dagenham Dock and the Metropolitan Outer Circle Railways in 1881, a new line from London to Eastbourne and a number of Irish light railways. He worked on a bill for the City and South London Railway, which was built between 1886 and 1890; here compressed air was used to prevent the inrush of water, a method for tunnelling which was generally adopted from then on. He invented apparatus for the application of water to excavate in front of the shield as well as for injecting cement-grout behind the lining of the tunnel.

He was joint engineer with Sir Douglas Fox for the construction of the Liverpool Overhead Railway, and held the same post with W.R. Galbraith on the Waterloo and City Railway; he was also associated with Sir John Fowler and Sir Benjamin Baker in the construction of the Central London Railway. He died, aged 52, before the completion of some of these projects.

Further Reading
Obituary, 1896, *Proceedings of the Institution of Mechanical Engineers*.
O. Green, 1987, *The London Underground: An Illustrated History*, London: Ian Allan (in association with the London Transport Museum).
P.P. Holman, 1990, *The Amazing Electric Tube: A History of the City and South London Railway*, London: London Transport Museum.
IMcN

Green, Charles
b. 31 January 1785 London, England
d. 26 March 1870 London, England

English balloonist who introduced the use of coal gas for balloons.

Charles Green lived in London at a time when gas mains were being installed to supply coal gas for the recently introduced gas lighting. He was interested in the exploits of balloonists but lacked the finance needed to construct a balloon and fill it with expensive hydrogen. He decided to experiment with coal gas, which was very much cheaper, albeit a little heavier, than hydrogen: a larger balloon would be needed to lift the same weight. Green made his first ascent on 19 July 1821 to celebrate the coronation of King George IV. His large balloon was prepared in Green Park, London, and filled from the gas main in Piccadilly. He made a spectacular ascent to 11,000 ft (3,350 m), thus proving the suitability of coal gas, which was readily available and cheap. Like many balloonists, Green was also a showman. He made ascents on horseback or with fireworks to attract spectators. He did, however, try out some new ideas, such as cemented fabric joints (instead of stitching) for a huge new balloon, the *Royal Vauxhall*. On its first flight, in

September 1836, this impressive balloon carried Green plus eight passengers. On 7 November 1836 Green and two friends ascended from Vauxhall Gardens, London, to make a long-distance flight. They landed safely in the Duchy of Nassau, Germany, having covered a record 480 miles (772 km) in eighteen hours. To help control the height of the balloon on this flight, Green fitted a long, heavy rope which trailed on the ground. If the balloon started to rise, then more of the 'trail rope' was lifted off the ground, resulting in an increase in the weight to be lifted and a reduction in the rate of ascent. This idea had been suggested earlier by Thomas Baldwin in 1785, but Green developed it and in 1840 proposed to use if for a flight across the Atlantic: he later abandoned this plan.

Charles Green made over five hundred ascents and died in bed at the age of 85, no small age for a balloonist.

Principal Honours and Distinctions
Member of the (Royal) Aeronautical Society, founded in 1866.

Bibliography
1836, *Authentic Narrative of the Great Balloon Voyage and Descent in Germany*, London (a pamphlet).

Further Reading
L.T.C. Rolt, 1966, *The Aeronauts*, London (provides a full account of Green's achievements).
J.E. Hodgson, 1924, *the History of Aeronautics in Great Britain*, London.
T. Monck Mason, 1838, *Aeronautica*, London.
JDS

Gregory, Sir Charles Hutton
b. 14 October 1817 Woolwich, England
d. 10 January 1898 London, England

English civil engineer, inventor of the railway semaphore signal.

Gregory's father was Professor of Mathematics at the Royal Military Academy, Woolwich. C.H. Gregory himself, after working for Robert **Stephenson**, was appointed Engineer to the London & Croydon Railway in 1839. On it, at New Cross in 1841, he installed a semaphore signal derived from signalling apparatus used by the Royal Navy; two hinged semaphore arms projected either side from the top of a post, signalling to drivers of trains in each direction of travel. In horizontal position each arm signified 'danger', an arm inclined at 45° meant 'caution' and the vertical position, in which the arms disappeared within a slot in the post, meant 'all right'. Gregory's signal was the forerunner of semaphore signals adopted on railways worldwide. In 1843 Gregory invented the stirrup frame: signal arms were connected to stirrups that were pushed down by the signalman's foot in order to operate them, while the points were operated by levers. The stirrups were connected together to prevent conflicting signals from being shown. This was a predecessor of interlocking. In 1846 Gregory became Engineer to the Bristol & Exeter Railway, where in 1848 he co-operated with W.B. **Adams** in the development and operation of the first self-propelled railcar. He later did civil engineering work in Italy and France, was Engineer to the Somerset Central and Dorset Central railways and became Consulting Engineer for the government railways in Ceylon (now Sri Lanka), Cape of Good Hope, Straits Settlements and Trinidad.

Principal Honours and Distinctions
Companion of the Order of St Michael and St George 1876. Knight Commander of the Order of St Michael and St George 1883. President, Institution of Civil Engineers 1867–8.

Bibliography
1841, *Practical Rules for the Management of a Locomotive Engine*, London (one of the earliest such textbooks).

Further Reading
Obituary, 1898, *Engineering* 65 (14 January).

See also **Saxby, John.**

PJGR

Gresley, Sir Herbert Nigel
b. 19 June 1876 Edinburgh, Scotland
d. 5 April 1941 Hertford, England

English mechanical engineer, designer of the A4-class 4–6–2 locomotive holding the world speed record for steam traction.

Gresley was the son of the Rector of Netherseale, Derbyshire; he was educated at Marlborough and by the age of 13 was skilled at making sketches of locomotives. In 1893 he became a pupil of F.W. **Webb** at Crewe works, London & North Western Railway, and in 1898 he moved to Horwich works, Lancashire & Yorkshire Railway, to gain drawing-office experience under J.A.F. **Aspinall**, subsequently becoming Foreman of the locomotive running sheds at Blackpool. In 1900 he transferred to the carriage and wagon department, and in 1904 he had risen to become its Assistant Superintendent. In 1905 he moved to the Great Northern Railway, becoming Superintendent of its carriage and wagon department at Doncaster under H.A. **Ivatt**. In 1906 he designed and produced a bogie luggage van with steel underframe, teak body, elliptical roof, bowed ends and buckeye couplings: this became the prototype for East Coast main-line coaches built over the next thirty-five years. In 1911 Gresley succeeded Ivatt as Locomotive, Carriage & Wagon Superintendent. His first locomotive was a mixed-traffic 2–6–0, his next a 2–8–0 for freight. From 1915 he worked on the design of a 4–6–2 locomotive for express passenger traffic: as with Ivatt's 4–4–2s, the trailing axle would allow the wide firebox needed for Yorkshire coal. He also devised a means by which two sets of valve gear could operate the valves on a three-cylinder locomotive and applied it for the first time on a 2–8–0 built in 1918. The system was complex, but a later simplified form was used on all subsequent Gresley three-cylinder locomotives, including his first 4–6–2 which appeared in 1922. In 1921, Gresley introduced the first British restaurant car with electric cooking facilities.

With the grouping of 1923, the Great Northern Railway was absorbed into the London & North Eastern Railway and Gresley was appointed Chief Mechanical Engineer. More 4–6–2s were built, the first British class of such wheel arrangement. Modifications to their valve gear, along lines developed by G.J. **Churchward**, reduced their coal consumption sufficiently to enable them to run non-stop between London and Edinburgh. So that enginemen might change over en route, some of the locomotives were equipped with corridor tenders from 1928. The design was steadily improved in detail, and by comparison an experimental 4–6–4 with a water-tube boiler that Gresley produced in 1929 showed no overall benefit. A successful high-powered 2–8–2 was built in 1934, following the introduction of third-class sleeping cars, to haul 500-ton passenger trains between Edinburgh and Aberdeen.

In 1932 the need to meet increasing road competition had resulted in the end of a long-standing agreement between East Coast and West Coast railways, that train journeys between London and Edinburgh by either route should be scheduled to take 8¼ hours. Seeking to accelerate train services, Gresley studied high-speed, diesel–electric railcars in Germany and petrol–electric railcars in France. He considered them for the London & North Eastern Railway, but a test run by a train hauled by one of his 4–6–2s in 1934, which reached 108 mph (174 km/h), suggested that a steam train could better the railcar proposals while its accommodation would be more comfortable. To celebrate the Silver Jubilee of King George V, a high-speed, streamlined train between London and Newcastle upon Tyne was proposed, the first such train in Britain. An improved 4–6–2, the A4 class, was designed with modifications to ensure free running and an ample reserve of power up hill. Its streamlined outline included a wedge-shaped front which reduced wind resistance and helped to lift the exhaust clear of the cab windows at speed. The first locomotive of the class, named *Silver Link*, ran at an average speed of 100 mph (161 km/h) for 43 miles (69 km), with a maximum speed of 112½ mph (181 km/h), on a seven-coach test train on 27 September 1935: the locomotive went into service hauling the Silver Jubilee express single-handed (since others of the class had still to be completed) for the first three weeks, a round trip of 536 miles (863 km) daily, much of it at 90 mph (145 km/h), without any mechanical troubles at all. Coaches for the Silver Jubilee had teak-framed, steel-panelled bodies on all-steel, welded underframes; windows were double glazed; and there was a pressure ventilation/heating system. Comparable trains were introduced between London Kings Cross and Edinburgh in 1937 and to Leeds in 1938.

Gresley did not hesitate to incorporate outstanding features from elsewhere into his locomotive designs and was well aware of the work of André **Chapelon** in France. Four A4s built in 1938 were equipped with Kylchap twin blast-pipes and double chimneys to improve performance still further. The first of these to be completed, no. 4468, *Mallard*, on 3 July 1938

ran a test train at over 120 mph (193 km/h) for 2 miles (3.2 km) and momentarily achieved 126 mph (203 km/h), the world speed record for steam traction. J. Duddington was the driver and T. Bray the fireman. The use of high-speed trains came to an end with the Second World War. The A4s were then demonstrated to be powerful as well as fast: one was noted hauling a 730-ton, 22-coach train at an average speed exceeding 75 mph (120 km/h) over 30 miles (48 km). The war also halted electrification of the Manchester–Sheffield line, on the 1,500 volt DC overhead system; however, anticipating eventual resumption, Gresley had a prototype main-line Bo-Bo electric locomotive built in 1941. Sadly, Gresley died from a heart attack while still in office.

Principal Honours and Distinctions
Knighted 1936. President, Institution of Locomotive Engineers 1927 and 1934. President, Institution of Mechanical Engineers 1936.

Further Reading
F.A.S. Brown, 1961, *Nigel Gresley, Locomotive Engineer*, Ian Allan (full-length biography).
John Bellwood and David Jenkinson, *Gresley and Stanier. A Centenary Tribute* (a good comparative account).

See also **Bulleid, Oliver Vaughan Snell**.

PJGR

Griffith, Alan Arnold
b. 13 June 1893 London, England
d. 13 October 1963 Farnborough, England

English research engineer responsible for many original ideas, including jet-lift aircraft.

Griffith was very much a 'boffin', for he was a quiet, thoughtful man who shunned public appearances, yet he produced many revolutionary ideas. During the First World War he worked at the Royal Aircraft Factory, Farnborough, where he carried out research into structural analysis. Because of his use of soap films in solving torsion problems, he was nicknamed 'Soap-bubble'.

During the 1920s Griffith carried out research into gas-turbine design at the Royal Aircraft Establishment (RAE; as the Royal Aircraft Factory had become). In 1929 he made proposals for a gas turbine driving a propeller (a turboprop), but the idea was shelved. In the 1930s he was head

of the Engine Department of the RAE and developed multi-stage axial compressors, which
were later used in jet engines. This work attracted
the attention of E.W. (later Lord) Hives of Rolls-
Royce who persuaded Griffith to join Rolls-
Royce in 1939. His first major project was a
'contra-flow' jet engine, which was a good idea
but a practical failure. However, Griffith's axial-
flow compressor experience played an important
part in the success of Rolls-Royce jet engines
from the *Avon* onwards. He also proposed the
bypass principle used for the *Conway*.

Griffith experimented with suction to control
the boundary layer on wings, but his main interest in the 1950s centred on vertical-take-off and
-landing aircraft. He developed the remarkable
'flying bedstead', which consisted of a framework
(the bedstead) in which two jet engines were
mounted with their jets pointing downwards,
thus lifting the machine vertically. It first flew in
1954 and provided much valuable data. The
Short *SC 1* aircraft followed, with four small jets
providing lift for vertical take-off and one conventional jet to provide forward propulsion. This
flew successfully in the late 1950s and early
1960s. Griffith proposed an airliner with lifting
engines, but the weight of the lifting engines
when not in use would have been a serious handicap. He retired in 1960.

Principal Honours and Distinctions
CBE 1948. FRS 1941. Royal Aeronautical Society Silver Medal 1955; Blériot Medal 1962.

Bibliography
Griffith produced many technical papers in his
early days; for example:
1926, *Aerodynamic Theory of Turbine Design*,
Farnborough.

Further Reading
D. Eyre, 1966, 'Dr A.A. Griffith, CBE, FRS',
Journal of the Royal Aeronautical Society (June)
(a detailed obituary).
F.W. Armstrong, 1976, 'The aero engine and its
progress: fifty years after Griffith', *Aeronauti-
cal Journal* (December).
O. Stewart, 1966, *Aviation: The Creative Ideas*,
London (provides brief descriptions of Grif-
fith's many projects).

JDS

Grimthorpe (of Grimthorpe), Edmund Beckett, Baron
b. 12 May 1816 Newark, Nottinghamshire,
England
d. 29 April 1905 St Albans, Hertfordshire,
England

*English lawyer and amateur horologist who was
the first successfully to apply the gravity
escapement to public clocks.*

Born Edmund Beckett Denison, he was educated at Eton and Trinity College, Cambridge,
where he studied mathematics, graduating in
1838. He was called to the Bar in 1841 and became a Queen's Counsel in 1854. He built up a
large and lucrative practice which gave him the
independence to pursue his many interests outside law. His interest in horology may have been
stimulated by a friend and fellow lawyer, J.M.
Bloxham, who interestingly had invented a gravity escapement with an affinity to the escapement
eventually used by Denison. Denison studied horology with his usual thoroughness and by 1850
he had published his *Rudimentary Treatise on
Clock and Watchmaking*. It was natural, therefore, that he should have been invited to be a
referee when a disagreement arose over the design of the clock for the new Houses of Parliament. Typically, he interpreted his brief very
liberally and designed the clock himself. The
most distinctive feature of the clock, in its final
form, was the incorporation of a gravity escapement. A gravity escapement was particularly desirable in a public clock as it enabled the
pendulum to receive a constant impulse (and
thus swing with a constant amplitude), despite
the variable forces that might be exerted by the
wind on the exposed hands. The excellent performance of the prestigious clock at Westminster
made Denison's form of gravity escapement *de
rigueur* for large mechanical public clocks produced in Britain and in many other countries. In
1874 he inherited his father's baronetcy, dropping the Denison name, but later adopted the
name Grimthorpe when he was created a Baron
in 1886.

Principal Honours and Distinctions
Peerage 1886. President, British Horological
Institute 1868–1905.

Bibliography
His highly idiosyncratic *A Rudimentary Treatise on Clocks and Watchmaking*, first published in 1850, went through eight editions, with slight changes of title, and became the most influential work in English on the subject of public clocks.

Further Reading
Vaudrey Mercer, 1977, *The Life and Letters of Edward John Dent*, London, pp. 650–1 (provides biographical information relating to horology; also contains a reliable account of Denison's involvement with the clock at Westminster).
A.L. Rawlings, 1948, *The Science of Clocks and Watches*, repub. 1974, pp. 98–102 (provides a technical assessment of Denison's escapement).

DV

Gropius, Walter Adolf
b. 18 May 1883 Berlin, Germany
d. 5 July 1969 Boston, USA

German co-founder of the modern movement of architecture.

A year after he began practice as an architect, Gropius was responsible for the pace-setting Fagus shoe-last factory at Alfeld-an-der-Leine in Germany, one of the few of his buildings to survive the Second World War. Today the building does not appear unusual, but in 1911 it was a revolutionary prototype, heralding the glass curtain walled method of non-load-bearing cladding that later became ubiquitous. Made from glass, steel and reinforced concrete, this factory initiated a new concept, that of the International school of modern architecture.

In 1919 Gropius was appointed to head the new School of Art and Design at Weimar, the Staatliches Bauhaus. The school had been formed by an amalgamation of the Grand Ducal schools of fine and applied arts founded in 1906. Here Gropius put into practice his strongly held views and he was so successful that this small college, which trained only a few hundred students in the limited years of its existence, became world famous, attracting artists, architects and students of quality from all over Europe.

Gropius's idea was to set up an institution where students of all the arts and crafts could work together and learn from one another. He abhorred the artificial barriers that had come to exist between artists and craftsmen and saw them all as interdependent. He felt that manual dexterity was as essential as creative design. Every Bauhaus student, whatever the individual's field of work or talent, took the same original workshop training. When qualified they were able to understand and supervise all the aesthetic and constructional processes that made up the scope of their work.

In 1924, because of political changes, the Weimar Bauhaus was closed, but Gropius was invited to go to Dessau to re-establish it in a new purpose-built school which he designed. This group of buildings became a prototype that designers of the new architectural form emulated. Gropius left the Bauhaus in 1928, only a few years before it was finally closed due to the growth of National Socialism. He moved to England in 1934, but because of a lack of architectural opportunities and encouragement he continued on his way to the USA, where he headed the Department of Architecture at Harvard University's Graduate School of Design from 1937 to 1952. After his retirement from there Gropius formed the Architect's Collaborative and, working with other architects such as Marcel **Breuer** and Pietro Belluschi, designed a number of buildings (for example, the US Embassy in Athens (1960) and the Pan Am Building in New York (1963)).

Bibliography
1984, *Scope of Total Architecture*, Allen & Unwin.

Further Reading
N. Pevsner, 1936, *Pioneers of the Modern Movement: From William Morris to Walter Gropius*, Penguin.
C. Jenck, 1973, *Modern Movements in Architecture*, Penguin.
H. Probst and C. Shädlich, 1988, *Walter Gropius*, Berlin: Ernst & Son.

DY

Grove, Sir William Robert
b. 11 July 1811 Swansea, Wales
d. 1 August 1896 London, England

Welsh chemist and physicist, inventor of the Grove electrochemical primary cell.

After education at Brasenose College, Oxford, Grove was called to the Bar in 1835. Instead of immediately practising, he became involved in electrical research, devising in 1839 the cell that bears his name. He became Professor of Experimental Philosophy at the London Institution from 1840 to 1845; it was during this period that he built up his high reputation among physicists. In 1846 he published *On the Correlation of Physical Forces*, which was based on a course of his lectures. He returned to the practice of law, becoming a judge in 1871, but retained his interest in scientific research during his sixteen-year occupancy of the Bench. He served as a member of the Council of the Royal Society in 1846 and 1847 and played a leading part in its reform. Contributing to the science of electrochemistry, he invented the Grove cell, which together with its modification by Bunsen became an important source of electrical energy during the middle of the nineteenth century, before mechanically driven generators became available. The Grove cell had a platinum electrode immersed in strong nitric acid, separated by a porous diaphragm from a zinc electrode in weak sulphuric acid. The hydrogen formed at the platinum electrode was immediately oxidized by the acid, turning it into water. This avoided the polarization which occurred in the early copper–zinc cells. It was a very powerful primary cell with a high voltage and a low internal resistance, but it produced objectionable fumes. Grove also invented his 'gas battery', the earliest fuel cell, in which a current resulted from the chemical energy released from combining oxygen and hydrogen. This was developed by **Rawcliffe** and others, and found applications as a power source in manned spacecraft.

Principal Honours and Distinctions
Knighted 1872. FRS 1840. Fellow of the Chemistry Society 1841. Royal Society Royal Medal 1847.

Bibliography
1846, *On the Correlation of Physical Forces*, London; 1874, 6th edn, with reprints of many of Grove's papers (his only book, an early view on the conservation of energy).
1839, 'On a small voltaic battery of great energy', *Philosophical Magazine* 15: 287–93 (his account of his cell).

Further Reading
Obituary, 1896, *Electrician* 37: 483–4.
K.R. Webb, 1961, 'Sir William Robert Grove (1811–1896) and the origin of the fuel cell', *Journal of the Royal Institute of Chemistry* 85: 291–3 (for the present-day significance of Grove's experiments).
C.C. Gillispie (ed.), 1972, *Dictionary of Scientific Biography*, Vol. V, New York, pp. 559–61.
GW

Guericke, Otto von
b. 20 November 1602 Magdeburg, Saxony, Germany
d. 11 May 1686 Hamburg, Germany

German engineer and physicist, inventor of the air pump and investigator of the properties of a vacuum.

Guericke was born into a patrician family in Magdeburg. He was educated at the University of Leipzig in 1617–20 and at the University of Helmstedt in 1620. He then spent two years studying law at Jena, and in 1622 went to Leiden to study law, mathematics, engineering and especially fortification. He spent most of his life in politics, for he was elected an alderman of Magdeburg in 1626. After the destruction of Magdeburg in 1631, he worked in Brunswick and Erfurt as an engineer for the Swedish government, and then in 1635 for the Electorate of Saxony. He was Mayor of Magdeburg for thirty years, between 1646 and 1676. He was ennobled in 1666 and retired from public office in 1681and went to Hamburg. It was through his attendances at international congresses and at princely courts that he took part in the exchange of scientific ideas.

From his student days he was concerned with the definition of space and posed three questions: can empty space exist or is space always filled? How can heavenly bodies affect each other across space and how are they moved? Is space, and so also the heavenly bodies, bounded or unbounded? In *c.*1647 Guericke made a suction pump for air and tried to exhaust a beer barrel, but he could not stop the leaks. He then tried a copper sphere, which imploded. He developed a series of spectacular demonstrations with his air pump. In 1654 at Rattisbon he used a vertical cylinder with a well-fitting piston connected over pulleys by a rope to fifty men, who could not stop the piston descending when the cylinder was exhausted. More famous were his copper hemispheres which, when exhausted, could not be drawn apart by two teams of eight horses. They were first demonstrated at Magdeburg in 1657 and at the court in Berlin in 1663. Through these experiments he discovered the elasticity of air and began to investigate its density at different heights. He heard of the work of **Torricelli** in 1653 and by 1660 had succeeded in making barometric forecasts. He published his famous work *New Experiments Concerning Empty Space* in 1672. Between 1660 and 1663 Guericke constructed a large ball of sulphur that could be rotated on a spindle. He found that, when he pressed his hand on it and it was rotated, it became strongly electrified; he thus unintentionally became the inventor of the first machine to generate static electricity. He attempted to reach a complete physical explanation of the world and the heavens with magnetism as a primary force and evolved an explanation for the rotation of the heavenly bodies.

Bibliography
1672, *Experimenta nova (ut vocantur) Magdeburgica de vacuo spatio* (New Experiments Concerning Empty Space).

Further Reading
F.W. Hoffmann, 1874, *Otto von Guericke* (a full biography).
T.I. Williams (ed.), 1969, *A Biographical Dictionary of Scientists*, London: A. & C. Black (contains a short account of his life).
Chambers Concise Dictionary of Scientists, 1989, Cambridge.
Dictionary of Scientific Biography, Vol. V, New York.
C. Singer (ed.), 1957, *A History of Technology*, Vols. III and IV, Oxford University Press (includes references to Guericke's inventions).
RLH

Guest, James John
b. 24 July 1866 Handsworth, Birmingham, England
d. 11 June 1956 Virginia Water, Surrey, England

English mechanical engineer, engineering teacher and researcher.

James John Guest was educated at Marlborough in 1880–4 and at Trinity College, Cambridge, graduating as fifth wrangler in 1888. He received practical training in several workshops and spent two years in postgraduate work at the Engineering Department of Cambridge University. After working as a draughtsman in the machine-tool, hydraulic and crane departments of Tangyes Ltd at Birmingham, he was appointed in 1896 Assistant Professor of Engineering at McGill University in Canada. After a short time he moved to the Polytechnic Institute at Worcester, Massachusetts, where he was for three years Professor of Mechanical Engineering and Head of the Engineering Department. In 1899 he returned to Britain and set up as a consulting engineer in Birmingham, being a partner in James J. Guest & Co. For the next fifteen years he combined this work with research on grinding phenomena. He also developed a theory of grinding which he first published in a paper at the British Association for the Advancement of Science in 1914 and elaborated in a paper to the Institution of Mechanical Engineers and in his book *Grinding Machinery* (1915). During the First World War, in 1916–17, he was in charge of inspection in the Staffordshire and Shropshire Area, Ministry of Munitions. In 1917 he returned to teaching as Reader in Graphics and Structural Engineering at University College London. His final appointment was about 1923 as Professor of Mechanical and Electrical Engineering, Artillery College, Woolwich, which later became the Military College of Science.

He carried out research on the strength of materials and contributed many articles on the subject to the technical press. He originated Guest's Law for a criterion of failure of materials under combined stresses, first published in 1900. He was a Member of the Institution of Mechanical Engineers in 1900–6 and from 1919 and contributed to their proceedings in many discussions and two major papers.

Bibliography
Of many publications by Guest, the most important are:
1900, 'Ductile materials under combined stress', *Proceedings of the Physical Society* 17: 202.
1915, *Grinding Machinery*, London.
1915, 'Theory of grinding, with reference to the selection of speeds in plain and internal work',

Proceedings of the Institution of Mechanical Engineers 89: 543.

1917, 'Torsional hysteresis of mild steel', *Proceedings of the Royal Society* A93: 313.

1918, with F.C. Lea, 'Curved beams', *Proceedings of the Royal Society* A95: 1.

1930, 'Effects of rapidly acting stress', *Proceedings of the Institution of Mechanical Engineers* 119: 1,273.

RTS

Guido d'Arezzo
b. *c.*995 Italy
d. 1050 Avellana, Italy

Italian music theorist who made important developments in musical notation.

Guido was originally a monk at the Benedictine Abbey of Pomposa, where he began to introduce innovations into the symbolic representation of music, which greatly helped in the training of choristers. Because of jealousies aroused by this work, he was obliged to leave and settled in Arezzo, capital of the province of that name in northern Italy. Around 1030 he went to Rome at the invitation of the Pope, John XIX, to explain his theories, after which he appears to have settled at the monastery of S. Croce di Fonte, Avellana, where he became prior some three years before his death. In an effort to make it easier for the choristers to maintain correct pitch and to learn the complex polyphonic chants then in development, Guido introduced two major innovations. The first was the use of a four-line staff on which the pitch of successive notes could be recorded. The second was a nomenclature for the first six notes of the major scale supposedly based on the initial syllables of a hymn said to have been composed by him, namely *ut* (later *do*), *re*, *mi*, *fa*, *so* and *la*. These had a dramatic effect on the learning and singing of music. He also apparently devised forms of parallel voices for plainsong.

Bibliography
Guido's work is recorded in his treatise, *c.*1026, *Micrologus*.

Further Reading
Works describing the development of music and musical notation in medieval times include:
W.C. Mickelson, 1977, *Hugo Riemann's History of Music Theory*, Lincoln: University of

Nebraska Press.
S. Sadie (ed.), 1980, *The New Grove Dictionary of Music and Musicians*, vol. 9, London: Macmillan, 803.

KF

Guillaume, Charles-Edouard
b. 15 February 1861 Fleurier, Switzerland
d. 13 June 1938 Sèvres, France

Swiss physicist who developed two alloys, 'invar' and 'elinvar', used for the temperature compensation of clocks and watches.

Guillaume came from a family of clock- and watchmakers. He was educated at the Gymnasium in Neuchâtel and at Zurich Polytechnic, from which he received his doctorate in 1883 for a thesis on electrolytic capacitors. In the same year he joined the International Bureau of Weights and Measures at Sèvres in France, where he was to spend the rest of his working life. He retired as Director in 1936. At the bureau he was involved in distributing the national standards of the metre to countries subscribing to the General Conference on Weights and Measures that had been held in 1889. This made him aware of the crucial effect of thermal expansion on the lengths of the standards and he was prompted to look for alternative materials that would be less costly than the platinum alloys which had been used. While studying nickel steels he made the surprising discovery that the thermal expansion of certain alloy compositions was less than that of the constituent metals. This led to the development of a steel containing about 36 per cent nickel that had a very low thermal coefficient of expansion. This alloy was subsequently named 'invar', an abbreviation of *inva*riable. It was well known that changes in temperature affected the timekeeping of clocks by altering the length of the pendulum, and various attempts had been made to overcome this defect, most notably the mercury-compensated pendulum of **Graham** and the gridiron pendulum of **Harrison**. However, an invar pendulum offered a simpler and more effective method of temperature compensation and was used almost exclusively for pendulum clocks of the highest precision.

Changes in temperature can also affect the timekeeping of watches and chronometers, but this is due mainly to changes in the elasticity or stiffness of the balance spring rather than to changes in the size of the balance itself. To compensate for this effect Guillaume developed another more complex nickel alloy, 'elinvar' (*el*asticity *invar*iable), whose elasticity remained almost constant with changes in temperature. This had two practical consequences: the construction of watches could be simplified (by using monometallic balances) and more accurate chronometers could be made.

Principal Honours and Distinctions

Nobel Prize for Physics 1920. Corresponding member of the Académie des Sciences. Grand Officier de la Légion d'honneur 1937. Physical Society Duddell Medal 1928. British Horological Institute Gold Medal 1930.

Bibliography

1897, 'Sur la dilation des aciers au nickel', *Comptes rendus hebdomadaires des séances de l'Académie des sciences* 124: 176.
1903, 'Variations du module d'élasticité des aciers au nickel', *Comptes rendus hebdomadaires des séances de l'Académie des sciences* 136: 498.
'Les aciers au nickel et leurs applications à l'horlogerie', in J. Grossmann, *Horlogerie théorique*, Paris, Vol. II, pp. 361–414 (describes the application of invar and elinvar to horology).
Sir Richard Glazebrook (ed.), 1923 'Invar and Elinvar', *Dictionary of Applied Physics*, 5 vols, London, Vol. V, pp. 320–7 (a succinct account in English).

Further Reading

R.M. Hawthorne, 1989, *Nobel Prize Winners, Physics, 1901–1937*, ed. F.N. Magill, Pasadena, Salem Press, pp. 244–51.

See also **Le Roy, Pierre**.

DV

Guinand, Pierre Louis

b. 20 April 1748 Brenets, Neuchâtel, Switzerland
d. 13 February 1824 Brenets, Neuchâtel, Switzerland

Swiss optical glassmaker.

Guinand received little formal education and followed his father's trade of joiner. He specialized in making clock cases, but after learning how to cast metals he took up the more lucrative work of making watch cases. When he was about 20 years old, in a customer's house he caught sight of an English telescope, a rarity in a Swiss mountain village. Intrigued, he obtained permission to examine it. This aroused his interest in optical matters and he began making spectacles and small telescopes.

Achromatic lenses were becoming known, their use being to remove the defect of chromatic aberration or coloured optical images, but there remained defects due to imperfections in the glass itself. Stimulated by offers of prizes by scientific bodies, including the Royal Society of London, for removing these defects, Guinand set out to remedy them. He embarked in 1784 on a long and arduous series of experiments, varying the materials and techniques for making glass. The even more lucrative trade of making bells for repeaters provided the funds for a furnace capable of holding 2 cwt (102 kg) of molten glass. By 1798 or so he had succeeded in making discs of homogeneous glass. He impressed the famous Parisian astronomer de Lalande with them and his glass became well enough known for scientists to visit him. In 1805 Fraunhofer persuaded Guinand to join his optical-instrument works at Benediktheurn, in Bavaria, to make lenses. After nine years, Guinand returned to Brenets with a pension, on condition he made no more glass and disclosed no details of his methods. After two years these conditions had become irksome and he relinquished the pension. On 19 February 1823 Guinand described his discoveries in his classic 'Memoir on the making of optical glass, more particularly of glass of high refractive index for use in the production of achromatic lenses', presented to the Société de Physique et d'Histoire Naturelle de Genève. This gives details of his experiments and investigations and discusses a suitable pot-clay stirrer and stirring mechanism for the molten glass, with temperature control, to overcome optical-glass defects such as bubbles, seeds, cords and colours. Guinand was hailed as the man in Europe who had achieved this and has thus rightly been called the founder of the era of optical glassmaking.

Further Reading

The fullest account in English of Guinand's life

and work is 'Some account of the late M. Guinand and of the discovery made by him in the manufacture of flint glass for large telescopes by F.R., extracted from the Bibliothèque Universelle des Sciences, trans. C.F. de B.', *Quart.J.Sci.Roy.Instn.Lond.* (1825) 19: 244–58.

M. von Rohr, 1924, 'Pierre Louis Guinand', *Zeitschrift für Instr.*, 46: 121, 139, with an English summary in *J.Glass. Tech.*, (1926) 10: abs. 150–1.

LRD

Guo Shoujing (Kuo Shou-Ching)
b. 1231 China
d. 1316 China

Chinese mathematician, astronomer and civil engineer.

First, from 1262, he was engaged in hydraulic-engineering works for Kublai Khan. He began astronomical and calendrical investigations in 1276, and became the greatest astronomer of the Yuan dynasty. He perfected interpolation formulae (a method of finite differences) and was the founder of the study of spherical trigonometry in China; this was applied to the circles of the heavenly sphere. He planned the Ji Zhou, the summit section of the Grand Canal through the Shandong foothills, in 1283. Although the canal had to await further improvement before it could become fully effective, it was nevertheless the world's first successful entirely artificial summit canal.

Guo Shoujing was responsible for the construction of the Tong Hui He (Channel of Communicating Grace) canal with twenty lock gates in 1293, in addition to the overhaul of the entire Grand Canal. He constructed a number of devices, including 40 ft (12 m) gnomons in 1276, with which he made some of the most accurate measurements of the sun's solstitial shadows, the results of which were collected in a book that is now lost. Between 1276 and 1279 he also constructed at least one water-driven mechanical escapement clock with sophisticated jack work, and the Beijing observatory and its equipment.

Further Reading
J. Needham, *Science and Civilisation in China*, Cambridge: Cambridge University Press, 1959–1971, vols III, pp. 48–50, 109–10, 294,

296, 299, 349, 350; IV.2, pp. 504–5; IV.3, pp. 312ff., 319, 355; *Heavenly Clockwork*, 1960, pp. 134, 136ff., 159, 160, 163; *Clerks and Craftsmen in China and the West*, 1970, pp. 2, 5, 9–10, 16, 96, 398.

LRD

Gurney, Sir Goldsworthy
b. 14 February 1793 Treator, near Padstow, Cornwall, England
d. 28 February 1875 Reeds, near Bude, Cornwall, England

English pioneer of steam road transport.

Educated at Truro Grammar School, he then studied under Dr Avery at Wadebridge to become a doctor of medicine. He settled as a surgeon in Wadebridge, spending his leisure time in building an organ and in the study of chemistry and mechanical science. He married Elizabeth Symons in 1814, and in 1820 moved with his wife to London. He delivered a course of lectures at the Surrey Institution on the elements of chemical science, attended by, amongst others, the young Michael **Faraday**. While there, Gurney made his first invention, the oxyhydrogen blowpipe. For this he received the Gold Medal of the Society of Arts. He experimented with lime and magnesia for the production of an illuminant for lighthouses with some success. He invented a musical instrument of glasses played like a piano.

In 1823 he started experiments related to steam and locomotion which necessitated taking a partner in to his medical practice, from which he resigned shortly after. His objective was to produce a steam-driven vehicle to run on common roads. His invention of the steam-jet of blast greatly improved the performance of the steam engine. In 1827 he took his steam carriage to Cyfarthfa at the request of Mr Crawshaw, and while there applied his steam-jet to the blast furnaces, greatly improving their performance in the manufacture of iron. Much of the success of George **Stephenson**'s steam engine, the *Rocket* was due to Gurney's steam blast.

In July 1829 Gurney made a historic trip with his road locomotive. This was from London to Bath and back, which was accomplished at a speed of 18 mph (29 km/h) and was made at the instigation of the Quartermaster-General of the Army. So successful was the carriage that Sir Charles Dance started to run a regular service with it between Gloucester and Cheltenham. This ran for three months without accident, until Parliament introduced prohibitive taxation on all self-propelled vehicles. A House of Commons committee proposed that these should be abolished as inhibiting progress, but this was not done. Sir Goldsworthy petitioned Parliament on the harm being done to him, but nothing was done and the coming of the railways put the matter beyond consideration. He devoted his time to finding other uses for the steam-jet: it was used for extinguishing fires in coal-mines, some of which had been burning for many years; he developed a stove for the production of gas from oil and other fatty substances, intended for lighthouses; he was responsible for the heating and the lighting of both the old and the new Houses of Parliament. His evidence after a colliery explosion resulted in an Act of Parliament requiring all mines to have two shafts. He was knighted in 1863, the same year that he suffered a stroke which incapacitated him. He retired to his house at Reeds, near Bude, where he was looked after by his daughter, Anna.

Principal Honours and Distinctions
Knighted 1863. Society of Arts Gold Medal.

IMcN

Gutenberg, Johann Gensfleisch zum

b. *c.*1394–9 Mainz, Germany
d. 3 February 1468 Mainz, Germany

German inventor of printing with movable type.

Few biographical details are known of Johann Gensfleisch zum Gutenberg, yet it has been said that he was responsible for Germany's most notable contribution to civilization. He was a goldsmith by trade, of a patrician family of the city of Mainz. He seems to have begun experiments on printing while a political exile in Strasbourg *c.*1440. He returned to Mainz between 1444 and 1448 and continued his experiments, until by 1450 he had perfected his invention sufficiently to justify raising capital for its commercial exploitation.

Circumstances were propitious for the invention of printing at that time. Rises in literacy and prosperity had led to the formation of a social class with the time and resources to develop a taste for reading, and the demand for reading matter had outstripped the ability of the scribes to satisfy it. The various technologies required were well established, and finally the flourishing textile industry was producing enough waste material, rag, to make paper, the only satisfactory and cheap medium for printing. There were others working along similar lines, but it was Gutenberg who achieved the successful adaptation and combination of technologies to arrive at a process by which many identical copies of a text could be produced in a wide variety of forms, of which the book was the most important. Gutenberg did make several technical innovations, however. The two-piece adjustable mould for casting types of varying width, from 'I' to 'M', was ingenious. Then he had to devise an oil-based ink suitable for inking metal type, derived from the painting materials developed by contemporary Flemish artists. Finally, probably after many experiments, he arrived at a metal alloy of distinctive composition suitable for casting type.

In 1450 Gutenberg borrowed 800 guldens from Johannes Fust, a lawyer of Mainz, and two years later Fust advanced a further 800 guldens, securing for himself a partnership in Gutenberg's business. But in 1455 Fust foreclosed and the bulk of Gutenberg's equipment passed to Peter Schöffer, who was in the service of Fust and later married his daughter. Like most early printers, Gutenberg seems not to have appreciated, or at any rate to have been able to provide for, the great dilemma of the publishing trade, namely the outlay of considerable capital in advance of each publication and the slowness of the return. Gutenberg probably retained only the type for the 42- and 36-line bibles and possibly the *Catholicon* of 1460, an encyclopedic work compiled in the thirteenth century and whose production pointed the way to printing's role as a means of spreading knowledge. The work concluded with a short descriptive piece, or colophon, which is probably by Gutenberg himself and is the only output of his mind that we have; it manages to omit the names of both author and printer.

Gutenberg seems to have abandoned printing after 1460, perhaps due to failing eyesight as well as for financial reasons, and he suffered further loss in the sack of Mainz in 1462. He received a kind of pension from the Archbishop in 1465, and on his death was buried in the Franciscan church in Mainz. The only major work to have issued for certain from Gutenberg's workshop is the great 42-line bible, begun in 1452 and completed by August 1456. The quality of this piece of printing is a tribute to Gutenberg's ability as a printer, and the soundness of his invention is borne out by the survival of the process as he left it to the world, unchanged for over three hundred years save in minor details.

Further Reading
A. Ruppel, 1967, *Johannes Gutenberg: sein Leben und sein Werk*, 3rd edn, Nieuwkoop: B. de Graaf (the standard biography).
A.M.L. de Lamartine, 1960, *Gutenberg, inventeur de l'imprimerie*, Tallone.
V. Scholderer, 1963, *Gutenberg, Inventor of Printing*, London: British Museum.
S.H. Steinberg, 1974, *Five Hundred Years of Printing*, 3rd edn, London: Penguin (provides briefer details).

LRD

H

Haber, Fritz

b. 9 December 1868 Breslau, Germany (now Wroclaw, Poland)
d. 29 January 1934 Basel, Switzerland

German chemist, inventor of the process for the synthesis of ammonia.

Haber's father was a manufacturer of dyestuffs, so he studied organic chemistry at Berlin and Heidelberg universities to equip him to enter his father's firm. But his interest turned to physical chemistry and remained there throughout his life. He became Assistant at the Technische Hochschule in Karlsruhe in 1894; his first work there was on pyrolysis and electrochemistry, and he published his *Grundrisse der technischen Electrochemie* in 1898. Haber became famous for thorough and illuminating theoretical studies in areas of growing practical importance. He rose through the academic ranks and was appointed a full professor in 1906. In 1912 he was also appointed Director of the Institute of Physical Chemistry and Electrochemistry at Dahlem, outside Berlin.

Early in the twentieth century Haber invented a process for the synthesis of ammonia. The English chemist and physicist Sir William **Crookes** (1832–1919) had warned of the danger of mass hunger because the deposits of Chilean nitrate were becoming exhausted and nitrogenous fertilizers would not suffice for the world's growing population. A solution lay in the use of the nitrogen in the air, and the efforts of chemists centred on ways of converting it to usable nitrate. Haber was aware of contemporary work on the fixation of nitrogen by the cyanamide and arc processes, but in 1904 he turned to the study of ammonia formation from its elements, nitrogen and hydrogen. During 1907–9 Haber found that the yield of ammonia reached an industrially viable level if the reaction took place under a pressure of 150–200 atmospheres and a temperature of 600°C ($1,112^{\circ}$F) in the presence of a suitable catalyst – first osmium, later uranium. He devised an apparatus in which a mixture of the gases was pumped through a converter, in which the ammonia formed was withdrawn while the unchanged gases were recirculated. By 1913, Haber's collaborator, Carl **Bosch** had succeeded in raising this laboratory process to the industrial scale. It was the first successful high-pressure industrial chemical process, and solved the nitrogen problem. The outbreak of the First World War directed the work of the institute in Dahlem to military purposes, and Haber was placed in charge of chemical warfare. In this capacity, he developed poisonous gases as well as the means of defence against them, such as gas masks. The synthetic-ammonia process was diverted to produce nitric acid for explosives. The great benefits and achievement of the Haber–Bosch process were recognized by the award in 1919 of the Nobel Prize in Chemistry, but on account of Haber's association with chemical warfare, British, French and American scientists denounced the award; this only added to the sense of bitterness he already felt at his country's defeat in the war. He concentrated on the theoretical studies for which he was renowned, in particular on pyrolysis and autoxidation, and both the Karlsruhe and the Dahlem laboratories became international centres for discussion and research in physical chemistry.

With the Nazi takeover in 1933, Haber found that, as a Jew, he was relegated to second-class status. He did not see why he should appoint staff on account of their grandmothers instead of their ability, so he resigned his posts and went into exile. For some months he accepted hospitality in Cambridge, but he was on his way to a new post in what is now Israel when he died suddenly in Basel, Switzerland.

Bibliography
1898, *Grundrisse der technischen Electrochemie.*
1927, *Aus Leben und Beruf.*

Further Reading
J.E. Coates, 1939, 'The Haber Memorial Lecture', *Journal of the Chemical Society:* 1,642–72.
M. Goran, 1967, *The Story of Fritz Haber*, Norman,

OK: University of Oklahoma Press (includes a complete list of Haber's works).

LRD

Hackworth, Timothy

b. 22 December 1786 Wylam, Northumberland, England
d. 7 July 1850 Shildon, Co. Durham, England

English engineer, pioneer in construction and operation of steam locomotives.

Hackworth trained under his father, who was Foreman Blacksmith at Wylam colliery, and succeeded him upon his death in 1807. Between 1812 and 1816 he helped to build and maintain the Wylam locomotives under William **Hedley**. He then moved to Walbottle colliery, but during 1824 he took temporary charge of Robert Stephenson & Co.'s works while George **Stephenson** was surveying the Liverpool & Manchester Railway and Robert **Stephenson** was away in South America. In May 1825 Hackworth was appointed to the Stockton & Darlington Railway (S & DR) 'to have superintendence of the permanent (i.e. stationary) and locomotive engines'. He established the workshops at Shildon, and when the railway opened in September he became in effect the first locomotive superintendent of a railway company. From experience of operating Robert Stephenson & Co.'s locomotives he was able to make many detail improvements, notably spring safety valves. In 1827 he designed and built the locomotive *Royal George*, with six wheels coupled and inverted vertical cylinders driving the rear pair. From the pistons, drive was direct by way of piston rods and connecting rods to crankpins on the wheels, the first instance of the use of this layout on a locomotive. *Royal George* was the most powerful and satisfactory locomotive on the S & DR to date and was the forerunner of Hackworth's type of heavy-goods locomotive, which was built until the mid-1840s.

For the Rainhill Trials in 1829 Hackworth built and entered the locomotive *Sans Pareil*, which was subsequently used on the Bolton & Leigh Railway and is now in the Science Museum, London. A working replica was built for the 150th anniversary of the Liverpool & Manchester Railway in 1980. In 1833 a further agreement with the S & DR enabled Hackworth, while remaining in charge of their locomotives, to set up a locomotive and engineering works on his own account. Its products eventually included locomotives for the London, Brighton & South Coast and York, Newcastle & Berwick Railways, as well as some of the earliest locomotives exported to Russia and Canada. Hackworth's son, John Wesley Hackworth, was also an engineer and invented the radial valve gear for steam engines that bears his name.

Further Reading
R. Young, 1975, *Timothy Hackworth and the Locomotive*, Shildon: Shildon 'Stockton & Darlington Railway' Silver Jubilee Committee; orig. pub. 1923, London (tends to emphasize Hackworth's achievements at the expense of other contemporary engineers).
L.T.C. Rolt, 1960, *George and Robert Stephenson*, London: Longmans (describes much of Hackworth's work and is more objective).
E.L. Ahrons, 1927, *The British Steam Railway Locomotive 1825–1925*, London: The Locomotive Publishing Co.

PJGR

Haddy, Arthur Charles

b. 16 May 1906 Newbury, Berkshire, England
d. December 1989

English electronics engineer who developed Full Frequency Range Recording for the Decca Record Company and was instrumental in the development of stereo records.

He developed recording equipment for the Crystallate Gramophone Company, becoming Chief Recording Engineer at Decca when Crystallate was taken over. Eventually he was made Technical Director of Decca Record Company Ltd, a position he held until 1980. The developments of good cutterheads accelerated due to contract work for the armed services during the Second World War, because an extended frequency range was needed. This necessitated the solution of the problem of surface noise, and the result became known publicly as the *ffrr* system. The experience gained enabled Haddy to pioneer European Long Play recording. Haddy started development of a practical stereo record system within the Decca group, and for economic reasons he eventually chose a solution developed outside his direct surveillance by Teldec. The foresight of Decca made the company an equal partner in the standards discussions during the late 1950s, when it was decided to use the American 45/45 system, which utilized the two sidewalls of the groove. The same foresight had led Decca to record their repertoire in stereo from 1954 in order to prepare for any commercialized distribution system. In 1967 Haddy also became responsible for cassette manufacture, which meant organizing the logistics of a tape-duplication plant.

Principal Honours and Distinctions
OBE 1976.

Bibliography
Haddy's patents are a good description of some of his technical achievements; for example:
UK patent no. 770,465 (greater playing time from a record by changing the groove pitch);
UK patent no. 807,301 (using feedback to linearize a cutterhead);
UK patent no. 810,106 (two-channel by simultaneous vertical and lateral modulation).

Further Reading
G.A. Briggs (ed.), 1961, *Audio Biographies*, Wharfedale Wireless Works, pp. 157–63.
H.E. Roys, 'The coming of stereo', *Jour. AES* 25 (10/11): 824–7 (an appreciation of Haddy's role in the standardization of stereo recording).

GB-N

Hadfield, Sir Robert Abbott

b. 28 November 1858 Attercliffe, Sheffield, Yorkshire, England
d. 30 September 1940 Kingston Hill, Surrey, England

English metallurgist and pioneer in alloy steels.

Hadfield's father, Robert, set up a steelworks in Sheffield in 1872, one of the earliest to specialize in steel castings. After his education in Sheffield, during which he showed an interest in chemistry, Hadfield entered his father's works. His first act was to set up a laboratory, where he began systematically experimenting with alloy steels in order to improve the quality of the products of the family firm. In 1883 Hadfield found that by increasing the manganese content to 12.5 per cent, with a carbon content of 1.4 per cent, the resulting alloy showed extraordinary resistance to ab-

rasive wear even though it was quite soft. It was soon applied in railway points and crossings, crushing and grinding machinery, and wherever great resistance to wear is required. Its lack of brittleness led to its use in steel helmets during the First World War. Hadfield's manganese steel was also non-magnetic, which was later of importance in the electrical industry. Hadfield's other great invention was that of silicon steel. Again after careful and systematic laboratory work, Hadfield found that a steel containing 3–4 per cent silicon and as little as possible of other elements was highly magnetic, which was to prove important in the electrical industry (e.g. reducing the weight and bulk of electrical transformers). Hadfield took over the firm on the death of his father in 1888, but he continued to lay great stress on the need for laboratory research to improve the quality and range of products. The steel-casting side of the business led to a flourishing armaments industry, and this, together with their expertise in alloy steels, made Hadfield's one of the great names in Sheffield and British steel until, sadly, it succumbed along with so many other illustrious names during the British economic recession of 1983. Hadfield had a keen interest in metallurgical history, particularly in his characteristically thorough examination of the alloys of iron prepared by **Faraday** at the Royal Institution. Hadfield was an enlightened employer and was one of the first to introduce the eight-hour day.

Principal Honours and Distinctions
Knighted 1908. Baronet 1917. FRS 1909.

Bibliography
A list of Hadfield's published papers and other works is published with a biographical account in *Obituary Notices of Fellows of the Royal Society* (1940) 10.
1925, *Metallurgy and Its Influence on Modern Progress*.
1931, *Faraday and His Metallurgical Researches*.
LRD

Hair, Thomas H.

fl. *c*.1830–75 northern England

English artist whose work was concerned with the industrial landscape.

Hair is best known for the folio volume *A Series*

of Views of the Collieries in the Counties of Northumberland and Durham, published in 1839. This is a volume of engravings after watercolours by T.H. Hair which show in its forty-two pictures particular collieries and details of the workings. The accompanying text by M. Ross describes the pictures and the activities of the various collieries in considerable detail. One of Hair's most famous paintings is 'Hartley Colliery after the Disaster' (1869). T.H. Hair's paintings and his book are important for they give an accurate picture of industrial Northumberland and Durham in the middle of the nineteenth century.

Bibliography
1839, *A Series of Views of the Collieries in the Counties of Northumberland and Durham*, London; reprinted 1969, Newton Abbot.

Further Reading
M. Hall, 1973, *The Artists of Northumbria*, Newcastle upon Tyne.

KM

Hales, Stephen

b. September 1677 Bekesbourne, Kent, England
d. 4 January 1761 Teddington, Middlesex, England

English physiologist and inventor, author of the first account of the measurement of blood pressure.

After attending Corpus Christi, Cambridge, he was admitted as a Fellow in 1702. During the ensuing years he was engaged in botanical, astronomical and chemical activities and research. He was appointed Minister at Teddington, Middlesex, in 1708 and remained in that post until his death. During these years, he continued to engage in a wide range of botanical and physiological activities involving studies of the nutrition of plants, blood pressure and the flow of blood in animals. He was also the inventor of improved ventilation by systems of partition and ducting, and the production of fresh water by distillation for ships at sea. The wide range of his interests did not preclude his care for his pastoral duties, and he was involved in the education of the Prince of Wales's children, although he declined a canonry of Windsor. In his writings he set a standard for the scientific method as related to principles based on facts and observation.

Principal Honours and Distinctions
FRS 1718. Copley Medal 1739. Académie Française 1753. Founding Member, Society of Arts; Vice-President 1755.

Bibliography
1727, *Vegetable Statisticks*, London.
1733, *Statistical Essays*, London.
1734, *A Friendly Admonition to the Drinkers of Brandy*, London.
1736, *Distilled Spirituous Liquors the Bane of the Nation*, London.
1739, *Philosophical Experiments*, London.
1740, *An Account of Some Experiments and Observations*, London.
1743, 1758, *A Description of Ventilators*, London.
1756, *An Account of a Useful Discovery to Distill*, London.

MG

Hall, Charles Martin

b. 6 December 1863 Thompson, Ohio, USA
d. 27 December 1914 USA

American metallurgist, inventor of the first feasible electrolytic process for the production of aluminium.

The son of a Congregationalist minister, Hall was educated at Oberlin College. There he was instructed in chemistry by Professor F.F. Jewett, a former student of the German chemist Friedrich Wöhler, who encouraged Hall to believe that there was a need for a cheap process for the manufacture of aluminium. After graduating in 1885, Hall set to work in his private laboratory exploring the method of fused salt electrolysis. On Wednesday 10 February 1886 he found that alumina dissolved in fused cryolite 'like sugar in water', and that the bath so produced was a good conductor of electricity. He contained the solution in a pure graphite crucible which also acted as an efficient cathode, and by 16 February 1886 had produced the first globules of metallic aluminium. With two backers, Hall was able to complete his experiments and establish a small pilot plant in Boston, but they withdrew after the US Patent Examiners reported that Hall's invention had been anticipated by a French patent, filed by Paul Toussaint **Héroult** in April 1886. Although

Hall had not filed until July 1886, he was permitted to testify that his invention had been completed by 16 February 1886 and on 2 April 1889 he was granted a seventeen-year monopoly in the United States. Hall now had the support of Captain A.E. Hunt of the Pittsburgh Testing Institute who provided the capital for establishing the Pittsburgh Reduction Company, which by 1889 was selling aluminium at $1 per pound compared to the $15 for sodium-reduced aluminium. Further capital was provided by the banker Andrew Mellon (1855–1937). Hall then turned his attention to Britain and began negotiations with Johnson Matthey, who provided land on a site at Patricroft near Manchester. Here the Aluminium Syndicate, owned by the Pittsburgh Reduction Company, began to produce aluminium in July 1890. By this time the validity of Hall's patent was being strongly contested by Héroult and also by the Cowles brothers, who attempted to operate the Hall process in the United States. Hall successfully sued them for infringement, and was confirmed in his patent rights by the celebrated ruling in 1893 of William Howard Taft, subsequently President of the USA. In 1895 Hall's company changed its name to the Pittsburgh Aluminium Company and moved to Niagara Falls, where cheap electrical power was available. In 1903 a legal compromise ended the litigation between the Hall and Héroult organizations. The American rights in the invention were awarded to Hall, and the European to Héroult. The Pittsburgh Aluminium Company became the Aluminium Company of America on 1 January 1907. On his death he left his estate, worth about $45 million, for the advancement of education.

Principal Honours and Distinctions
Chemical Society, London, Perkin Medal 1911.

Further Reading
H.N. Holmes, 1930, 'The story of aluminium', *Journal of Chemical Education*.
E.F. Smith, 1914, *Chemistry in America*.

ASD

Hall, Joseph
b. 1789
d. 1862

English ironmaker who invented the wet puddling process.

Hall was a practical man with no theoretical background: his active years were spent at Bloomfield Ironworks, Tipton, Staffordshire. Around 1816 he began experimenting in the production of wrought iron. At that time, blast-furnace or cast iron was converted to wrought iron by the dry puddling process invented by Henry **Cort** in 1784. In this process, the iron was decarburized (i.e. had its carbon removed) by heating it in a current of air in a furnace with a sand bed. Some of the iron combined with the silica in the sand to form a slag, however, so that no less than 2 tons of cast iron were needed to produce 1 ton of wrought. Hall found that if bosh cinder was charged into the furnace, a vigorous reaction occurred in which the cast iron was converted much more quickly than before, to produce better quality wrought iron, a ton of which could be formed by no more than 21 cwt (1,067 kg) of cast iron. Because of the boiling action, the process came to be known as pig boiling. Bosh cinder, essentially iron oxide, was formed in the water troughs or boshes in which workers cooled their tools used in puddling and reacted with the carbon in the cast iron. The advantages of pig boiling over dry puddling were striking enough for the process to be widely used by the late 1820s. By mid-century it was virtually the only process used for producing wrought iron, an essential material for mechanical and civil engineering during the Industrial Revolution. Hall reckoned that if he had patented his invention he would have 'made a million'. As luck would have it, the process that he did patent in 1838 left his finances unchanged: this was for the roasting of cinder for use as the base of the puddling furnace, providing better protection than the bosh cinder for the iron plates that formed the base.

Bibliography
1857, *The Iron Question Considered in Connection with Theory, Practice and Experience with Special Reference to the Bessemer Process*, London.

Further Reading
J. Percy, 1864, *Metallurgy. Iron and Steel*, London, pp. 670 ff.
W.K.V. Gale, *Iron and Steel*, London: Longmans, pp. 46–50.

LRD

Halske, Johann Georg

b. 30 July 1814 Hamburg, Germany
d. 18 March 1890 Berlin, Germany

German engineer who introduced precision methods into the manufacture of electrical equipment; co-founder of Siemens & Halske.

Halske moved to Berlin when he was a young man, and in 1844 was working for the university, at first independently and then jointly with F. Bötticher, developing and building electric medical appliances. In 1845 he met Werner von **Siemens** and together they became founder members of the Berlin Physics Society. It was in Halske's workshop that Siemens, assisted by the skill of the former, was able to work out his inventions in telegraphy. In 1847 the two men entered into partnership to manufacture telegraph equipment, laying the foundations of the successful firm of Siemens & Halske. At the outset, before Werner von Siemens gave up his army career, Halske acted as the sole manager of the firm and was also involved in testing the products. Inventions they developed included electric measuring instruments and railway signalling equipment, and they installed many telegraph lines, notably those for the Russian Government. When gutta-percha became available on the market, the two men soon developed an extrusion process for applying this new material to copper conductors. To the disappointment of Halske, who was opposed to mass production, the firm introduced series production and piece wages in 1857. The expansion of the business, particularly into submarine cable laying, caused some anxiety to Halske, who left the firm on amicable terms in 1867. He then worked for a few years developing the Arts and Crafts Museum in Berlin and became a town councillor.

Further Reading
S. von Weihr and H. Götzeler, 1983, *The Siemens Company. Its Historical Role in the Progress of Electrical Engineering 1847–1983*, Berlin (provides a full account).
Neue Deutsche Biographie, 1966, Vol. 7, Berlin, pp. 572–3.
S. von Weiher, 1972–3, 'The Siemens brothers, pioneers of the electrical age in Europe', *Transactions of the Newcomen Society* 45: 1–11.

GW

Halsted, William Stewart

b. 23 September 1852 Baltimore, Maryland, USA
d. 7 September 1922 Baltimore, Maryland, USA

American surgeon, originator of the surgical use of rubber gloves and silk ligatures.

After education at Yale University, he studied at the College of Physicians and Surgeons of New York, qualifying in 1877. Following internships in New York, he spent two postgraduate years in Germany and Austria, where he became acquainted with the German methods of surgical education. He returned to New York in 1880 to practise privately and also demonstrate anatomy at the College.

In 1884, when experimenting with cocaine as an anaesthetic, he became addicted; he underwent treatment for his addiction in 1886–7 and there is also some evidence of treatment for morphine addiction in 1892. As a consequence of these problems he moved to Johns Hopkins Hospital in Baltimore, where he was appointed Surgeon-in-Chief in 1890 and Professor of Surgery in 1892. In this role he devoted considerable time to laboratory study and made important contributions in the treatment of breast carcinoma, thyroid disease and aneurism. A perfectionist, his technical advances were an outcome of his approach to surgery, which was methodical and painstaking in comparison with the cavalier methods of some contemporaries.

Bibliography
1894, *Johns Hopkins Hospital Reports*, Baltimore (rubber gloves).
1924, *Surgical Papers by William Stewart Halsted,* ed. W.C. Berket, Baltimore.

Further Reading
W.G. McCallum, 1930, *William Stewart Halsted, Surgeon,* Baltimore.

MG

Hamilton, Harold Lee (Hal)

b. 14 June 1890 Little Shasta, California, USA
d. 3 May 1969 California, USA

American pioneer of diesel rail traction.

Orphaned as a child, Hamilton went to work for Southern Pacific Railroad in his teens, and then worked for several other companies. In his spare time he learned mathematics and physics from a retired professor. In 1911 he joined the White Motor Company, makers of road motor vehicles in Denver, Colorado, where he had gone to recuperate from malaria. He remained there until 1922, apart from an eighteenth-month break for war service.

Upon his return from war service, Hamilton found White selling petrol-engined railbuses with mechanical transmission, based on road vehicles, to railways. He noted that they were not robust enough and that the success of petrol railcars with electric transmission, built by General Electric since 1906, was limited as they were complex to drive and maintain. In 1922 Hamilton formed, and became President of, the Electro-Motive Engineering Corporation (later Electro-Motive Corporation) to design and produce petrol–electric railcars. Needing an engine larger than those used in road vehicles, yet lighter and faster than marine engines, he approached the Winton Engine Company to develop a suitable engine; in addition, General Electric provided electric transmission with a simplified control system. Using these components, Hamilton arranged for his petrol–electric railcars to be built by the St Louis Car Company, with the first being completed in 1924. It was the beginning of a highly successful series. Fuel costs were lower than for steam trains and initial costs were kept down by using standardized vehicles instead of designing for individual railways. Maintenance costs were minimized because Electro-Motive kept stocks of spare parts and supplied replacement units when necessary. As more powerful, 800 hp (600 kW) railcars were produced, railways tended to use them to haul trailer vehicles, although that practice reduced the fuel saving. By the end of the decade Electro-Motive needed engines more powerful still and therefore had to use cheap fuel. Diesel engines of the period, such as those that Winton had made for some years, were too heavy in relation to their power, and too slow and sluggish for rail use. Their fuel-injection system was erratic and insufficiently robust and Hamilton concluded that a separate injector was needed for each cylinder.

In 1930 Electro-Motive Corporation and Winton were acquired by General Motors in pursuance of their aim to develop a diesel engine suitable for rail traction, with the use of unit fuel injectors; Hamilton retained his position as President. At this time, industrial depression had combined with road and air competition to undermine railway-passenger business, and Ralph Budd, President of the Chicago, Burlington & Quincy Railroad, thought that traffic could be recovered by way of high-speed, luxury motor trains; hence the *Pioneer Zephyr* was built for the Burlington. This comprised a 600 hp (450 kW), lightweight, two-stroke, diesel engine developed by General Motors (model 201A), with electric transmission, that powered a streamlined train of three articulated coaches. This train demonstrated its powers on 26 May 1934 by running non-stop from Denver to Chicago, a distance of 1,015 miles (1,635 km), in 13 hours and 6 minutes, when the fastest steam schedule was 26 hours. Hamilton and Budd were among those on board the train, and it ushered in an era of high-speed diesel trains in the USA. By then Hamilton, with General Motors backing, was planning to use the lightweight engine to power diesel–electric locomotives. Their layout was derived not from steam locomotives, but from the standard American boxcar. The power plant was mounted within the body and powered the bogies, and driver's cabs were at each end. Two 900 hp (670 kW) engines were mounted in a single car to become an 1,800 hp (1,340 kW) locomotive, which could be operated in multiple by a single driver to form a 3,600 hp (2,680 kW) locomotive. To keep costs down, standard locomotives could be mass-produced rather than needing individual designs for each railway, as with steam locomotives. Two units of this type were completed in 1935 and sent on trial throughout much of the USA. They were able to match steam locomotive performance, with considerable economies: fuel costs alone were halved and there was much less wear on the track. In the same year, Electro-Motive began manufacturing diesel–electric locomotives at La Grange, Illinois, with design modifications: the driver was placed high up above a projecting nose, which improved visibility and provided protection in the event of collision on unguarded level crossings; six-wheeled bogies were introduced, to reduce axle loading and improve stability. The first production passenger locomotives emerged from La Grange in 1937, and by early 1939 seventy units were in service.

Meanwhile, improved engines had been developed and were being made at La Grange, and late in 1939 a prototype, four-unit, 5,400 hp (4,000 kW) diesel–electric locomotive for freight trains was produced and sent out on test from coast to coast; production versions appeared late in 1940. After an interval from 1941 to 1943, when Electro-Motive produced diesel engines for military and naval use, locomotive production resumed in quantity in 1944, and within a few years diesel power replaced steam on most railways in the USA.

Hal Hamilton remained President of Electro-Motive Corporation until 1942, when it became a division of General Motors, of which he became Vice-President.

Further Reading
F.M. Reck, 1948, *On Time: The History of the Electro-Motive Division of General Motors Corporation*, La Grange, Ill.: General Motors (describes Hamilton's career).

PJGR

Hammond, Robert
b. 19 January 1850 Waltham Cross, England
d. 5 August 1915 London, England

English engineer who established many of the earliest public electricity-supply systems in Britain.

After an education at Nunhead Grammar School, Hammond founded engineering businesses in Middlesbrough and London. Obtaining the first concession from the Anglo-American Brush Company for the exploitation of their system in Britain, he was instrumental in popularizing the Brush arc-lighting generator. Schemes using this system, which he established at Chesterfield, Brighton, Eastbourne and Hastings in 1881–2, were the earliest public electricity-supply ventures in Britain. On the invention of the incandescent lamp, high-voltage Brush dynamos were employed to operate both arc and incandescent lamps. The limitations of this arrangement led Hammond to become the sole agent for the **Ferranti** alternator, introduced in 1882. Commencing practice as a consulting engineer, Hammond was responsible for the construction of many electricity works in the United Kingdom, of which the most notable were those at Leeds,

Hackney (London) and Dublin, in addition to many abroad. Appreciating the need for trained engineers for the new electrical industry and profession then being created, in 1882 he established the Hammond Electrical Engineering College. Later, in association with Francis Ince, he founded Faraday House, a training school that pioneered the concept of 'sandwich courses' for engineers. Between 1883 and 1903 he paid several visits to the United States to study developments in electric traction and was one of the advisers to the Postmaster General on the acquisition of the telephone companies.

Bibliography
1884, *Electric Light in Our Homes*, London (one of the first detailed accounts of electric lighting).
1897, 'Twenty five years' developments in central stations', *Electrical Review* 41: 683–7 (surveys nineteenth-century public electricity supply).

Further Reading
F.W. Lipscomb, 1973, *The Wise Men of the Wires*, London (the story of Faraday House).
B. Bowers, 1985, biography, in *Dictionary of Business Biography*, Vol. III, ed. J. Jeremy, London, pp. 21–2 (provides an account of Hammond's business ventures).
J.D. Poulter, 1986, *An Early History of Electricity Supply*, London.

GW

Hancock, Thomas
b. 8 May 1786 Marlborough, Wiltshire, England
d. 26 March 1865 Stoke Newington, London, England

English founder of the British rubber industry.

After education at a private school in Marlborough, Hancock spent some time in 'mechanical pursuits'. He went to London to better himself and *c.*1819 his interest was aroused in the uses of rubber, which until then had been limited. His first patent, dated 29 April 1820, was for the application of rubber in clothing where some elasticity was useful, such as braces or slip-on boots. He noticed that freshly cut pieces of rubber could be made to adhere by pressure to form larger pieces. To cut up his imported and waste rubber into small pieces, Hancock developed his 'masticator'. This device consisted of a spiked roller revolving in a hollow cylinder. However, when rubber was fed in to the machine, the product was not the expected shredded rubber, but a homogeneous cylindrical mass of solid rubber, formed by the heat generated by the process and pressure against the outer cylinder. This rubber could then be compacted into blocks or rolled into sheets at his factory in Goswell Road, London; the blocks and sheets could be used to make a variety of useful articles. Meanwhile Hancock entered into partnership with Charles **Macintosh** in Manchester to manufacture rubberized, waterproof fabrics. Despite these developments, rubber remained an unsatisfactory material, becoming sticky when warmed and losing its elasticity when cold. In 1842 Hancock encountered specimens of vulcanized rubber prepared by Charles **Goodyear** in America. Hancock worked out for himself that it was made by heating rubber and sulphur, and obtained a patent for the manufacture of the material on 21 November 1843. This patent also included details of a new form of rubber, hardened by heating to a higher temperature, that was later called vulcanite, or ebonite. In 1846 he began making solid rubber tyres for road vehicles. Overall Hancock took out sixteen patents, covering all aspects of the rubber industry; they were a leading factor in the development of the industry from 1820 until their expiry in 1858.

Bibliography
1857, *Personal Narrative of the Origin and Progress of the Caoutchouc or Indiarubber Manufacture in England*, London.

Further Reading
H. Schurer, 1953, 'The macintosh: the paternity of an invention', *Transactions of the Newcomen Society* 28: 77–87.

LRD

Hancock, Walter

b. 16 June 1799 Marlborough, Wiltshire, England
d. 14 May 1852

English engineer and promoter of steam locomotion on common roads.

He was the sixth son of James Hancock, a cabinet-maker and merchant of Marlborough, Wiltshire. Initially Walter was apprenticed to a watchmaker and jeweller in London, but he soon turned his attention to engineering. In 1824 he invented a steam engine in which the cylinder and piston were replaced by two flexible bags of several layers of canvas and rubber solution, which were alternately filled with steam. The engine worked satisfactorily at Hancock's works in Stratford and its simplicity and lightness suggested its suitability for road carriages. Initial experiments were not very successful, but Hancock continued to experiment. After many trials in and around London, the *Infant* began a regular run between Stratford and London in February 1831. The following year he built the *Era* for the London and Brighton Steam Carriage Company. The *Enterprise* was next put on the road, by the London and Paddington Steam Carriage Company in April 1833. The *Autopsy* started to run from Finsbury Square to Pentonville in October of the same year and ran alternately with the *Erin* between the City and Paddington. Hancock's interest in steam road locomotion continued until about 1840, by which time he had built ten carriages. But by then public interest had declined and most of the companies involved had failed. Later, he turned his attention to indiarubber, working with his brother Thomas **Hancock**. In 1843 he obtained a patent for cutting rubber into sheets and for a method of preparing a solution of rubber.

Bibliography
1838, *Narrative of Twelve Years of Experiments (1824–1836) Demonstrative of the Practicability and Advantages of Employing Steam Carriages on Common Roads*, London.

IMcN

Handley Page, Sir Frederick

b. 15 November 1885 Cheltenham, England
d. 21 April 1962 London, England

English aviation pioneer, specialist in large aircraft and developer of the slotted wing for safer slow flying.

Frederick Handley Page trained as an electrical engineer but soon turned his attention to the more exciting world of aeronautics. He started by manufacturing propellers for aeroplanes and airships, and then in 1909 he founded a public company. His first aeroplane, the *Bluebird*, was not a success, but an improved version flew well. It was known as the 'Yellow Peril' because of its yellow doped finish and made a notable flight across London from Barking to Brooklands. In 1910 Handley Page became one of the first college lecturers in aeronautical engineering. During the First World War Handley Page concentrated on the production of large bombers. The *0/100* was a biplane with a wing span of 100 ft (30 m) and powered by two engines: it entered service in 1916. In 1918 an improved version, the *0/400*, entered service and a larger four-engined bomber made its first flight. This was the *V/1500*, which was designed to bomb Berlin, but the war ended before this raid took place. After the war, Handley Page turned his attention to airline operations with the great advantage of having at his disposal large bombers which could be adapted to carry passengers. Handley Page Air Transport Ltd was formed in 1919 and provided services to several European cities. Eventually this company became part of Imperial Airways, but Handley Page continued to supply them with large airliners. Probably the most famous was the majestic *HP 42* four-engined biplane, which set very high standards of comfort and safety. Safety was always important to Handley Page and in 1920 he developed a wing with a slot along the leading edge: this made slow flying safer by delaying the stall. Later versions used separate aerofoil-shaped slats on the leading edge that were sometimes fixed, sometimes retractable. The *HP 42* was fitted with these slats. From the 1930s Handley Page produced a series of bombers, such as the *Heyford*, *Hampden*, *Harrow* and, most famous of all, the *Halifax*, which played a major role in the Second World War. Then followed the *Victor* V-bomber of 1952 with its distinctive 'crescent' wing and high tailplane. Sir Frederick's last venture was the *Herald* short-haul airliner of 1955; designed to replace the ubiquitous Douglas *DC-3*, it was only a limited success.

Principal Honours and Distinctions
Knighted 1942. CBE 1918. Lord Lieutenant of the County of Middlesex 1956–60. Honorary Fellow of the Royal Aeronautical Society.

Bibliography
1950, 'Towards slower and safer flying, improved take-off and landing and cheaper airports', *Journal of the Royal Aeronautical Society*.

Further Reading
Two accounts of Handley Page's life and work were published in the *Journal of the Royal Aeronautical Society* December 1962 and July 1964.
D.C. Clayton, 1970, *Handley Page: An Aircraft Album*, London (for details of his aircraft).
C.H. Barnes, 1976, *Handley Page Aircraft since 1907*, London.

JDS

Hannart, Louis
fl. *c*.1863

Inventor of the first press stud for garments.

Fastenings are an essential component of the majority of garments. Until the middle of the nineteenth century, these relied on buttons or toggles passing through either button holes or loops of cord. The press stud stems from the invention by Louis Hannart in 1863 of an 'Improved clasp or fastener for gloves and other wearing apparel, for umbrellas, travelling bags . . .'.

Further Reading
I. McNeil (ed.), 1990, *An Encyclopaedia of the History of Technology*, London: Routledge, pp. 852–3 (provides a short account of fastenings).
RLH

Hansom, Joseph Aloysius
b. 26 October 1803 York, England
d. 29 June 1883 Fulham, London, England

English architect and inventor, originator of the Hansom cab.

In 1816 he was apprenticed to his father, who was a joiner. After a year his abilities in design and construction were so marked that it was decided that he would have more scope as an architect. He was accordingly apprenticed to a Mr Phillips in York, becoming a clerk to Phillips in 1820. While he served his time he also worked on his own account and taught at a night school. In 1825 he married Hannah Glover and settled in Halifax, where he became Assistant to another architect. In 1828 he became a partner of Edward Welch, with whom he built a number of churches in the north of England. He designed the Town Hall for Birmingham and was responsible for the constructional work until 1833, but he had to become bond because the builders caused him to become bankrupt. He was appointed Manager of the business affairs of Dempster Hemming of Caldicote Hall, which included the landed estates, banking and coal-mining. It was during this period that he designed the 'Patent Safety Cab' named after him and popular in Victorian days. The safety element consisted in lowering the centre of gravity by the use of the cranked axle. Hansom sold his rights for £10,000 to a company proposing to exploit the patent, but he was never paid, for the company got into difficulties; Hansom became its temporary Manager in 1839 and put matters right, for which he was paid £300, all he ever made out of the Hansom Cab. In 1842 he brought out the first issue of *The Builder*, but lack of capital caused him to retire from the journal. He devoted himself from then on to domestic and ecclesiastical architecture, designing many churches, colleges, convents and schools all over Britain and even in Australia and South America. Of note is St Walburga's church, Preston, Lancashire, whose spire is 306 ft (93 m) high. At various times he was in partnership with his younger brother, his eldest son, and with E.W. Pugin with whom he had a disagreement. He was a Catholic and much of his work was for the Catholic Church.

Further Reading
1882, *The Builder* (8 July).
1882, *Illustrated London News* (15 July).

IMcN

Hargreaves, James

b. *c.*1720–1 Oswaldtwistle, near Blackburn, England
d. April 1778 Nottingham, England

English inventor of the first successful machine to spin more than a couple of yarns of cotton or wool at once.

James Hargreaves was first a carpenter and then a hand-loom weaver at Stanhill, Blackburn, probably making Blackburn Checks or Greys from linen warps and cotton weft. An invention ascribed to him doubled production in the preparatory carding process before spinning. Two

or three cards were nailed to the same stock and the upper one was suspended from the ceiling by a cord and counterweight. Around 1762 Robert Peel (1750–1830) sought his assistance in constructing a carding engine with cylinders that may have originated with Daniel **Bourn**, but this was not successful. In 1764, inspired by seeing a spinning wheel that continued to revolve after it had been knocked over accidentally, Hargreaves invented his spinning jenny. The first jennies had horizontal wheels and could spin eight threads at once. To spin on this machine required a great deal of skill. A length of roving was passed through the clamp or clove. The left hand was used to close this and draw the roving away from the spindles which were rotated by the spinner turning the horizontal wheel with the right hand. The spindles twisted the fibres as they were being drawn out. At the end of the draw, the spindles continued to be rotated until sufficient twist had been put into the fibres to make the finished yarn. This was backed off from the tips of the spindles by reversing them and then, with the spindles turning in the spinning direction once more, the yarn was wound on by the right hand rotating the spindles, the left hand pushing the clove back towards them and one foot operating a pedal which guided the yarn onto the spindles by a faller wire. A piecer was needed to rejoin the yarns when they broke. At first Hargreaves's jenny was worked only by his family, but then he sold two or three of them, possibly to Peel. In 1768, local opposition and a riot in which his house was gutted forced him to flee to Nottingham. He entered into partnership there with Thomas James and established a cotton mill. In 1770 he followed **Arkwright**'s example and sought to patent his machine and brought an action for infringement against some Lancashire manufacturers, who offered £3,000 in settlement. Hargreaves held out for £4,000, but he was unable to enforce his patent because he had sold jennies before leaving Lancashire. Arkwright's 'water twist' was more suitable for the Nottingham hosiery industry trade than jenny yarn and in 1777 Hargreaves replaced his own machines with Arkwright's. When he died the following year, he is said to have left property valued at £7,000 and his widow received £400 for her share in the business. Once the jenny had been made public, it was quickly improved by other inventors and the number of spindles per machine increased. In 1784, there were reputed to be 20,000 jennies of 80 spindles each at work. The jenny greatly eased the shortage of cotton weft for weavers.

Bibliography
1770, British patent no. 962 (spinning jenny).

Further Reading
C. Aspin and S.D. Chapman, 1964, *James Har- greaves and the Spinning Jenny*, Helmshore Local History Society (the fullest account of Hargreaves's life and inventions).
For descriptions of his invention, see W. English, 1969, *The Textile Industry*, London; R.L. Hills, 1970, *Power in the Industrial Revol- ution*, Manchester; and W.A. Hunter, 1951–3, 'James Hargreaves and the invention of the spinning jenny', *Transactions of the Newcomen Society* 28.
A.P. Wadsworth and J. de L. Mann, 1931, *The Cotton Trade and Industrial Lancashire*, Man- chester (a good background to the whole of this period).

RLH

Harington, Sir John

b. 1561 Kelston (?), Somerset, England
d. 20 November 1612 Kelston, Somerset, Eng- land

English inventor of the valve-operated water-closet.

Harington was a writer and poet and was a god- son of Queen Elizabeth I. In 1596 he published a satire entitled *A New Discourse upon a Stale Subject called the Metamorphosis of Ajax*, which described the water-closet that he constructed for his home in Kelston, near Bath. Ajax was a whimsical reference to 'jakes', a euphemism for privy or closet. The use of the water-closet, he declared, 'would make unsavoury Places sweet, noisome Places wholesome and filthy Places cleanly'. The water-closet was illustrated in his book and was, in effect, a water-fed and -control- led close-stool. Water was pumped up into a cis- tern, which fed a closet pan, and was retained there by the operation of a valve. The water ac- tion was controlled by a handle set into the seat of the pan, thus causing the sewage to be dis- charged into a cesspool beneath. However, be- cause of the lack of adequate water supplies and

sewage systems, Harington's invention was not generally taken up until 1775, when Alexander Cumming patented it.

Further Reading
Lucinda Lambton, 1978, *Temples of Conveni- ence*: Gordon Fraser.

DY

Harris, Alanson

b. 1816 Ingersoll, Ontario, Canada
d. 1894 Canada

Canadian manufacturer of agricultural machinery and co-founder of the Massey Harris Company (later Massey Ferguson).

Alanson Harris was the first of ten children born to the wife of a circuit rider and preacher. His father's wanderings left Alanson at an early age in charge of the running of the family farm on the Grand River in Canada; also, his father's pref- erence was for tinkering with machines rather than for farming. However, when he was 13 Alanson had to go out to work in order to bring badly needed cash to augment the family in- come. He worked at a sawmill in the small village of Boston, becoming Boss Sawyer and then Foreman after ten years. In 1839 the family moved to Mount Pleasant, and the following year Alanson married Mary Morgan, the daughter of a well-to-do pioneer Welsh farmer. He entered into a brief partnership with his father to build a sawmill at Whiteman's Creek, but within a few months his father returned to preaching and Alanson became the sole proprie- tor. After a successful early period Alanson rec- ognized the signs of decline in the timber market, and in 1857 he sold the mill, moved to Beamsville, Niagara, and bought a small factory from which he produced the flop-over hay rake invented by his father. In 1863 he took his eldest son into partnership; the latter returned from a visit to the United States with the sole rights to produce the Kirby mower and reaper. The Cri- mean War created a market for corn, which gave a great boost to North American farming and, in its turn, to machinery production. This was rein- forced by the tariff agreements between the United States and Canada. By the 1880s Harris and **Massey** between them accounted for two thirds of the harvesting machines sold in Canada, and they also supplied machines abroad. By the end of the decade the mutual benefits of joining forces were apparent and by 1891 an agreement was reached, with Alanson Harris and A.H. Massey on the first board.

Further Reading

G. Quick and W. Buchele, 1978, *The Grain Harvesters*, American Society of Agricultural Engineers (refers to Harris and Massey Harris Company in its account of the development of harvest machinery).

M. Denison, 1949, *Harvest Triumphant: The Story of Massey Harris*, London (gives a more detailed account of Massey Harris Company).

AP

Harrison, James

b. 1816 Glasgow, Scotland
d. 3 September 1893 Geelong, Victoria, Australia

Scottish pioneer of the transport of frozen meat.

James Harrison emigrated to Australia in 1834, and in 1840 settled in Geelong as a journalist. At one time he was editor of the *Melbourne Age*. In 1850 he began to devote his attention to the development of an ice-making scheme, erecting the first factory at Rodey Point, Barwin, in that year. In 1851 the Brewery Glasgow & Co. in Bendigo, Victoria, installed the first Harrison refrigerator. He took out patents for his invention in 1856 and 1857, and visited London at about the same time. On his return to Australia he began experiments into the long-term freezing of meat. In 1873 he publicly exhibited the process in Melbourne and organized a banquet for the consumption of meat which had been in store for six months. In July of the same year the SS *Norfolk* sailed with a cargo of 20 tons of frozen mutton and beef, but this began to rot en route to London. The refrigeration plant was later put to use in a paraffin factory in London, but the failure ruined Harrison and took all his newspaper profits.

Further Reading

J.T. Critchell, 1912, *A History of the Frozen Meat Trade*, London (gives a brief account of Harrison's abortive but essential part in the transport of frozen meat).

AP

Harrison, John

b. 24 March 1693 Foulby, Yorkshire, England
d. 24 March 1776 London, England

English horologist who constructed the first timekeeper of sufficient accuracy to determine longitude at sea and invented the gridiron pendulum for temperature compensation.

John Harrison was the son of a carpenter and was brought up to that trade. He was largely self-taught and learned mechanics from a copy of Nicholas Saunderson's lectures that had been lent to him. With the assistance of his younger brother, James, he built a series of unconventional clocks, mainly of wood. He was always concerned to reduce friction, without using oil, and this influenced the design of his 'grasshopper' escapement. He also invented the 'gridiron' compensation pendulum, which depended on the differential expansion of brass and steel. The excellent performance of his regulator clocks, which incorporated these devices, convinced him that they could also be used in a sea clock to compete for the longitude prize. In 1714 the Government had offered a prize of £20,000 for a method of determining longitude at sea to within half a degree after a voyage to the West Indies. In theory the longitude could be found by carrying an accurate timepiece that would indicate the time at a known longitude, but the requirements of the Act were very exacting. The timepiece would have to have a cumulative error of no more than two minutes after a voyage lasting six weeks.

In 1730 Harrison went to London with his proposal for a sea clock, supported by examples of his grasshopper escapement and his gridiron pendulum. His proposal received sufficient encouragement and financial support, from George **Graham** and others, to enable him to return to Barrow and construct his first sea clock, which he completed five years later. This was a large and complicated machine that was made out of brass but retained the wooden wheelwork and the grasshopper escapement of the regulator clocks. The two balances were interlinked to counteract the rolling of the vessel and were controlled by helical springs operating in tension. It was the first timepiece with a balance to have temperature compensation. The effect of temperature change on the timekeeping of a balance is more pronounced than it is for a pendulum, as two effects are involved: the change in the size of the balance; and the change in the elasticity of the balance spring. Harrison compensated for both effects by using a gridiron arrangement to alter the tension in the springs. This timekeeper performed creditably when it was tested on a voyage to Lisbon, and the Board of Longitude agreed to finance improved models. Harrison's second timekeeper dispensed with the use of wood and had the added refinement of a remontoire, but even before it was tested he had embarked on a third machine. The balance of this machine was controlled by a spiral spring whose effective length was altered by a bimetallic strip to compensate for changes in temperature. In 1753 Harrison commissioned a London watchmaker, John Jefferys, to make a watch for his own personal use, with a similar form of temperature compensation and a modified verge escapement that was intended to compensate for the lack of isochronism of the balance spring. The timekeeping of this watch was surprisingly good and Harrison proceeded to build a larger and more sophisticated version, with a remontoire. This timekeeper was completed in 1759 and its performance was so remarkable that Harrison decided to enter it for the longitude prize in place of his third machine. It was tested on two voyages to the West Indies and on both occasions it met the requirements of the Act, but the Board of Longitude withheld half the prize money until they had proof that the timekeeper could be duplicated. Copies were made by Harrison and by Larcum Kendall, but the Board still continued to prevaricate and Harrison received the full amount of the prize in 1773 only after George III had intervened on his behalf.

Although Harrison had shown that it was possible to construct a timepiece of sufficient accuracy to determine longitude at sea, his solution was too complex and costly to be produced in quantity. It had, for example, taken Larcum Kendall two years to produce his copy of Harrison's fourth timekeeper, but Harrison had overcome the psychological barrier and opened the door for others to produce chronometers in quantity at an affordable price. This was achieved before the end of the century by **Arnold** and Earnshaw, but they used an entirely different design that owed more to **Le Roy** than it did to Harrison and which only retained Harrison's maintaining power.

Principal Honours and Distinctions
Royal Society Copley Medal 1749.

Bibliography
1767, *The Principles of Mr Harrison's Timekeeper, with Plates of the Same*, London.
1767, *Remarks on a Pamphlet Lately Published by the Rev. Mr Maskelyne Under the Authority of the Board of Longitude*, London.
1775, *A Description Concerning Such Mechanisms as Will Afford a Nice or True Mensuration of Time*, London.

Further Reading
R.T. Gould, 1923, *The Marine Chronometer: Its History and Development*, London; reprinted 1960, Holland Press.
— 1978, *John Harrison and His Timekeepers*, 4th edn, London: National Maritime Museum.
H. Quill, 1966, *John Harrison, the Man who Found Longitude*, London.
A.G. Randall, 1989, 'The technology of John Harrison's portable timekeepers', *Antiquarian Horology* 18: 145–60, 261–77.
J. Betts, 1993, *John Harrison* London (a good short account of Harrison's work).
S. Smiles, 1905, *Men of Invention and Industry*, London: John Murray, Chapter III.
Dictionary of National Biography, Vol. IX, pp. 35–6.

See also: **Burgi, Jost; Huygens, Christiaan.**

DV

Hartley, Ralph V.L.
b. 1889 USA
d. 1 May 1970 Summit, New Jersey, USA

American engineer who made contributions to radio communications.

Hartley obtained his BA in 1909 from the University of Utah, then gained a Rhodes Scholarship to Oxford University, England. After obtaining a further BA and a BSc in 1912 and 1913, respectively, he returned to the USA and took a job with the Western Electric Laboratories of the Bell Telephone Company, where he was in charge of radio-receiver development. In 1915 he invented the Hartley oscillator, analogous to that invented by **Colpitts**. Subsequently he worked on carrier telephony at Western Electric and then at Bell Laboratories. There he concentrated on information theory, building on the pioneering work of **Nyquist**, in 1926 publishing his law that related information capacity, frequency bandwidth and time. Forced to give up work in 1929 due to ill health, he returned to Bell in 1939 as a consultant on transmission problems. During the Second World War he worked on various projects, including the use of servo-mechanisms for radar and fire control, and finally retired in 1950.

Principal Honours and Distinctions
Institution of Electrical and Electronics Engineers Medal of Honour 1946.

Bibliography
29 May 1918, US patent no. 1,592,934 (plate modulator).
29 September 1919, US patent no. 1,419,562 (balanced modulator or detector).
1922, with T.C. Fry, 'Binaural location of complex sounds', *Bell Systems Technical Journal* (November).
1923, 'Relation of carrier and sidebands in radio transmission', *Proceedings of the Institute of Radio Engineers* 11: 34.
1924, 'The transmission unit', *Electrical Communications* 3: 34.
1926, 'Transmission limits of telephone lines', *Bell Laboratories Record* 1: 225.
1928, 'Transmission of information', *Bell Systems Technical Journal* (July).
1928, '"TU" becomes Decibel', *Bell Laboratories Record* 7: 137.
1936, 'Oscillations in systems with non-linear reactance', *Bell System Technology Journal* 15: 424.

Further Reading
M.D. Fagen (ed.), 1975, *A History of Engineering & Science in the Bell System*, Vol. 1: Bell Laboratories.

KF

Harwood, John
b. 1893 Bolton, England
d. 9 August 1964

English watchmaker, inventor and producer of the first commercial self-winding wrist watch.

John Harwood served an apprenticeship as a watch repairer in Bolton, and after service in the First World War he obtained a post with a firm of jewellers in Douglas, Isle of Man. He became interested in the self-winding wrist watch, not because of the convenience of not having to wind it, but because of its potential to keep the mainspring fully wound and to exclude dust and moisture from the watch movement. His experience at the bench had taught him that these were the most common factors to affect adversely the reliability of watches. Completely unaware of previous work in this area, in 1922 he started experimenting and two years later he had produced a serviceable model for which he was granted a patent in 1924. The watch operated on the pedometer principle, the mainspring being wound by a pivoted weight that oscillated in the watch case as a result of the motion of the arm. The hands of his watch were set by rotating the bezel surrounding the dial, dispensing with the usual winding/hand-setting stem which allowed dust and moisture to enter the watch case. He took the watch to Switzerland, but he was unable to persuade the watchmaking firms to produce it until he had secured independent finance to cover the cost of tooling. The Harwood Self-Winding Watch Company Ltd was set up in 1928 to market the watches, but although several thousand were produced the company became a victim of the slump and closed down in 1932. The first practical self-winding watch also operated on the pedometer principle and is attributed to Abraham-Louis Perrellet (1770). The method was refined by **Breguet** in France and by Recordon, who patented the device in England, but it proved troublesome and went out of fashion. There was a brief revival of interest in self-winding watches towards the end of the nineteenth century, but they never achieved great popularity until after the Second World War, when they used either self-winding mechanisms similar to that devised by Harwood or weights which rotated in the case.

Principal Honours and Distinctions
British Horological Institute Gold Medal 1957.

Bibliography
1 September 1924, Swiss patent no. 106,582.

Further Reading
A. Chapuis and E. Jaquet, 1956, *The History of the Self-Winding Watch*, London (provides

general information).

'How the automatic wrist watch was invented', 1957, *Horological Journal* 99: 612–61 (for specific information).

DV

Haupt, Hans
fl. *c.*1930 Berlin, Germany

German inventor of the telescopic umbrella.

Few biographical details are known of Hans Haupt, other than that he invented the telescopic umbrella in Berlin in 1930. His device gave protection from rain and sun similar to that provided by Samuel **Fox**'s lightweight steel-framed device of 1874, but it was much more compact when folded.

Further Reading
There is a brief mention in I. McNeil (ed.), 1990, *An Encyclopaedia of the History of Technology*, London: Routledge, p. 853; and in C. Singer (ed.), 1958, *A History of Technology*, Vol. IV, Oxford: Clarendon Press.

RLH

Hauron, Louis Ducos du
See **Ducos du Hauron, Louis**.

Havilland, Geoffrey de
See **de Havilland, Geoffrey**.

Haynes, Elwood
b. 14 October 1857 Portland, Indiana, USA
d. 13 April 1925 Kokomo, Indiana, USA

American inventor of Stellite cobalt-based alloys, early motor-car manufacturer and pioneer in stainless steels.

From his early years, Haynes was a practising Presbyterian and an active prohibitionist. He graduated in 1881 at Worcester, Massachusetts, and a spell of teaching in his home town was interrupted in 1884–5 while he attended the Johns Hopkins University in Baltimore. In 1886 he became permanently diverted by the discovery of natural gas in Portland. He was soon appointed Superintendent of the local gas undertaking, and then in 1890 he was hired by the Indiana Natural Gas & Oil Company. While continuing his gas-company employment until 1901, Haynes conducted numerous metallurgi-

cal experiments. He also designed an automobile: this led to the establishment of the Haynes–Apperson Company at Kokomo as one of the earliest motor-car makers in North America. From 1905 the firm traded as the Haynes Automobile Company, and before its bankruptcy in 1924 it produced more than 50,000 cars. After 1905, Haynes found the first 'Stellite' alloys of cobalt and chromium, and in 1910 he was publicizing the patented material. He then discovered the valuable hardening effect of tungsten, and in 1912 began applying the 'improved' Stellite to cutting tools. Three years later, the Haynes Stellite Company was incorporated, with Haynes as President, to work the patents. It was largely from this source that Haynes became a millionaire in 1920. In April 1912, Haynes's attempt to patent the use of chromium with iron to render the product rustless was unsuccessful. However, he re-applied for a US patent on 12 March 1915 and, although this was initially rejected, he persevered and finally obtained recognition of his modified claim. The American Stainless Steel Company licensed the patents of **Brearley** and Haynes jointly in the USA until the 1930s.

Principal Honours and Distinctions
John Scott Medal 1919 (awarded for useful inventions).

Bibliography
Haynes was the author of more than twenty published papers and articles, among them:
1907, 'Materials for automobiles', *Proceedings of the American Society of Mechanical Engineers* 29: 1,597–606;
1910, 'Alloys of nickel and cobalt with chromium', *Journal of Industrial Engineering and Chemistry* 2: 397–401;
1912–13, 'Alloys of cobalt with chromium and other metals', *Transactions of the American Institute of Mining Engineers* 44: 249–55;
1919–20, 'Stellite and stainless steel', *Proceedings of the Engineering Society of West Pennsylvania* 35: 467–74.
1 April 1919, US patent no. 1,299,404 (stainless steel).
The four US patents worked by the Haynes Stellite Company were:
17 December 1907, patent no. 873,745.
1 April 1913, patent no. 1,057,423.

1 April 1913, patent no. 1,057,828.
17 August 1915, patent no. 1,150,113.

Further Reading
R.D. Gray, 1979, *Alloys and Automobiles. The Life of Elwood Haynes*, Indianapolis: Indiana Historical Society (a closely documented biography).

JKA

Heald, James Nichols

b. 21 September 1864 Barre, Massachusetts, USA
d. 7 May 1931 Worcester, Massachusetts, USA

American mechanical engineer and machine-tool manufacturer who concentrated on grinding machines.

James N. Heald was the son of Leander S. Heald and was educated at the Worcester Polytechnic Institute, graduating with the degree of Bachelor of Science in 1884. He then joined the firm that had been established by his grandfather, Stephen Heald, in 1826; this was a machine shop and foundry then known as S. Heald & Son. When his grandfather died in 1888, James Heald took over the management of the business, which then became known as L.S. Heald & Son. He concentrated on the manufacture of grinding machines and in 1903 bought out his father's interest and organized the Heald Machine Company. James Heald then began the development of a series of grinding machines designed to meet the needs of the expanding automobile industry. Special machines were produced for grinding piston rings making use of the recently invented magnetic chuck, and for cylinder bores he introduced the planetary grinder. Heald was a member of the National Machine Tool Builders' Association and served as its Treasurer and on its Board of Directors. He was elected a member of the American Society of Mechanical Engineers in 1917 and was also a member of the Society of Automotive Engineers.

Further Reading
Robert S. Woodbury, 1959, *History of the Grinding Machine*, Cambridge, Mass (describes his grinding machines).
L.T.C. Rolt, 1965, *Tools for the Job*, London; repub. 1986 (describes his grinding machines).

RTS

Heathcote, John

b. 7 August 1783 Duffield, Derbyshire, England
d. 18 January 1861 Tiverton, Devonshire, England

English inventor of the bobbin-net lace machine.

Heathcote was the son of a small farmer who became blind, obliging the family to move to Long Whatton, near Loughborough, *c.*1790. He was apprenticed to W. Shepherd, a hosiery-machine maker, and became a frame-smith in the hosiery industry. He moved to Nottingham where he entered the employment of an excellent machine maker named Elliott. He later joined William Caldwell of Hathern, whose daughter he had married. The lace-making apparatus they patented jointly in 1804 had already been anticipated, so Heathcote turned to the problem of making pillow lace, a cottage industry in which women made lace by arranging pins stuck in a pillow in the correct pattern and winding around them thread contained on thin bobbins. He began by analysing the complicated hand-woven lace into simple warp and weft threads and found he could dispense with half the bobbins. The first machine he developed and patented, in 1808, made narrow lace an inch or so wide, but the following year he made much broader lace on an improved version. In his second patent, in 1809, he could make a type of net curtain, Brussels lace, without patterns. His machine made bobbin-net by the use of thin brass discs, between which the thread was wound. As they passed through the warp threads, which were arranged vertically, the warp threads were moved to each side in turn, so as to twist the bobbin threads round the warp threads. The bobbins were in two rows to save space, and jogged on carriages in grooves along a bar running the length of the machine. As the strength of this fabric depended upon bringing the bobbin threads diagonally across, in addition to the forward movement, the machine had to provide for a sideways movement of each bobbin every time the lengthwise course was completed. A high standard of accuracy in manufacture was essential for success. Called the 'Old Loughborough', it was acknowledged to be the most complicated machine so far produced. In partnership with a man named Charles Lacy, who supplied the necessary capital, a factory was established at Loughborough that proved highly successful; however, their fifty-five frames were destroyed by Luddites in 1816. Heathcote was awarded damages of £10,000 by the county of Nottingham on the condition it was spent locally, but to avoid further interference he decided to transfer not only his machines but his entire workforce elsewhere and refused the money. In a disused woollen factory at Tiverton in Devonshire, powered by the waters of the river Exe, he built 300 frames of greater width and speed. By continually making inventions and improvements until he retired in 1843, his business flourished and he amassed a large fortune. He patented one machine for silk cocoon-reeling and another for plaiting or braiding. In 1825 he brought out two patents for the mechanical ornamentation or figuring of lace. He acquired a sound knowledge of French prior to opening a steam-powered lace factory in France. The factory proved to be a successful venture that lasted many years. In 1832 he patented a monstrous steam plough that is reputed to have cost him over £12,000 and was claimed to be the best in its day. One of its stated aims was 'improved methods of draining land', which he hoped would develop agriculture in Ireland. A cable was used to haul the implement across the land. From 1832 to 1859, Heathcote represented Tiverton in Parliament and, among other benefactions, he built a school for his adopted town.

Bibliography
1804, with William Caldwell, British patent no. 2,788 (lace-making machine).
1808, British patent no. 3,151 (machine for making narrow lace).
1809, British patent no. 3,216 (machine for making Brussels lace).
1813, British patent no. 3,673.
1825, British patent no. 5,103 (mechanical ornamentation of lace).
1825, British patent no. 5,144 (mechanical ornamentation of lace).

Further Reading
V. Felkin, 1867, *History of the Machine-wrought Hosiery and Lace Manufacture*, Nottingham (provides a full account of Heathcote's early life and his inventions).
A. Barlow, 1878, *The History and Principles of Weaving by Hand and by Power*, London (provides more details of his later years).
W.G. Allen, 1958, *John Heathcote and His Heritage* (biography).
M.R. Lane, 1980, *The Story of the Steam Plough Works, Fowlers of Leeds*, London (for comments about Heathcote's steam plough).
W. English, 1969, *The Textile Industry*, London, and C. Singer (ed.), 1958, *A History of Technology*, Vol. V, Oxford: Clarendon Press (both describe the lace-making machine).

RLH

Heaviside, Oliver
b. 18 May 1850 London, England
d. 2 February 1925 Torquay, Devon, England

English physicist who correctly predicted the existence of the ionosphere and its ability to reflect radio waves.

Brought up in poor, almost Dickensian, circumstances, at the age of 13 years Heaviside, a nephew by marriage of Sir Charles **Wheatstone**, went to Camden House Grammar School. There he won a medal for science, but he was forced to leave because his parents could not afford the fees. After a year of private study, he began his working life in Newcastle in 1870 as a telegraph operator for an Anglo-Dutch cable company, but he had to give up after only four years because of increasing deafness. He therefore proceeded to spend his time studying theoretical aspects of electrical transmission and communication, and moved to Devon with his parents in 1889. Because the operation of many electrical circuits involves transient phenomena, he found it necessary to develop what he called operational calculus (which was essentially a form of the Laplace transform calculus) in order to determine the response to sudden voltage and current changes. In 1893 he suggested that the distortion that occurred on long-distance telephone lines could be reduced by adding loading coils at regular intervals, thus creating a matched-transmission line. Between 1893 and 1912 he produced a series of writings on electromagnetic theory, in one of which, anticipating a conclusion of Einstein's special theory of relativity, he put forward the idea that the mass of an electric charge increases with its velocity. When it was found that despite the curvature of the earth it was possible to communicate over very great distances using radio signals in the so-called 'short' wavebands, Heaviside suggested the presence of a conducting layer in the ionosphere that reflected the waves back to earth. Since a similar suggestion had been made almost at the same time by Arthur **Kennelly** of Harvard, this layer became known as the Kennelly–Heaviside layer.

Principal Honours and Distinctions
FRS 1891. Institution of Electrical Engineers Faraday Medal 1924. Honorary PhD Gottingen. Honorary Member of the American Association for the Advancement of Science.

Bibliography
1872, 'A method for comparing electro-motive forces', *English Mechanic* (July).
1873, *Philosophical Magazine* (February) (a paper on the use of the Wheatstone Bridge).
1889, *Electromagnetic Waves*.
1892, *Electrical Papers*.
1893–1912, *Electromagnetic Theory*.

Further Reading
I. Catt (ed.), 1987, *Oliver Heaviside, The Man*, St Albans: CAM Publishing.
P.J. Nahin, 1988, *Oliver Heaviside, Sage in Solitude: The Life and Works of an Electrical Genius of the Victorian Age*, Institute of Electrical and Electronics Engineers, New York.
J.B. Hunt, *The Maxwellians*, Ithaca: Cornell University Press.

See also **Appleton, Sir Edward Victor**.

KF

Hedley, William
b. 13 July 1779 Newburn, Northumberland, England
d. 9 January 1843 Lanchester, Co. Durham, England

English coal-mine manager, pioneer in the construction and use of steam locomotives.

The Wylam wagonway passed Newburn, and Hedley, who went to school at Wylam, must have been familiar with this wagonway from childhood. It had been built *c.*1748 to carry coal from Wylam Colliery to the navigable limit of the Tyne at Lemington. In 1805 Hedley was appointed viewer, or manager, of Wylam Colliery by Christopher Blackett, who had inherited the colliery and wagonway in 1800. Unlike most Tyneside wagonways, the gradient of the Wylam line was insufficient for loaded wagons to run down by gravity and they had to be hauled by horses. Blackett had a locomotive, of the type designed by Richard **Trevithick**, built at Gateshead as early as 1804 but did not take delivery, probably because his wooden track was not strong enough. In 1808 Blackett and Hedley relaid the wagonway with plate rails of the type promoted by Benjamin **Outram**, and in 1812, following successful introduction of locomotives at Middleton by John **Blenkinsop**, Blackett asked Hedley to investigate the feasibility of locomotives at Wylam. The expense of re-laying with rack rails was unwelcome, and Hedley experimented to find out the relationship between the weight of a locomotive and the load it could move relying on its adhesion weight alone. He used first a model test carriage, which survives at the Science Museum, London, and then used a full-sized test carriage laden with weights in varying quantities and propelled by men turning handles. Having apparently satisfied himself on this point, he had a locomotive incorporating the frames and wheels of the test carriage built. The work was done at Wylam by Thomas Waters, who was familiar with the 1804 locomotive, Timothy **Hackworth**, foreman smith, and Jonathan Forster, enginewright. This locomotive, with cast-iron boiler and single cylinder, was unsatisfactory: Hackworth and Forster then built another locomotive to Hedley's design, with a wrought-iron return-tube boiler, two vertical external cylinders and drive via overhead beams through pinions to the two axles. This locomotive probably came into use in the spring of 1814: it performed well and further examples of the type were built. Their axle loading, however, was too great for the track and from about 1815 each locomotive was mounted on two four-wheeled bogies, the bogie having recently been invented by William Chapman. Hedley eventually left Wylam in 1827 to devote himself to other colliery interests. He supported the construction of the Clarence Railway, opened in 1833, and sent his coal over it in trains hauled by his own locomotives. Two of his Wylam locomotives survive – *Puffing Billy* at the Science Museum, London, and *Wylam Dilly* at the Royal Museum of Scotland, Edinburgh – though how much of these is original and how much dates from the period 1827–32, when the Wylam line was re-laid with edge rails and the locomotives reverted to four wheels (with flanges), is a matter of mild controversy.

Further Reading
P.R.B. Brooks, 1980, *William Hedley Locomotive Pioneer*, Newcastle upon Tyne: Tyne & Wear Industrial Monuments Trust (a good recent short biography of Hedley, with bibliography).
R. Young, 1975, *Timothy Hackworth and the Locomotive*, Shildon: Shildon 'Stockton & Darlington Railway' Silver Jubilee Committee; orig. pub. 1923, London.
C.R. Warn, 1976, *Waggonways and Early Railways of Northumberland*, Newcastle upon Tyne: Frank Graham.

See also **Stephenson, George**.

PJGR

Heilmann, Josué (Joshua)
b. 1796 Alsace
d. 1848

Alsatian inventor of the first machine for combing cotton.

Josué Heilmann, of Mulhouse, was awarded 5,000 francs offered by the cotton spinners of Alsace for a machine that would comb cotton. It was a process not hitherto applied to this fibre and, when perfected, enabled finer, smoother and more lustrous yarns to be spun. The important feature of Heilmann's method was to use a grip or nip to hold the end of the sliver that was being combed. Two or more combs passed through the protruding fibres to comb them thoroughly, and a brush cylinder and knife cleared away the noils. The combed section was passed forward so that the part held in the nip could then be combed. The combed fibres were joined up with the length already finished. Heilmann obtained a British patent in 1846, but no machines were put to work until 1851. Six firms of cotton spinners in Lancashire paid £30,000 for the cotton-combing rights and Marshall's of Leeds paid £20,000 for the rights to comb flax. Heilmann's machine was used on the European continent for combing silk as well as flax, wool and cotton, so it proved to be very versatile. Priority of his patent was challenged in England because **Lister** had patented a combing machine with a gripper or nip in 1843; in 1852 the parties went to litigation and cross-suits were instituted. While Heilmann obtained a verdict of infringement against Lister for certain things, Lister also obtained one against Heilmann for other matters. After this outcome, Heilmann's patent was bought on speculation by Messrs Akroyd and Titus **Salt** for £30,000, but was afterwards resold to Lister for the same amount. In this way Lister was able to exploit his own patent through suppressing Heilmann's.

Bibliography
1846, British patent no. 11,103 (cotton-combing machine).

Further Reading
For descriptions of his combing machine see:
W. English, 1969, *The Textile Industry*, London;
T.K. Derry and T. I. Williams, 1960, *A Short History of Technology from the Earliest Times to AD 1900*, Oxford; and C. Singer (ed.), 1958, *A History of Technology*, Vol. IV, Oxford: Clarendon Press.

RLH

Heinkel, Ernst
b. 24 January 1888 Grünbach, Remstal, Germany
d. 30 January 1958 Stuttgart, Germany

German aeroplane designer who was responsible for the first jet aeroplane to fly.

The son of a coppersmith, as a young man Ernst Heinkel was much affected by seeing the **Zeppelin** *LZ 4* crash and burn out at Echterdringen, near Stuttgart. After studying engineering, in 1910 he designed his first aeroplane, but it crashed; he was more successful the following year when he made a flight in it, with an engine on hire from the **Daimler** company. After a period working for a firm near Munich and for LVG at Johannisthal, near Berlin, he moved to the Albatros Company of Berlin with a monthly salary of 425 marks. In May 1913 he moved to Lake Constance to work on the design of seaplanes and in May 1914 he moved again, this time to the Brandenburg Company, where he remained as a designer until 1922, when he founded his own company, Ernst Heinkel Flugzeugwerke. Following the First World War, German companies were not allowed to build military aircraft, which was frustrating for

Heinkel whose main interest was high-speed aircraft. His sleek *He 70* airliner, built for Lufthansa, was designed to carry four passengers at high speeds: indeed it broke many records in 1933. Lufthansa decided it needed a larger version capable of carrying ten passengers, so Heinkel produced his most famous aeroplane, the *He 111*. Although it was designed as a twin-engined airliner on the surface, secretly Heinkel was producing a bomber. The airliner version first flew on Lufthansa routes in 1936, and by 1939 almost 1,000 bombers were in service with the Luftwaffe. A larger four-engined bomber, the *He 177*, ran into development problems and it did not see service until late in the Second World War. Heinkel's quest for speed led to the *He 176* rocket-powered research aeroplane which flew on 20 June 1939, but Hitler and Goering were not impressed. The *He 178*, with Dr Hans von **Ohain**'s jet engine, made its historic first flight a few weeks later on 27 August 1939; this was almost two years before the maiden flight in Britain of the Gloster *E 28/39*, powered by **Whittle**'s jet engine. This project was a private venture by Heinkel and was carried out in great secrecy, so the world's first jet aircraft went almost unnoticed. Heinkel's jet fighters, the *He 280* and the *He 162*, were never fully operational. After the war, Heinkel in 1950 set up a new company which made bicycles, motor cycles and 'bubble' cars.

Bibliography

1956, *He 1000*, trans. M. Savill, London: Hutchinson (the English edition of his autobiography).

Further Reading

J. Stroud, 1966, *European Transport Aircraft since 1910*, London.
Jane's Fighting Aircraft of World War II, London: Jane's; reprinted 1989.
P. St J. Turner, 1970, *Heinkel: An Aircraft Album*, London.
H.J. Nowarra, 1975, *Heinkel und seine Flugzeuge*, Munich (a comprehensive record of his aircraft).

JDS/IMcN

Helmholtz, Hermann Ludwig Ferdinand von
b. 31 August 1821 Potsdam, Germany
d. 8 September 1894 Berlin, Germany

German physicist and man of science, inventor of the ophthalmoscope.

Constrained by poverty despite displaying considerable gifts, particularly in the realm of mathematics, he became a surgeon in the Prussian Army but was able to undertake research; in 1842 he wrote a thesis on the discovery of nerve cells in ganglia. He became Professor of Physiology in Königsberg (now Kaliningrad, Russia) in 1849, moving to a similar post in Bonn in 1855, to Heidelberg in 1858, and the Chair of Physic in Berlin in 1871. This latter included the directorship of the physicotechnical institute at Charlottenburg.

His investigations over the years encompassed almost the whole field of science, including physiology, physiological optics, physiological acoustics, chemistry, mathematics, electricity and magnetism, meteorology and theoretical mechanics. He also made important additions to the understanding of putrefaction and fermentation.

Helmholtz's contributions to the understanding of vision and optics ranged widely, but one of the most significant was the definitive development of the ophthalmoscope in 1851. Incorporating some of the aspects of **Babbage**'s original suggestions (which were not brought to practical fruition), his instrument inaugurated a new diagnostic era in ophthalmology, particularly when his method of direct ophthalmoscopy was supplemented by the indirect method of Ruete. His personal life was uneventful, in contrast to his inventive achievements, which were perhaps unequalled in scope in his century. Michael **Faraday**'s tribute, 'the absolute simplicity, modesty and untroubled purity of his disposition had a charm such as I have never encountered in another man', is therefore all the more to be valued.

Bibliography

1850, 'The ophthalmoscope', *Physikalische Gesellschaft*, Berlin.
1851, *Beschreibung eines Augen-Spiegels zur Untersuchung der Netzhaut im lebenden Auge*, Berlin.

1856–66, *Physiological Optics* (2 vols).

Further Reading
L. Konigsberger, 1906, trans. F.A. Welby, *Hermann von Helmholtz*, Oxford.

MG

Hennébique, François

b. 25 April 1842 Neuville-Saint-Vaast, near Arras, France
d. 20 March 1921 Paris, France

French engineer who contributed to the development of reinforced concrete.

Hennébique was an important leader in experimenting with various ways of reinforcing concrete with iron and steel. He set up his own firm in 1867, so acquiring valuable experience in the number of commissions that he carried out when using this material. He patented his own invention in 1892; this was for a method of using hooked connections for reinforcing-bars of iron and steel. England lagged behind France in developing the use of reinforced concrete as a structural material: it was Hennébique who was most influential in changing this situation. He had used his new method of reinforcement in the construction of the Spinning Mills at Tourcoing in France in 1895, and he was commissioned by Weaver & Co., who wished to build a new flour mill in Swansea: the mill was completed in 1898. Soon after, both Hennébique and **Coignet** established London offices for developing their constructional techniques in England.

Further Reading
Le Béton armé 1898–1921 (monthly journal published by the Hennébique Company in Paris).
P. Collins, 1959, *Concrete: A Vision of a New Architecture (a study of Auguste Perret and his predecessors)*, Faber.
C.C. Stanley, 1979, *Highlights in the History of Concrete*, Cement and Concrete Association.

DY

Henry, James J.

b. 22 June 1913 Ancon, Panama Canal Zone
d. 1986 USA

American naval architect, innovator in specialist cargo-ship design.

After graduating in 1935 from the Webb Institute of Naval Architecture, New York, Henry served in different government agencies until 1938 when he joined the fast expanding US Maritime Commission. He assisted in the design and construction of troop-carrying vessels, C1 cargo ships, and he supervised the construction of two wartime attack transports. At the end of hostilities, he set up as a consultant naval architect and by 1951 had incorporated the business as J.J. Henry & Company Inc. The opportunities that consultancy gave him were grasped eagerly; he became involved in the conversion of war-built tonnage to peaceful purposes (such as T2 tankers to ore carriers), the development of the new technologies of the carriage of liquefied gases at cryogenic temperatures and low pressures and, possibly the greatest step forward of all, the development of containerization. Containerization and the closely related field of barge transportation were to provide considerable business during the 1960s and the 1970s. The company designed the wonderful 33-knot container ships for Sea-Land and the auspicious Seabee barge carriers for the Lykes Brothers of New Orleans. James Henry's professional achievements were recognized internationally when he was elected President of the (United States) Society of Naval Architects and Marine Engineers in 1969. By then he had served on many boards and committees and was especially honoured to be Chairman of the Board of Trustees of his graduating college, the Webb Institute of Naval Architecture of New York.

FMW

Henry, Joseph

b. 17 December 1797 Albany, New York, USA
d. 13 May 1878 Washington, DC, USA

American scientist after whom the unit of inductance is named.

Sent to stay with relatives at the age of 6 because of the illness of his father, when the latter died in 1811 Henry was apprenticed to a silversmith and then turned to the stage. Whilst he was ill himself, a book on science fired his interest and he began studying at Albany Academy, working as a tutor to finance his studies. Initially intending to pursue medicine, he then spent some time as a surveyor before becoming Professor of Mathematics and Natural Philosophy at Albany Academy in 1826. There he became interested in the improvement of electromagnets and discovered that the use of an increased number of turns of wire round the core greatly increased their power; by 1831 he was able to supply to Yale a magnet capable of lifting almost a ton weight. During this time he also discovered the principles of magnetic induction and self-inductance. In the same year he made, but did not patent, a cable telegraph system capable of working over a distance of 1 mile (1.6 km). It was at this time, too, that he found that adiabatic expansion of gases led to their sudden cooling, thus paving the way for the development of refrigerators. For this he was recommended for, but never received, the Copley Medal of the Royal Society. Five years later he became Professor of Natural Philosophy at New Jersey College (later Princeton University), where he deduced the laws governing the operation of transformers and observed that changes in magnetic flux induced electric currents in conductors. Later he also observed that spark discharges caused electrical effects at a distance. He therefore came close to the discovery of radio waves. In 1836 he was granted a year's leave of absence and travelled to Europe, where he was able to meet Michael **Faraday**. It was with his help that in 1844 Samuel **Morse** set up the first patented electric telegraph, but, sadly, the latter seems to have reaped all the credit and financial rewards. In 1846 he became the first secretary of the Washington Smithsonian Institute and did much to develop government support for scientific research. As a result of his efforts some 500 telegraph stations across the country were equipped with meteorological equipment to supply weather information by telegraph to a central location, a facility that eventually became the US National Weather Bureau. From 1852 he was a member of the Lighthouse Board, contributing to improvements in lighting and sound warning systems and becoming its chairman in 1871. During the Civil War he was a technical advisor to President Lincoln. He was a founder of the National Academy of Science and served as its President for eleven years.

Principal Honours and Distinctions
President, American Association for the Advancement of Science 1849. President, National Academy of Science 1893–1904. In 1893, to honour his work on induction, the International Congress of Electricians adopted the henry as the unit of inductance.

Bibliography
1824, 'On the chemical and mechanical effects of steam'.
1825, 'The production of cold by the rarefaction of air'.
1832, 'On the production of currents & sparks of electricity & magnetism', *American Journal of Science* 22: 403.
'Theory of the so-called imponderables', *Proceedings of the American Association for the Advancement of Science* 6: 84.

Further Reading
Smithsonian Institution, 1886, *Joseph Henry, Scientific Writings*, Washington DC.

KF

Henson, William Samuel
b. 3 May 1812 Nottingham, England
d. 22 March 1888 New Jersey, USA

*English (naturalized American) inventor who patented a design for an 'aerial steam carriage' and combined with John **Stringfellow** to build model aeroplanes.*

William Henson worked in the lacemaking industry and in his spare time invented many mechanical devices, from a breech-loading cannon to an ice-machine. It could be claimed that he invented the airliner, for in 1842 he prepared a patent (granted in 1843) for an 'aerial steam carriage'. The patent application was not just a vague outline, but contained detailed drawings of a large monoplane with an enclosed fuselage to accommodate the passengers and crew. It was to be powered by a steam engine driving two pusher propellers aft of the wing. Henson had followed the lead give by Sir George **Cayley** in his basic layout, but produced a very much more advanced structural design with cambered wings strengthened by streamlined bracing wires: the intended wing-span was 150 ft (46 m). Henson probably discussed the design of the steam engine and boiler with his friend John Stringfellow (who was also in the lacemaking industry). Stringfellow joined Henson and others to found the Aerial Transit Company, which was set up to raise the finance needed to build Henson's machine. A great publicity campaign was mounted with artists' impressions of the 'aerial steam carriage' flying over London, India and even the pyramids. Passenger-carrying services to India and China were proposed, but the whole project was far too optimistic to attract support from financiers and the scheme foundered. Henson and Stringfellow drew up an agreement in December 1843 to construct models which would prove the feasibility of an 'aerial machine'. For the next five years they pursued this aim, with no real success. In 1848 Henson and his wife emigrated to the United States to further his career in textiles. He became an American citizen and died there at the age of 75.

Bibliography
Henson's diary is preserved by the Institute of Aeronautical Sciences in the USA. Henson's patent of 1842–3 is reproduced in Balantyne and Pritchard (1956) and Davy (1931) (see below).

Further Reading
H. Penrose, 1988, *An Ancient Air: A Biography of John Stringfellow*, Shrewsbury.
A.M. Balantyne and J.L. Pritchard, 1956, 'The lives and work of William Samuel Henson and John Stringfellow', *Journal of the Royal Aeronautical Society* (June) (an attempt to analyse conflicting evidence; includes a reproduction of Henson's patent).
M.J.B. Davy, 1931, *Henson and Stringfellow*, London (an earlier work with excellent drawings from Henson's patent).

JDS

Herbert, Sir Alfred Edward
b. 5 September 1866 Leicester, England
d. 26 May 1957 Kings Somborne, Hampshire, England

English mechanical engineer and machine-tool manufacturer.

Alfred Herbert was educated at Stoneygate School, Leicester, and served an apprenticeship with Joseph Jessop & Sons, also of Leicester, from 1881 to 1886. In 1887 he was engaged as Manager of a small engineering firm in Coventry, and before the end of that year he purchased the business in partnership with William Hubbard. They commenced the manufacture of machine-tools especially for the cycle industry. Hubbard

withdrew from the partnership in 1890 and Herbert continued on his own account, the firm being established as a limited liability company, Alfred Herbert Ltd, in 1894. A steady expansion of the business continued, especially after the introduction of their capstan lathe, and by 1914 it was the largest manufacturer of machine-tools in Britain. In addition to making machine-tools of all types for the home and export market, the firm acted as an agent for the import of specialist machine-tools from abroad. During the First World War Alfred Herbert was in 1915 appointed head of machine-tool production at the War Office and when the Ministry of Munitions was set up he was transferred to that Ministry as Controller of Machine Tools. He was President of the Machine Tools Trades Association from 1919 to 1934. He was elected a member of the Institution of Mechanical Engineers in 1892 and in 1921 was a founder member of the Institution of Production Engineers. Almost to the end of his long life he continued to take an active part in the direction of his company. He expressed his views on current events affecting industry in the technical press and in his firm's house journal.

Principal Honours and Distinctions
KBE 1917. Officier de la Légion d'honneur 1917. Order of St Stanislas of Russia 1918. Order of Leopold of Belgium 1918. Freeman of the City of Coventry 1933. President, Institution of Production Engineers 1927–9. Honorary Member, Institution of Mechanical Engineers 1941.

Bibliography
1948, *Shots at the Truth*, Coventry (a selection of his speeches and writings).

Further Reading
D.J. Jeremy (ed.), 1984–6, *Dictionary of Business Biography*, Vol. 3, London, pp. 174–7 (a useful account).
Obituary, 1957, *Engineering*, 183: 680.

RTS

Herbert, Edward Geisler
b. 23 March 1869 Dedham, near Colchester, Essex, England
d. 9 February 1938 West Didsbury, Manchester, England

English engineer, inventor of the Rapidor saw and the Pendulum Hardness Tester, and pioneer of cutting tool research.

Edward Geisler Herbert was educated at Nottingham High School in 1876–87, and at University College, London, in 1887–90, graduating with a BSc in Physics in 1889 and remaining for a further year to take an engineering course. He began his career as a premium apprentice at the Nottingham works of Messrs James Hill & Co, manufacturers of lace machinery. In 1892 he became a partner with Charles Richardson in the firm of Richardson & Herbert, electrical engineers in Manchester, and when this partnership was dissolved in 1895 he carried on the business in his own name and began to produce machine tools. He remained as Managing Director of this firm, reconstituted in 1902 as a limited liability company styled Edward G. Herbert Ltd, until his retirement in 1928. He was joined by Charles Fletcher (1868–1930), who as joint Managing Director contributed greatly to the commercial success of the firm, which specialized in the manufacture of small machine tools and testing machinery.

Around 1900 Herbert had discovered that hacksaw machines cut very much quicker when only a few teeth are in operation, and in 1902 he patented a machine which utilized this concept by automatically changing the angle of incidence of the blade as cutting proceeded. These saws were commercially successful, but by 1912, when his original patents were approaching expiry, Herbert and Fletcher began to develop improved methods of applying the rapid-saw concept. From this work the well-known *Rapidor* and *Manchester* saws emerged soon after the First World War. A file-testing machine invented by Herbert before the war made an autographic record of the life and performance of the file and brought him into close contact with the file and tool steel manufacturers of Sheffield. A tool-steel testing machine, working like a lathe, was introduced when high-speed steel had just come into general use, and Herbert became a prominent member of the Cutting Tools Research Committee of the Institution of Mechanical Engineers in 1919, carrying out many investigations for that body and compiling four of its Reports published between 1927 and 1933. He was the first to conceive the idea of the 'tool-work' thermo-couple which allowed cutting tool temperatures to be accurately measured. For this advance he was awarded the Thomas Hawksley Gold Medal of the Institution in 1926.

His best-known invention was the Pendulum Hardness Tester, introduced in 1923. This used a spherical indentor, which was rolled over, rather than being pushed into, the surface being examined, by a small, heavy, inverted pendulum. The period of oscillation of this pendulum provided a sensitive measurement of the specimen's hardness. Following this work Herbert introduced his 'Cloudburst' surface hardening process, in which hardened steel engineering components were bombarded by steel balls moving at random in all directions at very high velocities like gaseous molecules. This treatment superhardened the surface of the components, improved their resistance to abrasion, and revealed any surface defects. After bombardment the hardness of the superficially hardened layers increased slowly and spontaneously by a room-temperature ageing process. After his retirement in 1928 Herbert devoted himself to a detailed study of the influence of intense magnetic fields on the hardening of steels.

Herbert was a member of several learned societies, including the Manchester Association of Engineers, the Institute of Metals, the American Society of Mechanical Engineers and the Institution of Mechanical Engineers. He retained a seat on the Board of his company from his retirement until the end of his life.

Principal Honours and Distinctions
Manchester Association of Engineers Butterworth Gold Medal 1923. Institution of Mechanical Engineers Thomas Hawksley Gold Medal 1926.

Bibliography
E.G. Herbert obtained several British and American patents and was the author of many papers, which are listed in T.M. Herbert (ed.), 1939, 'The inventions of Edward Geisler Herbert: an autobiographical note', *Proceedings of the Institution of Mechanical Engineers* 141: 59–67.

ASD/RTS

Hero of Alexandria
fl. *c.*62 AD Alexandria

Alexandrian mathematician and mechanician.

Nothing is known of Hero, or Heron, apart from what can be gleaned from the books he wrote. Their scope and style suggest that he was a teacher at the museum or the university of Alexandria, writing textbooks for his students. The longest book, and the one with the greatest technological interest, is *Pneumatics*. Some of its material is derived from the works of the earlier writers **Ctesibius** of Alexandria and Philo of Byzantium, but many of the devices described were invented by Hero himself. The introduction recognizes that the air is a body and demonstrates the effects of air pressure, as when air must be allowed to escape from a closed vessel before water can enter. There follow clear descriptions of a variety of mechanical contrivances depending on the effects of either air pressure or heated gases. Most of the devices seem trivial, but such toys or gadgets were popular at the time and Hero is concerned to show how they work. Inventions with a more serious purpose are a fire pump and a water organ. One celebrated gadget is a sphere that is set spinning by jets of steam – an early illustration of the reaction principle on which modern jet propulsion depends.

Mechanics, known only in an Arabic version, is a textbook expounding the theory and practical skills required by the architect. It deals with a variety of questions of mechanics, such as the statics of a horizontal beam resting on vertical posts, the theory of the centre of gravity and equilibrium, largely derived from **Archimedes**, and the five ways of applying a relatively small force to exert a much larger one: the lever, winch, pulley, wedge and screw. Practical devices described include sledges for transporting heavy loads, cranes and a screw cutter.

Hero's *Dioptra* describes instruments used in surveying, together with an odometer or device to indicate the distance travelled by a wheeled vehicle. *Catoptrics*, known only in Latin, deals with the principles of mirrors, plane and curved, enunciating that the angle of incidence is equal to that of reflection. *Automata* describes two forms of puppet theatre, operated by strings and drums driven by a falling lead weight attached to a rope wound round an axle. Hero's mathematical work lies in the tradition of practical mathematics stretching from the Babylonians through Islam to Renaissance Europe. It is seen most clearly in his *Metrica*, a treatise on mensuration.

Of all his works, *Pneumatics* was the best known and most influential. It was one of the works of Greek science and technology assimilated by the Arabs, notably **Banu Musa ibn Shakir**, and was transmitted to medieval Western Europe.

Bibliography
All Hero's works have been printed with a German translation in *Heronis Alexandrini opera quae supersunt omnia*, 1899–1914, 5 vols, Leipzig. The book on pneumatics has been published as *The Pneumatics of Hero of Alexandria*, 1851, trans. and ed. Bennet Woodcroft, London (facs. repr. 1971, introd. Marie Boas Hall, London and New York).

Further Reading
A.G. Drachmann, 1948, 'Ktesibios, Philon and Heron: A Study in Ancient Pneumatics', *Acta Hist. Sci. Nat. Med. 4*, Copenhagen: Munksgaard.
T.L. Heath, 1921, *A History of Greek Mathematics*, Oxford (still useful for his mathematical work).

LRD

Héroult, Paul Louis Toussaint
b. 1863 Thury-Harcourt, Caen, France
d. 9 May 1914 Antibes, France

French metallurgist, inventor of the process of aluminium reduction by electrolysis.

Paul Héroult, the son of a tanner, at the age of 16, while still at school in Caen, read **Deville**'s book on aluminium and became obsessed with the idea of developing a cheap way of producing this metal. After his family moved to Gentilly-sur-Bièvre he studied at the Ecole Sainte-Barbe in Paris and then returned to Caen to work in the laboratory of his father's tannery. His first patent, filed in February and granted on 23 April 1886, described an invention almost identical to that of C.M. **Hall**: 'the electrolysis of alumina dissolved in molten cryolite into which the current is introduced through suitable electrodes. The cryolite is not consumed.' Early in 1887 Héroult attempted to obtain the support of Alfred Rangod Pechiney, the proprietor of the works at Salindres where Deville's process for making sodium-reduced aluminium was still being operated. Pechiney persuaded Héroult to modify his electrolytic process by using a cathode of molten copper, thus making it possible produce aluminium bronze rather than pure aluminium. Héroult then approached the Swiss firm J.G. Nehe Söhne, ironmasters, whose works at the Falls of Schaffhausen obtained power from the Rhine. They were looking for a new metallurgical process requiring large quantities of cheap hydroelectric power and Héroult's process seemed suitable. In 1887 they established the Société Metallurgique Suisse to test Héroult's process. Héroult became Technical Director and went to the USA to defend his patents against those of Hall. During his absence the Schaffhausen trials were successfully completed, and on 18 November 1888 the Société Metallurgique combined with the German AEG group, Oerlikon and Escher Wyss, to establish the Aluminium Industrie Aktiengesellschaft Neuhausen. In the early electrolytic baths it was occasionally found that arcs between the bath surface and electrode could develop if the electrodes were inadvertently raised. From this observation, Héroult and M. Killiani developed the electric arc furnace. In this, arcs were intentionally formed between the surface of the charge and several electrodes, each connected to a different pole of the AC supply. This furnace, the prototype of the modern electric steel furnace, was first used for the direct reduction of iron ore at La Praz in 1903. This work was undertaken for the Canadian Government, for whom Héroult subsequently designed a 5,000-amp single-phase furnace which was installed and tested at Sault-Sainte-Marie in Ontario and successfully used for smelting magnetite ore.

Further Reading

Aluminium Industrie Aktiengesellschaft Neuhausen, 1938, *The History of the Aluminium-Industrie-Aktien-Gesellschaft Neuhausen 1888–1938*, 2 vols, Neuhausen.

C.J. Gignoux, *Histoire d'une entreprise française*.

'The Hall-Héroult affair', 1961, *Metal Bulletin* (14 April): 1–4.

ASD

Herreshoff, Nathaniel Greene

b. 18 March 1848 Bristol, Rhode Island, USA
d. 2 June 1938 Bristol, Rhode Island, USA

American naval architect and designer of six successful America's Cup defenders.

Herreshoff, or, as he was known, Captain Nat, was seventh in a family of nine, four of whom became blind in childhood. Association with such problems may have sharpened his appreciation of shape and form; indeed, he made a lengthy European small-boat trip with a blind brother. While working on yacht designs, he used three-dimensional models in conjunction with the sheer draught on the drawing-board. With many of the family being boatbuilders, he started designing at the age of 16 and then decided to make this his career. As naval architecture was not then a graduating subject, he studied mechanical engineering at Massachusetts Institute of Technology. While still studying, c.1867, he broke new ground by preparing direct reading time handicapping tables for yachts up to 110 ft (33.5 m) long. After working with the Corliss Company, he set up the Herreshoff Manufacturing Company, in partnership with J.B. Herreshoff, as shipbuilders and engineers. Over the years their output included steam machinery, fishing vessels, pleasure craft and racing yachts. They built the first torpedo boat for US Navy and another for the Royal Navy, the only such acquisition in the late nineteenth century. Herreshoff designed six of the world's greatest yachts, of the America's Cup, between 1890 and 1920. His accomplishments included new types of lightweight wood fasteners, new systems of framing, hollow spars and better methods of cutting sails. He continued to work full-time until 1935 and his work was internationally acclaimed. He maintained cordial relations with his British rivals **Fife**, Nicholson and G.L. **Watson**, and enjoyed friendship with his compatriot Edward Burgess. Few will ever match Herreshoff as an all-round engineer and designer.

Principal Honours and Distinctions

Herreshoff was one of the very few, other than heads of state, to become an Honorary Member of the New York Yacht Club.

Further Reading

L.F. Herreshoff, 1953, *Capt. Nat Herreshoff. The*

Wizard of Bristol, White Plains, NY: Sheridan House; 2nd edn 1981.

FMW

Herschel, John Frederick William

b. 7 March 1792 Slough, England
d. 11 May 1871 Collingwood, England

English scientist who introduced 'hypo' (thiosulphate) as a photographic fixative and discovered the blueprint process.

The only son of Sir William Herschel, the famous astronomer, John graduated from Cambridge in 1813 and went on to become a distinguished astronomer, mathematician and chemist. He left England in November 1833 to set up an observatory near Cape Town, South Africa, where he embarked on a study of the heavens in the southern hemisphere. He returned to England in the spring of 1838, and between 1850 and 1855 Herschel served as Master of the Royal Mint. He made several notable contributions to photography, perhaps the most important being his discovery in 1819 that hyposulphites (thiosulphates) would dissolve silver salts. He brought this property to the attention of W.H.F. **Talbot**, who in 1839 was using a common salt solution as a fixing agent for his early photographs. After trials, Talbot adopted 'hypo', which was a far more effective fixative. It was soon adopted by other photographers and eventually became the standard photographic fixative, as it still is in the 1990s. After hearing of the first photographic process in January 1839, Herschel devised his own process within a week. In September 1839 he made the first photograph on glass. He is credited with introducing the words 'positive', 'negative' and 'snapshot' to photography, and in 1842 he invented the cyanotype or 'blueprint' process. This process was later to be widely adopted by engineers and architects for the reproduction of plans and technical drawings, a practice abandoned only in the late twentieth century.

Principal Honours and Distinctions
Knight of the Royal Hanoverian Guelphic Order 1831. Baronet 1838. FRS 1813. Copley Medal 1821.

Further Reading
Dictionary of National Biography, 1968, Vol. IX, pp. 714–19.
H.J.P. Arnold, 1977, *William Henry Fox Talbot*, London; Larry J. Schaaf, 1992, *Out of the Shadows: Herschel, Talbot and the Invention of Photography*, Newhaven and London (for details of his contributions to photography and his relationship with Talbot).

JW

Hertz, Heinrich Rudolph

b. 22 February 1857 Hamburg, Germany
d. 1 January 1894 Bonn, Germany

German physicist who was reputedly the first person to transmit and receive radio waves.

At the age of 17 Hertz entered the Gelehrtenschule of the Johaneums in Hamburg, but he left the following year to obtain practical experience for a year with a firm of engineers in Frankfurt am Main. He then spent six months at the Dresden Technical High School, followed by year of military service in Berlin. At this point he decided to switch from engineering to physics, and after a year in Munich he studied physics under **Helmholtz** at the University of Berlin, gaining his PhD with high honours in 1880. From 1883 to 1885 he was a privat-dozent at Kiel, during which time he studied the electromagnetic theory of James Clerk **Maxwell**. In 1885 he succeeded to the Chair in Physics at Karlsruhe Technical High School. There, in 1887, he constructed a rudimentary transmitter consisting of two 30 cm (12 in.) rods with metal balls separated by a 7.5 mm (0.3 in.) gap at the inner ends and metallic plates at the outer ends, the whole assembly being mounted at the focus of a large parabolic metal mirror and the two rods being connected to an induction coil. At the other side of his laboratory he placed a 70 cm (27½ in.) diameter wire loop with a similar air gap at the focus of a second metal mirror. When the induction coil was made to create a spark across the transmitter air gap, he found that a spark also occurred at the 'receiver'. By a series of experiments he was not only able to show that the invisible waves travelled in straight lines and were reflected by the parabolic mirrors, but also that the vibrations could be refracted like visible light and had a similar wavelength. By this first transmission and reception of radio waves he thus confirmed the theoretical predictions made by Maxwell some twenty years earlier. It was probably in his experiments with this apparatus in 1887 that Hertz also observed that the voltage at which a spark was able to jump a gap was significantly reduced by the presence of ultraviolet light. This so-called photoelectric effect was subsequently placed on a theoretical basis by Albert Einstein in 1905. In 1889 he became Professor of Physics at the University of Bonn, where he continued to investigate the nature of electric discharges in gases at low pressure until his death after a long and painful illness. In recognition of his measurement of radio and other waves, the international unit of frequency of an oscillatory wave, the cycle per second, is now universally known as the Hertz.

Principal Honours and Distinctions
Royal Society Rumford Medal 1890.

Bibliography
Much of Hertz's work, including his 1890 paper 'On the fundamental equations of electrodynamics for bodies at rest', is recorded in three collections of his papers which are available in English translations by D.E. Jones et al., namely *Electric Waves* (1893), *Miscellaneous Papers* (1896) and *Principles of Mechanics* (1899).

Further Reading
J.G. O'Hara and W. Pricha, 1987, *Hertz and the Maxwellians*, London: Peter Peregrinus.
J. Hertz, 1977, *Heinrich Hertz, Memoirs, Letters and Diaries*, San Francisco: San Francisco Press.
R. Appleyard, 1930, *Pioneers of Electrical Communication*.

See also **Heaviside, Oliver**.

KF

Hetzel, Max
b. 5 March 1921 Basle, Switzerland

Swiss electrical engineer who invented the tuning-fork watch.

Hetzel trained as an electrical engineer at the Federal Polytechnic in Zurich and worked for several years in the field of telecommunications before joining the Bulova Watch Company in 1950. At that time several companies were developing watches with electromagnetically maintained balances, but they represented very little advance on the mechanical watch and the mechanical switching mechanism was unreliable. In 1952 Hetzel started work on a much more radical design which was influenced by a transistorized tuning-fork oscillator that he had developed when he was working on telecommunications. Tuning forks, whose vibrations were maintained electromagnetically, had been used by scientists during the nineteenth century to measure small intervals of time, but Niaudet-**Breguet** appears to have been the first to use a tuning fork to control a clock. In 1866 he described a mechanically operated tuning-fork clock manufactured by the firm of Breguet, but it was not successful, possibly because the fork did not compensate for changes in temperature. The tuning fork only became a precision instrument during the 1920s, when elinvar forks were maintained in vibration by thermionic valve circuits. Their primary purpose was to act as frequency standards, but they might have been developed into precision clocks had not the quartz clock made its appearance very shortly afterwards. Hetzel's design was effectively a miniaturized version of these precision devices, with a transistor replacing the thermionic valve. The fork vibrated at a frequency of 360 cycles per second, and the hands were driven mechanically from the end of one of the tines. A prototype was working by 1954, and the watch went into production in 1960. It was sold under the tradename Accutron, with a guaranteed accuracy of one minute per month: this was a considerable improvement on the performance of the mechanical watch. However, the events of the 1920s were to repeat themselves, and by the end of the decade the Accutron was eclipsed by the introduction of quartz-crystal watches.

Principal Honours and Distinctions
Neuchâtel Observatory Centenary Prize 1958. Swiss Society for Chronometry Gold Medal 1988.

Bibliography
'The history of the "Accutron" tuning fork watch', 1969, *Swiss Watch & Jewellery Journal* 94: 413–5.

Further Reading
R. Good, 1960, 'The Accutron', *Horological Journal* 103: 346–53 (for a detailed technical description).
J.D. Weaver, 1982, *Electrical & Electronic Clocks & Watches*, London (provides a technical description of the tuning-fork watch in its historical context).

DV

Highs, Thomas
fl. 1760s England

English reedmaker who claimed to have invented both the spinning jenny and the waterframe.

The claims of Highs to have invented both the spinning jenny and the waterframe have been dismissed by most historians. Thomas Highs was a reedmaker of Leigh, Lancashire. In about 1763 he had as a neighbour John **Kay**, the clockmaker from Warrington, whom he employed to help him construct his machines. During this period they were engaged in making a spinning jenny, but after several months of toil, in a fit of despondency, they threw the machine through the attic window. Highs persevered, however, and made a jenny that could spin six threads. The comparatively sophisticated arrangements for drawing and twisting at the same time, as depicted by Guest (1823), suggest that this machine came after the one invented by James **Hargreaves**. Guest claims that Highs made this machine between 1764 and 1766 and in the following two years constructed another, in which the spindles were placed in a circle. In 1771 Highs moved to Manchester, where he constructed a double jenny that was displayed at the Manchester Exchange, and received a subscription of £200 from the cotton manufacturers. However, all this occurred after Hargreaves had constructed his jenny. In the trial of **Arkwright**'s patent during 1781, Highs gave evidence. He was recalled from Ireland, where he had been superintending the building of cotton-spinning machinery for Baron Hamilton's newly erected mill at Balbriggan, north of Dublin. Then in 1785, during the next trial of Arkwright's patent, Highs claimed that in 1767 he had made rollers for drawing out the cotton before spinning. This would have been for a different type of spinning machine, similar to the one later constructed by Arkwright. Highs was helped by John Kay and it

was these rollers that Kay subsequently built for Arkwright. If the drawing shown by Guest is correct, then Highs was working on the wrong principles because his rollers were spaced too far apart and were not held together by weights, with the result that the twist would have passed into the drafting zone, producing uneven drawing.

Further Reading
R. Guest, 1823, *A Compendious History of the Cotton-Manufacture: With a Disproval of the Claim of Sir Richard Arkwright to the Invention of its Ingenious Machinery*, Manchester (Highs's claim for the invention of his spinning machines).
R.S. Fitton, 1989, *The Arkwrights, Spinners of Fortune*, Manchester (an examination of Highs's claims).
R.L. Hills, 1970, *Power in the Industrial Revolution*, Manchester (discusses the technical problems of the invention).

RLH

Hipp, Matthäus
b. 25 October 1813 Blaubeuren, Germany
d. 3 May 1893 Zurich, Switzerland

German inventor and entrepreneur who produced the first reliable electric clock.

After serving an apprenticeship with a clockmaker in Blaubeuren, Hipp worked for various clockmakers before setting up his own workshop in Reutlingen in 1840. In 1842 he made his first electric clock with an ingenious toggle mechanism for switching the current, although he claimed that the idea had occurred to him eight years earlier. The switching mechanism was the Achilles' heel of early electric clocks. It was usually operated by the pendulum and it presented the designer with a dilemma: if the switch made a firm contact it adversely affected the timekeeping, but if the contact was lightened it sometimes failed to operate due to dirt or corrosion on the contacts. The Hipp toggle switch overcame this problem by operating only when the amplitude of the pendulum dropped below a certain value. As this occurred infrequently, the contact pressure could be increased to provide reliable switching without adversely affecting the timekeeping. It is an indication of the effectiveness of the Hipp toggle that it was used in clocks for over one hundred years and was adopted by many other makers in addition to Hipp and his successor Favag. It was generally preferred for its reliability rather than its precision, although a regulator made in 1881 for the observatory at Neuchâtel performed creditably. This regulator was enclosed in an airtight case at low pressure, eliminating errors due to changes in barometric pressure. This practice later became standard for observatory regulators such as those of **Riefler** and **Shortt**. The ability of the Hipp toggle to provide more power when the clock was subjected to an increased load made it particularly suitable for use in turret clocks, whose hands were exposed to the vagaries of the weather. Hipp also improved the operation of slave dials, which were advanced periodically by an electrical impulse from a master clock. If the electrical contacts 'chattered' and produced several impulses instead of a single sharp impulse, the slave dials would not indicate the correct time. Hipp solved this problem by producing master clocks which delivered impulses that alternated in polarity, and slave dials which only advanced when the polarity was changed in this way. Polarized impulses delivered every minute became the standard practice for slave dials used on the European continent. Hipp also improved **Wheatstone's** chronoscope, an instrument that was used for measuring very short intervals of time (such as those involved in ballistics).

Principal Honours and Distinctions
Honorary doctorate, University of Zurich 1875.

Further Reading
Neue deutsche Biographie, 1972, Vol. 9, Berlin, pp. 199–200.
'Hipp's sich selbst conrolirende Uhr', *Dinglers polytechnisches Journal* (1843), 88: 258–64 (the first description of the Hipp toggle).
F. Hope-Jones, 1949, *Electrical Timekeeping*, 2nd edn, London, pp. 62–6, 97–8 (a modern description in English of the Hipp toggle and the slave dial).
C.A. Aked, 1983, 'Electrical precision', *Antiquarian Horology* 14: 172–81 (describes the observatory clock at Neuchâtel).

DV

Hjorth, Soren
b. 13 October 1801 Vesterbygaard, Denmark
d. 28 August 1870 Copenhagen, Denmark

Danish engineer and inventor who first proposed the principle of the self-excited dynamo.

After passing a legal examination, Hjorth found employment in the state treasury in Copenhagen and in 1830 advanced to be Clerk of the Exchequer and Secretary. In 1834 he visited England to study the use of steam road and rail vehicles. Hjorth was involved in the formation of the first railway company in Denmark and became Technical Director of Denmark's first railway, a line between Copenhagen and Roskilde that opened in 1847. In 1848 he petitioned the Government for funds to visit England and have built there an electric motor of his own design with oscillating motion. This petition, supported by Hans Christian Oersted (1777–1851), was granted. A British patent was obtained for the machine, an example being exhibited at the 1851 Great Exhibition in London. Turning his attention to the generation of electricity, he conceived as early as May 1851 the dynamo electric principle with self-excitation that was incorporated in his patent in 1855. Unfortunately, Hjorth held the firm but mistaken belief that if he could use his dynamo to drive a motor he would obtain more power than was consumed in driving the dynamo. The theory of conservation of energy was being only slowly accepted at that time, and Hjorth, with little scientific training, was to be disappointed at the failure of his schemes. He worked with great perseverance and industry to the end of his life on the design of his electrical machines.

Bibliography
11 April 1855, British patent no. 806 (Hjorth's self-excited dynamo).
11 April 1855, British patent nos. 807 and 808 (reciprocating and rotary electric motors).

Further Reading
S. Smith, 1912, *Soren Hjorth*, Copenhagen (the most detailed biography).
1907, 'Soren Hjorth, discoverer of the dynamo-electric principle', *Electrical Engineering* 1: 957–8 (a short biography).
Catalogue of the 1851 Exhibition, 1851, London, pp. 1,359–60 (for a description of Hjorth's electromagnetic engine with oscillating motion.

GW

Hodgkinson, Eaton

b. 26 February 1789 Anderton, Cheshire, England
d. 18 June 1861 near Manchester, England

English engineer who devised a new form of cast-iron girder.

Eaton Hodgkinson's father, a farmer, died when he was 6 years old, but his mother was a resourceful woman who set up a business in Salford and ensured that her son received a sound schooling. Most important for his education, however, was his friendship with the Manchester scientific luminary Dr. Dalton, who instructed him in practical mathematics. These studies led Hodgkinson to devise a new form of cast-iron girder, carefully tested by experiments and which was widely adopted for fireproof structures in the nineteenth century. Following Dalton, Hodgkinson became an active member of the Manchester Philosophical Society, of which he was elected President in 1848. He also became an active member of the British Association for the Advancement of Science. Hodgkinson's work on cast-iron girders secured him a Fellowship of the Royal Society, and the Royal Medal of the Society, in 1841. It was Hodgkinson also who verified the mathematical value of the pioneering experiments carried out by William **Fairbairn** for Robert **Stephenson**'s proposed wrought-iron tube structure which, in 1849, became the Britannia Bridge over the Menai Straits. He received a Silver Medal for this work at the Paris Exhibition of 1858. Hodgkinson served as a member of the Royal Commission appointed to enquire into the application of iron to railway structures. In 1847 he was appointed Professor of the Mechanical Principles of Engineering at University College, London, but his health began to fail shortly after. He was elected an Honorary Member of the Institution of Civil Engineers in 1851. Described as 'singularly simple and guileless', he was widely admired and respected.

Principal Honours and Distinctions
President, Manchester Philosophical Society 1848. FRS 1841. Royal Society Medal 1841.

Further Reading
Dictionary of National Biography, London.
Proceedings of the Institution of Civil Engineers 21: 542–5.

AB

Hoe, Richard March

b. 12 September 1812 New York, USA
d. 7 June 1886 Florence, Italy

American inventor of the rotary printing press.

He was the son of Robert Hoe, a printer who improved the cylinder press invented by David **Napier**. At the age of 15 he entered his father's business, taking full control of it three years later. Newspaper publishers demanded ever-increasing speeds of output from the printing press, and Hoe was one of those who realized that the speed was limited by the reciprocating action of the flat-bed machine. In 1846 he constructed a rotary press in which a central cylinder carried the type and flat sheets of paper were fed to smaller impression cylinders ranged around it. This kind of press, with four impression cylinders, was first used to print the *Philadelphia Public Ledger* in 1847, and was able to print 8,000 papers per hour. Such presses reigned supreme for newspaper printing in many countries for twenty-five years: in 1857, for example, *The Times* had a ten-feeder machine making 20,000 impressions per hour. Even so, the quest for speed, now limited by the single-sheet feed, continued. William Bullock (1813–67) introduced continuous roll or web feed for the *Philadelphia Inquirer* in 1865, and the next year *The Times* followed suit with the web-fed Walter press. In 1871 Hoe devised a machine that combined all the advantages of the existing machines, producing a rotary, web, perfecting (printing on both sides of the paper at once) machine, first used in the office of the *New York Tribune*. Ten years later the Hoe Company devised a folding machine to fold the copies as they came off the press: the modern newspaper printing press had arrived. In addition to his contributions to the printing industry, Hoe was a good employer, arranging free evening classes and other welfare services for his apprentices.

Further Reading
R. Hoe, 1902, *A Short History of the Printing Press*, New York.
S.D. Tucker, *A History of R. Hoe & Co. New York*.

LRD

Hofmann, August Wilhelm von

b. 8 April 1818 Giessen, Germany
d. 2 May 1892 Berlin, Germany

German organic chemist.

The son of an architect, Hofmann began studying law and languages but was increasingly drawn to chemistry, attracted by **Liebig**'s teaching at Giessen. In 1841 Hofmann took his doctorate with a study of coal tar. He became *Privatdozent* at Bonn University in 1845, but later that year he was persuaded to take up the post of first Director of the Royal College of Chemistry in London, after tenure was guaranteed as a result of Prince **Albert**'s influence. He remained there for twenty years until he was offered professorships in chemistry at Bonn and Berlin. He accepted the latter. Hofmann continued the method of teaching chemistry, based on laboratory instruction, developed by Liebig at Giessen, and extended it to England and Berlin. A steady stream of well-trained chemists issued forth from Hofmann's tuition, concerning themselves especially with experimental organic chemistry and the industrial applications of chemistry. In 1848 one of his students, C.B. **Mansfield**, devised the method of fractional distillation of coal tar, to separate pure benzene, xylene and toluene, thus laying the foundations of the coal-tar industry. In 1856 another student, W.H. **Perkin**, prepared the first synthetic dyestuff, aniline purple, heralding the great dyestuffs industry, in which several other of his students distinguished themselves. Although keenly interested in the chemistry of dyestuffs, Hofmann did not pursue their large-scale preparation, but he stressed the importance of scientific research for success on a commercial scale. Hofmann's stimulus in this direction flagged after his return to Germany, and this was a factor in the failure of British industry to follow up their initial advantage and allow it to pass to Germany. In 1862 Hofmann prepared a dye from a derivative of triphenylmethane, which he called rosaniline. From this he derived a series of beautiful colours, ranging from blue to violet, which he patented as 'Hofmann's violets' the following year.

Principal Honours and Distinctions
Ennobled 1888.

Further Reading
J. Volhard and E. Fischer, 1902, *August Wilhelm von Hofmann, ein Lebensbild*, Berlin (the basic biography).

K.M. Hammond, 1967, bibliography, unpublished, (Diploma in Librarianship, London University (lists 373 items; deposited in University College, London)).

LRD

Holabird, William
b. 11 September 1854 American Union, New York, USA
d. 19 July 1923 Evanston, Illinois, USA

American architect who contributed to the development of steel framing, a type of structure that rendered possible the erection of the skyscraper.

The American skyscraper was, in the 1870s and 1880s, very much the creation of what came to be known as the Chicago school of architecture. It was the most important American contribution to the urban architectural scene. At this time conditions were ripe for this type of office development, and in the big cities, notably Chicago and New York, steeply rising land values provided the incentive to build high; the structural means to do so had been triggered by the then low costs of making quality iron and steel. The skyscraper appeared after the invention of the passenger lift by **Otis** and the pioneer steel-frame work of **Jenney**. In 1875 Holabird was working in Jenney's office in Chicago. By 1883 he had set up in private practice, joined by another young architect, Martin Roche (1855–1927), and together they were responsible for the Tacoma Building (1887–9) in Chicago. In this structure the two front façades were entirely non-load-bearing and were carried by an internal steel skeleton; only the rear walls were load-bearing. The design of the building was not revolutionary (this had to wait for L.H. **Sullivan**) but was traditional in form. It was the possibility of being able to avoid load-bearing outer walls that enabled a building to rise above some nine storeys, and the thirteen-storeyed Tacoma Building pointed the way to the future development of the skyscraper. The firm of Holabird & Roche continued in the following decades in Chicago to design and construct further high-quality, although lower, commercial buildings such as those in South Michigan Avenue and the McClurg Building. However, they are best remembered for their contribution in engineering to the development of high-rise construction.

Further Reading
F. Mujica, 1929, *History of the Skyscraper*, Paris: Archaeology and Architecture Press.
C.W. Condit, 1964, *The Chicago School of Architecture: A History of Commercial and Public Building in the Chicago Area 1875–1925*, Chicago: University of Chicago Press.
J.W. Rudd (compiler), 1966, *Holabird and Roche: Chicago Architects*, American Association of Architectural Bibliographers.

DY

Holden, Sir Isaac

b. 7 May 1807 Hurlet, between Paisley and Glasgow, Scotland
d. 13 August 1897

British developer of the wool-combing machine.

Isaac Holden's father, who had the same name, had been a farmer and lead miner at Alston in Cumbria before moving to work in a coal-mine near Glasgow. After a short period at Kilbarchan grammar school, the younger Isaac was engaged first as a drawboy to two weavers and then, after the family had moved to Johnstone, Scotland, worked in a cotton-spinning mill while attending night school to improve his education. He was able to learn Latin and bookkeeping, but when he was about 15 he was apprenticed to an uncle as a shawl-weaver. This proved to be too much for his strength so he returned to scholastic studies and became Assistant to an able teacher, John Kennedy, who lectured on physics, chemistry and history, which he also taught to his colleague. The elder Isaac died in 1826 and the younger had to provide for his mother and younger brother, but in 1828, at the age of 21, he moved to a teaching post in Leeds. He filled similar positions in Huddersfield and Reading, where in October 1829 he invented and demonstrated the lucifer match but did not seek to exploit it. In 1830 he returned because of ill health to his mother in Scotland, where he began to teach again. However, he was recommended as a bookkeeper to William Townend, member of the firm of Townend Brothers, Cullingworth, near Bingley, Yorkshire. Holden moved there in November 1830 and was soon involved in running the mill, eventually becoming a partner.

In 1833 Holden urged Messrs Townend to introduce seven wool-combing machines of Collier's designs, but they were found to be very imperfect and brought only trouble and loss. In 1836 Holden began experimenting on the machines until they showed reasonable success. He decided to concentrate entirely on developing the combing machine and in 1846 moved to Bradford to form an alliance with Samuel **Lister**. A joint patent in 1847 covered improvements to the Collier combing machine. The 'square motion' imitated the action of the hand-comber more closely and was patented in 1856. Five more patents followed in 1857 and others from 1858 to 1862. Holden recommended that the machines should be introduced into France, where they would be more valuable for the merino trade. This venture was begun in 1848 in the joint partnership of Lister & Holden, with equal shares of profits. Holden established a mill at Saint-Denis, first with Donisthorpe machines and then with his own 'square motion' type. Other mills were founded at Rheims and at Croix, near Roubaix. In 1858 Lister decided to retire from the French concerns and sold his share to Holden. Soon after this, Holden decided to remodel all their machinery for washing and carding the gill machines as well as perfecting the square comb. Four years of excessive application followed, during which time £20,000 was spent in experiments in a small mill at Bradford. The result fully justified the expenditure and the Alston Works was built in Bradford.

Holden was a Liberal and from 1865 to 1868 he represented Knaresborough in Parliament. Later he became the Member of Parliament for the Northern Division of the Riding, Yorkshire, and then for the town of Keighley after the constituencies had been altered. He was liberal in his support of religious, charitable and political objectives. His house at Oakworth, near Keighley, must have been one of the earliest to have been lit by electricity.

Principal Honours and Distinctions
Baronet 1893.

Bibliography
1847, with Samuel Lister, British patent no. 11,896 (improved Collier combing machine).
1856, British patent no. 1,058 ('square motion' combing machine).
1857, British patent no. 278

1857, British patent no. 279
1857, British patent no. 280
1857, British patent no. 281
1857, British patent no. 3,177
1858, British patent no. 597
1859, British patent no. 52
1860, British patent no. 810
1862, British patent no. 1,890
1862, British patent no. 3,394

Further Reading
J. Hogg (ed.), *c.*1888, *Fortunes Made in Business*, London (provides an account of Holden's life).
Obituary, 1897, *Engineer* 84.
Obituary, 1897, *Engineering* 64.
E.M. Sigsworth, 1973, 'Sir Isaac Holden, Bt: the first comber in Europe', in N.B. Harte and K.G. Ponting (eds), *Textile History and Economic History, Essays in Honour of Miss Julia de Lacy Mann*, Manchester.
W. English, 1969, *The Textile Industry*, London (provides a good explanation of the square motion combing machine).

RLH

Holland, John Philip

b. 29 February 1840 Liscanor, Co. Clare, Ireland
d. 12 August 1915 Newark, New Jersey, USA

Irish/American inventor of the successful modern submarine

Holland was educated first in his native town and later in Limerick, a seaport bustling with coastal trade ships. His first job was that of schoolteacher, and as such he worked in various parts of Ireland until he was about 32 years old. A combination of his burning patriotic zeal for Ireland and his interest in undersea technology (then in its infancy) made him consider designs for underwater warships for use against the British Royal Navy in the fight for Irish independence. He studied all known works on the subject and commenced drawing plans, but he was unable to make real headway owing to a lack of finance.

In 1873 he travelled to the United States, ultimately settling in New Jersey and continuing in the profession of teaching. His work on submarine design continued, but in 1875 he suffered a grave setback when the United States Navy turned down his designs. Help came from an unexpected source, the Irish Republican Brotherhood, or Fenian Society, which had been founded in Dublin and New York in 1858. Financial help enabled Holland to build a 4 m (13 ft) one-person craft, which was tested in 1878, and then a larger boat of 19 tonnes' displacement that was tested with a crew of three to depths of 20 m (65 ft) in New York's harbour in 1883. Known as the *Fenian Ram*, it embodied most of the principles of modern submarines, including weight compensation. The Fenians commandeered this boat, but they were unable to operate it satisfactorily and it was relegated to history.

Holland continued work, at times independently and sometimes with others, and continuously advocated submarines to the United States Navy. In 1895 he was successful in winning a contract for US$150,000 to build the US Submarine *Plunger* at Baltimore. With too much outside interference, this proved an unsatisfactory venture. However, with only US$5,000 of his capital left, Holland started again and in 1898 he launched the *Holland* at Elizabeth, New Jersey. This 16 m (52 ft) vessel was successful, and in 1900 it was purchased by the United States Government.

Six more boats were ordered by the Americans, and then some by the Russians and the Japanese. The British Royal Navy ordered five, which were built by Vickers Son and Maxim (now VSEL) at Barrow-in-Furness in the years up to 1903, commencing their long run of submarine building. They were licensed by another well-known name, the Electric Boat Company, which had formerly been the J.P. Holland Torpedo Boat Company.

Holland now had some wealth and was well known. He continued to work, trying his hand at aeronautical research, and in 1904 he invented a respirator for use in submarine rescue work. It is pleasing to record that one of his ships can be seen to this day at the Royal Navy Submarine Museum, Gosport: HM Submarine *Holland No. 1*, which was lost under tow in 1913 but salvaged and restored in the 1980s.

Principal Honours and Distinctions
Order of the Rising Sun, Japan, 1910.

Bibliography
1900, 'The submarine boat and its future', *North American Review* (December).
Holland wrote several other articles of a similar nature.

Further Reading
R.K. Morris, 1966, *John P. Holland 1841–1914, Inventor of the Modern Submarine*, Annapolis, MD: US Naval Institute.
F.W. Lipscomb, 1975, *The British Submarine*, London: Conway Maritime Press.
A.N. Harrison, 1979, *The Development of HM Submarines from Holland No. 1 (1901) to Porpoise (1930)*, Bath: MoD Ships Department (internal publication).

FMW

Holly, Birdsill

b. Auburn, New York, USA
d. 27 April 1894 Lockport, New York, USA

American inventor of water-pumping machinery and a steam heating system.

Holly was educated in mechanics and millwrighting work. He was an indefatigable inventor and took out over 150 patents for his ideas. He became Superintendent and later Proprietor of a millwrighting shop in Uniontown, Pennsylvania. Then at Seneca Falls, New York, he began manufacturing hydraulic machinery with the firm of Silsby, Race & Holly. He made the Silsby fire-engine famous through his invention in 1852 of a rotary pump which was later developed into a steam fire pump. In 1866 he introduced at Lockport, New York, a pressurized water-supply system using a pump rather than an elevated reservoir or standpipe. While this installation at Lockport was powered by a water-wheel, a second one in Dunkirk, New York, used steam-driven pumps, which had a significant effect on the history of steam pumping engines.

Further Reading
Obituary, 1894, *Engineering Record* 29.
Obituary, 1894, *Iron Age* 53.
I. McNeil (ed.), 1990, *An Encyclopaedia of the History of Technology*, London: Routledge (mentions his work on water supply).

RLH

Holmes, Frederic Hale

fl. 1850s–60s

British engineer who pioneered the electrical illumination of lighthouses in Great Britain.

An important application of the magneto generator was demonstrated by Holmes in 1853 when he showed that it might be used to supply an arc lamp. This had many implications for the future because it presented the possibility of making electric lighting economically successful. In 1856 he patented a machine with six disc armatures on a common axis rotating between seven banks of permanent magnets. The following year Holmes suggested the possible application of his invention to lighthouse illumination and a trial was arranged and observed by **Faraday**, who was at that time scientific adviser to Trinity House, the corporation entrusted with the care of lighthouses in England and Wales. Although the trial was successful and gained the approval of Faraday, the Elder Brethren of Trinity House imposed strict conditions on Holmes's design for machines to be used for a more extensive trial. These included connecting the machine directly to a slow-speed steam engine, but this resulted in a reduced performance. The experiments of Holmes and Faraday were brought to the attention of the French lighthouse authorities and magneto generators manufactured by Société Alliance began to be installed in some lighthouses along the coast of France. After noticing the French commutatorless machines, Holmes produced an alternator of similar type in 1867. Two of these were constructed for a new lighthouse at Souter Point near Newcastle and two were installed in each of the two lighthouses at South Foreland. One of the machines from South Foreland that was in service from 1872 to 1922 is preserved in the Royal Museum of Scotland, Edinburgh. A Holmes generator is also preserved in the Science Museum, London. Holmes obtained a series of patents for generators between 1856 and 1869, with all but the last being of the magneto-electric type.

Bibliography
7 March 1856, British patent no. 573 (the original patent for Holmes's invention).
1863, 'On magneto electricity and its application to lighthouse purposes', *Journal of the Society of Arts* 12: 39–43.

Further Reading
W.J. King, 1962, in *The Development of Electrical Technology in the 19th Century*, Washington, DC: Smithsonian Institution, Paper 30, pp. 351–63 (provides a detailed account of Holmes's generators).
J.N. Douglas, 1879, 'The electric light applied to lighthouse illumination', *Proceedings of the Institution of Civil Engineers* 57(3): 77–110 (describes trials of Holmes's machines).

GW

Holt, Benjamin

b. 1 January 1849 Concord, New Hampshire, USA
d. 5 December 1924 Stockton, California, USA

American machinery manufacturer responsible for the development of the Caterpillar tractor and for early developments in combine harvesters.

In 1864 Charles Henry Holt led three other brothers to California in response to the gold rush. In 1868 he founded C.H. Holt & Co. in San Francisco with the help of his brothers Williams and Ames. The company dealt in timber as well as wagon and carriage materials, as did the business they had left behind in Concord in the care of their youngest brother, Benjamin. In 1883 Benjamin joined the others in California and together they formed the Stockton Wheel Company with offices in San Francisco and Stockton. The brothers recognized the potential of combine harvesters and purchased a number of patents, enlarged their works and began to experiment. Their first combine was produced in 1886, and worked for forty-six days that year. With the stimulus of Benjamin Holt the company produced the first hillside combine in 1891 and introduced the concept of belt drive. The Holt harvesting machine produced in 1904 was the first to use an auxiliary gas engine. By 1889 Benjamin was sole family executive. In 1890 the company produced its first traction engine. He began experimenting with track-laying machines, building his first in 1904. It was this machine which earned the nickname 'Caterpillar', which has remained the company trade name to the present day. In 1906 the company produced its first gasoline-engined Caterpillar, and the first production model was introduced two years later. The development of Caterpillar tractors had a significant impact on the transport potential of the Allies during the First World War, and the Holt production of track-laying traction engines was of immense importance to the supply of the armed forces. In 1918 Benjamin Holt was still actively involved in the company, but he died in Stockton in 1920.

Further Reading
W.A. Payne (ed.), 1982, *Benjamin Holt: The Story of the Caterpillar Tractor*, Stockton, Calif: University of the Pacific (provides an illustrated account of the life of Holt and the company he formed).
R. Jones, 'Benjamin Holt and the Caterpillar tractor', *Vintage Tractor Magazine* 1st special vol.

AP

Holtzapffel, Charles

b. 1806 London, England
d. 11 April 1847 London, England

English mechanical engineer and author of Turning and Mechanical Manipulation.

Charles Holtzapffel was the son of John Holtzapffel, a native of Germany who settled in London *c*.1787 and set up as a manufacturer of lathes and tools for amateur mechanics. Charles Holtzapffel received a good English education and training in his father's workshop, and subsequently became a partner and ultimately succeeded to the business. He was engaged in the construction of machinery for printing banknotes, of lathes for cutting rosettes and for ornamental and plain turning. Holtzapffel is chiefly remembered for his monumental work entitled *Turning and Mechanical Manipulation, intended as a work of general reference and practical instruction on the lathe*. Publication began in 1843 and only the first two volumes were published in his lifetime. A third volume was edited by his widow from his notes and published shortly after his death. The fourth and fifth volumes were completed by his son, John Jacob **Holtzapffel**, more than thirty years later. Holtzapffel was an Associate of the Institution of Civil Engineers and served on its Council; he was also a member of the Society of Arts and Chairman of its Committee on Mechanics.

RTS

Holtzapffel, John Jacob

b. June 1836 London, England
d. 14 October 1897 Eastbourne, Sussex, England

English mechanical engineer and author of several volumes of Turning and Mechanical Manipulation.

John Jacob Holtzapffel was the second son of Charles **Holtzapffel** and was educated at King's College School, London, and at Cromwell House, Highgate. Following the death of his father in 1847 and of his elder brother, Charles, at the age of 10, he was called on at an early age to take part in the business of lathe-making and turning founded by his grandfather. He made many improvements to the lathe for ornamental turning, but he is now remembered chiefly for the continuation of his father's publication *Turning and Mechanical Manipulation.* J.J. Holtzapffel produced the fourth volume, on *Plain Turning*, in 1879, and the fifth, on *Ornamental Turning*, in 1884. In 1894 he revised and enlarged the third volume, but the intended sixth volume was never completed. J.J. Holtzapffel was admitted to the Turners' Company of London in 1862 and became Master in 1879. He was associated with the establishment of the Turners' Competition to encourage the art of turning and was one of the judges for many years. He was also an examiner for the City and Guilds of London Institute and the British Horological Institute. He was a member of the Society of Arts and a corresponding member of the Franklin Institute of Philadelphia. He was elected an Associate of the Institution of Civil Engineers in 1863 and became an Associate Member after reorganization of the classes of membership in 1878.

Principal Honours and Distinctions
Master, Turners' Company of London 1879.

Bibliography
1879, *Turning and Mechanical Manipulation,* Vol. IV: *Plain Turning*, London; 1884, Vol. V: *The Principles and Practice of Ornamental or Complex Turning*, London; reprinted 1894; reprinted 1973, New York.

RTS

Honnecourt, Villard de
See **Villard de Honnecourt**.

Hooke, Robert
b. 18 July 1635 Freshwater, Isle of Wight, England
d. 3 March 1703 London, England

English physicist, astronomer and mechanician.

Son of Revd John Hooke, minister of the parish, he was a sickly child who was subject to headaches which prevented protracted study. He devoted his time while alone to making mechanical models including a wooden clock. On the death of his father in October 1648 he was left £100 and went to London, where he became a pupil of Sir Peter Lely and then went to Westminster School under Dr Busby. There he learned the classical languages, some Hebrew and oriental languages while mastering six books of Euclid in one week. In 1653 he entered Christ Church College, Oxford, where he graduated MA in 1663, after studying chemistry and astronomy. In 1662 he was appointed Curator of Experiments to the Royal Society and was elected a Fellow in 1663. In 1665 his appointment was made permanent and he was given apartments in Gresham College, where he lived until his death in 1703. He was an indefatigable experimenter, perhaps best known for the invention of the universal joint named after him. The properties of the atmosphere greatly engaged him and he devised many forms of the barometer. He was the first to apply the spiral spring to the regulation of the balance wheel of the watch in an attempt to measure longitude at sea, but he did not publish his results until after **Huygens**'s reinvention of the device in 1675. Several of his 'new watches' were made by Thomas **Tompion**, one of which was presented to King Charles II. He is said to have invented, among other devices, thirty different ways of flying, the first practical system of telegraphy, an odometer, a hearing aid, an arithmetical machine and a marine barometer. Hooke was a small man, somewhat deformed, with long, lank hair, who went about stooped and moved very quickly. He was of a melancholy and mistrustful disposition, ill-tempered and sharp-tongued. He slept little, often working all night and taking a nap during the day. John Aubrey, his near-contemporary, wrote of Hooke, 'He is certainly the greatest Mechanick this day in the World.' He is said to have been the first to establish the true principle of the arch. His eyesight failed and he was blind for the last year of his life. He is best known for his *Micrographia, or some Physiological Descriptions of Minute Bodies*, first published in 1665. After the Great Fire of London, he exhibited a model for the rebuilding of the City. This was not accepted, but it did result in Hooke's appointment as one of two City Surveyors. This proved a lucrative post and through it Hooke amassed a fortune of some thousands of pounds, which was found intact after his death some thirty years later. It had never been opened in the interim period. Among the buildings he designed were the new Bethlehem (Bedlam) Hospital, the College of Physicians and Montague House.

Principal Honours and Distinctions
FRS 1663; Secretary 1677–82.

IMcN

Hoover, William Henry
b. 1849 New Berlin (now North Canton), Ohio, USA
d. 25 February 1932 North Canton, Ohio, USA

American founder of the Electric Suction Company, which manufactured and successfully marketed the first practical and portable suction vacuum cleaner.

Hoover was descended from a Swiss farming family called Hofer who emigrated from Basle and settled in Lancaster County, Pennsylvania, in the early eighteenth century. By 1832 the family had become tanners and lived near North Berlin in Ohio. In 1870 William Henry Hoover, who had studied at Mount Union College, bought the tannery with his brothers and soon expanded the business to make horse collars and saddlery. The firm expanded to become W.H. Hoover & Co. In the early years of the first decade of the twentieth century, horses were beginning to be replaced by the internal combustion engine, so Hoover needed a new direction for his firm. This he found in the suction vacuum cleaner devised in 1907 by J. Murray Spangler, a cousin of Hoover's wife. The first successful cleaner of this type had been operating in England since 1901 (see **Booth**), but was not a portable model. Attracted by the development of the small electric motor, Spangler produced a vertical cleaner with such a motor that sucked the dust through the machine and blew it into a bag attached to the handle. Spangler applied for a patent for his invention on 14 September in the same year; it was granted for a carpet sweeper and cleaner on 2 June 1908, but Spangler was unable to market it himself and sold the rights to Hoover. The Model O machine, which ran on small wheels, was immediately manufactured and marketed. Hoover's model was the first electric, one-person-operated, domestic vacuum cleaner and was instantly successful, although the main expansion of the business was delayed for some time until the greater proportion of houses were wired for electricity. The Hoover slogan, 'it beats as it sweeps as it cleans', came to be true in 1926 with the introduction of the Model 700, which was the first cleaner to offer triple-action cleaning, a process which beat, swept and sucked at the carpet. Further advances in the 1930s included the use of magnesium and the early plastics.

Further Reading
G. Adamson, 1969, *Machines at Home*, Lutterworth Press.
How it Works: The Universal Encyclopaedia of Machines, Paladin.
D. Yarwood, 1981, *The British Kitchen*, Batsford, Ch. 6.

DY

Hopkinson, John
b. 27 July 1849 Manchester, England
d. 27 August 1898 Petite Dent de Veisivi, Switzerland

English mathematician and electrical engineer who laid the foundations of electrical machine design.

After attending Owens College, Manchester, Hopkinson was admitted to Trinity College, Cambridge, in 1867 to read for the Mathematical Tripos. An appointment in 1872 with the lighthouse department of the Chance Optical Works in Birmingham directed his attention to electrical engineering. His most noteworthy contribution to lighthouse engineering was an optical system to produce flashing lights that distinguished between individual beacons. His extensive researches on the dielectric properties of glass were recognized when he was elected to a Fellowship of the Royal Society at the age of 29. Moving to London in 1877 he became established as a consulting engineer at a time when electricity supply was about to begin on a commercial scale. During the remainder of his life, Hopkinson's researches resulted in fundamental contributions to electrical engineering practice, dynamo design and alternating current machine theory. In making a critical study of the **Edison** dynamo he developed the principle of the magnetic circuit, a concept also arrived at by Gisbert **Kapp** around the same time. Hopkinson's improvement of the Edison dynamo by reducing the length of the field magnets almost doubled its output. In 1890, in addition to his consulting practice, Hopkinson accepted a post as the first Professor of Electrical Engineering and Head of the Siemens laboratory recently established at King's College, London. Although he was not involved in lecturing, the position gave him the necessary facilities and staff and student assistance to continue his researches. Hopkinson was consulted on many proposals for electric traction and electricity supply, including schemes in London, Manchester, Liverpool and Leeds. He also advised Mather and Platt when they were acting as contractors for the locomotives and generating plant for the City and South London tube railway. As early as 1882 he considered that an ideal method of charging for the supply of electricity should be based on a two-part tariff, with a charge related to maximum demand together with a charge for energy supplied. Hopkinson was one the foremost expert witnesses of his day in patent actions and was himself the patentee of over forty inventions, of which the three-wire system of distribution and the series–parallel connection of traction motors were his most successful. Jointly with his brother Edward, John Hopkinson communicated the outcome of his investigations to the Royal Society in a paper entitled 'Dynamo Electric Machinery' in 1886. In this he also described the later widely used 'back to back' test for determining the characteristics of two identical machines. His interest in electrical machines led him to more fundamental research on magnetic materials, including the phenomenon of recalescence and the disappearance of magnetism at a well-defined temperature. For his work on the magnetic properties of iron, in 1890 he was awarded the Royal Society Royal Medal. He was a member of the Alpine Club and a pioneer of rock climbing in Britain; he died, together with three of his children, in a climbing accident.

Principal Honours and Distinctions
FRS 1878. Royal Society Royal Medal 1890. President, Institution of Electrical Engineers 1890 and 1896.

Bibliography
7 July 1881, British patent no. 2,989 (series–parallel control of traction motors).
27 July 1882, British patent no. 3,576 (three-wire distribution).
1901, *Original Papers by the Late J. Hopkinson, with a Memoir*, ed. B. Hopkinson, 2 vols, Cambridge.

Further Reading
J. Greig, 1970, *John Hopkinson Electrical Engineer*, London: Science Museum and HMSO (an authoritative account).
—— 1950, 'John Hopkinson 1849–1898', *Engineering* 169: 34–7, 62–4.

GW

Hopper, Thomas
b. 1776 Rochester, Kent, England
d. 11 August 1856 London, England

English architect whose large practice produced Gothic Revival work.

Like so many of his contemporaries, Hopper made extensive use of cast iron, both structurally and decoratively. A notable example of this was his Conservatory, added to Carlton House in London in 1807–12 for the Prince of Wales: it was demolished in 1827–8. Constructed with cast iron and stained glass, the Conservatory took the form of slender, tall piers supporting an elaborate fan vault, the design of which was based upon that of the sixteenth-century Henry VII Chapel at Westminster Abbey.

Further Reading
H. Colvin, *Biographical Dictionary of English Architects, 1600–1840*, London: John Murray.
Henry Russell-Hitchcock, 1977, *Architecture, Nineteenth and Twentieth Centuries*, London: Penguin.

DY

Hornblower, Jonathan

b. 1753 Cornwall (?), England
d. 1815 Penryn, Cornwall, England

English mining engineer who patented an early form of compound steam engine.

Jonathan came from a family with an engineering tradition: his grandfather Joseph had worked under Thomas **Newcomen**. Jonathan was the sixth child in a family of thirteen whose names all began with 'J'. In 1781 he was living at Penryn, Cornwall and described himself as a plumber, brazier and engineer. As early as 1776, when he wished to amuse himself by making a small steam engine, he wanted to make something new and wondered if the steam would perform more than one operation in an engine. This was the foundation for his compound engine. He worked on engines in Cornwall, and in 1778 was Engineer at the Ting Tang mine where he helped **Boulton & Watt** erect one of their engines. He was granted a patent in 1781 and in that year tried a large-scale experiment by connecting together two engines at Wheal Maid. Very soon John Winwood, a partner in a firm of iron founders at Bristol, acquired a share in the patent, and in 1782 an engine was erected in a colliery at Radstock, Somerset. This was probably not very successful, but a second was erected in the same area. Hornblower claimed greater economy from his engines, but steam pressures at that time were not high enough to produce really efficient compound engines. Between 1790 and 1794 ten engines with his two-cylinder arrangement were erected in Cornwall, and this threatened Boulton & Watt's near monopoly. At first the steam was condensed by a surface condenser in the bottom of the second, larger cylinder, but this did not prove very successful and later a water jet was used. Although Boulton & Watt proceeded against the owners of these engines for infringement of their patent, they did not take Jonathan Hornblower to court. He tried a method of packing the piston rod by a steam gland in 1781 and his work as an engineer must have been quite successful, for he left a considerable fortune on his death.

Bibliography
1781, British patent no. 1,298 (compound steam engine).

Further Reading
R. Jenkins, 1979–80, 'Jonathan Hornblower and the compound engine', *Transactions of the Newcomen Society* 11.
J. Tann, 1979–80, 'Mr Hornblower and his crew, steam engine pirates in the late 18th century', *Transactions of the Newcomen Society* 51.
J. Farey, 1827, *A Treatise on the Steam Engine, Historical, Practical and Descriptive*, reprinted 1971, Newton Abbot: David & Charles (an almost contemporary account of the compound engine).
D.S.L. Cardwell, 1971, *From Watt to Clausius. The Rise of Thermodynamics in the Early Industrial Age*, London: Heinemann.
H.W. Dickinson, 1938, *A Short History of the Steam Engine*, Cambridge University Press.
R.L. Hills, 1989, *Power from Steam. A History of the Stationary Steam Engine*, Cambridge University Press.

RLH

Hornby, Frank

b. 15 May 1863 Liverpool, England
d. 21 September 1936 Liverpool, England

English toy manufacturer and inventor of Meccano kits.

Frank Hornby left school at the age of 16 and worked as a clerk, at first for his father, a provision merchant, and later for D.H. Elliott, an importer of meat and livestock, for whom he became Managing Clerk. As a youth he was interested in engineering and in his own small workshop he became a skilled amateur mechanic. He made toys for his children and *c.*1900 he devised a constructional toy kit consisting of perforated metal strips which could be connected by bolts and nuts. He filed a patent application in January 1901 and, having failed to interest established toy manufacturers, he set up a small business in partnership with his employer, D.H. Elliott, who provided financial support. The kits were sold at first under the name of Mechanics Made Easy, but by 1907 the name Meccano had been registered as a trade mark. The business expanded rapidly and in 1908 Elliott withdrew from the partnership and Hornby continued on his own account, the company being incorporated as Meccano Ltd. Although parts for Meccano were produced at first by various manufacturers, Hornby soon acquired premises to produce all the components under his own control, and between 1910 and 1913 he established his own factory on a 5-acre (2-hectare) site at Binn's Road, Liverpool. The *Meccano Magazine*, a monthly publication with articles of general engineering interest, developed from a newsletter giving advice on the use of Meccano, and from the first issue in 1916 until 1924 was edited by Frank Hornby. In 1920 he introduced the clockwork Hornby trains, followed by the electric version five years later. These were gauge '0' (1¼ in./32 mm); the smaller gauge '00', or Hornby Dublo, was a later development. Another product of Meccano Ltd was the series of model vehicles known as Dinky toys, introduced in 1934.

Frank Hornby served as a Member of Parliament for the Everton Division of Liverpool from 1931 to 1935.

Principal Honours and Distinctions
MP, 1931–5.

Further Reading
D.J. Jeremy (ed.), 1984–6, *Dictionary of Business Biography*, Vol. 3, London, 345–9 (a useful biography).
Proceedings of the Institution of Mechanical Engineers 127 (1934): 140–1 (describes the Binn's Road factory).

RTS

Hosking, William
b. 1800
d. 1861

Australian architect and engineer.

William Hosking was appointed Professor of 'the arts and construction' at King's College, London, in 1840. He was an architect and engineer who moved to England in 1819 after working as a builder in Sydney. He thus represents an unusually early example of the reverse migration of professional talent between Britain and its colonies. He exhibited drawings in London, becoming a Fellow of the Society of Antiquaries in 1830 and Fellow of the Royal Institution of British Architects in 1835. He was then caught up, like so many of his contemporaries with engineering ability, in railway building, working on the

West London Railway. From 1840 to his death in 1861 he occupied the Chair at King's College, making a pioneering contribution to the development of engineering education in Britain. He published his *Theory, Practice and Architecture of Bridges* in 1843, and contributed to the design for the British Museum reading room.

Principal Honours and Distinctions
Fellow of the Society of Antiquaries 1830. FRIBA 1835.

Bibliography
1843, *Theory, Practice and Architecture of Bridges*.

Further Reading
Dictionary of National Biography, London.

AB

Houldsworth, Henry
b. 1797 Manchester (?), England
d. 1868 Manchester (?), England

English cotton spinner who introduced the differential gear to roving frames in Britain.

There are two claimants for the person who originated the differential gear as applied to roving frames: one is J. Green, a tinsmith of Mansfield, in his patent of 1823; the other is A. **Arnold**, who had applied it in America and patented it in early 1823. This latter was the source for Houldsworth's patent in 1826. It seems that Arnold's gearing was secretly communicated to Houldsworth by Charles Richmond, possibly when Houldsworth visited the United States in 1822–3, but more probably in 1825 when Richmond went to England. In return, Richmond received information about parts of a cylinder printing machine from Houldsworth. In the working of the roving frame, as the rovings were wound onto their bobbins and the diameter of the bobbins increased, the bobbin speed had to be reduced to keep the winding on at the same speed while the flyers and drawing rollers had to maintain their initial speed. Although this could be achieved by moving the driving belt along coned pulleys, this method did not provide enough power and slippage occurred. The differential gear combined the direct drive from the main shaft of the roving frame with that from the cone drive, so that only the latter provided the difference between flyer and bobbin speeds, i.e. the winding speeds, thus taking away most of the power from that belt. Henry Houldsworth Senior (1774–1853) was living in Manchester when his son Henry was born, but by 1800 had moved to Glasgow. He built several mills, including a massive one at Anderston, Scotland, in which a **Boulton** & **Watt** steam engine was installed. Henry Houldsworth Junior was probably back in Manchester by 1826, where he was to become an influential cotton spinner as chief partner in his mills, which he moved out to Reddish in 1863–5. He was also a prominent landowner in Cheetham. When William **Fairbairn** was considering establishing the Association for the Prevention of Steam Boiler Explosions in 1854, he wanted to find an influential manufacturer and mill-owner and he made a happy choice when he turned to Henry Houldsworth for assistance.

Bibliography
1826, British patent no. 5,316 (differential gear for roving frames).

Further Reading
Details about Henry Houldsworth Junior are very sparse. The best account of his acquisition of the differential gear is given by D.J. Jeremy, 1981, *Transatlantic Industrial Revolution. The Diffusion of Textile Technologies Between Britain and America, 1790–1830*, Oxford.
W. English, 1969, *The Textile Industry*, London (an explanation of the mechanisms of the roving frame).
W. Pole, 1877, *The Life of Sir William Fairbairn, Bart.*, London (provides an account of the beginning of the Manchester Steam Users' Association for the Prevention of Steam-boiler Explosions).

RLH

Hounsfield, Sir Godfrey Newbold
b. 28 August 1919 Newark, Nottinghamshire, England

English scientist, inventor and developer of computer-assisted tomography (CAT) scanning technique of radiographic examination.

After an education in Newark and London in radiocommunications and radar, Hounsfield volunteered and served in the RAF during 1939–45. He was a lecturer at Cranwell Radar School

from *c*.1942 to 1945. From 1947 to 1951 he undertook further study in electrical and mechanical engineering, and in 1951 he joined Electrical and Musical Instruments (EMI) Ltd, where he led the design team for the first British all-transistor computer (EMIDEC, 1959). In 1969–72 he invented and developed the EMI computerized transverse axial tomography scanner system of X-ray examination; this, while applicable to other areas of the body, particularly permitted the elimination of difficulties presented since the earliest days of X-ray examination in the examination of the cranial contents.

Principal Honours and Distinctions
Knighted 1981. CBE 1976. FRS 1975. Nobel Prize for Medicine or Physiology (jointly with A.M. Cormack) 1979.

Bibliography
1973, 'Computerized transverse axial scanning (Tomography)', *British Journal of Radiology, American Journal of Roentgenology*.

MG

Houston, Sir Alexander Cruickshank
b. 18 September 1865 Settle, Yorkshire, England
d. 29 October 1933 London, England

English physician and bacteriologist, pioneer of the chlorination of water supplies.

Son of an Army surgeon-general, he graduated in Edinburgh in 1889. Specializing in public health and forensic matters, he worked from 1897 to 1905 for the Local Government Board on lead poisoning resulting from moorland water supplies. He also acted as Bacteriologist to the Royal Commission on Sewage Disposal from 1890 to 1905. In 1905 he was appointed Director of Water Examinations to the Metropolitan Water Board, with whom he served until his death. Shortly before he joined the Board, he was involved in the investigation of an outbreak of typhoid at Lincoln and was instrumental in establishing a chlorination plant of a rudimentary nature there, and also in organizing the comprehensive chlorinating system which was then applied to London's water supply. He also advised on water supplies in Egypt and Canada.

Knighted 1918. Commander of the Royal Victorian Order 1919. FRS 1931. Gunning Victoria Jubilee Prize, Edinburgh 1892.

Bibliography
1914, *Studies in Water Supply.*
1918, *Rural Water Supplies and their Purification.*
1953, *London's Water Supply, 1903–1953,* London: Metropolitan Water Board.

MG

Howden, James

b. 29 February 1832 Prestonpans, East Lothian, Scotland
d. 21 November 1913 Glasgow, Scotland

Scottish engineer and boilermaker, inventor of the forced-draught system for the boiler combustion chamber.

Howden was educated in Prestonpans. While aged only 14 or 15, he travelled across Scotland by canal to Glasgow, where he served an engineering apprenticeship with James Gray & Co. In 1853 he completed his time and for some months served with the civil engineers Bell and Miller, and then with Robert Griffiths, a designer of screw propellers for ships. In 1854, at the age of 22, Howden set up as a consulting engineer and designer. He designed a rivet-making machine from which he realized a fair sum by the sale of patent rights, this assisting him in converting the design business into a manufacturing one. His first contract for a marine engine came in 1859 for the compound steam engine and the watertube boilers of the Anchor Liner *Ailsa Craig*. This ship operated at 100 psi (approximately 7 kg/cm^2), well above the norm for those days. James Howden & Co. was formed in 1862. Despite operating in the world's most competitive market, the new company remained prosperous through the flow of inventions in marine propulsion. Shipbuilding was added to the company's list of services, but such work was subcontracted. Work was obtained from all the great shipping companies building in the Glasgow region, and with such throughput Howden's could afford research and experimentation. This led to the Howden hot-air forced-draught system, whereby furnace waste gases were used to heat the air being drawn into the combustion chambers. The first installation was on the *New York City*, built in 1885 for West Indian service. Howden's fertile mind brought about a fully enclosed high-speed marine steam engine in the 1900s and, shortly after, the Howden–Zoelly impulse steam turbine for land operation. Until his death, Howden worked on many technical and business problems: he was involved in the St Helena Whaling Company, marble quarrying in Greece and in the design of a recoilless gun for the Admiralty.

Principal Honours and Distinctions
Howden was the last surviving member of the group who founded the Institution of Engineers and Shipbuilders in Scotland in 1857.

Bibliography
Howden contributed several papers to the Institution of Engineers and Shipbuilders in Scotland.

Further Reading
C.W. Munn, 1986, 'James Howden', *Dictionary of Scottish Business Biography*, Vol. I, Aberdeen.

FMW

Howe, Elias

b. 9 July 1819 Spencer, Massachusetts, USA
d. 3 October 1867 Bridgeport, Connecticut, USA

American inventor of one of the earliest successful sewing machines.

Son of Elias Howe, a farmer, he acquired his mechanical knowledge in his father's mill. He left school at 12 years of age and was apprenticed for two years in a machine shop in Lowell, Massachusetts, and later to an instrument maker, Ari Davis in Boston, Massachusetts, where his master's services were much in demand by Harvard University. Fired by a desire to invent a sewing machine, he utilized the experience gained in Lowell to devise a shuttle carrying a lower thread and a needle carrying an upper thread to make lock-stitch in straight lines. His attempts were so rewarding that he left his job and was sustained first by his father and then by a partner. By 1845 he had built a machine that worked at 250 stitches per minute, and the following year he patented an improved machine. The invention of the sewing machine had an enormous impact on the textile industry, stimulating demand for cloth because making up garments became so much quicker. The sewing machine was one of the first mass-produced consumer durables and was essentially an American invention. William Thomas, a London manufacturer of shoes, umbrellas and corsets, secured the British rights and persuaded Howe to come to England to apply it to the making of shoes. This Howe did, but he quarrelled with Thomas after less than one year. He returned to America to face with his partner, G.W. Bliss, a bigger fight over his patent (see I.M. **Singer**), which was being widely infringed. Not until 1854 was the case settled in his favour. This litigation threatened the very existence of the new industry, but the Great Sewing Machine Combination, the first important patent-pooling arrangement in American history, changed all this. For a fee of $5 on every domestically-sold machine and $1 on every exported one, Howe contributed to the pool his patent of 1846 for a grooved eye-pointed needle used in conjunction with a lock-stitch-forming shuttle. Howe's patent was renewed in 1861; he organized and equipped a regiment during the Civil War with the royalties. When the war ended he founded the Howe Machine Company of Bridgeport, Connecticut.

Further Reading

Obituary, 1867, *Engineer* 24.

Obituary, 1867, *Practical Magazine* 5.

F.G. Harrison, 1892–3, *Biographical Sketches of Pre-eminent Americans* (provides a good account of Howe's life and achievements).

N. Salmon, 1863, *History of the Sewing Machine from the Year 1750, with a biography of Elias Howe*, London (tells the history of sewing machines).

F.B. Jewell, 1975, *Veteran Sewing Machines, A Collector's Guide*, Newton Abbot (a more modern account of the history of sewing machines).

C. Singer (ed.), 1958, *A History of Technology*, Vol. V, Oxford: Clarendon Press (covers the mechanical developments).

D.A. Hounshell, 1984, *From the American System to Mass Production 1800–1932. The Development of Manufacturing Technology in the United States*, Baltimore (examines the role of the American sewing machine companies in the development of mass-production techniques).

RLH

Howe, Frederick Webster

b. 28 August 1822 Danvers, Massachusetts, USA
d. 25 April 1891 Providence, Rhode Island, USA

American mechanical engineer, machine-tool designer and inventor.

Frederick W. Howe attended local schools until the age of 16 and then entered the machine shop of Gay & Silver at North Chelmsford, Massachusetts, as an apprentice and remained with that firm for nine years. He then joined Robbins, Kendall & Lawrence of Windsor, Vermont, as Assistant to Richard S. **Lawrence** in designing machine tools. A year later (1848) he was made Plant Superintendent. During his time with this firm, Howe designed a profiling machine which was used in all gun shops in the United States: a barrel-drilling and rifling machine, and the first commercially successful milling machine. Robbins & Lawrence took to the Great Exhibition of 1851 in London, England, a set of rifles built on the interchangeable system. The interest this created resulted in a visit of some members of the British Royal Small Arms Commission to America and subsequently in an order for 150 machine tools, jigs and fixtures from Robbins & Lawrence, to be installed at the small-arms factory at Enfield. From 1853 to 1856 Howe was in charge of the design and building of these machines. In 1856 he established his own armoury at Newark, New Jersey, but transferred after two years to Middletown, Connecticut, where he continued the manufacture of small arms until the outbreak of the Civil War. He then became Superintendent of the armoury of the Providence Tool Company at Providence, Rhode Island, and served in that capacity until the end of the war. In 1865 he went to Bridgeport, Connecticut, to assist Elias **Howe** with the manufacture of his sewing machine. After the death of Elias Howe, Frederick Howe returned to Providence to join the Brown & Sharpe Manufacturing Company. As Superintendent of that establishment he worked with Joseph R. **Brown** in the development of many of the firm's products, including machinery for the Wilcox & Gibbs sewing machine then being made by Brown & Sharpe. From 1876 Howe was in business on his own account as a consulting mechanical engineer and in his later years he was engaged in the development of shoe machinery and in designing a one-finger typewriter, which, however, was never completed. He was granted several patents, mainly in the fields of machine tools and firearms. As a designer, Howe was said to have been a perfectionist, making frequent improvements; when completed, his designs were always sound.

Further Reading
J.W. Roe, 1916, *English and American Tool Builders*, New Haven; repub. 1926, New York, and 1987, Bradley, Ill. (provides biographical details).
R.S. Woodbury, 1960, *History of the Milling Machine*, Cambridge, Mass. (describes Howe's contribution to the development of the milling machine).

RTS

Howe, William
b. 12 May 1803 Spencer, Massachusetts, USA
d. 19 September 1852 Springfield, Massachusetts, USA

American bridge engineer.

He was uncle of Elias **Howe** and spent his youth in the neighbourhood of his birthplace, primarily as a farmer. In 1838 he was commissioned to build a bridge at Warren, Massachusetts, for the Boston & Albany Railway. He worked on this for two years, incorporating some novel features for which he applied for patents. His design was a truss with wooden diagonals and vertical iron ties in single and double systems which was said to be an improvement on the Long type of truss, introduced by Colonel Stephen Long in 1830. Howe was the first to incorporate the rectangular truss frame. Soon after this, he was to use his patent truss over the Connecticut River at Springfield for the Western Railroad. So successful was he that he became engaged for the rest of his life in the design of bridges and roof trusses, which, together with selling royalties for the rights to his patents, brought to him a considerable fortune. Many Howe truss bridges were built until the introduction of the iron bridge. In 1846 he took out a third patent for an improvement in the original rectangular truss, consisting of a curved timber member rising from each buttress to the centre of the span and greatly adding to the strength.

Further Reading
Dictionary of American Biography, 1932–3, New York: Charles Scribner.

IMcN

Hsu Kuang-Chhi
See **Xu Guangqi**.

Hulls, Jonathan
b. 1699 Campden, Gloucestershire, England
d. after 1754

English inventor (supposed) of the steamboat.

Hulls was the first in Britain to attempt to employ steam in propelling a vessel in water. His experiment was made on the River Avon at Evesham in 1737, the main idea being to install a **Newcomen** engine, the only type then known, on a boat in front of the vessel it was intended to propel, and connected to it with a tow-rope. Six paddles in the stern of the tow boat were fastened to a cross axis connected by ropes to another shaft, which was turned by the engine. Hulls undoubtedly showed how to convert the rectilinear motion of a piston into rotary motion, which is an essential principle in steam locomotion, on land or water.

He is described as 'the inventor of the Steamboat' on a portrait that once hung at the Institution of Marine Engineers, and his patent for the steamboat is dated 21 December 1736. He published his *Description and Draught of a New-Invented Machine* ('for carrying vessels or ships out or into any harbour, port or river against wind and tide, or in a calm: for which His Majesty has granted Letters Patent for the sole benefit of the author for the space of 14 years', 1737); this rare book was reprinted in 1855. According to De Morgan, Hull's work probably gave the idea to **Symington**, as Symington's did to **Fulton**. Erasmus Darwin had him in mind when he wrote 'drag the slow barge'. In 1754 Hulls published *The Art of Measuring Made Easy by the Help of a New Sliding Scale*, which he patented in 1753 together with a machine for weighing gold coins. He also wrote *Maltmakers' Instructor*.

Further Reading
S. Smiles, *Boulton and Watt*, pp. 72–4.
De Morgan, *Budget of Paradoxes*.

IMcN

Humfrey, William

b. *c.*1515
d. 14 July 1579

English goldsmith and Assay Master of the Royal Mint who attempted to introduce brass production to England.

William Humfrey, goldsmith of the parish of St Vedast, was appointed Assay Master of the Royal Mint in 1561. At the Tower of London he assumed responsibility for the weight of silver and for production standards at a time of intense activity in recoining the debased coinage of the realm. Separation of copper from the debased silver involved liquation techniques which enabled purification of the recovered silver and copper. German co-operation in introducing these methods to England developed their interest in English copper mining, resulting in the formation of the Mines Royal Company. Shareholders in this government-led monopoly included Humfrey, whose assay of Keswick copper ore, mined with German expertise, was bitterly disputed. As a result of this dispute, Humfrey promoted the formation of a smaller monopoly, the Company of Mineral Battery Works, with plans to mine lead and especially the zinc carbonate ore, calamine, using it to introduce brassmaking and wire manufacture into England. Humfrey acquired technical assistance from further skilled German immigrants, relying particularly on Christopher Schutz of Annaberg in Saxony, who claimed experience in such matters. However, the brassmaking project set up at Tintern was abandoned by 1569 after failure to make a brass suitable for manufacturing purposes. The works changed its production to iron wire. Humfrey had meanwhile been under suspicion of embezzlement at the Tower in connection with his work there. He died intestate while involved in litigation regarding infringement of rights and privileges claimed from his introduction of new techniques in later lead-mining activities under the auspices of the Company of Mineral and Battery Works.

Further Reading
M.B. Donald, 1961, *Elizabethan Monopolies*, London: Oliver & Boyd (the most detailed account).
—— 1955, *Elizabethan Copper*, reprinted 1989, Michael Moon.

JD

Hunt, Robert

b. 6 September 1807 Devonport, Devon, England
d. 19 March 1887 England

English photographic pioneer and writer.

A chemist by training, Hunt took an early interest in photography and during the 1840s devised several original photographic processes and techniques. The properties of iron sulphate as a developing agent, widely used by wet-collodion photographers, were first described by Hunt in 1844. He was a prolific author and it was as a writer that he was most influential. In 1841 he published the first substantial English-language photographic manual, a work that was to run to six editions. Perhaps his most important work was his *Researches on Light*, first published in 1844, with a second edition containing considerable additional material appearing in 1854. In 1851 Hunt was appointed Professor of Mechanical Science at the Royal School of Mines in London. He was a founder member of the London (later Royal) Photographic Society in 1853.

Principal Honours and Distinctions
Member of the Royal Society 1854.

Further Reading
C. Thomas, 1988, *Views and Likenesses*, Truro: Royal Institution of Cornwall (a brief account of Hunt's life and work).
H. Gernsheim and A. Gernsheim, 1969, *The History of Photography*, rev. edn, London.

JW

Hunt, Walter

b. 29 July 1796 Martinsburg, New York, USA
d. 8 June 1859 New York, USA

American inventor and developer of the first repeating rifle.

Hunt displayed talent as an inventor at an early age. While in his late teens he designed a machine for spinning flax, and after taking out a patent on it in 1826 he went to New York in order to set up a company to manufacture it. The company failed, however, and he was forced to go into business as an estate agent in order to make a living. Nevertheless, he remained undeterred and continued to invent a wide range of objects, including an iron fire alarm for fire stations and engines (1827) and the safety pin (1849). However, either many of his ideas were before their time or he failed to market them properly: for example, in 1834 he invented a sewing machine with lockstitch, but failed to patent it and it was left to others, such as Merritt **Singer**, to reap the rewards. He also conceived the name 'fountain pen', but again more commercially minded people, Swan, **Parker** and Waterman, enjoyed the benefits. His paper collar, invented in 1854, only became popular after his death. Hunt is probably best remembered in the field of firearms. In 1849 he produced the first repeating rifle, which had a tubular magazine fixed under the barrel and fired special self-propelled or 'rocket' balls, for which Hunt had taken out a patent the previous year. Although this weapon never entered general manufacture, the design principles incorporated in it were later reflected in the Springfield, Winchester, Henry and Volcanic rifles, which began to appear towards the end of the following decade.

Further Reading
1974, *Webster's American Biographies* (a useful summary of Hunt's life and work).

CM

Hunter, John

b. 14 (registered 13) February 1728 East Kilbride, Lanarkshire, Scotland
d. 16 October 1793 London, England

Scottish surgeon and anatomist, pioneer of experimental methods in medicine and surgery.

The younger brother of William Hunter (1718–83), who was of great distinction but perhaps of slightly less achievement in similar fields, he owed much of his early experience to his brother; William, after a period at Glasgow University, moved to St George's Hospital, London. In his later teens, John assisted a brother-in-law with cabinet-making. This appears to have contributed to the lifelong mechanical skill which he displayed as a dissector and surgeon. This skill was particularly obvious when, after following William to London in 1748, he held post at a number of London teaching hospitals before moving to St George's in 1756. A short sojourn at Oxford in 1755 appears to have been unfruitful.

Despite his deepening involvement in the study of comparative anatomy, facilitated by the purchase of animals from the Tower menagerie and travelling show people, he accepted an appointment as a staff surgeon in the Army in 1760, participating in the expedition to Belle Isle and also serving in Portugal. He returned home with over 300 specimens in 1763 and, until his appointment as Surgeon to St George's in 1768, was heavily involved in the examination of this and other material, as well as in studies of foetal testicular descent, placental circulation, the nature of pus and lymphatic circulation. In 1772 he commenced lecturing on the theory and practice of surgery, and in 1776 he was appointed Surgeon-Extraordinary to George III.

He is rightly regarded as the founder of scientific surgery, but his knowledge was derived almost entirely from his own experiments and observations. His contemporaries did not always accept or understand the concepts which led to such aphorisms as, 'to perform an operation is to mutilate a patient we cannot cure', and his written comment to his pupil **Jenner**: 'Why think. Why not trie the experiment'. His desire to establish the aetiology of gonorrhoea led to him infecting himself, as a result of which he also contracted syphilis. His ensuing account of the characteristics of the disease remains a classic of medicine, although it is likely that the sequelae of the condition brought about his death at a relatively early age. From 1773 he suffered recurrent anginal attacks of such a character that his life 'was in the hands of any rascal who chose to annoy and tease him'. Indeed, it was following a contradiction at a board meeting at St George's that he died.

By 1788, with the death of Percival Pott, he had become unquestionably the leading surgeon in Britain, if not Europe. Elected to the Royal Society in 1767, the extraordinary variety of his collections, investigations and publications, as well as works such as the 'Treatise on the natural history of the human teeth' (1771–8), gives testimony to his original approach involving the fundamental and inescapable relation of structure and function in both normal and disease states. The massive growth of his collections led to his acquiring two houses in Golden Square to contain them. It was his desire that after his death his collection be purchased and preserved for the nation. It contained 13,600 specimens and had cost him £70,000. After considerable delay, Parliament voted inadequate sums for this purpose and the collection was entrusted to the recently rechartered Royal College of Surgeons of England, in whose premises this remarkable monument to the omnivorous and eclectic activities of this outstanding figure in the evolution of medicine and surgery may still be seen. Sadly, some of the collection was lost to bombing during the Second World War. His surviving papers were also extensive, but it is probable that many were destroyed in the early nineteenth century.

Principal Honours and Distinctions
FRS 1767. Copley Medal 1787.

Bibliography
1835–7, *Works*, ed. J.F. Palmer, *Philosophical Transactions of the Royal Society*, London.
MG

Hunter, Matthew Albert
b. 9 November 1878 Auckland Province, New Zealand
d. 24 March 1961 Troy, New York, USA

New Zealand/American technologist and academic who was a pioneer in the production of metallic titanium.

Hunter arrived in England in 1902, the seventh in the succession of New Zealand students nominated for the 1851 Exhibition science research scholarships (the third, in 1894, having been Ernest Rutherford). He intended to study the metallurgy of tellurides at the Royal School of Mines, but owing to the death of the professor concerned, he went instead to University College London, where his research over two years involved the molecular aggregation of liquified gases. In 1904–5 he spent a third year in Göttingen, Paris and Karlsruhe. Hunter then moved to the USA, beginning work in 1906 with the General Electric Company in Schenectady. His experience with titanium came as part of a programme to try to discover satisfactory lamp-filament materials. He and his colleagues achieved more success in producing moderately pure titanium than previous workers had done, but found the metal's melting temperature inadequate. However, his research formed the basis for the 'Hunter sodium process', a modern method for producing commercial quantities of titanium. In 1908 he was appointed Assistant Professor of

Electrochemistry and Physics at Rensselaer Polytechnic Institute in Troy, New York, where he was to remain until his retirement in 1949 as Dean Emeritus. In the 1930s he founded and headed the Institute's Department of Metallurgical Engineering. As a consultant, he was associated with the development of Invar, Managanin and Constantan alloys.

Principal Honours and Distinctions
1851 Great Exhibition science research scholar 1902–5. DSc London University 1904. American Die Casting Institute Doehler Award 1959. American Society for Metals Gold Medal 1959.

Bibliography
1910, 'Metallic titanium', *Journal of the American Chemistry Society* 32: 330–6 (describes his work relating to titanium production).

Further Reading
1961, 'Man of metals', *Rensselaer Alumni News* (December), 5–7: 32.
JKA

Huntsman, Benjamin
b. 1704 Barton-on-Humber, Lincolnshire, England
d. 21 June 1776 Sheffield, England

English inventor of crucible steelmaking.

Of Dutch descent, Hunstman was apprenticed to a clockmaker at Epworth, Lincolnshire. In 1725 he set up in Doncaster as a maker of clocks, locks and roasting jacks. He made improvements in his tools but found himself hampered by the poor quality of the steel available, then made by the cementation process, which yielded a steel with a non-uniform carbon content. Around 1740, Huntsman moved to Handsworth, now part of Sheffield, and began experimenting by heating varying compositions of fuel and flux with crude steel in a crucible, to obtain a steel of uniform composition. During the years 1745 to 1750 he attained his object, but not without many unsuccessful 'heats', as excavations of the site of his works now reveal. Although his steel was far better than that previously available, however, the conservative cutlers of Sheffield rejected it, claiming it was too hard to work; therefore Huntsman exported his product to France, where the cutlers promptly worked it into high-quality knives and razors that were exported to England. The Sheffield cutlers' attempts to prevent Huntsman from exporting his steel proved unsuccessful. Huntsman did not patent his process, preferring to retain his advantage by shrouding his work in secrecy, carrying out his melting at night to escape observation, but a rival cutler, Samuel Walker, gained admittance to Huntsman's works disguised as a tramp seeking food. As a result, Walker was able to make crucible steel at a handsome profit. Huntsman fought back and earned success through the sheer quality of his steel, and had to move to a larger site at Attercliffe in 1770. Crucible steelmaking remained important through the nineteenth century although, as it was a small-scale process, its application was restricted to engineers' cutting tools and the cutting edges of certain tools.

Further Reading

E.W. Hulme, 1945, 'The pedigree and career of Benjamin Huntsman, inventor in Europe of crucible steel', *Transactions of the Newcomen Society* 24: 37–48.

W.K.V. Gale, 1969, *Iron and Steel*, London: Longman.

LRD

Hurter, Ferdinand
b. 15 March 1844 Schaffhausen, Switzerland
d. 5 March 1898

Swiss chemist who, with Vero Charles Driffield, established the basis of modern sensitometry in England.

Ferdinand Hurter worked for three years as a dyer's apprentice before entering the Polytechnic in Zurich; he transferred to Heidelberg, where he graduated in 1866. A year later he secured an appointment as a chemist for the British alkali manufacturing company, Gaskell, Deacon & Co. of Widnes, Cheshire. In 1871 he was joined at the company by the young engineer Vero Charles Driffield, who was to become his co-worker. Driffield had worked for a professional photographer before beginning his engineering apprenticeship and it was in 1876, when Hurter sought to draw on this experience, that the partnership began. At this time the speed of the new gelatine halide dry plates was expressed in terms of the speed of a wet-collodion plate, an almost worthless concept as the speed of a collodion

plate was itself variable. Hurter and Driffield sought to place the study of photographic emulsions on a more scientific basis. They constructed an actinometer to measure the intensity of sunlight and in 1890 published the first of a series of papers on the sensitivity of photographic plates. They suggested methods of exposing a plate to lights of known intensities and measuring the densities obtained on development. They were able to plot curves based on density and exposure which became known as the H & D curve. Hurter and Driffield's work allowed them to express the characteristics of an emulsion with a nomenclature which was soon adopted by British plate manufacturers. From the 1890s onwards most British-made plates were identified with H & D ratings. Hurter and Driffield's partnership was ended by the former's death in 1898.

Further Reading

W.B. Ferguson (ed.), 1920, *The Photographic Researches of Ferdinand Hurter & Vero C. Driffield*, London: Royal Photographic Society reprinted in facsimile, with a new introd. by W. Clark, 1974, New York (a memorial volume; the most complete account of Hurter and Driffield's work, includes a reprint of all their published papers).

JW

Hutchinson, Sir Jonathan
b. 23 July 1828 Selby, Yorkshire, England
d. 26 June 1913 Haslemere, Surrey, England

English physician and surgeon, ophthalmologist, syphilologist, neuropathologist and inventor of the spirometer for the measurement of lung volumes.

Born of Quaker stock, he was educated at home and apprenticed in 1845 to Caleb Williams, apothecary and surgeon of York. It was during this period that he developed and described his spirometer, which he had used in testing 121 sailors, 24 pugilists and wrestlers and 4 giants and dwarfs.

In 1850 he left York to complete his medical training at St Bartholomew's Hospital. By 1859 he was on the staff of the London Hospital as well as the many other specialist hospitals, including the Royal London Ophthalmic, the Blackfriars Hospital for Skin Diseases and the Royal Lock, the multiplicity of which reflected the very wide variety of his interests and expertise.

By 1863, having obtained the Fellowship of the Royal College of Surgeons, he had been appointed full Surgeon to London Hospital and was also responsible for medical ophthalmology. In 1883 he was appointed Emeritus Professor, and for many years after was deeply involved in a wide variety of medical interests. A vivid and memorable teacher, his name has been given to a large number of conditions, particularly in the fields of syphilis and ophthalmology. His special gift was an acuity of observation coupled with the accumulation and collation of clinical facts.

Principal Honours and Distinctions
Knighted 1908. FRS 1882. Hunterian Professor, Royal College of Surgeons 1879–83; Hunterian Orator 1891.

Bibliography
1846, 'On the capacity of the lungs', *Med-Chi. Transactions*, London (describes his spirometer).
1878–84, *Illustrations of Clinical Surgery*, London.

Further Reading
Obituary, 1913, *Lancet* (June).
Obituary, 1913, *British Medical Journal* (June).
Lives of the Fellows of the Royal College of Surgeons, London: Royal College of Surgeons of England.

MG

Huygens, Christiaan
b. 14 April 1629 The Hague, the Netherlands
d. 8 June 1695 The Hague, the Netherlands

Dutch scientist who was responsible for two of the greatest advances in horology: the successful application of both the pendulum to the clock and the balance spring to the watch.

Huygens was born into a cultured and privileged class. His father, Constantijn, was a poet and statesman who had wide interests. Constantijn exerted a strong influence on his son, who was educated at home until he reached the age of 16. Christiaan studied law and mathematics at Leyden University from 1645 to 1647, and continued his studies at the Collegium Arausiacum in Breda until 1649. He then lived at The Hague, where he had the means to devote his time entirely to study. In 1666 he became a

Member of the Académie des Sciences in Paris and settled there until his return to The Hague in 1681. He also had a close relationship with the Royal Society and visited London on three occasions, meeting Newton on his last visit in 1689. Huygens had a wide range of interests and made significant contributions in mathematics, astronomy, optics and mechanics. He also made technical advances in optical instruments and horology.

Despite the efforts of **Burgi** there had been no significant improvement in the performance of ordinary clocks and watches from their inception to Huygens's time, as they were controlled by foliots or balances which had no natural period of oscillation. The pendulum appeared to offer a means of improvement as it had a natural period of oscillation that was almost independent of amplitude. Galileo **Galilei** had already pioneered the use of a freely suspended pendulum for timing events, but it was by no means obvious how it could be kept swinging and used to control a clock. Towards the end of his life Galileo described such a mechanism to his son Vincenzio, who constructed a model after his father's death, although it was not completed when he himself died in 1642. This model appears to have been copied in Italy, but it had little influence on horology, partly because of the circumstances in which it was produced and possibly also because it differed radically from clocks of that period. The crucial event occurred on Christmas Day 1656 when Huygens, quite independently, succeeded in adapting an existing spring-driven table clock so that it was not only controlled by a pendulum but also kept it swinging. In the following year he was granted a privilege or patent for this clock, and several were made by the clockmaker Salomon Coster of The Hague. The use of the pendulum produced a dramatic improvement in timekeeping, reducing the daily error from minutes to seconds, but Huygens was aware that the pendulum was not truly isochronous. This error was magnified by the use of the existing verge escapement, which made the pendulum swing through a large arc. He overcame this defect very elegantly by fitting cheeks at the pendulum suspension point, progressively reducing the effective length of the pendulum as the amplitude increased. Initially the cheeks were shaped empirically, but he was later able to show that they should have a cycloidal shape. The cheeks were not adopted universally because they introduced other defects, and the problem was eventually solved more prosaically by way of new escapements which reduced the swing of the pendulum. Huygens's clocks had another innovatory feature: maintaining power, which kept the clock going while it was being wound.

Pendulums could not be used for portable timepieces, which continued to use balances despite their deficiencies. Robert **Hooke** was probably the first to apply a spring to the balance, but his efforts were not successful. From his work on the pendulum Huygens was well aware of the conditions necessary for isochronism in a vibrating system, and in January 1675, with a flash of inspiration, he realized that this could be achieved by controlling the oscillations of the balance with a spiral spring, an arrangement that is still used in mechanical watches. The first model was made for Huygens in Paris by the clockmaker Isaac Thuret, who attempted to appropriate the invention and patent it himself. Huygens had for many years been trying unsuccessfully to adapt the pendulum clock for use at sea (in order to determine longitude), and he hoped that a balance-spring timekeeper might be better suited for this purpose. However, he was disillusioned as its timekeeping proved to be much more susceptible to changes in temperature than that of the pendulum clock.

Principal Honours and Distinctions

FRS 1663. Member of the Académie Royale des Sciences 1666.

Bibliography

For his complete works, see *Oeuvres complètes de Christiaan Huygens*, 1888–1950, 22 vols, The Hague.

1658, *Horologium*, The Hague; repub., 1970, trans. E.L. Edwardes, *Antiquarian Horology* 7: 35–55 (describes the pendulum clock).

1673, *Horologium Oscillatorium*, Paris; repub., 1986, *The Pendulum Clock or Demonstrations Concerning the Motion of Pendula as Applied to Clocks*, trans. R.J. Blackwell, Ames.

The balance spring watch was first described in *Journal des Sçavans* 25 February 1675, and translated in *Philosophical Transactions of the Royal Society* (1675) 4: 272–3.

Further Reading

H.J.M. Bos, 1972, *Dictionary of Scientific Biography*, ed. C.C. Gillispie, Vol. 6, New York, pp. 597–613 (for a fuller account of his life and scientific work, but note the incorrect date of his death).

R. Plomp, 1979, *Spring-Driven Dutch Pendulum Clocks, 1657–1710*, Schiedam (describes Huygens's application of the pendulum to the clock).

S.A. Bedini, 1991, *The Pulse of Time*, Florence (describes Galileo's contribution of the pendulum to the clock).

J.H. Leopold, 1982, 'L'Invention par Christiaan Huygens du ressort spiral réglant pour les montres', *Huygens et la France*, Paris, pp. 154–7 (describes the application of the balance spring to the watch).

A.R. Hall, 1978, 'Horology and criticism', *Studia Copernica* 16: 261–81 (discusses Hooke's contribution).

DV

Hyatt, John Wesley

b. 28 November 1837 Starkey, New York, USA
d. 10 May 1920 Short Hills, New Jersey, USA

American inventor and the first successful manufacturer of celluloid.

Leaving school at the age of 16, Hyatt spent ten years in the printing trade, demonstrating meanwhile a talent for invention. The offer of a prize of $10,000 for finding a substitute for ivory billiard balls stimulated Hyatt to experiment with various materials. After many failures, he arrived at a composition of paper flock, shellac and collodion, which was widely adopted. Noting the 'skin' left after evaporating collodion, he continued his experiments, using nitrocellulose as a base for plastic materials, yet he remained largely ignorant of both chemistry and the dangers of this explosive substance. Independently of **Parkes** in England, he found that a mixture of nitrocellulose, camphor and a little alcohol could, by heating, be made soft enough to mould but became hard at room temperature. Hyatt's first patent for the material, celluloid, was dated 12 July 1870 (US pat. 105338) and was followed by many others for making domestic and decorative articles of celluloid, replacing more expensive natural materials. Manufacture began at Albany in the winter of 1872–3. In

1881 Hyatt and his brother Isiah Smith floated the Hyatt Pure Water Company. By introducing purifying coagulants into flowing water, they avoided the expense and delay of allowing the water to settle in large tanks before filtration. Many towns and paper and woollen mills adopted the new process, and in 1891 it was introduced into Europe. During 1891–2, Hyatt devised a widely used type of roller bearing. Later inventions included a sugar-cane mill, a multi-stitch sewing machine and a mill for the cold rolling and straightening of steel shafts. It was characteristic of Hyatt's varied inventions that they achieved improved results at less expense.

Principal Honours and Distinctions
Society of Chemical Industry Perkin Medal 1914.

Bibliography
12 July 1870, US patent no. 105,338 (celluloid).

Further Reading
Obituary, 1920, *Chem. Metal. Eng.* (19 May).
J. Soc. Chem. Ind. for 16 March 1914 and *J. Ind. Eng. Chem.* for March 1914 carried accounts of Hyatt's achievements, on the occasion of his award of the Perkin Medal of the Society of Chemical Industry in that year.

LRD

I

Ibn Shakir, Banu Musa
See **Banu Musa ibn Shakir**.

I-Hsing
See **Yi-Xing**.

Ilgner, Karl
b. 27 July 1862 Neisse, Upper Silesia (now Nysa, Poland)
d. 18 January 1921 Berthelsdorf, Silesia

German electrical engineer, inventor of a transformer for electromotors.

Ilgner graduated from the Gewerbeakademie (the forerunner of the Technical University) in Berlin. As the representative of an electric manufacturing company in Breslau (now Wroclaw, Poland) from 1897, he was confronted with the fact that there were no appropriate drives for hoisting-engines or rolling-plants in steelworks. Two problems prevented the use of high-capacity electric motors in the mining as well as in the iron and steel industry: the reactions of the motors on the circuit at the peak point of stress concentration; and the complicated handling of the control system which raised the risks regarding safety. Having previously been head of the department of electrical power transmission in Hannover, he was concerned with the development of low-speed direct-current motors powered by gas engines.

It was Harry Ward Leonard's switchgear for direct-current motors (USA, 1891) that permitted sudden and exact changes in the speed and direction of rotation without causing power loss, as demonstrated in the driving of a rolling sidewalk at the Paris World Fair of 1900. Ilgner connected this switchgear to a large and heavy flywheel which accumulated the kinetic energy from the circuit in order to compensate shock loads. With this combination, electric motors did not need special circuits, which were still weak, because they were working continuously and were regulated individually, so that they could be used for driving hoisting-engines in mines, rolling-plants in steelworks or machinery for producing tools and paper. Ilgner thus made a notable advance in the general progress of electrification.

His transformer for hoisting-engines was patented in 1901 and was commercially used *inter alia* by **Siemens & Halske** of Berlin. Their first electrical hoisting-engine for the Zollern II/IV mine in Dortmund gained international reputation at the Düsseldorf exhibition of 1902, and is still preserved *in situ* in the original machine hall of the mine, which is now a national monument in Germany. Ilgner thereafter worked with several companies to pursue his conception, became a consulting engineer in Vienna and Breslau and had a government post after the First World War in Brussels and Berlin until he retired for health reasons in 1919.

Bibliography
1901, DRP no. 138, 387
1903, 'Der elektrische Antrieb von Reversier-Walzenstraßen', *Stahl und Eisen* 23: 769–71.

Further Reading
W. Kroker, 'Karl Ilgner', *Neue Deutsche Biographie*, Vol.X, pp. 134–5.
W. Philippi, 1924, *Elektrizität im Bergbau*, Leipzig (a general account).
K. Warmbold, 1925, 'Der Ilgner-Umformer in Förderanlagen', *Kohle und Erz* 22: 1031–36 (a detailed description).

WK

Ilyushin, Sergei Vladimirovich
b. 30 March 1894 Dilyalevo, Vologda, Russia
d. 9 February 1977 Moscow, Russia

Russian aircraft designer.

In 1914 he joined the Russian army, later transferring to the air service and gaining his pilot's licence in 1917. After fighting in the Red Army during the Civil War, he entered the Zhukovsky Air Force Engineering Academy in Moscow in 1922, graduating four years later. He joined the Engineering Technical Corps of the Red Air Force as a designer and eventually rose to the rank of Lieutenant-General. His first design success was the 1936 *DB-3* two engined bomber, which broke several world air records. In April 1938 he was injured in a forced landing that resulted in a permanently scarred forehead. His most significant design contribution during 1939ö45 was undoubtedly the *Il-2 Stormovik* ground-attack aircraft. This entered service in 1941 and was distinguished by the high degree of armoured protection afforded to the crew, enabling them to operate at very low levels above ground. It was also increasingly well armed and was known by the Germans as *der schwarze Tod* (Black Death). After the war Ilyushin concentrated primarily on four-engined airliners, producing the *Il-12* (1946), *Il-14* (1954) and *Il-18* (1957), but also designed the Soviet Union's first jet bomber, the *Il-28*. In 1948 he became Professor at the Zhukovsky Air Force Engineering Academy.

Principal Honours and Distinctions
Deputy to the Supreme Soviet 1937. Hero of Socialist Labour 1941, and two further awards of this. Order of Lenin. Winner of seven Stalin Prizes.

CM

Ingersoll, Simon
b. 3 March 1818 Stamford, Connecticut, USA
d. 24 July 1894 Stamford, Connecticut, USA

American mechanic, inventor of a rock drill

Ingersoll worked on his father's farm and spent much of his time carrying out all kinds of mechanical experiments until 1839, when he went to Long Island, New York, to work on another farm. Having returned home in 1858, he received several patents for different mechanical devices, but he did not know how to turn his inventive talent into economic profit. His patents were sold to others for money to continue his work and support his family. In 1870, working again on Long Island, he by chance came into contact with New York City's largest contractor, who urged him to design a mechanical rock drill in order to replace hand drills in the rock-excavation business. Within one year Ingersoll built several models and a full-size machine at the machine shop of Henry Clark Sergeant, who contributed several improvements. They secured a joint patent in 1871, which was soon followed by a patent for a rock drill with tappet-valve motion.

Although the Ingersoll Drill Company was established, he again sold the patent rights and went back to Stamford, where he continued his inventive work and gained several more patents for improving the rock drill. However, he never understood how to make a fortune from his patents, and he died almost penniless. His former partner, Sergeant, who had formed his own drill company on the basis of an entirely novel valve motion which led to compressed air being used as a power source, in 1888 established the Ingersoll–Sergeant Drill Company, which in 1905 merged with Rand Drill Company, which had been a competitor, to form the Ingersoll–Rand Company. This merger led to many achievements in manufacturing rock drills and air compressors at a time when there was growing demand for such machinery.

Further Reading
Dictionary of American Biography (articles on both Ingersoll and Sergeant).
W.L. Saunders, 1910, 'The history of the rock drill and of the Ingersoll-Rand Company', *Compressed Air Magazine*: 3,679–80 (a lively description of the way in which he was encouraged to design the rock drill).

WK

Inoue Masaru
b. 1 August 1843 Hagi, Choshu, Japan
d. 2 August 1910 London, England

Japanese 'Father of Japanese Railways'.

In the early 1860s, most travel in Japan was still by foot and the Japanese were forbidden by their government to travel abroad. Inoue was one of a small group of students who left Japan illegally in 1863 for London. There he studied English, mathematics and science, and afterwards mineralogy and railways. Inoue returned to Japan in 1868, when the new Meiji Government reopened the country to the outside world after some 200 years of isolation. Part of its policy, despite opposition, was to build railways; at Inoue's suggestion, the gauge of 3 ft 6 in. (1.07 m) was adopted. Initially capital, engineers, skilled labour and materials ranging from locomotives to pencils and stationery were all imported from Britain; Edmund Morel was the first Chief

Engineer. In 1871 Inoue was appointed Director of the Government Railway Bureau and he became the driving force behind railway development in Japan for more than two decades. The first line, from Tokyo to Yokohama, was opened in 1872, to be followed by others, some of them at first isolated. The number of foreigners employed, most of them British, peaked at 120 in 1877 and then rapidly declined as the Japanese learned to take over their tasks. In 1878, at Inoue's instance, construction of a line entirely by Japanese commenced for the first time, with British engineers as consultants only. It was ten years before Japanese Railways' total route was 70 miles (113 km) long; over the next ten years, this increased to 1,000 miles (1,600 km) and the system continued to grow rapidly. During 1892–3, a locomotive was built in Japan for the first time, under the guidance of Locomotive Superintendent R.F. Trevithick, grandson of the pioneer Richard **Trevithick**: it was a compound 2–4–2 tank engine, with many parts imported from Britain. Locomotive building in Japan then blossomed so rapidly that imports were discontinued, with rare exceptions, from 1911. Meanwhile Inoue had retired in 1893; he was on a visit to England at the time of his death.

Principal Honours and Distinctions
Viscount 1887.

Bibliography
1909, 'Japanese communications: railroads', in Count Shigenobu Okuma (ed.), *Fifty Years of New Japan* (English version ed. M.B. Huish), Smith, Elder, Ch. 18.

Further Reading
T. Richards and K.C. Rudd, 1991, *Japanese Railways in the Meiji Period 1868–1912*, Uxbridge: Brunel University (one of the few readily available accounts in English of the origins of Japanese Railways).

PJGR

Issigonis, Sir Alexander Arnold Constantine (Alec)
b. 18 November 1906 Smyrna (now Izmir), Turkey
d. 2 October 1988 Birmingham, England

British automobile designer whose work included the Morris Minor and the Mini series.

His father was of Greek descent but was a naturalized British subject in Turkey who ran a marine engineering business. After the First World War, the British in Turkey were evacuated by the Royal Navy, the Issigonis family among them. His father died en route in Malta, but the rest of the family arrived in England in 1922. Alec studied engineering at Battersea Polytechnic for three years and in 1928 was employed as a draughtsman by a firm of consulting engineers in Victoria Street who were working on a form of automatic transmission. He had occasion to travel frequently in the Midlands at this time and visited many factories in the automobile industry. He was offered a job in the drawing office at Humber and lived for a couple of years in Kenilworth. While there he met Robert Boyle, Chief Engineer of Morris Motors (see **Morris, William Richard**), who offered him a job at Cowley. There he worked at first on the design of independent front suspension. At Morris Motors, he designed the Morris Minor, which entered production in 1948 and continued to be manufactured until 1971. Issigonis disliked mergers, and after the merger of Morris with Austin to form the British Motor Corporation (BMC) he left to join Alvis in 1952. The car he designed there, a V8 saloon, was built as a prototype but was never put into production. Following his return to BMC to become Technical Director in 1955, his most celebrated design was the Mini series, which entered production in 1959. This was a radically new concept: it was unique for its combination of a transversely mounted engine in unit with the gearbox, front wheel drive and rubber suspension system. This suspension system, designed in cooperation with Alex **Moulton**, was also a fundamental innovation, developed from the system designed by Moulton for the earlier Alvis prototype. Issigonis remained as Technical Director of BMC until his retirement.

Further Reading
Peter King, 1989, *The Motor Men. Pioneers of the British Motor Industry*, London: Quiller Press.

IMcN

Ivatt, Henry Alfred

b. 16 September 1851 Cambridgeshire, England
d. 25 October 1923 Haywards Heath, Sussex, England

English locomotive engineer, noted for the introduction of 4–4–2-type locomotives to Britain.

H.A. Ivatt initially joined the London & North Western Railway as an apprentice at Crewe Works, and in 1877 moved to the Great Southern & Western Railway in Ireland, eventually succeeding J.A.F. **Aspinall** as Locomotive Engineer at its works in Inchicore, Dublin. In 1896 he moved back to England to become Locomotive Superintendent of the Great Northern Railway. Weights of express trains were increasing rapidly there, and in 1898 Ivatt introduced his 'Atlantic', or 4–4–2 type, the first locomotive of this wheel arrangement in Britain, which had originated in the USA only three years earlier. It was not until 1902, however, that he took full advantage of its potential, when he introduced an Atlantic with a wide firebox and a larger boiler. Both types were successful and even more so when superheated and fitted with piston valves some years later. The first locomotive of each type to be built is now preserved at the National Railway Museum in York.

Further Reading
E.L. Ahrons, 1927, *The British Steam Railway Locomotive 1825–1925*, The Locomotive Publishing Co.
C. Hamilton Ellis, 1959, *British Railway History, Vol. II: 1877–1947*, London: George Allen & Unwin, pp. 195 and 268–9.

See also: **Bulleid, Oliver Vaughan Snell**; **Gresley, Sir Herbert Nigel**.

PJGR

Ives, Frederic Eugene

b. 17 February 1856 Litchfield, Connecticut, USA
d. 27 May 1937 Philadelphia, Pennsylvania, USA

American printer who pioneered the development of photomechanical and colour photographic processes.

Ives trained as a printer in Ithaca, New York, and became official photographer at Cornell University at the age of 18. His research into photomechanical processes led in 1886 to methods of making halftone reproduction of photographs using cross-line screens. In 1881 he was the first to make a three-colour print from relief halftone blocks. He made significant contributions to the early development of colour photography, and from 1888 he published and marketed a number of systems for the production of additive colour photographs. He designed a beam-splitting camera in which a single lens exposed three negatives through red, green and blue filters. Black and white transparencies from these negatives were viewed in a device fitted with internal reflectors and filters, which combined the three colour separations into one full-colour image. This device was marketed in 1895 under the name Kromskop; sets of Kromograms were available commercially, and special cameras, or adaptors for conventional cameras, were available for photographers who wished to take their own colour pictures. A Lantern Kromskop was available for the projection of Kromskop pictures. Ives's system enjoyed a few years of commercial success before simpler methods of making colour photographs rendered it obsolete. Ives continued research into colour photography; his later achievements included the design, in 1915, of the Hicro process, in which a simple camera produced sets of separation negatives that could be printed as dyed transparencies in complementary colours and assembled in register on paper to produce colour prints. Later, in 1932, he introduced Polychrome, a simpler, two-colour process in which a bipack of two thin negative plates or films could be exposed in conventional cameras. Ives's interest extended into other fields, notably stereoscopy. He developed a successful parallax stereogram process in 1903, in which a three-dimensional image could be seen directly, without the use of viewing devices. In his lifetime he received many honours, and was a recipient of the Royal Photographic Society's Progress Medal in 1903 for his work in colour photography.

Further Reading
B. Coe, 1978, *Colour Photography: The First Hundred Years*, London
J.S. Friedman, 1944, *History of Colour Photography*, Boston.
G. Koshofer, 1981, *Farbfotografie*, Vol. I, Munich.
E.J. Wall, 1925, *The History of Three-Colour Photography*, Boston.

BC

Ives, Herbert Eugene

b. 1882 USA
d. 1953

American physicist and television pioneer.

Ives gained his PhD in physics from Johns Hopkins University, Baltimore, Maryland, and subsequently served in the US Signal Corps, eventually gaining experience in aerial photography. He then joined the Western Electric Engineering Department (later Bell Telephone Laboratories), *c.*1920 becoming leader of a group concerned with television-image transmission over telephone lines. In 1927, using a **Nipkow** disc, he demonstrated 50-line, 18 frames/sec pictures that could be displayed as either 2 in. x 2½ in. (5.1 cm x 6.4 cm) images suitable for a 'wirephone', or 2 ft x 2½ ft (61 cm x 76 cm) images for television viewing. Two years later, using a single-spiral disc and three separately modulated light sources, he was able to produce full-colour images.

Bibliography

1915, 'The transformation of colour mixture equations', *Journal of the Franklin Institute* 180: 673.
1923, 'do – Pt II', *Journal of the Franklin Institute* 195: 23.
1925, 'Telephone picture transmission', *Transactions of the Society of Motion Picture and Television Engineers* 23: 82.
1929, 'Television in colour', *Bell Laboratories Record* 7: 439.
1930, with A.L. Johnsrul, 'Television in colour by a beam-scanning method', *Journal of the Optical Society of America* 20: 11.

Further Reading

J.H. Udelson, 1982, *The Great Television Race: History of the Television Industry 1925–41*: University of Alabama Press.

See also **Baird, John Logie**; **Jenkins, Charles Francis**.

KF

Izod, Edwin Gilbert

b. 17 July 1876 Portsmouth, England
d. 2 October 1946 England

English engineer who devised the notched-bar impact test named after him.

After a general education at Vickery's School at Southsea, Izod (who pronounced his name Izzod, not Izod) started his career as a premium apprentice at the works of Maudslay, Sons and Field at Lambeth in January 1893. When in 1995 he was engaged in the installation of machinery in *HMS Renown* at Pembroke, he gained some notoriety for his temerity in ordering Rear Admiral J.A. Fisher, who had no pass, out of the main engine room. He subsequently worked at Portsmouth Dockyard where the battleships *Caesar* and *Gladiator* were being engined by Maudslay's. From 1898 to 1900 Izod worked as a Demonstrator in the laboratories of University College London, and he was then engaged by Captain H. Riall Sankey as his Personal Assistant at the Rugby works of Willans and Robinson. Soon after going to Rugby, Izod was asked by Sankey to examine a failed gun barrel and try to ascertain why it burst in testing. Conventional mechanical testing did not reveal any significant differences in the properties of good and bad material. Izod found, however, that, when specimens from the burst barrel were notched, gripped in a vice, and then struck with a hammer they broke in a brittle manner, whereas sounder material merely bent plastically. From these findings his well-known notched-bar impact test emerged. His address to the British Association in September 1903 described the test and his testing machine, and was subsequently published in *Engineering*. Izod never claimed any priority for this method of test, and generously acknowledged his predecessors in this field, Swedenborg, Fremont, Arnold and Bent Russell. The Izod Test was rapidly adopted by the English-speaking world, although Izod himself, being a busy man, did little to publicize his work, which was introduced to the engineering world largely through the efforts of Captain Sankey. Izod became Assistant Managing Director at Willans, and in 1910 was appointed Chief Consulting Mechanical and Electrical Engineer to the Central Mining Corporation at Johannesburg. He became Managing Director of the Rand Mines in 1918, and returned to the UK in 1927 to become the Managing Director of

Weymann Motor Bodies Ltd of Addlestone. As Chairman of this company he extended its activities considerably.

Principal Honours and Distinctions
MBE. Member of the Iron and Steel Institute.

Further Reading
1903, 'Testing brittleness of steel', *Engineering* (25 September): 431–2.

ASD

J

Jablochkoff, Paul

b. 14 September 1847 Serdobsk, Russia
d. April 1894 St Petersburg, Russia

Russian military engineer and inventor of an electric 'candle', the invention of which gave an immense impetus to electric lighting in the 1870s.

Jablochkoff studied at the Military Engineering College in St Petersburg. Having a scientific bent, he was sent to the Military Galvano Technical School. At the end of his military service in 1871 he was appointed Director General of the Moscow–Kursk telegraph lines for the Midi Railway Company. At this time he began to develop an interest in electric lighting, and in 1875 he left the Imperial Telegraph Service to devote his time exclusively to scientific pursuits. He found employment at the workshop of M Bréguet in Paris, where **Gramme** dynamos and Serrin arc lamps were being constructed. After some experimentation he found a means of producing a carbon arc that regulated itself without any mechanism. This lamp, the Jablochkoff candle, with two carbon rods placed parallel to each other and so close that an arc formed at the ends, could continue to burn until the rods were consumed. Plaster of Paris was used to separate the two electrodes and crumbled away as the carbon burned, thus exposing fresh carbon. These lamps were used in May 1878 in Paris to illuminate the avenue de l'Opéra, and later in Rome and London, and in essence were the first practical electric street lighting. Since there was no regulating mechanism, several candles could be placed in a single circuit. Despite inherent defects, such as the inability to restart the lamps after they were extinguished by wind or interruption of supply, they remained in use for some purposes for several years on account of their simplicity and cheapness. In 1877 Jablochkoff obtained the earliest patent to employ transformers to distribute current in an alternating-current circuit.

Bibliography

11 September 1876, British patent no. 3,552 (Jablochkoff's candle).

22 May 1877, British patent no. 1,996 (transformer or induction coil distribution).

Further Reading

W.J. King, 1962, *The Development of Electrical Technology in the 19th Century*, Washington, DC: Smithsonian Institution, Paper 30, pp. 393–407 (a detailed account).

W.E. Langdon, 1877, 'On a new form of electric light', *Journal of the Society of Telegraph Engineers* 6: 303–19 (an early report on Jablochkoff's system).

Engineering (1878) 26: 125–7.

GW

Jackson, John Hughlings

b. 4 April 1835 Providence Green, Yorkshire, England
d. 7 October 1911 London, England

English neurologist and neurophysiologist, discoverer of Jacksonian epilepsy and the neurological basis of speech defects; pioneer of the technique of the localization of the site of cerebral disease.

Jackson studied medicine at York and at St Bartholomew's Hospital, qualifying in 1856. For a while he practised in York and was dissuaded from abandoning medicine for philosophy by Jonathan **Hutchinson**. Upon his return to London, he was appointed Assistant Physician and later, in 1874, Physician to the London Hospital. He was also on the staff of Moorfields Eye Hospital and in 1874 was appointed to the National Hospital for the Paralysed and Epileptic in Queen's Square. It was particularly in connection with his association with cases at the latter that he was able to establish the association of designated areas of the brain with specific limbs and functions. He acknowledged that in the field of speech the work of Broca had shown the way.

Principal Honours and Distinctions

FRS 1878. Gulstonian Lecturer and Croonian Lecturer, College of Physicians.

Bibliography
1869, *Certain Points on the Study and Classification of Diseases of the Nervous System.*
1884, *Evolution and Dissolution of the Nervous System.*
1931–32, *Selected Writings* (ed. J. Taylor *et al.*).
MG

Jacobi, Moritz Hermann von

b. 21 September 1801 Potsdam, Germany
d. 27 February 1874 St Petersburg, Russia

German scientist who developed one of the first practical electric motors.

After studying architecture at Göttingen University, Jacobi turned his attention to physics and chemistry. In 1835 he was appointed a professor of civil engineering at the University of Dorpat (which later assumed the Estonian name of Tartu). Later, moving to St Petersburg, he became a member of the Imperial Academy of Sciences and commenced research on electricity and its practical applications. In December 1834 Jacobi presented a paper to the Academy of Sciences in Paris in which he stated that he had obtained rotation by electromagnetic methods in May of that year. Tsar Nicholas of Russia gave him a grant to prove that his electric motor had a practical application. Jacobi had a boat constructed that measured 28 ft in length and was propelled by paddles connected to an electric motor of his own design. Powered by Grove cells, it carried about fourteen passengers at a speed of almost 3 mph (5 km/h) on the River Neva. The weight of and possibly the fumes from the batteries contributed to the abandonment of the project. In 1839 Jacobi introduced electrotyping, i.e. the reproduction of forms by electrodeposition, which was one of the first commercial applications of electricity. In 1840 he reported the results of his investigations into the power of the electromagnet as a function of various parameters to the British Association.

Principal Honours and Distinctions
Member, Imperial Academy of Sciences, St Petersburg, 1847.

Bibliography
Jacobi's papers are listed in *Catalogue of Scientific Papers*, 1868, Vol. III, London: Royal Society, pp. 517–18.

1837, *Annals of Electricity* 1: 408–15 and 419–44 (describes his motor).

Further Reading
Biography, 1876, *Bulletin de l'Académie imperiale des sciences de St Petersburg* 21: 262–79.
E.H. Huntress, 1951, in *Proceedings of the American Academy of Arts and Sciences* 79: 22–3 (a short biography).
B. Bowers, 1982, *A History of Electric Light and Power*, London.
GW

Jacobs, Mary Phelps
See **Crosby, Caresse**.

Jacquard, Joseph-Marie

b. 7 July 1752 Lyons, France
d. 7 August 1834 Oullines, France

French developer of the apparatus named after him and used for selecting complicated patterns in weaving.

Jacquard was apprenticed at the age of 12 to bookbinding, and later to type-founding and cutlery. His parents, who had some connection with weaving, left him a small property upon their death. He made some experiments with pattern weaving, but lost all his inheritance; after marrying, he returned to type-founding and cutlery. In 1790 he formed the idea for his machine, but it was forgotten amidst the excitement of the French Revolution, in which he fought for the Revolutionists at the defence of Lyons. The machine he completed in 1801 combined earlier inventions and was for weaving net. He was sent to Paris to demonstrate it at the National Exposition and received a bronze medal. In 1804 Napoleon granted him a patent, a pension of 1,500 francs and a premium on each machine sold. This enabled him to study and work at the Conservatoire des Arts et Métiers to perfect his mechanism for pattern weaving. A method of selecting any combination of leashes at each shoot of the weft had to be developed, and Jacquard's mechanism was the outcome of various previous inventions. By taking the cards invented by **Falcon** in 1728 that were punched with holes like the paper of **Bouchon** in 1725, to select the needles for each pick, and by placing the apparatus above the loom where Vaucanson had put his mechanism, Jacquard combined the best features of earlier inventions. He was not entirely successful because his invention failed in the way it pressed the card against the needles; later modifications by Breton in 1815 and **Skola** in 1819 were needed before it functioned reliably. However, the advantage of Jacquard's machine was that each pick could be selected much more quickly than on the earlier draw looms, which meant that John **Kay**'s flying shuttle could be introduced on fine pattern looms because the weaver no longer had to wait for the drawboy to sort out the leashes for the next pick. Robert **Kay**'s drop box could also be used with different coloured wefts. The drawboy could be dispensed with because the foot-pedal operating the Jacquard mechanism could be worked by the weaver. Patterns could be changed quickly by replacing one set of cards with another, but the scope of the pattern was more limited than with the draw loom. Some machines that were brought into use aroused bitter hostility. Jacquard suffered physical violence, barely escaping with his life, and his machines were burnt by weavers at Lyons. However, by 1812 his mechanism began to be generally accepted and had been applied to 11,000 draw-looms in France. In 1819 Jacquard received a gold medal and a Cross of Honour for his invention. His machines reached England *c.*1816 and still remain the basic way of weaving complicated patterns.

Principal Honours and Distinctions
French Cross of Honour 1819. National Exposition Bronze Medal 1801.

Further Reading
A. Barlow, 1878, *The History and Principles of Weaving by Hand and by Power*, London.
C. Singer (ed.), 1958, *A History of Technology*, Vol. IV, Oxford: Clarendon Press.
R.L. Hills, 1970, *Power in the Industrial Revolution*, Manchester (covers the introduction of pattern weaving and the power loom).
RLH

Janney, Eli Hamilton
b. 12 November 1831 Loudóun County, Virginia, USA
d. 16 June 1912 Alexandria, Virginia, USA

American inventor of buckeye coupling for railway vehicles.

Early American railways used link-and-pin couplings, with consequent danger to life and limb of those who had to go between vehicles to couple and uncouple them. Many inventors tried to produce a coupling that would couple automatically and could be uncoupled from the trackside, and Janney was eventually successful in achieving this. He invented his device, which worked like the hooked fingers of two hands, in 1868, and after improvement it was adopted by the Pennsylvania Railroad in 1874. Janney formed the Janney Car Coupling Company, but it was not until 1888 that the Master Car Builders' Association made the Janney coupling standard on American railways. Automatic couplings were made compulsory in the USA by the Railroad Safety Appliance Act of 1893.

Bibliography
Janney took out five US patents for automatic couplings between 1868 and 1882.

Further Reading
J.F. Stover, 1961, *American Railroads*, Chicago: University of Chicago Press, pp. 152ö4.
PJGR

Jansky, Karl Guthe
b. 22 October 1905 Norman, Oklahoma, USA
d. 14 February 1950 Red Bank, New Jersey, USA

American radio engineer who discovered stellar radio emission.

Following graduation from the University of Wisconsin in 1928 and a year of postgraduate study, Jansky joined Bell Telephone Laboratories in New Jersey with the task of establishing the source of interference to telephone communications by radio. To this end he constructed a linear-directional short-wave antenna and eventually, in 1931, he concluded that the interference actually came from the stars, the major source being the constellation Sagittarius in the direction of the centre of the Milky Way. Although he continued to study the propagation of short radio waves and the nature of observed echoes, it was left to others to develop the science of radioastronomy and to use the creation of echoes for radiolocation. Although he received no scientific award for his discovery, Jansky's name is primarily honoured by its use as the unit of stellar radio-emission strength.

Bibliography

1935, 'Directional studies of atmospherics at high frequencies', *Proceedings of the Institute of Radio Engineers* 23: 1,158.

1935, 'A note on the sources of stellar interference', *Proceedings of the Institute of Radio Engineers.*

1937, 'Minimum noise levels obtained on short-wave radio receiving systems', *Proceedings of the Institute of Radio Engineers* 25: 1,517.

1941, 'Measurements of the delay and direction of arrival of echoes from nearby short-wave transmitters', *Proceedings of the Institute of Radio Engineers* 29: 322.

Further Reading

P.C. Mahon, 1975, *Bell Labs, Mission Communication. The Story of the Bell Labs.*

W.I. Sullivan (ed.), 1984, *The Early Years of Radio-Astronomy: Reflections 50 Years after Jansky's Discovery*, Cambridge: Cambridge University Press.

See also **Appleton, Sir Edward Victor**.

KF

Jazari, Ibn al-Razzaz al-

See **al-Jazari, Ibn al-Razzaz**.

Jeanneret, Charles-Edouard (Le Corbusier)

b. 6 October 1887 La Chaux-de-Fonds, Switzerland
d. 27 August 1965 Cap Martin, France

Swiss/French architect.

The name of Le Corbusier is synonymous with the International style of modern architecture and city planning, one utilizing functionalist designs carried out in twentieth-century materials with modern methods of construction. Charles-Edouard Jeanneret, born in the watch-making town of La Chaux-de-Fonds in the Jura mountain region, was the son of a watch engraver and dial painter. In the years before 1918 he travelled widely, studying building in many countries. He learned about the use of reinforced concrete in the studio of Auguste **Perret** and about industrial construction under Peter **Behrens**. In 1917 he went to live in Paris and spent the rest of his life in France; in 1920 he adopted the name of Le Corbusier, one derived from that of his ancestors (Le Corbesier), and ten years later became a French citizen.

Le Corbusier's long working life spanned a career divided into three distinct parts. Between 1905 and 1916 he designed a number of simple and increasingly modern houses; the years 1921 to 1940 were ones of research and debate; and the twenty years from 1945 saw the blossoming of his genius. After 1917 Le Corbusier gained a reputation in Paris as an architect of advanced originality. He was particularly interested in low-cost housing and in improving accommodation for the poor. In 1923 he published *Vers une architecture*, in which he planned estates of mass-produced houses where all extraneous and unnecessary features were stripped away and the houses had flat roofs and plain walls: his concept of 'a machine for living in'. These white boxes were lifted up on stilts, his *pilotis*, and double-height living space was provided internally, enclosed by large areas of factory glazing. In 1922 Le Corbusier exhibited a city plan, *La Ville contemporaine*, in which tall blocks made from steel and concrete were set amongst large areas of parkland, replacing the older concept of city slums with the light and air of modern living. In 1925 he published *Urbanisme*, further developing his socialist ideals. These constituted a major reform of the industrial-city pattern, but the ideas were not taken up at that time. The Depression years of the 1930s severely curtailed architectural activity in France. Le Corbusier designed houses for the wealthy there, but most of his work prior to 1945 was overseas: his Centrosoyus Administration Building in Moscow (1929–36) and the Ministry of Education Building in Rio de Janeiro (1943) are examples.

Immediately after the end of the Second World War Le Corbusier won international fame for his Unité d'habitation theme, the first example of which was built in the boulevard Michelet in Marseille in 1947–52. His answer to the problem of accommodating large numbers of people in a small space at low cost was to construct an immense all-purpose block of pre-cast concrete slabs carried on a row of massive central supports. The Marseille Unité contains 350 apartments in eight double storeys, with a storey for shops half-way up and communal facilities on the roof. In 1950 he published *Le Modulor*, which described a system of measurement based upon the human male figure. From this was derived a relationship of human and mathematical proportions; this concept, together with the extensive use of various forms of concrete, was fundamental to Le Corbusier's later work. In the world-famous and highly personal Pilgrimage Church of Notre Dame du Haut at Ronchamp (1950–5), Le Corbusier's work was in Expressionist form, a plastic design in massive rough-cast concrete, its interior brilliantly designed and lit. His other equally famous, though less popular, ecclesiastical commission showed a contrasting theme, of 'brutalist' concrete construction with uncompromisingly stark, rectangular forms. This is the Dominican Convent of Sainte Marie de la Tourette at Eveux-sur-l'Arbresle near Lyon, begun in 1956. The interior, in particular, is carefully worked out, and the lighting, from both natural and artificial sources, is indirect, angled in many directions to illuminate vistas and planes. All surfaces are carefully sloped, the angles meticulously calculated to give optimum visual effect. The crypt, below the raised choir, is painted in bright colours and lit from ceiling *oculi*. One of Le Corbusier's late works, the Convent is a *tour de force*.

Principal Honours and Distinctions
Honorary Doctorate Zurich University 1933. Honorary Member RIBA 1937. Chevalier de la Légion d'honneur 1937. American Institute of Architects Gold Medal 1961. Honorary Degree University of Geneva 1964.

Bibliography
His chief publications, all of which have been numerously reprinted and translated, are:
1923, *Vers une architecture*.
1935, *La Ville radieuse*.
1946, *Propos d'urbanisme*.
1950, *Le Modulor*.

Further Reading
P. Blake, 1963, *Le Corbusier: Architecture and Form*, Penguin.
R. Furneaux-Jordan, 1972, *Le Corbusier*, Dent.
W. Boesiger, 1970, *Le Corbusier*, 8 vols, Thames and Hudson.
—— 1987, *Le Corbusier: Architect of the Century*, Arts Council of Great Britain.

DY

Jenkins, Charles Francis
b. 1867 USA
d. 1934 USA

American pioneer of motion pictures and television.

During the early years of the motion picture industry, Jenkins made many innovations, including the development in 1894 of his own projector, the 'Phantoscope', which was widely used for a number of years. In the same year he also suggested the possibility of electrically transmitting pictures over a distance, an interest that led to a lifetime of experimentation. As a result of his engineering contributions to the practical realization of moving pictures, in 1915 the National Motion Picture Board of Trade asked him to chair a committee charged with establishing technical standards for the industry. This in turn led to his proposing the creation of a professional society for those engineers in the industry, and the following year the Society of Motion Picture Engineers (later to become the Society of Motion Picture and Television Engineers) was formed, with Jenkins as its first President. Soon after this he began experiments with mechanical television, using both the **Nipkow** hole-spiral disc and a low-definition system of his own, based on rotating bevelled glass discs (his so-called 'prismatic rings') and alkali-metal photocells. In the 1920s he gave many demonstrations of mechanical television, including a cable transmission of a crude silhouette of President Harding from Washington, DC, to Philadelphia in 1923 and a radio broadcast from Washington in 1928. The following year he formed the Jenkins Television Company to make television transmitters and receivers, but it soon went into debt and was acquired by the de Forest Company, from whom RCA later purchased the patents.

Principal Honours and Distinctions
First President, Society of Motion Picture Engineers 1916.

Bibliography
1923, 'Radio photographs, radio movies and radio vision', *Transactions of the Society of Motion Picture Engineers* 16: 78.
1923, 'Recent progress in the transmission of motion pictures by radio', *Transactions of the Society of Motion Picture Engineers* 17: 81.

1925, 'Radio movies', *Transactions of the Society of Motion Picture Engineers* 21: 7.

1930, 'Television systems', *Journal of the Society of Motion Picture Engineers* 15: 445.

1925, *Vision by Radio*.

Further Reading

J.H. Udelson, 1982, *The Great Television Race: A History of the American Television Industry, 1925–41*: University of Alabama Press.

R.W. Hubbell, 1946, *4,000 Years of Television*, London: G. Harrap & Sons.

1926, 'The Jenkins system', *Wireless World* 18: 642 (contains a specific account of Jenkins's work).

See also: **Baird, John Logie**; **Ives, Herbert Eugene**; **Zworykin, Vladimir Kosma**.

KF

Jenner, Edward

b. 17 May 1749 Berkeley, Gloucestershire, England

d. 26 January 1823 Berkeley, Gloucestershire, England

English medical practitioner, pioneer of vaccination against smallpox.

In 1770, following a local surgical apprenticeship in Gloucestershire, he became a resident pupil in London under John **Hunter**. In 1773 he returned to Berkeley to practise, but he continued correspondence with Hunter on a variety of topics of natural history, including the study of earthworms and hibernation.

From his apprentice days he had known of the country belief that an attack of cowpox would protect against smallpox. Soon after 1775 he had been in touch with Hunter, who gave him the celebrated advice to 'trie the experiment'. However, it was not until 14 May 1796 that he made the first vaccination from a case of cowpox. The practice of vaccination from mild cases of smallpox was already well established.

He was unable to undertake further observations until 1798, when he published the results of twenty-two more cases. The procedure gained wide acceptance and in 1802 he received a parliamentary award of £10,000; the Royal Jennerian Society for the promotion of smallpox vaccination was founded in 1803. In 1806 he was awarded a further £20,000. He received his first degree, of MD, from Oxford in 1813.

Bibliography

1798, *An Enquiry into the Cause and Effects of the Variolae Vaccinae*, London.

Further Reading

Crookshank, 1889, *Pathology and History of Vaccination*.

MG

Jenney, William Le Baron

b. 25 September 1832 Fairhaven, Massachusetts, USA

d. 15 June 1907 Los Angeles, California, USA

American architect and engineer who pioneered a method of steel-framed construction that made the skyscraper possible.

Jenney's Home Insurance Building in Chicago was completed in 1885 but demolished in 1931. It was the first building to rise above ten to twelve storeys and was possible because it did not require immensely thick walls on the lower storeys to carry the weight above. Using square-sectioned cast-iron wall piers, hollow cylindrical cast-iron columns on the interior and, across these, steel and cast-iron beams and girders, Jenney produced a load-bearing metal framework independent of the curtain walling. Beams and girders were united by ties as well as being bolted to the vertical members, so providing a strong framework to take the building load. Jenney went on to build in Chicago the Second Leiter Building (1889–91) and, in 1891, the Manhattan Building. He played a considerable part in the planning of the 1893 Chicago World's Fair. Jenney is accepted as having been the founder of the Chicago school of architecture, and he trained many of the later noted architects and builders of the city, such as William **Holabird**, Martin Roche and Louis **Sullivan**.

Further Reading

A. Woltersdorf, 1924, 'The father of the skeleton frame building', *Western Architecture* 33.

F.A. Randall, 1949, *History of the Development of Building Construction in Chicago*, Urbana: University of Illinois Press.

C. Condit, 1964, *The Chicago School of Architecture: A History of Commercial and Public*

Building in the Chicago Area 1875–1925, Chicago: University of Chicago Press.

DY

Jervis, John Bloomfield

b. 14 December 1795 Huntingdon, New York, USA
d. 12 January 1885 Rome, New York, USA

American pioneer of civil engineering and locomotive design.

Jervis assisted in the survey and construction of the Erie Canal, and by 1827 was Chief Engineer of the Delaware & Hudson Canal and, linked with it, the Carbondale Railroad. He instructed Horatio **Allen** to go to England to purchase locomotives in 1828, and the locomotive *Stourbridge Lion*, built by J.U. **Rastrick**, was placed on the railway in 1829. It was the first full-size locomotive to run in America, but the track proved too weak for it to be used regularly. In 1830 Jervis became Chief Engineer to the Mohawk & Hudson Rail Road, which was the first railway in New York State and was opened the following year. In 1832 the 4–2–0 locomotive *Experiment* was built to his plans by West Point Foundry: it was the first locomotive to have a leading bogie or truck. Jervis was subsequently associated with many other extensive canals and railways and pioneered economic analysis of engineering problems to enable, for example, the best choice to be made between two possible routes for a railroad.

Bibliography
1861, *Railway Property*, New York.

Further Reading
J.H. White Jr, 1979, *A History of the American Locomotive – Its Development: 1830–1880*, New York: Dover Publications Inc.
J.K. Finch, 1931, 'John Bloomfield Jervis, civil engineer', *Transactions of the Newcomen Society*, 11.

PJGR

Jessop, William

b. 23 January 1745 Plymouth, England
d. 18 November 1814

English engineer engaged in river, canal and dock construction.

William Jessop inherited from his father a natural ability in engineering, and because of his father's association with John **Smeaton** in the construction of Eddystone Lighthouse he was accepted by Smeaton as a pupil in 1759 at the age of 14. Smeaton was so impressed with his ability that Jessop was retained as an assistant after completion of his pupilage in 1767. As such he carried out field-work, making surveys on his own, but in 1772 he was recommended to the Aire and Calder Committee as an independent engineer and his first personally prepared report was made on the Haddlesey Cut, Selby Canal. It was in this report that he gave his first evidence before a Parliamentary Committee. He later became Resident Engineer on the Selby Canal, and soon after he was elected to the Smeatonian Society of Engineers, of which he later became Secretary for twenty years. Meanwhile he accompanied Smeaton to Ireland to advise on the Grand Canal, ultimately becoming Consulting Engineer until 1802, and was responsible for Ringsend Docks, which connected the canal to the Liffey and were opened in 1796. From 1783 to 1787 he advised on improvements to the River Trent, and his ability was so recognized that it made his reputation. From then on he was consulted on the Cromford Canal (1789–93), the Leicester Navigation (1791–4) and the Grantham Canal (1793–7); at the same time he was Chief Engineer of the Grand Junction Canal from 1793 to 1797 and then Consulting Engineer until 1805. He also engineered the Barnsley and Rochdale Canals. In fact, there were few canals during this period on which he was not consulted. It has now been established that Jessop carried the responsibility for the Pont-Cysyllte Aqueduct in Wales and also prepared the estimates for the Caledonian Canal in 1804. In 1792 he became a partner in the Butterley ironworks and thus became interested in railways. He proposed the Surrey Iron Railway in 1799 and prepared for the estimates; the line was built and opened in 1805. He was also the Engineer for the 10 mile (16 km) long Kilmarnock & Troon Railway, the Act for which was obtained in 1808 and was the first Act for a public railway in Scotland. Jessop's advice was sought on drainage works between 1785 and 1802 in the lowlands of the Isle of Axholme, Holderness, the Norfolk Marshlands, and the Axe and Brue area of the Somerset Levels. He was also consulted on harbour and dock improvements. These included Hull (1793), Portsmouth (1796), Folkestone (1806) and Sunderland (1807), but his greatest dock works were the West India Docks in London and the Floating Harbour at Bristol. He was Consulting Engineer to the City of London Corporation from 1796to 1799, drawing up plans for docks on the Isle of Dogs in 1796; in February 1800 he was appointed Engineer, and three years later, in September 1803, he was appointed Engineer to the Bristol Floating Harbour. Jessop was re-garded as the leading civil engineer in the country from 1785 until 1806. He died following a stroke in 1814.

Further Reading
C. Hadfield and A.W. Skempton, 1979, *William Jessop. Engineer*, Newton Abbot: David & Charles.

JHB

Jia Sixie (Chia Ssu-Hsieh)
b. sixth century AD China
d. sixth century AD China

Chinese writer on agricultural practice.

Jia Sixie was the author of the *Qi Min Yao Shu* (*Chhi Min Yao Shu*), the earliest complete Chinese agricultural treatise to have survived. The survey quotes from over 160 other texts and the author himself relates how he collected from a wide range of sources, including folk songs and the anecdotes of old men. Little is known of Jia Sixie. It is assumed that he was a middle-ranking official and that his agricultural experience derives from his own work in the Shantung re-gion. In addition to husbandry information, the treatise deals with the problems of running an agricultural estate. Details of experiments are also given, indicating that the text may have been aimed more at the estate owner than the peasant farmer. Culinary matters are also commented upon. Discussions of the range of crops available to the Chinese farmer, and of the rotational prac-tices implemented to make best use of those crops, give a clear indication that a much higher productivity was being achieved than in Europe at that time or for almost another thousand years. Crop diversity and rotations, as well as technologies such as green manuring and imple-ments such as rollers and seed-drills, were com-bined to achieve these substantial yields.

Further Reading
F. Bray, vol. VI.2 of J. Needham (ed.), *Science and Civilisation in China* (provides a compre-hensive discussion on Chinese agricultural practice, and an early chapter gives details of her sources).

AP

Jobard, Jean-Baptiste-Ambroise Marcelin
b. 14 May 1792 Baissey, Haute-Marne, France
d. 27 October 1861 Brussels, Belgium

French technologist, promoter of Belgian industry.

After attending schools in Langres and Dijon, Jobard worked in Groningen and Maastricht as a cadastral officer from 1811 onwards. After the Netherlands had been constituted as a new state in 1814, he became a Dutch citizen in 1815 and settled in Brussels. In 1825, when he had learned of the invention of lithography by Alois **Sene-felder**, he retired and established a renowned li-thographic workshop in Belgium, with considerable commercial profit. After the politi-cal changes which led to the separation of Bel-gium from the Netherlands in 1830, he devoted his activities to the progress of science and indus-try in this country, in the traditional idea of en-lightenment. His main aim was to promote all branches of the young economy, to which he contributed with ceaseless energy. He cultivated especially the transfer of technology in many ar-ticles he wrote on his various journeys, such as to Britain, France, Germany and Switzerland, and he continued to do so when he became the Di-rector of the Museum of Industry in Brussels in 1841, editing its *Bulletin* until his death. Jobard, as a member of societies for the encouragement of arts and industry in many countries, published on almost any subject and produced many inven-tions. Being a restless character by nature, and having, in addition, a strong attitude towards de-signing and constructing, he also contributed to mining technology in 1828 when he was the first European to practise successfully the Chinese method of rope drilling near Brussels.

Bibliography
1840, *Plan d'organisation du Musée de l'indus-trie, présenté au Ministre de l'interieur*, Brussels.

1844, *Machines à vapeur, arrêtes et instructions*, Brussels.

1846, *Comment la Belgique peut devenir industrielle, à propos de la Société d'exportation*, Brussels.

1846, *Constitution d'une noblesse industrielle à l'aide des marques de fabrique considérées comme blason de l'industrie et du commerce, dédié à la Société des inventeurs et protecteurs de l'industrie*, Brussels.

1855, *Discours prononcé à l'assemblée des industriels réunis pour l'adoption de la marque obligatoire*, Paris.

Further Reading

H. Blémont, 1991, article in *Dictionnaire de biographie française*, Paris, pp. 676–7 (for a short account of his life).

A. Siret, 1888–9, article in *Biographie nationale de belgique*, Vol. X, Brussels, col. 494–500 (provides an impressive description of his restless character and a selected bibliography of his many publications.

T. Tecklenburg, 1900, *Handbuch der Tiefbohrkunde*, 2nd edn, Vol. IV, Berlin, pp. 7–8 (contains detailed information on his method of rope drilling).

WK

Jobs, Steven Paul

b. 24 February 1955 San Francisco, California, USA

*American engineer who, with Stephen **Wozniak**, built the first home computer.*

Moving with his family to Mountain View, Palo Alto, in 1960, Jobs entered Homestead High School, Cupertino, in 1968. At about the same time he joined the Explorers' Club for young engineers set up by Hewlett-Packard Company. As a result of this contact, three years later he met up with Stephen Wozniak, who was working at Hewlett-Packard and helped him with the construction of the first home computer based on the 8-bit MOS Technology 6502 microprocessor. In 1973 he went to Reid College, Portland, Oregon, to study engineering, but he dropped out in the second semester and spent time in India. On his return he obtained a job with Atari to design video games, but he soon met up again with Wozniak, who had been unable to interest Hewlett-Packard in commercial development of his home computer. Together they therefore founded Apple Computer Company to make and market it, and found a willing buyer in the Byte Shop chain store. The venture proved successful, and with the help of a financial backer, Mike Markkula, a second version, the Apple II, was developed in 1976. With Jobs as Chairman, the company experienced a phenomenal growth and by 1983 had 4,700 employees and an annual turnover of US$983 million. The company then began to run into difficulties and John Sculley, a former president of Pepsi-Cola, was brought in to manage the business while Jobs concentrated on developing new computers, including the Apple Macintosh. Eventually a power struggle developed, and with Sculley now Chairman and Chief Executive, Jobs resigned in 1985 to set up his own computer company, NeXt.

Principal Honours and Distinctions

First National Technology Medal (with Wozniak) 1985.

Further Reading

J.S. Young, 1988, *Steve Jobs: The Journey is the Reward*: Scott Foresman & Co. (includes a biography and a detailed account of Apple Company).

M. Moritz, 1984, *The Little Kingdom. The Private Story of Apple Computers*.

KF

Johansson, Carl Edvard

b. 15 March 1864 Orebro, Sweden
d. 30 September 1943 Eskilstuna, Sweden

Swedish metrologist and inventor of measuring-gauge blocks.

Carl Edvard Johansson was first apprenticed to a shoemaker, but he soon abandoned that career. In 1882 he went to America to join his brother Arvid working at a sawmill in the summer; in winter the brothers obtained further general education at the Gustavus Adolphus College at St Peter, Minnesota. They returned to Sweden in November 1884 and in the following year Carl obtained employment with a small engineering firm which rented a workshop in the government small-arms factory at Eskilstuna. In his spare time he attended the Eskilstuna Technical College and in 1888 he was accepted as an apprentice armourer inspector. After completion of his apprenticeship he was appointed an armourer inspector, and it was in his work of inspection that he realized that the large number of gauges then required could be reduced if several accurate gauges could be used in combination. This was in 1896, and the first set of gauges was made for use in the rifle factory. With these, any dimension between 1 mm and 201 mm could be made up to the nearest 0.01 mm, the gauges having flat polished surfaces that would adhere together by 'wringing'. Johansson obtained patents for the system from 1901, but it was not until *c*.1907 that the sets of gauges were marketed generally. Gauges were made in inch units for Britain and America – slightly different as the standards were not then identical. Johansson formed his own company to manufacture the gauges in 1910, but he did not give up his post in the rifle factory until 1914. By the 1920s Johansson gauges were established as the engineering dimensional standards for the whole world; the company also made other precision measuring instruments such as micrometers and extensometers. A new company, C.E. Johansson Inc., was set up in America for manufacture and sales, and the gauges were extensively used in the American automobile industry. Henry **Ford** took a special interest and Johansson spent several years in a post with the Ford Motor Company in Detroit, Michigan, until he returned to Sweden in 1936.

Principal Honours and Distinctions
Honorary Doctorates, Gustavus Adolphus College, St Peter and Wayne University, Detroit. Swedish Engineering Society John Ericsson Gold Medal. American Society of Mechanical Engineers Gold Medal.

Further Reading
K.J. Hume, 1980, *A History of Engineering Metrology*, London, pp. 54–66 (a short biography).

RTS

Johnson, Clarence Leonard ('Kelly')

b. 27 February 1910 Michigan, USA
d. 21 December 1990 Burbank County, California, USA

American aircraft designer responsible for many outstanding Lockheed aircraft over a period of almost forty-eight years.

The large and successful Lockheed Aircraft Corporation grew out of a small company founded by Allan and Malcolm Loughhead (pronounced 'Lockheed') in 1913. The company employed many notable designers such as Jack Northrop, Jerry Vultee and Lloyd Stearman, but the most productive was 'Kelly' Johnson. After studying aeronautical engineering at the University of Michigan, Johnson joined Lockheed in 1933 and gained experience in all the branches of the design department. By 1938 he had been appointed Chief Research Engineer and became involved with the design of the *P-38 Lightning* twin-boom fighter and the *Constellation* airliner. In 1943 he set up a super-secret research and development organization called Advanced Development Projects, but this soon became known as the 'Skunk Works': the name came from a very mysterious factory which made potions from skunks in the popular comic strip *Li'l Abner*. The first aircraft designed and built by Johnson's small hand-picked team was the *XP-80 Shooting Star* prototype jet fighter, which was produced in just 143 days: it became the United States' first production jet fighter. At this stage the Skunk Works produced a prototype, then the main Lockheed factories took over the production run. The *F-104 Starfighter* and the *C-130 Hercules* transport were produced in this way and became widely used in many countries. In 1954 work began on the *U-2* reconnaissance aircraft which was so secret that production was carried out within the Skunk Works. This made the headlines in 1960 when one was shot down over Russia. Probably the most outstanding of Johnson's designs was the *SR-71 Blackbird* of 1964, a reconnaissance aircraft capable of flying at Mach 3 (three times the speed of sound). Johnson was not only a great designer, he was also an outstanding manager, and his methods – including his '14 Rules' – have been widely followed. He retired from the Lockheed board in 1980, having been involved in the design of some forty aircraft.

Principal Honours and Distinctions
National Medal of Freedom (the highest United States award for a civilian) 1964.

Further Reading
Obituary, 1991, *Aerospace* (Royal Aeronautical Society) (March).
B.R. Rich, 1989, 'The Skunk Works' management style: it's no secret', *Aerospace* (Royal

Aeronautical Society) (March) (Rich was Johnson's successor).

Details of Lockheed aircraft can be found in several publications, e.g.:

R.J. Francillon, 1982, *Lockheed Aircraft since 1913*, London.

JDS

Johnson, Eldridge Reeves

b. 18 February 1867 Wilmington, Delaware, USA

d. 14 November 1945 Moorestown, New Jersey, USA

American industrialist, founder and owner of the Victor Talking Machine Company; developer of many basic constructions in mechanical sound recording and the reproduction and manufacture of gramophone records.

He graduated from the Dover Academy (Delaware) in 1882 and was apprenticed in a machine-repair firm in Philadelphia and studied in evening classes at the Spring Garden Institute. In 1888 he took employment in a small Philadelphia machine shop owned by Andrew Scull, specializing in repair and bookbinding machinery. After travels in the western part of the US, in 1891 he became a partner in Scull & Johnson, Manufacturing Machinists, and established a further company, the New Jersey Wire Stitching Machine Company. He bought out Andrew Scull's interest in October 1894 (the last instalment being paid in 1897) and became an independent general machinist. In 1896 he had perfected a spring motor for the **Berliner** flat-disc gramophone, and he started experimenting with a more direct method of recording in a spiral groove: that of cutting in wax. Co-operation with Berliner eventually led to the incorporation of the Victor Talking Machine Company in 1901. The innumerable court cases stemming from the fact that so many patents for various elements in sound recording and reproduction were in very many hands were brought to an end in 1903 when Johnson was material in establishing cross-licencing agreements between Victor, Columbia Graphophone and **Edison** to create what is known as a patent pool. Early on, Johnson had a thorough experience in all matters concerning the development and manufacture of both gramophones and records. He made and patented many major contributions in all these fields, and his approach was very business-like in that the contribution to cost of each part or process was always a decisive factor in his designs. This attitude was material in his consulting work for the sister company, the Gramophone Company, in London before it set up its own factories in 1910. He had quickly learned the advantages of advertising and of providing customers with durable equipment and records. This motivation was so strong that Johnson set up a research programme for determining the cause of wear in records. It turned out to depend on groove profile, and from 1911 one particular profile was adhered to and processes for transforming the grooves of valuable earlier records were developed. Without precise measuring instruments, he used the durability as the determining factor. Johnson withdrew more and more to the role of manager, and the Victor Talking Machine Company gained such a position in the market that the US anti-trust legislation was used against it. However, a generation change in the Board of Directors and certain erroneous decisions as to product line started a decline, and in February 1926 Johnson withdrew on extended sick leave: these changes led to the eventual sale of Victor. However, Victor survived due to the advent of radio and the electrification of replay equipment and became a part of Radio Corporation of America. In retirement Johnson took up various activities in the arts and sciences and financially supported several projects; his private yacht was used in 1933 in work with the Smithsonian Institution on a deep-sea hydrographic and fauna-collecting expedition near Puerto Rico.

Bibliography

Johnson's patents were many, and some were fundamental to the development of the gramophone, such as:

US patent no. 650,843 (in particular a recording lathe);

US patent nos. 655,556, 655,556 and 679,896 (soundboxes);

US patent no. 681,918 (making the original conductive for electroplating);

US patent no. 739,318 (shellac record with paper label).

Further Reading

Mrs E.R. Johnson, 1913, 'Eldridge Reeves Johnson (1867–1945): Industrial pioneer', manuscript (an account of his early experience).

E. Hutto, Jr, 'Emile Berliner, Eldridge Johnson, and the Victor Talking Machine Company', *Journal of AES* 25 (10/11): 666–73 (a good but brief account based on company information).

E.R. Fenimore Johnson, 1974, *His Master's Voice was Eldridge R. Johnson*, Milford, Del. (a very personal biography by his only son).

GB-N

Johnson, Isaac Charles

b. 28 January 1811 Vauxhall, London, England

d. 29 November 1911 Gravesend (?), Kent, England

English contributor to the development of efficient hydraulic cements.

As a young man Johnson studied both chemistry and physics and gained some experience in the manufacture of cement before joining the firm of John Bazely White as Works Manager at Swanscombe in Kent in 1838. He spent some years investigating the production processes and left the firm to set up on his own in 1851 on the Limehouse Reach of the River Medway, moving later to Gateshead on the River Tyne. Johnson produced a cement that was a great improvement on that of **Parker** and of **Frost**: like William Aspdin (see **Aspdin, Joseph**), he made a true Portland cement by mixing chalk, clay and water, and then clinkering the mixture. He used local clay at Gateshead and had the chalk shipped from the Thames area. In 1872 Johnson patented an improved bottle kiln, called the Johnson Chamber Kiln; it was of horizontal design, which speeded up manufacturing processes.

Further Reading

A.J. Francis, *The Cement Industry 1796–1914: A History*, David & Charles.

DY

Johnson, Percival Norton

b. 29 September 1792 London, England

d. 1 June 1866 Stoke Fleming, Devon, England

English chemist, assayer, mining engineer and founder of the firm Johnson Matthey.

He was the son of John Johnson, then sole Commercial Assayer in London, from whom he inherited his aptitude for chemistry and metallurgy. At the age of 14 he was apprenticed to his father by the Worshipful Company of Goldsmiths. Ore samples then being analysed in Johnson's office introduced him to the new metal platinum, and resulted in a paper to *Philosophical Magazine* in 1812. Johnson established himself as a 'practical mineralogist' in Maiden Lane, London, in 1818 and in Hatton Garden after 1822. He was greatly assisted by a fellow metallurgist, Thomas Cock (1787–1842), who developed the platinum fabrication and pigment sides of the business. In 1827 Johnson was consulted by the Russian government about the exploitation of the rich platinum deposits that had been discovered in the Urals in 1819. Between 1829 and 1832 Johnson became the first in England to manufacture nickel, extracted from nickel-bearing material imported from Germany at his plant at Bow Common on the Regent's Canal. In 1832 he began to refine gold imported from the Imperial Brazilian Association by a process which separated without loss the metals silver, platinum, palladium, rhodium and iridium. This profitable activity continued until the Brazilian company was wound up in 1852. Since 1824, Johnson had been named 'assay master' by a number of mining companies. From 1843 until the mid-1850s he had a considerable mining interest in the West Country. Meanwhile, the Hatton Garden establishment continued to prosper. In 1839 he was joined by George Matthey, who particularly fostered the Russian platinum business, and in 1851 he was taken unto partnership and the firm became the celebrated Johnson Matthey. In the following year the firm was officially recognized as one of the four Assayers to the Bank of England appointed to handle the flood of gold dust then arriving in England from the Australian gold fields. Soon after, however, ill health compelled him to retire to his Devon country house.

Principal Honours and Distinctions
FRS 1846.

Bibliography
1812, 'Experiments which prove platina, when combined with gold and silver, to be soluble in nitric acid', *Philosophical Magazine* (1st series) 40 (171): 3–4.

Further Reading
D. McDonald, 1951, *Percival Norton Johnson*, London: Johnson Matthey (includes lists of his publications and his honours and awards).
—— 1964, *The Johnsons of Morden Lane*, London: Martins.
—— 1960, *A History of Platinum*, London: Johnson Matthey.

ASD

Johnson, Samuel Waite

b. 14 October 1831 Bramley, Leeds, England
d. 14 January 1912 Nottingham, England

English locomotive engineer, designer of Midland Railway's successful compound locomotives.

After an apprenticeship with E.B. Wilson, Leeds, Johnson worked successively for the Great Northern, Manchester Sheffield & Lincolnshire, Edinburgh & Glasgow and Great Eastern Railways before being appointed Locomotive Superintendent of the Midland Railway in 1873. There he remained for the rest of his working life, becoming notable for well-designed, well-finished locomotives. Of these, the most famous were his 4-2-2 express locomotives, introduced in 1887. The use of a single pair of driving-wheels was made possible at this late date by application of steam sanding gear (invented in 1886 by F. Holt) to enable them to haul heavy trains without slipping. In 1901, almost at the end of his career, he produced the first Midland compound 4-4-0, with a single internal high-pressure cylinder and two external low-pressure ones. The system had been devised by W.M. Smith, working on the North Eastern Railway under Wilson Worsdell. These locomotives were successful enough to be developed and built in quantity by Johnson's successors and were adopted as a standard locomotive by the London Midland & Scottish Railway after the grouping of 1923.

Principal Honours and Distinctions
President, Institution of Mechanical Engineers 1898.

Further Reading
C. Hamilton Ellis, 1958, *Twenty Locomotive Men*, Ian Allan, Ch. 11 (describes Johnson's career).
E.L. Ahrons, 1927, *The British Steam Railway Locomotive 1825–1925*, The Locomotive Publishing Co. (describes Johnson's locomotives).

PJGR

Johnson, Thomas

fl. 1800s England
d. after 1846

English developer of the sizing and beaming machine, and improver of the hand loom.

Thomas Johnson was an assistant to William **Radcliffe** *c.*1802 in his developments of the sizing machine and hand looms. Johnson is described by Edward Baines (1835) as 'an ingenious but dissipated young man to whom he [Radcliffe] explained what he wanted, and whose fertile invention suggested a great variety of expedients, so that he obtained the name of the "conjuror" among his fellow-workmen'. Johnson's genius, and Radcliffe's judgement and perseverance, at length produced the dressing-machine that was soon applied to power looms and made their use economic. Cotton warps had to be dressed with a starch paste to prevent them from fraying as they were being woven. Up to this time, the paste had had to be applied as the warp was unwound from the back of the loom, which meant that only short lengths could be treated and then left to dry, holding up the weaver. Radcliffe carried out the dressing and beaming in a separate machine so that weaving could proceed without interruption. Work on the dressing-machine was carried out in 1802 and patents were taken out in 1803 and 1804. These were made out in Johnson's name because Radcliffe was afraid that if his own name were used other people, particularly foreigners, would discover his secrets. Two more patents were taken out for improvements to hand looms. The first of these was a take-up motion for the woven cloth that automatically wound the cloth onto a roller as the weaver operated the loom. This was later incorporated by H. Horrocks into his own power loom design. Radcliffe and Johnson also developed the 'dandy-loom', which was a more compact form of hand loom and later became adapted for weaving by power. Johnson was the inventor of the first circular or revolving temples, which kept the woven cloth at the right width. In the patent specifications there is a patent in 1805 by Thomas Johnson and James Kay for an improved power loom and another in 1807 for a vertical type of power loom. Johnson could have been involved with further patents in the 1830s and 1840s for vertical power looms and dressing-machines, which would put his death after 1846.

Bibliography

1802, British patent no. 2,684 (dressing-machine).

1803, British patent no. 2,771 (dressing-machine).

1805, with James Kay, British patent no. 2,876 (power-loom).

1807, British patent no. 6,570 (vertical power-loom).

Further Reading

There is no general account of Johnson's life, but references to his work with Radcliffe may be found in A. Barlow, 1878, *The History and Principles of Weaving by Hand and by Power*, London; and in E. Baines, 1835, *History of the Cotton Manufacture in Great Britain*, London.

D.J. Jeremy, 1981, *Transatlantic Industrial Revolution. The Diffusion of Textile Technologies Between Britain and America, 1790–1830s*, Oxford (for the impact of the dressing-machine in America).

RLH

Johnston, William J.

fl. mid-nineteenth century Philadelphia, Pennsylvania, USA

American architect who was one of the pioneers during the mid-nineteenth century of metal framing for commercial building structures.

The Jayne Building, erected in Philadelphia in 1849–50, was begun by Johnston and completed by Thomas U. **Walter**, architect of the iron dome of the Washington Capitol. The seven-storey Philadelphia Building was iron-framed and clad in granite, and Johnston introduced a vertical type of architectural design reflecting the metal structural form beneath – a format later taken up for taller, skyscraper buildings by Louis **Sullivan** – but here the upper storey was eclectic, using Gothic tracery. The building was later demolished.

Further Reading

H. Russell-Hitchcock, 1958, *Architecture: 19th and 20th Centuries*, London: Penguin, Pelican History of Art series, 333.

N. Pevsner, 1975, *Pioneers of Modern Design*, London: Penguin, 24–25.

Society of Architectural Historians of Great Britain: Vol. 9, *Ante-Bellum Skyscraper*, and Vol. 10, *The Jayne Building Again*.

DY

Jolly-Bellin, Jean-Baptiste

fl. *c*.1850 France

French pioneer in dry-cleaning.

Until the mid-nineteenth century, washing with soap and water was the only way to clean clothes; with woollen fabrics in particular, it was more common to dye them to a darker colour to conceal the dirt. In about 1850, Jean-Baptiste Jolly-Bellin, a Paris tailor, spilt some camphene, a kind of turpentine, on an article belonging to his wife and found that the area stained by the spirit was cleaner than the rest. He opened up a business for 'Nettoyage à sec', the first dry-cleaning business. The garments had to be unstitched before being brushed with camphene and were then sewn together again.

Further Reading

I. McNeil (ed.), 1990, *An Encyclopaedia of the History of Technology*, London: Routledge (provides an account of the development of methods of cleaning garments).

RLH

Joly, John

b. 1857 Holywood, King's County (now County Down, Northwern Ireland), Ireland
d. 8 December 1933 Dublin, Eire

Irish pioneer of additive screen-plate colour photography.

Professor of Physics at Trinity College, Dublin, Joly developed a concept first suggested by **Ducos du Hauron**, creating in 1893 a process in which fine transparent red, green and blue lines, less than 0.1 mm wide, were ruled on a glass plate. The coloured inks were aniline dyes mixed with gum. This screen plate was held in close contact with a photographic negative plate which was exposed through the screen in a camera. The processed negative was printed onto a positive plate, and a viewing screen, similar to that used for taking, was bound up with it in careful register, to reproduce the original colours. The process was patented in 1894, and marketed in 1895. It was the first commercially successful additive screen-plate process to appear. While the results could be quite acceptable, the inadequate colour sensitivity of the negative plates then available limited the usefulness of this process. Professor Joly's other achievements included geological research and the treatment of cancer by radium.

Further Reading

J.S. Friedman, 1944, *History of Colour Photography*, Boston.
B. Coe, 1978, *Colour Photography: The First Hundred Years*, London.
G. Koshofer, 1981, *Farbfotografie*, Vol. I, Munich.

BC

Joubert, Jules François

b. 1834 Tours, France
d. 1910 Paris, France

French physicist, investigator of alternating-current wave-forms.

Joubert became Professor of Physics in the Collège Rollin, Paris, in 1874, a position he held until 1888. He was at one time General Secretary of the Société Française de Physique. In collaboration with **Pasteur** he began studies into the theories of germs and bacteria. In 1880 Joubert carried out research on wave-forms in alternating-current arc-lighting circuits. Reinventing a method previously used by earlier experimenters, including **Wheatstone**, he was, by a mechanical sampling technique, able to determine the voltage at different points in the cycle. By using a rotating contact on the alternator shaft, the angular position of which could be varied, the whole of the wave-form could be delineated. This successful technique was widely used for some thirty years.

Bibliography

1880, 'Sur les courants alternatifs et la force électromotive de l'arc électrique', *Journal of Physics* 9: 297–303 (describes his experiments).

Further Reading

'Investigation of alternating current arcs', *Elec-*

trician (1880) 5: 151–2 (a report on Joubert's method).
V.J. Phillips, 1987, *Waveforms*, Bristol (an extensive account of early methods of wave-form observation).
W. Bulloch, 1938, *The History of Bacteriology*, Oxford; 1979, repub. New York.

See also: **Duddell, William du Bois**.

GW

Joy, David

b. 3 March 1825 Leeds, England
d. 14 March 1903 Hampstead, London, England

English mechanical engineer, designer of the locomotive Jenny Lind and of Joy's valve gear for steam engines.

By the mid-1840s Joy was Chief Draughtsman at E.B. Wilson's locomotive works at Leeds. During that period, attempts by engineers to design ever larger and more powerful locomotives were producing ungainly types, such as the long-boiler and the Crampton, which were to prove blind alleys in locomotive development. Joy rediscovered the proper route with his *Jenny Lind* 2–2–2, built in 1847. His locomotive had minimal overhang, with the firebox between the driving and trailing axles; the driving axle supported inside frames which stopped short at the firebox, allowing the latter to be wide, while leading and trailing wheels were held by outside plate frames which had a degree of elasticity. The boiler was low-pitched, the steam pressure high at 120 psi (8.4 kg/cm^2). The result was a powerful locomotive which rode well and immediately became popular, a forerunner of many later designs. Joy subsequently had a varied career with successive railways and engineering firms. In the late 1850s he invented steam reversing gear for large, marine steam engines, a hydraulic organ blower and a pneumatic hammer. In 1879 he invented his radial valve gear for steam engines, which was adopted by F.W. **Webb** for the London & North Western Railway's locomotives and was also much used in marine steam engines.

Bibliography

1879, British patent no. 929 (valve gear).

Further Reading
Obituary, 1903, *Engineering* (20 March).
Obituary, 1903, *The Engineer* (20 March).
PJGR

Judson, Whitcomb L.
fl. 1891–1905 USA

American inventor of the zip fastener.

Whitcomb Judson was a mechanical engineer by profession. He filed his first patent application for a zip fastener in 1891 and took out a fifth in 1905. His invention was originally designed for shoes and consisted of separate fasteners with two interlocking parts which could be fastened either by hand or by a movable guide. In his last patent, he clamped the fastening elements to the edge of a fabric tape and patented a machine for manufacturing this. Through an earlier exploit, the Judson Pneumatic Street Railway Company, Judson knew Colonel Lewis Walker, who helped him to organize the Universal Fastener Company of Chicago to manufacture these fasteners, which at first were made by hand. One machine invented by Judson proved to be too complicated, but Judson's later fasteners were easier to adapt to machine production. The original company was reorganized as the Automatic Hook and Eye Company of Hoboken, New Jersey, and the new fasteners were sold under the name 'C-curity'. However, the garment manufacturers would not use them at first because the fasteners had defects, such as springing open at unexpected moments. The Automatic Hook and Eye Company brought in Gideon **Sundback**, who improved Judson's work and made the zip fastener successful.

Further Reading
J. Jewkes, D. Sawyers and R. Stillerman, 1969, *The Sources of Invention*, 2nd edn, London (for an account of the invention).
I. McNeil (ed.), 1990, *An Encyclopaedia of the History of Technology*, London: Routledge, pp. 852–3 (provides a brief account of fastenings).
RLH

Junghans, Siegfried
b. 1887
d. 1954

German pioneer of the continuous casting of metals.

Junghans was of the family that owned Gebrüder Junghans, one of the largest firms in the German watch- and clockmaking industry. From 1906 to 1918 he served in the German Army, after which he took a course in metallurgy and analytical chemistry at the Technical High School in Stuttgart. Junghans was then given control of the brassworks owned by his family. He wanted to make castings simply and cheaply, but he found that he lacked the normal foundry equipment. By 1927, formulating his ideas on continuous casting, he had conceived a way of overcoming this deficiency and began experiments. By the time the firm was taken over by Wieland-Werke AG in 1931, Junghans had achieved positive results. A test plant was erected in 1932, and commercial production of continuously cast metal followed the year after. Wieland told Junghans that a brassfounder who had come up through the trade would never have hit on the idea: it took an outsider like Junghans to do it. He was made Technical Director of Wielands but left in 1935 to work privately on the development of continuous casting for all metals. He was able to license the process for non-ferrous metals during 1936–9 in Germany and other countries, but the Second World War interrupted his work; however, the German government supported him and a production plant was built. In 1948 he was able to resume work on the continuous casting of steel, which he had been considering since 1936. He pushed on in spite of financial difficulties and produced the first steel by this process at Schorndorf in March 1949. From 1950 he made agreements with four firms to work towards the pilot plant stage, and this was achieved in 1954 at Mannesmann's Huckingen works. The aim of continuous casting is to bypass the conventional processes of casting molten steel into ingots, re-heating the ingots and shaping them by rolling them in a large mill. Essentially, in continuous casting, molten steel is drawn through the bottom of a ladle and down through a water-cooled copper mould. The unique feature of Junghans's process was the vertically reciprocating mould, which prevented the molten metal sticking as it passed through. A continuous length of steel is taken off and cooled until it is completely solidified into the required shape. The idea of continuous casting can be traced back to **Bessemer**, and although others tried to apply it later, they did not have any success. It was Junghans who, more than anybody, made the process a reality.

Further Reading
K. Sperth and A. Bungeroth, 1953, 'The Junghans method of continuous casting of steel', *Metal Treatment and Drop Forging*, Mayn.
J. Jewkes *et al.*, 1969, *The Sources of Invention*, 2nd edn, London: Macmillan, pp. 287 ff.

LRD

Junkers, Hugo

b. 3 February 1859 Rheydt, Germany
d. 3 February 1935 Munich, Germany

German aircraft designer, pioneer of all-metal aircraft, including the world's first real airliner.

Hugo Junkers trained as an engineer and in 1895 founded the Junkers Company, which manufactured metal products including gas-powered hot-water heaters. He was also Professor of Thermodynamics at the high school in Aachen. The visits to Europe by the **Wright** brothers in 1908 and 1909 aroused his interest in flight, and in 1910 he was granted a patent for a flying wing, i.e. no fuselage and a thick wing which did not require external bracing wires. Using his sheet-metal experience he built the more conventional Junkers *J 1* entirely of iron and steel. It made its first flight in December 1915 but was rather heavy and slow, so Junkers turned to the newly available aluminium alloys and built the *J 4* biplane, which entered service in 1917. To stiffen the thin aluminium-alloy skins, Junkers used corrugations running fore and aft, a feature of his aircraft for the next twenty years. Incidentally, in 1917 the German authorities persuaded Junkers and **Fokker** to merge, but the Junkers–Fokker Company was short-lived.

After the First World War Junkers very rapidly converted to commercial aviation, and in 1919 he produced a single-engined low-wing monoplane capable of carrying four passengers in an enclosed cabin. The robust all-metal *F 13* is generally accepted as being the world's first airliner and over three hundred were built and used worldwide: some were still in service eighteen years later. A series of low-wing transport aircraft followed, of which the best known is the *Ju 52*. The original version had a single engine and first flew in 1930; a three-engined version flew in 1932 and was known as the *Ju 52/3m*. This was used by many airlines and served with the Luftwaffe throughout the Second World War, with almost five thousand being built.

Junkers was always ready to try new ideas, such as a flap set aft of the trailing edge of the wing that became known as the 'Junkers flap'. In 1923 he founded a company to design and manufacture stationary diesel engines and aircraft petrol engines. Work commenced on a diesel aero-engine: this flew in 1929 and a successful range of engines followed later. Probably the most spectacular of Junkers's designs was his *G 38* airliner of 1929. This was the world's largest land-plane at the time, with a wing span of 44 m (144 ft). The wing was so thick that some of the thirty-four passengers could sit in the wing and look out through windows in the leading edge. Two were built and were frequently seen on European routes.

Bibliography
1923, 'Metal aircraft construction', *Journal of the Royal Aeronautical Society*, London.

Further Reading
G. Schmitt, 1988, *Hugh Junkers and His Aircraft*, Berlin.
1990, *Jane's Fighting Aircraft of World War I*, London: Jane's (provides details of Junkers's aircraft).
J. Stroud, 1966, *European Transport Aircraft since 1910*, London.
P. St J. Turner and H.J. Nowarra, 1971, *Junkers: An Aircraft Album*, London.

JDS

K

Kao, Charles Kuen
b. 4 November 1933 Shanghai, China

Chinese electrical engineer whose work on optical fibres did much to make optical communications a practical reality.

After the Second World War, Kao moved with his family to Hong Kong, where he went to St Joseph's College. To further his education he then moved to England, taking his 'A' Levels at Woolwich Polytechnic. In 1957 he gained a BSc in electrical engineering and then joined Standard Telephones and Cables Laboratory (STL) at Harlow. Following the discovery by others in 1960 of the semiconductor laser, from 1963 Kao worked on the problems of optical communications, in particular that of achieving attenuation in optical cables low enough to make this potentially very high channel capacity form of communication a practical proposition; this problem was solved by suitable cladding of the fibres. In the process he obtained his PhD from University College, London, in 1965. From 1970 until 1974, whilst on leave from STL, he was Professor of Electronics and Department Chairman at the Chinese University of Hong Kong, then in 1982–7 he was Chief Scientist and Director of Engineering with the parent company ITT in the USA. Since 1988 he has been Vice-Chancellor of Hong Kong University.

Principal Honours and Distinctions
Franklin Institute Stuart Ballantine Medal 1977. Institute of Electrical and Electronic Engineers Morris N. Liebmann Memorial Prize 1978; L.M. Ericsson Prize 1979. Institution of Electrical Engineers A.G. Bell Medal 1985; Faraday Medal 1989. American Physical Society International Prize for New Materials 1989.

Bibliography
1966, with G.A. Hockham, 'Dielectric fibre surface waveguides for optical frequencies', *Proceedings of the Institution of Electrical Engineers* 113: 1,151 (describes the major step in optical-fibre development).

1982, *Optical Fibre Systems. Technology, Design & Application*, New York: McGraw-Hill.
1988, *Optical Fibre*, London: Peter Peregrinus.

Further Reading
W.B. Jones, 1988, *Introduction to Optical Fibre Communications*: R&W Holt.

KF

Kaplan, Viktor
b. 27 November 1876 Mutz, Austria
d. 23 August 1834 Unterach, Austria

Austrian engineer, inventor of the Kaplan turbine.

Kaplan was educated at the Realschule in Vienna and went on to the Technische Hochschule to study machine construction, gaining his engineer's diploma in 1900. He spent a year in voluntary service in the Navy before entering Ganz & Co. at Lebersdorf, where he was engaged in the manufacture of diesel engines. In 1903 he turned to an academic career, first with a professorship in kinematics, theoretical machine studies and machine construction at the Technische Hochschule in Brunn (now Brno). In 1918 he became Professor of Water Turbine Construction, remaining as such until his early retirement for health reasons in 1931.

Kaplan's first publication on turbines, in 1908, was an extension of work carried out for his doctorate at the Technische Hochschule in Vienna and concerned the Francis-type turbine. Kaplan went on to develop and patent the form of water turbine that came to bear his name. It is a reaction turbine which uses a large flow on a low head and which is made like a ship's propeller with variable-pitch vanes running in a close-fitting casing. Its application was neglected at first, but since the 1920s it has become the basic turbine for most high-powered hydroelectric plant: the turbines have been capable of around 85 per cent efficiency and modern developments have raised this figure still further. Perhaps the most impressive application of the Kaplan turbine and its derivatives is the great tidal-power scheme in the estuary of the Rance by St-Malo in France, completed in 1966. The turbines probably have to meet a greater demand for flexibility than any others, for they must operate at constant speed with variable head, as the tide ebbs and flows.

LRD

Kapp, Gisbert Johann Eduard Karl
b. 2 September 1852 Mauer, Vienna, Austria
d. 10 August 1922 Birmingham, England

Austrian (naturalized British in 1881) engineer and a pioneer of dynamo design, being particularly associated with the concept of the magnetic circuit.

Kapp entered the Polytechnic School in Zurich in 1869 and gained a mechanical engineering diploma. He became a member of the engineering staff at the Vienna International Exhibition of 1873, and then spent some time in the Austrian navy before entering the service of Gwynne & Co. of London, where he designed centrifugal pumps and gas exhausters. Kapp resolved to become an electrical engineer after a visit to the Paris Electrical Exhibition of 1881 and in the following year was appointed Manager of the Crompton Co. works at Chelmsford. There he developed and patented the dynamo with compound field winding. Also at that time, with **Crompton**, he patented electrical measuring instruments with over-saturated electromagnets. He became a naturalized British subject in 1881.

In 1886 Kapp's most influential paper was published. This described his concept of the magnetic circuit, providing for the first time a sound theoretical basis for dynamo design. The theory was also developed independently by J. **Hopkinson**. After commencing practice as a consulting engineer in 1884 he carried out design work on dynamos and also electricity-supply and -traction schemes in Germany, Italy, Norway, Russia and Switzerland. From 1891 to 1894 much of his time was spent designing a new generating station in Bristol, officially as Assistant to W.H. **Preece**. There followed an appointment in Germany as General Secretary of the Verband Deutscher Electrotechniker. For some years he edited the *Electrotechnische Zeitschrift* and was also a part-time lecturer at the Charlottenberg Technical High School in Berlin. In 1904 Kapp was invited to accept the new Chair of Electrical Engineering at the University of Birmingham, which he occupied until 1919. He was the author of several books on electrical machine and transformer design.

Principal Honours and Distinctions
Institution of Civil Engineers Telford Medal 1886 and 1888. President, Institution of Electrical Engineers 1909.

Bibliography
10 October 1882, with R.E.B. Crompton, British patent no. 4,810; (the compound wound dynamo).
1886, 'Modern continuous current dynamo electric machines and their engines', *Proceedings of the Institution of Civil Engineers* 83: 123–54.

Further Reading
D.G. Tucker, 1989, 'A new archive of Gisbert Kapp papers', *Proceedings of the Meeting on History of Electrical Engineering*, IEE 4/1–4/11 (a transcript of an autobiography for his family).
D.G. Tucker, 1973, *Gisbert Kapp 1852–1922*, Birmingham: Birmingham University (includes a bibliography of his most important publications).

GW

Kay (of Bury), John
b. 16 July 1704 Walmersley, near Bury, Lancashire, England
d. 1779 France

English inventor of the flying shuttle.

John Kay was the youngest of five sons of a yeoman farmer of Walmersley, near Bury, Lancashire, who died before his birth. John was apprenticed to a reedmaker, and just before he was 21 he married a daughter of John Hall of Bury and carried on his trade in that town until 1733. It is possible that his first patent, taken out in 1730, was connected with this business because it was for an engine that made mohair thread for tailors and twisted and dressed thread; such thread could have been used to bind up the reeds used in looms. He also improved the reeds by making them from metal instead of cane strips so they lasted much longer and could be made to be much finer. His next patent in 1733, was a double one. One part of it was for a batting machine to remove dust from wool by beating it with sticks, but the patent is better known for its description of the flying shuttle. Kay placed boxes to receive the shuttle at either end of the reed or sley. Across the open top of these boxes was a metal rod along which a picking peg could slide and drive the shuttle out across the loom. The pegs at each end were connected by strings to a stick that was held in the right hand of the weaver and which jerked the shuttle out of the box. The shuttle had wheels to make it 'fly' across the warp more easily, and ran on a shuttle race to support and guide it. Not only was weaving speeded up, but the weaver could produce broader cloth without any aid from a second person. This invention was later adapted for the power loom. Kay moved to Colchester and entered into partnership with a baymaker named Solomon Smith and a year later was joined by William Carter of Ballingdon, Essex. His shuttle was received with considerable hostility in both Lancashire and Essex, but it was probably more his charge of 15 shillings a year for its use that roused the antagonism. From 1737 he was much involved with lawsuits to try and protect his patent, particularly the part that specified the method of winding the thread onto a fixed bobbin in the shuttle. In 1738 Kay patented a windmill for working pumps and an improved chain pump, but neither of these seems to have been successful. In 1745, with Joseph Stell of Keighley, he patented a narrow fabric loom that could be worked by power; this type may have been employed by **Gartside** in Manchester soon afterwards. It was probably through failure to protect his patent rights that Kay moved to France, where he arrived penniless in 1747. He went to the Dutch firm of Daniel Scalongne, woollen manufacturers, in Abbeville. The company helped him to apply for a French patent for his shuttle, but Kay wanted the exorbitant sum of £10,000. There was much discussion and eventually Kay set up a workshop in Paris, where he received a pension of 2,500 *livres*. However, he was to face the same problems as in England with weavers copying his shuttle without permission. In 1754 he produced two machines for making card clothing: one pierced holes in the leather, while the other cut and sharpened the wires. These were later improved by his son, Robert **Kay**. Kay returned to England briefly, but was back in France in 1758. He was involved with

machines to card both cotton and wool and tried again to obtain support from the French Government. He was still involved with developing textile machines in 1779, when he was 75, but he must have died soon afterwards. As an inventor Kay was a genius of the first rank, but he was vain, obstinate and suspicious and was destitute of business qualities.

Bibliography
1730, British patent no. 515 (machine for making mohair thread).
1733, British patent no. 542 (batting machine and flying shuttle).
1738, British patent no. 561 (pump windmill and chain pump).
1745, with Joseph Stell, British patent no. 612 (power loom).

Further Reading
B. Woodcroft, 1863, *Brief Biographies of Inventors or Machines for the Manufacture of Textile Fabrics*, London.
J. Lord, 1903, *Memoir of John Kay*, (a more accurate account).
Descriptions of his inventions may be found in A. Barlow, 1878, *The History and Principles of Weaving by Hand and by Power*, London; R.L. Hills, 1970, *Power in the Industrial Revolution*, Manchester; and C. Singer (ed.), 1957, *A History of Technology*, Vol. III, Oxford: Clarendon Press. The most important record, however, is in A.P. Wadsworth and J. de L. Mann, 1931, *The Cotton Trade and Industrial Lancashire*, Manchester.

RLH

Kay (of Warrington), John
fl. *c*.1770 England

English clockmaker who helped Richard Arkwright to construct his spinning machine.

John Kay was a clockmaker of Warrington. He moved to Leigh, where he helped Thomas **Highs** to construct his spinning machine, but lack of success made them abandon their attempts. Kay first met Richard **Arkwright** in March 1767 and six months later was persuaded by Arkwright to make one or more models of the roller spinning machine he had built under Highs's supervision. Kay went with Arkwright to Preston, where they continued working on the machine. Kay also went with Arkwright when he moved to Nottingham. It was around this time that he entered into an agreement with Arkwright to serve him for twenty-one years and was bound not to disclose any details of the machines. Presumably Kay helped to set up the first spinning machines at Arkwright's Nottingham mill as well as at Cromford. Despite their agreement, he seems to have left after about five years and may have disclosed the secret of Arkwright's crank and comb on the carding engine to others. Kay was later to give evidence against Arkwright during the trial of his patent in 1785.

Further Reading

R.S. Fitton, 1989, *The Arkwrights, Spinners of Fortune*, Manchester (the most detailed account of Kay's connections with Arkwright and his evidence during the later patent trials).

A.P. Wadsworth and J. de L. Mann, 1931, *The Cotton Trade and Industrial Lancashire*, Manchester (mentions Kay's association with Arkwright).

RLH

Kay, Robert

b. probably before 1747
d. 1801 Bury, Lancashire, England

English inventor of the drop box, whereby shuttles with different wefts could be stored and selected when needed.

Little is known about the early life of Robert Kay except that he may have moved to France with his father, John **Kay** of Bury in 1747 but must have returned to England and their home town of Bury soon after. He may have been involved with his father in the production of a machine for making the wire covering for hand cards to prepare cotton for spinning. However, John Aikin, writing in 1795, implies that this was a recent invention. Kay's machine could pierce the holes in the leather backing, cut off a length of wire, bend it and insert it through the holes, row after row, in one operation by a person turning a shaft. The machine preserved in the Science Museum, in London's South Kensington, is more likely to be one of Robert's machine than his father's, for Robert carried on business as a cardmaker in Bury from 1791 until his death in 1801. The flying shuttle, invented by his father, does not seem to have been much used by weavers of cot-

ton until Robert invented the drop box in 1760. Instead of a single box at the end of the sley, Robert usually put two, but sometimes three or four, one above another; the boxes could be raised or lowered. Shuttles with either different colours or different types of weft could be put in the boxes and the weaver could select any one by manipulating levers with the left hand while working the picking stick with the right to drive the appropriate shuttle across the loom. Since the selection could be made without the weaver having to pick up a shuttle and place it in the lath, this invention helped to speed up weaving, especially of multi-coloured checks, which formed a large part of the Lancashire output.

Between 1760 and 1763 Robert Kay may have written a pamphlet describing the invention of the flying shuttle and the attack on his father, pointing out how much his father had suffered and that there had been no redress. In February 1764 he brought to the notice of the Society of Arts an improvement he had made to the flying shuttle by substituting brass for wood, which enabled a larger spool to be carried.

Further Reading

A.P. Wadsworth and J. de L. Mann, 1931, *The Cotton Trade and Industrial Lancashire*, Manchester.

A. Barlow, 1878, *The History and Principles of Weaving by Hand and by Power*, London; and R.L. Hills, 1970, *Power in the Industrial Revolution*, Manchester (for details about the drop box).

RLH

Kegel, Karl

b. 19 May 1876 Magdeburg, Germany
d. 5 March 1959 Freiberg, Saxony, Germany

German professor of mining who established the mining of lignite as a discipline in the science of mining.

Within the long tradition of celebrated teachers at the Mining Academy in Freiberg, Kegel can be considered as probably the last professor teaching the science of mining who was able to cover all the different disciplines. As was the case with a number of his predecessors, he was able to combine theoretical research work with the teaching of students and to support his theories with the practical experience of industry. He has apprenticed at the Mansfeld copper mines, went to the School of Mines at Eisleben (1896–8), worked as an engineer with various mining companies and thereafter became a scholar of the Berlin Mining Academy (1901–4). For twelve years he taught at the Bochum School of Mining until, in 1918, he was appointed Professor of Mining at Freiberg. There, one year later, as a new approach, he introduced lectures on brown-coal mining and mineral economics. He remained Professor at Freiberg until his first retirement in 1941, although he was active again between 1945 and 1951.

In 1924 Kegel took over a department at the State Research Institute for Brown Coal in Freiberg which he extended into the Institute for Briquetting. In this field his main achievement lies in the initially questioned theory that producing briquettes from lignite is a molecular process rather than the result of bituminous factors. This perception, among others, led **Rammler** to produce coke from lignite in 1951. Kegel's merits result from having established all the aspects of mining and using lignite as an independent subdiscipline of mining science, based on substantial theories and an innovative understanding of applied technologies.

Bibliography

1912, *Bergmännische Wasserwirtschaft*, Halle (Saale).
1931, *Lehrbuch der Bergwirtschaft*, Berlin.
1941, *Bergmännische Gebirgsmechanik*, Halle (Saale).
1948, *Brikettierung der Braunkohle*, Halle (Saale).
1953, *Lehrbuch des Braunkohlentagebaus*, Halle (Saale).

Further Reading

E. Kroker, 'Karl Kegel', *Neue deutsche Biographie*, Vol. XI, p. 394 (a reliable short account).
Bergakademie Freiberg (ed.), 1976, *Karl Kegel 1876–1959. Festschrift aus Anlaß seines 100. Geburtstages*, Leipzig (contains substantial biographical information).

WK

Keller, Arthur

b. 18 August 1901 New York City, New York, USA
d. 1983

American engineer and developer of telephone switching equipment who was instrumental in the development of electromechanical recording and stereo techniques.

He obtained a BSc in electrical engineering at Cooper Union for the Advancement of Science and Art, New York, in 1923 and an MSc from Yale University, and he did postgraduate work at Columbia University. Most of the time he was also on the staff of the Bell Telephone Laboratories. The Bell Laboratories and its predecessors had a long tradition in research in speech and hearing, and in a team of researchers under H.C. Harrison, Keller developed a number of definite improvements in electrical pick-ups, gold-sputtering for matrix work and electrical disc recording equipment. From 1931 onwards the team at Bell Labs developed disc recording for moving pictures and entered into collaboration with Leopold Stokowski and the Philadelphia Orchestra concerning transmission and recording of high-fidelity sound over wires, and stereo techniques. Keller developed a stereo recording system for disc records independently of A.D. **Blumlein** that was used experimentally in the Bell Labs during the 1930s. During the Second World War Keller was in a team developing sonar (*sound navigation and ranging*) for the US Navy. After the war he concentrated on switching equipment for telephone exchanges and developed a miniature relay. In 1966 he retired from the Bell Laboratories, where he had been Director of several departments, ending as Director of the Switching Apparatus Laboratory. After retirement he was a consultant internationally, concerning electromechanical devices in particular. When, in 1980, the Bell Laboratories decided to issue LP re-recordings of a number of the experimental records made during the 1930s, Keller was brought in from retirement to supervise the project and decide on the selections.

Bibliography
Keller was inventor or co-inventor of forty patents, including:
US patent no. 2,114,471 (the principles of stereo disc recording); US patent no. 2,612,586

(tape guides with air lubrication); US patent no. 3,366,901 (a miniature crossbar switch).

Apart from a large number of highly technical papers, Keller also wrote the article 'Phonograph' in the 1950 and 1957 editions of *Encyclopaedia Britannica*.

1986, *Reflections of a Stereo Pioneer*, San Francisco: San Francisco Press (an honest, personal account).

GB-N

Keller, Friedrich Gottlieb

b. 27 June 1818 Hainichen, Saxony, Germany
d. 8 September 1895 Krippen, Bad Schandau, Germany

German inventor of wood-pulp paper.

The son of a master weaver, he originally wished to become an engineer, but while remaining in the parental home he had to follow his father's trade in the textile industry, becoming a master weaver himself in 1839 at Hainichen. He was a good observer and a keen model maker. It was at this stage, in the early 1840s, that he began experimenting with a new material for papermaking. Until then the raw material had been waste rag from the textile industry, but the ever-increasing demands of the mechanical printing presses, especially those producing newspapers, were beginning to outstrip supply. Keller tried using pine wood ground with a wet grindstone. The mass of fibres that resulted was then heated with water to form a thick brew which he then strained through a cloth. By this means Keller obtained a pulp that could be used for papermaking. He constructed a simple grinding machine that could disintegrate the wood without splinters; this was used to make paper in the Altchemnitzer paper mill, and the newspaper *Frankenberger Intelligenz- und Wochenblatt* was the first to be printed on wood-pulp paper. Keller could not secure state funds to promote his invention, so he approached an expert in papermaking, Heinrich Voelter, Technical Director of the Vereinigten Bautzener Papierfabrik. Voelter put up 700 thaler, and in August 1845 the state of Saxony granted a patent in both their names. In 1848 the first practical machine for grinding wood was produced, but four years later the patent expired. Unfortunately Keller could not afford the renewal fee, and it was Voelter who developed the process of wood-pulp papermak-

ing under his own name, leaving Keller behind. Without this invention, the output of paper from the mills could not have kept pace with the demands of the printing industry, and the mass readership that these technological developments made possible could not have been served. It is no fault of Keller's that wood-pulp paper contains within itself the seeds of its own deterioration and ultimate destruction, presenting librarians of today with an intractable problem of preservation. Keller's part in this technical breakthrough is established in his 'ideas' notebook covering the years 1841 and 1842, preserved in the museum at Hainichen.

Further Reading
Neue deutsche Biographie.
VDI Zeitschrift, Vol. 39, p. 1,238.
'Eine Erfindung von Weltruf', 1969, *VDI Nachrichten*, Vol. 29, p. 18.
Clapperton, *History of Papermaking Through the Ages* (provides details of the development of wood-pulp papermaking in its historical context).

LRD

Kelly, William

b. 1790s Lanark, Scotland

Scottish pioneer in attempts to make
Crompton's *spinning mule work automatically.*

William Kelly, a Larnack clockmaker, was Manager of David **Dale**'s New Lanark cotton-spinning mills. He was writing to **Boulton** & **Watt** in 1796 about the different ways in which he heated the mills and the New Institution. He must also have been responsible for supervising the millwrights' and mechanics' shops where much of the spinning machinery for the mills was constructed. At one time there were eighty-seven men employed in these shops alone. He devised a better method of connecting the water wheel to the line shafting which he reckoned would save a quarter of the water power required. Kelly may have been the first to apply power to the mule, for in 1790 he drove the spinning sequence from the line shafting, which operated the gear mechanism to turn the rollers and spindles as well as draw out the carriage. The winding on of the newly spun yarn still had to be done by hand. Then in 1792 he applied for a patent for a self-acting mule in which all the operations would be carried out by power. However, winding the yarn on in a conical form was a problem; he tried various ways of doing this, but abandoned his attempts because the mechanism was cumbersome and brought no economic advantage as only a comparatively small number of spindles could be operated. Even so, his semi-automatic mule became quite popular and was exported to America in 1803. Kelly was replaced as Manager at New Lanark by Robert **Owen** in 1800.

Bibliography
1792, British patent no. 1,879 (semi-automatic mule).

Further Reading
R.L. Hills, 1970, *Power in the Industrial Revolution*, Manchester (includes Kelly's own account of his development of the self-acting mule).
H. Catling, 1970, *The Spinning Mule*, Newton Abbot (describes some of Kelly's mule mechanisms).
J. Butt (ed.), 1971, *Robert Owen, Prince of Cotton Spinners*, Newton Abbot (provides more details about the New Lanark mills).

RLH

Kelvin (of Largs), Baron
See **Thomson, Sir William**.

Kemeny, John G.
b. before 1939

American mathematician and systems programmer, jointly responsible with Thomas Kurtz for the development of the high-level computer language BASIC.

Kemeny entered the USA as an immigrant in 1939. He subsequently became a mathematics lecturer at Dartmouth College, Hanover, New Hampshire, and later became a professor and then Chairman of the Mathematics Department; finally, in 1971, he became President of the College. In 1964, with Thomas Kurtz, he developed the high-level computer language known as BASIC (*B*eginners *A*ll-purpose *S*ymbolic *I*nstruction *C*ode). It was initially designed for use by students with a time-sharing minicomputer, but it soon became the standard language for microcomputers, frequently being embedded in

the computer as 'firmware' loaded into a read-only-memory (ROM) integrated circuit.

Bibliography
1963, *Programming for a Digital Computer*.
1964, with T.E. Kurtz, *BASIC Instruction Manual*.
1968, with T.E. Kurtz, 'Dartmouth time-sharing', *Science* 223.

Further Reading
R.L. Wexelblat (ed.), 1981, *History of Programming Languages*, New York: Academic Press.

KF

Kennedy, Sir Alexander Blackie William
b. 17 March 1847 Stepney, London, England
d. 1928

English marine engineer and educator.

Sir Alexander Kennedy was trained as a marine engineer. The son of a Congregational minister, he was educated at the City of London School and the School of Mines, Jermyn Street. He was then apprenticed to J. & W. Dudgeon of Millwall, marine engineers, and went on to become a draughtsman to Sir Charles Marsh Palmer of Jarrow (with whom he took part in the development of the compound steam-engine for marine use) and T.M. Tennant & Co. of Leith. In 1874 he was appointed Professor of Engineering at University College, London. He built up an influential School of Engineering, being the first in England to integrate laboratory work as a regular feature of instruction. The engineering laboratory that he established in 1878 has been described as 'the first of its kind in England' (Proceedings of the Institution of Civil Engineers). He and his students conducted important experiments on the strength and elasticity of materials, boiler testing and related subjects. He followed the teaching of Franz Reuleaux, whose *Kinematics of Machinery* he translated from the German.

While thus breaking new educational ground at University College, Kennedy concurrently established a very thriving private practice as a consulting engineer in partnership with Bernard Maxwell Jenkin (the son of Fleeming **Jenkin**), to pursue which he relinquished his academic posts in 1889. He planned and installed the whole electricity system for the Westminster Electric Supply Corporation, and other electricity companies. He was also heavily involved in the development of electrically powered transport systems. During the First World War he served on a panel of the Munitions Invention Department, and after the war he undertook to record photographically the scenes of desolation in his book *From Ypres to Verdun* (1921). Towards the end of his life, he pursued his interest in archaeology with the exploration of Petra, recorded in a monograph: *Petra. Its History and Monuments* (1925). He also joined the Institution of Mechanical Engineers in 1879, becoming the President of that body in 1894, and he joined the Institution of Electrical Engineers in 1890. Kennedy was thus something of an engineering polymath, as well as being an outstanding engineering educationalist.

Principal Honours and Distinctions
FRS 1887. Knighted 1905. Member, Institution of Civil Engineers 1879; President, 1906. President, Institution of Mechanical Engineers 1894.

Bibliography
1921, *From Ypres to Verdum.*
1925, *Petra. Its History and Monuments.*

Further Reading
DNB supplement.
1928–9, *Proceedings of the Institution of Civil Engineers* 221: 269–75.

AB

Kennedy, John
b. 4 July 1769 Knocknalling, Kirkcudbrightshire, Scotland
d. 30 October 1855 Ardwick Hall, Manchester, England

Scottish cotton spinner and textile machine maker.

Kennedy was the third son of his father, Robert, and went to the village school in Dalry. On his father's death, he was sent at the age of 14 to Chowbent, Lancashire, where he was apprenticed to William Cannan, a maker of textile machines such as carding frames, **Hargreaves**'s jennies and **Arkwright**'s waterframes. On completion of his apprenticeship in 1791, he moved

to Manchester and entered into partnership with Benjamin and William Sandford and James M'-Connel, textile machine makers and mule spinners. In 1795 this partnership was terminated and one was made with James M'Connel to form the firm M'Connel & Kennedy, cotton spinners.

Kennedy introduced improvements for spinning fine yarns and the firm of M'Connel & Kennedy became famous for the quality of these products, which were in great demand. He made the spindles turn faster during the second part of the mule carriage's outward draw, and from 1793 onwards he experimented with driving mules by steam engines. Like William **Kelly** at New Lanark, he succeeded in making the spinning sequences power-operated by 1800, although the spinner had to take over the winding on. This made the mule into a factory machine, but it still required skilled operators. He was also involved with Henry **Houldsworth**, Junior, in the improvement of the roving frame. In 1803 Kennedy joined the Manchester Literary & Philosophical Society, to which he presented several papers, including one in 1830 on 'A memoir of Samuel Crompton'. He retired from the spinning business in 1826, but continued his technical and mechanical pursuits. He was consulted about whether the Liverpool & Manchester Railway should have moving or stationary steam engines and was an umpire at the Rainhill Trials in 1829.

Further Reading
Dictionary of National Biography.
W. Fairbairn, obituary, *Manchester Memoirs*, Manchester Literary and Philosophical Society.
C.H. Lee, 1972, *A Cotton Enterprise 1795–1840. A History of M'Connel & Kennedy, Fine Cotton Spinners*, Manchester (an account of Kennedy's spinning business).
R.L. Hills, 1970, *Power in the Industrial Revolution*, Manchester (provides details of Kennedy's inventions on the mule).

RLH

Kennelly, Arthur Edwin
b. 17 December 1871 Colaba, Bombay, India
d. 18 June 1939 Boston, Massachusetts, USA

Anglo-American electrical engineer who predicted the ionosphere and developed mathematical analysis for electronic circuits.

As a young man, Kennelly worked as office boy for a London engineering society, as an electrician and on a cable-laying ship. In 1887 he went to work for Thomas **Edison** at West Orange, New Jersey, USA, becoming his chief assistant. In 1894, with Edwin J. Houston, he formed the Philadelphia company of Houston and Kennelly, but eight years later he took up the Chair of Electrical Engineering at Harvard, a post he held until his retirement in 1930. In 1902 he noticed that the radio signals received by **Marconi** in Nova Scotia from the transmitter in England were stronger than predicted and postulated a reflecting ionized layer in the upper atmosphere. Almost simultaneously the same prediction was made in England by **Heaviside**, so the layer became known as the Kennelly–Heaviside layer. Throughout most of his working life Kennelly was concerned with the application of mathematical techniques, particularly the use of complex theory, to the analysis of electrical circuits. With others he also contributed to an understanding of the high-frequency skin-effect in conductors.

Principal Honours and Distinctions

President, American Institute of Electrical Engineers 1898–1900. President, Institution of Electrical Engineers 1916. Institute of Electrical and Electronics Engineers Medal of Honour 1932; Edison Medal 1933.

Bibliography

1915, with F.A. Laws & P.H. Pierce 'Experimental research on the skin effect in conductors', *Transactions of the American Institute of Electrical Engineers* 34: 1,953.

1924, *Hyperbolic Functions as Applied to Electrical Engineering*.

1924, *Check Atlas of Complex Hyperbolic & Circular Functions* (both on mathematics for circuit analysis).

Further Reading

K. Davies, 1990, *Ionospheric Radio*, London: Peter Peregrinus.

See also **Appleton, Sir Edward Victor**.

KF

Kettering, Charles Franklin

b. 29 August 1876 near Londonsville, Ohio, USA
d. 25 November 1958 Dayton, Ohio, USA

American engineer and inventor.

Kettering gained degrees in mechanical and electrical engineering from Ohio State University. He was employed by the National Construction Register (NCR) of Dayton, Ohio, where he devised an electric motor for use in cash registers. He became Head of the Inventions Department of that company but left in 1909 to form, with the former Works Manager of NCR, Edward A. Deeds, the Dayton Engineering Laboratories (later called Delco), to develop improved lighting and ignition systems for automobiles. In the first two years of the new company he produced not only these but also the first self-starter, both of which were fitted to the Cadillac, America's leading luxury car. In 1914 he founded Dayton Metal Products and the Dayton Wright Airplane Company. Two years later Delco was bought by General Motors. In 1925 the independent research facilities of Delco were moved to Detroit and merged with General Motors' laboratories to form General Motors Research Corporation, of which Kettering was President and General Manager. (He had been Vice-President of General Motors since 1920.) In that position he headed investigations into methods of achieving maximum engine performance as well as into the nature of friction and combustion. Many other developments in the automobile field were made under his leadership, such as engine coolers, variable-speed transmissions, balancing machines, the two-way shock absorber, high-octane fuel, leaded petrol or gasoline, fast-drying lacquers, crank-case ventilators, chrome plating, and the high-compression automobile engine. Among his other activities were the establishment of the Charles Franklin Kettering Foundation for the Study of Chlorophyll and Photosynthesis at Antioch College, and the founding of the Sloan–Kettering Institute for Cancer Research in New York City. He sponsored the Fever Therapy Research Project at Miami Valley Hospital at Dayton, which developed the hypertherm, or artificial fever machine, for use in the treatment of disease. He resigned from General Motors in 1947.

IMcN

Kilby, Jack St Clair

b. 8 November 1923 Jefferson City, Missouri, USA

American engineer who filed the first patents for micro-electronic (integrated) circuits.

Kilby spent most of his childhood in Great Bend, Kansas, where he often accompanied his father, an electrical power engineer, on his maintenance rounds. Working in the blizzard of 1937, his father borrowed a 'ham' radio, and this fired Jack to study for his amateur licence (W9GTY) and to construct his own equipment while still a student at Great Bend High School. In 1941 he entered the University of Illinois, but four months later, after the attack on Pearl Harbor, he was enlisted in the US Army and found himself working in a radio repair workshop in India. When the war ended he returned to his studies, obtaining his BSEE from Illinois in 1947 and his MSEE from the University of Wisconsin. He then joined Centralab, a small electronics firm in Milwaukee owned by Globe-Union. There he filed twelve patents, including some for reduced titanate capacitors and for Steatite-packing of transistors, and developed a transistorized hearing-aid. During this period he also attended a course on transistors at Bell Laboratories. In May 1958, concerned to gain experience in the field of number processing, he joined Texas Instruments in Dallas. Shortly afterwards, while working alone during the factory vacation, he conceived the idea of making monolithic, or integrated, circuits by diffusing impurities into a silicon substrate to create P–N junctions. Within less than a month he had produced a complete oscillator on a chip to prove that the technology was feasible, and the following year at the IERE Show he demonstrated a germanium integrated-circuit flip-flop. Initially he was granted a patent for the idea, but eventually, after protracted litigation, priority was awarded to Robert **Noyce** of Fairchild. In 1965 he was commissioned by Patrick Haggerty, the Chief Executive of Texas Instruments, to make a pocket calculator based on integrated circuits, and on 14 April 1971 the world's first such device, the Pocketronic, was launched onto the market. Costing $150 (and weighing some 2½ lb or 1.1 kg), it was an instant success and in 1972 some 5 million calculators were sold worldwide. He left Texas Instruments in November 1970 to become an independent consultant and inventor, working on, amongst other things, methods of deriving electricity from sunlight.

Principal Honours and Distinctions

Franklin Institute Stuart Ballantine Medal 1966. Institute of Electrical and Electronics Engineers David Sarnoff Award 1966; Cledo Brunetti Award (jointly with Noyce) 1978; Medal of Honour 1986. National Academy of Engineering 1967. National Science Medal 1969. National Inventors Hall of Fame 1982. Honorary DEng Miami 1982, Rochester 1986. Honorary DSc Wisconsin 1988. Distinguished Professor, Texas A & M University.

Bibliography

6 February 1959, US patent no. 3,138,743 (the first integrated circuit (IC); initially granted June 1964).
US patent no. 3,819,921 (the Pocketronic calculator).

Further Reading

T.R. Reid, 1984, *Microchip. The Story of a Revolution and the Men Who Made It*, London: Pan Books (for the background to the development of the integrated circuit).
H. Queisser, 1988, *Conquest of the Microchip*, Cambridge, Mass.: Harvard University Press.

KF

Kind, Karl Gotthelf

b. 6 June 1801 Linda, near Freiberg, Germany
d. 9 March 1873 Saarbrücken, Germany

German engineer, pioneer in deep drilling.

The son of an ore miner in Saxony, Kind was engaged in his father's profession for some years before he joined **Glenck**'s drillings for salt at Stotternheim, Thuringia. There in 1835, after trying for five years, he self-reliantly put down a 340 m (1,100 ft) deep well; his success lay in his use of fish joints of a similar construction to those used shortly before by von **Oeynhausen** in Westphalia. In order to improve their operational possibilities in aquiferous wells, in 1842 he developed his own free-fall device between the rod and the drill, which enabled the chisel to reach the bottom of the hole without hindrance. His invention was patented in France. Four years later, at Mondorf, Luxembourg, he put down a

736 m (2,415 ft) deep borehole, the deepest in the world at that time.

Kind contributed further considerable improvements to deep drilling and was the first successfully to replace iron rods with wooden ones, on account of their buoyancy in water. The main reasons for his international reputation were his attempts to bore out shafts, which he carried out for the first time in the region of Forbach, France, in 1848. Three years later he was engaged in the Ruhr area by a Belgian- and English-financed mining company, later the Dahlbusch mining company in Gelsenkirchen, to drill a hole that was later enlarged to 4.4 m (14½ ft) and made watertight by lining. Although he had already taken out a patent for boring and lining shafts in 1849 in Belgium, his wooden support did not qualify. It was the Belgian engineer Joseph **Chaudron,** in charge of the mining company, who overcame the difficulty of making the bottom of the borehole watertight. In 1854 they jointly founded a shaft-sinking company in Brussels which specialized in aquiferous formations and operated internationally.

Principal Honours and Distinctions
Chevalier de la Légion d'honneur 1849.

Bibliography
1842, *Anleitung zum Abteufen von Bohrlöchern*, Luxembourg.

Further Reading
H.G. Conrad, 'Carl Gotthelf Kind', *Neue deutsche Biographie* 10: 613–14.
D. Hoffmann, 1959, *150 Jahre Tiefbohrungen in Deutschland*, Vienna and Hamburg, pp. 20–5 (assesses his technological achievements).
T. Tecklenburg, 1914, *Handbuch der Tiefbohrkunde*, 2nd end, Vol. VI, Berlin, pp. 36–9 (provides a detailed description of his equipment).
J. Chaudron, 1862, 'Über die nach dem Kindschen Erdbohrverfahren in Belgien ausgeführten Schachtbohrarbeiten', *Berg- und Hüttenmännische Zeitung* 21: 402–4, (describes his contribution to making Kind's shafts watertight).

WK

King, James Foster
b. 9 May 1862 Erskine, Scotland
d. 11 August 1947 Glasgow, Scotland

Scottish naval architect and classification society manager who made a significant contribution to the safety of shipping.

King was educated at the High School of Glasgow, and then served an apprenticeship with the Port Glasgow shipyard of Russell & Co. This was followed by experience in drawing offices in Port Glasgow, Hull and finally in Belfast, where he was responsible for the separate White Star Line drawing office of Harland & Wolff Ltd, which was then producing the plans for the Atlantic passenger liners *Majestic* and *Teutonic*. Following certain unpopular government shipping enactments in 1890, a protest from shipbuilders and shipowners in Ireland, Liverpool and the West of Scotland led to the founding of a new classification society to compete against Lloyd's Register of Shipping. It became known as the British Corporation Register and had headquarters in Glasgow. King was recruited to the staff and by 1903 had become Chief Surveyor, a position he held until his retirement thirty-seven years later. By then the Register was a world leader, with hundreds of thousands of tons of shipping on its books; it acted as consultant to many governments and international agencies. Throughout his working life, King did everything in his power to quantify the risks and problems of ship operation: his contribution to the Load Lines Convention of 1929 was typical, and few major enactments in shipping were designed without his approval. During the inter-war period the performance of the British Corporation outshone that of all rivals, for which King deserved full credit. His especial understanding was for steel structures, and in this respect he ensured that the British Corporation enabled owners to build ships of strengths equal to any others despite using up to 10 per cent less steel within the structure. In 1949 Lloyd's Register of Shipping and the British Corporation merged to form the largest and most influential ship classification society in the world.

Principal Honours and Distinctions
CBE 1920. Honorary Member, Institution of Engineers and Shipbuilders in Scotland 1941; North East Coast Institution of Engineers and

Shipbuilders (Newcastle) 1943; British Corporation 1940. Honorary Vice-President, Institution of Naval Architects.

Further Reading
G. Blake, 1960, *Lloyd's Register of Shipping 1760–1960*, London: Lloyd's Register.
F.M. Walker, 1984, *Song of the Clyde. A History of Clyde Shipbuilding*, Cambridge: PSL.
1947, *The British Corporation Register of Shipping and Aircraft 1890–1947, An Illustrated Record*, 1947, Glasgow.
1946, *The British Corporation Register. The War Years in Retrospect*, 1956, Glasgow.

FMW

Kirk, Alexander Carnegie
b. *c*.1830 Barry, Angus, Scotland
d. 5 October 1892 Glasgow, Scotland

Scottish marine engineer, advocate of multiple-expansion in steam reciprocating engines.

Kirk was a son of the manse, and after attending school at Arbroath he proceeded to Edinburgh University. Following graduation he served an apprenticeship at the Vulcan Foundry, Glasgow, before serving first as Chief Draughtsman with the Thames shipbuilders and engineers Maudslay Sons & Field, and later as Engineer of Paraffin Young's Works at Bathgate and West Calder in Lothian. He was credited with the inventions of many ingenious appliances and techniques for improving production in these two establishments. About 1866 Kirk returned to Glasgow as Manager of the Cranstonhill Engine Works, then moved to Elder's Shipyard (later known as the Fairfield Company) as Engineering Manager. There he made history in producing the world's first triple-expansion engines for the single-screw steamship *Propontis* in 1874. That decade was to confirm the Clyde's leading role as shipbuilders to the world and to establish the iron ship with efficient reciprocating machinery as the workhorse of the British Merchant Marine. Upon the death of the great Clyde shipbuilder Robert **Napier** in 1876, Kirk and others took over as partners in the shipbuilding yard and engine shops of Robert Napier & Sons. There in 1881 they built a ship that is acknowledged as one of the masterpieces of British shipbuilding: the SS *Aberdeen* for George Thompson's Aberdeen Line to the Far East. In this ship the fullest advantage was taken of high steam temperatures and pressures, which were expanded progressively in a three-cylinder configuration. The *Aberdeen*, in its many voyages from London to China and Japan, was to prove the efficiency of these engines that had been so carefully designed in Glasgow. In the following years Dr Kirk (he has always been known as Doctor, although his honorary LLD was only awarded by Glasgow University in 1888) persuaded the Admiralty and several shipping companies to accept not only triple-expansion machinery but also the use of mild steel in ship construction. The successful SS *Parisian*, built for the Allan Line of Glasgow, was one of these pioneer ships.

Principal Honours and Distinctions
Fellow of the Royal Society of Edinburgh.

FMW

Kirkaldy, David
b. 4 April 1820 Mayfield, Dundee, Scotland
d. 25 January 1897 London, England

Scottish engineer and pioneer in materials testing.

The son of a merchant of Dundee, Kirkaldy was educated there, then at Merchiston Castle School, Edinburgh, and at Edinburgh University. For a while he worked in his father's office, but with a preference for engineering, in 1843 he commenced an apprenticeship at the Glasgow works of Robert **Napier**. After four years in the shops he was transferred to the drawing office and in a very few years rose to become Chief. Here Kirkaldy demonstrated a remarkable talent both for the meticulous recording of observations and data and for technical drawing. His work also had an aesthetic appeal and four of his drawings of Napier steamships were shown at the Paris Exhibition of 1855, earning both Napier and Kirkaldy a medal. His 'as fitted' set of drawings of the Cunard Liner *Persia*, which had been built in 1855, is now in the possession of the National Maritime Museum at Greenwich, London; it is regarded as one of the finest examples of its kind in the world, and has even been exhibited at the Royal Academy in London.

With the impending order for the Royal Naval Ironclad *Black Prince* (sister ship to HMS *Warrior*, now preserved at Portsmouth) and for some high-pressure marine boilers and engines, there was need for a close scientific analysis of the physical properties of iron and steel. Kirkaldy, now designated Chief Draughtsman and Calculator, was placed in charge of this work, which included comparisons of puddled steel and wrought iron, using a simple lever-arm testing machine. The tests lasted some three years and resulted in Kirkaldy's most important publication, *Experiments on Wrought Iron and Steel* (1862, London), which gained him wide recognition for his careful and thorough work. Napier's did not encourage him to continue testing; but realizing the growing importance of materials testing, Kirkaldy resigned from the shipyard in 1861. For the next two and a half years Kirkaldy worked on the design of a massive testing machine that was manufactured in Leeds and installed in premises in London, at The Grove, Southwark. The works was open for trade in January 1866 and engineers soon began to bring him specimens for testing on the great machine: Joseph Cubitt (son of William **Cubitt**) brought him samples of the materials for the new Blackfriars Bridge, which was then under construction. Soon The Grove became too cramped and Kirkaldy moved to 99 Southwark Street, reopening in January 1874. In the years that followed, Kirkaldy gained a worldwide reputation for rigorous and meticulous testing and recording of results, coupled with the highest integrity. He numbered the most distinguished engineers of the time among his clients.

After Kirkaldy's death, his son William George, whom he had taken into partnership, carried on the business. When the son died in 1914, his widow took charge until her death in 1938, when the grandson David became proprietor. He sold out to Treharne & Davies, chemical consultants, in 1965, but the works finally closed in 1974. The future of the premises and the testing machine at first seemed threatened, but that has now been secured and the machine is once more in working order. Over almost one hundred years of trading in South London, the company was involved in many famous enquiries, including the analysis of the iron from the ill-fated Tay Bridge (see **Bouch, Sir Thomas**).

Principal Honours and Distinctions
Institution of Engineers and Shipbuilders in Scotland Gold Medal 1864.

Bibliography
1862, *Results of an Experimental Inquiry into the Tensile Strength and Other Properties of Wrought Iron and Steel* (originally presented as a paper to the 1860–1 session of the Scottish Shipbuilders' Association).

Further Reading
D.P. Smith, 1981, 'David Kirkaldy (1820–97) and engineering materials testing', *Transactions of the Newcomen Society* 52:49–65 (a clear and well-documented account).

LRD/FMW

Kirtley, Matthew
b. 6 February 1813 Tanfield, Co. Durham, England
d. 24 May 1873 Derby, England

English locomotive engineer, responsible for the introduction of the brick arch in fireboxes.

At the age of 13, Kirtley was a pupil of George **Stephenson** on the Stockton & Darlington Railway. He subsequently became a fireman and then a driver of locomotives: he drove the first locomotive to enter London on the London & Birmingham Railway. When the Midland Railway was formed in 1844 he was appointed Locomotive Superintendent. Ever since the Act of Parliament for the Liverpool & Manchester Railway had required that its locomotives consume their own smoke (probably as a reaction to the clouds of black smoke emitted by steamboats at Liverpool), the usual fuel for locomotives had been coke. Early multi-tubular boilers, with their small fireboxes and short tubes, were in any case unsuitable for coal because they did not allow the burning gases sufficient time to combust properly. Many engineers attempted to solve the problem with weird and complex boiler designs. Kirtley and Charles Markham, who was working under him, succeeded by inserting a deflector plate above the firedoor and an arch of firebricks in the front of the firebox: this helped to maintain the high temperatures needed and lengthened the route by which the gases travelled. The brick arch and deflector plate became the usual components of locomotive fireboxes, and expensive coke was replaced as fuel by coal.

Further Reading
J. Marshall, 1978, *A Biographical Dictionary of*

Railway Engineers, Newton Abbot: David & Charles.

E.L. Ahrons, 1927, *The British Steam Railway Locomotive 1825–1925*, London: The Locomotive Publishing Co. (describes the brick arch and Kirtley's locomotives).

PJGR

Klic, Karol (Klietsch, Karl)
b. 31 May 1841 Arnau, Bohemia (now Czech Republic)
d. 16 November 1826 Vienna, Austria

Czech inventor of photogravure and rotogravure.

Klic, sometimes known by the germanized form of his name Karl Klietsch, gained a knowledge of chemistry from his chemist father. However, he inclined towards the arts, preferring to mix paints rather than chemicals, and he trained in art at the Academy of Painting in Prague. His father thought to combine the chemical with the artistic by setting up his son in a photographic studio in Brno, but the arts won and in 1867 Klic moved to Vienna to practise as an illustrator and caricaturist. He also acquired skill as an etcher, and this led him to print works of art reproduced by photography by means of an intaglio process. He perfected the process *c.*1878 and, through it, Vienna became for a while the world centre for high-quality art reproductions. The prints were made by hand from flat plates, but Klic then proposed that the images should be etched onto power-driven cylinders. He found little support for rotary gravure, or rotogravure, on the European continent, but learning that Storey Brothers, textile printers of Lancaster, England, were working in a similar direction, he went there in 1890 to perfect his idea. Rotogravure printing on textiles began in 1893. They then turned to printing art reproductions on paper by rotogravure and in 1895 formed the Rembrandt Intaglio Printing Company. Their photogravures attracted worldwide attention when they appeared in the *Magazine of Art*. Klic saw photogravure as a small-scale medium for the art lover and not for mass-circulation publications, so he did not patent his invention and thought to control it by secrecy. That had the usual result, however, and knowledge of the process leaked out from Storey's, spreading to other countries in Europe and, from 1903, to the USA. Klic lived on in a modest way in Vienna, his later years troubled by failing sight. He hardly earned the credit for the invention, let alone the fortune reaped by others who used, and still use, photogravure for printing long runs of copy such as newspaper colour supplements.

Further Reading
Obituary, 1927, *Inland Printer* (January): 614.
Karol Klic. vynálezu hlubotisku, 1957, Prague (the only full-length biography; in Czech, with an introduction in English, French and German).
S.H. Horgan, 1925, 'The invention of photogravure', *Inland Printer* (April): 64 (contains brief details of his life and works).
G. Wakeman, 1973, *Victorian Book Illustration*, Newton Abbot: David & Charles, pp. 126–8.

LRD

Knight, John Peake
b. 1828
d. 1886

English railway engineer, inventor of the first road traffic lights in Britain.

Knight was initially employed as a clerk at the Midland Railway in Derby, and in 1846 he had a job in the audit office of the Brighton Railway. From 1854 to 1869 he was Superintendent of the South Eastern Railway and then became manager of the London, Brighton and South Coast Railway, a post he held until his death. During this period many improvements were put in hand, including the interlocking of signals, the block system, the incorporation of Westinghouse brakes (in 1878), Pullman cars (1877) and electric lighting.

In 1868 it was decided to erect the first set of traffic lights in London in Bridge Street, New Palace Yard, Westminster, and the authorities naturally sought the advice of an engineer familiar with railway practice. Thus John Knight was called in, and red and green lights mounted on the ends of semaphore arms were duly installed. Unfortunately, a fault in the gas supply of this set of lights caused an explosion which killed a police constable.

Principal Honours and Distinctions
Lieutenant-Colonel, Engineer and Railway Volunteer Staff Corps 1870–86. Associate, Institution of Civil Engineers 1872. Legion of Honour 1878.

Further Reading
Obituary, 1886, *The Engineer* 62.

IMcN

Knight, Margaret E.
b. 1838 Maine, USA
d. 1914 USA

American inventor.

Little is known of Knight's childhood, except that she was probably educated to high school level. She made her first invention at the age of 12, after seeing a woman cotton-mill worker injured when a dislodged shuttle fell on her. Knight set herself to design a mechanism that would shut down the machine if the thread broke and caused a shuttle to fly out. The device was widely used by cotton and woollen mills. Between that and her first patent in 1870, little is known of her activities; but she then embarked on a career of invention, achieving over 90 of them, earning herself the title 'the female **Edison**'. Perhaps her most notable invention was a machine for making paper bags with square or satchel bottoms, which proved to be of great benefit to shoppers until the advent of the plastic bag. It won her little financial reward, but a decoration from Queen Victoria. Her other two main inventions related to the manufacture of shoes and, around 1902, to a rotary automobile engine. She worked for various companies, assigning to them her patent rights, so that at her death her estate was valued at less than $300.

Further Reading
A. Stanley, 1993, *Mothers and Daughters of Invention*, Meruchen, NJ: Scarecrow Press.

LRD

Koch, Robert
b. 11 December 1843 Clausthal, Hannover, Germany
d. 28 May 1910 Baden-Baden, Germany

German bacteriologist and innovator of many bacteriological techniques, including the process of bacteria-free water filtration and the introduction of solid cultivation media.

Koch studied medicine at Göttingen and graduated MD in 1866. He served in the war of 1870, and in 1872 was appointed Medical Officer at Wollstein. It was there that he commenced his bacteriological researches which led to numerous technical advances and the culture of the anthrax bacillus in 1876.

Appointed in 1880 to the Imperial Health Office in Berlin, he perfected his methods and was appointed Professor of Hygiene in the University of Berlin in 1885. From 1886 he was editor of the *Zeitschrift für Hygiene und Infektionskrankheiten,* which was published in Leipzig. In 1891 he became Director of the Institute for Infectious Diseases, founded for him in Berlin. He had already discovered the tubercle bacillus in 1882 and the cholera vibrio in 1883. He travelled extensively in India, Africa and South Africa in connection with research into bubonic plague, malaria, rinderpest and sleeping sickness. His name will always be associated with Koch's postulates, the propositions which need to be satisfied before attributing a disease to a specific infective agent.

Principal Honours and Distinctions
Nobel Prize for Medicine or Physiology 1905.

Bibliography
1877, 'Verfahrungen zur Untersuchung zum Conservieren und Photographieren der Bacterien', *Beitr. Biol. Pflanzen.*

Further Reading
M. Kirchner, 1924, *Robert Koch.*

MG

Koenig, Friedrich
b. 17 April 1774 Eisleben, Thuringia, Germany
d. 17 January 1833 Oberzell, near Würzburg, Germany

German inventor of the machine printing press.

Koenig became a printer and bookseller. Around 1800 he was among those who conceived the idea of mechanizing the hand printing press, which apart from minor details had survived virtually unchanged through the first three and a half centuries of printing. In 1803, in Suhl, Saxony, he designed a press in which the flat forme, carrying the type, was mechanically inked and passed to and from the platen. Whether this machine was ever constructed is not known, but Koenig found little support for his ideas because of lack of technical and financial resources. So, in 1806, he went to England and was introduced to

Thomas Bensley, a book printer off Fleet Street in London. Bensley agreed to support Koenig and brought in two other printers to help finance Koenig's experiments. Another German, Andreas Bauer, an engineer, assisted Koenig and became largely responsible for the practical execution of Koenig's plans.

In 1810 they patented a press which was steam-driven but still used a platen. It was set to work in Bensley's office the following year but did not prove to be satisfactory. Koenig redesigned it, and in October 1811 he obtained a patent for a steam-driven press on an entirely new principle. In place of the platen, the paper was fixed around a hollow rotating cylinder, which impressed the paper on to the inked forme. In Bensley's office it was used for book printing, but its increased speed over the hand press appealed to newspaper proprietors and John Walter II of *The Times* asked Koenig to make a double-cylinder machine, so that the return stroke of the forme would be productive. A further patent was taken out in 1813 and the new machine was made ready to print the 29 November 1814 issue – in secrecy, behind closed doors, to forestall opposition from the pressmen working the hand presses. An important feature of the machine was that the inking rollers were not of the traditional leather or skin but a composite material made from glue, molasses and some soda. The inking could not have been achieved satisfactorily with the old materials. The editorial of that historic issue proclaimed, 'Our Journal of this day presents to the public the practical result of the greatest improvement connected with printing, since the discovery of the art itself.' Koenig's machine press could make 1,200 impressions an hour compared to 200 with the hand press; further improvements raised this figure to 1,500–2,000. Koenig's last English patent was in 1814 for an improved cylinder machine and a perfecting machine, which printed both sides of the paper. The steam-driven perfecting press was printing books in Bensley's office in February 1816. Koenig and Bauer wanted by that time to manufacture machine presses for other customers, but Bensley, now the principal shareholder, insisted that they should make machines for his benefit only. Finding this restriction intolerable, Koenig and Bauer returned to Germany: they became partners in a factory at Oberzell, near Würzburg, in 1817 and the firm

of Koenig and Bauer flourishes there to this day.

Further Reading
J. Moran, 1973, *Printing Presses*, London: Faber & Faber.
T. Goebel, 1956, *Friedrich Koenig und die Erfindung der Schnellpresse*, Würzburg.

LRD

Koepe, Friedrich
b. 1 July 1835 Bergkamen, Westphalia, Germany
d. 12 September 1922 Bochum, Germany

German mining engineer, inventor of the friction winder for shaft hoisting.

After attending the School of Mines at Bochum, from 1862 he worked as an overseer in the coal-mining district of Ibbenbüren until he joined a mining company in the Ruhr area. There, as head of the machine shop, he was mainly concerned with sinking new shafts. In 1873 he became the Technical Director of the Hannover mine, near Bochum, which belonged to **Krupp**. When the shaft hoisting was to be extended to a lower level Koepe conceived the idea of applying a friction winder to the hoist instead of a drum, in order to save weight and costs. His method involved the use of an endless rope to which the cages were fixed without a safety catch. The rope passed over pulleys instead of coiling and uncoiling on a drum, and he consequently proposed to have the motor erected on top of the shaft rather than beside it, as had been the practice until then.

Koepe's innovation turned out to be highly effective for hoisting heavy loads from deep shafts and was still popular in many countries in the 1990s, although the Krupp company did not accept it for a long time. He had severe personal problems with the company, and as Krupp refused to have his system patented he had to take it out in his own name in 1877. However, Krupp did not pay for the extension of the patent, nor did they pass the dossiers over to him, so the patent expired two years later. It was not until 1888 that a hoisting engine equipped with a friction winder was erected for the first time in a head gear, above the new Hannover II shaft. The following year Koepe left the Krupp company and settled as a freelance consulting engineer in Bochum; he was successful in having his system introduced by other mining companies. Ironically, in 1948 the world's first four-rope winding, based on his system, was installed at the Hannover mine.

Further Reading

For detailed biographical information and an assessment of his technological achievements see:

H. Arnold and W. Kroker, 1977, '100 Jahre Schachtförderung nach dem System Koepe', *Der Anschnitt* 29: 235–42.

F. Lange, 1952, *Die Vierseilförderung*, Essen.
WK

Kolff, Willem Johan

b. 14 February 1914 Leiden, the Netherlands

Dutch physician and inventor of the first effective artificial kidney.

Kolff studied at Leiden Medical School and qualified in 1938. While studying at Gröningen in 1938, in the utilization of cellulose sausage skin which had become available he designed an artificial kidney, developing the work of **Abel** in animal experiments.

At the outbreak of the Second World War he was banished to a provincial town. Even so, he succeeded in making some clandestine machines, one of which was effective in saving the life of a patient with acute renal failure. During 1950–67 he continued in general practice and at the University of Leiden, and in 1958–67 he was head of department and Professor of the Division of Artificial Organs at the University of Utah College of Medicine, Salt Lake City, USA. He was decorated for his services in the establishment of blood banks in Holland during the war.

Bibliography

1944, 'The artificial kidney: dialyser with great area', *Acta. Med. Scand.*

1962, 'First clinical experience with the artificial kidney', *Annals of Internal Medicine* 62.

1990, 'The invention of the artificial heart', *International Journal of Artificial Organs*.

Further Reading

Abel *et al.*, 1913, 'On the removal of diffusible substances form the circulating blood by means of dialysis', *Transactions of the Association of American Physicians* 28.
MG

Kompfner, Rudolph

b. 16 May 1909 Vienna, Austria
d. 3 December 1977 Stanford, California, USA

Austrian (naturalized English in 1949, American in 1957) electrical engineer primarily known for his invention of the travelling-wave tube.

Kompfner obtained a degree in engineering from the Vienna Technische Hochschule in 1931 and qualified as a Diplom-Ingenieur in Architecture two years later. The following year, with a worsening political situation in Austria, he moved to England and became an architectural apprentice. In 1936 he became Managing Director of a building firm owned by a relative, but at the same time he was avidly studying physics and electronics. His first patent, for a television pick-up device, was filed in 1935 and granted in 1937, but was not in fact taken up. In June 1940 he was interned on the Isle of Man, but as a result of a paper previously sent by him to the Editor of *Wireless Engineer* he was released the following December and sent to join the group at Birmingham University working on centimetric radar. There he worked on klystrons, with little success, but as a result of the experience gained he eventually invented the travelling-wave tube (TWT), which was based on a helical transmission line. After disbandment of the Birmingham team, in 1946 Kompfner moved to the Clarendon Laboratory at Oxford and in 1947 he became a British subject. At the Clarendon Laboratory he met J.R. **Pierce** of Bell Laboratories, who worked out the theory of operation of the TWT. After gaining his DPhil at Oxford in 1951, Kompfner accepted a post as Principal Scientific Officer at Signals Electronic Research Laboratories, Baldock, but very soon after that he was invited by Pierce to work at Bell on microwave tubes. There, in 1952, he invented the backward-wave oscillator (BWO). He was appointed Director of Electronics Research in 1955 and Director of Communications Research in 1962, having become a US citizen in 1957. In 1958, with Pierce, he designed Echo 1, the first (passive) satellite, which was launched in August 1960. He was also involved with the development of Telstar, the first active communications satellite, which was launched in 1962. Following his retirement from Bell in 1973, he continued to pursue research, alternately at Stanford, California, and Oxford, England.

Principal Honours and Distinctions
Physical Society Duddell Medal 1955. Franklin Institute Stuart Ballantine Medal 1960. Institute of Electrical and Electronics Engineers David Sarnoff Award 1960. Member of the National Academy of Engineering 1966. Member of the National Academy of Science 1968. Institute of Electrical and Electronics Engineers Medal of Honour 1973. City of Philadelphia John Scott Award 1974. Roentgen Society Silvanus Thompson Medal 1974. President's National medal of Science 1974. Honorary doctorates Vienna 1965, Oxford 1969.

Bibliography
1944, 'Velocity modulated beams', *Wireless Engineer* 17: 262.
1942, 'Transit time phenomena in electronic tubes', *Wireless Engineer* 19: 3.
1942, 'Velocity modulating grids', *Wireless Engineer* 19: 158.
1946, 'The travelling-wave tube', *Wireless Engineer* 42: 369.
1964, *The Invention of the TWT*, San Francisco: San Francisco Press.

Further Reading
J.R. Pierce, 1992, 'History of the microwave tube art', *Proceedings of the Institute of Radio Engineers*: 980.

KF

Korolov (Korolyev), Sergei Pavlovich
b. 12 January 1907 (30 December 1906 Old Style) Zhitomir, Ukraine
d. 14 January 1966 Moscow, Russia

Russian engineer and designer of air- and spacecraft.

His early life was spent in the Ukraine and he then studied at **Tupolev**'s aeroplane institute in Moscow. In the mid-1930s, just before his thirtieth birthday, he joined the GIRD (Group Studying Rocket Propulsion) under Frederick Zander, a Latvian engineer, while earning a living designing aircraft in Tupolev's bureau. In

1934 he visited **Konstantin Tsiolovsky**. Soon after this, under the Soviet Armaments Minister, Mikhail N. Tukhachevsky, who was in favour of rocket weapons, financial support was available for the GIRD and Korolov was appointed General-Engineer (1-star) in the Soviet Army. In June 1937 the Armaments Minister and his whole staff were arrested under Stalin, but Korolov was saved by Tupolev and sent to a *sharaska*, or prison, near Moscow where he worked for four years on rocket- and jet-propelled aircraft, among other things. In 1946 he went with his superior, Valentin Glushko, to Germany where he watched the British test-firing of possibly three V-2s at Altenwaide, near Cuxhaven, in 'Operation Backfire'. They were not allowed within the wire enclosure. He remained in Germany to supervise the shipment of V-2 equipment and staff to Russia (it is possible that he underwent a second term of imprisonment from 1948), the Germans having been arrested in October 1946. He kept working in Russia until 1950 or the following year. He supervised the first Russian ballistic missile, R-1, in late 1947. Stalin died in 1953 and Korolov was rehabilitated, but freedom under Nikita Kruschev was almost as restrictive as imprisonment under Stalin. Kruschev would only refer to him as 'the Chief Designer', never naming him, and would not let him go abroad or correspond with other rocket experts in the USA or Germany. Anything he published could only be under the name 'Sergeyev'. He continued to work on his R-7 without the approval that he sought for a satellite project. This was known as *semyorka*, or 'old number seven'. In January 1959 he added a booster stage to *semyorka*. He may have suffered confinement in the infamous Kolyma Gulag around this time. He designed all the Sputnik, Vostok and some of the Voshkod units and worked on the Proton space booster. In 1966 he underwent surgery performed by Dr Boris Petrovsky, then Soviet Minister of Health, for the removal, it is said, of tumours of the colon. In spite of the assistance of Dr Aleksandr Vishaevsky he bled to death on the operating table. The first moon landing (by robot) took place three weeks after his death and the first flight of the new Soyuz spacecraft a little later.

Further Reading
Y. Golanov, 1975, *Sergey Korolev. The Appren-*

ticeship of a Space Pioneer, Moscow: Mir.

A. Romanov, 1976, *Spacecraft Designers*, Moscow: Novosti Press Agency.

J.E. Oberg, 1981, *Red Star in Orbit*, New York: Random House.

IMcN

Krauss, Georg

b. 25 December 1826 Augsburg, Germany
d. 5 November 1906 Munich, Germany

German locomotive engineer, founder of the locomotive builders Krauss & Co.

Krauss entered the Maffei locomotive works, Munich, as a fitter and subsequently worked successively for the Bavarian State Railways and the Swiss North Eastern Railway, which he left in 1866 to found Locomotivfabrik Krauss in Munich. The firm became one of the most important locomotive builders in Germany. A second factory was established in Munich in 1872 and a third at Linz, Austria, in 1880: by the time of Krauss's death, these factories had built more than 5,500 locomotives. The second Munich factory was predominantly for small locomotives, and to increase the sales of these Krauss promoted the construction of many local railways in south Germany and Austria. The firm survived to amalgamate with Maffei and take the name Krauss–Maffei AG in 1940.

Further Reading
J. Marshall, 1978, *A Biographical Dictionary of Railway Engineers*, Newton Abbot: David & Charles.
Biographical note, 1985–6, *Transactions of the Newcomen Society* 57: 46.

PJGR

Krupp, Alfred

b. 26 April 1812 Essen, Germany
d. 14 July 1887 Bredeney, near Essen, Germany

German manufacturer of steel and armaments.

Krupp's father founded a small cast-steel works at Essen, but at his early death in 1826 the firm was left practically insolvent to his sons. Alfred's formal education ended at that point and he entered the ailing firm. The expansion of trade brought about by the Zollverein, or customs union, enabled him to increase output, and by 1843 he had 100 workers under him, making steel springs and machine parts. Five years later he was able to buy out his co-heirs, and in 1849 he secured his first major railway contract. The quality of his product was usefully advertised by displaying a flawless 2-ton steel ingot at the Great Exhibition of 1851. Krupp was then specializing in the manufacture of steel parts for railways and steamships, notably a weldless steel tire for locomotives, from which was derived the three-ring emblem of the Krupp concern. Krupp made a few cannon from 1847 but sold his first to the Khedive of Egypt in 1857. Two years later he won a major order of 312 cannon from the Prussian Government. With the development of this side of the business, he became the largest steel producer in Europe. In 1862 he adopted the **Bessemer** steelmaking process. The quality and design of his cannon were major factors in the victory of the Prussian artillery bombardment at Sedan in the Franco-Prussian War of 1870. Krupp expanded further during the boom years of the early 1870s and he was able to gain control of German coal and Spanish iron-ore supplies. He went on to manufacture heavy artillery, with a celebrated testing ground at Osnabrück. By this time he had a workforce of 21,000, whom he ruled with benevolent but strict control. His will instructed that the firm should not be divided.

Further Reading
P. Batty, 1966, *The House of Krupp* (includes a bibliography).
G. von Klass, 1954, *Krupp: The Story of an Industrial Empire*.

LRD

Krylov, Alexei Nicolaevitch

b. 15 August 1863 Visyoger, Siberia
d. 26 October 1945 Leningrad (now St Petersburg), Russia

Russian academician and naval architect, exponent of a rigorous mathematical approach to the study of ship motions.

After schooling in France and Germany, Krylov returned to St Petersburg (as it then was) and in 1878 entered the Naval College. Upon graduating, he started work with the Naval Hydrographic Department; the combination of his genius and breadth of interest became apparent, and from 1888 until 1890 he undertook simultaneously a two-year university course in mathematics and a naval architecture course at his old college. On completion of his formal studies, Krylov commenced fifty years of service to the academic bodies of St Petersburg, including eight years as Superintendent of the Russian Admiralty Ship Model Experiment Tank. For many years he was Professor of Naval Architecture in the city, reorganizing the methods of teaching of his profession in Russia. It was during this period that he laid the foundations of his remarkable research and published the first of his many books destined to become internationally accepted in the fields of waves, rolling, ship motion and vibration. Practical work was not overlooked: he was responsible for the design of many vessels for the Imperial Russian Navy, including the battleships *Sevastopol* and *Petropavlovsk*, and went on, as Director of Naval Construction, to test anti-rolling tanks aboard military vessels in the North Atlantic in 1913. Following the Revolution, Krylov was employed by the Soviet Union to re-establish scientific links with other European countries, and on several occasions he acted as Superintendent in the procurement of important technical material from overseas. In 1919 he was appointed Head of the Marine Academy, and from then on participated in many scientific conferences and commissions, mainly in the shipbuilding field, and served on the Editorial Board of the well-respected Russian periodical *Sudostroenie* (Shipbuilding). The breadth of his personal research was demonstrated by the notable contributions he made to the Russian development of the gyro compass.

Principal Honours and Distinctions
Member, Russian Academy of Science 1814. Royal Institution of Naval Architects Gold Medal 1898. State Prize of the Soviet Union (first degree). Stalin Premium for work on compass deviation.

Bibliography
Krylov published more than 500 books, papers and articles; these have been collected and published in twelve volumes by the Academy of Sciences of the USSR.
1942, *My Memories* (autobiography).

AK/FMW

Ktesibios of Alexandria
See **Ctesibius of Alexandria**.

Kungshu Phan
See **Gongshu Pan**.

Kuo Shou-Ching
See **Guo Shoujing**.

Kurtz, Thomas E.
b. USA

American mathematician who, with Kemeny developed BASIC, a high-level computer language.

Kurtz took his first degree in mathematics at the University of California in Los Angeles (UCLA), where he also gained experience in numerical methods as a result of working in the National Bureau of Standards Institute for Numerical Analysis located on the campus. In 1956 he obtained a PhD in statistics at Princeton, after which he took up a post as an instructor at Dartmouth College in Hanover, New Hampshire. There he found a considerable interest in computing was already in existence, and he was soon acting as the Dartmouth contact with the New England Regional Computer Center at Massachusetts Institute of Technology, an initiative partly supported by IBM. With Kemeny, he learned the Share Assembly Language then in use, but they were concerned about the difficulty of programming computers in assembly language and of teaching it to students and colleagues at Dartmouth. In 1959 the college obtained an LGP-30 computer and Kurtz became the first Director of the Dartmouth Computer Center. However, the small memory (4 k) of this 30-bit machine precluded its use with the recently available high-level language Algol 58. Therefore, with Kemeny, he set about developing a simple language and operating system that would use simple English commands and be easy to learn and use. This they called the *Beginners All-purpose Symbolic Instruction Code* (BASIC). At the same time they jointly supervised the design and development of a time-sharing system suitable for college use, so that by 1964, when Kurtz became an associate professor of mathematics, they had a fully operational BASIC system; by 1969 a sixth version was already in existence. In 1966 Kurtz left Dartmouth to become a Director of the Kiewit Computer Center, and then, in 1975, he became a Director of the Office of Academic Computing; in 1978 he returned to Dartmouth as Professor of Mathematics. He also served on various national committees.

Bibliography

1964, with J.G. Kemeny, *BASIC Instruction Manual*: Dartmouth College (for details of the development of BASIC etc.).
1968, with J.G. Kemeny 'Dartmouth time-sharing', *Science* 223.

Further Reading

R.L. Wexelblat, 1981, *History of Programming Languages*, London: Academic Press (a more general view of the development of computer languages).

KF

Kussmaul, Adolf

b. 22 February 1822 Baden, Karlsruhe, Germany
d. 28 May 1902 Heidelberg, Germany

German physician and surgeon, inventor of the oesophagoscope and gastroscope.

Coming from two generations of a medical family, Kussmaul entered Heidelberg University in 1840 and, after qualifying, served in the German–Danish war in 1848. After four years in country practice, he received an MD from Würzburg in 1854 and soon after was appointed to a teaching post in Heidelberg. He held further positions in Erlangen, Freiburg and finally Strasbourg.

His researches ranged over diabetic coma, rigor mortis, thoracocentesis and pericarditis, and in a paper on pyloric stenosis he described not only a stomach pump but also an oesophagoscope and a gastroscope and their use. He also made improvements to the ophthalmoscope. At the age of 66, on retirement from Strasbourg, he became Professor Emeritus at Heidelberg.

Bibliography

1855, 'Treatment of hypertrophy of the stomach through a new method using the stomach pump', *Deutsch. Arch. Klin. Med.* 6.

Further Reading

T. Bast, 1826, 'The life and times of Adolf Kussmaul', *Annals of Medical History* 8.

MG

L

Laënnec, René Théophile Hyacinthe

b. 16 February 1781 Quimper, France
d. 13 August 1826 Paris, France

French physician, inventor of the stethoscope.

Laënnec commenced his medical career assisting his uncle, a physician of Nantes, Brittany. On moving to Paris he studied under Corvisart, Napoleon's friend and personal physician, and Dupuytren. Appointed Physician to the Necker Hospital in 1816, his difficulties in examining an obese patient led him to make a roll of paper and, placing one end on the patient's chest and his ear to the other, he found that he could hear the heart sounds much more clearly; although auscultation had been practised in medicine since the time of Hippocrates (*fl.* 400 BC), its inconvenience and distastefulness made the stethoscope an instrument which soon gained wide acceptance. As a consequence, a large number of new auditory phenomena were reported in the immediately ensuing years. In his book, published in 1819, he described the instrument as 'a cylinder of wood an inch and a half in diameter and a foot long, perforated by a bore three lines wide and hollowed out into a funnel shape at one of its extremities'.

By now he had contracted tuberculosis and retired to Brittany to recover. In 1822 he accepted the Chair of Medicine in the College of France, but he suffered a relapse and died four years later, ironically of the same disease that his invention had done so much to facilitate the diagnosis of.

Bibliography
1819, *Traité de l'auscultation médiate*, Paris.

Further Reading
W. Hale-White, 1923, *Laënnec: Translation of Selected Papers from 'de l'Auscultation médiate', with a Biography,* London.
H. Saintignon, 1904, *Laënnec, sa vie et son oeuvre,* Paris.
Z. Cope, 1957, *Sidelights from the History of Medicine.*

MG

Laird, John

b. 1805 (?) Greenock, Scotland
d. 26 October 1874 Birkenhead, England

Scottish pioneer of large-scale iron shipbuilding.

When only 5 years old, Laird travelled with his family to Merseyside, where his father William Laird was setting up a ship-repair yard. Fourteen years later his father established the Birkenhead Ironworks for ship and engine repairs, which in later years was to achieve great things with John Laird at the helm. John Laird trained as a solicitor, but instead of going into practice he joined the family business. Between 1829 and 1832 they built three iron barges for inland use in Ireland; this form of construction had become less of a novelty and followed the example set by Thomas **Wilson** in 1819, but Laird was fired with enthusiasm for this mode of construction. New iron ships followed in rapid succession, with two of especial note: the paddle steamer *Lady Lansdown* of 1833, which was dismantled and later re-erected on the river Shannon, becoming one of Britain's first 'knock-down' contracts; and the early steamer *Robert F. Stockton,* which had a double **Ericsson** screw propeller and the first iron transverse watertight bulkheads. With the good name of the shipyard secure, they received orders from MacGregor Laird (John Laird's younger brother) for iron ships for the West African trade. This African connection was to grow and the yard's products were to include the *Ma Roberts* for Dr David Livingstone. Being of steel and with constant groundings on African rivers, this craft only lasted 18 months in steady operation. In 1858 a new yard dedicated to iron construction was opened at Monk's Ferry. In 1861 John Laird was returned as the first Member of Parliament for Birkenhead and his sons took over the day-to-day affairs of the business. Laird was to suffer acute embarrassment by questions at Westminster over the building in the Birkenhead Works of the United States Confederate raider *Alabama* in 1862. In 1874 he suffered serious injuries in a riding accident; his health declined and he died later that year.

Bibliography
1858, with Fairbairn, Forrester, Lang and Seaward, *Steam Navigation, Vessels of Iron and Wood, the Steam Engine, etc.* 2 vols, London: Weale.

FMW

Laithwaite, Eric Roberts

b. 14 June 1921 Atherton, Lancashire, England

English engineer, notable contributor to the development of linear electric motors.

Laithwaite's education at Kirkham Grammar School and Regent Street Polytechnic, London, was followed by service in the Royal Air Force. After entering Manchester University in 1946 and graduating in 1949, he joined the university staff and became Secretary to the Inaugural Conference of the Ferranti Mark I computer. In 1964 he moved to Imperial College of Science and Technology, London, and became Professor of Heavy Electrical Engineering. From 1967 to 1976 he also held the post of External Professor of Applied Electricity at the Royal Institution. Research into the use of linear induction motors as shuttle drives in weaving looms was followed by investigations into their application to conveyors in industrial processes and as high-speed propulsion units for railway vehicles. With considerable involvement in a tracked hovercraft project in the 1960s and 1970s, he proposed the concept of transverse flux and the magnetic river high-speed linear induction machine. Linear motors and electromagnetic levitation have been applied to high-speed propulsion in the United States, France and Japan.

Laithwaite has written five books and over one hundred papers on the subjects of linear motors and electromagnetic levitation. Two series of Christmas lectures were presented by him at the Royal Institution.

Principal Honours and Distinctions
Royal Society S.G. Brown Medal 1966. Institute of Electronic and Electrical Engineers Nikola Tesla Award 1986.

Bibliography
1966, *Induction Machines for Special Purposes*, London.
1970, *Propulsion Without Wheels*, London (discusses properties and applications of linear induction motors).
1977 (ed.), *Transport Without Wheels*, London (describes the design and applications of linear electric motors).
1987, *A History of Linear Electric Motors*, London (provides a general historical survey).

Further Reading
B. Bowers, 1982, *A History of Electric Light and Power*, London, pp. 261–4 (provides an account of early linear motors).
M. Poloujadoff, 1980, *The Theory of Linear Induction Motors*, Oxford (for a comparison of analytical methods recommended by various investigators).

GW

Lanchester, Frederick William

b. 28 October 1868 Lewisham, London, England
d. 8 March 1946 Birmingham, England

English designer and builder of the first all-British motor car.

The fourth of eight children of an architect, he spent his childhood in Hove and attended a private preparatory school, from where, aged 14, he went to the Hartley Institution (the forerunner of Southampton University). He was then granted a scholarship to the Royal College of Science, South Kensington, and also studied practical engineering at Finsbury Technical College, London. He worked first for a draughtsman and pseudo-patent agent, and was then appointed Assistant Works Manager of the Forward Gas Engine Company of Birmingham, with sixty men and a salary of £1 per week. He was then aged 21. His younger brother, George, was apprenticed to the same company. In 1889 and 1890 he invented a pendulum governor and an engine starter which earned him royalties. He built a flat-bottomed river craft with a stern paddle-wheel and a vertical single-cylinder engine with a wick carburettor of his own design. From 1892 he performed a number of garden experiments on model gliders relating to problems of lift and drag, which led him to postulate vortices from the wingtips trailing behind, much of his work lying behind the theory of modern aerodynamics. The need to develop a light engine for aircraft led him to car design.

In February 1896 his first experimental car took the road. It had a torsionally rigid chassis, a perfectly balanced and almost noiseless engine, dynamically stable steering, epicyclic gear for low speed and reverse with direct drive for high speed. It turned out to be underpowered and was therefore redesigned. Two years later an 8 hp, two-cylinder flat twin appeared which retained the principle of balancing by reverse rotation, had new Lanchester valve-gear and a new method of ignition based on a magneto generator. For the first time a worm and wheel replaced chain-drive or bevel-gear transmission. Lanchester also designed the machinery to make it. The car was capable of about 18 mph (29 km/h): future cars of his travelled at twice that speed. From 1899 to 1904 cars were produced for sale by the Lanchester Engine Company, which was formed in 1898. The company had to make every component except the tyres. Lanchester gave up the managership but remained as Chief Designer, and he remained in this post until 1914.

In 1907–8 his two-volume treatise *Aerial Flight* was published; it included consideration of skin friction, boundary-layer theory and the theory of stability. In 1909 he was appointed to the Government's Committee for Aeronautics and also became a consultant to the Daimler Company. At the age of 51 he married Dorothea Cooper. He remained a consultant to Daimler and worked also for Wolseley and Beardmore until 1929 when he started Lanchester Laboratories, working on sound reproduction. He also wrote books on relativity and on the theory of dimensions.

Principal Honours and Distinctions
FRS.

Bibliography
bht = 1907–8, *Aerial Flight*, 2 vols.

Further Reading
P.W. Kingsford, 1966, *F.W. Lanchester, Automobile Engineer*.
E.G. Semler (ed.), 1966, *The Great Masters. Engineering Heritage*, Vol. II, London: Institution of Mechanical Engineers/Heinemann.
IMcN

Land, Edwin Herbert

b. 7 May 1909 Bridgeport, Connecticut, USA
d. 1 March 1991 Cambridge, Massachusetts, USA

American scientist and inventor of the Polaroid instant-picture process.

Edwin Land's career began when, as a Harvard undergraduate in the late 1920s, he became interested in the possibility of developing a polarizing filter in the form of a thin sheet, to replace the crystal and stacked-glass devices then in use, which were expensive, cumbersome and limited in size. He succeeded in creating a material in which minute anisotropic iodine crystals were oriented in line, producing an efficient polarizer that was patented in 1929. After presenting the result of his researches in a Physics Department colloquium at Harvard, he left to form a partnership with George Wheelwright to manufacture the new material, which was seen to have applications as diverse as anti-glare car headlights, sunglasses, and viewing filters for stereoscopic photographs and films. In 1937 he founded the Polaroid Corporation and developed the Vectograph process, in which self-polarized photographic images could be printed, giving a stereoscopic image when viewed through polarizing viewers. Land's most significant invention, the instant picture, was stimulated by his three-year-old daughter. As he took a snapshot of her, she asked why she could not see the picture at once. He began to research the possibility, and on 21 February 1947 he demonstrated a system of one-step photography at a meeting of the Optical Society of America. Using the principle of diffusion transfer of the image, it produced a photograph in one minute. The Polaroid Land camera was launched on 26 November 1948. The original sepia-coloured images were soon replaced by black and white and, in 1963, by Polacolor instant colour film. The original peel-apart 'wet' process was superseded in 1972 with the introduction of the *SX-70* camera with dry picture units which developed in the light. The instant colour movie system Polavision, introduced in 1978, was less successful and was one of his few commercial failures.

Land died in March 1991, after a career in which he had been honoured by countless scientific and academic bodies and had received the Medal of Freedom, the highest civilian honour in America.

Principal Honours and Distinctions
Medal of Freedom.

BC

Landsteiner, Karl
b. 14 June 1868 Vienna, Austria
d. 26 June 1943 New York, USA

Austrian/American physician, physiologist and immunologist, discoverer of human blood groups.

He graduated in medicine from Vienna in 1891 and spent the next five years at various European universities. In 1923 he began to work at the Rockefeller Institute for Medical Research in New York. In 1900, while investigating the disintegration of red blood cells, he discovered the reaction of one person's cells to the serum of another. By 1909 he had developed the classification of four main blood groups, which has proved to be of fundamental importance, particularly in relation to the development of blood-transfusion techniques and blood banks, despite the later discovery of many subgroups as well as of the rhesus factor (1940) and its relation to miscarriages and neonatal disease.

He was involved in research in many other fields, including syphilis, thyroid disease, scarlet fever and typhus, but his main studies were centred on the chemistry of immunology and its significance in allergy.

Principal Honours and Distinctions
Nobel Prize for Medicine or Physiology 1930. Foreign member of the Royal Society.

Bibliography
1900, 'Zur Kenntnis der Antifermentium, Lytischen und Agglutinierenden Werkungen des Blutserums und der Lymphe', *Zbl. Bact.*

Further Reading
1962, *The Specificity of Serological Reactions*, New York.
1945–8, *Obituary Notices of Fellows of the Royal Society*.

MG

Langen, Eugen
b. 1839 Germany
d. 1895 Germany

German engineer and businessmen.

A sound engineering training combined with an inherited business sense were credentials that Langen put to good use in his association with internal-combustion engines. The sight of a working engine built by N.A. **Otto** in 1864 convinced Langen that this was a means to provide power in industry. Shortly afterwards, assisted by members of his family, he formed the company N.A. Otto and Cie, Cologne, the world's first engine factory. At the Paris Exhibition of 1867, the new Otto–Langen Atmospheric Gas Engine was awarded a Gold Medal, and in 1870 Crossley Bros of Manchester was appointed sole agent and manufacturer in Britain. Under Langen's guidance, the firm grew, and in 1872 it was renamed Die Gasmotoren Fabrik, employing Gottlieb **Daimler** and Wilhelm **Maybach**. Apart from running the business, Langen often played peacemaker when differences arose between Daimler and Otto. The success of the firm, known today as Klockner–Humboldt–Deutz, owed much to Langen's business and technical skills. Langen was a strong supporter of Otto's constant efforts to produce a better engine, and his confidence was justified by the appearance, in 1876, of Otto's four-stroke engine. The two men remained close friends until Otto's death in 1892.

Further Reading
Friederick Sass, 1962, *Geschichte des deutschen Verbrennungsmotorenbaues von 1860 bis 1918*, Berlin: Springen Verlag (a detailed account).
Gustav Goldbeck, 1964, *Kraft für die Welt: 100 Jahre Klockner–Humboldt–Deutz AG*, Dusseldorf (an account of the history and development of Klockner Humboldt).

KAB

Langley, Samuel Pierpont
b. 22 August 1834 Roxbury, Massachusetts, USA
d. 27 February 1906 Aiken, South Carolina, USA

American scientist who built an unsuccessful aeroplane in 1903, just before the success of the **Wright** *brothers.*

Professor Langley was a distinguished mathematician and astronomer who became Secretary of the Smithsonian Institution (US National Museum) in 1887. He was also interested in aviation and embarked on a programme of experiments with a whirling arm to test wings and with a series of free-flying models. In 1896 one of his steam-powered models made a flight of 4,199 ft (1,280 m): this led to a grant from the Government to subsidize the construction of a manned aeroplane. Langley commissioned Stephen M. Balzer, an automobile engine designer, to build a lightweight aero-engine and appointed his assistant, Charles M. Manly, to oversee the project. After many variations, including rotary and radical designs, two versions of the Balzer–Manly engine were produced, one quarter size and one full size. In August 1903 the small engine powered a model which thus became the first petrol-engined aeroplane to fly. Langley designed his full-size aeroplane (which he called an *Aerodrome*) with tandem wings and a cruciform tail unit. The Balzer–Manly engine drove two pusher propellers. Manly was to be the pilot as Langley was now almost 70 years old. Most early aviators tested their machines by making tentative hops, but Langley decided to launch his *Aerodrome* by catapult from the roof of a houseboat on the Potomac river. Two attempts were made and on both occasions the *Aerodrome* crashed into the river: catapult problems and perhaps a structural weakness were to blame. The second crash occurred on 8 December 1903 and it is ironic that the Wright brothers, with limited funds and no Government support, successfully achieved a manned flight just nine days later. Langley was heartbroken. After his death there followed a strange affair in 1914 when Glenn **Curtiss** took Langley's *Aerodrome*, modified it, and tried to prove that but for the faulty catapult it would have flown before the Wrights' *Flyer*. A brief flight was made with floats instead of the catapult, and it flew rather better after more extensive modifications and a new engine.

Bibliography
1897, *Langley Memoir on Mechanical Flight*, Part 1, Washington, DC: Smithsonian Institution;

1911, Part 2.

Further Reading
J. Gordon Vaeth, 1966, *Langley: Man of Science and Flight*, New York (biography).
Charles H. Gibbs-Smith, 1985, *Aviation*, London (includes an analysis of Langley's work).
Tom D. Crouch, 1981, *A Dream of Wings*, New York.
Robert B. Meyer Jr (ed.), 1971, *Langley's Aero Engine of 1903*, Washington, DC: Smithsonian Annals of Flight, No. 6 (provides details about the engine).

JDS

Langmuir, Irving
b. 31 January 1881 Brooklyn, New York, USA
d. 16 August 1957 Falmouth, Massachusetts, USA

American Nobel Prize winner in chemistry in 1932 who was responsible for a number of important scientific developments ranging from electric lamps, through a high-vacuum transmitting tube (for broadcasting) to a high-vacuum mercury pump for studies in atomic structure, in radar and the stimulation of artificial rainfall.

Langmuir took a degree in metallurgical engineering at Columbia University School of Mines, and then a PhD in chemistry at Göttingen University in Germany. For much of his life he carried out research in physical chemistry at the General Electric Research Laboratory at Schenechtady, New York, where he remained until his retirement in 1950. One important result of his work there led to a great improvement in artificial illumination of homes. This was his development in 1913 of a much more efficient electric light bulb, which was filled with argon gas and had a coiled filament. The idea of using an inert gas was an old one, but it was not a viable proposition until a filament that could be coiled became available. Overall, Langmuir's lamp was more reliable than previous designs and gave a brighter light.

Further Reading
Arthur A. Bright, 1949, *The Electric Lamp Industry*, New York: Macmillan.
Floyd A. Lewis, 1961, *The Incandescent Light*, New York: Shorewood.

DY

Lanston, Tolbert
b. 3 February 1844 Troy, Ohio, USA
d. 18 February 1913 Washington, DC, USA

American inventor of the Monotype typesetting machine.

Although reared in a farming community, Lanston was able to develop his mechanical talent. After serving in the American Civil War he secured a clerkship in the Pensions Office in Washington, where he remained for twenty-two years. He studied law in his spare time and was called to the Bar. At the same time, he invented a whole variety of mechanical devices, many of which he patented. Around 1883 Lanston began taking an interest in machines for composing printers' type, probably stimulated by Ottmar **Mergenthaler**, who was then in Washington and working in this field. Four years' work were rewarded on 7 June 1887 by the grant of a patent, followed by three more, for a machine 'to produce justified lines of type'. The machine, the Monotype, consisted of two components: first a keyboard unit produced a strip of paper tape with holes punched in patterns corresponding to the characters required; this tape controlled the matrices in the caster, the second and 'hot metal' component, from which types were ejected singly and fed to an assembly point until a complete line of type had been formed. Lanston resigned his post and set up the Lanston Type Machine Company in Washington. He laboured for ten years to convert the device defined in his patents into a machine that could be made and used commercially. In 1897 the perfected Monotype appeared. The company was reorganized as the Lanston Monotype Manufacturing Company of Philadelphia, and Lanston devoted himself to promoting and improving the machine. Monotype, with Mergenthaler's Linotype, steadily supplanted hand-setting and the various inadequate mechanical methods that were then in use, and by the 1920s they reigned supreme, until the 1960s, when they themselves began to be superseded by computer-controlled photosetting methods.

Principal Honours and Distinctions
Franklin Institute Cresson Gold Medal 1896.

Further Reading
Obituary, 1913, *American Printer* (March).
L.A. Legros and J.C. Grant, 1916, *Typographical Printing Surfaces*, London.
J. Moran, 1964, *The Composition of Reading Matter*, London.

LRD

Lartigue, Charles François Marie-Thérèse
b. 1834 Toulouse, France
d. 1907

French engineer and businessman, inventor of the Lartigue monorail.

Lartigue worked as a civil engineer in Algeria and while there invented a simple monorail for industrial or agricultural use. It comprised a single rail carried on trestles; vehicles comprised a single wheel with two tubs suspended either side, like panniers. These were pushed or pulled by hand or, occasionally, hauled by mule. Such lines were used in Algerian esparto-grass plantations.

In 1882 he patented a monorail system based on this arrangement, with important improvements: traction was to be mechanical; vehicles were to have two or four wheels and to be able to be coupled together; and the trestles were to have, on each side, a light guide rail upon which horizontal rollers beneath the vehicles would bear. Early in 1883 the Lartigue Railway Construction Company was formed in London and two experimental prototype monorails were subsequently demonstrated in public. One, at the Paris Agricultural Exhibition, had an electric locomotive that was built in two parts, one either side of the rail to maintain balance, hauling small wagons. The other prototype, in London, had a small, steam locomotive with two vertical boilers and was designed by Anatole **Mallet**. By now Lartigue had become associated with F.B. **Behr**. Behr was Managing Director of the construction company and of the Listowel & Ballybunion Railway Company, which obtained an Act of Parliament in 1886 to built a Lartigue monorail railway in the South West of Ireland between those two places. Its further development and successful operation are described in the article on Behr in this volume.

A much less successful attempt to establish a Lartigue monorail railway took place in France, in the département of Loire. In 1888 the council of the département agreed to a proposal put forward by Lartigue for a 10½ mile (17 km) long monorail between the towns of Feurs and Panissières: the agreement was reached on the casting vote of the Chairman, a contact of Lartigue. A concession was granted to successive companies with which Lartigue was closely involved, but construction of the line was attended by muddle, delay and perhaps fraud, although it was completed sufficiently for trial trains to operate. The locomotive had two horizontal boilers, one either side of the track. But the inspectors of the départment found deficiencies in the completeness and probable safety of the railway; when they did eventually agree to opening on a limited scale, the company claimed to have insufficient funds to do so unless monies owed by the départment were paid. In the end the concession was forfeited and the line dismantled. More successful was an electrically operated Lartigue mineral line built at mines in the eastern Pyrenees. It appears to have reused equipment from the electric demonstration line, with modifications, and included gradients as steep as 1 in 12. There was no generating station: descending trains generated the electricity to power ascending ones. This line is said to have operated for at least two years.

Bibliography
1882, French patent no. 149,301 (monorail system).
1882, British patent no. 2,764 (monorail system).

Further Reading
D.G. Tucker, 1984, 'F.B. Behr's development of the Lartigue monorail', *Transactions of the Newcomen Society* 55 (describes Lartigue and his work).
P.H. Chauffort and J.-L. Largier, 1981, 'Le monorail de Feurs à Panissières', *Chemin de fer régionaux et urbains* (magazine of the *Fédération des Amis des Chemins de Fer Secondaires*) 164 (in French; describes Lartigue and his work).

See also: **Brennan, Louis**; **Palmer, Henry Robinson**.

PJGR

Lascelles, William
fl. *c*.1895 England

English pioneer in methods of construction utilizing concrete panels.

In 1895 Lascelles patented a system of pre-cast concrete panels that were affixed to wooden framing. This type of construction was intended for low-cost housing, and a number of examples were constructed in the Croydon area of Surrey, where Lascelles lived. The panels, in the fashion of the day, were decoratively moulded with classical borders and floral or geometric patterning. They were large, being about 1½ in. (38 mm) thick and measuring about 3 ft x 2 ft 6 in. (91 cm x 76 cm), and were manufactured from Portland Cement mixed with powdered coke. The system was adopted by several architects.

Further Reading
Christopher C. Stanley, 1979, *Highlights in the History of Concrete*, Cement and Concrete Association.

DY

La Trobe Bateman, John Frederic
See **Bateman, John Frederick La Trobe**.

Lauste, Eugène Augustin
b. 1857 Montmartre, France
d. 1935

French inventor who devised the first practicable sound-on-film system.

Lauste was a prolific inventor who as a 22-year-old had more than fifty patents to his name. He joined **Edison**'s West Orange Laboratory as Assistant to W.K.L. **Dickson** in 1887; he was soon involved in the development of early motion pictures, beginning an association with the cinema that was to dominate the rest of his working life. He left Edison in 1892 to pursue an interest in petrol engines, but within two years he returned to cinematography, where, in association with Major Woodville Latham, he introduced small but significant improvements to film- projection systems. In 1900 an interest in sound recording, dating back to his early days with Edison, led Lauste to begin exploring the possibility of recording sound photographically on film alongside the picture. In 1904 he moved to England, where he continued his experiments, and by 1907 he had succeeded in photographing a sound trace and picture simultaneously, each image occupying half the width of the film.

Despite successful demonstrations of Lauste's system on both sides of the Atlantic, he enjoyed no commercial success. Handicapped by lack of capital, his efforts were finally brought to an end by the First World War. In 1906 Lauste had filed a patent for his sound-on-film system, which has been described by some authorities as the master patent for talking pictures. Although this claim is questionable, he was the first to produce a practicable sound-on-film system and establish the basic principles that were universally followed until the introduction of magnetic sound.

Bibliography
11 August 1906, with Robert R. Haines and John S. Pletts, British Patent no. 18,057 (sound-on-film system).

Further Reading
The most complete accounts of Lauste's work and the history of sound films can be found in the *Journal of the Society of Motion Picture (and Television) Engineers*.

For an excellent account of Lauste's work, see the Report of the Historical Committee, 1931, *Journal of the Society of Motion Picture Engineers* 16 (January): 105–9; and Merritt Crawford, 1941, *Journal of the Society of Motion Picture Engineers*, 17 (October) 632–44.

For good general accounts of the evolution of sound in the cinema, see:

E.I. Sponable, 1947, *Journal of the Society of Motion Picture Engineers* 48: 275–303 and 407–22; E.W. Kellog, 1955, *Journal of the Society of Motion Picture Engineers* 64: 291–302 and 356–74.

JW

Laval, Carl Gustaf Patrik de

b. 9 May 1845 Orsa, Sweden
d. 2 February 1913 Stockholm, Sweden

Swedish inventor of an advanced cream separator and a steam turbine.

Gustaf de Laval was educated at the Stockholm Technical Institute and Uppsala University. He proved to have an unfailing vigour and variety in his inventive talent, for his interests ranged from electric lighting and electrometallurgy to aerodynamics. In the 1890s he employed over one hundred engineers to develop his inventions, but he was best known for two: the cream separator and a steam turbine. In 1877 he invented the high-speed centrifugal cream separator, which was probably the greatest advance in butter-making up to that time. By 1880 the separators were being successfully marketed all over the world, for they were quickly adopted in larger dairies where they effected enormous savings in labour and space. He followed this with various devices for the dairy industry, including a vacuum milking machine perfected in 1913. In *c.*1882, de Laval invented a turbine on the principle of **Hero**'s engine, but he quickly turned his attention to the impulse type, which was like **Branca**'s, with a jet of steam impinging on a set of blades around the periphery of a wheel. He applied for a British patent in 1889. The steam was expanded in a single stage from the initial to the final pressure: to secure economy with the steam issuing at high velocity, the blades also had to rotate at high velocity. An early 5 hp (3.7 kW) turbine rotated at 30,000 rpm, so reduction gearing had to be introduced. Production started in Sweden in 1893 and in other countries at about the same time. In 1892 de Laval proposed employing one of his turbines of 15 hp (11 kW) in an experimental launch, but there is no evidence that it was ever actually installed in a vessel. However, his turbines were popular for powering electric generating sets for lighting textile mills and ships, and by 1900 were available in sizes up to 300 bhp (224 kW).

Bibliography
1889, British patent no. 7,143 (steam turbine).

Further Reading
T. Althin, 1943, *Life of de Laval*, Stockholm (a full biography).
T.I. Williams (ed.), 1969, *A Biographical Dictionary of Scientists*, London: A. & C. Black (contains a brief biography).
R.M. Neilson, 1902, *The Steam Turbine*, London: Longmans, Green & Co. (fully covers the development of de Laval's steam turbine).
H.W. Dickinson, 1938, *A Short History of the Steam Engine*, Cambridge University Press

(contains a short account of the development of the steam turbine).

R.L. Hills, 1989, *Power from Steam. A History of the Stationary Steam Engine*, Cambridge University Press (contains a short account).

RLH

Lavoisier, Antoine Laurent

b. 26 August 1743 Paris, France
d. 8 May 1794 Paris, France

French founder of the modern science of chemistry.

As well as receiving a formal education in law and literature, Lavoisier studied science under some of the leading figures of the day. This proved to be an ideal formation of the man in whom 'man of science' and 'public servant' were so intimately combined. His early work towards the first geological map of France and on the water supply of Paris helped to win him election to the Royal Academy of Sciences in 1768 at the youthful age of 25. In the same year he used some of his private income to buy a part-share in the 'tax farm', a private company which leased from the Government the right to collect certain indirect taxes.

In 1772 Lavoisier began his researches into the related phenomena of combustion, respiration and the calcination or oxidation of metals. This culminated in the early 1780s in the overthrow of the prevailing theory, based on an imponderable combustion principle called 'phlogiston', and the substitution of the modern explanation of these processes. At the same time, understanding of the nature of acids, bases and salts was placed on a sounder footing. More important, Lavoisier defined a chemical element in its modern sense and showed how it should be applied by drawing up the first modern list of the chemical elements. With the revolution in chemistry initiated by Lavoisier, chemists could begin to understand correctly the fundamental processes of their science. This understanding was the foundationo of the astonishing advance in scientific and industrial chemistry that has taken place since then. As an academician, Lavoisier was paid by the Government to carry out investigations into a wide variety of practical questions with a chemical bias, such as the manufacture of starch and the distillation of phosphorus. In 1775 Louis XVI ordered the setting up of the Gunpowder Commission to improve the supply and quality of gunpowder, deficiencies in which had hampered France's war efforts. Lavoisier was a member of the Commission and, as usual, took the leading part, drawing up its report and supervising its implementation. As a result, the industry became profitable, output increased so that France could even export powder, and the range of the powder increased by two-thirds. This was a material factor in France's war effort in the Revolution and the Napoleonic wars.

As if his chemical researches and official duties were not enough, Lavoisier began to apply his scientific principles to agriculture when he purchased an estate at Frechines, near Blois. After ten years' work on his experimental farm there, Lavoisier was able to describe his results in the memoir 'Results of some agricultural experiments and reflections on their relation to political economy' (Paris, 1788), which holds historic importance in agriculture and economics. In spite of his services to the nation and to humanity, his association with the tax farm was to have tragic consequences: during the reign of terror in 1794 the Revolutionaries consigned to the guillotine all the tax farmers, including Lavoisier.

Bibliography

1862–93, *Oeuvres de Lavoisier*, Vols I–IV, ed. J.B.A. Dumas; Vols V–VI, ed. E. Grimaux, Paris (Lavoisier's collected works).

Further Reading

D.I. Duveen and H.S. Klickstein, 1954, *A Bibliography of the Works of Antoine Laurent Lavoisier 1743–1794*, London: William Dawson (contains valuable biographical material).

D. McKie, 1952, *Antoine Lavoisier, Scientist, Economist, Social Reformer*, London: Constable (the best modern, general biography).

H. Guerlac, 1975, *Antoine Laurent Lavoisier, Chemist and Revolutionary*, New York: Charles Scribner's Sons (a more recent work).

LRD

Lawes, Sir John Bennet

b. 28 December 1814 Rothamsted, Hertfordshire, England
d. 31 August 1900 Rothamsted, Hertfordshire, England

English scientific agriculturalist.

Lawes's education at Eton and Oxford did little to inform his early taste for chemistry, which he developed largely on his own. By the age of 20 he had fitted up the best bedroom in his house as a fully equipped chemical laboratory. His first interest was in the making of drugs; it was said that he knew the *Pharmacopoeia* by heart. He did, however, receive some instruction from Anthony Todd Thomson of University College, London. His father having died in 1822, Lawes entered into possession of the Rothamsted estate when he came of age in 1834. He began experiments with plants with uses as drugs, but following an observation by a neighbouring farmer of the effect of bones on the growth of certain crops Lawes turned to experiments with bones dissolved in sulphuric acid on his turnip crop. The results were so promising that he took out a patent in 1842 for converting mineral and fossil phosphates into a powerful manure by the action of sulphuric acid. The manufacture of these superphosphates became a major industry of tremendous benefit to agriculture. Lawes himself set up a factory at Deptford in 1842 and a larger one in 1857 at Barking Creek, both near London. The profits from these and other chemical manufacturing concerns earned Lawes profits which funded his experimental work at Rothamsted. In 1843, Lawes set up the world's first agricultural experiment station. Later in the same year he was joined by Joseph Henry Gilbert, and together they carried out a considerable number of experiments of great benefit to agriculture, many of the results of which were published in the leading scientific journals of the day, including the *Philosophical Transactions of the Royal Society*. In all, 132 papers were published, most of them jointly with Gilbert. A main theme of the work on plants was the effect of various chemical fertilizers on the growth of different crops, compared with the effects of farm manure and of no treatment at all. On animal rearing, they studied particularly the economical feeding of animals.

The work at Rothamsted soon brought Lawes into prominence; he joined the Royal Agricultural Society in 1846 and became a member of its governing body two years later, a position he retained for over fifty years. Numerous distinctions followed and Rothamsted became a place of pilgrimage for people from many parts of the world who were concerned with the application of science to agriculture. Rothamsted's jubilee in 1893 was marked by a public commemoration headed by the Prince of Wales.

Principal Honours and Distinctions
Baronet 1882. FRS 1854. Royal Society Royal Medal (jointly with Gilbert) 1867.

Further Reading
Memoir with portrait published in *J. Roy. Agric. Soc. Memoranda of the origin, plan and results of the field and other experiments at Rothamsted*, issued annually by the Lawes Agricultural Trust Committee, with a list of Lawes's scientific papers.

LRD

Lawrence, Richard Smith
b. 22 November 1817 Chester, Vermont, USA
d. 10 March 1892 Hartford, Connecticut, USA

American gunsmith and inventor.

Richard S. Lawrence received only an elementary education and as a young man worked on local farms and later in a woodworking shop. His work there included making carpenters' and joiners' tools and he spent some of his spare time in a local gunsmith's shop. After a brief period of service in the Army, he obtained employment in 1838 with N. Kendall & Co. of Windsor, Vermont, making guns at the Windsor prison. Within six months he was put in charge of the work, continuing in this position until 1842 when the gun-making ceased; he remained at the prison for a time in charge of the carriage shop. In 1843 he opened a gun shop in Windsor in partnership with Kendall, and the next year S.E. Robbins, a businessman, helped them obtain a contract from the Federal Government for 10,000 rifles. A new company, Robbins, Kendall & Lawrence, was formed and a factory was built at Windsor. Three years later Kendall's share of the business was purchased by his partners and the firm became Robbins & Lawrence. Lawrence supervised the design and production and, to improve methods of manufacture, developed new machine tools with the aid of F.W. **Howe**. In 1850 Lawrence introduced the lubrication of bullets, which practice ensured the success of the breech-loading rifle. Also in 1850, the company undertook to manufacture railway cars, but this involved them in a considerable financial loss. The company took to the Great Exhibition of 1851 in London, England, a set of rifles built on the interchangeable system. The interest this created resulted in a visit of some members of the British Royal Small Arms Commission to America and subsequently an order for 150 machine tools, jigs and fixtures from Robbins & Lawrence, to be installed at the small-arms factory at Enfield. In 1852 the company contracted to manufacture Sharps rifles and carbines at a new factory to be built at Hartford, Connecticut. Lawrence moved to Hartford in 1853 to superintend the building and equipment of the plant. Shortly afterwards, however, a promised order for a large number of rifles failed to materialize and, following its earlier financial difficulties, Robbins & Lawrence was forced into bankruptcy. The Hartford plant was acquired by the Sharps Rifle Company in 1856 and Lawrence remained there as Superintendent until 1872. From then he was for many years Superintendent of Streets in the city of Hartford and he also served on the Water Board, the Board of Aldermen and as Chairman of the Fire Board.

Further Reading

J.W. Roe, 1916, *English and American Tool Builders*, New Haven; repub. 1926, New York; and 1987, Bradley, Ill. (provides biographical information and includes in an Appendix (pp. 281–94) autobiographical notes written by Richard S. Lawrence in 1890).

Merritt Roe Smith, 1974, 'The American Precision Museum', *Technology and Culture* 15 (3): 413–37 (for information on Robbins & Lawrence and products).

RTS

Leavers, John

See **Levers, John**.

Lebaudy, Paul

b. 1858 Enghien, France
d. 1937 Rosny-sur-Seine, France

French airship pioneer responsible for the first practical airship, in collaboration with his brother Pierre (1861–1924).

Soon after Alberto **Santos-Dumont** had made his first successful flight in a small airship, Paul and Pierre Lebaudy decided to construct a large airship. The two brothers were sugar manufacturers in Moisson, France, and in 1899 they commissioned their chief engineer, Henri Julliot, to build them a large airship. Julliot was conscientious and cautious, and consequently he spent many months studying the problems and working out a feasible design. The *Lebaudy I* was not completed until late in 1902 and made its first flight on 13 November. It was 57 m (187 ft) long and powered by a 30 kW (40 hp) **Daimler** petrol engine driving two propellers which enabled it to fly at 40 km/h (25 mph); it could overcome all but very strong winds. During the ensuing months, *Lebaudy I* made many successful flights, often carrying passengers, and usually returning to its base at Moisson. On 12 November 1903 it flew a distance of 62 km (38½ miles) in 1 hour 41 minutes, from Moisson to Paris, where it was put on display and attracted huge crowds. After being damaged, *Lebaudy I* was rebuilt as *Lebaudy II*, although it was often called *La Jaune* because of the yellow fabric of the envelope. In 1905 it made a flight lasting over 3 hours; few would argue that this was the first really successful airship.

Further Reading

Basil Clarke, 1961, *The History of Airships*, London.

Wilfrid de Fonvieille, 1911, *Histoire de la navigation aérienne*, Paris.

JDS

Leblanc, Nicolas

b. 6 December 1742 Ivey-le-Pré, France
d. 16 January 1806 Paris, France

French chemist, inventor of the Leblanc process for the manufacture of soda.

Orphaned at an early age, Leblanc was sent by his guardian, a doctor, to study medicine at the Ecole de Chirurgie in Paris. Around 1780 he entered the service of the Duke of Orléans as Surgeon. There he was able to pursue his interest in chemistry by carrying out research, particularly into crystallization; this bore fruit in a paper to the Royal Academy of Sciences in 1786, published in 1812 as a separate work entitled *Crystallotechnie*. At that time there was much concern that supplies of natural soda were becoming insufficient to meet the increasing demands of various industries, textile above all. In 1775 the Academy offered a prize of 2,400 *livres* for a means of manufacturing soda from sea salt. Several chemists studied the problem, but the prize was never awarded. However, in 1789 Leblanc reported in the *Journal de physique* for 1789 that he had devised a process, and he applied to his patron for support. The Duke had the process subjected to tests, and when these proved favourable he, with Leblanc and the referee, formed a company in February 1790 to exploit it. A patent was granted in 1791 and, with the manufacture of a vital substance at low cost based on a raw material, salt in unlimited supply, a bright prospect seemed to open out for Leblanc. The salt was treated with sulphuric acid to form salt-cake (sodium sulphate), which was then rotated with coal and limestone to form a substance from which the soda was extracted with water followed by evaporation. Hydrochloric acid was a valuable by-product, from which could be made calcium chloride, widely used in the textile and paper industries. The factory worked until 1793, but did not achieve regular production, and then disaster struck: Leblanc's principal patron, the Duke of Orléans, perished under the guillotine in the reign of terror; the factory was sequestered by the Revolutionary government and the agreement was revoked. Leblanc laboured in vain to secure adequate compensation. Eventually a grant was made towards the cost of restoring the factory, but it was quite inadequate, and in despair, Leblanc shot himself. However, his process proved to be one of the greatest inventions in the chemical industry, and was taken up in other countries and remained the leading process for the production of soda for a century. In 1855 his family tried again to vindicate his name and achieve compensation, this time with success.

Further Reading

A.A. Leblanc, 1884, *Nicolas Leblanc, sa vie, ses travaux et l'histoire de la soude artificielle*, Paris (the standard biography, by his grandson).
For more critical studies, see:
C.C. Gillispie, 1957, 'The discovery of the Leblanc process', *Isis* 48: 152–70;
J.G. Smith, 1970, 'Studies in certain chemical industries in revolutionary and Napoleonic France', unpublished PhD thesis, Leeds University.

LRD

Lebon, Philippe

b. 29 May 1767 Bruchey, near Joinville, France
d. 2 December 1804 Paris, France

French pioneer of gas lighting.

Lebon was the son of a court official under Louis XV. He entered the Ecole des Ponts et Chaussées and graduated in 1792, by which time he had acquired a considerable reputation as a scientific engineer. He is credited with the invention of the firetube steam boiler and of the superheater, and he also devised an engine to work by gas, but from 1792 until his untimely death he worked mainly on his experiments to produce an inflammable gas for lighting purposes. He submitted a paper on the subject in 1799 to the Institut National and received a patent in the same year. The patent covers the detailed making and application of gas for light, heat and power, and the recovery of by-products. It describes the production of the gas by the carbonization of coal, although Lebon in fact used only wood gas for his experiments and demonstrations. He began demonstrations in a private house in Paris, but these attracted little attention. He achieved wider public interest when he moved to the Hôtel Seignelay, where he started a series of public demonstrations in 1801, but he attracted little profit, and in fact lost his money in his experiments. He then set up a plant near Rouen to manufacture wood tar, but his career was brought to an end by his brutal murder in the Champs Elysées in Paris. William **Murdock** was working along similar lines in England, although Lebon knew nothing of his experiments. The German entrepreneur F.A. **Winsor** visited Lebon and managed to discover the essentials of his processes, which he turned to good account in England with the founding of the Gas, Light & Coke Company.

Further Reading

S.T. McCloy, 1952, *French Inventors of the Eighteenth Century*.
A. Fayol, 1943, *Philippe Lebon et le gaz d'éclairage*.

LRD

Le Chatelier, Henri Louis

b. 8 November 1850 Paris, France
d. 17 September 1926 Miribel-les-Echelle, France

French inventor of the rhodium–platinum thermocouple and the first practical optical pyrometer, and pioneer of physical metallurgy.

The son of a distinguished engineer, Le Chatelier entered the Ecole Polytechnique in 1869: after graduating in the Faculty of Mines, he was appointed Professor at the Ecole Supérieure des Mines in 1877. After assisting **Deville** with the purification of bauxite in unsuccessful attempts to obtain aluminium in useful quantities, Le Chatelier's work covered a wide range of topics and he gave much attention to the driving forces of chemical reactions. Between 1879 and 1882 he studied the mechanisms of explosions in mines, and his doctorate in 1882 was concerned with the chemistry and properties of hydraulic cements. The dehydration of such materials was studied by thermal analysis and dilatometry. Accurate temperature measurement was crucial and his work on the stability of thermocouples, begun in 1886, soon established the superiority of rhodium–platinum alloys for high-temperature measurement. The most stable combination, pure platinum coupled with a 10 per cent rhodium platinum positive limb, became known as Le Chatelier couple and was in general use throughout the industrial world until *c.*1922. For applications where thermocouples could not be used, Le Chatelier also developed the first practical optical pyrometer. From hydraulic cements he moved on to refractory and other ceramic materials which were also studied by thermal analysis and dilatometry. By 1888 he was systematically applying such techniques to metals and alloys. Le Chatelier, together with Osmond, Worth, Genet and Charpy, was a leading member of that group of French investigators who established the new science of physical metallurgy between 1888 and 1900. Le Chatelier was determining the recalescence points in steels in 1888 and was among the first to study intermetallic compounds in a systematic manner. To facilitate such work he introduced the inverted microscope, upon which metallographers still depend for the routine examination of polished and etched metallurgical specimens under incident light. The principle of mobile equilibrium, developed independently by Le Chatelier in 1885 and F. Braun in 1886, stated that if one parameter in an equilibrium situation changed, the equilibrium point of the system would move

in a direction which tended to reduce the effect of this change. This provided a useful qualitative working tool for the experimentalists, and was soon used with great effect by **Haber** in his work on the synthesis of ammonia.

Principal Honours and Distinctions
Grand Officier de la Légion d'honneur. Honorary Member of the Institute of Metals 1912. Iron and Steel Institute Bessemer Medal.

Further Reading
F. Le Chatelier, 1969, *Henri Le Chatelier.*
C.K. Burgess and H.L. Le Chatelier, *The Measurement of High Temperature.*

ASD

Leclanché, Georges
b. 1839 Paris, France
d. 14 September 1882 Paris, France

French chemist and inventor of the primary cell named after him, from which the electrochemical principles of the modern dry cell have been developed.

Leclanché was sent to England for his early education. Returning to France, he entered the Central School of Arts and Manufacture, from which he graduated as a chemical engineer in 1860. He spent some years with a railway company in setting up an electrical timing system, and this work led him to electrochemical research. Driven by political pressure into exile, he set up a small laboratory in Brussels to continue the studies of the behaviour of voltaic cells he had started in France. Many workers directed their efforts to constructing a cell with a single electrolyte and a solid insoluble depolarizer, but it was Leclanché who produced, in 1866, the prototype of a battery that was rugged, cheap and contained no highly corrosive liquid. With electrodes of carbon and zinc and a solution of ammonium chloride, polarization was prevented by surrounding the positive electrode with manganese dioxide. The Leclanché cell was adopted by the Belgian Government Telegraph Service in 1868 and rapidly came into general use wherever an intermittent current was needed; for example, in telegraph and later in telephone circuits. Carl Gassner in 1888 pioneered successful dry cells based on the Leclanché system, with the zinc anode serving as the container, and *c.*1890 commercial production of such cells began.

Bibliography
10 October 1866, British patent no. 2,623 (Leclanché cell).
1868, 'Pile au peroxyde de manganèse à seul liquide', *Les Mondes* 16: 532–3 (describes the Leclanché cell).

Further Reading
M. Barak, 1966, 'Georges Leclanché (1939–1882)', *IEE Electronics and Power* 12: 184–91 (a detailed account).
N.C. Cahoon and G.W. Heise (eds), 1976, *The Primary Battery*, Vol. II, New York, pp. 1–147 (describes subsequent developments),

GW

Le Corbusier

See **Jeanneret, Charles-Edouard**.

Lee, Edmund

d. mid-1763 Brock Mill, Wigan, England

English inventor of the fantail, used to turn windmills automatically to face the wind.

On 9 December 1745 Edmund Lee was granted letters patent for his invention of the windmill fantail. In the preamble to Lee's patent he is described as a smith of Brock Mill, near Wigan, where he ran a millwright's business. Brock Mill is known to have been a substantial water-powered iron forge by the River Douglas to the north of Wigan. The drawing accompanying the patent shows a tower mill with its tail pole reaching the ground, and this is connected to a frame or carriage supporting a seven-bladed wind wheel. This tail projected some distance from the back of the tower, and when the wind caught it and turned it the cap was turned to face the wind by means of the gears which linked the cap to the fantail. The next logical step from Lee's invention was to place the fantail at a high level on the cap or at the foot of the ladder of a post mill. There is also an inferred connection between the Lee fantail and the annular sail of the wind engine or of a windmill such as that at Haverhill in Suffolk.

Further Reading
Stephen Buckland, 1987, *Lee's Patent Windmill*, London

KM

Lee, Revd William

d. *c.*1615

English inventor of the first knitting machine, called the stocking frame.

It would seem that most of the stories about Lee's invention of the stocking frame cannot be verified by any contemporary evidence, and the first written accounts do not appear until the second half of the seventeenth century. The claim that he was Master of Arts from St John's College, Cambridge, was first made in 1607 but cannot be checked because the records have not survived. The date for the invention of the knitting machine as being 1589 was made at the same time, but again there is no supporting evidence. There is no evidence that Lee was Vicar of Calverton, nor that he was in Holy Orders at all. Likewise there is no evidence for the existence of the woman, whether she was girlfriend, fiancée or wife, who is said to have inspired the invention, and claims regarding the involvement of Queen Elizabeth I and her refusal to grant a patent because the stockings were wool and not silk are also without contemporary foundation. Yet the first known reference shows that Lee was the inventor of the knitting machine, for the partnership agreement between him and George Brooke dated 6 June 1600 states that 'William Lee hath invented a very speedy manner of making works usually wrought by knitting needles as stockings, waistcoats and such like'. This agreement was to last for twenty-two years, but terminated prematurely when Brooke was executed for high treason in 1603. Lee continued to try and exploit his invention, for in 1605 he described himself as 'Master of Arts' when he petitioned the Court of Aldermen of the City of London as the first inventor of an engine to make silk stockings. In 1609 the Weavers' Company of London recorded Lee as 'a weaver of silk stockings by engine'. These petitions suggest that he was having difficulty in establishing his invention, which may be why in 1612 there is a record of him in Rouen, France, where he hoped to have better fortune. If he had been invited there by Henry IV, his hopes were dashed by the assassination of the king soon afterwards. He was to supply four knitting machines, and there is further evidence that he was in France in 1615, but it is thought that he died in that country soon afterwards.

The machine Lee invented was probably the most complex of its day, partly because the need to use silk meant that the needles were very fine. Henson (1970) in 1831 took five pages in his book to describe knitting on a stocking frame which had over 2,066 pieces. To knit a row of stitches took eleven separate stages, and great care and watchfulness were required to ensure that all the loops were equal and regular. This shows how complex the machines were and points to Lee's great achievement in actually making one. The basic principles of its operation remained unaltered throughout its extraordinarily long life, and a few still remained in use commercially in the early 1990s.

Further Reading
J.T. Millington and S.D. Chapman (eds), 1989, *Four Centuries of Machine Knitting, Commemorating William Lee's Invention of the Stocking Frame in 1589*, Leicester (N. Harte examines the surviving evidence for the life of William Lee and this must be considered as the most up-to-date biographical information).
Dictionary of National Biography (this contains only the old stories).
Earlier important books covering Lee's life and invention are G. Henson, 1970, *History of the Framework Knitters*, reprint, Newton Abbot (orig. pub. 1831); and W. Felkin, 1967, *History of the Machine-wrought Hosiery and Lace Manufactures*, reprint, Newton Abbot (orig. pub. 1867).
M. Palmer, 1984, *Framework Knitting*, Aylesbury (a simple account of the mechanism of the stocking frame).
R.L. Hills, 'William Lee and his knitting machine', *Journal of the Textile Institute* 80 (2) (a more detailed account).
M. Grass and A. Grass, 1967, *Stockings for a Queen. The Life of William Lee, the Elizabethan Inventor*, London.

RLH

Leeuwenhoek, Antoni van
b. 24 October 1632 Delft, Netherlands
d. 1723 Delft, Netherlands

Dutch pioneer of microscopy.

He was the son of a basketmaker, Philip Tonisz Leeuwenhoek, and Grietje Jacobsdr van den Berch, a brewer's daughter. After the death of his father in 1637, his mother married the painter Jacob Jansz Molijn. He went to school at Warmond and, later to an uncle who was Sheriff of Benthuizen. In 1648 he went to Amsterdam, where he was placed in a linen-draper's shop owned by William Davidson, a Scottish merchant. In 1652 or 1653 he moved back to Delft, where in 1654 he married the daughter of a cloth-merchant, Barbara de Mey. They had five children, only one of whom survived (born 22 September 1656). At about this time he bought a house and shop in the Hippolytus buurt and set up in business as a draper and haberdasher. His wife died in 1666 and in 1671 he married Cornelia Swalmius, a Reformed Church minister's daughter. Lacking self-confidence and not knowing Latin, the scientific language of the day, he was reluctant to publish the results of his investigations into a multitude of natural objects. His observations were made with single-lens microscopes made by himself. (He made at least 387 microscopes with magnifications of between 30x and 266x.) Among the subjects he studied were the optic nerve of a cow, textile fibres, plant seeds, a spark from a tinderbox, the anatomy of mites and insects' blood corpuscles, semen and spermatozoa. It was the physician Reinier de Graaf who put him in touch with the Royal Society in London, with whom he corresponded for fifty years from 1673. One of his last letters, in 1723, to the Royal Society was about the histology of the rare disease of the diaphragm that he had studied in sheep and oxen and from which he died. In public service he was a chamberlain to the sheriffs of Delft, a surveyor and a wine-gauger, offices which together gave him an income of about 800 florins a year. Leeuwenhoek never wrote a book, but collections were published in Latin and in Dutch from his scientific letters, which numbered more than 250.

Principal Honours and Distinctions
FRS 1680.

Further Reading
L.C. Palm and H.A.M. Snelders, *Antoni van Leeuwenhoek 1632–1723: Studies in the Life and Work of the Delft Scientist, Commemorating the 350th Anniversary of his Birthday*.
B. Bracegirdle (ed.), *Beads of Glass: Leeuwenhoek and the Early Microscope*. (Catalogue of an exhibition in the Museum Boerhaave, November

1982 to May 1983, and in the Science Museum, May to October 1983).

IMcN

Le Gray, Gustave
b. 1820 Villiers-le-Bel, France
d. 1882 Cairo, Egypt

French painter and photographic innovator.

Le Gray studied painting, and to supplement his income as an artist he took up photography in the mid-1840s. He showed remarkable aptitude, and for a time he was at the forefront of innovation in France and pioneered a number of minor improvements. In 1847 he began gold-toning positive-paper prints, a practice widely adopted later. In 1850 independently of **Archer** in England, he experimented with collodion on glass as a carrying medium for silver salts. It was also in 1850 that Le Gray introduced his waxed-paper process, an improvement of **Talbot**'s calotype process which was favoured by many travelling photographers in the 1850s and 1860s. Le Gray published instruction manuals in photography that were well received. He travelled to Egypt to teach drawing in 1865, but his health deteriorated after a riding accident and he made no further significant contributions to photography.

Bibliography
1850, *Traité pratique de photographier sur papier et sur verre*, Paris 1851, 2nd edn, London: T. & R. Willats (his most significant publication).

Further Reading
J.M. Eder, 1945, *History of Photography*, trans. E. Epstean, New York.

JW

Lenoir, Jean Joseph Etienne
b. 1822 Mussey-la-Ville, Belgium
d. 1900 Verenna Saint-Hildar, France

Belgian (naturalized French in 1870) inventor of internal combustion engines, an electroplating process and railway telegraphy systems.

Leaving his native village for Paris at the age of 16, Lenoir became a metal enameller. Experiments with various electroplating processes provided a useful knowledge of electricity that showed in many of his later ideas. Electric ignition, although somewhat unreliable, was a feature of the Lenoir gas engine which appeared in 1860. Resembling the steam engine of the day, Lenoir engines used a non-compression cycle of operations, in which the gas–air mixture of about atmospheric pressure was being ignited at one-third of the induction stroke. The engines were double acting. About five hundred of Lenoir's engines were built, mostly in Paris by M. Hippolyte Marinoni and by Lefébvre; the Reading Ironworks in England built about one hundred. Many useful applications of the engine are recorded, but the explosive shock that occurred on ignition, together with the unreliable ignition systems, prevented large-scale acceptance of the engine in industry. However, Lenoir's effort and achievements stimulated much discussion, and N.A. **Otto** is reported to have carried out his first experiments on a Lenoir engine.

Principal Honours and Distinctions
Académie des Sciences Prix Montyon Prize 1870. Société d'Encouragement, Silver Prize of 12,000 francs. Légion d'honneur 1881 (for his work in telegraphy).

Bibliography
8 February 1860, British patent no. 335 (the first Lenoir engine).
1861, British patent no. 107 (the Lenoir engine).

Further Reading
Dugald Clerk, 1895, *The Gas and Oil Engine*, 6th edn, London, pp. 13–15, 30, 118, 203.
World Who's Who in Science, 1968 (for an account of Lenoir's involvement in technology).

KAB

Leonardo da Vinci
b. 15 April 1452 Vinci, near Florence, Italy.
d. 2 May 1519 St Cloux, near Amboise, France.

Italian scientist, engineer, inventor and artist.

Leonardo was the illegitimate son of a Florentine lawyer. His first sixteen years were spent with the lawyer's family in the rural surroundings of Vinci, which aroused in him a lifelong love of nature and an insatiable curiosity in it. He received little formal education but extended his knowledge through private reading. That gave him only a smattering of Latin, a deficiency that was to be a hindrance throughout his active life. At sixteen he was apprenticed in the studio of Andrea del Verrochio in Florence, where he received a training not only in art but in a wide variety of crafts and technical arts.

In 1482 Leonardo went to Milan, where he sought and obtained employment with Ludovico Sforza, later Duke of Milan, partly to sculpt a massive equestrian statue of Ludovico but the work never progressed beyond the full-scale model stage. He did, however, complete the painting which became known as the *Virgin of the Rocks* and in 1497 his greatest artistic achievement, *The Last Supper*, commissioned jointly by Ludovico and the friars of Santa Maria della Grazie and painted on the wall of the monastery's refectory. Leonardo was responsible for the court pageants and also devised a system of irrigation to supply water to the plains of Lombardy. In 1499 the French army entered Milan and deposed Leonardo's employer. Leonardo departed and, after a brief visit to Mantua, returned to Florence, where for a time he was employed as architect and engineer to Cesare Borgia, Duke of Romagna. Around 1504 he completed another celebrated work, the *Mona Lisa*.

In 1506 Leonardo began his second sojourn in Milan, this time in the service of King Louis XII of France, who appointed him 'painter and engineer'. In 1513 Leonardo left for Rome in the company of his pupil Francesco Melzi, but his time there was unproductive and he found himself out of touch with the younger artists active there, Michelangelo above all. In 1516 he accepted with relief an invitation from King François I of France to reside at the small château of St Cloux in the royal domain of Amboise. With the pension granted by François, Leonardo lived out his remaining years in tranquility at St Cloux.

Leonardo's career can hardly be regarded as a success or worthy of such a towering genius. For centuries he was known only for the handful of artistic works that he managed to complete and have survived more or less intact. His main activity remained hidden until the nineteenth and twentieth centuries, during which the contents of his notebooks were gradually revealed. It became evident that Leonardo was one of the greatest scientific investigators and inventors in the history of civilization. Throughout his working life he extended a searching curiosity over an extraordinarily wide range of subjects. The notes show careful investigation of questions of mechanical and civil engineering, such as power transmission by means of pulleys and also a form of chain belting. The notebooks record many devices, such as machines for grinding and polishing lenses, a lathe operated by treadle-crank, a rolling mill with conical rollers and a spinning machine with pinion and yard divider. Leonardo made an exhaustive study of the flight of birds, with a view to designing a flying machine, which obsessed him for many years.

Leonardo recorded his observations and conclusions, together with many ingenious inventions, on thousands of pages of manuscript notes, sketches and drawings. There are occasional indications that he had in mind the publication of portions of the notes in a coherent form, but he never diverted his energy into putting them in order; instead, he went on making notes. As a result, Leonardo's impact on the development of science and technology was virtually nil. Even if his notebooks had been copied and circulated, there were daunting impediments to their understanding. Leonardo was left-handed and wrote in mirror-writing: that is, in reverse from right to left. He also used his own abbreviations and no punctuation.

At his death Leonardo bequeathed his entire output of notes to his friend and companion Francesco Melzi, who kept them safe until his own death in 1570. Melzi left the collection in turn to his son Orazio, whose lack of interest in the arts and sciences resulted in a sad period of dispersal which endangered their survival, but in 1636 the bulk of them, in thirteen volumes, were assembled and donated to the Ambrosian Library in Milan. These include a large volume of notes and drawings compiled from the various portions of the notebooks and is now known as the *Codex Atlanticus*. There they stayed, forgotten and ignored, until 1796, when Napoleon's marauding army overran Italy and art and literary works, including the thirteen volumes of Leonardo's notebooks, were pillaged and taken to Paris. After the war in 1815, the French government agreed to return them but only the *Codex Atlanticus* found its way back to Milan; the rest remained in Paris. The appendix to one notebook, dealing with the flight of birds, was later regarded as of sufficient importance to stand on its own. Four small collections reached Britain at various times during the seventeenth and eight-eenth centuries; of these, the volume in the Royal Collection at Windsor Castle is notable for its magnificent series of anatomical drawings. Other collections include the *Codex Leicester* and *Codex Arundel* in the British Museum in London, and the *Madrid Codices* in Spain.

Towards the end of the nineteenth century, Leonardo's true stature as scientist, engineer and inventor began to emerge, particularly with the publication of transcriptions and translations of his notebooks. The volumes in Paris appeared in 1881–97 and the *Codex Atlanticus* was published in Milan between 1894 and 1904.

Principal Honours and Distinctions
'Premier peintre, architecte et mécanicien du Roi' to King François I of France, 1516.

Further Reading
E. MacCurdy, 1939, *The Notebooks of Leonardo da Vinci*, 2 vols, London; 2nd edn, 1956, London (the most extensive selection of the notes, with an English translation).
G. Vasari (trans. G. Bull), 1965, *Lives of the Artists*, London: Penguin, pp. 255–271.
C. Gibbs-Smith, 1978, *The Inventions of Leonardo da Vinci*, Oxford: Phaidon.
L.H. Heydenreich, Dibner and L. Reti, 1981, *Leonardo the Inventor*, London: Hutchinson.
I.B. Hart, 1961, *The World of Leonardo da Vinci*, London: Macdonald.

LRD/IMcN

Le Roy, Pierre
b. 24 November 1717 Paris, France
d. 25 August 1785 Viry-sur-Orge, France

French horologist who invented the detached détente escapement and the compensation balance.

Le Roy was born into a distinguished horological family: his father, Julien, was Clockmaker to the King. Pierre became Master in 1737 and continued to work with his father, taking over the business when his father died in 1759. However, he seems to have left the commercial side of the business to others so that he could concentrate on developing the marine chronometer. Unlike John **Harrison**, he believed that the solution lay in detaching the escapement from the balance, and in 1748 he submitted a proposal for the first detached escapement to the Académie des Sciences in Paris. He also differed from Harrison in his method of temperature compensation, which acted directly on the balance by altering its radius of gyration. This was achieved either by mounting thermometers on the balance or by using bimetallic strips which effectively reduced the diameter of the balance as the temperature rose (with refinements, this later became the standard method of temperature compensation in watches and chronometers). Le Roy had already discovered that for every spiral balance spring there was a particular length at which it would be isochronous, and this method of temperature compensation did not destroy that isochronism by altering the length, as other methods did. These innovations were incorporated in a chronometer with an improved detached escapement which he presented to Louis XV in 1766 and described in a memoir to the Académie des Sciences. This instrument contained the three essential elements of all subsequent chronometers: an isochronous balance spring, a detached escapement and a balance with temperature compensation. Its performance was similar to that of Harrison's fourth timepiece, and Le Roy was awarded prizes by the Académie des Sciences for the chronometer and for his memoir. However, his work was never fully appreciated in France, where he was overshadowed by his rival Ferdinand Berthoud. When Berthoud was awarded the coveted title of Horloger de la Marine, Le Roy became disillusioned and shortly afterwards gave up chronometry and retired to the country.

Principal Honours and Distinctions
Horloger du Roi 1760.

Bibliography
1748, 'Echappement à détente', *Histoire et mémoires de l'Académie Royale des Sciences*.
1770, *Mémoire sur la meilleure manière de mesurer le temps en mer*, Paris.

Further Reading
R.T. Gould, 1923, *The Marine Chronometer: Its History and Development*, London; reprinted 1960, Holland Press (still the standard work on the subject).

DV

Leschot, Georges Auguste

b. 24 March 1800 Geneva, Switzerland
d. 4 February 1884 Geneva, Switzerland

Swiss clockmaker, inventor of diamond drilling.

By about 1843, Leschot, who was renowned for designing machines to produce parts of clocks on an industrialized scale, had gathered that the fine, deep lines he found on an Egyptian red porphyry plate must have been cut by diamonds. He thus resurrected a technology that had been largely forgotten over the centuries, when in 1862 his son, who was engaged in constructing a railway line in Italy, was confronted with the problems of tunnelling through hard rock. In Paris he developed a drilling machine consisting of a casing that rotated in a similar way to the American rope drilling method. The crown of the machine was mounted with eight black diamonds, and inside the casing a stream of water circulated continuously to flush out the mud.

He took out his first patent in France in 1862, and followed it with further ones in many European countries and in America. He continued to concentrate on his watchmaker's profession and left the rights to his patents to his son. It was Leschot's ingenious idea of utilizing diamonds for drilling hard rock that was later applied in different mining processes. It influenced a series of further developments in many countries, including those of Alfred **Brandt** and Major Beaumont in England. In particular, the fact that the hollow casing produced a complete core was of importance for the increasing amount of petroleum prospecting in Pennsylvania after Edwin Laurentine **Drake**'s find of 1859, where M.C. Bullock sunk the first deep well (200 m) in the world by diamond drilling in 1870. The efforts of Per Anton **Crælius** in Sweden made diamond drilling a success worldwide.

Further Reading

D. Colladon, 1884, 'Notice sur les inventions mécaniques de M.G. Leschot, horloger', *Archives des Sciences Physiques et Naturelles* 3, XI (1): 297–313 (discusses the influences of Leschot's invention on other engineers in Europe).

D. Hoffmann, 1962, 'Die Erfindung der Diamantbohrmaschine vor 100 Jahren', *Der An-*

schnitt 14 (1): 15–19 (contains detailed biographical outlines).

WK

Lesseps, Ferdinand de

b. 19 November 1805 Versailles, France
d. 7 December 1894 La Chesnaye, near Paris, France

French diplomat and canal entrepreneur.

Ferdinand de Lesseps was born into a family in the diplomatic service and it was intended that his should be his career also. He was educated at the Lycée Napoléon in Paris. In 1825, aged 20, he was appointed an attaché to the French consulate in Lisbon. In 1828 he went to the Consulate-General in Tunis and in 1831 was posted from there to Egypt, becoming French Consul in Cairo two years later. For his work there during the plague in 1836 he was awarded the Croix de Chevalier in the Légion d'honneur. During this time he became very friendly with Said Mohammed and the friendship was maintained over the years, although there were no expectations then that Said would occupy any great position of authority.

De Lesseps then served in other countries. In 1841 he had thought about a canal from the Mediterranean to the Red Sea, and he brooded over the idea until 1854. In October of that year, having retired from the diplomatic service, he returned to Egypt privately. His friend Said became Viceroy and he readily agreed to the proposal to cut the canal. At first there was great international opposition to the idea, and in 1855 de Lesseps travelled to England to try to raise capital. Work finally started in 1859, but there were further delays following the death of Said Pasha in 1863. The work was completed in 1869 and the canal was formally opened by the Empress Eugenie on 20 November 1869. De Lesseps was fêted in France and awarded the Grand Croix de la Légion d'honneur.

He subsequently promoted the project of the Corinth Canal, but his great ambition in his later years was to construct a canal across the Isthmus of Panama. This idea had been conceived by Spanish adventurers in 1514, but everyone felt the problems and cost would be too great. De Lesseps, riding high in popularity and with his charismatic character, convinced the public of the scheme's feasibility and was able to raise vast sums for the enterprise. He proposed a sea-level canal, which required the excavation of a 350 ft (107 m) cut through terrain; this eventually proved impossible, but work nevertheless started in 1881.

In 1882 de Lesseps became first Président d'Honneur of the Syndicat des Entrepreneurs de Travaux Publics de France and was elected to the Chair of the French Academy in 1884. By 1891 the Panama Canal was in a disastrous financial crisis: a new company was formed, and because of the vast sums expended a financial investigation was made. The report led to de Lesseps, his son and several high-ranking government ministers and officials being charged with bribery and corruption, but de Lesseps was a very sick man and never appeared at the trial. He was never convicted, although others were, and he died soon after, at the age of 89, at his home.

Principal Honours and Distinctions
Croix de Chevalier de la Légion d'honneur 1836; Grand Croix 1869.

Further Reading
John S. Pudney, 1968, Suez. *De Lesseps' Canal,* London: Dent.
John Marlowe, 1964, *The Making of the Suez Canal,* London: Cresset.

JHB

Leupold, Jacob
b. 25 May 1674 Planitz, Germany
d. 12 January 1727 Leipzig, Germany

German scientist famous for his nine-volume work, which comes under the general title Theatrum Machinarum.

Leupold was essentially an academic of great learning in the tradition of the Renaissance. He was basically a scientist with a principal interest in the extraction of minerals, and in 1725 was made a Commissioner of Mines. He was also a member of the Academy of Berlin. The nine volumes of his work *Theatrum Machinarum* are detailed studies of the various disciplines, with existing practices illustrated in woodcuts. These nine volumes (see below, Bibliography) were brought to England by the younger members of the aristocracy returning from their Grand Tour. The large water-wheel created for raising water at Painshill, in Surrey, was a straight copy of the

relevant illustration in *Wasser-Bau-Kunst* (1724). The volume *Mühlen-Bau-Kunst* is a good reference book on German milling practice, which remains essentially unchanged in existing mills.

Bibliography
The nine volumes of *Theatrum Machinarum* were all reprinted in Hanover in the 1980s. The original dates of publication were as follows:
1722, *Schau-Platz der Rechen- und Mess-kunst;*
1724, *Schau-Platz der Wasser-Bau-Kunst;*
1724, *Schau-Platz der Wasser-Künste;*
1724, *Schau-Platz des Grundes der mechanischen Wissenschaften;*
1725, *Schau-Platz der Heb-Zeuge;*
1726, *Schau-Platz der Gewicht-Kunst und Waagen;*
1726, *Schau-Platz der Brücken und des Brücken-Baues;*
1729, *Zusatz zum Schau-Platz der Machinen und Instrumenten;*
1735, *Schau-Platz der Mühlen-Bau-Kunst.*

KM

Levavasseur, Léon
b. 8 January 1863 Cherbourg, France
d. 26 February 1922 Puteaux, France

French designer of Antoinette aeroplanes and engines.

Léon Levavasseur was an artist who became an electrical engineer and in 1902 Technical Director of a firm called Société Antoinette, headed by Jules Gastambide (Antoinette being the name of Gastambide's daughter). Levavasseur's first aeroplane, built in 1903, was a bird-like machine which did not fly. The engine showed promise, however, and Levavasseur developed it for use in motor boats from 1904. In 1906 he produced two Antoinette aero-engines, one of 24 hp (18 kW) and the other 50 hp (37 kW), which were used by Alberto **Santos-Dumont** and several other early designers. In February 1908 Levavasseur produced a tractor (propeller at the front) monoplane, the Gastambide–Mengin *I*, for two of his colleagues. Flown by a mechanic, this managed several short hops before it crash-landed. It was rebuilt and improved to become the Antoinette *II* and later in the year became the first monoplane to complete a circular flight.

Levavasseur then went on to produce a series of Antoinette monoplanes which, with the monoplanes of Louis **Blériot**, challenged the pusher biplanes of **Voisin** and **Farman**. The rivalry between the Antoinettes and Blériots made headlines in 1909 when they were being prepared to win the *Daily Mail* prize for the first flight across the English Channel. Hubert Latham took off in his Antoinette on 19 July 1909, but his engine failed and he had to be rescued from the sea. On 25 July Louis Blériot took off in his Blériot *No. XI* and won both the prize and worldwide acclaim. In 1911 Latham flew his Antoinette across the Golden Gate at San Francisco. The same year Levavasseur built a revolutionary streamlined three-seater monoplane with cantilever wings (no wire bracing), but this *Monobloc* Antoinette failed; with it the line of Antoinettes came to an end.

Further Reading

C.H. Gibbs-Smith, 1965, *The Invention of the Aeroplane 1799–1909*, London (provides details of the Antoinette monoplanes).

F. Peyrey, 1909, *Les Oiseaux artificiels*, Paris (a contemporary account of the early machines).

JDS

Lever, William Hesketh

b. 19 September 1851 Bolton, Lancashire, England
d. 7 May 1925 Hampstead, London, England

English manufacturer of soap.

William Hesketh Lever was the son of the retail grocer James Lever, who built up the large wholesale firm of Lever & Co. in the north-west of England. William entered the firm at the age of 19 as a commercial traveller, and in the course of his work studied the techniques of manufacture and the quality of commercial soaps available at the time. He decided that he would concentrate on the production of a soap that was not evil-smelling, would lather easily and be attractively packaged. In 1884 he produced Sunlight Soap, which became the trade mark for Lever & Co. He had each tablet wrapped, partly to protect the soap from oxygenization and thus prevent it from becoming rancid, and partly to display his brand name as a form of advertising. In 1885 he raised a large capital sum, purchased the Soap Factory in Warrington of Winser & Co.,

and began manufacture. His product contained oils from copra, palm and cotton blended with tallow and resin, and its quality was carefully monitored during production. In a short time it was in great demand and began to replace the previously available alternatives of home-made soap and poor-quality, unpleasant-smelling bars.

It soon became necessary to expand the firm's premises, and in 1887 Lever purchased fifty-six acres of land upon which he set up a new centre of manufacture. This was in the Wirral in Cheshire, near the banks of the River Mersey. Production at the new factory, which was called Port Sunlight, began in January 1889. Lever introduced a number of technical improvements in the production process, including the heating systems and the recovery of glycerine (which could later be sold) from the boiling process.

Like Sir Titus **Salt** of Saltaire before him, Lever believed it to be in the interest of the firm to house his workers in a high standard of building and comfort close to the factory. By the early twentieth century he had created Port Sunlight Village, one of the earliest and certainly the most impressive housing estates, for his employees. Architecturally the estate is highly successful, being built from a variety of natural materials and vernacular styles by a number of distinguished architects, so preventing an overall architectural monotony. The comprehensive estate comprises, in addition to the factory and houses, a church, an art gallery, schools, a cottage hospital, library, bank, fire station, post office and shops, as well as an inn and working men's institute, both of which were later additions. In 1894 Lever & Co. went public and soon was amalgamated with other soap firms. It was at its most successful high point by 1910.

Principal Honours and Distinctions
First Viscount Leverhulme of the Western Isles.

Further Reading
1985, *Dictionary of Business Biography*. Butterworth.
Ian Campbell Bradley, 1987, *Enlightened Entrepreneurs*, London: Weidenfeld & Nicolson.
DY

Levers (Leavers), John

fl. 1812–21 England
d. after 1821 Rouen, France

English improver of lace-making machines that formed the basis for many later developments.

John **Heathcote** had shown that it was possible to make lace by machine with his patents of 1808 and 1809. His machines were developed and improved by John Levers. Levers was originally a hosiery frame-smith and setter-up at Sutton-in-Ashfield but moved to Nottingham, where he extended his operations to the construction of point-net and warp-lace machinery. In the years 1812 and 1813 he more or less isolated himself in the garret of a house in Derby Road, where he assembled his lace-making machine by himself. He was helped by two brothers and a nephew who made parts, but they saw it only when it was completed. Financial help for making production machines came from the firm of John Stevenson & Skipwith, lace manufacturers in Nottingham. Levers never sought a patent, as he was under the mistaken impression that additions or improvements to an existing patented machine could not be protected. An early example of the machine survives at the Castle Museum in Nottingham. Although his prospects must have seemed good, for some reason Levers dissolved his partnership with Stevenson & Co. and continued to work on improving his machine. In 1817 he altered it from the horizontal to the upright position, building many of the machines each year. He was a friendly, kind-hearted man, but he seems to have been unable to apply himself to his business, preferring the company of musicians – he was a bandmaster of the local militia – and was soon frequently without money, even to buy food for his family. He emigrated in 1821 to Rouen, France, where he set up his lace machines and where he subsequently died; when or in what circumstances is unknown. His machine continued to be improved and was adapted to work with the **Jacquard** mechanism to select the pattern.

Further Reading

W. Felkin, 1967, *History of the Machine-wrought Hosiery and Lace Manufactures*, reprint, Newton Abbot (orig. pub. 1867) (the main account of the Levers machine).

W. English, 1969, *The Textile Industry*, London (a brief account of the Levers lace machine).

D.M. Smith, 1965, *Industrial Archaeology of the East Midlands*, Dawlish (includes an illustration of Levers's machine).

RLH

Lewis, Colonel Isaac Newton

b. 12 October 1858 New Salem, Pennsylvania, USA
d. 9 November 1931 Hoboken, New Jersey, USA

American soldier and weapons designer.

Lewis graduated from the US Military Academy, West Point, in 1884 and was commissioned into the Artillery. He soon displayed his technical aptitude and in 1891 patented an artillery ranging device. This was followed by further gunnery devices to improve artillery accuracy and a quick-firing field gun. He also displayed an interest in electricity and designed a car lighting system and wind-powered electric lighting.

In 1911 he patented the gun that bears his name. The significance of this compared with existing machine guns was its comparatively light weight, which enabled it to be carried and operated by one person. Even so, the US Army showed no interest and so Lewis, by now retired from the Army, moved to Europe and set up a factory to produce it at Liège in Belgium. At the outbreak of war he moved his operation to England and merged it with the Birmingham Small Arms Company. The Lewis gun became the British Army's standard light machine gun during the First World War and was also used on aircraft. The USA eventually had a change of heart and also used the Lewis gun.

CM

Lewis, John

fl. *c.*1815 England

English developer of a machine for shearing woollen cloth with rotary cutters.

To give a smooth surface to cloth such as the old English broadcloth, the nap was raised and then sheared off. Hand-operated shears of enormous size were used to cut the fibres that stuck up when the cloth was laid over a curved table top. Great skill was required to achieve a smooth finish. Various attempts, such as that in 1784 by James Harmer, a clergyman of Sheffield, were made to mechanize the process by placing several pairs of shears in a frame and operating them by cranks, but success was not achieved. Samuel G. Dow of Albany, New York, patented a rotary shearer in England in 1794, and there was Samuel **Dore** in the same year too. John Lewis never claimed that he invented the rotary cutter, and it is possible that he made have seen drawings or actual examples of these earlier machines. His claim in his patent of 1815 was that, for the first time, he brought together a number of desirable features in one machine for shearing cloth to achieve the first really successful example. The local story in the Stroudwater district in Gloucestershire is that Lewis obtained this idea from Budding, who as a lad worked for the Lewis family, clothiers at Brinscombe Mills; Budding invented a lawn mower with rotary barrel blades that works on the same principle, patenting it in 1830. In the shearing machine, the cloth was moved underneath the blades, which could be of the same width so that only one operation was needed for each side. Other inventors had similar ideas, and a Stroud engineer, Stephen Price, took out a patent a month after Lewis did. These machines spread quickly in the Gloucestershire textile industry, and by 1830 hand-shearing was extinct. John Lewis was the son of Joseph, who had inherited the Brinscombe Mills in 1790 but must have died before 1815, when his children mortgaged the property for £12,000. Joseph's three sons, George, William and John, worked the mill for a time, but in 1840 William was there alone.

Bibliography
1815, British patent no. 3,945 (rotary shearing machine).

Further Reading
J. de L. Mann, 1971, *The Cloth Industry in the West of England from 1660 to 1880*, Oxford (the best account of the introduction of the shearing machines).
J. Tann, 1967, *Gloucestershire Woollen Mills*, Newton Abbot (includes notes about the Brinscombe Mills).
K.G. Ponting, 1971, *The Woollen Industry of South-West England*, Bath; and H.A. Randall, 1965–6, 'Some mid-Gloucestershire engineers and inventors', *Transactions of the Newcomen Society* 38 (both mention Lewis's machine).

RLH

Li Bing (Li Ping)
fl. 309–240 BC China
d. soon after 240 BC China

Chinese hydraulic engineer who began the construction of the Guanxian irrigation system.

He was Governor of Szechuan. His outstanding achievement was to initiate the Guanxian (Kuanhsien) irrigation system, one of the world's greatest irrigation projects. North-west of Chengdu, capital of Szechuan province, the Min Jiang river tumbles from the Tibetan border country. It was distributed in some 735 miles (1,185 km) of channels into an irrigation system that fertilized half a million acres of good agricultural land and enabled a largely farming population of some 5 million to support themselves, with a regular water supply and free from drought and flood. In the ancient world, it can only be compared in scale with the works on the Nile in Ancient Egypt. The irrigation system was completed by his son Li Erlang *c.*230 BC. At the time, it earned both Li Bing and his son temples in their honour; it survives to this day and is still impressive.

Further Reading
J. Needham, *Science and Civilisation in China*, Cambridge: Cambridge University Press, 1971, vol. IV.3, pp. 249, 288ff., 296, 304, 329.

LRD

Li Chieh
See **Li Jie**.

Li Chun
fl. *c.*610 China

Chinese bridge builder who constructed the earliest segmental-arch long-span stone bridge.

Li Chun and his pupils founded a school and style of building that was to last for centuries. He was responsible for one of China's greatest engineering achievements, the world's earliest segmental-arch long-span stone bridge. It stretched across the Jiao Shui river flowing out of the Shansi mountains at the edge of the north China plain. The bridge had a span of 123 ft (37.5 m), with a rise of 23 ft 7 in. (7.19 m) above chord level and the spandrels were pierced with two arches on each side.

Further Reading
J. Needham, *Science and Civilisation in China*,

Cambridge: Cambridge University Press, 1965, Vols IV.2, p. 33; 1971, IV.3, pp. 172–3, 175, 177ff.

LRD

Liebig, Justus von

b. 12 May 1803 Darmstadt, Germany
d. 18 April 1873 Munich, Germany

German chemist, pioneer in the training of chemists and in agricultural chemistry.

As the son of a pharmacist, Leibig early acquired an interest in chemistry. In 1822 he pursued his chemical studies in Paris under Joseph Louis Gay-Lussac (1778–1850), one of the leading chemists of the time. Three years later he became Professor of Chemistry in the small university of Giessen, near Frankfurt, where he remained for over thirty years. It was there that he established his celebrated laboratory for training in practical chemistry. The laboratory itself and the instruction given by Liebig were a model for the training of chemists throughout Europe and a steady stream of well-qualified chemists issued forth from Giessen. It was the supply of well-trained chemists that proved to be the basis for Germany's later success in industrial chemistry. The university now bears Liebig's name, and the laboratory has been preserved as a museum in the same state that it was in after the extensions of 1839. Liebig's many and important researches into chemical theory and organic chemistry lie outside the scope of this *Dictionary*. From 1840 he turned to the chemistry of living things. In agriculture, he stressed the importance of fertilizers containing potassium and phosphorus, although he underrated the role of nitrogen. Liebig thereby exerted a powerful influence on the movement to provide agriculture with a scientific basis.

Further Reading

C. Paoloni, 1968, *Justus von Liebig: eine Bibliographie sämtlicher Veröffentlichungen*, Heidelberg: Carl Winter (includes a complete list of Liebig's papers and books, published collections of his letters and a list of secondary works about him).

A.W. Hofmann, 1876, *The Life Work of Liebig* (Faraday Lecture), London (a valuable reference).

J.R. Partington, 1964, *A History of Chemistry*, Vol. 4, London (a well-documented account of his work).

F.R. Moulton, 1942, *Liebig and After Liebig: A Century of Progress in Agricultural Chemistry*, Washington, DC: American Association for the Advancement of Science, publication 18 (for Liebig's work in agricultural chemistry).

J.B. Morrell, 1972, 'The chemist breeders', *Ambix* 19: 1–47 (for information about Liebig's laboratory).

LRD

Li Gao (Li Kao)

fl. 752/820 China

Chinese physicist, technologist and patron of engineers.

Li Gao was Prince of Cao (Tshao). He was interested in acoustics and carried out experiments on both hydrostatic and air pressure. He constructed 'trick' hydrostatic vessels that could take up different positions according to the amount of water in them. Such vessels had been known since the third century BC and were popular at court for over a thousand years: Li's were made of lacquered wood, *c.*790, probably in quantity. He made successful use of paddle warships operated by treadmills. Similar vessels may have been in use as early as the late fifth century, but this is not at all certain. Li Gao's ships are therefore the first practical achievement of an idea for ship propulsion that, probably independently, had been mooted but not realized in early Byzantine times in Europe. His experiments with this type of vessel were made during 782 to 785, while he was Governor of Hungchow. It was said that the ships 'went like the wind', faster than a charging horse.

Further Reading

J. Needham, *Science and Civilisation in China*, Cambridge: Cambridge University Press, 1962, Vols IV.1, pp. 38, 62; 1965, IV.2, pp. 417–18, 433, 435; *Clerks and Craftsmen in China and the West*, 1970, pp. 25, 127–8.

LRD

Li Jie (Li Chieh)

fl. 1085–1110 China

Chinese architect who revised the Chinese treatise on architectural method, Ying Zao Fa Shi.

435

He was a first-rate architect and from 1092 was an assistant in the Directorate of Buildings and Construction. He must have shown promise as an architect for he was commissioned to revise the old manuals of architecture. The work was completed in 1100 and printed three years later as the treatise for which he is best known, the *Ying Zao Fa Shi* (Treatise on Architectural Method). This work has been called the greatest and definitive treatise of any age in the millennial tradition of Chinese architecture. The work is noted for the comprehensive range of constructions covered and the thoroughness of its instruction to architects. The detailed instructions for the construction and shaping of woodwork are not found in European literature until the eighteenth century. The illustrations are fine and the excellence of the constructional drawings makes them the earliest working drawings. He was a distinguished practising builder, as well as a writer, for he erected administrative offices, palace apartments, gates and gate towers, together with the ancestral temples of the Sung dynasty as well as Buddhist temples.

Further Reading

J. Needham, *Science and Civilisation in China*, Cambridge: Cambridge University Press, 1965, Vols IV.2, pp. 49, 549, 551; 1971, IV.3, pp. 84–5, 107.

LRD

Li Kao
See **Li Gao**.

Lilienthal, Otto
b. 23 May 1848 Anklam, Prussia (now Germany)
d. 10 August 1896 Berlin, Germany

German glider pioneer, the first to make a controlled flight using wings.

Otto Lilienthal and his brother Gustav developed an interest in flying as boys, when they studied birds in flight, built models and even tried to fit wings to their arms. Gustav went on to become a successful architect while Otto, after a brilliant scholastic career, became a mechanical engineer. Otto was able to devote his spare time to the problems of flight, and Gustav helped when his work allowed. They considered man-powered and mechanically powered projects, but neither looked hopeful so they turned to gliding. Otto published his research work in a book, *Bird Flight as a Basis for Aviation*. By 1889 Otto Lilienthal was ready to test his first full-size gliders. No. 1 and No. 2 were not successful, but No. 3, built in 1891, showed promise. He gradually improved his designs and his launching sites as he gained experience. To take off he ran downhill carrying his hang-glider until it became airborne, then he controlled it by swinging his body weight in the appropriate direction. He even built an artificial mound near Berlin so that he could take off into the wind whichever way it was blowing.

In all, Lilienthal built some eighteen gliders with various wing shapes, including biplanes. By 1895 he was planning movable control surfaces (operated by head movement) and a powered version using a carbonic acid gas motor. Unfortunately, Lilienthal crashed and died of his injuries before these ideas could be tested. In all, he made over two thousand flights covering distances up to 300 m (300 yds. Many of these flights were recorded on photographs and so generated an interest in flying. Lilienthal's achievements also encouraged other pioneers, such as Percy Pilcher in Britain, and Octave **Chanute** and the **Wright** brothers in the United States.

Bibliography

1899, *Der Vogelflug als Grundlage der Fliegekunst*, Berlin, reprinted *c*.1977; repub. in English, 1911, as *Bird Flight as a Basis for Aviation*.

Further Reading

Charles H. Gibbs-Smith, 1985, *Aviation*, London (provides a detailed account of Lilienthal's gliders).
P.H. Lilienthal, 1978, 'Die Lilienthal Gebrüder', *Aerospace* (Royal Aeronautical Society) (January) (for more personal information).
'The Lilienthal and Pilcher gliders compared', *Flight* (1 January 1910 and 8 January 1910) (for details about and plans of a typical Lilienthal glider).

JDS

Lind, James
b. 1716 Edinburgh, Scotland
d. 13 July 1794 Gosport, England

Scottish physician and naval surgeon whose studies and investigations led to significant improvements in the living conditions on board ships; the author of the first treatise on the nature and prevention of scurvy.

Lind was registered in 1731 as an apprentice at the College of Surgeons in Edinburgh. By 1739 he was serving as a naval surgeon in the Mediterranean and during the ensuing decade he experienced conditions at sea off Guinea, the West Indies and in home waters. He returned to Edinburgh, taking his MD in 1748, and in 1750 was elected a Fellow of the College of Physicians of Edinburgh, becoming the Treasurer in 1757. In 1758 he was appointed Physician to the Naval Hospital at Haslar, Gosport, near Portsmouth, a post which he retained until his death.

He had been particularly struck by the devastating consequences of scurvy during Anson's circumnavigation of the globe in 1740. At least 75 per cent of the crews had been affected (though it should be borne in mind that a considerable number of them were pensioners and invalids when posted aboard). Coupled with his own experiences, this led to the publication of *A Treatise on the Scurvy*, in 1754. Demonstrating that this condition accounted for many more deaths than from all the engagements with the French and Spanish in the current wars, he made it clear that by appropriate measures of diet and hygiene the disease could be entirely eliminated.

Further editions of the treatise were published in 1757 and 1775, and the immense importance of his observations was immediately recognized. None the less, it was not until 1795 that an Admiralty order was issued on the supply of lime juice to ships. The efficacy of lime juice had been known for centuries, but it was Lind's observations that led to action, however tardy; that for economic reasons the relatively ineffective West Indian lime juice was supplied was in no way his responsibility. It is of interest that there is no evidence that Captain James Cook (1728–79) had any knowledge of Lind's work when arranging his own anti-scorbutic precautions in preparation for his historic first voyage.

Lind's other work included observations on typhus, the proper ventilation of ships at sea, and the distillation of fresh from salt water.

Bibliography
1754, *A Treatise on the Scurvy*, Edinburgh.
1757, *An Essay on the most effectual means of Preserving the Health of Seamen in the Royal Navy*, Edinburgh.
1767, *An Essay on Diseases incidental to Europeans in Hot Climates*, Edinburgh.

Further Reading
L. Roddis, 1951, *James Lind – Founder of Nautical Medicine*.
Records of the Royal Colleges of Surgeons of Edinburgh.
Records of the Royal College of Physicians of Edinburgh.

MG

Linde, Carl von

b. 11 June 1842 Berndorf, Bavaria, Germany
d. 16 November 1934 Munich, Germany

German refrigeration engineer.

He was educated at the Zurich Polytechnic, with Clausius being among his lecturers. He spent some time at a locomotive works and in 1868 went on to teach at the Munich Polytechnic. He became a director of a refrigeration company, where he was employed from 1879 until 1892, during which time he took out many patents in refrigeration technology. Among these was one for the ammonia compressor in 1876; this was probably the most important. His interests turned again to research and he went to the Munich Technische Hochschule, where he worked on the liquefaction of gases, including air. He designed plant for the liquefaction of air on a commercial scale, establishing the successful foundation of a whole new industry.

Bibliography
Aus meinem Leben und meiner Arbeit.

Further Reading
A.F. Burstall, *A History of Mechanical Engineering*.

IMcN

Linton, Hercules

b. 1 January 1836 Inverbervie, Kincardineshire, Scotland
d. 15 May 1900 Inverbervie, Kincardineshire, Scotland

Scottish naval architect and shipbuilder; designer of the full-rigged ship Cutty Sark.

Linton came from a north-east Scottish family with shipbuilding connections. After education at Arbuthnott and then Arbroath Academy, he followed his father by becoming an apprentice at the Aberdeen shipyard of Alex Hall in January 1855. Thus must have been an inspiring time for him as the shipyards of Aberdeen were at the start of their rise to world renown. Hall's had just introduced the hollow, lined Aberdeen Bow which heralded the great years of the Aberdeen Clippers. Linton stayed on with Hall's until around 1863, when he joined the Liverpool Underwriters' Register as a ship surveyor; he then worked for similar organizations in different parts of England and Scotland. Early in 1868 Linton joined in partnership with William Dundas Scott and the shipyard of Scott and Linton was opened on the banks of the River Leven, a tributary of the Clyde, at Dumbarton. The operation lasted for about three years until bankruptcy forced closure, the cause being the age-old shipbuilder's problem of high capital investment with slow cash flow. Altogether, nine ships were built, the most remarkable being the record-breaking composite-built clipper ship *Cutty Sark*. At the time of the closure the tea clipper was in an advanced state of outfitting and was towed across the water to Denny's shipyard for completion. Linton worked for a while with Gourlay Brothers of Dundee, and then with the shipbuilders Oswald Mordaunt, of Woolston near Southampton, before returning to the Montrose area in 1884. His wife died the following year and thereafter Linton gradually reduced his professional commitments.

Further Reading
Robert E. Brettle, 1969, *The Cutty Sark, Her Designer and Builder. Hercules Linton 1836–1900*, Cambridge: Heffer.
Frank C.G. Carr, 'The restoration of the Cutty Sark', *Transactions of the Royal Institution of Naval Architects* 108: 193–216.
Fred M. Walker, 1984, *Song of the Clyde. A History of Clyde Shipbuilding*, Cambridge: PSL.

FMW

Lioret, Henri Jules

b. 26 July 1848 Moret-sur-Loing, Seine-et-Marne, France
d. 1938

French clockmaker, developer of sound recording and reproducing equipment, and inventor of a celluloid cylinder.

His first connection with the phonograph principle was in the development of a miniature talking doll with a spring motor and interchangeable and indestructible celluloid cylinders in 1893 for the firm Emile Jumeau. He went on to develop commercial recording and reproducing equipment for celluloid cylinders, perfecting the process of embossing a piece of heated celluloid tube and supporting it by shrinking it onto a piece of metal tube. His training as a clockmaker enabled him to construct a functional clockwork phonograph at a time when other companies struggled with the conversion from manual or electrical to clockwork. He was unable to compete with cheap mass production and left the phonograph field in 1911. However, he continued in other acoustic fields, including moving pictures with sound and underwater sound ranging.

Bibliography
18 May 1893, French patent no. 230,177.

Further Reading
O. Read and W.L. Welch, 1959, *From Tin Foil to Stereo*, Indianapolis: Howard W. Sams, pp. 94–5.

GB-N

Li Ping
See **Li Bing**.

Lippershey, Hans (Johannes)
fl. sixteenth/seventeenth centuries the Netherlands

Dutch probable inventor of the telescope.

Lippershey was a spectacle maker of Middelburg, a contender for the invention of the telescope. It is said that about 1600 two children were playing about his workshop and chanced to place a convex and a concave lens in a line, and noted a great magnification of the nearby church. Lippershey confirmed this and started manufacture of 'instruments for seeing at a distance'. In 1608 he petitioned the States General of the Netherlands for a patent for thirty years. A committee appointed to look into the matter declared that the device was likely to be of use to the State and suggested the improvement of a binocular arrangement. Other Dutch glass-workers, however, put forward claims to have constructed similar instruments, and, in the confusion, the States General turned down Lippershey's plea and he received no financial reward or patent protection.

Further Reading
D.J. Boorstin, 1984, *The Discoverers*, London: J.M. Dent.

IMcN

Lippman, Gabriel
b. 16 August 1845 Hallerick, Luxembourg
d. 14 July 1921 at sea, in the North Atlantic

French physicist who developed interference colour photography.

Born of French parents, Lippman's work began with a distinguished career in classics, philosophy, mathematics and physics at the Ecole Normale in Luxembourg. After further studies in physics at Heidelberg University, he returned to France and the Sorbonne, where he was in 1886 appointed Director of Physics. He was a leading pioneer in France of research into electricity, optics, heat and other branches of physics.

In 1886 he conceived the idea of recording the existence of standing waves in light when it is reflected back on itself, by photographing the colours so produced. This required the production of a photographic emulsion that was effectively grainless: the individual silver halide crystals had to be smaller than the shortest wavelength of light to be recorded. Lippman succeeded in this and in 1891 demonstrated his process. A glass plate was coated with a grainless emulsion and held in a special plate-holder, glass towards the lens. The back of the holder was filled with mercury, which provided a perfect reflector when in contact with the emulsion. The standing waves produced during the exposure formed laminae in the emulsion, with the number of laminae being determined by the wavelength of the incoming light at each point on the image. When the processed plate was viewed under the correct lighting conditions, a theoreti-

cally exact reproduction of the colours of the original subject could be seen. However, the Lippman process remained a beautiful scientific demonstration only, since the ultra-fine- grain emulsion was very slow, requiring exposure times of over 10,000 times that of conventional negative material. Any method of increasing the speed of the emulsion also increased the grain size and destroyed the conditions required for the process to work.

Principal Honours and Distinctions
Royal Photographic Society Progress Medal 1897. Nobel Prize (for his work in interference colour photography) 1908.

Further Reading
J.S. Friedman, 1944, *History of Colour Photography*, Boston.
Brian Coe, 1978, *Colour Photography: The First Hundred Years*, London.
Gert Koshofer, 1981, *Farbfotografie*, Vol. I, Munich.

BC

Lister, Joseph, Baron Lister
b. 5 April 1827 Upton, Essex, England
d. 10 February 1912 Walmer, Kent, England

English surgeon, founder of the antiseptic and aseptic principles of surgical practice.

Of Quaker stock, his father also being a Fellow of the Royal Society, he studied medicine at University College, London. He qualified, and became a Fellow of the Royal College of Surgeons, in 1852. Wishing to pursue a surgical career, he moved to Edinburgh to study surgery under William Syme, whose daughter he married in 1852, the same year he was appointed Assistant Surgeon to the Edinburgh Royal Infirmary.

Until his appointment as Regius Professor of Surgery at Glasgow University and Glasgow Royal Infirmary in 1861, he was engaged in a wide variety of investigations into the nature of inflammation and the effects of irritants on wounds. Following his move to Glasgow, he became particularly involved in the major problems arising out of the vast increase in the number of surgical procedures brought about by the recent introduction of general anaesthesia. By 1865 his continuing study of wound inflammation and the microbial studies of Pasteur had led him to institute in the operating theatre a regime of surgical antisepsis involving the use of a carbolic acid spray coupled with the sterilization of instruments, the site of operation and the hands of the operator. Increasingly it was appreciated that the air was the least important origin of infection, and by 1887 the antiseptic approach had been superseded by the aseptic.

In 1869 he succeeded Syme in the Chair at Edinburgh and his methods were widely accepted abroad. In 1877 he moved to the Chair of Surgery at King's College Hospital, London, in the hope of encouraging acceptance of his work in the metropolis. As well as developing a variety of new surgical procedures, he was engaged for many years in the development of surgical ligatures, which had always been a potent stimulant of infection. His choice of catgut as a sterilizable, absorbable material paved the way for major developments in this field. The Lister Institute of Preventive Medicine was named in his honour in 1903.

Principal Honours and Distinctions

Created Baronet 1883. Baron 1897. Order of Merit 1902. President, Royal Society 1895–1900.

Bibliography

1870, 'On the effects of the antiseptic system of treatment upon the salubrity of a surgical hospital', *Lancet*.
1859, *Philosophical Transactions of the Royal Society*.
1863, *Croonian Lecture*.
1881, 1900, *Transactions of the International Medical Congress*.

Further Reading

R.J. Godlee, 1924, *Lord Lister*.
1927, *Lister Centenary Handbook*, London: Wellcome Historical Medical Museum.
H.C. Cameron, 1948, *Joseph Lister, the Friend of Man*.

MG

Lister, Samuel Cunliffe, 1st Baron Masham

b. 1 January 1815 Calverly Hall, Bradford, England
d. 2 February 1906 Swinton Park, near Bradford, England

English inventor of successful wool-combing and waste-silk spinning machines.

Lister was descended from one of the old Yorkshire families, the Cunliffe Listers of Manningham, and was the fourth son of his father Ellis. After attending a school on Clapham Common, Lister would not go to university; his family hoped he would enter the Church, but instead he started work with the Liverpool merchants Sands, Turner & Co., who frequently sent him to America. In 1837 his father built for him and his brother a worsted mill at Manningham, where Samuel invented a swivel shuttle and a machine for making fringes on shawls. It was here that he first became aware of the unhealthy occupation of combing wool by hand. Four years later, after seeing the machine that G.E. **Donisthorpe** was trying to work out, he turned his attention to mechanizing wool-combing. Lister took Donisthorpe into partnership after paying him £12,000 for his patent, and developed the Lister–Cartwright 'square nip' comber. Until this time, combing machines were little different from **Cartwright**'s original, but Lister was able to improve on this with continuous operation and by 1843 was combing the first fine botany wool that had ever been combed by machinery. In the following year he received an order for fifty machines to comb all qualities of wool. Further combing patents were taken out with Donisthorpe in 1849, 1850, 1851 and 1852, the last two being in Lister's name only. One of the important features of these patents was the provision of a gripping device or 'nip' which held the wool fibres at one end while the rest of the tuft was being combed. Lister was soon running nine combing mills. In the 1850s Lister had become involved in disputes with others who held combing patents, such as his associate Isaac **Holden** and the Frenchman Josué **Heilmann**. Lister bought up the Heilmann machine patents and afterwards other types until he obtained a complete monopoly of combing machines before the patents expired. His invention stimulated demand for wool by cheapening the product and gave a vital boost to the Australian wool trade. By 1856 he was at the head of a wool-combing business such as had never been seen before, with mills at Manningham, Bradford, Halifax, Keighley and other places in the West Riding, as well as abroad.

His inventive genius also extended to other fields. In 1848 he patented automatic compressed air brakes for railways, and in 1853 alone he took out twelve patents for various textile machines. He then tried to spin waste silk and made a second commercial career, turning what was called 'chassum' and hitherto regarded as refuse into beautiful velvets, silks, plush and other fine materials. Waste silk consisted of cocoon remnants from the reeling process, damaged cocoons and fibres rejected from other processes. There was also wild silk obtained from uncultivated worms. This is what Lister saw in a London warehouse as a mass of knotty, dirty, impure stuff, full of bits of stick and dead mulberry leaves, which he bought for a halfpenny a pound. He spent ten years trying to solve the problems, but after a loss of £250,000 and desertion by his partner his machine caught on in 1865 and brought Lister another fortune. Having failed to comb this waste silk, Lister turned his attention to the idea of 'dressing' it and separating the qualities automatically. He patented a machine in 1877 that gave a graduated combing. To weave his new silk, he imported from Spain to Bradford, together with its inventor Jose Reixach, a velvet loom that was still giving trouble. It wove two fabrics face to face, but the problem lay in separating the layers so that the pile remained regular in length. Eventually Lister was inspired by watching a scissors grinder in the street to use small emery wheels to sharpen the cutters that divided the layers of fabric. Lister took out several patents for this loom in his own name in 1868 and 1869, while in 1871 he took out one jointly with Reixach. It is said that he spent £29,000 over an eleven-year period on this loom, but this was more than recouped from the sale of reasonably priced high-quality velvets and plushes once success was achieved. Manningham mills were greatly enlarged to accommodate this new manufacture.

In later years Lister had an annual profit from his mills of £250,000, much of which was presented to Bradford city in gifts such as Lister Park, the original home of the Listers. He was connected with the Bradford Chamber of Commerce for many years and held the position of President of the Fair Trade League for some time. In 1887 he became High Sheriff of Yorkshire, and in 1891 he was made 1st Baron Masham. He was also Deputy Lieutenant in North and West Riding.

Principal Honours and Distinctions
Created 1st Baron Masham 1891.

Bibliography
1849, with G.E. Donisthorpe, British patent no. 12,712.
1850, with G.E. Donisthorpe, British patent no. 13,009.
1851, British patent no. 13,532.
1852, British patent no. 14,135.
1877, British patent no. 3,600 (combing machine).
1868, British patent no. 470.
1868, British patent no. 2,386.
1868, British patent no. 2,429.
1868, British patent no. 3,669.
1868, British patent no. 1,549.
1871, with J. Reixach, British patent no. 1,117.
1905, *Lord Masham's Inventions* (autobiography).

Further Reading
J. Hogg (ed.), *c.*1888, *Fortunes Made in Business*, London (biography).
W. English, 1969, *The Textile Industry*, London; and C. Singer (ed.), 1958, *A History of Technology*, Vol. IV, Oxford: Clarendon Press (both cover the technical details of Lister's invention).

RLH

Lithgow, James

b. 27 January 1883 Port Glasgow, Renfrewshire, Scotland
d. 23 February 1952 Langbank, Renfrewshire, Scotland

Scottish shipbuilder; creator of one of the twentieth century's leading industrial organizations.

Lithgow attended Glasgow Academy and then spent a year in Paris. In 1901 he commenced a shipyard apprenticeship with Russell & Co., where his father, William Lithgow, was sole proprietor. For years Russell's had topped the Clyde tonnage output and more than once had been the world's leading yard. Along with his brother Henry, Lithgow in 1908 was appointed a director, and in a few years he was Chairman and the yard was renamed Lithgows Ltd. By the outbreak of the First World War the Lithgow brothers were recognized as good shipbuilders and astute businessmen. In 1914 he joined the Royal Artillery; he rose to the rank of major and served with distinction, but his skills in administration were recognized and he was recalled home to become Director of Merchant Shipbuilding when British shipping losses due to submarine attack became critical. This appointment set a pattern, with public duties becoming predominant and the day-to-day shipyard business being organized by his brother. During the interwar years, Lithgow served on many councils designed to generate work and expand British commercial interests. His public appointments were legion, but none was as controversial as his directorship of National Shipbuilders Security Ltd, formed to purchase and 'sterilize' inefficient shipyards that were hindering recovery from the Depression. To this day opinions are divided on this issue, but it is beyond doubt that Lithgow believed in the task in hand and served unstintingly. During the Second World War he was Controller of Merchant Shipbuilding and Repairs and was one of the few civilians to be on the Board of Admiralty. On the cessation of hostilities, Lithgow devoted time to research boards and to the expansion of the Lithgow Group, which now included the massive Fairfield Shipyard as well as steel, marine engineering and other companies.

Throughout his life Lithgow worked for the Territorial Army, but he was also a devoted member of the Church of Scotland. He gave practical support to the Iona Community, no doubt influenced by unbounded love of the West Highlands and Islands of Scotland.

Principal Honours and Distinctions
Military Cross and mentioned in dispatches during the First World War. Baronet 1925. Grand Cross of the Order of the British Empire 1945. Commander of the Order of the Orange-Nassau (the Netherlands). CB 1947. Served as the employers' representative on the League of Nations International Labour Conference in the 1930s. President, British Iron and Steel Cofederation 1943.

Further Reading
J.M. Reid, 1964, *James Lithgow, Master of Work*, London: Hutchinson.

FMW

Lloyd Wright, Frank
See **Wright, Frank Lloyd**.

Lobnitz, Frederick
b. 7 September 1863 Renfrew, Scotland
d. 7 December 1932 Crookston, Renfrewshire, Scotland

Scottish shipbuilder, expert in dredge technology.

Lobnitz was the son of Henry Christian Lobnitz. His father was born in Denmark in 1831, and had worked for some years in both England and Scotland before becoming a naturalized British subject. Ultimately Henry joined the Clyde shipyard of James Henderson & Son and worked there until his death, by which time he was sole proprietor and the yard was called Lobnitz & Co. By this time the shipyard was the acknowledged world leader in rock-cutting machinery.

Frederick was given the opportunity to travel in Europe during the late 1870s and early 1880s. He studied at Bonn, Heidelberg and at the Zurich Polytechnic, and also served an apprenticeship at the Fairfield Shipyard of John **Elder** & Co. of Glasgow. One of his first tasks was to supervise the construction and commissioning of a subaqueous rock excavator, and then he was asked to direct rock excavations at the Suez Canal.

In 1888 Frederick Lobnitz was made a partner of the company by his father and was to remain with them until his death, at which time he was Chairman. By this time the shipyard was a private limited company and had continued to enhance its name in the specialized field of dredging. At that time the two greatest dredge builders in the world (and deadly rivals) were situated next to each other on the banks of the Clyde at Renfrew; in 1957 they merged as Simons–Lobnitz Ltd. In 1915 Lobnitz was appointed Deputy Director for Munitions in Scotland and one year later he became Director, a post he held until 1919. Having investigated the running of munitions factories in France, he released scarce labour for the war effort by staffing the plants under his control with female and unskilled labour.

Principal Honours and Distinctions
Knighted 1920. Officier de la Légion d'honneur.

Further Reading
Fred M. Walker, 1984, *Song of the Clyde. A History of Clyde Shipbuilding*, Cambridge: PSL.
Lobnitz & Co., n.d., *Romance of Dredging*.

FMW

Locke, Joseph

b. 9 August 1805 Attercliffe, Yorkshire, England
d. 18 September 1860 Moffat, Scotland

English civil engineer who built many important early main-line railways.

Joseph Locke was the son of a colliery viewer who had known George **Stephenson** in Northumberland before moving to Yorkshire: Locke himself became a pupil of Stephenson in 1823. He worked with Robert **Stephenson** at Robert Stephenson & Co.'s locomotive works and surveyed railways, including the Leeds & Selby and the Canterbury & Whitstable, for George Stephenson.

When George Stephenson was appointed Chief Engineer for construction of the Liverpool & Manchester Railway in 1826, the first resident engineer whom he appointed to work under him was Locke, who took a prominent part in promoting traction by locomotives rather than by fixed engines with cable haulage. The pupil eventually excelled the master and in 1835 Locke was appointed in place of Stephenson as Chief Engineer for construction of the Grand Junction Railway. He introduced double-headed rails carried in chairs on wooden sleepers, the prototype of the bullhead track that became standard on British railways for more than a century. By preparing the most detailed specifications, Locke was able to estimate the cost of the railway much more accurately than was usual at that time, and it was built at a cost close to the estimate; this made his name. He became Engineer to the London & Southampton Railway and completed the Sheffield, Ashton-under-Lyme & Manchester Railway, including the 3-mile (3.8 km) Woodhead Tunnel, which had been started by Charles **Vignoles**. He was subsequently responsible for many British main lines, including those of the companies that extended the West Coast Route northwards from Preston to Scotland. He was also Engineer to important early main lines in France, notably that from Paris to Rouen and its extension to Le Havre, and in Spain and Holland. In 1847 Locke was elected MP for Honiton.

Locke appreciated early in his career that steam locomotives able to operate over gradients steeper than at first thought practicable would be developed. Overall his monument is not great individual works of engineering, such as the famous bridges of his close contemporaries Robert Stephenson and I.K. **Brunel**, but a series of lines built economically but soundly through rugged country without such works; for example, the line over Shap, Cumbria.

Principal Honours and Distinctions
Officier de la Légion d'honneur, France. FRS. President, Institution of Civil Engineers 1858–9.

Further Reading
Obituary, 1861, *Minutes of Proceedings of the Institution of Civil Engineers* 20.
L.T.C. Rolt, 1962, *Great Engineers*, London: G. Bell & Sons, ch.6.
Industrial Heritage, 1991, Vol. 9 (2): 9.

See also **Brassey, Thomas**.

PJGR

Lodge, Sir Oliver Joseph

b. 12 June 1851 Penkhull, Staffordshire, England
d. 22 August 1940 Lake, near Salisbury, Wiltshire, England

*English physicist who perfected **Branly's** coherer; said to have given the first public demonstration of wireless telegraphy.*

At the age of 8 Lodge entered Newport Grammar School, and in 1863–5 received private education at Coombs in Suffolk. He then returned to Staffordshire, where he assisted his father in the potteries by working as a book-keeper. Whilst staying with an aunt in London in 1866–7, he attended scientific lectures and became interested in physics. As a result of this and of reading copies of *English Mechanic* magazine, when he was back home in Hanley he began to do experiments and attended the Wedgewood Institute. Returning to London *c.*1870, he studied initially at the Royal College of Science and then, from 1874, at University College, London (UCL), at the same time attending lectures at the Royal Institution.

In 1875 he obtained his BSc, read a paper to

443

the British Association on 'Nodes and loops in chemical formulae' and became a physics demonstrator at UCL. The following year he was appointed a physics lecturer at Bedford College, completing his DSc in 1877. Three years later he became Assistant Professor of Mathematics at UCL, but in 1881, after only two years, he accepted the Chair of Experimental Physics at the new University College of Liverpool. There began a period of fruitful studies of electricity and radio transmission and reception, including development of the lightning conductor, discovery of the 'coherent' effect of sparks and improvement of Branly's coherer, and, in 1894, what is said to be the first public demonstration of the transmission and reception (using a coherer) of wireless telegraphy, from Lewis's department store to the clock tower of Liverpool University's Victoria Building. On 10 May 1897 he filed a patent for selective tuning by self-inductance; this was before **Marconi**'s first patent was actually published and its priority was subsequently upheld.

In 1900 he became the first Principal of the new University of Birmingham, where he remained until his retirement in 1919. In his later years he was increasingly interested in psychical research.

Principal Honours and Distinctions
Knighted 1902. FRS 1887. Royal Society Council Member 1893. President, Society for Psychical Research 1901–4, 1932. President, British Association 1913. Royal Society Rumford Medal 1898. Royal Society of Arts Albert Medal 1919. Institution of Electrical Engineers Faraday Medal 1932. Fourteen honorary degrees from British and other universities.

Bibliography
1875, 'The flow of electricity in a plane', *Philosophical Magazine* (May, June and December).
1876, 'Thermo-electric phenomena', *Philosophical Magazine* (December).
1888, 'Lightning conductors', *Philosophical Magazine* (August).
1889, *Modern Views of Electricity* (lectures at the Royal Institution).
10 May 1897, 'Improvements in syntonized telegraphy without line wires', British patent no. 11,575, US patent no. 609,154.
1898, 'Radio waves', *Philosophical Magazine* (August): 227.
1931, *Past Years, An Autobiography*, London: Hodder & Stoughton.

Further Reading
W.P. Jolly, 1974, *Sir Oliver Lodge, Psychical Researcher and Scientist*, London: Constable.
E. Hawks, 1927, *Pioneers of Wireless*, London: Methuen.

See also **Hertz, Heinrich Rudolph**.

KF

Lombe, John
b. *c*.1693 probably Norwich, England
d. 20 November 1722 Derby, England

English creator of the first successful powered textile mill in Britain.

John Lombe's father, Henry Lombe, was a worsted weaver who married twice. John was the second son of the second marriage and was still a baby when his father died in 1695. John, a native of the Eastern Counties, was apprenticed to a trade and employed by Thomas **Cotchett** in the erection of Cotchett's silk mill at Derby, which soon failed however. Lombe went to Italy, or was sent there by his elder half-brother, Thomas, to discover the secrets of their throwing machinery while employed in a silk mill in Piedmont. He returned to England in 1716 or 1717, bringing with him two expert Italian workmen.

Thomas Lombe was a prosperous London merchant who financed the construction of a new water-powered silk mill at Derby which is said to have cost over £30,000. John arranged with the town Corporation for the lease of the island in the River Derwent, where Cotchett had erected his mill. During the four years of its construction, John first set up the throwing machines in other parts of the town. The machines were driven manually there, and their product helped to defray the costs of the mill. The silk-throwing machine was very complex. The water wheel powered a horizontal shaft that was under the floor and on which were placed gearwheels to drive vertical shafts upwards through the different floors. The throwing machines were circular, with the vertical shafts running through the middle. The doubled silk threads had previously been wound on bobbins which were placed on spindles with wire flyers at intervals around the outer circumference of the machine. The bobbins were free to rotate on the spindles while the spindles and flyers were driven by the periphery of a horizontal wheel fixed to the vertical shaft. Another horizontal wheel set a little above the first turned the starwheels, to which were attached reels for winding the silk off the bobbins below. Three or four sets of these spindles and reels were placed above each other on the same driving shaft. The machine was very complicated for the time and must have been expensive to build and maintain.

John lived just long enough to see the mill in operation, for he died in 1722 after a painful illness said to have been the result of poison administered by an Italian woman in revenge for his having stolen the invention and for the injury he was causing the Italian trade. The funeral was said to have been the most superb ever known in Derby.

Further Reading
Samuel Smiles, 1890, *Men of Invention and Industry*, London (probably the only biography of John Lombe).
Rhys Jenkins, 1933–4, 'Historical notes on some Derbyshire industries', *Transactions of the Newcomen Society* 14 (provides an acount of John Lombe and his part in the enterprise at Derby).
R.L. Hills, 1970, *Power in the Industrial Revolution*, Manchester (briefly covers the development of early silk-throwing mills).
W. English, 1969, *The Textile Industry*, London (includes a chapter on 'Lombe's Silk Machine').
P. Barlow, 1836, *Treatise of Manufactures and Machinery of Great Britain*, London (describes Lombe's mill and machinery, but it is not known how accurate the account may be).

RLH

Longbotham, John
b. mid-seventeenth century Halifax (?), Yorkshire, England
d. 1801

English canal engineer.

The nature of Longbotham's career before 1766 is unknown, although he was associated with **Smeaton** as a pupil and thus became acquainted with canal engineering. In 1766 he suggested a canal linking Leeds and Liverpool across the Pennines. The suggestion was accepted and in 1767–8 he surveyed the line of the Leeds & Liverpool Canal. This was approved by the promoters and by **Brindley**, who had been called in as an assessor. The Act was obtained in 1770 and Longbotham was first appointed as Clerk of Works under Brindley as Chief Engineer. As the latter did not take up the appointment, Longbotham became Chief Engineer and from 1770 to 1775 was responsible for the design of locks and aqueducts. He also prepared contracts and supervised construction. Meanwhile, in 1768 he had proposed a canal from the Calder and Hebble to Halifax. In 1773 he was elected to the Smeatonian Society of Civil Engineers. As soon as a part of the Leeds and Liverpool Canal was opened he started a passenger packet service, but in 1775, after completing both 50 miles (80 km) of the canal and the Bradford Canal, he was dismissed from his post because of discrepancies in his accounts. However, in the early 1790s he again advised the Leeds and Liverpool proprietors, who were in difficulties on the summit level. Longbotham had colliery interests in the Upholland area of Wigan, and in 1787 he surveyed a proposed route for the Lancaster Canal. In 1792 he was also associated with the Grand Western Canal. Details of his later life are scarce, but it is known that he died in poverty in 1801 and that the Leeds & Liverpool company paid his funeral expenses.

JHB

Loos, Adolf
b. 10 December 1870 Brno, Moravia (now in the Czech Republic)
d. 23 August 1933 Vienna, Austria

Austrian architect who was one of the earliest pioneers of the modern school in Europe.

Loos was the son of a sculptor and trained as a mason before studying architecture at Dresden College of Technology between 1890 and 1893. He then spent three years in America in such diverse areas as New York, Chicago, Philadelphia and St Louis. He became a devotee of America and of building there, and he was particularly impressed by the work of Louis **Sullivan**. He returned to Austria in 1896 and set up practice in Vienna. His early work there was in line with the current Sezessionist mode, but he quickly came to disassociate himself from this trend and increasingly insisted upon very plain and functionalist designs: by 1908 he is quoted as saying that 'the evolution of culture marches with the elimination of ornament from useful objects'. By this time Loos had become the pace-setter for modern ideas and was designing houses constructed from modern materials in as severe and cubic a style as Le Corbusier (Charles-Edouard **Jeanneret**) was soon to do. Adolf Loos made many designs, but only a small proportion were translated into building. Of his notable interiors the Kärtner Bau (1907) in Vienna had pride of place, while his Steiner Haus (1910) there is regarded as the earliest truly modern house in Europe. Cubic in form and with simplified fenestration, this was the forerunner of inter-war architecture. In 1920 Loos was appointed Chief Housing Architect for Vienna, but he resigned two years later. He spent some time in Paris mixing with avant-garde artists and architects and lectured for a time at the Sorbonne. His last commissions, after he had returned to Vienna in 1928, included some of his best work, notably the Müller House (1930) in Prague.

Further Reading
Benedetto Gravagnuolo, 1982, *Adolf Loos: Theory and Works*, Milan: Idea Books.
——1986, *The Architecture of Adolf Loos*, Arts Council Exhibition Book (with a Foreword by Sir John Summerson).
L. Münz and G. Künstet, 1964, *Der Architekt Adolf Loos*, Vienna and Munich: Anton Schroll.
DY

Lotz, Irmgard
See **Flügge-Lotz, Irmgard**.

Lovelace, Ada, Countess of
See **Byron, Ada Augusta, Countess of Lovelace**.

Lovelock, James Ephraim
b. 26 July 1919 Brixton, London, England

English biologist and philosopher, inventor of the microwave oven and electron capture detector.

Lovelock was brought up in Brixton in modest circumstances. At the age of 4 he was given a toy electrical set, which first turned his attention towards the study of science. From the Strand School, Brixton, he went on to the universities of Manchester and London, and after graduating in science, in 1941 he joined the National Institute for Medical Research, Mill Hill, as a staff scientist, remaining there for twenty years. During the early 1950s, he and his colleagues were engaged in research into freezing live animals and bringing them back to life by heating: Lovelock was struck by the intense pain this process caused the animals, and he sought a more humane method. He tried diathermy or internal heating through the effect of a continuous wave magnetron borrowed from the Navy. He found that the animals were brought back to life painlessly, and impressed with his success he tried baking a potato for his lunch in the apparatus and found that it cooked amazingly quickly compared with the one hour normally needed in an ordinary oven. Lovelock had invented the microwave oven, but its commercial possibilities were not at first realized.

In the late 1950s he invented the electron capture detector, which proved to be more sensitive than any other analytical equipment in detecting and measuring toxic substances. The apparatus therefore had obvious uses in testing the quality of the environment and so offered a tremendous boost to the 'green' movement. In 1961 he was invited to joint the US National Aeronautics and Space Administration (NASA) to employ the apparatus in an attempt to detect life in space.

In the early 1970s Lovelock relinquished his biological work in order to devote his attention to philosophical matters, specifically to develop his theory of the Universe, now widely celebrated as the 'Gaia theory'. In this controversial theory, Lovelock regards our planet and all its living beings, including humans, as a single living organism.

Principal Honours and Distinctions
CBE 1990. FRS 1974. Many academic awards and honorary degrees. Visiting Professor, University of Reading 1967–90.

Bibliography
1979, *Gaia*.
1983, *The Great Extinction*.
1988, *The Ages of Gaia*.
1991, *Gaia: The Practical Science of Planetary Medicine*.

LRD

Lowthian Bell, Sir Isaac
See **Bell, Sir Isaac Lowthian**.

Lubetkin, Berthold
b. 12 December 1901 Tiflis, Georgia
d. 23 October 1990 Bristol, England

Soviet émigré architect who, through the firm of Tecton, was influential in introducing architecture of the modern international style into England.

Lubetkin studied in Moscow, where in the years immediately after 1917 he met Vesnin and Rodchenko and absorbed the contemporary Constructivist ideas. He then moved on to Paris and worked with Auguste **Perret**, coming in on the ground floor of the modern movement. He went to England in 1930 and two years later formed the Tecton group, leading six young architects who had newly graduated from the Architectural Association in London. Lubetkin's early commissions in England were for animals rather than humans. He designed the gorilla house (1932) at the Regent's Park Zoological Gardens, after which came his award-winning Penguin Pool there, a sculptural blend of curved planes in reinforced concrete. He also worked at Whipsnade and at Dudley Zoo. The name of Tecton had quickly became synonymous with modern methods of design and structure, particularly the use of reinforced concrete; such work was not common in the 1930s in Britain. In 1938–9 the firm was responsible for another pace-setting design, the Finsbury Health Centre in London. Tecton was disbanded during the Second World War, and although it was reformed in the late 1940s it did not recover its initiative in leading the field of modern work. Lubetkin lived on to be an old man but his post-war career did not fulfil his earlier promise and brilliance. He was appointed Architect-Planner of the Peterlee New Town in 1948, but he resigned after a few years and no other notable commissions materialized. In 1982 the Royal Institute of British Architects belatedly remembered him with the award of their Gold Medal.

Principal Honours and Distinctions
RIBA Gold Medal 1982.

Further Reading
John Allan, 1992, *Architecture and the Tradition of Progress*, RIBA publications.
R. Furneaux Jordan, 1955, 'Lubetkin', *Architectural Review* 36–44.
P. Coe and M. Reading, 1981, *Lubetkin and Tecton*, University of Bristol Arts Council.

DY

Lucas, Anthony Francis
b. 9 September 1855 Spalato, Dalmatia, Austria-Hungary (now Split, Croatia)
d. 2 September 1921 Washington, DC, USA

Austrian (naturalized American) mining engineer who successfully applied rotary drilling to oil extraction.

A former Second Lieutenant of the Austrian navy (hence his later nickname 'Captain') and graduate of the Polytechnic Institute of Graz, Lucas decided to stay in Michigan when he visited his relatives in 1879. He changed his original name, Lucic, into the form his uncle had adopted and became a naturalized American citizen at the age of 30. He worked in the lumber industry for some years and then became a consulting mechanical and mining engineer in Washington, DC. He began working for a salt-mining company in Louisiana in 1893 and became interested in the geology of the Mexican Gulf region, with a view to prospecting for petroleum. In the course of this work he came to the conclusion that the hills in this elevated area, being geological structures distinct from the surrounding deposits, were natural reservoirs of petroleum. To prove his unusual theory he subsequently chose Spindle Top, near Beaumont, Texas, where in 1899 he began to bore a first oil-well. A second drill-hole, started in October 1900, was put through clay and quicksand. After many difficulties, a layer of rock containing marine shells was reached. When the 'gusher' came out on 10 January 1901, it not only opened up a new era in the oil and gas business, but it also led to the future exploration of the terrestrial crust.

Lucas's boring was a breakthrough for the rotary drilling system, which was still in its early days although its principles had been established by the English engineer Robert Beart in his patent of 1884. It proved to have advantages over the pile-driving of pipes. A pipe with a simple cutter at the lower end was driven with a constantly revolving motion, grinding down on the bottom of the well, thus gouging and chipping its way downward. To deal with the quicksand he adopted the use of large and heavy casings successively telescoped one into the other. According to **Fauvelle**'s method, water was forced through the pipe by means of a pump, so the well was kept full of circulating liquid during drilling, flushing up the mud. When the salt-rock was reached, a diamond drill was used to test the depth and the character of the deposit.

When the well blew out and flowed freely he developed a preventer in order to save the oil and, even more importantly at the time, to shut the well and to control the oil flow. This assembly, patented in 1903, consisted of a combined system of pipes, valves and casings diverting the stream into a horizontal direction.

Lucas's fame spread around the world, but as he had to relinquish the larger part of his interest to the oil company supporting the exploration, his financial reward was poor. One year after his success at Spindle Top he started oil exploration in Mexico, where he stayed until 1905, when he resumed his consulting practice in Washington, DC.

Bibliography
1899, 'Rock-salt in Louisiana', *Transactions of the American Institution of Mining Engineers* 29: 462–74.
1902, 'The great oil-well near Beaumont, Texas', *Transactions of the American Institution of Mining Engineers* 31: 362–74.

Further Reading
R.S. McBeth, 1918, *Pioneering the Gulf Coast*, New York (a very detailed description of Lucas's important accomplishments in the development of the oil industry).
R.T. Hill, 1903, 'The Beaumont oil-field, with notes on other oil-fields of the Texas region', *Transactions of the American Institution of Mining Engineers* 33: 363–405; *Transactions of the American Institution of Mining Engineers* 55: 421–3 (contain shorter biographical notes).

WK

Ludwig, Karl Friedrich Wilhelm
b. 29 December 1816 Wittenhausen, Breslau, Germany (now Wrocław, Poland)
d. 23 April 1895 Leipzig, Saxony, Germany

German physiologist, inventor of the kymograph for the measurement of blood pressure, early experimenter in tissue grafting.

He graduated MD from Marburg and in 1846 was appointed Professor of Comparative Anatomy. He later held the Chairs of Anatomy and Physiology at Zurich, in 1849, and of Physiology and Zoology at Vienna, in 1855. In 1865 he was appointed to the Chair of Physiology at Leipzig and founded the Physiological Institute named after him.

Renowned as a teacher, who often published under his pupils' names, his field of research was wide-ranging and he was an inspiration to many future distinguished names. In 1847 he invented the kymograph, an instrument which permitted the recording of variations in blood pressure. He supplemented this in 1867 with the 'Stromuhr', with which the volume of blood passing through a blood vessel could be measured. He was also much involved in the elucidation of kidney function, and the kidney tubules are named after him.

Bibliography
1847, 'Beiträge zur Kenntnis des Einflußes der Respirationsbewegungen auf den Blutlauf im Aortensystem' *Arch. Anat. Physiol. wiss. Med.*
1865, *Die Physiologischen leistungen des Blutdrucks*, Leipzig.

Further Reading
1852–6, *Textbook of Human Physiology*.

MG

Lumière, Auguste
b. 19 October 1862 Besançon, France
d. 10 April 1954 Lyon, France

French scientist and inventor.

Auguste and his brother Louis Lumière (b. 5 October 1864 Besançon, France; d. 6 June 1948 Bandol, France) developed the photographic plate-making business founded by their father, Charles Antoine **Lumière**, at Lyons, extending production to roll-film manufacture in 1887. In the summer of 1894 their father brought to the factory a piece of **Edison** kinetoscope film, and said that they should produce films for the French owners of the new moving-picture machine. To do this, of course, a camera was needed; Louis was chiefly responsible for the design, which used an intermittent claw for driving the film, inspired by a sewing-machine mechanism. The machine was patented on 13 February 1895, and it was shown on 22 March 1895 at the Société d'Encouragement pour l'Industrie Nationale in Paris, with a projected film showing workers leaving the Lyons factory. Further demonstrations followed at the Sorbonne, and in Lyons during the Congrès des Sociétés de Photographie in June 1895. The Lumières filmed the delegates returning from an excursion, and showed the film to the Congrès the next day. To bring the *Cinématographe*, as it was called, to the public, the basement of the Grand Café in the Boulevard des Capuchines in Paris was rented, and on Saturday 28 December 1895 the first regular presentations of projected pictures to a paying public took place. The half-hour shows were an immediate success, and in a few months Lumière *Cinématographes* were seen throughout the world.

The other principal area of achievement by the Lumière brothers was colour photography. They took up **Lippman**'s method of interference colour photography, developing special grainless emulsions, and early in 1893 demonstrated their results by lighting them with an arc lamp and projecting them on to a screen. In 1895 they patented a method of subtractive colour photography involving printing the colour separations on bichromated gelatine glue sheets, which were then dyed and assembled in register, on paper for prints or bound between glass for transparencies. Their most successful colour process was based upon the colour-mosaic principle. In 1904 they described a process in which microscopic grains of potato starch, dyed red, green and blue, were scattered on a freshly varnished glass plate. When dried the mosaic was coated with varnish and then with a panchromatic emulsion. The plate was exposed with the mosaic towards the lens, and after reversal processing a colour transparency was produced. The process was launched commercially in 1907 under the name Autochrome; it was the first fully practical single-plate colour process to reach the public, remaining on the market until the 1930s, when it was followed by a film version using the same principle.

Auguste and Louis received the Progress Medal of the Royal Photographic Society in 1909 for their work in colour photography. Auguste was also much involved in biological science and, having founded the Clinique Auguste Lumière, spent many of his later years working in the physiological laboratory.

Further Reading
Guy Borgé, 1980, *Prestige de la photographie*, Nos. 8, 9 and 10, Paris.
Brian Coe, 1978, *Colour Photography: The First Hundred Years*, London
—— 1981, *The History of Movie Photography*, London.
Jacques Deslandes, 1966, *Histoire comparée du cinéma*, Vol. I, Paris.
Gert Koshofer, 1981, *Farbfotografie*, Vol. I, Munich.

BC

Lumière, Charles Antoine
b. 13 March 1840 Ormoy, France
d. 16 April 1911

French photographer and photographic manufacturer.

Orphaned when his parents died of cholera, at the age of 14 he was taken by his elder sister to live in Marcilly-le-Hayer. Apprenticed to a joiner, he was also interested in chemistry and physics, but his great love was drawing and painting. The leading water-colourist Auguste Constantin took him into his Paris home as an apprentice and taught him the whole business of painting. He was able to earn his living as a sign-painter, and numbered among his clients several photographers. This led to an interest in photography, which caused him to abandon the safe trade of sign-painter for that of photographer.

Lumière took a post with a photographer in Besançon in 1862. He set up business on his own account in 1865 and moved to Lyons *c.*1870, joining his friend and fellow photographer Emile Lebeau. The business prospered; in 1879 he installed an electricity generator in his studio to run the newly invented Van de Weyde electric arc lamp, permitting portraiture in all weathers and at all times. With the arrival of the dry-plate process *c.*1880, the Lumière business looked to employ the new medium. His second son, Louis Lumière (b. 5 October 1864 Besançon, France; d. 6 June 1948 Bandol, France; see under **Lumière, Auguste**), fresh from college, experimented with emulsions with which his

12-year-old sister coated glass plates. While still running the studio, Antoine started marketing the plates, which were the first to be made in France, and production was soon up to 4,000 plates a day. Under his guidance A. Lumière et ses Fils acquired a worldwide reputation for the quality and originality of its products.

After his retirement from business, when he handed it over to his sons, Auguste (see **Lumière, Auguste**) and Louis, he took up painting again and successfully exhibited in several Salons. He was a Chevalier of the Légion d'honneur, a recognition of his participation in the 1893 World's Colombian Exposition in Chicago.

Further Reading
Guy Borgé, 1980, *Prestige de la photographie*, Nos. 8 and 9, Paris.

BC

Lundstrom, Johan E.
fl. *c*.1855 Sweden

Swedish scientist credited with the invention of the safety match, first produced in 1855.

Lundstrom's safety match replaced the friction match, popularly called the 'strike-anywhere' match because all the ingredients for ignition were contained in the match head so that any abrasive surface would suffice for striking. These matches ignited easily, in fact too readily, so causing numerous accidents.

It was Professor Anton von **Schrötter**'s discovery of amorphous red phosphorus in 1845 that led to the invention of Lundstrom's safety match. The substance was much less dangerous to handle than the yellow phosphorus that was earlier in use and which had so badly damaged the health of match-factory workers who had to handle it.

In Lundstrom's safety match the chemical constituents for ignition were divided between the match head and the striking surface of the matchbox, so markedly reducing the chances of spontaneous combustion. Lundstrom's patent mixtures were:

Match-head: 32 parts potassium nitrate, 12 parts potassium bichromate, 32 parts red lead, 24 parts sulphide of antimony.

Rubbing Surface: 8 parts red phosphorous, 9 parts sulphide of antimony.

Further Reading
W.T. O'Dea, 1964, *Making Fire*, London: Science Museum, HMSO (illustrated booklet).
See also the Bryant & May permanent exhibition in the Domestic Appliances Gallery of the Science Museum, London.

DY

M

McAdam, John Loudon

b. 21 September 1756 Ayr, Ayrshire, Scotland
d. 26 November 1836 Moffat, Dumfriesshire, Scotland

Scottish road builder, inventor of the macadam road surface.

McAdam was the son of one of the founders of the first bank in Ayr. As an infant, he nearly died in a fire which destroyed the family's house of Laywyne, in Carsphairn parish; the family then moved to Blairquhan, near Straiton. Thence he went to the parish school in Maybole, where he is said to have made a model section of a local road. In 1770, when his father died, he was sent to America where he was brought up by an uncle who was a merchant in New York. He stayed in America until the close of the revolution, becoming an agent for the sale of prizes and managing to amass a considerable fortune. He returned to Scotland where he settled at Sauchrie in Ayrshire. There he was a magistrate, Deputy-Lieutenant of the county and a road trustee, spending thirteen years there. In 1798 he moved to Falmouth in Devon, England, on his appointment as agent for revictualling of the Royal Navy in western ports.

He continued the series of experiments started in Ayrshire on the construction of roads. From these he concluded that a road should be built on a raised foundation with drains formed on either side, and should be composed of a number of layers of hard stone broken into angular fragments of roughly cubical shape; the bottom layer would be larger rocks, with layers of progressively smaller rocks above, all bound together with fine gravel. This would become compacted and almost impermeable to water by the action of the traffic passing over it. In 1815 he was appointed Surveyor-General of Bristol's roads and put his theories to the test.

In 1823 a Committee of the House of Commons was appointed to consider the use of 'macadamized' roads in larger towns; McAdam gave evidence to this committee, and it voted to give him £10,000 for his past work. In 1827 he was appointed Surveyor-General of Roads and moved to Hoddesdon, Hertfordshire. From there he made yearly visits to Scotland and it was while returning from one of these that he died, at Moffat in the Scottish Borders. He had married twice, both times to American women; his first wife was the mother of all seven of his children.

McAdam's method of road construction was much cheaper than that of Thomas Telford, and did much to ease travel and communications; it was therefore adopted by the majority of Turnpike Trusts in Britain, and the macadamization process quickly spread to other countries.

Bibliography

1819, *A Practical Essay on the Scientific Repair and Preservation of Roads*.
1820, *Present State of Road-Making*.

Further Reading

R. Devereux, 1936, *John Loudon McAdam: A Chapter from the History of Highways*, London: Oxford University Press.

IMcN

MacArthur, John Stewart

b. December 1856 Hutchesontown, Glasgow, Scotland
d. 16 March 1920 Pollokshields, Glasgow, Scotland

Scottish industrial chemist who introduced the 'cyanide process' for the commercial extraction of gold from its ores.

MacArthur served his apprenticeship in the laboratory of **Tennant**'s Tharsis Sulphur and Copper Company in Glasgow. In 1886 he was appointed Technical Manager of the Tennant-run Cassel Gold Extracting Company. By 1888 he was advocating a treatment scheme in which gold was dissolved from crushed rock by a dilute solution of alkali cyanide and then precipitated onto finely divided zinc. During the next few years, with several assistants, he was extremely active in promoting the new gold-extraction technique in various parts of the world. In 1894 significant sums in royalty payments were received, but by 1897 the patents had been successfully contested; henceforth the Cassel Company concentrated on the production and marketing of the essential sodium cyanide reagent.

MacArthur was Managing Director of the Cassel Company from 1892 to 1897; he resigned as a director in December 1905. In 1907 he created the Antimony Recovery Syndicate, and in 1911 he set up a small plant at Runcorn, Cheshire, to produce radium salts. In 1915 this radium-extraction activity was transferred to Balloch, south of Loch Lomond, where it was used until some years after his death.

Principal Honours and Distinctions
Institution of Mining and Metallurgy Gold Medal 1902.

Bibliography
10 August 1888, jointly with R.W. Forrest and W. Forrest, British patent no. 14,174.
13 July 1889, jointly with R.W. Forrest and W. Forrest, British patent no. 10,223.
1905, 'Gold extraction by cyanide: a retrospect', *Journal of the Society of Chemical Industry* (15 April): 311–15.

Further Reading
D.I. Harvie, 1989, 'John Stewart MacArthur: pioneer gold and radium refiner', *Endeavour* (NS) 13 (4): 179–84 (draws on family documents not previously published).

JKA

McCormick, Cyrus
b. 1809 Walnut Grove, Virginia, USA
d. 1884 USA

American inventor of the first functionally and commercially successful reaping machine; founder of the McCormick Company, which was to become one of the founding companies of International Harvester.

Cyrus McCormick's father, a farmer, began to experiment unsuccessfully with a harvesting machine between 1809 and 1816. His son took up the challenge and gave his first public demonstration of his machine in 1831. It cut a 4 ft swathe, but, wanting to perfect the machine, he waited until 1834 before patenting it, by which time he

felt that his invention was threatened by others of similar design. In the same year he entered an article in the *Mechanic's Magazine*, warning competitors off his design. His main rival was Obed Hussey who contested McCormick's claim to the originality of the idea, having patented his own machine six months before McCormick.

A competition between the two machines was held in 1843, the judges favouring McCormick's, even after additional trials were conducted after objections of unfairness from Hussey. The rivalry continued over a number of years, being avidly reported in the agricultural press. The publicity did no harm to reaper sales, and McCormick sold twenty-nine machines in 1843 and fifty the following year.

As the westward settlement movement progressed, so the demand for McCormick's machine grew. In order to be more central to his markets, McCormick established himself in Chicago. In partnership with C.M. Gray he established a factory to produce 500 harvesters for the 1848 season. By means of advertising and offers of credit terms, as well as production-line assembly, McCormick was able to establish himself as sole owner and also control all production, under the one roof. By the end of the decade he dominated reaper production but other developments were to threaten this position; however, foreign markets were appearing at the same time, not least the opportunities of European sales stimulated by the Great Exhibition in 1851. In the trials arranged by the Royal Agricultural Society of England the McCormick machine significantly outperformed that of Hussey's, and as a result McCormick arranged for 500 to be made under licence in England.

In 1874 McCormick bought a half interest in the patent for a wire binder from Charles Withington, a watchmaker from Janesville, Wisconsin, and by 1885 a total of 50,000 wire binders had been built in Chicago. By 1881 McCormick was producing twine binders using **Appleby**'s twine knotter under a licence agreement, and by 1885 the company was producing only twine binders. The McCormick Company was one of the co-founders of the International Harvester Company in 1901.

Bibliography
1972, *The Century of the Reaper*, Johnson Reprint (the original is in the New York State Library).

Further Reading
Graeme Quick and Wesley Buchele, 1978, *The Grain Harvesters*, American Society of Agricultural Engineers (deals in detail with McCormick's developments).
G.H. Wendell, 1981, *150 Years of International Harvester*, Crestlink (though more concerned with the machinery produced by International Harvester, it gives an account of its originating companies).
T.W. Hutchinson, 1930, *Cyrus Hall McCormick, Seedtime 1809–1856*; —— 1935, *Cyrus Hall McCormick, Harvest 1856–1884* (both attempt to unravel the many claims surrounding the reaper story).
Herbert N. Casson, 1908, *The Romance of the Reaper*, Doubleday Page (deals with McCormick, Deering and the formation of International Harvester).

AP

McCoy, Elijah

b. 1843 Colchester, Ontario, Canada
d. 1929 Detroit, Michigan (?), USA

African-American inventor of steam-engine lubricators.

McCoy was born into a community of escaped African-American slaves. As a youth he went to Scotland and served an apprenticeship in Edinburgh in mechanical engineering. He returned to North America and ended up in Ypsilanti, Michigan, seeking employment at the headquarters of the Michigan Central Railroad Company. In spite of his training, the only job McCoy could obtain was that of locomotive fireman. Still, that enabled him to study at close quarters the problem of lubricating adequately the moving parts of a steam locomotive. Inefficient lubrication led to overheating, delays and even damage. In 1872 McCoy patented the first of his lubricating devices, applicable particularly to stationary engines. He assigned his patent rights to W. and S.C. Hamlin of Ypsilanti, from which he derived enough financial resources to develop his invention. A year later he patented an improved hydrostatic lubricator, which could be used for both stationary and locomotive engines, and went on to make further improvements. McCoy's lubricators were widely taken up by other railroads and his employers promoted him from the footplate to the task of giving instruc-

tion in the use of his lubricating equipment. Many others had been attempting to achieve the same result and many rival products were on the market, but none was superior to McCoy's, which came to be known as 'the Real McCoy', a term that has since acquired a wider application than to engine lubricators. McCoy moved to Detroit, Michigan, as a patent consultant in the railroad business. Altogether, he took out over fifty patents for various inventions, so that he became one of the most prolific of nineteenth-century black inventors, whose activities had been so greatly stimulated by the freedoms they acquired after the American Civil War. His more valuable patents were assigned to investors, who formed the Elijah McCoy Manufacturing Company. McCoy himself, however, was not a major shareholder, so he seems not to have derived the benefit that was due to him.

Further Reading
P.P. James, 1989, *The Real McCoy: African-American Invention and Innovation 1619–1930*, Washington: Smithsonian Institution, pp. 73–5.

LRD

MacCready, Paul

b. 29 September 1925 New Haven, Connecticut, USA

American designer of man-powered aeroplanes, one of which flew across the English Channel in 1979.

As a boy, Paul MacCready was an enthusiastic builder of flying model aeroplanes; he became US National Junior Champion in 1941. He learned to fly and became a pilot with the US Navy in 1943. he developed an interest in gliding in 1945 and became National Soaring Champion in 1948 and 1949. After graduating from the California Institute of Technology (Cal Tech) as a meteorologist, he set up Meteorological Research Inc. In 1953 MacCready became the first American to win the World Gliding Championship. When hang-gliders became popular in the early 1970s MacCready studied their performance and compared them with soaring birds: he came to the conclusion that man-powered flight was a possibility. In an effort to generate an interest in man-powered flight, a cash prize had been offered in Britain by Henry

Kremer, a wealthy industrialist and fitness enthusiast. A man-powered aircraft had to complete a one-mile (1.6 km) figure-of-eight course in order to win. However, the figure-of-eight proved to be a major obstacle and the prize money was increased over the years to £50,000. In 1976 MacCready and his friend Dr Peter Lissaman set to work on their computer and came up with their optimum design for a man-powered aircraft. The *Gossamer Condor* had a wing span of 96 ft (27.4 m), about the same as a Douglas *DC-9* airliner, yet it weighed just 70 lb (32 kg). It was a tail-first design with a pedal-driven pusher propeller just behind the pilot. Bryan Allen, a biologist, pilot and racing cyclist, joined the team to provide the muscle-power. After over two hundred flights they were ready to make an attempt on the prize, and on 23 August 1977 they succeeded where many had failed, in 7 minutes. Kremer then offered £100,000 for the first man-powered flight across the English Channel. Many thought this would be impossible, but MacCready and his team set about the task of designing a new machine based on their *Condor*, which they called the *Gossamer Albatross*. Bryan Allen also had a major task: getting fit for a flight which might take three hours of pedalling. The weather was more of a problem than in California, and after a long delay the *Gossamer Albatross* took off, on 12 June 1979. After pedalling for 2 hours 49 minutes, Bryan Allen landed in France: it was seventy years since **Blériot**'s flight, although Blériot was much quicker.

Principal Honours and Distinctions
World Gliding Champion 1953.

Bibliography
1979, 'The Channel crossing and the future', *Man Powered Aircraft Symposium*, London: Royal Aeronautical Society.

Further Reading
M. Grosser, 1981, *Gossamer Odyssey*, London (provides a brief biography and detailed accounts of the two aircraft).
M.F. Jerram, 1980, *Incredible Flying Machines*, London (a short survey of pedal planes).
Articles by Ron Moulton on the *Gossamer Albatross* appeared in *Aerospace* (Royal Aeronautical Society) London, August/September 1979, and the *Aeromodeller*, London, September 1979.

JDS

MacGregor, Robert
b. 1873 Hebburn-on-Tyne, England
d. 4 October 1956 Whitley Bay, England

English naval architect who, working with others, significantly improved the safety of life at sea.

On leaving school in 1894, MacGregor was apprenticed to a famous local shipyard, the Palmers Shipbuilding and Iron Company of Jarrow-on-Tyne. After four years he was entered for the annual examination of the Worshipful Company of Shipwrights, coming out top and being nominated Queen's Prizeman. Shortly thereafter he moved around shipyards to gain experience, working in Glasgow, Hull, Newcastle and then Dunkirk. His mastery of French enabled him to obtain in 1906 the senior position of Chief Draughtsman at an Antwerp shipyard, where he remained until 1914. On his return to Britain, he took charge of the small yard of Dibbles in Southampton and commenced a period of great personal development and productivity. His fertile mind enabled him to register no fewer than ten patents in the years 1919 to 1923.

In 1924 he started out on his own as a naval architect, specializing in the coal trade of the North Sea. At that time, colliers had wooden hatch covers, which despite every caution could be smashed by heavy seas, and which in time of war added little to hull integrity after a torpedo strike. The International Loadline Committee of 1932 noted that 13 per cent of ship losses were through hatch failures. In 1927, designs for self-trimming colliers were developed, as well as designs for steel hatch covers. In 1928 the first patents were under way and the business was known for some years as MacGregor and King. During this period, steel hatch covers were fitted to 105 ships.

In 1937 MacGregor invited his brother Joseph (*c*.1883–1967) to join him. Joseph had wide experience in ship repairs and had worked for many years as General Manager of the Prince of Wales Dry Docks in Swansea, a port noted for its coal exports. By 1939 they were operating from Whitley Bay with the name that was to become world famous: MacGregor and Company (Naval Architects) Ltd. The new company worked in association with the shipyards of Austin's of Sunderland and Burntisland of Fife, which were then developing the 'flatiron' colliers for the upriver London coal trade. The MacGregor business gained a great boost when the massive coastal fleet of William Cory & Son was fitted with steel hatches.

In 1945 the brothers appointed Henri Kummerman (b. 1908, Vienna; d. 1984, Geneva) as their sales agent in Europe. Over the years, Kummerman effected greater control on the MacGregor business and, through his astute business dealings and his well-organized sales drives worldwide, welded together an international company in hatch covers, cargo handling and associated work. Before his death, Robert MacGregor was to see mastery of the design of single-pull steel hatch covers and to witness the acceptance of MacGregor hatch covers worldwide. Most important of all, he had contributed to great increases in the safety and the quality of life at sea.

Further Reading

L.C. Burrill, 1931, 'Seaworthiness of collier types', *Transactions of the Institution of Naval Architechts*.

S. Sivewright, 1989, *One Man's Mission – 20,000 Ships*, London: Lloyd's of London Press.

See also **Ayre, Sir Amos**.

FMW

Ma Chun

See **Ma Jun**.

Macintosh, Charles

b. 29 December 1766 Glasgow, Scotland
d. 25 July 1843 Dunchattan, near Glasgow, Scotland

Scottish inventor of rubberized waterproof clothing.

As the son of the well-known and inventive dyer George Macintosh, Charles had an early interest in chemistry. At the age of 19 he gave up his work as a clerk with a Glasgow merchant to manufacture sal ammoniac (ammonium chloride) and developed new processes in dyeing. In 1797 he started the first Scottish alum works, finding the alum in waste shale from coal mines. His first works was at Hurlet, Renfrewshire, and was followed later by others. He then formed a partnership with Charles **Tennant**, the proprietor of a chemical works at St Rollox, near

Glasgow, and sold 'lime bleaching liquor' made with chlorine and milk of lime from their bleach works at Darnley. A year later the use of dry lime to make bleaching powder, a process worked out by Macintosh, was patented. Macintosh remained associated with Tennant's St Rollox chemical works until 1814. During this time, in 1809, he had set up a yeast factory, but it failed because of opposition from the London brewers.

There was a steady demand for the ammonia that gas works produced, but the tar was often looked upon as an inconvenient waste product. Macintosh bought all the ammonia and tar that the Glasgow works produced, using the ammonia in his establishment to produce cudbear, a dyestuff extracted from various lichens. Cudbear could be used with appropriate mordants to make shades from pink to blue. The tar could be distilled to produce naphtha, which was used as a flare. Macintosh also became interested in iron-making. In 1825 he took out a patent for converting malleable iron into steel by taking it to white heat in a current of gas with a carbon content, such as coal gas. However, the process was not commercially successful because of the difficulty keeping the furnace gas-tight. In 1828 he assisted J.B. **Neilson** in bringing hot blast into use in blast furnaces; Neilson assigned Macintosh a share in the patent, which was of dubious benefit as it involved him in the tortuous litigation that surrounded the patent until 1843.

In June 1823, as a result of experiments into the possible uses of naphtha obtained as a by-product of the distillation of coal tar, Macintosh patented his process for waterproofing fabric. This comprised dissolving rubber in naphtha and applying the solution to two pieces of cloth which were afterwards pressed together to form an impermeable compound fabric. After an experimental period in Glasgow, Macintosh commenced manufacture in Manchester, where he formed a partnership with H.H. Birley, B. Kirk and R.W. Barton. Birley was a cotton spinner and weaver and was looking for ways to extend the output of his cloth. He was amongst the first to light his mills with gas, so he shared a common interest with Macintosh.

New buildings were erected for the production of waterproof cloth in 1824-5, but there were considerable teething troubles with the process, particularly in the spreading of the rubber solution onto the cloth. Peter **Ewart** helped to install the machinery, including a steam engine supplied by Boulton & Watt, and the naphtha was supplied from Macintosh's works in Glasgow. It seems that the process was still giving difficulties when Thomas **Hancock**, the foremost rubber technologist of that time, became involved in 1830 and was made a partner in 1834. By 1836 the waterproof coat was being called a 'mackintosh' [sic] and was gaining such popularity that the Manchester business was expanded with additional premises. Macintosh's business was gradually enlarged to include many other kinds of indiarubber products, such as rubber shoes and cushions.

Principal Honours and Distinctions
FRS 1823.

Further Reading
G. Macintosh, 1847, *Memoir of Charles Macintosh*, London (the fullest account of Charles Macintosh's life).
T. Hancock, 1957, *Narrative of the Indiarubber Manufacture*, London.
H. Schurer, 1953, 'The macintosh: the paternity of an invention', *Transactions of the Newcomen Society* 28: 77–87 (an account of the invention of the mackintosh).

RLH/LRD

McKay, Donald

b. 4 September 1810 Shelburne, Nova Scotia, Canada
d. 20 September 1880 Hamilton, Massachusetts, USA

American shipbuilder of Western Ocean packets and clippers.

Of Scottish stock, McKay was the son of a farmer and the grandson of a loyalist officer who had left the United States after the War of Independence. After some elementary shipwright training in Nova Scotia, McKay travelled to New York to apprentice to the great American shipbuilder Isaac Webb, then building some of the outstanding ships of the nineteenth century. At the age of 21 and a fully fledged journeyman, McKay again set out and worked in various shipyards before joining William Currier in 1841 to establish a yard in Newburyport, Massachusetts. He moved on again in 1843 to form another venture, the yard of McKay and Pickett in the same locality.

In 1844 McKay came to know Enoch Train of Boston, then proprietor of a fleet of fast clipper ships on the USA-to-Liverpool run. He persuaded McKay to set out on his own and promised to support him with orders for ships. The partnership with Pickett was dissolved amicably and Donald McKay opened the yard in East Boston, from which some of the world's fastest ships were to be launched. McKay's natural ability as a shipwright had been enhanced by the study of mathematics and engineering drawing, something he had learned from his wife Albenia Boole, the daughter of another shipbuilder. He was not too proud to learn from other masters on the East Coast such as William H. Webb and John Willis Griffiths. The first ships from East Boston included the *Washington Irvine* of 1845 and the *Anglo Saxon* of 1846; they were well built and had especially comfortable emigrant accommodation. However, faster ships were to follow, almost all three-masted, fully rigged ships with very fine or 'extreme' lines, including the *Flying Cloud* for the Californian gold rush of 1851, the four-masted barque *Great Republic*; then, *c*.1854, the *Lightning* was ordered by James Baines of Liverpool for his Black Ball Line. The *Lightning* holds to this day the speed record for a square-rigged ship's daily run. As the years passed the shipbuilding scene changed, and while McKay's did build some iron ships for the US Navy, they became much less profitable and in 1875 the yard closed down, with McKay retiring to take up farming.

Further Reading
Frank C. Bowen, 1952, 'Shipbuilders of other days, Donald McKay of Boston', *Shipbuilding and Shipping Record* (18 September).

FMW

McKay, Hugh Victor

b. *c*.1866 Drummartin, Victoria, Australia
d. 21 May 1926 Australia

Australian inventor and manufacturer of harvesting and other agricultural equipment.

A farmer's son, at the age of 17 McKay developed modifications to the existing stripper harvester and created a machine that would not only strip the seed from standing corn, but was able to produce a threshed, winnowed and clean sample in one operation. The prototype was produced in 1884 and worked well on the two acres of wheat that had been set aside on the family farm. By arrangement with a Melbourne plough maker, five machines were made and sold for the 1885 season. In 1886 the McKay Harvester Company was formed, with offices at Ballarat, from which the machines, built by various companies, were sold. The business expanded quickly, selling sixty machines in 1888, and eventually rising to the production of nearly 2,000 harvesters in 1905. The name 'Sunshine' was given to the harvester, and the 'Sun' prefix was to appear on all other implements produced by the company as it diversified its production interests. In 1902 severe drought reduced machinery sales and left 2,000 harvesters unsold. McKay was forced to look to export markets to dispose of his surplus machines. By 1914 a total of 10,000 machines were being exported annually. During the First World War McKay was appointed to the Business Board of the Defence Department. Increases in the scale of production resulted in the company moving to Melbourne, where it was close to the port of entry of raw materials and was able to export the finished article more readily. In 1909 McKay produced one of the first gas-engined harvesters, but its cost prevented it from being more than an experimental prototype. By this time McKay was the largest agricultural machinery manufacturer in the Southern hemisphere, producing a wide range of implements, including binders. In 1916 McKay hired Headlie Taylor, who had developed a machine capable of harvesting fallen crops. The jointly developed machine was a major success, coming as it did in what would otherwise have been a disastrous Australian harvest. Further developments included the 'Sun Auto-header' in 1923, the first of the harvesting machines to adopt the 'T' configuration to be seen on modern harvesters. The Australian market was expanding fast and a keen rivalry developed between McKay and Massey Harris. Confronted by the tariff regulations with which the Australian Government had protected its indigenous machinery industry since 1906, Massey Harris sold all its Australian assets to the H.V. McKay company in 1930. Twenty-three years later Massey Ferguson acquired the old Sunshine works and was still operating from there in the 1990s.

Despite a long-running history of wage dis-putes with his workforce, McKay established a retiring fund as well as a self-help fund for distressed cases. Before his death he created a charitable trust and requested that some funds should be made available for the 'aerial experiments' which were to lead to the establishment of the Flying Doctor Service.

Principal Honours and Distinctions
CBE.

Further Reading
Graeme Quick and Wesley Buchele, 1978, *The Grain Harvesters*, American Society of Agricultural Engineers (devotes a chapter to the unique development of harvesting machinery which took place in Australia).

AP

Mackenzie, Sir James
b. 12 April 1853 Scone, Perthshire, Scotland
d. 26 January 1925 London, England

Scottish physician and clinical researcher, inventor of the 'polygraph' for the investigation of normal and abnormal cardiac rhythms.

Mackenzie graduated in medicine from Edinburgh University in 1878. The next year he moved to a practice in Burnley, Lancashire, where he began the exhaustive clinical studies into irregularities of cardiac rhythm that he was to continue for the rest of his life. In 1907 he moved to London and in 1913 was appointed physician to the London Hospital.

It was while engaged in the heavy industrial practice in Burnley that he developed, with the aid of a Lancashire watchmaker, the 'polygraph' apparatus, which by recording vascular pulses permitted analysis of cardiac function and performance. He also investigated herpes zoster (shingles) and was a pioneer in the treatment of heart disease with digitalis. He himself suffered from angina pectoris for the last fifteen years of his life and his views on the condition were published in a book in 1923. When shown the electrocardiogram (ECG) machine of **Einthoven**, he expressed reservations as to its future utility.

Principal Honours and Distinctions
Knighted 1915. FRS 1915.

Bibliography
1902, *The Study of the Pulse*, Edinburgh.
1908, *Diseases of the Heart*, London.
1925, *Heart*, London.

Further Reading
M. Wilson, 1926, *The Beloved Physician: Sir James Mackenzie*.

MG

Macmillan, Kirkpatrick
b. 1810
d. 1878

Scottish inventor and builder of the first pedal-operated bicycle.

Macmillan was the blacksmith at the village of Courthill, Dumfriesshire, Scotland. Before 1839, bicycles were of the *draisienne* or hobby-horse type, which were propelled by the rider's feet pushing alternately on the ground. Macmillan was the first to appreciate that two wheels placed in line could be balanced while being propelled by means of treadles and cranks fitted to one of the axles. His machine, completed in 1839, had wooden wheels shod with iron tyres, and a curved wooden frame which was forked to take the rear axle; the front, steering wheel was carried in an iron fork. The axles ran in brass bearings. Cranks were keyed to the rear axle which was driven by rods connected to two swinging arms; these were pivotted from the frame near the pivot of the front fork, and had foot treadles at their lower ends. Macmillan frequently rode this machine the 22.5 km (14 miles) from Courthill to Dumfries. In 1842 he was fined five shillings at the Gorbals Police Court for knocking over a child at the end of a 64 km (40 mile) ride from Courthill to Glasgow.

Although several people copied Macmillan's machine over the next twenty years and it anticipated the rear-driven safety bicycle by some forty years, it did not prove popular.

Further Reading
C.F. Caunter, 1955, *The History and Development of Cycles*, London: HMSO.

IMcN

McNaught, William
b. 27 May 1813 Sneddon, Paisley, Scotland
d. 8 January 1881 Manchester, England

Scottish patentee of a very successful form of compounding beam engine with a high-pressure cylinder between the fulcrum of the beam and the connecting rod.

Although born in Paisley, McNaught was educated in Glasgow where his parents had moved in 1820. He followed in his father's footsteps and became an engineer through an apprenticeship with Robert **Napier** at the Vulcan Works, Washington Street, Glasgow. He also attended science classes at the Andersonian University in the evenings and showed such competence that at the age of 19 he was offered the position of being in charge of the Fort-Gloster Mills on the Hoogly river in India. He remained there for four years until 1836, when he returned to Scotland because the climate was affecting his health.

His father had added the revolving cylinder to the steam engine indicator, and this greatly simplified and extended its use. In 1838 William joined him in the business of manufacturing these indicators at Robertson Street, Glasgow. While advising textile manufacturers on the use of the indicator, he realized the need for more powerful, smoother-running and economical steam engines. He provided the answer by placing a high-pressure cylinder midway between the fulcrum of the beam and the connecting rod on an ordinary beam engine. The original cylinder was retained to act as the low-pressure cylinder of what became a compound engine. This layout not only reduced the pressures on the bearing surfaces and gave a smoother-running engine, which was one of McNaught's aims, but he probably did not anticipate just how much more economical his engines would be; they often gave a saving of fuel up to 40 per cent. This was because the steam pipe connecting the two cylinders acted as a receiver, something lacking in the Woolf compound, which enabled the steam to be expanded properly in both cylinders. McNaught took out his patent in 1845, and in 1849 he had to move to Manchester because his orders in Lancashire were so numerous and the scope was much greater there than in Glasgow. He took out further patents for equalizing the stress on the working parts, but none was as important as his original one, which was claimed to have been one of the greatest improvements since the steam engine left the hands of James **Watt**. He was one of the original promoters of the Boiler Insurance and Steam Power Company and was elected Chairman in 1865, a position he retained until a short time before his death.

Bibliography
1845, British patent no. 11,001 (compounding beam engine).

Further Reading
Obituary, *Engineer* 51.
Obituary, *Engineering* 31.
R.L. Hills, 1989, *Power from Steam. A History of the Stationary Steam Engine*, Cambridge University Press (the fullest account of McNaught's proposals for compounding).

RLH

McNeill, Sir James McFadyen

b. 19 August 1892 Clydebank, Scotland
d. 24 July 1964 near Glasgow, Scotland

Scottish naval architect, designer of the Cunard North Atlantic Liners Queen Mary and Queen Elizabeth.

McNeill was born in Clydebank just outside Glasgow, and was to serve that town for most of his life. After education at Clydebank High School and then at Allan Glen's in Glasgow, in 1908 he entered the shipyard of John Brown & Co. Ltd as an apprentice. He was encouraged to matriculate at the University of Glasgow, where he studied naval architecture under the (then) unique Glasgow system of 'sandwich' training, alternately spending six months in the shipyard, followed by winter at the Faculty of Engineering. On graduating in 1915, he joined the Army and by 1918 had risen to the rank of Major in the Royal Field Artillery.

After the First World War, McNeill returned to the shipyard and in 1928 was appointed Chief Naval Architect. In 1934 he was made a local director of the company. During the difficult period of the 1930s he was in charge of the technical work which led to the design, launching and successful completion of the great liners *Queen Mary* and *Queen Elizabeth*. Some of the most remarkable ships of the mid-twentieth century were to come from this shipyard, including the last British battleship, HMS *Vanguard*, and the Royal Yacht *Britannia*, completed in 1954. From 1948 until 1959, Sir James was Managing Director of the Clydebank part of the company

and was Deputy Chairman by the time he retired in 1962. His public service was remarkable and included chairmanship of the Shipbuilding Conference and of the British Ship Research Association, and membership of the Committee of Lloyd's Register of Shipping.

Principal Honours and Distinctions
Knight Commander of the Royal Victorian Order 1954. CBE 1950. FRS 1948. President, Institution of Engineers and Shipbuilders in Scotland 1947–9. Honorary Vice-President, Royal Institution of Naval Architects. Military Cross (First World War).

Bibliography
1935, 'Launch of the quadruple-screw turbine steamer *Queen Mary*', *Transactions of the Institution of Naval Architects* 77: 1–27 (in this classic paper McNeill displays complete mastery of a difficult subject; it is recorded that prior to launch the estimate for travel of the ship in the River Clyde was 1,194 ft (363.9 m), and the actual amount recorded was 1,196 ft (364.5 m)!).

FMW

MacNeill, Sir John Benjamin

b. 1793 (?) Mount Pleasant, near Dundalk, Louth, Ireland
d. 2 March 1880

Irish railway engineer and educator.

Sir John MacNeill became a pupil of Thomas **Telford** and served under him as Superintendent of the Southern Division of the Holyhead Road from London to Shrewsbury. In this capacity he invented a 'Road Indicator' or dynamometer. Like other Telford followers, he viewed the advent of railways with some antipathy, but after the death of Telford in 1834 he quickly became involved in railway construction and in 1837 he was retained by the Irish Railway Commissioners to build railways in the north of Ireland (Vignoles received the commission for the south). Much of his subsequent career was devoted to schemes for Irish railways, both those envisaged by the Commissioners and other private lines with more immediately commercial objectives. He was knighted in 1844 on the completion of the Dublin & Drogheda Railway along the east coast of Ireland. In 1845 MacNeill lodged plans for over 800 miles (1,300 km) of Irish railways. Not all of these were built, many falling victim to Irish poverty in the years after the Famine, but he maintained a large staff and became financially embarrassed. His other schemes included the Grangemouth Docks in Scotland, the Liverpool & Bury Railway, and the Belfast Waterworks, the latter completed in 1843 and subsequently extended by Bateman.

MacNeill was an engineer of originality, being the person who introduced iron-lattice bridges into Britain, employing the theoretical and experimental work of Fairbairn and Eaton **Hodgkinson** (the Boyne Bridge at Drogheda had two such spans of 250 ft (76 m) each). He also devised the Irish railway gauge of 5 ft 2 in. (1.57 m). Consulted by the Board of Trinity College, Dublin, regarding a School of Engineering in 1842, he was made an Honorary LLD of the University and appointed the first Professor of Civil Engineering, but he relinquished the chair to his assistant, Samuel **Downing,** in 1846. MacNeill was a large and genial man, but not, we are told, 'of methodical and business habit': he relied heavily on his subordinates. Blindness obliged him to retire from practice several years before his death. He was an early member of the Institution of Civil Engineers, joining in 1827, and was elected a Fellow of the Royal Society in 1838.

Principal Honours and Distinctions
FRS 1838.

Further Reading
Dictionary of National Biography.
Proceedings of the Institution of Civil Engineers 73: 361–71.

AB

Maddox, Richard Leach
b. 1816 Bath, England
d. 1902 Southampton, England

English physician, amateur photographer and photomicrographer, inventor of the first practicable gelatine silver halide emulsion.

Maddox studied medicine, but dogged by ill health he travelled widely, eventually settling in Constantinople (now Istanbul), where he married in 1849. After further migrations, Maddox returned to England in the 1870s. He had become interested in photography and was awarded medals for his photomicrographs. Searching for a substitute for collodion to hold the sensitive silver salts, Maddox devised a gelatine bromide emulsion that gave acceptable results, and he published details in 1871. Gelatine had been tried by earlier experimenters, but the results were poor; the plates made by Maddox were slow and lacked density, but they pointed the way to the modern gelatine halide emulsions which continued to form the basis of photographic emulsions in the 1990s.

Bibliography
1871, *British Journal of Photography* 8 (September): 422–3 (first published details of Maddox's emulsion).

Further Reading
J.M. Eder, 1945, *History of Photography*, trans E. Epstean, New York.
H. Gernsheim and A, Gernsheim, 1969, *The History of Photography*, rev. edn, London: Phandon.

JW

Maiman, Theodore Harold
b. 11 July 1927 Los Angeles, California, USA

American physicist who developed the laser.

The son of an electrical engineer, Theodore H. Maiman graduated with the degree of BS in engineering physics from the University of Colorado in 1949. He then went on to do postgraduate work at Stanford University, where he gained an MS in electrical engineering in 1951 and a PhD in physics in 1955 for work on spectroscopy using microwave-optical techniques. He then joined the Hughes Research Laboratories, where he worked on the stimulated emission of microwave energy. In this field Charles H. **Townes** had developed the maser (an acronym of *m*icrowave *a*mplification by *s*timulated *e*mission of *r*adiation) and in a paper in 1958 with Arthur L. **Schawlow** he had suggested the possibility of a further development into optical frequencies, or, of an optical maser, later known as a laser (an acronym of *l*ight *a*mplification by *s*timulated *e*mission of *r*adiation). Maiman was the first to achieve this when in May 1960 he operated a ruby laser and coherent light was produced for the first time. In 1962 he founded his own company, Korad Corporation, for research, development and manufacture of high-power lasers. He founded Maiman Associates in 1968, acting as consultant on lasers and optics. He was a co-founder of the Laser Video Corporation in 1972, and in 1976 he became Vice-President for advanced technology at TRW Electronics.

Principal Honours and Distinctions
Franklin Institute Stuart Ballantine Medal 1962. American Electrical Society/American Astronautical Society Award 1965. American Physical Society Oliver E. Buckley Solid State Physics Prize 1966. Fannie and John Hertz Foundation Award for Applied Physical Science 1966. American Optical Society R.W. Wood Prize 1976.

Bibliography
1980, entry in *McGraw-Hill Modern Scientists and Engineers*, Part 2, New York, pp. 271–2 (autobiographical).

RTS

Ma Jun (Ma Chun)
fl. 220–265 China

Chinese engineer and inventor.

Ma Jun was active at the court of Emperor Ming Ti and achieved several useful inventions in a number of fields. First, he made improvements in the silk-weaving loom by simplifying the heddles and treadles, thereby enabling a greater variety of patterns to be woven. Second, he constructed a 'south pointing carriage', which was a two-wheeled cart with a train of gears arranged so that whichever direction the vehicle turned, the figure mounted on top of it would always point south. This may seem trivial, but the carriage may have had useful applications, possibly in surveying. During the period 227 to 239, Ma Jun also made a square-pallet chain pump, usually attributed to Bi Lan (186 AD), Loyang, that was used to irrigate parks and gardens. Other inventions included rotary ballistae and mechanical toys that were worked by water power, such as puppets operated by horizontal jack wheels.

Further Reading
J. Needham, *Science and Civilisation in China*, Cambridge: Cambridge University Press,

1965, Vol. IV,2, pp. 39–42, 286–8, 295, 303, 346, 350, 524, 532–3.

LRD

Mallet, Jules Théodore Anatole
b. 1837 Geneva, Switzerland
d. November 1919 Nice, France

Swiss engineer, inventor of the compound steam locomotive and the Mallet articulated locomotive.

Mallet's family moved to Normandy while he was still a child. After working as a civil engineer, in 1867 he turned to machinery, particularly to compound steam engines. He designed the first true compound steam locomotives, which were built for the Bayonne–Biarritz Railway in 1876. They were 0–4–2 tank locomotives with one high-pressure and one low-pressure cylinder. A starting valve controlled by the driver admitted high-pressure steam to the low-pressure cylinder while the high-pressure cylinder exhausted to the atmosphere. At that time it was thought impracticable in a narrow-gauge locomotive to have more than three coupled axles in rigid frames. Mallet patented his system of articulation in 1884 and the first locomotives were built to that design in 1888: they were 0–4–4–0 tanks with two sets of frames. The two rear pairs of wheels carried the rear set of frames and were driven by two high-pressure cylinders; the two front pairs, which were driven by the high-pressure cylinders, carried a separate set of frames that was allowed sideplay, with a centre of rotation between the low-pressure cylinders. In contrast to the patent locomotive of Robert **Fairlie**, no flexible connections were required to carry steam at boiler pressure. The first Mallet articulated locomotives were small, built to 60 cm (23.6 in.) gauge: the first standard-gauge Mallets were built in 1890, for the St Gotthard Railway, and it was only after the type was adopted by American railways in 1904 that large Mallet locomotives were built, with sizes increasing rapidly to culminate in some of the largest steam locomotives ever produced. In the late 1880s Mallet also designed monorail locomotives, which were built for the system developed by C.F.M.-T. **Lartigue**.

Bibliography
1884, French patent no. 162,876 (articulated locomotive).

461

Further Reading

J.T. van Riemsdijk, 1970, 'The compound locomotive, Part I', *Transactions of the Newcomen Society* 43 (describes Mallet's work on compounding).

L. Wiener, 1930, *Articulated Locomotives*, London: Constable (describes his articulated locomotives).

For the Mallet family, see *Historisch-Biographisches Lexikon der Schweiz*.

See also: **Bousquet, Gaston du**; **Vauclain, Samuel Matthews**; **Webb, Francis William**.

PJGR

Malouin, Paul-Jacques

b. 29 June 1701 Caen, France
d. 3 January 1778 Versailles, France

French medical practitioner who suggested producing tin plate with zinc.

Setting out to study law, Malouin turned to scientific studies, settling in Paris to teach and practice medicine. He retained his scientific interest in the field of chemistry, producing memoirs on zinc and tin, and .as early as 1742 suggested that a type of tin plate might instead be produced with zinc. A method of zinc-coating hammered-iron saucepans was introduced briefly at Rouen in the early 1780s.

His contribution to early volumes of **Diderot**'s *Encyclopédie* included those on 'Alchemy', 'Antimony', 'Acid' and 'Alkali'. Malouin also applied his scientific knowledge to articles on milling and baking for the Academy in *Descriptions des arts et métiers*.

Principal Honours and Distinctions
Elected to Academy 1742. FRS 1753.

Further Reading

Dumas, 1831, *Treatise de chimie appliqué aux arts* 3, 218.

J.R. Partington, 1961, *A History of Chemistry*, Vol. III (refers to Malouin's work in chemistry).

John Percy, 1864, *Metallurgy: Iron and Steel*, London: John Murray, 155 (provides brief references to his theories on zinc coatings).

See also **Craufurd, Henry William**.

JD

Mannesmann, Reinhard

b. 13 May 1856 Remscheid, Bleidinghausen, Germany
d. 22 February 1922 Remscheid, Bleidinghausen, Germany

German metallurgical engineer.

Reinhard Mannesmann and his four brothers developed the engineering works at Remscheid that had been founded by their father. With his brother Max, Reinhard devised c.1885 a method of producing seamless tubes by a rolling process. Factories for manufacturing tubes by this process were established at Remscheid, at Bous in the Saar district and at Komotau in Bohemia. Further developments of the process were patented by the brothers in the years following the initial patent of 1885. The British patent rights for the Mannesmann process were purchased by the Landore Siemens Steel Company in 1888, and the Mannesmann Tube Company was established at Landore in South Wales. This company went into liquidation in 1899 after ten years of production and the Tube Works was then purchased by the Mannesmann family, and a new company, the British Mannesmann Tube Company, was formed. Reinhard and Max Mannesmann took up residence near the Landore works and the business prospered so that by 1914 Landore was employing 1,500 men and producing 35,000 tons of tubing each year. The company was taken over during the First World War by the Custodian of Enemy Property, and after the war a new tube works which had been planned in 1914 was built at Newport, Monmouthshire. The Mannesmann family were able to resume control in 1926 for some ten years, but in 1938 the company became part of the Stewarts & Lloyds organization.

Further Reading

G. Evans, 1934, *Manufacture of Seamless Tubes Ferrous and Non-Ferrous*, London; 1940, *Proceedings of the Institution of Mechanical Engineers* 143: 62–3 (both provide technical details of the Mannesmann process for forming seamless tubes).

RTS

Mansart, Nicolas François

b. 23 January 1598 Paris, France
d. 23 September 1666 Paris, France

French architect believed by many historians to be the greatest French architect of all time.

Mansart was a classical architect who designed in High Renaissance style in France. Chief architect to Louis XIII, he was responsible for a number of fine châteaux and hôtels such as the Château de Maisons (1642–51) near Paris and the Hôtel Carnavalet (1660) in Paris. He was also the architect of the magnificent Paris church of Val de Grâce (begun in 1645).

The mansard roof, which has two different slopes of pitch, one steeper than the other, was named after Mansart (with a small change of spelling for euphony). It was a type of roof that was very popular in France from the early seventeenth century onwards and was revived under Napoleon III in the nineteenth century. However, although Mansart popularized this style of roof, he did not invent it; indeed, it was used in earlier works by both Pierre Lescot and Jacques Lemercier.

Further Reading
R. Blomfield, 1911, *A History of French Architecture*, Vol II, Bell (the standard work).
A. Braham and P. Smith, 1974, *François Mansart*, Zwemmer.
A. Blunt, 1941, *François Mansart and the Origins of French Classical Architecture*, The Warburg Institute.

DY

Mansfield, Charles Blachford
b. 8 May 1819 Rowner, Hampshire, England
d. 26 February 1855 London, England

English chemist, founder of coal-tar chemistry.

Mansfield, the son of a country clergyman, was educated privately at first, then at Winchester College and at Cambridge; ill health, which dogged his early years, delayed his graduation until 1846. He was first inclined to medicine, but after settling in London, chemistry seemed to him to offer the true basis of the grand scheme of knowledge he aimed to establish. After completing the chemistry course at the Royal College of Chemistry in London, he followed the suggestion of its first director, A.W. von **Hofmann**, of investigating the chemistry of coal tar. This work led to a result of great importance for industry by demonstrating the valuable substances that could be extracted from coal tar. Mansfield obtained pure benzene, and toluene by a process for which he was granted a patent in 1848 and published in the Chemical Society's journal the same year. The following year he published a pamphlet on the applications of benzene.

Blessed with a private income, Mansfield had no need to support himself by following a regular profession. He was therefore able to spread his brilliant talents in several directions instead of confining them to a single interest. During the period of unrest in 1848, he engaged in social work with a particular concern to improve sanitation. In 1850, a description of a balloon machine in Paris led him to study aeronautics for a while, which bore fruit in an influential book, *Aerial Navigation* (London, 1851). He then visited Paraguay, making a characteristically thorough and illuminating study of conditions there. Upon his return to London in 1853, Mansfield resumed his chemical studies, especially on salts. He published his results in 1855 as *Theory of Salts*, his most important contribution to chemical theory.

Mansfield was in the process of preparing specimens of benzene for the Paris Exhibition of 1855 when a naphtha still overflowed and caught fire. In carrying it to a place of safety, Mansfield sustained injuries which unfortunately proved fatal.

Bibliography
1851, *Aerial Navigation*, London.
1855, *Theory of Salts*, London.

Further Reading
E.R. Ward, 1969, 'Charles Blachford Mansfield, 1819–1855, coal tar chemist and social reformer', *Chemistry and Industry* 66: 1,530–7 (offers a good and well-documented account of his life and achievements).

LRD

Marconi, Marchese Gugliemo
b. 25 April 1874 Bologna, Italy
d. 20 July 1937 Rome, Italy

Italian radio pioneer whose inventiveness and business skills made radio communication a practical proposition.

Marconi was educated in physics at Leghorn and at Bologna University. An avid experimenter, he worked in his parents' attic and, almost certainly aware of the recent work of **Hertz** and others, soon improved the performance of coherers and spark-gap transmitters. He also discovered for himself the use of earthing and of elevated metal plates as aerials. In 1895 he succeeded in transmitting telegraphy over a distance of 2 km (1¼ miles), but the Italian Telegraph authority rejected his invention, so in 1896 he moved to England, where he filed the first of many patents. There he gained the support of the Chief Engineer of the Post Office, and by the following year he had achieved communication across the Bristol Channel.

The British Post Office was also slow to take up his work, so in 1897 he formed the Wireless Telegraph & Signal Company to work independently. In 1898 he sold some equipment to the British Army for use in the Boer War and established the first permanent radio link from the Isle of Wight to the mainland. In 1899 he achieved communication across the English Channel (a distance of more than 31 miles or 50 km), the construction of a wireless station at Spezia, Italy, and the equipping of two US ships to report progress in the America's Cup yacht race, a venture that led to the formation of the American Marconi Company. In 1900 he won a contract from the British Admiralty to sell equipment and to train operators. Realizing that his business would be much more successful if he could offer his customers a complete radio-communication service (known today as a 'turnkey' deal), he floated a new company, the Marconi International Marine Communications Company, while the old company became the Marconi Wireless Telegraph Company.

His greatest achievement occurred on 12 December 1901, when **Morse** telegraph signals from a transmitter at Poldhu in Cornwall were received at St John's, Newfoundland, a distance of some 2,100 miles (3,400 km), with the use of an aerial flown by a kite. As a result of this, Marconi's business prospered and he became internationally famous, receiving many honours for his endeavours, including the Nobel Prize for Physics in 1909. In 1904, radio was first used to provide a daily bulletin at sea, and in 1907 a transatlantic wireless telegraphy service was inaugurated. The rescue of 1,650 passengers from the shipwreck of SS *Republic* in 1909 was the first of many occasions when wireless was instrumental in saving lives at sea, most notable being those from the *Titanic* on its maiden voyage in April 1912; more lives would have been saved had there been sufficient lifeboats. Marconi was one of those who subsequently pressed for greater safety at sea. In 1910 he demonstrated the reception of long (8 km or 5 miles) waves from Ireland in Buenos Aires, but after the First World War he began to develop the use of short waves, which were more effectively reflected by the ionosphere. By 1918 the first link between England and Australia had been established, and in 1924 he was awarded a Post Office contract for short-wave communication between England and the various parts of the British Empire.

With his achievements by then recognized by the Italian Government, in 1915 he was appointed Radio-Communications Adviser to the Italian armed forces, and in 1919 he was an Italian delegate to the Paris Peace Conference. From 1921 he lived on his yacht, the *Elettra*, and although he joined the Fascist Party in 1923, he later had reservations about Mussolini.

Principal Honours and Distinctions
Nobel Prize for Physics (jointly with K.F. **Braun**) 1909. Russian Order of St Anne. Commander of St Maurice and St Lazarus. Grand Cross of the Order of the Crown (i.e. Knight) of Italy 1902. Freedom of Rome 1903. Honorary DSc Oxford. Honorary LLD Glasgow. Chevalier of the Civil Order of Savoy 1905. Royal Society of Arts Albert Medal. Honorary knighthood (GCVO) 1914. Institute of Electrical and Electronics Engineers Medal of Honour 1920. Chairman, Royal Society of Arts 1924. Created Marquis (Marchese) 1929. Nominated to the Italian Senate 1929. President, Italian Academy 1930. Rector, University of St Andrews, Scotland, 1934.

Bibliography
1896, 'Improvements in transmitting electrical impulses and in apparatus thereof', British patent no. 12,039.
1 June 1898, British patent no. 12,326 (transformer or 'jigger' resonant circuit).
1901, British patent no. 7,777 (selective tuning).
1904, British patent no. 763,772 ('four circuit' tuning arrangement).

Further Reading
D. Marconi, 1962, *My Father, Marconi.*
W.J. Baker, 1970, *A History of the Marconi Company*, London: Methuen.

KF

Marcus, Siegfried

b. 18 September 1831 Malchin, Mecklenburg
d. 30 June 1898 Vienna, Austria

German inventor, builder of the world's first self-propelled vehicle driven by an internal combustion engine.

Marcus was apprenticed as a mechanic and was employed in the newly founded enterprise of Siemens & Halske in Berlin. He then went to Vienna and, from 1853, was employed in the workshop of the Imperial Court Mechanic, Kraft, and in the same year he was a mechanic in the Royal and Imperial Institute of Physics of the University of Vienna. In 1860 he became independent of the Imperial Court, but he installed an electrical bell system for the Empress Elizabeth and instructed the Crown Prince Rudolf in natural science.

Marcus was granted thirty-eight patents in Austria, as well as many foreign patents. The magnetic electric ignition engine, for which he was granted a patent in 1864, brought him the biggest financial reward; it was introduced as the 'Viennese Ignition' engine by the Austrian Navy and the pioneers of the Prussian and Russian armies. The engine was exhibited at the World Fair in Paris in 1867 together with the 'Thermoscale' which was also constructed by Marcus; this was a magnetic/electric rotative engine for electric lighting and field telegraphy.

Marcus's reputation is due mainly to his attempts to build a new internal combustion engine. By 1870 he had assembled a simple, direct-working internal combustion engine on a primitive chassis. This was, in fact, the first petrol-engined vehicle with electric ignition, and tradition records that when Marcus drove the vehicle in the streets of Vienna it made so much noise that the police asked him to remove it; this he did and did not persist with his experiments. Thus ended the trials of the world's first petrol-engined vehicle; it was running in 1875, ten years before **Daimler** and **Benz** were carrying out their early trials in Stuttgart.

Further Reading
Austrian Dictionary of National Biography.

IMcN

Marey, Etienne-Jules

b. 5 March 1830 Beaune, France
d. 15 May 1904 Paris, France

French physiologist and pioneer of chronophotography.

At the age of 19 Marey went to Paris to study medicine, becoming particularly interested in the problems of the circulation of the blood. In an early communication to the Académie des Sciences he described a much improved device for recording the pulse, the sphygmograph, in which the beats were recorded on a smoked plate. Most of his subsequent work was concerned with methods of recording movement: to study the movement of the horse, he used pneumatic sensors on each hoof to record traces on a smoked drum; this device became known as the Marey recording tambour. His attempts to study the wing movements of a bird in flight in the same way met with limited success since the recording system interfered with free movement. Reading in 1878 of **Muybridge**'s work in America using sequence photography to study animal movement, Marey considered the use of photography himself. In 1882 he developed an idea first used by the astronomer Janssen: a camera in which a series of exposures could be made on a circular photographic plate. Marey's 'photographic gun' was rifle shaped and could expose twelve pictures in approximately one second on a circular plate. With this device he was able to study wing movements of birds in free flight. The camera was limited in that it could record only a small number of images, and in the summer of 1882 he developed a new camera, when the French government gave him a grant to set up a physiological research station on land provided by the Parisian authorities near the Porte d'Auteuil. The new design used a fixed plate, on which a series of images were recorded through a rotating shutter. Looking rather like the results provided by a modern stroboscope flash device, the images were partially superimposed if the subject was slow moving, or separated if it was fast. His human subjects were dressed all in white and moved against a black background. An alternative was to dress the subject in black, with highly reflective strips and points along limbs and at joints, to produce a graphic record of the relationships of the parts of the body during action. A one-second-sweep timing clock was included in the scene to enable the precise interval between exposures to be assessed. The fixed-plate cameras were used with considerable success, but the number of individual records on each plate was still limited. With the appearance of **Eastman**'s Kodak roll-film camera in France in September 1888, Marey designed a new camera to use the long rolls of paper film. He described the new apparatus to the Académie des Sciences on 8 October 1888, and three weeks later showed a band of images taken with it at the rate of 20 per second. This camera and its subsequent improvements were the first true cinematographic cameras. The arrival of Eastman's celluloid film late in 1889 made Marey's camera even more practical, and for over a decade the Physiological Research Station made hundreds of sequence studies of animals and humans in motion, at rates of up to 100 pictures per second.

Marey pioneered the scientific study of movement using film cameras, introducing techniques of time-lapse, frame-by-frame and slow-motion analysis, macro- and micro-cinematography, superimposed timing clocks, studies of airflow using smoke streams, and other methods still in use in the 1990s. Appointed Professor of Natural History at the Collège de France in 1870, he headed the Institut Marey founded in 1898 to continue these studies. After Marey's death in 1904, the research continued under the direction of his associate Lucien Bull, who developed many new techniques, notably ultra-high-speed cinematography.

Principal Honours and Distinctions
Foreign member of the Royal Society 1898. President, Académie des Sciences 1895.

Bibliography
1860–1904, *Comptes rendus de l'Académie des Sciences de Paris*.
1873, *La Machine animale*, Paris
1874, *Animal Mechanism*, London.
1893, *Die Chronophotographie*, Berlin.
1894, *Le Mouvement*, Paris.
1895, *Movement*, London.
1899, *La Chronophotographie*, Paris.

Further Reading
1905, *Travaux de l'Association de l'Institut Marey*, Paris.
Brian Coe, 1981, *History of Movie Photography*, London.
—— 1992, *Muybridge and the Chronophotographers*, London.
Jacques Deslandes, 1966, *Histoire comparée du cinéma*, Vol. I, Paris.

See also **Demenÿ, Georges**.

BC/MG

Marrison, Warren Alvin
b. 21 May 1896 Inverary, Canada
d. 27 March 1980 Palo Verdes Estates, California, USA

Canadian (naturalized American) electrical engineer, pioneer of the quartz clock.

Marrison received his high-school education at Kingston Collegiate Institute, Ontario, and in 1914 he entered Queen's University in Kingston. He graduated in Engineering Physics in 1920, his college career having been interrupted by war service in the Royal Flying Corps. During his service in the Flying Corps he worked on radio, and when he returned to Kingston he established his own transmitter. This interest in radio was later to influence his professional life.

In 1921 he entered Harvard University, where he obtained an MA, and shortly afterwards he joined the Western Electric Company in New York to work on the recording of sound on film. In 1925 he transferred to Western Electric's Bell Laboratory, where he began what was to become his life's work: the development of frequency standards for radio transmission. In 1922 **Cady** had used the elastic vibration of a quartz crystal to control the frequency of a valve oscillator, but at that time there was no way of counting and displaying the number of vibrations as the frequency was too high. In 1927 Marrison succeeded in dividing the frequency electronically until it was low enough to drive a synchronous motor. Although his purpose was to determine the frequency accurately by counting the number of vibrations that occurred in a given time, he had incidentally produced the first quartz-crystal-ontrolled clock. The results were sufficiently encouraging for him to build an improved version the following year, specifically as a time and frequency standard.

Principal Honours and Distinctions
British Horological Institute Gold Medal
1947. Clockmakers' Company Tompion
Medal 1955.

Bibliography
1928, with J.W. Horton, 'Precision measurement of frequency', *Proceedings of the Institute of Radio Engineers* 16: 137–54 (provides details of the original quartz clock, although it was not described as such).
1930, 'The crystal clock', *Proceedings of the National Academy of Sciences* 16: 496–507 (describes the second clock).

Further Reading
W.R. Topham, 1989, 'Warren A. Marrison – pioneer of the quartz revolution', *NAWCC Bulletin* 31 (2): 126–34.
J.D. Weaver, 1982, *Electrical and Electronic Clocks and Watches*, London (a technical assessment of his work on the quartz clock).

DV

Marsden, Samuel
b. 1764 Farsley, Yorkshire, England
d. 1838 Australia

English farmer whose breeding programme established the Australian wool industry.

Although his father was a farmer, at the age of 10 Samuel Marsden went to work as a blacksmith, and continued in that trade for ten years. He then decided to go into the Church, was educated at Hull Grammar School and Cambridge, and was ordained in 1793. He then emigrated to Australia, where he took up an appointment as Assistant Chaplain to the Colony. He was stationed at Parramatta, where he was granted 100 acres and bought a further 128 acres himself. In 1800 he became Principal Chaplain, and by 1802 he farmed the third largest farm in the colony. Initially he was able to obtain only two Marino rams and was forced to crossbreed with imported Indian stock. However, with this combination he was able to improve wool quality dramatically, and this stock provided the basis of his breeding stock. In 1807 he returned to Britain, taking 160 lb of wool with him. This was woven into 40 yards (36.5 m) of cloth in a mill near Leeds, and from this Marsden had a suit made which he wore

when he visited George III. The latter was so impressed with the cloth that he presented Marsden with five Marino ewes in lamb, with which he returned to Australia. By 1811 he was sending more than 5,000 lb of wool back to the UK each year. In 1814 Marsden concentrated more on Church matters and made the first of seven missionary visits to New Zealand. He made the last of these excursions the year before his death.

Principal Honours and Distinctions
Vice-President, New South Wales Agricultural Society (on its foundation) 1821.

Further Reading
Michael Ryder, 1983, *Sheep and Man*, Duckworth (a definitive study on sheep history that deals in detail with Marsden's developments).

AP

Marsh, Sylvester
b. 30 September 1803 Campton, New Hampshire, USA
d. 30 December 1884 Concord, New Hampshire, USA

American pioneer of mountain rack railways.

Marsh, a businessman whose interests successively included packing pork and dealing in corn, was inspired by a rack railway built in 1847 up the 1 in 16.5 Jefferson incline, Indiana, to design and build a line to the 6,293 ft (1,918 m) summit of Mount Washington, New Hampshire. The gradient averaged 1 in 4 and Marsh installed a rack made from wrought iron with rungs fastened between upright bearers that were deep enough for the teeth of a locomotive's driving pinion to engage with two rungs at a time; counter-pressure brakes controlled a locomotive's descent. The Mount Washington Cog Railway was the first mountain rack railway: it opened in 1869 and even now continues to operate with steam locomotives.

Bibliography
Marsh took out four US patents relating to rack railways between 1861 and 1870.

Further Reading
O.J. Morris, 1951, *The Snowdon Mountain Railway*, Shepperton: Ian Allan.
P.B. Whitehouse, J.B. Snell and J.B. Hollingsworth,

1978, *Steam for Pleasure*, London: Routledge & Kegan Paul.
J.R. Day and B.G. Wilson, 1957, *Unusual Railways*, F. Muller.

See also **Riggenbach, Niklaus**.

PJGR

Marshall, William
b. baptized 28 July 1745 Yorkshire, England
d. 1818 Pickering, Yorkshire, England

English commentator and writer on agriculture who established the first agricultural college in Britain.

Little is known for certain about William Marshall's early life, other than that he was baptized at Sinnington in the West Riding of Yorkshire. On his own account he was involved in trade in the West Indies from the age of 15 for a period of fourteen years. It is assumed that he was financially successful in this, for on his return to England in 1774 he was able to purchase Addisham Farm in Surrey. Having sacked his bailiff he determined to keep a minute book relating to all transactions on the farm, which he was now managing for himself. On these entries he made additional comments. The publication of these writings was the beginning of a substantial review of agriculture in Britain and a criticism of existing practices. From 1779 he acted as agent on a Norfolk estate, and his five years in that position resulted in *The Rural Economy of Norfolk*, the first of a series of county reviews that he was to write, intending the somewhat ambitious task of surveying the whole country. By 1808 Marshall had accumulated sufficient capital to be able to purchase a substantial property in the Vale of Cleveland, where he lived for the rest of his life. At the time of his death he was engaged in the erection of a building to serve as an agricultural college; the same building is now a rural-life museum.

Bibliography
Other titles in his *Rural Economy* series included *Yorkshire* in 1788, *Gloucester* in 1789, *The Midland Counties* in 1790, *The West of England* in 1796, and *The Southern Counties* two years later. Further titles included *Experiments and Observations Concerning Agriculture and the Weather* in 1779, *Observations on the Different Breeds of Sheep* in 1792, *The General View of the Agriculture of Central Highland Scotland* in 1794, and *Planting and Rural Ornament* in 1796. He also wrote *On the Enclosure of Commonable and Intermixed Lands* in 1801, *On the Landed Property of England, an Elementary Practical Treatise* in 1804, and *On the Management of Landed Estates* in 1806. He was not asked to write any of the County Surveys produced by the Board of Agriculture, despite his own claims to the origin of the idea. Instead in 1817 he wrote *A Review and Complete Abstract of the Reports of the Board of Agriculture* as his own criticism of them.

Further Reading
Joan Thirsk, 1989, *The Agrarian History of England and Wales*, Vol. VI (deals with the years 1750 to 1850, the period associated with Marshall).
Pamela Horn, 1982, *William Marshall (1745–1818) and the Georgian Countryside*, Beacon (gives a more specific account).

AP

Martin, C.
fl. *c.*1861 Belgium

Belgian maker of one of the most popular types of tape condensers.

The object of condensing, the last process in carding, is to obtain a roving, or slightly twisted yarn which is the same thickness and weight throughout its length. In a tape condenser, the web of fibres from the last swift of the carder is divided into the requisite number of ribbons, which are supported on tapes before being rubbed into round rovings and wound onto bobbins ready for spinning.

It was Martin who introduced in 1861 what became the most common type of condenser on the European continent. It divided the web by a combined tearing and cutting action between leather tapes and a pair of rigid rollers. As its division of the web was more minute than with earlier machines, its product was more suitable for fine yarns, so it was accepted rapidly in Belgium and France but much more slowly in England and the United States.

Further Reading
C. Singer (ed.), 1958, *A History of Technology*, Vol. V, Oxford: Clarendon Press (includes an account of this invention).
L.J. Mills (ed.), 1928, *The Textile Educator*, Vol. III, London; and W.E. Morton, 1937, *An Introduction to the Study of Spinning*, London (both provide an explanation of the condenser system).

RLH

Martin, Sir James

b. 1893 Co. Down, Northern Ireland
d. 5 January 1981 England

Irish military aircraft engineer, inventor of the ejector seat.

Martin acquired a general knowledge of engineering as an industrial worker in Belfast. In 1929 he established the Martin Aircraft Company, which was merged five years later with another concern to form the Martin–Baker Aircraft Company at Denham, Buckinghamshire. They became known for designing and constructing efficient, lightweight military aircraft, and Martin supervised personally every aspect of the work of his factory. During the Second World War they developed a number of aircraft weapons, including an explosive device carried on a bomber's wings for cutting the cables of barrage balloons, the flat-feed system for the 20 mm Hispano cannon used on British fighter planes and the twelve-gun pack mounted in the nose of the Havoc night fighter. Martin began devising means of rapid escape from a disabled fighter plane. First came a quick-release canopy for the Spitfire, followed by an improved form sliding on guides set in the fuselage. Then came the Martin–Baker seat, which ejected the pilot from his plane by an explosive charge. Ground tests were made to determine the rates of acceleration that could be tolerated by the pilot, and the first test in the air with a pilot took place in July 1946 at a speed of 320 mph (515 km/h) and an altitude of 8,000 ft (2,400 m). Its first use in a genuine emergency was in May 1949.

After the Second World War, the firm specialized in making components, particularly the ejector seat, rather than complete aircraft. The higher speeds and altitudes of supersonic jet aircraft made it necessary to modify the ejector seat: a device to hold the pilot's legs together, to pre-vent their being broken, was incorporated. In addition, with the Institute of Aviation Medicine, Martin developed a face blind to prevent skin damage at low temperatures. Another modification was to allow the seat to fall freely for the first 10,000 ft (3,000 m) to enable the pilot to reach breathable air more quickly; in October 1959 a successful demonstration took place at 1,250 mph (2,000 km/h) and 40,000 ft (12,000 m) altitude. During the inventor's lifetime, it is estimated that his ejector seat saved the lives of some 4,700 airmen.

Principal Honours and Distinctions
Knighted 1965. Barbour Air Safety Award 1958. Cumberbatch Air Safety Trophy 1959. Royal Aero Club Gold Medal 1964.

Further Reading
Obituary, 1981, *The Times*.

LRD

Martin, Pierre Emile

b. 18 August 1824 Bourges, France
d. 23 May 1915 Fourchambault, France

French metallurgist, pioneer of open-hearth steelmaking.

His father Emile owned an iron- and steelworks at Sireuil, near Angoulême, and, through this, Pierre became interested in improving the steelmaking process. In England, C.W. **Siemens** had developed the regenerative principle of waste-heat recovery that produced a much higher furnace temperature. In 1863, the Martins applied this process in an open-hearth furnace built under licence from Siemens, with the aid of his engineers. They melted a mixture of pig- and wrought iron to produce steel with the required carbon content. Martin exhibited the product at the Paris Exhibition of 1867 and was awarded a gold medal. The open-hearth process was for a long time known as the Siemens–Martin process, but Martin did not share in the profits which others gained from its successful adoption. He had difficulty in obtaining patent rights as it was claimed that the principles of the process were already known and in use. The costs of litigation brought Martin to the brink of poverty, from which relief came only late in life, when in 1907 the Comité des Forges de France opened a subscription for him that was generously supported.

A week before his death, the Iron and Steel Institute of London bestowed on him their Bessemer gold medal.

Principal Honours and Distinctions
Iron and Steel Institute Bessemer Gold Medal 1915.

Further Reading
Obituary, 1915, *Journal of the Iron and Steel Institute* 91: 466.

LRD

Martinville, Edouard-Léon Scott de
See **Scott de Martinville, Edouard-Léon**.

Marton, Ladislaus (Laslo)
b. 15 August 1901 Budapest Hungary

Hungarian physicist, pioneer of the development and practical application of the electron microscope.

He studied and obtained his degree at Zurich in 1924 and undertook research there until 1925, when he moved to Budapest to work at the Tungsram Lamp Company. He moved to the University of Brussels in 1928, and during the ensuing ten years was involved in the construction and development of a focusing electron microscope. With the second of these he was able to take micrographs of cells in 1932 and of a bacterium in 1937.

In 1941 he moved to the USA to work with Radio Corporation of America (RCA).

Principal Honours and Distinctions
International Union Against Cancer Medal 1938. Verhagen Medical, Brussels 1947. US Department of Commerce Gold Medal 1955.

Bibliography
1947, *Advances in Electronics and Electron Physics*.
1957, *Methods of Experimental Physics*.
1968, *Early History of the Electron Microscope*.

Further Reading
Watt, 1984, *Principles and Practice of Electron Microscopy*, Cambridge.
M. Hayat, 1973–80, *Principles and Techniques of Electron Microscopy*.

MG

Martyn, Sir Richard
b. 1543
d. July 1617

English goldsmith, Warden and later Master of the Royal Mint, entrepreneur and shareholder in Elizabethan metal industries.

Martyn became a leading shareholder in the Company of Mineral and Battery Works, the Elizabethan monopoly established in 1565 under the initiative William **Humfrey**. Its purpose was to mine lead and zinc ores and to introduce production of brass and manufacture of brass wire to England, activities in which he took an active interest. Appointed Warden of the Royal Mint in 1572, Martyn's responsibilities included the receipt of bullion and dispatch of freshly minted coins. He reported unfavourably on a new invention for producing 'milled' coins by a screw press which embossed the two faces simultaneously. Considerable friction arose from his criticism of the then Master of the Mint. He was later subject to criticism himself on the irregularity of coin weights produced at the Mint. In 1580 Martyn leased Tintern wireworks, property of the Mineral and Battery Company, which was by then producing iron wire after earlier failing in the production of brass. Two years later he sought rights from the company to mine the zinc ore calamine and to make brass. When this was granted in 1587, he formed a partnership with others including William Brode, a London goldsmith who had been experimenting with the making of brass. Production started on a small scale using imported copper at Queen's Mill, Isleworth, largely financed by Martyn. Brode soon disagreed with his partners and with the Mineral and Battery Works Company and Martyn withdrew. After long and acrimonious disputes the works closed completely in 1605.

Principal Honours and Distinctions
Alderman 1578. Knighted and appointed Lord Mayor of London 1589. Prime Warden of the Goldsmiths' Company 1592. Joint Master of the Mint with his son, Richard, 1599.

Further Reading
M.B. Donald, 1961, *Elizabethan Monopolies*, London: Oliver & Boyd (provides a comprehensive account).

JD

Masaru, Inoue
See **Inoue Masaru**.

Masham, 1st Baron
See **Lister, Samuel Cunliffe**.

Massey, Daniel
b. 1798 Vermont, USA
d. 1856 Canada

American agricultural machinery manufacturer and co-founder of the Massey Harris Company (now Massey Ferguson).

In about 1800 Daniel Massey's family moved to Upper Canada. At the age of 6 he was sent back to stay with his grandparents in Waterton, USA, where he attended school for three years. He returned to his parents in 1807, and for the next twelve years he remained on his father's farm.

At the age of 19 he forfeited his rights to his inheritance and rented land further west, which he began to clear. By the age of 21 he owned 200 acres, and during the next twelve years he bought, cleared and sold a further 1,200 acres. In 1820 he married Lucina Bradley from Watertown and returned with her to Canada.

In 1830 he decided to settle down to farming and brought one of the first US threshing machines into Canada. From frequent visits to his family in the US he would return with new farm equipment, and in 1844 he handed his farm over to his eldest son so that he could concentrate on the development of his farm workshop. In 1845 he formed a brief partnership with R.F. Vaughan, who owned a small factory in Durham County near Lake Ontario. He began the production of ploughs, harrows, scufflers and rollers at a time when the Canadian Government was imposing heavy import duties on agricultural equipment being brought in from the USA. His business flourished and within six months he bought out his partner.

In 1848 he bought another foundry in Newcastle, together with 50 acres of land, and in 1851 his son Hart joined him in the business. The following year Hart returned from the USA with the sole rights to manufacture the Ketchum mower and the Burrell reaper.

The advent of the railway four years later opened up wider markets, and from these beginnings the Massey Company was to represent Canada at the Paris Exhibition of 1867. The European market was secured by the successes of the Massey reaper in the 'World' trials held in France in 1889. Two years later the company merged with the Harris Company of Canada, to become the Massey Harris Company. Daniel Massey retired from the company four years after his son joined it, and he died the following year.

Further Reading
Graeme Quick and Wesley Buchele, 1978, *The Grain Harvesters*, American Society of Agricultural Engineers (gives an account of harvest machinery development, in which Massey Harris played a vital role).
Merrill Denison, 1949, *Harvest Triumphant: The Story of Massey Harris*, London.

AP

Matteucci, Felice
b. 1803 Italy
d. 1887 Italy

Italian engineer, co-inventor of internal-combustion engines.

A distinguished hydraulic engineer, Matteucci is more widely known for his work on early internal-combustion engines. In 1851, during a land-reclamation project in Florence, he became acquainted with Eugenio **Barsanti**. Together they succeeded in designing and producing a number of the first type of gas engines to produce a vacuum within a closed cylinder, atmospheric pressure then being utilized to produce the power stroke. The principle was demonstrated by **Cecil** in 1820 and was used by Samuel **Brown** in 1827 and by N.A. **Otto** in 1867. The company Società Promotrice del Nuovo Motore Barsanti e Matteucci was formed in 1860, but ill health forced Matteucci to resign in 1862, and in 1864 Barsanti, whilst negotiating mass production of engines with Cockerill of Seraing, Belgium, contracted typhoid and later died. Efforts to continue the business in Italy subsequently failed and Matteucci returned to his engineering practice.

Bibliography
13 May 1852, British Provisional Patent no. 1,072 (the Barsanti and Matteucci engine).
12 June 1857, British patent no. 1,655 (contained many notable improvements to the design).

Further Reading
The Engineer (1858) 5: 73–4 (for an account of
the Italian engine).
Vincenzo Vannacci, 1955, *L'invenzione del mo-
tore a scoppio realizzota dai toscani Barsanti e
Matteucci 1854–1954*, Florence.

KAB

Matzeliger, Jan

b. 1852 Surinam
d. 1889 Lynn, Massachusetts, (?) USA

*African-American inventor of the shoe-lasting
machine.*

He served an apprenticeship as a machinist in his
native country, Surinam. As a young man he emigrated to New England in the USA, but he was
unable to secure employment in his trade. To
survive, he took various odd jobs, including sewing soles on to shoes in a factory at Lynn, Massachusetts, a centre of the shoemaking industry.
Much of the shoemaking process had already
been mechanized, but lasting remained laborious, painstaking hand work. Matzeliger
turned his undoubted inventive powers to mechanizing this operation. It took him four years to
achieve a working model of a mechanical last that
could be patented. By this time his health and
finances had been undermined by the struggle to
reach this stage; to raise funds he had to dispose
of two-thirds of his rights in his patent to two
local investors. Eventually he demonstrated a
trial model of his lasting machine and successfully
lasted seventy-five pairs of shoes. Not satisfied
with that, Matzeliger went on to produce two
improved machines, protected by further patent-
s. Finally, the United Shoe Machine Company
bought up his patents, but that relief came too
late to prevent Matzeliger from dying in poor
circumstances. The mechanization of shoe lasting made a significant contribution to the manufacture of shoes, raising production and reducing
costs. It also effectively extinguished the final element of skilled hand work required in shoemaking, earning him considerable unpopularity
among the workers who were about to be displaced, and resulting in the machine being dero-
gatorily nicknamed 'Niggerhead'.

Further Reading
P.P. James, 1989, *The Real McCoy: African-
American Invention and Innovation 1619–*

1930, Washington, DC: Smithsonian Institution, pp. 70–2.

LRD

Maudslay, Henry

b. 22 August 1771 Woolwich, Kent, England
d. 15 February 1831 Lambeth, London, England

English precision toolmaker and engineer.

Henry Maudslay was the third son of an ex-sol-
dier and storekeeper at Woolwich Arsenal. At the
age of 12 he was employed at the Arsenal filling
cartridges; two years later he was transferred to
the woodworking department, adjacent to the
smithy, to which he moved when 15 years old.
He was a rapid learner, and three years later Joseph **Bramah** took him on for the construction
of special tools required for the mass-production
of his locks. Maudslay was thus employed for the
next eight years. He became Bramah's foreman,
married his housekeeper, Sarah Tindale, and, unable to better himself, decided to leave and set up
on his own. He soon outgrew his first premises
in Wells Street and moved to Margaret Street, off
Oxford Street, where some examples of his workmanship were displayed in the window. These
caught the attention of a visiting Frenchman, de
Bacquancourt; he was a friend of Marc Isambard
Brunel, who was then in the early stages of designing the block-making machinery later installed at Portsmouth dockyard.

Brunel wanted first a set of working models, as
he did not think that the Lords of the Admiralty
would be capable of understanding engineering
drawings; Maudslay made these for him within
the next two years. Sir Samuel **Bentham**, Inspector-General of Naval Works, agreed that Brunel's
system was superior to the one that he had gone
some way in developing; the Admiralty approved, and an order was placed for the complete
plant. The manufacture of the machinery occupied Maudslay for the next six years; he was assisted by a draughtsman whom he took on from
Portsmouth dockyard, Joshua Field (1786–
1863), who became his partner in Maudslay, Son
and Field. There were as many as eighty employees at Margaret Street until, in 1810, larger
premises became necessary and a new works was
built at Lambeth Marsh where, eventually, there
were up to two hundred workers. The new factory was flanked by two houses, one of which was

occupied by Maudslay, the other by Field. The firm became noted for its production of marine steam-engines, notably Maudslay's table engine which was first introduced in 1807.

Maudslay was a consummate craftsman who was never happier than when working at his bench or at a machine tool; he was also one of the first engineers to appreciate the virtues of standardization. Evidence of this appreciation is to be found in his work in the development of the Bramah lock and then on the machine tools for the manufacture of ship's blocks to Marc Brunel's designs; possibly his most important contribution was the invention in 1797 of the metal lathe. He made a number of surface plates of the finest quality. The most celebrated of his numerous measuring devices was a micrometer-based machine which he termed his 'Lord Chancellor' because, in the machine shop, it represented the 'final court of appeal', measuring to one-thousandth of an inch.

Further Reading
1934–5, 'Maudslay, Sons & Field as general engineers', *Transactions of the Newcomen Society* 15, London.
1963, *Engineering Heritage*, Vol. 1, London: Institution of Mechanical Engineers.
L.T.C. Rolt, 1965, *Tools for the Job*, London: Batsford.
W. Steeds, 1969, *A History of Machine Tools 1700–1910*, Oxford: Oxford University Press.
IMcN

Maughan, Benjamin Waddy
fl. *c*.1868 London, England

English inventor of the first gas geyser.

Maughan was a decorative painter in the Clerkenwell district of London. He invented the first instantaneous domestic water-heater, which did not utilize solid fuel. He christened his device a geyser, taking the name from the Icelandic word *geysir*, which is the name of a specific hot spring there and means 'gusher'. He patented the geyser on 23 December 1868. In his design the cold water entered from the top of the apparatus, then flowed downwards by means of constricting wires to be heated by hot gases rising from the burner below. Hot water then flowed into the bath or sink. No flue was fitted to conduct tainted air and gases from the bathroom. An impressive example of Maughan's geyser is on display in the Science Museum in London. The fittings are of brass and the casing is painted in marbled green. it stands on three curved legs and displays the Royal Arms.

Bibliography
1868, 'Improvements in apparatus for the heating of water and other liquids, applicable for baths and other purposes', British patent no. 3,917 (provides a very long account of the details of the invention and its purpose).
DY

Mavor, Henry Alexander
b. 1858 Stranraer, Scotland
d. 16 July 1915 Mauchline, Ayrshire, Scotland

Scottish engineer who pioneered the use of electricity for lighting, power and the propulsion of ships.

Mavor came from a distinguished Scottish family with connections in medicine, industry and the arts. On completion of his education at Glasgow University, he joined R.J. Crompton & Co.; then in 1883, along with William C. Muir, he established the Glasgow firm which later became well known as Mavor and Coulson. It pioneered the supply of electricity to public undertakings and equipped the first two generating stations in Scotland. Mavor and his fellow directors appreciated the potential demand by industry in Glasgow for electricity. Two industries were especially well served; first, the coal-mines, where electric lighting and power transformed efficiency and safety beyond recognition; and second, marine engineering. Here Mavor recognized the importance of the variable-speed motor in working with marine propellers which have a tighter range of efficient working speeds. In 1911 he built a 50 ft (15 m) motor launch, appropriately named *Electric Arc*, at Dumbarton and fitted it with an alternating-current motor driven by a petrol engine and dynamo. Within two years British shipyards were building electrically powered ships, and by the beginning of the First World War the United States Navy had a 20,000-ton collier with this new form of propulsion.

Principal Honours and Distinctions
Vice-President, Institution of Engineers and Shipbuilders in Scotland 1894–6.

Bibliography
Mavor published several papers on electric power supply, distribution and the use of electricity for marine purposes in the *Transactions of the Institution of Engineers and Shipbuilders in Scotland* between the years 1890 and 1912.

Further Reading
Mavor and Coulson Ltd, 1911, *Electric Propulsion of Ships*, Glasgow.

FMW

Maxim, Sir Hiram Stevens

b. 5 February 1840 Brockway's Mills, Maine, USA
d. 24 November 1916 Streatham, London, England

American (naturalized British) inventor; designer of the first fully automatic machine gun and of an experimental steam-powered aircraft.

Maxim was born the son of a pioneer farmer who later became a wood turner. Young Maxim was first apprenticed to a carriage maker and then embarked on a succession of jobs before joining his uncle in his engineering firm in Massachusetts in 1864. As a young man he gained a reputation as a boxer, but it was his uncle who first identified and encouraged Hiram's latent talent for invention.

It was not, however, until 1878, when Maxim joined the first electric-light company to be established in the USA, as its Chief Engineer, that he began to make a name for himself. He developed an improved light filament and his electric pressure regulator not only won a prize at the first International Electrical Exhibition, held in Paris in 1881, but also resulted in his being made a Chevalier de la Légion d'honneur. While in Europe he was advised that weapons development was a more lucrative field than electricity; consequently, he moved to England and established a small laboratory at Hatton Garden, London. He began by investigating improvements to the Gatling gun in order to produce a weapon with a faster rate of fire and which was more accurate. In 1883, by adapting a Winchester carbine, he successfully produced a semi-automatic weapon, which used the recoil to cock the gun automatically after firing. The following year he took this concept a stage further and produced a fully automatic belt-fed weapon. The recoil drove barrel and breechblock to the vent. The barrel then halted, while the breechblock, now unlocked from the former, continued rearwards, extracting the spent case and recocking the firing mechanism. The return spring, which it had been compressing, then drove the breechblock forward again, chambering the next round, which had been fed from the belt, as it did so. Keeping the trigger pressed enabled the gun to continue firing until the belt was expended. The Maxim gun, as it became known, was adopted by almost every army within the decade, and was to remain in service for nearly fifty years. Maxim himself joined forces with the large British armaments firm of Vickers, and the Vickers machine gun, which served the British Army during two world wars, was merely a refined version of the Maxim gun.

Maxim's interests continued to occupy several fields of technology, including flight. In 1891 he took out a patent for a steam-powered aeroplane fitted with a pendulous gyroscopic stabilizer which would maintain the pitch of the aeroplane at any desired inclination (basically, a simple autopilot). Maxim decided to test the relationship between power, thrust and lift before moving on to stability and control. He designed a lightweight steam-engine which developed 180 hp (135 kW) and drove a propeller measuring 17 ft 10 in. (5.44 m) in diameter. He fitted two of these engines into his huge flying machine test-rig, which needed a wing span of 104 ft (31.7 m) to generate enough lift to overcome a total weight of 4 tons. The machine was not designed for free flight, but ran on one set of rails with a second set to prevent it rising more than about 2 ft (61 cm). At Baldwyn's Park in Kent on 31 July 1894 the huge machine, carrying Maxim and his crew, reached a speed of 42 mph (67.6 km/h) and lifted off its rails. Unfortunately, one of the restraining axles broke and the machine was extensively damaged. Although it was subsequently repaired and further trials carried out, these experiments were very expensive. Maxim eventually abandoned the flying machine and did not develop his idea for a stabilizer, turning instead to other projects. At the age of almost 70 he returned to the problems of flight and designed a biplane with a petrol engine: it was built in 1910 but never left the ground.

In all, Maxim registered 122 US and 149 British patents on objects ranging from mousetraps to automatic spindles. Included among them was a 1901 patent for a foot-operated suction cleaner. In 1900 he became a British subject and he was knighted the following year. He remained a larger-than-life figure, both physically and in character, until the end of his life.

Principal Honours and Distinctions
Chevalier de la Légion d'Honneur 1881. Knighted 1901.

Bibliography
1908, *Natural and Artificial Flight*, London.
1915, *My Life*, London: Methuen (autobiography).

Further Reading
Obituary, 1916, *Engineer* (1 December).
Obituary, 1916, *Engineering* (1 December).
P.F. Mottelay, 1920, *The Life and Work of Sir Hiram Maxim*, London and New York: John Lane.
Dictionary of National Biography, 1912–1921, 1927, Oxford: Oxford University Press.

See also **Pilcher, Percy Sinclair**.

CM/JDS

Maxwell, James Clerk
b. 13 June 1831 Edinburgh, Scotland
d. 5 November 1879 Cambridge, England

Scottish physicist who formulated the unified theory of electromagnetism, the kinetic theory of gases and a theory of colour.

Maxwell attended school at the Edinburgh Academy and at the age of 16 went on to study at Edinburgh University. In 1850 he entered Trinity College, Cambridge, where he graduated four years later as Second Wrangler with the award of the Smith's Prize. Two years later he was appointed Professor at Marischal College, Aberdeen, where he married the Principal's daughter. In 1860 he moved to King's College London, but on the death of his father five years later, Maxwell returned to the family home in Scotland, where he continued his researches as far as the life of a gentleman farmer allowed. This rural existence was interrupted in 1874 when he was persuaded to accept the chair of Cavendish Professor of Experimental Physics at Cambridge. Unfortunately, in 1879 he contracted the cancer

that brought his brilliant career to an untimely end. While at Cambridge, Maxwell founded the Cavendish Laboratory for research in physics. A succession of distinguished physicists headed the laboratory, making it one of the world's great centres for notable discoveries in physics.

During the mid-1850s, Maxwell worked towards a theory to explain electrical and magnetic phenomena in mathematical terms, culminating in 1864 with the formulation of the fundamental equations of electromagnetism (Maxwell's equations). These equations also described the propagation of light, for he had shown that light consists of transverse electromagnetic waves in a hypothetical medium, the 'ether'. This great synthesis of theories uniting a wide range of phenomena is worthy to set beside those of Sir Isaac Newton and Einstein. Like all such syntheses, it led on to further discoveries. Maxwell himself had suggested that light represented only a small part of the spectrum of electromagnetic waves, and in 1888 **Hertz** confirmed the discovery of another small part of the spectrum, radio waves, with momentous implications for the development of telecommunication technology. Maxwell contributed to the kinetic theory of gases, which by then were viewed as consisting of a mass of randomly moving molecules colliding with each other and with the walls of the containing vessel. From 1869 Maxwell applied statistical methods to describe the molecular motion in mathematical terms. This led to a greater understanding of the behaviour of gases, with important consequences for the chemical industry.

Of more direct technological application was Maxwell's work on colour vision, begun in 1849, showing that all colours could be derived from the three primary colours, red, yellow and blue. This enabled him in 1861 to produce the first colour photograph, of a tartan. Maxwell's discoveries about colour vision were quickly taken up and led to the development of colour printing and photography.

Bibliography
Most of his technical papers are reprinted in *The Scientific Papers of J. Clerk Maxwell*, 1890, ed. W.D. Niven, Cambridge, 2 vols; reprinted 1952, New York.
Maxwell published several books, including *Theory of Heat*, 1870, London (1894, 11th edn, with notes by Lord Rayleigh) and *Theory of*

Electricity and Magnetism, 1873, Oxford (1891, ed. J.J. Thomson, 3rd edn).

Further Reading
L. Campbell and W. Garnett, 1882, *The Life of James Clerk Maxwell*, London (the standard biography).
J.J. Thomson (ed.), 1931, *James Clerk Maxwell 1831–1931*, Cambridge.
J.G. Crowther, 1932, *British Scientists of the Nineteenth Century*, London.

LRD

Maybach, Wilhelm
b. 9 February 1846 Heilbronn, Württemberg, Germany
d. 14 December 1929 Stuttgart, Germany

German engineer and engine designer, inventor of the spray carburettor.

Orphaned at the age of 10, Maybach was destined to become one of the world's most renowned engine designers. From 1868 he was apprenticed as a draughtsman at the Brüderhaus Engineering Works in Reurlingen, where his talents were recognized by Gottlieb **Daimler**, who was Manager and Technical Director. Nikolaus **Otto** had by then developed his atmospheric engine and reorganized his company, Otto & **Langen**, into Gasmotorenfabrik Deutz, of which he appointed Daimler Manager. After employment at a machine builders in Karlsruhe, in 1872 Maybach followed Daimler to Deutz where he worked as a partner on the design of high-speed engines: his engines ran at up to 900 rpm, some three times as fast as conventional engines of the time. Maybach made improvements to the timing, carburation and other features. In 1881 Daimler left the Deutz Company and set up on his own as a freelance inventor, moving with his family to Bad Cannstatt; in April 1882 Maybach joined him as Engineer and Designer to set up a partnership to develop lightweight high-speed engines suitable for vehicles. A motor cycle appeared in 1885 and a modified horse-drawn carriage was fitted with a Maybach engine in 1886. Other applications to small boats, fire-engine pumps and small locomotives quickly followed, and the Vee engine of 1890 that was fitted into the French Peugeot automobiles had a profound effect upon the new sport of motor racing. In 1895 Daimler won the first international motor race and the same year Maybach became Technical Director of the Daimler firm. In 1899 Emil Jellinek, Daimler agent in France and also Austro-Hungarian consul, required a car to compete with Panhard and Levassor, who had been victorious in the Paris–Bordeaux race; he wanted more power and a lower centre of gravity, and turned to Maybach with his requirements, the 35 hp Daimler–Simplex of 1901 being the outcome. Its performance and road holding superseded those of all others at the time; it was so successful that Jellinek immediately placed an order for thirty-six cars. His daughter's name was Mercedes, after whom, when the merger of Daimler and Benz came about, the name Mercedes–Benz was adopted.

In his later years, Maybach designed the engine for the **Zeppelin** airships. He retired from the Daimler Company in 1907.

Principal Honours and Distinctions
Society of German Engineers Grashof Medal (its highest honour). In addition to numerous medals and titles from technical institutions, Maybach was awarded an honorary doctorate from the Stuttgart Institute of Technology.

Further Reading
F. Schidberger, *Gottlieb Daimler, Wilhelm Maybach and Karl Benz*, Stuttgart: Daimler Benz AG.
1961, *The Annals of Mercedes–Benz Motor Vehicles and Engines*, 2nd edn, Stuttgart: Daimler Benz AG.
E. Johnson, 1986, *The Dawn of Motoring*.

KAB/IMcN

Meek, Marshall
b. 22 April 1925 Auchtermuchty, Fife, Scotland

Scottish naval architect and leading twentieth-century exponent of advanced maritime technology.

After early education at Cupar in Fife, Meek commenced training as a naval architect, taking the then popular sandwich apprenticeship of alternate half years at the University of Glasgow (with a Caird Scholarship) and at a shipyard, in his case the Caledon of Dundee. On leaving Dundee he worked for five years with the British Ship Research Association before joining Alfred

Holt & Co., owners of the Blue Funnel Line. During his twenty-five years at Liverpool, he rose to Chief Naval Architect and Director and was responsible for bringing the cargo-liner concept to its ultimate in design. When the company had become Ocean Fleets, it joined with other British shipowners and looked to Meek for the first purpose-built containership fleet in the world. This required new ship designs, massive worldwide investment in port facilities and marketing to win public acceptance of freight containers, thereby revolutionizing dry-cargo shipping. Under the houseflag of OCL (now POCL), this pioneer service set the highest standards of service and safety and continues to operate on almost every ocean.

In 1979 Meek returned to the shipbuilding industry when he became Head of Technology at British Shipbuilders. Closely involved in contemporary problems of fuel economy and reduced staffing, he held the post for five years before his appointment as Managing Director of the National Maritime Institute. He was deeply involved in the merger with the British Ship Research Association to form British Maritime Technology (BMT), an organization of which he became Deputy Chairman.

Marshall Meek has held many public offices, and is one of the few to have been President of two of the United Kingdom's maritime institutions. He has contributed over forty papers to learned societies, has acted as Visiting Professor to Strathclyde University and University College London, and serves on advisory committees to the Ministry of Defence, the Department of Transport and Lloyd's Register of Shipping. While in Liverpool he served as a Justice of the Peace.

Principal Honours and Distinctions
CBE 1989. Fellow of the Royal Academy of Engineering 1990. President, Royal Institution of Naval Architects 1990–3; North East Coast Institution of Engineers and Shipbuilders 1984–6. Royal Designer for Industry (RDI) 1986. Royal Institution of Naval Architects Silver Medal (on two occasions).

Bibliography
1970, 'The first OCL containerships', *Transactions of the Royal Institution of Naval Architects.*

FMW

Mees, Charles Edward Kenneth
b. 1882 Wellingborough, England
d. 1960 USA

Anglo-American photographic scientist and Director of Research at the Kodak Research Laboratory.

The son of a Wesleyan minister, Mees was interested in chemistry from an early age and studied at St Dunstan's College in Catford, where he met Samuel E. Sheppard, with whom he went on to University College London in 1900. They worked together on a thesis for BSc degrees in 1903, developing the work begun by **Hurter** and Driffield on photographic sensitometry. This and other research papers were published in 1907 in the book *Investigations on the Theory of the Photographic Process*, which became a standard reference work. After obtaining a doctorate in 1906, Mees joined the firm of Wratten & Wainwright (see **F.C.L. Wratten**), manufacturers of dry plates in Croydon; he started work on 1 April 1906, first tackling the problem of manufacturing colour-sensitive emulsions and enabling the company to market the first fully panchromatic plates from the end of that year.

During the next few years Mees ran the commercial operation of the company as Managing Director and carried out research into new products, including filters for use with the new emulsions. In January 1912 he was visited by George **Eastman**, the American photographic manufacturer, who asked him to go to Rochester, New York, and set up a photographic research laboratory in the Kodak factory there. Wratten was prepared to release Mees on condition that Eastman bought the company; thus, Wratten and Wainwright became part of Kodak Ltd, and Mees left for America. He supervised the construction of a building in the heart of Kodak Park, and the building was fully equipped not only as a research laboratory, but also with facilities for coating and packing sensitized materials. It also had the most comprehensive library of photographic books in the world. Work at the laboratory started at the beginning of 1913, with a staff of twenty recruited from America and England, including Mees's collaborator of earlier years, Sheppard. Under Mees's direction there flowed from the Kodak research Laboratory a constant stream of discoveries, many of them leading to new products. Among these were the 16 mm amateur film-making system launched in 1923; the first amateur colour-movie system, Kodacolor, in 1928; and 8 mm home movies, in 1932. His support for the young experimenters Mannes and **Godowsky**, who were working on colour photography, led to their joining the Research Laboratory and to the introduction of the first multi-layer colour film, Kodachrome, in 1935. Eastman had agreed from the beginning that as much of the laboratory's work as possible should be published, and Mees himself wrote prolifically, publishing over 200 articles and ten books. While he made significant contributions to the understanding of the photographic process, particularly through his early research, it is his creation and organization of the Kodak Research Laboratory that is his lasting memorial. His interests were many and varied, including Egyptology, astronomy, marine biology and history. He was a Fellow of the Royal Society.

Principal Honours and Distinctions
FRS.

Bibliography
1961, *From Dry Plates to Ektachrome Film*, New York (partly autobiographical).

BC

Mège Mouriés, Hippolyte
See **Mouriés, Hippolyte Mège**.

Meikle, Andrew
b. 1719 Scotland
d. 27 November 1811

Scottish millwright and inventor of the threshing machine.

The son of the millwright James Meikle, who is credited with the introduction of the winnowing machine into Britain, Andrew Meikle followed in his father's footsteps. His inventive inclinations were first turned to developing his father's idea, and together with his own son George he built and patented a double-fan winnowing machine.

However, in the history of agricultural development Andrew Meikle is most famous for his invention of the threshing machine, patented in 1784. He had been presented with a model of a threshing mill designed by a Mr Ilderton of Northumberland, but after failing to make a full-scale machine work, he developed the concept further. He eventually built the first working threshing machine for a farmer called Stein at Kilbagio. The patent revolutionized farming practice because it displaced the back-breaking and soul-destroying labour of flailing the grain from the straw. The invention was of great value in Scotland and in northern England when the land was becoming underpopulated as a result of heavy industrialization, but it was bitterly opposed in the south of England until well into the nineteenth century. Although the introduction of the threshing machine led to the 'Captain Swing' riots of the 1830s, in opposition to it, it shortly became universal.

Meikle's provisional patent in 1785 was a natural progression of earlier attempts by other millwrights to produce such a machine. The published patent is based on power provided by a horse engine, but these threshing machines were often driven by water-wheels or even by windmills. The corn stalks were introduced into the machine where they were fed between cast-iron rollers moving quite fast against each other to beat the grain out of the ears. The power source, whether animal, water or wind, had to cause the rollers to rotate at high speed to knock the grain out of the ears. While Meikle's machine was at first designed as a fixed barn machine powered by a water-wheel or by a horse wheel, later threshing machines became mobile and were part of the rig of an agricultural contractor.

In 1788 Meikle was awarded a patent for the invention of shuttered sails for windmills. This patent is part of the general description of the threshing machine, and whilst it was a practical application, it was superseded by the work of Thomas **Cubitt**.

At the turn of the century Meikle became a manufacturer of threshing machines, building appliances that combined the threshing and winnowing principles as well as the reciprocating 'straw walkers' found in subsequent threshing machines and in conventional combine harvesters to the present day. However, he made little financial gain from his invention, and a public subscription organized by the President of the Board of Agriculture, Sir John Sinclair, raised £1,500 to support him towards the end of his life.

Bibliography

1831, *Threshing Machines* in *The Dictionary of Mechanical Sciences, Arts and Manufactures*, London: Jamieson, Alexander.

7 March 1768, British patent no. 896, 'Machine for dressing wheat, malt and other grain and for cleaning them from sand, dust and smut'.

9 April 1788, British patent no. 1,645, 'Machine which may be worked by cattle, wind, water or other power for the purpose of separating corn from the straw'.

Further Reading

J.E. Handley, 1953, *Scottish Farming in the 18th Century*, and 1963, *The Agricultural Revolution in Scotland* (both place Meikle and his invention within their context).

G. Quick and W. Buchele, 1978, *The Grain Harvesters*, American Society of Agricultural Engineers (gives an account of the early development of harvesting and cereal treatment machinery).

KM/AP

Meisenbach, Georg

b. 1841 Nuremberg, Germany
d. 12 December 1912 Munich, Germany

German engraver, inventor of the first commercially exploitable halftone printing process.

Trained in Nuremberg as a copper-plate engraver, Meisenbach moved to Munich in 1873 and established the first zincographic engraving business in Germany. In 1879 he began experimenting with halftone reproductions and in May 1882 he took out a German patent which described a single-line screen made from the proof of an engraved plate ruled with lines. The screen was then placed before a photographic positive of a picture and the two were photographed together. Approximately half-way through the exposure the screen was turned 90 degrees so that the lines crossed. A halftone negative was thus produced, from which could be made a zinc printing block. The full details of the process were not revealed in the patent so that trade competition would be limited. It was the first commercially practicable halftone process. Ill health forced Meisenbach to retire from the business in 1891, by which time his process was being superseded by **Ives's** cross-line process.

Bibliography

9 May 1882, German patent no. 22,444 (halftone printing process).

1882, British patent no. 2,156.

Further Reading

J.M. Eder, 1945, *History of Photography*, trans. E. Epstean, New York.

G. Wakeman, 1973, *Victorian Book Illustration* (a popular account of the introduction of halftone to England).

JW

Mendelsohn, Erich

b. 21 March 1887 Allenstein, East Prussia
d. 15 September 1953 San Francisco, California, USA

German architect, a pioneering innovator in the modern International style of building that developed in Germany during the early 1920s.

In some examples of his work Mendelsohn envisaged bold, sculptural forms, dramatically expressed in light and shade, which he created with extensive use of glass, steel and concrete. Characteristic of his type of early Expressionism was his design for the Einstein Tower (1919), a physical laboratory and observatory that was purpose built for Professor Einstein's research work at Neubabelsburg near Berlin in 1921. As its shape suggests, this structure was intended to be made from poured concrete but, due to technical problems, it was erected in stucco-faced steel and brickwork. Equally dramatic and original were Mendelsohn's department stores, for example the pace-setting Schocken Stores at Stuttgart (1926) and Chemnitz (1928), the Petersdorff Store at Breslau (1927) (now Wrocaw in Poland), and a very different building, the Columbus Haus in Berlin (1929–31). One of his most original designs was also in this city, that for the complex on the great boulevard, the Kurfürstendamm, which included the Universum Cinema (1928). Mendelsohn moved to England in 1933, a refugee from Nazism, and there entered into partnership with another émigré, Serge Chermayeff from Russia. Together they were responsible for a building on the seafront at Bexhill-on-Sea, the De La Warr arts and entertainments pavilion (1935–6). This long, low, glass, steel and concrete structure was ahead of its time in England and comprised a theatre and restaurant; in the centre of the façade, facing the sea, is its chief architectural feature, a semicircular glazed staircase. Soon Mendelsohn moved on to Palestine, where he was responsible for the Government Hospital at Haifa (1937) and the Hadassah University Medical Centre in Jerusalem (1936); in both cases he skilfully adapted his mode to different climatic needs. He finally settled in the USA in 1941, where his most notable buildings are the Maimonides Hospital in San Francisco and the synagogues and Jewish community centres which he built in a number of American cities.

Further Reading
Arnold Whittick, 1964, *Erich Mendelsohn*, Leonard Hill Books (the standard work).

DY

Mengoni, Giuseppe
b. 1829 Bologna, Italy
d. 1877

Italian architect who designed one of the most impressive of the great ferrovitreous shopping arcades of the nineteenth century, that of the Galleria Vittorio Emmanuele II in the centre of Milan.

The Milan Galleria (1865–77), unsurpassed among existing arcades of this type, has a cruciform plan, its lofty arms barrel-vaulted and the crossing covered by a domed octagon. The entrance to the arcade, from the Piazza del Duomo, takes the form of an imposing classical triumphal arch. The whole urban scheme involved the enlargement of the cathedral square and alterations to the Piazza della Scala, which is situated at the opposite end of the arcaded gallery. The stone, iron and glass structure is of high quality, with careful attention to detail. In good restorative condition, the Galleria has always provided an important function in the life of the centre of the city of Milan.

DY

Menzies, Michael
b. end of the seventeenth century Lanarkshire, Scotland (?)
d. 13 December 1766 Edinburgh, Scotland

Scottish inventor and lawyer.

Menzies was admitted as a member of the Faculty of Advocates on 31 January 1719. It is evident from his applications for patents that he was more concerned with inventions than the law, however. He took out his first patent in 1734 for a threshing machine in which a number of flails were attached to a horizontal axis, which was moved rapidly forwards and backwards through half a revolution, essentially imitating the action of an ordinary flail. The grain to be threshed was placed on either side.

Though not a practical success, Menzies's invention seems to have been the first for the mechanical threshing of grain. His idea of imitating non-mechanized action also influenced his invention of a coal cutter, for which he took out a patent in 1761 and which copied miners' tools for obtaining coal. He proposed to carry heavy chains down the pit so that they could be used to give motion to iron picks, saws or other chains with cutting implements. The chains could be set into motion by a steam-engine, by water- or windmills, or by horses gins. Although it is quite obvious that this apparatus could not work, Menzies was the first to have thought of mechanizing coal production in the style that was in use in the late twentieth century. Subsequent to Menzies's proposal, many inventors at varying intervals followed this direction until the problem was finally solved one century later by, among others, W.E. **Garforth**.

Menzies had successfully used the power of a steam-engine on the Wear eight years beforehand, when he obtained a patent for raising coal. According to his device a descending bucket filled with water raised a basket of coals, while a steam-engine pumped the water back to the surface; the balance-tub system, in various forms, quickly spread to other coalfields. Menzies's patent from 1750 for improved methods of carrying the coals from the coalface to the pit-shaft had also been of considerable influence: this device employed self-acting inclined planes, whereon the descending loaded wagons hauled up the empty ones.

Further Reading
The article entitled 'Michael Menzies' in the *Dictionary of National Biography* neglects Menzies's inventions for mining. A comprehensive evaluation of his influence on coal cutting is given in the introductory chapter of S.F. Walker, 1902, *Coal-Cutting by Machinery*, London.

WK

Mercer, John

b. 21 February 1791 Great Harwood, Lancashire, England
d. 30 November 1866 Oakenshaw, Lancashire, England

English pioneer in textile chemistry.

Mercer began work at the age of 9 as a bobbin-winder and then a hand-loom weaver. He had no formal education in chemistry but taught himself and revealed remarkable ability in both theoretical and applied aspects of the subject. He became the acknowledged 'father of textile chemistry' and the Royal Society elected him Fellow in 1850. His name is remembered in connection with the lustrous 'mercerized' cotton which, although not developed commercially until 1890, arose from his discovery, *c.*1844, of the effect of caustic soda on cotton linters. He also discovered that cotton could be dissolved in a solution of copper oxide in ammonia, a phenomenon later exploited in the manufacture of artificial silk. As a youth, Mercer experimented at home with dyeing processes and soon acquired sufficient skill to set up as an independent dyer. Most of his working life was, however, spent with the calico-printing firm of Oakenshaw Print Works in which he eventually became a partner, and it was there that most of his experimental work was done. The association was a very appropriate one, for it was a member of this firm's staff who first recognized Mercer's potential talent and took the trouble in his spare time to teach him reading, writing and arithmetic. Mercer developed manganese-bronze colours and researched into catalysis and the ferrocyanides. Among his innovations was the chlorination of wool in order to make it print as easily as cotton. It was many years later that it was realized that this treatment also conferred valuable shrink-resisting qualities. Becoming interested in photochemistry, he devised processes for photographic printing on fabric. Queen Victoria was presented with a handkerchief printed in this way when she visited the Great Exhibition of 1851, of which Mercer was a juror. A photograph of Mercer himself on cloth is preserved in the Museum of Science and Industry in Manchester. He presented papers to the British Association and was a member of the Chemical Society.

Principal Honours and Distinctions
FRS 1850.

Further Reading
Obituary, *Manchester Memoirs*, Manchester Literary and Philosophical Society.
Dictionary of National Biography.
E.A. Parnell, 1886. *The Life and Labours of John Mercer, F.R.S.*, London (biography).
1867, biography, *Journal of the Chemical Society.*
A.E. Musson and E. Robinson, 1969, *Science and Technology in the Industrial Revolution*, Manchester (includes a brief reference to Mercer's work).

RLH

Mergenthaler, Ottmar

b. 11 May 1854 Hachtel, Germany
d. 28 October 1899 Baltimore, Maryland, USA

German/American inventor of the Linotype typesetting machine.

Mergenthaler came from a family of teachers, but following a mechanical bent he was apprenticed to a clockmaker. Having served his time, Mergenthaler emigrated to the USA in 1872 to avoid military service. He immediately secured work in Washington, DC, in the scientific instrument shop of August Hahl, the son of his former master. He steadily acquired a reputation for skill and ingenuity, and in 1876, when Hahl transferred his business to Baltimore, Mergenthaler went too. Soon after, they were commissioned to remedy the defects in a model of a writing machine devised by James O. Clephane of Washington. It produced print by typewriting, which was then multiplied by lithography. Mergenthaler soon corrected the defects and Clephane ordered a full-size version. This was completed in 1877 but did not work satisfactorily. Nevertheless, Mergenthaler was moved to engage in the long battle to mechanize the typesetting stage of the printing process. Clephane suggested substituting stereotyping for lithography in his device, but in spite of their keen efforts Mergenthaler and Hahl were again unsuccessful and they abandoned the project. In spare moments Mergenthaler continued his search for a typesetting machine. Late in 1883 it occurred to him to stamp matrices into type bars and to cast type metal into them in the same machine. From this idea, the Linotype machine developed and was

481

completed by July 1884. It worked well and a patent was granted on 26 August that year, and Clephane and his associates set up the National Typographic Company of West Virginia to manufacture it. The *New York Tribune* ordered twelve Linotypes, and on 3 July 1886 the first of these set part of that day's issue. During the previous year the company had passed into the hands of a group of newspaper owners; increasing differences with the Board led to Mergenthaler's resignation in 1888, but he nevertheless continued to improve the machine, patenting over fifty modifications. The Linotype, together with the Monotype of Tolbert **Lanston**, rapidly supplanted earlier typesetting methods, and by the 1920s it reigned supreme, the former being used more for newspapers, the latter for book work.

Principal Honours and Distinctions

Franklin Institute John Scott Medal, Elliott Cresson Medal.

Bibliography

1898, *Ottmar Mergenthaler and the Invention of Linotype*, New York.

Further Reading

J. Moran, 1964, *The Composition of Reading Matter*, London.

LRD

Merica, Paul Dyer

b. 17 March 1889 Warsaw, Indiana, USA
d. 20 October 1957 Tarrytown, New York, USA

American physical metallurgist who elucidated the mechanism of the age-hardening of alloys.

Merica graduated from the University of Wisconsin in 1908. Before proceeding to the University of Berlin, he spent some time teaching in Wisconsin and in China. He obtained his doctorate in Berlin in 1914, and in that year he joined the US National Bureau of Standards (NBS) in Washington. During his five years there, he investigated the causes of the phenomenon of age-hardening of the important new alloy of aluminium, Duralumin.

This phenomenon had been discovered not long before by Dr Alfred Wilm, a German research metallurgist. During the early years of the twentieth century, Wilm had been seeking a suit-

able light alloy for making cartridge cases for the Prussian government. In the autumn of 1909 he heated and quenched an aluminium alloy containing 3.5 per cent copper and 0.5 per cent magnesium and found its properties unremarkable. He happened to test it again some days later and was impressed to find its hardness and strength were much improved: Wilm had accidentally discovered age-hardening. He patented the alloy, but he made his rights over to Durener Metallwerke, who marketed it as Duralumin. This light and strong alloy was taken up by aircraft makers during the First World War, first for **Zeppelin**s and then for other aircraft.

Although age-hardened alloys found important uses, the explanation of the phenomenon eluded metallurgists until in 1919 Merica and his colleagues at the NBS gave the first rational explanation of age-hardening in light alloys. When these alloys were heated to temperatures near their melting points, the alloying constituents were taken into solution by the matrix. Quenching retained the alloying metals in supersaturated solid solution. At room temperature very small crystals of various intermetallic compounds were precipitated and, by inserting themselves in the aluminium lattice, had the effect of increasing the hardness and strength of the alloy. Merica's theory stimulated an intensive study of hardening and the mechanism that brought it about, with important consequences for the development of new alloys with special properties.

In 1919 Merica joined the International Nickel Company as Director of Research, a post he held for thirty years and followed by a three-year period as President. He remained in association with the company until his death.

Bibliography

1919, 'Heat treatment and constitution of Duralumin', *Sci. Papers, US Bureau of Standards*, no. 37; 1932, 'The age-hardening of metals', *Transactions of the American Institution of Min. Metal* 99: 13–54 (his two most important papers).

Further Reading

Z. Jeffries, 1959, 'Paul Dyer Merica', *Biographical Memoirs of the National Academy of Science* 33: 226–39 (contains a list of Merica's publications and biographical details).

LRD

Meritens, Baron Auguste de

b. 1834
d. 1898 Pontoise, France

French engineer who improved the design of magneto-electric generators successfully used for lighthouse illumination.

Founding the firm of Messrs A. de Meritens of Paris to build magneto-electric generators for electric arc lighting, de Meritens revised the arrangement of the Holmes and Alliance machines. By employing a distributed rotor winding on laminated cores in place of individual bobbins, the wave-form was improved and a continuous output was achieved, as distinct from a series of short-duration pulses. The rotor windings were carried on the periphery of spoked wheels which revolved below the poles of stationary compound permanent magnets. These generators came to prominence in 1880; in France they quickly replaced the Alliance machines in lighthouses, and Trinity House also installed them in Britain. Two examples remained in continuous service at the Lizard lighthouse in Cornwall from 1881 to 1950, and one still survives there as an exhibit. Before being installed, this machine was shown at the Paris Electrical Exhibition of 1881. An electric candle invented by de Meritens was a variation on that of **Jablochkoff** and he is credited with being the first to suggest the use of a carbon electrode as one pole for electric-arc welding, with the metal to be welded serving as the other pole. Baron de Meritens died tragically in great poverty.

Bibliography

10 April 1878, French patent no. 123,766 (improved magneto-electric generator).
17 September 1878, British patent no. 3,658 (improved magneto-electric generator).

Further Reading

Engineering (1878) 28: 372 (a description of the original de Meritens machine).
J. Hopkinson, 1886–7, *Proceedings of the Institution of Civil Engineers* 87 (1): 243–60 (a report on machines in service).

GW

Merivale, John Herman

b. mid-nineteenth century
d. after 1895

English mining educator

J.H. Merivale had the distinction of being elected to the first English professorship in mining when a chair in this subject was endowed by a group of prominent coal-mine owners at the Durham College of Science, Newcastle upon Tyne (then the University of Durham, but subsequently to become the nucleus of the University of Newcastle). He was the son of Dean Merivale, a distinguished Roman historian, and had been educated at Winchester. He had been the first student to register to train as a mining engineer at the school of science in Durham. He served as Professor for fifteen years, resigning in 1895 to become Manager of the Broomhill collieries. About a hundred students attended his classes in 1887–8, and the College acquired a reputation for supplying more Government Inspectors of Mines than any other institution.

Further Reading

R.A. Buchanan, 1989, *The Engineers*, p. 173.
C.E. Whiting, 1932, *University of Durham*, p. 197.

AB

Merritt, William Hamilton

b. 3 July 1793 Bedford, Winchester County, New York, USA ·
d. 5 July 1862 aboard a vessel on the Cornwall Canal, Canada

American-born Canadian merchant, entrepreneur and promoter of the First and Second Welland Canals bypassing the Niagara Falls and linking Lakes Ontario and Erie.

Although he was born in the USA, his family moved to Canada in 1796. Educated in St Catharines and Niagara, he received a good training in mathematics, navigation and surveying. He served with distinction in the 1812–14 war, although he was captured by the Americans in 1814. After the war he established himself in business operating a sawmill, a flour mill, a small distillery, a potashery, a cooperage and a smithy, as well as running a general store. By 1818 he was one of the leading figures in the area and realized that for real economic progress it was essential to improve communications in the Niagara peninsula; in that year he surveyed a route for a waterway that would carry boats.

In *c*.1820 he began discussions with neighbouring landowners and businessmen, who, on 19 January 1824 together obtained a charter for building the first Welland Canal to link Lakes Ontario and Erie. They were greatly influenced by the realization that the completion of the Erie Canal would attract trade through the United States instead of through Canada. Construction began on 30 November 1824, largely with redundant labour from the Erie Canal. Merritt foresaw the need for financial support and for publicity to sustain interest in the project. Accordingly he started a newspaper, the *Farmer's Journal and Welland Canal Intelligencer*, which was published until 1835. He also visited York (now Toronto), the capital of Upper Canada, and obtained some support, but the Government was reluctant to assist financially. He was more successful in raising money in New York. Then in 1828 he visited England to see **Telford** and persuaded both Telford and the Duke of Wellington, among others, to purchase shares. The Canal opened on 30 November 1829. In 1832 Merritt became a member of the Legislative Assembly of Upper Canada, and after the Union of the Canadas in 1841 he was elected to the new Assembly, later serving as Minister of Public Works and then as President of the Assembly. He advocated improvements to the St Lawrence River and also promoted railways. He pioneered a bridge across the Niagara River that was opened in 1849 and later carried a railway. He was not a canal engineer, but he did pioneer communications in developing territory.

Further Reading
R.M. Styran and R.R. Taylor, 1988, *The Welland Canals. The Growth of Mr Merritt's Ditch*, Erin, Ont.: Boston Mills Press.

JHB

Merz, Charles Hesterman
b. 5 October 1874 Gateshead, England
d. 14 October 1940 London, England

English engineer who pioneered large-scale integration of electricity-supply networks, which led to the inauguration of the British grid system.

Merz was educated at Bootham School in York and Armstrong College in Newcastle. He served an apprenticeship with the Newcastle Electric Supply Company at their first power station, Pandon Dene, and part of his training was at Robey and Company of Lincoln, steam engine builders, and the British Thomson-Houston Company, electrical equipment manufacturers. After working at Bankside in London and at Croydon, he became Manager of the Croydon supply undertaking. In 1898 he went to Cork on behalf of BTH to build and manage a tramway and electricity company. It was there that he met William McLellan, who later joined him in establishing a firm of consulting engineers. Merz, with his vision of large-scale electricity supply, pioneered an integrated traction and electricity scheme in north-eastern England. He was involved in the reorganization of electricity schemes in many countries and established a reputation as a leading parliamentary witness. Merz was appointed Director of Experiments and Research at the Admiralty, where his main contribution was the creation of an organization of outstanding engineers and scientists during the First World War. In 1925 he was largely responsible for a report of the Weir Committee which led to the Electricity (Supply) Act of 1926, the formation of the Central Electricity Board and the construction of the National Grid. The choice of 132 kV as the original grid voltage was that of Merz and his associates, as was the origin of the term 'grid'. Merz and his firm produced many technical innovations, including the first power-system control room and Merz–Price and Merz–Hunter forms of cable and transformer protection.

Principal Honours and Distinctions
Institution of Electrical Engineers Faraday Medal 1931.

Bibliography
1903–4, with W. McLennan, 'Power station design', *Journal of the Institution of Electrical Engineers* 33: 696–742 (a classic on its subject).
1929, 'The national scheme of electricity supply in Great Britain', *Proceedings of the British Association*, Johannesburg.

Further Reading
J. Rowland, 1960, *Progress in Power. The Contribution of Charles Merz and His Associates to Sixty Years of Electrical Development*

1899–1959, London (the most detailed account).

L. Hannah, 1979, *Electricity Before Nationalisation*, London.

——, 1985, *Dictionary of Business Biography*, ed. J. Jeremy, London, pp. 221–7 (a short account).

GW

Messel, Rudolf

b. 14 January 1848 Darmstadt, Germany
d. 18 April 1920 London, England

German industrial chemist.

Messel served three years as an apprentice to the chemical manufacturers E. Lucius of Frankfurt before studying chemistry at Zürich, Heidelberg and Tübingen. In 1870 he travelled to England to assist the distinguished chemist Sir Henry Roscoe, but was soon recalled to Germany on the outbreak of the Franco-Prussian War. After hostilities ceased, Messel returned to London to join the firm of manufacturers of sulphuric acid Dunn, Squire & Company of Stratford, London. The firm amalgamated with Spencer Chapman, and after Messel became its Managing Director in 1878 it was known as Spencer, Chapman & Messel Ltd.

Messel's principal contribution to chemical technology was the invention of the contact process for the manufacture of sulphuric acid. Earlier processes for making this essential product, now needed in ever-increasing quantities by the new processes for making dyestuffs, fertilizers and explosives, were based on the oxidation of sulphur dioxide by oxides of nitrogen, developed by Joshua **Ward** and John **Roebuck**. Attempts to oxidize the dioxide to the trioxide with the oxygen in the air in the presence of a suitable catalyst had so far failed because the catalyst had become 'poisoned' and ineffective; Messel avoided this by using highly purified gases. The contact process produced a concentrated form of sulphuric acid called oleum. Until the outbreak of the First World War, Messel's firm was the principal manufacturer, but then the demand rose sharply, so that other firms had to engage in its manufacture. Production thereby increased from 20,000 to 450,000 tons per year.

Principal Honours and Distinctions

FRS 1912. President, Society of Chemical Industry 1911–12, 1914.

Further Reading

1931, Special jubilee issue, *Journal of the Society of the Chemical Industry* (July).

G.T. Morgan and D.D. Pratt, 1938, *The British Chemical Industry*, London.

LRD

Messerschmitt, Willi E.

b. 26 June 1898 Frankfurt-am-Main, Germany
d. 17 September 1978 Munich, Germany

German aircraft designer noted for successful fighters such as the Bf 109, one of the world's most widely produced aircraft.

Messerschmitt studied engineering at the Munich Institute of Tchnology and obtained his degree in 1923. By 1926 he was Chief Designer at the Bayerische Flugzeugwerke in Augsburg. Due to the ban on military aircraft in Germany following the First World War, his early designs included gliders, light aircraft, and a series of high-wing airliners. He began to make a major impact on German aircraft design once Hitler came to power and threw off the shackles of the Treaty of Versailles, which so restricted Germany's armed forces. In 1932 he bought out the now-bankrupt Bayerische Flugzeugwerke, but initially, because of enmity between himself and the German aviation minister, was not invited to compete for an air force contract for a single-engined fighter. However, in 1934 Messerschmitt designed the *Bf 108 Taifun*, a small civil aircraft with a fighter-like appearance. This displayed the quality of his design and the German air ministry was forced to recognize him. As a result, he unveiled the famous *Bf 109* fighter which first flew in August 1935; it was used during the Spanish Civil War in 1936–9, and was to become one of the foremost combat aircraft of the Second World War. In 1938, after several name changes, the company became Messerschmitt Aktien-Gesellschaft (and hence a change of prefix from *Bf* to *Me*). During April 1939 a Messerschmitt aircraft broke the world air-speed record at 755.14 km/h (469.32 mph): it was entered in the FAI records as a *Bf 109R*, but was more accurately a new design designated *Me 209V-1*.

During the Second World War, the *Bf 109* was progressively improved, and eventually almost 35,000 were built. Other successful fighters followed, such as the twin-engined *Me 110* which also served as a bomber and night fighter. The

Messerschmitt *Me 262* twin-engined jet fighter, the first jet aircraft in the world to enter service, flew during the early years of the war, but it was never given a high priority by the High Command and only a small number were in service when the war ended. Another revolutionary Messerschmitt AG design was the *Me 163 Komet*, the concept of Professor Alexander Lippisch who had joined Messerschmitt's company in 1939; this was the first rocket-propelled fighter to enter service. It was a small tailless design capable of 880 km/hr (550 mph), but its duration under power was only about 10 minutes and it was very dangerous to fly. From late 1944 onwards it was used to intercept the United States Air Force bombers during their daylight raids. At the other end of the scale, Messerschmitt produced the *Me 321 Gigant*, a huge transport glider which was towed behind a flight of three *Me 110*s. Later it was equipped with six engines, but it was an easy target for allied fighters. This was a costly white elephant, as was his high-speed twin-engined *Me 210* fighter-bomber project which nearly made his company bankrupt. Nevertheless, he was certainly an innovator and was much admired by Hitler, who declared that he had 'the skull of a genius', because of the *Me 163 Komet* rocket-powered fighter and the *Me 262*.

At the end of the war Messerschmitt was detained by the Americans for two years. In 1952 Messerschmitt became an aviation adviser to the Spanish government, and his *Bf 109* was produced in Spain as the Hispano *Buchon* for a number of years and was powered by Rolls-Royce *Merlin* engines. A factory was also constructed in Egypt to produce aircraft to Messerschmitt's designs. His German company, banned from building aircraft, produced prefabricated houses, sewing machines and, from 1953 to 1962, a series of bubble-cars: the *KR 175* (1953–55) and the *KR 200* (1955–62) were single-cylinder three-wheeled bubble-cars, and the *Tiger* (1958–62) was a twin-cylinder, 500cc four-wheeler. In 1958 Messerschmitt resumed aircraft construction in Germany and later became the Honorary Chairman of the merged Messerschmitt–Bölkow–Blohm company (now part of the Franco-German Eurocopter company).

Further Reading

A. van Ishoven, 1975, *Messerschmitt. Aircraft Designer*, London.
J. Richard Smith, 1971, *Messerschmitt. An Aircraft Album*, London.
Anthony Pritchard, 1975, *Messerschmitt*, London (describes Messerschmitt aircraft).

JDS/CM

Metcalf, John
b. 1717 Knaresborough, Yorkshire, England
d. 1810

English pioneer road builder.

The son of poor working parents, at the age of 6 an attack of smallpox left him blind; however, this did not restrict his future activities, which included swimming and riding. He learned the violin and was much employed as the fiddle-player at country parties. He saved enough money to buy a horse on which he hunted. He took part in bowls, wrestling and boxing, being a robust six foot two inches tall. He rode to Whitby and went thence by boat to London and made other trips to York, Reading and Windsor. In 1740 Colonel Liddell offered him a seat in his coach from London to Harrogate, but he declined and got there more quickly on foot. He set up a one-horse chaise and a four-wheeler for hire in Harrogate, but the local innkeepers set up in competition in the public hire business. He went into the fish business, buying at the coast and selling in Leeds and other towns, but made little profit so he took up his violin again. During the rebellion of 1745 he recruited for Colonel Thornton and served to fight at Hexham, Newcastle and Falkirk, returning home after the Battle of Culloden. He then started travelling between Yorkshire, where be bought cotton and worsted stockings, and Aberdeen, where he sold horses. He set up a twice-weekly service of stage wagons between Knaresborough and York.

In 1765 an Act was passed for a turnpike road between Harrogate and Boroughbridge and he offered to build the Master Surveyor, a Mr Ostler, three miles (5 km) of road between Minskip and Fearnly, selling his wagons and his interest in the carrying business. The road was built satisfactorily and on time. He then quoted for a bridge at Boroughbridge and for a turnpike road between Knaresborough and Harrogate. He built many other roads, always doing the survey of the route on his own. The roads crossed bogs on a base of ling and furze. Many of his roads outside Yorkshire were in Lancashire, Cheshire and Derbyshire. In all he built some 180 miles (290 km) of road, for which he was paid some £65,000.

He worked for thirty years on road building, retiring in old age to a cotton business in Stockport where he had six spinning jennies and a carding engine; however, he found there was little profit in this so he gave the machinery to his son-in-law. The last road he built was from Haslington to Accrington, but due to the rise in labour costs brought about by the demand from the canal boom, he only made £40 profit on a £3,000 contract; the road was completed in 1792, when he retired to his farm at Spofforth at the age of 75. There he died, leaving a wife, four children, twenty grandchildren and ninety great-grandchildren. His wife was the daughter of the landlord of the Granby Inn, Knaresborough.

Further Reading
S. Smiles, *Lives of the Engineers, Metcalfe*, Telford: John Murray.

IMcN

Meusnier, Jean Baptiste Marie
b. 1754 Tours, France
d. 1793 Mainz, Germany

French designer of the 'dirigible balloon' (airship).

Just a few days after the first balloon flight by the relatively primitive **Montgolfier** hot-air balloon, a design for a sophisticated steerable or 'dirigible' balloon was proposed by a young French army officer. On 3 December 1783, Lieutenant (later General) Jean Baptiste Marie Meusnier of the Corps of Engineers presented to the Académie des Sciences a paper entitled *Mémoire sur l'équilibre des machines aérostatiques*. This outlined Meusnier's ideas and so impressed the learned members of the Academy that they commissioned him to make a more complete study. This was published in 1784 and contained sixteen water-colour drawings of the proposed airship, which are preserved by the Musée de l'Air in Paris.

Meusnier's 'machine aérostatique' was ellipsoidal in shape, in contrast to those of his unsuccessful contemporaries who tried to make spherical balloons steerable, often using oars for propulsion. Meusnier's proposed airship was 79.2 m (260 ft) long with the crew in a slim boat slung below the envelope (in case of a landing on water); it was steered by a large sail-like rudder at the rear end. Between the envelope and the boat were three propellers, which were to be manually driven as there was no suitable engine available; this was the first design for a propeller-driven aircraft. The most important innovation was a *ballonnet*, a balloon within the main envelope that was pressurized with air supplied by bellows in the boat. Varying the amount of air in the *ballonnet* would compensate for changes in the volume of hydrogen gas in the main envelope when the airship changed altitude. The *ballonnet* would also help to maintain the external shape of the main envelope.

General Meusnier was killed in action in 1793 and it was almost one hundred years from the date of his publication that his idea of *ballonnets* was put into practice, by Dupuy de Lome in 1872, and later by Renard and Krebs.

Bibliography
1784, *Mémoire sur l'équilibre des machines aérostatiques*, Paris; repub. Paris: Musée de l'Air.

Further Reading
L.T.C. Rolt, 1966, *The Aeronauts*, London (paperback 1985).
Basil Clarke, 1961, *The History of Airships*, London.

JDS

Michaux, Pierre
b. 1813
d. 1883

French bicycle maker and developer, in partnership with his son Ernest (1849–89).

Pierre Michaux has been variously described as a cabinet-maker, a locksmith and a carriage-repairer. He probably combined all these occupations. He had a workshop near the Champs Elysées in Paris in 1861 where he set up a business in the manufacture of bicycles. His machines, which became known as *Michaulines*, were largely built of wood but had the great advantage over the *draisienne* that the rider's feet rested on a pair of pedals connected to the axle of the front wheel. In the late 1850s solid rubber tyres were added to the wheels. In 1865 Michaux et Cie built about four hundred *Michaulines*. By 1866–7 they had developed a new model with a wrought-iron frame and a larger front wheel. This machine was shown at the World Exhibition held in Paris in 1867 and the company received many orders, including one from the invalid Napoleon III. The Prince Imperial also had a *Michauline*. Late in the 1860s the Olivier brothers invested 100,000 francs in Michaux et Cie, allowing the firm to move to a 2½-acre (1-hecare) factory near the Arc de Triomphe. Soon afterwards, Michaux *père* accepted a 200,000 franc payment and left the firm, which continued to flourish. In the early 1870s the Olivier brothers were building as many as two hundred machines each day. By 1870 they employed 500 workers using fifty-seven forges. There were in addition about sixty other bicycle makers in Paris and fifteen in provincial France.

The 1867 *Michauline* had a metal backbone and a lever-shoe brake; the saddle was mounted on a single leaf spring; slotted cranks allowed the effective crank length to be adjusted; and the machine weighed 59 lb (27 kg).

Further Reading
Science Museum, 1955, *Cycles: History and Development*, London: HMSO.
J. McGunn, 1987, *On Your Bicycle: An Illustrated History of Cycling*, London: John Murray.

IMcN

Mies van der Rohe, Ludwig
b. 27 March 1886 Aachen, Germany
d. 17 August 1969 Chicago, USA

German architect, third of the great trio of long-lived, second-generation modernists who established the international style in the inter-war years and brought it to maturity (See **Jeanneret** *(Le Corbusier) and* **Gropius**).

Mies van der Rohe was the son of a stonemason and his early constructional training came from his father. As a young man he gained experience of the modern school from study of the architecture of the earlier leaders, notably Peter **Behrens**, Hendrik Berlage and Frank Lloyd **Wright**. He commenced architectural practice in 1913 and soon after the First World War was establishing his own version of modern architecture. His

building materials were always of the highest quality, of marble, stone, glass and, especially, steel. He stripped his designs of all extraneous decoration: more than any of his contemporaries he followed the theme of elegance, functionalism and an ascetic concentration on essentials. He believed that architectural design should not look backwards but should reflect the contemporary achievement of advanced technology in both its construction and the materials used, and he began early in his career to act upon these beliefs. Typical was his early concrete and glass office building of 1922, after which, more importantly, came his designs for the German Pavilion at the Barcelona Exposition of 1929. These designs included his famous Barcelona chair, made from chrome steel and leather in a geometrical design, one which has survived as a classic and is still in production. Another milestone was his Tugendhat House in Brno (1930), a long, low, rectilinear structure in glass and steel that set a pattern for many later buildings of this type. In 1930 Mies followed his colleagues as third Director of the Bauhaus, but due to the rise of National Socialism in Germany it was closed in 1933. He finally left Germany for the USA in 1937, and the following year he took up his post as Director of Architecture in Chicago at what is now known as the Illinois Institute of Technology and where he remained for twenty years. In America Mies van der Rohe continued to develop his work upon his original thesis. His buildings are always recognizable for their elegance, fine proportions, high-quality materials and clean, geometrical forms; nearly all are of glass and steel in rectangular shapes. The structure and design evolved according to the individual needs of each commission, and there were three fundamental types of design. One type was the single or grouped high-rise tower, built for apartments for the wealthy, as in his Lake Shore Drive Apartments in Chicago (1948–51), or for city-centre offices, as in his Seagram Building in New York (1954–8, with Philip Johnson) or his Chicago Federal Centre (1964). Another form was the long, low rectangle based upon the earlier Tugendhat House and seen again in the New National Gallery in Berlin (1965–8). Third, there were the grouped schemes when the commission called for buildings of varied purpose on a single, large site. Here Mies van der Rohe achieved a variety and interest in the different shapes and heights of buildings set out in spatial harmony of landscape. Some examples of this type of scheme were housing estates (Lafayette Park Housing Development in Detroit, 1955–6), while others were for educational, commercial or shopping requirements, as at the Toronto Dominion Centre (1963–9).

Further Reading
L. Hilbersheimer, 1956, *Ludwig Mies van der Rohe*, Chicago: P. Theobald.
Peter Blake, 1960, *Mies van der Rohe, Architecture and Structure*, Penguin, Pelican.
Arthur Drexler, 1960, *Ludwig Mies van der Rohe*, London: Mayflower.
Philip Johnson, 1978, *Mies van der Rohe*, Secker and Warburg.

DY

Mignet, Henri
b. 19 October 1893 Saintes, France
d. 31 August 1965 Bordeaux, France

French inventor of the Pou-du-Ciel or Flying Flea, a small aeroplane for the do-it-yourself constructor, popular in the 1930s.

Throughout the history of aviation there have been many attempts to produce a cheap and simple aeroplane for 'the man in the street'. The tiny *Demoiselle* built by Alberto **Santos-Dumont** in 1909 or the **de Havilland** *Moth* of 1925 are good examples, but the one which very nearly achieved this aim was Henri Mignet's *Flying Flea* of 1933. Mignet was a self-taught designer of light aircraft, which often incorporated his unorthodox ideas. His *Pou-du-Ciel* ('Sky Louse' or 'Flying Flea') was unorthodox. The materials used in construction were conventional wood and fabric, but the control system departed from the usual wing plus tailplane (with elevators). The *Flea* had two wings in tandem. The rear wing was fixed, while the forward wing was hinged to allow the angle of incidence, and hence its lift, to be increased or decreased. Reducing the forward wing's lift would cause the *Flea* to dive. After Mignet's first flight, on 6 September 1933, and the publication of his book *Le Sport de l'air*, which explains how to build a *Pou-du-Ciel*, a *Pou*-building craze started in France. Mignet's book was translated into English and 6,000 copies were sold in a month. During 1935 the craze spread to Britain, where a *Flying Flea*

could be built for £50–£90, including the engine. After several fatal crashes, the aircraft was banned in 1936. A design fault in the control system was to blame, and although this was remedied the wave of popular enthusiasm vanished. Mignet continued to design light aircraft and during the Second World War he was working on a *Pou-Maquis* for use by the French Resistance but the war ended before the aircraft was ready. During the post-war years a series of *Flying Flea* derivatives appeared, but their numbers were small. However, the home-build movement in general has grown in recent years, a fact which would have pleased Henri Mignet, the 'Patron Saint of Homebuilders'.

Principal Honours and Distinctions
Chevalier de la Légion d'honneur. Médaille de l'Aéronautique.

Bibliography
1935, *The Flying Flea: How to Build and Fly it*, London (English edn).

Further Reading
Ken Ellis and Geoff Jones, 1990, *Henri Mignet and His Flying Flea*, Yeovil (a full account).
Geoff Jones, 1992, *Building and Flying Your Own Plane*, Yeovil (describes the *Flying Flea* and its place in the homebuild story).

JDS

Mikhailov, Petr
See **Peter the Great**.

Mikoyan, Artem Ivanovich
b. 5 August 1905 Sanain, Armenia
d. 9 December 1970 Moscow, Russia

Armenian aircraft designer.

Mikoyan graduated from the Zhukovsky Military Aircraft Academy in 1936. His first major design project was in response to an official requirement, issued in December 1940, for a single-engined fighter with performance equating to those then in service with the British, French and German air forces. In conjunction with M.L. Gurevich, a mathematician, and in a bare four months, he produced a flying prototype, with a top speed of 401 mph (645 km/h), that entered service as the *MiG-1* in 1941. The Mikoyan and Gurevich *MiG-3* and *MiG-5* followed, and they then designed the *MiG-7* high-altitude fighter; however, the latter never came into service on account of the decline of the German air force.

The Second World War MiG fighters were characterized by high speed, good protection and armament, but they had poor manoeuvrability. In 1945, however, Mikoyan began to study Western developments in jet-powered aircraft. The result was a series of jet fighters, beginning with the *MiG-9A*, through the *MiG-11*, to the *MiG-15* that gave the Allied air forces such a shock when it first appeared during the Korean War. The last in the series in which Mikoyan himself was involved was the *MiG-23*, which entered service in 1967. The MiG series lived on after both his and Gurevich's (1976) deaths, with one of the latest models being the *MiG-31*.

Principal Honours and Distinctions
Deputy to the Supreme Soviet 1950, 1954, 1958. Corresponding Member of the Soviet Academy of Sciences 1953. Member of the Council of Nationalities 1962. Three Stalin Prizes and other decorations.

CM

Miller, Patrick
b. 1731 Glasgow, Scotland
d. 9 December 1815 Dalswinton, Dumfriesshire, Scotland

Scottish merchant and banker, early experimenter in powered navigation and in ship form.

In his own words, Patrick Miller was 'without a sixpence' in his early youth; this is difficult to prove one way or another as he ended his life as Director and Deputy Governor of the Bank of Scotland. One thing is clear however, that from his earliest days, in common with most of his counterparts of the late eighteenth century, he was interested in experimental and applied science. Having acquired a substantial income from other sources, Miller was able to indulge his interest in ships and engineering. His first important vessel was the trimaran *Edinburgh*, designed by him and launched at Leith in 1786. Propulsion was man-powered using paddle wheels positioned in the spaces between the outer and central hulls. This led to several trials of similar craft on the Forth in the 1780s, and ultimately to the celebrated Dalswinton Loch

trials. In 1785 Miller had purchased the Dumfriesshire estate of Dalswinton and commenced a series of experiments on agricultural development and other matters. With the help of William **Symington** he built a double-hull steamship with internal paddle wheels which was tested on the Loch in 1788. The 7.6 m (25 ft) long ship travelled at 5 mph (8 km/h) on her trials, and according to unsubstantiated tradition carried a group of well-known people including the poet Robert Burns (1759–1796).

Miller carried out many more important experiments and in 1796 obtained a patent for the design of shallow-drafted ships able to carry substantial cargo on flat bottoms. His main achievement may have been to stimulate William Symington, who at the beginning of the nineteenth century went on to design and build two of the world's first important steamships, each named *Charlotte Dundas*, for service on the Forth and Clyde Canal.

Further Reading
H. Philip Spratt, 1958, *The Birth of the Steamboat*, London: Griffiths.
W.S. Harvey and G. Downs-Rose, 1980, *William Symington, Inventor and Engine Builder*, London: Northgate.
F.M. Walker, 1984, *Song of the Clyde. A History of Clyde Shipbuilding*, Cambridge: PSL.

FMW

Miller, Robert
fl. 1790s Scotland

Scottish pioneer of improvements to the power loom.

After Edmund **Cartwright** many people contributed to the development of the power loom. Among them was Robert Miller of Dumbartonshire, Scotland. In 1796 he took out a patent for an improved protector which stopped the loom altogether when the shuttle failed to enter its box, thus preventing breakage of the warp threads. The same patent contained the specification for his 'wiper' loom. The wipers, or cams, worked the picking stick to drive the shuttle across, a feature found on most later looms. He also moved the sley by a cam in one direction and by springs in the other. His looms were still working in 1808 and may have formed the basis for power looms built in Lowell in the USA.

Bibliography
1796, British patent no. 2,122.

Further Reading
R.L. Hills, 1970, *Power in the Industrial Revolution*, Manchester (provides the most detailed account of Miller's loom, with illustrations).
A. Barlow, 1878, *The History and Principles of Weaving by Hand and by Power*, London.
W. English, 1969, *The Textile Industry*, London.
D.J. Jeremy, 1981, *Transatlantic Industrial Revolution. The Diffusion of Textile Technologies Between Britain and America, 1790–1830s*, Oxford (illustrates Miller's influence in America).

RLH

Millington, John

b. 1779
d. 1868

English engineer and educator.

John Millington was Professor of Mechanics at the Royal Institution, London, from 1817 to 1829. He gave numerous courses on natural philosophy and mechanics and supported the introduction of coal gas for lighting. In 1823 he testified to a Select Committee of the House of Commons that the spread of gas lighting would greatly benefit the preservation of law and order, and with the same utilitarian and penal inclination he devised a treadmill for use in the Bedfordshire House of Correction. Millington was appointed the first Professor of Engineering and the Application of Mechanical Philosophy to the Arts at the newly founded University of London in 1828, but he speedily resigned from the post, preferring to go to Mexico in 1829. Like **Trevithick** and Robert **Stephenson** before him, he was attracted to the New World by the possibility of using new techniques to reopen old mines, and he became an engineer to some Mexican mining projects. In 1837 he went to Williamsburg in the United States, being appointed Professor of Chemistry, and it was there that he died in 1868. Millington wrote extensively on scientific subjects.

Further Reading
Dictionary of National Biography.
M. Berman, *The Royal Institution*, pp. 46, 98–9.
AB

Mitchell, Charles

b. 20 May 1820 Aberdeen, Scotland
d. 22 August 1895 Jesmond, Newcastle upon Tyne, England

Scottish industrialist whose Tyneside shipyard was an early constituent of what became the Vickers Shipbuilding Group.

Mitchell's early education commenced at Ledingham's Academy, Correction Wynd, Aberdeen, and from there he became a premium apprentice at the Footdee Engineering Works of Wm Simpson & Co. Despite being employed for around twelve hours each day, Mitchell matriculated at Marischal College (now merged with King's College to form the University of Aberdeen). He did not graduate, although in 1840 he won the chemistry prize. On the completion of his apprenticeship, like Andrew Leslie (founder of Hawthorn Leslie) and other young Aberdonians he moved to Tyneside, where most of his working life was spent. From 1842 until 1844 he worked as a draughtsman for his friend Coutts, who had a shipyard at Low Walker, before moving on to the drawing offices of **Maudslay** Sons and Field of London, then one of the leading shipbuilding and engineering establishments in the UK. While in London he studied languages, acquiring a skill that was to stand him in good stead in later years. In 1852 he returned to the North East and set up his own iron-ship building yard at Low Walker near Newcastle. Two years later he married Anne Swan, the sister of the two young men who were to found the company now known as Swan Hunter Ltd. The Mitchell yard grew in size and reputation and by the 1850s he was building for the Russian Navy and Merchant Marine as well as advising the Russians on their shipyards in St Petersburg. In 1867 the first informal business arrangement was concluded with Armstrongs for the supply of armaments for ships; this led to increased co-operation and ultimately in 1882 to the merger of the two shipyards as Sir W.G. Armstrong Mitchell & Co. At the time of the merger, Mitchell had launched 450 ships in twenty-nine years. In 1886 the new company built the SS *Gluckauf*, the world's first bulk oil tanker. After ill health in 1865 Mitchell reduced his workload and lived for a while in Surbiton, London, but returned to Tyneside to a new house at Jesmond. In his later years he was a generous benefactor to many good causes in Tyneside and Aberdeen, to the Church and to the University of Aberdeen.

Further Reading

D.F. McGuire, 1988, *Charles Mitchell 1820–1895, Victorian Shipbuilder*, Newcastle upon Tyne: City Libraries and Arts.

J.D. Scott, 1962, *Vickers. A History*, London: Weidenfeld & Nicolson (a recommended overview of the Vickers Group).

FMW

Mitchell, Reginald Joseph

b. 20 May 1895 Talke, near Stoke-on-Trent, Staffordshire, England
d. 11 June 1937 Southampton, England

English aircraft designer.

He was the son of a headmaster who, when Mitchell was aged 6 years, set up his own printing business. Mitchell was apprenticed at the age of 16 to a locomotive builder in Stoke and also studied engineering, mechanics, mathematics and drawing at night-school. With the outbreak of war in 1914 he became increasingly interested in aircraft and in 1916 joined the Supermarine Aviation Works at Southampton. Such was his talent for aviation design that within three years he had risen to be Chief Engineer Designer. Initially Mitchell's work was concentrated on flying boats, but with the resurrection after the First World War of the biennial Schneider Trophy races for seaplanes he turned his attention increasingly to high-speed floatplanes. He first achieved success with his *S-5* in the 1927 race at Venice and followed it up with further victories in 1929 and 1931 with the *S-6* and *S-6B*, enabling Britain to win the trophy outright (See also **Royce, Sir Frederick Henry**). Using the experience gained from the Schneider Trophy races, Mitchell now began to design fighter aircraft. He was dissatisfied with his first attempt, which was to produce a fighter to an Air Ministry specification, and started afresh on his own. The result was the Supermarine Spitfire, which was to become one of the outstanding aircraft of the Second World War. Sadly, he died of cancer before his project came to full fruition, with the Spitfire not entering Royal Air Force service until June 1938. The success of Mitchell's designs was due to his ability to combine good engineering with aerodynamic grace.

Principal Honours and Distinctions

Royal Aeronautical Society Silver Medal 1927. CBE 1931.

Further Reading

Ralph Barker, 1971, *The Schneider Trophy Races*, London: Chatto & Windus.

CM

Mitscherlich, Alexander

b. 28 May 1836 Berlin, Germany
d. 31 May 1918 Oberstdorf, Germany

German inventor of sulphite wood pulp for papermaking.

Mitscherlich had an impeccable scientific background; his father was the celebrated chemist Eilhardt Mitscherlich, discoverer of the law of isomorphism, and his godfather was Alexander von Humboldt. At first his progress at school failed to live up to this auspicious beginning and his father would only sanction higher studies if he first qualified as a teacher so as to assure a means of livelihood. Alexander rose to the occasion and went on to gain his doctorate at the age of 25 in the field of mineralogical chemistry. He worked for a few years as Assistant to the distinguished chemists Wöhler in Göttingen and Wurtz in Paris. On his father's death in 1863, he succeeded him as teacher of chemistry in the University of Berlin. In 1868 he accepted a post in the newly established Forest Academy in Hannoversch-Munden, teaching chemistry, physics and geology. The post offered little financial advantage, but it left him more time for research. It was there that he invented the process for producing sulphite wood pulp.

The paper industry was seeking new raw materials. Since the 1840s pulp had been produced mechanically from wood, but it was unsuitable for making fine papers. From the mid-1860s several chemists began tackling the problem of separating the cellulose fibres from the other constituents of wood by chemical means. The American Benjamin C. Tilghman was granted patents in several countries for the treatment of wood with acid or bisulphite. Carl Daniel Ekman in Sweden and Karl Kellner in Austria also made sulphite pulp, but the credit for devising the process that came into general use belongs to Mitscherlich. His brother Oskar came to him at the Academy with plans for producing pulp by the action of soda, but the results were inferior, so Mitscherlich substituted calcium bisulphite and in the laboratory obtained good results. To extend this to a large-scale process, he was forced to set up his own mill, where he devised the characteristic towers for making the calcium bisulphite, in which water trickling down through packed lime met a rising current of sulphur dioxide. He was granted a patent in Luxembourg in 1874 and a German one four years later. The sulphite process did not make him rich, for there was considerable opposition to it; government objected to the smell of sulphur dioxide, forestry authorities were anxious about the inroads that might be made into the forests and his patents were contested. In 1883, with the support of an inheritance from his mother, Mitscherlich resigned his post at the Academy to devote more time to promoting his invention. In 1897 he at last succeeded in settling the patent disputes and achieving recognition as the inventor of sulphite pulp. Without this raw material, the paper industry could never have satisfied the insatiable appetite of the newspaper presses.

Further Reading
H. Voorn 'Alexander Mitscherlich, inventor of sulphite wood pulp', *Paper Maker* 23 (1): 41–4.

LRD

Moissan, Ferdinand-Frédéric-Henri
b. 28 September 1852 Paris, France
d. 20 February 1907 Paris, France

French chemist, the first to isolate fluorine, and a pioneer in high-temperature technology.

His family, of modest means, moved in 1864 to Meaux, where he attended the municipal college; he returned to Paris before completing his education and apprenticed himself to a pharmacist. In 1872 he began work as a laboratory assistant at the Musée d'Histoire Naturelle, while continuing studies in chemistry. He qualified as a pharmacist at the Ecole Supérieure de Pharmacie in 1879, and by this time he had decided that his main interest was inorganic chemistry. His early investigations concerned the oxides of iron and related metals; his work attracted the favourable attention of Sainte-Claire **Deville** and was the subject of his doctoral thesis. In 1882 Moissan married Léonie Lugan, whose father

provided generous financial support, enabling him to pursue his researches with greater freedom and security. He became, successively, Professor of Toxicology at the Ecole in 1886 and of Inorganic Chemistry in 1899. In 1884 Moissan began both his investigation of the compounds of fluorine and his attempts to isolate the highly reactive element itself. Previous attempts by chemists had ended in failure and sometimes injury. Moissan's health, too, was affected, but in June 1886 he succeeded in isolating fluorine by electrolysing potassium fluoride in hydrogen fluoride at $-50°C$ ($-58°F$) in platinum apparatus. He was then able to prepare further compounds of fluorine, some of technological importance, such as carbon tetrafluoride. At the same time, Moissan turned his attention to the making of artificial diamonds. To achieve this, he devised his celebrated electric-arc furnace; this was first demonstrated in December 1892 and consisted of two lime blocks placed one above the other, with a cavity for a crucible and two grooves for carbon electrodes, and could attain a temperature of $3,500°C$ ($6,332°F$). It seemed at first that he had succeeded in making diamonds, but this attempt is now regarded as a failure. Nevertheless, with the aid of his furnace he was able to produce and study many substances of technological importance, including refractory oxides, borides and carbides, and such metals as manganese, chromium, uranium, tungsten, vanadium, molybdenum, titanium and zirconium; many of these materials had useful applications in the chemical and metallurgical industries (e.g. calcium carbide became the main source of acetylene).

Principal Honours and Distinctions
Nobel Prize in Chemistry 1906.

Bibliography
There are several listings of his more than 300 publications, such as Lebeau, cited below. Major works are *Le Four électrique* (1897, Paris) and *Le Fluor et ses composés* (1900, Paris).

Further Reading
Centenaire de l'Ecole supérieure de pharmacie de l'Université de Paris 1803–1903, 1904, Paris, pp. 249–57.
B. Harrow, 1927, *Eminent Chemists of Our Time*,

2nd edn, New York, pp. 135–54, 374–88.
P. Lebeau, 1908, 'Notice sur la vie et les travaux de Henri Moissan', *Bulletin Soc. chim. de France* (4 ser.) 3: i–xxxviii.

LRD

Mole, Lancelot de

b. 13 March 1880 Adelaide, Australia
d. 6 May 1950 Sydney, Australia

Australian engineer and early tank designer.

De Mole's father was an architect and surveyor and he himself followed a similar avenue as a draughtsman working on mining, surveying and engineering projects in Australia. It was in 1911, while surveying in particularly rough terrain in Western Australia, that he first conceived the idea of the tank as a tracked, armoured vehicle capable of traversing the most difficult ground. He drew up detailed plans and submitted them to the War Office in London the following year, but although they were rejected, not all the plans were returned to him. When war broke out in 1914 he tried without success to interest the Australian authorities, even after he had constructed a model at their request. A further blow came in 1916, when the first tanks, built by the British, appeared on the battlefields of France and looked remarkably similar in design to his own. Believing that he could play a significant role in further tank development, but lacking the funds to travel to Britain, de Mole eventually succeeded, after an initial rejection by a medical board, in enlisting in the Australian Army, which got him to England at the beginning of 1918. He immediately took his model to the British Inventions Committee, who were sufficiently impressed to pass it to the Tank Board, who promptly mislaid it for six weeks. Meanwhile, in March 1918, Private de Mole was ordered to France and was unable to take matters further. On his return to England in early 1919 he made a formal claim for a reward for his invention, but this was turned down on the grounds that no direct link could be established between his design and the first tanks that were built. Even so, the Inventions Committee did authorize a sum of money to cover his expenses, and in 1920 de Mole was a made a Commander of the Order of the British Empire.

Returning to Australia, de Mole worked as an engineer in the design branch of the Sydney Water Board. He continued to invent, but none of his designs, which covered a wide range of items, were ever taken up.

Principal Honours and Distinctions
CBE 1920.

Further Reading
Australian Dictionary of Biography, 1918, Vol. 8.
A.J. Smithers, 1986, *A New Excalibur: The Development of the Tank 1909–1939*, London: Leo Cooper (for illustrations of the model of his tank).
Mention of his invention is made in a number of books on the history of the tank.

CM

Möller, Anton

fl. *c.*1580 Danzig, Poland

Polish may have been involved with the invention of the ribbon loom.

Around 1586, Anton Möller related that he saw in Danzig a loom on which four to six pieces of ribbon could be woven at once. Some accounts say he may have invented this loom, which required no skill to use beyond the working of a bar. The city council was afraid that a great many workers might be reduced to begging because of this invention, so they had it suppressed and the inventor strangled or drowned. It seems to have been in use in London *c.*1616 and at Leiden in Holland by 1620, but its spread was handicapped both by popular rioting and by restrictive legislation. By 1621 the capacity of the loom had been increased to twenty-four ribbons, and it was later increased to fifty. It made its appearance in Lancashire around 1680 and the way the shuttles were operated could have given John **Kay** the inspiration for his flying shuttle.

Further Reading
A. Barlow, 1878, *The History and Principles of Weaving by Hand and by Power*, London (includes a good description and illustration of the invention).
T.K. Derry and T.I. Williams, 1960, *A Short History of Technology from the Earliest Times to AD 1900*, Oxford; C. Singer (ed.), 1957, *A History of Technology*, Vol. III, Oxford:

Clarendon Press (both provide brief accounts of the introduction of the ribbon loom).

RLH

Momma (Mumma), Jacob

b. early seventeenth century Germany
d. 1679 England

German (naturalized English) immigrant skilled in the manufacture and production of brass, who also mined and smelted copper.

The protestant Momma family were well known in Aachen, the seventeenth-century centre of German brass production. Subjected to religious pressures, some members of the family moved to nearby Stolberg, while others migrated to Sweden, starting brass manufacture there. Jacob travelled to England, establishing brassworks with two German partners at Esher in Surrey in 1649; theirs was the only such works in England to survive for more than a few years during the seventeenth century.

Jacob, naturalized English by 1660, is often referred to in England as Mummer or another variant of his name. He became respected, serving as a juror, and was appointed a constable in 1661. During the 1660s Momma was engaged in mining copper at Ecton Hill, Staffordshire, where he was credited with introducing gunpowder to English mining technology. He smelted his ore at works nearby in an effort to secure copper supplies, but the whole project was brief and unprofitable.

The alternative imported copper required for his brass came mainly from Sweden, its high cost proving a barrier to viable English brass production. In 1662 Momma petitioned Parliament for some form of assistance. A year later he pleaded further for higher tariffs against brass-wire imports as protection from the price manipulation of Swedish exporters. He sought support from the Society of Mineral and Battery Works, the Elizabethan monopoly (see **Dockwra, William**) claiming jurisdiction over the country's working of brass, but neither petition succeeded. Despite these problems with the high cost of copper supplies in England, Momma continued his business and is recorded as still paying hearth tax on his twenty brass furnaces up to 1664. Although these were abandoned before his death and he claimed to have lost £6,000 on his brassworks, his wire mills survived him for a few years under the management of his son.

Further Reading
J. Morton, 1985, *The rise of the modern copper and brass industry: 1690 to 1750*, unpublished thesis: University of Birmingham, 16–25.
J. Day, 1984, 'The continental origins of Bristol Brass', *Industrial Archaeology Review* 8/1: 32–56.
John Robey, 1969, 'Ecton copper mines in the seventeenth century', *Bulletin of the Peak District Mines Historic Society* 4 (2): 145–55 (the most comprehensive published account).

JD

Monckhoven, Désiré Charles Emanuel van

b. 1834 Ghent, Belgium
d. 1882

Belgian chemist, photographic researcher, inventor and author.

Born in Belgium of German stock, Monckhoven spoke German and French with equal fluency. He originally studied chemistry, but devoted the greater part of his working life to photography. His improved solar enlarger of 1864 was seen by his contemporaries as one of the significant innovations of the day. In 1867 he moved to Vienna, where he became involved in portrait photography, but returned to Ghent in 1870. In 1871 he announced his discovery of a practicable collodion dry-plate process, and later in the decade he conducted research into the carbon printing process. In 1879 Monckhoven constructed a comprehensively equipped laboratory where he commenced a series of experiments on gelatine dry-plate emulsions, including some which yielded the discovery that the ripening of silver bromide was greatly accelerated by ammonia; this allowed the production of emulsions of much greater sensitivity. He was a prolific author, and his 1852 book on photography, *Traité général de photographie*, published when he was only 18, became one of the standard texts of his day.

Bibliography
1852, *Traité général de photographie*, Paris.

Further Reading
J.M. Eder, 1945, *History of Photography*, trans. E. Epstean, New York.

JW

Mond, Ludwig

b. 7 March 1839 Cassel, Germany
d. 11 December 1909 London, England

German (naturalized English) industrial chemist.

Born into a prosperous Jewish merchant family, Mond studied at the Polytechnic in Cassel and then under the distinguished chemists Hermann Kolbe at Marburg and **Bunsen** at Heidelberg from 1856. In 1859 he began work as an industrial chemist in various works in Germany and Holland. At this time, Mond was pursuing his method for recovering sulphur from the alkali wastes in the **Leblanc** soda-making process. Mond came to England in 1862 and five years later settled permanently, in partnership with John Hutchinson & Co. at Widnes, to perfect his process, although complete success eluded him. He became a naturalized British subject in 1880.

In 1872 Mond became acquainted with Ernest **Solvay**, the Belgian chemist who developed the ammonia–soda process which finally supplanted the Leblanc process. Mond negotiated the English patent rights and set up the first ammonia–soda plant in England at Winnington in Cheshire, in partnership with John Brunner. After overcoming many difficulties by incessant hard work, the process became a financial success and in 1881 Brunner, Mond & Co. was formed, for a time the largest alkali works in the world. In 1926 the company merged with others to form Imperial Chemical Industries Ltd (ICI). The firm was one of the first to adopt the eight-hour day and to provide model dwellings and playing fields for its employees.

From 1879 Mond took up the production of ammonia and this led to the Mond producer-gas plant, patented in 1883. The process consisted of passing air and steam over coal and coke at a carefully regulated temperature. Ammonia was generated and, at the same time, so was a cheap and useful producer gas. Mond's major discovery followed the observation in 1889 that carbon monoxide could combine with nickel in its ore at around 60°C to form a gaseous compound, nickel carbonyl. This, on heating to a higher temperature, would then decompose to give pure nickel. Mond followed up this unusual way of producing and purifying a metal and by 1892 had succeeded in setting up a pilot plant to perfect a large-scale process and went on to form the Mond Nickel Company.

Apart from being a successful industrialist, Mond was prominent in scientific circles and played a leading role in the setting up of the Society of Chemical Industry in 1881. The success of his operations earned him great wealth, much of which he donated for learned and charitable purposes. He formed a notable collection of pictures which he bequeathed to the National Gallery.

Principal Honours and Distinctions
FRS 1891.

Bibliography
1885, 'On the origin of the ammonia-soda process', *Journal of the Society of Chemical Industry* 4: 527–9.
1895, 'The history of the process of nickel extraction', *Journal of the Society of Chemical Industry* 14: 945–6.

Further Reading
J.M. Cohen, 1956, *The Life of Ludwig Mond*, London: Methuen.
Obituary, 1918, *Journal of the Chemical Society* 113: 318–34.
F.C. Donnan, 1939, *Ludwig Mond 1839–1909*, London (a valuable lecture).

LRD

Monell, Ambrose

b. 1874 New York, USA
d. 2 May 1921 Beacon, New York, USA

American metallurgist who gave his name to a successful nickel–copper alloy.

After graduating from Columbia University in 1896, Monell became a metallurgical engineer to the Carnegie Steel Company, rising in six years to be Assistant to the President. In 1900, while Manager of the company's open-hearth steelworks at Pittsburg, he patented a procedure for making high-carbon steel in basic conditions on the hearth of a fixed/stationary furnace; the method was intended to refine pig-iron containing substantial proportions of phosphorus and to do so relatively quickly. The process was introduced at the Homestead Works of the Carnegie Steel Company in February 1900, where it continued in use for some years. In April 1902 Monell was among those who launched the

International Nickel Company of New Jersey in order to bring together a number of existing nickel interests; he became the new company's President. In 1904–5, members of the company's metallurgical staff produced an alloy of about 70 parts nickel and 30 copper which seemed to show great commercial promise on account of its high resistance to corrosion and its good appearance. Monell agreed to the suggestion that the new alloy should be given his name; for commercial reasons it was marketed as 'Monel metal'. In 1917, following the entry of the USA into the First World War, Monell was commissioned Colonel in the US Army (Aviation) for overseas service, relinquishing his presidency of the International Nickel Company but remaining as a director. At the time of his death he was also a director in several other companies in the USA.

Bibliography
1900, British patent no. 5506 (taken out by O. Imray on behalf of Monell).
Monell insinuated an account of his steel-making procedure at a meeting of the Iron and Steel Institute held in London and reported in *The Journal of the Iron and Steel Institute* (1900) 1: 71–80; some of the comments made by other speakers, particularly B. Talbot, were adverse. The following year (1901) Monell produced a general historical review: 'A summary of development in open-hearth steel', *Iron Trade Review* 14 (14 November): 39–47.

Further Reading
A.J. Wadhams, 1931, 'The story of the nickel industry', *Metals and Alloys* 2 (3): 166–75 (mentions Monell among many others, and includes a portrait (p. 170)).

See also: **Stanley, Robert Crooks**; **Talbot, Benjamin**.

JKA

Monier, Joseph
b. 1823 France
d. 1906 Paris, France

French gardener and one of the principal inventors of reinforced concrete.

Monier was a commercial gardener who in the course of his work was struck with the idea of inserting iron reinforcement in concrete tubs such as were used for growing orange trees. He patented this idea in 1867 and exhibited his invention the same year at the Paris Exposition. It soon occurred to him to apply the same principles to other engineering structures such as railway sleepers, pipes, floors, arches and bridges. In 1878 he took out a French patent for reinforced concrete beams and held numerous other patents for the material. Although he was not the only one to realize the benefits of combining a concrete girder or slab to resist compressive forces with iron or steel wires or rods to resist tensile stresses, 'Das System Monier' was known as such by 1887 throughout Europe.

Further Reading
J.W. De Courcy, 1987, 'The emergence of reinforced concrete', *Structural Engineer* 65A: 316.

IMcN

Monro, Philip Peter
b. 27 May 1946 London, England

English biologist, inventor of a water-purification process by osmosis.

Monro's whole family background is engineering, an interest he did not share. Instead, he preferred biology, an enthusiasm aroused by reading the celebrated *Science of Life* by H.G. and G.P. Wells and Julian Huxley. Educated at a London comprehensive school, Monro found it necessary to attend evening classes while at school to take his advanced level science examinations. Lacking parental support, he could not pursue a degree course until he was 21 years old, and so he gained valuable practical experience as a research technician. He resumed his studies and took a zoology degree at Portsmouth Polytechnic. He then worked in a range of zoology and medical laboratories, culminating after twelve years as a Senior Experimental Officer at Southampton Medical School. In 1989 he relinquished his post to devote himself full time to developing his inventions as Managing Director of Hampshire Advisory and Technical Services Ltd (HATS). Also in 1988 he obtained his PhD from Southampton University, in the field of embryology.

Monro had meanwhile been demonstrating a talent for invention, mainly in microscopy. His most important invention, however, is of a water-purification system. The idea for it came from Michael Wilson of the Institute of Dental Surgery in London, who evolved a technique for osmotic production of sterile oral rehydration solutions, of particular use in treating infants suffering from diarrhoea in third-world countries. Monro broadened the original concept to include dried food, intravenous solutions and even dried blood. The process uses simple equipment and no external power and works as follows: a dry sugar/salts mixture is sealed in one compartment of a double bag, the common wall of which is a semipermeable membrane. Impure water is placed in the empty compartment and the water transfers across the membrane by the osmotic force of the sugar/salts. As the pores in the membrane exclude all viruses, bacteria and their toxins, a sterile solution is produced.

With the help of a research fellowship granted for humanitarian reasons at King Alfred College, Winchester, the invention was developed to functional prototype stage in 1993, with worldwide patent protection. Commercial production was expected to follow, if sufficient financial backing were forthcoming. The process is not intended to replace large installations, but will revolutionize the small-scale production of sterile water in scattered third-world communities and in disaster areas where normal services have been disrupted.

HATS was awarded First Prize in the small business category and was overall prize winner in the Toshiba Year of Invention, received a NatWest/BP award for technology and a Prince of Wales Award for Innovation.

Bibliography
1993, with M. Wilson and W.A.M. Cutting, 'Osmotic production of sterile oral rehydration solutions', *Tropical Doctor* 23: 69–72.

LRD

Montferrand, Auguste Ricard de

b. 1786
d. 1858

French architect who was responsible for the rebuilding of the Cathedral of St Isaac in St Petersburg (1817–57).

As a young man Montferrand is believed to have spent some time working on Pierre Vignon's Church of the Madeleine in Paris. He went to Russia in the early nineteenth century, arriving in 1816 in St Petersburg, where he worked as a draughtsman. The following year a competition was held to rebuild the great Cathedral of St Isaac in the city, and Montferrand submitted a variety of eclectic designs which gained him the task of designing the cathedral. A succession of plans were prepared and altered over the years and it was 1842 before the design was finally agreed. Though French, Montferrand produced a very Russian building, immensely large and monumental and with an interior superbly rich in the variety of its materials: the monolithic columns of red Finnish granite, their capitals and bases gilded; the marbles of many colours; lapis lazuli; malachite; mosaics; paintings; and sculpture. St Isaac is a classical building on Greek cross plan with a large central dome carried on a Corinthian, colonnaded drum with smaller cupolas set around it. Below are façades with four weighty Corinthian porticoes, pedimented and sculptured. Noteworthy, and characteristic of the time, was Montferrand's masonry dome, which was supported by a framework of cast-iron girders; this was the first use of such a large-scale structure of this type in Russia.

Further Reading
George Heard Hamilton, 1954, *The Art and Architecture of Russia*, Penguin, Pelican History of Art.

DY

Montgolfier, Joseph-Michel

b. 26 August 1740 Vidalon-lès-Annonay, France
d. 26 June 1810 Balaruc-les-Bains, France

French ballooning pioneer who, with his brother Jacques-Etienne (b. 6 January 1745 Vidalon-lès-Annonay, France; d. 2 August 1799, Serriers, France), built the first balloon to carry passengers on a 'free' flight.

Joseph-Michel and Jacques-Etienne Montgolfier were papermakers of Annonay, near Lyon. Joseph made the first experiments after studying smoke rising from a fire and assuming that the smoke contained a gas which was lighter than air: of course, this lighter-than-air gas was just hot air. Using fine silk he made a small balloon with an aperture in its base, then, by burning paper beneath this aperture, he filled the balloon with hot air and it rose to the ceiling. Jacques-Étienne joined his brother in further experiments and they progressed to larger hot-air balloons until, by October 1783, they had constructed one large enough to lift two men on tethered ascents. In the same month Joseph-Michel delivered a paper at the University of Lyon on his experiments for a propulsive system by releasing gas through an opening in the side of a balloon; unfortunately, there was not enough pressure for an effective jet. Then, on 21 November 1783, the scientist Pilâtre de Rozier and the Marquis d'Arlandes ascended on a 'free' flight in a Montgolfier balloon. They departed from the grounds of a château in the Bois de Boulogne in Paris on what was to be the world's first aerial journey, covering 9 km (5½ miles) in 25 minutes.

Ballooning became a popular spectacle with initial rivalry between the hot-air *Montgolfières* and the hydrogen-filled *Charlières* of J.A.C. **Charles**. Interest in hot-air balloons subsided, but was revived in the 1960s by an American, Paul E. **Yost**. His propane-gas burner to provide hot-air was a great advance on the straw-burning fire-basket of the Montgolfiers.

Principal Honours and Distinctions
Légion d'honneur.

Further Reading
C.C. Gillispie, 1983, *The Montgolfier Brothers and the Invention of Aviation 1783–1784*, Princeton, NJ (one of the publications to commemorate the bicentenary of the Montgolfiers).
L.T.C. Rolt, 1966, *The Aeronauts*, London (describes the history of balloons).
C. Dollfus, 1961, *Balloons*, London.

JDS

Moon, William
b. 18 December 1818 Horsmonden, Kent, England
d. 10 October 1894 Brighton, England

English inventor of the first effective embossed reading type for use by the blind and visually handicapped.

Having lost the sight of one eye from scarlet fever at the age of 4, by the time he was 22 he had become completely blind. Dissatisfied with the existing Frères system of embossed letters, he established that the twenty-six letters of the alphabet could be encompassed in only nine variously positioned symbols. These were sufficiently adaptable so that by the time of his death they had been utilized for 476 languages and dialects. Although superseded for more general use by Braille, the Moon system is still in current use for those with defective touch sense and other disabilities. With the assistance of his son, who became a physician, and his daughter, who continued the work after his death, he established a centre in Brighton where the production of Moon transcriptions in still carried on.

Principal Honours and Distinctions
Fellow of the Royal Geographical Society 1852. Fellow of the Society of Arts 1857. LLD University of Philadelphia 1871.

Bibliography
1868, *Blindness, Its Consequences and Complications*, Brighton.
1873, *Light for the Blind*, Brighton.

Further Reading
Rutherford, 1898, *William Moon and his Work for the Blind*.

MG

Moore, Hiram
b. 19 July 1801 New England, USA
d. *c.*1874 Wisconsin, USA

American farmer and inventor who developed the first combine harvester.

Hiram Moore was the son of a New England stonemason. In 1831 he moved to West Michigan to farm, and he and his two brothers settled in Climax in Kalamazoo County.

Stimulated by a conversation with his neighbour, John Hascall, Moore made a model harvesting machine, which he patented in 1834. By the following year he had built a full-scale machine, but it broke down very quickly. In 1835 he successfully harvested 3 acres left standing for the purpose. Each year alterations and additions were made to the machine, and by 1839 over 50 acres were successfully harvested and threshed in the one operation by the Moore–Hascall machine.

During further developments which took place in the 1840s, Moore sold much of his interest to Senator Lucius Lyon. By the late 1840s this source of funding was no longer available, and attempts to extend the patent became embroiled in similar attempts by **McCormick** and Hussey and were blocked by rural pressures stemming from the fear that high machinery prices would ensue if the patents continued.

Discouraged, Moore moved to Brandon, Wisconsin, where he farmed 600 acres. He was still developing various machines, but was no longer actively involved in the development of the combine harvester. He continued to work his own machine, with which he would cut just a few acres each year.

Further Reading
Graeme Quick and Wesley Buchele, 1978, *The Grain Harvesters*, American Society of Agricultural Engineers (describes Hiram Moore's achievements in detail).

AP

Morland, Sir Samuel
b. 1625 Sulhampton, near Reading, Berkshire, England
d. 26 December 1695 Hammersmith, near London, England

English mathematician and inventor.

Morland was one of several sons of the Revd Thomas Morland and was probably initially educated by his father. He went to Winchester School from 1639 to 1644 and then to Magdalene College, Cambridge, where he graduated BA in 1648 and MA in 1652. He was appointed a tutor there in 1650. In 1653 he went to Sweden in the ambassadorial staff of Bulstrode Whitelocke and remained there until 1654. In that year he was appointed Clerk to Mr Secretary Thurloe, and in 1655 he was accredited by Oliver Cromwell to the Duke of Savoy to appeal for the Waldenses. In 1657 he married Susanne de Milleville of Boissy, France, with whom he had three children. In 1660 he went over to the Royalists, meeting King Charles at Breda, Holland. On 20 May, the King knighted him, creating him baron, for revealing a conspiracy against the king's life. He was also granted a pension of £500 per year. In 1661, at the age of 36, he decided to devote himself to mathematics and invention.

He devised a mechanical calculator, probably based on the pattern of Blaise **Pascal**, for adding and subtracting: this was followed in 1666 by one for multiplying and other functions. A Perpetual Calendar or Almanack followed; he toyed with the idea of a 'gunpowder engine' for raising water; he developed a range of speaking trumpets, said to have a range of $\frac{1}{2}$ to 1 mile (0.8–1.6 km) or more; also iron stoves for use on board ships, and improvements to barometers.

By 1675 he had started selling a range of pumps for private houses, for mines or deep wells, for ships, for emptying ponds or draining low ground as well as to quench fire or wet the sails of ships. The pumps cost from £5 to £63, and the great novelty was that he used, instead of packing around the cylinder sealing against the bore of the cylinder, a neck-gland or seal around the outside diameter of the piston or piston-rod. This revolutionary step avoided the necessity of accurately boring the cylinder, replacing it with the need to machine accurately the outside diameter of the piston or rod, a much easier operation. Twenty-seven variations of size and materials were included in his schedule of 'Pumps or Water Engines of Isaac Thompson of Great Russel Street', the maker of Morland's design. In 1681 the King made him 'Magister mechanicorum', or Master of Machines. In that year he sailed for France to advise Louis XIV on the waterworks being built at Marly to supply the Palace of Versailles. About this time he had shown King Charles plans for a pumping engine 'worked by fire alone'. He petitioned for a patent for this, but did not pursue the matter.

In 1692 he went blind. In all, he married five times. While working for Cromwell he became an expert in ciphers, in opening sealed letters and in their rapid copying.

Principal Honours and Distinctions
Knighted 1660.

Bibliography
1685, *Elevation des eaux*.

Further Reading
H.W. Dickinson, 1970, *Sir Samuel Morland: Diplomat and Inventor*, Cambridge: Newcomen Society/Heffers.

IMcN

Morris, William Richard, Viscount Nuffield

b. 10 October 1877 Worcester, England
d. 22 August 1963 Nuffield Place, England

English industrialist, car manufacturer and philanthropist.

Morris was the son of Frederick Morris, then a draper. He was the eldest of a family of seven, all of whom, except for one sister, died in childhood. When he was 3 years old, his father moved to Cowley, near Oxford, where he attended the village school. After a short time with a local bicycle firm he set up on his own at the age of 16 with a capital of £4. He manufactured pedal cycles and by 1902 he had designed a motor cycle and was doing car-repair work. By 1912, at the Motor Show, he was able to announce his first car, the 8.9 hp, two-seater Morris Oxford with its characteristic 'bull-nose'. It could perform at up to 50 mph (80 km/h) and 50 mpg (5.65 1/100 km). It cost £165.

Though untrained, Morris was a born engineer as well as a natural judge of character. This enabled him to build up a reliable team of assistants in his growing business, with an order for four hundred cars at the Motor Show in 1912. Much of his business was built up in the assembly of components manufactured by outside suppliers. In he moved out of his initial premises by New College in Longwall and bought land at Cowley, where he brought out his second model, the 11.9 hp Morris Oxford. This was after the First World War, during which car production was reduced to allow the manufacture of tanks and munitions. He was awarded the OBE in 1917 for his war work. Morris Motors Ltd was incorporated in 1919, and within fifteen months sales of cars had reached over 3,000 a year. By 1923 he was producing 20,000 cars a year, and in 1926 50,000, equivalent to about one-third of Britain's output. With the slump, a substantial overdraft, and a large stock of unsold cars, Morris took the bold decision to cut the prices of cars in stock, which then sold out within three weeks. Other makers followed suit, but Morris was ahead of them.

Morris was part-founder of the Pressed Steel Company, set up to produce car bodies at Cowley. A clever operation with the shareholding of the Morris Motors Company allowed Morris a substantial overall profit to provide expansion capital. By 1931 his 'empire' comprised, in addition to Morris Motors, the MG Car Company, the Wolseley Company, the SU Carburettor Company and Morris Commercial Cars. In 1936, the value of Morris's financial interest in the business was put at some £16 million.

William Morris was a frugal man and uncomplicated, having little use for all the money he made except to channel it to charitable purposes. It is said that in all he gave away some £30 million during his lifetime, much of it invested by the recipients to provide long-term benefits. He married Elizabeth Anstey in 1904 and lived for thirty years at Nuffield Place. He lived modestly, and even after retirement, when Honorary President of the British Motor Corporation, the result of a merger between Morris Motors and the Austin Motor Company, he drove himself to work in a modest 10 hp Wolseley. His generosity benefited many hospitals in London, Oxford, Birmingham and elsewhere. Oxford Colleges were another class of beneficiary from his largesse.

Principal Honours and Distinctions
Viscount 1938; Baron (Lord Nuffield) 1934; Baronet 1929; OBE 1917; GBE 1941; CH 1958. FRS 1939. He was a doctor of seven universities and an honorary freeman of seven towns.

Further Reading
R. Jackson, 1964, *The Nuffield Story*.
P.W.S. Andrews and E. Brunner, *The Life of Lord Nuffield*.

IMcN

Morrison, William Murray

b. 7 October 1873 Birchwood, Inverness-shire, Scotland
d. 21 May 1948 London, England

Scottish pioneer in the development of the British aluminium industry and Highlands hydroelectric energy.

After studying at the West of Scotland Technical College in Glasgow, in January 1895 Morrison was appointed Engineer to the newly formed British Aluminium Company Limited (BAC); it was with this organization that he spent his entire career. The company secured the patent rights to the **Héroult** and **Bayer** processes. It constructed a 200 tonne per year electrolytic plant at Foyers on the shore of Loch Ness, together with an adjacent 5000 kW hydroelectric scheme, and it built an alumina factory at Larne Harbour in north-eastern Ireland. Morrison was soon Manager at Foyers, and he became the company's Joint Technical Adviser. In 1910 he was made General Manager, and later he was appointed Managing Director. Morrison successfully brought about improvements in all parts of the production process; between 1915 and 1930 he increased the size of individual electrolytic cells by a factor of five, from 8,000 to 40,000 amperes. Soon after 1901, BAC built a second works for electrolytic reduction, at Kinlochleven in Argyllshire, where the primary design originated from Morrison. In the 1920s a third plant was erected at Fort William, in the lee of Ben Nevis, with hydroelectric generators providing some 75 MW. Alumina factories were constructed at Burntisland on the Firth of Forth and, in the 1930s, at Newport in Monmouthshire. Rolling mills were developed at Milton in Staffordshire, Warrington, and Falkirk in Stirlingshire, this last coming into use in the 1940s, by which time the company had a primary-metal output of more than 30,000 tonnes a year. Morrison was closely involved in all of these developments. He retired in 1946 as Deputy Chairman of BAC.

Principal Honours and Distinctions
Commander of the Order of St Olav of Norway 1933 (BAC had manufacturing interests in Norway). Knighted 1943. Vice-Chairman, British Non-Ferrous Metals Research Association, Faraday Society, Institute of Metals. Institute of Metals Platinum Medal 1942.

Bibliography
1939, 'Aluminium and highland water power', *Journal of the Institute of Metals* 65: 17–36 (seventeenth autumn lecture),

See also **Hall, Charles Martin**.

JKA

Morse, Samuel Finley Breeze

b. 27 April 1791 Charlestown, Massachusetts, USA
d. 2 April 1872 New York City, New York, USA

American portrait painter and inventor, best known for his invention of the telegraph and so-called Morse code.

Following early education at Phillips Academy, Andover, at the age of 14 years Morse went to Yale College, where he developed interests in painting and electricity. Upon graduating in 1810 he became a clerk to a Washington publisher and a pupil of Washington Allston, a well-known American painter. The following year he travelled to Europe and entered the London studio of another American artist, Benjamin West, successfully exhibiting at the Royal Academy as well as winning a prize and medal for his sculpture. Returning to Boston and finding little success as a 'historical-style' painter, he built up a thriving portrait business, moving in 1818 to Charleston, South Carolina, where three years later he established the (now defunct) South Carolina Academy of Fine Arts. In 1825 he was back in New York, but following the death of his wife and both of his parents that year, he embarked on an extended tour of European art galleries. In 1832, on the boat back to America, he met Charles T. Jackson, who told him of the discovery of the electromagnet and fired his interest in telegraphy to the extent that Morse immediately began to make suggestions for electrical communications and, apparently, devised a form of printing telegraph. Although he returned to his painting and in 1835 was appointed the first Professor of the Literature of Art and Design at the University of New York City, he began to spend more and more time experimenting in telegraphy. In 1836 he invented a relay as a means of extending the cable distance over which telegraph signals could be sent. At this time he became acquainted with Alfred **Vail**, and the following year, when the US government published the requirements for a national telegraph service, they set out to produce a workable system, with finance provided by Vail's father (who, usefully, owned an ironworks). A patent was filed on 6 October 1837 and a successful demonstration using the so-called Morse code was given on 6 January 1838; the work was, in fact, almost certainly largely that of Vail. As a result of the demonstration a Bill was put forward to Congress for $30,000 for an experimental line between Washington and Baltimore. This was eventually passed and the line was completed, and on 24 May 1844 the first message, 'What hath God wrought', was sent between the two cities. In the meantime Morse also worked on the insulation of submarine cables by means of pitch tar and indiarubber.

With success achieved, Morse offered his invention to the Government for $100,000, but this was declined, so the invention remained in private hands. To exploit it, Morse founded the Magnetic Telephone Company in 1845, amalgamating the following year with the telegraph company of a Henry O'Reilly to form Western Union. Having failed to obtain patents in Europe, he now found himself in litigation with others in the USA, but eventually, in 1854, the US Supreme Court decided in his favour and he soon became very wealthy. In 1857 a proposal was made for a telegraph service across the whole of the USA; this was completed in just over four months in 1861. Four years later work began on a link to Europe via Canada, Alaska, the Aleutian Islands and Russia, but it was abandoned with the completion of the transatlantic cable, a venture in which he also had some involvement. Showered with honours, Morse became a generous philanthropist in his later years. By 1883 the company he had created was worth $80 million and had a virtual monopoly in the USA.

Principal Honours and Distinctions
LLD, Yale 1846. Fellow of the Academy of Arts and Sciences 1849. Celebratory Banquet, New York, 1869. Statue in New York Central Park 1871. Austrian Gold Medal of Scientific Merit. Danish Knight of the Danneborg. French Légion d'honneur. Italian Knight of St Lazaro and Mauritio. Portuguese Knight of the Tower and Sword. Turkish Order of Glory.

Bibliography
E.L. Morse (ed.), 1975, *Letters and Journals*, New York: Da Capo Press (facsimile of a 1914 edition).

Further Reading
J. Munro, 1891, *Heroes of the Telegraph* (discusses his telegraphic work and its context).
C. Mabee, 1943, *The American Leonardo: A Life of Samuel Morse*; reprinted 1969 (a detailed biography).

KF

Morton, William Thomas Green
b. 1819 Charlton, Massachusetts, USA
d. 1868 New York, USA

American dentist, pioneer of inhalation anaesthesia using ether.

He received his dental training at Baltimore College of Dental Surgery and by 1842 was in a short-lived partnership with Horace **Wells**. Following the latter's successful dental anaesthesia using nitrous oxide in 1844 and his later failures of general anaesthesia, Morton embarked on a period of medical training at Massachusetts Medical College. The use of ether had been suggested by an acquaintance, Charles Jackson, a chemist and geologist, and in 1846 Morton commenced his investigations with a dog, himself and two assistants as subjects. The first major operation under ether general anaesthesia was performed at the Massachusetts General Hospital in October 1846. The technique speedily gained widespread acceptance in America and Europe. Morton's later life was bedevilled by prolonged acrimony over the question of priority of the discovery.

Bibliography
1847, *Remarks on the Proper Mode of Administering Sulphuric Ether by Inhalation*, Boston.

Further Reading
W.J. Morton, 1905, *Memoranda Relating to the Discovery of Surgical Anaesthesia*.
B.M. Duncum, 1947, *Development of Inhalational Anaesthesia*.

MG

Moulton, Alexander
b. 9 April 1920 Stratford-on-Avon

English inventor of vehicle suspension systems and the Moulton bicycle.

He spent his childhood at The Hall in Bradford-on-Avon. He was educated at Marlborough College, and in 1937 was apprenticed to the Sentinel Steam Wagon Company of Shrewsbury. About that same time he went to King's College, Cambridge, where he took the Mechanical Sciences Tripos. It was then wartime, and he did research on aero-engines at the Bristol Aeroplane Company, where he became Personal Assistant to Sir Roy Fedden. He left Bristol's in 1945 to join his family firm, Spencer & Moulton, of which he eventually became Technical Director and built up the Research Department. In 1948 he invented his first suspension unit, the 'Flexitor', in which an inner shaft and an outer shell were separated by an annular rubber body which was bonded to both.

In 1848 his great-grandfather had founded the family firm in an old woollen mill, to manufacture vulcanized rubber products under Charles **Goodyear**'s patent. The firm remained a family business with Spencer's, consultants in railway engineering, until 1956 when it was sold to the Avon Rubber Company. He then formed Moulton Developments to continue his work on vehicle suspensions in the stables attached to The Hall. Sponsored by the British Motor Corporation (BMC) and the Dunlop Rubber Company, he invented a rubber cone spring in 1951 which was later used in the BMC Mini (see **Issigonis, Sir Alexander Arnold Constantine**): by 1994 over 4 million Minis had been fitted with these springs, made by Dunlop. In 1954 he patented the Hydrolastic suspension system, in which all four wheels were independently sprung with combined rubber springs and damper assembly, the weight being supported by fluid under pressure, and the wheels on each side being interconnected, front to rear. In 1962 he formed Moulton Bicycles Ltd, having designed an improved bicycle system for adult use. The conventional bicycle frame was replaced by a flat-sided oval steel tube F-frame on a novel rubber front and rear suspension, with the wheel size reduced to 41 cm (16 in.) with high-pressure tyres. Raleigh Industries Ltd having refused his offer to produce the Moulton Bicycle under licence, he set up his own factory on his estate, producing 25,000 bicycles between 1963 and 1966. In 1967 he sold out to Raleigh and set up as Bicycle Consultants Ltd while continuing the suspension development of Moulton Developments Ltd. In the 1970s the combined firms employed some forty staff, nearly 50 per cent of whom were graduates.

He won the Queen's Award for Industry in 1967 for technical innovation in Hydrolastic car suspension and the Moulton Bicycle. Since that time he has continued his innovative work on suspensions and the bicycle. In 1983 he introduced the AM bicycle series of very sophisticated space-frame design with suspension and 43 cm (17 in.) wheels; this machine holds the world speed record fully formed at 82 km/h (51 mph). The current Rover 100 and MGF use his Hydragas interconnected suspension. By 1994 over 7 million cars had been fitted with Moulton suspensions. He has won many design awards and prizes, and has been awarded three honorary doctorates of engineering. He is active in engineering and design education.

Principal Honours and Distinctions
Queen's Award for Industry 1967; CBE; RDI. Fellow of the Royal Academy of Engineering.

Further Reading
P.R. Whitfield, 1975, *Creativity in Industry*, London: Penguin Books.

IMcN

Mouriés, Hippolyte Mège
b. 24 October 1817 Draguignan, France
d. 1880 France

French inventor of margarine.

The son of a schoolmaster, Mouriés became a chemist's assistant in his home town at the age of 16. He then spent a period of training in Aix-en-Provence, and in 1838 he moved to Paris, where he became Assistant to the Resident Pharmacist at the Hotel Dieu Hospital. He stayed there until 1846 but never sat his final exams. His main success during this period was with the drug Copahin, which was used against syphilis; he invented an oral formulation of the drug by treating it with nitric acid. In the 1840s he took out various patents relating to tanning and to sugar extraction, and in the 1850s he turned his attention to food research. He developed a health chocolate with his calcium phosphate protein, and also developed a method that made it possible to gain 14 per cent more white bread from a given quantity of wheat. He lectured on this process in Berlin and Brussels and was awarded two gold medals. After 1862 he concentrated his research on fats. His margarine process was based on the cold saponification of milk in fat emulsions and was patented in both France and Britain in 1869. These experiments were carried out at the Ferme Impériale de La Faisanderie in Vincennes, the personal property of the Emperor, and it is therefore likely that they were State-funded. He sold his knowledge to the

Dutch firm Jurgens in 1871, and between 1873 and 1874 he also sold his British, American and Prussian rights. His final patent, in 1875, was for canned meat.

Principal Honours and Distinctions
Napoleon III awarded him the Légion d'honneur for his work on wheat and bread.

Further Reading
J.H. van Stuyvenberg (ed.), *Margarine: An Economic, Social and Scientific History, 1869–1969* (provides a brief outline of the life of Mouriés in a comprehensive history of his discovery.

AP

Moxon, Joseph
b. 8 August 1627 Wakefield, Yorkshire, England
d. 1700

English publisher of mathematical and technical books.

Moxon acquired a knowledge of mathematics, map making and many technical arts, to which, as a result of some time spent in Holland, he added a knowledge of languages. By 1657 he was established in Cornhill in London, 'at the sign of Atlas', where he published and sold 'all manner of mathematical books or instruments and maps whatsoever'. Soon after 1660, Moxon was appointed Hydrographer to King Charles II, i.e. map and chart printer and seller. By this time his shop was on Ludgate Hill, and in 1683 it had moved to the west side of Fleet Ditch, but retained its name 'at the sign of Atlas'. Moxon's most important publishing venture was a series of handbooks, never completed, entitled *Mechanick Exercises or the Doctrine of Handy-Works*. It was begun in 1677 and was intended to be published monthly and cover the whole range of practical techniques, such as metal-turning and woodworking. However, the series was suspended after a year or so due to the effects of the Popish Plot, which 'took off the minds of my few customers from buying'. He resumed publication with the most important of these works, *Mechanick Exercises on the Whole Art of Printing*, which appeared in 1683–4. Although printing had been invented more than two centuries earlier, this is the first detailed account in any language of printing, and includes all aspects of the process: type casting, setting, and construction and operation of the press itself, together with the organization of the printing shop. It served as the basis of future handbooks throughout the age of the hand press.

Principal Honours and Distinctions
FRS 1678.

Bibliography
1683–4, *Mechanick Exercises on the Whole Art of Printing*; reprinted 1958, eds H. Davies and H. Carter, London: Oxford University Press (this facsimile reprint includes the most detailed account of Moxon's life and work, with full bibliographical details of the book itself).

LRD

Musa ibn Shakir, Banu
See **Banu Musa ibn Shakir**.

Mudge, Thomas
b. 1715 Exeter, England
d. 14 November 1794 Walworth, England

English clock- and watchmaker who invented the lever escapement that was ultimately used in all mechanical watches.

Thomas Mudge was the son of a clergyman and schoolmaster who, recognizing his son's mechanical aptitude, apprenticed him to the eminent London clock- and watchmaker George **Graham**. Mudge became free of the Clockmakers' Company in 1738 and set up on his own account after Graham's death in 1751. Around 1755 he formed a partnership with William Dutton, another apprentice of Graham. The firm produced conventional clocks and watches of excellent quality, but Mudge had also established a reputation for making highly innovative individual pieces. The most significant of these was the watch with a detached-lever escapement that he completed in 1770, although the idea had occurred to him as early as 1754. This watch was purchased by George III for Queen Charlotte and is still in the Royal Collection. Shortly afterwards Mudge moved to Plymouth, to devote his time to the perfection of the marine chronometer, leaving the London business in the hands of Dutton. The chronometers he produced were comparable in performance to those of John **Harrison**, but like them they were too complicated and expensive to be produced in quantity.

Mudge's patron, Count Bruhl, recognized the potential of the detached-lever escapement, but Mudge was too involved with his marine chronometers to make a watch for him. He did, however, provide Bruhl with a large-scale model of his escapement, from which the Swiss expatriate Josiah Emery was able to make a watch in 1782. Over the next decade Emery made a limited number of similar watches for wealthy clients, and it was the performance of these watches that demonstrated the worth of the escapement. The detached-lever escapement took some time to be adopted universally, but this was facilitated in the nineteenth century by the development of a cheaper form, the pin lever. By the end of the century the detached-lever escapement was used in one form or another in practically all mechanical watches and portable clocks. If a watch is to be a good timekeeper the balance must be free to swing with as little interference as possible from the escapement. In this respect the cylinder escapement is an improvement on the verge, although it still exerts a frictional force on the balance. The lever escapement is a further improvement because it detaches itself from the balance after delivering the impulse which keeps it oscillating.

Principal Honours and Distinctions
Clockmaker to George III 1776.

Further Reading
T. Mudge, Jr, 1799, *A Description with Plates of the Time-Keeper Invented by the Late Mr. Thomas Mudge*, London (contains a tract written by his father and the text of his letters to Count Bruhl).
C. Clutton and G. Daniels, 1986, *Watches*, 4th edn, London (provides further biographical information and a good account of the history of the lever watch).
R. Good, 1978, *Britten's Watch & Clock Maker's Handbook Dictionary and Guide*, 16th edn, London, pp. 190–200 (provides a good technical description of Mudge's lever escapement and its later development).

DV

Muller, Paul Hermann
b. 12 January 1899 Olten, Solothurn, Switzerland
d. 13 October 1965 Basle, Switzerland

Swiss chemist, inventor of the insecticide DDT.

Muller was educated in Basle and his interest in chemistry was stimulated when he started work as a laboratory assistant in the chemical factory of Dreyfus & Co. After further laboratory work, he entered the University of Basle in 1919, achieving his doctorate in 1925. The same year, he entered the dye works of J.R. Geigy AG as a research chemist. He spent the rest of his career there, rising to the position of Deputy Head of Pest Control Research. From 1935 he began the search for an insecticide that was fast acting and persistent, but harmless to plants and warm-blooded animals. In 1940 he patented the use of a compound known since 1873, dichlorodiphenyltrichloroethane, or DDT. It could be easily and cheaply manufactured and was highly effective. Muller obtained a Swiss patent for DDT in 1940 and it went into commercial production two years later. One useful application of DDT at the end of the Second World War was in killing lice to prevent typhus epidemics. It was widely used and an important factor in farmers' post-war success in raising food production, but after twenty years or so, some species of insects were found to have developed resistance to its action, thus limiting its effectiveness. Worse, it was found to be harmful to other animals, which gave rise to anxieties about its persistence in the food chain. By the 1970s its use was banned or strictly limited in developed countries. Nevertheless, in its earlier career it had conferred undoubted benefits and was highly valued, as reflected by the award of a Nobel Prize in Medicine or Physiology in 1948.

Principal Honours and Distinctions
Nobel Prize in Medicine or Physiology 1948.

Bibliography
Muller described DDT and related compounds in two papers in *Helvetica chimica acta* for 1944 and 1946.

Further Reading
Obituary, 1965, *Nature* 208: 1,043–4.

LRD

Mumma, Jacob

See **Momma, Jacob**.

Murchland, William

fl. 1889 Kilmarnock, Scotland

Scottish inventor of a vacuum milking machine.

The milking machine patented in 1889 by William Murchland, a sanitary engineer from Kilmarnock, applied a continuous suction to the teat of a cow by means of a vacuum produced by draining water from a sealed system. He first began experiments in response to a shortage of experienced milkers in his region. The apparatus was first erected on the farms of a Mr Shaw at Haining Mains and a John Spier of Newton, near Glasgow. The latter carried out a season of milking on his herd of 35 cows, but despite numerous modifications was unhappy with the yield and the veterinary problems encountered. The concept needed the addition of Shield's pulsator before it performed satisfactorily and without damage to the cow.

Further Reading

John Spier, 1982, 'A Season's experiment of a mechanical milking apparatus', *Transactions of the Highland and Agricultural Society of Scotland*, pp. 19–33 (provides an account of Murchland's experiences).

AP

Murdock (Murdoch), William

b. 21 August 1754 Cumnock, Ayrshire, Scotland
d. 15 November 1839 Handsworth, Birmingham, England

Scottish engineer and inventor, pioneer in coal-gas production.

He was the third child and the eldest of three boys born to John Murdoch and Anna Bruce. His father, a millwright and joiner, spelled his name Murdock on moving to England. He was educated for some years at Old Cumnock Parish School and in 1777, with his father, he built a 'wooden horse', supposed to have been a form of cycle. In 1777 he set out for the Soho manufactory of **Boulton** & **Watt**, where he quickly found employment, Boulton supposedly being impressed by the lad's hat. This was oval and made of wood, and young William had turned it

himself on a lathe of his own manufacture. Murdock quickly became Boulton & Watt's representative in Cornwall, where there was a flourishing demand for steam-engines. He lived at Redruth during this period.

It is said that a number of the inventions generally ascribed to James Watt are in fact as much due to Murdock as to Watt. Examples are the piston and slide valve and the sun-and-planet gearing. A number of other inventions are attributed to Murdock alone: typical of these is the oscillating cylinder engine which obviated the need for an overhead beam.

In about 1784 he planned a steam-driven road carriage of which he made a working model. He also planned a high-pressure non-condensing engine. The model carriage was demonstrated before Murdock's friends and travelled at a speed of 6–8 mph (10–13 km/h). Boulton and Watt were both antagonistic to their employees' developing independent inventions, and when in 1786 Murdock set out with his model for the Patent Office, having received no reply to a letter he had sent to Watt, Boulton intercepted him on the open road near Exeter and dissuaded him from going any further.

In 1785 he married Mary Painter, daughter of a mine captain. She bore him four children, two of whom died in infancy, those surviving eventually joining their father at the Soho Works. Murdock was a great believer in pneumatic power: he had a pneumatic bell-push at Sycamore House, his home near Soho. The patternmakers lathe at the Soho Works worked for thirty-five years from an air motor. He also conceived the idea of a vacuum piston engine to exhaust a pipe, later developed by the London Pneumatic Despatch Company's railway and the forerunner of the atmospheric railway.

Another field in which Murdock was a pioneer was the gas industry. In 1791, in Redruth, he was experimenting with different feedstocks in his home-cum-office in Cross Street: of wood, peat and coal, he preferred the last. He designed and built in the backyard of his house a prototype generator, washer, storage and distribution plant, and publicized the efficiency of coal gas as an illuminant by using it to light his own home. In 1794 or 1795 he informed Boulton and Watt of his experimental work and of its success, suggesting that a patent should be applied for. James Watt Junior was now in the firm and was against patenting the idea since they had had so much trouble with previous patents and had been involved in so much litigation. He refused Murdock's request and for a short time Murdock left the firm to go home to his father's mill. Boulton & Watt soon recognized the loss of a valuable servant and, in a short time, he was again employed at Soho, now as Engineer and Superintendent at the increased salary of £300 per year plus a 1 per cent commission. From this income, he left £14,000 when he died in 1839.

In 1798 the workshops of Boulton and Watt were permanently lit by gas, starting with the foundry building. The 180 ft (55 m) façade of the Soho works was illuminated by gas for the Peace of Paris in June 1814. By 1804, Murdock had brought his apparatus to a point where Boulton & Watt were able to canvas for orders. Murdock continued with the company after the death of James Watt in 1819, but retired in 1830 and continued to live at Sycamore House, Handsworth, near Birmingham.

Principal Honours and Distinctions
Royal Society Rumford Gold Medal 1808.

Further Reading
S. Smiles, 1861, *Lives of the Engineers*, Vol. IV: *Boulton and Watt*, London: John Murray.
H.W. Dickinson and R. Jenkins, 1927, *James Watt and the Steam Engine*, Oxford: Clarendon Press.
J.A. McCash, 1966, 'William Murdoch. Faithful servant' in E.G. Semler (ed.), *The Great Masters. Engineering Heritage*, Vol. II, London: Institution of Mechanical Engineers/Heinemann.

IMcN

Murphy, John Benjamin
b. 21 December 1857 Appleton, Wisconsin, USA
d. 11 August 1916 Mackinac, Michigan, USA

American surgeon, pioneer of intestinal anastomosis and proponent of joint replacement.

Murphy qualified in 1879 at Rush Medical College. After postgraduate study in Vienna, he returned to Chicago and was appointed Professor of Surgery at Northwestern University. He pioneered surgical techniques in the pneumothoracic, biliary and gastrointestinal systems with the invention of the Murphy 'button' for intestinal anastomosis. He also originated a procedure for the replacement of infected joints utilizing a living graft of fascial tissue. He was described by W.J. Mayo as 'the surgical genius of our century'.

Principal Honours and Distinctions
Knight Commander of the Order of St Gregory 1910. Hon. Fellow, Royal College of Surgeons 1913. Laetare Medal, Notre Dame University 1902.

Bibliography
1897, 'Resection of arteries and veins injured in continuity', *Medical Record*, New York.

Further Reading
Kelly & Burrage, 1928, *The Surgical Clinics of John B. Murphy MD at Mercy Hospital*, Chicago.

MG

Murray, John Mackay
b. 25 June 1902 Glasgow, Scotland
d. 5 August 1966 Maplehurst, Sussex, England

Scottish naval architect who added to the understanding of the structural strength of ships.

Murray was educated in Glasgow at Allan Glen's School and then at the University, from which he graduated in naval architecture in 1922. He served an apprenticeship simultaneously with Barclay Curle & Co., rising to the rank of Assistant Shipyard Manager before leaving in 1927 to join Lloyd's Register of Shipping. After an initial year in Newcastle, he joined the head office in London, which was to be base for the remainder of his working life. Starting with plan approval, he worked his way to experimental work on ship structures and was ultimately given the massive task of revising Lloyd's Rules and placing them on a scientific basis. During the Second World War he acted as liaison officer between Lloyd's and the Admiralty. Throughout his career he presented no fewer than twenty-two papers on ship design, and of these nearly half dealt with hull longitudinal strength. This work won him considerable acclaim and several awards and was of fundamental importance to the shipping industry. The Royal Institution of Naval Architects honoured Murray in 1960 by inviting him to present one of the only two papers read at their centenary meeting: 'Merchant ships 1860–1960'. At Lloyd's Register he rose to Chief Ship Surveyor, and at the time of his death was Honorary Vice-President of the Royal Institution of Naval Architects.

Principal Honours and Distinctions
MBE 1946. Honorary Vice-President, Royal Institution of Naval Architects. Royal Institution of Naval Architects Froude Gold Medal. Institute of Marine Engineers Silver Medal. Premium of the Institution of Engineers and Shipbuilders in Scotland.

FMW

Murray, Matthew
b. 1765 near Newcastle upon Tyne, England
d. 20 February 1826 Holbeck, Leeds, England

English mechanical engineer and steam engine, locomotive and machine-tool pioneer.

Matthew Murray was apprenticed at the age of 14 to a blacksmith who probably also did millwrighting work. He then worked as a journeyman mechanic at Stockton-on-Tees, where he had experience with machinery for a flax mill at Darlington. Trade in the Stockton area became slack in 1788 and Murray sought work in Leeds, where he was employed by John Marshall, who owned a flax mill at Adel, located about 5 miles (8 km) from Leeds. He soon became Marshall's chief mechanic, and when in 1790 a new mill was built in the Holbeck district of Leeds by Marshall and his partner Benyon, Murray was responsible for the installation of the machinery. At about this time he took out two patents relating to improvements in textile machinery.

In 1795 he left Marshall's employment and, in partnership with David Wood (1761–1820), established a general engineering and millwrighting business at Mill Green, Holbeck. In the following year the firm moved to a larger site at Water Lane, Holbeck, and additional capital was provided by two new partners, James Fenton (1754–1834) and William Lister (1796–1811). Lister was a sleeping partner and the firm was known as Fenton, Murray & Wood and was organized so that Fenton kept the accounts, Wood was the administrator and took charge of the workshops, while Murray provided the technical expertise. The factory was extended in 1802 by the construction of a fitting shop of circular form, after which the establishment became known as the 'Round Foundry'.

In addition to textile machinery, the firm soon began the manufacture of machine tools and steam-engines. In this field it became a serious rival to **Boulton & Watt**, who privately acknowledged Murray's superior craftsmanship, particularly in foundry work, and resorted to some industrial espionage to discover details of his techniques. Murray obtained patents for improvements in steam engines in 1799, 1801 and 1802. These included automatic regulation of draught, a mechanical stoker and his short-D slide valve. The patent of 1801 was successfully opposed by Boulton & Watt. An important contribution of Murray to the development of the steam engine was the use of a bedplate so that the engine became a compact, self-contained unit instead of separate components built into an engine-house.

Murray was one of the first, if not the very first, to build machine tools for sale. However, this was not the case with the planing machine, which he is said to have invented to produce flat surfaces for his slide valves. Rather than being patented, this machine was kept secret, although it was apparently in use before 1814.

In 1812 Murray was engaged by John Blenkinsop (1783–1831) to build locomotives for his rack railway from Middleton Colliery to Leeds (about $3\frac{1}{2}$ miles or 5.6 km). Murray was responsible for their design and they were fitted with two double-acting cylinders and cranks at right angles, an important step in the development of the steam locomotive. About six of these locomotives were built for the Middleton and other colliery railways and some were in use for over twenty years. Murray also supplied engines for many early steamboats. In addition, he built some hydraulic machinery and in 1814 patented a hydraulic press for baling cloth.

Murray's son-in-law, Richard Jackson, later became a partner in the firm, which was then styled Fenton, Murray & Jackson. The firm went out of business in 1843.

Principal Honours and Distinctions
Society of Arts Gold Medal 1809 (for machine for hackling flax).

Further Reading
L.T.C. Rolt, 1962, *Great Engineers*, London (contains a good short biography).
E. Kilburn Scott (ed.), 1928, *Matthew Murray, Pioneer Engineer*, Leeds (a collection of essays and source material).
C.F. Dendy Marshall, 1953, *A History of Railway Locomotives Down to the End of the Year 1831*, London.
L.T.C. Rolt, 1965, *Tools for the Job*, London; repub. 1986 (provides information on Murray's machine-tool work).
Some of Murray's correspondence with Simon Goodrich of the Admiralty has been published in *Transactions of the Newcomen Society* 3 (1922–3); 6 (1925–6); 18 (1937–8); and 32 (1959–60).

RTS

Mushet, Robert Forester

b. 8 April 1811 Coleford, Gloucestershire, England
d. 19 January 1891 Cheltenham, Gloucestershire, England

English steelmaker who invented the first alloy steel.

Mushet acquired his metallurgical knowledge in his father's ironworks at Coleford in the Forest of Dean. In 1848 his attention seems to have been drawn to the use of manganese in ironworking, in the form of spiegeleisen, an alloy of iron and manganese derived from a Prussian iron ore consisting essentially of a double carbonate of iron and manganese. This alloy came into its own in 1856 with the invention of the **Bessemer** steelmaking process, for Mushet found that if molten spiegeleisen was added to the Bessemer iron the quality of the product was greatly improved. Mushet patented this process, but when he failed to pay the stamp duty due in 1859 his rights lapsed. Bessemer independently discovered the use of spiegeleisen, although Mushet continued to maintain his priority.

Mushet's most important discovery was that of tungsten steel, the forerunner of a long line of alloy steels. While working a small crucible steelworks at Coleford, he was asked by a Scottish manufacturer to make a hard-metal tool, but he found that the metal was unsatisfactory. After experiments, he found that an alloy steel containing about 8 per cent tungsten possessed remarkable properties. It proved to be self-hardening, i.e. after forging and being allowed to cool, it was found to have become hardened, without the need for the heat treatment that was normally required. Also, unlike other hardened steels, it did not lose its hardness when heated even to dull-red heat. It would thus remain hard in a cutting tool that had run hot through deep cutting. Mushet's tungsten steel was brought into use in 1868 and was of great benefit to engineers, who were making increasing demands on cutting machines.

Further Reading
Biographical notice, 1878, *Journal of the Iron and Steel Institute*: 1–4.

LRD

Muspratt, James

b. 12 August 1793 Dublin, Ireland
d. 4 May 1886 Seaforth Hall, near Liverpool, England

British industrial chemist.

Educated in Dublin, Muspratt was apprenticed at the age of 14 to a wholesale chemist and druggist, with whom he remained for three or four years. Muspratt then went in search of the Napoleonic War and found it first in Spain and finally as Second Officer on a naval vessel. Finding the life unpleasantly harsh, he left his ship off Swansea and returned to Dublin around 1814. Soon afterwards, he received an inheritance, much reduced and delayed by litigation in Chancery. He began manufacturing chemicals in a small way and from 1818 set up as a manufacturer of prussiate of potash. In 1823, Muspratt took advantage of the removal of the salt tax to establish the first plant in England for the large-scale manufacture of soda by the **Leblanc** process. His first soda works was on the outskirts of Liverpool, but when this proved inadequate, he established a larger factory at St Helens, Lancashire, where the raw materials lay close at hand. This district has remained an important centre of the British chemical industry ever since. Although the plant was successful commercially, there were environmental problems. The equipment for condensing the hydrochloric acid gas produced were inadequate and this caused extensive damage to local vegetation, so that Muspratt had to contend with legal action lasting from 1832 to 1850. Eventually Muspratt moved his alkali manufacture to Widnes, which also became a great centre for the chemical industry.

Further Reading

Obituary, 1886, *Journal of the Society of Chemical Industry* 5:314.

J.F. Allen, 1890, *Memoir of James Muspratt*, London.

LRD

Muybridge, Eadweard

b. 9 April 1830 Kingston upon Thames, England

d. 8 May 1904 Kingston upon Thames, England

English photographer and pioneer of sequence photography of movement.

He was born Edward Muggeridge, but later changed his name, taking the Saxon spelling of his first name and altering his surname, first to Muygridge and then to Muybridge. He emigrated to America in 1851, working in New York in bookbinding and selling as a commission agent for the London Printing and Publishing Company. Through contact with a New York daguerreotypist, Silas T. Selleck, he acquired an interest in photography that developed after his move to California in 1855. On a visit to England in 1860 he learned the wet-collodion process from a friend, Arthur Brown, and acquired the best photographic equipment available in London before returning to America. In 1867, under his trade pseudonym 'Helios', he set out to record the scenery of the Far West with his mobile dark-room, christened 'The Flying Studio'.

His reputation as a photographer of the first rank spread, and he was commissioned to record the survey visit of Major-General Henry W. Halleck to Alaska and also to record the territory through which the Central Pacific Railroad was being constructed. Perhaps because of this latter project, he was approached by the President of the Central Pacific, Leland Stanford, to attempt to photograph a horse trotting at speed. There was a long-standing controversy among racing men as to whether a trotting horse had all four hooves off the ground at any point; Stanford felt that it did, and hoped than an 'instantaneous' photograph would settle the matter once and for all. In May 1872 Muybridge photographed the horse 'Occident', but without any great success

because the current wet-collodion process normally required many seconds, even in a good light, for a good result. In April 1873 he managed to produce some better negatives, in which a recognizable silhouette of the horse showed all four feet above the ground at the same time.

Soon after, Muybridge left his young wife, Flora, in San Francisco to go with the army sent to put down the revolt of the Modoc Indians. While he was busy photographing the scenery and the combatants, his wife had an affair with a Major Harry Larkyns. On his return, finding his wife pregnant, he had several confrontations with Larkyns, which culminated in his shooting him dead. At his trial for murder, in February 1875, Muybridge was acquitted by the jury on the grounds of justifiable homicide; he left soon after on a long trip to South America.

He again took up his photographic work when he returned to North America and Stanford asked him to take up the action-photography project once more. Using a new shutter design he had developed while on his trip south, and which would operate in as little as 1/1,000 of a second, he obtained more detailed pictures of 'Occident' in July 1877. He then devised a new scheme, which Stanford sponsored at his farm at Palo Alto. A 50 ft (15 m) long shed was constructed, containing twelve cameras side by side, and a white background marked off with vertical, numbered lines was set up. Each camera was fitted with Muybridge's high-speed shutter, which was released by an electromagnetic catch. Thin threads stretched across the track were broken by the horse as it moved along, closing spring electrical contacts which released each shutter in turn. Thus, in about half a second, twelve photographs were obtained that showed all the phases of the movement.

Although the pictures were still little more than silhouettes, they were very sharp, and sequences published in scientific and photographic journals throughout the world excited considerable attention. By replacing the threads with an electrical commutator device, which allowed the release of the shutters at precise intervals, Muybridge was able to take series of actions by other animals and humans. From 1880 he lectured in America and Europe, projecting his results in motion on the screen with his Zoopraxiscope projector. In August 1883 he received a grant of $40,000 from the University of Pennsylvania to carry on his work there. Using the vastly improved gelatine dry-plate process and new, improved multiple-camera apparatus, during 1884 and 1885 he produced over 100,000 photographs, of which 20,000 were reproduced in *Animal Locomotion* in 1887. The subjects were animals of all kinds, and human figures, mostly nude, in a wide range of activities. The quality of the photographs was extremely good, and the publication attracted considerable attention and praise.

Muybridge returned to England in 1894; his last publications were *Animals in Motion* (1899) and *The Human Figure in Motion* (1901). His influence on the world of art was enormous, overturning the conventional representations of action hitherto used by artists. His work in pioneering the use of sequence photography led to the science of chronophotography developed by **Marey** and others, and stimulated many inventors, notably Thomas **Edison** to work which led to the introduction of cinematography in the 1890s.

Bibliography
1887, *Animal Locomotion*, Philadelphia.
1893, *Descriptive Zoopraxography*, Pennsylvania.
1899, *Animals in Motion*, London.
1901, *The Human Figure in Motion*, London.

Further Reading
1973, *Eadweard Muybridge: The Stanford Years*, Stanford.
G. Hendricks, 1975, *Muybridge: The Father of the Motion Picture*, New York.
R. Haas, 1976, *Muybridge: Man in Motion*, California.
B. Coe, 1992, *Muybridge and the Chromophotographers*, London.

BC

Mylne, Robert
b. 1733 Edinburgh, Scotland
d. 1811

Scottish engineer, architect and bridge-builder.

Mylne was the eldest son of Thomas Mylne, Surveyor to the City of Edinburgh. Little is known of his early education. In 1754, at the age of 21, he left Edinburgh by sea and journeyed to Rome, where he attended the Academy of St Luke. There he received the first prize for architecture. In 1759 he left Rome to travel back to England, where he arrived in time for the competition then going ahead for the design and building of a new bridge across the Thames at Blackfriars. Against 68 other competitors, Mylne won the competition; the work took some ten years to complete.

In 1760 he was appointed Engineer and Architect to the City of London, and in 1767 Joint Engineer to the New River Company together with Henry Mill, who died within a few years to leave Mylne to become Chief Engineer in 1770. Thus for the next forty years he was in charge of all the works for the New River Company between Clerkenwell and Ware, the opposite ends of London's main water supply. By 1767 he had also been appointed to a number of other important posts, which included Surveyor to Canterbury Cathedral and St Paul's Cathedral. In addition to undertaking his responsibilities for these great public buildings, he designed many private houses and villas all over the country, including several buildings for the Duke of Argyll on the Inverary Castle estate.

Mylne was also responsible for the design of a great number of bridges, waterworks and other civil engineering works throughout Britain. Called in to advise on the Norwich city waterworks, he fell out with Joseph **Bramah** in a somewhat spectacular dispute.

For much of his life Mylne lived at the Water House at the New River Head at Islington, from which he could direct much of the work on that waterway that came under his supervision. He also had residences in New Bridge Street and, as Clerk of Works, at Greenwich Hospital. Towards the end of his life he built himself a small house at Amwell, a country retreat at the outer end of the New River. He kept a diary from 1762 to 1810 which includes only brief memoranda but which shows a remarkable diligence in travelling all over the country by stagecoach and by post-chaise. He was a freemason, as were many of his family; he married Mary Home on 10 September 1770, with whom he had ten children, four of whom survived into adulthood.

Principal Honours and Distinctions
Fellow of the Royal Society 1767.

Further Reading
Dictionary of National Biography, London.
A.E. Richardson, 1955, *Robert Mylne, 1733–1811, Engineer and Architect*, London: Batsford.

IMcN

N

Nadar

See **Tournachon, Gaspard Félix**.

Napier, David

b. 1785 Scotland
d. 1873

Scottish engineer who devised printing machinery incorporating important improvements.

Born in Scotland, Napier moved to London to set up an engineering workshop in St Giles. In 1824 he was commissioned by Thomas Curson Hansard (1776–1833), who from 1803 began printing the debates in the Houses of Parliament, to make a perfecting press, i.e. one that printed on both sides of the paper. Known as the *Nay-Peer*, it was the first to incorporate grippers in order to improve register (the correct positioning of the paper on the inked type); the grippers took hold of a sheet of paper as it was fed on to the impression cylinder. Napier made several machines for Hansard, hand-powered at first but steam-powered from 1832. Napier did not patent the *Nay-Peer*, but in 1828 he took out a patent for a four-feeder press with a single impression cylinder, which had the then-usual 'stop and start' action while the bed carrying the inked type passed to and fro beneath it. To speed output, two years later Napier patented a press with two cylinders revolving in the same direction in place of the single-stop cylinder. Also in 1830, the firm of Napier and Son introduced an improved form of bed and platen press, which became the most popular of its kind; one remained in use at Oxford University Press into the twentieth century. Another invention of Napier's, in 1825, was an automatic inking device, with which turning the rounce or mechanism for moving the type bed under the platen activated inking rollers working on the type. Napier is credited with being the first to introduce the printing machine to Ireland, for the *Dublin Evening Post*. His cylinder machine was the first of its kind in North America, where it was seen by **Hoe** and others.

Further Reading
J. Moran, 1973, *Printing Presses*, London: Faber & Faber (contains details of Napier's printing machines).

LRD

Napier (Neper), John

b. 1550 Merchiston Castle, Edinburgh, Scotland
d. 4 April 1617 Merchiston Castle, Edinburgh, Scotland

Scottish mathematician and theological writer noted for his discovery of logarithms, a powerful aid to mathematical calculations.

Born into a family of Scottish landowners, at the early age of 13 years Napier went to the University of St Andrews in Fife, but he apparently left before taking his degree. An extreme Protestant, he was active in the struggles with the Roman Catholic Church and in 1594 he dedicated to James VI of Scotland his *Plaine Discovery of the Whole Revelation of St John*, an attempt to promote the Protestant case in the guise of a learned study. About this time, as well as being involved in the development of military equipment, he devoted much of his time to finding methods of simplifying the tedious calculations involved in astronomy. Eventually he realized that by representing numbers in terms of the power to which a 'base' number needed to be raised to produce them, it was possible to perform multiplication and division and to find roots, by the simpler processes of addition, substraction and integer division, respectively.

A description of the principle of his 'logarithms' (from the Gk. *logos*, reckoning, and *arithmos*, number), how he arrived at the idea and how they could be used was published in 1614 under the title *Mirifici Logarithmorum Canonis Descriptio*. Two years after his death his *Mirifici Logarithmorum Canonis Constructio* appeared, in which he explained how to calculate the logarithms of numbers and gave tables of them to eight significant figures, a novel feature being the use of the decimal point to distinguish the integral and fractional parts of the logarithm. As originally conceived, Napier's tables of logarithms were calculated using the natural number e (= 2.71828. . .) as the base, not directly, but in effect according to the formula: Naperian $\log x = 10^7(\log_e 10^7 - \log_e x)$ so that the original Naperian logarithm of a number decreased as the number increased. However, prior to his death he had readily acceded to a suggestion by Henry **Briggs** that it would greatly facilitate their use if logarithms were simply defined as the value to which the decimal base 10 needed to be raised to realize the number in question. He was almost certainly also aware of the work of Joost **Burgi**.

No doubt as an extension of his ideas of logarithms, Napier also devised a means of manually performing multiplication and division by means of a system of rods known as Napier's Bones, a forerunner of the modern slide-rule, which evolved as a result of successive developments by Edmund Gunther, William Oughtred and others. Other contributions to mathematics by Napier include important simplifying discoveries in spherical trigonometry. However, his discovery of logarithms was undoubtedly his greatest achievement.

Bibliography

Napier's '*Descriptio*' and his '*Constructio*' were published in English translation as *Description of the Marvelous Canon of Logarithms* (1857) and W.R. MacDonald's *Construction of the Marvelous Canon of Logarithms* (1889), which also catalogues all his works. His *Rabdologiae, seu Numerationis per Virgulas Libri Duo* (1617) was published in English as *Divining Rods, or Two Books of Numbering by Means of Rods* (1667).

Further Reading

D. Stewart and W. Minto, 1787, *An Account of the Life Writings and Inventions of John Napier of Merchiston* (an early account of Napier's work).
C.G. Knott (ed.), 1915, *Napier Tercentenary Memorial Volume* (the fullest account of Napier's work).

KF

Napier, Robert

b. 18 June 1791 Dumbarton, Scotland
d. 23 June 1876 Shandon, Dunbartonshire, Scotland

Scottish shipbuilder, one of the greatest shipbuilders of all time, known as the 'father' of Clyde shipbuilding.

Educated at Dumbarton Grammar School, Robert Napier had been destined for the Church but persuaded his father to let him serve an apprenticeship as a blacksmith under him. For a while he worked in Edinburgh, but then in 1815 he commenced business in Glasgow, the city that he served for the rest of his life. Initially his workshop was in Camlachie, but it was moved in 1836 to a riverside factory site at Lancefield in the heart of the City and again in 1841 to the Old Shipyard in the Burgh of Govan (then independent of the City of Glasgow). The business expanded through his preparedness to build steam machinery, beginning in 1823 with the engines for the paddle steamer *Leven*, still to be seen a few hundred metres from Napier's grave in Dumbarton. His name assured owners of quality, and business expanded after two key orders: one in 1836 for the Honourable East India Company; and the second two years later for the Royal Navy, hitherto the preserve of the Royal Dockyards and of the shipbuilders of south-east England. Napier's shipyard and engine shops, then known as Robert Napier and Sons, were to be awarded sixty Admiralty contracts in his lifetime, with a profound influence on ship and engine procurement for the Navy and on foreign governments, which for the first time placed substantial work in the United Kingdom.

Having had problems with hull subcontractors and also with the installation of machinery in wooden hulls, in 1843 Napier ventured into shipbuilding with the paddle steamer *Vanguard*, which was built of iron. The following year the Royal Navy took delivery of the iron-hulled *Jackall*, enabling Napier to secure the contract for the *Black Prince*, Britain's second ironclad and sister ship to HMS *Warrior* now preserved at Portsmouth. With so much work in iron Napier instigated studies into metallurgy, and the published work of David **Kirkaldy** bears witness to his open-handedness in assisting the industry. This service to industry was even more apparent in 1866 when the company laid out the Skelmorlie Measured Mile on the Firth of Clyde for ship testing, a mile still in use by ships of all nations.

The greatest legacy of Robert Napier was his training of young engineers, shipbuilders and naval architects. Almost every major Scottish shipyard, and some English too, was influenced by him and many of his early foremen left to set up rival establishments along the banks of the River Clyde. His close association with Samuel Cunard led to the setting up of the company now known as the Cunard Line. Napier designed and engined the first four ships, subcontracting the hulls of this historic quartet to other shipbuilders on the river. While he contributed only 2 per cent to the equity of the shipping line, they came back to him for many more vessels, including the magnificent paddle ship *Persia*, of 1855.

It is an old tradition on the Clyde that the smokestacks of ships are made by the engine-builders. The Cunard Line still uses red funnels with black bands, Napier's trademark, in honour of the engineer who set them going.

Principal Honours and Distinctions
Knight Commander of the Dannebrog (Denmark). President, Institution of Mechanical Engineers 1864. Honorary Member of the Glasgow Society of Engineers 1869.

Further Reading
James Napier, 1904, *The Life of Robert Napier*, Edinburgh, Blackwood.
J.M. Halliday, 1980–1, 'Robert Napier. The father of Clyde shipbuilding', *Transactions of the Institution of Engineers and Shipbuilders in Scotland* 124.
Fred M. Walker, 1984, *Song of the Clyde. A History of Clyde Shipbuilding*, Cambridge: PSL.

See also: **Fairbairn, Sir William**; **Thomson, Sir William**.

FMW

Nash, John
b. *c.*1752 (?) London, England
d. 13 May 1835 Cowes, Isle of Wight

English architect and town planner.

Nash's name is synonymous with the great scheme carried out for his patron, the Prince Regent, in the early nineteenth century: the development of Marylebone Park from 1811 constituted a 'garden city' for the wealthy in the centre of London. Although only a part of Nash's great scheme was actually achieved, an immense amount was carried out, comprising the Regent's Park and its surrounding terraces, the Regent's Street, including All Souls' Church, and the Regent's Palace in the Mall. Not least was Nash's exotic Royal Pavilion at Brighton.

From the early years of the nineteenth century, Nash and a number of other architects took advantage of the use of structural materials developed as a result of the Industrial Revolution; these included wrought and cast iron and various cements. Nash utilized iron widely in the Regent Street Quadrant, Carlton House Terrace and at the Brighton Pavilion. In the first two of these his iron columns were masonry clad, but at Brighton he unashamedly constructed iron column supports, as in the Royal Kitchen, and his ground floor to first floor cast-iron staircase, in which he took advantage of the malleability of the material to create a 'Chinese' bamboo design, was particularly notable. The great eighteenth-century terrace architecture of Bath and much of the later work in London was constructed in stone, but as nineteenth-century needs demanded that more buildings needed to be erected at lower cost and greater speed, brick was used more widely for construction; this was rendered with a cement that could be painted to imitate stone. Nash, in particular, employed this method at Regent's Park and used a stucco made from sand, brickdust, powdered limestone and lead oxide that was suited for exterior work.

Further Reading
Terence Davis, 1960, *The Architecture of John Nash*, Studio.
—— 1966, *John Nash: The Prince Regent's Architect*, Country Life.
Sir John Summerson, 1980, *John Nash: Architect to King George IV*, Allen & Unwin.

DY

Nasmyth, James Hall
b. 19 August 1808 Edinburgh, Scotland
d. 7 May 1890 London, England

Scottish mechanical engineer and inventor of the steam-hammer.

James Nasmyth was the youngest son of Alexander Nasmyth (1758–1840), the portrait and landscape painter. According to his autobiography he was named James Hall after his father's friend, the geologist Sir James Hall (1761–1832), but he seems never to have used his second name in official documents. He received an elementary education at Edinburgh High School, but left at the age of 12. He attended evening classes at the Edinburgh School of Arts for the instruction of Mechanics between 1821 and 1825, and gained experience as a mechanic at an early age in his father's workshop. He shared these early experiences with his brother George, who was only a year or so older, and in the 1820s the brothers built several model steam engines and a steam-carriage capable of carrying eight passengers on the public roads. In 1829 Nasmyth obtained a position in London as personal assistant to Henry **Maudslay**, and after Maudslay's death in February 1831 he remained with Maudslay's partner, Joshua **Field**, for a short time. He then returned to Edinburgh, where he and his brother George started in a small way as general engineers. In 1834 they moved to a small workshop in Manchester, and in 1836, with the aid of financial backing from some Manchester businessmen, they established on a site at Patricroft, a few miles from the city, the works which became known as the Bridgewater Foundry. They were soon joined by a third partner, Holbrook Gaskell (1813–1909), who looked after the administration of the business, the firm then being known as Nasmyths Gaskell & Co. They specialized in making machine tools, and Nasmyth invented many improvements so that they soon became one of the leading manufacturers in this field. They also made steam locomotives for the rapidly developing railways. James Nasmyth's best-known invention was the steam-hammer, which dates from 1839 but was not patented until 1842. The self-acting control gear was probably the work of Robert **Wilson** and ensured the commercial success of the invention. George Nasmyth resigned from the partnership in 1843 and in 1850 Gaskell also resigned, after which the firm continued as James Nasmyth & Co. James Nasmyth himself retired at the end of 1856 and went to live at Penshurst, Kent, in a house which he named 'Hammerfield' where he devoted his time mainly to his hobby of astronomy. Robert Wilson returned to become Managing Partner of the firm, which later became Nasmyth, Wilson & Co. and retained that style until its closure in 1940. Nasmyth's claim to be the sole inventor of the steam-hammer has been disputed, but his patent of 1842 was not chal-

lenged and the fourteen-year monopoly ensured the prosperity of the business so that he was able to retire at the age of 48. At his death in 1890 he left an estate valued at £243,805.

Bibliography
1874, with J. Carpenter, *The Moon Considered as a Planet, a World, and a Satellite*, London.
1883, *Autobiography*, ed. Samuel Smiles, London.

Further Reading
R. Wailes, 1963, 'James Nasmyth – Artist's Son', *Engineering Heritage*, vol. I, London, 106–11 (a short account).
J.A. Cantrell, 1984, *James Nasmyth and the Bridgewater Foundry: A Study of Entrepreneurship in the Early Engineering Industry*, Manchester (a full-length critical study).
—— 1984–5, 'James Nasmyth and the steam hammer', *Transactions of the Newcomen Society* 56: 133–8.

RTS

Need, Samuel

b. 1718
d. 14 April 1781 Bread Street, Cheapside, London, England

English manufacturer of hosiery who helped to finance Arkwright's spinning machine and early cotton mills.

Samuel Need was apprenticed as a framework knitter and entered the hosiery trade *c.*1742. He was a Dissenter and later became an Independent Congregationalist. He married Elizabeth Gibson of Hacking, Middlesex, who survived him and died in 1781. He had a warehouse in Nottingham, where he was made a burgess in 1739–40. In 1747 he bought a mill there and had a house adjoining it, but in 1777 he bought an estate at Arnold, outside the city. From about 1759 he supported Jedediah **Strutt** and William Woollat in their development of Strutt's invention of the rib attachment to the knitting machine. Need became a partner with Strutt in 1762 over the patent and then they shared a joint hosiery business. When **Arkwright** sought financial assistance from Ichabod and John Wright, the Nottingham bankers, to develop his spinning mill in that town, the Wrights turned him over to Samuel Need. Need, having profited so much from the successful patent with Strutt, was ready to exploit another; on 19 January 1770 Need and Strutt, on payment of £500, became co-partners with Arkwright, **Smalley** and **Thornley** for the remainder of Arkwright's patent. In Need, Arkwright had secured the patronage of the leading hosier in Nottingham. Need was leader of the Hosiers' Federation in 1779 when the framework knitters petitioned Parliament to better their conditions. He gave evidence against the workers' demands and, when their bill failed, the Nottingham workers attacked first his Nottingham house and then the one at Arnold.

Need was to remain a partner with Arkwright until his death in 1781. He was involved in the mill at Cromford and also with some later ones, such as the Birkacre mill near Chorley, Lancashire, in 1777. He made a fortune and died at his home in London.

Further Reading
M.L. Walker, 1963, *A History of the Family of Need of Arnold, Nottinghamshire*, London (a good biography).
R.S. Fitton, 1989, *The Arkwrights, Spinners of Fortune*, Manchester (covers Need's relationship with Arkwright).
R.S. Fitton and A.P. Wadsworth, 1958, *The Strutts and the Arkwrights, 1758–1830*, Manchester.
S.D. Chapman, 1967, *The Early Factory Masters*, Newton Abbot (describes his wider contacts with the Midlands hosiery industry).

RLH

Neilson, James Beaumont
b. 22 June 1792 Shettleston, near Glasgow, Scotland
d. 18 January 1865 Queenshill, Kirkcudbrightshire, Scotland

Scottish inventor of hot blast in ironmaking.

After leaving school before the age of 14 Neilson followed his father in tending colliery-steam engines. He continued in this line while apprenticed to his elder brother and afterwards rose to engine-wright at Irvine colliery. That failed and Neilson obtained work as Foreman at the first gasworks to be set up in Glasgow. After five years he became Manager and Engineer to the works, remaining there for thirty years. He introduced a number of improvements into gas manufacture,

such as the use of clay retorts, iron sulphate as a purifier and the swallow-tail burner. He had meanwhile benefited from studying physics and chemistry at the Andersonian University in Glasgow.

Neilson is best known for introducing hot blast into ironmaking. At that time, ironmasters believed that cold blast produced the best results, since furnaces seemed to make more and better iron in the winter than the summer. Neilson found that by leading the air blast through an iron chamber heated by a coal fire beneath it, much less fuel was needed to convert the iron ore to iron. He secured a patent in 1828 and managed to persuade Clyde Ironworks in Glasgow to try out the device. The results were immediately favourable, and the use of hot blast spread rapidly throughout the country and abroad. The equipment was improved, raising the blast temperature to around 300°C (572°F), reducing the amount of coal, which was converted into coke, required to produce a tonne of iron from 10 tonnes to about 3. Neilson entered into a partnership with Charles **Macintosh** and others to patent and promote the process. Successive, and successful, lawsuits against those who infringed the patent demonstrates the general eagerness to adopt hot blast. Beneficial though it was, the process did not become really satisfactory until the introduction of hot-blast stoves by E.A. **Cowper** in 1857.

Principal Honours and Distinctions
FRS 1846.

Further Reading
S. Smiles, *Industrial Biography*, Ch. 9 (offers the most detailed account of Neilson's life).
Proc. Instn. Civ. Engrs., vol. 30, p.451.
J. Percy, 1851, *Metallurgy: Iron and Steel* (provides a detailed history of hot blast).
W.K.V. Gale, 1969, *Iron and Steel*, London: Longmans (provides brief details).

LRD

Neper, John
See **Napier, John**.

Neri, Antonio Ludovic
b. 29 February 1576 Florence, Italy
d. 1614 Florence, Italy

Italian glassmaker.

Neri entered the Church and by 1601 was a priest in the household of Alamanno Bertolini in Florence. There he met the Portuguese Sir Emanuel Ximenes, with whom he shared an interest in chemistry. The two later corresponded and the twenty-seven letters extant from Ximenes, who was living in Antwerp, are the main source of information about Neri's life. At the same time, Neri was working as a craftsman in the Medici glasshouse in Florence and then in their works at Pisa. These glasshouses had been flourishing since the fifteenth century with the help of Muranese glassmakers imported from Venice. Ximenes persuaded Neri to spend some time with the glassmakers in Antwerp, probably from 1603/4, for the correspondence breaks off at that point. A final letter in March 1611 refers to Neri's recent return to Florence. In the following year, Neri published the work by which he is known, the *L'arte vetraria*, the first general treatise on glassmaking. Neri's plan for a further book describing his chemical and medical experiments was thwarted by his early death. *L'arte* belongs to the medieval tradition of manuscript recipe books. It is divided into seven books, the first being the most interesting, dealing with the materials of glassmaking and their mixing and melting to form crystal and other colourless glasses. Other sections deal with coloured glasses and the making of enamels for goldsmiths' use. Although it was noted by Galileo **Galilei** (1564–1642), the book made little impression for half a century, the second edition not appearing until 1661. The first Venice edition came out two years later, with a second in 1678. Due to a decline in scientific activity in Italy at this time, *L'arte* had more influence elsewhere in Europe, especially England, Holland and France. It began to make a real impact with the appearance in 1662 of the English translation by Christopher Merrett (1614–95), physician, naturalist and founder member of the Royal Society. This edition included Merrett's annotations, descriptions of the tools used by English glassmakers and a translation of **Agricola**'s short account of glassmaking in his *De re metallica* of 1556. Later translations were based on the Merrett translation rather than the Italian original. **Ravenscroft** probably used Neri's account of lead glass as a starting point for his own researches in the 1670s.

Bibliography
1612, *L'arte vetraria*, 7 vols; reprinted 1980, ed. R. Barovier, Milan: Edizioni Polifilo (the introd., in Italian, England and French, contains the most detailed account of Neri's life and work).

LRD

Nervi, Pier Luigi
b. 21 June 1891 Sondrio, Italy
d. 9 January 1979 (?), Italy

Italian engineer who played a vital role in the use and adaptation of reinforced concrete as a structural material from the 1930s to the 1970s.

Nervi early established a reputation in the use of reinforced concrete with his stadium in Florence (1930–2). This elegant concrete structure combines graceful curves with functional solidity and is capable of seating some 35,000 spectators. The stadium was followed by the aircraft hangars built for the Italian Air Force at Orvieto and Ortebello, in which he spanned the vast roofs of the hangars with thin-shelled vaults supported by precast concrete beams and steel-reinforced ribs. The structural strength and subtle curves of these ribbed roofs set the pattern for Nervi's techniques, which he subsequently varied and elaborated on to solve problems that arose in further commissions.

Immediately after the Second World War Italy was short of supplies of steel for structural purposes so, in contrast to the USA, Britain and Germany, did not for some years construct any quantity of steel-framed rectangular buildinngs used for offices, housing or industrial use. It was Nervi who led the way to a ferroconcrete approach, using a new type of structure based on these materials in the form of a fine steel mesh sprayed with cement mortar and used to roof all kinds of structures. It was a method that resulted in expressionist curves instead of rectangular blocks, and the first of his great exhibition halls at Turin (1949), with a vault span of 240 ft (73 m), was an early example of this technique. Nervi continued to create original and beautiful ferroconcrete structures of infinite variety: for example, the hall at the Lido di Roma, Ostia; the *terme* at Chianciano; and the three buildings that he designed for the Rome Olympics in 1960. The Palazzetto dello Sport is probably the most famous of these, for which he co-operated with the architect Annibale Vitellozzi to construct a small sports palace seating 5,000 spectators under a concrete 'big top' of 194 ft (59 m) diameter, its enclosing walls supported by thirty-six guy ropes of concrete; inside, the elegant roof displays a floral quality. In 1960 Nervi returned to Turin to build his imaginative Palace of Labour for the centenary celebrations of Garibaldi and Victor Emmanuel in the city. This vast hall, like the Crystal Palace in England a century earlier (see **Paxton**), had to be built quickly and be suitable for later adaptation. It was therefore constructed partly in steel, and the metal supporting columns rose to palm-leaf capitals reminiscent of those in ancient Nile palaces.

Nervi's aim was always to create functional buildings that simultaneously act by their aesthetic qualities as an effective educational influence. Functionalism for Nervi never became 'brutalism'. In consequence, his work is admired by the lay public as well as by architects. He collaborated with many of the outstanding architects of the day: with Gio Ponti on the Pirelli Building in Milan (1955–9); with Zehrfuss and Breuer on the Y-plan UNESCO Building in Paris (1953–7); and with Marcello Piacentini on the 16,000-seat Palazzo dello Sport in Rome. Nervi found time to write a number of books on building construction and design, lectured in the Universities of Rio de Janiero and Buenos Aires, and was for many years Professor of Technology and Technique of Construction in the Faculty of Architecture at the University of Rome. He continued to design new structures until well into the 1970s.

Principal Honours and Distinctions
RIBA Royal Gold Medal 1960. Royal Institute of Structural Engineers Gold Medal 1968. Honorary Degree Edinburgh University, Warsaw University, Munich University, London University, Harvard University. Member International Institute of Arts and Letters, Zurich; American Academy of Arts and Sciences; Royal Academy of Fine Arts, Stockholm.

Bibliography
1956, *Structures*, New York: Dodge.
1945, *Scienza o Arte del Costruire?*, Rome: Bussola.

Further Reading
P. Desideri *et al.*, 1979, *Pier Luigi Nervi*, Bologna: Zanichelli.
A.L. Huxtable, 1960, *Masters of World Architecture; Pier Luigi Nervi*, New York: Braziller.

DY

Newcomen, Thomas
b. January or February 1663 Dartmouth, Devon, England
d. 5 August 1729 London, England

English inventor and builder of the world's first successful stationary steam-engine.

Newcomen was probably born at a house on the quay at Dartmouth, Devon, England, the son of Elias Newcomen and Sarah Trenhale. Nothing is known of his education, and there is only dubious evidence of his apprenticeship to an ironmonger in Exeter. He returned to Dartmouth and established himself there as an 'ironmonger'. The term 'ironmonger' at that time meant more than a dealer in ironmongery: a skilled craftsman working in iron, nearer to today's 'blacksmith'. In this venture he had a partner, John Calley or Caley, who was a plumber and glazier. Besides running his business in Dartmouth, it is evident that Newcomen spent a good deal of time travelling round the mines of Devon and Cornwall in search of business.

Eighteenth-century writers and others found it impossible to believe that a provincial ironmonger could have invented the steam-engine, the concept of which had occupied the best scientific brains in Europe, and postulated a connection between Newcomen and **Savery** or **Papin**, but scholars in recent years have failed to find any evidence of this. Certainly Savery was in Dartmouth at the same time as Newcomen but there is nothing to indicate that they met, although it is possible. The most recent biographer of Thomas Newcomen is of the opinion that he was aware of Savery and his work, that the two men had met by 1705 and that, although Newcomen could have taken out his own patent, he could not have operated his own engines without infringing Savery's patent. In the event, they came to an agreement by which Newcomen was enabled to sell his engines under Savery's patent.

The first recorded Newcomen engine is dated 1712, although this may have been preceded by a good number of test engines built at

Dartmouth, possibly following a number of models. Over one hundred engines were built to Newcomen's design during his lifetime, with the first engine being installed at the Griff Colliery near Dudley Castle in Staffordshire.

On the death of Thomas Savery, on 15 May 1715, a new company, the Proprietors of the Engine Patent, was formed to carry on the business. The Company was represented by Edward Elliot, 'who attended the Sword Blade Coffee House in Birchin Lane, London, between 3 and 5 o'clock to receive enquiries and to act as a contact for the committee'. Newcomen was, of course, a member of the Proprietors.

A staunch Baptist, Newcomen married Hannah Waymouth, who bore him two sons and a daughter. He died, it is said of a fever, in London on 5 August 1729 and was buried at Bunhill Fields.

Further Reading

L.T.C. Rolt and J.S. Allen, 1977, *The Steam Engine of Thomas Newcomen*, Hartington: Moorland Publishing Company (the definitive account of his life and work).

IMcN

Niepce, Joseph Nicéphore

b. 1765 France
d. 5 July 1833 Chalon, France

French inventor who was the first to produce permanent photographic images with the aid of a camera.

Coming from a prosperous family, Niepce was educated in a Catholic seminary and destined for the priesthood. The French Revolution intervened and Niepce became an officer in an infantry regiment. An attack of typhoid fever in Italy ended his military career, and he returned to France and was married. Returning to his paternal home in Chalon in 1801, he joined with his brother Claude to construct an ingenious engine called the *pyréolophore*, which they patented in 1807. The French Government also encouraged the brothers in their attempts to produce large quantities of indigo-blue dye from wood, a venture that was ultimately unsuccessful.

Nicéphore began to experiment with lithography, which led him to take an interest in the properties of light-sensitive materials. He pursued this interest after Claude moved to Paris in

1816 and is reported to have made negative images in a camera obscura using paper soaked in silver chloride. Niepce went on to experiment with bitumen of judea, a substance that hardened on exposure to light. In 1822, using bitumen of judea on glass, he produced a heliograph from an engraving. The first images from nature may have been made as early as 1824, but the world's earliest surviving photographic image was made in 1826. A view of the courtyard of Niepce's home in Chalon was captured on a pewter plate coated with bitumen of judea; an exposure of several hours was required, the softer parts of the bitumen being dissolved away by a solvent to reveal the image.

In 1827 he took examples of his work to London where he met Francis Bauer, Secretary of the Royal Society. Nothing came of this meeting, but on returning to France Niepce continued his work and in 1829 entered into a formal partnership with L.J.M. **Daguerre** with a view to developing their mutual interest in capturing images formed by the camera obscura. However, the partnership made only limited progress and was terminated by Niepce's death in 1833. It was another six years before the announcement of the first practicable photographic processes was made.

Bibliography

1973, *Joseph Nicéphore Niepce lettres 1816–7*, Pavillon de Photographie du Parc Naturel, Régional de Brotonne.
1974, *Joseph Nicéphore Niepce correspondences 1825–1829*, Pavillon de Photographie du Parc Naturel, Régional de Brotonne.

Further Reading

J.M. Eder, 1945, *History of Photography*, trans. E. Epstean, New York (provides a full account of Niepce's life and work).
H. Gernsheim and A. Gernsheim, 1969, *The History of Photography*, rev. edn, London (provides a full account of Niepce's life and work).

JW

Niepce de St Victor, Claude Félix Abel

b. 1805 Saint-Cyr, France
d. 1870 France

French soldier and photographic scientist, inventor of the first practicable glass negative process.

A cousin of the photographic pioneer J.N. **Niepce**, he attended the military school of Saumur, graduating in 1827. Niepce de St Victor had wide scientific interests, but came to photography indirectly from experiments he made on fading dyes in military uniforms. He was transferred to the Paris Municipal Guard in 1845 and was able to set up a chemical laboratory to conduct research. From photographic experiments performed in his spare time, Niepce de St Victor devised the first practicable photographic process on glass in 1847. Using albumen derived from the white of eggs as a carrier for silver iodide, he prepared finely detailed negatives which produced positive prints far sharper than those made with the paper negatives of **Talbot**'s calotype process. Exposure times were rather long, however, and the albumen-negative process was soon displaced by the wet-collodion process introduced in 1851, although albumen positives on glass continued to be used for high-quality stereoscopic views and lantern slides. In 1851 Niepce de St Victor described a photographic colour process, and between 1853 and 1855 he developed his famous cousin's bitumen process into a practicable means of producing photographically derived printing plates. He then went on to investigate the use of uranium salts in photography. He presented twenty-six papers to the Académie des Sciences between 1847 and 1862.

Bibliography
1847, *Comptes Rendus* 25 (25 October): 586 (describes his albumen-on-glass process).

Further Reading
J.M. Eder, 1945, *History of Photography*, trans. E. Epstean, New York (provides details of his contributions to photography).

JW

Nightingale, Florence
b. 15 May 1820 Florence, Italy
d. 13 August 1910 London, England

English nurse, pioneer of the reform of nursing, hospital organization and technology.

Dedicated to the relief of suffering, Florence Nightingale spent her early years visiting civil and military hospitals all over Europe. She then attended a course of formal training at Kaiserwerth in Germany and with the Sisters of St Vincent de Paul in Paris.

She had returned to London and was managing, after having reformed, a hostel for invalid gentlewomen when in 1854 the appalling conditions of the wounded in Turkey during the Crimean War led to her taking a party of thirty-eight nurses out to Scutari. The application of principles of hygiene and sanitation resulted in dramatic improvements in conditions and on her return to England in 1856 she applied the large sums which had been raised in her honour to the founding in 1861 of the St Thomas's School of Nursing.

From this base she acted as adviser, goad and promoter of sound nursing common sense for the remainder of a long life marred by a chronic invalidism quite out of keeping with the rigorousness of her role in the nursing field. It was not only in the training and conduct of nursing that her influence was primal. Many concepts of hospital technology relating to hygiene, ventilation and ward design are to be attributed to her forthright common sense. The 'Nightingale ward', for a time the target of progressive reformers, has been shown still to have abiding virtues.

Principal Honours and Distinctions
Order of Merit 1907.

Bibliography
1858, *Notes on Nursing*.
1899, *Notes on Hospitals*.

Further Reading
C. Woodham-Smith, 1949, *Florence Nightingale*, London.

MG

Nipkow, Paul Gottlieb
b. 22 August 1860 Lauenburg, Pommern (now Lebork, Poland)
d. 24 August 1940 Berlin, Germany

Polish electrical engineer who invented the Nipkow television scanning disc.

In 1884, while still a student engineer, Nipkow

patented a mechanical television pick-up device using a disc with a spiral of twenty-four holes rotating at 600 rpm in front of a selenium cell. He also proposed a display on an identical synchronous disc in conjunction with a light-modulator based on the **Faraday** effect. Unfortunately it was not possible to realize a working system at the time because of the slow response of selenium cells and the lack of suitable electronic-signal amplifiers; he was unable to pay the extension fees and so the patent lapsed. Others took up the idea, however, and in 1907 pictures were sent between London and Paris by wire. Subsequently, the principle was used by **Baird**, **Ives**, and **Jenkins**.

For most of his working life after obtaining his doctorate, Nipkow was employed as an engineer by a company that made railway-signalling equipment, but his pioneering invention was finally recognized in 1934 when he was made Honorary President of the newly formed German Television Society.

Principal Honours and Distinctions
President, German Television Society 1934.

Bibliography
1884, German patent no. 30,105 (Nipkow's pioneering method of television image-scanning).

Further Reading
R.W. Hubbell, 1946, *4,000 Years of Television*, London: G. Harrap & Co.

KF

Nobel, Alfred Bernhard
b. 21 October 1833 Stockholm, Sweden
d. 10 December 1896 San Remo, Italy

Swedish industrialist, inventor of dynamite, founder of the Nobel Prizes.

Alfred's father, Immanuel **Nobel**, builder, industrialist and inventor, encouraged his sons to follow his example of inventiveness. Alfred's education was interrupted when the family moved to St Petersburg, but was continued privately and was followed by a period of travel. He thus acquired a good knowledge of chemistry and became an excellent linguist.

During the Crimean War, Nobel worked for his father's firm in supplying war materials. The cancellation of agreements with the Russian Government at the end of the war bankrupted the firm, but Alfred and his brother Immanuel continued their interest in explosives, working on improved methods of making nitroglycerine. In 1863 Nobel patented his first major invention, a detonator that introduced the principle of detonation by shock, by using a small charge of nitroglycerine in a metal cap with detonating or fulminating mercury. Two years later Nobel set up the world's first nitroglycerine factory in an isolated area outside Stockholm. This led to several other plants and improved methods for making and handling the explosive. Yet Nobel remained aware of the dangers of liquid nitroglycerine, and after many experiments he was able in 1867 to take out a patent for dynamite, a safe, solid and pliable form of nitroglycerine, mixed with kieselguhr. At last, nitroglycerine, discovered by **Sobrero** in 1847, had been transformed into a useful explosive; Nobel began to promote a worldwide industry for its manufacture. Dynamite still had disadvantages, and Nobel continued his researches until, in 1875, he achieved blasting gelatin, a colloidal solution of nitrocellulose (gun cotton) in nitroglycerine. In many ways it proved to be the ideal explosive, more powerful than nitroglycerine alone, less sensitive to shock and resistant to moisture. It was variously called Nobel's Extra Dynamite, blasting gelatin and gelignite. It immediately went into production.

Next, Nobel sought a smokeless powder for military purposes, and in 1887 he obtained a nearly smokeless blasting powder using nitroglycerine and nitrocellulose with 10 per cent camphor. Finally, a progressive, smokeless blasting powder was developed in 1896 at his San Remo laboratory.

Nobel's interests went beyond explosives into other areas, such as electrochemistry, optics and biology; his patents amounted to 355 in various countries. However, it was the manufacture of explosives that made him a multimillionaire. At his death he left over £2 million, which he willed to funding awards 'to those who during the preceding year, shall have conferred the greatest benefit on mankind'.

Bibliography
1875, *On Modern Blasting Agents*, Glasgow (his only book).

Further Reading

H. Schuck *et al.*, 1962, *Nobel, the Man and His Prizes*, Amsterdam.

E. Bergengren, 1962, *Alfred Nobel, the Man and His Work*, London and New York (includes a supplement on the prizes and the Nobel institution).

LRD

Nobel, Immanuel

b. 1801 Gävle, Sweden
d. 3 September 1872 Stockholm, Sweden

Swedish inventor and industrialist, particularly noted for his work on mines and explosives.

The son of a barber-surgeon who deserted his family to serve in the Swedish army, Nobel showed little interest in academic pursuits as a child and was sent to sea at the age of 16, but jumped ship in Egypt and was eventually employed as an architect by the pasha. Returning to Sweden, he won a scholarship to the Stockholm School of Architecture, where he studied from 1821 to 1825 and was awarded a number of prizes. His interest then leaned towards mechanical matters and he transferred to the Stockholm School of Engineering. Designs for linen-finishing machines won him a prize there, and he also patented a means of transforming rotary into reciprocating movement. He then entered the real-estate business and was successful until a fire in 1833 destroyed his house and everything he owned. By this time he had married and had two sons, with a third, Alfred (of Nobel Prize fame; see Alfred **Nobel**), on the way. Moving to more modest quarters on the outskirts of Stockholm, Immanuel resumed his inventions, concentrating largely on India rubber, which he applied to surgical instruments and military equipment, including a rubber knapsack.

It was talk of plans to construct a canal at Suez that first excited his interest in explosives. He saw them as a means of making mining more efficient and began to experiment in his backyard. However, this made him unpopular with his neighbours, and the city authorities ordered him to cease his investigations. By this time he was deeply in debt and in 1837 moved to Finland, leaving his family in Stockholm. He hoped to interest the Russians in land and sea mines and, after some four years, succeeded in obtaining financial backing from the Ministry of War, enabling him

to set up a foundry and arms factory in St Petersburg and to bring his family over. By 1850 he was clear of debt in Sweden and had begun to acquire a high reputation as an inventor and industrialist. His invention of the horned contact mine was to be the basic pattern of the sea mine for almost the next 100 years, but he also created and manufactured a central-heating system based on hot-water pipes. His three sons, Ludwig, Robert and Alfred, had now joined him in his business, but even so the outbreak of war with Britain and France in the Crimea placed severe pressures on him. The Russians looked to him to convert their navy from sail to steam, even though he had no experience in naval propulsion, but the aftermath of the Crimean War brought financial ruin once more to Immanuel. Amongst the reforms brought in by Tsar Alexander II was a reliance on imports to equip the armed forces, so all domestic arms contracts were abruptly cancelled, including those being undertaken by Nobel. Unable to raise money from the banks, Immanuel was forced to declare himself bankrupt and leave Russia for his native Sweden. Nobel then reverted to his study of explosives, particularly of how to adapt the then highly unstable nitroglycerine, which had first been developed by Ascanio **Sobrero** in 1847, for blasting and mining. Nobel believed that this could be done by mixing it with gunpowder, but could not establish the right proportions. His son Alfred pursued the matter semi-independently and eventually evolved the principle of the primary charge (and through it created the blasting cap), having taken out a patent for a nitroglycerine product in his own name; the eventual result of this was called dynamite. Father and son eventually fell out over Alfred's independent line, but worse was to follow. In September 1864 Immanuel's youngest son, Oscar, then studying chemistry at Uppsala University, was killed in an explosion in Alfred's laboratory: Immanuel suffered a stroke, but this only temporarily incapacitated him, and he continued to put forward new ideas. These included making timber a more flexible material through gluing crossed veneers under pressure and bending waste timber under steam, a concept which eventually came to fruition in the form of plywood.

In 1868 Immanuel and Alfred were jointly awarded the prestigious Letterstedt Prize for their work on explosives, but Alfred never forgave his father for retaining the medal without offering it to him.

Principal Honours and Distinctions

Imperial Gold Medal (Russia) 1853. Swedish Academy of Science Letterstedt Prize (jointly with son Alfred) 1868.

Bibliography

Immanuel Nobel produced a short handwritten account of his early life 1813–37, which is now in the possession of one of his descendants. He also had published three short books during the last decade of his life – *Cheap Defence of the Country's Roads* (on land mines), *Cheap Defence of the Archipelagos* (on sea mines), and *Proposal for the Country's Defence* (1871) – as well as his pamphlet (1870) on making wood a more physically flexible product.

Further Reading

No biographies of Immanuel Nobel exist, but his life is detailed in a number of books on his son Alfred.

CM

Noble, James
fl. 1850s England

English inventor of the most generally used wool-combing machine.

For many years James Noble had been experimenting with combing machines and had taken out patents, but it was not until he was nearly 50 that he invented a really successful one. In 1853 he took out patents for the machine with which his name has become associated. His invention differed from all others in that the combing and clearing away of the noil was done by and through circles revolving in the same direction with practically the same surface speed. It consisted of a large horizontal revolving circle of vertical pins onto which the wool fibres were fed, and inside this were smaller circles of heated pins revolving at the same speed and which also caught the fibres. The combing occurred at the point where the circles separated. Further rollers drew the fibres off the pins of the other circles. The Noble comb became the machine mostly used for wool combing because of its mechanical simplicity, adaptability for varying classes of wool, superior output and economy, for it required little supervision.

Bibliography

1853, British patent no. 890 (wool-combing machine).
1853, British patent no. 894 (wool-combing machine).

Further Reading

L.J. Mills, 1927, *The Textile Educator*, London (for a full description of the Noble comb).
W. English, 1969, *The Textile Industry*, London (provides a good short account of the principles of Noble's machine).

RLH

North, Simeon
b. 13 July 1765 Berlin, Connecticut, USA
d. 25 August 1852 Middletown, Connecticut, USA

American manufacturer of small arms.

Like his father and grandfather, Simeon North began his working life as a farmer. In 1795 he started a business making scythes in an old mill adjoining his farm. He had apparently already been making some pistols for sale, and in March 1799 he secured his first government contract, for 500 horse-pistols to be delivered within one year. This was followed by further contracts for 1,500 in 1800, 2,000 in 1802, and others; by 1813 he had supplied at least 10,000 pistols and was employing forty or fifty men. In a contract for 20,000 pistols in 1813 there was a provision, which North himself recommended, that parts should be interchangeable. It is probable that he had employed the concept of interchangeability at least as early as his more famous contemporary Eli **Whitney**. To meet this contract he established a new factory at Middletown, Connecticut, but his original works at Berlin continued to be used until 1843. His last government order for pistols was in 1828, but from 1823 he obtained a series of contracts for rifles and carbines, with the last (1850) being completed in 1853, after his death. In developing machine tools to carry out these contracts, North was responsible for what was probably the earliest milling machine, albeit in a relatively primitive form, *c.*1816 or even as early as 1808. In 1811 he was elected Lieutenant-Colonel of the 6th Connecticut

Regiment; although he resigned after only two years, he was generally known thereafter as Colonel North.

Further Reading
S.N.D. North and R.H. North, 1913, *Simeon North: First Official Pistol Maker of the United States*, Concord, NH (the fullest account).
J.W. Roe, 1916, *English and American Tool Builders*, New Haven; reprinted 1926, New York, and 1987, Bradley, Ill.
Merrit Roe Smith, 1973, 'John H. Hall, Simeon North, and the milling machine: the nature of innovation among antebellum arms makers', *Technology and Culture* 14: 573–91.

RTS

Northrop, James H.
fl. 1890s Keighley, Yorkshire, England

English-born American inventor of the first successful loom to change the shuttles automatically when the weft ran out.

Although attempts had been continuing since about 1840 to develop a loom on which the shuttles were changed automatically when the weft was exhausted, it was not until J.H. Northrop invented his cop-changer and patented it in the United States in 1894 that the automatic loom really became a serious competitor to the ordinary power loom. Northrop was born at Keighley in Yorkshire but emigrated to America, where he developed his loom. In about 1891 he appears to have been undecided whether to work on the shuttle-changing system or the cop-changing system, for in that year he took out three patents, one of which was for a shuttle changer and the other two for cop-changers.

A communication from W.F. Draper, Northrop's employer, was used in 1894 as a patent in Britain for a cop- or bobbin-changing automatic loom, which was in fact the Northrop loom. A further five patents for stop motions were taken out in 1895, and yet another in 1896. In one shuttle-box, a feeler was pushed through a hole in the side of the shuttle each time the shuttle entered the box. When the cop of weft was full, the loom carried on working normally. If lack of weft enabled the feeler to enter beyond a certain point, a device was activated which pushed a full cop down into the place of the old one. The full cops were contained in a rotary magazine, ready for insertion.

The full Northrop loom comprised several basic inventions in addition to the cop-changer, namely a self-threading shuttle, a weft-fork mechanism to stop the loom, a warp let-off mechanism and a warp-stop motion. The Northrop loom revolutionized cotton weaving in America and the Northrop system became the basis for most later automatic looms. While Northrop looms were made in America and on the European continent, they never achieved much popularity in Britain, where finer cloth was usually woven.

Further Reading
W.A. Hanton, 1929, *Automatic Weaving*, London (describes the Northrop loom and has good illustrations of the mechanism).
W. English, 1969, *The Textile Industry*, London (explains the Northrop system).
C. Singer (ed.), 1958, *A History of Technology*, Vol. V, Oxford: Clarendon Press.

RLH

Norton, Charles Hotchkiss
b. 23 November 1851 Plainville, Connecticut, USA
d. 27 October 1942 Plainville, Connecticut, USA

American mechanical engineer and machine-tool designer.

After an elementary education at the public schools of Plainville and Thomaston, Connecticut, Charles H. Norton started work in 1866 at the Seth Thomas Clock Company in Thomaston. He was soon promoted to machinist, and further progress led to his successive appointments as Foreman, Superintendent of Machinery and Manager of the department making tower clocks. He designed many public clocks.

In 1886 he obtained a position as Assistant Engineer with the Brown & Sharpe Manufacturing Company at Providence, Rhode Island, and was engaged in redesigning their universal grinding machine to give it more rigidity and make it more suitable for use as a production machine. In 1890 he left to become a partner in a newly established firm, Leland, Faulconer & Norton Company at Detroit, Michigan, designing and building machine tools. He withdrew from this firm in 1895 and practised as a consulting mechanical engineer for a short time before returning to Brown & Sharpe in 1896. There he designed a grinding machine incorporating larger and wider grinding wheels so that heavier cuts could be made to meet the needs of the mass-production industries, especially the automobile industry. This required a heavier and more rigid machine and greater power, but these ideas were not welcomed at Brown & Sharpe and in 1900 Norton left to found the Norton Grinding Company in Worcester, Massachusetts. Here he was able to develop heavy-production grinding machines, including special machines for grinding crankshafts and camshafts for the automobile industry.

In setting up the Norton Grinding Company, Charles H. Norton received financial support from members of the Norton Emery Wheel Company (also of Worcester and known after 1906 as the Norton Company), but he was not related to the founder of that company. The two firms were completely independent until 1919 when they were merged. From that time Charles H. Norton served as Chief Engineer of the machinery division of the Norton Company, until 1934 when he became their Consulting Engineer.

Principal Honours and Distinctions
City of Philadelphia, John Scott Medal 1925.

Bibliography
Norton was granted more than one hundred patents and was author of *Principles of Cylindrical Grinding*, 1917, 1921, Worcester, Mass.

Further Reading
Robert S. Woodbury, 1959, *History of the Grinding Machine*, Cambridge, Mass. (contains biographical information and details of the machines designed by Norton).

RTS

Noyce, Robert
b. 12 December 1927 Burlington, Iowa, USA

American engineer responsible for the development of integrated circuits and the microprocessor chip.

Noyce was the son of a Congregational minister whose family, after a number of moves, finally settled in Grinnell, some 50 miles (80 km) east of Des Moines, Iowa. Encouraged to follow his interest in science, in his teens he worked as a baby-sitter and mower of lawns to earn money for his hobby. One of his clients was Professor of Physics at Grinnell College, where Noyce enrolled to study mathematics and physics and eventually gained a top-grade BA. It was while there that he learned of the invention of the transistor by the team at Bell Laboratories, which included John Bardeen, a former fellow student of his professor. After taking a PhD in physical electronics at the Massachusetts Institute of Technology in 1953, he joined the Philco Corporation in Philadelphia to work on the development of transistors. Then in January 1956 he accepted an invitation from William **Shockley**, another of the Bell transistor team, to join the newly formed Shockley Transistor Company, the first electronic firm to set up shop in Palo Alto, California, in what later became known as 'Silicon Valley'.

From the start things at the company did not go well and eventually Noyce and Gordon Moore and six colleagues decided to offer themselves as a complete development team; with the aid of the Fairchild Camera and Instrument Company, the Fairchild Semiconductor Corporation was born. It was there that in 1958, contemporaneously with Jack K. **Wilby** at Texas Instruments, Noyce had the idea for monolithic integration of transistor circuits. Eventually, after extended patent litigation involving study of laboratory notebooks and careful examination of the original claims, priority was assigned to Noyce. The invention was most timely. The Apollo Moon-landing programme announced by President Kennedy in May 1961 called for lightweight sophisticated navigation and control computer systems, which could only be met by the rapid development of the new technology, and Fairchild was well placed to deliver the micrologic chips required by NASA.

In 1968 the founders sold Fairchild Semiconductors to the parent company. Noyce and Moore promptly found new backers and set up the Intel Corporation, primarily to make high-density memory chips. The first product was a 1,024-bit random access memory (1 K RAM) and by 1973 sales had reached $60 million. However, Noyce and Moore had already realized that it was possible to make a complete microcomputer by putting all the logic needed to go with the memory chip(s) on a single integrated circuit (IC) chip in the form of a general purpose central processing unit (CPU). By 1971 they had produced the Intel 1004 microprocessor, which sold for US$200, and within a year the 8008 followed. The personal computer (PC) revolution had begun!

Noyce eventually left Intel, but he remained active in microchip technology and subsequently founded Sematech Inc.

Principal Honours and Distinctions
Franklin Institute Stuart Ballantine Medal 1966. National Academy of Engineering 1969. National Academy of Science. Institute of Electrical and Electronics Engineers Medal of Honour 1978; Cledo Brunetti Award (jointly with Kilby) 1978. Institution of Electrical Engineers Faraday Medal 1979. National Medal of Science 1979. National Medal of Engineering 1987.

Bibliography
1955, 'Base-widening punch-through', *Proceedings of the American Physical Society*.
30 July 1959, US patent no. 2,981,877.

Further Reading
T.R. Reid, 1985, *Microchip: The Story of a Revolution and the Men Who Made It*, London: Pan Books.

KF

Nuffield, Viscount
See **Morris, William Richard.**

Nyquist, Harry
b. 7 February 1889 Nilsby, Sweden
d. 4 April 1976 Texas, USA

Swedish-American engineer who established the formula for thermal noise in electrical circuits and the stability criterion for feedback amplifiers.

Nyquist (original family name Nykvist) emigrated from Sweden to the USA when he was 18 years old and settled in Minnesota. After teaching for a time, he studied electrical engineering at the University of North Dakota, gaining his first and Master's degrees in 1915 and 1916, and his PhD from Yale in 1917. He then joined the American Telegraph & Telephone Company, moving to its Bell Laboratories in 1934 and remaining there until his retirement in 1954. A prolific inventor, he made many contributions to communication engineering, including the invention of vestigial-sideband transmission. In the late 1920s he analysed the behaviour of analogue and digital signals in communication circuits, and in 1928 he showed that the thermal noise per unit bandwidth is given by $4\,kT$, where k is Boltzmann's constant and T the absolute temperature. However, he is best known for the Nyquist Criterion, which defines the conditions necessary for the stable, oscillation-free operation of amplifiers with a closed feedback loop. The problem of how to realize these conditions was investigated by his colleague Hendrik **Bode**.

Principal Honours and Distinctions
Franklin Institute Medal 1960. Institute of Electrical and Electronics Engineers Medal of Honour 1960; Mervin J. Kelly Award 1961.

Bibliography
1924, 'Certain factors affecting telegraph speed', *Bell System Technical Journal* 3: 324.
1928, 'Certain topics in telegraph transmission theory', *Transactions of the American Institute of Electrical Engineers* 47: 617.
1928, 'Thermal agitation of electric charge in conductors', *Physical Review* 32: 110.
1932, 'Regeneration theory', *Bell System Technical Journal* 11: 126.
1940, with K. Pfleger, 'Effect of the quadrature component in single-sideband transmission', *Bell System Technical Journal* 19: 63.

Further Reading
Bell Telephone Laboratories, 1975, *Mission Communications*.

See also **Shannon, Claude Elwood**.

KF

O

Oberth, Hermann Julius

b. 25 June 1894 Nagyszeben, Transylvania (now Sibiu, Romania)
d. 29 December 1989 Nuremberg, Germany

*Austro-Hungarian lecturer who is usually regarded, with Robert **Goddard**, as one of the 'fathers' of modern astronautics.*

The son of a physician, Oberth originally studied medicine in Munich, but his education was interrupted by the First World War and service in the Austro-Hungarian Army. Wounded, he passed the time by studying astronautics. He apparently simulated weightlessness and worked out the design for a long-range liquid-propelled rocket, but his ideas were rejected by the War Office; after the war he submitted them as a dissertation for a PhD at Heidelberg University, but this was also rejected. Consequently, in 1923, whilst still an unknown mathematics teacher, he published his ideas at his own expense in the book *The Rocket into Interplanetary Space*. These included a description of how rockets could achieve a sufficient velocity to escape the gravitational field of the earth. As a result he gained international prestige almost overnight and learned of the work of Robert Goddard and Konstantin **Tsiolkovsky**. After correspondence with the Goddard and Tsiolkovsky, Oberth published a further work in 1929, *The Road to Space Travel*, in which he acknowledged the priority of Goddard's and Tsiolkovski's calculations relating to space travel; he went on to anticipate by more than thirty years the development of electric and ionic propulsion and to propose the use of giant mirrors to control the weather. For this he was awarded the annual Hirsch Prize of 10,000 francs. From 1925 to 1938 he taught at a college in Mediasch, Transylvania, where he carried out experiments with petroleum and liquid-air rockets. He then obtained a lecturing post at Vienna Technical University, moving two years later to Dresden University and becoming a German citizen. In 1941 he became assistant to the German rocket engineer Werner von **Braun** at the rocket development centre at Peenemünde, and in 1943 he

began work on solid propellants. After the Second World War he spent a year in Switzerland as a consultant, then in 1950 he moved to Italy to develop solid-propellant anti-aircraft rockets for the Italian Navy. Five years later he moved to the USA to carry out advanced rocket research for the US Army at Huntsville, Alabama, and in 1958 he retired to Feucht, near Nuremberg, Germany, where he wrote his autobiography.

Principal Honours and Distinctions
French Astronautical Society REP-Hirsch Prize 1929. German Society for Space Research Medal 1950. Diesel German Inventors Medal 1954. American Astronautical Society Award 1955. German Federal Republic Award 1961. Institute of Aviation and Astronautics Medal 1969.

Bibliography
1923, *Die Rakete zu den Planetenraumen*; repub. 1934 as *The Rocket into Interplanetary Space* (autobiography).
1929, *Wege zur Raumschiffahrt* [*Road to Space Travel*].
1959, *Stoff und Leben* [*Material and Life*].

Further Reading
R. Spangenburg and D. Moser, 1990, *Space People from A to Z*, New York: Facts on File.
H. Wulforst, 1991, *The Rocketmakers: The Dreamers who made Spaceflight a Reality*, New York: Crown Publishers.

KF/IMcN

Oeynhausen, Karl von

b. 4 February 1795 Grevenburg, near Höxter, Germany
d. 1 February 1865 Grevenburg, near Höxter, Germany

German mining officer who introduced fish joints to deep-drilling.

The son of a mining officer, Oeynhausen started his career in the Prussian administration of the mining industry in 1816, immediately after he had finished his studies in natural sciences and mathematics at the University of Göttingen. From 1847 until his retirement he was a most effective head of state mines inspectorates, first in Silesia (Breslau; now Wroclaw, Poland), later in Westphalia (Dortmund). During his working life he served in all the important mining districts of Prussia, and travelled to mining areas in other parts of Germany, Belgium, France and Britain. In the 1820s, after visiting **Glenck**'s well-known saltworks near Wimpfen, he was commissioned to search for salt deposits in Prussian territory, where he discovered the thermal springs south of Minden which later became the renowned spa carrying his name.

With deeper drills, the increased weight of the rods made it difficult to disengage the drill on each stroke and made the apparatus self-destructive on impact of the drill. Oeynhausen, from 1834, used fish joints, flexible connections between the drill and the rods. Not only did they prevent destructive impact, but they also gave a jerk on the return stroke that facilitated disengagements. He never claimed to have invented the fish joints: in fact, they appeared almost simultaneously in Europe and in America at that time, and had been used since at least the seventeenth century in China, although they were unknown in the Western hemisphere.

Using fish joints meant the start of a new era in deep-drilling, allowing much deeper wells to be sunk than before. Five weeks after Oeynhausen, K.G. **Kind** operated with a different kind of fish joint, and in 1845 another Prussian mining officer, Karl Leopold Fabian (1782–1855), Director of the salt inspectorate at Schönebeck, Elbe, improved the fish joints by developing a special device between the rod and the drill to enable the chisel, strengthened by a sinker bar, to fall onto the bottom of the hole without hindrance with a higher effect. The free-fall system became another factor in the outstanding results of deep-drilling in Prussia in the nineteenth century.

Principal Honours and Distinctions
Honorary PhD, University of Berlin 1860.

Bibliography
1822, *Versuch einer geognostischen Beschreibung von Oberschlesien*, Essen.
1824, 'Über die geologische Ähnlichkeit des steinsalzführenden Gebirges in Lothringen und im südlichen Deutschland mit einigen Gegenden auf beiden Ufern der Weser', *Karstens Archiv für Bergbau und Hüttenwesen* 8: 52–84.
1847, 'Bemerkungen über die Anfertigung und den Effekt der aus Hohleisen zusammengesetzten Bohrgestänge', *Archiv fur Mineralogie, Geognosie, Bergbau und Hüttenkunde* 21: 135–60.
1832–3, with H. von Dechen, *Über den Steinkohlenbergbau in England*, 2 parts, Berlin.

Further Reading
von Gümbel, 'K. v. Oeynhausen', *Allgemeine deutsche Biographie* 25: 31–3.
W. Serlo, 1927, 'Bergmannsfamilien. Die Familien Fabian und Erdmann', *Glückauf*: 492–3.
D. Hoffmann, 1959, *150 Jahre Tiefbohrungen in Deutschland*, Vienna and Hamburg (a careful elaboration of the single steps and their context with relation to the development of deep-drilling).

WK

Ohain, Hans Joachim Pabst von
b. 14 December 1911 Dessau, Germany

German engineer who designed the first jet engine to power an aeroplane successfully.

Von Ohain studied engineering at the University of Göttingen, where he carried out research on gas-turbine engines, and centrifugal compressors in particular. In 1935 he patented a design for a jet engine (in Britain, Frank **Whittle** patented his jet-engine design in 1930). Von Ohain was recruited by the **Heinkel** company in 1936 to develop an engine for a jet aircraft. Ernst Heinkel was impressed by von Ohain's ideas and gave the project a high priority. The first engine was bench tested in September 1937. A more powerful version was developed and tested in air, suspended beneath a Heinkel dive-bomber, during the spring of 1939. A new airframe was designed to house the revolutionary power plant and designated the Heinkel *He 178*. A short flight was made on 24 August 1939 and the first recognized flight on 27 August. This important achievement received only a lukewarm response from the German authorities. Von Ohain's turbojet engine had a centrifugal compressor and developed a thrust of 380 kg (837 lb). An improved, more powerful, engine was developed and installed in a new twin-engined fighter design, the *He 280*. This flew on 2 April 1941 but never progressed beyond the prototype stage. By this time two other German companies, BMW and **Junkers**, were constructing successful turbojets with axial compressors: luckily for the Allies, Hitler was reluctant to pour his hard-pressed resources into this new breed of jet fighters. After the war, von Ohain emigrated to the United States and worked for the Air Force there.

Bibliography
1929, 'The evolution and future of aeropropulsion system', *The Jet Age. 40 Years of Jet Aviation*, Washington, DC: National Air & Space Museum, Smithsonian Institution.

Further Reading
Von Ohain's work is described in many books covering the history of aviation, and aero engines in particular, for example:
R. Schlaifer and S.D. Heron, 1950, *Development of Aircraft Engines and Fuels*, Boston.
G.G. Smith, 1955, *Gas Turbines and Jet Propulsion*.
Grover Heiman, 1963, *Jet Pioneers*.

JDS

Ohm, Georg Simon
b. 16 March 1789 Erlangen, near Nuremberg, Germany
d. 6 July 1854 Munich, Germany

German physicist who laid the foundations of electrical science with his discovery of Ohm's Law.

Given the same first name as his father, Johann, at his baptism, Ohm was generally known by the name of Georg to avoid confusion. While still a child he became interested in science and learned many of his basic skills from his father, a mechanical engineer. After basic education he attended the Gymnasium at Erlangen for a year, then in 1805 he entered the University of Erlangen. Probably for financial reasons, he left after three terms in 1806 and obtained a post as a mathematics tutor at a school in Gottstadt, Switzerland, where he may well have begun to experiment with electrical circuits. In 1811 he returned to Erlangen. He appears to have obtained his doctorate in the same year. After studying physics for a year, he became a tutor at the

Studienanstalt (girls' secondary school) at Bamberg in Bavaria. There, in 1817, he wrote a book on the teaching of geometry in schools, as a result of which King Freidrich Wilhelm III of Prussia had him appointed Oberlehrer (Senior Master) in Mathematics and Physics at the Royal Consistory in Cologne. He continued his electrical experiments and in 1826 was given a year's leave of absence to concentrate on this work, which culminated the following year in publication of his 'Die galvanische Kette', in which he demonstrated his now-famous Law, that the current in a resistor is proportional to the applied voltage and inversely proportional to the resistance. Because he published only a theoretical treatment of his Law, without including the supporting experimental evidence, his conclusions were widely ignored and ridiculed by the eminent German scientists of his day; bitterly disappointed, he was forced to resign his post at the Consistory. Reduced to comparative poverty he took a position as a mathematics teacher at the Berlin Military School. Fortunately, news of his discovery became more widely known, and in 1833 he was appointed Professor at the Nuremberg Polytechnic School. Two years later he was given the Chair of Higher Mathematics at the University of Erlangen and the position of State Inspector of Scientific Education. Honoured by the Royal Society of London in 1841 and 1842, in 1849 he became Professor of Physics at Munich University, a post he held until his death.

Principal Honours and Distinctions
Royal Society Copley Medal 1841. FRS 1842.

Bibliography
1817, 'Grundlinien zu einer zweckmässigen Behandlung der Geometrie als hohern Bildungsmittels an vorbereitenden Lehranstalt'.
1827, 'Die galvanische Kette, mathematische bearbeit'.

Further Reading
F.E. Terman, 1943, *Radio Engineers' Handbook*, New York: McGraw-Hill, Section 3 (for circuit theory based on Ohm's Law).

See also **Thévénin, Léon Charles**.

KF

Olds, Ransom Eli

b. 1864 Geneva, Ohio, USA
d. 1950 Lansing, Michigan, USA

American pioneer motor manufacturer.

He began his working life in 1885 as a book-keeper in his father's machine shop in Lansing, Michigan, where he became a partner soon after. Encouraged by his success in making a small steam engine, heated by an ordinary gasoline stove burner, he built a three-wheeled, self-pro-pelled vehicle in 1887. Increasingly interested in the internal combustion engine, he adopted it for a further vehicle which he completed in 1896. The following year he founded the Olds Motor Vehicle Company and, to take the place of the family machine shop, the Olds Gasoline Machine Works. In 1899 the assets of the motor-vehicle company were diverted into a new com-pany, the Olds Motor Works, and operations were transferred to Detroit. In 1904 he resigned and founded the Reo M Car Company (an acro-nym of his initials) and organized several subsi-diary companies as suppliers of components. After 1915 he tended to drop out to give more time to other interests such as the Ideal Power Lawn Mower Company, set up to manufacture a mower he had invented, the Capital National Bank and R.E. Olds and Co., an investment company.

Further Reading
Dictionary of American Biography, 3rd edn, New
 York: Charles Scribner.

IMcN

Osborne, Adam

b. 6 February 1939 Bangkok, Thailand

*British computer pioneer, producer of the first
practical portable microcomputer.*

Born of British parents, Osborne spent some time in India before moving to the UK. He ob-tained a BSc in chemical engineering at Birming-ham University in 1961, then worked for a number of companies in the USA before obtain-ing a PhD at the University of Delaware. He was then employed by the Shell Oil Company, near San Francisco, California, but he resigned in 1971 to write and to study computing. In 1975 he published a book on microcomputers that sold 20,000 copies in less than a year. He then

set up a publishing firm, Osborne and Associates, which he sold to McGraw-Hill in 1979. Sub-sequently, he formed the Osborne Computer Company and in March 1981 he introduced the Osborne I, the first portable microcomputer. Features of this innovative machine, which sold for under US$2,000, were a full-size keyboard, a CRT (cathode ray tube) display, dual floppy-disk drives, a CP/M operating system, Wordstar word-processing, SuperCalc (a financial-analysis package) and interpretive and compiled BASIC. By late 1982 the company had over 1,000 em-ployees and sales had reached US$70 million, but within a year the company was bankrupt, a débâcle that Osborne later described in a book. Following this he returned to publishing with the formation of Paperback Software Interna-tional.

Bibliography
1975, *An Introduction to Microcomputers*: Adam
 Osborne & Associates.
1984, *Hypergrowth: The Rise and Fall of the Osborne Computer Co.*

KF

Otis, Elisha Graves

b. 3 August 1811 Halifax, Vermont, USA
d. 8 April 1861 Yonkers, New York, USA

*American mechanic and inventor of the safety
passenger elevator.*

Otis was educated in public schools and worked in a variety of jobs in the trucking and construc-tion industries as well as in a machine shop, a carriage makers, a grist mill, and a saw mill and in a bedstead factory. It was when supervisor of construction of a new bedstead factory at Yon-kers in 1852 that he developed the innovative safety features of an elevator that was to be the foundation of his later success. If the ropes or cables of a hoist should break, springs would force pawls on the lift cage to engage the rat-cheted guide rails fitted into the sides of the shaft and so stop the lift. In 1853 he was planning to leave his job to join the California Gold Rush but representatives of two New York City firms who had seen his Safety Elevator and were impressed with the safety devices requested that he make them replicas. He purchased space in the Yonkers plant and began manufacture of the lifts. De-mand was small at first until in 1854 he exhibited at the American Institute Fair in New York City with an impressive performance. Standing on top of the lift cage, he ordered the rope supporting it to be cut. The safety pawls engaged and the cage stopped its downward movement. From then on orders gradually increased and in 1857 he installed the first safety lift for passengers in the Haughtwout Store in New York City. The invention immediately became popular and started a revolution in architecture and the construction industry, leading to the design and building of skyscrapers, as previously buildings were limited to six or seven storeys, because of the stairs people had to climb. Otis patented several other devices, the most important of which was for a steam elevator which established the future of the Otis Elevator Company. He died at Yonkers in 1861, leaving his business to his sons.

Further Reading
Scribner's and Webster's Dictionaries of Biography.

IMcN/DY

Otto, Nikolaus August
b. 10 June 1832 Holzhausen, Nassau (now in Germany)
d. 26 January 1891 Cologne, Germany

German engineer, developer of the four-stroke internal combustion engine.

Otto's involvement in internal combustion engines was first prompted by his interest in **Lenoir**'s coal-gas engine of 1860. He built his first engine in 1861; in 1864, Otto's engine came to the attention of Eugen **Langen**, who arranged for the capital to set up the world's first engine company, N.A. Otto and Company, in Cologne. In 1867 the Otto-Langen free-piston internal combustion engine was exhibited at the Paris Exposition, where it won the gold medal. The company continued to expand, and five years after the Paris triumph its name was changed to the Gasmotoren Fabrik; amongst Otto's colleagues at this time were Gottlieb **Daimler** and Wilhelm **Maybach**.

Otto is most famous for the development of the four-stroke cycle which was to bear his name. He patented his version of this in 1876, although the principle of the four-stroke cycle had been patented by Alphonse **Beau de Rochas** fourteen years previously; Otto was the first, however, to

put the principle into practice with the 'Otto Silent Engine'. Many thousands of Otto four-stroke engines had already been built by 1886, when a German patent lawyer successfully claimed that Otto had infringed the Beau de Rochas patent, and Otto's patent was declared invalid.

Principal Honours and Distinctions
Médaille d'or, Paris Exposition 1867 (for the Otto-Langen engine).

Further Reading
1989, *History of the Internal Combustion Engine*, Detroit: Society of Automotive Engineers.
I. McNeil (ed.), 1990, *An Encyclopaedia of the History of Technology*, London and New York: Routledge, 306–7.

IMcN

Outram, Benjamin
b. 1 April 1764 Alfreton, England
d. 22 May 1805 London, England

English ironmaster and engineer of canals and tramroads, protagonist of angled plate rails in place of edge rails.

Outram's father was one of the principal promoters of the Cromford Canal, Derbyshire, and Benjamin Outram became Assistant to the canal's Engineer, William **Jessop**. In 1789 Outram was appointed Superintendent in charge of construction, and his responsibilities included the 2,978 yd (2,723 m) Butterley Tunnel; while the tunnel was being driven, coal and iron ore were encountered. Outram and a partner purchased the Butterley Hall estate above the tunnel and formed Outram & Co. to exploit the coal and iron: a wide length of the tunnel beneath the company's furnace was linked to the surface by shafts to become in effect an underground wharf. **Jessop** soon joined the company, which grew and prospered to eventually become the long-lived Butterley Company.

As a canal engineer, Outram's subsequent projects included the Derby, Huddersfield Narrow and Peak Forest Canals. On the Derby Canal he built a small iron aqueduct, which though designed later than the Longdon Aqueduct of Thomas **Telford** was opened earlier, in 1796, to become the first iron aqueduct.

It is as a tramroad engineer that Outram is best

known. In 1793 he completed a mile-long (1.6 km) tramroad from Outram & Co.'s limestone quarry at Crich to the Cromford Canal, for which he used plate rails of the type recently developed by John **Curr**. He was, however, able to use a wider gauge – 3 ft 6 in. (1.07 m) between the flanges – and larger wagons than Curr had been able to use underground in mines. It appears to have been Outram's idea to mount the rails on stone blocks, rather than wooden sleepers.

Outram then engineered tramroads to extend the lines of the Derby and Peak Forest Canals. He encouraged construction of such tramroads in many parts of Britain, often as feeders of traffic to canals. He acted as Engineer, and his company often provided the rails and sometimes undertook the entire construction of a line. Foreseeing that lines would be linked together, he recommended a gauge of 4 ft 2 in. (1.27 m) between the flanges as standard, and for twenty years or so Outram's plateways, with horses or gravity as motive power, became the usual form of construction for new railways. However, experience then showed that edge rails, weight for weight, could carry greater load, and were indeed almost essential for the introduction of steam locomotives.

Further Reading

R.B. Schofield, 1986, 'The design and construction of the Cromford Canal, 1788–1794', *Transactions of the Newcomen Society* 57 (provides good coverage of Outram's early career).

P.J. Riden, 1973, 'The Butterley Company and railway construction, 1790–1830', *Transport History* 6 (1) (covers Outram's development of tramroads).

R.A. Mott, 1969, 'Tramroads of the eighteenth century and their originator: John Curr', *Transactions of the Newcomen Society* 42.

'Dowie' (A.R. Cowlishaw, J.H. Price and R.G.P. Tebb), 1971, *The Crich Mineral Railways*, Crich: Tramway Publications.

PJGR

Owen, Robert

b. 14 May 1771 Newtown, Montgomeryshire, Wales
d. 17 November 1858 Newtown, Montgomeryshire, Wales

Welsh cotton spinner and social reformer.

Robert Owen's father was also called Robert and was a saddler, ironmonger and postmaster of Newtown in Montgomeryshire. Robert, the younger, injured his digestion as a child by drinking some scalding hot 'flummery', which affected him for the rest of his life. He developed a passion for reading and through this visited London when he was 10 years old. He started work as a pedlar for someone in Stamford and then went to a haberdasher's shop on old London Bridge in London. Although he found the work there too hard, he stayed in the same type of employment when he moved to Manchester.

In Manchester Owen soon set up a partnership for making bonnet frames, employing forty workers, but he sold the business and bought a spinning machine. This led him in 1790 into another partnership, with James M'Connel and John **Kennedy** in a spinning mill, but he moved once again to become Manager of Peter Drinkwater's mill. These were all involved in fine spinning, and Drinkwater employed 500 people in one of the best mills in the city. In spite of his youth, Owen claims in his autobiography (1857) that he mastered the job within six weeks and soon improved the spinning. This mill was one of the first to use Sea Island cotton from the West Indies. To have managed such an enterprise so well Owen must have had both managerial and technical ability. Through his spinning connections Owen visited Glasgow, where he met both David **Dale** and his daughter Anne Caroline, whom he married in 1799. It was this connection which brought him to Dale's New Lanark mills, which he persuaded Dale to sell to a Manchester consortium for £60,000. Owen took over the management of the mills on 1 January 1800.

Although he had tried to carry out social reforms in the manner of working at Manchester, it was at New Lanark that Owen acquired fame for the way in which he improved both working and living conditions for the 1,500-strong workforce. He started by seeing that adequate food and groceries were available in that remote site and then built both the school and the New Institution for the Formation of Character, which opened in January 1816. To the pauper children from the Glasgow and Edinburgh slums he gave a good education, while he tried to help the rest of the workforce through activities at the Institution. The 'silent monitors' hanging on the textile machines, showing the performance of their operatives, are famous, and many came to see his social experiments. Owen was soon to buy out his original partners for £84,000.

Among his social reforms were his efforts to limit child labour in mills, resulting in the Factory Act of 1819. He attempted to establish an ideal community in the USA, to which he sailed in 1824. He was to return to his village of 'Harmony' twice more, but broke his connection in 1828. The following year he finally withdrew from New Lanark, where some of his social reforms had been abandoned.

Bibliography
1857, *The Life of Robert Owen, Written by Himself*, London.

Further Reading
G.D.H. Cole, 1965, *Life of Robert Owen* (biography).
J. Butt (ed.), 1971, *Robert Owen, Prince of Cotton Spinners*, Newton Abbot; S. Pollard and J. Salt (eds), 1971, *Robert Owen, Prophet of the Poor. Essays in Honour of the Two-Hundredth Anniversary of His Birth*, London (both describe Owen's work at New Lanark).

RLH

Owens, Michael Joseph

b. 1 January 1859 Mason County, Virginia, USA
d. 27 December 1923 Toledo, Ohio, USA

American inventor of the automatic glass bottle making machine.

To assist the finances of a coal miner's family, Owens entered a glassworks at Wheeling, Virginia, at the tender age of 10, stoking coal into the 'glory hole' or furnace where glass was resoftened at various stages of the hand-forming process. By the age of 15 he had become a glassblower.

In 1888 Owens moved to the glassworks of Edward Drummond Libbey at Toledo, Ohio, where within three months he was appointed Superintendent and, not long after, a branch manager. In 1893 Owens supervised the company's famous exhibit at the World's Columbian Exposition at Chicago. He had by then begun experiments that were to lead to the first automatic bottle-blowing machine. He first used a piston pump to suck molten glass into a mould, and then transferred the gathered glass over another mould into which the bottle was blown by reversing the pump. The first patents were taken out in 1895, followed by others incorporating improvements and culminating in the patent of 8 November 1904 for an essentially perfected machine. Eventually it was capable of producing four bottles a second, thus effecting a revolution in bottle making. Owens, with Libbey and others, set up the Owens Bottle Machine Company in 1903, which Owens himself managed from 1915 to 1919, becoming Vice-President from 1915 until his death. A plant was also established in Manchester in 1905.

Besides this, Owens and Libbey first assisted Irving W. Colburn with his experiments on the continuous drawing of flat sheet glass and then in 1912 bought the patents, forming the Owens–Libbey Sheet Glass Company. In all, Owens was granted forty-five US patents, mainly relating to the manufacture and processing of glass. Owens's undoubted inventive genius was hampered by a lack of scientific knowledge, which he made good by judicious consultation.

Further Reading
1923, *Michael J. Owens* (privately printed) (a series of memorial articles reprinted from various sources).
G.S. Duncan, 1960, *Bibliography of Glass*, Sheffield: Society of Glass Manufacturers (cites references to Owens's papers and patents).

LRD

P

Pääbo, Max

b. Estonia
fl. 1950s Sweden

Estonian inventor of one of the most successful looms, in which the weft is sent across the warp by a jet of air.

The earliest patent for using a jet of air to propel a shuttle across a loom was granted to J.C. Brooks in 1914. A different method was tried by E.H. Ballou in 1929, but the really important patent was taken out by Max Pääbo, a refugee from Estonia. He exhibited his machine in Sweden in 1951, weaving cotton cloth 80 cm (31½ in.) wide at a speed of 350 picks per minute, but it was not widely publicized until 1954. One shown in Manchester in 1958 ran at 410 picks per minute while weaving 90 cm (35½ in.) cloth. His looms were called 'Maxbo' after him. They had no shuttle; instead a jet of air drove a measured amount of weft drawn from a supply package across the warp threads. Efficient control of the airstream was the main reason for its success; not only was weaving much quicker, but it was also much quieter than traditional methods, and as the warp was nearly vertical the looms took up little space. Manufacture of these looms in Sweden ceased in 1962, but development continued in other countries.

Further Reading
J.J. Vincent, 1980, *Shuttleless Looms*, Manchester (a good account of the development of modern looms).

RLH

Page, Charles Grafton

b. 25 January 1812 Salem, Massachusetts, USA
d. 5 May 1868 Washington, DC, USA

American scientist and inventor of electric motors.

Page graduated from Harvard in 1832 and subsequently attended Boston Medical School. He began to practise in Salem and also engaged in experimental research in electricity, discovering the improvement effected by substituting bundles of iron wire for solid bars in induction coils. He also created a device which he termed a Dynamic Multiplier, the prototype of the auto-transformer. Following a period in medical practice in Virginia, in 1841 he became one of the first two principal examiners in the United States Patent Office. He also held the Chair of Chemistry and Pharmacy at Columbian College, later George Washington University, between 1844 and 1849.

A prolific inventor, Page completed several large electric motors in which reciprocating action was converted to rotary motion, and invested an extravagant sum of public money in a foredoomed effort to develop a 10-ton electric locomotive powered by primary batteries. This was unsuccessfully demonstrated in April 1851 on the Washington–Baltimore railway and seriously damaged his reputation. Page approached Thomas **Davenport** with an offer of partnership, but Davenport refused.

After leaving the Patent Office in 1852 he became a patentee himself and advocated the reform of the patent procedures. Page returned to the Patent Office in 1861, and later persuaded Congress to pass a special Act permitting him to patent the induction coil. This was the cause, after his death, of protracted and widely publicized litigation.

Bibliography
A number of Page's papers were reprinted in Sturgeon's *Annals of Electricity*, London, 1837–9.
1867, *History of Induction: The American Claim to the Induction Coil and its Electrostatic Developments*, Washington, DC.

Further Reading
R.C. Post, 1976, Physics, Patents and Politics, New York (a biography which treats Page as a focal point for studying the American patent system).
—— 1976, 'Stray sparks from the induction coil: the Volta prize and the Page patent, *Proceedings*

of the Institute of Electrical Engineers 64: 1,279–86 (a short account).

W.J. King, 1962, *The Development of Electrical Technology in the 19th Century*, Washington, DC: Smithsonian Institution, Paper 28.

GW

Page, Frederick Handley
See **Handley Page, Frederick**.

Paget, Arthur
fl. 1850s Loughborough, England

English inventor of one of the first circular, power-driven knitting machines.

The family firm of Paget's of Loughborough was of long standing in hosiery manufacture. They were well aware of the importance of modernizing their factory with the latest improvements in machinery, as well as developing their own inventions. They discovered Marc **Brunel**'s circular knitting machine *c.*1844 and constructed many on that principle, with modifications that performed very well. Arthur Paget took out three patents. The first, was in 1857, was for making the machine self-acting so that it could be driven by power. In his patent of 1859 he introduced modifications on the earlier patent, and his third patent, in 1860, described further alterations. These machines produced excellent work with speed and accuracy.

Bibliography
1857, British patent no. 930.
1859, British patent no. 830.
1860, British patent no. 624.

Further Reading
W. Felkin, 1967, *History of the Machine-wrought Hosiery and Lace Manufactures*, reprint, Newton Abbot (orig. pub. 1867) (includes a description of Paget's inventions).

RLH

Palladius, Rutilius Taurus
fl. late fourth century AD Italy and/or Gaul

Roman writer on agricultural matters.

Palladius produced a fourteen-volume manual dealing with agricultural practice. The first volume is an introduction to the twelve calendar volumes, completed by a poem on grafting. Although much of what he wrote was taken from other sources, there is still a significant amount of new material within his account. Of particular interest was his description of the harvesting machine known as 'Vallus'.

Bibliography
Opus Agriculturae de veterinaria medicina de insitione.

Further Reading
Studies in English are unfortunately rare. Edited Latin edn, 1975, ed. R.H. Rodgers.
R. Harris, 1882, article in *American Journal of Philology* 3: 411–21 (argues that Palladius must have lived in Gaul, because the length he ascribes to his sundial places his latitude thereabouts).

AP

Palmer, Henry Robinson
b. 1795 Hackney, London, England
d. 12 September 1844

English civil engineer and monorail pioneer.

Palmer was an assistant to Thomas **Telford** for ten years from 1816. In 1818 he arranged a meeting of young engineers from which the Institution of Civil Engineers originated. In the early 1820s he invented a monorail system, the first of its kind, in which a single rail of wood, with an iron strip spiked on top to form a running surface, was supported on posts. Wagon bodies were supported pannier fashion from a frame attached to grooved wheels and were propelled by men or horses. An important object was to minimize friction, and short lines were built on this principle at Deptford and Cheshunt. In 1826 Palmer was appointed Resident Engineer to the London Docks and was responsible for the construction of many of them. He was subsequently consulted about many important engineering works.

Principal Honours and Distinctions
FRS 1831. Vice-President, Institution of Civil Engineers.

Bibliography
1821, British patent no. 4,618 (monorail).
1823, *Description of a Railway on a New Principle* ..., London (describes his monorail).

Further Reading

Obituary, 1845, *Minutes of Proceedings of the Institution of Civil Engineers* 4.

C. von Oeynhausen and H. von Dechen, 1971, *Railways in England 1826 and 1827*, London: Newcomen Society (a contemporary description of the monorails).

M.J.T. Lewis, 1970, *Early Wooden Railways*, London: Routledge & Kegan Paul.

See also **Lartigue, Charles François Marie-Thérèse**.

PJGR

Palmer, John

b. 1743 Bath, Avon, England
d. 1818 Bath, Avon, England

English pioneer in mail transport.

He was the son of a brewer and maltster and part-owner of a theatre in Bath. In his early 20s his father sent him to London to organize the petition for a licence for the Orchard Street theatre, which was granted in 1768. He then organized a series of post-chaises to transport actors between this and another theatre in Bristol in which his father also had an interest. By 1782 he had ready a plan for a countrywide service of mail coaches to replace the existing arrangements of conveying the mail by post-boys and -girls mounted on horseback who were by law compelled to carry the mail 'at a Rate of Six Miles in the Hour at least' on penalty of one month's hard labour if found loitering. Lord Camden, Member of Parliament for Bath, put Palmer's plan before Prime Minister Pitt, who approved of it. An experimental run was tried on 2 August 1782, a coach leaving Bristol at 4 pm and arriving in London at 8 am the next morning, to return the following night from London at 8 pm and reaching Bristol at 10 am. In March 1785 the Norwich Mail Coach was started and during that year services were started to Portsmouth, Dover, Exeter, Leeds, Manchester, Liverpool, Birmingham, Shrewsbury, Chester, Holyhead, Worcester, South Wales and Milford Haven. A feature of importance was that each mail coach was accompanied by an armed guard. In August 1786 Palmer was appointed Surveyor and Comptroller-General of the Post Office at a salary of £1,500 per annum and a bonus depending on all revenue over £300,000 each year. The popularity of the new service is shown by the fact that by 1813 his 2½ per cent bonus came to £50,000. Due to the intrigues of his deputy, he was removed from office, but he was given a pension of £3,000 a year. He received the freedom of some eighteen towns, was made Mayor of Bath and represented that constituency in Parliament four times.

Further Reading

E. Vale, 1960, *The Mail-Coach Men*, London: Cassell.

IMcN

Papanicolaou, George Nicolas

b. 13 May 1883 Kimi, Greece
d. 19 February 1962 Miami, Florida, USA

Greek physician and pathological anatomist, developer of the Papanicolaou cytological smear test (Pap test).

Of a medical family, he graduated at Athens in 1904. After postgraduate study at Jena, Freiburg and Munich, he returned to Greece and turned to an academic career. After a year at the Oceanographic Institute at Monaco and a period in Paris, he again returned to Greece and in 1911 served in the army in the Balkan War.

In 1913 he emigrated to the United States and was appointed to the pathology department of New York Hospital and Cornell Medical College. He became Emeritus Professor of Clinical Anatomy at Cornell in 1951. In 1961 he moved to Florida to head the Miami Cancer Institute, but he died shortly thereafter.

Almost all his research was devoted to the physiology of reproduction and exfoliative cytology, and from his studies in 1917 on vaginal discharge in animals he developed his human studies culminating in cancer diagnostic tests, which after some early scepticism soon gained wide acceptance as a routine screening technique. There are laboratories at both Cornell and Miami that are named after him.

Bibliography

1943, with H. Traut, *Diagnosis of Uterine Cancer by the Vaginal Smear*, New York.

1954, *Atlas of Exfoliative Cytology*, Cambridge, Mass.

Further Reading
D.E. Carmichael, 1973, *The Pap Smear: Life of George N. Papanicolaou*, Springfield, Ill.

MG

Papin, Denis

b. 22 August 1647 Blois, Loire et Cher, France
d. 1712 London, England

French mathematician and physicist, inventor of the pressure-cooker.

Largely educated by his father, he worked for some time for **Huygens** at Leyden, then for a time in London where he assisted Robert Boyle with his experiments on the air pump. He supposedly invented the double-acting air pump. He travelled to Venice and worked there for a time, but was back in London in 1684 before taking up the position of Professor of Mathematics at the University of Marburg (in 1669 or 1670 he became a Doctor of Medicine at Angers), where he remained from 1687 to 1695. Then followed a period at Cassel, where he was employed by the Duke of Hesse. In this capacity he was much involved in the application of steam-power to pumping water for the Duke's garden fountains. Papin finally returned to London in 1707. He is best known for his 'digester', none other than the domestic pressure-cooker. John Evelyn describes it in his diary (12 April 1682):

'I went this Afternoone to a Supper, with severall of the R. Society, which was all dressed (both fish and flesh) in Monsieur Papins Digestorie; by which the hardest bones of Biefe itself, & Mutton, were without water, or other liquor, & with less than 8 ounces of Coales made as soft as Cheeze, produc'd an incredible quantity of Gravie.... This Philosophical Supper raised much mirth among us, & exceedingly pleased all the Companie.'

The pressure-cooker depends on the increase in the boiling point of water with increase of pressure. To avoid the risk of the vessel exploding, Papin devised a weight-loaded lever-type safety valve.

There are those who would claim that Papin preceded **Newcomen** as the true inventor of the steam engine. There is no doubt that as early as 1690 Papin had the idea of an atmospheric engine, in which a piston in a cylinder is forced upwards by expanding steam and then returned by the weight of the atmosphere upon the piston, but he lacked practical engineering skill such as was necessary to put theory into practice. The story is told of his last trip from Cassel, when returning to England. It is said that he built his own steamboat, intending to make the whole journey by this means, ending with a triumphal journey up the Thames. However, boatmen on the river Weser, thinking that the steamboat threatened their livelihood, attacked it and broke it up. Papin had to travel by more orthodox means. Papin is said to have co-operated with Thomas **Savery** in the development of the latter's steam engine, on which he was working *c.*1705.

Further Reading
Charles-Armand Klein, 1987, *Denis Papin: Illustre savant blaisois*, Chambray, France: CLD.
A.P.M. Fleming and H.R.S. Brocklehurst, 1925, *A History of Engineering*.
Sigvar Strandh, 1979, *Machines*, Mitchell Beazley.

IMcN

Paré, Ambroise

b. 1510 Laval, Maine, France
d. 20 December 1590 Paris, France

French physician, surgeon and anatomist recognized as the founder of the rational approach to the practice of surgery and the treatment of wounds.

After a barber-surgeon apprenticeship in Paris, Paré was appointed Resident Surgeon to the Hôtel-Dieu in 1533. From 1537 he served as a military surgeon in the Wars of Religion under Henri II, François II, Charles IX and Henri III. His immense experience of battlefield surgery led him to initiate new treatments of wounds and amputations, replacing the destructive and infecting procedures then practised. His first book, published in 1549, advocated the use of simple ointments and ligatures for amputations.

During the following years he experienced many adventures and vicissitudes and survived the St Bartholomew's Day massacre probably as a result of royal intervention. His numerous surgical and anatomical discoveries and innovations appeared in two major sets of works published in 1564 and 1572. In 1574 he was appointed *premier chirurgien, conseiller et valet-de-chambre* to Henri II, and a further collection of writings was published in 1575.

His attempts to unite French surgeons under his leadership were consistently opposed by the Faculty of Physicians, who not only objected to his writing in French rather than Latin, but also to his refutation of such therapies as 'mummies and unicorn's horn'.

Of his many contributions to medicine, his insistence on rational treatments is outstanding, and two aphorisms are representative: 'Then I resolved never again to so cruelly burn the poor wounded by gunshot'; 'I removed the stone but God cured the patient'.

Bibliography
1564, *Dix livres de chirurgerie*, Paris.
1572, *Cinq livres de chirurgerie*, Paris.
1575, *Les Oeuvres de M. Ambroise Paré*, Paris.

Further Reading
T. Johnson, 1649, *The Works of That Famous Chirurgien Ambroise Parey*, London.

MG

Parker, George Safford

b. 1 November 1863 Shullsberg, Wisconsin, USA
d. 19 July 1937 USA

American perfector of the fountain pen and founder of the Parker Pen Company.

Parker was born of English immigrant stock and grew up on his parents' farm in Iowa. He matriculated at Upper Iowa University and then joined the Valentine School of Telegraphy at Jamesville, Wisconsin: within a year he was on the staff. He supplemented his meagre schoolmaster's pay by selling fountain pens to his students. He found that the pens needed constant attention, and his students were continually bringing them back to him for repair. The more he sold, the more he repaired. The work furnished him, first, with a detailed knowledge of the design and construction of the fountain pen and then with the thought that he could make a better pen himself. He gave up his teaching career and in 1888 began experimenting. He established his own company and in the following year he registered his first patent. The Parker Pen Company was formally incorporated on 8 March 1892.

In the following years he patented many improvements, including the Lucky Curve pen and ink-feed system, patented in 1894. That was the real breakthrough for Parker and the pen was an immediate success. It solved the problem that had bedevilled the fountain pen before and since, by incorporating an ink-feed system that ensured a free and uniform flow of ink to where it was wanted, the nib, and not to other undesirable places.

Parker established a reputation for manufacturing high-quality pens that looked good and worked well and reliably. The pens were in demand worldwide and the company grew.

During the First World War, Parker introduced the Trench Pen for use on the Western Front. A tablet of pigment was inserted in a blind cap at the end of the pen. When this tablet was placed in the barrel and the barrel was filled with water, the pen was ready for use.

Later developments included the *Duofold* pen, designed and launched in 1920. It had an enlarged ink capacity, a red barrel and a twenty-five-year guarantee on the nib. It became immensely popular with the public and was the flagship product throughout the 1920s and early 1930s, until the *Vacumatic* was launched in 1933.

Parker handed over control of the company to this two sons, Kenneth and Russell, during the 1920s, remaining President until his retirement in 1933.

Further Reading
Obituary, 1937, *Jamesville Gazette* 19 July (an appreciation by the architect Frank Lloyd **Wright** was published simultaneously).
No biography has appeared, but Parker gave details of his career in an article in *Systems Review*, October 1926.

LRD

Parker, James

fl. 1790s Northfleet, Kent, England

English patentee of Roman Cement.

James Parker was a vicar at Northfleet in Kent. In experiments of an almost accidental nature he calcined some nodules of clay found on the beach on the Isle of Sheppey. From these he developed a cement which he called Roman, because he believed that this was the type of material the Romans made in ancient times, and which proved to be the basis of the cement industry in Britain, Parker's cement was better than any other so far produced, and was suited to engineering and architectural uses.

Bibliography
27 July 1796, British patent no. 2,120 (Roman Cement).

Further Reading
A.J. Francis, 1977, *The Cement Industry 1796–1914: A History*, David & Charles.

DY

Parkes, Alexander
b. 29 December 1813 Birmingham, England
d. 29 June 1890 West Dulwich, England

English chemist and inventor who made the first plastic material.

After serving apprentice to brassfounders in Birmingham, Parkes entered Elkington's, the celebrated metalworking firm, and took charge of their casting department. They were active in introducing electroplating and Parkes's first patent, of 1841, was for the electroplating of works of art. The electrodeposition of metals became a lifelong interest. Notably, he achieved the electroplating of fragile objects, such as flowers, which he patented in 1843. When Prince **Albert** visited Elkington's, he was presented with a spider's web coated with silver. Altogether, Parkes was granted sixty-six patents over a period of forty-six years, mainly relating to metallurgy.

In 1841 he patented a process for waterproofing textiles by immersing them in a solution of indiarubber in carbon disulphide. Elkingtons manufactured such fabrics until they sold the process to Mackintosh Company, which continued making them for many years. While working for Elkingtons in south Wales, Parkes developed the use of zinc for desilvering lead. He obtained a patent in 1850 for this process, which was one of his most important inventions and became widely used.

The year 1856 saw Parkes's first patent on pyroxylin, later called Xylonite or celluloid, the first plastic material. Articles made of Parkesine, as it came to be called, were shown at the International Exhibition in London in 1862, and he was awarded a medal for his work. Five years later, Parkesine featured at the Paris Exhibition. Even so, Parkes's efforts to promote the material commercially, particularly as a substitute for ivory, remained stubbornly unsuccessful.

Bibliography
1850, British patent no. 13118 (the desilvering of lead).
1856, British patent no. 235 (the first on Parkesine).
1865, Parkes gave an account of his invention of Parkesine in *J.Roy.Arts*, (1865), 14, 81–.

Further Reading
Obituary, 1890, *Engineering*, (25 July): 111.
Obituary, 1890, *Mining Journal* (26 July): 855.

LRD

Parkhurst, Edward G.
b. 29 August 1830 Thompson, Connecticut, USA
d. 31 July 1901 Hartford, Connecticut, USA

American mechanical engineer and inventor.

Little is known of the early training of Edward G. Parkhurst, but at the time of Civil War (1861–5) he was employed by the Savage Arms Company of Middletown, Connecticut. In 1869 he joined the **Pratt** & **Whitney** Company of Hartford, Connecticut, as Assistant Superintendent and later took charge of their gun department. He was the inventor of many improvements in machine tools and armaments. Among these was an automatic rod feeder for turret lathes, in which movement of a single lever enabled bar stock to be fed through the lathe spindle and gripped by a collet chuck while the machine was in motion. This was patented in August 1871 and was followed by other patents, particularly for improvements in machine guns and their accessories. Parkhurst retired from Pratt & Whitney *c*.1895 but was afterwards associated with the American Ordnance Company and the Bethlehem Steel Company. He was a founder member of the American Society of Mechanical Engineers in 1880 and served his home city of Hartford as Councillor and Alderman. In 1900 he contributed to the journal *American Machinist* some articles of reminiscences dealing with the early history of the American machine-tool industry and, in particular, the earliest milling machines and the origin of the turret lathe.

RTS

Parry, George

fl. 1800–1850 Wales

Welsh ironmaker and inventor of the bell and hopper for blast furnaces.

Until the mid-nineteenth century, blast furnaces were open at the top to facilitate loading of the iron ore, fuel and flux (the charge). However, that arrangement allowed the hot gases produced in the furnace to escape, whereas they could have been used to heat boilers or the incoming air blast. Attempts had been made to capture the fugitive gases, but they had all failed until George Parry devised his bell and hopper equipment for closing the throat or top of the furnace. He fixed an inverted cone or hopper inside the throat and arranged inside it a cast-iron bell that could be raised or lowered. When in the raised position, it was in contact with the underside of the hopper, thus sealing the furnace. The hot gases could then be led off through a large pipe to do useful work. The charge was dropped onto the bell, and when enough had accumulated there the bell was lowered, allowing the charge to fall into the furnace. The gas escaped only for the brief period that the bell was lowered. The advantages of this arrangement were soon realized by other ironmasters and it was quite rapidly, and then generally, adopted. The device was still in use in the 1990s, with modifications.

Bibliography

1858, 'On the principal causes of derangements in blast furnaces', *Proceedings of the South Wales Institute of Engineers* 1: 26–39 (describes his improvements to the blast furnace), 28 ff. (relates to the improvements in the charging arrangements).

Further Reading

W.K.V. Gale, 1969, *Iron and Steel*, London: Longmans, p. 52.

LRD

Parseval, August von

b. 1861
d. 22 February 1942 Berlin, Germany

German designer of tethered observation balloons and non-rigid airships.

Major von Parseval and his colleague Captain von Sigsfeld were serving in the German army during the 1890s when improved military observation from the air was being pursued. Tethered observation balloons, raised and lowered by a winch, had been used since 1794, but in strong winds a spherical balloon became very unstable. Manned kites were being developed by 'Colonel' S. F. **Cody**, in Britain, and others, but kites were a problem if the wind dropped. A very successful compromise was achieved in 1897 by von Parseval and von Sigsfeld, who developed a kite-balloon, the *Drachen* ('Dragon'), which was elongated like an airship and fitted with large inflated fins. It was attached to its tethering cable in such a way that it flew with a positive incidence (nose up) to the wind, thus producing some lift – like a kite. The combination of these factors made the kite-balloon very stable. Other countries followed suit and a version designed by the Frenchman Albert Caquot was widely used during the First World War for observing the results of artillery fire. Caquot balloons were also used around London as a barrage to obstruct enemy aircraft, and 'barrage balloons' were widely used during the Second World War. After working at a government balloon factory in Berlin where non-rigid airships were built, von Parseval designed his own non-rigid airship. The *Parseval I* which flew in 1906 was small, but larger and faster non-rigids followed. These were built by Luftfahrzeug-Gesellschaft m.b.H. of Berlin founded in 1908 to build and operate Parseval airships. The British Admiralty ordered three Parseval airships, two to be built by Vickers of Barrow (who had built the rigid airship *R 1 Mayfly* in 1911), and one to be built in Berlin. This one was flown from Berlin to Farnborough in 1913 and joined the Vickers-built Parseval in the Naval Air Service. During the First World War, Parseval airships had the unique distinction of serving on both sides. Three small Parseval airships were built between 1929 and 1932 for use in advertising.

Further Reading

A. Hildebrandt, 1908, *Airships Past and Present*, London (describes the kite-balloon).
Fred Gütschow, 1985, *Das Luftschiff*, Stuttgart (includes a record of all the airships).
Basil Clarke, 1961, *The History of Airships*, London (provides limited coverage of von Parseval's work).
Basil Collier, 1974, *The Airship: A History*, London (provides limited coverage of von Parseval's work).

JDS

Parsons, Sir Charles Algernon

b. 13 June 1854 London, England
d. 11 February 1931 on board *Duchess of Rich-mond*, Kingston, Jamaica

English eingineer, inventor of the steam turbine and developer of the high-speed electric generator.

The youngest son of the Earl of Rosse, he came from a family well known in scientific circles, the six boys growing up in an intellectual atmosphere at Birr Castle, the ancestral home in Ireland, where a forge and large workshop were available to them. Charles, like his brothers, did not go to school but was educated by private tutors of the character of Sir Robert Ball, this type of education being interspersed with overseas holiday trips to France, Holland, Belgium and Spain in the family yacht. In 1871, at the age of 17, he went to Trinity College, Dublin, and after two years he went on to St John's College, Cambridge. This was before the Engineering School had opened, and Parsons studied mechanics and mathematics.

In 1877 he was apprenticed to W.G. Armstrong & Co. of Elswick, where he stayed for four years, developing an epicycloidal engine that he had designed while at Cambridge. He then moved to Kitson & Co. of Leeds, where he went half shares in a small experimental shop working on rocket propulsion for torpedoes.

In 1887 he married Katherine Bethell, who contracted rheumatic fever from early-morning outdoor vigils with her husband to watch his torpedo experiments while on their honeymoon! He then moved to a partnership in Clarke, Chapman & Co. at Gateshead. There he joined the electrical department, initially working on the development of a small, steam-driven marine lighting set. This involved the development of either a low-speed dynamo, for direct coupling to a reciprocating engine, or a high-speed engine, and it was this requirement that started Parsons on the track of the steam turbine. This entailed many problems such as the running of shafts at speeds of up to 40,000 rpm and the design of a DC generator for 18,000 rpm. He took out patents for both the turbine and the generator on 23 April 1884. In 1888 he dissolved his partnership with Clarke, Chapman & Co. to set up his own firm in Newcastle, leaving his patents with the company's owners. This denied him the use of the axial-flow turbine, so

Parsons then designed a radial-flow layout; he later bought back his patents from Clarke, Chapman & Co. His original patent had included the use of the steam turbine as a means of marine propulsion, and Parsons now set about realizing this possibility. He experimented with 2 ft (61 cm) and 6 ft (183 cm) long models, towed with a fishing line or, later, driven by a twisted rubber cord, through a single-reduction set of spiral gearing.

The first trials of the *Turbinia* took place in 1894 but were disappointing due to cavitation, a little-understood phenomenon at the time. He used an axial-flow turbine of 2,000 shp running at 2,000 rpm. His work resulted in a far greater understanding of the phenomenon of cavitation than had hitherto existed. Land turbines of up to 350 kW (470 hp) had meanwhile been built. Experiments with the *Turbinia* culminated in a demonstration which took place at the great Naval Review of 1897 at Spithead, held to celebrate Queen Victoria's Diamond Jubilee. Here, the little *Turbinia* darted in and out of the lines of heavy warships and destroyers, attaining the unheard of speed of 34.5 knots. The following year the Admiralty placed their first order for a turbine-driven ship, and passenger vessels started operation soon after, the first in 1901. By 1906 the Admiralty had moved over to use turbines exclusively. These early turbines had almost all been direct-coupled to the ship's propeller shaft. For optimum performance of both turbine and propeller, Parsons realized that some form of reduction gearing was necessary, which would have to be extremely accurate because of the speeds involved. Parsons's Creep Mechanism of 1912 ensured that any errors in the master wheel would be distributed evenly around the wheel being cut.

Parsons was also involved in optical work and had a controlling interest in the firm of Ross Ltd of London and, later, in Sir Howard Grubb & Sons. He he was an enlightened employer, originating share schemes and other benefits for his employees.

Principal Honours and Distinctions
Knighted. Order of Merit 1927.

Further Reading
A.T. Bowden, 1966, 'Charles Parsons: Purveyor of power', in E.G. Semler (ed.), *The Great*

Masters. *Engineering Heritage*, Vol. II, London: Institution of Mechanical Engineers/Heinemann.

IMcN

Pascal, Blaise

b. 19 June 1623 Clermont Ferrand, France
d. 19 August 1662 Paris, France

French mathematician, physicist and religious philosopher.

Pascal was the son of Etienne Pascal, President of the Court of Aids. His mother died when he was 3 years old and he was brought up largely by his two sisters, one of whom was a nun at Port Royal. They moved to Paris in 1631 and again to Rouen ten years later. He received no formal education. In 1654 he was involved in a carriage accident in which he saw a mystical vision of God and from then on confined himself to philosophical rather than scientific matters. In the field of mathematics he is best known for his work on conic sections and on the laws of probability. As a youth he designed a calculating machine of which, it is said, some seventy were made. His main contribution to technology was his elucidation of the laws of hydrostatics which formed the basis of all hydrostatic machines in subsequent years. Pascal, however, did not put these laws to any practical use: that was left to the English cabinet-maker and engineer Joseph **Bramah** more than a century later. Suffering from indifferent health, Pascal persuaded his brother-in-law Périer to repeat the experiments of Evangelista Torricelli on the pressure of the atmosphere. This involved climbing the 4,000 ft (1,220 m) of the Puy de Dôme, a mountain close to Clermont, with a heavy mercury-in-glass barometer. The experiment was reported in the 1647 pamphlet 'Expériences nouvelles touchant le vide'. The Hydrostatic Law was laid down by Pascal in *Traité de l'équilibre des liqueurs*, published a year after his death. In this he established the fact that in a fluid at rest the pressure is transmitted equally in all directions.

Bibliography
1647, 'Expériences nouvelles touchant le vide'.
1663, *Traité de l'équilibre des liqueurs*.

Further Reading
J. Mesnard, 1951, *Pascal, His Life and Works*.
I. McNeil, 1972, *Hydraulic Power*, London: Longmans.

IMcN

Pasley, General Sir Charles William

b. 8 September 1780 Eskdalemuir, Dumfriesshire, Scotland
d. 19 April 1861 London, England

Scottish Colonel-Commandant, Royal Engineers.

At first he was educated by Andrew Little of Langholm. At the age of 14 he was sent to school at Selkirk, where he stayed for two years until joining the Royal Military Academy at Woolwich in August 1796. He was commissioned as Second Lieutenant in the Royal Artillery and transferred to the Royal Engineers on 1 April 1798. He served at Minorca, Malta, Naples, Sicily, Calabria and in the siege of Copenhagen and in other campaigns. He was promoted First Captain in 1807, and was on the staff of Sir John Moore at the battle of Coruna. He was wounded at the siege of Flushing in 1809 and was invalided for a year, employing his time in learning German.

In November 1810 he published his *Essay on Military Policy and Institutions of the British Empire*, which ran through four editions. In 1811 he was in command of a company of Royal Military Artificers at Plymouth and there he devised a method of education by which the NCOs and troops could teach themselves without 'mathematical masters'. His system was a great success and was adopted at Chatham and throughout the corps. In 1812 he was appointed Director of the School of Military Engineering at Chatham. He remained at Chatham until 1841, when he was appointed Inspector-General of Railways. During this period he organized improved systems of sapping, mining, telegraphing, pontooning and exploding gunpowder on land or under water, and prepared pamphlets and courses of instruction in these and other subjects. In May 1836 he started what is probably the most important work for which he is remembered. This was a book on *Limes, Calcareous Cements, Mortar, Stuccos and Concretes*. The general adoption of Joseph **Aspdin**'s Portland Cement was largely due to Pasley's recommendation of the material.

He was married twice: first in 1814 at Chatham to Harriet Cooper; and then on 30 March

1819 at Rochester to Martha Matilda Roberts, with whom he had six children – she died in 1881.

Principal Honours and Distinctions
KCB 1846. FRS 1816. Honorary DCL, Oxford University 1844.

Bibliography
1810, *Essay on Military Policy and Institutions of the British Empire.*
Limes, Calcareous Cements, Mortar, Stuccos and Concretes.

Further Reading
Porter, *History of the Corps of Royal Engineers.*
DNB.
Proceedings of the Royal Society.

IMcN

Pasteur, Louis
b. 27 December 1822 Dôle, France
d. 28 September 1895 Paris, France

French chemist, founder of stereochemistry, developer of microbiology and immunology, and exponent of the germ theory of disease.

Sustained by the family tanning business in Dôle, near the Swiss border, Pasteur's school career was undistinguished, sufficing to gain him entry into the teacher-training college in Paris, the Ecole Normale. There the chemical lectures by the great organic chemist J.B.A. Dumas (1800–84) fired Pasteur's enthusiasm for chemistry which never left him. Pasteur's first research, carried out at the Ecole, was into tartaric acid and resulted in the discovery of its two optically active forms resulting from dissymmetrical forms of their molecules. This led to the development of stereochemistry. Next, an interest in alcoholic fermentation, first as Professor of Chemistry at Lille University in 1854 and then back at the Ecole from 1857, led him to deny the possibility of spontaneous generation of animal life. Doubt had previously been cast on this, but it was Pasteur's classic research that finally established that the putrefaction of broth or the fermentation of sugar could not occur spontaneously in sterile conditions, and could only be caused by airborne micro-organisms. As a result, he introduced pasteurization or brief, moderate heating to kill pathogens in milk, wine and other foods. The

suppuration of wounds was regarded as a similar process, leading **Lister** to apply Pasteur's principles to revolutionize surgery. In 1860, Pasteur himself decided to turn to medical research. His first study again had important industrial implications, for the silk industry was badly affected by diseases of the silkworm. After prolonged and careful investigation, Pasteur found ways of dealing with the two main infections. In 1868, however, he had a stroke, which prevented him from active carrying out experimentation and restricted him to directing research, which actually was more congenial to him. Success with disease in larger animals came slowly. In 1879 he observed that a chicken treated with a weakened culture of chicken-cholera bacillus would not develop symptoms of the disease when treated with an active culture. He compared this result with **Jenner**'s vaccination against smallpox and decided to search for a vaccine against the cattle disease anthrax. In May 1881 he staged a demonstration which clearly showed the success of his new vaccine. Pasteur's next success, finding a vaccine which could protect against and treat rabies, made him world famous, especially after a person was cured in 1885. In recognition of his work, the Pasteur Institute was set up in Paris by public subscription and opened in 1888. Pasteur's genius transcended the boundaries between science, medicine and technology, and his achievements have had significant consequences for all three fields.

Bibliography
Pasteur published over 500 books, monographs and scientific papers, reproduced in the magnificent *Oeuvres de Pasteur*, 1922–39, ed. Pasteur Vallery-Radot, 7 vols, Paris.

Further Reading
P. Vallery-Radot, 1900, *La vie de Louis Pasteur*, Paris: Hachette; 1958, *Louis Pasteur. A Great Life in Brief*, English trans., New York (the standard biography).
E. Duclaux, 1896, *Pasteur: Histoire d'un esprit*, Paris; 1920, English trans., Philadelphia (perceptive on the development of Pasteur's thought in relation to contemporary science).
R. Dobos, 1950, *Louis Pasteur, Free Lance of Science*, Boston, Mass.; 1955, French trans.

LRD

Pattinson, Hugh Lee

b. 25 December 1796 Alston, Cumberland,
England
d. 11 November 1858 Scot's House, Gateshead, England

English inventor of a silver-extraction process.

Born into a Quaker family, he was educated at
private schools; his studies included electricity
and chemistry , with a bias towards metallurgy.
Around 1821 Pattinson became Clerk and Assistant to Anthony Clapham, a soap-boiler of Newcastle upon Tyne. In 1825 he secured
appointment as Assay Master to the lords of the
manor of Alston. There he was able to pursue the
subject of special interest to him, and in January
1829 he devised a method of separating silver
from lead ore; however, he was prevented from
developing it because of a lack of funds.

Two years later he was appointed Manager of
Wentworth Beaumont's lead-works. There he
was able to continue his researches, which culminated in the patent of 1833 enshrining the invention by which he is best known: a new process for
extracting silver from lead by skimming crystals
of pure lead with a perforated ladle from the
surface of the molten silver-bearing lead, contained in a succession of cast-iron pots. The molten metal was stirred as it cooled until one pot
provided a metal containing 300 oz. of silver to
the ton (8,370 g to the tonne). Until that time,
it was unprofitable to extract silver from lead ores
containing less than 8 oz. per ton (223 g per
tonne), but the Pattinson process reduced that
to 2–3 oz. (56–84 g per tonne), and it therefore
won wide acceptance. Pattinson resigned his
post and went into partnership to establish a
chemical works near Gateshead. He was able to
devise two further processes of importance, one
an improved method of obtaining white lead and
the other a new process for manufacturing magnesia alba, or basic carbonate of magnesium.
Both processes were patented in 1841.

Pattinson retired in 1858 and devoted himself
to the study of astronomy, aided by a 7½ in. (19
cm) equatorial telescope that he had erected at
his home at Scot's House.

Principal Honours and Distinctions
Vice-President, British Association Chemical
Section 1838. Fellow of the Geological Society,
Royal Astronomical Society and Royal Society
1852.

Bibliography
Pattinson wrote eight scientific papers, mainly on
  mining, listed in *Royal Society Catalogue of
  Scientific Papers*, most of which appeared in
  the *Philosophical Magazine*.

Further Reading
J. Percy, *Metallurgy* (volume on lead): 121–44
  (fully describes Pattinson's desilvering process).
Lonsdale, 1873, *Worthies of Cumberland*, pp.
  273–320 (contains details of his life).
T.K. Derry and T.I. Williams, 1960, *A Short
  History of Technology*, Oxford: Oxford University Press.

LRD

Paul, Lewis

d. April 1759 Brook Green, London, England

*English inventor of hand carding machines and
partner with **Wyatt** in early spinning machines.*

Lewis Paul, apparently of French Huguenot extraction, was quite young when his father died.
His father was Physician to Lord Shaftsbury, who
acted as Lewis Paul's guardian. In 1728 Paul
made a runaway match with a widow and apparently came into her property when she died a
year later. He must have subsequently remarried.
In 1732 he invented a pinking machine for making the edges of shrouds out of which he derived
some profit.

Why Paul went to Birmingham is unknown,
but he helped finance some of Wyatt's earlier
inventions. Judging by the later patents taken
out by Paul, it is probable that he was the one
interested in spinning, turning to Wyatt for help
in the construction of his spinning machine because he had no mechanical skills. The two men
may have been involved in this as early as 1733,
although it is more likely that they began this
work in 1735. Wyatt went to London to construct a model and in 1736 helped to apply for a
patent, which was granted in 1738 in the name
of Paul. The patent shows that Paul and Wyatt
had a number of different ways of spinning in
mind, but contains no drawings of the machines.
In one part there is a description of sets of rollers
to draw the cotton out more finely that could

have been similar to those later used by Richard **Arkwright**. However, it would seem that Paul and Wyatt followed the other main method described, which might be called spindle drafting, where the fibres are drawn out between the nip of a pair of rollers and the tip of the spindle; this method is unsatisfactory for continuous spinning and results in an uneven yarn.

The spinning venture was supported by Thomas Warren, a well-known Birmingham printer, Edward Cave of *Gentleman's Magazine*, Dr Robert James of fever-powder celebrity, Mrs Desmoulins, and others. Dr Samuel Johnson also took much interest. In 1741 a mill powered by two asses was equipped at the Upper Priory, Birmingham, with, machinery for spinning cotton being constructed by Wyatt. Licences for using the invention were sold to other people including Edward Cave, who established a mill at Northampton, so the enterprise seemed to have great promise. A spinning machine must be supplied with fibres suitably prepared, so carding machines had to be developed. Work was in hand on one in 1740 and in 1748 Paul took out another patent for two types of carding device, possibly prompted by the patent taken out by Daniel **Bourn**. Both of Paul's devices were worked by hand and the carded fibres were laid onto a strip of paper. The paper and fibres were then rolled up and placed in the spinning machine. In 1757 John Dyer wrote a poem entitled *The Fleece*, which describes a circular spinning machine of the type depicted in a patent taken out by Paul in 1758. Drawings in this patent show that this method of spinning was different from Arkwright's. Paul endeavoured to have the machine introduced into the Foundling Hospital, but his death in early 1759 stopped all further development. He was buried at Paddington on 30 April that year.

Bibliography

1738, British patent no. 562 (spinning machine).
1748, British patent no. 636 (carding machine).
1758, British patent no. 724 (circular spinning machine).

Further Reading

G.J. French, 1859, *The Life and Times of Samuel Crompton*, London, App. This should be read in conjunction with R.L. Hills, 1970, *Power in the Industrial Revolution*, Manchester, which shows that the roller drafting system on Paul's later spinning machine worked on the wrong principles.
A.P. Wadsworth and J. de L. Mann, 1931, *The Cotton Trade and Industrial Lancashire, 1600–1780*, Manchester (provides good coverage of the partnership of Paul and Wyatt and the early mills).
E. Baines, 1835, *History of the Cotton Manufacture in Great Britain*, London (this publication must be mentioned, but is now out of date).
A. Seymour-Jones, 1921, 'The invention of roller drawing in cotton spinning', *Transactions of the Newcomen Society* 1 (a more modern account).

RLH

Paul, Robert William

b. 3 October 1869 Highbury, London, England
d. 28 March 1943 London, England

English scientific instrument maker, inventor of the Unipivot electrical measuring instrument, and pioneer of cinematography.

Paul was educated at the City of London School and Finsbury Technical College. He worked first for a short time in the Bell Telephone Works in Antwerp, Belgium, and then in the electrical instrument shop of Elliott Brothers in the Strand until 1891, when he opened an instrument-making business at 44 Hatton Garden, London. He specialized in the design and manufacture of electrical instruments, including the Ayrton Mather galvanometer. In 1902, with a purpose-built factory, he began large batch production of his instruments. He also opened a factory in New York, where uncalibrated instruments from England were calibrated for American customers. In 1903 Paul introduced the Unipivot galvanometer, in which the coil was supported at the centre of gravity of the moving system on a single pivot. The pivotal friction was less than in a conventional instrument and could be used without accurate levelling, the sensitivity being far beyond that of any pivoted galvanometer then in existence.

In 1894 Paul was asked by two entrepreneurs to make copies of **Edison**'s kinetoscope, the pioneering peep-show moving-picture viewer, which had just arrived in London. Discovering that Edison had omitted to patent the machine in England, and observing that there was considerable demand for the machine from showpeople, he began production, making six before the end of the year. Altogether, he made about sixty-six units, some of which were exported. Although Edison's machine was not patented, his films were certainly copyrighted, so Paul now needed a cinematographic camera to make new subjects for his customers. Early in 1895 he came into contact with Birt **Acres**, who was also working on the design of a movie camera. Acres's design was somewhat impractical, but Paul constructed a working model with which Acres filmed the Oxford and Cambridge Boat Race on 30 March, and the Derby at Epsom on 29 May. Paul was unhappy with the inefficient design, and developed a new intermittent mechanism based on the principle of the Maltese cross. Despite having signed a ten-year agreement with Paul, Acres split with him on 12 July 1895, after having unilaterally patented their original camera design on 27 May. By the early weeks of 1896, Paul had developed a projector mechanism that also used the Maltese cross and which he demonstrated at the Finsbury Technical College on 20 February 1896. His Theatrograph was intended for sale, and was shown in a number of venues in London during March, notably at the Alhambra Theatre in Leicester Square. There the renamed Animatographe was used to show, among other subjects, the Derby of 1896, which was won by the Prince of Wales's horse 'Persimmon' and the film of which was shown the next day to enthusiastic crowds. The production of films turned out to be quite profitable: in the first year of the business, from March 1896, Paul made a net profit of £12,838 on a capital outlay of about £1,000. By the end of the year there were at least five shows running in London that were using Paul's projectors and screening films made by him or his staff.

Paul played a major part in establishing the film business in England through his readiness to sell apparatus at a time when most of his rivals reserved their equipment for sole exploitation. He went on to become a leading producer of films, specializing in trick effects, many of which he pioneered. He was affectionately known in the trade as 'Daddy Paul', truly considered to be the 'father' of the British film industry. He continued to appreciate fully the possibilities of cinematography for scientific work, and in collaboration with Professor Silvanus P. Thompson films were made to illustrate various phenomena to students.

Paul ended his involvement with film making in 1910 to concentrate on his instrument business; on his retirement in 1920, this was amalgamated with the Cambridge Instrument Company. In his will he left shares valued at over £100,000 to form the R.W. Paul Instrument Fund, to be administered by the Institution of Electrical Engineers, of which he had been a member since 1887. The fund was to provide instruments of an unusual nature to assist physical research.

Principal Honours and Distinctions
Fellow of the Physical Society 1920. Institution of Electrical Engineers Duddell Medal 1938.

Bibliography
17 March 1903, British patent no. 6,113 (the Unipivot instrument).
1931, 'Some electrical instruments at the Faraday Centenary Exhibition 1931', *Journal of Scientific Instruments* 8: 337–48.

Further Reading
Obituary, 1943, *Journal of the Institution of Electrical Engineers* 90 (1): 540–1.
P. Dunsheath, 1962, *A History of Electrical Engineering*, London: Faber & Faber, pp. 308–9 (for a brief account of the Unipivot instrument).
John Barnes, 1976, *The Beginnings of Cinema in Britain*, London.
Brian Coe, 1981, *The History of Movie Photography*, London.

BC/GW

Paxton, Sir Joseph
b. 3 August 1801 Milton Bryant, Bedfordshire, England
d. 8 June 1865 Sydenham, London, England

English designer of the Crystal Palace, the first large-scale prefabricated ferrovitreous structure.

The son of a farmer, he had worked in gardens since boyhood and at the age of 21 was employed as Undergardener at the Horticultural Society Gardens in Chiswick, from where he went on to become Head Gardener for the Duke of Devonshire at Chatsworth. It was there that he developed his methods of glasshouse construction, culminating in the Great Conservatory of 1836–40, an immense structure some 277 ft (84.4 m) long, 123 ft (37.5 m) wide and 67 ft (20.4 m) high. Its framework was of iron and its roof of glass, with wood to contain the glass panels; it is now demolished. Paxton went on to landscape garden design, fountain and waterway engineering, the laying out of the model village of Edensor, and to play a part in railway and country house projects.

The structure that made Paxton a household name was erected in Hyde Park, London, to house the Great Exhibition of 1851 and was aptly dubbed, by *Punch*, the Crystal Palace. The idea of holding an international exhibition for industry had been mooted in 1849 and was backed by Prince **Albert** and Henry Cole. The money for this was to be raised by public subscription and 245 designs were entered into a competition held in 1850; however, most of the concepts, received from many notable architects and engineers, were very costly and unsuitable, and none were accepted. That same year, Paxton published his scheme in the *Illustrated London News* and it was approved after it received overwhelming public support.

Paxton's Crystal Palace, designed and erected in association with the engineers **Fox** and Henderson, was a prefabricated glasshouse of vast dimensions: it was 1,848 ft (563.3 m) long, 408 ft (124.4 m) wide and over 100 ft (30.5 m) high. It contained 3,300 iron columns, 2,150 girders, 24 miles (39 km) of guttering, 600,000 ft^3 (17,000 m^3) of timber and 900,000 ft^2 (84,000 m^2) of sheet glass made by Chance Bros. of Birmingham. One of the chief reasons why it was accepted by the Royal Commission Committee was that it fulfilled the competition proviso that it should be capable of being erected quickly and subsequently dismantled and re-erected elsewhere. The Crystal Palace was to be erected at a cost of £79,800, much less than the other designs. Building began on 30 July 1850, with a labour force of some 2,000, and was completed on 31 March 1851. It was a landmark in construction at the time, for its size, speed of construction and its non-eclectic design, and, most of all, as the first great prefabricated building: parts were standardized and made in quantity,

and were assembled on site. The exhibition was opened by Queen Victoria on 1 May 1851 and had received six million visitors when it closed on 11 October. The building was dismantled in 1852 and reassembled, with variations in design, at Sydenham in south London, where it remained until its spectacular conflagration in 1936.

Principal Honours and Distinctions
Knighted 1851. MP for Coventry 1854–65. Fellow Linnaean Society 1853; Horticultural Society 1826. Order of St Vladimir, Russia, 1844.

Further Reading
P. Beaver, 1986, *The Crystal Palace: A Portrait of Victorian Enterprise*, Phillimore.
George F. Chadwick, 1961, *Works of Sir Joseph Paxton 1803–1865*, Architectural Press.

DY

Pennington, William
fl. 1750 England

English patentee of a machine for making holes in the leather backing used for card clothing.

Prior to the spinning process, the raw cotton or wool must be prepared. One stage of the preparation is carding, in which the mass of fibres is drawn out and disentangled before being rolled up into a sliver or rollrag. At first natural teazels were mounted on boards. The wool was caught round their hooks and pulled out as the hand cards were drawn across each other. It is not known when iron wire hooks inserted through a leather backing were substituted for teazels, but in 1750 William Pennington took out a patent, for a machine to make the holes in the leather backing so that the bent wires could be inserted more easily and more regularly. Soon after this a machine for making the complete card clothing was made by Robert **Kay**.

Bibliography
1750, British patent no. 657.

Further Reading
R.L. Hills, 1970, *Power in the Industrial Revolution*, Manchester (includes a brief account of the development of card-clothing machines).

RLH

Percy, John

b. 23 March 1817 Nottingham, England
d. 19 June 1889 London, England

English metallurgist, first Professor of
Metallurgy at the School of Mines, London.

After a private education, Percy went to Paris in
1834 to study medicine and to attend lectures on
chemistry by Gay-Lussac and Thenard. After
1838 he studied medicine at Edinburgh, obtaining his MD in 1839. In that year he was appointed Professor of Chemistry at Queen's
College, Birmingham, moving to Queen's Hospital at Birmingham in 1843. During his time at
Birmingham, Percy became well known for his
analysis of blast furnace slags, and was involved
in the manufacture of optical glass. On 7 June
1851 Percy was appointed Metallurgical Professor and Teacher at the Museum of Practical Geology established in Jermyn Street, London, and
opened in May 1851. In November of 1851,
when the Museum became the Government
(later Royal) School of Mines, Percy was appointed Lecturer in Metallurgy. In addition to
his work at Jermyn Street, Percy lectured on metallurgy to the Advanced Class of Artillery at
Woolwich from 1864 until his death, and from
1866 he was Superintendent of Ventilation at
the Houses of Parliament. He served from 1861
to 1864 on the Special Committee on Iron set
up to examine the performance of armour-plate
in relation to its purity, composition and structure.

Percy is best known for his metallurgical text
books, published by John Murray. Volume I of
Metallurgy, published in 1861, dealt with fuels,
fireclays, copper, zinc and brass; Volume II, in
1864, dealt with iron and steel; a volume on lead
appeared in 1870, followed by one on fuels and
refractories in 1875, and the first volume on gold
and silver in 1880. Further projected volumes on
iron and steel, noble metals, and on copper, did
not materialize. In 1879 Percy resigned from his
School of Mines appointment in protest at the
proposed move from Jermyn Street to South
Kensington. The rapid growth of Percy's metallurgical collection, started in 1839, eventually
forced him to move to a larger house. After his
death, the collection was bought by the South
Kensington (later Science) Museum. Now comprising 3,709 items, it provides a comprehensive
if unselective record of nineteenth-century metallurgy, the most interesting specimens being
those of the first sodium-reduced aluminium
made in Britain and some of the first steel produced by Bessemer in Baxter House. Metallurgy
for Percy was a technique of chemical extraction,
and he has been criticized for basing his system
of metallurgical instruction on this assumption.
He stood strangely aloof from new processes of
steel making such as that of Gilchrist and
Thomas, and tended to neglect early developments in physical metallurgy, but he was the first
in Britain to teach metallurgy as a discipline in its
own right.

Principal Honours and Distinctions
FRS 1847. President, Iron and Steel Institute
1885, 1886.

Bibliography
1861–80, *Metallurgy*, 5 vols, London: John
Murray.

Further Reading
S.J. Cackett, 1989, 'Dr Percy and his metallurgical collection', *Journal of the Hist. Met. Society*
23 (2): 92–8.

RLH

Perga, Apollonius of
See **Apollonius of Perga**.

Perkin, Sir William Henry

b. 12 March 1838 London, England
d. 14 July 1907 Sudbury, England

English chemist, discoverer of aniline dyes, the
first synthetic dyestuffs.

He early showed an aptitude for chemistry and
in 1853 entered the Royal College of Chemistry
as a student under A.W. von **Hofmann**, the first
Professor at the College. By the end of his first
year, he had carried out his first piece of chemical
research, on the action of cyanogen chloride on
phenylamine, which he published in the *Journal*
of the Chemical Society (1857). He became honorary assistant to von Hofmann in 1857; three
years previously he had set up his own chemical
laboratory at home, where he had discovered the
first of the azo dyes, aminoazonapththalene. In
1856 Perkin began work on the synthesis of
quinine by oxidizing a salt of allyl toluidine with
potassium dichromate. Substituting aniline, he

obtained a dark-coloured precipitate which proved to possess dyeing properties: Perkin had discovered the first aniline dye. Upon receiving favourable reports on the new material from manufacturers of dyestuffs, especially Pullars of Perth, Perkin resigned from the College and turned to the commercial exploitation of his discovery. This proved highly successful. From 1858, the dye was manufactured at his Greenford Green works as 'Aniline Purple' or 'Tyrian Purple'. It was later to be referred to by the French as *mauve*. Perkin's discovery led to the development of the modern dyestuffs industry, supplanting dyes from the traditional vegetable sources. In 1869, he introduced two new methods for making the red dye alizarin, in place of the process that involved the use of the madder plant (*Rubia tinctorum*). In spite of German competition, he dominated the British market until the end of 1873. After eighteen years in chemical industry, Perkin retired and devoted himself entirely to the pure chemical research which he had been pursuing since the 1850s. He eventually contributed ninety papers to the Chemical Society and further papers to other bodies, including the Royal Society. For example, in 1867 he published his synthesis of unsaturated organic acids, known as 'Perkin's synthesis'. Other papers followed, on the structure of 'Aniline Purple'. In 1881 Perkin drew attention to the magnetic-rotatory power of some of the substances he had been dealing with. From then on, he devoted particular attention to the application of this phenomenon to the determination of chemical structure.

Perkin won wide recognition for his discoveries and other contributions to chemistry. The half-centenary of his great discovery was celebrated in July 1906 and later that year he received a knighthood.

Principal Honours and Distinctions

Knighted 1906. FRS 1866. President, Chemical Society 1883–5. President, Society of Chemical Industry 1884–5. Royal Society Royal Medal 1879; Davy Medal 1889.

Bibliography

26 August 1856, British patent no. 1984 (Aniline Purple).
1867, 'The action of acetic anhydride upon the hydrides of salicyl, etc.', *Journal of the Chemi-*

cal Society 20: 586 (the first description of Perkin's synthesis).

Further Reading

S.M. Edelstein, 1961, biography in *Great Chemists*, ed. E. Farber, New York: Interscience, pp. 757–72 (a reliable, short account).
R. Meldola, 1908, *Journal of the Chemical Society* 93: 2,214–57 (the most detailed account).

LRD

Perkins, Jacob
b. 9 July 1766 Newburyport, Massachusetts, USA
d. 30 July 1849 London, England

American inventor of a nail-making machine and a method of printing banknotes, investigator of the use of steam at very high pressures.

Perkins's occupation was that of a gold- and silversmith; while he does not seem to have followed this after 1800, however, it gave him the skills in working metals which he would continue to employ in his inventions. He had been working in America for four years before he patented his nail-making machine in 1796. At the time there was a great shortage of nails because only hand-forged ones were available. By 1800, other people had followed his example and produced automatic nail-making machines, but in 1811 Perkins' improved machines were introduced to England by J.C. **Dyer**. Eventually Perkins had twenty-one American patents for a range of inventions in his name.

In 1799 Perkins invented a system of engraving steel plates for printing banknotes, which became the foundation of modern siderographic work. It discouraged forging and was adopted by many banking houses, including the Federal Government when the Second United States Bank was inaugurated in 1816. This led Perkins to move to Philadelphia. In the intervening years, Perkins had improved his nail-making machine, invented a machine for graining morocco leather in 1809, a fire-engine in 1812, a letter-lock for bank vaults and improved methods of rolling out spoons in 1813, and improved armament and equipment for naval ships from 1812 to 1815.

It was in Philadelphia that Perkins became interested in the steam engine, when he met Oliver **Evans**, who had pioneered the use of high-pressure steam. He became a member of the American Philosophical Society and conducted experiments on the compressibility of water before a committee of that society. Perkins claimed to have liquified air during his experiments in 1822 and, if so, was the real discoverer of the liquification of gases. In 1819 he came to England to demonstrate his forgery-proof system of printing banknotes, but the Bank of England was the only one which did not adopt his system.

While in London, Perkins began to experiment with the highest steam pressures used up to that time and in 1822 took out his first of nineteen British patents. This was followed by another in 1823 for a 10 hp (7.5 kW) engine with only 2 in. (51 mm) bore, 12 in. (305 mm) stroke but a pressure of 500 psi (35 kg/cm^2), for which he claimed exceptional economy. After 1826, Perkins abandoned his drum boiler for iron tubes and steam pressures of 1,500 psi (105 kg/cm^2), but the materials would not withstand such pressures or temperatures for long. It was in that same year that he patented a form of uniflow cylinder that was later taken up by L.J. **Todd**. One of his engines ran for five days, continuously pumping water at St Katherine's docks, but Perkins could not raise more finance to continue his experiments.

In 1823 one his high-pressure hot-water systems was installed to heat the Duke of Wellington's house at Stratfield Saye and it acquired a considerable vogue, being used by Sir John Soane, among others. In 1834 Perkins patented a compression ice-making apparatus, but it did not succeed commercially because ice was imported more cheaply from Norway as ballast for sailing ships. Perkins was often dubbed 'the American inventor' because his inquisitive personality allied to his inventive ingenuity enabled him to solve so many mechanical challenges.

Further Reading

Historical Society of Pennsylvania, 1943, biography which appeared previously as a shortened version in the *Transactions of the Newcomen Society* 24.

D. Bathe and G. Bathe, 1943–5, 'The contribution of Jacob Perkins to science and engineering', *Transactions of the Newcomen Society* 24.

D.S.L. Cardwell, 1971, *From Watt to Clausius. The Rise of Thermodynamics in the Early Industrial Age*, London: Heinemann (includes com-

ments on the importance of Perkins's steam engine).

A.F. Dufton, 1940–1, 'Early application of engineering to warming of buildings', *Transactions of the Newcomen Society* 21 (includes a note on Perkins's application of a high-pressure hot-water heating system).

RLH

Perret, Auguste

b. 12 February 1874 Ixelles, near Brussels, Belgium
d. 26 February 1954 Le Havre (?), France

French architect who pioneered and established building design in reinforced concrete in a style suited to the modern movement.

Auguste Perret belonged to the family contracting firm of A. & G. Perret, which early specialized in the use of reinforced concrete. His eight-storey building at 25 *bis* Rue Franklin in Paris, built in 1902–3, was the first example of frame construction in this material and established its viability for structural design. Both ground plan and façade are uncompromisingly modern, the simplicity of the latter being relieved by unobtrusive faience decoration. The two upper floors, which are set back, and the open terrace roof garden set a pattern for future schemes. All of Perret's buildings had reinforced-concrete structures and this was clearly delineated on the façade designs. The concept was uncommon in Europe at the time, when eclecticism still largely ruled, but was derived from the late nineteenth-century skyscraper façades built by Louis **Sullivan** in America. In 1905–6 came Perret's Garage Ponthieu in Paris; a striking example of exposed concrete, it had a central façade window glazed in modern design in rich colours. By the 1920s ferroconcrete was in more common use, but Perret still led the field in France with his imaginative, bold use of the material. His most original structure is the Church of Notre Dame at Le Raincy on the outskirts of Paris (1922–3). The imposing exterior with its tall tower in diminishing stages is finely designed, but the interior has magnificence. It is a wide, light church, the segmented vaulted roof supported on slender columns. The whole structure is in concrete apart from the glass window panels, which extend the full height of the walls all around the church. They provide a symphony of colour culminating in deep blue behind the altar. Because of the slenderness of the columns and the richness of the glass, this church possesses a spiritual atmosphere and unimpeded sight and sound of and from the altar for everyone. It became the prototype for churches all over Europe for decades, from Moser in prewar Switzerland to Spence's postwar Coventry Cathedral.

In a long working life Perret designed buildings for a wide range of purposes, adhering to his preference for ferroconcrete and adapting its use according to each building's needs. In the 1940s he was responsible for the railway station at Amiens, the Atomic Centre at Saclay and, one of his last important works, the redevelopment after wartime damage of the town centre of Le Havre. For the latter, he laid out large open squares enclosed by prefabricated units, which display a certain monotony, despite the imposing town hall and Church of St Joseph in the Place de L'Hôtel de Ville.

Principal Honours and Distinctions
Président des Réunions Internationales des Architectes. American Society of the French Legion of Honour Gold Medal 1950. Elected after the Second World War to the Institut de France. First President of the International Union of Architects on its creation in 1948. RIBA Royal Gold Medal 1948.

Further Reading
P. Blater, 1939, 'Work of the architect A. Perret', *Architektura SSSR* (Moscow) 7:57 (illustrated article).
1848 'Auguste Perret: a pioneer in reinforced concrete', *Civil Engineers' Review*, pp. 296–300.
Peter Collins, 1959, *Concrete: The Vision of a New Architecture: A Study of Auguste Perret and his Precursors*, Faber & Faber.
Marcel Zahar, 1959, *D'Une Doctrine d'Architecture: Auguste Perret*, Paris: Vincent Fréal.

DY

Perry, John
b. 14 February 1850 Garvagh, Co. Londonderry, Ireland (now Northern Ireland)
d. 4 August 1920 London, England

Irish engineer, mathematician and technical-education pioneer.

Educated at Queens College, Belfast, Perry became Physics Master at Clifton College in 1870 until 1874. This was followed by a brief period of study under Sir William **Thomson** in Glasgow. He was then appointed Professor of Engineering at the Imperial College of Japan in Tokyo, where he formed a remarkable research partnership with W.E. **Ayrton**. On his return to England he became Professor of Engineering and Mathematics at City and Guilds College, Finsbury. Perry was the co-inventor with Ayrton of many electrical measuring instruments between 1880 and 1890, including an energy meter incorporating pendulum clocks and the first practicable portable ammeter and voltmeter, the latter being extensively used until superseded by instruments of greater accuracy. An optical indicator for high-speed steam engines was among Perry's many patents. Having made a notable contribution to education, particularly in the teaching of mathematics, he turned his attention in the latter period of his life to the improvement of the gyrostatic compass.

Principal Honours and Distinctions
FRS 1885. President, Institution of Electrical Engineers 1900. Whitworth Scholar 1870.

Bibliography
28 April 1883, jointly with Ayrton, British patent no. 2,156 (portable ammeter and voltmeter).
1900, *England's Neglect of Science*, London (for Perry's collected papers on technical education).

Further Reading
Obituary, 1920, *Journal of the Institution of Electrical Engineers* 58: 901–2.
D.W. Jordan, 1985, 'The cry for useless knowledge: education for a new Victorian technology', *Proceedings of the Institution of Electrical Engineers* 132 (Part A): 587–601.

GW

Peter the Great (Pyotr Alekseyevich Romanov)

b. 10 June 1672 (30 May 1672 Old Style) Moscow, Russia
d. 8 February 1725 (28 January 1725 Old Style) St Petersburg, Russia

Russian Tsar (1682–1725), Emperor of all the Russias (1721–5), founder of the Russian Navy, shipbuilder and scientist; as a shipbuilder he was known by the pseudonym Petr Mikhailov.

Peter the Great was a man with a single-minded approach to problems and with passionate and lifelong interests in matters scientific, military and above all maritime. The unusual and dominating rule of his vast lands brought about the age of Russian enlightenment, and ensured that his country became one of the most powerful states in Europe.

Peter's interest in ships and shipbuilding started in his childhood; c.1687 he had an old English-built day sailing boat repaired and launched, and on it he learned the rudiments of sailing and navigation. This craft (still preserved in St Petersburg) became known as the 'Grandfather of the Russian Navy'. In the years 1688 to 1693 he established a shipyard on Lake Plestsheev and then began his lifelong study of shipbuilding by visiting and giving encouragement to the industry at Archangelsk on the White Sea and Voronezh in the Sea of Azov. In October 1696, Peter took Azov from the Turks, and the Russian Fleet ever since has regarded that date as their birthday. Setting an example to the young aristocracy, Peter travelled to Western Europe to widen his experience and contacts and also to learn the trade of shipbuilding. He worked in the shipyards of Amsterdam and then at the Naval Base of Deptford on the Thames.

The war with Sweden concentrated his attention on the Baltic and, to establish a base for trading and for the Navy, the City of St Petersburg was constructed on marshland. The Admiralty was built in the city and many new shipyards in the surrounding countryside, one being the Olonez yard which in 1703 built the frigate *Standart*, the first for the Baltic Fleet, which Peter himself commanded on its first voyage. The military defence of St Petersburg was effected by the construction of Kronstadt, seawards of the city.

Throughout his life Peter was involved in ship design and it is estimated that one thousand ships were built during his reign. He introduced the building of standard ship types and also, centuries ahead of its time, the concept of prefabrication, unit assembly and the building of part hulls in different places. Officially he was the de-

signer of the ninety-gun ship *Lesnoe* of 1718, and this may have influenced him in instituting Rules for Shipbuilders and for Seamen. In 1716 he commanded the joint fleets of the four naval powers: Denmark, Britain, Holland and Russia.

He established the Marine Academy, organized and encouraged exploration and scientific research, and on his edict the St Petersburg Academy of Science was opened. He was not averse to the recruitment of foreigners to key posts in the nation's service. Peter the Great was a remarkable man, with the unusual quality of being a theorist and an innovator, in addition to the endowments of practicality and common sense.

Further Reading
Robert K. Massie, 1981, *Peter the Great: His Life and Work*, London: Gollancz.
Henri Troyat, 1979, *Pierre le Grand*; pub. in English 1988 as *Peter the Great*, London: Hamish Hamilton (a good all-round biography).

AK/FMW

Pettit Smith, Sir Francis
See **Smith, Sir Francis Pettit**.

Petty, Sir William
b. 26 May 1623 Romsey, Hampshire, England
d. 16 December 1687 London, England

English scientist, medical practitioner, researcher and founder member of the Royal Society of London.

Despite coming from modest circumstances, Petty had an illustrious career, which started with college in France at the age of 13, followed by service on a small coastal ship and then studies at the medical schools of Leyden and Paris. In 1651 he was appointed Professor of Anatomy at Oxford, and by this time was attending meetings of fellow scientists and philosophers which culminated in the founding of the Royal Society of London for Improving Natural Knowledge. In 1652 Petty was sent to Ireland as Physician-General for the Army; he was soon involved in many matters of an intellectual and experimental nature. He took responsibility for the first proper survey of the country and produced maps and an Irish atlas, *Hiberniae Delineatio*, published in 1685. His investigations into political economics had a profound effect on seventeenth-century thinking. Of equal importance were his radical proposals for ship design; he presented many papers on naval architecture to the Royal Society and at one time suggested floating harbours similar to the Mulberry harbours of nearly three centuries later. In 1662 he built the pioneer catamaran *Invention II* (described at the time as a double-bottomed ship!), which was capable of lifting 5 tons of cargo.

Principal Honours and Distinctions
Knighted 1661.

Further Reading
P.G. Dale, 1987, *Sir W. P. of Romsey*, Romsey: LTVAS Group.

FMW

Petzval, Josef Max
b. 1807 Spisska-Beila, Hungary
d. 17 September 1891 Vienna, Austria

Hungarian mathematician and photographic-lens designer, inventor of the first 'rapid' portrait lens.

Although born in Hungary, Petzval was the son of German schoolteacher. He studied engineering at the University of Budapest and after graduation was appointed to the staff as a lecturer. In 1835 he became the University's Professor of Higher Mathematics. Within a year he was offered a similar position at the more prestigious University of Vienna, a chair he was to occupy until 1884.

The earliest photographic cameras were fitted with lenses originally designed for other optical instruments. All were characterized by small apertures, and the long exposures required by the early process were in part due to the 'slow' lenses. As early as 1839, Petzval began calculations with the idea of producing a fast achromatic objective for photographic work. For technical advice he turned to the Viennese optician Peter **Voigtländer**, who went on to make the first Petzval portrait lens in 1840. It had a short focal length but an extremely large aperture for the day, enabling exposure times to be reduced to at least one tenth of that required with other contemporary lenses. The Petzval portrait lens was to become the basic design for years to come and was probably the single most important develop-

ment in making portrait photography possible; by capturing public imagination, portrait photography was to drive photographic innovation during the early years.

Petzval later fell out with Voigtländer and severed his connection with the company in 1845. When Petzval was encouraged to design a landscape lens in the 1850s, the work was entrusted to another Viennese optician, Dietzler. Using some early calculations by Petzval, Voigtländer was able to produce a similar lens, which he marketed in competition, and an acrimonious dispute ensued. Petzval, embittered by the quarrel and depressed by a burglary which destroyed years of records of his optical work, abandoned optics completely in 1862 and devoted himself to acoustics. He retired from his professorship on his seventieth birthday, respected by his colleagues but unloved, and lived the life of a recluse until his death.

Principal Honours and Distinctions
Member of the Hungarian Academy of Science 1873.

Further Reading
J.M. Eder, 1945, *History of Photography*, trans. E. Epstean, New York (provides details of Petzval's life and work; Eder claims he was introduced to Petzval by mutual friends and succeeded in obtaining personal data).
Rudolf Kingslake, 1989, *A History of the Photographic Lens*, Boston (brief biographical details).
L.W. Sipley, 1965, *Photography's Great Inventors*, Philadelphia (brief biographical details).

JW

Phillips, Edouard
b. 21 May 1821 Paris, France
d. 14 December 1889 Pouligny-Saint-Martin, France

French engineer and mathematician who achieved isochronous oscillations of a balance by deriving the correct shape for the balance spring.

Phillips was educated in Paris, at the Ecole Polytechnic and the Ecole des Mines. In 1849 he was awarded a doctorate in mathematical sciences by the University of Paris. He had a varied career in industry, academic and government institutions, rising to be Inspector-General of Mines in 1882.

It was well known that the balance of a watch or chronometer fitted with a simple spiral or helical spring was not isochronous, i.e. the period of the oscillation was not entirely independent of the amplitude. Watch- and chronometer-makers, notably **Breguet** and **Arnold**, had devised empirical solutions to the problem by altering the curvature of the end of the balance spring. In 1858 Phillips was encouraged to tackle the problem mathematically, and two years later he published a complete solution for the helical balance spring and a partial solution for the more complex spiral spring. Eleven years later he was able to achieve a complete solution for the spiral spring by altering the curvature of both ends of the spring. Phillips published a series of typical curves that the watch- or chronometer-maker could use to shape the ends of the balance spring.

Principal Honours and Distinctions
Académie des Sciences 1868. Chairman, Jury on Mechanics, Universal Exhibition 1889.

Bibliography
1861, 'Mémoire sur l'application de la Théorie du Spiral Réglant', *Annales des Mines* 20: 1–107.
1878, *Comptes Rendus* 86: 26–31.
An English translation (by J.D. Weaver) of both the above papers was published by the Antiquarian Horological Society in 1978 (Monograph No. 15).

Further Reading
J.D. Weaver, 1989, 'Edouard Phillips: a centenary appreciation', *Horological Journal* 132: 205–6 (a good short account).
F.J. Britten, 1978, *Britten's Watch and Clock Maker's Handbook*, 16th edn, rev. R. Good (a description of the practical applications of the balance spring).

DV

Phillips, Horatio Frederick
b. 2 February 1845 London, England
d. 15 July 1926 Hampshire, England

English aerodynamicist whose cambered two-surface wing sections provided the foundations for aerofoil design.

At the age of 19, Phillips developed an interest in flight and constructed models with lightweight engines. He spent a large amount of time and money over many years, carrying out practical research into the science of aerodynamics. In the early 1880s he built a wind tunnel with a working section of 15 in. by 10 in. (38 cm by 25 cm). Air was sucked through the working section by an adaptation of the steam injector used in boilers and invented by Henry **Giffard**, the airship pioneer. Phillips tested aerofoils based on the cross-section of bird's wings, with a greater curvature on the upper surface than the lower. He measured the lift and drag and showed that the major component of lift came from suction on the upper surface, rather than pressure on the lower. He took out patents for his aerofoil sections in 1884 and 1891. In addition to his wind-tunnel test, Phillips tested his wing sections on a whirling arm, as used earlier by **Cayley**, **Wenham** and **Lilienthal**. After a series of tests using an arm of 15 ft (4.57 m) radius, Phillips built a massive whirling arm driven by a steam engine. His test pieces were mounted on the end of the arm, which had a radius of 50 ft (15.24 m), giving them a linear speed of 70 mph (113 km/h). By 1893 Phillips was ready to put his theories to a more practical test, so he built a large model aircraft driven by a steam engine and tethered to run round a circular track. It had a wing span of 19 ft (5.79 m), but it had fifty wings, one above the other. These wings were only 10 in. (25 cm) wide and mounted in a frame, so it looked rather like a venetian blind. At 40 mph (64 km/h) it lifted off the track. In 1904 Phillips built a full-size multi-wing aeroplane with twenty wings which just lifted off the ground but did not fly. He built another multi-wing machine in 1907, this time with four 'venetian blind' frames in tandem, giving it two hundred wings! Phillips made a short flight of almost 500 ft (152 m) which could be claimed to be the first powered aeroplane flight in England by an Englishman. He retired from flying at the age of 62.

Bibliography
1900, 'Mechanical flight and matters relating thereto', *Engineering* (reprint).
1891–3, 'On the sustentation of weight by mechanical flight', *Aeronautical Society of Great Britain* 23rd Report.

Further Reading
J. Laurence Pritchard, 1957, 'The dawn of aerodynamics', *Journal of the Royal Aeronautical*

Society (March) (good descriptions of Phillips's early work and his wind tunnel).

J.E. Hodgson, 1924, *The History of Aeronautics in Great Britain*, London.

F.W. Brearey, 1891–3, 'Remarks on experiments made by Horatio Phillips', *Aeronautical Society of Great Britain* 23rd Report.

JDS

Piccard, Auguste

b. 28 January 1884 Basel, Switzerland
d. 24 March 1962 Lausanne, Switzerland

Swiss physicist who developed balloons to explore the upper atmosphere.

Auguste Piccard and his twin brother, Jean-Félix, studied together in Zurich and qualified as a physicist and a chemist, respectively. In 1913 they made a sixteen-hour balloon flight together, and in 1915 they joined the balloon section of the Swiss Army. Auguste moved to Brussels as Professor of Applied Physics in 1922 and he carried out research into cosmic radiation. He realized that he needed to ascend into the rarefied air of the stratosphere in order to study these cosmic rays. His target was 16,000 m (52,500 ft), but no one had ever ventured to this height before.

Not surprisingly, Auguste Piccard turned to a balloon for his experiments, and during 1930 he designed a hydrogen balloon with a spherical gondola to house the crew. This gondola was sealed and pressurized with air, just as a modern airliner has a pressurized cabin. With Belgian finance, Piccard was able to build his balloon, and on 27 May 1931 he and his colleague Paul Kipfer reached a height of 15,781 m (51,775 ft). Although this was a world record and created great public interest, Piccard was a scientist rather than a record breaker, and as he needed further information he prepared for another ascent. His new gondola was equipped with radio and improved scientific equipment. On 18 August 1932 it ascended from Zurich and reached a height of 16,201 m (53,152 ft).

Jean-Félix was also interested in high-altitude balloon flights and in 1934, together with his wife, he ascended through a clouded sky and reached 17,550 m (57,579 ft). Jean-Félix also tested a gondola lifted by ninety-eight small balloons, and he developed frost-resistant windows. Other balloonists followed with record-breaking high-altitude flights, but Auguste Piccard, aided by his son Jacques, turned his attention to exploration of the depths of the ocean.

Bibliography
1950, *Between Earth and Sky*, London.
1956, *In Balloon and Bathyscaph*, London.

Further Reading
D.H. de Vorkin, 1990, *Race to the Stratosphere*, Berlin (the first chapters describe the work of the Piccard twins).
Pierre de Latil and Jean Rivoire, 1962, *Le Professeur Auguste Piccard*, France.

JDS

Pickard, James

fl. *c.*1780 Birmingham, England

English patentee of the application of the crank to steam engines.

James Pickard, the Birmingham button maker, also owned a flour mill at Snow Hill, in 1780, where Matthew **Wasborough** installed one of his rotative engines with ratchet gear and a flywheel. In August 1780, Pickard obtained a patent (no. 1263) for an application to make a rotative engine with a crank as well as gearwheels, one of which was weighted to help return the piston in the atmospheric cylinder during the dead stroke and overcome the dead centres of the crank. Wasborough's flywheel made the counterweight unnecessary, and engines were built with this and Pickard's crank. Several Birmingham business people seem to have been involved in the patent, and William Chapman of Newcastle upon Tyne was assigned the sole rights of erecting engines on the Wasborough–Pickard system in the counties of Northumberland, Durham and York. Wasborough was building engines in the south until his death the following year. The patentees tried to bargain with **Boulton** & **Watt** to exchange the use of the crank for that of the separate condenser, but Boulton & Watt would not agree, probably because James Watt claimed that one of his workers had stolen the idea of the crank and divulged it to Pickard. To avoid infringing Pickard's patent, Watt patented his sun-and-planet motion for his rotative engines.

Bibliography
August 1780, British patent no. 1,263 (rotative engine with crank and gearwheels).

Further Reading
J. Farey, 1827, *A Treatise on the Steam Engine, Historical, Practical and Descriptive*, reprinted 1971, Newton Abbot: David & Charles (contains an account of Pickard's crank).
R.L. Hills, 1989, *Power from Steam. A History of the Stationary Steam Engine*, Cambridge University Press (provides an account of Pickard's crank).
R.A. Buchanan, 1978–9, 'Steam and the engineering community in the eighteenth century', *Transactions of the Newcomen Society* 50 ('Thomas Newcomen. A commemorative symposium') (provides details about the development of his engine).

RLH

Pierce, George Washington

b. 11 January 1872 Austin, Texas, USA
d. 25 August 1956 Franklin, New Hampshire, USA

American physicist who made various contributions to electronics, particularly crystal oscillators.

Pierce entered the University of Texas in 1890, gaining his BSc in physics in 1893 and his MSc in 1894. After teaching and doing various odd jobs, in 1897 he obtained a scholarship to Harvard, obtaining his PhD three years later. Following a period at the University of Leipzig, he returned to the USA in 1903 to join the teaching staff at Harvard, where he soon established new courses and began to gain a reputation as a pioneer in electronics, including the study of crystal rectifiers and publication of a textbook on wireless telegraphy. In 1912, with **Kennelly**, he conceived the idea of motional impedance. The same year he was made first Director of Harvard's Cruft High-Tension Electrical Laboratory, a post he held until his retirement. In 1917 he was appointed Professor of Physics, and for the remainder of the First World War he was also involved in work on submarine detection at the US Naval Base in New London. In 1921 he was appointed Rumford Professor of Physics and became interested in the work of Walter **Cady** on crystal-controlled circuits. As a result of this he patented the Pierce crystal oscillator in 1924. Having discovered the magnetostriction property of nickel and nichrome, in 1928 he also invented the magnetostriction oscillator. The

mercury-vapour discharge lamp is also said to have been his idea. He became Gordon McKay Professor of Physics and Communications in 1935 and retired from Harvard in 1940, but he remained active for the rest of his life with the study of sound generation by birds and insects.

Principal Honours and Distinctions
President, Institute of Radio Engineers 1918–19. Institute of Electrical and Electronics Engineers Medal of Honour 1929.

Bibliography
1910, *Principles of Wireless Telegraphy*.
1914, US patent no. 1,450,749 (a mercury vapour tube control circuit).
1919, *Electrical Oscillations and Electric Waves*.
1922, 'The piezo-electric Resonator', *Proceedings of the Institute of Radio Engineers* 10: 83.

Further Reading
F.E. Terman, 1943, *Radio Engineers' Handbook*, New York: McGraw-Hill (for details of piezo-electric crystal oscillator circuits).

KF

Pierce, John Robinson

b. 27 March 1910 Des Moines, Iowa, USA

American scientist and communications engineer said to be the 'father' of communication satellites.

From his high-school days, Pierce showed an interest in science and in science fiction, writing under the pseudonym of J.J. Coupling. After gaining Bachelor's, Master's and PhD degrees at the California Institute of Technology (CalTech) in Pasadena in 1933, 1934 and 1936, respectively, Pierce joined the Bell Telephone Laboratories in New York City in 1936. There he worked on improvements to the travelling-wave tube, in which the passage of a beam of electrons through a helical transmission line at around 7 per cent of the speed of light was made to provide amplification at 860 MHz. He also devised a new form of electrostatically focused electron-multiplier which formed the basis of a sensitive detector of radiation. However, his main contribution to electronics at this time was the invention of the Pierce electron gun – a method of producing a high-density electron beam. In the Second World War he worked with

McNally and Shepherd on the development of a low-voltage reflex klystron oscillator that was applied to military radar equipment.

In 1952 he became Director of Electronic Research at the Bell Laboratories' establishment, Murray Hill, New Jersey. Within two years he had begun work on the possibility of round-the-world relay of signals by means of communication satellites, an idea anticipated in his early science-fiction writings (and by Arthur C. **Clarke** in 1945), and in 1955 he published a paper in which he examined various possibilities for communications satellites, including passive and active satellites in synchronous and non-synchronous orbits. In 1960 he used the National Aeronautics and Space Administration 30 m (98½ ft) diameter, aluminium-coated Echo 1 balloon satellite to reflect telephone signals back to earth. The success of this led to the launching in 1962 of the first active relay satellite (Telstar), which weighed 170 lb (77 kg) and contained solar-powered rechargeable batteries, 1,000 transistors and a travelling-wave tube capable of amplifying the signal 10,000 times. With a maximum orbital height of 3,500 miles (5,600 km), this enabled a variety of signals, including full bandwidth television, to be relayed from the USA to large receiving dishes in Europe.

From 1971 until his 'retirement' in 1979, Pierce was Professor of Electrical Engineering at CalTech, after which he became Chief Technologist at the Jet Propulsion Laboratories, also in Pasadena, and Emeritus Professor of Engineering at Stanford University.

Principal Honours and Distinctions
Institute of Electrical and Electronics Engineers Morris N. Liebmann Memorial Award 1947; Edison Medal 1963; Medal of Honour 1975. Franklin Institute Stuart Ballantine Award 1960. National Medal of Science 1963. Danish Academy of Science Valdemar Poulsen Medal 1963. Marconi Award 1974. National Academy of Engineering Founders Award 1977. Japan Prize 1985. Arthur C. Clarke Award 1987. Honorary DEng Newark College of Engineering 1961. Honorary DSc Northwest University 1961, Yale 1963, Brooklyn Polytechnic Institute 1963. Editor, *Proceedings of the Institute of Radio Engineers* 1954–5.

Bibliography
23 October 1956, US patent no. 2,768,328 (his development of the travelling-wave tube, filed on 5 November 1946).
1947, with L.M. Field, 'Travelling wave tubes', *Proceedings of the Institute of Radio Engineers* 35: 108 (describes the pioneering improvements to the travelling-wave tube).
1947, 'Theory of the beam-type travelling wave tube', *Proceedings of the Institution of Radio Engineers* 35: 111.
1950, *Travelling Wave Tubes*.
1956, *Electronic Waves and Messages*.
1962, *Symbols, Signals and Noise*.
1981, *An Introduction to Information Theory: Symbols, Signals and Noise*: Dover Publications.
1990, with M.A. Knoll, *Signals: Revolution in Electronic Communication*: W.H. Freeman.

KF

Pihl, Carl Abraham

b. 16 January 1825 Stavanger, Norway
d. 14 September 1897 Kristiania (now Oslo), Norway

Norwegian railway engineer, protagonist of narrow-gauge railways.

Pihl trained as an engineer at Göteborg, Sweden, and then moved to London, where he worked under Robert **Stephenson** during 1845 and 1846. In 1850 he returned to Norway and worked with the English contractors building the first railway in Norway, the Norwegian Trunk Railway from Kristiania to Eidsvold, for which the English standard gauge was used. Subsequently he worked in England for a year, but in 1856 joined the Norwegian government's Road Department, which was to have responsibility for railways. In 1865 a distinct Railway Department was set up, and Pihl became Director for State Railway Construction. Because of the difficulties of the terrain and limited traffic, Pihl recommended that in the case of two isolated lines to be built the outlay involved in ordinary railways would not be justified, and that they should be built to the narrow gauge of 3 ft 6 in. (1.07 m). His recommendation was accepted by the Government in 1857 and the two lines were built to this gauge and opened during 1861–4. Six of their seven locomotives, and all their rolling stock, were imported from Britain. The lines cost £3,000 and £5,000 per mile, respectively; a standard-gauge line built in the same period cost £6,400 per mile.

Subsequently, many hundreds of miles of Norwegian railways were built to 3 ft 6 in. (1.07 m) gauge under Pihl's direction. They influenced construction of railways to this gauge in Australia, Southern Africa, New Zealand, Japan and elsewhere. However, in the late 1870s controversy arose in Norway over the economies that could in fact be gained from the 3 ft 6 in. (1,07 m) gauge. This controversy in the press, in discussion and in the Norwegian parliament became increasingly acrimonious during the next two decades; the standard-gauge party may be said to have won with the decision in 1898, the year after Pihl's death, to build the Bergen–Oslo line to standard gauge.

Principal Honours and Distinctions
Knight of the Order of St Olaf 1862; Commander of the Order of St Olaf 1877. Commander of the Royal Order of Vasa 1867. Royal Order of the Northern Star 1882.

Further Reading
P. Allen and P.B. Whitehouse, 1959, *Narrow Gauge Railways of Europe*, Ian Allan (describes the Norwegian Battle of the Gauges).
A biographical article on Pihl appears (in Norwegian) in *Norsk Biografisk Leksikon*.

See also **Fox, Sir Charles**; **Inoue, Masaru**; **Spooner, Charles Easton**.

PJGR

Pilcher, Percy Sinclair
b. 16 January 1867 Bath, England
d. 2 October 1899 Stanford Hall, Northamptonshire, England

English designer and glider aeronaut.

He was educated at HMS Britannia Royal Naval College, Dartmouth, from 1880 to 1882. He sailed on HMS *Duke of Wellington*, *Agincourt*, *Northampton* and other ships and resigned from the navy on 18 April 187 after seven years at sea. In June 1887 he was apprenticed at Randolph, Elder & Co.'s shipyard at Govan, and was then an apprentice moulder at Cairn & Co., Glasgow. For some time he 'studied' at London University (though there is no official record of his doing

so) while living with his sister at Phillbeck Gardens, South Kensington. In May 1890 he was working for John H. Biles, Manager of the Southampton Naval Works Ltd. Biles was later appointed Professor of Naval Architecture at Glasgow University with Pilcher as his Assistant Lecturer. In 1895 he was building his first glider, the Bat, which was built mainly of Riga pine and weighed 44 lb (20 kg). In succeeding months he travelled to Lichterfelde to study the gliders made by the German **Lilienthal** and built a further three machines, the Beetle, the Gull and the Hawk. In 1896 he applied for his only aeronautical patent, for 'Improved flying and soaring machines', which was accepted on March 1897. In April 1896 he resigned his position at Glasgow University to become Assistant to Sir Hiram **Maxim**, who was also doing experiments with flying machines at his Nordenfeld Guns and Ammunition Co. Ltd at Crayford. He took up residence in Artillery Mansions, Victoria Street, later taken over by Vickers Ltd. Maxim had a hangar at Upper Lodge Farm, Austin Eynsford, Kent: using this, Pilcher reached a height of 12 ft (3.66 m) in 1899 with a cable launch. He planned to build a 2 hp (1.5 kW) petrol engine

In September 1899 he went to stay with Lord Braye at Stanford Hall, Northamptonshire, where many people came to see his flying machine, a triplane. The weather was far from ideal, windy and raining, but Pilcher would not disappoint them. A bracing wire broke, the tail collapsed and the pilot crashed to the ground suffering two broken legs and concussion. He did not regain consciousness and died the following day. He was buried in Brompton Cemetery.

Bibliography
1896, British patent no. 9144 'Improved flying and soaring machines'.

Further Reading
P. Jarrett, 1987, *Another Icarus. Percy Pilcher and the Quest for Flight*, Washington, DC: Smithsonian Institution Press.
A. Welch and L. Welch, 1965, *The Story of Gliding*, London: John Murray.

IMcN

Pilkington, Sir Lionel Alexander Bethune (Alastair)

b. 7 January 1920 Calcutta, India

English inventor of the float-glass process.

Pilkington was educated at Sherborne School and Trinity College, Cambridge, where he graduated in mechanical science. He spent one year at Cambridge followed by war service, which lasted until 1945. He returned to complete his degree and then joined Pilkington, the well-known glass manufacturer at St Helens' Lancashire, in 1947. Sir Alastair is not, however, related to the Pilkington family of glassmakers.

The forming of perfectly flat glass that retained its fire finish had eluded glassmakers for centuries. Until the 1950s the only way of making really flat glass was to form plate glass by continuous casting between steel rollers. This destroyed the fire finish, which had to be restored by expensive grinding and polishing. The process entailed the loss of 20 per cent of good glass. The idea of floating glass on molten metal occurred to Sir Alastair in October 1952, and thereafter he remained in charge of development until commercial success had been achieved. The idea of floating molten glass on molten tin had been patented in the United States as early as 1902, but had never been pursued. The Pilkington process in essence was to float a ribbon of molten glass on a bath of molten tin in an inert atmosphere of nitrogen, to prevent oxidation of the tin. It was patented in Britain in 1957 and in the USA two years later. The first production glass issued from the plant in May 1957, although the first good glass did not appear until July 1958. The process was publicly announced the following year and was quickly taken up by the industry. It is now the universal method for manufacturing high quality flat glass.

Having seen through the greatest single advance in glassmaking and one of the most important technological developments this century, Sir Alastair became Chairman of Pilkingtons until 1980 and President thereafter.

Principal Honours and Distinctions
Knighted 1970. FRS 1969. Honorary Fellow of Trinity College, Cambridge, 1991.

Bibliography
1969, 'Float glass process – the review lecture', Royal Society (13 February).

1975, 'Floating windows', *Proceedings of the Royal Institution*, Vol. 48.
1976, 'Float glass – evolution and revolution over 60 years', *Glass Technology*, Vol. 17, no. 5.
1963, 'The development of float glass', *Glass Industry*, (February).

Further Reading
J. Jewkes *et al.*, 1969, *The Sources of Invention*, 2nd ed., London: Macmillan.

LRD

Pi Sheng
See **Bi Sheng**.

Pixii, Antoine Hippolyte
b. 1808 France
d. 1835

French instrument maker who devised the first machine to incorporate the basic elements of a modern electric generator.

Mechanical devices to transform energy from a mechanical to an electrical form followed shortly after **Faraday**'s discovery of induction. One of the earliest was Pixii's magneto generator. Pixii had been an instrument maker to Arago and **Ampère** for a number of years and his machine was first announced to the Academy of Sciences in Paris in September 1832. In this hand-driven generator a permanent magnet was rotated in close proximity to two coils on soft iron cores, producing an alternating current. Subsequently Pixii adapted to a larger version of his machine a 'see-saw' switch or commutator devised by Ampère, in order to obtain a unidirectional current. The machine provided a current similar to that obtained with a chemical cell and was capable of decomposing water into oxygen and hydrogen. It was the prototype of many magneto-electric machines which followed.

Principal Honours and Distinctions
Academy of Sciences, Paris, Gold Medal 1832.

Further Reading
B. Bowers, 1982, *A History of Electric Light and Power*, London, pp. 70–2 (describes the development of Pixii's generator).
C. Jackson, 1833, 'Notice of the revolving electric magnet of Mr Pixii of Paris', *American Journal of Science* 24: 146–7.

GW

Planté, Raimond Louis Gaston

b. 22 April 1834 Orthez, France
d. 21 May 1889 Paris, France

French physicist and inventor of a secondary electric cell from which was developed the widely used lead–acid storage battery.

After a scientific training at the Conservatoire des Arts et Métiers, Planté obtained an appointment as a Laboratory Assistant to Becquerel. Later, when he was employed as a chemist in the Parisian electroplating firm of Christofle et Cie, he carried out investigations into polarization in electrical cells, which led to his discovery of the lead–acid accumulator in 1859. This cell, with lead plates in an electrolyte of dilute sulphuric acid, had the characteristics of a storage device for electrical energy. Its performance was improved considerably if it was repeatedly charged and discharged, the active material being formed electrochemically from the lead of the plate itself. At the time of its discovery the Planté cell had little practical application and it was not until satisfactory dynamos were introduced that its commercial exploitation was possible. The cell was improved by **Faure** and later by **Swan** and others. The lead–acid cell became considerably important in the early days of electricity supply and later for electric traction and automobile use. The results of Planté's researches were communicated to the Academy of Sciences and published in various scientific periodicals. He devoted the last few years of his life to the study of atmospheric electricity.

Principal Honours and Distinctions
Chevalier de la Légion d'honneur 1881. Société d'Encouragement pour l'Industrie Nationale Médaille d'Ampère.

Bibliography
1860, 'Nouvelle Pile secondaire d'une grande puissance', *Comptes rendus* 50: 640–2.
See *Recherches sur l'électricité*, Paris, 1879.

Further Reading
G. Wood Vinal, 1955, *Storage Batteries*, 4th edn, London (describes developments subsequent to Planté's work).
E.W. Wade, 1902, *Secondary Batteries*, London.
GW

Plimsoll, Samuel

b. 10 February 1824 Bristol, England
d. 8 June 1898 Folkestone, Kent, England

English inventor of the Plimsoll Line on ships.

Plimsoll was educated privately and at Dr Eadon's school in Sheffield. On leaving school he became Clerk to a solicitor and then to a brewery, where he rose to become Manager. In 1851 he acted as an honorary secretary to the Great Exhibition. Two years later he went to London and set up as a coal merchant: he published two pamphlets on the coal trade in 1862. After several unsuccessful attempts, he managed to be elected as Member of Parliament for Derby in 1868, in the Radical interest. He concerned himself with mercantile shipping and in 1870 he began his campaign to improve safety at sea, particularly by the imposition of a load-line on vessels to prevent dangerous overloading. In 1871 he introduced a resolution into the House of Commons and also a bill, the Government also having proposed one on the same subject, but strong opposition from the powerful shipping-business interest forced a withdrawal. Plimsoll published a pamphlet, *Our Seamen*, bitterly attacking the shipowners. This aroused public feeling and controversy, and under pressure the Government appointed a Royal Commission in 1873, under the chairmanship of the Duke of Somerset, to examine the matter. Their report did not support Plimsoll's proposal for a load-line, but that did not prevent him from bringing forward his own bill, which was narrowly defeated by only three votes. The Government then introduced its own merchant shipping bill in 1875, but it was so mauled by the Opposition that the Prime Minister, Disraeli, threatened to withdraw it. That provoked a violent protest from Plimsoll in the House, including a description of the shipowners which earned him temporary suspension from the House. He was allowed to return after an apology, but the incident served to heighten public feeling for the seamen. The Government were obliged to hustle through the Merchant Shipping Act 1876, which ensured, among other things, that ships should be marked with what has become universally known as the Plimsoll Line; Plimsoll himself became known as 'The Seamen's Friend'.

In 1880 he relinquished his parliamentary seat at Derby, but he continued his campaign to improve conditions for seamen and to ensure that the measures in the Act were properly carried out.

LRD

Pliny the Elder (Gaius Plinius Secundus)

b. *c*.23 AD Como, Italy
d. 25 August 79 AD near Pompeii, Italy

Roman encyclopedic writer on the natural world.

Pliny was well educated in Rome, and for ten years or so followed a military career with which he was able to combine literary work, writing especially on historical subjects. He completed his duties *c*.57 AD and concentrated on writing until he resumed his official career in 69 AD with administrative duties. During this last phase he began work on his only extant work, the thirty-seven 'books' of his *Historia Naturalis* (Natural History), each dealing with a broad subject such as astronomy, geography, mineralogy, etc. His last post was the command of the fleet based at Misenum, which came to an end when he sailed too near Vesuvius during the eruption that engulfed Pompeii and he was overcome by the fumes.

Pliny developed an insatiable curiosity about the natural world. Unlike the Greeks, the Romans made few original contributions to scientific thought and observation, but some made careful compilations of the learning and observations of Greek scholars. The most notable and influential of these was the *Historia Naturalis*. To the ideas about the natural world gleaned from earlier Greek authors, he added information about natural history, mineral resources, crafts and some technological processes, such as the extraction of metals from their ores, reported to him from the corners of the Empire. He added a few observations of his own, noted during travels on his official duties. Not all the reports were reliable, and the work often presents a tangled web of fact and fable. Gibbon described it as an immense register in which the author has 'deposited the discoveries, the arts, and the errors of mankind'. Pliny was indefatigable in his relentless note-taking, even dictating to his secretary while dining.

During the Dark Ages and early Middle Ages in Western Europe, Pliny's *Historia Naturalis* was the largest known collection of facts about the natural world and was drawn upon freely by a succession of later writers. Its influence survived the influx into Western Europe, from the twelfth century, of translations of the works of Greek and Arab scholars. After the invention of printing in the middle of the fifteenth century, Pliny was the first work on a scientific subject to be printed, in 1469. Many editions followed and it may still be consulted with profit for its insights into technical knowledge and practice in the ancient world.

Bibliography
The standard Latin text with English translation is that edited by H. Rackham *et al.* (1942–63, Loeb Classical Library, London: Heinemann, 10 vols). The French version is by A. Ernout *et al.* (1947– ,Belles Lettres, Paris).

Further Reading
The editions mentioned above include useful biographical and other details. For special aspects of Pliny, see K.C. Bailey, 1929–32, *The Elder Pliny's Chapters on Chemical Subjects*, London, 2 vols.

LRD

Poelzig, Hans

b. 1869 Berlin, Germany
d. June 1936 Berlin, Germany

German teacher and practising architect, the most notable individualistic exponent of the German Expressionist movement in the modern school.

In the last decade of the nineteenth century and in the first of the twentieth, Poelzig did not, like most of his colleagues in Germany and Austria, follow the *Jugendstil* theme or the eclectic or fundamentalist lines: he set a path to individualism. In 1898 he began a teaching career at the Breslau (now Wroclaw, Poland) Academy of Arts and Crafts, remaining there until 1916. He early introduced workshop practice into the curriculum, presaging **Gropius**'s Bauhaus ideas by many years; the school's workshop produced much of the artisan needs for a number of his buildings. From Breslau Poelzig moved to Dresden, where he was appointed City Architect. It was there that he launched his Expressionist line: which was particularly evident in the town hall and concert hall in the city. The structure for which Poelzig is best known and with which his name will always be associated is the Großes Schauspielhaus in Berlin; he had returned to his native city after the First World War and this great theatre was his first commission there. Using modern materials, he created a fabulous interior to seat 5,000 spectators. It was in the form of a vast amphitheatre with projecting stage and with the curving area roofed by a cavernous, stalactited dome, the Arabic-style stalactites of which were utilized by Poelzig for acoustic purposes. In the 1920s Poelzig went on to design cinemas, a field for which Expressionism was especially suited; these included the Capitol Cinema in Berlin and the Deli in Breslau. For his later industrial commissions – for example, the administrative building for the chemical firm I.G. Farben in Frankfurt – he had perforce to design in more traditional modern manner.

Poelzig died in 1936, which spared him, unlike many of his contemporaries, the choice of emigrating or working for National Socialism.

Further Reading
Dennis Sharp, 1966, *Modern Architecture and Expressionism*, Longmans.
Theodor Heuss, 1966, *Hans Poelzig: Lebensbild eines Baumeister*, Tübingen, Germany: Wunderlich.

DY

Poitevin, Alphonse Louise
b. 1819 Conflans, France
d. 1882 Conflans, France

French chemical engineer who established the essential principles of photolithography, carbon printing and collotype printing.

Poitevin graduated as a chemical engineer from the Ecole Centrale in Paris in 1843. He was appointed as a chemist with the Salines National de l'Est, a post which allowed him time for research, and he soon became interested in the recent invention of photography. He conducted a series of electrolytic experiments on daguerreotype plates in 1847 and 1848 which led him to propose a method of photochemical engraving on plates coated with silver or gold. In 1850 he joined the firm of Periere in Lyons, and the same year travelled to Paris. During the 1850s, Poitevin conducted a series of far-reaching experiments on the reactions of chromates with

light, and in 1855 he took out two important patents which exploited the light sensitivity of bichromated gelatine. Poitevin's work during this period is generally recognized as having established the essential principles of photolithography, carbon printing and collotype printing, key steps in the development of modern photomechanical printing. His contribution to the advancement of photography was widely recognized and honours were showered upon him. Particularly welcome was the greater part of the 10,000 franc prize awarded by the Duke of Lynes, a wealthy art lover, for the discovery of permanent photographic printing processes. This sum was not sufficient to allow Poitevin to stop working, however, and in 1869 he resumed his career as a chemical engineer, first managing a glass works and then travelling to Africa to work in silver mines. Upon the death of his father he returned to his home town, where he remained until his own death in 1882.

Principal Honours and Distinctions
Chevalier de la Légion d'honneur 1865. Paris Exposition Internationale Gold Medal for Services to Photography, 1878.

Bibliography
December 1855, British patent nos 2,815, 2,816.

Further Reading
G. Tissandiers, 1876, *A History and Handbook of Photography*, trans. J. Thomson.
J.M. Eder, 1945, *History of Photography*, trans. E. Epstean, New York.
H. Gernsheim and A. Gernsheim, 1969, *The History of Photography*, rev. edn, London.

JW

Pole, William
b. 22 April 1814 Birmingham, England
d. 1900

English engineer and educator.

Although primarily an engineer, William Pole was a man of many and varied talents, being amongst other things an accomplished musician (his doctorate was in music) and an authority on whist. He served an apprenticeship at the Horsley Company in Birmingham, and moved to London in 1836, when he was employed first as

Manager to a gasworks. In 1844 he published a study of the Cornish pumping engine, and he also accepted an appointment as the first Professor of Engineering in the Elphinstone College at Bombay. He spent three pioneering years in this post, and undertook the survey work for the Great Indian Peninsular Railway. Before returning to London in 1848 he married Matilda Gauntlett, the daughter of a clergyman.

Back in Britain, Pole was employed by James Simpson, J.M. Rendel and Robert **Stephenson**, the latter engaging him to assist with calculations on the Britannia Bridge. In 1858 he set up his own practice. He kept a very small office, choosing not to delegate work to subordinates but taking on a bewildering variety of commissions for government and private companies. In the first category, he made calculations for government officials of the main drainage of the metropolis and for its water supply. He lectured on engineering to the Royal Engineers' institution at Chatham, and served on a Select Committee to enquire into the armour of warships and fortifications. He became a member of the Royal Commission on the Railways of Great Britain and Ireland (the Devonshire Commission, 1867) and reported to the War Office on the Martini-Henry rifle. He also advised the India Office about examinations for engineering students. The drafting and writing up of reports was frequently left to Pole, who also made distinguished contributions to the official *Lives* of Robert Stephenson (1864), I.K. **Brunel** (1870) and William **Fairbairn** (1877). For other bodies, he acted as Consulting Engineer in England to the Japanese government, and he assisted W.H. Barlow in calculations for a bridge at Queensferry on the Firth of Forth (1873). He was consulted about many urban water supplies.

Pole joined the Institution of Civil Engineers as an Associate in 1840 and became a Member in 1856. He became a Member of Council, Honorary Secretary (succeeding Manby in 1885–96) and Honorary Member of the Institution. He was interested in astronomy and photography, he was fluent in several languages, was an expert on music, and became the world authority on whist. In 1859 he was appointed Professor of Civil Engineering at University College London, serving in this office until 1867. Pole, whose dates coincided closely with those of Queen Victoria, was one of the great Victorian engineers:

he was a polymath, able to apply his great abilities to an amazing range of different tasks. In engineering history, he deserves to be remembered as an outstanding communicator and popularizer.

Bibliography
1843, 'Comparative loss by friction in beam and direct-action engines', *Proceedings of the Institution of Civil Engineers* 2: 69.

Further Reading
Dictionary of National Biography, London.
Proceedings of the Institution of Civil Engineers 143: 301–9.

AB

Polhem, Christopher
b. 18 December 1661 Tingstade, Gotland, Sweden
d. 1751

Swedish engineer and inventor.

He was the eldest son of Wolf Christopher Polhamma, a merchant. The father died in 1669 and the son was sent by his stepfather to an uncle in Stockholm who found him a place in the Deutsche Rechenschule. After the death of his uncle, he was forced to find employment, which he did with the Biorenklou family near Uppsala where he eventually became a kind of estate bailiff. It was during this period that he started to work with a lathe, a forge and at carpentry, displaying great technical ability. He realized that without further education he had little chance of making anything of his life, and accordingly, in 1687, he registered at the University of Uppsala where he studied astronomy and mathematics, remaining there for three years. He also repaired two astronomical pendulum clocks as well as the decrepit medieval clock in the cathedral. After a year's work he had this clock running properly: this was his breakthrough. He was summoned to Stockholm where the King awarded him a salary of 500 dalers a year as an encouragement to further efforts. Around this time, one of increasing mechanization and when mining was Sweden's principal industry, Pohlem made a model of a hoist frame for mines and the Mines Authority encouraged him to develop his ideas. In 1693 Polhem completed the Blankstot hoist at the Stora Kopparberg mine, which attracted great interest on the European continent.

From 1694 to 1696 Polhem toured factories, mills and mines abroad in Germany, Holland, England and France, studying machinery of all kinds and meeting many foreign engineers. In 1698 he was appointed Director of Mining Engineering in Sweden, and in 1700 he became Master of Construction in the Falu Mine. He installed the Karl XII hoist there, powered by moving beams from a distant water-wheel. His plan of 1697 for all the machinery at the Falu mine to be driven by three large and remote water-wheels was never completed.

In 1707 he was invited by the Elector of Hanover to visit the mines in the Harz district, where he successfully explained many of his ideas which were adopted by the local engineers. In 1700, in conjunction with Gabriel Stierncrona, he founded the Stiersunds Bruk at Husby in Southern Dalarna, a factory for the mass production of metal goods in iron, steel and bronze. Simple articles such as pans, trays, bowls, knives, scissors and mirrors were made there, together with the more sophisticated Polhem lock and the Stiersunds clock. Production was based on water power. Gear cutting for the clocks, shaping hammers for plates, file cutting and many other operations were all water powered, as was a roller mill for the sheet metal used in the factory. He also designed textile machinery such as stocking looms and spinning frames and machines for the manufacture of ribbons and other things.

In many of his ideas Polhem was in advance of his time and Swedish country society was unable to absorb them. This was largely the reason for the Stiersund project being only a partial success. Polhem, too, was of a disputatious nature, self-opinionated almost to the point of conceit. He was a prolific writer, leaving over 20,000 pages of manuscript notes, drafts, essays on a wide range of subjects, which included building, brick-making, barrels, wheel-making, bell-casting, organ-building, methods of stopping a horse from bolting and a curious tap 'to prevent serving maids from sneaking wine from the cask', the construction of ploughs and threshing machines. His major work, *Kort Berattelse om de Fornamsta Mechaniska Inventioner* (A Brief Account of the Most Famous Inventions), was printed in 1729 and is the main source of knowledge about his technological work. He is also known for his 'mechanical alphabet', a collection of some eighty wooden models of mechanisms

for educational purposes. It is in the National Museum of Science and Technology in Stockholm.

Bibliography
1729, *Kort Berattelse om de Fornamsta Mechaniska Inventioner* (A Brief Account of the Most Famous Inventions).

Further Reading
1985, *Christopher Polhem, 1661–1751, 'The Swedish Daedalus'* (catalogue of a travelling exhibition from the Swedish Institute in association with the National Museum of Science and Technology), Stockholm.

IMcN

Pollio, Vitruvius
See **Vitruvius Pollio**.

Poncelet, Jean Victor
b. 1 July 1788 Metz, France
d. 22 December 1867 Paris, France

French mathematician and military and hydraulic engineer.

Poncelet studied mathematics at the Ecole Polytechnique in Paris from 1807 to 1810. He joined the Army, gaining admission to the Corps of Engineers. He worked on the fortifications on the Isle of Walcheren in Holland, and in 1812 he found himself on the Russian front, engulfed in the disastrous defeat of the French at Krasnoi. Poncelet was left for dead on the field, but he was found by the Russians and taken to Saratov, where he was imprisoned for two years. He had ample opportunity there to ponder mathematical problems, a mental process from which stemmed his pioneering advances in projective geometry.

After his release he returned to this native city of Metz, where he undertook routine military engineering and teaching tasks. These left him time to pursue his mathematical studies in projective geometry. This bore fruit in a series of publications, most notably the first volume of his *Traité des propriétés projectives des figures* (1822, Paris), the first book to be devoted to the new discipline of projective geometry. With his election to the Académie des Sciences in 1834, Poncelet moved to Paris and devoted much of his time to developing courses in applied mechanics in the Faculty of Science, resulting in a number of books, especially the *Introduction à la mécanique industrielle, physique ou expérimentale* (1841, Paris: Metz). In 1848 he had attained the rank of general and was made Commandant of the Ecole Polytechnique, a post he held for two years. After his retirement in 1850 he was deeply involved in the industrial machines and tools division at both the Great Exhibition in London in 1851 and the similar exhibition in Paris in 1855.

Most of Poncelet's work in applied mechanics and technology was conceived during the period 1825–40. His technological innovations were centred on hydraulic engineering, and in 1826 he invented an inward-flow turbine. At the same time he directed his attention to the vertical undershot water-wheel, with wooden blades set radially and substituted curved metal blades: he used tight-fitting masonry and floors in the wheel pits so that all the water would be swept into the spaces between the blades. In addition, he ensured that the water flowing from the blades fell clear of the wheel and did not run in tail water. This greatly improved the efficiency of the water–wheel.

Bibliography

H. Tribout, 1936, *Un Grand Savant: le général Jean-Victor Poncelet*, Paris, pp. 204–20 (the most complete list of his published works).

Further Reading

I. Didion, 1870, 'Notice sur la vie et les ouvrages du général J.-V. Poncelet', *Mémoires de l'Académie de Metz* 50: 101–59.

M. Daumas (ed), 1968, *Histoire des techniques*, Vol. 3, Paris (briefly describes his technological work).

LRD

Poniatoff, Alexander Mathew

b. 25 March 1892 Kazan District, Russia
d. 24 October 1980

Russian (naturalized American in 1932) electrical engineer responsible for the development of the professional tape recorder and the first commercially-successful video tape recorder (VTR).

Poniatoff was educated at the University of Kazan, the Imperial College in Moscow, and the Technische Hochschule in Karlsruhe, gaining degrees in mechanical and electrical engineering.

He was in Germany when the First World War broke out, but he managed to escape back to Russia, where he served as an Air Force pilot with the Imperial Russian Navy. During the Russian Revolution he was a pilot with the White Russian Forces, and escaped into China in 1920; there he found work as an assistant engineer in the Shanghai Power Company. In 1927 he immigrated to the USA, becoming a US citizen in 1932. He obtained a post in the research and development department of the General Electric Company in Schenectady, New York, and later at Dalmo Victor, San Carlos, California. During the Second World War he was involved in the development of airborne radar for the US Navy.

In 1944, taking his initials to form the title, Poniatoff founded the AMPEX Corporation to manufacture components for the airborne radar developed at General Electric, but in 1946 he turned to the production of audio tape recorders developed from the German wartime Telefunken Magnetophon machine (the first tape recorder in the truest sense). In this he was supported by the entertainer Bing Crosby, who needed high-quality replay facilities for broadcasting purposes, and in 1947 he was able to offer a professional-quality product and the business prospered.

With the rapid post-war boom in television broadcasting in the USA, a need soon arose for a video recorder to provide 'time-shifting' of live TV programmes between the different US time zones. Many companies therefore endeavoured to produce a video tape recorder (VTR) using the same single-track, fixed-head, longitudinal-scan system used for audio, but the very much higher bandwidth required involved an unacceptably high tape-speed. AMPEX attempted to solve the problem by using twelve parallel tracks and a machine was demonstrated in 1952, but it proved unsatisfactory.

The development team, which included Charles Ginsburg and Ray **Dolby**, then devised a four-head transverse-scan system in which a quadruplex head rotating at 14,400 rpm was made to scan across the width of a 2 in. (5 cm) tape with a tape-to-head speed of the order of 160 ft/sec (about 110 mph; 49 m/sec or 176 km/h) but with a longitudinal tape speed of only 15 in./sec (0.38 m/sec). In this way, acceptable picture quality was obtained with an acceptable tape consumption. Following a public demonstration on 14 April 1956, commercial production of studio-quality machines began to revolutionize the production and distribution of TV programmes, and the perfecting of time-base correctors which could stabilize the signal timing to a few nanoseconds made colour VTRs a practical proposition. However, AMPEX did not rest on its laurels and in the face of emerging competition from helical scan machines, where the tracks are laid diagonally on the tape, the company was able to demonstrate its own helical machine in 1957. Another development was the Videofile system, in which 250,000 pages of facsimile could be recorded on a single tape, offering a new means of archiving information. By 1986, quadruplex VTRs were obsolete, but Poniatoff's role in making television recording possible deserves a place in history.

Poniatoff was President of AMPEX Corporation until 1955 and then became Chairman of the Board, a position he held until 1970.

Further Reading
A. Abrahamson, 1953, 'A short history of television recording', Part I, *JSMPTE* 64: 73; 1973, Part II, *Journal of the Society of Motion Picture and Television Engineers*, 82: 188 (provides a fuller background).
Audio Biographies, 1961, ed. G.A. Briggs, Wharfedale Wireless Works, pp. 255–61 (contains a few personal details about Poniatoff's escape from Germany to join the Russian Navy).
E. Larsen, 1971, *A History of Invention*.
Charles Ginsburg, 1981, 'The horse or the cowboy. Getting television on tape', *Journal of the Royal Television Society* 18: 11 (a brief account of the AMPEX VTR story).

KF/GB-N

Ponton, Mungo
b. 1801 Balgreen, Scotland
d. 1880 Clifton, England

Scottish discoverer of the light sensitivity of potassium bichromate.

Employed as Secretary of the Bank of Scotland, Ponton was an amateur photographer and described details of experiments on the effect of light on potassium bichromate in May 1839, only months after the announcement of the first practicable photographic processes. In a paper communicated to the Society of Arts for Scotland (of which he was Vice-President), Ponton suggested that paper soaked in a solution of potassium bichromate could be used as a cheap substitute for paper coated with silver salts. Although Ponton's descriptions were received with interest, potassium bichromate was not widely employed at the time; his work was to be exploited later, however, in the development of permanent photographic and photomechanical printing processes.

Bibliography
For the original announcement of Ponton's work, see *Edinburgh New Philosophical Journal* 1839, p. 169.

Further Reading
J.M. Eder, 1945, *History of Photography*, trans. E. Epstean, New York.
H. Gernsheim and A. Gernsheim, 1969, *The History of Photography*, rev. edn, London.

JW

Popescu, Elena
b. 1877 Romania
d. 5 September 1944 Bucharest (?), Romania

Romanian inventor of the Romanian needle threader.

Popescu came from a fairly prosperous family. Outwardly she led a conventional life as wife of an army officer and mother of nine children; yet, as her unpublished diaries reveal, even when caught up in the fighting in the First World War she led an intense inner life isolated from her surroundings and hardly guessed at even by many members of her family. She seems to have had a mechanical turn of mind, for at the age of 14 she achieved the invention which should have earned her some fame. One day, when home for the school holidays, she saw an elderly servant struggling to thread a needle. Popescu resolved to devise some means of making life easier for the servant. She tried using various materials, including animal and human hair and plant fibres, but finally settled on fine steel wire fashioned into a kind of crochet needle. This did not work too well at first, until its shape had been modified with use. Helped by a mechanically minded younger brother, she made two or three further threaders, which immediately impressed the neighbouring needlewomen. Fired by success, she made 20 or 30 more, but then her return to school occupied her mind to the exclusion of needle threaders. Some twenty years later, when visiting a haberdasher's shop in Bucharest, she noticed on sale a needle threader very similar to her own, advertised as 'recently invented in the USA'.

Further Reading
A. Stanley, 1993, *Mothers and Daughters of Invention*, Meruchen, NJ: Scarecrow Press, 581–3, 912–6.

LRD

Popoff, Andrei Alexandrovitch
b. 21 September 1821 Russia
d. 6 March 1898 Russia

Russian admiral and naval constructor involved in the building of unusual warships.

After graduating from the Naval School Popoff served in the Russian Navy, ultimately commanding the cruiser *Meteor*. During the Crimean War he was Captain of a steamship and was later Manager of Artillery Supplies at Sevastopol. At the conclusion of the war he was appointed to supervise the construction of all steamships and so started his real career in naval procurement. For the best part of thirty years he oversaw the Russian naval building programme, producing many new ships at St Petersburg. Probably the finest was the battleship *Petr Veliki* (Peter the Great), of 9,000 tons displacement, built at Galernii Island in 1869. With some major refits the ship remained in the fleet until 1922. Two remarkable ships were produced at St Petersburg, the *Novgorod* and the *Vice Admiral Popoff* in 1874 and 1876, respectively. Their hull form was almost circular in the hope of creating stable and steady gun platforms and to lessen the required depth of water for their duties as defence ships in the shallow waters of the Black Sea and the Sea of Azov. Despite support for the idea from Sir Edward Reed of the Royal Navy, the designs failed owing to unpleasant oscillations and poor manoeuvring qualities. One further attempt was made to find a successful outcome to this good idea in the construction of the Russian Imperial Yacht *Livadia* at Elder's Glasgow shipyard in 1880: for many reasons the *Livadia* never fulfilled her purpose. Despite their great advantages, the age of the Popoffkas was over. Popoff had a remarkable effect on Russian shipbuilding

and warship design. He had authority, and used it wisely at a time when the Russian shipbuilding industry was developing quickly.

Principal Honours and Distinctions
Honorary Associate of the Institution of Naval Architects, London.

Further Reading
Fred T. Jane, 1899, *The Imperial Russian Navy*, London.

AK/FMW

Popov, Aleksandr Stepanovich
b. 16 March 1859 Bogoslavsky, Zamod, Ural District, Russia
d. 13 January 1906 St Petersburg, Russia

Russian physicist and electrical engineer acclaimed by the former Soviet Union as the inventor of radio.

Popov, the son of a village priest, received his early education in a seminary, but in 1877 he entered the University of St Petersburg to study mathematics. He graduated with distinction in 1883 and joined the faculty to teach mathematics and physics. Then, increasingly interested in electrical engineering, he became an instructor at the Russian Navy Torpedo School at Krondstadt, near St Petersburg, where he later became a professor. On 7 May 1895 he is said to have transmitted and received **Morse** code radio signals over a distance of 40 m (130 ft) in a demonstration given at St Petersburg University to the Russian Chemical Society, but in a paper published in January 1896 in the *Journal of the Russian Physical and Chemical Society*, he in fact described the use of a coherer for recording atmospheric disturbances such as lightning, together with the design of a modified coherer intended for reception at a distance of 5 km (3 miles). Subsequently, on 26 November 1897, after **Marconi**'s own radio-transmission experiments had been publicized, he wrote a letter claiming priority for his discovery to the English-language journal *Electrician*, in the form of a translated précis of his original paper, but neither the original Russian paper nor the English précis made specific claims of either a receiver or a transmitter as such. However, by 1898 he had certainly developed some form of ship-to-shore radio for the Russian Navy. In 1945, long after the Russian revolution, the communist regime supported his claim to be the inventor of radio, but this is a matter for much debate and the priority of Marconi's claim is generally acknowledged outside the USSR.

Bibliography
1896, *Journal of the Russian Physical and Chemical Society* (his original paper in Russian).
1897, *Electrician* 40: 235 (the English précis).

Further Reading
C. Susskind, 1962, 'Popov and the beginnings of radiotelegraphy', *Proceedings of the Institute of Radio Engineers* 50: 2,036.
—— 1964, Marconi, Popov and the dawn of radiocommunication', *Electronics and Power*, London: Institution of Electrical Engineers, 10: 76.

KF

Porsche, Ferdinand

b. 3 September 1875 Maffersdorf, Austria
d. 30 January 1952 Stuttgart, Baden-Württemberg, Germany

Austrian automobile engineer, designer of the Volkswagen car.

At the age of fifteen, Porsche built a complete electrical installation for his home. In 1894 he went to technical school in Vienna. Four years later he became Manager of the test department of the Bela Egger concern, which later became part of the Brown Boveri organization where he became the first Assistant in the calculating section. In 1899 he joined the long-established coachbuilders Jacob Lohner, and in 1902 a car of his design with mixed drive won the 1,000 kg (2,200 lb) class in the Exelberg races. In 1905 he joined the Austro-Daimler Company as Technical Director; his subsequent designs included an 85 hp mixed-drive racing car in 1907 and in 1912 an air-cooled aircraft engine which came to be known in later years as the 'great-grandfather' of the Volkswagen engine. In 1916, he became Managing Director of Austro-Daimler.

In 1921 he designed his first small car, which, appearing under the name of Sasch, won its class in the 1922 Targa Florio, a gruelling road-race in Italy. In 1923 Porsche left Austro-Daimler and joined the Daimler Company in Untertürkheim, near Stuttgart, Germany. In 1929 he joined the firm of Steyr in Austria as a director and chief engineer, and in 1930 he set up his own independent design office in Stuttgart. In 1932 he visited Russia, and in the same year completed the design calculations for the Auto-Union racing car.

In 1934, with his son Ferry (b. 1909), he prepared a plan for the construction of the German 'people's car', a project initiated by Adolf Hitler and his Nazi regime; in June of that year he signed a contract for the design work on the Volkswagen. Racing cars of his design were also successful in 1934: the rear-engined Auto-Union won the German Grand Prix, and another Auto-Union car took the Flying Kilometre speed record at 327 km/h (203.2 mph). In 1935 Daimler-Benz started pre-production on the Volkswagen. The first trials of the cars took place in the autumn of 1936, and the following year thirty experimental cars were built by Daimler-Benz. In that year, Porsche visited the United States, where he met Henry **Ford**; in October an Auto-Union took the Flying Five Kilometre record at 404.3 km/h (251.2 mph). On 26 May 1938, the foundation stone of the Volkswagen factory was laid in Wolfsburg, near Braunschweig, Germany.

In October 1945 Ferdinand Porsche was arrested by a unit of the United States Army and taken to Hessen; the French army removed him to Baden-Baden, then to Paris and later to Dijon. During this time he was consulted by Renault engineers regarding the design of their *4CV* and designed a diesel-engined tractor. He was finally released on 5 August 1947. His last major work before his death was the approval of the design for the Cisitalia Grand Prix car.

Principal Honours and Distinctions
Poetting Medal 1905. Officer's Cross of Franz Josef 1916. Honorary PhD, Vienna Technical University 1916. Honorary PhD, University of Stuttgart 1924.

Further Reading
K. Ludvigsen, 1983, *Porsche: Excellence Was Expected: The Complete History of the Sports and Racing Cars*, London: Frederick Muller.
T. Shuler and G. Borgeson, 1985, 'Origin and Evolution of the VW Beetle', *Automobile Quarterly* (May).
M. Toogood, 1991, *Porsche – Germany's Legend*, London: Apple Press.

IMcN

Porta, Giovanni Battista (Giambattista) della

b. between 3 October and 15 November 1535
Vico Equense, near Naples, Italy
d. 4 February 1615 Naples, Italy

Italian natural philosopher who published many scientific books, one of which covered ideas for the use of steam.

Giambattista della Porta spent most of his life in Naples, where some time before 1580 he established the Accademia dei Segreti, which met at his house. In 1611 he was enrolled among the Oziosi in Naples, then the most renowned literary academy. He was examined by the Inquisition, which, although he had become a lay brother of the Jesuits by 1585, banned all further publication of his books between 1592 and 1598.

His first book, the *Magiae Naturalis*, which covered the secrets of nature, was published in 1558. He had been collecting material for it since the age of 15 and he saw that science should not merely represent theory and contemplation but must arrive at practical and experimental expression. In this work he described the hardening of files and pieces of armour on quite a large scale, and it included the best sixteenth-century description of heat treatment for hardening steel. In the 1589 edition of this work he covered ways of improving vision at a distance with concave and convex lenses; although he may have constructed a compound microscope, the history of this instrument effectively begins with Galileo. His theoretical and practical work on lenses paved the way for the telescope and he also explored the properties of parabolic mirrors.

In 1563 he published a treatise on cryptography, *De Furtivis Literarum Notis*, which he followed in 1566 with another on memory and mnemonic devices, *Arte del Ricordare*. In 1584 and 1585 he published treatises on horticulture and agriculture based on careful study and practice; in 1586 he published *De Humana Physiognomonia*, on human physiognomy, and in 1588 a treatise on the physiognomy of plants. In 1593 he published his *De Refractione* but, probably because of the ban by the Inquisition, no more were produced until the *Spiritali* in 1601 and his translation of Ptolemy's *Almagest* in 1605. In 1608 two new works appeared: a short treatise on military fortifications; and the *De Distilla-*

tione. There was an important work on meteorology in 1610. In 1601 he described a device similar to Hero's mechanisms which opened temple doors, only Porta used steam pressure instead of air to force the water out of its box or container, up a pipe to where it emptied out into a higher container. Under the lower box there was a small steam boiler heated by a fire. He may also have been the first person to realize that condensed steam would form a vacuum, for there is a description of another piece of apparatus where water is drawn up into a container at the top of a long pipe. The container was first filled with steam so that, when cooled, a vacuum would be formed and water drawn up into it. These are the principles on which Thomas **Savery**'s later steam- engine worked.

Further Reading

Dictionary of Scientific Biography, 1975, Vol. XI, New York: C. Scribner's Sons (contains a full biography).

H.W. Dickinson, 1938, *A Short History of the Steam Engine*, Cambridge University Press (contains an account of his contributions to the early development of the steam-engine).

C. Singer (ed.), 1957, *A History of Technology*, Vol. III, Oxford University Press (contains accounts of some of his other discoveries).

I. Asimov (ed.), 1982, *Biographical Encyclopaedia of Science and Technology*, 2nd edn., New York: Doubleday.

G. Sarton, 1957, *Six wings: Men of Science in the Renaissance*, London: Bodley Head, pp. 85–8.

RLH/IMcN

Porter, Charles Talbot

b. 18 January 1826 Auburn, New York, USA
d. 1910 USA

American inventor of a stone dressing machine, an improved centrifugal governor and a high-speed steam engine.

Porter graduated from Hamilton College, New York, in 1845, read law in his father's office, and in the autumn of 1847 was admitted to the Bar. He practised for six or seven years in Rochester, New York, and then in New York City. He was drawn into engineering when aged about 30, first through a client who claimed to have invented a revolutionary type of engine and offered Porter the rights to it as payment of a debt.

Having lent more money, Porter saw neither the man nor the engine again. Porter followed this with a similar experience over a patent for a stone dressing machine, except this time the machine was built. It proved to be a failure, but Porter set about redesigning it and found that it was vastly improved when it ran faster. His improved machine went into production. It was while trying to get the steam engine that drove the stone dressing machine to run more smoothly that he made a discovery that formed the basis for his subsequent work.

Porter took the ordinary **Watt** centrifugal governor and increased the speed by a factor of about ten; although he had to reduce the size of the weights, he gained a motion that was powerful. To make the device sufficiently responsive at the right speed, he balanced the centrifugal forces by a counterweight. This prevented the weights flying outwards until the optimum speed was reached, so that the steam valves remained fully open until that point and then the weights reacted more quickly to variations in speed. He took out a patent in 1858, and its importance was quickly recognized. At first he manufactured and sold the governors himself in a specially equipped factory, because this was the only way he felt he could get sufficient accuracy to ensure a perfect action. For marine use, the counterweight was replaced by a spring.

Higher speed had brought the advantage of smoother running and so he thought that the same principles could be applied to the steam engine itself, but it was to take extensive design modifications over several years before his vision was realized. In the winter of 1860–1, J.F. **Allen** met Porter and sketched out his idea of a new type of steam inlet valve. Porter saw the potential of this for his high-speed engine and Allen took out patents for it in 1862. The valves were driven by a new valve gear designed by Pius Fink. Porter decided to display his engine at the International Exhibition in London in 1862, but it had to be assembled on site because the parts were finished in America only just in time to be shipped to meet the deadline. Running at 150 rpm, the engine caused a sensation, but as it was non-condensing there were few orders. Porter added condensing apparatus and, after the failure of Ormerod Grierson & Co., entered into an agreement with Joseph **Whitworth** to build the engines. Four were exhibited at the 1867 Paris Exposition Universelle, but Whitworth and Porter fell out and in 1868 Porter returned to America.

Porter established another factory to build his engine in America, but he ran into all sorts of difficulties, both mechanical and financial. Some engines were built, and serious production was started *c*.1874, but again there were further problems and Porter had to leave his firm. High-speed engines based on his designs continued to be made until after 1907 by the Southwark Foundry and Machine Company, Philadelphia, so Porter's ideas were proved viable and led to many other high-speed designs.

Bibliography
1908, *Engineering Reminiscences*, New York: J. Wiley & Sons; reprinted 1985, Bradley, Ill.: Lindsay (autobiography; the main source of information about his life).

Further Reading
R.L. Hills, 1989, *Power from Steam. A History of the Stationary Steam Engine*, Cambridge University Press (examines his governor and steam engine).
O. Mayr, 1974, 'Yankee practice and engineering theory; Charles T. Porter and the dynamics of the high-speed engine', *Technology and Culture* 16 (4) (examines his governor and steam engine).

RLH

Pötsch, Friedrich Hermann

b. 12 December 1842 Biendorf, near Köthen, Germany
d. 9 June 1902 Dresden, Germany

German mine surveyor, inventor of the freezing process for sinking shafts.

Pötsch was the son of a forest officer and could not easily attend school, with the consequences that it took him a long time to obtain the scholarly education needed to enable him to begin work on a higher level with the mining administration in the duchy of Anhalt in 1868. Seven years later, he was licensed as a Prussian mining surveyor and in this capacity he worked with the mining inspectorate of Aschersleben. During that time he frequently came across shafts for brown-coal mines which had been sunk down to watery strata but then had to be abandoned. His solution to the problem was to freeze the quicksand with a solution of chloride; this was better than the previous attempts in England to instal cooling coils at the bottom of the shaft. Pötsch's conception implied the construction of ice walls with the means of boreholes and refrigerators. By his method a set of boreholes was driven through the watery strata, the smaller pipes contained within the main bore pipes, providing a channel through which calcium chloride was pumped, returning through the longer pipe until the ground was frozen solid. He obtained a patent in 1883 and many leading international journals reported on the method the same year.

In 1884 he established the Internationale Gesselschaft für Schacht-, Brücken- und Tunnelbau in Magdeburg and he also became Director of the Poetsch-Sooy-Smith Freezing Company in New Jersey, which constructed the first freezing shaft in America in 1888.

However, Pötsch was successful only for a short period of time and, being a clumsy entrepreneur, he had to dissolve his company in 1894. Unfortunately, his decision to carry out the complete shaft-sinking business did not allow him to concentrate on solving upcoming technical problems of his new process. It was Louis Gebhardt (1861–1924), his former engineer, who took care of development, especially in co-operation with French mining engineers, and thus provided the basis for the freezing process becoming widely used for shaft-sinking in complicated strata ever since.

Bibliography
1886, *Das Gefrierverfahren. Methode für schnelles, sicheres und lotrechtes Abteufen von Schächten im Schwimmsande und überhaupt im wasserreichen Gebirge; für Herstellung tiefgehender Brückenpfeiler und für Tunnel-Bauten in rolligem und schwimmendem Gebirge*, Freiberg.
1889, *Geschichtliches über die Entstehung und Herausbildung des Gefrierverfahrens*, Magdeburg.
1895, *Das Gefrierverfahren und das kombinierte Schachtabbohr- und Gefrierverfahren* (Patent Pötsch), Freiberg.

Further Reading
D. Hoffmann, 1962, *Acht Jahrzehnte Gefrierverfahren nach Pötsch*, Essen: Glückauf (the most substantial biography; also covers technological aspects).
G. Gach, 1986, *In Schacht und Strecke*, Essen: Glückauf, pp. 31–53 (provides information on the development of specialized mining companies in Germany originating in the freezing process).

WK

Poulsen, Valdemar
b. 23 November 1869 Copenhagen, Denmark
d. 23 July 1942 Gentofte, Denmark

Danish engineer who developed practical magnetic recording and the arc generator for continuous radio waves.

From an early age he was absorbed by phenomena of physics to the exclusion of all other subjects, including mathematics. When choosing his subjects for the final three years in Borgedydskolen in Christianshavn (Copenhagen) before university, he opted for languages and history. At the University of Copenhagen he embarked on the study of medicine in 1889, but broke it off and was apprenticed to the machine firm of A/S Frichs Eftf. in Aarhus. He was employed between 1893 and 1899 as a mechanic and assistant in the laboratory of the Copenhagen Telephone Company KTAS. Eventually he advanced to be Head of the line fault department. This suited his desire for experiment and measurement perfectly. After the invention of the telegraphone in 1898, he left the laboratory and with responsible business people he created Aktieselskabet Telegrafonen, Patent Poulsen in order to develop it further, together with Peder Oluf Pedersen (1874–1941). Pedersen brought with him the mathematical background which eventually led to his professorship in electronic engineering in 1922.

The telegraphone was the basis for multinational industrial endeavours after it was demonstrated at the 1900 World's Exhibition in Paris. It must be said that its strength was also its weakness, because the telegraphone was unique in bringing sound recording and reproduction to the telephone field, but the lack of electronic amplifiers delayed its use outside this and the dictation fields (where headphones could be used) until the 1920s. However, commercial interest was great enough to provoke a number of court cases concerning patent infringement, in which Poulsen frequently figured as a witness.

In 1903–4 Poulsen and Pedersen developed the arc generator for continuous radio waves which was used worldwide for radio transmitters in competition with **Marconi**'s spark-generating system. The inspiration for this work came from the research by William **Duddell** on the musical arc. Whereas Duddell had proposed the use of the oscillations generated in his electric arc for telegraphy in his 1901 UK patent, Poulsen contributed a chamber of hydrogen and a transverse magnetic field which increased the efficiency remarkably. He filed patent applications on these constructions from 1902 and the first publication in a scientific forum took place at the International Electrical Congress in St Louis, Missouri, in 1904.

In order to use continuous waves efficiently (the high frequency constituted a carrier), Poulsen developed both a modulator for telegraphy and a detector for the carrier wave. The modulator was such that even the more primitive spark-communication receivers could be used. Later Poulsen and Pedersen developed frequency-shift keying.

The Amalgamated Radio-Telegraph Company Ltd was launched in London in 1906, combining the developments of Poulsen and those of De Forest Wireless Telegraph Syndicate. Poulsen contributed his English and American patents. When this company was liquidated in 1908, its assets were taken over by Det Kontinentale Syndikat for Poulsen Radio Telegrafi, A/S in Copenhagen (liquidated 1930–1). Some of the patents had been sold to C. Lorenz AG in Berlin, which was very active.

The arc transmitting system was in use worldwide from about 1910 to 1925, and the power increased from 12 kW to 1,000 kW. In 1921 an exceptional transmitter rated at 1,800 kW was erected on Java for communications with the Netherlands. More than one thousand installations had been in use worldwide. The competing systems were initially spark transmitters (Marconi) and later rotary converters (**Westinghouse**). Similar power was available from valve transmitters only much later.

From *c*.1912 Poulsen did not contribute actively to further development. He led a life as a well-respected engineer and scientist and served on several committees. He had his private laboratory and made experiments in the composition of matter and certain resonance phenomena; however, nothing was published. It has recently been suggested that Poulsen could not have been unaware of Oberlin **Smith**'s work and publication in 1888, but his extreme honesty in technical matters indicates that his development was indeed independent. In the case of the arc generator, Poulsen was always extremely frank about the inspiration he gained from earlier developers' work.

Bibliography
1899, British patent no. 8,961 (the first British telegraphone patent).
1903, British patent no. 15,599 (the first British arc-generator patent).
His scientific publications are few, but fundamental accounts of his contribution are:
1900, 'Das Telegraphon', *Ann. d. Physik* 3: 754–60;
1904, 'System for producing continuous oscillations', *Trans. Int. El. Congr. St. Louis*, Vol. II, pp. 963–71.

Further Reading
A. Larsen, 1950, *Telegrafonen og den Traadløse*, Ingeniørvidenskabelige Skrifter no. 2, Copenhagen (provides a very complete, although somewhat confusing, account of Poulsen's contributions; a list of his patents is given on pp. 285–93).
F.K. Engel, 1990, *Documents on the Invention of Magnetic Recording in 1878*, New York: Audio Engineering Society, reprint no. 2,914 (G2) (it is here that doubt is expressed about whether Poulsen's ideas were developed independently).

GB-N

Pouncy, John
b. 1820 England
d. 1894 Dorchester (?), Dorset, England

English photographer and pioneer of the gum bichromate permanent printing process.

A professional photographer working from a studio in Dorchester, Pouncy had a long interest in 'permanent' photographs. In 1857 he published two volumes of photolithographed views of Dorset. He was later to devise a number of variations of the photolithographic process.

Pouncy is best remembered for his pigment

process, patented in 1858, using vegetable carbon, gum arabic and potassium bichromate. His prints exhibited at the London Photographic Society the same year were greatly admired. However, Pouncy's gum bichromate process was, in fact, covered by earlier patents filed by **Poitevin**, but this did not deter Pouncy from submitting his prints to the Duke of Lyne's competition for permanent photographs in 1859. For the excellence of his work, Pouncy was awarded the lesser part of the major prize won by Poitevin. Although Pouncy's work was not original, he pioneered the carbon process in England and can be considered the practical founder of the different technique of gum bichromate printing.

Bibliography
10 April 1858, British patent no. 780 (gum bichromate permanent printing process).

Further Reading
John Werge, 1890, *The Evolution of Photography*, London (an interesting contemporary account of Pouncy's work).
J.M. Eder, 1945, *History of Photography*, trans. E. Epstean, New York.
H. Gernshiem and A. Gernsheim, 1969, *The History of Photography*, rev. edn, London.
G. Wakeman, 1973, *Victorian Book Illustration*, Great Britain (a good popular account of Pouncy's work).

JW

Pounder, Cuthbert Coulson
b. 10 May 1891 Hartlepool, England
d. 18 December 1982 Belfast (?), Northern Ireland

English marine engineer and exponent of the slow-speed diesel engine.

Pounder served an apprenticeship with Richardsons Westgarth, marine engineers in north east England. Shortly after, he moved to Harland & Wolff of Belfast and there fulfilled his life's work. He rose to the rank of Director but is remembered for his outstanding leadership in producing the most advanced steam and diesel machinery installations of their time. Harland & Wolff were the main licensees for the Burmeister & Wain marine diesel system, and the Copenhagen company made most of the decisions on design; however, Pounder often found himself in the hot seat and once had the responsibility of concurring with the shipyard's decision to build three Atlantic liners with the largest diesel engines in the world, well beyond the accepted safe levels of extrapolation. With this, Belfast secured worldwide recognition as builders of diesel-driven liners. During the German occupation of Denmark (1940–5), the engineering department at Belfast worked on its own and through systematic research and experimentation built up a database of information that was invaluable in the postwar years.

Pounder was instrumental in the development of airless injection diesel fuel pumps. He was a stalwart supporter of all research and development, and while at Belfast was involved in the building of twelve hundred power units. While in his twenties, Pounder began a literary career which continued for sixty years. The bulk of his books and papers were on engineering and arguably the best known is his work on marine diesel engines, which ran to many editions. He was Chairman of Pametrada, the marine engineering research council of Great Britain, and later of the machinery committee of the British Ship Research Association. He regarded good relations within the industry as a matter of paramount importance.

Principal Honours and Distinctions
President, Institute of Marine Engineers; Denny Gold Medal 1839, 1959. Institution of Mechanical Engineers Ackroyd Stewart Award; James Clayton Award.

Further Reading
Michael Moss and John R. Hume, 1986, *Shipbuilders to the World*, Belfast: Blackstaff.

FMW

Praed, William
b. 24 June 1747 Trevethoe, Leland, St Ives, Cornwall, England
d. 9 October 1833 Trevethoe, Leland, St Ives, Cornwall, England

English banker and Member of Parliament.

Born into a wealthy Cornish family, he was educated at Eton and Magdalen College, Oxford. He was elected Member of Parliament for St Ives in 1774, but it was alleged that his father, who was a banker, had acted as agent for both his son and Drummond, the other candidate for the same party, in the course of which he advanced money to voters 'on their notes payable with interest to the bank of Truro (Praed's bank)' but with the understanding that repayment would not be demanded from those who had voted for Praed and Drummond. Praed's election was therefore declared void on 8 May 1775. He was re-elected in 1780, by which time St Ives was virtually a Praed family monopoly. He served in successive Parliaments until 1806 and then represented Banbury until 1808. Meanwhile, in 1779 he had become a partner in his father's Truro bank, *c.*1801 founded the London bank of Praed & Co. at 189 Fleet Street.

While in Parliament, he was instrumental in obtaining and carrying into effect the Bill for the Grand Junction Canal from Braunston to London. He was elected Chairman of the company formed for constructing the canal and proved an excellent choice, serving the company faithfully for nearly thirty years until his resignation in 1821. Upon his marriage to Elizabeth Tyringham in 1778 he made his home at Tyringham Hall in Buckinghamshire and so was very much in the Grand Junction Canal Company's area. London's Praed Street, in which Paddington Station stands, is named in his honour and the canal basin is at the rear of this street. His monument in Tyringham Church bears a relief illustrating a pair of lock gates and a canal boat.

Further Reading
Alan H. Faulkner, 1972, *The Grand Junction Canal*, Newton Abbot: David & Charles.
L.S. Presnell, 1956, *Country Banking in the Industrial Revolution*, Oxford: Clarendon Press, pp. 295–6.
G.C. Boase and W.P. Courtney, 1874, *Bibliotheca Cornubiensis*, Vol. II, London: Longmans, p. 524.

JHB

Pratt, Francis Ashbury

b. 15 February 1827 Woodstock, Vermont, USA
d. 10 February 1902 Hartford, Connecticut, USA

American mechanical engineer and machine-tool manufacturer.

Francis A. Pratt served an apprenticeship as a machinist with Warren Aldrich, and on completing it in 1848 he entered the Gloucester Machine Works as a journeyman machinist. From 1852 to 1854 he worked at the Colt Armory in Hartford, Connecticut, where he met his future partner, Amos **Whitney**. He then became Superintendent of the Phoenix Iron Works, also at Hartford and run by George S. Lincoln & Company. While there he designed the well-known 'Lincoln' miller, which was first produced in 1855. This was a development of the milling machine built by Robbins & Lawrence and designed by F.W. **Howe**, and incorporated a screw drive for the table instead of the rack and pinion used in the earlier machine.

Whitney also moved to the Phoenix Iron Works, and in 1860 the two men started in a small way doing machine work on their own account. In 1862 they took a third partner, Monroe Stannard, and enlarged their workshop. The business continued to expand, but Pratt and Whitney remained at the Phoenix Iron Works until 1864 and in the following year they built their first new factory. The Pratt & Whitney Company was incorporated in 1869 with a capital of $350,000, F.A. Pratt being elected President. The firm specialized in making machine tools and tools particularly for the armament industry. In the 1870s Pratt made no less than ten trips to Europe gaining orders for equipping armouries in many different countries. Pratt & Whitney was one of the leading firms developing the system of interchangeable manufacture which led to the need to establish national standards of measurement. The Rogers–Bond Comparator, developed with the backing of Pratt & Whitney, played an important part in the establishment of these standards, which formed the basis of the gauges of many various types made by the firm. Pratt remained President of the company until 1898, after which he served as their Consulting Engineer for a short time before retiring from professional life. He was granted a number of patents relating to machine tools. He was a founder member of the American Society of Mechanical Engineers in 1880 and was elected a vice-president in 1881. He was an alderman of the city of Hartford.

Principal Honours and Distinctions
Vice-President, American Society of Mechanical Engineers 1881.

Further Reading
J.W. Roe, 1916, *English and American Tool Builders*, New Haven; reprinted 1926, New York, and 1987, Bradley, Ill. (describes the origin and development of the Pratt & Whitney Company).

RTS

Pratt, Thomas Willis

b. 4 July 1812 Boston, Massachusetts, USA.
d. 10 July 1875 Boston, Massachusetts, USA.

American civil engineer, inventor of the Pratt truss.

The son of Caleb and Sally Pratt, Thomas Pratt attended public school in Boston before going on to the Rensselaer School (now the Rensselaer Polytechnic Institute) in Troy, New York. While at school, his spare time was spent assisting his father, a well-known architect, in his practice. He is said to have drawn a complete set of plans for a substantial house when only 12 years old. At the conclusion of his studies, he was offered a teaching position at Rensselaer but turned it down as he was planning an engineering career; he became a government assistant on the construction of dry docks at Charleston, South Carolina, and Norfolk, Virginia.

After this experience of government work, he turned to railroad construction, first with the Boston and Lowell and Boston and Maine railroads, followed by many others. In this work, he became involved in bridge construction, mostly as consulting engineer. His best-known bridge was that over the Merrimack River at Newburyport, Massachusetts, which he built with six long timber spans and a metal drawspan. He also invented a new method of ship propulsion, a form of steam boiler, an equalizer for drawbridge supports and an improved form of combined timber and steel truss; he is best known, however, for the Pratt truss. This did not truly come into its own until the inception of all-metal construction for bridges, by which time it was too late for Pratt to gain much financial reward from it.

Further Reading
D.B. Steinman and S.R. Watson, 1941, *Bridges and their Builders*, New York: Dover Books.
D. Malone (ed.), *Dictionary of American Biography*, New York: Charles Scribner.

IMcN

Pravaz, Charles Gabriel

b. 24 March 1791 Isère, France
d. 24 June 1853 Lyon, France

French physician, orthopaedic innovator, inventor of the hypodermic syringe and developer of galvanocautery.

Pravaz was educated at the Ecole Polytechnique and served in Napoleon's army until 1814. He qualified in medicine in 1824, practised in Paris and then moved to Lyon, where he founded the orthopaedic Institut de Lyon. In 1853 he produced the first practical hypodermic syringe, and developed galvanocautery.

Principal Honours and Distinctions
Légion d'honneur.

Bibliography
1829, *Recherches sur la possibilité de prévenir l'absorption des virus et des venirs par l'emploi des moyens physiques*.
1853, 'Sur un nouveau moyen d'opérer la coagulation du sang dans les artères', *C. P. Acad. Sci. Paris*.

Further Reading
G. Despierres, 1985, 'Un Lyonnais méconnu', *La Cohorte 7*.

MG

Preece, Sir William Henry

b. 15 February 1834 Bryn Helen, Gwynedd, Wales
d. 6 November 1913 Penrhos, Gwynedd, Wales

Welsh electrical engineer who greatly furthered the development and use of wireless telegraphy and the telephone in Britain, dominating British Post Office engineering during the last two decades of the nineteenth century.

After education at King's College, London, in 1852 Preece entered the office of Edwin Clark with the intention of becoming a civil engineer, but graduate studies at the Royal Institution under **Faraday** fired his enthusiasm for things electrical. His earliest work, as connected with telegraphy and in particular its application for securing the safe working of railways; in 1853 he obtained an appointment with the Electric and National Telegraph Company. In 1856 he became

Superintendent of that company's southern district, but four years later he moved to telegraph work with the London and South West Railway. From 1858 to 1862 he was also Engineer to the Channel Islands Telegraph Company. When the various telegraph companies in Britain were transferred to the State in 1870, Preece became a Divisional Engineer in the General Post Office (GPO). Promotion followed in 1877, when he was appointed Chief Electrician to the Post Office. One of the first specimens of **Bell**'s telephone was brought to England by Preece and exhibited at the British Association meeting in 1877. From 1892 to 1899 he served as Engineer-in-Chief to the Post Office. During this time he made a number of important contributions to telegraphy, including the use of water as part of telegraph circuits across the Solent (1882) and the Bristol Channel (1888). He also discovered the existence of inductive effects between parallel wires, and with **Fleming** showed that a current (thermionic) flowed between the hot filament and a cold conductor in an incandescent lamp.

Preece was distinguished by his administrative ability, some scientific insight, considerable engineering intuition and immense energy. He held erroneous views about telephone transmission and, not accepting the work of Oliver **Heaviside**, made many errors when planning trunk circuits. Prior to the successful use of Hertzian waves for wireless communication Preece carried out experiments, often on a large scale, in attempts at wireless communication by inductive methods. These became of historic interest only when the work of **Maxwell** and **Hertz** was developed by Guglielmo **Marconi**. It is to Preece that credit should be given for encouraging Marconi in 1896 and collaborating with him in his early experimental work on radio telegraphy.

While still employed by the Post Office, Preece contributed to the development of numerous early public electricity schemes, acting as Consultant and often supervising their construction. At Worcester he was responsible for Britain's largest nineteenth-century public hydro-electric station. He received a knighthood on his retirement in 1899, after which he continued his consulting practice in association with his two sons and Major Philip **Cardew**. Preece contributed some 136 papers and printed lectures to scientific journals, ninety-nine during the period 1877 to 1894.

Principal Honours and Distinctions
CB 1894. Knighted (KCB) 1899. FRS 1881. President, Society of Telegraph Engineers, 1880. President, Institution of Electrical Engineers 1880, 1893. President, Institution of Civil Engineers 1898–9. Chairman, Royal Society of Arts 1901–2.

Bibliography
Preece produced numerous papers on telegraphy and telephony that were presented as Royal Institution Lectures (see *Royal Institution Library of Science*, 1974) or as British Association reports.
1862–3, 'Railway telegraphs and the application of electricity to the signaling and working of trains', *Proceedings of the ICE* 22: 167–93.
Eleven editions of *Telegraphy* (with J. Sivewright), London, 1870, were published by 1895.
1883, 'Molecular radiation in incandescent lamps', *Proceedings of the Physical Society* 5: 283.
1885, 'Molecular shadows in incandescent lamps'. *Proceedings of the Physical Society* 7: 178.
1886, 'Electric induction between wires and wires', *British Association Report*.
1889, with J. Maier, *The Telephone*.
1894, 'Electric signalling without wires', *RSA Journal*.
1898, 'Aetheric telegraphy', *Proceedings of the Institution of Electrical Engineers*.

Further Reading
J.J. Fahie, 1899, *History of Wireless Telegraphy 1838–1899*, Edinburgh: Blackwood.
E. Hawkes, 1927, *Pioneers of Wireless*, London: Methuen.
E.C. Baker, 1976, *Sir William Preece, F.R.S. Victorian Engineer Extraordinary*, London (a detailed biography with an appended list of his patents, principal lectures and publications).
D.G. Tucker, 1981–2, 'Sir William Preece (1834–1913)', *Transactions of the Newcomen Society* 53: 119–36 (a critical review with a summary of his consultancies).

GW/KF

Presbyter, Theophilus

See **Theophilus Presbyter**.

Pretsch, Paul

b. 1808 Vienna, Austria
d. 1873 Vienna, Austria

Austrian printer and inventor of photogalvanography, one of the earliest commercial photomechanical printing processes.

The son of a goldsmith, Pretsch learned the printing trade in Vienna, where he worked until 1831. He then took up a series of posts in Germany, Belgium and Holland before returning to Vienna, where in 1842 he joined the Imperial State Printing Office. The office was equipped with a photographic studio, and Pretsch was encouraged to explore applications of photography to printing and the graphic arts. In 1851 he was sent to London to take responsibility for the Austrian printing exhibits of the Great Exhibition. This event proved to be a significant international show case for photography and Pretsch saw a great number of recent innovations and made many useful contacts. On returning to Vienna, he began to develop a process for producing printing plates from photographs. Using **Talbot**'s discovery that bichromated gelatine swells in water after exposure to light, he electrotyped the relief image obtained. In 1854 Pretsch resigned from his post in Vienna and travelled back to London, where he patented his process, calling it photogalvanography. He went on to form a business, the Photo-Galvano-Graphic Company, to print and market his pictures.

The Photographic Manager of the company was the celebrated photographer Roger Fenton, recently returned from his exploits on the battlefields of the Crimea. In 1856 the company issued a large serial work, *Photographic Art Treasures*, illustrated with Pretsch's pictures, which created considerable interest. The venture did not prove a commercial success, however, and although further plates were made and issued, Fenton found other interests to pursue and Pretsch was left to try to apply some of his ideas to lithography. This too had no successful outcome, and in 1863 Pretsch returned to Vienna. He was reappointed to a post at the Imperial State Printing Office, but his health failed and he made no further progress with his processes.

Bibliography
9 November 1854, British patent no. 2,373.
11 August 1855, British patent no. 1,824.

Further Reading
J.M. Eder, 1945, *History of Photography*, trans. E. Epstean, New York.
H. Gernsheim and A. Gernsheim, 1969, *The History of Photography*, rev. edn, London.
H.J.P. Arnold, 1977, *William Henry Fox Talbot*, London (an account of the relationship with Talbot's process).

JW

Priestman, William Dent

b. 23 August 1847 Sutton, Hull, England
d. 7 September 1936 Hull, England

English oil engine pioneer.

William was the second son and one of eleven children of Samuel Priestman, who had moved to Hull after retiring as a corn miller in Kirkstall, Leeds, and who in retirement had become a director of the North Eastern Railway Company. The family were strict Quakers, so William was sent to the Quaker School in Bootham, York. He left school at the age of 17 to start an engineering apprenticeship at the Humber Iron Works, but this company failed so the apprenticeship was continued with the North Eastern Railway, Gateshead. In 1869 he joined the hydraulics department of Sir William Armstrong & Company, Newcastle upon Tyne, but after a year there his father financed him in business at a small, run down works, the Holderness Foundry, Hull. He was soon joined by his brother, Samuel, their main business being the manufacture of dredging equipment (grabs), cranes and winches. In the late 1870s William became interested in internal combustion engines. He took a sublicence to manufacture petrol engines to the patents of Eugène Etève of Paris from the British licensees, Moll and Dando. These engines operated in a similar manner to the non-compression gas engines of **Lenoir**. Failure to make the two-stroke version of this engine work satisfactorily forced him to pay royalties to Crossley Bros, the British licensees of the **Otto** four-stroke patents.

Fear of the dangers of petrol as a fuel, reflected by the associated very high insurance premiums, led William to experiment with the use of lamp oil as an engine fuel. His first of many patents was for a vaporizer. This was in 1885, well before Ackroyd **Stuart**. What distinguished the Priestman engine was the provision of an air pump which pressurized the fuel tank, outlets at the top and bottom of which led to a fuel atomizer injecting continuously into a vaporizing chamber heated by the exhaust gases. A spring-loaded inlet valve connected the chamber to the atmosphere, with the inlet valve proper between the chamber and the working cylinder being cam-operated. A plug valve in the fuel line and a butterfly valve at the inlet to the chamber were operated, via a linkage, by the speed governor; this is believed to be the first use of this method of control. It was found that vaporization was only partly achieved, the higher fractions of the fuel condensing on the cylinder walls. A virtue was made of this as it provided vital lubrication. A starting system had to be provided, this comprising a lamp for preheating the vaporizing chamber and a hand pump for pressurizing the fuel tank.

Engines of 2–10 hp (1.5–7.5 kW) were exhibited to the press in 1886; of these, a vertical engine was installed in a tram car and one of the horizontals in a motor dray. In 1888, engines were shown publicly at the Royal Agricultural Show, while in 1890 two-cylinder vertical marine engines were introduced in sizes from 2 to 10 hp (1.5–7.5 kW), and later double-acting ones up to some 60 hp (45 kW). First, clutch and gearbox reversing was used, but reversing propellers were fitted later (Priestman patent of 1892). In the same year a factory was established in Philadelphia, USA, where engines in the range 5–20 hp (3.7–15 kW) were made. Construction was radically different from that of the previous ones, the bosses of the twin flywheels acting as crank discs with the main bearings on the outside.

On independent test in 1892, a Priestman engine achieved a full-load brake thermal efficiency of some 14 per cent, a very creditable figure for a compression ratio limited to under 3 : 1 by detonation problems. However, efficiency at low loads fell off seriously owing to the throttle governing, and the engines were heavy, complex and expensive compared with the competition.

Decline in sales of dredging equipment and bad debts forced the firm into insolvency in 1895 and receivers took over. A new company was formed, the brothers being excluded. However, they were able to attend board meetings, but to exert no influence. Engine activities ceased in about 1904 after over 1,000 engines had been made. It is probable that the Quaker ethics of the brothers were out of place in a business that was becoming increasingly cut-throat. William spent the rest of his long life serving others.

Further Reading

C. Lyle Cummins, 1976, *Internal Fire*, Carnot Press.

C. Lyle Cummins and J.D. Priestman, 1985, 'William Dent Priestman, oil engine pioneer and inventor: his engine patents 1885–1901', *Proceedings of the Institution of Mechanical Engineers* 199: 133.

Anthony Harcombe, 1977, 'Priestman's oil engine', *Stationary Engine Magazine* 42 (August).

JB

Pritchard, Thomas Farnolls

b. probably Shrewsbury, England
d. 23 December 1777 Shrewsbury, England

English architect and builder renowned for designing the first cast-iron bridge in England.

In 1775 Pritchard designed the Ironbridge bridge, which was built over the River Severn by Abraham **Darby** of Coalbrookdale in 1777–9. It is constructed of five parallel arch ribs almost 200 ft (61 m) in length. The spandrels are filled by circles and ogee arch heads, while the roadway above is made from cast-iron plates 2½ in. (64 mm) thick. The bridge, which weighs 400 tons, was made in the Coalbrookdale foundry and took only three months to erect.

DY

Prony, Baron de

See **Riche, Gaspard-Clair-François-Marie**.

Pullman, George Mortimer

b. 3 March 1831 Brocton, New York, USA
d. 19 October 1897 Chicago, Illinois, USA

American inventor of the Pullman car.

Pullman was initially a cabinet-maker in Albion, New York, and then became a road-works contractor in Chicago. Observing a need for improved sleeping accommodation on trains, he arranged in 1858 with the Chicago & Alton Railroad to convert two of their coaches into sleeping cars by incorporating upper berths hinged to the sides of the car. These and a third car entered service in 1859 and were popular with passengers, but other railways were reluctant to adopt them.

Pullman moved to the Colorado mining area and kept a general store, but in 1863 he returned to Chicago. With Ben Field he spent a year building the car *Pioneer*, which not only incorporated the folding upper berths but also had seats arranged to convert into lower berths. When *Pioneer* entered service, the travelling public was enthusiastic: Pullman and Field built more cars, and an increasing number of railways arranged to operate them under contract. In 1867 Pullman and Field organized the Pullman Palace Car Company, which grew to have five car-building plants. Pullman introduced a combined sleeping/restaurant car in 1867 and the dining car in 1868.

In 1872 James Allport, General Manager of the Midland Railway in Britain, toured the USA and was impressed by Pullman cars. He arranged with Pullman for the American company to ship a series of Pullman cars to Britain in parts for Midland to assemble at its works at Derby. The first, a sleeping car, was completed early in 1874 and entered service on the Midland Railway. Several others followed the same year, including the first Pullman Parlor Car, a luxury coach for day rather than overnight use, to enter service in Europe. Pullman formed the Pullman Palace Car Company (Europe), and although the Midland Railway purchased the Pullman cars running on its system a few years later, Pullman cars were used on many other railways in Britain (notably the London Brighton & South Coast Railway) and on the continent of Europe. In 1881 the Pullman Parlor Car *Globe*, running in Britain, became the first vehicle to be illuminated by electric light.

Bibliography
1864, jointly with Field, US patent no. 42,182 (upper berth).
1865, jointly with Field, US patent no. 49,992 (the seat convertible into a lower berth).

Further Reading
Dictionary of American Biography
C. Hamilton Ellis, 1965, *Railway Carriages in the British Isles*, London: George Allen & Unwin, Ch. 6 (describes the introduction of Pullman cars to Europe).

PJGR

Pupin, Michael Idvorsky
b. 4 October 1858 Idvor, Banat, Serbia
d. 12 March 1935 New York, USA

Serbian/American applied physicist involved in the development of fluoroscopy and radiological diagnosis.

Pupin's early education was in Prague and then he emigrated alone to America in 1874. After five years of farm and factory jobs accompanied by night study, he gained admission to Columbia University, New York, in 1879. He graduated in 1883 and after a period at Cambridge University, England, worked under **Helmholtz** in Berlin. He received his doctorate in 1889.

He returned to Columbia and, apart from his involvement in X-ray diagnosis in 1896, was engaged in practical work in connection with problems in telegraphy and telephony, radio transmitters and electrical network theory. In 1901 he was appointed Professor of Electromechanics, a post that he held for thirty years. He acted as an adviser on behalf of Yugoslavia at the 1919 Peace Conference.

Principal Honours and Distinctions
Member of the National Academy of Sciences. Pulitzer Prize.

Bibliography
1896, 'A few remarks on experiments with roentgen rays', *Electricity*, New York.
1924, *From Immigrant to Inventor* (autobiography).
1938, *Biographical Memoirs*, National Academy of Sciences, Washington, DC.

MG

Purvis, Frank Prior
b. 18 April 1850 London, England
d. 20 February 1940 Seaford Downs, England

English naval architect.

Despite being one of the youngest entrants to

the South Kensington School of Naval Architecture, Purvis obtained both a Whitworth Exhibition and a Scholarship. Upon graduating he commenced a career in shipbuilding that involved him in military, civil and research work in Scotland, England and Japan. Initially he worked in Robert **Napier**'s shipyard on the River Clyde, and then in the London drawing offices of Sir Edward Reed, before joining the staff of the Admiralty, where he assisted William **Froude** in his classic ship experiments at Torquay. After a short spell with Sir William Pearce at Govan, Purvis joined William Denny and Bros and with his recently gained knowledge of hydrodynamics helped set up the world's first commercial ship model tank at Dumbarton. His penultimate appointment was that of Shipbuilding Partner in the Scottish shipyard of Blackwood and Gordon.

In 1901 he became Professor of Naval Architecture at the Imperial University of Tokyo (succeeding Percy Hillhouse, who had become Naval Architect of Fairfield and later became Professor at Glasgow University) and it was in this role that Purvis was to achieve distinction through developing a teaching course of the highest order. It is accepted that his influence on the Japanese shipbuilding industry was profound. After nineteen years of service he retired to the United Kingdom.

Bibliography

Purvis presented several papers to the Institution of Naval Architects and to the Institution of Engineers and Shipbuilders in Scotland, and in 1900 he assisted in the preparation of the Ships and Shipbuilding supplement to *Encyclopaedia Britannica*.

FMW

Q

Qiao Weiyue (Chiao Wei-Yo)

fl. *c*.980/987 China

Chinese canal engineer who constructed pound-lock gates on the Huai section of the Grand Canal.

Qiao held office as Assistant Transport Commissioner of Huainan *c*.984. In the course of his duties he constructed true pound-lock gates on the Huai section of the Grand Canal as a means of preventing tax frauds on grain, which resulted from the frequent wrecking of grain-carrying boats on the canal's double slipways. The pound locks included suspended lock gates (portcullis gates), implying some mechanism for raising and lowering them. The locks were covered over by a shed-like roof and were large enough to accommodate several barges at a time. Qiao's pound locks were the first in any civilization: they probably resembled those illustrated in the work of the Italian writer Vittorio **Zonca** on machines of the seventeenth century.

Further Reading
J. Needham, *Science and Civilisation in China*, Cambridge: Cambridge University Press, 1971, vol. IV.3, pp. 350–2, 357, 660(i).

LRD

Quincke, Heinrich Irenaeus

b. 28 August 1842 Frankfurt an der Oder, Germany
d. 19 May 1922 Frankfurt am Main, Germany

German physician, inventor of the technique of lumbar puncture.

Quincke trained in medicine at Berlin, Würzburg and Heidelberg Universities. Following three years as a postgraduate at the University of Berlin, he was appointed Professor of Internal Medicine at Berne. Five years later he was appointed to the Chair in Kiel that he held for the next thirty years.

During this time his researches included the study of angioneurotic oedema, blood pressure and the systemic responses to carotid sinus stimulation. His studies of lumbar puncture procedures in animals led to the use of the technique in humans, and in 1911 he reported on the results of using the procedure twenty-two times in ten patients.

Bibliography
1902, *Die Technik der Lumbarpunktion*.
1890, 'Lumbar Puncture in Hydrocephalus', *Klin. Wschr.*

MG

R

Radcliffe, William
b. 1761 Mellor, Cheshire, England
d. 1842 Mellor, Cheshire, England

English inventor of the sizing machine.

Radcliffe was brought up in the textile industry and learned carding and spinning as a child. When he was old enough, he became a weaver. It was a time when there were not enough weavers to work up all the yarn being spun on the recently invented spinning machines, so some yarn was exported. Radcliffe regarded this as a sin; meetings were held to prohibit the export, and Radcliffe promised to use his best endeavours to discover means to work up the yarn in England. He owned a mill at Mellor and by 1801 was employing over 1,000 hand-loom weavers. He wanted to improve their efficiency so they could compete against power looms, which were beginning to be introduced at that time.

His first step was to divide up as much as possible the different weaving processes, not unlike the plan adopted by **Arkwright** in spinning. In order to strengthen the warp yarns made of cotton and to reduce their tendency to fray during weaving, it was customary to apply an adhesive substance such as starch paste. This was brushed on as the warp was unwound from the back beam during weaving, so only short lengths could be treated before being dried. Instead of dressing the warp in the loom as was hitherto done, Radcliffe had it dressed in a separate machine, relieving the weaver of the trouble and saving the time wasted by the method previously used. Radcliffe employed a young man names Thomas **Johnson**, who proved to be a clever mechanic. Radcliffe patented his inventions in Johnson's name to avoid other people, especially foreigners, finding out his ideas. He took out his first patent, for a dressing machine, in March 1803 and a second the following year. The combined result of the two patents was the introduction of a beaming machine and a dressing machine which, in addition to applying the paste to the yarns and then drying them, wound them onto a beam ready for the loom. These machines

enabled the weaver to work a loom with fewer stoppages; however, Radcliffe did not anticipate that his method of sizing would soon be applied to power looms as well and lead to the commercial success of powered weaving. Other manufacturers quickly adopted Radcliffe's system, and Radcliffe himself soon had to introduce power looms in his own business.

Radcliffe improved the hand looms themselves when, with the help of Johnson, he devised a cloth taking-up motion that wound the woven cloth onto a roller automatically as the weaver operated the loom. Radcliffe and Johnson also developed the 'dandy loom', which was a more compact form of hand loom and was also later adapted for weaving by power. Radcliffe was among the witnesses before the Parliamentary Committee which in 1808 awarded Edmund **Cartwright** a grant for his invention of the power loom. Later Radcliffe was unsuccessfully to petition Parliament for a similar reward for his contributions to the introduction of power weaving. His business affairs ultimately failed partly through his own obstinacy and his continued opposition to the export of cotton yarn. He lived to be 81 years old and was buried in Mellor churchyard.

Bibliography
1811, *Exportation of Cotton Yarn and Real Cause of the Distress that has Fallen upon the Cotton Trade for a Series of Years Past*, Stockport.
1828, *Origin of the New System of Manufacture, Commonly Called 'Power-Loom Weaving'*, Stockport (this should be read, even though it is mostly covers Radcliffe's political aims).

Further Reading
A. Barlow, 1870, *The History and Principles of Weaving by Hand and by Power*, London (provides an outline of Radcliffe's life and work).
W. English, 1969, *The Textile Industry*, London (a general background of his inventions).
R.L. Hills, 1970, *Power in the Industrial Revolution*, Manchester (a general background).
D.J. Jeremy, 1981, *Transatlantic Industrial Revolution. The Diffusion of Textile Technologies*

Between Britain and America, 1790–1830s, Oxford (discusses the spread of the sizing machine in America).

RLH

Railton, Reid Anthony

b. 24 June 1895 Alderley Edge, Cheshire, England
d. 1 September 1977 Berkeley, California, USA.

English designer of record-breaking automobiles and motor boats.

Railton was educated at Rugby School and Manchester University. From 1915 to 1917 he served an apprenticeship with Leyland Motors, after which he served in the Motor Boat Section of the Royal Naval Volunteer Reserve (RNVR). Having obtained his Royal Aeronautical Club (RAeC) pilot's certificate in 1918, he went to the United States to study factory layout. He was Assistant to the Chief Engineer of Leyland Motors from 1921 to 1923, when he became Managing Director of Arab Motors Limited of Letchworth, Hertfordshire.

Railton was engineering consultant to Sir Malcolm Campbell, and was responsible for Campbell's Bluebird II boat which set a water speed record of 228.1 km/h (141.7 mph) in 1939. He was the designer of John R. Cobb's Napier Railton car which broke the speed record for automobiles on 16 September 1947 with an average speed of 634.3 km/h (394.2 mph); this record stood until 1964, when it was broken by Sir Malcolm Campbell's son Donald. Railton was also responsible for Cobb's boat, Crusader, which was the first to exceed 200 mph (322 km/h).

Railton presented many papers to the Institution of Automobile Engineers, the Institution of Mechanical Engineers and the Society of Automotive Engineers in the United States. In his later years, he lived in Berkeley, California.

Further Reading
1971–80, *Who Was Who*, London: A. & C. Black.

IMcN

Raky, Anton

b. 5 January 1868 Seelenberg, Taunus, Germany
d. 22 August 1943 Berlin, Germany

German inventor of rapid percussion drilling, entrepreneur in the exploration business.

While apprenticed at the drilling company of E. Przibilla, Raky already called attention by his reflections towards developing drilling methods and improving tools. Working as a drilling engineer in Alsace, he was extraordinarily successful in applying an entire new hydraulic boring system in which the rod was directly connected to the chisel. This apparatus, driven by steam, allowed extremely rapid percussions with very low lift.

With some improvements, his boring rig drilled deep holes at high speed and at least doubled the efficiency of the methods hitherto used. His machine, which was also more reliable, was secured by a patent in 1895. With borrowed capital, he founded the Internationale Bohrgesellschaft in Strasbourg in the same year, and he began a career in the international exploration business that was unequalled as well as breathtaking. Until 1907 the total depth of the drillings carried out by the company was 1,000 km.

Raky's rapid drilling was unrivalled and predominant until improved rotary drilling took over. His commercial sense in exploiting the technical advantages of his invention by combining drilling with producing the devices in his own factory at Erkelenz, which later became the headquarters of the company, and in speculating on the concessions for the explored deposits made him by far superior to all of his competitors, who were provoked into contests which they generally lost. His flourishing company carried out drilling in many parts of the world; he became the initiator of the Romanian oil industry and his extraordinary activities in exploring potash and coal deposits in different parts of Germany, especially in the Ruhr district, provoked the government in 1905 into stopping granting claims to private companies. Two years later, he was forced to withdraw from his holding company because of his restless and eccentric character. He turned to Russia and, during the First World War, he was responsible for the reconstruction of the destroyed Romanian oilfields. Thereafter, partly financed by mining companies, he continued explorations in several European countries, and in Germany he was pioneering again with exploring oilfields, iron ore and lignite deposits which later grew in economic value. Similar to **Glenck** a generation before, he was a daring entrepreneur who took many risks and opened new avenues of exploration, and he was constantly having to cope with a weak financial position, selling concessions and shares, most of them to Preussag and Wintershall; however, this could not prevent his business from collapse in 1932. He finally gave up drilling in 1936 and died a poor man.

Principal Honours and Distinctions
Dr-Ing. (Hon.) Bergakademie Clausthal 1921.

Further Reading
G.P.R. Martin, 1967, 'Hundert Jahre Anton Raky', *Erdöl-Erdgas-Zeitschrift*, 83: 416–24 (a detailed description).
D. Hoffmann, 1959, *150 Jahre Tiefbohrungen in Deutschland*, Vienna and Hamburg: 32–4 (an evaluation of his technologial developments).

WK

Rammler, Erich

b. 9 July 1901 Tirpersdorf, near Oelsnitz, Germany
d. 6 November 1986 Freiberg, Saxony, Germany

German mining engineer, developer of metallurgic coke from lignite.

A scholar of the Mining Academy in Freiberg, who in his dissertation dealt with the fineness of coal dust, Rammler started experiments in 1925 relating to firing this material. In the USA this process, based on coal, had turned out to be very effective in large boiler furnaces. Rammler endeavoured to apply the process to lignite and pursued general research work on various thermochemical problems as well as methods of grinding and classifying. As producing power from lignite was of specific interest for the young Soviet Union, with its large demand from its new power stations and its as-yet unexploited lignite deposits, he soon came into contact with the Soviet authorities. In his laboratory in Dresden, which he had bought from the freelance metallurgist Paul Otto Rosin after his emigration and under whom he had been working since he left the Academy, he continued his studies in refining coal and soon gained an international reputation. He opened up means of producing coke from lignite for use in metallurgical processes.

His later work was of utmost importance after the Second World War when several countries in Eastern Europe, especially East Germany with its large lignite deposits, established their own iron and steel industries. Accordingly, the Soviet administration supported his experiments vigorously after he joined Karl **Kegel**'s Institute for Briquetting in Freiberg in 1945. Through his numerous books and articles, he became the internationally leading expert on refining lignite and Kegel's successor as head of the Institute and Professor at the Bergakademie. Six years later, he produced for the first time high-temperature coke from lignite low in ash and sulphur for smelting in low-shaft furnaces. Rammler was widely honoured and contributed decisively to the industrial development of his country; he demonstrated new technological processes when, under austere conditions, economical and ecological considerations were neglected.

Bibliography
Rammler, whose list of publications comprises more than 600 titles on various matters of his main scientific concern, also was the co-author (with E. Wächtler) of two articles on the development of briquetting brown coal in Germany, both published in 1985, *Freiberger Forschungshefte*, D 163 and D 169, Leipzig.

Further Reading
E. Wächtler, W. Mühlfriedel and W. Michel, 1976, *Erich Rammler*, Leipzig, (substantial biography, although packed with communist propaganda).
M. Rasch, 1989, 'Paul Rosin – Ingenieur, Hochschullehrer und Rationalisierungsfachmann'. *Technikgeschichte* 56: 101–32 (describes the framework within which Rammler's primary research developed).

WK

Ramsbottom, John

b. 11 September 1814 Todmorden, Lancashire, England
d. 20 May 1897 Alderley Edge, Cheshire, England

English railway engineer, inventor of the reversing rolling mill.

Ramsbottom's initial experience was gained at the locomotive manufacturers Sharp, Roberts & Co. At the age of 28 he was Manager of the Longsight works of the Manchester & Birmingham Railway, which, with other lines, became part of the London & North Western Railway (L & NWR) in 1846. Ramsbottom was appointed Locomotive Superintendent of its north-eastern division. Soon after 1850 came his first major invention, that of the split-ring piston, consisting of cast-iron rings fitted round the piston to ensure a steam-tight fit in the cylinder. This proved to be successful, with a worldwide application. In 1856 he introduced sight-feed lubrication and the form of safety valve that bears his name. In 1857 he became Locomotive Superintendent of the L & NWR at Crewe, producing two notable classes of locomotives: 2–4–0s for passenger traffic; and 0–6–0s for goods. They were of straightforward design and robust construction, and ran successfully for many years. His most spectacular railway invention was the water trough between the rails which enabled locomotives to replenish their water tanks without stopping.

As part of his policy of making Crewe works as independent as possible, Ramsbottom made several metallurgical innovations. He installed one of the earliest Bessemer converters for steelmaking. More important, in 1866 he coupled the engine part of a railway engine to a two-high rolling mill so that the rolls could be run in either direction, and quickly change direction, by means of the standard railway link reversing gear. This greatly speeded up the rolling of iron or steel into the required sections. He eventually retired in 1871.

Further Reading
J.N. Weatwood, 1977, *Locomotive Designers in the Age of Steam*, London: Sidgwick & Jackson, pp. 43–7.
W.K.V. Gale, 1969, *Iron and Steel*, London: Longmans, p. 80 (provides brief details of his reversing mill).
F.C. Hammerton, 1937, *John Ramsbottom, the Father of the Modern Locomotive*, London.

LRD

Ramsden, Jesse

b. 6 October 1735 (?) Halifax, Yorkshire, England
d. 5 November 1800 Brighton, Sussex, England

English instrument-maker who developed machines for accurately measuring angular and linear scales.

Jesse Ramsden was the son of an innkeeper but received a good general education: after attending the free school at Halifax, he was sent at the age of 12 to his uncle for further study, particularly in mathematics. At the age of 16 he was appriced to a cloth-worker in Halifax and on completion of the apprenticeship in 1755 he moved to London to work as a clerk in a cloth warehouse. In 1758 he became an apprentice in the workshop of a London mathematical instrument-maker named Burton. He quickly gained the skill, particularly in engraving, and by 1762 he was able to set up on his own account. He married in 1765 or 1766 the youngest daughter of the optician John Dollond FRS (1706–61) and received a share of Dollond's patent for making achromatic lenses.

Ramsden's experience and reputation increased rapidly and he was generally regarded as the leading instrument-maker of his time. He opened a shop in the Haymarket and transferred to Piccadilly in 1775. His staff increased to about sixty workers and apprentices, and by 1789 he had constructed nearly 1,000 sextants as well as theodolites, micrometers, balances, barometers, quadrants and other instruments.

One of Ramsden's most important contributions to precision measurement was his development of machines for obtaining accurate division of angular and linear scales. For this work he received a premium from the Commissioners of the Board of Longitude, who published his descriptions of the machines. For the trigonometrical survey of Great Britain, initiated by General William Roy FRS (1726–90) and continued by the Board of Ordnance, Ramsden supplied a 3 ft (91 cm) theodolite and steel measuring chains, and was also engaged to check the glass tubes used to measure the fundamental base line.

Principal Honours and Distinctions
FRS 1786; Royal Society Copley Medal 1795. Member, Imperial Academy of St Petersburg 1794. Member, Smeatonian Society of Civil Engineers 1793.

Bibliography
1774, *Description of a New Universal Equatorial Instrument*, London; repub. 1791.
1777, *Description of an Engine for Dividing Mathematical Instruments*, London.
1779, *Description of an Engine for Dividing Straight Lines on Mathematical Instruments*, London.

1779, 'Description of two new micrometers', *Philosophical Transactions of the Royal Society* 69: 419–31.

1782, 'A new construction of eyeglasses for such telescopes as may be applied to mathematical instruments', *Philosophical Transactions of the Royal Society* 73: 94–99.

Further Reading
R.S. Woodbury, 1961, *History of the Lathe to 1850*, Cleveland, Ohio; W. Steeds, 1969, *A History of Machine Tools 1700–1910*, Oxford (both provide a brief description of Ramsden's dividing machines).

RTS

Ramus, Revd C.M.

fl. 1870s Sussex, England

English pioneer designer of hydroplanes.

While Rector of Playden, near Rye in Sussex, in 1870 the Reverend C.M. Ramus designed the first hydroplane form seen in the United Kingdom. It is understood that he produced a reasonably flat-bottomed model that was just under 1 m (3 ft 3 in.) in length but had one step.

The idea was submitted to the Admiralty and tested by William **Froude** at the Ship Model Testing Tank at Torquay. While the results were significant at the time, it was some years before this hull form became advanced enough to be used commercially.

Bibliography
1878, *The Polyspenic Ship and Speed at Sea*.

Further Reading
P. Du Cane, 1951, *High Speed Small Craft*, London: Temple Press.
D. Phillips-Birt, 1957, *The Naval Architecture of Small Craft*, London: Hutchinson.

FMW

Randall, Sir John Turton

b. 23 March 1905 Newton-le-Willows, Lancashire, England
d. 16 June 1984 Edinburgh, Scotland

*English physicist and biophysicist, primarily known for the development, with **Boot** of the cavity magnetron.*

Following secondary education at Ashton-in-Makerfield Grammar School, Randall entered Manchester University to read physics, gaining a first class BSc in 1925 and his MSc in 1926. From 1926 to 1937 he was a research physicist at the General Electric Company (GEC) laboratories, where he worked on luminescent powders, following which he became Warren Research Fellow of the Royal Society at Birmingham University, studying electronic processes in luminescent solids. With the outbreak of the Second World War he became an honorary member of the university staff and transferred to a group working on the development of centrimetric radar. With Boot he was responsible for the development of the cavity magnetron, which had a major impact on the development of radar.

When Birmingham resumed its atomic research programme in 1943, Randall became a temporary lecturer at the Cavendish Laboratory in Cambridge. The following year he was appointed Professor of Natural Philosophy at the University of St Andrews, but in 1946 he moved again to the Wheatstone Chair of Physics at King's College, London. There his developing interest in biophysical research led to the setting up of a multi-disciplinary group in 1951 to study connective tissues and other biological components, and in 1950–5 he was joint Editor of *Progress in Biophysics*. From 1961 until his retirement in 1970 he was Professor of Biophysics at King's College and for most of that time he was also Chairman of the School of Biological Sciences. In addition, for many years he was honorary Director of the Medical Research Council Biophysics Research Unit.

After he retired he returned to Edinburgh and continued to study biological problems in the university zoology laboratory.

Principal Honours and Distinctions
Knighted 1962. FRS 1946. FRS Edinburgh 1972. DSc Manchester 1938. Royal Society of Arts Thomas Gray Memorial Prize 1943. Royal Society Hughes Medal 1946. Franklin Institute John Price Wetherill Medal 1958. City of Pennsylvania John Scott Award 1959. (All jointly with Boot for the cavity magnetron.)

Bibliography
1934, *Diffraction of X-Rays by Amorphous Solids, Liquids & Gases* (describes his early work).
1953, editor, *Nature & Structure of Collagen*.

1976, with H. Boot, 'Historical notes on the cavity magnetron', *Transactions of the Institute of Electrical and Electronics Engineers* ED-23: 724 (gives an account of the cavity-magnetron development at Birmingham).

Further Reading

M.H.F. Wilkins, *'John Turton Randall'* – *Biographical Memoirs of Fellows of the Royal Society*, London: Royal Society.

KF

Rankine, William John Macquorn
b. 5 July 1820 Edinburgh, Scotland
d. 1872

Scottish engineer and educator

Rankine was educated at Ayr Academy and Glasgow High School, although he appears to have learned much of his basic mathematics and physics through private study. He attended Edinburgh University and then assisted his father, who was acting as Superintendent of the Edinburgh and Dalkeith Railway. This introduction to engineering practice was followed in 1838 by his appointment as a pupil to Sir John **MacNeill**, and for the next four years he served under Mac-Neill on his Irish railway projects. While still in his early twenties, Rankine presented pioneering papers on metal fatigue and other subjects to the Institution of Civil Engineers, for which he won a prize, but he appears to have resigned from the Civils in 1857 after an argument because the Institution would not transfer his Associate Membership into full Membership. From 1844 to 1848 Rankine worked on various projects for the Caledonian Railway Company, but his interests were becoming increasingly theoretical and a series of distinguished papers for learned societies established his reputation as a leading scholar in the new science of thermodynamics. He was elected Fellow of the Royal Society in 1853. At the same time, he remained intimately involved with practical questions of applied science, in shipbuilding, marine engineering and electric telegraphy, becoming associated with the influential coterie of fellow Scots such as the **Thomson** brothers, **Napier**, **Elder**, and Lewis **Gordon**. Gordon was then the head of a large and successful engineering practice, but he was also Regius Professor of Engineering at the University of Glasgow, and when he retired from

the Chair to pursue his business interests, Rankine, who had become his Assistant, was appointed in his place.

From 1855 until his premature death in 1872, Rankine built up an impressive engineering department, providing a firm theoretical basis with a series of text books that he wrote himself and most of which remained in print for many decades. Despite his quarrel with the Institution of Civil Engineers, Rankine took a keen interest in the institutional development of the engineering profession, becoming the first President of the Institution of Engineers and Shipbuilders in Scotland, which he helped to establish in 1857. Rankine campaigned vigorously for the recognition of engineering studies as a full university degree at Glasgow, and he achieved this in 1872, the year of his death. Rankine was one of the handful of mid-nineteenth century engineers who virtually created engineering as an academic discipline.

Principal Honours and Distinctions

FRS 1853. First President, Institution of Engineers and Shipbuilders in Scotland, 1857.

Bibliography

1858, *Manual of Applied Mechanics*.
1859, *Manual of the Steam Engine and Other Prime Movers*.
1862, *Manual of Civil Engineering*.
1869, *Manual of Machinery and Millwork*.

Further Reading

1873, *Proceedings of the Institution of Civil Engineers* 21.
J. Small, 1957, 'The institution's first president', *Proceedings of the Institution of Engineers and Shipbuilders in Scotland*: 687–97.
H. B. Sutherland, 1972, *Rankine. His Life and Times*.

AB

Ransome, Frederick
b. 18 June 1818 Rushmere, Suffolk, England
d. 19 April 1893 London, England

English engineer and inventor of a type of artificial stone.

Frederick Ransome was the son of James Ransome (1782–1849) and grandson of Robert **Ransome**, founder of the well-known Ipswich firm of engineers. He did not become a partner in the family firm, but devoted his life to experiments to develop an artificial stone. These experiments were recorded in a paper which he presented to the Institution of Civil Engineers in 1848 and in a long series of over thirty patents dating from 1844. The material so formed was a sandstone, the particles of which were bonded together by a silicate of lime. It could be moulded into any required form while in its initial soft state, and when hard was suitable for surface-dressing or carving. It was used for many public buildings, but time proved it unsuitable for outside work. Ransome also used his artificial stone to make grinding wheels by incorporating emery powder in the mixture. These were found to be much superior to those made of natural stone. Another use of the artificial stone was in a porous form which could be used as a filter. In later years Ransome turned his attention to the manufacture of Portland cement and of a cheaper substitute incorporating blast-furnace slag. He also invented a rotary kiln for burning the cement, the first of these being built in 1887. It was 26 ft (7.9 m) long and 5 ft (1.5 m) in diameter; although reasonably successful, the development of such kilns of much greater length was carried out in America rather than England. Ransome was elected an Associate of the Institution of Civil Engineers in 1848 and served as an Associate of Council in 1868–9.

Bibliography

1848, 'On the manufacture of artificial stone with a silica base', *Minutes of the Proceedings of the Institution of Civil Engineers* 7: 57.

RTS

Ransome, Robert

b. 1753 Wells, Norfolk, England
d. 1830 England

English inventor of a self-sharpening ploughshare and all-metal ploughs with interchangeable parts.

The son of a Quaker schoolmaster, Ransome served his apprenticeship with a Norfolk iron manufacturer and then went into business on his own in the same town, setting up one of the first brass and iron foundries in East Anglia. At an early stage of his career he was selling into Norfolk and Suffolk, well beyond the boundaries to

be expected from a local craftsman. He achieved this through the use of forty-seven agents acting on his behalf. In 1789, with one employee and £200 capital, he transferred to Ipswich, where the company was to remain and where there was easier access to both raw materials and his markets. It was there that he discovered that cooling one part of a metal share during its casting could result in a self-sharpening share, and he patented the process in 1785.

Ransome won a number of awards at the early Bath and West shows, a fact which demonstrates the extent of his markets. In 1808 he patented an all-metal plough made up of interchangeable parts, and the following year was making complete ploughs for sale. With interchangeable parts he was able to make composite ploughs suitable for a wide variety of conditions and therefore with potential markets all over the country.

In 1815 he was joined by his son James, and at about the same time by William Cubitt. With the expertise of the latter the firm moved into bridge building and millwrighting, and was therefore able to withstand the agricultural depression which began to affect other manufacturers from about 1815. In 1818, under Cubitt's direction, Ransome built the gas-supply system for the town of Ipswich. In 1830 his grandson James Ransome joined the firm, and it was under his influence that the agricultural side was developed. There was a great expansion in the business after 1835.

Further Reading

J.E. Ransome, 1865, *Ploughs and Ploughing* at the Royal Agricultural College at Cirencester in 1865, in which he outlined the accepted theories of the day.

J.B. Passmore, 1930, *The English Plough*, Reading: University of Reading (provides a history of plough development from the eighth century to the inter-war period).

Ransome's Royal Records 1789–1939, produced by the company;

D.R. Grace and D.C. Phillips, 1975, *Ransomes of Ipswich*, Reading: Institute of Agricultural History, Reading University (both provide information about Ransome in a more general account about the company and its products; Reading University holds the company archives).

AP

Rastrick, John Urpeth

b. 26 January 1780 Morpeth, England
d. 1 November 1856 Chertsey, England

English engineer whose career spanned the formative years of steam railways, from constructing some of the earliest locomotives to building great trunk lines.

John Urpeth Rastrick, son of an engineer, was initially articled to his father and then moved to Ketley Ironworks, Shropshire, c.1801. In 1808 he entered into a partnership with John Hazledine at Bridgnorth, Shropshire: Hazledine and Rastrick built many steam engines to the designs of Richard **Trevithick**, including the demonstration locomotive *Catch-Me-Who-Can*. The firm also built iron bridges, notably the bridge over the River Wye at Chepstow in 1815–16.

Between 1822 and 1826 the Stratford & Moreton Railway was built under Rastrick's direction. Malleable iron rails were laid, in one of the first instances of their use. They were supplied by James Foster of Stourbridge, with whom Rastrick went into partnership after the death of Hazledine. In 1825 Rastrick was one of a team of engineers sent by the committee of the proposed Liverpool & Manchester Railway (L & MR) to carry out trials of locomotives built by George **Stephenson** on the Killingworth Waggonway. Early in 1829 the directors of the L & MR, which was by then under construction, sent Rastrick and James Walker to inspect railways in North East England and report on the relative merits of steam locomotives and fixed engines with cable haulage. They reported, rather hesitantly, in favour of the latter, particularly the reciprocal system of Benjamin **Thompson**. In consequence the Rainhill Trials, at which Rastrick was one of the judges, were held that October. In 1829 Rastrick constructed the Shutt End colliery railway in Worcestershire, for which Foster and Rastrick built the locomotive *Agenoria*; this survives in the National Railway Museum. Three similar locomotives were built to the order of Horatio **Allen** for export to the USA.

From then until he retired in 1847 Rastrick found ample employment surveying railways, appearing as a witness before Parliamentary committees, and supervising construction. Principally, he surveyed the southern part of the Grand Junction Railway, which was built for the most part by Joseph **Locke**, and the line from Manchester to Crewe which was eventually built as the Manchester & Birmingham Railway. The London & Brighton Railway (Croydon to Brighton) was his great achievement: built under Rastrick's supervision between 1836 and 1840, it included three long tunnels and the magnificent Ouse Viaduct. In 1845 he was Engineer to the Gravesend & Rochester Railway, the track of which was laid through the Thames & Medway Canal's Strood Tunnel, partly on the towpath and partly on a continuous staging over the water.

Principal Honours and Distinctions
FRS 1837.

Bibliography
1829, with Walker, *Report ... on the Comparative Merits of Locomotive and Fixed Engines*, Liverpool.

Further Reading
C.F. Dendy Marshall, 1953, *A History of Railway Locomotives Down to the End of the Year 1831*, The Locomotive Publishing Co.
R.E. Carlson, 1969, *The Liverpool & Manchester Railway Project 1821–1831*, Newton Abbot: David & Charles.
C. Hadfield and J. Norris, 1962, *Waterways to Stratford*, Newton Abbot: David & Charles (covers Stratford and Moreton Railway).

See also **Stephenson, Robert**.

PJGR

Rateau, Auguste Camille-Edmond

b. 13 October 1863 Royan, France
d. 13 January 1930 Neuilly-sur-Seine, France

French constructor of turbines, inventor of the turbo compressor and a centrifugal fan for mine ventilation.

A don of the Ecole Polytechnique and the Ecole Supérieure des Mines in Paris, Rateau joined the French Corps des Mines in 1887. Between 1888 and 1898 he taught applied mechanics and electrotechnics at the Ecole des Mines in St-Etienne. Trying to apply the results of his research to practise, he became into contact with commercial firms, before he was appointed Professor of Industrial Electricity at the Ecole Supérieure des Mines in Paris in 1902. He held this position until 1910, although he founded the Société Anonyme Rateau in Paris in 1903 which by the time of his death had subsidiaries in most of the industrial centres of Europe. By the middle of the nineteenth century, when the increasing problems of ventilation in coal mines had become evident and in many countries had led to several unsatisfactory mechanical constructions, Rateau concentrated on this problem soon after he began working in St-Etienne. The result of his research was the design of a centrifugal fan in 1887 with which he established the principles of mechanical ventilation on a general basis that led to future developments and helped, together with the ventilator invented by Capell in England, to pave the way for the use of electricity in mine ventilation.

Rateau continued the study of fluid mechanics and the applications of rotating engines, and after he had published widely on this subject he began to construct many steam turbines, centrifugal compressors and centrifugal pumps. The multicellular Rateau turbine of 1901 became the prototype for many others constructors. During the First World War, when he was very active in the French armaments industry, he developed the invention of the automatic supercharger for aircraft engines and later diesel engines.

Principal Honours and Distinctions
Académie des Sciences, Prix Fourneyron 1899, Prix Poncelet 1911, Member 1918.

Bibliography
1892, *Considérations sur les turbo-machines et en particulier sur les ventilateurs*, St-Etienne.
1900, *Traité des turbo-machines*, Paris.
1907, *Ventilateurs centrifuges à haute pression*, Paris.
1908, *Développement des turbines à vapeur d'échappement*, Paris.
1917, *Notice sur les travaux scientifiques et techniques*, Paris.

Further Reading
H.H. Suplee, 1930, obituary, *Mechanical Engineering* 52: 570–1.
L. Leprince-Ringuet (ed.), 1951, *Les inventeurs célèbres*, Geneva: 151–2 (a comprehensive description of his life and the importance of his turbines).

WK

Ravenscroft, George
b. 1632 Alconbury, Huntingdonshire, England
d. 7 June 1683 Barnet, Hertfordshire, England

English inventor of lead-crystal glass.

George's father James was a successful lawyer and merchant, engaging in overseas trade. A devout but necessarily circumspect Catholic, James sent his sons to the English College at Douai, now in northern France. Leaving there in 1651, George began to learn his father's business and spent some fifteen years in Venice. He took an increasingly important part in it, doubtless dealing in Venice's leading products of lace and glass. By 1666 he was back in England and, perhaps because the supply of Venetian glass was beginning to decline, he started to manufacture glass himself. In 1673 he set up a glassworks in the Savoy in London and succeeded so well that in the following year he petitioned the King for the grant of a patent to make glassware. This was granted on 16 May 1674, stimulating the Glass Sellers' Company to enter into an agreement with Ravenscroft to buy the glassware he produced. Later in 1674 the company allowed Ravenscroft to establish a second glasshouse at Henley-on-Thames. At first his ware was beset with 'crizzling', i.e. numerous fine surface cracks. The Glass Sellers probably urged Ravenscroft to cure this defect, and this he achieved in 1675 by replacing crushed flint with increasing amounts of lead oxide, rising finally to a content of 30 per cent. He thereby obtained a relatively soft, heavy glass with high refractive index and dispersive power. This made it amenable to deep cutting, to produce the brilliant prismatic effects of cut glass. At about the same time, the Duke of Buckingham, a considerable promoter of the glass industry, agreed that Ravenscroft should manage his works at Vauxhall for the making of plate glass for mirrors. Ravenscroft terminated his agreement with the Glass Sellers in 1678, the date of the last evidence of his activities as a maker of crystal glass, and the patent expired in 1681. His new glass had immediately rivalled the best Venetian crystal glass and has been a valued product ever since.

Further Reading
R.F. Moody, 1988, 'The life of George Ravenscroft', *Glass Technology* 29 (1): 198–210; *Glass Technology* 30 (5): 191–2 (additional notes on his life).

LRD

Rawcliffe, Gordon Hindle
b. 2 June 1910 Sheffield, England
d. 3 September 1979 Bristol, England

*English scientist and inventor of the multi-speed
induction motor using the pole amplitude
modulation principle.*

After graduating from Keble College, Oxford,
Rawcliffe joined the Metropolitan Vickers Electrical Company in 1932 as a college apprentice,
and later became a design engineer. This was followed by a period as a lecturer at Liverpool
University, where he was able to extend his
knowledge of the principles underlying the design and operation of electrical machines. In
1941 he became Head of the Electrical Engineering Department at the Robert Gordon Technical College, Aberdeen, and Lecturer in charge
of Electrical Engineering at Aberdeen University. In 1944 Rawcliffe was appointed to the
Chair of Electrical Engineering at the University
of Bristol, where he remained until his retirement
in 1975. The reputation of his department was
enhanced by the colleagues he recruited.

After 1954 he began research into polyphase
windings, the basis of alternating-current machinery, and published papers concerned with
the dual problems of frequency changing and
pole changing. The result of this research was the
discovery in 1957 of a technique for making
squirrel-cage induction motors run at more than
one speed. By reversing current in one part of the
winding, the pole distribution and number were
changed, and with it the speed of rotation.

Rawcliffe's name became synonymous with
pole amplitude modulation, or PAM, the name
given to this technique. Described by Rawcliffe
as a new philosophy of windings, the technique
led to a series of research papers, patents and
licensing agreements in addition to consultancies
to advise on application problems. Commercial
exploitation of the new idea throughout Western
Europe, the United Kingdom and the United
States followed. In total he contributed twenty-
five papers to the *Proceedings of the Institution of
Electrical Engineers* and some sixty British patent
applications were filed.

Principal Honours and Distinctions
FRS 1972. Royal Society S.G. Brown Medal
1978.

Bibliography
21 August 1958, British patent no. 900,600
(pole amplitude modulation).
1958, with R.F. Burbridge and W. Fong, 'Induction motor speed changing by pole amplitude
modulation', *Proceedings of the Institution of
Electrical Engineers* 105 (Part A): 411–19 (the
first description of pole amplitude modulation).

Further Reading
*Biographical Memoirs of Fellows of the Royal So-
ciety*, 1981, Vol. XXVII, London, pp. 479–503
(includes lists of Rawcliffe's patents and principal papers published).

GW

Reason, Richard Edmund
b. 21 December 1903 Exeter, Devon, England
d. 20 March 1987 Great Bowden, Leicestershire, England

*English metrologist who developed instruments
for measuring machined-surface roughness.*

Richard Edmund Reason was educated at Tonbridge School and the Royal College of Science
(Imperial College), where he studied under Professor A.F.C. Pollard, Professor of Technical Optics. After graduating in 1925 he joined Taylor,
Taylor and Hobson Ltd, Leicester, manufacturers of optical, electrical and scientific instruments, and remained with that firm throughout
his career. One of his first contributions was in
the development, with E.F. Fincham, of the Fincham Coincidence Optometer. At this time the
firm, under William **Taylor**, was mainly concerned with optical instruments and lens manufacture, but in the 1930s Reason was also
engaged in developing means for measuring the
roughness of machined surfaces. The need for
establishing standards and methods of measurement of surface finish was called for when the
subcontracting of aero-engine components became necessary during the Second World War.
This led to the development by Reason of an
instrument in which a stylus was moved across
the surface and the profile recorded electronically. This was called the Talysurf and was first
produced in 1941. Further development followed, and from 1947 Reason tackled the problem of measuring roundness, producing the first
Talyrond machine in 1949. The technology developed for these instruments was used in the

production of others such as the Talymin Comparator and the Talyvel electronic level. Reason was also associated with the development of optical projection systems to measure the profile of parts such as gear teeth, screw threads and turbine blades. He retired in 1968 but continued as a consultant to the company. He served for many years on committees of the British Standards Institution on surface metrology and was a representative of Britain at the International Standards Organization.

Principal Honours and Distinctions

OBE 1967. FRS 1971. Honorary DSc University of Birmingham 1969. Honorary DSc Leicester University 1971.

Further Reading

D.J. Whitehouse, 1990, *Biographical Memoirs of Fellows of the Royal Society* 36, London, pp. 437–62 (an illustrated obituary notice listing Reason's eighty-nine British patents, published between 1930 and 1972, and his twenty-one publications, dating from 1937 to 1966).

K.J. Hume, 1980, *A History of Engineering Metrology*, London, 113–21 (contains a shorter account of Reason's work).

RTS

Reichenbach, Georg Friedrich von

b. 24 August 1772 Durlach, Baden, Germany
d. 21 May 1826 Munich, Germany

German engineer.

While he was attending the Military School at Mannheim, Reichenbach drew attention to himself due to the mathematical instruments that he had designed. On the recommendation of Count Rumford in Munich, the Bavarian government financed a two-year stay in Britain so that Reichenbach could become acquainted with modern mechanical engineering. He returned to Mannheim in 1793, and during the Napoleonic Wars he was involved in the manufacture of arms. In Munich, where he was in the service of the Bavarian state from 1796, he started producing precision instruments in his own time. His basic invention was the design of a dividing machine for circles, produced at the end of the eighteenth century. The astronomic and geodetic instruments he produced excelled all the others for their precision. His telescopes in particular,

being perfect in use and of solid construction, soon brought him an international reputation. They were manufactured at the Mathematic-Mechanical Institute, which he had jointly founded with Joseph Utzschneider and Joseph Liebherr in 1804 and which became a renowned training establishment. The glasses and lenses were produced by Joseph Fraunhofer who joined the company in 1807.

In the same year he was put in charge of the technical reorganization of the salt-works at Reichenhall. After he had finished the brine-transport line from Reichenhall to Traunstein in 1810, he started on the one from Berchtesgaden to Reichenhall which was an extremely difficult task because of the mountainous area that had to be crossed. As water was the only source of energy available he decided to use water-column engines for pumping the brine in the pipes of both lines. Such devices had been in use for pumping purposes in different mining areas since the middle of the eighteenth century. Reichenbach knew about the one constructed by Joseph Karl Hell in Slovakia, which in principle had just been a simple piston-pump driven by water which did not work satisfactorily. Instead he constructed a really effective double-action water-column engine; this was a short time after Richard **Trevithick** had constructed a similar machine in England. For the second line he improved the system and built a single-action pump. All the parts of it were made of metal, which made them easy to produce, and the pumps proved to be extremely reliable, working for over 100 years.

At the official opening of the line in 1817 the Bavarian king rewarded him generously. He remained in the state's service, becoming head of the department for roads and waterways in 1820, and he contributed to the development of Bavarian industry as well as the public infrastructure in many ways as a result of his mechanical skill and his innovative engineering mind.

Further Reading

Bauernfeind, 'Georg von Reichenbach' *Allgemeine deutsche Biographie* 27: 656–67 (a reliable nineteenth-century account).

W.Dyck, 1912, *Georg v. Reichenbach*, Munich.

K. Matschoss, 1941, *Grosse Ingenieure*, Munich and Berlin, 3rd edn. 121–32 (a concise description of his achievements in the development of optical instruments and engineering).

WK

Reis, (Johann) Philipp

b. 7 January 1834 Geinherusen, Hesse-Kassel, Germany
d. 14 January 1874 Friedrichsdorf, Germany

German schoolteacher and inventor who constructed an early form of telephone.

Reis entered the Garniers Institute in Friedrichsdorf in 1844 and then the Hassels Institute in Frankfurt. There he developed an interest in science, but on leaving school in 1850 he was apprenticed to the colour trade by his uncle. This involved study at the trade school and Dr Poppe's Institute in Frankfurt; while there he joined the Frankfurt Physical Society. Following military service in 1855 he studied to be a teacher. After his graduation he obtained a post at Garniers, where he began to pursue experiments with electricity and the development of hearing aids. In 1859 he sent a paper on the radiation of electricity to the editor of *Annalen der Physik*, but this was rejected, as was a later submission. Undeterred, he continued his experiments and by 1861 he had designed several instruments for the transmission of sound. The transmitter consisted of a membrane on which rested a metal strip that made contact with a metal point and completed an electrical circuit under the action of sound. The receiver consisted of an iron needle surrounded by a coil and resting on a sounding box, the operation probably being achieved by magnetostriction. The invention, which he described in a lecture to the Frankfurt Physical Society on 26 October 1861 and in a published paper, could produce tones and probably also speech, but was largely rejected by the scientific fraternity. The claim to produce speech was discounted in subsequent court cases that upheld the patents of Alexander **Bell**.

Principal Honours and Distinctions
On 8 December 1878 a monument to Reis was erected in the Friedrichsdorf Cemetery by the Physical Society of Frankfurt.

Bibliography
1860–1, 'Über Telephone durch den galvanischen Strom, *Jahresbericht der Physikalische* 57.

Further Reading
J. Munro, 1891, *Heroes of the Telegraph*.
Silvanus P. Thompson, 1883, *Philipp Reis. Inventor of the Telephone*.
B.B. Bauer, 1962, 'A century of the microphone', *Proceedings of the Institute of Radio Engineers*: 720.

KF

Renard, Charles

b. 23 November 1847 Damblain, Vosges, France
d. 13 April 1905 Chalais-Meudon, France

French pioneer of military aeronautics who, with A.C. Krebs, built an airship powered by an electric motor.

Charles Renard was a French army officer with an interest in aviation. In 1873 he constructed an unusual unmanned glider with ten wings and an automatic stabilizing device to control rolling. This operated by means of a pendulum device linked to moving control surfaces. The model was launched from a tower near Arras, but unfortunately it spiralled into the ground. The control surfaces could not cope with the basic instability of the design, but as an idea for automatic flight control it was ahead of its time.

Following a Commission report on the military use of balloons, carrier pigeons and an optical telegraph, an aeronautical establishment was set up in 1877 at Chalais-Meudon, near Paris, under the direction of Charles Renard, who was assisted by his brother Paul. The following year Renard and a colleague, Arthur Krebs, began to plan an airship. They received financial help from Léon Gambetta, a prominent politician who had escaped from Paris by balloon in 1870 during the siege by the Prussians. Renard and Krebs studied earlier airship designs: they used the outside shape of Paul Haenlein's gas-engined airship of 1872 and included **Meusnier**'s internal air-filled *ballonnets*. The gas-engine had not been a success so they decided on an electric motor. Renard developed lightweight pile batteries while Krebs designed a motor, although this was later replaced by a more powerful **Gramme** motor of 6.5 kW (9 hp). *La France* was constructed at Chalais-Meudon and, after a two-month wait for calm conditions, the airship finally ascended on 9 August 1884. The motor was switched on and the flight began. Renard and Krebs found their airship handled well and after twenty-three minutes they landed back at their base. *La France* made several successful flights, but its speed of only 24 km/h (15 mph) meant that flights could be made only in calm weather. Parts of *La France*, including the electric motor, are preserved in the Musée de l'Air in Paris.

Renard remained in charge of the establishment at Chalais-Meudon until his death. Among other things, he developed the 'Train Renard', a train of articulated road vehicles for military and civil use, of which a number were built between 1903 and 1911. Towards the end of his life Renard became interested in helicopters, and in 1904 he built a large twin-rotor model which, however, failed to take off.

Bibliography
1886, *Le Ballon dirigeable La France*, Paris (a description of the airship).

Further Reading
Descriptions of Renard and Kreb's airship are given in most books on the history of lighter-than-air flight, e.g.
L.T.C. Rolt, 1966, *The Aeronauts*, London; pub. in paperback 1985.
C. Bailleux, *c*.1988, *Association pour l'Histoire de l'Electricité en France*, (a detailed account of the conception and operations of *La France*).
1977, *Centenaire de la recherche aéronautique à Chalais-Meudon*, Paris (an official memoir on the work of Chalais-Meudon with a chapter on Renard).

JDS

Rennie, John

b. 7 June 1761 Phantassie, East Linton, East Lothian, Scotland
d. 4 October 1821 Stamford Street, London, England

Scottish civil engineer.

Born into a prosperous farming family, he early demonstrated his natural mechanical and structural aptitude. As a boy he spent a great deal of time, often as a truant, near his home in the workshop of Andrew **Meikle**. Meikle was a millwright and the inventor of a threshing machine. After local education and an apprenticeship with Meikle, Rennie went to Edinburgh University until he was 22. He then travelled south and met James **Watt**, who in 1784 offered him the post of Engineer at the Albion Flour Mills, London, which was then under construction. Rennie designed all the mill machinery, and it was while there that he began to develop an interest in canals, opening his own business in 1791 in Blackfriars. He carried out work on the Kennet and Avon Canal and in 1794 became Engineer for the company. He meanwhile carried out other surveys, including a proposed extension of the River Stort Navigation to the Little Ouse and a Basingstoke-to-Salisbury canal, neither of which were built. From 1791 he was also engaged on the Rochdale Canal and the Lancaster Canal, as well as the great masonry aqueduct carrying the latter canal across the river Lune at Lancaster. He also surveyed the Ipswich and Stowmarket and the Chelmer and Blackwater Navigations. He advised on the Horncastle Canal in 1799 and on the River Ancholme in 1799, both of which are in Lincolnshire. In 1802 he was engaged on the Royal Canal in Ireland, and in the same year he was commissioned by the Government to prepare a plan for flooding the Lea Valley as a defence on the eastern approach to London in case Napoleon invaded England across the Essex marshes. In 1809 he surveyed improvements on the Thames, and in the following year he was involved in a proposed canal from Taunton to Bristol. Some of his schemes, particularly in the Fens and Lincolnshire, were a combination of improvements for both drainage and navigation. Apart from his canal work he engaged extensively in the construction and development of docks and harbours including the East and West India Docks in London, Holyhead, Hull, Ramsgate and the dockyards at Chatham and Sheerness. In 1806 he proposed the great breakwater at Plymouth, where work commenced on 22 June 1811.

He was also highly regarded for his bridge construction. These included Kelso and Musselburgh, as well as his famous Thames bridges: London Bridge (uncompleted at the time of his death), Waterloo Bridge (1810–17) and Southwark Bridge (1815–19). He was elected a Fellow of the Royal Society in 1798.

Principal Honours and Distinctions
FRS 1798.

Further Reading
C.T.G. Boucher, 1963, *John Rennie 1761–1821*, Manchester University Press.
W. Reyburn, 1972, *Bridge Across the Atlantic*, London: Harrap.

JHB

Renold, Hans

b. 31 July 1852 Aarau, Switzerland
d. 2 May 1943 Grange-over-Sands, Lancashire, England

Swiss (naturalized British 1881) mechanical engineer, inventor and pioneer of the precision chain industry.

Hans Renold was educated at the cantonal school of his native town and at the Polytechnic in Zurich. He worked in two or three small workshops during the polytechnic vacations and served an apprenticeship of eighteen months in an engineering works at Neuchâtel, Switzerland. After a short period of military service he found employment as a draughtsman in an engineering firm at Saint-Denis, near Paris, from 1871 to 1873. In 1873 Renold moved first to London and then to Manchester as a draughtsman and inspector with a firm of machinery exporters. From 1877 to 1879 he was a partner in his own firm of machine exporters. In 1879 he purchased a small firm in Salford making chain for the textile industry. At about this time J.K. Starley introduced the 'safety' bicycle, which, however, lacked a satisfactory drive chain. Renold met this need with the invention of the bush roller chain, which he patented in 1880. The new chain formed the basis of the precision chain industry: the business expanded and new premises were acquired in Brook Street, Manchester, in 1881. In the same year Renold became a naturalized British subject.

Continued expansion of the business necessitated the opening of a new factory in Brook Street in 1889. The factory was extended in 1895, but by 1906 more accommodation was needed and a site of 11½ acres was acquired in the Manchester suburb of Burnage: the move to the new building was finally completed in 1914. Over the years, further developments in the techniques of chain manufacture were made, including the invention in 1895 of the inverted tooth or silent chain. Renold made his first visit to America in 1891 to study machine-tool developments and designed for his own works special machine tools, including centreless grinding machines for dealing with wire rods up to 10 ft (3 m) in length.

The business was established as a private limited company in 1903 and merged with the Coventry Chain Company Ltd in 1930. Good industrial relations were always of concern to Renold and he established a 48-hour week as early as 1896, in which year a works canteen was opened. Joint consultation with shop stewards date2 from 1917. Renold was elected a Member of the Institution of Mechanical Engineers in 1902 and in 1917 he was made a magistrate of the City of Manchester.

Principal Honours and Distinctions
Honorary DSc University of Manchester 1940.

Further Reading
Basil H. Tripp, 1956, *Renold Chains: A History of the Company and the Rise of the Precision Chain Industry 1879–1955*, London.
J.J. Guest, 1915, *Grinding Machinery*, London, pp. 289, 380 (describes grinding machines developed by Renold).

RTS

Reynolds, Edwin

b. 1831 Mansfield, Connecticut, USA
d. 1909 Milwaukee, Wisconsin, USA

American contributor to the development of the Corliss valve steam engine, including the 'Manhattan' layout.

Edwin Reynolds grew up at a time when formal engineering education in America was almost unavailable, but through his genius and his experience working under such masters as G.H. **Corliss** and William Wright, he developed into one of the best mechanical engineers in the country. When he was Plant Superintendent for the Corliss Steam Engine Company, he built the giant Corliss valve steam engine displayed at the 1876 Centennial Exhibition. In July 1877 he left the Corliss Steam Engine Company to join Edward Allis at his Reliance Works, although he was offered a lower salary. In 1861 Allis had moved his business to the Menomonee Valley, where he had the largest foundry in the area. Immediately on his arrival with Allis, Reynolds began designing and building the 'Reliance–Corliss' engine, which becamea symbol of simplicity, economy and reliability. By early 1878 the new engine was so successful that the firm had a six- month back-log of orders. In 1888 he built the first triple-expansion waterworks-pumping engine in the United States for the city of Milwaukee, and in the same year he patented a new design of blowing engine for blast furnaces. He followed this in March 1892 with the first steam engine sets coupled directly to electric generators when Allis–Chalmers contracted to build two Corliss cross-compound engines for the Narragansett Light Company of Providence, Rhode Island. In 1893, one of the impressive attractions at the World's Columbian Exposition in Chicago was the 3,000 hp (2,200 kW) quadruple-expansion Reynolds–Corliss engine designed by Reynolds, who continued to make significant improvements and gained worldwide recognition of his outstanding achievements in engine building.

Reynolds was asked to go to New York in 1898 for consultation about some high-horse-power engines for the Manhattan transport system. There, 225 railway locomotives were to be replaced by electric trains, which would be supplied from one generating station producing 60,000 hp (45,000 kW). Reynolds sketched out his ideas for 10,000 hp (7,500 kW) engines while on the train. Because space was limited, he suggested a four-cylinder design with two horizontal-high-pressure cylinders and two vertical, low-pressure ones. One cylinder of each type was placed on each side of the flywheel generator, which with cranks at 135° gave an exceptionally smooth-running compact engine known as the 'Manhattan'. A further nine similar engines that were superheated and generated three-phase current were supplied in 1902 to the New York Interborough Rapid Transit Company. These were the largest reciprocating steam engines built for use on land, and a few smaller ones with a similar layout were installed in British textile mills.

Further Reading
Concise Dictionary of American Biography, 1964, New York: C. Scribner's Sons (contains a brief biography).
R.L. Hills, 1989, *Power from Steam. A History of the Stationary Steam Engine*, Cambridge University Press (provides a brief account of the Manhattan engines)

Part of the information for this biography is derived from a typescript in the Smithsonian Institution, Washington, DC: T.H. Fehring, 'Technological contributions of Milwaukee's Menomonee Valley industries'.

RLH

Reynolds, Osborne
b. 23 April 1842 Belfast, Ireland
d. 1912 Watchet, Somerset, England

English engineer and educator.

Osborne Reynolds's father, a clergyman and schoolteacher, had been a Fellow of Queens' College, Cambridge; it was to Queens' that the young Reynolds went to study mathematics, graduating as 7th Wrangler in 1867, and going on in his turn to become a Fellow of the College. Reynolds had developed an interest in practical applications of physics and engineering, and for a short time he entered the office of the London civil engineers Lawson and Mansergh. In 1868 he was appointed to the new Chair of Engineering at Owens College, Manchester, and he remained in this post for thirty-seven years, until he retired in 1905. During this period he presided over a department that grew steadily in size and reputation, and undertook prolonged research projects into phenomena such as lubrication, the laws governing the flow of water in pipes, turbulence and other physical features with practical applications. He was elected a Fellow of the Royal Society in 1877, being nominated Royal Medallist in 1888. In 1883 he became a Member of the Institution of Civil Engineers, and in 1885 he was awarded the Telford Premium of the Institution. He served as Secretary of the Manchester Literary and Philosophical Society from 1874 to 1883, and was appointed President in 1888–9 and Dalton Medallist in 1903. He was President of Section G of the British Association for the History of Science in 1887, and in 1884 he received the degree of LLD from Glasgow University. Among his many students at Owens College was J.J. (later Sir Joseph) Thomson (1856–1940), who entered the college in 1871. Reynolds's collected scientific papers were published in 1900–3.

Principal Honours and Distinctions
FRS 1877. Institution of Civil Engineers Telford

Premium 1885. President, Manchester Literary and Philosophical Society 1888–9. Manchester Literary and Philosophical Society, Dalton Medal 1903.

Further Reading
Dictionary of National Biography Supplement.
D.M. McDowell and J.D. Jackson (eds), 1970, *Osborne Reynolds and Engineering Science Today*, Manchester: Manchester University Press.

AB

Reynolds, Richard
b. 1 November 1735 Bristol, England
d. 10 September 1816 Cheltenham, Gloucestershire, England

English ironmaster who invented iron rails.

Reynolds was born into a Quaker family, his father being an iron merchant and a considerable customer for the products of the Darbys (see Abraham **Darby**) of Coalbrookdale in Shropshire. After education at a Quaker boarding school in Pickwick, Wiltshire, Reynolds was apprenticed to William Fry, a grocer of Bristol, from whom he would have learned business methods. The year before the expiry of his apprenticeship in 1757, Reynolds was being sent on business errands to Coalbrookdale. In that year he met and married Hannah Darby, the daughter of Abraham **Darby** II. At the same time, he acquired a half-share in the Ketley ironworks, established not long before, in 1755. There he supervised not only the furnaces at Ketley and Horsehay and the foundry, but also the extension of the railway, linking this site to Coalbrookdale itself.

On the death of Abraham Darby II in 1763, Reynolds took charge of the whole works during the minority of Abraham **Darby** III. During this period, the most notable development was the introduction by the Cranage brothers of a new way of converting pig-iron to wrought iron, a process patented in 1766 that used coal in a reverberatory furnace. This, with other processes for the same purpose, remained in use until superseded by the puddling process patented by Henry **Cort** in 1783 and 1784. Reynolds's most important innovation was the introduction of cast-iron rails in 1767 on the railway around Coalbrookdale. A useful network had been in operation for some time with wooden rails, but these wore out quickly and were expensive to maintain. Reynolds's iron rails were an immediate improvement, and some 20 miles (32 km) were laid within a short time. In 1768 Abraham Darby III was able to assume control of the Coalbrookdale works, but Reynolds had been extending his own interest in other ironworks and various other concerns, earning himself considerable wealth. When Darby was oppressed with loan repayments, Reynolds bought the Manor of Madely, which made him Landlord of the Coalbrookdale Company; by 1780 he was virtually banker to the company.

Further Reading
H.M. Rathbone, 1852, *Letters of Richard Reynolds with a Memoir of his Life*, London.
A. Raistrick, 1989, *Dynasty of Iron Founders*, 2nd edn, Ironbridge Gorge Museum Trust (contains many details of Reynolds's life).

LRD

Ricardo, Sir Harry Ralph
b. 26 January 1885 London, England
d. 18 May 1974 Graffham, Sussex, England

English mechanical engineer; researcher, designer and developer of internal combustion engines.

Harry Ricardo was the eldest child and only son of Halsey Ricardo (architect) and Catherine Rendel (daughter of Alexander Rendel, senior partner in the firm of consulting civil engineers that later became Rendel, Palmer and Tritton). He was educated at Rugby School and at Cambridge. While still at school, he designed and made a steam engine to drive his bicycle, and by the time he went up to Cambridge in 1903 he was a skilled craftsman. At Cambridge, he made a motor cycle powered by a petrol engine of his own design, and with this he won a fuel-consumption competition by covering almost 40 miles (64 km) on a quart (1.14 l) of petrol. This brought him to the attention of Professor Bertram Hopkinson, who invited him to help with research on turbulence and pre-ignition in internal combustion engines. After leaving Cambridge in 1907, he joined his grandfather's firm and became head of the design department for mechanical equipment used in civil engineering. In 1916 he was asked to help with the problem of loading tanks on to railway trucks. He was then given the task of designing and organizing the manufacture of engines for tanks, and the success of this enterprise encouraged him to set up his own establishment at Shoreham, devoted to research on, and design and development of, internal combustion engines.

Leading on from the work with Hopkinson were his discoveries on the suppression of detonation in spark-ignition engines. He noted that the current paraffinic fuels were more prone to detonation than the aromatics, which were being discarded as they did not comply with the existing specifications because of their high specific gravity. He introduced the concepts of 'highest useful compression ratio' (HUCR) and 'toluene number' for fuel samples burned in a special variable compression-ratio engine. The toluene number was the proportion of toluene in heptane that gave the same HUCR as the fuel sample. Later, toluene was superseded by iso-octane to give the now familiar octane rating. He went on to improve the combustion in side-valve engines by increasing turbulence, shortening the flame path and minimizing the clearance between piston and head by concentrating the combustion space over the valves. By these means, the compression ratio could be increased to that used by overhead-valve engines before detonation intervened. The very hot poppet valve restricted the advancement of all internal combustion engines, so he turned his attention to eliminating it by use of the single sleeve-valve, this being developed with support from the Air Ministry. By the end of the Second World War some 130,000 such aero-engines had been built by Bristol, Napier and Rolls-Royce before the piston aero-engine was superseded by the gas turbine of **Whittle**. He even contributed to the success of the latter by developing a fuel control system for it.

Concurrent with this was work on the diesel engine. He designed and developed the engine that halved the fuel consumption of London buses. He invented and perfected the 'Comet' series of combustion chambers for diesel engines, and the Company was consulted by the vast majority of international internal combustion engine manufacturers.

He published and lectured widely and fully deserved his many honours; he was elected FRS in 1929, was President of the Institution of Mechanical Engineers in 1944–5 and was knighted in 1948. This shy and modest, though very determined man was highly regarded by all who came into contact with him. It was said that research into internal combustion engines, his family and boats constituted all that he would wish from life.

Principal Honours and Distinctions
Knighted 1948. FRS 1929. President, Institution of Mechanical Engineers 1944–5.

Bibliography
1968, *Memo & Machines. The Pattern of My Life*, London: Constable.

Further Reading
Sir William Hawthorne, 1976, 'Harry Ralph Ricardo', *Biographical Memoirs of Fellows of the Royal Society 22*.

JB

Richard of Wallingford, Abbot
b. 1291/2 Wallingford, England
d. 23 May 1336 St Albans, Hertfordshire, England

English cleric, mathematician and astronomer who produced the earliest mechanical clock of which there is detailed knowledge.

Richard, the son of a blacksmith, was adopted by the Prior of Wallingford when his father died and educated at Oxford. He then joined the monastery at St Albans and was ordained as a priest in 1317. After a further period at Oxford studying mathematics and astronomy he returned to St Albans as Abbot in 1327. Shortly after he had been elected Abbot he started work on a very elaborate astronomical clock. The escapement and the striking mechanism of this clock were unusual. The former was a variation on the verge escapement, and the hour striking (up to twenty-four) was controlled by a series of pins laid out in a helical pattern on a drum. However, timekeeping was of secondary importance as the main purpose of the clock was to show the motion of the Sun, Moon and planets (the details of the planet mechanism are lost) and to demonstrate eclipses. This was achieved in a very precise manner by a series of ingenious mechanisms, such as the elliptical wheel that was used to derive the variable motion of the sun.

Richard died of leprosy, which he had contracted during a visit to obtain papal confirmation of his appointment, and the clock was completed after his death. The last recorded reference to it was made by John Leyland, shortly before the dissolution of the monasteries. It is now known only from incomplete manuscript copies of Richard's treatise. A modern reconstruction has been made based upon J.D. North's interpretation of the manuscript.

Bibliography

For the drafts of Richard's Treatise on the Clock, with translation and commentary, see J.D. North, 1976, *Richard of Wallingford*, 3 vols, Oxford.

Further Reading

See J.D. North's definitive work above: for biographical information see Vol. 2, pp. 1–16. Most of the shorter accounts appeared before the publication of North's treatise and are therefore of more limited use.

G. White, 1978, 'Evolution of the epicyclic gear – part 2', *Chartered Mechanical Engineer* (April): 85–8 (an account of Richard's use of epicyclic gearing).

DV

Riche, Gaspard-Clair-François-Marie, Baron de Prony

b. *c.*1755 France
d. *c.*1839

French mathematician who used the method of differences to calculate logarithms and trigonometric functions.

Whilst Directeur of the Bureau du Cadastre, Prony was made responsible for a project to determine the trigonometric functions of the centesimal units of $90°$, i.e. the right angle was successively divided into 100 grades containing 100 minutes, which in turn each consisted of 100 seconds. This work produced tables (known as the Table de Cadastre) of the natural sines to twenty-two decimal places and the logarithms of sines and tangents to fourteen places. Although the tables as calculated were never published, tables based on them (presumably derived for the more familiar degree, minute and second sub-divisions of a right-angle by interpolation) have since appeared.

See also **Briggs, Henry; Burgi, Jost; Napier, John**.

KF

Rickman, Thomas

b. 8 June 1776 Maidenhead, England
d. 4 January 1841 Birmingham, England

English architect who published the first serious study of the development of the styles of medieval architecture.

Thomas Rickman trained first in medicine and then, after practising for a short while, became an insurance clerk. During his thirties, having taught himself draughtsmanship, he travelled the country drawing, and recording some 3,000 medieval churches. He became deeply interested in and knowledgeable about ecclesiastical medieval architecture and in 1817 he began architectural practice. Rickman was responsible for a great deal of collegiate and ecclesiastical building. His understanding of true medieval materials and construction was much greater than that of his contemporaries, but like them he saw nothing incongruous about using modern materials such as plaster and cast iron for vault supports and tracery, so changing the structural proportions from medieval precepts. Characteristic of his work was St George Edgbaston (1819–22; demolished 1960) and Hartlebury Church (1836–7). Rickman is known primarily for his book *An Attempt to Discriminate the Styles of English Architecture from the Conquest to the Reformation*, in which he suggested classifying periods of architecture as Norman, Early English, Decorated and Perpendicular. These terms are still largely accepted even today.

Further Reading

H. Colvin, 1978, *A Biographical Dictionary of English Architects 1600–1840*, John Murray.

DY

Rickover, Admiral Hyman George

b. 27 January 1900 Russian Poland
d. 8 July 1986 Arlington, Virginia, USA

Polish/American naval officer, one of the principal architects of the United States nuclear submarine programme.

Born in Poland, Rickover was brought to the United States early in his life by his father, who settled in Chicago as a tailor. Commissioned into the US Navy in 1922, he specialized in electrical engineering (graduating from the US Naval Postgraduate School, Columbia, in 1929), qualified as a Submariner in 1931 and then held various posts until appointed Head of the Electrical Section of the Bureau of Ships in 1939. He held this post until the end of the Second World War.

Rickover was involved briefly in the 'Manhattan' atomic bomb project before being assigned to an atomic energy submarine project in 1946. Ultimately he was made responsible for the development and building of the world's first nuclear submarine, the USS *Nautilus.* He was convinced of the need to make the nuclear submarine an instrument of strategic importance, and this led to the development of the ballistic missile submarine and the Polaris programme.

Throughout his career he was no stranger to controversy; indeed, his remaining on the active service list as a full admiral until the age of 82 (when forced to retire on the direct intervention of the Navy Secretary) indicates a man beyond the ordinary. He imposed his will on all around him and backed it with a brilliant and clear-thinking brain; his influence was even felt by the Royal Navy during the building of the first British nuclear submarine, HMS *Dreadnought.* He made many friends, but he also had many detractors.

Principal Honours and Distinctions
US Distinguished Service Medal with Gold Star. Honorary CBE. US Congress Special Gold Medal 1959. Numerous awards and honorary degrees.

Bibliography
Rickover wrote several treatises on education and on the education of engineers. He also wrote on several aspects of the technical history of the US Navy.

Further Reading
W.R. Anderson and C. Blair, 1959, *Nautilus 90 North,* London: Hodder & Stoughton.
E.L. Beach, 1986, *The United States Navy,* New York: Henry Holt.

FMW

Ridley, John
b. 1806 West Boldon, Co. Durham, England
d. 1887 Malvern, England

English developer of the stripper harvester which led to a machine suited to the conditions of Australia and South America.

John Ridley was a preacher in his youth, and then became a mill owner before migrating to Australia with his wife and daughters in 1839. Intending to continue his business in the new colony, he took with him a 'Grasshopper' overbeam steam-engine made by James Watt, together with milling equipment. Cereal acreages were insufficient for the steam power he had available, and he expanded into saw milling as well as farming 300 acres. Aware of the Adelaide trials of reaping machines, he eventually built a prototype using the same principles as those developed by Wrathall Bull. After a successful trial in 1843 Ridley began the patent procedure in England, although he never completed the project. The agricultural press was highly enthusiastic about his machine, but when trials took place in 1855 the award went to a rival. The development of the stripper enabled a spectacular increase in the cereal acreage planted over the next decade. Ridley left Australia in 1853 and returned to England. He built a number of machines to his design in Leeds; however, these failed to perform in the much damper English climate. All of the machines were exported to South America, anticipating a substantial market to be exploited by Australian manufacturers.

Principal Honours and Distinctions
In 1913 a Ridley scholarship was established by the faculty of Agriculture at Adelaide University.

Further Reading
G. Quick and W. Buchele, 1978, *The Grain Harvesters,* American Society of Agricultural Engineers (includes a chapter devoted to the Australian developments).
A.E. Ridley, 1904, *A Backward Glance* (describes Ridley's own story).
G.L. Sutton, 1937, *The Invention of the Stripper* (a review of the disputed claims between Ridley and Bull).
L.J. Jones, 1980, 'John Ridley and the South Australian stripper', *The History of Technology,* pp. 55–103 (a more detailed study).
—— 1979, 'The early history of mechanical harvesting', *The History of Technology,* pp. 4, 101–48 (discusses the various claims to the first invention of a machine for mechanical harvesting).

AP

Ridley, Nicholas Harold Lloyd

b. 10 July 1906 Leicester, England

English ophthalmic surgeon, pioneer of intra-ocular lens implants.

Following a medical education at Cambridge and St Thomas's Hospital, London, he was appointed at an early age to the post of Surgeon to Moorfields Eye Hospital (Royal London Ophthalmic Hospital). During the Second World War he served abroad in Africa as an ophthalmic specialist and became an authority on onchocerciasis (river blindness) and filiariasis.

His experience of the inertness of plastic material retained inside the eye in injured aircraft personnel led him to investigate the possibility of replacing cataractous lenses with intra-ocular plastic lenses. After his appointment as Consultant Ophthalmologist to St Thomas's in 1946, the first lens implant procedure was successfully carried out in 1949. The implantation of glass lenses in the treatment of myopia had been attempted in Germany at the end of the nineteenth century, but the weight of the material had militated against a successful outcome.

It was some time before the new procedure, which owed much to his surgical dexterity, became widely accepted, but the work of Strampelli, Binkhorst and others led to its wider application; intra-ocular implants are now a standard element of the surgical treatment of cataract.

Principal Honours and Distinctions
FRS 1986. Royal Society Galen Medal 1986; Crook Gold Medal 1988.

Bibliography
1951, 'Intraocular acrylic lenses', *Trans. Ophth. Soc. UK.*
1964, 'Intraocular lenses – past, present and future', *Trans. Ophth. Soc. UK.*

Further Reading
S. Duke-Elder, 1969, *System of Ophthalmology*, Vol. 9, London.

MG

Riefler, Sigmund

b. 9 August 1847 Maria Rain, Germany
d. 21 October 1912 Munich, Germany

German engineer who invented the precision clock that bears his name.

Riefler's father was a scientific-instrument maker and clockmaker who in 1841 had founded the firm of Clemens Riefler to make mathematical instruments. After graduating in engineering from the University of Munich Sigmund worked as a surveyor, but when his father died in 1876 he and his brothers ran the family firm. Sigmund was responsible for technical development and in this capacity he designed a new system of drawing-instruments which established the reputation of the firm. He also worked to improve the performance of the precision clock, and in 1889 he was granted a patent for a new form of escapement. This escapement succeeded in reducing the interference of the clock mechanism with the free swinging of the pendulum by impulsing the pendulum through its suspension strip. It proved to be the greatest advance in precision timekeeping since the introduction of the dead-beat escapement about two hundred years earlier. When the firm of Clemens Riefler began to produce clocks with this escapement in 1890, they replaced clocks with **Graham**'s dead-beat escapement as the standard regulator for use in observatories and other applications where the highest precision was required. In 1901 a movement was fitted with electrical rewind and was encapsulated in an airtight case, at low pressure, so that the timekeeping was not affected by changes in barometric pressure. This became the standard practice for precision clocks. Although the accuracy of the Riefler clock was later surpassed by the **Shortt** free-pendulum clock and the quartz clock, it remained in production until 1965, by which time over six hundred instruments had been made.

Principal Honours and Distinctions
Franklin Institute John Scott Medal 1894. Honorary doctorate, University of Munich 1897. Vereins zur Förderung des Gewerbefleisses in Preussen Gold Medal 1900.

Bibliography
1907, *Präzisionspendeluhren und Zeitdienstanlagen für Sternwarten*, Munich (for a complete bibliography see D. Riefler below).

Further Reading
D. Riefler, 1981, *Riefler-Präzisionspendeluhren*, Munich (the definitive work on Riefler and his clock).
A.L. Rawlings, 1948, *The Science of Clocks and Watches*, 2nd edn; repub. 1974 (a technical assessment of the Riefler escapement in its historical context).

See also **Marrison, Warren**.

DV

Riggenbach, Niklaus
b. 21 May 1817 Gebweiler, Alsace
d. 25 July 1899 Olten, Switzerland

Swiss locomotive engineer and pioneer of mountain rack railways.

Riggenbach came from a Basle family and was educated in Basle, Lyons and Paris, where he was so impressed by the new railway to Saint-Germain that he decided to devote himself to work in that field. He worked for Kessler's locomotive works in Karlsruhe, which built the first locomotives for the Zurich–Baden Railway. This was the first railway in Switzerland and when it was opened in 1847 Riggenbach drove the first train. He subsequently became Locomotive Superintendent of the Swiss Central Railway, and the problems of operating a steeply graded line solely by adhesion led him to develop a rack railway which incorporated a ladder rack similar to that of Sylvester **Marsh**. However, it was only after the Swiss Consul in Washington had reported enthusiastically on the Mount Washington Cog Railway that Riggenbach and associates were able to get a concession for their first line, which was laid up the Rigi mountain and was opened in 1871. That same year Riggenbach opened a quarry railway operated for the first time by a mixture of rack and adhesion. From this start, rack railways were built widely in Switzerland and to a lesser extent in many other parts of the world. His Rigi railway continues to operate.

Bibliography
Riggenbach patented his rack railway in 1863.

Further Reading
Riggenbach's type of counter-pressure brakes is described in *Transactions of the Newcomen So-*

ciety 55: 13.
M. Dietschy, 1971, 'Le Chemin de fer du Rigi à 100 ans', *Chemins de fer régionaux et urbains* 106.
O.J. Morris, 1951, *The Snowdon Mountain Railway*, Ian Allan.

See also **Abt, Roman**.

PJGR

Riley, James
b. 1840 Halifax, England
d. 15 July 1910 Harrogate, England

English steelmaker who promoted the manufacture of low-carbon bulk steel by the open-hearth process for tin plate and shipbuilding; pioneer of nickel steels.

After working as a millwright in Halifax, Riley found employment at the Ormesby Ironworks in Middlesbrough until, in 1869, he became manager of the Askam Ironworks in Cumberland. Three years later, in 1872, he was appointed Blast-furnace Manager at the pioneering Siemens Steel Company's works at Landore, near Swansea in South Wales. Using Spanish ore, he produced the manganese-rich iron (spiegeleisen) required as an additive to make satisfactory steel. Riley was promoted in 1874 to be General Manager at Landore, and he worked with William **Siemens** to develop the use of the latter's regenerative furnace for the production of open-hearth steel. He persuaded Welsh makers of tin plate to use sheets rolled from low-carbon (mild) steel instead of from charcoal iron and, partly by publishing some test results, he was instrumental in influencing the Admiralty to build two naval vessels of mild steel, the *Mercury* and the *Iris*.

In 1878 Riley moved north on his appointment as General Manager of the Steel Company of Scotland, a firm closely associated with Charles **Tennant** that was formed in 1872 to make steel by the Siemens process. Already by 1878, fourteen Siemens melting furnaces had been erected, and in that year 42,000 long tons of ingots were produced at the company's Hallside (Newton) Works, situated 8 km (5 miles) south-east of Glasgow. Under Riley's leadership, steelmaking in open-hearth furnaces was initiated at a second plant situated at Blochairn. Plates and sections for all aspects of shipbuilding, including boilers, formed the main products; the company also supplied the greater part of the steel for the Forth (Railway) Bridge. Riley was associated with technical modifications which improved the performance of steelmaking furnaces using Siemens's principles. He built a gas-fired cupola for melting pig-iron, and constructed the first British 'universal' plate mill using three-high rolls (Lauth mill).

At the request of French interests, Riley investigated the properties of steels containing various proportions of nickel; the report that he read before the Iron and Steel Institute in 1889 successfully brought to the notice of potential users the greatly enhanced strength that nickel could impart and its ability to yield alloys possessing substantially lower corrodibility.

The Steel Company of Scotland paid dividends in the years to 1890, but then came a lean period. In 1895, at the age of 54, Riley moved once more to another employer, becoming General Manager of the Glasgow Iron and Steel Company, which had just laid out a new steelmaking plant at Wishaw, 25 km (15 miles) south-east of Glasgow, where it already had blast furnaces. Still the technical innovator, in 1900 Riley presented an account of his experiences in introducing molten blast-furnace metal as feed for the open-hearth steel furnaces. In the early 1890s it was largely through Riley's efforts that a West of Scotland Board of Conciliation and Arbitration for the Manufactured Steel Trade came into being; he was its first Chairman and then its President.

In 1899 James Riley resigned from his Scottish employment to move back to his native Yorkshire, where he became his own master by acquiring the small Richmond Ironworks situated at Stockton-on-Tees. Although Riley's 1900 account to the Iron and Steel Institute was the last of the many of which he was author, he continued to contribute to the discussion of papers written by others.

Principal Honours and Distinctions
President, West of Scotland Iron and Steel Institute 1893–5. Vice-President, Iron and Steel Institute, 1893–1910. Iron and Steel Institute (London) Bessemer Gold Medal 1887.

Bibliography
1876, 'On steel for shipbuilding as supplied to

the Royal Navy', *Transactions of the Institute of Naval Architects* 17: 135–55.
1884, 'On recent improvements in the method of manufacture of open-hearth steel', *Journal of the Iron and Steel Institute* 2: 43–52 plus plates 27–31.
1887, 'Some investigations as to the effects of different methods of treatment of mild steel in the manufacture of plates', *Journal of the Iron and Steel Institute* 1: 121–30 (plus sheets II and III and plates XI and XII).
27 February 1888, 'Improvements in basic-hearth steel making furnaces', British patent no. 2,896.
27 February 1888, 'Improvements in regenerative furnaces for steel-making and analogous operations', British patent no. 2,899.
1889, 'Alloys of nickel and steel', *Journal of the Iron and Steel Institute* 1: 45–55.

Further Reading
A. Slaven, 1986, 'James Riley', in *Dictionary of Scottish Business Biography 1860–1960, Volume 1: The Staple Industries* (ed. A. Slaven and S. Checkland), Aberdeen: Aberdeen University Press, 136–8.
'Men you know', *The Bailie* (Glasgow) 23 January 1884, series no. 588 (a brief biography, with portrait).
J.C. Carr and W. Taplin, 1962, *History of the British Steel Industry*, Harvard University Press (contains an excellent summary of salient events).

JKA

Rillieux, Norbert
b. 1800 New Orleans, Louisiana, USA
d. 1894 France

African-American inventor of a sugar-evaporation process.

A free black, he was the son of Vincent Rillieux, a white engineer, and Constance Vivant, a quadroon. The family was prosperous enough to send him to France to be educated, at the Ecole Centrale in Paris. There he studied engineering and later taught mechanical engineering, developing a special interest in thermodynamics and steam-power. In 1830 he devised a vacuum evaporation system with industrial possibilities, but he was unable to interest any French firms in the device. He therefore returned to New Orleans and obtained his first patent in 1843. Two years later he was able to have the evaporation system installed on a plantation to refine sugar. It soon demonstrated its worth, for planters were able to recoup the cost of the plant within a year through raised production and reduced operating costs. It came to be the generally accepted method for processing sugar-cane juice, and the price of refined sugar fell so that white sugar ceased to be a luxury food for the rich.

Rillieux's patents protected him from repeated efforts to counterfeit the process, which thus earned him considerable wealth. However, because of increasing hostility and discriminatory laws against blacks in New Orleans, he did not long enjoy it and he returned to France, taking up the study of egyptology.

Further Reading
P.P. James, 1989, *The Real McCoy: African-American Invention and Innovation 1619–1930*, Washington, DC: Smithsonian Institution, pp. 41–3.

LRD

Riquet, Pierre Paul

b. 29 June 1604 Béziers, Hérault, France
d. 1 October 1680 buried at Toulouse, France

French canal engineer and constructor of the Canal du Midi.

Pierre Paul Riquet was the son of a wealthy lawyer whose ancestors came from Italy. In his education at the Jesuit College in Béziers he showed obvious natural ability in science and mathematics, but he received no formal engineering training. With his own and his wife's fortunes he was able to purchase a château at Verfeil, near Toulouse. In 1630 he was appointed a collector of the salt tax in Languedoc and in a short time became Lessee General (Fermier Général) of this tax for the whole province. This entailed constant travel through the district, with the result that he became very familiar with this part of the country. He also became involved in military contracting. He acquired a vast fortune out of both activities. At this time he pondered the possibility of building a canal from Toulouse to the Mediterranean beyond Béziers and, after further investigation as to possible water supplies, he wrote to Colbert in Paris on 16 November 1662 advocating the construction of the canal.

Although the idea proved acceptable it was not until 27 May 1665 that Riquet was authorized to direct operations, and on 14 October 1666 he was given authority to construct the first part of the canal, from Toulouse to Trebes. Work started on 1 January 1667. By 1669 he had between 7,000 and 8,000 men employed on the work. Unhappily, Riquet died just over six months before the canal was completed, the official opening beingon 15 May 1681.

Although Riquet's fame rightly rests on the Canal du Midi, probably the greatest work of its time in Europe, he was also consulted about and was responsible for other projects. He built an aqueduct on more than 100 arches to lead water into the grounds of the château of his friend the marquis de Castres. The plans for this work, which involved considerable practical difficulties, were finalized in 1670, and water flowed into the château grounds in 1676. Also in 1676, Riquet was commissioned to lead the waters of the river Ourcq into Paris; he drew up plans, but he was too busy to undertake the construction and on his death the work was shelved until Napoleon's time. He was responsible for the creation of the port of Sète on the Mediterranean at the end of the Canal du Midi. He was also consulted on the supply of water to the Palace of Versailles and on a proposed route which later became the Canal de Bourgogne. Riquet was a very remarkable man: when he started the construction of the canal he was well over 60 years old, an age at which most people are retiring, and lived almost to its completion.

Further Reading
L.T.C. Rolt, 1973, *From Sea to Sea*, London: Allen Lane; rev. ed. 1994, Bridgwater: Internet Ltd.
Jean-Denis Bergasse, 1982–7, *Le Canal de Midi*, 4 vols, Hérault: — Vol. I: *Pierre Paul Riquet et le Canal du Midi dans les arts et la littérature*; Vol II: *Trois Siècles de batellerie et de voyage*; Vol. III: *Des Siècles d'aventures humaine*; Vol. IV: *Grands Moments et grands sites*.

JHB

Rittinger, Peter von

b. 23 January 1811 Neutitschein, Moravia (now Novy Jicin, Czech Republic)
d. 7 December 1872 Vienna, Austria

Austrian mining engineer, improver of the processing of minerals.

After studying law, philosophy and politics at the University of Olmütz (now Olomouc), in 1835 Rittinger became a fellow of the Mining Academy in Schemnitz (now Banská Štiavnica), Slovakia. In 1839, the year he finished at the academy, he published a book on perspective drawing. The following year, he became Inspector of Mills at the ore mines in Schemnitz, and in 1845 he was engaged in coal mining in Bohemia and Moravia. In 1849 he joined the mining administration at Joachimsthal (now Jáchymov), Bohemia. In these early years he contributed his first important innovations for the mining industry and thus fostered his career in the government's service. In 1850 he was called to Vienna to become a high-ranked officer in various ministries. He was responsible for the construction of buildings, pumping installations and all sorts of machinery in the mining industry; he reorganized the curricula of the mining schools, was responsible for the mint and became head of the department of mines, forests and salt-works in the Austrian empire.

During all his years of public service, Rittinger continued his concern with technological innovations. He improved the processing of ores by introducing in 1844 the rotary washer and the box classifier, and later his continuously shaking concussion table which, having been exhibited at the Vienna World Fair of 1873, was soon adopted in other countries. He constructed water-column pumps, invented a differential shaft pump with hydraulic linkage to replace the heavy iron rods and worked on centrifugal pumps. He was one of the first to be concerned with the transfer of heat, and he developed a system of using exhaust steam for heating in salt-works. He kept his eye on current developments abroad, using his function as official Austrian commissioner to the world exhibitions, on which he published frequently as well as on other matters related to technology. With his systematic handbook on mineral processing, first published in 1867, he emphasized his international reputation in this specialized field of mining.

Principal Honours and Distinctions
Knighted 1863. Order of the Iron Crown 1863. Honorary Citizen of Joachimsthal 1864. President, Austrian Chamber of Engineers and Architects 1863–5.

Bibliography
1849, *Der Spitzkasten-Apparat statt Mehlrinnen und Sümpfen ... bei der nassen Aufbereitung*, Freiberg.
1854, *Theoretisch-praktische Anleitung zur Räder-Verzahnung*, Vienna.
1855, *Theoretisch-praktische Abhandlung über ein für alle Gattungen von Flüssigkeiten anwendbares neues Abdampfverfahren*, Vienna.
1861, *Theorie und Bau der Rohrturbinen*, Prague.
1867, *Lehrbuch der Aufbereitungskunde*, Berlin (with supplements, 1870–73).

Further Reading
H. Kunnert, 1972, 'Peter Ritter von Rittinger. Lebensbild eines grossen Montanisten', *Der Anschnitt* 24: 3–7 (a detailed description of his life, based on source material).
J. Steiner, 1972, 'Der Beitrag von Peter Rittinger zur Entwicklung der Aufbereitungstechnik'. *Berg- und hüttenmännische Monatshefte* 117: 471–6 (an evaluation of Rittinger's achievements for the processing of ores).

WK

Riva-Rocci, Scipione
b. 7 August 1863 Almese, Piedmont, Italy
d. 15 March 1937 Rapallo, Liguria, Italy

Italian physician, inventor and developer of the mercury sphygmomanometer for the measurement of blood pressure.

After graduating in medicine and surgery in 1888 from the University of Turin, he was appointed Assistant Lecturer at the University under **Forlanini**. In 1893 he followed Forlanini to Pavia, where for twenty-eight years he was Director and Head Physician of the Ospedale di Varese. From 1908 until 1921 he was also Lecturer in Paediatrics. He invented the sphygmomanometer in 1896 and its use was greatly encouraged by the support of **Cushing**, who visited Pavia in 1901 and was convinced of its value in the monitoring of anaesthesia, particularly in connection with intracranial surgery.

Bibliography
1896, 'Un nuovo sfigmomanometro', *Gazzetta*

Medica di Torino 447.

Further Reading
J.F. Fulton, 1946, *Harvey Cushing: A Biography*, Springfield, Ill.

MG

Robert, Nicolas Louis

b. 2 December 1761 Paris, France
d. 8 August 1828 Dreux, France

French inventor of the papermaking machine.

Robert was born into a prosperous family and received a fair education, after which he became a lawyer's clerk. In 1780, however, he enlisted in the Army and joined the artillery, serving with distinction in the West Indies, where he fought against the English. When dissatisfied with his prospects, Robert returned to Paris and obtained a post as proof-reader to the firm of printers and publishers owned by the Didot family. They were so impressed with his abilities that they promoted him, *c.*1790, to 'clerk inspector of workmen' at their paper mill at Essonnes, south of Paris, under the control of Didot St Leger.

It was there that Robert conceived the idea of a continuous papermaking machine. In 1797 he made a model of it and, after further models, he obtained a patent in 1798. The paper was formed on a continuously revolving wire gauze, from which the sheets were lifted off and hung up to dry. Didot was at first scathing, but he came round to encouraging Robert to make a success of the machine. However, they quarrelled over the financial arrangements and Robert left to try setting up his own mill near Rouen. He failed for lack of capital, and in 1800 he returned to Essonnes and sold his patent to Didot for part cash, part proceeds from the operation of the mill. Didot left for England to enlist capital and technical skills to exploit the invention, while Robert was left in charge at Essonnes. It was the **Fourdrinier** brothers and Bryan **Donkin** who developed the papermaking machine into a form in which it could succeed. Meanwhile the mill at Essonnes under Robert's direction had begun to falter and declined to the point where it had to be sold. He had never received the full return from the sale of his patent, but he managed to recover his rights in it. This profited him little, for Didot obtained a patent in France for the Fourdrinier machine and had two examples

erected in 1814 and the following year, respectively, neatly side-tracking Robert, who was now without funds or position. To support himself and his family, Robert set up a primary school in Dreux and there passed his remaining years. Although it was the Fourdrinier papermaking machine that was generally adopted, it is Robert who deserves credit for the original initiative.

Further Reading
R.H. Clapperton, 1967, *The Papermaking Machine*, Oxford: Pergamon Press, pp. 279–83 (provides a full description of Robert's invention and patent, together with a biography).

LRD

Roberts, Richard

b. 22 April 1789 Carreghova, Llanymynech, Montgomeryshire, Wales
d. 11 March 1864 London, England

Welsh mechanical engineer and inventor.

Richard Roberts was the son of a shoemaker and tollkeeper and received only an elementary education at the village school. At the age of 10 his interest in mechanics was stimulated when he was allowed by the Curate, the Revd Griffith Howell, to use his lathe and other tools. As a young man Roberts acquired a considerable local reputation for his mechanical skills, but these were exercised only in his spare time. For many years he worked in the local limestone quarries, until at the age of 20 he obtained employment as a pattern-maker in Staffordshire. In the next few years he worked as a mechanic in Liverpool, Manchester and Salford before moving in 1814 to London, where he obtained employment with Henry **Maudslay**. In 1816 he set up on his own account in Manchester. He soon established a reputation there for gear-cutting and other general engineering work, especially for the textile industry, and by 1821 he was employing about twelve men. He built machine tools mainly for his own use, including, in 1817, one of the first planing machines.

One of his first inventions was a gas meter, but his first patent was obtained in 1822 for improvements in looms. His most important contribution to textile technology was his invention of the self-acting spinning mule, patented in 1825. The normal fourteen-year term of this patent was extended in 1839 by a further seven years. Between 1826 and 1828 Roberts paid several visits to Alsace, France, arranging cotton-spinning machinery for a new factory at Mulhouse. By 1826 he had become a partner in the firm of Sharp Brothers, the company then becoming Sharp, Roberts & Co. The firm continued to build textile machinery, and in the 1830s it built locomotive engines for the newly created railways and made one experimental steam-carriage for use on roads. The partnership was dissolved in 1843, the Sharps establishing a new works to continue locomotive building while Roberts retained the existing factory, known as the Globe Works, where he soon after took as partners R.G. Dobinson and Benjamin Fothergill (1802–79). This partnership was dissolved *c.*1851, and Roberts continued in business on his own for a few years before moving to London as a consulting engineer.

During the 1840s and 1850s Roberts produced many new inventions in a variety of fields, including machine tools, clocks and watches, textile machinery, pumps and ships. One of these was a machine controlled by a punched-card system similar to the **Jacquard** loom for punching rivet holes in plates. This was used in the construction of the Conway and Menai Straits tubular bridges. Roberts was granted twenty-six patents, many of which, before the Patent Law Amendment Act of 1852, covered more than one invention; there were still other inventions he did not patent. He made his contribution to the discussion which led up to the 1852 Act by publishing, in 1830 and 1833, pamphlets suggesting reform of the Patent Law.

In the early 1820s Roberts helped to establish the Manchester Mechanics' Institute, and in 1823 he was elected a member of the Literary and Philosophical Society of Manchester. He frequently contributed to their proceedings and in 1861 he was made an Honorary Member. He was elected a Member of the Institution of Civil Engineers in 1838. From 1838 to 1843 he served as a councillor of the then-new Municipal Borough of Manchester. In his final years, without the assistance of business partners, Roberts suffered financial difficulties, and at the time of his death a fund for his aid was being raised.

Principal Honours and Distinctions
Member, Institution of Civil Engineers 1838.

Further Reading
There is no full-length biography of Richard Roberts but the best account is H.W. Dickinson, 1945–7, 'Richard Roberts, his life and inventions', *Transactions of the Newcomen Society* 25: 123–37.
W.H. Chaloner, 1968–9, 'New light on Richard Roberts, textile engineer (1789–1864)', *Transactions of the Newcomen Society* 41: 27–44.

RTS

Robinson, George J.
b. 1712 Scotland
d. 1798 England

*Scottish manufacturer who installed the first **Boulton & Watt** rotative steam-engine in a textile mill.*

George Robinson is said to have been a Scots migrant who settled at Burwell, near Nottingham, in 1737, but there is no record of his occupation until 1771, when he was noticed as a bleacher. By 1783 he and his son were describing themselves as 'merchants and thread manufacturers' as well as bleachers. For their thread, they were using the system of spinning on the water-frame, but it is not known whether they held a licence from **Arkwright**. Between 1776 and 1791, the firm G.J. & J. Robinson built a series of six cotton mills with a complex of dams and aqueducts to supply them in the relatively flat land of the Leen valley, near Papplewick, to the north of Nottingham. By careful conservation they were able to obtain considerable power from a very small stream. Castle mill was not only the highest one owned by the Robinsons, but it was also the highest mill on the stream and was fed from a reservoir. The Robinsons might therefore have expected to have enjoyed uninterrupted use of the water, but above them lived Lord Byron in his estate of Newstead Priory. The fifth Lord Byron loved making ornamental ponds on his property so that he could have mock naval battles with his servants, and this tampered with the water supplies so much that the Robinsons found they were unable to work their mills.

In 1785 they decided to order a rotative steam engine from the firm of Boulton & Watt. It was erected by John **Rennie**; however, misfortune seemed to dog this engine, for parts went astray to Manchester and when the engine was finally running at the end of February 1786 it was found to be out of alignment so may not have been very successful. At about the same time, the lawsuit against Lord Byron was found in favour of the Robinsons, but the engine continued in use for at least twelve years and was the first of the type which was to power virtually all steam-driven mills until the 1850s to be installed in a textile mill. It was a low-pressure double-acting condensing beam engine, with a vertical cylinder, parallel motion connecting the piston to one end of a rocking beam, and a connecting rod at the other end of the beam turning the flywheel. In this case Watt's sun and planet motion was used in place of a crank.

Further Reading
R.L. Hills, 1970, *Power in the Industrial Revolution*, Manchester (for an account of the installation of this engine).
D.M. Smith, 1965, *Industrial Archaeology of the East Midlands*, Newton Abbot (describes the problems which the Robinsons had with the water supplies to power their mills).
S.D. Chapman, 1967, *The Early Factory Masters*, Newton Abbot (provides details of the business activities of the Robinsons).
J.D. Marshall, 1959, 'Early application of steam power: the cotton mills of the Upper Leen', *Transactions of the Thoroton Society of Nottinghamshire* 60 (mentions the introduction of this steam-engine).

RLH

Rochas, Alphonse Eugène Beau de
See **Beau de Rochas, Alphonse Eugène**.

Roe, Sir Edwin Alliott Verdon
b. 26 April 1877 Manchester, England
d. 4 January 1958 London, England

English designer of one of the most successful biplanes of all time, the Avro 504.

A.V. Roe served an apprenticeship at a railway works, studied marine engineering at Kings College London, served at sea as an engineer, and then took a job in the motor-car industry. His hobby was flying: after studying bird-flight, he built several flying models and in 1907 one of these won a prize offered by the *Daily Mail*. With the prize money he built a full-size aeroplane loosely based on the *Flyer* of the **Wright** brothers, with whom he had corresponded. In September, Roe took his biplane to the motor-racing circuit at Brooklands, in Surrey, but it made only a few hops and his activities were not welcomed. Roe then moved to Essex, where he assembled his new aeroplane under the arch of a railway bridge. This was a triplane design with the engine at the front (a 'tractor'), and during 1909 it made several flights (this triplane is preserved by the Science Museum in London).

In 1910 Roe and his brother Humphrey founded A.V. Roe & Co. in Manchester, they described it the 'Aviator's Storehouse'. During the next three years Roe designed and built aeroplanes in Manchester, then transported them to Brooklands to fly (the authorities now made him more welcome). One of the most significant of these was his *Type D* tractor biplane of 1911, which led to the Avro *504* two-seater trainer of 1913. This was one of the most successful trainers of all time, as around 10,000 were built. In November 1914 a flight of Avro *504*s carried out the first-ever bombing raid when they attacked German airship sheds as Friedrichshafen. A.V. Roe produced the first aeroplanes with enclosed cabins during 1912: the *Type F* monoplane and *Type G* biplane. After the war, his *Avian* was used for several record-breaking flights. In 1928 he sold his interest in the company bearing his name and joined forces with Saunders Ltd of Cowes, on the Isle of Wight, to found Saunders–Roe Ltd. 'Saro' produced a series of flying boats, from the four-seat *Cutty Sark* of 1929 to the large, and ill-fated, *Princess* of 1952.

Principal Honours and Distinctions
Knighted 1929 (in 1933 he incorporated his mother's name to become Sir Alliott Verdon-Roe). Honorary Fellow of the Royal Aeronautical Society 1948.

Bibliography
1939, *The World of Wings and Things*, London.

Further Reading
L.J. Ludovic, 1956, *the Challenging Sky*.
A.J. Jackson, 1908, *Avro Aircraft since 1908*, London (a detailed account).

JDS

Roebling, John Augustus

b. 12 July 1806 Mühlhausen, Prussia.
d. 22 July 1869 Brooklyn, New York, USA

German/American bridge engineer and builder.

The son of Polycarp Roebling, a tobacconist, he studied mathematics at Dr Unger's Pedagogium in Erfurt and went on to the Royal Polytechnic Institute in Berlin, from which he graduated in 1826 with honours in civil engineering. He spent the next three years working for the Prussian government on the construction of roads and bridges. With his brother and a group of friends, he emigrated to the United States, sailing from Bremen on 23 May 1831 and docking in Philadelphia eleven weeks later. They bought 7,000 acres (2,800 hectares) in Butler County, western Pennsylvania, and established a village, at first called Germania but later known as Saxonburg. Roebling gave up trying to establish himself as a farmer and found work for the state of Pennsylvania as Assistant Engineer on the Beaver River canal and others, then surveying a railroad route across the Allegheny Mountains. During his canal work, he noted the failings of the hemp ropes that were in use at that time, and recalled having read of wire ropes in a German journal; he built a rope-walk at his Saxonburg farm, bought a supply of iron wire and trained local labour in the method of wire twisting.

At this time, many canals crossed rivers by means of aqueducts. In 1844, the Pennsylvania Canal aqueduct across the Allegheny River was due to be renewed, having become unsafe. Roebling made proposals which were accepted by the canal company: seven wooden spans of 162 ft (49 m) each were supported on either side by a 7 in. (18 cm) diameter cable, Roebling himself having to devise all the machinery required for the erection. He subsequently built four more suspension aqueducts, one of which was converted to a toll bridge and was still in use a century later.

In 1849 he moved to Trenton, New Jersey, where he set up a new wire rope plant. In 1851 he started the construction (completed in 1855) of an 821 ft (250 m) long suspension railroad bridge across the Niagara River, 245 ft (75 m) above the rapids; each cable consisted of 3,640 wrought iron wires. A lower deck carried road traffic. He also constructed a bridge across the Ohio River between Cincinnati and Covington,

a task which was much protracted due to the Civil War; this bridge was finally completed in 1866.

Roebling's crowning achievement was to have been the design and construction of the bridge over the Hudson River between Brooklyn and Staten Island, New York, but he did not live to see its completion. It had a span of 1,595 ft (486 m), designed to bear a load of 18,700 tons (19,000 tonnes) with a headroom of 135 ft (41 m). The work of building had barely started when, at the Brooklyn wharf, a boat crushed Roebling's foot against the timbering and he died of tetanus three weeks later. His son, Washington Augustus **Roebling**, then took charge of this great work.

Further Reading

D.B. Steinman and S.R. Watson, 1941, *Bridges and their Builders*, New York: Dover Books.
D. McCullough, 1982, *The Great Bridge: The Epic Story of the Building of the Brooklyn Bridge*, New York: Simon & Schuster.

IMcN

Roebling, Washington Augustus

b. 26 May 1837 Saxonburg, Pennsylvania, USA.
d. 21 July 1926 Trenton, New Jersey, USA.

American civil engineer.

The son of John Augustus **Roebling**, he graduated in 1857 from the Rensselaer Polytechnic Institute as a civil engineer, and joined his father in his suspension bridge construction work. He served in the Civil War as a colonel of engineers in the Union Army, and in 1867, two years after the end of the war, he went to Europe to study new methods of sinking underwater foundations by means of compressed air. These new methods were employed in the construction of the Brooklyn Bridge, of which he took charge on his father's death in 1869. Timber pneumatic caissons were used, with a maximum pressure of 34 psi (2.4 kg/cm^2) above atmospheric pressure. Two years after work on the piers had started in the caissons, Roebling, who had been working constantly with the men on the foundations of the piers, was carried unconscious out of the caisson, a victim of decompression sickness, then known as "caisson disease". He was paralysed and lost the use of his voice. From then on he directed the rest of the work from the sickroom of his nearby house, his wife, Emily Warren Roebling, helping with his instructions and notes and carrying them out to the workforce; she even read a statement from him to the American Society of Civil Engineers. The erection of the cables, which were of steel, began in August 1876 and took twenty-six months to complete. In 1881 eleven trustees and Emily Warren Roebling walked across temporary planking, but the decking of the total span was not completed until 1885, fourteen years after construction of the bridge had started. The Brooklyn Bridge was Roebling's last major work, although following the death of his nephew in 1921 he was forced to head again the management of Roebling & Company, though aged 84 and an invalid.

Further Reading

D.B. Steinman and S.R. Watson, 1941, *Bridges and their Builders*, New York: Dover Books.

D. McCullough, 1982, *The Great Bridge: The Epic Story of the Building of the Brooklyn Bridge*, New York: Simon & Schuster.

IMcN

Roebuck, John

b. 1718 Sheffield, England
d. 17 July 1794

English chemist and manufacturer, inventor of the lead-chamber process for sulphuric acid.

The son of a prosperous Sheffield manufacturer, Roebuck forsook the family business to pursue studies in medicine at Edinburgh University. There he met Dr Joseph Black (1727–99), celebrated Professor of Chemistry, who aroused in Roebuck a lasting interest in chemistry. Roebuck continued his studies at Leyden, where he took his medical degree in 1742. He set up in practice in Birmingham, but in his spare time he continued chemical experiments that might help local industries.

Among his early achievements was his new method of refining gold and silver. Success led to the setting up of a large laboratory and a reputation as a chemical consultant. It was at this time that Roebuck devised an improved way of making sulphuric acid. This vital substance was then made by burning sulphur and nitre (potassium nitrate) over water in a glass globe. The scale of the process was limited by the fragility of the glass. Roebuck substituted 'lead chambers', or vessels consisting of sheets of lead, a metal both cheap and resistant to acids, set in wooden frames. After the first plant was set up in 1746, productivity rose and the price of sulphuric acid fell sharply. Success encouraged Roebuck to establish a second, larger plant at Prestonpans, near Edinburgh. He preferred to rely on secrecy rather than patents to preserve his monopoly, but a departing employee took the secret with him and the process spread rapidly in England and on the European continent. It remained the standard process until it was superseded by the contact process towards the end of the nineteenth century. Roebuck next turned his attention to ironmaking and finally selected a site on the Carron river, near Falkirk in Scotland, where the raw materials and water power and transport lay close at hand. The Carron ironworks began producing iron in 1760 and became one of the great names in the history of ironmaking. Roebuck was an early proponent of the smelting of iron with coke, pioneered by Abraham **Darby** at Coalbrookdale. To supply the stronger blast required, Roebuck consulted John **Smeaton**, who *c.*1760 installed the first blowing cylinders of any size.

All had so far gone well for Roebuck, but he now leased coal-mines and salt-works from the Duke of Hamilton's lands at Borrowstonness in Linlithgow. The coal workings were plagued with flooding which the existing **Newcomen** engines were unable to overcome. Through his friendship with Joseph Black, patron of James **Watt**, Roebuck persuaded Watt to join him to apply his improved steam-engine to the flooded mine. He took over Black's loan to Watt of £1,200, helped him to obtain the first steam-engine patent of 1769 and took a two-thirds interest in the project. However, the new engine was not yet equal to the task and the debts mounted. To satisfy his creditors, Roebuck had to dispose of his capital in his various ventures. One creditor was Matthew **Boulton**, who accepted Roebuck's two-thirds share in Watt's steam-engine, rather than claim payment from his depleted estate, thus initiating a famous partnership. Roebuck was retained to manage Borrowstonness and allowed an annuity for his continued support until his death in 1794.

Further Reading
Memoir of John Roebuck in *J. Roy. Soc. Edin.*, vol. 4 (1798), pp. 65–87.
S. Gregory, 1987, 'John Roebuck, 18th century entrepreneur', *Chem. Engr.* 443: 28–31.
LRD

Rogallo, Francis Melvin
b. 1912 USA

American engineer who patented a flexible-winged hand-glider in 1948.

After the hang-gliders of pioneers such as Lilienthal, Pilcher and Chanute in the 1890s, this form of flying virtually disappeared for seventy years. It was reintroduced in the late 1960s based on Francis Rogallo's flexible wing, patented in the United States in 1948. Rogallo's wing was very basic: it consisted of a fabric delta wing with a solid boom along each leading edge and one along the centre line. Between these booms, the fabric was free to billow out into two partial cones. Variations of the Rogallo flexible wing were investigated in the 1960s by Ryans as a means of recovering space vehicles (e.g. Saturn booster), and by North American for the recovery of Gemini spacecraft. In 1963 a version with a 155 kW (210 hp) engine was tested by the US services as a potential lightweight transport vehicle. None of these made a great impact and the Rogallo wing became popular as a hang-glider c.1970. The pilot was suspended in a harness below a lightweight Rogallo wing. A framework attached to the wing structure allowed the pilot to move his or her body in any direction relative to the wing. Thus, if they wished to dive, they would move their weight forward, which made the glider nose-heavy. This was a great improvement over the earlier hang-gliders, in which the upper part of the pilot's body was held in a fixed position and control was achieved by swinging the legs. Rogallo-wing hang-gliders became very popular as they were relatively cheap and easy to transport. Once the sport developed, powered 'microlights' made their appearance and a new branch of popular flying was established.

Further Reading
Ann Welsh, 1977, 'Hang glider development', *Aerospace* (Royal Aeronautical Society) (August/September).
JDS

Rohe, Ludwig Mies van der
See **Mies van der Rohe, Ludwig**.

Rolls, The Hon. Charles Stewart
b. 28 August 1877 London, England.
d. 12 July 1910 Bournemouth, Hampshire, England.

English motorist, aviator and automobile manufacturer.

The son of a baron, Rolls drove cars such as Panhards and Mors from 1895. He was educated at Cambridge University, and set up in business selling French and Belgian cars. Henry **Royce**'s third car was built for a director of Royce Ltd, Henry Edwards, who was a friend of Rolls. A meeting was arranged between Royce and Rolls and, in 1904, they formed a partnership. From 1907, Rolls was selling the 40/50 hp Rolls–Royce *Ghost* from his London showroom; in 1908, the factory moved to Derby. Rolls took up flying and crossed the English Channel in a balloon in 1906, and in June 1910 he crossed it by plane. In the following month, he was killed when the plane he was piloting crashed.

Further Reading
J.J. Fucini and S. Fucini, 1985, *Entrepreneurs*, Boston: C.K. Hall & Co.
IMcN

Romanov, Pyotr Alekseyevich
See **Peter the Great**.

Rondelet, Jean-Baptiste
b. 1734 Lyons, France
d. 1829

French architect particularly interested in the scientific and mathematical basis of architectural structure, and who at an early date introduced reinforced concrete into supporting piers in his buildings.

From 1795 Rondelet was Professor at the Ecole Centrale des Travaux Publics and while there was responsible for a major treatise on building construction: this was his *Traité théorique et pratique de l'art de bâtir*, published in four volumes in 1802–17. From 1806 he taught at the Ecole Spéciale d'Architecture, which was soon afterwards merged with the Ecole Polytechnique. It was when Rondelet took over the work of completing the Panthéon in Paris, after the death of Jacques-Germain Soufflot, that he had the opportunity of putting some of his particular structural ideas into practice. In 1755 the King had appointed Soufflot architect of the great new church to be dedicated to the patron saint of the city, Sainte Geneviève. In this neo-classical structure based upon Greek cross plan, Soufflot intended four slender piers, each encased in three engaged columns, to support the pendentives for the dome to rise over the crossing. It was a fine and elegant building on a large scale, but by the early nineteenth century, when the church had become a pantheon, cracks were appearing in the masonry. When Rondelet succeeded as architect after Soufflot's death, he strengthened and enlarged the piers, employing a faced concrete structure reinforced with metal. He used a metal-reinforced mortar with rubble aggregate.

Bibliography
An article by Rondelet appears in:
1989, *Le Panthéon: Symbole des Révolutions*, pp. 308–10 (book of the Exhibition at the Hôtel de Sully, Paris), ed. Picard, Caisse Nationale des Monuments Historiques et des Sites en France.

Further Reading
M.N. Mathuset-Bandouin, 1980, 'Biographie de Jean Rondelet', *Soufflot et son temps*, Caisse Nationale des Monuments Historiques et des Sites en France, 155ő7.

DY

Röntgen, Wilhelm Conrad

b. 27 March 1845 Lennep, Prussia (now Remscheid, Germany)
d. 10 February 1923 Munich, Germany

German physicist who discovered X-rays.

Expelled from school and so unable to attend university, Röntgen studied engineering at Zurich Polytechnic. After graduation he obtained a post as assistant to the distinguished German physicist Kundt and eventually secured an appointment at the University of Würzburg in Bavaria. He was successively Professor of Physics at the universities of Strasbourg (1876), Giessen (1879), Würzburg (1888) and Munich (1900–20), but he died in abject poverty. At various times he studied piezo-electricity; heat absorp-

tion by and the specific heat of gases; heat conduction in crystals; elasticity; and the capillary action of fluids. In 1895, whilst experimenting with the **Crookes** tube, a partially evacuated tube invented some seven years earlier, he observed that when a high voltage was applied across the tube, a nearby piece of barium platinocyanide produced light. He theorized that when the so-called cathode rays produced by the tube (electrons, as we now know) struck the glass wall, some unknown radiation occurred that was able to penetrate light materials and affect photographic plates. These he called X-rays (they also became known as Röntgen rays), but he believed (erroneously) that they bore no relation to light rays. For this important discovery he was awarded the Nobel Prize for Physics, but, sadly, he died in abject poverty during the hyperinflation of the 1920s.

Principal Honours and Distinctions
First Nobel Prize for Physics 1901.

Bibliography
1895, 'A new kind of radiation', *Meeting of the Würzburg Physical-Medical Society* (December) (reported Röntgen's discovery of X-rays).

Further Reading
O. Glasser, 1945, *Dr. W.C. Röntgen* (biography).

KF

Root, Elisha King

b. 10 May 1808 Ludlow, Massachusetts, USA
d. 31 August 1865 Hartford, Connecticut, USA

American mechanical engineer and inventor.

After an elementary education, Elisha K. Root was apprenticed as a machinist and worked in that occupation at Ware and Chicopee Falls, Massachusetts. In 1832 he went to Collinsville, Connecticut, to join the Collins Company, manufacturers of axes. He started as a lathe hand but soon became Foreman and, in 1845, Superintendent. While with the company, he devised and patented special-purpose machinery for forming axes which transformed the establishment from a primitive workshop to a modern factory.

In 1849 Root was offered positions by four different manufacturers and accepted the post of

Superintendent of the armoury then being planned at Hartford, Connecticut, by Samuel **Colt** for the manufacture of his revolver pistol, which he had invented in 1835. Initial acceptance of the revolver was slow, but by the mid-1840s Colt had received sufficient orders to justify the establishment of a new factory and Root was engaged to design and install the machinery. The principle of interchangeable manufacture was adopted, and Root devised special machines for boring, rifling, making cartridges, etc., and a system of jigs, fixtures, tools and gauges. One of these special machines was a drop hammer that he invented and patented in 1853 and which established the art of die-forging on a modern basis. He was also associated with F.A. **Pratt** in the design of the 'Lincoln' milling machine in 1855.

When Colt died in 1862, Root became President of the company and continued in that capacity until his own death. It was said that he was one of the ablest and most highly paid mechanics from New England and that he was largely responsible for the success of both the Collins and the Colt companies.

Further Reading

J.W. Roe, 1916, *English and American Tool Builders*, New Haven; reprinted 1926, New York, and 1987, Bradley, Ill. (describes Root's work at the Colt Armory).

Paul Uselding, 1974, 'Elisha K. Root, Forging, and the "American System"', 'Elisha K. Root, forging, and the "American System"', *Technology and Culture* 15: 543–68 (provides further biographical details, his work with the Collins Company and a list of his patents).

RTS

Rosenhain, Walter

b. 24 August 1875 Berlin, Germany
d. 17 March 1934 Kingston Hill, Surrey, England

German metallurgist, first Superintendent of the Department of Metallurgy and Metallurgical Chemistry at the National Physical Laboratory, Teddington, Middlesex.

His family emigrated to Australia when he was 5 years old. He was educated at Wesley College, Melbourne, and attended Queen's College, University of Melbourne, graduating in physics and engineering in 1897. As an 1851 Exhibitioner he then spent three years at St John's College, Cambridge, under Sir Alfred Ewing, where he studied the microstructure of deformed metal crystals and abandoned his original intention of becoming a civil engineer. Rosenhain was the first to observe the slip-bands in metal crystals, and in the Bakerian Lecture delivered jointly by Ewing and Rosenhain to the Royal Society in 1899 it was shown that metals deformed plastically by a mechanism involving shear slip along individual crystal planes. From this conception modern ideas on the plasticity and recrystallization of metals rapidly developed. On leaving Cambridge, Rosenhain joined the Birmingham firm of Chance Brothers, where he worked for six years on optical glass and lighthouse-lens systems. A book, *Glass Manufacture*, written in 1908, derives from this period, during which he continued his metallurgical researches in the evenings in his home laboratory and published several papers on his work.

In 1906 Rosenhain was appointed Head of the Metallurgical Department of the National Physical Laboratory (NPL), and in 1908 he became the first Superintendent of the new Department of Metallurgy and Metallurgical Chemistry. Many of the techniques he introduced at Teddington were described in his *Introduction to Physical Metallurgy*, published in 1914. At the outbreak of the First World War, Rosenhain was asked to undertake work in his department on the manufacture of optical glass. This soon made it possible to manufacture optical glass of high quality on an industrial scale in Britain. Much valuable work on refractory materials stemmed from this venture. Rosenhain's early years at the NPL were, however, inseparably linked with his work on light alloys, which between 1912 and the end of the war involved virtually all of the metallurgical staff of the laboratory. The most important end product was the well-known 'Y' Alloy (4% copper, 2% nickel and 1.5% magnesium) extensively used for the pistons and cylinder heads of aircraft engines. It was the prototype of the RR series of alloys jointly developed by Rolls Royce and High Duty Alloys. An improved zinc-based die-casting alloy devised by Rosenhain was also used during the war on a large scale for the production of shell fuses.

After the First World War, much attention was devoted to beryllium, which because of its strength, lightness, and stiffness would, it was hoped, become the airframe material of the future. It remained, however, too brittle for practical use. Other investigations dealt with impurities in copper, gases in aluminium alloys, dental alloys, and the constitution of alloys. During this period, Rosenhain's laboratory became internationally known as a centre of excellence for the determination of accurate equilibrium diagrams.

Principal Honours and Distinctions
FRS 1913. President, Institute of Metals 1828–30. Iron and Steel Institute Bessemer Medal, Carnegie Medal.

Bibliography
1908, *Glass Manufacture*.
1914, *An Introduction to the Study of Physical Metallurgy*, London: Constable.
Rosenhain published over 100 research papers.

Further Reading
J.L. Haughton, 1934, 'The work of Walter Rosenhain', *Journal of the Institute of Metals* 55 (2): 17–32.

ASD

Rosing, Boris
fl. *c*.1907 St Petersburg, Russia

Russian scientist who made early experiments in television.

In 1907, while Professor at St Petersburg Technological Institute, Rosing proposed the use of the **Braun** tube as a television display in conjunction with a photoelectric cell and double mirror-drum scanning system as a pick-up device. Four years later he was apparently able to transmit faint and very crude static pictures.

Bibliography
1907, British patent no. 27,570.

Further Reading
C.J. Hylander & R. Harding, 1941, *An Introduction to Television*.
R.W. Hubbell, 1946, *4,000 Years of Television*, London: G. Harrap & Sons.

See also **Baird, John Logie**; **Ives, Herbert Eugene**; **Jenkins, Charles Francis**; **Zworykin, Vladimir Kosma**.

KF

Ross, Andrew
b. 1798 London, England
d. 1859

English optical-instrument maker, founder of a photographic-lens making dynasty.

Apprenticed to the optical-instrument maker Gilbert at the age of 14, Ross rose to become Manager of the factory before leaving to found his own business in 1830. He soon earned a reputation for fine craftsmanship and was the first optician in England to produce achromatic microscope objectives. He had an early involvement with photography, perhaps before the public announcements in 1839, for he supplied lenses and instruments to **Talbot**. On hearing of **Petzval**'s portrait lens, he made a high-aperture portrait lens to his own design for the first professional calotypist, Henry Collan. It was unsuccessful, however, and Ross did little more photographic work of note, although his son Thomas and his son-in-law and one-time apprentice, John Henry **Dallmeyer**, made significant contributions to English photographic optics. Both Thomas and Dallmeyer were left large sums of money on Andrew's death, and independently they established successful businesses; they were to become the two most important suppliers of photographic lenses in England.

Further Reading
Rudolf Kingslake, 1989, *A History of the Photographic Lens*, Boston (a brief biography of Ross).
J.M. Eder, 1945, *History of Photography*, trans. E. Epstean, New York.
H.J.P. Arnold, 1977, *William Henry Fox Talbot*, London.

JW

Rowland, Thomas Fitch
b. 15 March 1831 New Haven, Connecticut, USA
d. 13 December 1907 New York City, USA

American engineer and manufacturer, inventor of off-shore drilling.

The son of a grist miller, Rowland worked in various jobs until 1859 when he established his own business for the construction of wooden and iron steamships and for structural iron works, in Greenpoint, Long Island, New York. In 1860 he founded the Continental Works and during the American Civil War he started manu-facturing gun carriages and mortar beds. He fitted out many vessels for the navy, and as a con-tractor for John Ericsson he built heavily ar-moured war vessels.

He continued shipbuilding, but later diversified his business. He devoted great attention to the de-sign of gas-works, constructing innovative storage facilities all over the United States, and he was con-cerned with the improvement of welding iron and steel plates and other processes in the steel industry. In the late 1860s he also began the manufacture of steam-engines and boilers for use in the new but expanding oil industry. In 1869 he took out a pat-ent for a fixed platform for drilling for oil off-shore up to a depth of 15 m (49 ft). With this idea, just ten years after Edwin **Drake**'s success in on-shore oil drilling in Titusville, Pennsylvania, Rowland pioneered the technology of off-shore drilling for petroleum in which the United States later became the leading nation.

Principal Honours and Distinctions
American Society of Civil Engineers: Director 1871–3, Vice-President 1886–7, Honorary Member 1899.

Further Reading
'Thomas Fitch Rowland', *Dictionary of American Biography*.
1909, 'Memoir', *Transactions of the American Society of Civil Engineers* 62: 547–9.

WK

Royce, Sir Frederick Henry
b. 27 March 1863 Alwalton, Huntingdon-shire, England.
d. 22 April 1933 West Wittering, Sussex, Eng-land.

English engineer and industrialist.

Royce was the younger son of a flour miller. His father's death forced him to earn his own living from the age of 10 selling newspapers, as a post office messenger boy, and in other jobs. At the age of 14, he became an apprentice at the Great Northern Railway's locomotive works, but was unable to complete his apprenticeship due to a shortage of money. He moved to a tool company in Leeds, then in 1882 he became a tester for the London Electric Light & Power Company and attended classes at the City & Guilds Technical

College. In the same year, the company made him Chief Electrical Engineer for the lighting of the streets of Liverpool.

In 1884, at the age of 21, he founded F.H. Royce & Co (later called Royce Ltd, from 1894 to 1933) with a capital of £70, manufacturing arc lamps, dynamos and electric cranes. In 1903, he bought a 10 hp Deauville car which proved noisy and unreliable; he therefore designed his own car. By the end of 1903 he had produced a two-cylinder engine which ran for many hundreds of hours driving dynamos; on 31 March 1904, a 10 hp Royce car was driven smoothly and silently from the works in Cooke Street, Manchester. This car so impressed Charles S. **Rolls**, whose London firm were agents for high-class con-tinental cars, that he agreed to take the entire output from the Manchester works. In 1906 they jointly formed Rolls–Royce Ltd and at the end of that year Royce produced the first 40/50 hp *Sil-ver Ghost*, which remained in production until 1925 when it was replaced by the *Phantom* and *Wraith*. The demand for the cars grew so great that in 1908 manufacture was transferred to a new factory in Derby.

In 1911 Royce had a breakdown due to over-work and his lack of attention to taking regular meals. From that time he never returned to the works but continued in charge of design from a drawing office in his home in the south of France and later at West Wittering, Sussex, England. During the First World War he designed the *Fal-con*, *Hawk* and *Condor* engines as well as the V12 *Eagle*, all of which were liquid-cooled. Later he designed the 36.7-litre Rolls–Royce *R* engines for the Vickers Supermarine *S.6* and *S.6B* sea-planes which were entered for the Schneider Trophy (which they won in 1929 and 1931, the *S.5* having won in 1927 with a Napier *Lion* en-gine) and set a world speed record of 408 mph (657 km/h) in 1931; the 1941 *Griffon* engine was derived from the *R*.

Royce was an improver rather than an innova-tor, though he did invent a silent form of valve gear, a friction-damped slipper flywheel, the Royce carburettor and a spring drive for timing gears. He was a modest man with a remarkable memory who concentrated on perfecting the de-tail of every component. He married Minnie Punt, but they had no children. A bust of him at the Derby factory is captioned simply 'Henry Royce, Mechanic'.

Further Reading
R. Bird, 1995, *Rolls Royce Heritage*, London: Osprey.

IMcN

Ruggles, Stephen

fl. 1820s–1850s Boston, Massachusetts, USA

American maker of the first successful jobbing platen press.

Ruggles, a Bostonian, made a cylinder press in 1827 and also a card press, but neither was manufactured. In 1839 he completed his 'Engine' press, the first self-inking, treadle-driven jobbing platen press. The machine presses that had been developed from **Koenig** and Bauer *c.*1810 were suitable for large-scale printing but less so for the small miscellaneous work of the jobbing printer. For these needs, the bed and platen press was developed. The bed (carrying the type) and the platen (which pressed the paper onto the inked type) were pivoted and brought together like the jaws of a nutcracker instead of moving on a separate carriage. With automatic inking and treadle operation, the press offered a rapid and simple action for the small printer. In Ruggles's first press of this kind, the bed and platen were still horizontal, the bed being uppermost. If the type became loose, however, it fell onto the platen, so in 1851 Ruggles constructed a new version in which bed and platen were vertical. Later designers modified the form of the press, but it was the Ruggles that opened up a new era for the jobbing printer.

Further Reading
J. Moran, 1973, *Printing Presses*, London: Faber & Faber (provides details of Ruggles's machines).

LRD

Russell, John Scott

b. 9 May 1808 Parkhead, near Glasgow, Scotland
d. 8 June 1882 Isle of Wight, England

Scottish engineer, naval architect and academic.

A son of the manse, Russell was originally destined for the Church and commenced studies at the University of St Andrews, but shortly afterwards he transferred to Glasgow, graduating MA in 1825 when only 17 years old. He began work as a teacher in Edinburgh, working up from a school to the Mechanics Institute and then in 1832 to the University, where he took over the classes in natural philosophy following the death of the professor. During this period he designed and advised on the application of steam power to road transport and to the Forth and Clyde Canal, thereby awakening his interest in ships and naval architecture.

Russell presented papers to the British Association over several years, and one of them, *The Wave Line Theory of Ship Form* (although now superseded), had great influence on ship designers of the time and helped to establish the formal study of hydromechanics. With a name that was becoming well known, Russell looked around for better opportunities, and on narrowly missing appointment to the Chair of Mathematics at Edinburgh University he joined the up-and-coming Clyde shipyard of Caird & Co., Greenock, as Manager in 1838.

Around 1844 Russell and his family moved to London; following some business problems he was in straitened circumstances. However, appointment as Secretary to the Committee setting up the Great Exhibition of 1851 eased his path into London's intellectual society and allowed him to take on tasks such as, in 1847, the purchase of Fairbairn's shipyard on the Isle of Dogs and the subsequent building there of I.K. **Brunel**'s *Great Eastern* steamship. This unhappy undertaking was a millstone around the necks of Brunel and Russell and broke the health of the former. With the yard failing to secure the order for HMS *Warrior*, the Royal Navy's first ironclad, Russell pulled out of shipbuilding and for the remainder of his life was a designer, consultant and at times controversial, but at all times polished and urbane, member of many important committees and societies. He is remembered as one of the founders of the Institution of Naval Architects in 1860. His last task was to design a Swiss Lake steamer for Messrs Escher Wyss, a company that coincidentally had previously retained Sir William **Fairbairn**.

Principal Honours and Distinctions
FRS 1847.

Bibliography
John Scott Russell published many papers under the imprint of the British Association, the

Royal Society of Arts and the Institution of Naval Architects. His most impressive work was the mammoth three-volume work on shipbuilding published in London in 1865 and entitled *The Modern System of Naval Architecture*. Full details and plans of the *Great Eastern* are included.

Further Reading
G.S. Emmerson, 1977, *John Scott Russell, a Great Victorian Engineer and Naval Architect*, London: Murray

FMW

S

Saint-Claire Deville, Henri Etienne

See **Deville, Henri Etienne Sainte-Claire**.

St Victor, Claude Félix Abel Niepce de

See **Niepce de St Victor, Claude Félix Abel**.

Salomans, Sir David Lionel

b. 1851
d. 1925

English pioneer of electricity and the automobile in England.

Salomans inherited his baronetcy from his uncle, Sir David Salomans (1797–1873), who had been Member of Parliament for Greenwich and the first Jewish Lord Mayor of London. He was the archetypal amateur engineer and inventor of the Victorian age, indulging in such interests as photography, motoring, electricity, woodworking, polariscopy and astronomy. His house, 'Broomhill', near Tunbridge Wells in Kent, was one of the first to be lit by electricity and is said to have been the first to use electricity for cooking. He acted as architect for the building of the stables, the water tower and the 150-seat theatre at his home. In 1874 he was granted a patent for an automatic railway signalling system. He was the founder in 1895 of the first motoring organization in Great Britain, the Self Propelled Traffic Association, forerunner of the Royal Automobile Club (RAC). He was also the organizer of the first motor show to be held in Britain, on 15 October 1895. It is said that, in spite of being the Mayor of Tunbridge Wells, Salomans defied the law and drove without the obligatory pedestrian with a red flag preceding his vehicle; this requirement was removed with the later Light (Road) Locomotives Act, which raised the speed limit to 12 mph (19 km/h).

Further Reading
Various papers may be consulted from the Sir David Salomans Society.

See also **Simms, Frederick**.

IMcN

Salt, Sir Titus

b. 20 September 1803 Morley, Yorkshire, England
d. 29 December 1876 Saltaire, Yorkshire, England

English industrialist, social reformer and entrepreneur who made his fortune by overcoming the problems of utilizing alpaca wool in the production of worsted, and established the early model town at Saltaire.

Titus Salt arrived in Bradford with his father, who was a wool merchant in the town, in 1822. He soon set up his own company and it was there that he experimented with the textile worsted. Alpaca wool comes from an animal of the camel family that resembles the llama, and flocks of domesticated breeds of the animal had been raised in the high Andes since the days of the Incas. The wool was introduced into Europe via Spain and, later, Germany and France. The first attempts to spin and weave the yarn in England were made in 1808, but despite experimentation over the years the material was difficult to work. It was in 1836 that Salt evolved his method of utilizing a cotton warp with part alpaca weft. The method proved a great success and Bradford gained a reputation as a manufacturing centre for alpaca wool, exporting both yarn and cloth in quantity, especially to the USA. By 1850 Salt, who owned six mills, was Bradford's biggest employer and was certainly its richest citizen. He decided to move out of the city and built a new mill works, the architects of which were Lockwood and Mawson, on the banks of the River Aire a few miles from the city. Around the works, between 1851 and 1871, he built houses, a hospital, library, church, institute and almshouses for his workers. The buildings were solid, good-standard structures of local stone and the houses were pleasantly situated, with their amenities making them seem palaces compared to the slums in which other Bradford textile workers lived at the time. The collection of buildings was the first example in Britain of a 'model new town', and was, indeed still is, a remarkable prototype of its

619

kind. Apart from being a philanthropist and social reformer, Salt was also concerned with taking advantage of the technical developments of his time. His mill works, which eventually covered ten acres of land, was of fashionably Italianate architectural style (its chimney even a copy of the campanile of the Church of Santa Maria Gloriosa in Venice), although its structure was of iron framing. The weaving shed held 1,200 looms and had capacity for 3,000 workers, who produced 30,000 yards of cloth per day. Water from the river was used to produce steam to power the matchinery used in the manufacturing processes of scouring, dyeing and finishing. For the export of goods, the nearby Leeds–Liverpool Canal linked the works to Britain's chief ports, and the Midland Railway (an extension of the Leeds–Bradford line which opened in 1846) was of great use for the same purpose.

Principal Honours and Distinctions
Created Baronet 1869.

Further Reading
Dictionary of National Biography.
Visitors Guide to Saltaire, Bradford City Council.
DY

Samuda, Joseph d'Aguilar
b. 21 May 1813 London, England
d. 27 April 1885 London, England

English shipbuilder and promoter of atmospheric traction for railways.

Joseph Samuda studied as a engineer under his elder brother Jacob and formed a partnership with him in 1832 as builders of marine steam engines. In 1838, with Samuel Clegg, they took out a patent for an atmospheric railway system. In this system a cast-iron tube, with a continuous sealed slot along the top, was laid between the rails; trains were attached to a piston within the tube by an arm, the slot being opened and resealed before and behind it. The tube ahead of the piston was exhausted by a stationary steam engine and the train propelled by atmospheric pressure. The system appeared to offer clean, fast travel and was taken up by noted contemporary railway engineers such as I.K. **Brunel** and C.B. **Vignoles**, but it eventually proved a failure as no satisfactory means of sealing the slot could at that time be found. It did, however, lead to experi-

ments in the 1860s with underground, pneumatic-tube railways, in which the vehicle would be its own piston, and Samuda Bros. supplied cast-iron tubes for such a line.

Meanwhile, Samuda Bros. had commenced building iron steamships in 1843, and although Jacob Samuda lost his life in 1844 as the result of an accident aboard one of the earliest built, the firm survived to become noted London builders of steamships of many types over the ensuing four decades. Joseph Samuda became a founder member of the Institution of Naval Architects in 1860, and was MP for Tavistock from 1865 to 1868 and for Tower Hamlets from 1868 to 1880.

Bibliography
1838, jointly with Jacob Samuda and Samuel Clegg, British patent no. 7,920 (atmospheric traction).
1861–2, 'On the form and materials for iron plated ships', *Minutes of Proceedings of the Institution of Civil Engineers* 21.

Further Reading
Obituary, *Minutes of Proceedings of the Institution of Civil Engineers* 81: 334 (provides good coverage of his career).
C. Hadfield, 1967, *Atmospheric Railways*, Newton Abbot: David & Charles (includes a discussion of his railway work).
PJGR

Sanctorius, Santorio
b. 29 March 1561 Capodistria, Italy (now Koper, Slovenia)
d. 22 February 1636 Venice, Italy

Italian physician, founder of quantitative measurement in medicine.

Sanctorius graduated in Padua in 1582 and became Professor of Theoretical Medicine there in 1611. In 1629 he moved to Venice and devoted himself to scientific study. The first to use a thermometer to measure body temperature, he also invented a pulsimeter, a hygrometer, a water-bed and numerous other instruments. By constructing scales in which he was able to live, he was able to make measurements of changes in weight in daily living (see **Floyer**), including what he described as 'insensible perspiration', or basal metabolism.

Bibliography
1614, *Ars de statica medicina.*
1625, *Commentaria in primam fen primi libri canonis,* Avicenna.

Further Reading
A. Castiglioni, 1947, *History of Medicine,* London.

MG

Saniter, Ernest Henry
b. 1863 Middlesbrough, England
d. 2 November 1934 Rotherham, Yorkshire

English chemist and metallurgist who introduced a treatment to remove sulphur from molten iron.

Saniter spent three years as a pupil in J.E. Stead's chemical laboratory in Middlesbrough, and then from 1883 was employed in the same town as Assistant Chemist at the new North-Eastern Steelworks. In 1890 he became Chief Chemist to the Wigan Coal and Iron Company in Lancashire. There he devised a desulphurizing treatment for molten iron and steel, based upon the presence of abundant lime together with calcium chloride. Between 1898 and 1904 he was in the Middlesbrough district once more, employed by Dorman Long & Co. and Bell Brothers in experiments which led to the establishment of Teesside's first large-scale basic open-hearth steel plant. Calcium fluoride (fluorspar), mentioned in Saniter's 1892 patent, soon came to replace the calcium chloride; with this modification, his method retained wide applicability throughout the era of open-hearth steel. In 1904 Saniter became chief metallurgist to Steel, Peech & Tozer Limited of Sheffield, and he remained in this post until 1928. Throughout the last forty years of his life he participated in the discussion of steelmaking developments and practices.

Principal Honours and Distinctions
Vice-President, Iron and Steel Institute 1927–34. Iron and Steel Institute (London) Bessemer Gold Medal 1910.

Bibliography
1892, 'A new process for the purification of iron and steel from sulphur', *Journal of the Iron and Steel Institute* 2: 216–22.
1893, 'A supplementary paper on a new process for desulphurising iron and steel', *Journal of the Iron and Steel Institute* 1: 73–7.
29 October 1892, British patent no. 8,612.
15 October 1892, British patent no. 8,612A.
29 July 1893, British patent no. 17, 692.
28 October 1893, British patent no. 23,534.

Further Reading
K.C. Barraclough, 1990, *Steelmaking: 1850–1900* 458, London: Institute of Metals, 271–8.

JKA

Sant'Elia, Antonio
b. 30 April 1880 Como, Italy
d. 10 October 1916 Monfalcone, Italy

Italian architectural designer and town planner.

Sant 'Elia studied in Milan and in Bologna. In 1912 he began work in Milan, where he became part of the futurist movement in architecture. In the short time before the outbreak of the First World War, Sant 'Elia began to create his designs for the city of the future; he was a talented draughtsman and made hundreds of imaginative drawings to illustrate his ideas.

Fascinated by the possibilities of technology and by building in the USA, he was a visionary of future modern architecture. He planned cities for Italy, and in 1914 many of his drawings were shown at an exhibition of the *Nuove Tendenze* group in Milan. His *Città Nuova* was included; it envisaged electric power, skyscrapers, pedestrian precincts and traffic moving on overhead roadways at two and three different levels – a separation of pedestrian and wheeled traffic put forward by Leonardo da Vinci four centuries earlier in his sketchbooks. Sant'Elia was a socialist and developed his schemes as part of his suggestions for an ideal society.

He was killed in action in 1916, but his drawings have survived and have influenced later work.

Further Reading
F. Tentori, 1955, *Le Origini Liberty di Antonio Sant 'Elia,* Rome.
—— 1955, *L'Architettura Chronache e Storia,* Rome.
Rayner Banham, 1981, 'Antonio Sant 'Elia', *Architectural Design.*

DY

Santos-Dumont, Alberto

b. 20 July 1873 Cabangu, Rocha Dias, Brazil
d. 23 July 1932 d. Santos, São Paulo, Brazil

Brazilian pioneer in airship and aeroplane flights.

Alberto Santos-Dumont, the son of a wealthy Brazilian coffee planter, was sent to Paris to study engineering but developed a passion for flying. After several balloon flights he turned his attention to powered airships. His first small airship, powered by a motorcycle engine, flew in 1898. A series of airships followed and his flights over Paris – and his narrow escapes – generated much public interest. A large cash prize had been offered for the first person to fly from Saint-Cloud around the Eiffel Tower and back inside thirty minutes. Santos-Dumont made two attempts in his airship *No. 5*, but engine failures caused him to crash, once in a tree and once on a hotel roof. Undismayed, he prepared airship *No. 6* and on 19 October 1901 he set out and rounded the Tower, only to suffer yet another engine failure. This time he managed to restart the engine and claim the prize. This flight created a sensation in Paris and beyond. Santos-Dumont continued to create news with a series of airship exploits, and by 1906 he had built a total of fourteen airships. In 1904 Santos-Dumont visited the United States and met Octave **Chanute**, who described to him the achievements of the **Wright** brothers. On his return to Paris he set about designing an aeroplane which was unlike any other aeroplane of the period. It had box-kite-like wings and tail, and flew tail-first (a canard) powered by an Antoinette engine at the rear. It was built for him by Gabriel **Voisin** and was known as the '14 *bis*' because it was air-tested suspended beneath airship *No. 14*. It made its first free take-off on 13 September 1906, and then a series of short hops, including one of 220 m (720 ft) which won Santos-Dumont an Aero-Club prize and recognition for the first aeroplane flight in Europe; indeed, it was the first officially witnessed aeroplane flight in the world. Santos-Dumont's most successful aeroplane was his *No. 20* of 1909, known as the *Demoiselle*: a tiny machine popular with sporting pilots. About this time, however, Santos-Dumont became ill and had to abandon his aeronautical activities. Although he had not made any great technical breakthroughs, Santos-Dumont had played a major role in arousing public interest in flying.

Principal Honours and Distinctions
Aéro Club de France Grand Prix de l'Aéronautique 1901. Chevalier de la Légion d'honneur 1904.

Bibliography
1904, *Dans l'air*, Paris; 1904, pub. as *My Airships* (repub. 1973, New York: Dover).

Further Reading
Peter Wykeham, 1962, *Santos-Dumont, A Study in Obsession*, London.
F.H. da Costa, *c.*1971, *Alberto Santos-Dumont, O Pai da Aviação*; pub. in English as *Alberto Santos Dumont, Father of Aviation*, Rio de Janeiro.

JDS

Sarnoff, David

b. 27 February 1891 Uzlian, Minsk (now in Belarus)
d. 12 December 1971 New York City, New York, USA

Russian/American engineer who made a major contribution to the commercial development of radio and television.

As a Jewish boy in Russia, Sarnoff spent several years preparing to be a Talmudic Scholar, but in 1900 the family emigrated to the USA and settled in Albany, New York. While at public school and at the Pratt Institute in Brooklyn, New York, he helped the family finances by running errands, selling newspapers and singing the liturgy in the synagogue. After a short period as a messenger boy with the Commercial Cable Company, in 1906 he became an office boy with the Marconi Wireless Telegraph Company of America (see G. **Marconi**). Having bought a telegraph instrument with his first earnings, he taught himself **Morse** code and was made a junior telegraph operator in 1907. The following year he became a wireless operator at Nantucket Island, then in 1909 he became Manager of the Marconi station at Sea Gate, New York. After two years at sea he returned to a shore job as wireless operator at the world's most powerful station at Wanamaker's store in Manhattan. There, on 14 April 1912, he picked up the distress signals from the sinking liner *Titanic*, remaining at his post for three days.

Rewarded by rapid promotion (Chief Radio Inspector 1913, Contract Manager 1914, Assistant

Traffic Manager 1915, Commercial Manager 1917) he proposed the introduction of commercial radio broadcasting, but this received little response. Consequently, in 1919 he took the job of Commercial Manager of the newly formed Radio Corporation of America (RCA), becoming General Manager in 1921, Vice-President in 1922, Executive Vice-President in 1929 and President in 1930. In 1921 he was responsible for the broadcasting of the Dempsey–Carpentier title-fight, as a result of which RCA sold $80 million worth of radio receivers in the following three years. In 1926 he formed the National Broadcasting Company (NBC). Rightly anticipating the development of television, in 1928 he inaugurated an experimental NBC television station and in 1939 demonstrated television at the New York World Fair. Because of his involvement with the provision of radio equipment for the armed services, he was made a lieutenant-colonel in the US Signal Corps Reserves in 1924, a full colonel in 1931 and, while serving as a communications consultant to General Eisenhower during the Second World War, Brigadier General in 1944.

With the end of the war, RCA became a major manufacturer of television receivers and then invested greatly in the ultimately successful development of shadowmask tubes and receivers for colour television. Chairman and Chief Executive from 1934, Sarnoff held the former post until his retirement in 1970.

Principal Honours and Distinctions
French Croix de Chevalier d'honneur 1935, Croix d'Officier 1940, Croix de Commandant 1947. Luxembourg Order of the Oaken Crown 1960. Japanese Order of the Rising Sun 1960. US Legion of Merit 1946. UN Citation 1949. French Union of Inventors Gold Medal 1954.

See also **Zworykin, Vladimir Kosma**.

KF

Sauerbrun, Charles de, Baron von Drais

b. 1785
d. 1851

German popularizer of the first form of manumotive vehicle, the hobby-horse.

An engineer and agriculturalist who had to travel long distances over rough country, he evolved an improved design of velocipede. The original device appears to have been first shown in the gardens of the Palais Royal by the comte de Sivrac in 1791, a small wooden 'horse' fitted with two wheels and propelled by the rider's legs thrusting alternately against the ground. It was not possible to turn the front wheel to steer the machine, a small variation from the straight being obtained by the rider leaning sideways. It is not known if de Sivrac was the inventor of the machine: it is likely that it had been in existence, probably as a child's toy, for a number of years. Its original name was the *celerifère*, but it was renamed the *velocifère* in 1793. The Baron's Draisienne was an improvement on this primitive machine; it had a triangulated wooden frame, an upholstered seat, a rear luggage seat and an armrest which took the thrust of the rider as he or she pushed against the ground. Furthermore, it was steerable. In some models there was a cord-operated brake and a prop stand, and the seat height could be adjusted. At least one machine was fitted with a milometer. Drais began limited manufacture and launched a long marketing and patenting campaign, part of which involved sending advertising letters to leading figures, including a number of kings.

The Draisienne was first shown in public in April 1817: a ladies' version became available in 1819. Von Drais took out a patent in Baden on 12 January 1818 and followed with a French patent on 17 February. Three- and four-wheeled versions became available so the two men could take the ladies for a jaunt.

Drais left his agricultural and forestry work and devoted his full time to the 'Running Machine' business. Soon copies were being made and sold in Italy, Germany and Austria. In London, a Denis Johnson took out a patent in December 1818 for a 'pedestrian curricle' which was soon nicknamed the dandy horse.

Further Reading
C.A. Caunter, 1955, *Cycles: History and Development*, London: Science Museum and HMSO.

IMcN

Saulnier, Raymond

b. late eighteenth century France
d. mid-twentieth century

French designer of aircraft, associated with Louis Blériot and later the Morane–Saulnier company.

When Louis Blériot made his historic flight across the English Channel in 1909, the credit for the success of the flight naturally went to the pilot. Few people thought about the designer of the successful aeroplane, and those who did assumed it was Blériot himself. Blériot did design several of the aeroplanes bearing his name, but the cross-Channel *No. XI* was mainly designed by his friend Raymond Saulnier, a fact not broadcast at the time.

In 1911 the Morane–Saulnier company was founded in Paris by Léon (1885–1918) and Robert (1886–1968) Morane and Raymond Saulnier, who became Chief Designer. Flying a Morane–Saulnier, Roland Garros made a record-breaking flight to a height of 5,611 m (18,405 ft) in 1912, and the following year he made the first non-stop flight across the Mediterranean. Morane-Saulnier built a series of 'parasol' monoplanes which were very widely used during the early years of the First World War. With the wing placed above the fuselage, the pilot had an excellent downward view for observation purposes, but the propeller ruled out a forward-firing machine gun. During 1913–4, Raymond Saulnier was working on an idea for a synchronized machine gun to fire between the blades of the propeller. He could not overcome certain technical problems, so he devised a simple alternative: metal deflector plates were fitted to the propeller, so if a bullet hit the blade it did no harm. Roland Garros, flying a *Type L Parasol*, tested the device in action during April 1915 and was immediately successful. This opened the era of the true fighter aircraft. Unfortunately, Garros was shot down and the Germans discovered his secret weapon: they improved on the idea with a fully synchronized machine gun fitted to the **Fokker** *E 1* monoplane. The Morane–Saulnier company continued in business until 1963, when it was taken over by the Potez Group.

Further Reading
Jane's Fighting Aircraft of World War I, 1990, London: Jane's (reprint) (provides plans and details of 1914–18 Morane–Saulnier aeroplanes).

JDS

Savery, Thomas

b. *c*.1650 probably Shilston, near Modbury, Devonshire, England
d. *c*.15 May 1715 London, England

English inventor of a partially successful steam-driven pump for raising water.

Little is known of the early years of Savery's life and no trace has been found that he served in the Army, so the title 'Captain' is thought to refer to some mining appointment, probably in the West of England. He may have been involved in the Glorious Revolution of 1688, for later he was well known to William of Orange. From 1705 to 1714 he was Treasurer for Sick and Wounded Seamen, and in 1714 he was appointed Surveyor of the Water Works at Hampton Court, a post he held until his death the following year. He was interested in mechanical devices; amongst his early contrivances was a clock.

He was the most prolific inventor of his day, applying for seven patents, including one in 1649, for polishing plate glass which may have been used. His idea for 1697 for propelling ships with paddle-wheels driven by a capstan was a failure, although regarded highly by the King, and was published in his first book, *Navigation Improved* (1698). He tried to patent a new type of floating mill in 1707, and an idea in 1710 for baking sea coal or other fuel in an oven to make it clean and pure.

His most famous invention, however, was the one patented in 1698 'for raising water by the impellent force of fire' that Savery said would drain mines or low-lying land, raise water to supply towns or houses, and provide a source of water for turning mills through a water-wheel. Basically it consisted of a receiver which was first filled with steam and then cooled to create a vacuum by having water poured over the outside. The water to be pumped was drawn into the receiver from a lower sump, and then high-pressure steam was readmitted to force the water up a pipe to a higher level. It was demonstrated to the King and the Royal Society and achieved some success, for a few were installed in the London area and a manufactory set up at Salisbury Court in London. He published a book, *The Miner's Friend*, about his engine in 1702, but although he made considerable improvements, due to excessive fuel consumption and materials which could not withstand the steam pressures involved, no engines were installed in mines as Savery had hoped. His patent was extended in 1699 until 1733 so that it covered the atmospheric engine of Thomas **Newcomen** who was forced to join Savery and his other partners to construct this much more practical engine.

Principal Honours and Distinctions
FRS 1706.

Bibliography
1698, *Navigation Improved.*
1702, *The Miner's Friend.*

Further Reading
The entry in the *Dictionary of National Biography* (1897, Vol. L, London: Smith Elder & Co.) has been partially superseded by more recent research. The *Transactions of the Newcomen Society* contain various papers; for example, Rhys Jenkins, 1922–3, 'Savery, Newcomen and the early history of the steam engine', Vol. 3; A. Stowers, 1961–2, 'Thomas Newcomen's first steam engine 250 years ago and the initial development of steam power', Vol. 34; A. Smith, 1977–8, 'Steam and the city: the committee of proprietors of the invention for raising water by fire, 1715–1735, Vol. 49; and J.S.P. Buckland, 1977–8, 'Thomas Savery, his steam engine workshop of 1702', Vol. 49. Brief accounts may be found in H.W. Dickinson, 1938, *A Short History of the Steam Engine*, Cambridge University Press, and R.L. Hills, 1989, *Power from Steam. A History of the Stationary Steam Engine*, Cambridge University Press. There is another biography in T.I. Williams (ed.), 1969, *A Biographical Dictionary of Scientists*, London: A. & C. Black.

RLH

Saxby, John
b. 17 August 1821 Hurstpierpoint, Sussex, England
d. 22 April 1913 Hassocks, Sussex, England

English railway signal engineer, pioneer of interlocking.

In the mid-1850s Saxby was a foreman in the Brighton Works of the London Brighton & South Coast Railway, where he had no doubt become familiar with construction of semaphore signals of the type invented by C.H. **Gregory**; the London–Brighton line was one of the first over which these were installed. In the 1850s points and signals were usually worked independently, and it was to eliminate the risk of accident from conflicting points and signal positions that Saxby in 1856 patented an arrangement by which related points and signals would be operated simultaneously by a single lever.

Others were concerned with the same problem. In 1855 Vignier, an employee of the Western Railway of France, had made an interlocking apparatus for junctions, and in 1859 Austin Chambers, who worked for the North London Railway, installed at Kentish Town Junction an interlocking lever frame in which a movement that depended upon another could not even commence until the earlier one was completed. He patented it early in 1860; Saxby patented his own version of such an apparatus later the same year. In 1863 Saxby left the London Brighton & South Coast Railway to enter into a partnership with J.S. Farmer and established Saxby & Farmer's railway signalling works at Kilburn, London. The firm manufactured, installed and maintained signalling equipment for many prominent railway companies. Its interlocking frames made possible installation of complex track layouts at increasingly busy London termini possible.

In 1867 Saxby & Farmer purchased Chambers's patent of 1860, Later developments by the firm included effective interlocking actuated by lifting a lever's catch handle, rather than by the lever itself (1871), and an improved locking frame known as the 'gridiron' (1874). This was eventually superseded by tappet interlocking, which had been invented by James Deakin of the rival firm Stevens & Co. in 1870 but for which patent protection had been lost through non-renewal.

Saxby & Farmer's equipment was also much used on the European continent, in India and in the USA, to which it introduced interlocking. A second manufacturing works was set up in 1878 at Creil (Oise), France, and when the partnership terminated in 1888 Saxby moved to Creil and managed the works himself until he retired to Sussex in 1900.

Bibliography
1856, British patent no. 1,479 (simultaneous operation of points and signals).

1860, British patent no. 31 (a true interlocking mechanism).

1867, jointly with Farmer, British patent no. 538 (improvements to the interlocking mechanism patented in 1860).

1870, jointly with Farmer, British patent no. 569 (the facing point lock by plunger bolt).

1871, jointly with Farmer, British patent no. 1,601 (catch-handle actuated interlocking)

1874, jointly with Farmer, British patent no. 294 (gridiron frame).

Further Reading
Westinghouse Brake and Signal Company, 1956, *John Saxby (1821–1913) and His Part in the Development of Interlocking and of the Signalling Industry*, London (published to mark the centenary of the 1856 patent).

PJGR

Saxe-Coburg-Gotha, Prince Albert of
See **Albert, Prince Consort**.

Schanck, John
b. 1740 Fife, Scotland
d. 1823

Scottish admiral, builder of small ships with revolutionary form, pioneer of sliding keels.

Schanck first went to sea in the merchant service, but in 1758 he was transferred to the Royal Navy. After four years as an able seaman, he was made a midshipman (a rare occurrence in those days), and by perseverance was commissioned Lieutenant in 1776 and appointed to command a small vessel operating in the St Lawrence. Being known as an inventive and practical officer, he was soon placed in charge of shipbuilding operations for the British on the Great Lakes and quickly constructed a small fleet that operated on Lake Champlain and elsewhere. He was promoted Captain in 1783. In earlier years Schanck had built a small sliding-keel yacht and sailed it in Boston Harbor. The Admiralty accepted the idea and tested two similar small craft, one with and the other without sliding keels. The success of the keels encouraged the authorities to build further craft of increasing size, culminating in the *Lady Nelson*, which carried out many surveys in Australian waters at the end of the eighteenth century. Service with the Army and the transport board followed, when his special knowledge and skill were used to the full in the waterways of the Netherlands. Schanck rose to the rank of full Admiral, and advised not only the British Government on coastal defence but other groups on many aspects of hull design.

Further Reading
John Charnock, 1800, *A History of Marine Architecture, etc.*, London.

FMW

Schawlow, Arthur Leonard
b. 5 May 1921 Mount Vernon, New York, USA

American physicist involved in laser-spectroscopy research.

When Arthur L. Schawlow was 3 years old his family moved to Canada: it was in Toronto that he received his education, graduating from the University of Toronto with a BA in physics in 1941. He was awarded an MA in 1942, taught classes for military personnel at the University until 1944 and worked for a year on radar equipment. He returned to the University of Toronto in 1945 to carry out research on optical spectroscopy and received his PhD in 1949. From 1949 to 1951 he held a postgraduate fellowship at Columbia University, where he worked with Charles H. **Townes** on microwave spectroscopy. From 1951 to 1961 he was a research physicist at the Bell Telephone Laboratories, working mainly on superconductivity, but he maintained his association with Townes, who had pioneered the maser (an acronym of *m*icrowave *a*mplification by *s*timulated *e*mission of *r*adiation). In a paper published in *Physical Review* in December 1958, Townes and Schawlow suggested the possibility of a development into optical frequencies or an optical maser, later known as a laser (an acronym of *l*ight *a*mplification by *s*timulated *e*mission of *r*adiation). In 1960 the first such device was made by Theodore H. **Maiman**.

In 1960 Schawlow returned to Columbia University as a visiting professor and in the following year was appointed Professor of Physics at Stanford University, where he continued his researches in laser spectroscopy. He is a member of the National Academy of Sciences, the American Physical Society, the Optical Society of America and the Institute of Electrical and Electronic Engineers.

Principal Honours and Distinctions
Nobel Prize for Physics 1981. Franklin Institute Stuart Ballantine Medal 1962. Institute of Physics of London Thomas Young Medal and Prize 1963. Institute of Electrical and Electronics Engineers Morris N. Liebmann Memorial Prize 1964. Optical Society of America Frederick Ives Medal 1976. Honorary degrees from the State University of Ghent, the University of Bradford and the University of Toronto.

Bibliography
Schawlow is the author of many scientific papers and, with Charles H. Townes, of *Microwave Spectroscopy* (1955).

Further Reading
T. Wasson (ed.), 1987, *Nobel Prize Winners*, New York, pp. 930–3 (contains a short biography).

RTS

Scheutz, George

b. 23 September 1785 Jonkoping, Sweden
d. 27 May 1873 Stockholm, Sweden

*Swedish lawyer, journalist and self-taught engineer who, with his son Edvard Raphael Scheutz (b. 13 September 1821 Stockholm, Sweden; d. 28 January 1881 Stockholm, Sweden) constructed a version of the **Babbage** Difference Engine.*

After early education at the Jonkoping elementary school and the Weixo Gymnasium, George Scheutz entered the University of Lund, gaining a degree in law in 1805. Following five years' legal work, he moved to Stockholm in 1811 to work at the Supreme Court and, in 1814, as a military auditor. In 1816, he resigned, bought a printing business and became editor of a succession of industrial and technical journals, during which time he made inventions relating to the press. It was in 1830 that he learned from the *Edinburgh Review* of Babbage's ideas for a difference engine and started to make one from wood, pasteboard and wire. In 1837 his 15-year-old student son, Edvard Raphael Scheutz, offered to make it in metal, and by 1840 they had a working machine with two five-digit registers, which they increased the following year and then added a printer. Obtaining a government grant in 1851, by 1853 they had a fully working machine, now known as Swedish Difference Engine No. 1, which with an experienced operator could generate 120 lines of tables per hour and was used to calculate the logarithms of the numbers 1 to 10,000 in under eighty hours. This was exhibited in London and then at the Paris Great Exhibition, where it won the Gold Medal. It was subsequently sold to the Dudley Observatory in Albany, New York, for US$5,000 and is now in a Chicago museum.

In England, the British Registrar-General, wishing to produce new tables for insurance companies, and supported by the Astronomer Royal, arranged for government finance for construction of a second machine (Swedish Difference Engine No. 2). Comprising over 1,000 working parts and weighing 1,000 lb (450 kg), this machine was used to calculate over 600 tables. It is now in the Science Museum.

Principal Honours and Distinctions
Member of the Swedish Academy of Sciences, Paris Exhibition Medal of Honour (jointly with Edvard) 1856. Annual pension of 1,200 marks per annum awarded by King Carl XV 1860.

Bibliography
1825, 'Kranpunpar. George Scheutz's patent of 14 Nov 1825', *Journal for Manufacturer och Hushallning* 8.
1855, with E.S. Scheutz, *Machine à calcul qui présente les résultats en les imprimant elle-même*, Stockholm.

Further Reading
R.C. Archibald, 1947, 'P.G. Scheutz, publicist, author, scientific mechanic and Edvard Scheutz, engineer. Biography and Bibliography', *MTAC* 238.
U.C. Merzbach, 1977, 'George Scheutz and the first printing calculator', *Smithsonian Studies in History and Technology* 36: 73.
M. Lindgren, 1990, *Glory and Failure (the Difference Engines of Johan Muller, Charles Babbage and George & Edvard Scheutz)*, Cambridge, Mass.: MIT Press.

KF

Schickhard(t), Wilhelm

b. 22 April 1592 Herrenberg, Stuttgart, Germany
d. 24 October 1635 Tübingen, Germany

German polymath who described, and apparently built, a calculating 'clock', possibly the first mechanical adding-machine.

At an early age Schickard won a scholarship to the monastery school at Tübingen and then progressed to the university, where he obtained his BA and MA in theology in 1609 and 1611, respectively. He then specialized in oriental languages and eventually became Professor of Hebrew, Oriental Languages, Mathematics, Astronomy and Geography at Tübingen. Between 1613 and 1619 he was also deacon or pastor to a number of churches in the area. In 1617 he met Johannes **Kepler**, who, impressed by his ability, asked him to draw up tables of figures for his *Harmonica Mundi* (1619). As a result of this, Schickard designed and constructed a mechanical adding-machine that he called a calculating clock. This he described in a letter of 20 September 1623 to Kepler, but a subsequent letter of 25 February 1624 reported its destruction by fire. After his death, probably from bubonic plague, his papers and the letter to Kepler were discovered in the regional library in Stuttgart in 1930 by Franz Hamme, who described them to the 1957 Mathematical Congress. As a result, a Dr Baron von Freytag Lovinghoff, who was present at that meeting, built a reconstruction of Schickard's machine in 1960.

Further Reading

F. Hamme, 1958, 'Nicht Pascal sondern der Tübingen Prof. Wilhelm Schickard erfund die Rechenmaschin', *Buromarkt* 20: 1,023 (describes the papers and letter to Kepler).

B. von F. Lovinghoff, 1964, 'Die erste Rechenmaschin: Tübingen 1623', *Humanismus und Technik* 9: 45.

—— 1973, 'Wilhelm Schickard und seine Rechenmaschin von 1625', in M. Graef (ed.), *350 Jahre Rechenmaschin*.

M.R. Williams, 1985, *History of Computing Technology*, London: Prentice-Hall.

See also **Pascal, Blaise**.

KF

German engineer, inventor of an effective means of superheating steam in locomotive boilers.

Schmidt was educated at Dresden Technical High School and worked as an assistant to a locksmith. He experimented with steam engines worked at extremely high pressures and developed ideas for using superheated steam. Two early types of locomotive superheater that he designed were tried out in Prussia in the late 1890s, but his firetube type, which was eventually successful, was first used in Belgium in 1901. Within ten years of its introduction, superheating using Schmidt-type superheaters was standard practice on large locomotives worldwide.

In the superheater, steam from the boiler is passed through tubular elements within the firetubes before passing to the cylinders. This raises the steam's temperature without increasing its pressure: advantages of doing so include increasing the volume of steam produced and reducing condensation in the cylinders, with consequent economies of fuel and water. Schmidt superheaters were first used in Britain in 1906 by George Hughes, Locomotive Superintendent of the Lancashire & Yorkshire Railway, on two goods locomotives, and then by D. Earle Marsh on the London Brighton & South Coast Railway; hefitted them to 4–4–2 express tank locomotives in 1908. These were conspicuously successful in comparative trials with equivalent non-superheated locomotives from the London & North Western Railway.

Further Reading

J. Marshall, 1978, *A Biographical Dictionary of Railway Engineers*, Newton Abbot: David & Charles.

P. Ransome-Wallis (ed.), 1959, *The Concise Encyclopaedia of World Railway Locomotives*, London: Hutchinson, p. 501 (with references to superheaters, pp. 286, 392–4).

C. Hamilton Ellis, 1959, *British Railway History*, Vol. II: 1877–1947, George Allen & Unwin, pp. 268–71 (for the introduction of superheating to Britain).

PJGR

Schmidt, Wilhelm

b. 18 February 1858 Wegeleben, Saxony, Germany
d. 16 February 1924 Bethel, Westphalia, Germany

Schrötter, Anton von

b. 26 November 1802 Olmütz, Austria (now Olomouc, Czech Republic)
d. 15 April 1875 Vienna, Austria

Austrian scientist known particularly for his discovery in 1845 of red phosphorus, which led to the later development of the safety match.

Anton von Schrötter was the son of an apothecary. At the age of 20 he began his studies at the University of Vienna, first in medicine but later in science and mathematics. He specialized in chemistry and then set up a laboratory in Graz. From 1843 he was a professor of chemistry at the Technische Hochschule in Vienna. Von Schrötter published many papers on various aspects of chemistry, particularly in the field of metallurgy, but it was his demonstration at the Vienna Academy in 1847, which showed that red phosphorus was truly an allotropic form of the element phosphorus, that made him best known. His suggestion that it would be advisable to use such amorphous phosphorus in match manufacture led to **Lundström**'s later development of the safety match and ended the appalling toll that had long been taken on the health of match-factory workers, many of whom had suffered maiming and even death caused by white phosphorus entering the body via defective teeth when they sucked match-heads.

Principal Honours and Distinctions
Académie Française Prix Montyon 1856. Légion d'Honneur at Paris Exhibition 1855. General Secretary, Vienna Academy of Sciences 1850–75.

Further Reading
Moritz Kohn, 1944, 'The discovery of red phosphorus (1847)', *Journal of Chemical Education* 21.
1975, *Dictionary of Science Biography*, New York: Charles Scribner.

DY

Scott de Martinville, Edouard-Léon

b. 25 April 1817 Paris, France
d. 29 April 1879 Paris, France

French amateur phonetician, who developed a recorder for sound waves.

He was the descendant of a Scottish family who emigrated to France in 1688. He trained as a printer and later became a proof corrector in printing houses catering predominantly for scientific publishers. He became interested in shorthand systems and eventually turned his interest to making a permanent record of sounds in air. At the time it was already known (Young, Duhamel, Wertheim) to record vibrations of bodies. He made a theoretical study and deposited under sealed wrapper a note in the Académie des Sciences on 26 January 1857. He approached the scientific instrument maker Froment and was able to pay for the manufacture of one instrument due to support from the Société d'Encouragement à l'Industrie Nationale. This funding body obtained a positive report from the physicist Lissajous on 6 January 1858. A new model phonautograph was constructed in collaboration with the leading scientific instrument maker in Paris at the time, Rudolph Koenig, and a contract was signed in 1859. The instrument was a success, and Koenig published a collection of traces in 1864.

Although the membrane was parallel to the rotating surface, a primitive lever system generated lateral movements of a bristle which scratched curves in a thin layer of lampblack on the rotating surface. The curves were not necessarily representative of the vibrations in the air. Scott did not imagine the need for reproducing a recorded sound; rather, his intention was to obtain a trace that would lend itself to mathematical analysis and visual recognition of sounds. Obviously the latter did not require the same degree of linearity as the former. When Scott learned that similar apparatus had been built independently in the USA, he requested that his sealed wrapper be opened on 15 July 1861 in order to prove his scientific priority. The contract with Koenig left Scott without influence over his instrument, and eventually he became convinced that everyone else, including **Edison** in the end, had stolen his invention. Towards the end of his life he became interested mainly in the history of printing, and he was involved in the publishing of a series of books about books.

Bibliography
25 March 1857, amended 29 July 1859, French patent no. 31,470.

Further Reading
P. Charbon, 1878, *Scott de Martinville*, Paris: Hifi Stereo, pp. 199–205 (a good biography produced at the time of the centenary of the Edison phonograph).
V.J. Philips, 1987, *Waveforms*, Bristol: Adam Hilger, pp. 45–8 (provides a good account of

the importance of his contributions to accurate measurements of temporal phenomena).

GB-N

Séguin, Louis
b. 1869
d. 1918

French co-designer, with his brother Laurent Séguin (b. 1883 Rhône, France; d. 1944), of the extremely successful Gnome rotary engines.

Most early aero-engines were adaptations of automobile engines, but Louis Séguin and his brother Laurent set out to produce a genuine aero-engine. They decided to build a 'rotary' engine in which the crankshaft remained stationary and the cylinders rotated: the propeller was attached to the cylinders. The idea was not new, for rotary engines had been proposed by engineers from James **Watt** to Samuel P. **Langley**, rival of the **Wright** brothers. (An engine with stationary cylinders and a rotating crankshaft-plus-propeller is classed as a 'radial'.) Louis Séguin formed the Société des Moteurs Gnome in 1906 to build stationary industrial engines. Laurent joined him to develop a lightweight engine specifically for aeronautical use. They built a five-cylinder air-cooled radial engine in 1908 and then a prototype seven-cylinder rotary engine. Later in the year the Gnome *Oméga* rotary, developing 50 hp (37 kW), was produced. This was test-flown in a Voisin biplane during June 1909. The Gnome was much lighter than its conventional rivals and surprisingly reliable in view of the technical problems of supplying rotating cylinders with the petrol–air mixture and a spark to ignite it. It was an instant success.

Gnomes were mass-produced for use during the First World War. Both sides built and flew rotary engines, which were improved over the years until, by 1917, their size had grown to such an extent that a further increase was not practicable. The gyroscopic effects of a large rotating engine became a serious handicap to manoeuvrability, and the technical problems inherent in a rotary engine were accentuated.

Bibliography
1912, *L'Aérophile* 20 (4) (Louis Séguin's description of the Gnome).

Further Reading
C.F. Taylor, 1971, 'Aircraft Propulsion', *Smithsonian Annals of Flight* 1(4) (an account of the evolution of aircraft piston engines).
A. Nahum, 1987, *the Rotary Aero-Engine*, London.

JDS

Seguin, Marc
b. 20 April 1786 Annonay, Ardèche, France
d. 24 February 1875 Annonay, Ardèche, France

French engineer, inventor of multi-tubular firetube boiler.

Seguin trained under Joseph **Montgolfier**, one of the inventors of the hot-air balloon, and became a pioneer of suspension bridges. In 1825 he was involved in an attempt to introduce steam navigation to the River Rhône using a tug fitted with a winding drum to wind itself upstream along a cable attached to a point on the bank, with a separate boat to transfer the cable from point to point. The attempt proved unsuccessful and was short-lived, but in 1825 Seguin had decided also to seek a government concession for a railway from Saint-Etienne to Lyons as a feeder of traffic to the river. He inspected the Stockton & Darlington Railway and met George **Stephenson**; the concession was granted in 1826 to Seguin Frères & Ed. Biot and two steam locomotives were built to their order by Robert Stephenson & Co. The locomotives were shipped to France in the spring of 1828 for evaluation prior to construction of others there; each had two vertical cylinders, one each side between front and rear wheels, and a boiler with a single large-diameter furnace tube, with a watertube grate. Meanwhile, in 1827 Seguin, who was still attempting to produce a steamboat powerful enough to navigate the fast-flowing Rhône, had conceived the idea of increasing the heating surface of a boiler by causing the hot gases from combustion to pass through a series of tubes immersed in the water. He was soon considering application of this type of boiler to a locomotive. He applied for a patent for a multi-tubular boiler on 12 December 1827 and carried out numerous experiments with various means of producing a forced draught to overcome the perceived obstruction caused by the small tubes. By May 1829 the steam-navigation venture had collapsed, but

Seguin had a locomotive under construction in the workshops of the Lyons–Saint-Etienne Railway: he retained the cylinder layout of its Stephenson locomotives, but incorporated a boiler of his own design. The fire was beneath the barrel, surrounded by a water-jacket: a single large flue ran towards the front of the boiler, whence hot gases returned via many small tubes through the boiler barrel to a chimney above the fire-door. Draught was provided by axle-driven fans on the tender.

Seguin was not aware of the contemporary construction of *Rocket*, with a multi-tubular boiler, by Robert **Stephenson**; *Rocket* had its first trial run on 5 September 1829, but the precise date on which Seguin's locomotive first ran appears to be unknown, although by 20 October many experiments had been carried out upon it. Seguin's concept of a multi-tubular locomotive boiler therefore considerably antedated that of Henry **Booth**, and his first locomotive was completed about the same date as *Rocket*. It was from *Rocket*'s boiler, however, rather than from that of Seguin's locomotive, that the conventional locomotive boiler was descended.

Bibliography

22 February 1828, French patent no. 3,744 (multi-tubular boiler).

1839, *De l'Influence des chemins de fer et de l'art de les tracer et de les construire*, Paris.

Further Reading

F. Achard and L. Seguin, 1928, 'Marc Seguin and the invention of the tubular boiler', *Transactions of the Newcomen Society* 7 (traces the chronology of Seguin's boilers).

—— 1928, 'British railways of 1825 as seen by Marc Seguin', *Transactions of the Newcomen Society* 7.

J.B. Snell, 1964, *Early Railways*, London: Weidenfeld & Nicolson.

J.-M. Combe and B. Escudié, 1991, *Vapeurs sur le Rhône*, Lyons: Presses Universitaires de Lyon.

PJGR

Sellers, William

b. 19 September 1824 Upper Darby, Pennsylvania, USA
d. 24 January 1905 Philadelphia, Pennsylvania, USA

American mechanical engineer and inventor.

William Sellers was educated at a private school that had been established by his father and other relatives for their children, and at the age of 14 he was apprenticed for seven years to the machinist's trade with his uncle. At the end of his apprenticeship in 1845 he took charge of the machine shop of Fairbanks, Bancroft & Co. in Providence, Rhode Island. In 1848 he established his own factory manufacturing machine tools and mill gearing in Philadelphia, where he was soon joined by Edward Bancroft, the firm becoming Bancroft & Sellers. After Bancroft's death the name was changed in 1856 to William Sellers & Co. and Sellers served as President until the end of his life. His machine tools were characterized by their robust construction and absence of decorative embellishments. In 1868 he formed the Edgemoor Iron Company, of which he was President. This company supplied the structural ironwork for the Centennial Exhibition buildings and much of the material for the Brooklyn Bridge. In 1873 he reorganized the William Butcher Steel Works, renaming it the Midvale Steel Company, and under his presidency it became a leader in the production of heavy ordnance. It was at the Midvale Steel Company that Frederick W. **Taylor** began, with the encouragement of Sellers, his experiments on cutting tools.

In 1860 Sellers obtained the American rights of the patent for the Giffard injector for feeding steam boilers. He later invented his own improvements to the injector, which numbered among his many other patents, most of which related to machine tools. Probably Sellers's most important contribution to the engineering industry was his proposal for a system of screw threads made in 1864 and later adopted as the American national standard.

Sellers was a founder member in 1880 of the American Society of Mechanical Engineers and was also a member of many other learned societies in America and other countries, including, in Britain, the Institution of Mechanical Engineers and the Iron and Steel Institute.

Principal Honours and Distinctions

Chevalier de la Légion d'honneur 1889. President, Franklin Institute 1864–7.

Further Reading
J.W. Roe, 1916, *English and American Tool Builders*, New Haven; reprinted 1926, New York, and 1987, Bradley, Ill. (describes Sellers's work on machine tools).
Bruce Sinclair, 1969, 'At the turn of a screw: William Sellers, the Franklin Institute, and a standard American thread', *Technology and Culture* 10: 20–34 (describes his work on screw threads).

RTS

Semmelweis, Ignaz Philipp
b. 1 July 1818 Budapest, Austro-Hungary
d. 17 August 1865 Budapest, Austro-Hungary

Hungarian physician whose regime of chemical cleansing of the hands radically reduced the mortality associated with puerperal sepsis.

Originally a law student, he abandoned that discipline for medicine and graduated at Vienna in 1844. He was immediately appointed Assistant Professor in the midwifery department under Johann Klein. At this time there was a maternal mortality rate from sepsis of not less than 16 per cent in the students' wards, although the rate was not as high in the midwives' wards. The death of a colleague from a dissection wound led Semmelweis to associate the infection in the lying-in wards with inadequate cleaning of the hands of doctors who went straight from the dissecting room to attend deliveries.

In 1847 he instituted a regime of hand washing with chlorinated lime water, and by the end of the year the mortality in the students' ward had fallen to 1 per cent, less than that in the midwives' ward. However, Klein refused to accept the implications of these findings, and Semmelweis was dismissed from Vienna in 1849.

He was able to obtain a further post in Budapest in 1850, and during the ensuing six years he effected a similar reduction in puerperal mortality by the same methods. Of an impatient and irascible character, in 1865 he was committed to a mental institution, dying shortly afterwards from septicaemia arising in a dissection wound suffered before his admission.

Bibliography
1861, *Die Aetiologie der Begriff und die Prophylaxis des Kind betfeibers*, Vienna.

Further Reading
A. Castiglioni, 1947, *History of Medicine*, London.

MG

Sendzimir, Tadeusz
fl. twentieth century USA

American metallurgist, inventor of the planetary rolling mill.

The principle of the Sendzimir or planetary rolling mill was first conceived by an English engineer named Picken, but that did not lead to practical development. The principle was taken up independently in the USA by Sendzimir, who put forward his own ideas in 1948 and obtained a patent the same year. By 1952 he had reached agreements with Picken and other workers to license the construction of a plant completely under the control of Sendzimir and his associates. This type of rolling mill was developed primarily for the cold rolling of steel strip. Cold rolling requires higher pressures to be exerted by the rolls, which therefore must be harder than in hot rolling. In the Sendzimir mill the two hard work rolls are backed up by a cluster of heavier rolls of various sizes to prevent distortion of the work rolls. One advantage of this arrangement is that the work rolls can be quite small, so that they can be removed by hand when they need replacement. The Sendzimir mill is in wide use, particularly for rolling stainless steel. The first such mill was installed at Peugeot's in France in 1950, with two sets of planetary rolls for the hot rolling of 16 in. (41 cm) wide steel strip. The second was in the USA in 1951, and a third, larger one followed at Ductile Steels Ltd at Willenhall, Wolverhampton, England, in 1953.

Further Reading
E.C. Larke, 1957, *The Rolling of Strip, Sheet and Plate*, London: Chapman & Hall, pp. 53 ff. (gives some details of planetary mills, with a little historical background).

LRD

Senefelder, Alois
b. 6 November 1771 Prague, Bohemia (now Czech Republic)
d. 26 February 1834 Munich, Germany

German inventor of lithography.

Soon after his birth, Senefelder's family moved to Mannheim, where his father, an actor, had obtained a position in the state theatre. He was educated there, until he gained a scholarship to the university of Ingolstadt. The young Senefelder wanted to follow his father on to the stage, but the latter insisted that he study law. He nevertheless found time to write short pieces for the theatre. One of these, when he was 18 years old, was an encouraging success. When his father died in 1791, he gave up his studies and took to a new life as poet and actor. However, the wandering life of a repertory actor palled after two years and he settled for the more comfortable pursuit of playwriting. He had some of his work printed, which acquainted him with the art of printing, but he fell out with his bookseller. He therefore resolved to carry out his own printing, but he could not afford the equipment of a conventional letterpress printer. He began to explore other ways of printing and so set out on the path that was to lead to an entirely new method.

He tried writing in reverse on a copper plate with some acid-resisting material and etching the plate, to leave a relief image that could then be inked and printed. He knew that oily substances would resist acid, but it required many experiments to arrive at a composition of wax, soap and charcoal dust dissolved in rainwater. The plates wore down with repeated polishing, so he substituted stone plates. He continued to etch them and managed to make good prints with them, but he went on to make the surprising discovery that etching was unnecessary. If the image to be printed was made with the oily composition and the stone moistened, he found that only the oily image received the ink while the moistened part rejected it. The printing surface was neither raised (as in letterpress printing) nor incised (as in intaglio printing): Senefelder had discovered the third method of printing.

He arrived at a workable process over the years 1796 to 1799, and in 1800 he was granted an English patent. In the same year, lithography (or 'writing on stone') was introduced into France and Senefelder himself took it to England, but it was some time before it became widespread; it was taken up by artists especially for high-quality printing of art works. Meanwhile, Senefelder improved his techniques, finding that other materials, even paper, could be used in place of stone. In fact, zinc plates were widely used from the 1820s, but the name 'lithography' stuck. Although he won world renown and was honoured by most of the crowned heads of Europe, he never became rich because he dissipated his profits through restless experimenting.

With the later application of the offset principle, initiated by **Barclay**, lithography has become the most widely used method of printing.

Bibliography
1911, *Alois Senefelder, Inventor of Lithography*, trans. J.W. Muller, New York: Fuchs & Line (Senefelder's autobiography).

Further Reading
W. Weber, 1981, *Alois Senefelder, Erfinder der Lithographie*, Frankfurt-am-Main: Polygraph Verlag.
M. Tyman, 1970, *Lithography 1800–1950*, London: Oxford University Press (describes the invention and its development; with biographical details).

LRD

Seppings, Robert

b. 11 December 1767 near Fakenham, Norfolk, England
d. 25 April 1840 Taunton, Somerset, England

English naval architect who as Surveyor to the Royal Navy made fundamental improvements in wooden ship construction.

After the death of his father, Seppings at the age of 14 moved to his uncle's home in Plymouth, where shortly after (1782) he was apprenticed to the Master Shipwright. His indentures were honoured fully by 1789 and he commenced his climb up the professional ladder of the ship construction department of the Royal Dockyards. In 1797 he became Assistant Master Shipwright at Plymouth, and in 1804 he was appointed Master Shipwright at Chatham. In 1813 Sir William Rule, Surveyor to the Navy, retired and the number of surveyors was increased to three, with Seppings being appointed the junior. Later he was to become Surveyor to the Royal Navy, a post he held until his retirement in 1832. Seppings introduced many changes to ship construction in the early part of the nineteenth century. It is likely that the introduction of these innovations required positive and confident management, and their acceptance tells us much about Seppings.

The best-known changes were the round bow and stern in men-of-war and the alteration to framing systems.

The Seppings form of diagonal bracing ensured that wooden ships, which are notorious for hogging (i.e. drooping at the bow and stern), were stronger and therefore able to be built with greater length. This change was complemented by modifications to the floors, frames and futtocks (analogous to the ribs of a ship). These developments were to be taken further once iron composite construction (wooden sheathing on iron frames) was adopted in the United Kingdom mid-century.

Principal Honours and Distinctions
FRS. Knighted (by the Prince Regent aboard the warship *Royal George*) 1819.

Bibliography
Throughout his life Seppings produced a handful of pamphlets and published letters, as well as two papers that were published in the *Philosophical Transactions of the Royal Society* (1814 and 1820).

Further Reading
A description of the thinking in the Royal Navy at the beginning of the nineteenth century can be found in:
J. Fincham, 1851, *A History of Naval Architecture*, London;
B. Lavery, 1989, *Nelson's Navy. The Ships, Men and Organisation 1793–1815*, London: Conway.
T. Wright, 1982, 'Thomas Young and Robert Seppings: science and ship construction in the early nineteenth century', *Transactions of the Newcomen Society* 53: 55–72.
Seppings's work can be seen aboard the frigate *Unicorn*, launched in Chatham in 1824 and now on view to the public at Dundee. Similarly, his innovations in ship construction can be readily understood from many of the models at the National Maritime Museum, Greenwich.

FMW

Shakir, Banu Musa ibn
See **Banu Musa ibn Shakir**.

Shannon, Claude Elwood
b. 30 April 1916 Gaylord, Michigan, USA

American mathematician, creator of information theory.

As a child, Shannon tinkered with radio kits and enjoyed solving puzzles, particularly cryptographic ones. He graduated from the University of Michigan in 1936 with a Bachelor of Science in mathematics and electrical engineering, and earned his Master's degree from the Massachusetts Institute of Technology (MIT) in 1937. His thesis on applying Boolean algebra to switching circuits has since been acclaimed as possibly the most significant this century. Shannon earned his PhD in mathematics from MIT in 1940 with a dissertation on the mathematics of genetic transmission.

Shannon spent a year at the Institute for Advanced Study in Princeton, then in 1941 joined Bell Telephone Laboratories, where he began studying the relative efficiency of alternative transmission systems. Work on digital encryption systems during the Second World War led him to think that just as ciphers hide information from the enemy, 'encoding' information could also protect it from noise. About 1948, he decided that the amount of information was best expressed quantitatively in a two-value number system, using only the digits 0 and 1. John Tukey, a Princeton colleague, named these units 'binary digits' (or, for short, 'bits'). Almost all digital computers and communications systems use such on–off, or two-state logic as their basis of operation.

Also in the 1940s, building on the work of H. **Nyquist** and R.V.L. **Hartley**, Shannon proved that there was an upper limit to the amount of information that could be transmitted through a communications channel in a unit of time, which could be approached but never reached because real transmissions are subject to interference (noise). This was the beginning of information theory, which has been used by others in attempts to quantify many sciences and technologies, as well as subjects in the humanities, but with mixed results. Before 1970, when integrated circuits were developed, Shannon's theory was not the preferred circuit-and-transmission design tool it has since become.

Shannon was also a pioneer in the field of artificial intelligence, claiming that computing machines could be used to manipulate symbols as well as do calculations. His 1953 paper on computers and automata proposed that digital computers were capable of tasks then thought exclusively the province of living organisms. In 1956 he left Bell Laboratories to join the MIT faculty as Professor of Communications Science.

On the lighter side, Shannon has built many devices that play games, and in particular has made a scientific study of juggling.

Principal Honours and Distinctions
National Medal of Science. Institute of Electrical and Electronics Engineers Medal of Honor, Kyoto Prize.

Bibliography
His seminal paper (on what has subsequently become known as information theory) was entitled 'The mathematical theory of communications', first published in *Bell System Technical Journal* in 1948; it is also available in a monograph (written with Warren Weaver) published by the University of Illinois Press in 1949, and in *Key Papers in the Development of Information Theory*, ed. David Slepian, IEEE Press, 1974, 1988. For readers who want all of Shannon's works, see N.J.A. Sloane and A.D. Wyner, 1992, *The Collected Papers of Claude E. Shannon.*

HO

Shaw, Percy
b. 1889 Yorkshire, England
d. 1975

English inventor of the 'catseye' reflecting roadstud.

Little is known of Shaw's youth, but in the 1930s he was running a comparatively successful business repairing roads. One evening in 1933, he was driving to his home in Halifax, West Yorkshire; it was late, dark and foggy and only the reflection of his headlights from the tram-tracks guided him and kept him on the road. He decided to find or make an alternative to tramlines, which were not universal and by that time were being taken up as trams were being replaced with diesel buses.

Shaw needed a place to work and bought the old Boothtown Mansion, a cloth-merchant's house built in the mid-eighteenth century. There he devoted himself to the production of a prototype of the reflecting roadstud, inspired by the reflective nature of a cat's eyes. Shaw's design consisted of a prism backed by an aluminium mirror, set in pairs in a rubber casing; when traffic passed over the stud, the prisms would be wiped clean as the casing was depressed. In 1934, Shaw obtained permission from the county surveyor to lay, at his own expense, a short stretch of catseyes on a main highway near his home: fifty were laid at Brightlington crossroads, an accident blackspot near Bradford. This was inspected by a number of surveyors in 1936. The first order for catseyes had already been placed in 1935, for a pedestrian crossing in Baldon, Yorkshire.

There were alternative designs in existence, particularly in France, and in 1937 the Ministry of Transport laid an 8 km (5 mile) stretch in Oxfordshire with sample lengths of different types of studs. After two years, most of them had fractured, become displaced or ceased to reflect; only the product of Shaw's company, Reflecting Roadstuds Ltd, was still in perfect condition. The outbreak of the Second World War brought blackout regulations, which caused a great boost to sales of reflecting roadstuds; orders reached some 40,000 per week. Production was limited, however, due to the shortage of rubber supplies after the Japanese overran South-East Asia; until the end of the war, only about 12,000 catseyes were produced a year.

Over fifty million catseyes have been installed in Britain, where on average there are about two hundred and fifty catseyes in each kilometre of road, if laid in a single line. The success of Shaw's invention brought him great wealth, although he continued to live in the same house, without curtains – which obstructed his view – or carpets – which harboured odours and germs. He had three Rolls–Royce cars, and four television sets which were permanently switched on while he was at home, each tuned to a different channel.

Principal Honours and Distinctions
OBE 1965.

Further Reading
E. de Bono (ed.), 1979, *Eureka*, London: Thames & Hudson.
'Percy's bright idea', *En Route* (the magazine of the Caravan Club), reprinted in *The Police Review*, 23 March 1983.

IMcN

Shen Gua (Shen Kua)
fl. eleventh century China

Chinese writer on the compass.

Shen Gua gave the first clear description in any language of the magnetic compass and magnetic declination in his *Meng Qi Bi Tan* (*c.*1088). The text also describes north- and south-pointing needles, just over a century before the earliest Western accounts.

Bibliography
c.1088, *Meng Qi Bi Tan.*

Further Reading
J. Needham, *Science and Civilisation in China*, Cambridge: Cambridge University Press, 1962, Vol. IV.1, pp. 249–51.

LRD

Shih Lu
See **Shi Lu**.

Shillibeer, George
fl. early nineteenth century

English coachbuilder who introduced the omnibus to London.

Little is known of Shillibeer's early life except that he was for some years resident in France. He served as a midshipman in the Royal Navy before joining the firm of Hatchetts in Long Acre, London, to learn coachbuilding. He set up as a coachbuilder in Paris soon after the end of the Napoleonic Wars, and prospered. Early in the 1820s Jacques Laffite ordered two improved buses from Shillibeer. Their success prompted Shillibeer to sell up his business and return to London to start a similar service. His first two buses in London ran for the first time on 4 July 1829, from the Yorkshire Stingo at Paddington to the Bank, a distance of 9 miles (14 km) which had taken three hours by the existing short-stagecoaches. Shillibeer's vehicle was drawn by three horses abreast, carried twenty-two passengers at a charge of one shilling for the full journey or sixpence for a part-journey. These fares were a third of that charged for an inside seat on a short-stagecoach. The conductors were the sons of friends of Shillibeer from his naval days. He was soon earning £1,000 per week, each bus making twelve double journeys a day.

Dishonesty was rife among the conductors, so Shillibeer fitted a register under the entrance step to count the passengers; two of the conductors who had been discharged set out to wreck the register and its inventor. Expanded routes were soon being travelled by a larger fleet but the newly formed Metropolitan Police force complained that the buses were too wide, so the next buses had only two horses and carried sixteen passengers inside with two on top. Shillibeer's partner, William Morton, failed as competition grew. Shillibeer sold out in 1834 when he had sixty buses, six hundred horses and stabling for them. He started a long-distance service to Greenwich, but a competing railway opened in 1835 and income declined; the Official Stamp and Tax Offices seized the omnibuses and the business was bankrupted. Shillibeer then set up as an undertaker, and prospered with a new design of hearse which became known as a 'Shillibeer'.

Further Reading
A. Bird, 1969, *Road Vehicles*, London: Longmans Industrial Archaeology Series.

IMcN

Shi Lu (Shih Lu)
fl. late third century BC China

Chinese canal builder who constructed the oldest contour transport canal.

The background to Shi's work was the victorious campaign waged by the Qin emperor against the state of Yue. He scored a triumph by constructing the Ling Qu or 'magic canal', by far the oldest contour transport canal in any civilization and which took the emperor's barges and warships across a mountain range. The canal joined the Xiang and Li rivers and included thirty-six lock gates.

Further Reading
J. Needham, *Science and Civilisation in China*, Cambridge: Cambridge University Press, 1971, Vol. IV.3, pp. 299, 300, 303ff., 375.

LRD

Shipman, M.D.
fl. *c.*1886 USA

American patentee of a stud fastener in 1886.

From the late nineteenth century, a variety of press fasteners began to appear. In 1885 H. **Bauer** patented a spring-and-stud fastener, and the following year M.D. Shipman patented a similar design in the United States.

Further Reading
I. McNeil (ed.), 1990, *An Encyclopaedia of the History of Technology*, London: Routledge, pp. 852–3 (for a brief account of fastenings).

See also **Hannart, Louis**.

RLH

Shockley, William Bradford

b. 13 February 1910 London, England
d. 12 August 1989, Palo Alto, California, USA.

*American physicist who developed the junction transistor from the point contact transistor and was joint winner (with John **Bardeen** and Walter H. **Brattain**) of the 1956 Nobel Prize for physics.*

The son of a mining engineer, Shockley graduated from the California Institute of Technology in 1932 and in 1936 obtained his PhD at the Massachusetts Institute of Technology. In that year, he joined the staff of Bell Telephone Laboratories.

Since the early days of radio, crystals of silicon or similar materials had been used to rectify alternating current supply until these were displaced by thermionic valves or tubes. Shockley, with Bardeen and Brattain, found that crystals of germanium containing traces of certain impurities formed far better rectifiers than crystals of the material in its pure form. The resulting device, the transistor, could also be used to amplify the current; its name is derived from its ability to transfer current across a resistor. The transistor, being so much smaller than the thermionic valve which it replaced, led to the miniaturization of electronic appliances. Another advantage was that a transistorized device needed no period of warming up, such as was necessary with a thermionic valve before it would operate. The dispersal of the heat generated by a multiplicity of thermionic valves such as were present in early computers was another problem obviated by the advent of the transistor.

Shockley was responsible for much development in the field of semiconductors. He was De-

puty Director of the Weapons Systems Evaluation Group of the US Department of Defense (1954–5), and in 1963 he was appointed the first **Poniatoff** Professor of Engineering Science at Stanford University, California. During the late 1960s Shockley became a controversial figure for expressing his unorthodox views on genetics, such as that black people were inherently less intelligent than white people, and that the population explosion spread 'bad' genes at the expense of 'good' genes; he supported the idea of a sperm bank from Nobel Prize winners, voluntary sterilization and the restriction of interracial marriages.

Principal Honours and Distinctions
Nobel Prize for Physics 1956.

Further Reading
I. Asimov (ed.), 1982, *Biographical Encyclopedia of Science and Technology*, New York: Doubleday & Co.

IMcN

Shoenberg, Isaac

b. 1 March 1880 Kiev, Ukraine
d. 25 January 1963 Willesden, London, England

*Russian engineer and friend of Vladimir **Zworykin**; Director of Research at EMI, responsible for creating the team that successfully developed the world's first all-electronic television system.*

After his initial engineering education at Kiev Polytechnic, Shoenberg went to London to undertake further studies at the Royal College of Science. In 1905 he returned to Russia and rose to become Chief Engineer of the Russian Wireless Telegraphy Company. He then returned to England, where he was a consultant in charge of the Patent Department and then joint General Manager of the Marconi Wireless Telegraphy Company (see **Marconi**). In 1929 he joined the Columbia Graphophone Company, but two years later this amalgamated with the Gramophone Company, by then known as His Master's voice (HMV), to form EMI (Electric and Musical Industries), a company in which the Radio Corporation of America (RCA) had a significant shareholding. Appointed Director of the new company's Research Laboratories in 1931,

Shoenberg gathered together a team of highly skilled engineers, including **Blumlein**, Browne, Willans, McGee, Lubszynski, Broadway and White, with the objective of producing an all-electronic television system suitable for public broadcasting. A 150-line system had already been demonstrated using film as the source material; a photoemissive camera tube similar to Zworykin's iconoscope soon followed. With alternate demonstrations of the EMI system and the mechanical system of Baird arranged with the object of selecting a broadcast system for the UK, Shoenberg took the bold decision to aim for a 405-line 'high-definition' standard, using interlaced scanning based on an RCA patent and further developed by Blumlein. This was so successful that it was formally adopted as the British standard in 1935 and regular broadcasts, the first in the world, began in 1937. It is a tribute to Shoenberg's vision and the skills of his team that this standard was to remain in use, apart from the war years, until finally superseded in 1985.

Principal Honours and Distinctions
Knighted 1954. Institution of Electrical Engineers Faraday Medal 1954.

Further Reading
A.D. Blumlein et al., 1938, 'The Marconi-EMI television system', *Journal of the Institution of Electrical Engineers* 83: 729 (provides a description of the development of the 405-line system).
For more background information, see *Proceedings of the International Conference on the History of Television. From Early Days to the Present*, November 1986, Institution of Electrical Engineers Publication No. 271.

See also: **Baird, John Logie**; **Campbell-Swinton, Alan Archibald**.

KF

Sholes, Christopher Latham
b. 14 February 1819 Mooresburg, Pennsylvania, USA
d. 17 February 1890 USA

American inventor of the first commercially successful typewriter.

Sholes was born on his parents' farm, of a family that had originally come from England. After leaving school at 14, he was apprenticed for four years to the local newspaper, the *Danville Intelligencer*. He moved with his parents to Wisconsin, where he followed his trade as journalist and printer, within a year becoming State Printer and taking charge of the House journal of the State Legislature. When he was 20 he left home and joined his brother in Madison, Wisconsin, on the staff of the *Wisconsin Enquirer*. After marrying, he took the editorship of the *Southport Telegraph*, until he became Postmaster of Southport. His experiences as journalist and postmaster drew him into politics and, in spite of the delicate nature of his health and personality, he served with credit as State Senator and in the State Assembly. In 1860 he moved to Milwaukee, where he became Editor of the local paper until President Lincoln offered him the post of Collector of Customs at Milwaukee.

That position at last gave Sholes time to develop his undoubted inventive talents. With a machinist friend, Samuel W. Soule, he obtained a patent for a paging machine and another two years later for a machine for numbering the blank pages of a book serially. At the small machine shop where they worked, there was a third inventor, Carlos Glidden. It was Glidden who suggested to Sholes that, in view of his numbering machine, he would be well equipped to develop a letter printing machine. Glidden drew Sholes's attention to an account of a writing machine that had recently been invented in London by John Pratt, and Sholes was so seized with the idea that he devoted the rest of his life to perfecting the machine. With Glidden and Soule, he took out a patent for a typewriter on 23 June 1868 followed by two further patents for improvements. Sholes struggled unsuccessfully for five years to exploit his invention; his two partners gave up their rights in it and finally, on 1 March 1873, Sholes himself sold his rights to the Remington Arms Company for $12,000. With their mechanical skills and equipment, Remingtons were able to perfect the Sholes typewriter and put it on the market. This, the first commercially successful typewriter, led to a revolution not only in office work, but also in work for women, although progress was slow at first. When the New York Young Women's Christian Association bought six Remingtons in 1881 to begin classes for young women, eight turned up for the first lesson; and five years later it was estimated that there were 60,000 female typists in the USA. Sholes said, 'I feel that I have done something for the women who have always had to work so hard. This will more easily enable them to earn a living.'

Sholes continued his work on the typewriter, giving Remingtons the benefit of his results. His last patent was granted in 1878. Never very strong, Sholes became consumptive and spent much of his remaining nine years in the vain pursuit of health.

Bibliography
23 June 1868, US patent no. 79,265 (the first typewriter patent).

Further Reading
M.H. Adler, 1973, *The Writing Machine*, London: Allen & Unwin.

LRD

Short, Hugh Oswald
b. 16 January 1883 Derbyshire, England
d. 4 December 1969 Haslemere, England

English co-founder, with his brothers Horace Short (1872–1917) and Eustace (1875–1932), of the first company to design and build aeroplanes in Britain.

Oswald Short trained as an engineer; he was largely self-taught but was assisted by his brothers Eustace and Horace. In 1898 Eustace and the young Oswald set up a balloon business, building their first balloon in 1901. Two years later they sold observation balloons to the Government of India, and further orders followed. Meanwhile, in 1906 Horace designed a high-altitude balloon with a spherical pressurized gondola, an idea later used by Auguste **Piccard**, in 1931. Horace, a strange genius with a dominating character, joined his younger brothers in 1908 to found Short Brothers. Their first design, based on the **Wright** *Flyer*, was a limited success, but *No. 2* won a *Daily Mail* prize of £1,000. In the same year, 1909, the Wright brothers chose Shorts to build six of their new *Model A* biplanes. Still using the basic Wright layout, Horace designed the world's first twin-engined aeroplane to fly successfully: it had one engine forward of the pilot, and one aft. During the years before the First World War the Shorts turned to tractor biplanes and specialized in floatplanes for the Admiralty.

Oswald established a seaplane factory at Rochester, Kent, during 1913–14, and an airship works at Cardington, Bedfordshire, in 1916. Short Brothers went on to build the rigid airship *R 32*, which was completed in 1919. Unfortunately, Horace died in 1917, which threw a greater responsibility onto Oswald, who became the main innovator. He introduced the use of aluminium alloys combined with a smooth 'stressed-skin' construction (unlike **Junkers**, who used corrugated skins). His sleek biplane the *Silver Streak* flew in 1920, well ahead of its time, but official support was not forthcoming. Oswald Short struggled on, trying to introduce his all-metal construction, especially for flying boats. He eventually succeeded with the biplane *Singapore*, of 1926, which had an all-metal hull. The prototype was used by Sir Alan **Cobham** for his flight round Africa. Several successful all-metal flying boats followed, including the *Empire* flying boats (1936) and the ubiquitous *Sunderland* (1937). The *Stirling* bomber (1939) was derived from the *Sunderland*. The company was nationalized in 1942 and Oswald Short retired the following year.

Principal Honours and Distinctions
Honorary Fellow of the Royal Aeronautical Society. Freeman of the City of London. Oswald Short turned down an MBE in 1919 as he felt it did not reflect the achievements of the Short Brothers.

Bibliography
1966, 'Aircraft with stressed skin metal construction', *Journal of the Royal Aeronautical Society* (November) (an account of the problems with patents and officialdom).

Further Reading
C.H. Barnes, 1967, *Shorts Aircraft since 1900*, London; reprinted 1989 (a detailed account of the work of the Short brothers).

JDS

Shortt, William Hamilton
b. 28 September 1881
d. 4 February 1971

British railway engineer and amateur horologist who designed the first successful free-pendulum clock.

Shortt entered the Engineering Department of the London and South Western Railway as an engineering cadet in 1902, remaining with the company and its successors until he retired in 1946. He became interested in precision horology in 1908, when he designed an instrument for recording the speed of trains; this led to a long and fruitful collaboration with Frank Hope-Jones, the proprietor of the Synchronome Company. This association culminated in the installation of a free-pendulum clock, with an accuracy of the order of one second per year, at Edinburgh Observatory in 1921. The clock's performance was far better than that of existing clocks, such as the **Riefler**, and a slightly modified version was produced commercially by the Synchronome Company. These clocks provided the time standard at Greenwich and many other observatories and scientific institutions across the world until they were supplanted by the quartz clock.

The period of a pendulum is constant if it swings freely with a constant amplitude in a vacuum. However, this ideal state cannot be achieved in a clock because the pendulum must be impulsed to maintain its amplitude and the swings have to be counted to indicate time. The free-pendulum clock is an attempt to approach this ideal as closely as possible. In 1898 R.J. Rudd used a slave clock, synchronized with a free pendulum, to time the impulses delivered to the free pendulum. This clock was not successful, but it provided the inspiration for Shortt's clock, which operates on the same principle. The Shortt clock used a standard Synchronome electric clock as the slave, and its pendulum was kept in step with the free pendulum by means of the 'hit and miss' synchronizer that Shortt had patented in 1921. This allowed the pendulum to swing freely (in a vacuum), apart from the fraction of a second in which it received an impulse each half-minute.

Principal Honours and Distinctions
Master of the Clockmakers' Company 1950. British Horological Society Gold Medal 1931. Clockmakers' Company Tompion Medal 1954. Franklin Institute John Price Wetherill Silver Medal.

Bibliography
1929, 'Some experimental mechanisms, mechanical and otherwise, for the maintenance of vibration of a pendulum', *Horological Journal* 71: 224–5.

Further Reading
Obituary, 1971, *Proceedings of the Institution of Civil Engineers* 56: 396–7.
F. Hope-Jones, 1949, *Electrical Timekeeping*, 2nd edn, London (a detailed but not entirely impartial account of the development of the free-pendulum clock).

See also **Marrison, Warren**.

DV

Shrapnel, General Henry
b. 3 June 1761 Bradford-on-Avon, England
d. 13 March 1842 Southampton, England

English professional soldier and inventor of shrapnel ammunition.

The youngest of nine children, Shrapnel was commissioned into the Royal Artillery in July 1779. His early military service was in Newfoundland and it was on his return to England in 1784 that he began to interest himself in artillery ammunition. His particular concern was to develop a round that would be more effective against infantry than the existing solid cannonball and canister round. The result was a hollow, spherical shell filled with lead musket balls and fitted with a bursting charge and fuse. His development of the shell was interrupted by active service in the Low Countries in 1793–4, during which he was wounded, and duty in the West Indies. Nevertheless, in 1803 the British Army adopted his shell, which during the next twelve years played a significant part on the battlefield.

In 1804 Shrapnel was appointed Assistant Inspector of Artillery and made further contributions to the science of gunnery, drawing up a series of range tables to improve accuracy of fire, inventing the brass tangent slide for better sighting of guns, and improving the production of howitzers and mortars by way of the invention of parabolic chambers. His services were recognized in 1814 by a Treasury grant of £1,200 per annum for life. He was promoted Major-General in 1819 and appointed a Colonel-Commandant of the Royal Artillery in 1827, and in the 1830s there was talk of him being made a baronet, but nothing came of it. Shrapnel remains a current military term, although modern bursting shells rely on the fragmentation of the casing of the projectile for their effect rather than his original concept of having shot inside them.

Principal Honours and Distinctions
Colonel-Commandant of the Royal Artillery 1827.

Further Reading
Dictionary of National Biography, 1897, Vol. 52, London: Smith, Elder.

CM

Sickels, Frederick Ellsworth

b. 20 September 1819 Gloucester County, New Jersey, USA
d. 8 March 1895 Kansas City, Missouri, USA

American inventor of a steam-inlet cut-off valve mechanism for engines and steam steering apparatus for ships.

Sickels was educated in New York City, where his father was a practising physician. As he showed mechanical aptitude, at the age of 16 he joined the Harlem Railroad as a rod man, and a year later became a machinist in the Allaire Works in New York, studying physics and mechanics in his spare time. He perfected his cut-off mechanism for drop valves in 1841 and patented it the following year. The liberating mechanism allowed the valve to fall quickly onto its seat and so eliminated 'wire-drawing' of the steam, and Sickels arranged a dashpot to prevent the valve hitting the seat violently. Through further improvements patented in 1843 and 1845, he gained a considerable fortune, but he subsequently lost it through fighting patent infringements because his valve gear was copied extensively.

In 1846 he turned his attention to using a steam engine to assist the steering in ships. He filed a patent application in 1849 and completed a machine in 1854, but he could not find any ship owner willing to try it until 1858, when it was fitted to the *August*. A patent was granted in 1860, but as no American ship owners showed interest Sickels went to England, where he obtained three British patents; once again, however, he found no interest. He returned to the United States in 1867 and continued his fruitless

efforts until he was financially ruined. He patented improved compound engines in 1875 and also contributed improvements in sinking pneumatic piles. He turned to civil engineering and engaged in railway and bridge construction in the west. In about 1890 he was made Consulting Engineer to the National Water Works Company of New York and in 1891 became Chief Engineer of its operations at Kansas City.

Further Reading
Dictionary of American Biography, 1935, Vol. XVII, New York: C. Scribner's Sons.
C.T. Porter, 1908, *Engineering Reminiscences*, reprinted 1985, Bradley, Ill.: Lindsay Publications (comments on his cut-off valve gear).
H.G. Conway, 1955–6, 'Some notes on the origins of mechanical servo systems', *Transactions of the Newcomen Society* 29 (comments on his steam steering apparatus).

RLH

Siemens, Sir Charles William

b. 4 April 1823 Lenthe, Germany
d. 19 November 1883 London, England

German/British metallurgist and inventor, pioneer of the regenerative principle and open-hearth steelmaking.

Born Carl Wilhelm, he attended craft schools in Lübeck and Magdeburg, followed by an intensive course in natural science at Göttingen as a pupil of **Weber**. At the age of 19 Siemens travelled to England and sold an electroplating process developed by his brother Werner **Siemens** to Richard **Elkington**, who was already established in the plating business. From 1843 to 1844 he obtained practical experience in the Magdeburg works of Count Stolburg. He settled in England in 1844 and later assumed British nationality, but maintained close contact with his brother Werner, who in 1847 had co-founded the firm Siemens & Halske in Berlin to manufacture telegraphic equipment. William began to develop his regenerative principle of waste-heat recovery and in 1856 his brother Frederick (1826–1904) took out a British patent for heat regeneration, by which hot waste gases were passed through a honeycomb of fire-bricks. When they became hot, the gases were switched to a second mass of fire-bricks and incoming air and fuel gas were led through the hot bricks. By alternating the two gas flows, high temperatures could be reached and considerable fuel economies achieved. By 1861 the two brothers had incorporated producer gas fuel, made by gasifying low-grade coal.

Heat regeneration was first applied in ironmaking by **Cowper** in 1857 for heating the air blast in blast furnaces. The first regenerative furnace was set up in Birmingham in 1860 for glassmaking. The first such furnace for making steel was developed in France by Pierre **Martin** and his father, Emile, in 1863. Siemens found British steelmakers reluctant to adopt the principle so in 1866 he rented a small works in Birmingham to develop his open-hearth steelmaking furnace, which he patented the following year. The process gradually made headway; as well as achieving high temperatures and saving fuel, it was slower than **Bessemer**'s process, permitting greater control over the content of the steel. By 1900 the tonnage of open-hearth steel exceeded that produced by the Bessemer process.

In 1872 Siemens played a major part in founding the Society of Telegraph Engineers (from which the Institution of Electrical Engineers evolved), serving as its first President. He became President for the second time in 1878. He built a cable works at Charlton, London, where the cable could be loaded directly into the holds of ships moored on the Thames. In 1873, together with William Froude, a British shipbuilder, he designed the *Faraday*, the first specialized vessel for Atlantic cable laying. The successful laying of a cable from Europe to the United States was completed in 1875, and a further five transatlantic cables were laid by the *Faraday* over the following decade.

The Siemens factory in Charlton also supplied equipment for some of the earliest electric-lighting installations in London, including the British Museum in 1879 and the Savoy Theatre in 1882, the first theatre in Britain to be fully illuminated by electricity. The pioneer electric-tramway system of 1883 at Portrush, Northern Ireland, was an opportunity for the Siemens company to demonstrate its equipment.

Principal Honours and Distinctions
Knighted 1883. FRS 1862. Institution of Civil Engineers Telford Medal 1853. President, Institution of Mechanical Engineers 1872. President, Society of Telegraph Engineers 1872 and 1878. President, British Association 1882.

Bibliography
27 May 1879, British patent no. 2,110 (electric-arc furnace).
1889, *The Scientific Works of C. William Siemens*, ed. E.F. Bamber, 3 vols, London.

Further Reading
W. Poles, 1888, *Life of Sir William Siemens*, London; repub. 1986 (compiled from material supplied by the family).
S. von Weiher, 1972–3, 'The Siemens brothers. Pioneers of the electrical age in Europe', *Transactions of the Newcomen Society* 45: 1–11 (a short, authoritative biography).
S. von Weihr and H. Goetler, 1983, *The Siemens Company. Its Historical Role in the Progress of Electrical Engineering 1847–1980*, English edn, Berlin (a scholarly account with emphasis on technology).

GW

Siemens, Dr Ernst Werner von

b. 13 December 1816 Lenthe, near Hanover, Germany
d. 6 December 1892 Berlin, Germany

German pioneer of the dynamo, builder of the first electric railway.

Werner von Siemens was the eldest of a large family and after the early death of his parents took his place at its head. He served in the Prussian artillery, being commissioned in 1839, after which he devoted himself to the study of chemistry and physics. In 1847 Siemens and J.G. **Halske** formed a company, Telegraphen-Bauanstalt von Siemens und Halske, to manufacture a dial telegraph which they had developed from an earlier instrument produced by Charles **Wheatstone**. In 1848 Siemens obtained his discharge from the army and he and Halske constructed the first long-distance telegraph line on the European continent, between Berlin and Frankfurt am Main.

Werner von Siemens's younger brother, William **Siemens**, had settled in Britain in 1844 and was appointed agent for the Siemens & Halske company in 1851. Later, an English subsidiary company was formed, known from 1865 as Siemens Brothers. It specialized in manufacturing and laying submarine telegraph cables: the specialist cable-laying ship *Faraday*, launched for the purpose in 1874, was the prototype of later cable ships and in 1874–5 laid the first cable to run direct from the British Isles to the USA. In charge of Siemens Brothers was another brother, Carl, who had earlier established a telegraph network in Russia.

In 1866 Werner von Siemens demonstrated the principle of the dynamo in Germany, but it took until 1878 to develop dynamos and electric motors to the point at which they could be produced commercially. The following year, 1879, Werner von Siemens built the first electric railway, and operated it at the Berlin Trades Exhibition. It comprised an oval line, 300 m (985 ft) long, with a track gauge of 1 m (3 ft 3½ in.); upon this a small locomotive hauled three small passenger coaches. The locomotive drew current at 150 volts from a third rail between the running rails, through which it was returned. In four months, more than 80,000 passengers were carried. The railway was subsequently demonstrated in Brussels, and in London, in 1881. That same year Siemens built a permanent electric tramway, 1½ miles (2½ km) long, on the outskirts of Berlin. In 1882 in Berlin he tried out a railless electric vehicle which drew electricity from a two-wire overhead line: this was the ancestor of the trolleybus.

In the British Isles, an Act of Parliament was obtained in 1880 for the Giant's Causeway Railway in Ireland with powers to work it by 'animal, mechanical or electrical power'; although Siemens Brothers were electrical engineers to the company, of which William Siemens was a director, delays in construction were to mean that the first railway in the British Isles to operate regular services by electricity was that of Magnus **Volk**.

Principal Honours and Distinctions
Honorary doctorate, Berlin University 1860. Ennobled by Kaiser Friedrich III 1880, after which he became known as von Siemens.

Further Reading
S. von Weiher, 1972, 'The Siemens brothers, pioneers of the electrical age in Europe', *Transactions of the Newcomen Society* 45 (describes the Siemens's careers).
C.E. Lee, 1979, 'The birth of electric traction', *Railway Magazine* (May) (describes Werner

Siemens's introduction of the electric railway).
Transactions of the Newcomen Society (1979) 50: 82–3 (describes Siemens's and Halske's early electric telegraph instruments).
Transactions of the Newcomen Society (1961) 33: 93 (describes the railless electric vehicle).
PJGR

Sikorsky, Igor Ivanovich
b. 25 May 1889 Kiev, Ukraine
d. 26 October 1972 Easton, Connecticut, USA

Russian/American pioneer of large aeroplanes, flying boats, and helicopters.

Sikorsky trained as an engineer but developed an interest in aviation at the age of 19 when he was allowed to spend several months in Paris to meet French aviators. He bought an Anzani aero-engine and took it back to Russia, where he designed and built a helicopter. In his own words, 'It had one minor technical problem – it would not fly – but otherwise it was a good helicopter'.

Sikorsky turned to aeroplanes and built a series of biplanes: by 1911 the *S-5* was capable of flights lasting an hour. Following this success, the Russian–Baltic Railroad Car Company commissioned Sikorsky to build a large aeroplane. On 13 May 1913 Sikorsky took off in the *Grand*, the world's first four-engined aeroplane. With a wing span of 28 m (92 ft) it was also the world's largest, and was unique in that the crew were in an enclosed cabin with dual controls. The even larger *Ilia Mourometz* flew the following year and established many records, including the carriage of sixteen people. During the First World War many of these aircraft were built and served as heavy bombers.

Following the revolution in Russia during 1917, Sikorsky emigrated first to France and then the United States, where he founded his own company. After building the successful *S-38* passenger-carrying amphibian, the Sikorsky Aviation Corporation became part of the United Aircraft Corporation and went on to produce several large flying boats. Of these, the four-engined *S-42* was probably the best known, for its service to Hawaii in 1935 and trial flights across the Atlantic in 1937.

In the late 1930s Sikorsky once again turned his attention to helicopters, and on 14 September 1939 his *VS-300* made its first tentative hop,

643

with Sikorsky at the controls. Many improvements were made and on 6 May 1941 Sikorsky made a record-breaking flight of over 1 1/2 hours. The Sikorsky design of a single main lifting rotor combined with a small tail rotor to balance the torque effect has dominated helicopter design to this day. Sikorsky produced a long series of outstanding helicopter designs which are in service throughout the world.

Principal Honours and Distinctions
Chevalier de la Légion d'honneur 1960. Presidential Certificate of Merit 1948. Aeronautical Society Silver Medal 1949.

Bibliography
1971, 'Sixty years in flying', *Aeronautical Journal* (Royal Aeronautical Society) (November) (interesting and amusing).
1938, *The Story of the Winged S.*, New York; 1967, rev. edn.

Further Reading
D. Cochrane et al., 1990, *The Aviation Careers of Igor Sikorsky*, Seattle.
K.N. Finne, 1988, *Igor Sikorsky: The Russian Years*, ed. C.J. Bobrow and V. Hardisty, Shrewsbury; orig. pub. in Russian, 1930.
F.J. Delear, 1969, *Igor Sikorsky: His Three Careers in Aviation*, New York.

JDS

Simms, Frederick
b. 1863 Hamburg, Germany
d. 1944

English engineer and entrepreneur who imported the first internal combustion engines into Britain.

Simms was born of English parents in Hamburg. He met Gottlieb **Daimler** at an exhibition in Bremen in 1890, where he had gone to exhibit an aerial cableway that he had designed to provide passenger transport over rivers and valleys; in the previous year, he had invented and patented an automatic railway ticket machine, the principle of which is still in use worldwide. He obtained a licence to develop the Daimler engine throughout the British Empire (excluding Canada). He had great trouble in arranging any demonstration of the Daimler engine as authorities were afraid of the risk of fire and ex-

plosion with petroleum spirit, particularly at indoor venues. He succeeded eventually in operating a boat with an internal combustion engine between Charing Cross and Westminster piers on the River Thames in 1891. He then rented space under a railway arch at Putney Bridge station for installing Daimler engines in boats. With Sir David **Salomans** he was responsible for organizing the first motor show in Britain in 1895; four cars were on show. Simms became a director of the main Daimler company, and was a consultant to the Coventry Daimler Company. He was the founder of the Automobile Club of Great Britain and Ireland, a forerunner of the Royal Automobile Club (RAC), as well as the Society of Motor Manufacturers and Traders.

Further Reading
E. Johnson, 1986, *The Dawn of Motoring*, London: Mercedes-Benz UK Ltd.

IMcN

Simpson, Sir James Young
b. 7 June 1811 Bathgate, Linlithgowshire, Scotland
d. 6 May 1870 Edinburgh, Scotland

Scottish obstetrician, pioneer of the use of chloroform in labour.

The seventh and youngest son of a baker, after entering Edinburgh University at the tender age of 14 he graduated in 1832 and when only 28 was appointed Professor of Midwifery at Edinburgh University. Following the introduction of ether as a general anaesthetic (see W.T.G. **Morton**) he was the first to use it in midwifery. Aware of its disadvantages, he experimented on himself, and on 4 November 1847 he discovered the anaesthetic properties of chloroform. However, there were both medical and religious objections to its use, until in 1853 it was administered to Queen Victoria at the birth of Prince Leopold.

Widely recognized as a great obstetrician, he also founded the modern practice of gynaecology, introducing new diagnostic methods and techniques of investigation. He was also an enthusiastic archaeologist.

Principal Honours and Distinctions
Created Baronet 1866. Physician to the Queen in Scotland 1847.

Bibliography
1847, 'Discovery of a new anaesthetic agent more efficient than sulphuric ether', *Lancet*.
Obstetric Memoirs and Contributions, Edinburgh.

Further Reading
J. Duns, 1873, *Memoir of J.Y. Simpson*.

MG

Simpson, Thomas

b. 20 August 1710 Market Bosworth, Leicestershire, England
d. 14 May 1761 Market Bosworth, Leicestershire, England

English mathematician and author of Simpson's Rules.

Despite domestic difficulties, Simpson managed to study and teach mathematics and allied subjects throughout his life. His interest in celestial phenomena was aroused by the solar eclipse of 1724. Around 1736 he started to work in London as a weaver, teaching mathematics in his spare time. The genius of his prolific work was recognized and various honours came his way, culminating in his appointment in 1743 to the Chair of Mathematics at the Royal Academy, Woolwich. In that same year he published a paper relating to 'the means of approximating the areas of curves, by means of equidistant ordinates'. This method, now known as Simpson's first and second rules, enabled engineers to calculate areas under curves and volumes bounded by shapes made up of a regular envelope of curves. Shipbuilders and naval architects were to find this one of the greatest developments in the history of ship design.

Principal Honours and Distinctions
FRS 1745. Member of the Royal Academy of Stockholm 1740.

FMW

Sinclair, Sir Clive Marles

b. 30 July 1940

English electronic engineer and inventor.

The son of G.W.C. Sinclair, a machine tool engineer, the young Sinclair's education was disrupted by the failure of his father's business. Aged 12 he left Boxgrove preparatory school and went through twelve more schools before leaving St George's School, Weybridge, at the age of 17. His first job was as an editorial assistant on a hobbyist's magazine, *Practical Wireless*, and his next as an editor at Bernard Books, writing a series of technical manuals. In 1961 he registered Sinclair Radionics and in the following year announced its first product, a micro-amplifier. This was the first of a series of miniaturized radio products that he put on the market while retaining his editorial job. In 1972 he launched the Sinclair *Executive* calculator, selling originally at £79.95 but later at £24.95. In 1976, the *Black Watch*, an electronic watch with digital light-emitting diode (LED) display, was marketed, to be followed by the *TV1A*, a miniature television with a 2 in. (5 cm) monochrome screen. During the latter part of this period, Sinclair Radionics was supported by investment from the UK National Enterprise Board, who appointed an outside managing director; after making a considerable loss, they closed the company in 1979. However, Sinclair Electronics had already been set up and started to market the UK's first cheap computer kit, the *MK 14*, which was followed by the *ZX 80* and later the *ZX 81*. Price was kept at a minimum by the extensive use of existing components, though this was a restriction on performance. The small memory was enhanced from one kilobyte to seventeen kilobytes with the addition of a separate memory unit. In January 1985 Sinclair produced the Sinclair *C5*, a small three-wheeled vehicle driven by a washing-machine engine, intended as a revolutionary new form of personal transport; perceived as unsafe and impractical, it did not prove popular, and the failure of this venture resulted in a contraction of Sinclair's business activities. Later in 1985, a rival electronics company, Amstrad, paid £35,000,000 for all rights to existing Sinclair computer products.

In March 1992, the irrepressible Sinclair launched his latest brainchild, the *Zike* electric bicycle; a price of £499 was forecast. This machine, powered by an electric motor but with pedal assistance, had a top speed of 19 km/h (12 mph) and, on full power, would run for up to one hour. Its lightweight nickel-cadmium battery could be recharged either by a generator or by free-wheeling. Although more practical than the *C5*, it did not bring Sinclair success on the scale of his earlier micro-electronic products.

Principal Honours and Distinctions
Knighted 1983.

Further Reading
I. Adamson and R. Kennedy, 1986, *Sinclair and the 'Sunrise' Technology*, Harmondsworth: Penguin.

IMcN

Singer, Isaac Merritt

b. 27 October 1811 Pittstown, New York, USA
d. 23 July 1875 Torquay, Devonshire, England

American inventor of a sewing machine, and pioneer of mass production.

The son of a millwright, Singer was employed as an unskilled labourer at the age of 12, but later gained wide experience as a travelling machinist. He also found employment as an actor. On 16 May 1839, while living at Lockport, Illinois, he obtained his first patent for a rock-drilling machine, but he soon squandered the money he made. Then in 1849, while at Pittsburgh, he secured a patent for a wood- and metal-carving machine that he had begun five years previously; however, a boiler explosion in the factory destroyed his machine and left him penniless.

Near the end of 1850 Singer was engaged to redesign the Lerow & Blodgett sewing machine at the Boston shop of Orson C. Phelps, where the machine was being repaired. He built an improved version in eleven days that was sufficiently different for him to patent on 12 August 1851. He formed a partnership with Phelps and G.B. Zieber and they began to market the invention. Singer soon purchased Phelps's interest, although Phelps continued to manufacture the machines. Then Edward **Clark** acquired a one-third interest and with Singer bought out Zieber. These two, with Clark's flair for promotion and marketing, began to create a company which eventually would become the largest manufacturer of sewing machines exported worldwide, with subsidiary factories in England.

However, first Singer had to defend his patent, which was challenged by an earlier Boston inventor, Elias **Howe**. Although after a long lawsuit Singer had to pay royalties, it was the Singer machine which eventually captured the market because it could do continuous stitching. In 1856 the Great Sewing Machine Combination, the first important pooling arrangement in American history, was formed to share the various patents so that machines could be built without infringements and manufacture could be expanded without fear of litigation. Singer contributed his monopoly on the needle-bar cam with his 1851 patent. He secured twenty additional patents, so that his original straight-needle vertical design for lock-stitching eventually included such refinements as a continuous wheel-feed, yielding presser-foot, and improved cam for moving the needle-bar. A new model, introduced in 1856, was the first to be intended solely for use in the home.

Initially Phelps made all the machines for Singer. Then a works was established in New York where the parts were assembled by skilled workers through filing and fitting. Each machine was therefore a 'one-off' but Singer machines were always advertised as the best on the market and sold at correspondingly high prices. Gradually, more specialized machine tools were acquired, but it was not until long after Singer had retired to Europe in 1863 that Clark made the change to mass production. Sales of machines numbered 810 in 1853 and 21,000 ten years later.

Bibliography
12 August 1851, US patent no. 8,294 (sewing machine),

Further Reading
Biographies and obituaries have appeared in *Appleton's Cyclopedia of America*, Vol. V; *Dictionary of American Biography*, Vol XVII; *New York Times* 25 July 1875; *Scientific American* (1875) 33; and *National Cyclopaedia of American Biography*.
D.A. Hounshell, 1984, *From the American System to Mass Production 1800–1932. The Development of Manufacturing Technology in the United States*, Baltimore (provides a thorough account of the development of the Singer sewing machine, the competition it faced from other manufacturers and production methods).

RLH

Skinner, Halcyon

b. 6 March 1824 Mantua, Ohio, USA
d. 28 November 1900 USA

American inventor of a machine for making Royal Axminster and other carpets.

Halcyon was the son of Joseph and Susan Skinner. When he was 8 years old, his parents moved to Stockbridge in Massachusetts, where he obtained education locally and worked on farms. In 1838 his father moved to West Farms, New York, where Halcyon helped his father make violins and guitars for seven years. He then worked as a general carpenter for eight years until he was hired in 1849 by Alexander Smith, a carpet manufacturer. Skinner designed and constructed a hand loom that could weave figured instead of striped carpets, and by 1851 Smith had one hundred of these at work. Skinner was retained by Smith for forty years as a mechanical expert and adviser.

Weaving carpets by power started in the 1850s on enormous and complex machines. Axminster carpets had traditionally been produced in a similar way to those made by hand in Persia, with the tufts of woollen yarn being knotted around vertical warp threads. To mechanize this process proved very difficult, but Skinner patented a loom in 1856 to weave Axminster carpets although, it was not working successfully until 1860. Then in 1864 he developed a loom for weaving ingrain carpets, and *c.*1870 he altered some imported English looms for weaving tapestry carpets to double their output.

His most important invention was conceived in 1876 and patented on 16 January 1877. This was the Moquette or Royal Axminster loom, which marked yet another important step forward and enabled the use of an unlimited number of colours in carpet designs. This type of loom became known as the Spool Axminster because of the endless chain of spools carrying lengths of coloured yarns, wound in a predetermined order, from which short pieces could be cut and inserted as the tufts. It put Smith's company, Alexander Smith & Sons, Yonkers, New York, in the lead among American carpet manufacturers. This type of loom was introduced to Britain in 1878 by Tomkinson & Adam and spread rapidly. Skinner virtually retired in 1889 but continued to live in Yonkers.

Further Reading
Biography, *American Machinist* 23.
Dictionary of American Biography, Vol. XVII.
G. Robinson, 1966, *Carpets*, London (for the

history and techniques of carpet weaving).
A. Barlow, 1878, *The History and Principles of Weaving by Hand and by Power*, London (includes a section on pile weaving which covers some types of carpets).

RLH

Skola
fl. *c.*1819 France

French improver of the Jacquard mechanism for pattern weaving.

Jacquard hand looms surviving from the 1830s show a mechanism similar to those still used in the 1990s, with all the operations being carried out by the weaver: the flying shuttle, invented by John **Kay**, is driven across with the right hand, while the left hand rests on the sley and beats in the weft and also selects the appropriate shuttle from Robert **Kay**'s drop box. The right foot presses down on a pedal which operates the Jacquard mechanism. The single downwards movement of the foot has to be translated into two different motions to operate the Jacquard. First, the correct card has to be moved horizontally against the needles to select the desired pattern, then the appropriate needles have to be lifted vertically. Jacquard's invention failed in the way it pressed the card against the needles, but Skola was able to improve this in 1819, probably with the addition of a part called the 'swan neck'. It was Skola's Jacquard machine which truly rendered the process of weaving more economical and productive because the weaver now could operate the Jacquard mechanism with no help, so dispensing with the drawboy. The speed of selecting the pattern with this mechanism also meant that the weaver could use the flying shuttle, with an additional increment in weaving speeds.

Further Reading
R.L. Hills, 1970, *Power in the Industrial Revolution*, Manchester (includes a description of the development of the Jacquard mechanism).
A. Barlow, 1878, *The History and Principles of Weaving by Hand and by Power*, London (for illustrations of the perfected mechanism).

RLH

Slater, Samuel

b. 9 June 1768 Belper, Derbyshire, England
d. 21 April 1835 USA

Anglo-American manufacturer who established the first American mill to use Arkwright's spinning system.

Samuel's father, William, was a respected independent farmer who died when his son was aged 14; the young Slater was apprenticed to his father's friend, Jedediah **Strutt** for six and a half years at the beginning of 1783. He showed mathematical ability and quickly acquainted himself thoroughly with cotton-spinning machinery made by **Arkwright**, **Hargreaves** and **Crompton**. After completing his apprenticeship, he remained for a time with the Strutts to act as Supervisor for a new mill.

At that time it was forbidden to export any textile machinery or even drawings or data from England. The emigration of textile workers was forbidden too, but in September 1789 Slater left for the United States in disguise, having committed the details of the construction of the cotton-spinning machinery to memory. He reached New York and was employed by the New York Manufacturing Company.

In January 1790 he met Moses Brown in Providence, Rhode Island, and on 5 April 1790 he signed a contract to construct Arkwright's spinning machinery for Almy & Brown. It took Slater more than a year to get the machinery operational because of the lack of skilled mechanics and tools, but by 1793 the mill was running under the name of Almy, Brown & Slater. In October 1791 Slater had married Hannah Wilkinson, and in 1798 he set up his own mill in partnership with his father-in-law, Orziel Wilkinson. This mill was built in Pawtucket, near the first mill, but other mills soon followed in Smithville, Rhode Island, and elsewhere. Slater was the Incorporator, and for the first fifteen years was also President of the Manufacturer's Bank in Pawtucket. It was in his business role and as New England's first industrial capitalist that Slater made his most important contributions to the emergence of the American textile industry.

Further Reading
G.S. White, 1836, *Memoirs of Samuel Slater,* Philadelphia (the earliest account of his life).
Dictionary of American Biography, Vol. XVII.
Scientific American 63.
P.E. Rivard, 1974, *Samuel Slater, Father of American Manufactures*, Slater Mill.
D.J. Jeremy, 1981, *Transatlantic Industrial Revolution. The Diffusion of Textile Technologies Between Britain and America, 1790–1830s*, Oxford (covers Slater's activities in the USA very fully).

RLH

Small, James

b. *c.*1742 Scotland
d. 1793 Scotland

Scottish engineer who was first to apply scientific experiment and calculation to the design of ploughs.

James Small served his apprenticeship as a wright and blacksmith at Hutton in Berwickshire, and then travelled for a time in England. It is possible that he learned his trade from the ploughwright Pashley, who ran the 'Manufactory' in Rotherham. On his return to Scotland he settled at Blackadder Mount, Berwickshire, and there began to make his ploughs. He used a spring balance to determine the draft of the plough and fashioned the mouldboard from a soft wood so that the wear would show quickly on its surface. Repeated trials indicated the best shape to be adopted, and he had his mouldboards cast at the Carron Ironworks. At trials held at Dalkeith, Small's plough, pulled by two horses, outperformed the old Scotch plough hauled by as many as eight oxen, and his ploughs were soon to be found in all areas of the country. He established workshops in Leith Walk, where he made ploughs and other implements. It was in Edinburgh in 1784 that he published *Treatise on Ploughs*, in which he set out his methods and calculations. He made no attempt to patent his ideas, feeling that they should be available to all, and the book provided sufficient information for it to be used by his rivals. As a result he died a poor man at the age of 52. His family were supported with a £1,500 subscription raised on their behalf by Sir John Sinclair, President of the Board of Agriculture.

Bibliography
1784, *A Treatise on Ploughs and Wheel Carriages.*

Further Reading
J.B. Passmore, 1930, *The English Plough*, Reading: University of Reading (provides a history of plough development from the eighth century, and deals in detail with Small's work).

AP

Smalley, John

b. *c.*1729 England
d. 28 January 1782 Holywell, Wales.

English helped Arkwright to build and finance the waterframe.

John Smalley of Preston was the second son of John, a chapman of Blackburn. He was a distant relative of Richard **Arkwright** through marrying, in 1751, Elizabeth Baxter, whose mother Ellen was the widow of Arkwright's uncle, Richard. In the Preston Guild Rolls of 1762 he was described as a grocer and painter, and he was also Landlord of the Bull Inn. The following year he became a bailiff of Preston and in 1765 he became a Corporation steward. On 14 May 1768 Arkwright, Smalley and David **Thornley** became partners in a cotton-spinning venture in Nottingham. They agreed to apply for a patent for Arkwright's invention of spinning by rollers, and Smalley signed as a witness. It is said that Smalley provided much of the capital for this new venture as he sold his business at Preston for about £1,600, but this was soon found to be insufficient and the partnership had to be enlarged to include Samuel **Need** and Jedediah **Strutt**.

Smalley may have helped to establish the spinning mill at Nottingham, but by 28 February 1771 he was back in Preston, for on that day he was chosen a 'Councilman in the room of Mr. Thomas Jackson deceased' (Fitton 1989:38). He attended meetings for over a year, but either in 1772 or the following year he sold the Bull Inn, and certainly by August 1774 the Smalleys were living in Cromford, where he became Manager of the mill. He soon found himself at loggerheads with Arkwright; however, Strutt was able to smooth the dispute over for a while. Things came to a head in January 1777 when Arkwright was determined to get rid of Smalley, and the three remaining partners agreed to buy out Smalley's share for the sum of £10,751.

Although he had agreed not to set up any textile machinery, Smalley moved to Holywell in North Wales, where in the spring of 1777 he built a cotton-spinning mill in the Greenfield valley. He prospered there and his son was later to build two more mills in the same valley. Smalley used to go to Wrexham to sell his yarn, and there met John Peers, a leather merchant, who was able to provide a better quality leather for covering the drawing rollers which came to be used in Lancashire. Smalley died in 1782, shortly before Arkwright could sue him for infringement of his patents.

Further Reading
R.S. Fitton, 1989, *The Arkwrights, Spinners of Fortune*, Manchester (draws together the fullest details of John Smalley).
R.L. Hills, 1969, *Power in the Industrial Revolution*, Manchester (includes details of the agreement with Arkwright).
A.H. Dodd, 1971, *The Industrial Revolution in North Wales*, Cardiff; E.J. Foulkes, 1964, 'The cotton spinning factories of Flintshire, 1777–1866', *Flintshire Historical Society Journal* 21 (provide more information about his cotton mill at Holywell).

RLH

Smeaton, John

b. 8 June 1724 Austhorpe, near Leeds, Yorkshire, England
d. 28 October 1792 Austhorpe, near Leeds, Yorkshire, England

English mechanical and civil engineer.

As a boy, Smeaton showed mechanical ability, making for himself a number of tools and models. This practical skill was backed by a sound education, probably at Leeds Grammar School. At the age of 16 he entered his father's office; he seemed set to follow his father's profession in the law. In 1742 he went to London to continue his legal studies, but he preferred instead, with his father's reluctant permission, to set up as a scientific instrument maker and dealer and opened a shop of his own in 1748. About this time he began attending meetings of the Royal Society and presented several papers on instruments and mechanical subjects, being elected a Fellow in 1753. His interests were turning towards engineering but were informed by scientific principles grounded in careful and accurate observation.

In 1755 the second Eddystone lighthouse, on a reef some 14 miles (23 km) off the English coast at Plymouth, was destroyed by fire. The President of the Royal Society was consulted as to a suitable engineer to undertake the task of constructing a new one, and he unhesitatingly suggested Smeaton. Work began in 1756 and was completed in three years to produce the first great wave-swept stone lighthouse. It was constructed of Portland stone blocks, shaped and pegged both together and to the base rock, and bonded by hydraulic cement, scientifically developed by Smeaton. It withstood the storms of the English Channel for over a century, but by 1876 erosion of the rock had weakened the structure and a replacement had to be built. The upper portion of Smeaton's lighthouse was re-erected on a suitable base on Plymouth Hoe, leaving the original base portion on the reef as a memorial to the engineer.

The Eddystone lighthouse made Smeaton's reputation and from then on he was constantly in demand as a consultant in all kinds of engineering projects. He carried out a number himself, notably the 38 mile (61 km) long Forth and Clyde canal with thirty-nine locks, begun in 1768 but for financial reasons not completed until 1790. In 1774 he took charge of the Ramsgate Harbour works.

On the mechanical side, Smeaton undertook a systematic study of water- and windmills, to determine the design and construction to achieve the greatest power output. This work issued forth as the paper 'An experimental enquiry concerning the natural powers of water and wind to turn mills' and exerted a considerable influence on mill design during the early part of the Industrial Revolution. Between 1753 and 1790 Smeaton constructed no fewer than forty-four mills.

Meanwhile, in 1756 he had returned to Austhorpe, which continued to be his home base for the rest of his life. In 1767, as a result of the disappointing performance of an engine he had been involved with at New River Head, Islington, London, Smeaton began his important study of the steam-engine. Smeaton was the first to apply scientific principles to the steam-engine and achieved the most notable improvements in its efficiency since its invention by **Newcomen**, until its radical overhaul by James **Watt**. To compare the performance of engines quantitatively, he introduced the concept of 'duty', i.e. the weight of water that could be raised 1 ft (30 cm) while burning one bushel (84 lb or 38 kg) of coal. The first engine to embody his improvements was erected at Long Benton colliery in Northumberland in 1772, with a duty of 9.45 million pounds, compared to the best figure obtained previously of 7.44 million pounds. One source of heat loss he attributed to inaccurate boring of the cylinder, which he was able to improve through his close association with Carron Ironworks near Falkirk, Scotland.

Principal Honours and Distinctions
FRS 1753.

Bibliography
1759, 'An experimental enquiry concerning the natural powers of water and wind to turn mills', *Philosophical Transactions of the Royal Society*.
Towards the end of his life, Smeaton intended to write accounts of his many works but only completed *A Narrative of the Eddystone Lighthouse*, 1791, London.

Further Reading
S. Smiles, 1874, *Lives of the Engineers: Smeaton and Rennie*, London.
A.W. Skempton, (ed.), 1981, *John Smeaton FRS*, London: Thomas Telford.
L.T.C. Rolt and J.S. Allen, 1977, *The Steam Engine of Thomas Newcomen*, 2nd edn, Hartington: Moorland Publishing, esp. pp. 108–18 (gives a good description of his work on the steam-engine).

LRD

Smirke, Sydney
b. 1798 London, England
d. 8 December 1877 Tunbridge Wells, England

English architect who created the circular reading room in the British Museum in London.

Apart from his considerable architectural practice, Sydney Smirke was responsible, in particular, for two structures in which he utilized the increasingly popular combination of iron and glass, their popularity stemming not least from the fire hazard in urban centres. In 1834 he adapted James Wyatt's Pantheon, the famous concert and masquerade hall in Oxford Street that had been opened in 1772, refitting the building as a shopping centre.

Smirke is best known for his creation of the circular reading room in London's British Museum, which had been designed by his brother Sir Robert Smirke (1823–47). The reading room was designed within a central courtyard, conceived as a circular domed structure by the Chief Librarian and Keeper of the Department of Printed Books, Antonio Panizzi, and executed by Smirke; he covered the courtyard with a cast-iron domed structure (1854–7).

Principal Honours and Distinctions

RA 1859. Royal Academy Professor of Architecture 1861–5. FRS. RIBA Royal Gold Medal 1860.

Further Reading

Roger Dixon and Stefan Muthesius, 1978, *Victorian Architecture*, Thames & Hudson.

J. Mordaunt-Crook, 1977, *Seven Victorian Architects*, Pennsylvania State University Press.

DY

Smith, Charles Shaler

b. 1836 Pittsburgh, Pennsylvania, USA
d. 1886 St Louis, Missouri, USA

American bridge engineer.

Smith's early career started as an assistant to Albert Fink; he later became a divisional engineer for the Louisville and Nashville Railroad. During the Civil War, he served as a Captain of Engineers in the Confederate Army. In 1886 he went into partnership with Benjamin H. and Charles H. Latrobe in the Baltimore Bridge Company; his greatest achievement was the Kentucky Railroad Bridge built for the Cincinnati Southern Railroad in 1876–7. The cantilever that he used for this bridge was entirely novel, and soon became the standard type of construction for long spans. He is also well known for the Lachine bridge across the St Lawrence River near Montreal, Quebec, which was started in 1880 and was, for many years, the only continuous-span bridge of any importance in North America.

Further Reading

1964, *Concise Dictionary of American Biography*, New York: Charles Scribner.

IMcN

Smith, Sir Francis Pettit

b. 9 February 1808 Copperhurst Farm, near Hythe, Kent, England
d. 12 February 1874 South Kensington, London, England

English inventor of the screw propeller.

Smith was the only son of Charles Smith, Postmaster at Hythe, and his wife Sarah (née Pettit). After education at a private school in Ashford, Kent, he took to farming, first on Romney Marsh, then at Hendon, Middlesex. As a boy, he showed much skill in the construction of model boats, especially in devising their means of propulsion. He maintained this interest into adult life and in 1835 he made a model propelled by a screw driven by a spring. This worked so well that he became convinced that the screw propeller offered a better method of propulsion than the paddle wheels that were then in general use. This notion so fired his enthusiasm that he virtually gave up farming to devote himself to perfecting his invention. The following year he produced a better model, which he successfully demonstrated to friends on his farm at Hendon and afterwards to the public at the Adelaide Gallery in London. On 31 May 1836 Smith was granted a patent for the propulsion of vessels by means of a screw.

The idea of screw propulsion was not new, however, for it had been mooted as early as the seventeenth century and since then several proposals had been advanced, but without successful practical application. Indeed, simultaneously but quite independently of Smith, the Swedish engineer John **Ericsson** had invented the ship's propeller and obtained a patent on 13 July 1836, just weeks after Smith. But Smith was completely unaware of this and pursued his own device in the belief that he was the sole inventor.

With some financial and technical backing, Smith was able to construct a 10 ton boat driven by a screw and powered by a steam engine of about 6 hp (4.5 kW). After showing it off to the public, Smith tried it out at sea, from Ramsgate round to Dover and Hythe, returning in stormy weather. The screw performed well in both calm and rough water. The engineering world seemed opposed to the new method of propulsion, but the Admiralty gave cautious encouragement in 1839 by ordering that the 237 ton *Archimedes* be equipped with a screw. It showed itself superior to the *Vulcan*, one of the fastest paddle-driven ships in the Navy. The ship was put through its paces in several ports, including Bristol, where Isambard Kingdom **Brunel** was constructing his *Great Britain*, the first large iron ocean-going vessel. Brunel was so impressed that he adapted his ship for screw propulsion.

Meanwhile, in spite of favourable reports, the Admiralty were dragging their feet and ordered further trials, fitting Smith's four-bladed propeller to the *Rattler*, then under construction and completed in 1844. The trials were a complete success and propelled their lordships of the Admiralty to a decision to equip twenty ships with screw propulsion, under Smith's supervision.

At last the superiority of screw propulsion was generally accepted and virtually universally adopted. Yet Smith gained little financial reward for his invention and in 1850 he retired to Guernsey to resume his farming life. In 1860 financial pressures compelled him to accept the position of Curator of Patent Models at the Patent Museum in South Kensington, London, a post he held until his death. Belated recognition by the Government, then headed by Lord Palmerston, came in 1855 with the grant of an annual pension of £200. Two years later Smith received unofficial recognition when he was presented with a national testimonial, consisting of a service of plate and nearly £3,000 in cash subscribed largely by the shipbuilding and engineering community. Finally, in 1871 Smith was honoured with a knighthood.

Principal Honours and Distinctions
Knighted 1871.

Further Reading
Obituary, 1874, *Illustrated London News* (7 February).
1856, *On the Invention and Progress of the Screw Propeller*, London (provides biographical details).
Smith and his invention are referred to in papers in *Transactions of the Newcomen Society*, 14 (1934): 9; 19 (1939): 145–8, 155–7, 161–4, 237–9.

LRD

Smith, J.
fl. 1830s Scotland

Scottish inventor of the first endless chain of flats for carding.

Carding by hand required a pair of hand cards. The lump of tangled fibres was teased out by pulling one card across the other to even out the fibres and transfer them onto one of the cards from which they could be rolled up into a rollag or slubbing. When **Arkwright** began to use cylinder cards, the fibres were teased out as they passed from one cylinder to the next. In order to obtain a greater carding area, he soon introduced smaller cylinders and placed strips of flat card above the periphery of the main cylinder. These became clogged with short fibres and dirt, so they had to be lifted off and cleaned or 'stripped' at intervals. The first to invent a self-stripping card was Archibald Buchanan, at the Catrine mills in Ayrshire, with his patent in 1823. In his arrangement each flat was turned upside down and stripped by a rotary brush. This was improved by Smith in 1834 and patented in the same year. Smith fixed the flats on an endless chain so that they travelled around the periphery of the top of the main cylinder. Just after the point where they left the cylinder, Smith placed a rotary brush and a comb to clear the brush. In this way each flat in turn was properly and regularly cleaned.

Smith was an able mechanic and Managing Partner of the Deanston mills in Scotland. He visited Manchester, where he was warmly received on the introduction of his machine there at about the same time as he patented it in Scotland. The carding engine he designed was complex, for he arranged a double feed to obtain greater production. While this part of his patent was not developed, his chain or endless flats became the basis used in later cotton carding engines. He took out at least half a dozen other patents for textile machinery. These included two in 1834, the first for a self-acting mule and the second with J.C. **Dyer** for improvements to winding on to spools. There were further spinning patents in 1839 and 1844 and more for preparatory machinery including carding in 1841 and 1842. He was also interested in agriculture and invented a subsoil plough and other useful things.

Bibliography

1834, British patent no. 6,560 (self-stripping card).

1834, British patent no. 656 (self-acting mule).

1839, British patent no. 8,054.

1841, British patent no. 8,796 (carding machine).

1842, British patent no. 9,313 (carding machine).

1844, British patent no. 10,080.

Further Reading

E. Leigh, 1875, *The Science of Modern Cotton Spinning*, Manchester (provides a good account of Smith's carding engine).

W. English, 1969, *The Textile Industry*, London (covers the development of the carding engine).

RLH

Smith, Oberlin

b. 22 March 1840 Cincinnati, Ohio, USA
d. 18 July 1926

American mechanical engineer, pioneer in experiments with magnetic recording.

Of English descent, Smith embarked on an education in mechanical engineering, graduating from West Jersey Academy, Bridgeton, New Jersey, in 1859. In 1863 he established a machine shop in Bridgeton, New Jersey, that became the Ferracute Machine Company in 1877, eventually specializing in the manufacture of presses for metalworking. He seems to have subscribed to design principles considered modern even in the 1990s, 'always giving attention to the development of artistic form in combination with simplicity, and with massive strength where required' (bibliographic reference below). He was successful in his business, and developed and patented a large number of mechanical constructions.

Inspired by the advent of the phonograph of **Edison**, in 1878 Smith obtained the tin-foil mechanical phonograph, analysed its shortcomings and performed some experiments in magnetic recording. He filed a caveat in the US Patent Office in order to be protected while he 'reduced the invention to practice'. However, he did not follow this trail. When there was renewed interest in practical sound recording and reproduction in 1888 (the constructions of **Berliner**

and Bell & Tainter), Smith published an account of his experiments in the journal *Electrical World*. In a corrective letter three weeks later it is clear that he was aware of the physical requirements for the interaction between magnetic coil and magnetic medium, but his publications also indicate that he did not as such obtain reproduction of recorded sound.

Smith did not try to develop magnetic recording, but he felt it imperative that he be given credit for conceiving the idea of it. When accounts of Valdemar **Poulsen**'s work were published in 1900, Smith attempted to prove some rights in the invention in the US Patent Office, but to no avail.

He was a highly respected member of both his community and engineering societies, and in later life became interested in the anti-slavery cause that had also been close to the heart of his parents, as well as in the YMCA movement and in women's suffrage.

Bibliography

Apart from numerous technical papers, he wrote the book *Press Working of Metals*, 1896. His accounts on the magnetic recording experiments were 'Some possible forms of phonograph', *Electrical World* (8 September 1888): 161 ff, and 'Letter to the Editor', *Electrical World* (29 September 1888): 179.

Further Reading

F.K. Engel, 1990, *Documents on the Invention of Magnetic Recording in 1878*, New York: Audio Engineering Society, Reprint no. 2,914 (G2) (a good overview of the material collected by the Oberlin Smith Society, Bridgeton, New Jersey, in particular as regards the recording experiments; it is here that it is doubted that Valdemar Poulsen developed his ideas independently).

GB-N

Smith, Willoughby

b. 16 April 1828 Great Yarmouth, England
d. 17 July 1891 Eastbourne, England

English engineer of submarine telegraph cables who observed that light reduced the resistance of selenium.

Smith joined the Gutta Percha Company, London, in 1848 and successfully experimented with the use of gutta-percha, a natural form of latex, for the insulation of conducting wires. As a result, he was made responsible for the laying of the first cross-Channel cable between Dover and Calais in 1850. Four years later he laid the first Mediterranean cable between Spezia, Italy, and Corsica and Sardinia, later extending it to Algeria. On its completion he became Manager of the Gutta Percha works, which in 1864 became the Telegraph and Construction Company. In 1865 he assisted on board the *Great Eastern* with the laying of the transatlantic cable by **Bright**.

Clearly his management responsibilities did not stop him from experimenting practically. In 1866 he discovered that the resistance of a selenium rod was reduced by the action of incident light, an early discovery of the photoelectric effect more explicitly observed by **Hertz** and subsequently explained by Einstein. In 1883 he read a paper to the Society of Telegraph Engineers (later the Institution of Electrical Engineers), suggesting the possibility of wireless communication with moving trains, an idea that was later successfully taken up by others, and in 1888 he demonstrated the use of water as a practical means of communication with a lighthouse. Four years later, after his death, the system was tried between Alum Bay and the Needles in the Isle of Wight, and it was used subsequently for the Fastnet Rock lighthouse some 10 miles (16 km) off the south-west coast of Ireland.

Principal Honours and Distinctions
Founder and Council Member of the Society of Telegraph Engineers 1871; President 1873.

Bibliography
The effect of light on the resistance of selenium was reported in a letter to the Vice-Chairman of the Society of Telegraph Engineers on 4 February 1873.
7 June 1897, British patent no. 8,159 (the use of water, instead of cable, as a conductor).
2 November 1888, article in *Electrician* (describes his idea of using water as a conductor, rather than cable).

Further Reading
E. Hawkes, 1927, *Pioneers of Wireless*, London: Methuen.
C.T. Bright, 1898, *Submarine Cables, Their History, Construction and Working*.

See also **Field, Cyrus West**.

KF

Snellen, Hermann
b. 18 February 1834 Zeist, near Utrecht, the Netherlands
d. 18 January 1908 Utrecht, the Netherlands

Dutch ophthalmologist who developed scientifically based visual testing types.

Snellen took his degree in medicine at Utrecht in 1857, and after continued study was appointed Lecturer in Ophthalmology and Surgeon to the Hospital for Diseases of the Eye. In 1877 he succeeded Franciscus Cornelius Donders, an outstanding figure in the development of the understanding of the optics and physiology of vision, as Professor. He held this post until 1899 when he was succeeded by his son.

Although involved in virtually all aspects of the speciality, he particularly laid the basis for the scientific recording of visual acuity with the publication of his *Optotypes* in 1862. Optotypes were based on the concept of an average standard of vision permitting the discrimination of separate objects which subtended an angle of one minute of arc on the retina. While the concept does not take into account aspects of vision such as perception, it has stood the test of time in terms of practicality, even when abstract figures such as Landolt's rings replace the lines of single letters of the original.

Snellen originated many other advances of a surgical nature, his procedure for eyelid deformity is still practised, and he developed the use of glass in the manufacture of artificial eyes.

Principal Honours and Distinctions
Honorary Member and Bowman Lecturer, Ophthalmological Society, UK.

Bibliography
1862, *Optotypes/Ad visum determinandum*, Utrecht.
1874, *Des Functionem Sprungen*.
1862, *Scala tipografica per mesurare il visus*.
Numerous papers in *Graefes Archiv für Augenkinde* and the *Graefe-Saemisch Handbuch*.

Further Reading
S. Duke-Elder, 1969, *System of Ophthalmology*, London.
1973, *The Foundations of Ophthalmology*, Vol. 5.
MG

Snodgrass, Neil
fl. late 1790s Scotland

Scottish inventor of the scutcher for opening and cleaning raw cotton.

Raw cotton arrived in Britain in tightly packed bales. Before spinning, the fibres had to be opened out, and dirt, seeds and bits of plant had to be removed. This was an unpleasant and fatiguing job usually carried out by women and children. By 1800 it could be done by two machines. The first stage in opening was the 'willow' and then the cotton was passed through the 'scutcher' to open it further and give it a more effective cleaning. These machines reduced the labour of the operation to about one-twentieth of what it had been. The scutching machine was constructed by Snodgrass and first used at Houston's mill in Johnstone, near Paisley, in 1797. It was derived from the threshing machine invented by Andrew **Meikle** of Phantassie in 1786. In the scutcher, revolving bars beat the cotton to separate the fibres from the trash. As the dirt fell out, the cotton was blown forward by a fan and was rolled up into a lap at the end of the machine. Scutchers were not introduced to Manchester until 1808 or 1809 and further improvements were soon made to them.

Further Reading
R.L. Hills, 1970, *Power in the Industrial Revolution*, Manchester (covers the development of the scutcher).
W. English, 1970, *The Textile Industry*, London (provides a brief account).
RLH

Soane, Sir John
b. 20 September 1753 Whitchurch, England
d. 20 January 1837 London, England

English architect whose highly personalized architectural style foreshadowed the modern architecture of a century later.

Between 1777 and 1780 Soane studied in Italy on a Travelling Scholarship, working in Rome but also making extensive excursions further south to Paestum and Sicily to study the early and more severely simple Greek temples there.

His architectural career began in earnest with his appointment as Surveyor to the Bank of England in 1788. He held this post until 1833 and during this time developed his highly individual style, which was based upon a wide range of classical sources extending from early Greek to Byzantine themes. His own work became progressively more linear and austere, his domes and arches shallower and more segmental. During the 1790s and early 1800s Soane redesigned several halls in the Bank, notably the Bank Stock Office, which in 1791 necessitated technological experimentation.

The redesigning was required because of security problems which limited window openings to high-level positions and a need for fireproof construction because the site was so restricted. Soane solved the difficulties by introducing light through lunettes set high in the walls and through a Roman-style *oculus* in the centrally placed shallow dome. He utilized hollow terracotta pots as a lightweight material in the segmental vaulting.

Sadly, the majority of Soane's work in the Bank interior was lost in the rebuilding during the 1930s, but Soane went on to develop his architectural style in his houses and churches as well as in a quantity of public buildings in Whitehall and Westminster.

Principal Honours and Distinctions
Knighted 1831. Fellow Society of Antiquaries 1795. RA 1802. Royal Academy Professor of Architecture 1806. FRS 1821.

Further Reading
Sir John Summerson, 1952, *Sir John Soane, 1753–1837*, Art and Technics.
Dorothy Stroud, 1961, *The Architecture of Sir John Soane*, Studio.
DY

Sobrero, Ascanio
b. 12 October 1812 Cassale, Monteferrato, Italy
d. 26 May 1888 Turin, Italy

Italian chemist, inventor of nitroglycerine.

Sobrero initially studied medicine, qualifying as

both a physician and surgeon, and then went on to study chemistry in Turin, Paris and Giessen. In 1847 he created nitroglycerine by slowly adding glycerine to a mixture of nitric and sulphuric acids. The explosive injured both him and a number of others in the laboratory, and he was so horrified by its power and its potential effect on warfare that he refused to exploit his discovery; its introduction into general use thus had to wait for Immanuel and Alfred **Nobel**. In 1849 Sobrero was appointed Professor of Applied Chemistry at the Technical Institute, Turin, and he later became Professor of Pure Chemistry as well. He retired in 1882.

Bibliography
He was the author of numerous scientific papers reflecting his wide-ranging interests in chemistry.

CM

Soemmerring, Samuel Thomas von

b. 28 January 1755 Torun, Poland (later Thorn, Prussia)
d. 2 March 1830 Frankfurt, Germany

German physician who devised an early form of electric telegraph.

Soemmerring appears to have been a distinguished anatomist and physiologist who in 1805 became a member of the Munich Academy of Sciences. Whilst experimenting with electric currents in acid solutions in 1809, he observed the bubbles of gases produced by the dissociation process. Using this effect at the receiver, he devised a telegraph consisting of twenty-six parallel wires (one for each letter of the alphabet) and was able to transmit messages over a distance of 2 miles (3 km), but the idea was not commercially viable. In 1812, with the help of Schilling, he experimented with soluble indiarubber as a possible cable insulator.

Principal Honours and Distinctions
Knight of the Order of St Anne of Russia 1818. Hon. Member of St Petersburg Imperial Academy of Sciences 1819. FRS 1827.

Bibliography
Soemmerring's 'electrolytic' telegraph was described in a paper read before the Munich Academy of Sciences on 29 August 1809.

Further Reading
J.J. Fahie, 1884, *A History of Electric Telegraphy to the Year 1837*, London: E&F Spon.
E. Hawkes, 1927, *Pioneers of Wireless*, London: Methuen.

See also **Morse, Samuel Finley Breeze**.

KF

Solvay, Ernest

b. 16 April 1838 Rebcq, near Brussels, Belgium
d. 26 May 1922 Brussels, Belgium

Belgian manufacturer, first successfully to produce soda by the ammonia–soda process.

From the beginning of the nineteenth century, soda had been manufactured by the **Leblanc** process. Important though it was, serious drawbacks had shown themselves early on. The worst was the noxious alkali waste left after the extraction of the soda, in such large quantities that two tons of waste were produced for one of soda. The first attempt to work out an alternative process was by the French scientist and engineer A.J. Fresnel, but it failed. The process consisted essentially of passing carbon dioxide into a solution of ammonia in brine (sodium chloride). The product, sodium bicarbonate, could easily be converted to soda by heating. For over half a century, practical difficulties, principally the volatility of the ammonia, dogged the process and a viable solution eluded successive chemists, including James **Muspratt** and William Deacon.

Finally, Ernest Solvay and his brother Alfred tackled the problem, and in 1861 they filed a Belgian patent for improvements, notably the introduction of a carbonating tower, which made the process continuous. The first works were set up at Couillet in 1863, but four further years of hard work were still needed to overcome teething troubles. Once the Solvay ammonia–soda process was working well, it made rapid strides. It was introduced into Britain in 1872 under licence to Ludwig **Mond** and four years later Solvay opened the large Dombaske works in France.

Solvay was a member of the Belgian Senate and a Minister of State. International institutes of physics, chemistry and sociology are named after him.

Further Reading
P. Heger and C. Lefebvre, 1919, *La vie d'Ernest Solvay*.
Obituary, 1922, *Ind. Eng. Chem.*: 1,156.

LRD

Somerset, Edward, 2nd Marquis of Worcester

b. 1601
d. 3 April 1667 Lambeth (?), London, England

English inventor of a steam-operated pump for raising water, described in his work A Century of . . . Inventions.

Edward Somerset became 6th Earl and 2nd Marquis of Worcester and Titular Earl of Glamorgan. He was educated privately and then abroad, visiting Germany, Italy and France. He was made Councillor of Wales in 1633 and Deputy Lord Lieutenant of Monmouthshire in 1635. On the outbreak of the Civil War, he was commissioned to levy forces against the Scots in 1640. He garrisoned Raglan Castle for the King and was employed by Charles I to bring troops in from Ireland. He was declared an enemy of the realm by Parliament and was banished, remaining in France for some years. On the Restoration, he recovered most of his estates, principally in South Wales, and was able to devote most of his time to mechanical studies and experiments.

Soon after 1626, he had employed the services of a skilled Dutch or German mechanic, Caspar Kaltoff, to make small-scale models for display to interested people. In 1638 he showed Charles I a 14 ft (4.3 m) diameter wheel carrying forty weights that was claimed to have solved the problem of perpetual motion. He wrote his *Century of the Names and Scantlings of Such Inventions as at Present I Can Call to Mind to have Tried and Perfected* in 1655, but it was not published until 1663: no. 68 describes 'An admirable and most forcible way to drive up water by fire', which has been claimed as an early steam-engine. Before the Civil War he made experiments at Raglan Castle, and after the war he built one of his engines at Vauxhall, London, where it raised water to a height of 40 ft (12 m). An Act of Parliament enabling Worcester to receive the benefit and profits of his water-commanding engine for ninety-nine years did not restore his fortunes. Descriptions of this invention are so vague that it cannot be reconstructed.

Bibliography
1655, *Century of the Names and Scantlings of Such Inventions as at Present I Can Call to Mind to have Tried and Perfected*.

Further Reading
H. Dircks, 1865, *The Life, Times and Scientific Labours of the Second Marquis of Worcester*.
Dictionary of National Biography, 1898, Vol. L, London: Smith Elder & Co. (mainly covers his political career).
H.W. Dickinson, 1938, *A Short History of the Steam Engine*, Cambridge University Press (discusses his steam engine invention).
W.H. Thorpe, 1932–3, 'The Marquis of Worcester and Vauxhall', *Transactions of the Newcomen Society* 13.

RLH

Sommeiller, Germain

b. 15 March 1815 St Jeoire, Haute-Savoie, France
d. 11 July 1874 St Jeoire, Haute-Savoie, France

French civil engineer, builder of the Mont Cénis tunnel in the Alps.

Having been employed in railway construction in Sardinia, Sommeiller was working as an engineer at the University of Turin when, in 1857, he was commissioned to take charge of the French part in the construction of the 13 km (8 mile) tunnel under Mont Cénis between Modane, France, and Bardonècchia, Italy. This was to be the first long-distance tunnel through rock in the Alps driven from two headings with no intervening shafts; it is a landmark in the history of technology thanks to the use of a number of pioneering techniques in its construction.

As steam power was unsuitable because of the difficulties in transmitting power over long distances, Sommeiller developed ideas for the use of compressed-air machinery, first mooted by Daniel Colladon of Geneva in 1855; this also solved the problems of ventilation. He also decided to adapt the principle of his compressed-air ram to supply extra power to locomotives on steep gradients. In 1860 he took out a patent in France for a combined compressor-pump, and in 1861 his first percussion drill, mounted on a carriage, was introduced. Although it was of little use at first, Sommeiller improved his drill through trial and error, including the use of the diamond drill-crowns patented by Georges Auguste **Le-schot** in 1862. The invention of dynamite by Alfred **Nobel** contributed decisively to the speedy completion of the tunnel by the end of 1870, several years ahead of schedule.

Further Reading
A. Schwenger-Lerchenfeld, 1884, *Die Überschie-nung der Alpen*, Berlin; reprint 1983, Berlin: Moers, pp. 60–77 (explains how the use of compressed air for rock drilling in the Mont Cénis tunnel was a complex process of innova-tions to which several engineers contributed).
W. Bersch, 1898, *Mit Schlägel und Eisen*, Vienna: reprint 1985 (with introd. by W. Kroker), Düsseldorf, pp. 242–4.

WK

Song Yingxing (Sung Ying-Hsing)
b. 1600 China
d. *c.*1650

Chinese writer on technology and industry.

Song was an outstanding encyclopedist in the field of technology and industrial processes. He produced the *Tian Gong Kai Wu* (The Exploita-tion of the Works of Nature) of 1637, China's greatest technological classic, which dealt with agriculture and industry rather than engineering. It covered a wide range of subjects, including hydraulic devices and irrigation, silk and other textiles, salt and sugar technology, ceramics, pearls and jade, papermaking and ink, metallurgy of iron, bronze, silver, tin and lead, and trans-port. The work incorporated the finest Chinese illustrations on these subjects. Strangely, it fell into obscurity and it was a copy preserved in Japan that became the basis for later editions.

Bibliography
1637, *Tian Gong Kai Wu.*

Further Reading
J. Needham, *Science and Civilisation in China*, Cambridge: Cambridge University Press, 1965–86, Vols IV.2, pp. 171–2, 559; IV.3, many scattered references for it is an essential source of information about Chinese technol-ogy.

LRD

Sopwith, Sir Thomas ('Tommy') Octave Murdoch
b. 18 January 1888 London, England
d. 27 January 1989 Stockbridge, Hampshire, England

English aeronautical engineer and industrialist.

Son of a successful mining engineer, Sopwith did not shine at school and, having been turned down by the Royal Navy as a result, attended an engineering college. His first interest was motor cars and, while still in his teens, he set up a busi-ness in London with a friend in order to sell them; he also took part in races and rallies.

Sopwith's interest in aviation came initially through ballooning, and in 1906 he purchased his own balloon. Four years later, inspired by the recent flights across the Channel to France and after a joy-ride at Brooklands, he bought an *Avis* monoplane, followed by a larger biplane, and taught himself to fly. He was awarded the Royal Aero Society's Aviator Certificate No. 31 on 21 November 1910, and he quickly distinguished himself in flying competitions on both sides of the Atlantic and started his own flying school. In his races he was ably supported by his friend Fred Sigrist, a former motor engineer. Among the people Sopwith taught to fly were an Australian, Harry Hawker, and Major Hugh Trenchard, who later became the 'father' of the RAF.

In 1912, depressed by the poor quality of the aircraft on trial for the British Army, Sopwith, in conjunction with Hawker and Sigrist, bought a skating rink in Kingston-upon-Thames and, as-sisted by Fred Sigrist, started to design and build his first aircraft, the Sopwith *Hybrid*. He sold this to the Royal Navy in 1913, and the following year his aviation manufacturing company became the Sopwith Aviation Company Ltd. That year a seaplane version of his Sopwith *Tabloid* won the Schneider Trophy in the second running of this speed competition. During 1914–18, Sopwith concentrated on producing fighters (or 'scouts' as they were then called), with the *Pup*, the *Camel*, the 1½ *Strutter*, the *Snipe* and the Sop-with *Triplane* proving among the best in the war. He also pioneered several ideas to make flying easier for the pilot, and in 1915 he patented his adjustable tailplane and his 1½ Strutter was the first aircraft to be fitted with air brakes. During the four years of the First World War, Sopwith

Aviation designed thirty-two different aircraft types and produced over 16,000 aircraft.

The end of the First World War brought recession to the aircraft industry and in 1920 Sopwith, like many others, put his company into receivership; none the less, he immediately launched a new, smaller company with Hawker, Sigrist and V.W. Eyre, which they called the H.G. Hawker Engineering Company Ltd to avoid any confusion with the former company. He began by producing cars and motor cycles under licence, but was determined to resume aircraft production. He suffered an early blow with the death of Hawker in an air crash in 1921, but soon began supplying aircraft to the Royal Air Force again. In this he was much helped by taking on a new designer, Sydney **Camm**, in 1923, and during the next decade they produced a number of military aircraft types, of which the *Hart* light bomber and the *Fury* fighter, the first to exceed 200 mph (322 km/h), were the best known. In the mid-1930s Sopwith began to build a large aviation empire, acquiring first the Gloster Aircraft Company and then, in quick succession, Armstrong–Whitworth, Armstrong–Siddeley Motors Ltd and its aero-engine counterpart, and A.V. Roe, which produced Avro aircraft. Under the umbrella of the Hawker Siddeley Aircraft Company (set up in 1935) these companies produced a series of outstanding aircraft, ranging from the Hawker *Hurricane*, through the Avro *Lancaster* to the Gloster *Meteor*, Britain's first in-service jet aircraft, and the Hawker *Typhoon*, *Tempest* and *Hunter*. When Sopwith retired as Chairman of the Hawker Siddeley Group in 1963 at the age of 75, a prototype jump-jet (the *P-1127*) was being tested, later to become the *Harrier*, a far cry from the fragile biplanes of 1910.

Sopwith also had a passion for yachting and came close to wresting the America's Cup from the USA in 1934 when sailing his yacht *Endeavour*, which incorporated a number of features years ahead of their time; his greatest regret was that he failed in his attempts to win this famous yachting trophy for Britain. After his retirement as Chairman of the Hawker Siddeley Group, he remained on the Board until 1978. The British aviation industry had been nationalized in April 1977, and Hawker Siddeley's aircraft interests merged with the British Aircraft Corporation to become British Aerospace (BAe). Nevertheless, by then the Group had built up a wide range of companies in the field of mechanical and electrical engineering, and its board conferred on Sopwith the title Founder and Life President.

Principal Honours and Distinctions
Knighted 1953. CBE 1918.

Bibliography
1961, 'My first ten years in aviation', *Journal of the Royal Aeronautical Society* (April) (a very informative and amusing paper).

Further Reading
A. Bramson, 1990, *Pure Luck: The Authorized Biography of Sir Thomas Sopwith, 1888–1989*, Wellingborough: Patrick Stephens.
B. Robertson, 1970, *Sopwith. The Man and His Aircraft*, London (a detailed publication giving plans of all the Sopwith aircraft).

CM/JDS

Sorocold, George
b. probably Ashton-in-Makerfield, England
fl. *c.*1685–1715

English civil engineer who set up numerous water-driven pumping plants.

He began to practise in Derbyshire and South Yorkshire and later moved to London, where his most important work was carried out. Little is known of his birth or, indeed, of the date of his death, although it is thought that he may have been born in Ashton-in-Makerfield.

His first known work was a water-driven pumping plant in Derby erected in 1693 to supply water to houses and to points in the town through pipes from the pumps by the river Derwent. These water-driven pumping plants and the delivery of water to various towns were the result of entrepreneurial development by groups of 'adventurers'. Sorocold went on to set up many more pumping plants, including those at Leeds Bridge (1694–5), Macclesfield, Wirksworth, Yarmouth, Portsmouth, Norwich and King's Lynn.

His best-known work was the installation of a pumping plant at the north end of London Bridge to replace a sixteenth-century plant. This consisted of four water-wheels placed between the starlings of the bridge. As the bridge is situated on the tidal Thames, the water-wheels were

659

contrived so that their shafts could be raised or lowered to meet the state of the tidal flow. Whilst the waterworks designed by Sorocold are well known, it is clear that he had come to be regarded as a consulting engineer. One scheme that was carried through was the creation of a navigation between the river Trent and Derby on the line of the river Derwent. He appeared as a witness for the Derwent Navigation Act in 1703. He also held a patent for 'A new machine for cutting and sawing all sorts of boards, timber and stone, and twisting all kinds of ropes, cords and cables by the strength of horses of water': this illustrates that his knowledge of power sources was predominant in his practice.

Further Reading
R. Jenkins, 1936, 'George Sorocold. A chapter in the history of public water supply', *The Collected Papers of Rhys Jenkins*, Newcomen Society.
H. Beighton, 1731, article in *The Philosophical Transactions* (provides details of the London Bridge Waterworks).

KM

Spence, Peter
b. 19 February 1806 Brechin, Forfarshire, Scotland
d. 5 July 1883 Manchester, England

Scottish industrial chemist.

Spence was first apprenticed to a grocer and then joined his uncle's business. When that failed, he found work in a Dundee gasworks. During his spare time he had been studying chemistry, and in 1834 he established a small chemical works in London, which was none too successful. It was after a move to Burgh, near Carlisle, that his prospects brightened, with an improved method for making alum, a substance much used in the dyeing and textile industries. Spence obtained a patent in 1845 for extracting the substance from alum-containing shale by treating the burned shale and iron pyrites with sulphuric acid. He set up a plant at Pendleton, near Manchester, and enlarged the scale of his operation to become the largest manufacturer of alum in the world. The most profitable product was a crude form of alum known as aluminoferric. This came to be much in demand by the paper industry and in the treatment of sewage, an activity of growing im-

portance in mid-Victorian Britain.

Not all of Spence's ventures met with success; his attempts to exploit the phosphate deposits on the island of Redmonds in the West Indies lost heavily. He was an active citizen of Manchester, with a strongly Nonconformist tendency. He supported the cause against atmospheric pollution, although he himself was successfully prosecuted for pollution from his alum works at Pendleton; that prompted a move to Miles Platting, also near Manchester. In 1900, his firm became part of Laporte Industries Ltd.

Further Reading
J. Fenwick Allen, 1907, *Some Founders of the Chemical Industry*, London.
Proc. Manchester Lit. Phil. Soc. (1883–4) 23: 121.

LRD

Spencer, Christopher Miner
b. 10 June 1833 Manchester, Connecticut, USA
d. 14 January 1922 Hartford, Connecticut, USA

American mechanical engineer and inventor.

Christopher M. Spencer served an apprenticeship from 1847 to 1849 in the machine shop at the silk mills of Cheney Brothers in his native town and remained there for a few years as a journeyman machinist. In 1853 he went to Rochester, New York, to obtain experience with machinery other than that used in the textile industry. He then spent some years with the Colt Armory at Hartford, Connecticut, before returning to Cheney Brothers, where he obtained his first patent, which was for a silk-winding machine.

Spencer had long been interested in firearms and in 1860 he obtained a patent for a repeating rifle. The Spencer Repeating Rifle Company was organized for its manufacture, and before the end of the American Civil War about 200,000 rifles had been produced. He patented a number of other improvements in firearms and in 1868 was associated with Charles E. Billings (1835–1920) in the Roper Arms Company, set up at Amherst, Massachusetts, to manufacture Spencer's magazine gun. This was not a success, however, and in 1869 they moved to Hartford, Connecticut, and formed the Billings & Spencer Company. There they developed the technology of the drop hammer and Spencer continued his inventive work, which included an automatic turret lathe for producing metal screws. The patent that he obtained for this in 1873 inexplicably failed to protect the essential feature of the machine which provided the automatic action, with the result that Spencer received no patent right on the most valuable feature of the machine.

In 1874 Spencer withdrew from active connection with Billings & Spencer, although he remained a director, and in 1876 he formed with others the Hartford Machine Screw Company. However, he withdrew in 1882 to form the Spencer Arms Company at Windsor, Connecticut, for the manufacture of another of his inventions, a repeating shotgun. But this company failed and Spencer returned to the field of automatic lathes, and in 1893 he organized the Spencer Automatic Machine Screw Company at Windsor, where he remained until his retirement.

Further Reading

J.W. Roe, 1916, *English and American Tool Builders*, New Haven; reprinted 1926, New York, and 1987, Bradley, Ill. (briefly describes his career and his automatic lathes).
L.T.C. Rolt, 1965, *Tools for the Job*, London; repub. 1986 (gives a brief description of Spencer's automatic lathes).

RTS

Sperry, Elmer Ambrose

b. 21 October 1860 Cincinnatus, Cortland County, New York, USA
d. 16 June 1930 Brooklyn, New York, USA

American entrepreneur who invented the gyrocompass.

Sperry was born into a farming community in Cortland County. He received a rudimentary education at the local school, but an interest in mechanical devices was aroused by the agricultural machinery he saw around him. His attendance at the Normal School in Cortland provided a useful theoretical background to his practical knowledge. He emerged in 1880 with an urge to pursue invention in electrical engineering, then a new and growing branch of technology. Within two years he was able to patent and demonstrate his arc lighting system, complete with its own generator, incorporating new methods of regulating its output. The Sperry Electric Light,

Motor and Car Brake Company was set up to make and market the system, but it was difficult to keep pace with electric-lighting developments such as the incandescent lamp and alternating current, and the company ceased in 1887 and was replaced by the Sperry Electric Company, which itself was taken over by the General Electric Company.

In the 1890s Sperry made useful inventions in electric mining machinery and then in electric street- or tramcars, with his patent electric brake and control system. The patents for the brake were important enough to be bought by General Electric. From 1894 to 1900 he was manufacturing electric motor cars of his own design, and in 1900 he set up a laboratory in Washington, where he pursued various electrochemical processes.

In 1896 he began to work on the practical application of the principle of the gyroscope, where Sperry achieved his most notable inventions, the first of which was the gyrostabilizer for ships. The relatively narrow-hulled steamship rolled badly in heavy seas and in 1904 Ernst Otto Schuck, a German naval engineer, and Louis **Brennan** in England began experiments to correct this; their work stimulated Sperry to develop his own device. In 1908 he patented the active gyrostabilizer, which acted to correct a ship's roll as soon as it started. Three years later the US Navy agreed to try it on a destroyer, the USS *Worden*. The successful trials of the following year led to widespread adoption. Meanwhile, in 1910, Sperry set up the Sperry Gyroscope Company to extend the application to commercial shipping.

At the same time, Sperry was working to apply the gyroscope principle to the ship's compass. The magnetic compass had worked well in wooden ships, but iron hulls and electrical machinery confused it. The great powers' race to build up their navies instigated an urgent search for a solution. In Germany, Anschutz-Kämpfe (1872–1931) in 1903 tested a form of gyrocompass and was encouraged by the authorities to demonstrate the device on the German flagship, the *Deutschland*. Its success led Sperry to develop his own version: fortunately for him, the US Navy preferred a home-grown product to a German one and gave Sperry all the backing he needed. A successful trial on a destroyer led to widespread acceptance in the US Navy, and

Sperry was soon receiving orders from the British Admiralty and the Russian Navy.

In the rapidly developing field of aeronautics, automatic stabilization was becoming an urgent need. In 1912 Sperry began work on a gyrostabilizer for aircraft. Two years later he was able to stage a spectacular demonstration of such a device at an air show near Paris.

Sperry continued research, development and promotion in military and aviation technology almost to the last. In 1926 he sold the Sperry Gyroscope Company to enable him to devote more time to invention.

Principal Honours and Distinctions
John Fritz Medal 1927. President, American Society of Mechanical Engineers 1928.

Bibliography
Sperry filed over 400 patents, of which two can be singled out:
1908, US patent no. 434,048 (ship gyroscope);
1909, US patent no. 519,533 (ship gyrocompass set).

Further Reading
T.P. Hughes, 1971, *Elmer Sperry, Inventor and Engineer*, Baltimore: Johns Hopkins University Press (a full and well-documented biography, with lists of his patents and published writings).

LRD

Spode, Josiah
b. 1754 Stoke-on-Trent, England
d. 16 July 1827 Penkhull, Staffordshire, England

English potter, inventor of bone china and ironstone.

After learning the potter's trade in his father's works, Spode set up in business on his own. He especially favoured blue-printed ware, in particular willow-pattern. He also improved the jasper, Egyptian black and cream ware that were produced by a number of potters at the time. He employed William Copeland, a traveller in the trade, to market his products and together they established a base in London. He later took Copeland into partnership to manage the London end of the business. In 1800 Spode began to make porcelain and introduced bone ash and

feldspar into the paste, increasing the transparency of the ware; it came to be known as that most characteristically English of ware, bone china. In 1805 he introduced an opaque ware under the name of ironstone, much of which was exported to France, where it supplanted faience ware.

The Prince of Wales visited Spode's pottery in 1806 and he was appointed a potter to the King. In 1812 Spode installed a steam-engine in his works and effected many other improvements. Spode was called 'the most successful china manufacturer of his time'; this seems fair, for he won both fame and fortune.

Further Reading
A. Hayden, 1925, *Spode and His Successors: A History of the Pottery 1765–1865*, London.

LRD

Spooner, Charles Easton
b. 1818 Maentwrog, Merioneth (now Gwynedd), Wales
d. 18 November 1889 Portmadoc (now Porthmadog), Wales

English engineer, pioneer of narrow-gauge steam railways.

At the age of 16 Charles Spooner helped his father, James, to build the Festiniog Railway, a horse-and-gravity tramroad; they maintained an even gradient and kept costs down by following a sinuous course along Welsh mountainsides and using a very narrow gauge. This was probably originally 2 ft 1 in. (63.5 cm) from rail centre to rail centre; with the introduction of heavier, and therefore wider, rails the gauge between them was reduced and was eventually standardized at 1 ft 11½ in (60 cm). After James Spooner's death in 1856 Charles Spooner became Manager and Engineer of the Festiniog Railway and sought to introduce steam locomotives. Widening the gauge was impracticable, but there was no precedent for operating a public railway of such narrow gauge by steam. Much of the design work for locomotives for the Festiniog Railway was the responsibility of C.M. Holland, and many possible types were considered: eventually, in 1863, two very small 0–4–0 tank locomotives, with tenders for coal, were built by George **England**.

These locomotives were successful, after initial problems had been overcome, and a passenger train service was introduced in 1865 with equal success. The potential for economical operation offered by such a railway attracted widespread attention, the more so because it had been effectively illegal to build new passenger railways in Britain to other than standard gauge since the Gauge of Railways Act of 1846.

Spooner progressively improved the track, alignment, signalling and rolling stock of the Festiniog Railway and developed it from a tramroad to a miniaturized main line. Increasing traffic led to the introduction in 1869 of the 0–4–4–0 double-Fairlie locomotive *Little Wonder*, built to the patent of Robert **Fairlie**. This proved more powerful than two 0–4–0s and impressive demonstrations were given to engineers from many parts of the world, leading to the widespread adoption of narrow-gauge railways. Spooner himself favoured a gauge of 2 ft 6 in. (76 cm) or 2 ft 9 in. (84 cm). Comparison of the economy of narrow gauges with the inconvenience of a break of gauge at junctions with wider gauges did, however, become a continuing controversy, which limited the adoption of narrow gauges in Britain.

Bogie coaches had long been used in North America but were introduced to Britain by Spooner in 1872, when he had two such coaches built for the Festiniog Railway. Both of these and one of its original locomotives, though much rebuilt, remain in service.

Spooner, despite some serious illnesses, remained Manager of the Festiniog Railway until his death.

Bibliography
1869, jointly with G.A. Huddart, British patent no. 1,487 (improved fishplates).
1869, British patent no. 2,896 (rail-bending machinery).
1871, *Narrow Gauge Railways*, E. & F.N. Spon (includes his description of the Festiniog Railway, reports of locomotive trials and his proposals for narrow-gauge railways).

Further Reading
J.I.C. Boyd, 1975, *The Festiniog Railway*, Blandford: Oakwood Press; C.E. Lee, 1945, *Narrow-Gauge Railways in North Wales*, The Railway Publishing Co. (both give good descriptions of Spooner and the Festiniog Railway).
C. Hamilton Ellis, 1965, *Railway Carriages in the British Isles*, London: George Allen & Unwin, pp. 181–3.

Pihl, Carl Abraham.

PJGR

Sprague, Frank Julian
b. 25 July 1857 Milford, Connecticut, USA
d. 25 October 1934 New York, USA

American electrical engineer and inventor, a leading innovator in electric propulsion systems for urban transport.

Graduating from the United States Naval Academy, Annapolis, in 1878, Sprague served at sea and with various shore establishments. In 1883 he resigned from the Navy and obtained employment with the Edison Company; but being convinced that the use of electricity for motive power was as important as that for illumination, in 1884 he founded the Sprague Electric Railway and Motor Company. Sprague began to develop reliable and efficient motors in large sizes, marketing 15 hp (11 kW) examples by 1885. He devised the method of collecting current by using a wooden, spring-loaded rod to press a roller against the underside of an overhead wire. The installation by Sprague in 1888 of a street tramway on a large scale in Richmond, Virginia, was to become the prototype of the universally adopted trolley system with overhead conductor and the beginning of commercial electric traction. Following the success of the Richmond tramway the company equipped sixty-seven other railways before its merger with Edison General Electric in 1890. The Sprague traction motor supported on the axle of electric streetcars and flexibly mounted to the bogie set a pattern that was widely adopted for many years.

Encouraged by successful experiments with multiple-sheave electric elevators, the Sprague Elevator Company was formed and installed the first set of high-speed passenger cars in 1893–4. These effectively displaced hydraulic elevators in larger buildings. From experience with control systems for these, he developed his system of multiple-unit control for electric trains, which other engineers had considered impracticable. In Sprague's system, a master controller situated in the driver's cab operated electrically at a distance the contactors and reversers which controlled the motors distributed down the train. After years of experiment, Sprague's multiple-unit control was put into use for the first time in 1898 by the Chicago South Side Elevated Railway: within fifteen years multiple-unit operation was used worldwide.

Principal Honours and Distinctions

President, American Institute of Electrical Engineers 1892–3. Franklin Institute Elliot Cresson Medal 1904, Franklin Medal 1921. American Institute of Electrical Engineers Edison Medal 1910.

Bibliography

1888, 'The solution of municipal rapid transit', *Trans. AIEE* 5: 352–98. See 'The multiple unit system for electric railways', *Cassiers Magazine*, (1899) London, repub. 1960, 439–460.
1934, 'Digging in "The Mines of the Motor"', *Electrical Engineering* 53, New York: 695–706 (a short autobiography).

Further Reading

Lionel Calisch, 1913, *Electric Traction*, London: The Locomotive Publishing Co., Ch. 6 (for a near-contemporary view of Sprague's multiple-unit control).
D.C. Jackson, 1934, 'Frank Julian Sprague', *Scientific Monthly* 57: 431–41.
H.C. Passer, 1952, 'Frank Julian Sprague: father of electric traction', in *Men of Business*, ed. W. Miller, Cambridge, Mass., pp. 212–37 (a reliable account).
—— 1953, *The Electrical Manufacturers: 1875–1900*, Cambridge, Mass.
P. Ransome-Wallis (ed.), 1959, *The Concise Encyclopaedia of World Railway Locomotives*, London: Hutchinson, p. 143..
John Marshall, 1978, *A Biographical Dictionary of Railway Engineers*, Newton Abbot: David & Charles.

GW/PJGR

Staite, William Edwards

b. 19 April 1809 Bristol, England
d. 26 September 1854 Caen, France

English inventor who did much to popularize electric lighting in early Victorian England and demonstrated the first self-regulating arc lamp.

Before devoting the whole of his attention to the electric light, Staite was a partner in a business of iron merchants and patented a method of obtaining extracts and essences. From 1834 he attempted to produce a continuous light by electricity. The first public exhibition of Staite's arc lamp incorporating a fixed-rate clockwork mechanism was given in 1847 to the Sunderland Literary and Philosophical Society. He also demonstrated an incandescent lamp with an iridio-platinum filament. Sir Joseph Wilson **Swan** recorded that it was attending lectures by Staite in Sunderland, Newcastle and Carlisle that started him on the quest which many years later was to lead to his incandescent lamp.

In association with William Petrie (1821–1904), Staite made an important advance in the development of arc lamps by introducing automatic regulation of the carbon rods by way of an electromagnet. This was the first of many self-regulating arc lamps that were invented during the nineteenth century employing this principle. A contributory factor in the success of Staite's lamp was the semi enclosure of the arc in a transparent vessel that reduced the consumption of carbons, a feature not used again until the 1890s. His patents included processes for preparing carbons and the construction of primary cells for arc lighting. An improved lamp used by Staite in a theatrical production at Her Majesty's Theatre, London, in April 1849 may be considered the first commercial success of the electric light in England. In spite of the limitations imposed by the use of primary cells as the only available source of power, serious interest in this system of electric lighting was shown by railway companies and dock authorities. However, after he had developed a satisfactory arc lamp, an end to these early experiments was brought about by Staite's death.

Bibliography

3 July 1847, British patent no. 1,1783 (electromagnetic regulation of an arc lamp).
His manuscript 'History of electric light' is in the Institution of Electrical Engineers archives.

Further Reading

J.J. Fahie, 1902, 'Staite and Petrie's electric light 1846–1853', *Electrical Engineer* 30: 297–301, 337–40, 374–6 (a detailed reliable account).

G. Woodward, 1989, 'Staite and Petrie: pioneers of electric lighting', *Proceedings of the Institution of Electrical Engineers* 136 (Part A): 290–6

GW

Stalkartt, Marmaduke

b. 6 April 1750 London (?), England
d. 24 September 1805 Calcutta, India

English naval architect and author of a noted book on shipbuilding.

For a man who contributed much to the history of shipbuilding in Britain, surprisingly little is known of his life and times. The family are reputedly descendants of Danish or Norwegian shipbuilders who emigrated to England around the late seventeenth century. It is known, however, that Marmaduke was the fourth child of his father, Hugh Stalkartt, but the second child of Hugh's second wife.

Stalkartt is believed to have served an apprenticeship at the Naval Yard at Deptford on the Thames. He had advanced sufficiently by 1796 for the Admiralty to send him to India to establish shipyards dedicated to the construction of men-of-war in teak. The worsening supply of oak from England, and to a lesser extent Scotland, coupled with the war with France was making ship procurement one of the great concerns of the time. The ready supply of hardwoods from the subcontinent was a serious attempt to overcome this problem. For some years one of the shipyards in Calcutta was known as Stalkartt's Yard and this gives some credence to the belief that Stalkartt left the Navy while overseas and started his own shipbuilding organization.

Bibliography

1781, *Naval Architecture; or, the Rudiments and Rules of Shipbuilding*, repub. 1787, 1803 (an illustrated textbook).

FMW

Stanhope, Charles, 3rd Earl

b. 3 August 1753 London, England
d. 15 December 1816 Chevening, Kent, England

English politician, scientist and inventor.

Stanhope's schooling at Eton was interrupted in 1764 when the family moved to Geneva; there, he soon showed a talent for scientific pursuits. In 1771 he contributed a paper on the pendulum to the Swedish Academy, which awarded him a prize for it. After his return to London in 1774, he threw himself into politics, earning himself not only a reputation for promoting the liberty of the individual, but also unpopularity for championing the French Revolution.

Stanhope is best known for his inventions in printing. In 1800 he introduced the first successful iron press, known by his name. Its iron frame enabled a whole forme to be printed at one pull, thus speeding up production. The press retained the traditional screw but incorporated a system of levers which increased the pressure on the platen up to the moment of contact with the type, so that fine, sharp impressions were obtained and the work of the pressman was made easier. Stanhope's process for moulding and reproducing formes, known as stereotyping, became important when curved formes were required for cylinder presses. His invention of logotypes for casting type, however, proved a failure. Throughout his political activities, Stanhope devoted time and money to scientific and mechanical matters. Of these, the development of steamships is noteworthy. He took out patents in 1790 and 1807, and in 1796 he constructed the *Kent* for the Admiralty, but it was unsuccessful. In 1810, however, he claimed that a vessel 110 ft (33.5 m) long and 7 ft (2.1 m) in draught 'outsailed the swiftest vessels in the Navy'.

Further Reading

G. Stanhope, 1914, *The Life of Charles, Third Earl Stanhope*, London.

H. Hart, 1966, *Charles Earl Stanhope and the Oxford University Press*, London: Printing Historical Society (a reprint of a paper, originally published in 1896, describing Stanhope's printing inventions; with copious quotations from Stanhope's own writings, together with an essay on the Stanhope press by James Moran).

LRD

Stanier, Sir William Arthur

b. 27 May 1876 Swindon, England
d. 27 September 1965 London, England

English Chief Mechanical Engineer of the London Midland & Scottish Railway, the locomotive stock of which he modernized most effectively.

Stanier's career started when he was Office Boy at the Great Western Railway's Swindon works. He was taken on as a pupil in 1892 and steady promotion elevated him to Works Manager in 1920, under Chief Mechanical Engineer George **Churchward**. In 1923 he became Principal Assistant to Churchward's successor, C.B. Collett. In 1932, at the age of 56 and after some forty years' service with the Great Western Railway (GWR), W.A. Stanier was appointed Chief Mechanical Engineer of the London Midland & Scottish Railway (LMS). This, the largest British railway, had been formed by the amalgamation in 1923 of several long-established railways, including the London & North Western and the Midland, that had strong and disparate traditions in locomotive design. A coherent and comprehensive policy had still to emerge; Stanier did, however, inherit a policy of reducing the number of types of locomotives, in the interest of economy, by the withdrawal and replacement of small classes, which had originated with constituent companies.

Initially as replacements, Stanier brought in to the LMS a series of highly successful standard locomotives; this practice may be considered a development of that of G.J. Churchward on the GWR. Notably, these new locomotives included: the class 5, mixed-traffic 4–6–0; the 8F heavy-freight 2–8–0; and the 'Duchess' 4–6–2 for express passenger trains. Stanier also built, in 1935, a steam-turbine-driven 4–6–2, which became the only steam-turbine locomotive in Britain to have an extended career in regular service, although the economies it provided were insufficient for more of the type to be built. From 1932–3 onwards, and initially as part of a programme to economize on shunting costs by producing a single-manned locomotive, the LMS started to develop diesel shunting locomotives. Stanier delegated much of the responsibility for these to C.E. Fairburn. From 1939 diesel–electric shunting locomotives were being built in quantity for the LMS: this was the first instance of adoption of diesel power on a large scale by a British main-line railway. In a remarkably short time, Stanier transformed LMS locomotive stock, formerly the most backward of the principal British railways, to the point at which it was second to none. He was seconded to the Government as Scientific Advisor to the Ministry of Production in 1942, and retired two years later.

Principal Honours and Distinctions
Knighted 1943. FRS 1944. President, Institution of Mechanical Engineers 1941.

Bibliography
1955, 'George Jackson Churchward', *Transactions of the Newcomen Society* 30 (Stanier provides a unique view of the life and work of his former chief).

Further Reading
O.S. Nock, 1964, *Sir William Stanier, An Engineering Biography*, Shepperton: Ian Allan (a full-length biography).
John Bellwood and David Jenkinson, 1976, *Gresley and Stanier. A Centenary Tribute*, London: HMSO (a comparative account).
C. Hamilton Ellis, 1970, *London Midland & Scottish*, Shepperton: Ian Allan.

PJGR

Stanley, Robert Crooks

b. 1 August 1876 Little Falls, New Jersey, USA
d. 12 February 1951 USA

American mining engineer and metallurgist, originator of Monel Metal.

Robert, the son of Thomas and Ada (Crooks) Stanley, helped to finance his early training at the Stevens Institute of Technology, Hoboken, New Jersey, by working as a manual training instructor at Montclair High School. After graduating in mechanical engineering from Stevens in 1899, and as a mining engineer from the Columbia School of Mines in 1901, he accepted a two-year assignment from the S.S. White Dental Company to investigate platinum-bearing alluvial deposits in British Columbia. This introduced him to the International Nickel Company (Inco), which had been established on 29 March 1902 to amalgamate the major mining companies working the newly discovered cupro-nickel deposits at Sudbury, Ontario. Ambrose Monell,

President of Inco, appointed Stanley as Assistant Superintendent of its American Nickel Works at Camden, near Philadelphia, in 1903. At the beginning of 1904 Stanley was General Superintendent of the Orford Refinery at Bayonne, New Jersey, where most of the output of the Sudbury mines was treated.

Copper and nickel were separated there from the bessemerized matte by the celebrated 'tops and bottoms' process introduced thirteen years previously by R.M. Thompson. It soon occurred to Stanley that such a separation was not invariably required and that, by reducing directly the mixed matte, he could obtain a natural cupronickel alloy which would be ductile, corrosion resistant, and no more expensive to produce than pure copper or nickel. His first experiment, on 30 December 1904, was completely successful. A railway wagon full of bessemerized matte, low in iron, was calcined to oxide, reduced to metal with carbon, and finally desulphurized with magnesium. Ingots cast from this alloy were successfully forged to bars which contained 68 per cent nickel, 23 per cent copper and about 1 per cent iron. The new alloy, originally named after Ambrose Monell, was soon renamed Monel to satisfy trademark requirements. A total of 300,000 ft^2 (27,870 m^2) of this white, corrosion-resistant alloy was used to roof the Pennsylvania Railway Station in New York, and it also found extensive applications in marine work and chemical plant. Stanley greatly increased the output of the Orford Refinery during the First World War, and shortly after becoming President of the company in 1922, he established a new Research and Development Division headed initially by A.J. Wadham and then by Paul D. **Merica**, who at the US Bureau of Standards had first elucidated the mechanism of age-hardening in alloys. In the mid- 1920s a nickel-ore body of unprecedented size was identified at levels between 2,000 and 3,000 ft (600 and 900 m) below the Frood Mine in Ontario. This property was owned partially by Inco and partially by the Mond Nickel Company. Efficient exploitation required the combined economic resources of both companies. They merged on 1 January 1929, when Mond became part of International Nickel. Stanley remained President of the new company until February 1949 and was Chairman from 1937 until his death.

Principal Honours and Distinctions
American Society for Metals Gold Medal. Institute of Metals Platinum Medal 1948.

Further Reading
F.B. Howard-White, 1963, *Nickel*, London: Methuen (a historical review).

ASD

Starr, Albert
b. 1 June 1926 New York, USA

American cardiac surgeon, co-inventor of the Starr–Edwards artificial heart valve.

Starr graduated MM from the Columbia College of Physicians and Surgeons, New York. Following residencies at Johns Hopkins, Baltimore, Bellevue and the Presbyterian Hospitals, New York, he was appointed Professor and Chief of the Cardiopulmonary Division at the University of Oregon Medical School in 1965. Extensive research into the construction and use of artificial heart valves ensued following the first successful valve replacement in 1960.

Bibliography
1961, 'Mitral replacement: clinical experiments with a ball valve prosthesis', *Annals of Surgery*.
1960, *Total Mitral Valve Replacement: Fixation and Thrombosis*.
1985, 'Mitral replacement: clinical experience with a ball valve prosthesis. Twenty five years later', *Annals of Surgery* 202 (with Cobanoglu *et al.*).

MG

Starrett, Laroy S.
b. 25 April 1836 China, Maine, USA
d. 23 April 1922 St Petersburg, Florida, USA

American inventor and tool manufacturer.

As a youth, Laroy S. Starrett worked on his father's farm and later on other farms, and after a few years acquired his own 600-acre stock farm at Newburyport, Massachusetts, which he operated for four years. He had an interest in mechanics and in 1865 invented and patented a device for chopping meat. He arranged for this to be manufactured by the Athol Machine Company at Athol, Massachusetts, and it was so successful that three years later he sold his farm and purchased a controlling interest in the company. He reorganized the company for the manufacture of his meat chopper and two other inventions of his, a washing machine and a butter worker, which he had also patented in 1865. In 1877 Starrett invented the combination square and in 1880 he established the L.S. Starrett Company in Athol for manufacturing it and other small tools, such as steel rules and tapes, callipers, dividers, micrometers and depth gauges, etc. The business expanded and by 1906 he was employing over 1,000 people. He established agencies in Britain and other countries, and Starrett tools were sold throughout the world.

Further Reading
K.J. Hume, 1980, *A History of Engineering Metrology*, London, 133–4 (provides a short account of L.S. Starrett and his company).

RTS

Staudinger, Hermann
b. 23 March 1881 Worms, Germany
d. 8 September 1965 Freiberg im Breisgau, Germany

German chemist, founder of polymer chemistry.

Staudinger studied chemistry at the universities of Halle, Darmstadt and Munich, originally as a preparation for botanical studies, but chemistry claimed his full attention. He followed an academic career, with professorships at Karlsruhe in 1908, Zurich in 1912 and Freiberg from 1926 until his retirement in 1951. Staudinger began his work as an organic chemist by following well-established lines of research, but from 1920 he struck out in a new direction. Until that time, rubber and other apparently non-crystalline materials with high molecular weight were supposed to consist of a disordered collection of small molecules. Staudinger investigated the structure of rubber and realized that it was made up of very large molecules with many basic groups of atoms held together by normal chemical bonds. Substances formed in this way are known as 'polymers'. Staudinger's views first met with opposition, but he developed methods of determining the molecular weights of these 'high polymers'. Finally, the introduction of X-ray crystallographic investigation of chemical structure confirmed his views. This discovery has proved to be the basis of a new branch of chemistry with momentous consequences for indus-

try. From it stemmed the synthetic rubber, plastics, fibres, adhesives and other industries, with all their multifarious applications in everyday life. The Staudinger equation, linking viscosity with molecular weight, is still widely used, albeit with some reservations, in the polymer industry.

During the 1930s, Staudinger turned his attention to biopolymers and foresaw the discovery some twenty years later that these macromolecules were the building blocks of life. In 1953 he belatedly received the Nobel Prize in Chemistry.

Principal Honours and Distinctions
Nobel Prize in Chemistry 1953.

Bibliography
1961, *Arbeitserinnerungen*, Heidelberg; pub. in English, 1970 as *From Organic Chemistry to Macromolecules*, New York (includes a comprehensive bibliography of 644 items).

Further Reading
E. Farber, 1963, *Nobel Prize Winners in Chemistry*, New York.
R.C. Olby, 1970, 'The macromolecular concept and the origins of molecular biology', *J. Chem. Ed.* 47: 168–74.

LRD

Steers, Thomas
b. *c.*1672 Kent, England
d. buried November 1750 Liverpool, England

English dock and canal engineer.

An Army officer serving at the Battle of the Boyne in 1690 and later in the Low Countries, Steers thus gained experience in water control and development, canals and drainage. After his return to England he was associated with George **Sorocold** in the construction of Howland Great Dock, Rotherhithe, London, opened in 1699 and the first wet dock built in England. He was again associated with Sorocold in planning the first of Liverpool's wet docks and subsequently was responsible for its construction. On its completion, he became Dockmaster in 1717.

In 1712 he surveyed the River Douglas for navigation, and received authorization to make it navigable from the Ribble estuary to Wigan in 1720. Although work was started by Steers, the undertaking was hit by the collapse of the South Sea Bubble and Steers was no longer associated with it when it was restarted in 1738. In 1721 he proposed making the Mersey and Irwell navigable.

In 1736 he surveyed and engineered the first summit-level canal in the British Isles, between Portadown and Newry in Ulster, thus providing through-water communication between Lough Neagh and the Irish Sea. The canal was completed in 1741. He also carried out a survey of the river Boyne. Also in 1736, he surveyed the Worsley Brook in South Lancashire to provide navigation from Worsley to the Mersey. This was done on behalf of Scroop, 1st Duke of Bridgewater; an Act was obtained in 1737, but no work was started on the scheme at that time. It was left to Francis **Egerton**, the 3rd Duke, to initiate the Bridgewater Canal to provide water transport for coal from the Worsley pits direct to Manchester. In 1739 Steers was elected Mayor of Liverpool. The following year, jointly with John Eyes of Liverpool, he surveyed a possible navigation along the Calder from its junction with the Aire & Calder at Wakefield to the Hebble and so through to Halifax, but, owing to opposition at the time, the construction of the Calder & Hebble Navigation had to wait until after Steers's death. In the opinion of Professor A.W. Skempton, Steers was the most distinguished civil engineer before **Smeaton**'s time.

Further Reading

Henry Peet, 1932, *Thomas Steers. The Engineer of Liverpool's First Dock*; reprinted with App. from *Transactions of the Historic Society of Lancashire and Cheshire* 82: 163–242.

JHB

Steinheil, Carl August von
b. 1801 Roppoltsweiler, Alsace
d. 1870 Munich, Germany

German physicist, founder of electromagnetic telegraphy in Austria, and photographic innovator and lens designer.

Steinheil studied under Gauss at Göttingen and Bessel at Königsberg before jointing his parents at Munich. There he concentrated on optics before being appointed Professor of Physics and Mathematics at the University of Munich in 1832. Immediately after the announcement of the first practicable photographic processes in 1839, he began experiments on photography in association with another professor at the University, Franz von Kobell. Steinheil is reputed to

have made the first daguerreotypes in Germany; he certainly constructed several cameras of original design and suggested minor improvements to the daguerreotype process. In 1849 he was employed by the Austrian Government as Head of the Department of Telegraphy in the Ministry of Commerce. Electromagnetic telegraphy was an area in which Steinheil had worked for several years previously, and he was now appointed to supervise the installation of a working telegraphic system for the Austrian monarchy. He is considered to be the founder of electromagnetic telegraphy in Austria and went on to perform a similar role in Switzerland.

Steinheil's son, Hugo Adolph, was educated in Munich and Augsburg but moved to Austria to be with his parents in 1850. Adolph completed his studies in Vienna and was appointed to the Telegraph Department, headed by his father, in 1851. Adolph returned to Munich in 1852, however, to concentrate on the study of optics. In 1855 the father and son established the optical workshop which was later to become the distinguished lens- manufacturing company C.A. Steinheil Söhne. At first the business confined itself almost entirely to astronomical optics, but in 1865 the two men took out a joint patent for a wide-angle photographic lens claimed to be free of distortion. The lens, called the 'periscopic', was not in fact free from flare and not achromatic, although it enjoyed some reputation at the time. Much more important was the achromatic development of this lens that was introduced in 1866 and called the 'Aplanet'; almost simultaneously a similar lens, the 'Rapid Rentilinear', was introduced by **Dallmeyer** in England, and for many years lenses of this type were fitted as the standard objective on most photographic cameras. During 1866 the elder Steinheil relinquished his interest in lens manufacturing, and control of the business passed to Adolph, with administrative and financial affairs being looked after by another son, Edward. After Carl Steinheil's death Adolph continued to design and market a series of high-quality photographic lenses until his own death.

Further Reading

J.M. Eder, 1945, *History of Photography*, trans. E. Epstean, New York (a general account of the Steinheils's work).

Most accounts of photographic lens history will

give details of the Steinheils's more important work. See, for example, Chapman Jones, 1904, *Science and Practice of Photography*, 4th edn, London: and Rudolf Kingslake, 1989, *A History of the Photographic Lens*, Boston.

JW

Stephenson, George

b. 9 June 1781 Wylam, Northumberland, England

d. 12 August 1848 Tapton House, Chesterfield, England

English engineer, 'the father of railways'.

George Stephenson was the son of the fireman of the pumping engine at Wylam colliery, and horses drew wagons of coal along the wooden rails of the Wylam wagonway past the house in which he was born and spent his earliest childhood. While still a child he worked as a cowherd, but soon moved to working at coal pits. At 17 years of age he showed sufficient mechanical talent to be placed in charge of a new pumping engine, and had already achieved a job more responsible than that of his father. Despite his position he was still illiterate, although he subsequently learned to read and write. He was largely self-educated.

In 1801 he was appointed Brakesman of the winding engine at Black Callerton pit, with responsibility for lowering the miners safely to their work. Then, about two years later, he became Brakesman of a new winding engine erected by Robert Hawthorn at Willington Quay on the Tyne. Returning collier brigs discharged ballast into wagons and the engine drew the wagons up an inclined plane to the top of 'Ballast Hill' for their contents to be tipped; this was one of the earliest applications of steam power to transport, other than experimentally.

In 1804 Stephenson moved to West Moor pit, Killingworth, again as Brakesman. In 1811 he demonstrated his mechanical skill by successfully modifying a new and unsatisfactory atmospheric engine, a task that had defeated the efforts of others, to enable it to pump a drowned pit clear of water. The following year he was appointed Enginewright at Killingworth, in charge of the machinery in all the collieries of the 'Grand Allies', the prominent coal-owning families of Wortley, Liddell and Bowes, with authorization also to work for others. He built many stationary engines and he closely examined locomotives of John **Blenkinsop**'s type on the Kenton & Coxlodge wagonway, as well as those of William **Hedley** at Wylam.

It was in 1813 that Sir Thomas Liddell requested George Stephenson to build a steam locomotive for the Killingworth wagonway: *Blucher* made its first trial run on 25 July 1814 and was based on Blenkinsop's locomotives, although it lacked their rack-and-pinion drive. George Stephenson is credited with building the first locomotive both to run on edge rails and be driven by adhesion, an arrangement that has been the conventional one ever since. Yet *Blucher* was far from perfect and over the next few years, while other engineers ignored the steam locomotive, Stephenson built a succession of them, each an improvement on the last.

During this period many lives were lost in coalmines from explosions of gas ignited by miners' lamps. By observation and experiment (sometimes at great personal risk) Stephenson invented a satisfactory safety lamp, working independently of the noted scientist Sir Humphry **Davy** who also invented such a lamp around the same time.

In 1817 George Stephenson designed his first locomotive for an outside customer, the Kilmarnock & Troon Railway, and in 1819 he laid out the Hetton Colliery Railway in County Durham, for which his brother Robert was Resident Engineer. This was the first railway to be worked entirely without animal traction: it used inclined planes with stationary engines, self-acting inclined planes powered by gravity, and locomotives.

On 19 April 1821 Stephenson was introduced to Edward Pease, one of the main promoters of the Stockton & Darlington Railway (S & DR), which by coincidence received its Act of Parliament the same day. George Stephenson carried out a further survey, to improve the proposed line, and in this he was assisted by his 18-year-old son, Robert **Stephenson**, whom he had ensured received the theoretical education which he himself lacked. It is doubtful whether either could have succeeded without the other; together they were to make the steam railway practicable.

At George Stephenson's instance, much of the S & DR was laid with wrought-iron rails recently developed by John Birkinshaw at Bedlington Ironworks, Morpeth. These were longer than cast-iron rails and were not brittle: they made a track well suited for locomotives. In June 1823 George and Robert Stephenson, with other partners, founded a firm in Newcastle upon Tyne to build locomotives and rolling stock and to do general engineering work: after its Managing Partner, the firm was called Robert Stephenson & Co.

In 1824 the promoters of the Liverpool & Manchester Railway (L & MR) invited George Stephenson to resurvey their proposed line in order to reduce opposition to it. William James, a wealthy land agent who had become a visionary protagonist of a national railway network and had seen Stephenson's locomotives at Killingworth, had promoted the L & MR with some merchants of Liverpool and had carried out the first survey; however, he overreached himself in business and, shortly after the invitation to Stephenson, became bankrupt. In his own survey, however, George Stephenson lacked the assistance of his son Robert, who had left for South America, and he delegated much of the detailed work to incompetent assistants. During a devastating Parliamentary examination in the spring of 1825, much of his survey was shown to be seriously inaccurate and the L & MR's application for an Act of Parliament was refused. The railway's promoters discharged Stephenson and had their line surveyed yet again, by C.B. **Vignoles**.

The Stockton & Darlington Railway was, however, triumphantly opened in the presence of vast crowds in September 1825, with Stephenson himself driving the locomotive *Locomotion*, which had been built at Robert Stephenson & Co.'s Newcastle works. Once the railway was at work, horse-drawn and gravity-powered traffic shared the line with locomotives: in 1828 Stephenson invented the horse dandy, a wagon at the back of a train in which a horse could travel over the gravity-operated stretches, instead of trotting behind.

Meanwhile, in May 1826, the Liverpool & Manchester Railway had successfully obtained its Act of Parliament. Stephenson was appointed Engineer in June, and since he and Vignoles proved incompatible the latter left early in 1827. The railway was built by Stephenson and his staff, using direct labour. A considerable controversy arose *c.*1828 over the motive power to be used: the traffic anticipated was too great for horses, but the performance of the reciprocal system of cable haulage developed by Benjamin **Thom-**

pson appeared in many respects superior to that of contemporary locomotives. The company instituted a prize competition for a better locomotive and the Rainhill Trials were held in October 1829.

Robert Stephenson had been working on improved locomotive designs since his return from America in 1827, but it was the L & MR's Treasurer, Henry **Booth**, who suggested the multi-tubular boiler to George Stephenson. This was incorporated into a locomotive built by Robert Stephenson for the trials: *Rocket* was entered by the three men in partnership. The other principal entrants were *Novelty*, entered by John Braithwaite and John **Ericsson**, and *Sans Pareil*, entered by Timothy **Hackworth**, but only *Rocket*, driven by George Stephenson, met all the organizers' demands; indeed, it far surpassed them and demonstrated the practicability of the long-distance steam railway. With the opening of the Liverpool & Manchester Railway in 1830, the age of railways began.

Stephenson was active in many aspects. He advised on the construction of the Belgian State Railway, of which the Brussels–Malines section, opened in 1835, was the first all-steam railway on the European continent. In England, proposals to link the L & MR with the Midlands had culminated in an Act of Parliament for the Grand Junction Railway in 1833: this was to run from Warrington, which was already linked to the L & MR, to Birmingham. George Stephenson had been in charge of the surveys, and for the railway's construction he and J.U. **Rastrick** were initially Principal Engineers, with Stephenson's former pupil Joseph **Locke** under them; by 1835 both Stephenson and Rastrick had withdrawn and Locke was Engineer-in-Chief. Stephenson remained much in demand elsewhere: he was particularly associated with the construction of the North Midland Railway (Derby to Leeds) and related lines. He was active in many other places and carried out, for instance, preliminary surveys for the Chester & Holyhead and Newcastle & Berwick Railways, which were important links in the lines of communication between London and, respectively, Dublin and Edinburgh.

He eventually retired to Tapton House, Chesterfield, overlooking the North Midland. A man who was self-made (with great success) against colossal odds, he was ever reluctant, regrettably, to give others their due credit, although in retirement, immensely wealthy and full of honour, he was still able to mingle with people of all ranks.

Principal Honours and Distinctions
President, Institution of Mechanical Engineers, on its formation in 1847. Order of Leopold (Belgium) 1835. Stephenson refused both a knighthood and Fellowship of the Royal Society.

Bibliography
1815, jointly with Ralph Dodd, British patent no. 3,887 (locomotive drive by connecting rods directly to the wheels).
1817, jointly with William Losh, British patent no. 4,067 (steam springs for locomotives, and improvements to track).

Further Reading
L.T.C. Rolt, 1960, *George and Robert Stephenson*, Longman (the best modern biography; includes a bibliography).
S. Smiles, 1874, *The Lives of George and Robert Stephenson*, rev. edn, London (although sycophantic, this is probably the best nineteenth-century biography).

PJGR

Stephenson, John

b. 4 July 1809 County Armagh, Ireland.
d. 31 July 1893 New Rochelle, New York, USA.

Irish/American pioneer of tramways for urban transport, builder and innovator of streetcars.

Stephenson's parents emigrated to the United States when he was 2 years old; he was educated in public schools in New York, where his parents had settled, and at a Wesleyan seminary. He became a clerk in a store at 16, but in 1828 he apprenticed himself to a coachbuilder, Andrew Wade, of Broome Street, New York. His apprenticeship lasted two years, during which time he learned mechanical drawing in the evenings and started to design vehicles. He was employed for a year on carriage repair work and in 1831 he opened his own coach repair business. Within a year he had built New York's first omnibus; this was bought by Abraham Brower, Stephenson's former employer, who started the city's first bus service. Brower immediately ordered a further three buses from Stephenson, and a further

horse-drawn car was ordered by the New York & Harlem Railroad. He built the car used at the opening of the railroad on 26 November 1832, the first street railway in the world. Orders followed for cars for many street railroads in other cities in the eastern States, and business prospered until the financial panic of 1837. Stephenson's factory was forced to close but he managed to pay off his creditors in the next six years and started in business again, building only omnibuses and coaches to become recognized as the world's foremost builder of streetcars. His first car had four flanged wheels, and a body of three compartments slung on leather straps from an unsprung chassis. He built horse-drawn cars, cable cars, electric and open cars; by 1891 his factory had 500 employees and was producing some twenty-five cars a week. His first patent had been dated 23 April 1833 and was followed by some ten others. During the Civil War, his factory was turned over to the manufacture of pontoons and gun carriages. He married Julia Tiemann in 1833; they had two sons and a daughter. He lived at New Rochelle, New York, from 1865 until his death.

Further Reading
'The original carbuilder', 1891, *New York Tribune*, 10 September.
D. Malone (ed.), *Dictionary of American Biography*, Vol. 9, New York: Charles Scribner.

IMcN

Stephenson, Robert

b. 16 October 1803 Willington Quay, Northumberland, England
d. 12 October 1859 London, England

English engineer who built the locomotive Rocket and constructed many important early trunk railways.

Robert Stephenson's father was George **Stephenson**, who ensured that his son was educated to obtain the theoretical knowledge he lacked himself. In 1821 Robert Stephenson assisted his father in his survey of the Stockton & Darlington Railway and in 1822 he assisted William James in the first survey of the Liverpool & Manchester Railway. He then went to Edinburgh University for six months, and the following year Robert Stephenson & Co. was named after him as Managing Partner when it was formed by himself, his father and others. The firm was to build stationary engines, locomotives and railway rolling stock; in its early years it also built paper-making machinery and did general engineering.

In 1824, however, Robert Stephenson accepted, perhaps in reaction to an excess of parental control, an invitation by a group of London speculators called the Colombian Mining Association to lead an expedition to South America to use steam power to reopen gold and silver mines. He subsequently visited North America before returning to England in 1827 to rejoin his father as an equal and again take charge of Robert Stephenson & Co. There he set about altering the design of steam locomotives to improve both their riding and their steam-generating capacity. *Lancashire Witch*, completed in July 1828, was the first locomotive mounted on steel springs and had twin furnace tubes through the boiler to produce a large heating surface. Later that year Robert Stephenson & Co. supplied the Stockton & Darlington Railway with a wagon, mounted for the first time on springs and with outside bearings. It was to be the prototype of the standard British railway wagon. Between April and September 1829 Robert Stephenson built, not without difficulty, a multi-tubular boiler, as suggested by Henry **Booth** to George Stephenson, and incorporated it into the locomotive *Rocket* which the three men entered in the Liverpool & Manchester Railway's Rainhill Trials in October. *Rocket*, was outstandingly successful and demonstrated that the long-distance steam railway was practicable.

Robert Stephenson continued to develop the locomotive. *Northumbrian*, built in 1830, had for the first time, a smokebox at the front of the boiler and also the firebox built integrally with the rear of the boiler. Then in *Planet*, built later the same year, he adopted a layout for the working parts used earlier by steam road-coach pioneer Goldsworthy **Gurney**, placing the cylinders, for the first time, in a nearly horizontal position beneath the smokebox, with the connecting rods driving a cranked axle. He had evolved the definitive form for the steam locomotive.

Also in 1830, Robert Stephenson surveyed the London & Birmingham Railway, which was authorized by Act of Parliament in 1833. Stephenson became Engineer for construction of the 112-mile (180 km) railway, probably at that date the greatest task ever undertaken in of civil engineering. In this he was greatly assisted by G.P. Bidder, who as a child prodigy had been known as 'The Calculating Boy', and the two men were to be associated in many subsequent projects. On the London & Birmingham Railway there were long and deep cuttings to be excavated and difficult tunnels to be bored, notoriously at Kilsby. The line was opened in 1838.

In 1837 Stephenson provided facilities for W.F. **Cooke** to make an experimental electric-telegraph installation at London Euston. The directors of the London & Birmingham Railway company, however, did not accept his recommendation that they should adopt the electric telegraph and it was left to I.K. **Brunel** to instigate the first permanent installation, alongside the Great Western Railway. After Cooke formed the Electric Telegraph Company, Stephenson became a shareholder and was Chairman during 1857-8.

Earlier, in the 1830s, Robert Stephenson assisted his father in advising on railways in Belgium and came to be increasingly in demand as a consultant. In 1840, however, he was almost ruined financially as a result of the collapse of the Stanhope & Tyne Rail Road; in return for acting as Engineer-in-Chief he had unwisely accepted shares, with unlimited liability, instead of a fee.

During the late 1840s Stephenson's greatest achievements were the design and construction of four great bridges, as part of railways for which he was responsible. The High Level Bridge over the Tyne at Newcastle and the Royal Border Bridge over the Tweed at Berwick were the links needed to complete the East Coast Route from London to Scotland. For the Chester & Holyhead Railway to cross the Menai Strait, a bridge with spans as long as 460 ft (140 m) was needed: Stephenson designed them as wrought-iron tubes of rectangular cross-section, through which the trains would pass, and eventually joined the spans together into a tube 1,511 ft (460 m) long from shore to shore. Extensive testing was done beforehand by shipbuilder William Fairbairn to prove the method, and as a preliminary it was first used for a 400 ft (122 m) span bridge at Conway.

In 1847 Robert Stephenson was elected MP for Whitby, a position he held until his death, and he was one of the exhibition commissioners for the Great Exhibition of 1851. In the early 1850s he was Engineer-in-Chief for the

Norwegian Trunk Railway, the first railway in Norway, and he also built the Alexandria & Cairo Railway, the first railway in Africa. This included two tubular bridges with the railway running on top of the tubes. The railway was extended to Suez in 1858 and for several years provided a link in the route from Britain to India, until superseded by the Suez Canal, which Stephenson had opposed in Parliament. The greatest of all his tubular bridges was the Victoria Bridge across the River St Lawrence at Montreal: after inspecting the site in 1852 he was appointed Engineer-in-Chief for the bridge, which was 1¼ miles (2 km) long and was designed in his London offices. Sadly he, like Brunel, died young from self-imposed overwork, before the bridge was completed in 1859.

Principal Honours and Distinctions
FRS 1849. President, Institution of Mechanical Engineers 1849. President, Institution of Civil Engineers 1856. Order of St Olaf (Norway). Order of Leopold (Belgium). Like his father, Robert Stephenson refused a knighthood.

Further Reading
L.T.C. Rolt, 1960, *George and Robert Stephenson*, London: Longman (a good modern biography).

J.C. Jeaffreson, 1864, *The Life of Robert Stephenson*, London: Longman (the standard nineteenth-century biography).

M.R. Bailey, 1979, 'Robert Stephenson & Co. 1823–1829', *Transactions of the Newcomen Society* 50 (provides details of the early products of that company).

J. Kieve, 1973, *The Electric Telegraph*, Newton Abbot: David & Charles.

See also: **Pihl, Carl Abraham**; **Seguin, Marc**.

PJGR

Stevens, John
b. 1749 New York, New York, USA
d. 6 March 1838 Hoboken, New Jersey, USA

American pioneer of steamboats and railways.

Stevens, a wealthy landowner with an estate at Hoboken on the Hudson River, had his attention drawn to the steamboat of John Fitch in 1786, and thenceforth devoted much of his time

and fortune to developing steamboats and mechanical transport. He also had political influence and it was at his instance that Congress in 1790 passed an Act establishing the first patent laws in the USA. The following year Stevens was one of the first recipients of a US patent. This referred to multi-tubular boilers, of both watertube and firetube types, and antedated by many years the work of both Henry **Booth** and Marc **Seguin** on the latter.

A steamboat built in 1798 by John Stevens, Nicholas J. Roosevelt and Stevens's brother-in-law, Robert R. Livingston, in association was unsuccessful, nor was Stevens satisfied with a boat built in 1802 in which a simple rotary steam-engine was mounted on the same shaft as a screw propeller. However, although others had experimented earlier with screw propellers, when John Stevens had the *Little Juliana* built in 1804 he produced the first practical screw steamboat. Steam at 50 psi (3.5 kg/cm^2) pressure was supplied by a watertube boiler to a single-cylinder engine which drove two contra-rotating shafts, upon each of which was mounted a screw propeller. This little boat, less than 25 ft (7.6 m) long, was taken backwards and forwards across the Hudson River by two of Stevens's sons, one of whom, R.L. **Stevens**, was to help his father with many subsequent experiments. The boat, however, was ahead of its time, and steamships were to be driven by paddle wheels until the late 1830s.

In 1807 John Stevens declined an invitation to join with Robert **Fulton** and Robert R. Livingston in their development work, which culminated in successful operation of the PS *Clermont* that summer; in 1808, however, he launched his own paddle steamer, the *Phoenix*. But Fulton and Livingston had obtained an effective monopoly of steamer operation on the Hudson and, unable to reach agreement with them, Stevens sent *Phoenix* to Philadelphia to operate on the Delaware River. The intervening voyage over 150 miles (240 km) of open sea made *Phoenix* the first ocean-going steamer.

From about 1810 John Stevens turned his attention to the possibilities of railways. He was at first considered a visionary, but in 1815, at his instance, the New Jersey Assembly created a company to build a railway between the Delaware and Raritan Rivers. It was the first railway charter granted in the USA, although the line it authorized remained unbuilt. To demonstrate the feasibility of the steam locomotive, Stevens built an experimental locomotive in 1825, at the age of 76. With flangeless wheels, guide rollers and rack-and-pinion drive, it ran on a circular track at his Hoboken home; it was the first steam locomotive to be built in America.

Bibliography
1812, *Documents Tending to Prove the Superior Advantages of Rail-ways and Steam-carriages over Canal Navigation.*
He took out patents relating to steam-engines in the USA in 1791, 1803, and 1810, and in England, through his son John Cox Stevens, in 1805.

Further Reading
H.P. Spratt, 1958, *The Birth of the Steamboat*, Charles Griffin (provides technical details of Stevens's boats).
J.T. Flexner, 1978, *Steamboats Come True*, Boston: Little, Brown (describes his work in relation to that of other steamboat pioneers).
J.R. Stover, 1961, *American Railroads*, Chicago: University of Chicago Press.
Transactions of the Newcomen Society (1927) 7: 114 (discusses tubular boilers).
J.R. Day and B.G. Wilson, 1957, *Unusual Railways*, F. Muller (discusses Stevens's locomotive).

See also: **Allen, Horatio**; **Cooper, Peter**.

PJGR

Stevens, Robert Livingston

b. 18 October 1787 Hoboken, New Jersey, USA
d. 20 April 1856 Hoboken, New Jersey, USA

American engineer, pioneer of steamboats and railways.

R.L. Stevens was the son of John **Stevens** and was given the technical education his father lacked. He assisted his father with the *Little Juliana* and the *Phoenix*, managed the commercial operation of the *Phoenix* on the Delaware River, and subsequently built many other steamboats.

In 1830 he and his brother Edwin A. Stevens obtained a charter from the New Jersey Legislature for the Camden & Amboy Railroad & Transportation Company, and he visited Britain to obtain rails and a locomotive. Railway track in the USA then normally comprised longitudinal timber rails with running surfaces of iron straps, but Stevens designed rails of flat-bottom section, which were to become standard, and had the first batch rolled in Wales. He also designed hook-headed spikes for them, and 'iron tongues', which became fishplates. From Robert Stephenson & Co. (see Robert **Stephenson**) he obtained the locomotive *John Bull*, which was similar to the Liverpool & Manchester Railway's *Samson*. The Camden & Amboy Railroad was opened in 1831, but *John Bull*, a 0–4–0, proved over sensitive to imperfections in the track; Stevens and his mechanic, Isaac Dripps, added a two-wheeled non-swivelling 'pilot' at the front to guide it round curves. The locomotive survives at the Smithsonian Institution, Washington, DC.

Further Reading
H.P. Spratt, 1958, *The Birth of the Steamboat*, Charles Griffin.
J.H. White Jr, 1979, *A History of the American Locomotive – Its Development: 1830–1880*, New York: Dover Publications Inc.
J.F. Stover, 1961, *American Railroads*, Chicago: University of Chicago Press.

See also: **Adams, William Bridges** (fishplates); **Vignoles, Charles Blacker** (flat-bottom rail).

PJGR

Stevens, Stanley Smith

b. 4 November 1906 Ogden, Utah, USA
d. 18 January 1973 Cambridge, Massachusetts, USA

American psychophysicist, proponent of 'Stevens Law' of sensory magnitude, and developer of the technology of hearing and acoustics.

Of Mormon origins, Stevens graduated PhD in physiology from Harvard in 1933. After a further fellowship in physiology and a research fellowship in physics, he became an instructor in experimental psychology. At the beginning of the Second World War he founded the Psycho-Acoustic Laboratory at Harvard, which grew into the Laboratory of Psychophysics, and in 1962 he became the first Professor of Psychophysics.

Originally his research concentrated on sound and communication, but it later enlarged to embrace the whole range of sensory phenomena. It was his earlier studies that established the law relating sensory magnitude to stimulus magnitude. His studies of the loudness scale and its relationship to the decibel scale were significant in the development of the electronic hearing aid.

Principal Honours and Distinctions
National Academy of Sciences 1946. Society of Experimental Psychologists Warren Medal 1943. American Psychological Association Science Award 1960.

Bibliography
1938, *Hearing: Its Psychology and Physiology*.

Further Reading
1951, *Handbook of Experimental Psychology*.
MG

Stevenson, Robert
b. 8 June 1772 Glasgow, Scotland
d. 12 July 1850 Edinburgh, Scotland

Scottish lighthouse designer and builder.

After his father's death when he was only 2 years old, Robert Stevenson was educated at a school for children from families in reduced circumstances. However, *c.*1788 his mother married again, to Thomas Smith, Engineer to the Northern Lighthouse Board. Stevenson then served an apprenticeship under his new stepfather. The Board, which is still an active force in the 1990s, was founded in 1786 to oversee the lights and buoyage in some of the wildest waters in Western Europe, the seas around the coasts of Scotland and the Isle of Man.

After studies at Anderson's College (now the University of Strathclyde) and later at Edinburgh University, Stevenson assumed responsibility in the field for much of the construction work sanctioned by the Board. After some years he succeeded Smith as Engineer to the Board and thereby the long connection between the Northern Lights and the Stevenson family commenced.

Stevenson became Engineer to the Board when he was about 30 years old, remaining in that office for the best part of half a century. During these years he improved catoptric lighting, adopted the central lamp refracting system and invented the intermittent flashing light. While these developments were sufficient to form a just memorial to the man, he was involved

in greater endeavours in the construction of around twenty lighthouses, most of which had ingenious forms of construction. The finest piece was the Bell Rock Lighthouse, built on a reef off the Scottish East Coast. This enterprise took five years to complete and can be regarded as the most important construction of his life.

His interests fitted in with those of the other great men living in and around Edinburgh at the time, and included oceanography, astronomy, architecture and antiquarian studies. He designed several notable bridges, proposed a design for the rails for railways and also made a notable study of marine timber borers. He contributed to *Encyclopaedia Britannica* and to many journals.

His grandson, born in the year of his death, was the famous author Robert Louis Stevenson (1850–94).

Principal Honours and Distinctions
FRS Edinburgh.

Further Reading
Sir Walter Scott, 1982, *Northern Lights*, Hawick.
FMW

Stibitz, George R.
b. 20 April 1904 York, Pennsylvania, USA

American mathematician responsible for the conception of the Bell Laboratories 'Complex' computer.

Stibitz spent his early years in Dayton, Ohio, and obtained his first degree at Denison University, Granville, Ohio, his MS from Union College, Schenectady, New York, in 1927 and his PhD in mathematical physics from Cornell University, Ithaca, New York, in 1930. After working for a time for General Electric, he joined Bell Laboratories to work on various communications problems. In 1937 he started to experiment at home with telephone relays as the basis of a calculator for addition, multiplication and division. Initially this was based on binary arithmetic, but later he used binary-coded decimal (BCD) and was able to cope with complex numbers. In November 1938 the ideas were officially taken up by Bell Laboratories and, with S.B. Williams as Project Manager, Stibitz built a complex-number computer known as 'Complex', or Relay I, which became operational on 8 January 1940.

With the outbreak of the Second World War,

he was co-opted to the National Defence Research Council to work on anti-aircraft (AA) gun control, and this led to Bell Laboratories Relay II computer, which was completed in 1943 and which had 500 relays, bi-quinary code and self-checking of errors. A further computer, Relay III, was used for ballistic simulation of actual AA shell explosions and was followed by more machines before and after Stibitz left Bell after the end of the war. Stibitz then became a computer consultant, involved in particular with the development of the UNIVAC computer by John Mauchly and J. Presper Eckert.

Principal Honours and Distinctions
Institute of Electrical and Electronics Engineers Emanuel R. Priore Award 1977.

Bibliography
1957, with J.A. Larrivee, *Mathematics and Computers*, New York: McGraw-Hill.
1967, 'The Relay computer at the Bell Laboratories', *Datamation* 35.

Further Reading
E. Loveday, 1977, 'George Stibitz and the Bell Labs Relay computer', *Datamation* 80.
M.R. Williams, 1985, *A History of Computing Technology*, London: Prentice-Hall.

KF

Strachey, Christopher
b. 16 November 1916 England
d. 18 May 1975 Oxford, England

English physicist and computer engineer who proposed time-sharing as a more efficient means of using a mainframe computer.

After education at Gresham's School, London, Strachey went to King's College, Cambridge, where he completed an MA. In 1937 he took up a post as a physicist at the Standard Telephone and Cable Company, then during the Second World War he was involved in radar research. In 1944 he became an assistant master at St Edmunds School, Canterbury, moving to Harrow School in 1948. Another change of career in 1951 saw him working as a Technical Officer with the National Research and Development Corporation, where he was involved in computer software and hardware design. From 1958 until 1962 he was an independent consultant in computer design, and during this time

(1959) he realized that as mainframe computers were by then much faster than their human operators, their efficiency could be significantly increased by 'time-sharing' the tasks of several operators in rapid succession. Strachey made many contributions to computer technology, being variously involved in the design of the Manchester University MkI, Elliot and Ferranti Pegasus computers. In 1962 he joined Cambridge University Mathematics Laboratory as a senior research fellow at Churchill College and helped to develop the programming language CPL. After a brief period as Visiting Lecturer at the Massachusetts Institute of Technology, he returned to the UK in 1966 as Reader in Computation and Fellow of Wolfson College, Oxford, to establish a programming research group. He remained there until his death.

Principal Honours and Distinctions
Distinguished Fellow of the British Computer Society 1972.

Bibliography
1961, with M.R. Wilkes, 'Some proposals for improving the efficiency of Algol 60', *Communications of the ACM* 4: 488.
1966, 'Systems analysis and programming', *Scientific American* 25: 112.
1976, with R.E. Milne, *A Theory of Programming Language Semantics*.

Further Reading
J. Alton, 1980, *Catalogue of the Papers of C. Strachey 1916–1975*.
M. Campbell-Kelly, 1985, 'Christopher Strachey 1916–1975. A biographical note', *Annals of the History of Computing* 7: 19.
M.R. Williams, 1985, *A History of Computing Technology*, London: Prentice-Hall.

See also: **Wilkes, Maurice Vincent**; **Williams, Sir Frederic Calland**.

KF

Stratingh, Sibrandus
b. 9 April 1785 Adorp, The Netherlands
d. 15 February 1841 Groningen, The Netherlands

Dutch chemist and physician, maker of early electric motors.

Stratingh spent five years working for a relative who was a chemist in Groningen, and studied pharmacy under Professor Driessen. Encouraged to become a medical student, he qualified as a doctor of medicine in 1809. Later becoming a professor of chemistry at Groningen, he was honoured by a personal visit from the King to his laboratory in 1837. In 1835, assisted by Christopher Becker, an instrument maker, he built a table-top model of an electrically propelled vehicle. The motor, with wound armature and field coils, was geared to a wheel of a small carriage which also carried a single voltaic cell. A full-scale road vehicle was never built, but in 1840 he succeeded in making an electrically powered boat.

Principal Honours and Distinctions
Cross of the Netherlands Lion 1831.

Bibliography
1841, *De nagedachtenis van S. Stratingh Ez. gevierd in het Genootschap: ter bevordering der natuurkundige wetenschappen te Groningen*, Groningen (a memorial volume that includes a list of his works).

Further Reading
B. Bowers, 1982, *A History of Electric Light and Power*, London, p. 45 (provides a brief account of Stratingh's electric vehicle).

GW

Stringfellow, John
b. 6 December 1799 Sheffield, England
d. 13 December 1883 Chard, England

English inventor and builder of a series of experimental model aeroplanes.

After serving an apprenticeship in the lace industry, Stringfellow left Nottingham in about 1820 and moved to Chard in Somerset, where he set up his own business. He had wide interests such as photography, politics, and the use of electricity for medical treatment. Stringfellow met William Samuel **Henson**, who also lived in Chard and was involved in lacemaking, and became interested in his 'aerial steam carriage' of 1842–3. When support for this project foundered, Henson and Stringfellow drew up an agreement 'Whereas it is intended to construct a model of an Aerial Machine'. They built a large model with a wing span of 20 ft (6 m) and powered by a steam engine, which was probably the work of Stringfellow. The model was tested on a hillside near Chard, often at night to avoid publicity, but despite many attempts it never made a successful flight. At this point Henson emigrated to the United States. From 1848 Stringfellow continued to experiment with models of his own design, starting with one with a wing span of 10 ft (3 m). He decided to test it in a disused lace factory, rather than in the open air. Stringfellow fitted a horizontal wire which supported the model as it gained speed prior to free flight. Unfortunately, neither this nor later models made a sustained flight, despite Stringfellow's efficient lightweight steam engine. For many years Stringfellow abandoned his aeronautical experiments, then in 1866 when the (Royal) Aeronautical Society was founded, his interest was revived. He built a steam-powered triplane, which was demonstrated 'flying' along a wire at the world's first Aeronautical Exhibition, held at Crystal Palace, London, in 1868. Stringfellow also received a cash prize for one of his engines, which was the lightest practical power unit at the Exhibition. Although Stringfellow's models never achieved a really successful flight, his designs showed the way for others to follow. Several of his models are preserved in the Science Museum in London.

Principal Honours and Distinctions
Member of the (Royal) Aeronautical Society 1868.

Bibliography
Many of Stringfellow's letters and papers are held by the Royal Aeronautical Society, London.

Further Reading
Harald Penrose, 1988, *An Ancient Air: A Biography of John Stringfellow*, Shrewsbury.
A.M. Balantyne and J. Laurence Pritchard, 1956, 'The lives and work of William Samuel Henson and John Stringfellow', *Journal of the Royal Aeronautical Society* (June) (an attempt to analyse conflicting evidence).
M.J.B. Davy, 1931, *Henson and Stringfellow*, London (an earlier work with excellent drawings from Henson's patent).
'The aeronautical work of John Stringfellow, with some account of W.S. Henson', *Aeronau-*

tical Classics No. 5 (written by John Stringfellow's son and held by the Royal Aeronautical Society in London).

JDS

Strowger, Almon Brown

b. 19 October 1839 Penfield, New York, USA
d. 26 May 1902 St Petersburg, Florida, USA

American soldier, teacher and undertaker who developed the first commercially successful automatic telephone-switching system.

Enlisting in the 8th New York Cavalry on his twenty-second birthday at the beginning of the American Civil War, Strowger reached the rank of Second Lieutenant. After the war he taught in a number of schools, including that where he had been a pupil, then bought an undertaking business in North Topeka, Kansas. After the death of his wife, he remarried and moved the business to Kansas City.

In 1887, suspecting that the local telephone operator was diverting his potential clients to a rival, he devised a cardboard mock-up of an automatic switching mechanism comprising ten layers of ten contacts, in which electromagnets would be used to lift and rotate the contact wiper arm and thus connect the caller to any one of 100 telephone destinations. Two years later he filed a patent for a 1,000-line automatic exchange.

With the help of his nephew he made a 100-line working demonstration and eventually, with the aid of financial backers, the Strowger Automatic Exchange Company was established on 30 October 1891; its first exchange was installed in La Porte, Indiana, in 1892. By the end of 1896 Strowger exchanges had been established in a number of other towns. That year the Strowger engineers introduced the dial system to replace the confusing push-button mechanism, an innovation that was to survive until relatively recently, and the following year saw development of a 'trunking' system. In failing health, Strowger retired to Florida, but the company flourished and eventually became part of General Telephones and Electronics (GTE).

Principal Honours and Distinctions
Strowger's pioneering development was commemorated in 1949 by the telephone industry placing a bronze plaque on his grave in St Petersburg, Florida.

Bibliography
12 March 1889, US patent no. 447,918.

Further Reading
R.J. Chaphuis, 1982, *100 Years of Telephone Switching 1878–1978*. Part I: *Manual and Electromechanical Switching 1878–1960*.

KF

Strutt, Jedediah

b. 26 July 1726 South Normanton, near Alfreton, Derbyshire, England
d. 7 May 1797 Derby, England

English inventor of a machine for making ribbed knitting.

Jedediah Strutt was the second of three sons of William, a small farmer and maltster at South Normanton, near Alfreton, Derbyshire, where the only industry was a little framework knitting. At the age of 14 Jedediah was apprenticed to Ralph Massey, a wheelwright near Derby, and lodged with the Woollats, whose daughter Elizabeth he later married in 1755. He moved to Leicester and in 1754 started farming at Blackwell, where an uncle had died and left him the stock on his farm. It was here that he made his knitting invention.

William **Lee**'s knitting machine remained in virtually the same form as he left it until the middle of the eighteenth century. The knitting industry moved away from London into the Midlands and in 1730 a Nottingham workman, using Indian spun yarn, produced the first pair of cotton hose ever made by mechanical means. This industry developed quickly and by 1750 was providing employment for 1,200 frameworkers using both wool and cotton in the Nottingham and Derby areas. It was against this background that Jedediah Strutt obtained patents for his Derby rib machine in 1758 and 1759.

The machine was a highly ingenious mechanism, which when placed in front of an ordinary stocking frame enabled the fashionable ribbed stockings to be made by machine instead of by hand. To develop this invention, he formed a partnership first with his brother-in-law, William Woollat, and two leading Derby hosiers, John Bloodworth and Thomas Stamford. This partnership was dissolved in 1762 and another was formed with Woollat and the Nottingham hosier Samuel **Need**. Strutt's invention was followed by a succession of innovations which enabled frame-work knitters to produce almost every kind of mesh on their machines. In 1764 the stocking frame was adapted to the making of eyelet holes, and this later lead to the production of lace. In 1767 velvet was made on these frames, and two years later brocade. In this way Strutt's original invention opened up a new era for knitting. Although all these later improvements were not his, he was able to make a fortune from his invention. In 1762 he was made a freeman of Nottingham, but by then he was living in Derby. His business at Derby was concerned mainly with silk hose and he had a silk mill there.

It was partly his need for cotton yarn and partly his wealth which led him into partnership with Richard **Arkwright**, John **Smalley** and David **Thornley** to exploit Arkwright's patent for spinning cotton by rollers. Together with Samuel Need, they financed the Arkwright partnership in 1770 to develop the horse-powered mill in Nottingham and then the water-powered mill at Cromford. Strutt gave advice to Arkwright about improving the machinery and helped to hold the partnership together when Arkwright fell out with his first partners. Strutt was also involved, in London, where he had a house, with the parliamentary proceedings over the passing of the Calico Act in 1774, which opened up the trade in British-manufactured all-cotton cloth.

In 1776 Strutt financed the construction of his own mill at Belper, about seven miles (11 km) further down the Derwent valley below Cromford. This was followed by another at Milford, a little lower on the river. Strutt was also a partner with Arkwright and others in the mill at Birkacre, near Chorley in Lancashire. The Strutt mills were developed into large complexes for cotton spinning and many experiments were later carried out in them, both in textile machinery and in fireproof construction for the mills themselves. They were also important training schools for engineers.

Elizabeth Strutt died in 1774 and Jedediah never married again. The family seem to have lived frugally in spite of their wealth, probably influenced by their Nonconformist background. He had built a house near the mills at Milford, but it was in his Derby house that Jedediah died in 1797. By the time of his death, his son William had long been involved with the business and became a more important cotton spinner than Jedediah.

Bibliography

1758, British patent no. 722 (Derby rib machine).

1759, British patent no. 734 (Derby rib machine).

Further Reading

For the involvement of Strutt in Arkwright's spinning ventures, there are two books, the earlier of which is R.S. Fitton and A.P. Wadsworth, 1958, *The Strutts and the Arkwrights, 1758–1830*, Manchester, which has most of the details about Strutt's life. This has been followed by R.S. Fitton, 1989, *The Arkwrights, Spinners of Fortune*, Manchester.

R.L. Hills, 1970, *Power in the Industrial Revolution*, Manchester (for a general background to the textile industry of the period).

W. Felkin, 1967, *History of the Machine-wrought Hosiery and Lace Manufactures*, reprint, Newton Abbot (orig. pub. 1867) (covers Strutt's knitting inventions).

RLH

Stuart, Herbert Akroyd

b. 1864 Halifax, England
d. 1927 Perth, Australia

English inventor of an oil internal-combustion engine.

Stuart's involvement with engines covered a period of less than ten years and was concerned with a means of vaporizing the heavier oils for use in the so-called oil engines. Leaving his native Yorkshire for Bletchley in Buckinghamshire, Stuart worked in his father's business, the Bletchley Iron and Tin Plate works. After finishing grammar school, he worked as an assistant in the Mechanical Engineering Department of the City and Guilds of London Technical College. He also formed a connection with the Finsbury Technical College, where he became acquainted with Professor William Robinson, a distinguished engineer eminent in the field of internal-combustion engines.

Resuming work at Bletchley, Stuart carried out experiments with engines. His first patent was concerned with new methods of vaporizing the fuel, scavenging systems and improvement of speed control. Two further patents, in 1890, specified substantial improvements and formed the basis of later engine designs. In 1891 Stuart joined forces with R. Hornsby and Sons of Grantham, a firm founded in 1815 for the manufacture of machinery and steam engines. Hornsby acquired all rights to Stuart's engine patents, and their superior technical resources ensured substantial improvements to Stuart's early design. The Hornsby–Ackroyd engines, introduced in 1892, were highly successful and found wide acceptance, particularly in agriculture. With failing health, Stuart's interest in his engine work declined, and in 1899 he emigrated to Australia, where in 1903 he became a partner in importing gas engines and gas-producing plants. Following his death in 1927, under the terms of his will he was interred in England; sadly, he also requested that all papers and materials pertaining to his engines be destroyed.

Bibliography

July 1886, British patent no. 9,866 (fuel vapourization methods, scavenging systems and improvement of speed control; the patent describes Stuart as Mechanical Engineer of Bletchley Iron Works).

1890, British patent no. 7,146 and British patent no. 15,994 (describe a vaporizing chamber connected to the working cylinder by a small throat).

Further Reading

D. Clerk, 1895, *The Gas and Oil Engine*, 6th edn, London, pp. 420–6 (provides a detailed description of the Hornsby–Ackroyd engine and includes details of an engine test).

T. Hornbuckle and A.K. Bruce, 1940, *Herbert Akroyd Stuart and the Development of the Heavy Oil Engine*, London: Diesel Engine Users' Association, p. 1.

KAB

Stuart, James

b. 2 January 1843 Balgonie, Fife, Scotland
d. 12 October 1913 Norwich, Norfolk, England

Scottish engineer and educator.

James Stuart established the teaching of engineering as a university discipline at Cambridge. He was born at Balgonie in Fife, where his father managed a linen mill. He attended the University of St Andrews and then studied mathematics at Cambridge University. In 1867 he took up a post as Assistant Tutor at Trinity College, Cambridge, where his skills as a teacher were quickly recognized. The University was at that time adapting itself to the new systems of instruction recommended by the Royal Commission on university reform in the 1850s, and Stuart took an active part in the organization of a new structure of inter-collegiate lecture courses. He made an even more significant contribution to the establishment of extramural courses from which the Cambridge University extension lecture programme developed. This began in 1867, when Stuart took adult classes in Manchester and Crewe. The latter, in particular, brought him into close contact with those involved in practical mechanics and stimulated his interest in the applied sciences. In 1875 he was elected to the newly created Chair of Mechanism and Engineering in Cambridge, and he set out energetically to recruit students and to build up a flourishing unit with its own workshop and foundry, training a new generation of engineers in the applied sciences.

In November 1884 Stuart was elected to Parliament and embarked on an active but somewhat undistinguished career in politics as a radical Liberal, becoming amongst other things a keen supporter of the women's suffrage movement. This did not endear him to his academic colleagues, and the Engineering School suffered from neglect by Stuart until he resigned the Chair in 1890. By the time he left, however, the University was ready to recognize Engineering as a Tripos subject and to accept properly equipped teaching laboratories, so that his successor J.A. Ewing was able to benefit from Stuart's pioneering work. Stuart continued his political activities and was appointed a Privy Councillor in 1909. He married Elizabeth Colman after resigning the Chair, and on the death of his father-in-law in 1898 he moved to Norwich to take on the direction of the family mustard firm, J. & J. Colman Ltd.

Further Reading
Hilken, 1967, *Engineering at Cambridge*, Ch. 3, pp. 58–106.

AB

Stumpf, Johann
fl. *c.*1900 Germany

German inventor of a successful design of uniflow steam engine.

In 1869 Stumpf was commissioned by the Pope Manufacturing Company of Hertford, Connecticut, to set up two triple-expansion, vertical, **Corliss** pumping engines. He tried to simplify this complicated system and started research with the internal combustion engine and the steam turbine particularly as his models. The construction of steam turbines in several stages where the steam passed through in a unidirectional flow was being pursued at that time, and Stumpf wondered whether it would be possible to raise the efficiency of a reciprocating steam engine to the same thermal level as the turbine by the use of the uniflow principle.

Stumpf began to investigate these principles without studying the work of earlier pioneers like L.J. **Todd**, which he later thought would have led him astray. It was not until 1908, when he was Professor at the Institute of Technology in Berlin-Charlottenburg, that he patented his successful 'una-flow' steam engine. In that year he took out six British patents for improvements in details on his original one Stumpf fully realized the thermal advantages of compressing the residual steam and was able to evolve systems of coping with excessive compression when starting. He also placed steam-jackets around the ends of the cylinder. Stumpf's first engine was built in 1908 by the Erste Brünner Maschinenfabrik-Gesellschaft, and licences were taken out by many other manufacturers, including those in Britain and the USA. His engine was developed into the most economical type of reciprocating steam engine.

Bibliography
1912, *The Una-Flow Steam Engine*, Munich: R. Oldenbourg (his own account of the una-flow engine).

Further Reading
H.W. Dickinson, 1938, *A Short History of the Steam Engine*, Cambridge University Press; R.L. Hills, 1989, *Power from Steam. A History of the Stationary Steam Engine*, Cambridge University Press (both discuss Stumpf's engine).
H.J. Braun, 'The National Association of German-American Technologists and technology transfer between Germany and the United States, 1844–1930', *History of Technology* 8 (provides details of Stumpf's earlier work).

RLH

Sturgeon, William
b. 22 May 1783 Whittington, Lancashire, England
d. 4 December 1850 Prestwich, Manchester, England

English inventor and lecturer, discoverer of the electromagnet, and inventor of the first electric motor put to practical use.

After leaving an apprenticeship as a shoemaker, Sturgeon enlisted in the militia. Self-educated during service as a private in the Royal Artillery, he began to construct scientific apparatus. When he left the army in 1820 Sturgeon became an industrious writer, contributing papers to the *Philosophical Magazine*. In 1823 he was appointed Lecturer in Natural Science at the East India Company's Military College in Addiscombe. His invention in 1823 of an electromagnet with a horseshoe-shaped, soft iron core provided a much more concentrated magnetic field than previously obtained. An electric motor he designed in 1832 embodied his invention of the first metallic commutator. This was used to rotate a meat-roasting jack. Over an extended period he conducted researches into atmospheric electricity and also introduced the practice of amalgamating zinc in primary cells to prevent local action.

Sturgeon became Lecturer at the Adelaide Gallery, London, in 1832, an appointment of short duration, terminating when the gallery closed. In 1836 he established a monthly publication, *The Annals of Electricity, Magnetism and Chemistry; and Guardian of Experimental Science*, the first journal in England to be devoted to the subject. It was to this journal that James Prescot Joule contributed the results of his own researches in electromagnetism. Due to lack of financial support the publication ceased in 1843 after ten volumes had been issued. At the age of 57 Sturgeon became Superintendent of the Victoria Gallery of Practical Science in Manchester; after this gallery closed, the last five years of his life were spent in considerable poverty.

Principal Honours and Distinctions
Society of Arts Silver Medal 1825.

Bibliography
1836, *Annals of Electricity* 1: 75–8 (describes his motor).
All his published papers were collected in *Scientific Researches, Experimental and Theoretical in Electricity, Magnetism and Electro-Chemistry*, 1850, Bury; 1852, London.

Further Reading
J.P. Joule, 1857, biography, in *Memoirs of the Literary and Philosophical Society* 14, Manchester: 53–8.
Biography, 1895, *Electrician* 35: 632–5 (includes a list of Sturgeon's published work).
P. Dunsheath, 1957, *A History of Electrical Engineering*, London: Faber & Faber.

GW

Sullivan, Louis Henry

b. 3 September 1856 Boston, Massachusetts, USA
d. 14 April 1924 Chicago, Illinois, USA

American architect whose work came to be known as the 'Chicago School of Architecture' and who created a new style of architecture suited specifically to steel-frame, high-rise structures.

Sullivan, a Bostonian, studied at the Massachusetts Institute of Technology. Soon he joined his parents, who had moved to Chicago, and worked for a while in the office of William Le Baron **Jenney**, the pioneer of steel-frame construction. After spending some time studying at the Ecole des Beaux Arts in Paris, in 1875 Sullivan returned to Chicago, where he later met and worked for the Danish architect Dankmar Adler, who was practising there. In 1881 the two architects became partners, and during the succeeding fifteen years they produced their finest work and the buildings for which Sullivan is especially known.

During the early 1880s in Chicago, load-bearing, metal-framework structures that made lofty skyscrapers possible had been developed (see Jenney and **Holabird**). Louis H. Sullivan initiated building design to stress and complement the metal structure rather than hide it. Moving onwards from H.H. Richardson's treatment of his Marshall Field Wholesale Store in Chicago, Sullivan took the concept several stages further. His first outstanding work, built with Adler in 1886–9, was the Auditorium Building in Chicago. The exterior, in particular, was derived largely from Richardson's Field Store, and the building – now restored – is of bold but simple design, massively built in granite and stone, its form stressing the structure beneath. The architects' reputation was established with this building.

The firm of Sullivan & Adler established itself during the early 1890s, when they built their most famous skyscrapers. Adler was largely responsible for the structure, the acoustics and function, while Sullivan was responsible for the architectural design, concerning himself particularly with the limitation and careful handling of ornament. In 1892 he published his ideas in *Ornament in Architecture*, where he preached restraint in its quality and disposition. He established himself as a master of design in the building itself, producing a rhythmic simplicity of form, closely related to the structural shape beneath. The two great examples of this successful approach were the Wainwright Building in St Louis, Missouri (1890–1) and the Guaranty Building in Buffalo, New York (1894–5). The Wainwright Building was a ten-storeyed structure built in stone and brick and decorated with terracotta. The vertical line was stressed throughout but especially at the corners, where pilasters were wider. These rose unbroken to an Art Nouveau type of decorative frieze and a deeply projecting cornice above. The thirteen-storeyed Guaranty Building is Sullivan's masterpiece, a simple, bold, finely proportioned and essentially modern structure. The pilaster verticals are even more boldly stressed and decoration is at a minimum. In the twentieth century the almost free-standing supporting pillars on the ground floor have come to be called *pilotis*. As late as the 1920s, particularly in New York, the architectural style and decoration of skyscrapers remained traditionally eclectic, based chiefly upon Gothic or classical forms; in view of this, Sullivan's Guaranty Building was far ahead of its time.

Bibliography
Article by Louis H. Sullivan. Address delivered to architectural students June 1899, published in *Canadian Architecture* Vol. 18 (7): 52–3.

Further Reading
Hugh Morrison, 1962, *Louis Sullivan: Prophet of Modern Architecture.*
Willard Connely, 1961, *Louis Sullivan as He Lived*, New York: Horizon Press.

DY

Sundback, Gideon
fl. 1910 USA

American engineer who improved zip fasteners so they became both a practical and a commercial proposition.

The zip fastener was originally patented in the USA in 1896 by W.L. **Judson** of Chicago. At first it was used only in boots and shoes and was not a success because it tended to jam or spring open. It was expensive, for it was made largely by hand. Eventually the Automatic Hook and Eye Company of Hoboken, New Jersey, took on Dr Gideon Sundback, a Swedish electrical engineer who had settled in the United States in 1905. After several years' work Sundback filed a patent application and his model was sold as a novelty item but was still unsatisfactory in use. In 1912 he invented a hookless fastener which looked promising but also was impractical in use. Finally, in 1913, he invented a fastener which in all important essentials was the modern zip fastener and, in addition, he invented the machinery to produce it. However, clothing manufacturers continued to oppose its introduction until in 1918 a contractor making flying suits for the United States Navy placed an order for 10,000 fasteners and in 1923 B.F. Goodrich & Co. put zips in the galoshes that they manufactured. Success was assured from then on.

Further Reading
J. Jewkes, D. Sawers and R. Stillerman, 1969, *The Sources of Invention*, 2nd edn, London (discusses the invention).
I. McNeil (ed.), 1990, *An Encyclopaedia of the History of Technology*, London: Routledge pp. 852–3 (for an account of the development of fastenings).

RLH

Sung Ying-Hsing
See **Song Yingxing**.

Su Song (Su Sung)
b. 1020 China
d. 1101 China

Chinese astronomer and maker of a mechanical clock.

Su Song had a model armillary sphere in his home, which enabled him to study and understand the instrument, but he could not receive an imperial command to make a full-size one before holding an official position. This he attained, and he moved in high official circles in Imperial China; his official appointments included Ambassador, Minister of State and Deputy Imperial Tutor. At the same time he was an outstanding astronomer and calendrical scientist. With the assistance of Han Gonglian, he constructed a water-driven mechanical escapement clock and clocktower in 1088, which he described in detail in his *Xin Yi Xian Fa Yao,* completed in 1094; this book was noteworthy for illustrations of the armillary sphere and its component parts. The tower included an armillary sphere and celestial globe with clock drive. By applying clockwork to the observational side of the sphere, Su Song anticipated the clockwork drive of the telescope introduced by Robert **Hooke** six centuries later.

Su Song was also the pharmaceutical naturalist of the *Tu Jing Ben Cao* of 1061.

Bibliography
1094, *Xin Yi Xian Fa Yao.*

Further Reading
J. Needham, *Science and Civilisation in China*, Cambridge: Cambridge University Press, 1959–86, Vols III, pp. 208, 361–6; VI.1, 140, 174, 227, 252, 281, 335, 475, 477; *Heavenly Clockwork*, 1960, pp. 2–60, 64, 68, 70, 93–4, 115–18, 123–4, 133, 160, 162; *Clerks and Craftsmen in China and the West,* 1970, pp. 9, 6–7, 11–12, 91, 130–1, 192, 210ff., 221–3, 235, 280, 406.

LRD

Sutton, Thomas
b. 1819 England
d. 1875 Jersey, Channel Islands

English photographer and writer on photography.

In 1841, while studying at Cambridge, Sutton became interested in photography and tried out the current processes, daguerreotype, calotype and cyanotype among them. He subsequently settled in Jersey, where he continued his photographic studies. In 1855 he opened a photographic printing works in Jersey, in partnership with L.-D. **Blanquart-Evrard**, exploiting the latter's process for producing developed positive prints. He started and edited one of the first photographic periodicals, *Photographic Notes*, in 1856; until its cessation in 1867, his journal presented a fresher view of the world of photography than that given by its London-based rivals. He also drew up the first dictionary of photography in 1858.

In 1859 Sutton designed and patented a wide-angle lens in which the space between two meniscus lenses, forming parts of a sphere and sealed in a metal rim, was filled with water; the lens so formed could cover an angle of up to 120 degrees at an aperture of f12. Sutton's design was inspired by observing the images produced by the water-filled sphere of a 'snowstorm' souvenir brought home from Paris! Sutton commissioned the London camera-maker Frederick Cox to make the Panoramic camera, demonstrating the first model in January 1860; it took panoramic pictures on curved glass plates 152 x 381 mm in size. Cox later advertised other models in a total of four sizes. In January 1861 Sutton handed over manufacture to Andrew **Ross**'s son Thomas Ross, who produced much-improved lenses and also cameras in three sizes. Sutton then developed the first single-lens reflex camera design, patenting it on 20 August 1961: a pivoted mirror, placed at 45 degrees inside the camera, reflected the image from the lens onto a ground glass-screen set in the top of the camera for framing and focusing. When ready, the mirror was swung up out of the way to allow light to reach the plate at the back of the camera. The design was manufactured for a few years by Thomas Ross and J.H. **Dallmeyer**.

In 1861 James Clerk **Maxwell** asked Sutton to prepare a series of photographs for use in his lecture 'On the theory of three primary colours', to be presented at the Royal Institution in London on 17 May 1861. Maxwell required three photographs to be taken through red, green and blue filters, which were to be printed as lantern slides and projected in superimposition through three projectors. If his theory was correct, a colour reproduction of the original subject would be produced. Sutton used liquid filters: ammoniacal copper sulphate for blue, copper chloride for the green and iron sulphocyanide for the red. A fourth exposure was made through lemon-yellow glass, but was not used in the final demonstration. A tartan ribbon in a bow was used as the subject; the wet-collodion process in current use required six seconds for the blue exposure, about twice what would have been needed without the filter. After twelve minutes no trace of image was produced through the green filter, which had to be diluted to a pale green: a twelve-minute exposure then produced a serviceable negative. Eight minutes was enough to record an image through the red filter, although since the process was sensitive only to blue light, nothing at all should have been recorded. In 1961, R.M. Evans of the Kodak Research Laboratory showed that the red liquid transmitted ultraviolet radiation, and by an extraordinary coincidence many natural red dye-stuffs reflect ultraviolet. Thus the red separation was made on the basis of non-visible radiation rather than red, but the net result was correct and the projected images did give an identifiable reproduction of the original. Sutton's photographs enabled Maxwell to establish the validity of his theory and to provide the basis upon which all subsequent methods of colour photography have been founded.

JW/BC

Svaty, Vladimir
fl. 1950 Czechoslovakia

Czech inventor of a loom across which the weft was projected by a jet of water.

Since the 1930s people have been experimenting with ways of inserting the weft during weaving without using a massive shuttle. This would save wasting the energy that a shuttle requires to accelerate it through the warp and which is only to be lost when the shuttle is stopped in its box. Around 1950, the Czech engineer Vladimir Svaty had been working on air-jet looms, in which the weft was wafted across the loom by a jet of air. He then switched his interest to water-jet looms, and in 1955, at the Brussels exhibition, the first water-jet loom was displayed to a surprised world. In 1959 the Czechs had installed 150 of these looms at Semily in Czechoslovakia, weaving cloth 41 in. (104 cm) wide at 350 picks per minute. Water-jet looms are suitable only for certain types of synthetic fibres which are not affected by the wet. They are compact, quiet, mechanically simple and free from weft vibration. They find their most appropriate use in weaving simple fabrics from water-insensitive, continuous-filament yarn, which they can produce economically and with the highest quality.

Further Reading
J.J. Vincent, 1980, *Shuttleless Looms*, Manchester (written with inside knowledge of the problems; the author tried to develop a shuttleless loom himself).

RLH

Swan, Sir Joseph Wilson
b. 31 October 1828 Sunderland, England
d. 27 May 1914 Warlingham, Surrey, England

English chemist, inventor in Britain of the incandescent electric lamp and of photographic processes.

At the age of 14 Swan was apprenticed to a Sunderland firm of druggists, later joining John Mawson who had opened a pharmacy in Newcastle. While in Sunderland Swan attended lectures at the Athenaeum, at one of which W.E. **Staite** exhibited electric-arc and incandescent lighting. The impression made on Swan prompted him to conduct experiments that led to his demonstration of a practical working lamp in 1879. As early as 1848 he was experimenting with carbon as a lamp filament, and by 1869 he had mounted a strip of carbon in a vessel exhausted of air as completely as was then possible; however, because of residual air, the filament quickly failed.

Discouraged by the cost of current from primary batteries and the difficulty of achieving a good vacuum, Swan began to devote much of his attention to photography. With Mawson's support the pharmacy was expanded to include a photographic business. Swan's interest in making permanent photographic records led him to patent the carbon process in 1864 and he discovered how to make a sensitive dry plate in place of the inconvenient wet collodian process hitherto in use. He followed this success with the invention of bromide paper, the subject of a British patent in 1879.

Swan resumed his interest in electric lighting.

Sprengel's invention of the mercury pump in 1865 provided Swan with the means of obtaining the high vacuum he needed to produce a satisfactory lamp. Swan adopted a technique which was to become an essential feature in vacuum physics: continuing to heat the filament during the exhaustion process allowed the removal of absorbed gases. The inventions of **Gramme**, **Siemens** and **Brush** provided the source of electrical power at reasonable cost needed to make the incandescent lamp of practical service. Swan exhibited his lamp at a meeting in December 1878 of the Newcastle Chemical Society and again the following year before an audience of 700 at the Newcastle Literary and Philosophical Society. Swan's failure to patent his invention immediately was a tactical error as in November 1879 **Edison** was granted a British patent for his original lamp, which, however, did not go into production. Parchmentized thread was used in Swan's first commercial lamps, a material soon superseded by the regenerated cellulose filament that he developed. The cellulose filament was made by extruding a solution of nitro-cellulose in acetic acid through a die under pressure into a coagulating fluid, and was used until the ultimate obsolescence of the carbon-filament lamp. Regenerated cellulose became the first synthetic fibre, the further development and exploitation of which he left to others, the patent rights for the process being sold to Courtaulds.

Swan also devised a modification of **Planté**'s secondary battery in which the active material was compressed into a cellular lead plate. This has remained the central principle of all improvements in secondary cells, greatly increasing the storage capacity for a given weight.

Principal Honours and Distinctions
Knighted 1904. FRS 1894. President, Institution of Electrical Engineers 1898. First President, Faraday Society 1904. Royal Society Hughes Medal 1904. Chevalier de la Légion d'-Honneur 1881.

Bibliography
2 January 1880, British patent no. 18 (incandescent electric lamp).
24 May 1881, British patent no. 2,272 (improved plates for the Planté cell).
1898, 'The rise and progress of the electrochemical industries', *Journal of the Institution of*

Electrical Engineers 27: 8–33 (Swan's
Presidential Address to the Institution of Electrical Engineers).

Further Reading
M.E. Swan and K.R. Swan, 1968, *Sir Joseph
Wilson Swan F.R.S.*, Newcastle upon Tyne (a
detailed account).
R.C. Chirnside, 1979, 'Sir Joseph Swan and the
invention of the electric lamp', IEE *Electronics
and Power* 25: 96–100 (a short, authoritative
biography).

GW

Sykes, Adrian F.
fl. 1920s Britain

*English engineer who developed several early
mechanical and electromechanical recording
systems.*

The BBC used the Round-Sykes microphone.

In 1928 Sykes collaborated with W.D. Stern-
berg of British Homophone to exploit his patents on recording systems.

Sykes's contribution to sound recording lies in
the thorough analysis of the basic phenomena in
the mechanical side of recording. These analyses
are expressed by his many patent applications
which merged into complete specifications. His
basic patent on electromechanical recording
caused a fair amount of litigation in Germany.

GB-N

Symington, William
b. 1764 Leadhills, Lanarkshire, Scotland
d. 22 March 1831 Wapping, London, England

Scottish pioneer of steam navigation.

Symington was the son of the Superintendent of
the Mines Company in Lanarkshire, and attended the local school. When he was 22 years
old he was sent by Gilbert Meason, Manager of
the Wanlockhead mines, to Edinburgh University. In 1779 he was working on the assembly of
a **Watt** engine as an apprentice to his brother,
George, and in 1786 he started experiments to
modify a Watt engine in order to avoid infringing
the separate condenser patent. He sought a patent for his alternative, which was paid for by
Meason. He constructed a model steam road carriage which was completed in 1786; it was shown
in Edinburgh by Meason, attracting interest but

inadequate financial support. It had a horizontal
cylinder and was non-condensing. No full-sized
engine was ever built but the model secured the
interest of Patrick Miller, an Edinburgh banker,
who ordered an engine from Symington to drive
an experimental boat, 25 ft (7.6 m) long with a
dual hull, which performed satisfactorily on Dalswinton Loch in 1788. In the following year Miller ordered a larger engine for a bigger boat
which was tried on the Forth & Clyde Canal in
December 1789, the component parts having
been made by the Carron Company. The engine
worked perfectly but had the effect of breaking
the paddle wheels. These were repaired and further trials were successful but Miller lost interest
and his experiments lapsed. Symington devoted
himself thereafter to building stationary engines.
He built other engines for mine pumping at San-
quhar and Leadhills before going further afield.
In all, he built over thirty engines, about half of
them being rotary. In 1800–1 he designed the
engine for a boat for Lord Dundas, the *Charlotte
Dundas*; this was apparently the first boat of that
name and sailed on both the Forth and Clyde
rivers. A second *Charlotte Dundas* with a horizontal cylinder was to follow and first sailed in
January 1803 for the Forth & Clyde Canal Company. The speed of the boat was only 2 mph (3
km/h) and much was made by its detractors of
the damage said to be caused to the canal banks
by its wash. Lord Dundas declined to authorize
payment of outstanding accounts; Symington received little reward for his efforts. He died in the
house of his son-in-law, Dr Robert Bowie, in
Wapping, amidst heated controversy about the
true inventor of steam navigation.

Further Reading
W.S. Harvey and G. Downs-Rose, 1980, *William Symington, Inventor and Engine-Builder*,
London: Mechanical Engineering Publications.

IMcN

Syracuse, Archimedes of
See **Archimedes of Syracuse**.

Szilard, Leo
b. 11 February 1898 Budapest, Hungary
d. 30 May 1964 La Jolla, California, USA

Szilard, Leo

Hungarian (naturalized American in 1943) nuclear- and biophysicist .

The son of an engineer, Szilard, after service in the Austro-Hungarian army during the First World War, studied electrical engineering at the University of Berlin. Obtaining his doctorate there in 1922, he joined the faculty and concentrated his studies on thermodynamics. He later began to develop an interest in nuclear physics, and in 1933, shortly after Hitler came to power, Szilard emigrated to Britain because of his Jewish heritage.

In 1934 he conceived the idea of a nuclear chain reaction through the breakdown of beryllium into helium and took out a British patent on it, but later realized that this process would not work. In 1937 he moved to the USA and continued his research at the University of Columbia, and the following year Hahn and Meitner discovered nuclear fission with uranium; this gave Szilard the breakthrough he needed. In 1939 he realized that a nuclear chain reaction could be produced through nuclear fission and that a weapon with many times the destructive power of the conventional high-explosive bomb could be produced. Only too aware of the progress being made by German nuclear scientists, he believed that it was essential that the USA should create an atomic bomb before Hitler. Consequently he drafted a letter to President Roosevelt that summer and, with two fellow Hungarian émigrés, persuaded Albert Einstein to sign it. The result was the setting up of the Uranium Committee.

It was not, however, until December 1941 that active steps began to be taken to produce such a weapon and it was a further nine months before the project was properly co-ordinated under the umbrella of the Manhattan Project. In the meantime, Szilard moved to join Enrico **Fermi** at the University of Chicago and it was here, at the end of 1942, in a squash court under the football stadium, that they successfully developed the world's first self-sustaining nuclear reactor. Szilard, who became an American citizen in 1943, continued to work on the Manhattan Project. In 1945, however, when the Western Allies began to believe that only the atomic bomb could bring the war against Japan to an end, Szilard and a number of other Manhattan Project scientists objected that it would be immoral to use it against populated targets.

Although he would continue to campaign against nuclear warfare for the rest of his life, Szilard now abandoned nuclear research. In 1946 he became Professor of Biophysics at the University of Chicago and devoted himself to experimental work on bacterial mutations and biochemical mechanisms, as well as theoretical research on ageing and memory.

Principal Honours and Distinctions
Atoms for Peace award 1959.

Further Reading
Kosta Tsipis, 1985, *Understanding Nuclear Weapons*, London: Wildwood House, pp. 16–19, 26, 28, 32 (a brief account of his work on the atomic bomb).
A collection of his correspondence and memories was brought out by Spencer Weart and Gertrud W. Szilard in 1978.

CM

T

Tagliacocci, Gaspard

b. 1546 Bologna, Italy
d. 7 November 1599 Bologna, Italy

Italian physician, surgeon and anatomist, first exponent of plastic surgery and other cosmetic surgery techniques.

He studied at Bologna University and took his degree in medicine at the age of 24. He was later appointed Professor of Surgery and of Anatomy. In his writings he appears to have preceded some of the work of **Paré** and gives a detailed account of rhinoplasty facilitated by the deployment of strips of skin. He also described a type of artificial eye resembling Paré's ekblepharon. His surgical skill appears to have been highly regarded by his contemporaries.

Bibliography
1598, *Chirurgerie Nova de Narium, Aurium, Labiorum que Defecta per Institutionem Cutis ex Humero, arte hactenus omnibus ignota sarciendo*, Frankfurt.

Further Reading
H. Reichner, 1950, *The Life and Times of Gaspere Tagliacozzi*.

MG

Tainter, Charles Sumner

b. 1854
d. 1940

American scientific instrument maker, co-developer of practical cylinder recording.

He manufactured 'philosophical devices' in Cambridge, Massachusetts, and was approached by Alexander Graham **Bell** in connection with the construction of toys using sound recordings. A more formal co-operation was agreed, and after Bell's receipt of the French Volta prize in 1880 he financed the Volta Laboratory Association in Washington, DC. He founded this in 1881 together with a cousin and Tainter to develop a practical sound-recording and -reproducing system. Another area that was developed was the transmission of sound by means of modulated light and reception via a selenium cell.

The advances in sound recording and reproduction were very positive, and T.A. **Edison** was approached in mid-1885 in order to establish co-operation in the further development of a cylinder instrument. In early 1886 the Volta Graphophone Company was incorporated in Virginia, and an experimental laboratory was established in Washington, DC. The investors were connected with the secretarial services at the House of Representatives and needed the development for increasing efficiency in debate reporting. In mid-1887 Edison, against the advice of his collaborators, declined co-operation and went ahead on his own. There is no doubt that Tainter's skill in developing functional equipment and the speed with which he was able to work in the crucial years provoked other developments in the field, in particular the perfection of the Edison phonograph and the development of the disc record by **Berliner**.

Bibliography
Tainter's patents were numerous; those on sound recording were the most important, because they incorporated so many fundamental ideas, and included US patent no. 341,214 (with C.A. Bell), and US patent no. 375,579 (a complete dictation outfit).

Further Reading
V.K. Chew, 1981, *Talking Machines*, London: Science Museum and HMSO, pp. 9–12 (provides a good overview, not only of Tainter's contribution, but also of early sound recording and reproduction).

GB-N

Talbot, Benjamin

b. 19 September 1864 Wellington, Shropshire, England
d. 16 December 1947 Solberge Hall, Northallerton, Yorkshire, England

English steelmaker and businessman who introduced a technique for producing steel 'continuously' in large tilting basic-lined open-hearth furnaces.

After spending some years at his father's Castle Ironworks and at Ebbw Vale Works, Talbot travelled to the USA in 1890 to become Superintendent of the Southern Iron and Steel Company of Chattanooga, Tennessee, where he initiated basic open-hearth steelmaking and a preliminary slag washing to remove silicon. In 1893 he moved to Pennsylvania as Steel Superintendent at the Pencoyd works; there, six years later, he began his 'continuous' steelmaking process. Returning to Britain in 1900, Talbot marketed the technique: after ten years it was in successful use in Britain, continental Europe and the USA; it promoted the growth of steel production.

Meanwhile its originator had joined the Cargo Fleet Iron Company Limited on Teesside, where he was made Managing Director in 1907. Twelve years later he assumed, in addition, the same position in the allied South Durham Steel and Iron Company Limited. While remaining Managing Director, he was appointed Deputy Chairman of both companies in 1925, and Chairman in 1940. The companies he controlled survived the depressed 1920s and 1930s and were significant contributors to British steel output, with a capacity of more than half a million tonnes per year.

Principal Honours and Distinctions
President, Iron and Steel Institute 1928, and (British) National Federation of Iron and Steel Manufacturers. Iron and Steel Institute (London) Bessemer Gold Medal 1908. Franklin Institute (Philadelphia), Elliott Cresson Gold Medal, and John Scott Medal 1908.

Bibliography
1900, 'The open-hearth continuous steel process', *Journal of the Iron and Steel Institute* 57 (1): 33–61.
1903, 'The development of the continuous open-hearth process', *Journal of the Iron and Steel Institute* 63 (1): 57–73.
1905, 'Segregation in steel ingots', *Journal of the Iron and Steel Institute* 68 (2): 204–23.
1913, 'The production of sound steel by lateral compression of the ingot whilst its centre is liquid', *Journal of the Iron and Steel Institute* 87 (1): 30–55.

Further Reading
G. Boyce, 1986, entry in *Dictionary of Business Biography*, Vol. V, ed.J. Jeremy, Butterworth.
W.G. Willis, 1969, *South Durham Steel and Iron Co. Ltd*, South Durham Steel and Iron Company Ltd (includes a few pages specifically on Talbot, and a portrait photo).
J.C. Carr and W. Taplin, 1962, *History of the British Steel Industry*, Cambridge, Mass.: Harvard University Press (mentions Talbot's business attitudes).

JKA

Talbot, William Henry Fox
b. 11 February 1800 Melbury, England
d. 17 September 1877 Lacock, Wiltshire, England

English scientist, inventor of negative–positive photography and practicable photo engraving.

Educated at Harrow, where he first showed an interest in science, and at Cambridge, Talbot was an outstanding scholar and a formidable mathematician. He published over fifty scientific papers and took out twelve English patents. His interests outside the field of science were also wide and included Assyriology, etymology and the classics. He was briefly a Member of Parliament, but did not pursue a parliamentary career.

Talbot's invention of photography arose out of his frustrating attempts to produce acceptable pencil sketches using popular artist's aids, the camera discura and camera lucida. From his experiments with the former he conceived the idea of placing on the screen a paper coated with silver salts so that the image would be captured chemically. During the spring of 1834 he made outline images of subjects such as leaves and flowers by placing them on sheets of sensitized paper and exposing them to sunlight. No camera was involved and the first images produced using an optical system were made with a solar microscope. It was only when he had devised a more sensitive paper that Talbot was able to make camera pictures; the earliest surviving camera negative dates from August 1835. From the beginning, Talbot noticed that the lights and shades of his images were reversed. During 1834 or 1835 he discovered that by placing this reversed image on another sheet of sensitized paper and again exposing it to sunlight, a picture was produced with lights and shades in the correct disposition. Talbot had discovered the basis of modern photography, the photographic negative, from which could be produced an unlimited number of positives. He did little further work until the announcement of **Daguerre**'s process in 1839 prompted him to publish an account of his negative–positive process. Aware that his photogenic drawing process had many imperfections, Talbot plunged into further experiments and in September 1840, using a mixture incorporating a solution of gallic acid, discovered an invisible latent image that could be made visible by development. This improved calotype process dramatically shortened exposure times and allowed Talbot to take portraits. In 1841 he patented the process, an exercise that was later to cause controversy, and between 1844 and 1846 produced *The Pencil of Nature*, the world's first commercial photographically illustrated book.

Concerned that some of his photographs were prone to fading, Talbot later began experiments to combine photography with printing and engraving. Using bichromated gelatine, he devised the first practicable method of photo engraving, which was patented as Photoglyphic engraving in October 1852. He later went on to use screens of gauze, muslin and finely powdered gum to break up the image into lines and dots, thus anticipating modern photomechanical processes.

Talbot was described by contemporaries as the 'Father of Photography' primarily in recognition of his discovery of the negative–positive process, but he also produced the first photomicrographs, took the first high-speed photographs with the aid of a spark from a Leyden jar, and is credited with proposing infra-red photography. He was a shy man and his misguided attempts to enforce his calotype patent made him many enemies. It was perhaps for this reason that he never received the formal recognition from the British nation that his family felt he deserved.

Principal Honours and Distinctions
FRS March 1831. Royal Society Rumford Medal 1842. Grand Médaille d'Honneur, L'Exposition Universelle, Paris, 1855. Honorary Doctorate of Laws, Edinburgh University, 1863.

Bibliography
1839, 'Some account of the art of photographic drawing', *Royal Society Proceedings* 4: 120–1; *Phil. Mag.*, XIV, 1839, pp. 19–21.
8 February 1841, British patent no. 8842 (calotype process).
1844–6, *The Pencil of Nature*, 6 parts, London (Talbot'a account of his invention can be found in the introduction; there is a facsimile edn, with an intro. by Beamont Newhall, New York, 1968.

Further Reading
H.J.P. Arnold, 1977, *William Henry Fox Talbot*, London.
D.B. Thomas, 1964, *The First Negatives*, London (a lucid concise account of Talbot's photograph work).
J. Ward and S. Stevenson, 1986, *Printed Light*, Edinburgh (an essay on Talbot's invention and its reception).
H. Gernsheim and A. Gernsheim, 1977, *The History of Photography*, London (a wider picture of Talbot, based primarily on secondary sources).

JW

Taliedo, Conte di
See **Caproni, Giovanni Battista**.

Taylor, Albert Hoyt
b. 1 January 1874 Chicago, Illinois, USA
d. 11 December 1961 Claremont, California, USA

American radio engineer whose work on radio-detection helped lay the foundations for radar.

Taylor gained his degree in engineering from Northwest University, Evanston, Illinois, then spent a time at the University of Göttingen. On his return to the USA he taught successively at Michigan State University, at Lansing, and at the universities of Wisconsin at Madison and North Dakota at Grand Forks. From 1923 until 1945 he supervised the Radio Division at the US Naval Research Laboratories. There he carried out studies of short-wave radio propagation and confirmed **Heaviside**'s 1925 theory of the reflection characteristics of the ionosphere. In the 1920s and 1930s he investigated radio echoes, and in 1933, with L.C. Young and L.A. Hyland, he filed a patent for a system of radio-detection that contributed to the subsequent development of radar.

Principal Honours and Distinctions
Institute of Electrical and Electronics Engineers Morris N. Liebmann Memorial Award 1927. President, Institute of Radio Engineers 1929. Institute of Electrical and Electronics Engineers Medal of Honour 1942.

Bibliography
1926, with E.O. Hulbert, 'The propagation of radio waves over the earth', *Physical Review* 27: 189.
1936, 'The measurement of RF power', *Proceedings of the Institute of Radio Engineers* 24: 1,342.

Further Reading
S.S. Swords, 1986, *Technical History of the Beginnings of Radar*, London: Peter Peregrinus.

See also **Watson-Watt, Sir Robert Alexander**.
KF

Taylor, David Watson
b. 4 March 1864 Louisa County, Virginia, USA
d. 29 July 1940 Washington, DC, USA

American hydrodynamicist and Rear Admiral in the United States Navy Construction Corps.

Taylor's first years were spent on a farm in Virginia, but at the age of 13 he went to Randolph-Macon College, graduating in 1881, and from there to the US Naval Academy, Annapolis. He graduated at the head of his class, had some sea time, and then went to the Royal Naval College in Greenwich, England, where in 1888 he again came top of the class with the highest-ever marks of any student, British or overseas.

On his return to the United States he held various posts as a constructor, ending this period at the Mare Island Navy Yard in California. In 1894 he was transferred to Washington, where he joined the Bureau of Construction and started to interest the Navy in ship model testing. Under his direction, the first ship model tank in the United States was built at Washington and for fourteen years operated under his control. The work of this establishment gave him the necessary information to write the highly acclaimed

text *The Speed and Power of Ships*, which with revisions is still in use. By the outbreak of the First World War he was one of the world's most respected naval architects, and had been retained as a consultant by the British Government in the celebrated case of the collision between the White Star Liner *Olympic* and HMS *Hawke*.

In December 1914 Taylor became a Rear-Admiral and was appointed Chief Constructor of the US Navy. His term of office was extremely stressful, with over 1,000 ships constructed for the war effort and with the work of the fledgling Bureau for Aeronautics also under his control. The problems were not over in 1918 as the Washington Treaty required drastic pruning of the Navy and a careful reshaping of the defence force.

Admiral Taylor retired from active service at the beginning of 1923 but retained several consultancies in aeronautics, shipping and naval architecture. For many years he served as consultant to the ship-design company now known as Gibbs and Cox. Many honours came his way, but the most singular must be the perpetuation of his name in the David Taylor Medal, the highest award of the Society of Naval Architects and Marine Engineers in the United States. Similarly, the Navy named its ship test tank facility, which was opened in Maryland in 1937, the David W. Taylor Model Basin.

Principal Honours and Distinctions
President, Society of Naval Architects and Marine Engineers 1925–7. United States Distinguished Service Medal. American Society of Civil Engineers John Fritz Medal. Institution of Naval Architects Gold Medal 1894 (the first American citizen to receive it). Society of Naval Architects and Marine Engineers David W. Taylor Medal 1936 (the first occasion of this award).

Bibliography
Resistance of Ships and Screw Propulsion.
1911, *The Speed and Power of Ships*, New York: Wiley.
Taylor gave many papers to the Maritime Institutions of both the United States and the United Kingdom.

FMW

Taylor, Frederick Winslow

b. 20 March 1856 Germantown, Pennsylvania, USA
d. 21 March 1915 Philadelphia, Pennsylvania, USA

American mechanical engineer and pioneer of scientific management.

Frederick W. Taylor received his early education from his mother, followed by some years of schooling in France and Germany. Then in 1872 he entered Phillips Exeter Academy, New Hampshire, to prepare for Harvard Law School, as it was intended that he should follow his father's profession. However, in 1874 he had to abandon his studies because of poor eyesight, and he began an apprenticeship at a pump-manufacturing works in Philadelphia learning the trades of pattern-maker and machinist. On its completion in 1878 he joined the Midvale Steel Company, at first as a labourer but then as Shop Clerk and Foreman, finally becoming Chief Engineer in 1884. At the same time he was able to resume study in the evenings at the Stevens Institute of Technology, and in 1883 he obtained the degree of Mechanical Engineer (ME). He also found time to take part in amateur sport and in 1881 he won the tennis doubles championship of the United States.

It was while with the Midvale Steel Company that Taylor began the systematic study of workshop management, and the application of his techniques produced significant increases in the company's output and productivity. In 1890 he became Manager of a company operating large paper mills in Maine and Wisconsin, until 1893 when he set up on his own account as a consulting engineer specializing in management organization. In 1898 he was retained exclusively by the Bethlehem Steel Company, and there continued his work on the metal-cutting process that he had started at Midvale. In collaboration with J. Maunsel White (1856–1912) he developed high-speed tool steels and their heat treatment which increased cutting capacity by up to 300 per cent. He resigned from the Bethlehem Steel Company in 1901 and devoted the remainder of his life to expounding the principles of scientific management which became known as 'Taylorism'. The Society to Promote the Science of Management was established in 1911, renamed the Taylor Society after his death. He was an active member of the American Society of Mechanical Engineers and was its President in 1906; his presidential address 'On the Art of Cutting Metals' was reprinted in book form.

Principal Honours and Distinctions
Paris Exposition Gold Medal 1900. Franklin Institute Elliott Cresson Gold Medal 1900. President, American Society of Mechanical Engineers 1906. Hon. ScD, University of Pennsylvania 1906. Hon. LLD, Hobart College 1912.

Bibliography
F.W. Taylor was the author of about 100 patents, several papers to the American Society of Mechanical Engineers, *On the Art of Cutting Metals* (1907, New York) and *The Principles of Scientific Management* (1911, New York) and, with S.E. Thompson, 1905 *A Treatise on Concrete*, New York, and *Concrete Costs*, 1912, New York.

Further Reading
The standard biography is Frank B. Copley, 1923, *Frederick W. Taylor, Father of Scientific Management*, New York (reprinted 1969, New York) and there have been numerous commentaries on his work: see, for example, Daniel Nelson, 1980, *Frederick W. Taylor and the Rise of Scientific Management*, Madison, Wis.

RTS

Taylor, John

b. 16 August 1703 Norwich, England
d. 17 September 1772 Prague, Bohemia

English oculist and exponent of surgical treatment of squint and cataract.

In 1722, employed as an apothecary's assistant, he studied surgery and especially diseases of the eye under Cheselden at St Thomas's Hospital, London. He returned to Norwich to practise, but in 1727 he assumed the role of itinerant surgeon oculist, with a particular reputation for putting eyes straight; at first he covered the major part of the British Isles and then he extended his activities to Europe.

He obtained MDs from Basle in 1733, and from Liège and Cologne in 1734. In 1736 he was appointed Oculist to George II. It is likely that he was responsible for Johann Sebastian

Bach's blindness, and Gibbon was one of his patients. The subject of considerable obloquy on account of his self-advertisement in the crudest and most bombastic terms, it is none the less certain that he had developed a technique, probably related to couching, which was considerably in advance of that of other practitioners and at least offered a prospect of assistance where none had been available.

Dr Johnson declared him 'an instance of how far impudence will carry ignorance'. Without justification, he styled himself 'Chevalier'. He is said, not improbably having regard to his age, to have become blind himself later in life. His son carried on his practice.

Bibliography
1727, *An Account of the Mechanism of the Eye*, Norwich.
1736, *Treatise on the Chrystalline Humour of the Human Eye*, London.
1739, *De vera causi strabismi*, Lisbon.

Further Reading
1761, *The History of the Travels and Adventures of the Chevalier John Taylor, Ophthalmiater*, London.

MG

Taylor, William
b. 11 June 1865 London, England
d. 28 February 1937 Laughton, Leicestershire, England

English mechanical engineer and metrologist, originator of standard screw threads for lens mountings and inventor of 'Dimple' golf balls.

William Taylor served an apprenticeship from 1880 to 1885 in London with Paterson and Cooper, electrical engineers and instrument makers. He studied at the Finsbury Technical College under Professors W.E. Ayrton (1847–1908) and John Perry (1850–1920). He remained with Paterson and Cooper until 1887, when he joined his elder brother, who had set up in Leicester as a manufacturer of optical instruments. The firm was then styled T.S. & W. Taylor and a few months later, when H.W. Hobson joined them as a partner, it became Taylor, Taylor and Hobson, as it was known for many years.

William Taylor was mainly responsible for technical developments in the firm and he de-signed the special machine tools required for making lenses and their mountings. However, his most notable work was in originating methods of measuring and gauging screw threads. He proposed a standard screw-thread for lens mountings that was adopted by the Royal Photographic Society, and he served on screw thread committees of the British Standards Institution and the British Association. His interest in golf led him to study the flight of the golf ball, and he designed and patented the 'Dimple' golf ball and a mechanical driving machine for testing golf balls.

He was an active member of the Institution of Mechanical Engineers, being elected Associate Member in 1894, Member in 1901 and Honorary Life Member in 1936. He served on the Council from 1918 and was President in 1932. He took a keen interest in engineering education and advocated the scientific study of materials, processes and machine tools, and of management. His death occurred suddenly while he was helping to rescue his son's car from a snowdrift.

Principal Honours and Distinctions
OBE 1918. FRS 1934. President, Institution of Mechanical Engineers 1932.

Further Reading
K.J. Hume, 1980, *A History of Engineering Metrology*, London, 110–21 (a short account of William Taylor and of Taylor, Taylor and Hobson).

RTS

Telford, Thomas
b. 9 August 1757 Glendinning, Dumfriesshire, Scotland.
d. 2 September 1834 London, England.

Scottish civil engineer.

Telford was the son of a shepherd, who died when the boy was in his first year. Brought up by his mother, Janet Jackson, he attended the parish school at Westerkirk. He was apprenticed to a stonemason in Lochmaben and to another in Langholm. In 1780 he walked from Eskdale to Edinburgh and in 1872 rode to London on a horse that he was to deliver there. He worked for Sir William Chambers as a mason on Somerset House, then on the Eskdale house of Sir James Johnstone. In 1783–4 he worked on the new

Commissioner's House and other buildings at Portsmouth dockyard.

In late 1786 Telford was appointed County Surveyor for Shropshire and moved to Shrewsbury Castle, with work initially on the new infirmary and County Gaol. He designed the church of St Mary Magdalene, Bridgnorth, and also the church at Madley. Telford built his first bridge in 1790–2 at Montford; between 1790 and 1796 he built forty-five road bridges in Shropshire, including Buildwas Bridge. In September 1793 he was appointed general agent, engineer and architect to the Ellesmere Canal, which was to connect the Mersey and Dee rivers with the Severn at Shrewsbury; William **Jessop** was Principal Engineer. This work included the Pont Cysyllte aqueduct, a 1,000 ft (305 m) long cast-iron trough 127 ft (39 m) above ground level, which entailed an on-site ironworks and took ten years to complete; the aqueduct is still in use today. In 1800 Telford put forward a plan for a new London Bridge with a single cast-iron arch with a span of 600 ft (183 m) but this was not built.

In 1801 Telford was appointed engineer to the British Fisheries Society 'to report on Highland Communications' in Scotland where, over the following eighteen years, 920 miles (1,480 km) of new roads were built, 280 miles (450 km) of the old military roads were realigned and rebuilt, over 1,000 bridges were constructed and much harbour work done, all under Telford's direction. A further 180 miles (290 km) of new roads were also constructed in the Lowlands of Scotland. From 1804 to 1822 he was also engaged on the construction of the Caledonian Canal: 119 miles (191 km) in all, 58 miles (93 km) being sea loch, 38 miles (61 km) being Lochs Lochy, Oich and Ness, 23 miles (37 km) having to be cut.

In 1808 he was invited by King Gustav IV Adolf of Sweden to assist Count Baltzar von Platen in the survey and construction of a canal between the North Sea and the Baltic. Telford surveyed the 114 mile (183 km) route in six weeks; 53 miles (85 km) of new canal were to be cut. Soon after the plans for the canal were completed, the King of Sweden created him a Knight of the Order of Vasa, an honour that he would have liked to have declined. At one time some 60,000 soldiers and seamen were engaged on the work, Telford supplying supervisors, machinery – including an 8 hp steam dredger from the Donkin works and machinery for two small paddle boats – and ironwork for some of the locks. Under his direction an ironworks was set up at Motala, the foundation of an important Swedish industrial concern which is still flourishing today. The Gotha Canal was opened in September 1832.

In 1811 Telford was asked to make recommendations for the improvement of the Shrewsbury to Holyhead section of the London–Holyhead road, and in 1815 he was asked to survey the whole route from London for a Parliamentary Committee. Construction of his new road took fifteen years, apart from the bridges at Conway and over the Menai Straits, both suspension bridges by Telford and opened in 1826. The Menai bridge had a span of 579 ft (176 m), the roadway being 153 ft (47 m) above the water level.

In 1817 Telford was appointed Engineer to the Exchequer Loan Commission, a body set up to make capital loans for deserving projects in the hard times that followed after the peace of Waterloo. In 1820 he became the first President of the Engineers Institute, which gained its Royal Charter in 1828 to become the Institution of Civil Engineers. He was appointed Engineer to the St Katharine's Dock Company during its construction from 1825 to 1828, and was consulted on several early railway projects including the Liverpool and Manchester as well as a number of canal works in the Midlands including the new Harecastle tunnel, 3,000 ft (914 m) long.

Telford led a largely itinerant life, living in hotels and lodgings, acquiring his own house for the first time in 1821, 24 Abingdon Street, Westminster, which was partly used as a school for young civil engineers. He died there in 1834, after suffering in his later years from the isolation of deafness. He was buried in Westminster Abbey.

Principal Honours and Distinctions
FRSE 1803. Knight of the Order of Vasa, Sweden 1808. FRS 1827. First President, Engineers Insitute 1820.

Further Reading
L.T.C. Rolt, 1979, *Thomas Telford*, London: Penguin.
C. Hadfield, 1993, *Thomas Telford's Temptation*, London: M. & M. Baldwin.

IMcN

Temple, Lewis
b. 1800 Richmond, Virginia, USA
d. 1854 New Bedford, Massachusetts, USA

African-American inventor of the toggle harpoon for whaling.

An African-American blacksmith, he emigrated as a young man to New Bedford, Massachusetts, and set up a shop at Coffin's Wharf that was devoted to whalecraft. In 1845 he was able to establish a blacksmith's shop at Walnut Street Wharf. There, in 1848, Temple introduced his toggle harpoon. This was found to be more effective than the barb attached to a rope used up until then, and was rapidly taken up by the whaling industry. As Temple did not patent his device, many other blacksmiths were able to make it and he gained little financial return from his invention. Injuries sustained in an accident in 1853 undermined his health and he died the following year.

Further Reading
P.P. James, 1989, *The Real McCoy: African-American Invention and Innovation 1619–1930*, Washington, DC: Smithsonian Institution, pp. 35–7.

LRD

Tennant, Charles
b. 3 May 1768 Ochiltree, Ayrshire, Scotland
d. 1 October 1838 Glasgow, Scotland

Scottish inventor of bleaching powder.

After education at the local school, Tennant went to Kilbachan to learn the manufacture of silk. He then went on to Wellmeadow, where he acquired a knowledge of the old bleaching process, which enabled him to establish his own bleachfield at Darnly. The process consisted of boiling the fabric in weak alkali and then laying it flat on the ground to expose it to sun and air for several months. This process, expensive in time and space, would have formed an intolerable bottleneck in the rapidly expanding textile industry, but a new method was on the way. The French chemist **Berthollet** demonstrated in 1786 the use of chlorine as a bleaching agent and James **Watt** learned of this while on a visit to Paris. On his return to Glasgow, Watt passed details of the new process on to Tennant, who set about devising his own version of it. First he ob-

tained a bleaching liquor by passing chlorine through a stirred mixture of lime and water. He was granted a patent for this process in 1798, but it was promptly infringed by bleachers in Lancashire. Tennant's efforts to enforce the patent were unsuccessful as it was alleged that others had employed a similar process some years previously. Nevertheless, the Lancashire bleachers had the good grace to present Tennant with a service of plate in recognition of the benefits he had brought to the industry.

In 1799 Tennant improved on his process by substituting dry slaked lime for the liquid, to form bleaching powder. This was patented the same year and proved to be a vital element in the advance of the textile industry. The following year, Tennant established his chemical plant at St Rollox, outside Glasgow, to manufacture bleaching powder and alkali substances. The plant prospered and became for a time the largest chemical works in Europe.

Further Reading
L.F. Haber, 1958, *The Chemical Industry During the Nineteenth Century*, London: Oxford University Press.
F.S. Taylor, 1957, *A History of Industrial Chemistry*, London: Heinemann.
Walker, 1862, *Memoirs of Distinguished Men of Science of Great Britain Living in 1807–1808*, London, p. 186.

LRD

Terragni, Giuseppe
b. 1904 Meda, near Milan, Italy
d. 1943 Como (?), Italy

Italian architect, leader of the modern school in Italy in the inter-war years.

As early as 1926 Terragni helped to found the *gruppo sette*, the seven architects who joined the *Movimento Italiano per l'Archittetura Razionale*. These architects enunciated a new architectural theme based upon simplicity, a clean use of quality materials and an end to eclecticism. They were all young, strongly imbued with the ideals of the Bauhaus (see **Gropius**) and of Frank Lloyd **Wright** in America. Terragni's best and most typical work is the Casa del Popolo (originally built as the Casa del Fascio) in Como (1932–6), a streamline, simple, high-quality building reminiscent of the contemporary work of Le

Corbusier (Charles-Edouard **Jeanneret**). Unfortunately his career was cut short when he was killed in action during the Second World War.

Further Reading
Mario Labò, 1947, *Giuseppe Terragni*, Milan: Il Balcone.
Bruno Zevi, 1980, *Giuseppe Terragni*, Bologna: Zanichelli.

DY

Tesla, Nikola
b. 9 July 1856 Smiljan, Croatia
d. 7 January 1943 New York, USA

Serbian (naturalized American) engineer and inventor of polyphase electrical power systems.

While at the technical institute in Graz, Austria, Tesla's attention was drawn to the desirability of constructing a motor without a commutator. He considered the sparking between the commutator and brushes of the **Gramme** machine when run as a motor a serious defect. In 1881 he went to Budapest to work on the telegraph system and while there conceived the principle of the rotating magnetic field, upon which all polyphase induction motors are based. In 1882 Tesla moved to Paris and joined the Continental Edison Company. After building a prototype of his motor he emigrated to the United States in 1884, becoming an American citizen in 1889. He left Edison and founded an independent concern, the Tesla Electric Company, to develop his inventions.

The importance of Tesla's first patents, granted in 1888 for alternating-current machines, cannot be over-emphasized. They covered a complete polyphase system including an alternator and induction motor. Other patents included the polyphase transformer, synchronous motor and the star connection of three-phase machines. These were to become the basis of the whole of the modern electric power industry. The Westinghouse company purchased the patents and marketed Tesla motors, obtaining in 1893 the contract for the Niagara Falls two-phase alternators driven by 5,000 hp (3,700 kW) water turbines.

After a short period with Westinghouse, Tesla resigned to continue his research into high-frequency and high-voltage phenomena using the Tesla coil, an air-cored transformer. He lectured in America and Europe on his high-frequency

devices, enjoying a considerable international reputation. The name 'tesla' has been given to the SI unit of magnetic-flux density. The induction motor became one of the greatest advances in the industrial application of electricity. A claim for priority of invention of the induction motor was made by protagonists of Galileo Ferraris (1847–1897), whose discovery of rotating magnetic fields produced by alternating currents was made independently of Tesla's. Ferraris demonstrated the phenomenon but neglected its exploitation to produce a practical motor. Tesla himself failed to reap more than a small return on his work and later became more interested in scientific achievement than commercial success, with his patents being infringed on a wide scale.

Principal Honours and Distinctions
American Institute of Electrical Engineers Edison Medal 1917. Tesla received doctorates from fourteen universities.

Bibliography
1 May 1888, American patent no. 381,968 (initial patent for the three-phase induction motor).
1956, *Nikola Tesla, 1856–1943, Lectures, Patents, Articles*, ed. L.I. Anderson, Belgrade (selected works, in English).
1977, *My Inventions*, repub. Zagreb (autobiography).

Further Reading
M. Cheney, 1981, *Tesla: Man Out of Time*, New Jersey (a full biography).
C. Mackechnie Jarvis, 1969, in IEE *Electronics and Power* 15: 436–40 (a brief treatment).
T.C. Martin, 1894, *The Inventions, Researches and Writings of Nikola Tesla*, New York (covers his early work on polyphase systems).

GW

Theophilus Presbyter
fl. late eleventh/early twelfth century

German author of the most detailed medieval treatise relating to technology.

The little that is known of Theophilus is what can be inferred from his great work, *De diversis artibus*. He was a Benedictine monk and priest living in north-west Germany, probably near an important art centre. He was an educated man, conversant with scholastic philosophy and at the same time a skilled, practising craftsman. Even his identity is obscure: Theophilus is a pseudonym, possibly for Roger of Helmarshausen, for the little that is known of both is in agreement.

Evidence in *De diversis* suggests that it was probably composed during 1110 to 1140. White (see Further Reading) goes on to suggest late 1122 or early 1123, on the grounds that Theophilus only learned of St Bernard of Clairvaulx's diatribe against lavish church ornamentation during the writing of the work, for it is only in the preface to Book 3 that Theophilus seeks to justify his craft. St Bernard's *Apologia* can be dated late 1122. No other medieval work on art combines the comprehensive range, orderly presentation and attention to detail as does *De diversis*. It has been described as an encyclopedia of medieval skills and crafts. It also offers the best and often the only description of medieval technology, including the first direct reference to papermaking in the West, the earliest medieval account of bell-founding and the most complete account of organ building. Many metallurgical techniques are described in detail, such as the making of a crucible furnace and bloomery hearth.

The treatise is divided into three books, the first on the materials and art of painting, the second on glassmaking, including stained glass, glass vessels and the blown-cylinder method for flat glass, and the final and longest book on metalwork, including working in iron, copper, gold and silver for church use, such as chalices and censers. The main texts are no mere compilations, but reveal the firsthand knowledge that can only be gained by a skilled craftsman. The prefaces to each book present perhaps the only medieval expression of an artist's ideals and how he sees his art in relation to the general scheme of things. For Theophilus, his art is a gift from God and every skill an act of praise and piety. Theophilus is thus an indispensable source for medieval crafts and technology, but there are indications that the work was also well known at the time of its composition and afterwards.

Bibliography

The Wolfenbüttel and Vienna manuscripts of *De diversis* are the earliest, both dating from the first half of the twelfth century, while the British Library copy, in an early thirteenth-century hand, is the most complete. Two incomplete copies from the thirteenth century held at Cambridge and Leipzig offer help in arriving at a definitive edition.

There are several references to *De diversis* in sixteenth-century printed works, such as Cornelius Agrippa (1530) and Josias Simmler (1585). The earliest printed edition of *De diversis* was prepared by G.H. Lessing in 1781 with the title, much used since, *Diversarium artium schedula*.

There are two good recent editions: *Theophilus: De diversis artibus. The Various Arts*, 1964, trans. with introd. by C.R. Dodwell, London: Thomas Nelson, and *On Diverse Arts. The Treatise of Theophilus*, 1963, trans. with introd. and notes by J.G. Harthorne and C.S. Smith, Chicago University Press.

Further Reading

Lynn White, 1962, 'Theophilus redivivus', *Technology and Culture* 5: 224–33 (a comparative review of *Theophilus* (op. cit.) and *On Diverse Arts* (op. cit.)).

LRD

Thévénin, Léon Charles

b. 30 March 1857 Paris, France
d. 21 September 1926 Paris, France

*French telegraph engineer who extended **Ohm**'s Law to the analysis of complex electrical circuits.*

Following a basic education, Thévénin entered the Ecole Polytechnique in Paris, graduating in 1876. In 1878 he joined the Corps of Telegraph Engineers (which subsequently became the French PTT). There he initially worked on the development of long-distance underground telegraph lines, but he later switched to working on power lines. Appointed a teaching inspector at the Ecole Supérieure in 1882, he became increasingly interested in the problems of measurement in electrical circuits. As a result of studying Kirchoff's Laws, which were essentially derived from Ohm's Law, he developed his now-famous theorem which made it possible to calculate the currents in more complex electrical circuits.

As well as becoming Head of the Bureau des Lignes, up until his death he also found time for teaching other subjects outside the Ecole, including a course in mechanics at the Institut National Agronomique. In 1896 he was appointed

Director of the Telegraph Engineering School, then, in 1901, Engineer-in-Chief of the telegraph workshops. He retired in 1914.

Bibliography
1883, 'Extension of Ohm's Law to complex electrical circuits', *Comptes rendus* 97: 159 (describes Thévénin's Theorem).

Further Reading
F.E. Terman, 1943, *Radio Engineers' Handbook*, New York: McGraw-Hill, Section 3 (summarizes the relevant circuit theory).

KF

Thimmonier, Barthélémy

b. 1793 Saint-Etienne, France
d. 1857

French inventor of the first sewing machine.

The sewing machine is probably the most universal and the most important machine in clothing manufacture, being used both industrially and domestically. It was also the first domestic consumer durable and was the first mass-produced machine to appear in the home. The first practical sewing machine was built during 1828 and 1829 by Barthélémy Thimmonier, a working tailor of Saint-Etienne in France. He came from a modest family and had never received any training as a mechanic, so his invention is all the more remarkable. He took out a patent in 1830 in his own name and that of Ferrand, a tutor of the Saint-Etienne School of Mines who had helped him financially. It was a chain-stitch machine made largely of wood and operated by a foot pedal with a large flywheel. The needle moved up and down through the cloth, which was placed on a platform below it. A second, hooked needle under the platform made a loop in the thread, which was caught when the first needle descended again.

In 1841, Thimmonier was appointed to a senior position in a large Paris clothing factory engaged in the production of French army uniforms. He soon had eighty machines in use, but a mob of hand-sewers broke in, smashed the machines and nearly killed Thimmonier. In 1845, he had developed his machine so that it could make 200 stitches per minute and formed a partnership with Jean-Marie Magnin to build them commercially. However, the abdication of Louis Philippe on 21 February 1848 ended his hopes, even though patents were taken out in the UK and the USA in that year. The English patent was in Magnin's name, and Thimmonier died impoverished in 1857. His machine was perfected by many later inventors.

Bibliography
1830, with Ferrand, (chain-stitch machine).

Further Reading
A. Matagran, 1931, 'Barthélémy Thimmonier (1793–1857), inventeur de la machine à coudre', *Bull. Soc. Enc. Industr. nat.* 130 (biography in French).
J. Meyssin, 1914, *Histoire de la machine à coudre: portrait et biographie de l'inventeur B. Thimmonier*, 5th edn, Lyons (biography in French).
M. Daumas, (ed.), 1968, *Histoire générale des techniques*, Vol. III: *L'Expansion du machinisme*, Paris (includes a description of Thimmonier's machine, with a picture).
N. Salmon, 1863, *History of the Sewing Machine from the Year 1750* (tells the history of the sewing machine).
F.B. Jewell, 1975, *Veteran Sewing Machines. A Collector's Guide*, Newton Abbot (a more modern account).

RLH

Thomas, Hugh Owen

b. 1833 Anglesey, North Wales
d. 6 January 1891 Liverpool, England

Welsh orthopaedic surgeon, a founder of modern orthopaedics and inventor of Thomas's splints.

Eldest son of a bone-setter, he studied at University College London, Edinburgh and Paris and became a member of the Royal College of Surgeons in 1857. Three years later he commenced practice in Liverpool, but he was never appointed to the staff of a hospital. Over the next twenty years he not only developed his own approach to orthopaedic practice, but also promoted a number of advances in other aspects of medicine such as epilepsy.

Of a mechanical (as well as musical) bent of mind, he had his own workshop and over some twenty years developed his pattern of splints for fractures. In 1877 Rushton Parker, later Professor of Surgery at Liverpool, expressed his admiration of the splints. This led to the publication of their details and shortly after to their wide acceptance.

Thomas's nephew Robert Jones was collaborating with him on a book on orthopaedics at the time of his death and went on to continue the tradition of what has been called the Liverpool School of orthopaedics.

Principal Honours and Distinctions
Honorary MD University of St Louis *c.*1880.

Bibliography
1875, *Diseases of the Hip, Knee and Ankle-joints.*

Further Reading
A.W. Beasley, 1982, 'The origins of orthopaedics', *Journal of the Royal Society of Medicine* 75.

MG

Thomas, Sidney Gilchrist
b. 16 April 1850 London, England
d. 1 February 1885 Paris, France

English inventor of basic steelmaking.

Thomas was educated at Dulwich College and from the age of 17, for the next twelve years, he made his living as a police-court clerk, although he studied chemistry in his spare time as an evening student at Birkbeck College, London. While there, he heard of the difficulties encountered by the **Bessemer** steelmaking process, which at that time was limited to using phosphorus-free iron. Any of this element present in the iron was oxidized to phosphoric acid, which would not react with the acidic lining in the converter, with the result that it would remain in the iron and render it too brittle to use. Unfortunately, phosphoric iron ores are more common than those free of this harmful element. Thomas was attracted by the view that a fortune awaited anyone who could solve this problem, and was not discouraged by the failure of several august figures in the industry, including **Siemens** and Lowthian **Bell**.

Thomas's knowledge of chemistry taught him that whereas an acidic lining allowed the phosphorus to remain in the iron, a basic lining would react with it to form part of the slag, which could then be tapped off. His experiments to find a suitable material were conducted in difficult conditions, in his spare time with meagre apparatus.

Finally he found that a converter lined with dolomite, a form of limestone, would succeed, and he appealed to his cousin Percy Carlyle Gilchrist, Chemist at the Blaenavon Ironworks in Monmouthshire, for help in carrying out pilot-scale trials. In 1879 he gave up his police-court job to devote himself to the work, and in the same year they patented the Thomas–Gilchrist process. The first licence to use it was granted to Bolckow, Vaughan & Co. of Middlesborough, and there the first steel was made in a basic Bessemer converter on 4 April 1879. The process was rapidly taken up and spread widely in Europe and beyond and was applied to other furnaces. Thomas made a fortune, but his health did not long allow him to enjoy it, for he died at the early age of 34.

Bibliography
1891, *Memoir and Letters of Sidney Gilchrist Thomas*, ed. R.W. Burnis, London.

Further Reading
L.G. Thompson, 1940, *Sidney Gilchrist Thomas, an Invention and Its Consequences*, London: Faber.
T.G. Davies, 1978, *Blaenavon and Sidney Gilchrist Thomas*, Sheffield: Historical Metallurgy Society.

LRD

Thomas, William
fl. 1850 London, England

English patentee of the lock-stitch sewing machine in Britain.

William Thomas, of Cheapside, London, was a manufacturer of shoes, umbrellas and corsets. He paid Elias **Howe** a sum of £250 to secure the British rights of Howe's 1846 patent for the lock-stitch sewing machine. Thomas persuaded Howe to go from the USA to England and apply his machine to the manufacture of shoes and corsets. Howe was to receive £3 per week, and in addition Thomas was to patent the machine in Britain and pay Howe £3 for every machine sold under the British patent. Patents for sewing machines were taken out in the name of W. Thomas in 1846 and 1848, and again in 1849. Howe did travel to Britain but quarrelled with Thomas after less than a year and returned to the USA. In 1853 Thomas started selling his own lock-stitch machine. There are patents in the name of W.F. Thomas for sewing machines, making button-holes bindings, etc., dating from 1853 through to 1864.

Bibliography
1846, British patent no. 11,464 (sewing machine).
1848, British patent no. 12,221 (sewing machine).
1849, British patent no. 12,736 (sewing machine).
1853, British patent no. 1,026.
1855, British patent no. 2,079.
1856, British patent no. 740.
1856, British patent no. 2,978.
1860, British patent no. 1,631.
1864, British patent no. 1,609.

Further Reading
F.G. Harrison, 1892–3, *Biographical Sketches of Pre-eminent Americans* (includes an account of Howe's life).
F.B. Jewell, 1975, *Veteran Sewing Machines. A Collector's Guide*, Newton Abbot (makes brief mention of Thomas).

RLH

Thomé de Gamond, Aimé
See **Gamond, Aimé Thomé de**.

Thompson, A.
fl. *c*.1801 London, England

English patentee of one of the first significant machines for heckling flax.

The flax plant passes through many stages before its fibres are prepared for spinning. The woody pith surrounding the fibres is first softened by rotting or 'retting', and is then removed by beating or 'scutching'. This leaves the fibres in a tight bunch, as they have grown to form the stem of the plant. Hackling or heckling, the next process, separates the fibres from each other. In hand processes this was done by pulling the fibres across a board of steel spikes, or sometimes a form of comb was pulled through them.

In 1795 Sellers and Standage patented a method of heckling in which the flax was pulled by hand through stationary vertical teeth, but much more significant was the patent of 1801 of A. Thompson of London. The length of the fibres in a bundle of flax will vary considerably, therefore the distance between the point where the fibres pass out to be combed and the point where they can be put through another roller or gripper must be greater than the longest fibres, requiring some method of support in between. Thompson used a pair of chain gills for this purpose. These consist of rows of teeth mounted on a continuous chain or belt which moves around while the fibres pass through the teeth in the vertical position. The longer fibres are pulled through the teeth by the drawing rollers at the front, while the shorter ones are held steady by the teeth and presented to the rollers later; thus the teeth both support the fibres and heckle them at the same time. Following this process the fibres can be drawn and spun.

Bibliography
1801, British patent no. 2,533 (flax-heckling machine).

Further Reading
W. English, 1969, *The Textile Industry*, London (describes Thompson's machine, with an illustration).
L.J. Mills (ed.), 1927, *The Textile Educator*, London (includes a description of later flax-heckling machines).

RLH

Thompson, Benjamin
b. 11 April 1779 Eccleshall, Yorkshire, England
d. 19 April 1867 Gateshead, England

English coal owner and railway engineer, inventor of reciprocal cable haulage.

After being educated at Sheffield Grammar School, Thompson and his elder brother established Aberdare Iron Works, South Wales, where he gained experience in mine engineering from the coal- and ironstone-mines with which the works were connected. In 1811 he moved to the North of England as Managing Partner in Bewicke's Main Colliery, County Durham, which was replaced in 1814 by a new colliery at nearby Ouston. Coal from this was carried to the Tyne over the Pelew Main Wagonway, which included a 1,992 yd (1,821 m) section where horses had to haul loaded wagons between the top of one cable-worked incline and the foot of the next. Both inclines were worked by stationary steam engines, and by installing a rope with a record length of nearly 1½ miles (2.4 km), in 1821 Thompson arranged for the engine of the upper incline to haul the loaded wagons along the intervening section also. To their rear was attached the rope from the engine of the lower incline, to be used in due course to haul the empties back again.

He subsequently installed this system of 'reciprocal working' elsewhere, in particular in 1826 over five miles (8 km) of the Brunton & Shields Railroad, a colliery line north of the Tyne, where trains were hauled at an average speed of 6 mph (10 km/h) including rope changes. This performance was better than that of contemporary locomotives. The directors of the Liverpool & Manchester Railway, which was then being built, considered installing reciprocal cable haulage on their line, and then decided to stage a competition to establish whether an improved steam locomotive could do better still. This competition became the Rainhill Trials of 1829 and was decisively won by *Rocket*, which had been built for the purpose.

Thompson meanwhile had become prominent in the promotion of the Newcastle & Carlisle Railway, which, when it received its Act in 1829, was the longest railway so far authorized in Britain.

Bibliography

1821, British patent no. 4602 (reciprocal working).
1847, *Inventions, Improvements and Practice of Benjamin Thompson*, Newcastle upon Tyne: Lambert.

Further Reading

W.W. Tomlinson, 1914, *The North Eastern Railway*, Newcastle upon Tyne: Andrew Reid (includes a description of Thompson and his work).
R. Welford, 1895, *Men of Mark twixt Tyne and Tweed*, Vol. 3, 506–6.
C.R. Warn, 1976, *Waggonways and Early Railways of Northumberland*, Newcastle upon Tyne: Frank Graham.
—— *c.*1981, *Rails between Wear & Tyne*, Newcastle upon Tyne: Frank Graham.

See also: **Rastrick, John Urpeth**; **Stephenson, Robert**.

PJGR

Thomson, Elihu

b. 29 March 1853 Manchester, England
d. 13 March 1937 Swampscott, Massachusetts, USA

English (naturalized) American electrical engineer and inventor.

Thomson accompanied his parents to Philadelphia in 1858; he received his education at the Central High School there, and afterwards remained as a teacher of chemistry. At this time he constructed several dynamos after studying their design, and was invited by the Franklin Institute to give lectures on the subject. After observing an arc-lighting system operating commercially in Paris in 1878, he collaborated with Edwin J. Houston, a senior colleague at the Central High School, in working out the details of such a system. An automatic regulating device was designed which, by altering the position of the brushes on the dynamo commutator, maintained a constant current irrespective of the number of lamps in use. To overcome the problem of commutation at the high voltages necessary to operate up to forty arc lamps in a series circuit, Thomson contrived a centrifugal blower which suppressed sparking. The resulting system was efficient and reliable with low operating costs. Thomson's invention of the motor meter in 1882 was the first of many such instruments for the measurement of electrical energy. In 1886 he invented electric resistance welding using low-voltage alternating current derived from a transformer of his own design. Thomson's work is recorded in his technical papers and in the 700-plus patents granted for his inventions.

The American Electric Company, founded to exploit the Thomson patents, later became the Thomson–Houston Company, which was destined to be a leader in the electrical manufacturing industry. They entered the field of electric power in 1887, supplying railway equipment and becoming a major innovator of electric railways. Thomson–Houston and Edison General Electric were consolidated to form General Electric in 1892. Thomson remained associated with this company throughout his career.

Principal Honours and Distinctions

Chevalier and Officier de la Légion d'honneur 1889. American Academy of Arts and Sciences Rumford Medal 1901. American Institute of

Electrical Engineers Edison Medal 1909. Royal Society Hughes Medal 1916. Institution of Electrical Engineers Kelvin Medal 1923, Faraday Medal 1927.

Bibliography
1934, 'Some highlights of electrical history', *Electrical Engineering* 53: 758–67 (autobiography).

Further Reading
D.O. Woodbury, 1944, *Beloved Scientist*, New York (a full biography).
H.C. Passer, 1953, *The Electrical Manufacturers: 1875–1900*, Cambridge, Mass. (describes Thomson's industrial contribution).
K.T. Compton, 1940, *Biographical Memoirs of Elihu Thomson*, Washington, DCovides an abridged list of Thomson's papers and patents).

GW

Thomson, James

b. 16 February 1822 Belfast, Ireland (now Northern Ireland)
d. 8 May 1892 Glasgow, Scotland

Irish civil engineer noted for his work in hydraulics and for his design of the 'Vortex' turbine.

James Thomson was a pupil in several civil-engineering offices, but the nature of the work was beyond his physical capacity and from 1843 onwards he devoted himself to theoretical studies. Hhe first concentrated on the problems associated with the expansion of liquids when they reach their freezing point: water is one such example. He continued this work with his younger brother, Lord Kelvin (see **Thomson, Sir William**).

After experimentation with a 'feathered' paddle wheel as a young man, he turned his attention to water power. In 1850 he made his first patent application, 'Hydraulic machinery and steam engines': this patent became his 'Vortex' turbine design. He settled in Belfast, the home of the MacAdam–Fourneyron turbine, in 1851, and as a civil engineer became the Resident Engineer to the Belfast Water Commissioners in 1853. In 1857 he was appointed Professor of Civil Engineering and Surveying at Queen's College, Belfast.

Whilst it is understood that he made his first

turbine models in Belfast, he came to an arrangement with the Williamson Brothers of Kendal to make his turbine. In 1856 Williamsons produced their first turbine to Thomson's design and drawings. This was the Vortex Williamson Number 1, which produced 5 hp (3.7 kW) under a fall of 31 ft (9.4 m) on a 9 in. (23 cm) diameter supply. The rotor of this turbine ran in a horizontal plane. For several years the Williamson catalogue described their Vortex turbine as 'designed by Professor James Thomson'.

Thomson continued with his study of hydraulics and water flow both at Queen's College, Belfast, and, later, at Glasgow University, where he became Professor in 1873, succeeding Macquorn Rankine, another famous engineer. At Glasgow, James Thomson studied the flow in rivers and the effects of erosion on river beds. He was also an authority on geological formations such as the development of the basalt structure of the Giant's Causeway, north of Belfast.

James Thomson was an extremely active engineer and a very profound teacher of civil engineering. His form of water turbine had a long life before being displaced by the turbines designed in the twentieth century.

Bibliography
1850, British patent no. 13,156 'Hydraulic machinery and steam engines'.

Further Reading
Gilkes, 1956, *One Hundred Years of Water Power*, Kendal.

KM

Thomson, Sir William, Lord Kelvin

b. 26 June 1824 Belfast, Ireland (now Northern Ireland)
d. 17 December 1907 Largs, Scotland

Irish physicist and inventor who contributed to submarine telegraphy and instrumentation.

After education at Glasgow University and Peterhouse, Cambridge, a period of study in France gave Thomson an interest in experimental work and instrumentation. He became Professor of Natural Philosophy at Glasgow in 1846 and retained the position for the rest of his career, establishing the first teaching laboratory in Britain.

Among his many contributions to science and

engineering was his concept, introduced in 1848, of an 'absolute' zero of temperature. Following on from the work of Joule, his investigations into the nature of heat led to the first successful liquefaction of gases such as hydrogen and helium, and later to the science of low-temperature physics.

Cable telegraphy gave an impetus to the scientific measurement of electrical quantities, and for many years Thomson was a member of the British Association Committee formed in 1861 to consider electrical standards and to develop units; these are still in use. Thomson first became Scientific Adviser to the Atlantic Telegraph Company in 1857, sailing on the *Agamemnon* and *Great Eastern* during the cable-laying expeditions. He invented a mirror galvanometer and more importantly the siphon recorder, which, used as a very sensitive telegraph receiver, provided a permanent record of signals. He also laid down the design parameters of long submarine cables and discovered that the conductivity of copper was greatly affected by its purity. A major part of the success of the Atlantic cable in 1866 was due to Thomson, who received a knighthood for his contribution.

Other instruments he designed included a quadrant electrostatic voltmeter to measure high voltages, and his 'multi-cellular' instrument for low voltages. They could be used on alternating or direct current and were free from temperature errors. His balances for precision current measurement were widely used in standardizing laboratories.

Thomson was a prolific writer of scientific papers on subjects across the whole spectrum of physics; between 1855 and 1866 he published some 110 papers, with a total during his life of over 600. In 1892 he was raised to the peerage as Baron Kelvin of Largs. By the time of his death he was looked upon as the 'father' of British physics, but despite his outstanding achievements his later years were spent resisting change and progress.

Principal Honours and Distinctions
Knighted 1866. Created Lord Kelvin of Largs 1892. FRS 1851. President, Royal Society 1890–4. An original member of the Order of Merit 1902. President, Society of Telegraph Engineers 1874. President, Institution of Electrical Engin-

eers 1889 and 1907. Royal Society Royal Medal 1856, Copley Medal 1883.

Bibliography
1872, *Reprints of Papers on Electrostatics and Magnetism*, London; 1911, *Mathematical and Physical Papers*, 6 vols, Cambridge (collections of Thomson's papers).

Further Reading
Silvanus P. Thompson, 1910, *The Life of William Thomson, Baron Kelvin of Largs*, 2 vols, London (an uncritical biography).
D.B. Wilson, 1987, *Kelvin and Stokes: A Comparative Study in Victorian Physics*, Bristol (provides a present-day commentary on all aspects of Thomson's work).
J.G. Crowther, 1962, *British Scientists of the 19th Century*, London, pp. 199–257 (a short critical biography).

GW

Thornley, David
b. *c.*1741 Liverpool (?), England
d. 27 January 1772 Nottingham, England

English partner in Arkwright's cotton-spinning venture.

On 4 November 1766 David Thornley married Mary, daughter of Joseph Brown, roper, at St Peter's, Liverpool. In *Gore's Dictionary* for 1767 Thornley is described as 'merchant' and his wife as 'milliner' of Castle Street, Liverpool. David Thornley was distantly related to Richard **Arkwright** and certainly by 1768 Thornley had begun his active association with Arkwright when he joined him in Preston, an event recorded in the inquiry into the qualifications of those who had voted in the Burgoyne election. Thornley may have helped Arkwright with the technical development of his spinning machine.

On 14 May 1768, Arkwright, **Smalley** and Thornley became partners in the cotton-spinning venture at Nottingham for a term of fourteen years, or longer if a patent could be obtained. Each partner was to have three one-ninth shares and was to advance such money as might be necessary to apply for a patent as well as to develop the spinning machine. Profits were to be divided equally as often as convenient and the partners were to devote their whole time to the business after a period of two years. However, it seems that in 1769 the partners had difficulty in raising the necessary money to finance the patent, and Thornley had to reduce his stake in the partnership to a one-ninth share. By this time Thornley must have moved to Nottingham, where Arkwright established his first mill. On 19 January 1770, additional finance was provided by two new partners, Samuel **Need** and Jedediah **Strutt**, and alterations were made to the mill buildings that the partners had leased to work the spinning machines by horse power. Arkwright and Thornley were to be responsible for the day-to-day management of the mill, receiving £25 per annum for these duties. Thornley appears to have remained at Nottingham to supervise the mill, while the other partners moved to Cromford to establish the much larger enterprise there. It was at Nottingham that David Thornley died in January 1772, and his share in the partnership was bought from his wife, Mary, by Arkwright. Mary returned to her millinery business in Liverpool.

Further Reading

Until copies of the original agreements between Arkwright's partners were presented to the University of Manchester Institute of Science and Technology, Thornley's existence was unknown. The only account of his life is given in R.S. Fitton, 1989, *The Arkwrights, Spinners of Fortune*, Manchester. The 'Articles of Agreement', 19 June 1769, are printed in R.L. Hills, 1970, *Power in the Industrial Revolution*, Manchester. This book also includes part of Arkwright's agreement with his later partners which mentions Thornley's death and covers the technical aspects of the cotton-spinning invention.

RLH

Tideman, Bruno Joannes

b. 7 August 1834 Amsterdam, The Netherlands
d. 11 February 1883 Amsterdam, The Netherlands

Dutch naval architect and constructor, early hydrodynamicist.

The first thirty years of Tideman's life followed the normal pattern for a naval architect: study at the Breda Military Academy, work in the Royal Dockyards of Vlissingen as a constructor and then experience in the United Kingdom 'standing by' an armoured vessel being built for the Dutch at Birkenhead. Tideman took the opportunity to acquaint himself with current developments in British shipyards and to study the work of Macquorn **Rankine** at Glasgow University.

On his return to the Netherlands he was given the task of adapting the Royal Dockyard of Amsterdam for ironclad construction and from 1870 iron ships were built there. From 1868 until 1873 he taught shipbuilding at what was then the Delft Polytechnic, but resigned on his appointment as Chief Naval Constructor of Holland.

Through representations to appropriate authority he assisted in founding the great shipyard Koninklijke Maatschappij 'De Schelde' and in the setting up of Dutch ferry services across the North Sea. His interest in ship design and in the pioneering work of William **Froude** led to the founding of the world's second ship model test tank in 1876 in a sheltered part of the Royal Amsterdam Dockyard. The design was based on Froude's Torquay Tank.

As Scotland's first tank was not opened until 1883, he attracted work from the Clyde, including the testing of the Russian Imperial Yacht *Livadia* built by Elder's of Glasgow. This contract was so critical that it was agreed that a quarter-size model be tested on Loch Lomond. Throughout his life he was respected as an all-round engineer and consultancy work flowed in, the vast bulk of it from Britain. Continual trying to improve standards, Tideman was working on a development plan for Dutch shipbuilding at the time of his death.

Further Reading
J.M. Dirkzwager, 1970, *Bruno Joannes Tideman 1834–1883. Grondlegger van de Moderne Scheepsbouw in Nederland*, Leiden.

FMW

Ting Huan

See **Ding Huan**.

Titt, John Wallis

b. 1841 Cheriton, Wiltshire, England
d. May 1910 Warminster, Wiltshire, England

English agricultural engineer and millwright who developed a particular form of wind engine.

John Wallis Titt grew up on a farm which had a working post-mill, but at 24 years of age he joined the firm of Wallis, Haslam & Stevens, agricultural engineers and steam engine builders in Basingstoke. From there he went to the millwrighting firm of Brown & May of Devizes, where he worked for five years.

In 1872 he founded his own firm in Warminster, where his principal work as an agricultural engineer was on hay and straw elevators. In 1876 he moved his firm to the Woodcock Ironworks, also in Warminster. There he carried on his work as an agricultural engineer, but he also had an iron foundry. By 1884 the firm was installing water pumps on estates around Warminster, and it was about that time that he built his first wind engines. Between 1884 and 1903, when illness forced his retirement, his wind engines were built primarily with adjustable sails. These wind engines, under the trade marks 'Woodcock' and 'Simplex', consisted of a lattice tower with the sails mounted on a a ring at the top. The sails were turned to face the wind by means of a fantail geared to the ring or by a wooden vane. The important feature lay in the sails, which were made of canvas on a wood-and-iron frame mounted in a ring. The ends of the sail frames were hinged to the sail circumferences. In the middle of the sail a circular strap was attached so that all the frames had the same aspect for a given setting of the bar. The importance lies in the adjustable sails, which gave the wind engine the ability to work in variable winds.

Whilst this was not an original patent of John Wallis Titt, he is known to be the only maker of wind engines in Britain who built his business on this highly efficient form of sail. In design terms it derives from the annular sails of the conventional windmills at Haverhill in Suffolk and Roxwell in Essex. After his retirement, his sons reverted to the production of the fixed-bladed galvanized-iron wind engine.

Further Reading
J.K. Major, 1977, *The Windmills of John Wallis Titt*, The International Molinological Society.
E. Lancaster Burne, 1906, 'Wind power', *Cassier's Magazine* 30: 325–6.

KM

Tizard, Sir Henry Thoms
b. 23 August 1885 Gillingham, Kent, England
d. 9 October 1959 Fareham, Hampshire, England

English scientist and administrator who made many contributions to military technology.

Educated at Westminster College, in 1904 Tizard went to Magdalen College, Oxford, gaining Firsts in mathematics and chemistry. After a period of time in Berlin with Nernst, he joined the Royal Institution in 1909 to study the colour changes of indicators. From 1911 until 1914 he was a tutorial Fellow of Oriel College, Oxford, but with the outbreak of the First World War he joined first the Royal Garrison Artillery, then, in 1915, the newly formed Royal Flying Corps, to work on the development of bomb-sights. Successively in charge of testing aircraft, a lieutenant-colonel in the Ministry of Munitions and Assistant Controller of Research and Experiments for the Royal Air Force, he returned to Oxford in 1919 and the following year became Reader in Chemical Thermodynamics; at this stage he developed the use of toluene as an aircraft-fuel additive.

In 1922 he was appointed an assistant secretary at the government Department of Industrial and Scientific Research, becoming Principal Assistant Secretary in 1922 and its Permanent Director in 1927; during this time he was also a member of the Aeronautical Research Committee, being Chairman of the latter in 1933–43. From 1929 to 1942 he was Rector of Imperial College. In 1932 he was also appointed Chairman of a committee set up to investigate possible national air-defence systems, and it was largely due to his efforts that the radar proposals of **Watson-Watt** were taken up and an effective system made operational before the outbreak of the Second World War. He was also involved in various other government activities aimed at applying technology to the war effort, including the dambuster and atomic bombs.

President of Magdalen College in 1942–7, he then returned again to Whitehall, serving as Chairman of the Advisory Council on Scientific Policy and of the Defence Research Policy Committee. Finally, in 1952, he became Pro-Chancellor of Southampton University.

Principal Honours and Distinctions
Air Force Cross 1918. CB 1927. KCB 1937.
GCB 1949. American Medal of Merit 1947. FRS
1926. Ten British and Commonwealth Univer-
sity honorary doctorates. Hon. Fellowship of the
Royal Aeronautical Society. Royal Society of Arts
Gold Medal. Franklin Institute Gold Medal.
President, British Association 1948. Trustee of
the British Museum 1937–59.

Bibliography
1911, 'The sensitiveness of indicators', *British
Association Report* (describes Tizard's work on
colour changes in indicators).

Further Reading
1961, *Biographical Memoirs of Fellows of the Royal
Society* VII, London: Royal Society.

KF

Todd, Leonard Jennett
fl. 1885 London, England

*English (?) patentee of steam engines
incorporating the uniflow principle.*

In a uniflow system, the steam enters a steam
engine cylinder at one end, pushes the pistons
along, and exhausts through a ring of ports at the
centre of the cylinder that are uncovered by
movement of the piston. The piston is returned
by steam then entering the other end of the cylinder, moving the piston arrangement back, and
again making its exit through the central ports.
This gave the thermodynamic advantage of the
cylinder ends remaining hot and the centre
colder with reheating the ends of the cylinder
through compression of the residual steam. The
principle was first patented by Jacob **Perkins** in
England in 1827 and was tried in America in
1856.

Little is known about Todd. The addresses
given in his patent specifications show that he
was living first at South Hornsey and then Stoke
Newington, both in Middlesex (now in London). No obituary notices have been traced. He
took out a patent in 1885 for a 'terminal exhaust
engine' and followed this with two more in 1886
and 1887. His aim was to 'produce a double
acting steam engine which shall work more efficiently, which shall produce and maintain within
itself an improved gradation of temperature extending from each of its two Hot Inlets to its

common central Cold Outlet'. His later patents
show the problems he faced with finding suitable
valve gears and the compression developing during the return stroke of the piston. It was this last
problem, particularly when starting a condensing
engine, that probably defeated him through excessive compression pressures. There is some evidence that he hoped to apply his engines to
railway locomotives.

Bibliography
1885, British patent no. 7,301 (terminal exhaust
engine).
1886, British patent no. 2,132.
1887, British patent no. 6,666.

Further Reading
R.L. Hills, 1989, *Power from Steam. A History of
the Stationary Steam Engine*, Cambridge
University Press (provides the fullest dis-
cussion of his patents).
H.W. Dickinson, 1938, *A Short History of the
Steam Engine*, Cambridge University Press.
J. Stumpf, 1912, *The Una-Flow Steam Engine*,
Munich: R. Oldenbourg.

RLH

Tompion, Thomas
baptized 25 July 1639 Ickwell Green, England
d. 20 November 1713 London, England

*English clock- and watchmaker of great skill and
ingenuity who laid the foundations of his
country's pre-eminence in that field.*

Little is known about Tompion's early life except
that he was born into a family of blacksmiths.
When he was admitted into the Clockmakers'
Company in 1671 he was described as a 'Great
Clockmaker', which meant a maker of turret
clocks, and as these clocks were made of wrought
iron they would have required blacksmithing
skills. Despite this background, he also rapidly
established his reputation as a watchmaker. In
1674 he moved to premises in Water Lane at the
sign of 'The Dial and Three Crowns', where his
business prospered and he remained for the rest
of his life. Assisted by journeymen and up to
eleven apprentices at any one time, the output
from his workshop was prodigious, amounting
to over 5,000 watches and 600 clocks. In his
lifetime he was famous for his watches, as these
figures suggest, but although they are of high

quality they do not differ markedly from those produced by other London watchmakers of that period. He is now known more for the limited number of elaborate clocks that he produced, such as the equation clock and the spring-driven clock of a year's duration, which he made for William III. Around 1711 he took into partnership his nephew by marriage, George **Graham**, who carried on the business after his death.

Although Tompion does not seem to have been particularly innovative, he lived at a time when great advances were being made in horology, which his consummate skill as a craftsman enabled him to exploit. In this he was greatly assisted by his association with Robert **Hooke**, for whom Tompion constructed a watch with a balance spring in 1675; at that time Hooke was trying to establish his priority over **Huygens** for this invention. Although this particular watch was not successful, it made Tompion aware of the potential of the balance spring and he became the first person in England to apply Huygens's spiral spring to the balance of a watch. Although Thuret had constructed such a watch somewhat earlier in France, the superior quality of Tompion's wheel work, assisted by Hooke's wheel-cutting engine, enabled him to dominate the market. The anchor escapement (which reduced the amplitude of the pendulum's swing) was first applied to clocks around this time and produced further improvements in accuracy which Tompion and other makers were able to utilize. However, the anchor escapement, like the verge escapement, produced recoil (the clock was momentarily driven in reverse). Tompion was involved in attempts to overcome this defect with the introduction of the dead-beat escapement for clocks and the horizontal escapement for watches. Neither was successful, but they were both perfected later by George Graham.

Principal Honours and Distinctions
Master of the Clockmakers' Company 1703.

Bibliography
1695, with William Houghton and Edward Barlow, British patent no. 344 (for a horizontal escapement).

Further Reading
R.W. Symonds, 1951, *Thomas Tompion, His Life and Work*, London (a comprehensive but now slightly dated account).
H.W. Robinson and W. Adams (eds), 1935, *The Diary of Robert Hooke* (contains many references to Tompion).
D. Howse, 1970, 'The Tompion clocks at Greenwich and the dead-beat escapement', *Antiquarian Horology* 7: 18–34, 114–33.

DV

Torricelli, Evangelista
b. 15 October 1608 Faenza, Italy
d. 25 October 1647 Florence, Italy

Italian physicist, inventor of the mercury barometer and discoverer of atmospheric pressure.

Torricelli was the eldest child of a textile artisan. Between 1625 and 1626 he attended the Jesuit school at Faenza, where he showed such outstanding aptitude in mathematics and philosophy that his uncle was persuaded to send him to Rome to a school run by Benedetto Castelli, a mathematician and engineer and a former pupil of Galileo **Galilei**. Between 1630 and 1641, Torricelli was possibly Secretary to Giovanni Ciampoli, Galileo's friend and protector. In 1641 Torricelli wrote a treatise, *De motu gravium*, amplifying Galileo's doctrine on the motion of projectiles, and Galileo accepted him as a pupil. On Galileo's death in 1642, he was appointed as mathematician and philosopher to the court of Grand Duke Ferdinando II of Tuscany. He remained in Florence until his early death in 1647, possibly from typhoid fever. He wrote a great number of mathematical papers on conic sections, the cycloid, the logarithmic curve and other subjects, which made him well known.

By 1642 Torricelli was producing good lenses for telescopes; he subsequently improved them, and attained near optical perfection. He also constructed a simple microscope with a small glass sphere as a lens. Galileo had looked at problems of raising water with suction pumps, and also with a siphon in 1630. Torricelli brought up the subject again in 1640 and later produced his most important invention, the barometer. He used mercury to fill a glass tube that was sealed at one end and inverted it. He found that the height of mercury in the tube adjusted itself to a well-defined level of about 76 cm (30 in.), higher than the free surface outside. He realized that this must be due to the pressure of the air on the outside surface and predicted that it would fall with increasing altitude. He thus demonstrated the pressure of the atmosphere and the existence of a vacuum on top of the mercury, publishing his findings in 1644. He later noticed that changes in the height of the mercury were related to changes in the weather.

Bibliography
1641, *De motu gravium*.

Further Reading
T.I. Williams (ed.), 1969, *A Biographical Dictionary of Scientists*, London: A. & C. Black.
Chambers Concise Dictionary of Scientists, 1989, Cambridge.
A Dictionary of Scientific Biography, 1976, Vol. XIII, New York: C. Scribner's Sons.
A. Stowers, 1961–2, 'Thomas Newcomen's first steam engine 250 years ago and the initial development of steam power', *Transactions of the Newcomen Society* 34 (provides an account of his mercury barometer).
W.E. Knowles Middleton, 1964, *The History of the Barometer*, Baltimore.

RLH

Tossach, William
b. *c.*1700 probably Perthshire, Scotland
d. after 1771 Alloa, Scotland

Scottish surgeon, the first to report a case of artificial respiration by mouth.

Little is known of Tossach (a Tossach matriculated at Glasgow University in 1727), but in 1771 he published an account of the resuscitation of a miner, James Blair, who had been rescued from a coal-mine fire. Tossach found 'there was not the least pulse in either heart or arteries and not the least breathing could be observed; so that he was in all appearance dead, I applied my mouth close to his, and blowed my breath as strong as I could: but having neglected to close his nostrils all the air came out of them: Wherefore taking hold of them with one hand and holding my other on his breast at the left pap I blew again my breath as strong as I could, raising his chest fully with it; and immediately I felt six or seven very quick beats of the heart.' Blair recovered consciousness in an hour and walked home within four.

Bibliography
1771, 'A man dead in appearance recovered by distending the lungs with air', *Medical Essays and Observations*, Edinburgh.

Further Reading
1794, *Transactions of the Royal Humane Society from 1774–1784*, London.
J.P. Griffin, 1990, 'The origins of the Royal Humane Society', *Journal of the Royal Society of Medicine* 83.

MG

Tournachon, Gaspard Félix (Nadar)
b. 1820
d. 1910 Paris, France

French photographer and photographic innovator, pioneer of balloon photography.

He began his photographic career as a daguerreotypist and at an early date called himself 'Nadar', the name by which he was known for the rest of his life. Between 1855 and 1858 he made captive balloon ascents with the idea of producing a topographic map of Paris from aerial photographs. Nadar was also one of the first photographers to take successful photographs with the aid of artificial illuminants; using **Bunsen** batteries to power electric arc lamps, he was able to take views of the underground catacombs in Paris during 1861 and 1862. This exercise captured the imagination of the Paris public, and Nadar's work was widely acclaimed. In December 1863 he exhibited portraits taken by electric light, and later used magnesium illuminants to photograph underground canal construction. For many years Nadar practised as a photographer with his son Paul, a relationship that was sometimes stormy. Paul eventually took the name Nadar for himself and was, in turn, to become one of France's most celebrated photographers.

Bibliography
29 October 1858, British patent no. 2,425 (balloon photography).

Further Reading
J.M. Eder, 1945, *History of Photography*, trans. E. Epstean, New York.
H. Gernsheim and A. Gernsheim, 1969, *The History of Photography*, rev. edn, London.

JW

Town, Ithiel

b. 1784 Thompson, Connecticut, USA
d. 1844 New Haven, Connecticut, USA

American architect and bridge builder.

Town studied in Boston, Massachusetts, under Asher Benjamin. His first important work was the Center Church on New Haven Green, and in 1814 he was commissioned to build Trinity Church, also on New Haven Green. He designed many more public buildings in many cities, including the Customs House on Wall Street, New York, and the Indiana State Capitol in Indianapolis. He patented the 'Town lattice' for truss bridges in 1820, which established his reputation as a bridge builder; he also built a number of covered bridges. He entered into partnership with Martin E. Thompson in 1827–8 and with Alexander J. Davis in 1829–43. He was a collector of books on architecture and fine arts, using the money from his bridge building to acquire what was said to be the best collection in the country.

Principal Honours and Distinctions
Founder, National Academy of Design.

Further Reading
1975, *Webster's American Biographies.*

IMcN

Townes, Charles Hard

b. 28 July 1915 Greenville, South Carolina, USA

American physicist who developed the maser and contributed to the development of the laser.

Charles H. Townes entered Furman University, Greenville, at the early age of 16 and in 1935 obtained a BA in modern languages and a BS in physics. After a year of postgraduate study at Duke University, he received a master's degree in physics in 1936. He then went on to the California Institute of Technology, where he obtained a PhD in 1939. From 1939 to 1947 he worked at the Bell Telephone Laboratories, mainly on airborne radar, although he also did some work on radio astronomy. In 1948 he joined Columbia University as Associate Professor of Physics and in 1950 was appointed a full professor. He was Director of the University's Radiation Laboratory from 1950 to 1952, and from 1952 to 1955 he was Chairman of the Physics Department.

To meet the need for an oscillator generating very short wavelength electromagnetic radiation, Townes in 1951 realized that use could be made of the different natural energy levels of atoms and molecules. The practical application of this idea was achieved in his laboratory in 1953 using ammonia gas to make the device known as a maser (an acronym of *m*icrowave *a*mplification by *s*timulated *e*mission of *r*adiation). The maser was developed in the next few years and in 1958, in a joint paper with his brother-in-law Arthur L. **Schawlow**, Townes suggested the possibility of a further development into optical frequencies or an optical maser, later known as a laser (an acronym of *l*ight *a*mplification by *s*timulated *e*mission of *r*adiation). Two years later the first such device was made by Theodore H. **Maiman**.

In 1959 Townes was given leave from Columbia University to serve as Vice-President and Director of Research at the Institute for Defense Analyses until 1961. He was then appointed Provost and Professor of Physics at the Massachusetts Institute of Technology. In 1967 he became University Professor of Physics at the University of California, where he has extended his research interests in the field of microwave and infra-red astronomy. He is a member of the National Academy of Sciences, the Institute of Electrical and Electronics Engineers and the American Astronomical Society.

Principal Honours and Distinctions
Nobel Prize for Physics 1964. Foreign Member, Royal Society of London. President, American Physical Society 1967. Townes has received many awards from American and other scientific societies and institutions and honorary degrees from more than twenty universities.

Bibliography
Townes is the author of many scientific papers and, with Arthur L. Schawlow, of *Microwave Spectroscopy* (1955).
1980, entry, *McGraw-Hill Modern Scientists and Engineers*, Part 3, New York, pp. 227–8 (autobiography).
1991, entry, *The Nobel Century*, London, p. 106 (autobiography).

Further Reading
T. Wasson (ed.), 1987, *Nobel Prize Winners*, New York, pp. 1,071–3 (contains a short biography).

RTS

Townsend, Matthew
b. Leicester (?), England
d. after 1867 USA

English inventor of the latch needle for making seamless hose, and developer of ribbed knitting on circular machines.

Townsend, who described himself in his first patent as a framework knitter and afterwards as a hosier of Leicester, took out a patent in 1847 for the application of a 'machine like that of a point net frame to an ordinary stocking-frame'. He described needles and hooks of a peculiar shape which were able to take the work off the knitting machine, reverse the loops and return them again so that ribbed knitting could be made on circular machines. These became popular for knitting stockings which, although not fully fashioned, had sufficient strength to fit the leg. In 1854 he took out a patent for making round hose with heels and toes fashioned on other machines. In yet another patent, in 1856, he described a method of raising looped pile on knitted fabrics for making 'terry' towelling fabrics. He could use different coloured yarns in the fabric that were controlled by a **Jacquard** mechanism. It was in the same year, 1856, in a further patent that he described his tumbler or latch needles as well as the making of figured patterns in knitting on both sides of the fabric with a Jacquard mechanism. The latch needles were self-acting, being made to move up and down or backwards and forwards by the action of cams set in the cylindrical body of the machine. Normally the needle worked in a vertical or inclined position with the previous loop on the shank below the latch. Weft yarn was placed in the hook of the needle. The needle was drawn down between fixed plates which formed a new loop with the weft. At the same time, the original loop already on the shank of the needle moved along the shank and closed the latch so that it could pass over the newly formed loop in the needle hook and fall over the end of the needle incorporating the new loop on its way to make the next row of stitches. The latch needle obviated the need for loop wheels and pressers and thus simplified the knitting mechanism. Townsend's invention was the forerunner of an entirely new generation of knitting machines, but it was many years before its full potential was realized, the bearded needle of William Lee being preferred because the hinge of the latch could not be made as fine as the bearded needle.

Townsend was in the first rank of skilful manufacturers of fancy Leicester hosiery and had a good practical knowledge of the machinery used in his trade. Having patented his needles, he seems not to have succeeded in getting them into very profitable or extensive use, possibly because he fixed the royalty too high. His invention proved to be most useful and profitable in the hands of others, for it gave great impetus to the trade in seamless hose. For various reasons he discontinued his business in Leicester. He emigrated to the USA, where, after some initial setbacks, he began to reap the rewards of his skill.

Bibliography
1847, British patent no. 11,899 (knitting machine).
1854, British patent no. 1,523 (seamless hose).
1856, British patent no. 1,157 ('terry' towelling fabrics).
1856, British patent no. 1,858 (latch needles and double-sided patterns on fabrics).

Further Reading
F.A. Wells, 1935, *The British Hosiery and Knitwear Industry*, London (mentions Townsend briefly).
W. Felkin, 1967, *History of the Machine-wrought Hosiery and Lace Manufactures*, reprint, Newton Abbot (orig. pub. 1867) (a better account of Townsend).

RLH

Townshend, Charles, 2nd Viscount
b. 1674 England
d. 1738 England

English landowner and improver.

Charles Townshend succeeded his father as 2nd Viscount Townshend at the age of 15. In his early life he played a prominent political role: he was Lord Privy Seal under William III; served as a commissioner to treat for the Union between Scotland and England; and, with Marlborough, signed the treaty of Gertruydenberg in 1709. He was Secretary of State under both George I and George II, and was for a time Lord Lieutenant of Ireland.

In 1730 he retired from political life to Raynham, in Norfolk, and devoted himself to the care of his estate and to experiments in agricultural husbandry. He paid particular attention to the rotation of crops and the cultivation of turnips and clover. His efforts on the light soil of his estate brought substantial returns, and those of his tenants and neighbours who followed his example also prospered. His particular zeal for the merits of the turnip earned him the nickname of 'Turnip Townshend'.

He is popularly credited with the introduction of the Norfolk Four Course Rotation, but this had certainly been long practised in his area. However, the success of his farming practice and the wide publicity that he gave to it were important factors in the improvement of British agriculture during the mid-eighteenth century.

Further Reading
R.E. Prothero, 1892, article in *Journal of the Royal Agricultural Society of England*: 1–3.
—— 1912, *English Farming Past and Present*, London, pp. 172–5 (places Townshend within his context).

AP

Train, George Francis
b. 24 March 1829 Boston, Massachusetts, USA
d. 1904

American entrepreneur who introduced tramways to the streets of London.

He was the son of a merchant, Oliver Train, who had settled in New Orleans, Louisiana. His mother and sister died in a yellow fever epidemic and he was sent to live on his grandmother's farm at Waltham, Massachusetts, where he went to the district school. He left in 1843 and was apprenticed in a grocery store in nearby Cambridge, where, one day, a relative named Enoch Train called to see him. George Train left and went to join his relative's shipping office across the river in Boston; Enoch Train, among other enterprises, ran a packet line to Liverpool and, in 1850, sent George to England to manage his Liverpool office. Three years later, George Train went to Melbourne, Australia, and established his own shipping firm; he is said to have

earned £95,000 in his first year there. In 1855 he left Australia to travel in Europe and the Levant where he made many contacts. In the late 1850s and early 1860s he was in England seeking capital for American railroads and promoting the construction of street railways or trams in Liverpool, London and Staffordshire. In 1862 he was back in Boston, where he was put in jail for disturbing a public meeting; in 1870, he achieved momentary fame for travelling around the world in eighty days.

Further Reading
D. Malone (ed.), 1932–3, *Dictionary of American Biography*, Vol. 5, New York: Charles Scribner.

IMcN

Tralles, Anthemios of
See **Anthemios of Tralles**.

Traquair, Harry Moss
b. 13 September 1875 Edinburgh, Scotland
d. 14 November 1954 Edinburgh, Scotland

Scottish ophthalmologist, originator of techniques for the assessment of the visual fields and their neurological significance.

Traquair graduated in medicine at Edinburgh in 1901. After a period in Germany and South Africa occasioned by tuberculosis, a recurrence of which led to his death, he specialized in ophthalmology and filled a succession of appointments at the Royal Infirmary, Edinburgh, until his retirement in 1943 from his post as Senior Ophthalmic Surgeon.

Apart from a wide involvement in the full range of the speciality, he was particularly concerned, in association with neurologists and neurosurgeons, with the assessment and diagnosis of affections of the intracranial visual pathways. He refined the previously haphazard methods of field charting into perimetry, an exact and repeatable diagnostic routine. His work constituted an essential element in the development of modern surgical neurology.

Principal Honours and Distinctions
President, Royal College of Surgeons of Edinburgh 1939–41. Middlemore Prize 1920. Nettleship Medal 1922. Doyne Medal 1923. Mackenzie Medal 1939.

Bibliography
1949, *Clinical Perimetry* (6th edn).

Further Reading
S. Duke-Elder, 1969, *System of Ophthalmology*, Vol. 12, London.

MG

Treadgold, Arthur Newton Christian

b. August 1863 Woolsthorpe, Grantham, Lincolnshire, England
d. 23 March 1951 London, England

English organizer of the Yukon gold fields in Canada, who introduced hydraulic mining.

A direct descendant of Sir Isaac Newton, Treadgold worked as a schoolmaster, mostly at Bath College, for eleven years after completing his studies at Oxford University. He gained a reputation as an energetic teacher who devoted much of his work to sport, but he resigned his post and returned to Oxford; here, in 1897, he learned of the gold rush in the Klondike in the Canadian northwest. With a view to making his own fortune, he took a course in geology at the London Geological College and in 1898 set off for Dawson City, in the Yukon Territory. Working as a correspondent for two English newspapers, he studied thoroughly the situation there; he decided to join the stampede, but as a rather sophisticated gold hustler.

As there were limited water resources for sluicing or dredging, and underground mining methods were too expensive, Treadgold conceived the idea of hydraulic mining. He designed a ditch-and-siphon system for bringing large amounts of water down from the mountains; in 1901, after three years of negotiation with the Canadian government in Ottawa, he obtained permission to set up the Treadgold Concession to cover the water supply to the Klondike mining claims. This enabled him to supply giant water cannons which battered the hillsides, breaking up the gravel which was then sluiced. Massive protests by the individual miners in the Dawson City region, which he had overrun with his system, led to the concession being rescinded in 1904. Two years later, however, Treadgold began again, forming the Yukon Gold Company, initially in partnership with Solomon Guggenheim; he started work on a channel, completed in 1910, to carry water over a distance of 115 km (70 miles) down to Bonanza Creek. In 1919 he founded the Granville Mining Company, which was to give him control of all the gold-mining operations in the southern Klondike region. When he returned to London in the following year, the company began to fail, and in 1920 he went bankrupt with liabilities totalling more than $2 million. After the Yukon Consolidated Gold Corporation had been formed in 1923, Treadgold returned to the Klondike in 1925 in order to acquire the assets of the operating companies; he gained control and personally supervised the operations. But the company drifted towards disaster, and in 1930 he was dismissed from active management and his shares were cancelled by the courts; he fought for their reinstatement right up until his death.

Further Reading
L. Green, 1977, *The Gold Hustlers*, Anchorage, Alaska (describes this outstanding character and his unusual gold-prospecting career).

WK

Trembley, Abraham

b. 3 September 1710 Geneva, Switzerland
d. 12 May 1784 Petit Sacconex, Switzerland

Swiss philosopher and experimental zoologist, pioneer of tissue grafting.

Educated at Geneva, he later became a tutor to Count Bentinck's family near Leiden. It was during this time, from 1733 to 1743, that he undertook the studies of the organism *Hydra* that led, in October 1742, to the first permanent graft of animal tissues. His work covered the whole range of possibilities in tissue regeneration and grafting, but he was also engaged in other studies of the protozoa and *c.*1760 he made the first observations of cell division. In 1750 he was entrusted with the care of the son and heir of the Duke of Richmond and in 1757, having escorted the young duke all over the European continent, he was able to retire in comfort to the country at Petit Sacconex.

The advice and counsel of Réaumur was of considerable support to him, bearing in mind that many including Voltaire found it impossible to accept that an animal could be multiplied by cutting it into pieces.

Principal Honours and Distinctions
FRS 1743.

Bibliography
1744, *Mémoires pour servir à l'histoire d'un genre de polypes d'eau douce, à bras en forme des cornes*, Leiden.

Further Reading
J.R. Baker, 1952, *Abraham Trembley of Geneva: Scientist and Philosopher, 1710–1784*.

MG

Trésaguet, Pierre Marie Jérôme

b. 1716 Nevers, France
d. 1796 France

French civil engineer, best known for his system of road construction.

Born into a family of engineers, Trésaguet made his career in the Corps des Ponts et Chaussées, becoming Inspector-General of the Corps in 1775. He is best known for his improved method of road construction, which involved the use of carefully placed stones in the base with layers of progressively smaller sizes towards the surface. He also emphasized the importance of good drainage as well as regular maintenance. His system was generally adopted throughout France and in neighbouring European countries.

Further Reading
M. Magnusson (ed.), 1990, *Chambers Biographical Dictionary*, Edinburgh: W. & R. Chambers.

IMcN

Trevithick, Richard

b. 13 April 1771 Illogan, Cornwall, England
d. 22 April 1833 Dartford, Kent, England

English engineer, pioneer of non-condensing steam-engines; designed and built the first locomotives.

Trevithick's father was a tin-mine manager, and Trevithick himself, after limited formal education, developed his immense engineering talent among local mining machinery and steam-engines and found employment as a mining engineer. Tall, strong and high-spirited, he was the eternal optimist.

About 1797 it occurred to him that the separate condenser patent of James **Watt** could be avoided by employing 'strong steam', that is steam at pressures substantially greater than atmospheric, to drive steam-engines: after use, steam could be exhausted to the atmosphere and the condenser eliminated. His first winding engine on this principle came into use in 1799, and subsequently such engines were widely used. To produce high-pressure steam, a stronger boiler was needed than the boilers then in use, in which the pressure vessel was mounted upon masonry above the fire: Trevithick designed the cylindrical boiler, with furnace tube within, from which the Cornish and later the Lancashire boilers evolved.

Simultaneously he realized that high-pressure steam enabled a compact steam-engine/boiler unit to be built: typically, the Trevithick engine comprised a cylindrical boiler with return fire-tube, and a cylinder recessed into the boiler. No beam intervened between connecting rod and crank. A master patent was taken out.

Such an engine was well suited to driving vehicles. Trevithick built his first steam-carriage in 1801, but after a few days' use it overturned on a rough Cornish road and was damaged beyond repair by fire. Nevertheless, it had been the first self-propelled vehicle successfully to carry passengers. His second steam-carriage was driven about the streets of London in 1803, even more successfully; however, it aroused no commercial interest. Meanwhile the Coalbrookdale Company had started to build a locomotive incorporating a Trevithick engine for its tramroads, though little is known of the outcome; however, Samuel Homfray's ironworks at Penydarren, South Wales, was already building engines to Trevithick's design, and in 1804 Trevithick built one there as a locomotive for the Penydarren Tramroad. In this, and in the London steam-carriage, exhaust steam was turned up the chimney to draw the fire. On 21 February the locomotive hauled five wagons with 10 tons of iron and seventy men for 9 miles (14 km): it was the first successful railway locomotive.

Again, there was no commercial interest, although Trevithick now had nearly fifty stationary engines completed or being built to his design under licence. He experimented with one to power a barge on the Severn and used one to power a dredger on the Thames. He became Engineer to a project to drive a tunnel beneath the Thames at Rotherhithe and was only narrowly defeated, by quicksands. Trevithick then set up, in 1808, a circular tramroad track in London and upon it demonstrated to the admission-fee-paying public the locomotive *Catch me who can*, built to his design by John Hazledine and J.U. **Rastrick**.

In 1809, by which date Trevithick had sold all his interest in the steam-engine patent, he and Robert Dickinson, in partnership, obtained a patent for iron tanks to hold liquid cargo in ships, replacing the wooden casks then used, and started to manufacture them. In 1810, however, he was taken seriously ill with typhus for six months and had to return to Cornwall, and early in 1811 the partners were bankrupt; Trevithick was discharged from bankruptcy only in 1814.

In the meantime he continued as a steam engineer and produced a single-acting steam engine in which the cut-off could be varied to work the engine expansively by way of a three-way cock actuated by a cam. Then, in 1813, Trevithick was approached by a representative of a company set up to drain the rich but flooded silver-mines at Cerro de Pasco, Peru, at an altitude of 14,000 ft (4,300 m). Low-pressure steam engines, dependent largely upon atmospheric pressure, would not work at such an altitude, but Trevithick's high-pressure engines would. Nine engines and much other mining plant were built by Hazledine and Rastrick and despatched to Peru in 1814, and Trevithick himself followed two years later. However, the war of independence was taking place in Peru, then a Spanish colony, and no sooner had Trevithick, after immense difficulties, put everything in order at the mines then rebels arrived and broke up the machinery, for they saw the mines as a source of supply for the Spanish forces. It was only after innumerable further adventures, during which he encountered and was assisted financially by Robert **Stephenson**, that Trevithick eventually arrived home in Cornwall in 1827, penniless.

He petitioned Parliament for a grant in recognition of his improvements to steam-engines and boilers, without success. He was as inventive as ever though: he proposed a hydraulic power transmission system; he was consulted over steam engines for land drainage in Holland; and he suggested a 1,000 ft (305 m) high tower of gilded cast iron to commemorate the Reform Act of 1832. While working on steam propulsion of ships in 1833, he caught pneumonia, from which he died.

Bibliography
Trevithick took out fourteen patents, solely or in partnership, of which the most important are:
1802, *Construction of Steam Engines*, British patent no. 2,599.
1808, *Stowing Ships' Cargoes*, British patent no. 3,172.

Further Reading
H.W. Dickinson and A. Titley, 1934, *Richard Trevithick. The Engineer and the Man*, Cambridge; F. Trevithick, 1872, *Life of Richard Trevithick*, London (these two are the principal biographies).
E.A. Forward, 1952, 'Links in the history of the locomotive', *The Engineer* (22 February), 226 (considers the case for the Coalbrookdale locomotive of 1802).

See also **Blenkinsop, John**.

PJGR

Trueta, Joseph
b. 28 October 1897 Barcelona, Spain
d. 19 January 1977 Barcelona, Spain

Spanish surgeon who specialized in the treatment of trauma and invented the 'Trueta' technique of wound management.

Trueta studied medicine at Barcelona University and graduated in 1921. He held successive surgical appointments until in 1929 he was appointed to the Caja de Provisión y Socorro, an organization handling 40,000 cases of injury per year. In 1935, soon after becoming Chief Surgeon in Catalonia, he was confronted by the special problems presented by the casualties of the Spanish Civil War.

With a Nationalist victory imminent in 1939, he moved to England where his special skills were recognized, and at the outbreak of the Second World War he was appointed to the Wingfield Hospital and the Radcliffe Infirmary at Oxford. After an interregnum at the end of the war, in 1949 he was appointed Nuffield Professor of Orthopaedic Surgery at Oxford, and held this post until his retirement in 1965, when he was able to return to Spain.

His technique of wound management stressed

the importance of wound cleansing, excision of non-viable tissue, drainage and immobilization, and was particularly timely in that the advent of penicillin permitted the practical pursuit of new concepts in the treatment not only of the soft tissues, but also of bone infection. He was engaged in many other research projects, in particular those concerned with 'crush syndrome' and its renal implications.

Bibliography
1939, *Treatment of Wounds and Fractures with special reference to the closed method,* London.
1943, *The Principles and Practice of War Surgery with special reference to the Biological Method of Treatment of Wounds and Fractures,* London.
1980, *Trueta: Surgeon in War and Peace,* trans. M. Strubell and M. Strubell, London (autobiography).

MG

Tsai Lun
See **Cai Lun**.

Tseng Kung-Liang
See **Zeng Gonglian**.

Tshai Lun
See **Cai Lun**.

Tsiolkovsky (Ziolkowski), Konstantin Eduardovich
b. 17 September 1857 (5 September 1857, Old Style) Izhevskoye, Russia.
d. 19 September 1935 Kaluga, Russia.

Russian pioneer space theorist.

The son of a Polish lumberjack who had settled in Russia, Tsiolkovsky was a largely self-educated schoolteacher who was practically deaf from childhood. In spite of this handicap, he studied the problems of space and spaceflight and arrived at most of the correct theoretical solutions. In 1883 he noted that the gas escaping from a vehicle moving into space would drive the containing vehicle away from it. He wrote a remarkable series of technical articles and papers including, in 1903, a seminal article, 'Exploration of Space with Reactive Devices'. His aerodynamic experiments did not receive any significant recognition from the Academy of Sciences, and his design for an all-metal dirigible was largely ignored at the

1914 Aeronautics Congress in St Petersburg. However, from the inception of the Soviet Union until his death, Tsiolkovsky continued his research with state support, and on 9 November 1921 he was granted a pension for life by the Council of the People's Commissars. He has rightly been described as the 'Grandfather of Spaceflight' and as a fine theoretical engineer who established most of the principles upon which rocket technology is based.

Principal Honours and Distinctions
Elected to the Socialist Academy (later the Academy of Sciences of the USSR) 1919.

Further Reading
T. Osman, 1983, *Space History,* London: Michael Joseph.
R. Spangenburg and D. Moser, 1990, *Space People,* New York: Facts on File.

IMcN

Tull, Jethro
b. 30 March 1674 Basildon, Essex, England
d. February 1741 Hungerford, Berkshire, England

English farmer who developed and publicized a system of row crop husbandry.

Jethro Tull was born into an English landowning family. He was educated at St John's College, Oxford, but left without a degree at the age of 17. He then spent three years on the Grand Tour before returning to study law at Gray's Inn in London. After six years he was admitted to the Bar, but he never practised, moving instead to one of his father's farms near Oxford.

Because of labour problems he chose to plant sainfoin (*Onobrychis viciaefolia*) as a forage crop because it required less frequent reseeding than grass. The seed itself was expensive and of poor fertility, so he began to experiment. He discovered that the depth of sowing as well as the planting rate influenced germination and the rate of growth. he found the optimum rate could be gained with one plant per ft^2, a much lower density than could be achieved by broadcasting. His experiments created labour problems. He is traditionally and incorrectly credited with the invention of the seed drill, but he did develop and use a drill on his own farm to achieve the planting rate and depth he needed without having to rely on his workforce.

In 1711 Tull became ill and went to France, having first sold his original farm and moved to 'Properous', near Hungerford. In France he developed a husbandry technique that used a horse hoe to stir the soil between the rows of plants achieved with his drill. He incorrectly believed that his increased yields were the result of nutrients released from the soil by this method, whereas they were more likely to have been the result of a reduction in weed competition as a result of the repeated cultivation.

Bibliography
1731, *The New Horse-Hoeing Husbandry, or an Essay on the Principals of Tillage and Vegetation* (sets out the ideas and innovations for which he was already well known).

Further Reading
T.H. Marshall, 1929, 'Jethro Tull and the new husbandry of the 18th century', *Economic History Review* 11: 41–60 (the relevance and significance of Tull's work was already under discussion before his death; Marshall discusses the controversy).
G.E. Fussell, 1973, *Jethro Tull. His Influence on Mechanised Agriculture* (presents a pro-Tull account).

AP

Tupolev, Andrei Nikolayevich
b. 10 November 1888 Pastomazovo, Russia
d. 23 December 1972 Moscow, Russia

Russian aircraft designer.

In 1909 he entered the Moscow Higher Technical School and became a pupil of Nikolai Zhukovsky, who was known as 'the father of Russian aviation'. Graduating in 1918, he helped Zhukovsky to set up the Zhukovsky Central Aerohydrodynamic Institute and was made Assistant Director. He was appointed Head of the Institute's Design Department in 1922: his work was concentrated on wind tunnels and gliders, but later included aerodynamic calculations and the construction of all-metal aircraft. His first significant design project was the twin-engined *Ant-29* fighter prototype, which appeared in the early 1930s and eventually entered service as the *SB-2*. However, Tupolev and his wife fell victim to Stalin's purges in 1937: she was sent to a labour camp and he was imprisoned, but in 1943 both were rehabilitated and Tupolev was able to resume his design work. He devoted his attention to long-range strategic bombers, the first of these being the *Tu-4*, a copy of the US *B-29*, followed by the *Tu-70* bomber. He also designed the *Tu-104* airliner, and in 1967 he produced the world's first supersonic airliner, the *Tu-144*. Tupolev also became interested in fast-attack naval craft and designed a number of torpedo launches, and he rose to the rank of Lieutenant-General in the Soviet air force's Engineering and Technical Service.

Principal Honours and Distinctions
Honoured Scientist and Technologist RSFSR 1933. Hero of Socialist Labour 1945. Member of the Supreme Soviet 1950–58. Member of the Soviet Academy of Sciences 1953. Lenin Prize 1957. Stalin Prize.

CM

Türck, Ludwig
b. 22 July 1810 Vienna, Austria
d. 25 February 1868 Vienna, Austria

Austrian neurologist, developer of the techniques of laryngoscopy.

The son of a wealthy jeweller, he attended medical school in Vienna and qualified in 1836. Until 1844 he was engaged in research into the anatomy and physiology of the nervous system. In 1844, while on a visit to Paris, he came to the attention of Baron Türckheim, Director of the General Hospital in Vienna. The consequence was the establishment of a special division of the hospital for nervous diseases, with Türck in charge.

In 1857 he was appointed Chief Physician to the largest hospital in Vienna and at the same time he became aware of the invention in 1855 by Manuel García, a music teacher of Paris, of a practical laryngoscope. Türck adapted the apparatus to clinical purposes and proceeded to establish the diagnostic and therapeutic techniques required for its efficient use. Some conflict over priority ensued following a publication by Johann Nepomuk Czermak in 1858, but eventually a professional declaration asserted Türck's priority.

Bibliography

1862, *Recherches cliniques sur diverses maladies du larynx, de la trachée et du pharynx étudiées à l'aide du laryngoscope*, Paris.

Papers in *Allgemein. Wien. med. Zeit.* 1856–68.

MG

Further Reading

J. Hix, 1974, *The Glass House*, Cambridge, Mass.: MIT Press, pp. 122–7 (the Palm House at Kew).

U. Kulturmann, 1979, *Architecture and Urbanism*, Tokyo, pp. 76–81 (the Palm House at Kew).

DY

Turner, Richard

b. 1798 probably Dublin, Ireland
d. 1881

Irish engineer of ferrovitreous structures such as glasshouses and roofs of railway terminus buildings. Lime Street Station, Liverpool, erected 1849–50, was a notable example of the latter.

Turner's first glasshouse commission was for the Palm House at the Botanic Gardens in Belfast, begun in 1839; this structure was designed by Charles Lanyon, Turner being responsible for the ironwork construction. The Belfast Palm House was followed in 1843 by the Palm House for the Royal Dublin Society, but the structure for which Turner is best known is the famous Palm House in the Royal Botanic Gardens at Kew Gardens in London. This was originally designed in 1844 by the architect Decimus Burton, but his concept was rejected and Turner was asked to design a new one. Burton tried again, basing his new design upon that of Turner but also incorporating features that made it more similar to the famous Great Conservatory by **Paxton** at Chatsworth. Finally, Turner was contracted to build the Palm Stove in collaboration with Burton. Completed in 1848, the Kew Palm House is the finest example of the glasshouses of that era. This remarkable structure is simple but impressive: it is 362 ft (110 m) long and is covered by 45,000 ft^2 (4,180 m^2) of greenish glass. Inside, in the central taller part, a decorative, cast-iron, spiral staircase gives access to an upper gallery, from where tall plants may be clearly viewed; the roof rises to 62 ft (19 m). The curving, glazed panels, set in ribs of wrought iron, rise from a low masonry wall. The ingenious method of construction of these ribs was patented by Turner in 1846. It consists of wrought-iron tie rods inserted into hollow cast-iron tubes; these can be tightened after the erection of the building is complete, so producing a stable, balanced structure not unlike the concept of a timber-trussed roof. The Palm Stove has only recently undergone extensive adaptation to modern needs.

Türr, Istvan (Stephen, Etienne)

b. 10 August 1825 Baja, Hungary
d. 3 May 1908 Budapest, Hungary

Hungarian army officer and canal entrepreneur.

He entered the Austro-Hungarian Imperial Army in 1842 and, as a lieutenant, fought against the Piedmontese in 1848. In January 1849 he deserted to the Piedmontese and tried to form a Hungarian legion against Austria. Defeated at Novara he fled to London and intrigued with Kossuth and Pulszky against Austria. In 1852 he was Kossuth's agent in Italy and was involved with Mazzini in the Milan rising of 1853. He was expelled from Italy and joined the Turkish army as a volunteer until 1854. The Crimean War saw him as a British agent procuring horses in the Balkans for the British forces, but he was caught by the Austrians and sentenced to death as a deserter. Through English intervention the sentence was commuted to banishment. He was ill until 1859, but then returned to Genoa and offered his services to Garibaldi, becoming his Aide-de-Camp in the invasion of Sicily in 1860. On the unification of Italy he joined the regular Italian army as a general, and from 1870 was Honorary Aide-de-Camp to King Victor Emanuel II.

From then on he was more interested in peaceful projects. Jointly with Lucien Wyse, he obtained a concession in 1875 from the Columbian government to build a canal across Panama and formed the Société Civile Internationale du Canal Interocéanique du Darien. In 1879 he sold the concession to de **Lesseps**, and with the money negotiated a concession from King George of Greece for building the Corinth Canal. A French company undertook the work in April 1882, but financial problems led to the collapse of the company in 1889, at the same time as de Lesseps's financial storm. A Greek company then took over and completed the canal in 1893.

The canal was formally opened on 6 August 1893 by King George on his royal yacht; the king paid tribute to General Türr, who was accompanying him, saying that he had completed the work the Romans had begun. The general's later years were devoted to peace propaganda and he attended every peace conference held during those years.

JHB

Tu Shih
See **Du Shi**.

Tuve, Merle Antony
b. 27 June 1901 Canton, South Dakota, USA
d. 20 May 1982 Bethesda, Maryland, USA

American physicist and geophysicist who developed radio exploration of the ionosphere and made contributions to seismology and atomic physics.

After BS and AM degrees from the University of Minnesota, Tuve gained a PhD in physics from Johns Hopkins University in 1926. He then joined the Department of Terrestrial Magnetism at the Carnegie Institute, Washington, DC, where with Breit he established by experiment the existence and characteristics of the ionosphere. He also studied gamma and beta rays, artificial radioactivity and atomic transmutation, verified the existence of the neutron and measured nuclear binding forces. During the Second World War he performed military research, producing a proximity fuse for use against the V1 flying bomb. He returned to Carnegie in 1946 as Director of the Department of Terrestrial Magnetism, where he remained until 1966, making many contributions to the study of the earth and space.

Principal Honours and Distinctions
American Association for the Advancement of Science Prize for atomic and nuclear research 1931. National Academy of Science 1946. Research Corporation Award 1947. Comstock Prize 1948. National Academy of Science Barnard Medal 1955. Presidential Medal of Merit and Distinguished Service Member of the Carnegie Institute 1966.

Bibliography
1926, with G. Breit, 'A test of the existence of the conducting layer', *Physical Review* 28: 554 (gives an account of the early ionospheric studies).

See also **Appleton, Sir Edward Victor**.

KF

Tu Yu
See **Du Yu**.

Twiss, William
b. 1745
d. 14 March 1827 Hardon Grange, Bingley, Yorkshire, England.

English army officer and military engineer.

William Twiss entered the Ordnance Department at the age of 15, and in 1762, aged 17, he was appointed Overseer of Works at Gibraltar. At the end of the Seven Years War, in 1763, he was commissioned Ensign in the Engineers, and further promotion followed while he still remained in Gibraltar. In 1771, as a Lieutenant, he returned to England to be employed on Portsmouth's dockyard fortifications. In 1776 he was posted to Canada, where he was soon appointed Controller of Works for the building of a British fleet for Lake Champlain. He was involved in military operations in the American War of Independence and in 1777 was present at the capture of Fort Ticonderoga (New York State). He was taken prisoner shortly afterwards, but was soon exchanged, and a year later he was promoted Captain.

In 1779 he was given the task of constructing a short canal at Coteau du Lac, Quebec, to bypass rough water at this point in the St Lawrence River between Montreal and Pointe Maligne. This was probably the first locked canal in North America. In 1781, following his appointment as Chief Engineer for all military works in Canada, he supervised further navigational improvements on the St Lawrence with canals at Les Cèdres and the Cascades. In parallel with these projects, he was responsible for an amazing variety of works in Canada, including hospitals, windmills, storehouses, barracks, fortifications, roads, bridges, prisons, ironworks and dams. He was also responsible for a temporary citadel in Quebec.

In 1783 he returned to England, and from 1794–1810 he served as Lieutenant-Governor of the Royal Military Academy at Woolwich, although in 1799 he was sent to Holland as Commanding Engineer to the Duke of York. In 1802 he was promoted Colonel and was in Ireland reporting on the defences there. He became Colonel Commandant, Royal Engineers, in 1809, and retired two years later. In retirement he was promoted Lieutenant-General in 1812 and General in 1825.

Further Reading
W. Porter, 1889–1915, *History of the Corps of Royal Engineers*, London: Longmans.

JHB

Tyer, Edward

b. 6 February 1830 Kennington, London, England
d. 25 December 1912 Tunbridge Wells, England

English railway signal engineer, inventor of electric train-tablet system for the operation of single-line railways.

Use of the electric telegraph for the safe operation of railways was first proposed by W.F. **Cooke** in the late 1830s, but its application to this purpose and the concurrent replacement of the time-interval system of working, by the block system, comprised a matter of gradual evolution over several decades. In 1851 Tyer established a business making electrical apparatus for railways, and the block instruments invented by him in 1855 were an important step forward. A simple code of electric-bell rings (for up trains; for down trains, there was a distinctive gong) was used by one signalman to indicate to another in advance that a train was entering the section between them, and the latter signalman then operated a galvanometer telegraph instrument in the box of the former to indicate 'train on line', holding it so until the train arrived.

Even more important was the electric train-tablet apparatus. During the 1870s, single-line railways were operated either by telegraphed train orders, misuse of which led to two disastrous head-on collisions, or by 'train staff and ticket', which lacked flexibility since no train could enter one end of a section while the train staff was at the other. At the request of Currer, an official of the Caledonian Railway, Tyer designed and produced his apparatus, in which a supply of discs, or 'tablets', was contained in two instruments, one located at each end of a section, and linked electrically: only one tablet at a time could be extracted from the instruments, serving as an authority for a train to enter the section from one end or the other.

Bibliography
1855, British patent no. 2,895 (block instruments).
1861, British patent no. 3,015 (block instruments).
1878, British patent for electric train-tablet apparatus.

Further Reading
C. Hamilton Ellis, 1959, *British Railway History*, Vol. II: 1877–1947, London: George Allen & Unwin, p. 199 (describes the development of the tablet apparatus).
P.J.G. Ransom, 1990, *The Victorian Railway and How It Evolved*, London: Heinemann, pp. 157–8 and 164 (describes the block instruments and tablet apparatus).

PJGR

U

Unwin, William Cawthorne

b. 12 December 1838 Coggeshall, near Colchester, Essex, England
d. 1933

English engineer and educator.

Unwin made an important contribution to the establishment of engineering at the University of London. His family were of Huguenot stock, and his father was a Congregational minister. Unwin was educated at the City of London Corporation School and at New College, St John's Wood. At a time when the older universities were still effectively closed to Dissenters, he matriculated with Honours in Chemistry in the London University Matriculation Examination in 1858, and he subsequently graduated BSc from London in 1861. He served as Scientific Assistant to William **Fairbairn** in Manchester from 1856 to 1862, going on to manage engineering work of various sorts. He was appointed Instructor at the Royal School of Naval Architecture and Marine Engineering (1869–72), and then he became Professor of Hydraulics and Mechanical Engineering at the Royal Indian Engineering College (1872–84). From 1884 to 1904 he was Professor of Civil and Mechanical Engineering at the Central Institution of the City & Guilds of London, which was incorporated into the University of London in 1900. Unwin's research interests included hydraulics and water power, which led to him taking a leading part in the Niagara Falls hydroelectric scheme; the strength of materials, involving the stability of masonry dams; and the development of the internal combustion engine.

Principal Honours and Distinctions
FRS 1886.

Further Reading
DNB Supplement.
E.G. Walker, 1938, *Life and Work of William Cawthorne Unwin.*

AB

V

Vail, Alfred Lewis

b. 25 September 1807 Morristown, New Jersey, USA
d. 18 January 1859 Morristown, New Jersey, USA

American telegraph pioneer and associate of Samuel Morse; widely credited with the invention of 'Morse' code.

After leaving school, Vail was initially employed at his father's ironworks in Morristown, but he then decided to train for the Presbyterian ministry, graduating from New York City University in 1836. Unfortunately, he was then obliged to abandon his chosen career because of ill health. He accidentally met Samuel Morse not long afterwards, and he became interested in the latter's telegraph experiments; in return for a share of the rights, he agreed to construct apparatus and finance the filing of US and foreign patents. Working in Morristown with Morse and Leonard Gale, and with financial backing from his father, Vail constructed around his father's plant a telegraph with 3 miles (4.8 km) of wire. It is also possible that he, rather than Morse, was largely responsible for devising the so-called Morse code, a series of dot and dash codes representing the letters of the alphabet, and in which the simplest codes were chosen for those letters found to be most numerous in a case of printer's type. This system was first demonstrated on 6 January 1838 and there were subsequent public demonstrations in New York and Philadelphia. Eventually Congress authorized an above-ground line between Washington and Baltimore, and on 24 May 1844 the epoch-making message 'What hath God wrought?' was transmitted.

Vail remained with Morse for a further four years, but he gradually lost interest in telegraphy and resigned, receiving no credit for his important contribution.

Bibliography
The Magnetic Telegraph.

Further Reading
1845, *American Electrotelegraph* 135.
J.J. Fahie, 1884, *A History of the Electric Telegraph to the Year 1837*, London: E&F Spon.

KF

Varian, Russell Harrison

b. 24 April 1898 Washington, DC, USA
d. 28 July 1959 Juneau, Alaska, USA

American physicist who, with his brother Sigurd Varian and others, developed the klystron.

After attending schools in Palo Alto and Halcyon, Russell Varian went to Stanford University, gaining his BA in 1925 and his MA in 1927 despite illness and being dyslexic. His family being in need of financial help, he first worked for six months for Bush Electric in San Francisco and then for an oil company in Texas, returning to San Francisco in 1930 to join Farnsworth's Television Laboratory. After a move to Philadelphia, in 1933 the laboratory closed and Russell tried to take up a PhD course at Stanford but was rejected, so he trained as a teacher. However, although he did some teaching at Stanford it was not to be his career, for in 1935 he joined his brothers Sigurd and Eric in the setting up of a home laboratory.

There, with William Hansen, a former colleague of Russell's at Stanford, they worked on the development of microwave oscillators, based on some of the latter's ideas. By 1937 they had made sufficient progress on an electron velocity-bunching tube, which they called the klystron, to obtain an agreement with the university to provide laboratory facilities in return for a share of any proceeds. By August that year they were able to produce continuous power at a wavelength of 13 cm. Clearly needing greater resources to develop and manufacture the tube, and with a possible war looming, a deal was struck with the Sperry Gyroscope Company to finance the work, which was transferred to the East Coast.

In 1946, after the death of his first wife, Russell returned to Palo Alto, and in 1948 the brothers and Hansen founded Varian Associates to make microwave tubes for transmitters and linear accelerators and nuclear magnetic-resonance detectors. Subsequent research also resulted in the development of a satellite-borne magnetometer for measuring the earth's magnetic field.

Principal Honours and Distinctions
Honorary DSc Brooklyn Polytechnic Institute 1943. Franklin Institute Medal.

Bibliography
1939, with S.F. Varian, 'High frequency oscillator and amplifier', *Journal of Applied Physics* 10: 321 (describes the klystron).

Further Reading
J.R. Pierce, 1962, 'History of the microwave tube art', *Proceedings of the Institute of Radio Engineers* 979 (provides background to development of the klystron).
D. Varian, 1983, *The Inventor and the Pilot* (biographies of the brothers).

See also **Varian, Sigurd Fergus**.

KF

Varian, Sigurd Fergus
b. 4 May 1901 Syracuse, New York, USA
d. 18 October 1961 Puerto Vallarta, Mexico

American electrical engineer who, with his brother Russell, developed the klystron microwave tube.

Sigurd Varian left school in 1920 and entered California Polytechnic to study engineering, but he soon dropped out and trained as an electrician, taking up employment with the Southern Californian Edison Company. As a result of working on an airfield he developed an interest in flying. He took lessons and in 1924 bought a First World War biplane and became a 'barnstorming' pilot, giving flying displays and joyrides, etc., to earn his living. Beset by several prolonged bouts of tuberculosis, he used his periods of recuperation to study aerial navigation and to devise navigation instruments. In 1929 he took a permanent job as a pilot for Pan American in Mexico, but in 1935 he went to California to work on electron tubes with his younger brother, Eric. They were soon joined by Russell, and with William Hansen they developed the klystron. For details of this part of his life and the founding of

Varian Associates, see under Russell **Varian**. In later years, his health increasingly poor, he lived in semi-retirement in Mexico, where he died in a plane crash while flying himself home.

Principal Honours and Distinctions
Franklin Institute Medal.

Bibliography
1939, with R.S. Varian, 'High frequency oscillator and amplifier', *Journal of Applied Physics* 10: 321 (describes the klystron).

Further Reading
J.R. Pierce, 1962, 'History of the microwave tube art', *Proceedings of the Institute of Radio Engineers* 979 (provides background to development of the klystron).
D. Varian, 1983, *The Inventor and the Pilot* (biographies of the brothers).

KF

Vauban, Sébastien de
b. 15 May 1633 St-Léger-de-Fougeret, Château Chinon, Nièvre, France
d. 20 March 1707 Paris, France

French civil and military engineer.

Born of impecunious parents, Vauban joined Condé's regiment as a cadet in 1651, at the age of 17, although he had apparently acquired some knowledge of mathematics and fortifications in the Carmelite College of Semur-en-Auxois. In the war of the Fronde he was captured by the Royal troops in 1653 and was converted to the king's service. He was soon recognized as having engineering ability and was given the task of repairing the fortifications of Sainte-Menehould. During the next few years he was engaged on fortification repairs and assisting at sieges, including Ypres, Gravelines and Oudenarde in 1658. Vauban found favour with the king, Louis XIV, and was responsible for the fortifications of Lille, which had been captured in 1667; he commenced the defensive structures of the citadel and the town in 1668. These were completed in 1674 and consisted of a vast pentagonal fort with bastions and further detached works surrounded by water defences. In 1692 he was present at the siege of Namur and was responsible for its capture. He was then put in charge of re-establishing and improving the defences. He next developed a line of fortresses along the French border. He later was abandoned by the king, whom he had served so well, and, with his advice being ignored by the French forces, they suffered defeat after defeat in Marlborough's wars.

Meanwhile he had been called in to inspect the recently completed Canal du Midi and subsequently made recommendations for its improvement. These included the extension of the Montagne Noire feeder, and the construction of the Cesse and Orbiel aqueducts which were carried out to his design and under his supervision in 1686–7. In 1700 he was consulted on and produced a plan for a canal across France from north to south, providing a barge waterway from Nîmes to Dunkirk, but this was not carried out.

In 1703 he was created maréchal de France, and two years later he devised vast schemes for the development of the canal system in Flanders. Owing to determined opposition from the local people, these schemes were abandoned and not revived until 1770, by which time the locals were prepared to accept them.

Further Reading
Sir Reginald Blomfield, 1938, *Sébastien le Prestre de Vauban, 1633–1707*, Methuen.
D. Halévy, 1924, *Vauban. Builder of Fortresses*, trans. C.J.C. Street, Geoffrey Bles.

JHB

Vauclain, Samuel Matthews
b. 18 May 1856 Philadelphia, USA
d. 4 February 1940 Rosemont, Pennsylvania, USA

American locomotive builder, inventor of the Vauclain compound system.

Vauclain entered the service of the Pennsylvania Railroad in 1872 as an apprentice in Altoona workshops and moved to the Baldwin Locomotive Works in 1883. He remained with the latter for fifty-seven years, becoming President in 1919 and Chairman of the Board in 1929.

The first locomotive to his pattern of compound was built in 1889. There were four cylinders: on each side of the locomotive a high-pressure cylinder and a low-pressure cylinder were positioned one above the other, their pistons driving a common cross-head. They shared, also, a common piston valve. Large two-cylinder compound locomotives had been found

to suffer from uneven distribution of power between the two sides of the locomotive: Vauclain's system overcame this problem while retaining the accessibility of a locomotive with two outside cylinders. It was used extensively in the USA and other parts of the world, but not in Britain. Among many other developments, in 1897 Vauclain was responsible for the construction of the first locomotives of the 2–8–2 wheel arrangement.

Bibliography
1930, *Steaming Up* (autobiography).

Further Reading
Obituary, 1941, *Transactions of the Newcomen Society* 20: 180.
J.T. van Reimsdijk, 1970, 'The compound locomotive. Part 1: 1876 to 1901', *Transactions of the Newcomen Society* 43: 9 (describes Vauclain's system of compounding).

See also: **Baldwin, Matthias William**; **Mallet, Jules Théodore Anatole**.

PJGR

Vermuyden, Sir Cornelius
b. c.1590 St Maartensdijk, Zeeland, the Netherlands
d. 4 February 1656 probably London, England

Dutch/British civil engineer responsible for many of the drainage and flood-protection schemes in low-lying areas of England in the seventeenth century.

At the beginning of the seventeenth century, several wealthy men in England joined forces as 'adventurers' to put their money into land ventures. One such group was responsible for the draining of the Fens. The first need was to find engineers who were versed in the processes of land drainage, particularly when that land was at, or below, sea level. It was natural, therefore, to turn to the Netherlands to find these skilled men. Joachim Liens was one of the first of the Dutch engineers to go to England, and he started work on the Great Level; however, no real progress was made until 1621, when Cornelius Vermuyden was brought to England to assist in the work.

Vermuyden had grown up in a district where he could see for himself the techniques of embanking and reclaiming land from the sea. He acquired a reputation of expertise in this field, and by 1621 his fame had spread to England. In that year the Thames had flooded and breached its banks near Havering and Dagenham in Essex. Vermuyden was commissioned to repair the breach and drain neighbouring marshland, with what he claimed as complete success. The Commissioners of Sewers for Essex disputed this claim and whthheld his fee, but King Charles I granted him a portion of the reclaimed land as compensation.

In 1626 Vermuyden carried out his first scheme for drainage works as a consultant. This was the drainage of Hatfield Chase in South Yorkshire. Charles I was, in fact, Vermuyden's employer in the drainage of the Chase, and the work was undertaken as a means of raising additional rents for the Royal Exchequer. Vermuyden was himself an 'adventurer' in the undertaking, putting capital into the venture and receiving the title to a considerable proportion of the drained lands. One of the important elements of his drainage designs was the principal of 'washes', which were flat areas between the protective dykes and the rivers to carry flood waters, to prevent them spreading on to nearby land. Vermuyden faced bitter opposition from those whose livelihoods depended on the marshlands and who resorted to sabotage of the embankments and violence against his imported Dutch workmen to defend their rights. The work could not be completed until arbiters had ruled out on the respective rights of the parties involved. Disagreements and criticism of his engineering practices continued and he gave up his interest in Hatfield Chase. The Hatfield Chase undertaking was not a great success, although the land is now rich farmland around the river Don in Doncaster. However, the involved financial and land-ownership arrangements were the key to the granting of a knighthood to Cornelius Vermuyden in January 1628, and in 1630 he purchased 4,000 acres of low-lying land on Sedgemoor in Somerset.

In 1629 Vermuyden embarked on his most important work, that of draining the Great Level in the fenlands of East Anglia. Francis Russell, 4th Earl of Bedford, was given charge of the work, with Vermuyden as Engineer; in this venture they were speculators and partners and were recompensed by a grant of land. The area which contains the Cambridgeshire tributaries of the Great Ouse were subject to severe and usually annual flooding. The works to contain the rivers in their flood period were important. Whilst the rivers were contained with the enclosed flood plain, the land beyond became highly sought-after because of the quality of the soil. The fourteen 'adventurers' who eventually came into partnership with the Earl of Bedford and Vermuyden were the financiers of the scheme and also received land in accordance with their input into the scheme. In 1637 the work was claimed to be complete, but this was disputed, with Vermuyden defending himself against criticism in a pamphlet entitled *Discourse Touching the Great Fennes* (1638; 1642, London). In fact, much remained to be done, and after an interruption due to the Civil War the scheme was finished in 1652. Whilst the process of the Great Level works had closely involved the King, Oliver Cromwell was equally concerned over the success of the scheme. By 1655 Cornelius Vermuyden had ceased to have anything to do with the Great Level. At that stage he was asked to account for large sums granted to him to expedite the work but was unable to do so; most of his assets were seized to cover the deficiency, and from then on he subsided into obscurity and poverty.

While Cornelius Vermuyden, as a Dutchman, was well versed in the drainage needs of his own country, he developed his skills as a hydraulic engineer in England and drained acres of derelict flooded land.

Principal Honours and Distinctions
Knighted 1628.

Further Reading
L.E. Harris, 1953, *Vermuyden and the Fens*, London: Cleaver Hume Press.
J. Korthals-Altes, 1977, *Sir Cornelius Vermuyden: The Lifework of a Great Anglo-Dutchman in Land-Reclamation and Drainage*, New York: Alto Press.

KM/LRD

Vernier, Pierre
b. *c.*1580 Ornans, Franche-Comté, France
d. 14 September 1637 Ornans, Franche-Comté, France

French mathematician, inventor of the vernier caliper, an instrument for making highly accurate linear measurements.

He was educated by his father, Claude Vernier, and from an early age studied all kinds of instruments, both in practice and in theory. The Spanish government employed him on several commissions, before he was elected commandant of the Château d'Ornans and later Director-General of Finances and Counsellor for the county of Bourgogne. In 1631 he wrote *La Construction, l'usage et les propriétés du quadrant nouveau de mathématiques* ('The Construction, Uses and Properties of a New Mathematical Quadrant'), which contained tables of trigonometric sines and a method of calculating the angles of a triangle from the lengths of its sides, as well as a description of his new measuring instrument which became known as the vernier caliper.

Bibliography
1631, *La Construction, l'usage et les propriétés du quadrant nouveau de mathématiques*, Brussels.

Further Reading
Rosenkilde and Bagger (eds), 1969, *Nouvelle biographie générale*, Copenhagen.

IMcN

Vignoles, Charles Blacker

b. 31 May 1793 Woodbrook, Co. Wexford, Ireland
d. 17 November 1875 Hythe, Hampshire, England

English surveyor and civil engineer, pioneer of railways.

Vignoles, who was of Huguenot descent, was orphaned in infancy and brought up in the family of his grandfather, Dr Charles Hutton FRS, Professor of Mathematics at the Royal Military Academy, Woolwich. After service in the Army he travelled to America, arriving in South Carolina in 1817. He was appointed Assistant to the state's Civil Engineer and surveyed much of South Carolina and subsequently Florida. After his return to England in 1823 he established himself as a civil engineer in London, and obtained work from the brothers George and John Rennie.

In 1825 the promoters of the Liverpool & Manchester Railway (L & MR) lost their application for an Act of Parliament, discharged their engineer George **Stephenson** and appointed the Rennie brothers in his place. They in turn employed Vignoles to resurvey the railway, taking a route that would minimize objections. With Vignoles's route, the company obtained its Act in 1826 and appointed Vignoles to supervise the start of construction. After Stephenson was reappointed Chief Engineer, however, he and Vignoles proved incompatible, with the result that Vignoles left the L & MR early in 1827.

Nevertheless, Vignoles did not sever all connection with the L & MR. He supported John Braithwaite and John **Ericsson** in the construction of the locomotive *Novelty* and was present when it competed in the Rainhill Trials in 1829. He attended the opening of the L & MR in 1830 and was appointed Engineer to two railways which connected with it, the St Helens & Runcorn Gap and the Wigan Branch (later extended to Preston as the North Union); he supervised the construction of these.

After the death of the Engineer to the Dublin & Kingstown Railway, Vignoles supervised construction: the railway, the first in Ireland, was opened in 1834. He was subsequently employed in surveying and constructing many railways in the British Isles and on the European continent; these included the Eastern Counties, the Midland Counties, the Sheffield, Ashton-under-Lyme & Manchester (which proved for him a financial disaster from which he took many years to recover), and the Waterford & Limerick. He probably discussed rail of flat-bottom section with R.L. **Stevens** during the winter of 1830–1 and brought it into use in the UK for the first time in 1836 on the London & Croydon Railway: subsequently rail of this section became known as 'Vignoles rail'. He considered that a broader gauge than 4 ft 8½ in. (1.44 m) was desirable for railways, although most of those he built were to this gauge so that they might connect with others. He supported the atmospheric system of propulsion during the 1840s and was instrumental in its early installation on the Dublin & Kingstown Railway's Dalkey extension. Between 1847 and 1853 he designed and built the noted multi-span suspension bridge at Kiev, Russia, over the River Dnieper, which is more than half a mile (800 m) wide at that point.

Between 1857 and 1863 he surveyed and then supervised the construction of the 155-mile (250 km) Tudela & Bilbao Railway, which crosses the Cantabrian Pyrenees at an altitude of 2,163 ft (659 m) above sea level. Vignoles outlived his most famous contemporaries to become the grand old man of his profession.

Principal Honours and Distinctions
Fellow of the Royal Astronomical Society 1829. FRS 1855. President, Institution of Civil Engineers 1869–70.

Bibliography
1830, jointly with John Ericsson, British patent no. 5,995 (a device to increase the capability of steam locomotives on grades, in which rollers gripped a third rail).
1823, *Observations upon the Floridas*, New York: Bliss & White.
1870, *Address on His Election as President of the Institution of Civil Engineers*.

Further Reading
K.H. Vignoles, 1982, *Charles Blacker Vignoles: Romantic Engineer*, Cambridge: Cambridge University Press (good modern biography by his great-grandson).

See also **Samuda, Joseph d'Aguilar**.

PJGR

Villard de Honnecourt

b. *c*.1200 Honnecourt-sur-Escaut, near Cambrai, France
d. mid-13th century (?) France

French architect-engineer.

Villard was one of the thirteenth-century architect-engineers who were responsible for the design and construction of the great Gothic cathedrals and other churches of the time. Their responsibilities covered all aspects of the work, including (in the spirit of the Roman architect **Vitruvius**) the invention and construction of mechanical devices. In their time, these men were highly esteemed and richly rewarded, although few of the inscriptions paying tribute to their achievements have survived. Villard stands out among them because a substantial part of his sketchbook has survived, in the form of thirty-

three parchment sheets of drawings and notes, now kept in the Bibliothèque Nationale in Paris.

Villard's professional career lasted roughly from 1225 to 1250. As a boy, he went to work on the building of the Cistercian monastery at Vaucelles, not far from Honnecourt, and afterwards he was apprenticed to the masons' lodge at Cambrai Cathedral, where he began copying the drawings and layouts on the tracing-house floor. All his drawings are, therefore, of the plans, elevations and sections of cathedrals. These buildings have long since been destroyed, but his drawings, perhaps among his earliest, bear witness to their architecture. He travelled widely in France and recorded features of the great works at Reims, Laon and Chartres. These include the complex system of passageways built into the fabric of a great cathedral; Villard comments that one of their purposes was 'to allow circulation in case of fire'.

Villard was invited to Hungary and reached there *c*.1235. He may have been responsible for the edifice dedicated to St Elizabeth of Hungary, canonized in 1235, at Kassa (now Košice, Slovakia). Villard probably returned to France *c*.1240, at least before the Tartar invasion of Hungary in 1241.

His sketchbook, which dates to *c*.1235, stands as a memorial to Villard's skill as a draughtsman, a student of perspective and a mechanical engineer. He took his sketchbook with him on his travels, and used ideas from it in his work abroad. It contains architectural designs, geometrical constructions for use in building, surveying exercises and drawings for various kinds of mechanical devices, for civil or military use. He was transmitting details from the highly developed French Gothic masons to the relatively underdeveloped eastern countries. The notebooks were annotated for the use of pupils and other master masons, and the notes on geometry were obviously intended for pupils. The prize examples are the pages in the book, clearly Villard's own work, related to mechanical devices. Whilst he, like many others of the period and after, played with designs for perpetual-motion machines, he concentrated on useful devices. These included the first Western representation of a perpetual-motion machine, which at least displays a concern to derive a source of energy: this was a water-powered sawmill, with automatic feed of the timber into the mill. This has been described as the first industrial automatic power-machine to involve two motions, for it not only converts the rotary motion of the water-wheel to the reciprocating motion of the saw, but incorporates a means of keeping the log pressed against the saw. His other designs included water-wheels, watermills, the Archimedean screw and other curious devices.

Bibliography

Of several facsimile reprints with notes there are *Album de Villard de Honnecourt,* 1858, ed. J.B. Lassus, Paris (repr. 1968, Paris: Laget), and *The Sketchbook of Villard de Honnecourt,* 1959, ed. T. Bowie, Bloomington: Indiana University Press.

Further Reading

J. Gimpel, 1977, 'Villard de Honnecourt: architect and engineer', *The Medieval Machine,* London: Victor Gollancz, ch. 6, pp. 114–46.
—— 1988, *The Medieval Machine, the Industrial Revolution of the Middle Ages,* London.
R. Pernord, J. Gimpel and R. Delatouche, 1986, *Le Moyen age pour quoi fayre,* Paris.

KM/LRD

Vinci, Leonardo da
See **Leonardo da Vinci**.

Vitruvius Pollio
b. early first century BC
d. *c.*25 BC

Roman writer on architecture and engineering subjects.

Nothing is known of Vitruvius apart from what can be gleaned from his only known work, the treatise *De architectura.* He seems to have been employed in some capacity by Julius Caesar and continued to serve under his heir, Octavianus, later Emperor Augustus, to whom he dedicated his book. It was written towards the end of his life, after Octavianus became undisputed ruler of the Empire by his victory at Actium in 31 BC, and was based partly on his own experience and partly on earlier, Hellenistic, writers.

The *De architectura* is divided into ten books. The first seven books expound the general principles of architecture and the planning, design and construction of various types of building, public and domestic, including a consideration of techniques and materials. Book 7 deals with interior decoration, including stucco work and painting, while Book 8 treats water supply, from the location of sources to the transport of water by aqueducts, tunnels and pipes. Book 9, after a long and somewhat confused account of the astronomical theories of the day, describes various forms of clock and sundial. Finally, Book 10 deals with mechanical devices for handling building materials and raising and pumping water, for which Vitruvius draws on the earlier Greek authors **Ctesibius** and **Hero**.

Although this may seem a motley assembly of subjects, to the Roman architect and builder it was a logical compendium of the subjects he was expected to know about. At the time, Vitruvius' rigid rules for the design of buildings such as temples seem to have had little influence, but his accounts of more practical matters of building materials and techniques were widely used. His illustrations to the original work were lost in antiquity, for no later manuscript includes them. Through the Middle Ages, manuscript copies were made in monastic scriptoria, although the architectural style in vogue had little relevance to those in Vitruvius: these came into their own with the Italian Renaissance. Alberti, writing the first great Renaissance treatise on architecture from 1452 to 1467, drew heavily on *De architectura*; those who sought to revive the styles of antiquity were bound to regard the only surviving text on the subject as authoritative. The appearance of the first printed edition in 1486 only served to extend its influence.

During the sixteenth and seventeenth centuries, Vitruvius was used as a handbook for constructing machines and instruments. For the modern historian of technology and architecture the work is a source of prime importance, although it must be remembered that the illustrations in the early printed editions are of contemporary reproductions of ancient devices using the techniques of the time, rather than authentic representations of ancient technology.

Bibliography

Of the several critical editions of *De architectura* there are the Teubner edition, 1899. ed. V. Rose, Leipzig; the Loeb Classical Library edition, 1962, ed. F. Granger, London: Heinemann, (with English trans. and notes); and the Collection Guillaume Budé with French trans. and full commentary, 10 vols, Paris (in progress).

Further Reading
Apart from the notes to the printed editions, see also:
H. Plommer, 1973, *Vitruvius and Later Roman Building Manuals*, London.
A.G. Drachmann, 1963, *The Mechanical Technology of Greek and Roman Antiquity*, Copenhagen and London.
S.L. Gibbs, 1976, *Greek and Roman Sundials*, New Haven and London.

LRD

Voelcker, John Augustus

b. 24 June 1854 Cirencester, England
d. 1937 England

English agricultural chemist.

John Augustus Voelcker, as the son of Dr John Christopher **Voelcker**, grew up in an atmosphere of scientific agriculture and would have had contact with the leading agriculturists of the day. He was educated at University College School and then University College, London, where he obtained both a BA and a BSc Following in his father's footsteps, he studied for his PhD at Giessen University in Germany. At college he enjoyed athletics, an interest he was to pursue for the rest of his life. He decided to take up agricultural chemistry and was to succeed to all the public offices once held by his father, from whom he also took over the directorship of Woburn Farm. The experimental farm had been started in 1876 and was used to study the residual effects of chemicals in the soil. The results of these studies were used as the basis for compensation awards to tenant farmers giving up their farms. Voelcker broadened the range of studies to include trace elements in the soil, but by 1921 the Royal Agricultural Society of England had decided to give up the farm. This was a blow to Voelcker and occurred just before experiments elsewhere highlighted the importance of these elements to healthy plant growth. He continued the research at his own expense until the Rothampsted Experimental Station took over the farm in 1926. Aside from his achievements in Britain, Voelcker undertook a study tour of India in 1890, the report on which led to the appointment of an Agricultural Chemist, and the establishment of a scientific service for the Indian subcontinent.

Principal Honours and Distinctions
President, Royal Society of Public Analysts. Member of Council, Chemical Society, and Institute of Chemistry. Chairman, Farmers' Club.

Bibliography
Most of his publications were in the *Journal of the Royal Agricultural Society of England*, for which he wrote an annual report, and in another series of reports relating to Woburn Farm. *The Improvements of Indian Agriculture* was the result of his tour in 1890.

Further Reading
J.H. Gilbert, 1937, obituary, *Journal of the Royal Agricultural Society of England*, pp. 464–8.
Sir E. John Russell, *A History of Agricultural Science in Great Britain*.

AP

Voelcker, John Christopher

b. 24 September 1822 Frankfurt am Main, Germany
d. 5 December 1884 England

German analytical chemist resident in England whose reports on feedstuffs and fertilizers had a considerable influence on the quality of these products.

The son of a merchant in the city of his birth, John Christopher had delicate health and required private tuition to overcome the loss of his early years of schooling. At the age of 22 he went to study chemistry at Göttingen University and then worked for a short time for **Liebig** at Giessen. In 1847 he obtained a post as Analyst and Consulting Chemist at the Agricultural Chemistry Association of Scotland's Edinburgh office, and two years later he became Professor of Chemistry at the Royal Agricultural College in Cirencester, retaining this post until 1862. In 1855 he was appointed Chemist to the Bath and West Agricultural Society, and in that capacity organized lectures and field trials, and in 1857 he also became Consulting Chemist to the Royal Agricultural Society of England. Initially he studied the properties of farmyard manure and also the capacity of the soil to absorb ammonia, potash and sodium. As Consulting Chemist to farmers he analysed feedstuffs and manures; his assessments of artificial manures did much to force improvements in standards. During the

1860s he worked on milk and dairy products. He published the results of his work each year in the *Journal of the Royal Agricultural Society of England*. In 1877 he became involved in the field trials initiated and funded by the Duke of Bedford on his Woburn farm, and he continued his association with this venture until his death.

Principal Honours and Distinctions
FRS. Founder and Vice-President, Institute of Chemistry of Great Britain and Northern Ireland 1877. Member Chemical Society 1849; he was a member of Council as well as its Vice-President at the time of his death. Member of the Board of Studies, Royal Agricultural College, Cirencester; Honorary Professor from 1882.

Bibliography
His papers are to be found in the *Journal of the Royal Agricultural Society of England*, for which he began to write reports in 1855, and also in the *Journal of the Bath and West Society*.

Further Reading
J.H. Gilbert, 1844, obituary, *Journal of the Royal Agricultural Society of England*, pp. 308–21 (a detailed account).
Sir E. John Russell, *A History of Agricultural Science in Great Britain*.

See also **Voelcker, John Augustus**.

AP

Voigt, Paul Gustavus Adolphus Helmuth

b. 9 December 1901 Forest Hill, London, England
d. 9 February 1981 Brighton, Ontario, Canada

English/Canadian electronics engineer, developer of electromechanical recording and reproductions systems, amplifiers and loudspeakers.

He received his education at Dulwich College and in 1922 graduated with a BSc from University College, London. He had an early interest in the application of valve amplifiers, and after graduating he was employed by J.E. Hough, Edison Bell Works, to develop a line of radio-receiving equipment. However, he became interested in the mechanical (and later electrical) side of recording and from 1925 developed principles and equipment. In particular he developed capacitor microphones, not only for in-house work but also commercially, until the mid-1930s. The Edison Bell company did not survive the Depression and closed in 1933. Voigt founded his own company, Voigt Patents Ltd, concentrating on loudspeakers for cinemas and developing horn loudspeakers for domestic use. During the Second World War he continued to develop loudspeaker units and gramophone pick-ups, and in 1950 he emigrated to Toronto, Canada, but his company closed. Voigt taught electronics, and from 1960 to 1969 he was employed by the Radio Regulations Laboratory in Ottawa. After retirement he worked with theoretical cosmology and fundamental interactions.

Bibliography
Most of Voigt's patents are concerned with improvements in the magnetic circuit in dynamic loudspeakers and centring devices for diaphragms. However, UK patent nos. 278,098, 404,037 and 447,749 may be regarded as particularly relevant. In 1940 Voigt contributed a remarkable paper on the principles of equalization in mechanical recording: 'Getting the best from records, part 1 – the recording characteristic', *Wireless World* (February): 141–4.

Further Reading
Personal accounts of experiences with Voigt may be found in 'Paul Voigt's contribution to Audio', *British Kinematography Sound and Television* (October 1970): 316–27, which also includes a list of his patents.

GB-N

Voigtländer, Peter Wilhelm Friedrich

b. 1812 Vienna, Austria
d. 1878

Austrian manufacturer of the first purpose-designed photographic objective; key member of a dynasty of optical instrument makers.

Educated at the Polytechnic Institute in Vienna, Voigtländer travelled widely before taking over the family business in 1837. The business had been founded by Voigtländer's grandfather in 1756, and was continued by his father, Johann Friedrich, the inventor of the opera glass, and by the 1830s enjoyed one of the highest reputations in Europe. When **Petzval** made the calculations for the first purpose-designed photographic objective in 1840, it was inevitable that he should go to Peter Voigtländer for advice. The business went on to manufacture Petzval's lens, which was also fitted to an all-metal camera of totally original design by Voigtländer.

The Petzval lens was an extraordinary commercial success and Voigtländer sold specimens all over the world. Unfortunately Petzval had no formal agreement with Voigtländer and made little financial gain from his design, a fact which was to lead to dispute and separation; the Voigtländer concern continued to prosper, however. To meet the increasing demand for his products, Peter Voigtländer built a new factory in Brunswick and closed the business in Vienna. The closure is seen by at least one commentator as the death blow to Vienna's optical industry, a field in which it was once preeminent. The Voigtländer dynasty continued long after Peter's death and the name enjoyed a reputation for high-quality photographic equipment well into the twentieth century.

Principal Honours and Distinctions
Hereditary Peerage bestowed by the Emperor of Austria 1868.

Further Reading
L.W. Sipley, 1965, *Photography's Great Inventors*, Philadelphia (a brief biography).
J.M. Eder, 1945, *History of Photography*, trans. E. Epstean, New York.

JW

Voisin, Gabriel

b. 5 February 1880 Belleville-sur-Saône, France
d. 25 December 1973 Ozenay, France

French manufacturer of aeroplanes in the early years of aviation.

Gabriel Voisin was one of a group of aviation pioneers working in France *c.*1905. One of the leaders of this group was a rich lawyer-sportsman, Ernest Archdeacon. For a number of years they had been building gliders based on those of the **Wright** brothers. Archdeacon's glider of 1904 was flown by Voisin, who went on to assist in the design and manufacture of gliders for Archdeacon and Louis **Blériot**, including successful float-gliders. Gabriel Voisin was joined by

his brother Charles in 1905 and they set up the first commercial aircraft factory. As the Voisins had limited funds, they had to seek customers who could afford to indulge in the fashionable hobby of flying. One was **Santos-Dumont**, who commissioned Voisin to build his '14 *bis*' aeroplane in 1906.

Early in 1907 the Voisins built their first powered aeroplane, but it was not a success. Later that year they completed a biplane for a Paris sculptor, Léon Delagrange, and another for Henri **Farman**. The basic Voisin was a biplane with the engine behind the pilot and a 'pusher' propeller. Pitching was controlled by biplane elevators forward of the pilot and rudders were fitted to the box kite tail, but there was no control of roll. Improvements were gradually introduced by the Voisins and their customers, such as Farman. Incidentally, to flatter their clients the Voisins often named the aircraft after them, thus causing some confusion to historians. Many Voisins were built up until 1910, when the company's fortunes sank. Competition was growing, the factory was flooded, and Charles left. Gabriel started again, building robust biplanes of steel construction. Voisin bombers were widely used during the First World War, and a subsidiary factory was built in Russia.

In August 1917, Voisin sold his business when the French Air Ministry decided that Voisin aeroplanes were obsolete and that the factory should be turned over to the building of engines. After the war he started another business making prefabricated houses, and then turned to manufacturing motor cars. From 1919 to 1939 his company produced various models, mainly for the luxury end of the market but also including a few sports and racing cars. In the early 1950s he designed a small two-seater, which was built by the Biscuter company in Spain. The Voisin company finally closed in 1958.

Principal Honours and Distinctions
Chevalier de la Légion d'honneur 1909. Académie des Sciences Gold Medal 1909.

Bibliography
1961, *Mes dix milles cerfs-volants*, France; repub. 1963 as *Men, Women and 10,000 Kites*, London (autobiography; an eminent reviewer said, 'it contains so many demonstrable absurdities, untruths and misleading statements, that one

does not know how much of the rest one can believe').

1962, *Mes Mille et un voitures*, France (covers his cars).

Further Reading
C.H. Gibbs-Smith, 1965, *The Invention of the Aeroplane 1799–1909*, London (includes an account of Voisin's contribution to aviation and a list of his early aircraft).
Jane's Fighting Aircraft of World War I, London; reprinted 1990 (provides details of Voisin's 1914–18 aircraft).
E. Chadeau, 1987, *L'Industrie aéronautique en France 1900–1950, de Blériot à Dassault*, Paris.
G.N. Georgano, 1968, *Encyclopedia of Motor Cars 1885 to the Present*, New York (includes brief descriptions of Voisin's cars).

JDS

Volk, Magnus

b. 19 October 1851 Brighton, England
d. 20 May 1937 Brighton, England

English pioneer in the use of electric power; built the first electric railway in the British Isles to operate a regular service.

Volk was the son of a German immigrant clock-maker and continued the business with his mother after his father died in 1869, although when he married in 1879 his profession was de-scribed as 'electrician'. He installed Brighton's first telephone the same year and in 1880 he in-stalled electric lighting in his own house, using a Siemens Brothers dynamo (see **Siemens, Dr Ernst Werner von**) driven by a Crossley gas en-gine. This was probably one of the first half-dozen such installations in Britain. Magnus Volk & Co. became noted electrical manufacturers and contractors, and, *inter alia*, installed electric light in Brighton Pavilion in place of gas.

By 1883 Volk had moved house. He had kept the dynamo and gas engine used to light his pre-vious house, and he also had available an electric motor from a cancelled order. After approaching the town clerk of Brighton, he was given per-mission for a limited period to build and operate a 2 ft (61 cm) gauge electric railway along the foreshore. Using the electrical equipment he al-ready had, Volk built the line, a quarter of a mile (400 m) long, in eight weeks. The car was built by a local coachbuilder, with the motor under the seat; electric current at 50 volts was drawn from one running rail and returned through the other.

The railway was opened on 4 August 1883. It operated regularly for several months and then, permission to run it having been renewed, it was rebuilt for the 1884 season to 2 ft 9 in. (84 cm) gauge, with improved equipment. Despite storm damage from time to time, Volk's Electric Rail-way, extended in length, has become an endur-ing feature of Brighton's sea front. In 1887 Volk made an electric dogcart, and an electric van which he built for the Sultan of Turkey was prob-ably the first motor vehicle built in Britain for export. In 1896 he opened the Brighton & Rot-tingdean Seashore Electric Tramroad, with very wide-gauge track laid between the high- and low-tide lines, and a long-legged, multi-wheel car to run upon it, through the water if necessary. This lasted only until 1901, however. Volk sub-sequently became an early enthusiast for aircraft.

Further Reading
C. Volk, 1971, *Magnus Volk of Brighton*, Chi-chester: Phillimore (his life and career as de-scribed by his son).
C.E. Lee, 1979, 'The birth of electric traction', *Railway Magazine* (May).

PJGR

Volta, Alessandro Giuseppe Anto-nio Anastasio

b. 18 February 1745 Como, Italy
d. 5 March 1827 Como, Italy

Italian physicist, discoverer of a source of continuous electric current from a pile of dissimilar metals.

Volta had an early command of English, French and Latin, and also learned to read Dutch and Spanish. After completing studies at the Royal Seminary in Como he was involved in the study of physics, chemistry and electricity. He became a teacher of physics in his native town and in 1779 was appointed Professor of Physics at the University of Pavia, a post he held for forty years.

With a growing international reputation and a wish to keep abreast of the latest developments, in 1777 he began the first of many travels abroad. A journey started in 1781 to Switzerland, Ger-many, Belgium, Holland, France and England lasted about one year. By 1791 he had been elected to membership of many learned societies, including those in Zurich, Berlin, Berne and Paris. Volta's invention of his pile resulted from a controversy with Luigi Galvani, Professor of Anatomy at the University of Bologna. Galvani discovered that the muscles of frogs' legs contracted when touched with two pieces of different metals and attributed this to a phenomenon of the animal tissue. Volta showed that the excitation was due to a chemical reaction resulting from the contact of the dissimilar metals when moistened. His pile comprised a column of zinc and silver discs, each pair separated by paper moistened with brine, and provided a source of continuous current from a simple and accessible source. The effectiveness of the pile decreased as the paper dried and Volta devised his crown of cups, which had a longer life. In this, pairs of dissimilar metals were placed in each of a number of cups partly filled with an electrolyte such as brine. Volta first announced the results of his experiments with dissimilar metals in 1800 in a letter to Sir Joseph Banks, President of the Royal Society. This letter, published in the *Transactions of the Royal Society*, has been regarded as one of the most important documents in the history of science. Large batteries were constructed in a number of laboratories soon after Volta's discoveries became known, leading immediately to a series of developments in electrochemistry and eventually in electromagnetism. Volta himself made little further contribution to science. In recognition of his achievement, at a meeting of the International Electrical Congress in Paris in 1881 it was agreed to name the unit of electrical pressure the 'volt'.

Principal Honours and Distinctions

FRS 1791. Royal Society Copley Medal 1794. Knight of the Iron Crown, Austria, 1806. Senator of the Realm of Lombardy 1809.

Bibliography

1800, *Philosophical Transactions of the Royal Society* 18: 744–6 (Volta's report on his discovery).

Further Reading

G. Polvani, 1942, *Alessandro Volta*, Pisa (the best account available).

B. Dibner, 1964, *Alessandro Volta and the Electric Battery*, New York (a detailed account).

C.C. Gillispie (ed.), 1976, *Dictionary of Scientific Biography*, Vol. XIV, New York, pp. 66–82 (includes an extensive biography).

F. Soresni, 1988, *Alessandro Volta*, Milan (includes illustrations of Volta's apparatus, with brief text).

GW

W

Walker, Madame C.J.
b. 1867 Louisiana, USA
d. 1919 USA

African-American inventor of hair and cosmetic treatments.

She was born Sarah Breedlove in rural Louisiana, but she moved to St Louis, Mississippi, and settled there, first earning a living as a washerwoman. That occupation did not satisfy her for long, however; she saw a need among black women to smarten their appearance to improve their chances in city life, and by 1905 she had concocted a mixture that could straighten and groom black women's hair. She began to market her product in Denver, Colorado, under her married name, Madame C.J. Walker. After five further years of intensive marketing and persuading black women that they needed this product, she was able to establish her headquarters in Indianapolis for the national distribution of her hair and cosmetic products. She also set up beauty salons, which were especially successful in Harlem, New York.

Further Reading
P.P. James, 1989, *The Real McCoy: African-American Invention and Innovation 1619–1930*, Washington, DC: Smithsonian Institution, pp. 85–6.

LRD

Wallace, Sir William
b. 25 August 1881 Leicester, England
d. 27 May 1963 Edinburgh, Scotland

English engineer, developer of the Denny–Brown fin stabilizer for ships.

Wallace was brought up just outside Glasgow, and educated at Paisley Grammar School and later at the Anderson College in Glasgow. The next few years were typical of the early years in the life of many young engineers: he served an apprenticeship at the Paisley shipyard of Bow, MacLachlan, before joining the British and Burmese Steam Navigation Company (Paddy Henderson's Line) as a junior engineer. After some years on the Glasgow to Rangoon service, he rose to the rank of Chief Engineer early in life and then came ashore in 1911.

He joined the old established Edinburgh engineering company of Brown Brothers as a draughtsman, but by 1917 had been promoted Managing Director. He was appointed Chairman in 1946. During his near thirty years at the helm, he experimented widely and was the engineering force behind the development of the Denny–Brown ship stabilizer which was jointly pursued by Brown Brothers and the Dumbarton shipyard of William **Denny** & Brothers. The first important installation was on the cross-channel steamer *Isle of Sark*, built at Dumbarton for the Southern Railway in 1932. Over the years countless thousands of these installations have been fitted on liners, warships and luxury yachts. Brown Brothers produced many other important engineering innovations at this time, including the steam catapult for aircraft carriers.

In later years Sir William (now knighted) took an active part in the cultural life of Edinburgh and of Scotland. From 1952 to 1954 he served as President of the Institution of Engineers and Shipbuilders in Scotland.

Principal Honours and Distinctions
Knighted 1951. CBE 1944. Fellow of the Royal Society of Edinburgh. President, Institution of Engineers and Shipbuilders in Scotland 1952–4; Gold Medal.

Bibliography
1954–5 'Experiences in the stabilization of ships', *Transactions of the Institution of Engineers and Shipbuilders in Scotland* 98: 197–266.

FMW

Wallingford, Abbot Richard of
See **Richard of Wallingford, Abbot**.

Wallis, Sir Barnes Neville
b. 26 September 1887 Ripley, Derbyshire, England
d. 30 October 1979 Leatherhead, Surrey, England

English aeronautical designer and inventor.

Wallis was apprenticed first at Thames Engineering Works, and then, in 1908, at John Samuel White's shipyard at Cowes. In 1913, the Government, spurred on by the accelerating development of the German Zeppelins (see **Zeppelin,** Ferdinand von), ordered an airship from Vickers; Wallis was invited to join the design team. Thus began his long association with aeronautical design and with Vickers. This airship, and the R80 that followed it, were successfully completed, but the military lost interest in them.

In 1924 the Government initiated a programme for the construction of two airships to settle once and for all their viability for long-distance air travel. The R101 was designed by a Government-sponsored team, but the R100 was designed by Wallis working for a subsidiary of Vickers. The R100 took off on 29 July 1930 for a successful round trip to Canada, but the R101 crashed on its first flight on 4 October, killing many of its distinguished passengers. The shock of this disaster brought airship development in Britain to an abrupt end and forced Wallis to direct his attention to aircraft.

In aircraft design, Wallis is known for his use of geodesic construction, which combined lightness with strength. It was applied first to the single-engined 'Wellesley' and then the twin-engined 'Wellington' bomber, which first flew in 1936. With successive modifications, it became the workhorse of RAF Bomber Command during the Second World War until the autumn of 1943, when it was replaced by four-engined machines. In other areas, it remained in service until the end of the war and, in all, no fewer than 11,461 were built.

Wallis is best known for his work on bomb design, first the bouncing bomb that was used to breach the Möhne and Eder dams in the Ruhr district of Germany in 1943, an exploit immortalized in the film *Dambusters*. Encouraged by this success, the authorities then allowed Wallis to realize an idea he had long urged, that of heavy, penetration bombs. In the closing stages of the war, *Tallboy*, of 12,000 lb (5,400 kg), and the 10-ton *Grand Slam* were used to devastating effect.

After the Second World War, Wallis returned to aeronautical design and was given his own department at Vickers to promote his ideas, principally on variable-geometry or swing-wing aircraft. Over the next thirteen years he battled towards the prototype stage of this revolutionary concept. That never came, however; changing conditions and requirements and increasing costs led to the abandonment of the project. Bitterly disappointed, Wallis continued his researches into high-speed aircraft until his retirement from Vickers (by then the British Aircraft Corporation), in 1971.

Principal Honours and Distinctions
Knighted 1968. FRS 1945.

Further Reading
J. Morpurgo, 1972, *Barnes Wallis: A Biography*, London: Longman (a readable account, rather biased in Wallis's favour).
C.J. Heap, 1987, *The Papers of Sir Barnes Wallis (1887–1979) in the Science Museum Library*, London: Science Museum; with a biographical introd. by L.R. Day.

LRD

Walschaert, Egide

b. 20 January 1820 Mechlin, Belgium
d. 18 February 1901 Saint-Lilles, Brussels, Belgium

Belgian inventor of Walschaert's valve gear for steam engines.

Walschaert was appointed Foreman of the Brussels Midi workshops of the Belgian State Railways in 1844, when they were opened, and remained in this position until 1885. He invented his valve gear the year he took up his appointment and was allowed to fit it to a 2–2–2 locomotive in 1848, the results being excellent. It was soon adopted in Belgium and to a lesser extent in France, but although it offered accessibility, light weight and mechanical efficiency, railways elsewhere were remarkably slow to take it up. It was first used in the British Isles in 1878, on a 0–4–4 tank locomotive built to the patent of Robert **Fairlie**, but was not used again there until 1890. By contrast, Fairlie had already used Walchaert's valve gear in 1873, on locomotives for New Zealand, and when New Zealand Railways started to build their own locomotives in 1889 they perpetuated it. The valve gear was only introduced to the USA following a visit by an executive of the Baldwin Locomotive Works to New Zealand ten years later. Subsequently it came to be used almost everywhere there were steam locomotives. Walschaert himself invented other improvements for steam engines, but none with lasting effect.

Further Reading
P. Ransome-Wallis (ed.), 1959, *The Concise Encyclopaedia of World Railway Locomotives*, London: Hutchinson (includes both a brief biography of Walschaert (p. 502) and a technical description of his valve gear (p. 298)).
E.L. Ahrons, 1927, *The British Steam Railway Locomotive 1825–1925*, London: The Locomotive Publishing Co., pp. 224 and 289 (describes the introduction of the valve gear to Britain).
J.B. Snell, 1964, *Early Railways*, London: Weidenfeld & Nicolson, 103.

PJGR

Walter, Thomas Ustick

b. 4 September 1804 Philadelphia, Pennsylvania, USA
d. 30 October 1887 Philadelphia, Pennsylvania, USA

American architect, best known for his construction of the great iron dome of the United States Capitol in Washington.

Much of Walter's work was in neo-classical style, of which the Founders' Hall at Girard College in Philadelphia, built 1833–47, is a fine example. On the exterior this is a large-scale Corinthian temple of peripteral octastyle form. Inside, Walter showed his awareness of modern needs with his brick fireproof vaulting. In 1851 Walter was appointed by President Millard Fillmore as Architect to the Capitol in Washington, DC, to enlarge the building to accommodate the greater needs of the day. Between this time and 1865 Walter extended the side wings considerably to provide more space for the House of Representatives and the Senate and, to balance the composition of this much longer elevation, built a new great dome. In style, the dome and drum resemble those of **Wren**'s St Paul's Cathedral in London, but the scale is much greater and the internal construction largely of cast iron: internally the dome measures 98 ft (29.9 m) in diameter and has a total height of 222 ft (67.7 m).

Principal Honours and Distinctions
Founder American Institute of Architects 1857; President from 1876.

Further Reading
M. Whiffen and F. Koeper, 1981, *American Architecture 1607–1976*, Cambridge, Mass.: MIT.

DY

Walton, Frederick

fl. 1860s Chiswick, Middlesex, England

English inventor and early manufacturer of linoleum.

Walton's linoleum consisted of a burlap base coated with a cement made from linseed oil, gum, resin and colour pigments. The linseed oil was oxidized in order to produce a rubbery consistency, and this was achieved either by adding the oil to the burlap in a series of coats, allowing each coat to dry in a heated room and so absorb the oxygen from the atmosphere, or by inserting the product into a steam-heated container, thereby hastening the process. The coated fabric was then calendered so that the heat and pressure of the rollers would soften the coating mixture, making it adhere firmly to the fabric backing. On 19 December 1863 Walton applied for a patent for the manufacture of his invention at British Grove Works in Chiswick, Middlesex. The patent was granted on 31 May 1864 for 'Improvements in the Manufacture of Floor Cloths and Coverings and Similar Fabrics and in Pavements'. Later in 1864 Walton set up a factory in Staines.

The term linoleum derives from the Latin words *linum*, meaning linen thread, and *oleum*, meaning oil. Linoleum was made in rolls in ever-increasing quantity until about 1950, by which time it was being replaced by synthetic vinyl-type coverings.

Further Reading
See 'Linoleum' in *Children's Britannica*, Chicago, Ill.: Encyclopaedia Britannica, and in *Encyclopaedia Americana*, Danbury, Conn.: Americana.

DY

Wang Zhen (Wang Chen)

b. 14th century China
d. 14th century China

Chinese writer on agricultural affairs and practice.

Wang Zhen was a native of Shandong Province and was employed as a Government official. He wrote the *Wang Zhen Nung Shu c.*1313 as a text to be used by local officials in their instruction of the peasantry. The text was also used as a means of spreading information on potentially useful developments from one region to another.

Curious inaccuracies in the text indicate that Wang Zhen's knowledge of agriculture was not firsthand, but rather that his texts are the distillation of information derived from interviews with farmers. In this the text differs from the other major Chinese texts, which are clearly the work of individuals with personal knowledge of the subject about which they were writing.

Further Reading
F. Bray, Vol. VI.2 in J. Needham (ed.), *Science and Civilisation in China* (discusses her sources in an introductory chapter).

AP

Wankel, Felix
b. 13 August 1902 Lahr, Black Forest, Germany
d. 9 October 1988 Lindau, Bavaria, Germany

German internal combustion engineer, inventor of the Wankel rotary engine.

Wankel was first employed at the German Aeronautical Research Establishment, where he worked on rotary valves and valve sealing techniques in the early 1930s and during the Second World War. In 1951 he joined NSU Motorenwerk AG, a motor manufacturer based at Neckarsulm, near Stuttgart, and began work on his rotary engine; the idea for this had first occurred to Wankel as early as 1929. He had completed his first design by 1954, and in 1957 his first prototype was tested. The Wankel engine has a three-pointed rotor, like a prism of an equilateral triangle but with the sides bowed outwards. This rotor is geared to a driveshaft and rotates within a closely fitting and slightly oval-shaped chamber so that, on each revolution, the power stroke is applied to each of the three faces of the rotor as they pass a single spark plug. Two or more rotors may be mounted coaxially, their power strokes being timed sequentially. The engine has only two moving parts, the rotor and the output shaft, making it about a quarter less in weight compared with a conventional piston engine; however, its fuel consumption is high and its exhaust emissions are relatively highly pollutant. The average Wankel engine speed is 5,500 rpm. The first production car to use a Wankel engine was the NSU *Ro80*, though this was preceded by the experimental NSU Spyder prototype, an open two-seater. The Japanese company Mazda is the only other automobile manufacturer to have fitted a Wankel engine to a production car, although licences were taken by Alfa Romeo, Peugeot–Citroën, Daimler–Benz, Rolls–Royce, Toyota, Volkswagen–Audi (the company that bought NSU in the mid-1970s) and many others; Daimler–Benz even produced a Mercedes *C-111* prototype with a three-rotor Wankel engine. The American aircraft manufacturer Curtiss–Wright carried out research for a Wankel aero-engine which never went into production, but the Austrian company Rotax produced a motorcycle version of the Wankel engine which was fitted by the British motorcycle manufacturer Norton to a number of its models.

While Wankel became director of his own research establishment at Lindau, on Lake Constance in southern Germany, Mazda continued to improve the rotary engine and by the time of Wankel's death the Mazda RX-7 coupé had become a successful, if not high-selling, Wankel-engined sports car.

Further Reading
N. Faith, 1975, *Wankel: The Curious Story Behind the Revolutionary Rotary Engine*, New York: Stein & Day.

IMcN

Ward, Joshua
b. 1685
d. 21 November 1761 London, England

English doctor and industrial chemist.

Ward is perhaps better described as a 'quack' than a medical doctor. His remedies, one containing a dangerous quantity of antimony, were dubious to say the least. A fraudulent attempt to enter Parliament in 1717 forced him to leave the country quickly. After his pardon in 1733, he returned to London and established a successful practice. His medical prowess is immortalized in

Hogarth's picture *The Harlot's Progress*.

Sulphuric acid had been an important chemical for centuries and Ward found that he needed large quantities of it to make his remedies. He set up works to manufacture it at Twickenham, near London, in 1736 and then at Richmond three years later. His process consisted of burning a mixture of saltpetre (nitre; potassium nitrate) and sulphur in the neck of a large glass globe containing a little water. Dilute sulphuric acid was thereby formed, which was concentrated by distillation. Although the method was not new, having been described in the seventeenth century by the German chemist Johann **Glauber**, Ward was granted a patent for his process in 1749. An important feature was the size of the globes, which had no less than fifty gallons' capacity, which must have entailed considerable skill on the part of the glassblowers. Through the adoption of Ward's process, the price of this essential commodity fell from £2 per pound to only 2 shillings. It provided the best method of manufacture until the advent of the lead-chamber process invented by John **Roebuck**.

Further Reading

A. Clow and N. Clow, 1952, *The Chemical Revolution: A Contribution to Social Technology*, London: Batchworth.

C. Singer *et al.* (eds), 1958, *A History of Technology*, 7 vols, Oxford: Clarendon Press, Vol. IV.

LRD

Warren, Henry Ellis
b. 21 May 1872 Boston, Massachusetts, USA
d. 21 September 1957 Ashland, Massachusetts, USA

American electrical engineer who invented the mains electric synchronous clock.

Warren studied electrical engineering at the Boston Institute of Technology (later to become the Massachusetts Institute of Technology) and graduated in 1894. In 1912 he formed the Warren Electric Clock Company to make a battery-powered clock that he had patented a few years earlier. The name was changed to the Warren Telechron (time at a distance) Company after he had started to produce synchronous clocks.

In 1840 Charles **Wheatstone** had produced an electric master clock that produced an alternating current with a frequency of one cycle per second and which was used to drive slave dials. This system was not successful, but when **Ferranti** introduced the first alternating current power generator at Deptford in 1895 Hope-Jones saw in it a means of distributing time. This did not materialize immediately because the power generators did not control the frequency of the current with sufficient accuracy, and a reliable motor whose speed was related to this frequency was not available. In 1916 Warren solved both problems: he produced a reliable self-starting synchronous electric motor and he also made a master clock which could be used at the power station to control accurately the frequency of the supply. Initially the power-generating companies were reluctant to support the synchronous clock because it imposed a liability to control the frequency of the supply and the gain was likely to be small because it was very frugal in its use of power. However, with the advent of the grid system, when several generators were connected together, it became imperative to control the frequency; it was realized that although the power consumption of individual clocks was small, collectively it could be significant as they ran continuously. By the end of the 1930s more than half the clocks sold in the USA were of the synchronous type. The Warren synchronous clock was introduced into Great Britain in 1927, following the setting up of a grid system by the Electricity Commission.

Principal Honours and Distinctions

Franklin Institute John Price Wetherill Medal. American Institute of Electrical Engineers Lamme Medal.

Bibliography

The patents for the synchronous motor are US patent nos. 1,283,432, 1,283,433 and 1,283,435, and those for the master clock are 1,283,431, 1,409,502 and 1,502,493 of 29 October 1918 onwards.

1919, 'Utilising the time characteristics of alternating current', *Transactions of the American Institute of Electrical Engineers* 38: 767–81 (Warren's first description of his system).

Further Reading

J.M. Anderson, 1991, 'Henry Ellis Warren and his master clocks', *National Association of Watch and Clock Collectors Bulletin* 33: 375–95 (provides biographical and technical details).

DV

Wasborough, Matthew

b. 1753 Bristol, England
d. 21 October 1781 Bristol, England

English patentee of an application of the flywheel to create a rotative steam engine.

A single-cylinder atmospheric steam engine had a power stroke only when the piston descended the cylinder: a means had to be found of returning the piston to its starting position. For rotative engines, this was partially solved by the patent of Matthew Wasborough in 1779. His father was a partner in a Bristol brass-founding and clock-making business in Narrow Wine Street where he was joined by his son. Wasborough proposed to use some form of ratchet gear to effect the rotary motion and added a flywheel, the first time one was used in a steam engine, 'in order to render the motion more regular and uniform'. He installed one engine to drive the lathes in the Bristol works and another at James **Pickard**'s flour mill at Snow Hill, Birmingham, where Pickard applied his recently patented crank to it. It was this Wasborough–Pickard engine which posed a threat to **Boulton** & **Watt** trying to develop a rotative engine, for Wasborough built several engines for cornmills in Bristol, woollen mills in Gloucestershire and a block factory at Southampton before his early death. Matthew Boulton was told that Wasborough was 'so intent upon the study of engines as to bring a fever on his brain and he dyed in consequence thereof.... How dangerous it is for a man to wade out of his depth' (Jenkins 1936:106).

Bibliography

1779, British patent no. 1,213 (rotative engine with flywheel).

Further Reading

J. Tann, 1978–9, 'Makers of improved Newcomen engines in the late 18th century, and R.A. Buchanan, 1978–9, 'Steam and the engineering community in the eighteenth century', *Transactions of the Newcomen Society* 50 ('Thomas Newcomen. A commemorative symposium') (both papers discuss Wasborough's engines).

R.L. Hills, 1989, *Power from Steam. A History of the Stationary Steam Engine*, Cambridge University Press (examines his patent).

R. Jenkins (ed.), 1936, *Collected Papers*, 106 (for Matthew Boulton's letter of 30 October 1781).

RLH

Waterhouse, Major-General James

b. 1841
d. 28 September 1922

English military man and photographer.

Waterhouse spent most of his career in the Indian Army. In 1861–2 he was commissioned to photograph the tribes of central India, and over the next few years visited many parts of the subcontinent. In November 1866, after working for five months in the Great Trigonometrical Survey learning the process of photozincography (an early photomechanical process used chiefly for map making), he took charge of photographic operations at the Surveyor-General's office in Calcutta, a post he held until retiring in 1897. During this time he developed many improvements in the photomechanical methods used for reproduction in his office. He also experimented with methods of colour-sensitizing photographic materials, experimenting with eosine dye and publishing in 1875 the fact that this made silver halide salts sensitive to yellow light. He also discovered that gelatine dry plates could be made sensitive to red and infra-red illumination by treatment with alizarine blue solution.

He continued his researches upon his retirement and return to England in 1897, and made a special study of the early history of the photographic process. His work on dye sensitizing brought him the Progress Medal of the Royal Photographic Society, and the Vienna Photographic Society awarded him the **Voigtländer** Medal for researches in scientific photography. One invention often erroneously attributed to him is the Waterhouse stop, the use of a series of perforated plates as a means of adjusting the aperture of a photographic lens. This was described in 1858 by a *John* Waterhouse, being his only contribution to photography.

BC

Watkins, Alfred

b. 1854 Hereford, England
d. 7 April 1935 Hereford, England

English photographer who developed the first practical exposure-measuring system.

His first patent was granted on 27 January 1890 and described a method of measuring the 'actinic' value of light as a means of determining exposure. A strip of sensitized paper which darkened on exposure to light was used, and the time taken for it to darken to match a standard tint was measured. This time could be used to calculate the necessary exposure time, taking into account the speed of the plate, shutter speed and aperture. Watkins marketed a number of these actinometer designs, of which the most popular was the Watkins Bee Meter, which was in a pocketwatch form, introduced in 1903 and remaining on sale until 1939. Watkins was concerned that photographers recognize that exposure measurement had to take into account the effect of development time and temperature. In 1893 he devised the concept of the 'Watkins Factor': he showed that when plates were developed by inspection, as was the practice at the time, a fixed relationship existed between the time of the first appearance of the image and the total time required to give a fully developed negative. The Watkins Factor was the figure that the first time must be multiplied by to give the second time. Watkins published tables of factors for different brands of plates and for different developers, and marketed various aids such as specially calibrated thermometers and clocks, as aids in using 'Factorial Development' to give consistent negatives. After the early years of the twentieth century Watkins gave up direct participation in photography and devoted his time to a variety of interests, including the plotting of ley lines in England.

BC

Watson, George Lennox

b. 1851 Glasgow, Scotland
d. 12 November 1904 Glasgow, Scotland

Scottish designer of some of the world's largest sailing and powered yachts, principal technical adviser to the Royal National Lifeboat Institution.

Almost all of Watson's life was spent in or around the City of Glasgow; his formal education was at the city's High School and at the age of 16 he entered the yard and drawing offices of Robert **Napier**'s Govan Shipyard. Three years later he crossed the River Clyde and started work in the design office of the Pointhouse Shipyard of A. &

J. Inglis, and there received the necessary grounding of a naval architect. Dr John Inglis, the Principal of the firm, encouraged Watson, ensured that he was involved in advanced design work and allowed him to build a yacht in a corner of the shipyard in his spare time.

At the early age of 22 Watson set up as a naval architect with his own company, which is still in existence 120 years later. In 1875, assisted by two carpenters, Watson built the 5-ton yacht *Vril* to his own design. This vessel was the first with an integral heavy lead keel and its success ensured that design contracts flowed to him for new yachts for the Clyde and elsewhere. His enthusiasm and increasing skill were recognized and soon he was working on the ultimate: the America's Cup challengers *Thistle*, *Valkyrie II*, *Valkyrie III* and *Shamrock II*. The greatest accolade was the contract for the design of the J Class yacht *Britannia*, built by D. & W. Henderson of Glasgow in 1893 for the Prince of Wales.

The company of G.L. Watson became the world's leading designer of steam yachts, and it was usual for it to offer a full design service as well as supervise construction in any part of the world. Watson took a deep interest in the work of the Royal National Lifeboat Institution and was its technical consultant for many years. One of his designs, the *Watson Lifeboat*, was a stalwart in its fleet for many years. In public life he lectured, took an active part in the debates on yacht racing and was recognized as Britain's leading designer.

Bibliography
1881, *Progress in Yachting and Yacht-Building*, Glasgow Naval and Marine Engineering Catalogue, London and Glasgow: Collins.
1894, *The Evolution of the Modern Racing Yacht*, Badminton Library of Sports and Pastimes, Vol. 1, London: Longmans Green, pp. 54–109.

Further Reading
John Irving, 1937, *The King's Britannia. The Story of a Great Ship*, London: Seeley Service.

FMW

Watson-Watt, Sir Robert Alexander

b. 13 April 1892 Brechin, Angus, Scotland
d. 6 December 1973 Inverness, Scotland

Scottish engineer and scientific adviser known for his work on radar.

Following education at Brechin High School, Watson-Watt entered University College, Dundee (then a part of the University of St Andrews), obtaining a BSc in engineering in 1912. From 1912 until 1921 he was Assistant to the Professor of Natural Philosophy at St Andrews, but during the First World War he also held various posts in the Meteorological Office. During this time, in 1916 he proposed the use of cathode ray oscillographs for radio-direction-finding displays. He joined the newly formed Radio Research Station at Slough when it was opened in 1924, and 3 years later, when it amalgamated with the Radio Section of the National Physical Laboratory, he became Superintendent at Slough. At this time he proposed the name 'ionosphere' for the ionized layer in the upper atmosphere. With E.V. **Appleton** and J.F. Herd he developed the 'squegger' hard-valve transformer-coupled timebase and with the latter devised a direction-finding radio-goniometer.

In 1933 he was asked to investigate possible aircraft counter-measures. He soon showed that it was impossible to make the wished-for radio 'death-ray', but had the idea of using the detection of reflected radio-waves as a means of monitoring the approach of enemy aircraft. With six assistants he developed this idea and constructed an experimental system of radar (*RA*dio *Dete*ction *And Ranging*) in which arrays of aerials were used to detect the reflected signals and deduce the bearing and height. To realize a practical system, in September 1936 he was appointed Director of the Bawdsey Research Station near Felixstowe and carried out operational studies of radar. The result was that within two years the East Coast of the British Isles was equipped with a network of radar transmitters and receivers working in the 7–14 metre band – the so-called 'chain-home' system – which did so much to assist the efficient deployment of RAF Fighter Command against German bombing raids on Britain in the early years of the Second World War.

In 1938 he moved to the Air Ministry as Director of Communications Development, becoming Scientific Adviser to the Air Ministry and Ministry of Aircraft Production in 1940, then Deputy Chairman of the War Cabinet Radio Board in 1943. After the war he set up Sir Robert Watson-Watt & Partners, an industrial consultant firm. He then spent some years in relative retirement in Canada, but returned to Scotland before his death.

Principal Honours and Distinctions
Knighted 1942. CBE 1941. FRS 1941. US Medal of Merit 1946. Royal Society Hughes Medal 1948. Franklin Institute Elliot Cresson Medal 1957. LLD St Andrews 1943. At various times: President, Royal Meteorological Society, Institute of Navigation and Institute of Professional Civil Servants; Vice-President, American Institute of Radio Engineers.

Bibliography
1923, with E.V. Appleton & J.F. Herd, British patent no. 235,254 (for the 'squegger').
1926, with J.F. Herd, 'An instantaneous direction reading radio goniometer', *Journal of the Institution of Electrical Engineers* 64: 611.
1933, *The Cathode Ray Oscillograph in Radio Research*.
1935, *Through the Weather Hours* (autobiography).
1936, 'Polarisation errors in direction finders', *Wireless Engineer* 13: 3.
1958, *Three Steps to Victory*.
1959, *The Pulse of Radar*.
1961, *Man's Means to his End*.

Further Reading
S.S. Swords, 1986, *Technical History of the Beginnings of Radar*, Stevenage: Peter Peregrinus.

KF

Watt, James
b. 19 January 1735 Greenock, Renfrewshire, Scotland
d. 19 August 1819 Handsworth Heath, Birmingham, England

Scottish engineer and inventor of the separate condenser for the steam engine.

The sixth child of James Watt, merchant and general contractor, and Agnes Muirhead, Watt was a weak and sickly child; he was one of only two to survive childhood out of a total of eight, yet, like his father, he was to live to an age of over 80. He was educated at local schools, including Greenock Grammar School where he was an uninspired pupil. At the age of 17 he was sent to live with relatives in Glasgow and then in 1755 to London to become an apprentice to a mathematical instrument maker, John Morgan of Finch Lane, Cornhill. Less than a year later he returned to Greenock and then to Glasgow, where he was appointed mathematical instrument maker to the University and was permitted in 1757 to set up a workshop within the University grounds. In this position he came to know many of the University professors and staff, and it was thus that he became involved in work on the steam engine when in 1764 he was asked to put in working order a defective **Newcomen** engine model. It did not take Watt long to perceive that the great inefficiency of the Newcomen engine was due to the repeated heating and cooling of the cylinder. His idea was to drive the steam out of the cylinder and to condense it in a separate vessel. The story is told of Watt's flash of inspiration as he was walking across Glasgow Green one Sunday afternoon; the idea formed perfectly in his mind and he became anxious to get back to his workshop to construct the necessary apparatus, but this was the Sabbath and work had to wait until the morrow, so Watt forced himself to wait until the Monday morning.

Watt designed a condensing engine and was lent money for its development by Joseph Black, the Glasgow University professor who had established the concept of latent heat. In 1768 Watt went into partnership with John **Roebuck**, who required the steam engine for the drainage of a coal-mine that he was opening up at Bo'ness, West Lothian. In 1769, Watt took out his patent for 'A New Invented Method of Lessening the Consumption of Steam and Fuel in Fire Engines'. When Roebuck went bankrupt in 1772, Matthew **Boulton**, proprietor of the Soho Engineering Works near Birmingham, bought Roebuck's share in Watt's patent. Watt had met Boulton four years earlier at the Soho works, where power was obtained at that time by means of a water-wheel and a steam engine to pump the water back up again above the wheel. Watt moved to Birmingham in 1774, and after the patent had been extended by Parliament in 1775 he and Boulton embarked on a highly profitable partnership. While Boulton endeavoured to keep the business supplied with capital, Watt continued to refine his engine, making several improvements over the years; he was also involved

frequently in legal proceedings over infringements of his patent.

In 1794 Watt and Boulton founded the new company of Boulton & Watt, with a view to their retirement; Watt's son James and Boulton's son Matthew assumed management of the company. Watt retired in 1800, but continued to spend much of his time in the workshop he had set up in the garret of his Heathfield home; principal amongst his work after retirement was the invention of a pantograph sculpturing machine.

James Watt was hard-working, ingenious and essentially practical, but it is doubtful that he would have succeeded as he did without the business sense of his partner, Matthew Boulton. Watt coined the term 'horsepower' for quantifying the output of engines, and the SI unit of power, the watt, is named in his honour.

Principal Honours and Distinctions
FRS 1785. Honorary LLD, University of Glasgow 1806. Foreign Associate, Académie des Sciences, Paris 1814.

Further Reading
H.W. Dickinson and R. Jenkins, 1927, *James Watt and the Steam Engine*, Oxford: Clarendon Press.
L.T.C. Rolt, 1962, *James Watt*, London: B.T. Batsford.
R. Wailes, 1963, *James Watt, Instrument Maker* (*The Great Masters: Engineering Heritage*, Vol. 1), London: Institution of Mechanical Engineers.

IMcN

Watts, Philip
b. 30 May 1846 Portsmouth, England
d. 15 March 1926 probably London, England

English naval architect, shipbuilding manager and ultimately Director of Naval Construction.

Since he had a long family connection with the naval base at Portsmouth, it is not surprising that Watts started to serve his apprenticeship there in 1860. He was singled out for advanced training and then in 1866 was one of three young men selected to attend the Royal School of Naval Architecture at South Kensington in London. On completing his training he joined the technical staff, then had a period as a ship overseer before going to assist William **Froude** for two years, an arrangement which led to a close friendship between Watts and the two Froudes. Some interesting tasks followed: the calculations for HM Armoured Ram *Polyphemus*; the setting up of a 'calculating' section within the Admiralty; and then work as a constructor at Chatham Dockyard. In 1885 the first major change of direction took place: Watts resigned from naval service to take the post of General Manager of the Elswick shipyard of Sir W.G. Armstrong. This was a wonderful opportunity for an enthusiastic and highly qualified man, and Watts rose to the challenge. Elswick produced some of the finest warships at the end of the nineteenth century and its cruisers, such as the *Esmeralda* of the Chilean Navy, had a legendary name.

In 1902 he was recalled to the Navy to succeed Sir William **White** as Director of Naval Construction (DNC). This was one of the most exciting times ever in warship design and it was during Watts's tenure of the post that the Dreadnought class of battleship was produced, the submarine service was developed and the destroyer fleet reached high levels of performance. It has been said that Watts's distinct achievements as DNC were greater armament per ton displacement, higher speeds and better manoeuvring, greater protection and, almost as important, elegance of appearance. Watt retired in 1912 but remained a consultant to the Admiralty until 1916, and then joined the board of Armstrong Whitworth, on which he served until his death.

Principal Honours and Distinctions
Knighted 1905. FRS 1900. Chairman, Board of Trade's Load Line Committee 1913. Vice-President, Society for Nautical Research (upon its founding), and finally Chairman for the *Victory* preservation and technical committee. Honorary Vice-President, Institution of Naval Architects 1916. Master of the Worshipful Company of Shipwrights 1915.

Bibliography
Watts produced many high-quality technical papers, including ten papers to the Institution of Naval Architects.

FMW

Waymouth, Bernard
b. unknown
d. 25 November 1890 London, England

English naval architect, ship surveyor and designer of the clipper ship Thermopylae.

Waymouth had initial training in shipbuilding at one of the Royal Dockyards before going on to work at a privately owned shipyard. With this all-round experience he was accepted in 1854 by Lloyd's Register of Shipping as a surveyor, and was to serve the Society well during a period of great change in ship design. In 1864 he was charged with the task of framing the Rules for the Construction of Composite Built Vessels, i.e. ships with main structural members such as keel, frames and deck beams of iron and with the hull sheathing or planking of timber. Although long superseded, these rules were of considerable consequence at the time and they were accompanied by beautiful drawings executed by Harry J. Cornish, who became Chief Ship Surveyor of Lloyd's from 1900 until 1909. In 1870 revolutionary proposals were made for iron ships that led to the adoption of a new form of rules where the scantlings or size of individual parts were related to the overall dimensions of the vessel. The symbol 100A1 was then adopted for the first time.

Waymouth was more than a theoretical naval architect: in the late 1860s he was commissioned by the shipbuilders Walter Hood to design the famous Aberdeen Clipper *Thermopylae*. This was one of the fastest sailing ships of the nineteenth century and, along with its Clyde-built counterpart *Cutty Sark*, proved the efficacy of composite construction for these specialist vessels.

Waymouth was appointed Principal Surveyor of Lloyd's in 1870 and was Secretary of the Society from 1872 until his death at work in 1890. He was a member of the Royal Commission on Tonnage and of the Enquiry into the loss of HMS *Atlanta*, and at the time of his death was Vice-President of the Institution of Naval Architects.

Principal Honours and Distinctions
Vice-President, Institution of Naval Architects.

Further Reading
Annals of Lloyd's Register, 1934, London.

FMW

Webb, Francis William
b. 21 May 1836 Tixall, Staffordshire, England
d. 4 June 1906 Bournemouth, England

English locomotive engineer who pioneered compound locomotives in Britain and the use of steel for boilers.

Webb was a pupil at Crewe Works, London & North Western Railway (LNWR), under F. Trevithick (son of Richard **Trevithick**), and was subsequently placed in charge of the works under Trevithick's successor, J. Ramsbottom. After a brief spell away from the LNWR, Webb returned in 1871 and was made Chief Mechanical Engineer, a post he held until his retirement in 1904.

Webb's initial designs included the highly successful 'Precedent' or 'Jumbo' class 2–4–0, from which the example *Hardwicke* (now preserved by the National Railway Museum, York) achieved an average speed of 67.2 mph (108.1 km/h) between Crewe and Carlisle in 1895. His 0–6–0 'coal engines' were straightforward and cheap and were built in large numbers. In 1879 Webb, having noted the introduction of compound locomotives in France by J.T.A. **Mallet**, rebuilt an existing 2–2–2 locomotive as a two-cylinder compound. Then in 1882, seeking fuel economy and the suppression of coupling rods, he produced a compound locomotive to his own design, the 2–2,2–0 *Experiment*, in which two outside high-pressure cylinders drove the rear driving-wheels, and a single inside large-diameter low-pressure cylinder drove the front driving-wheels. This was followed by a large number of compound locomotives: three successive classes of 2–2,2–0s; some 2–2,2–2s; some 4–4–0s; and some 0–8–0s for goods traffic. Although these were capable of good performance, their overall value was controversial: Webb, who was notoriously autocratic, may never have been fully informed of their defects, and after his retirement most were quickly scrapped. Webb made many other innovations during his career, one of the most important being the construction of boilers from steel rather than wrought iron.

Further Reading
C. Hamilton Ellis, 1958, *Twenty Locomotive Men*, Shepperton: Ian Allan, Ch. 14 (describes Webb's career).
E.L. Ahrons, 1927, *The British Steam Railway Locomotive 1825–1925*, London: The Locomotive Publishing Co., Chs 18 and 20 (includes a critique of Webb's compound locomotives).

See also: **Bousquet, Gaston du**; **Gresley, Sir Herbert Nigel**; **Joy, David**; **Worsdell, Thomas William**.

PJGR

Weber, Wilhelm Eduard
b. 24 October 1804 Wittenberg, Germany
d. 23 June 1891 Göttingen, Germany

German physicist, the founder of precise measurement of electrical quantities.

Weber began scientific experiments at an early age and entered the University of Halle, where he came under the influence of J.S.C. Schweigger, inventor of the galvanometer. Completing his education with a dissertation on the theory of organ pipes and making important contributions to the science of acoustics, he was awarded a lectureship and later an assistant professorship at Halle. Weber was offered the Chair of Physics at Göttingen in 1831 and jointly with Gauss began investigations into the precision measurement of magnetic quantities. In 1841 he invented the electrodynamometer type of electrical measuring instrument. This was a development of the galvanometer in which, instead of a needle, a small coil was suspended within an outer coil. A current flowing through both coils tended to turn the inner coil, the sine of the angle through which the suspending wires were twisted being proportional to the square of the strength of the current. A variation of the electrodynamometer was capable of measuring directly the power in electrical circuits.

The introduction by Weber of a system of absolute units for the measurement of electrical quantities was a most important step in electrical science. He had a considerable influence on the British Association committees on electrical standards organized in 1861 to promote a coherent system of electrical units. Weber's ideas also led him to define elementary electric particles, ascribing mass and charge to them. His name was used for a time before 1883 as the unit of electric current, until the name 'ampere' was proposed by **Helmholtz**. Since 1948 the term 'weber' has been used for the SI unit of magnetic flux.

Principal Honours and Distinctions
FRS 1850. Royal Society Copley Medal 1859.

Bibliography
1892–4, *William Weber's Werke*, 6 vols, Berlin.

Further Reading
P. Lenard, 1954, *Great Men of Science*, London, pp. 263–70 (a reliable, short biography).
C.C. Gillispie (ed.), 1976, *Dictionary of Scientific Biography*, Vol. XIV, New York, pp. 203–9 (discusses his theoretical contributions).
S.P. Bordeau, 1982, *Volts to Herz*, Minneapolis, pp. 172 and 181 (discusses Weber's influence on contemporary scientists).

GW

Wedgwood, Josiah

baptized 12 July 1730 Burslem, Staffordshire, England
d. 3 January 1795 Etruria Hall, Staffordshire, England

English potter and man of science.

Wedgwood came from prolific farming stock who, in the seventeenth century, had turned to pot-making. At the age of 9 his education was brought to an end by his father's death and he was set to work in one of the family potteries. Two years later an attack of smallpox left him with a weakness in his right knee which prevented him from working the potter's wheel. This forced his attention to other aspects of the process, such as design and modelling. He was apprenticed to his brother Thomas in 1744, and in 1752 was in partnership with Thomas Whieldon, a leading Staffordshire potter, until probably the first half of 1759, when he became a master potter and set up in business on his own account at Ivy House Works in Burslem.

Wedgwood was then able to exercise to the full his determination to improve the quality of his ware. This he achieved by careful attention to all aspects of the work: artistic judgement of form and decoration; chemical study of the materials; and intelligent management of manufacturing processes. For example, to achieve greater control over firing conditions, he invented a pyrometer, a temperature-measuring device by which the shrinkage of prepared clay cylinders in the furnace gave an indication of the temperature. Wedgwood was the first potter to employ steam power, installing a **Boulton** & **Watt** engine for crushing and other operations in 1782. Beyond the confines of his works, Wedgwood concerned himself in local issues such as improvements to the road and canal systems to facilitate transport of raw materials and products.

During the first ten years, Wedgwood steadily improved the quality of his cream ware, known as 'Queen's ware' after a set of ware was presented to Queen Charlotte in 1762. The business prospered and his reputation grew. In 1766 he was able to purchase an estate on which he built new works, a mansion and a village to which he gave the name Etruria. Four years after the Etruria works were opened in 1769, Wedgwood began experimenting with a barium compound combined in a fine-textured base allied to a true porcelain. The result was Wedgwood's most original and distinctive ware similar to jasper, made in a wide variety of forms.

Wedgwood had many followers and imitators but the merit of initiating and carrying through a large-scale technical and artistic development of English pottery belongs to Wedgwood.

Principal Honours and Distinctions
FRS 1783.

Bibliography
Wedgwood contributed five papers to the *Philosophical Transactions of the Royal Society*, two in 1783 and 1790 on chemical subjects and three in 1782, 1784 and 1786 on his pyrometer.

Further Reading
Meteyard, 1865, *Life of Josiah Wedgwood*, London (biography).
A. Burton, 1976, *Josiah Wedgwood: Biography*, London: André Deutsch (a very readable account).

LRD

Wedgwood, Ralph

fl. late eighteenth/early nineteenth century
London, England

English inventor of carbon paper.

Wedgwood was descended from Thomas Wedgwood, the father of Josiah **Wedgwood**, the founder of the famous pottery firm. In 1806, he patented an apparatus for making copies of handwritten documents, Wedgwood's Stylographic Writer. It was originally developed with the intention of helping the blind to write and had a metal stylus instead of a quill pen: a piece of paper that had been soaked in printer's ink and then dried was placed between two sheets of paper, and wires placed across the page guided the stylus in the hand of the blind writer.

A few years later Wedgwood developed this apparatus into a way of making a copy of a letter at the time of writing. He used impregnated paper, which he called carbonic or carbonated paper, the first known reference to carbon paper. It was placed between a sheet of good quality writing paper and one of thin, transparent paper. By writing with the stylus on the thin paper, a good copy appeared on the lower sheet, while a reverse copy appeared on the underside of the other, which could be read right way round through the transparent paper. In its final form, the Manifold Stylographic Writer was put on sale, elegantly presented between marbled covers. Eventually a company was established to make and sell the writer, and by 1818 it was in the name of Wedgwood's son, R. Wedgwood Jun. of Rathbone Place, Oxford Street, London. Many of the writers were sold, although they never came into general use in offices, which preferred battalions of Dickensian Bob Cratchits armed with quill pens. Wedgwood himself did not share in the family prosperity, for his pathetic letters to his daughter show that he had to hawk his apparatus to raise the price of his next meal.

Further Reading
W.B. Proudfoot, 1972, *The Origin of Stencil Duplicating*, London: Hutchinson.

LRD

Weldon, Walter
b. 31 October 1832 Loughborough, England
d. 20 September 1885 Burstow, Surrey, England

English industrial chemist.

It was intended that Weldon should enter his father's factory in Loughborough, but he decided instead to turn to journalism, which he pursued with varying success in London. His *Weldon's Register of Facts and Occurrences in Literature, Science, and Art* ran for only four years, from 1860 to 1864, but the fashion magazine *Weldon's Journal*, which he published with his wife, was more successful. Meanwhile Weldon formed an interest in chemistry, although he had no formal training in that subject. He devoted himself

to solving one of the great problems of industrial chemistry at that time. The **Leblanc** process for the manufacture of soda produced large quantities of hydrochloric acid in gas form. By this time, this by-product was being converted, by oxidation with manganese dioxide, to chlorine, which was much used in the textile and paper industries as a bleaching agent. The manganese ended up as manganese chloride, from which it was difficult to convert back to the oxide, for reuse in treating the hydrochloric acid, and it was an expensive substance. Weldon visited the St Helens district of Lancashire, an important centre for the manufacture of soda, to work on the problem. During the three years from 1866 to 1869, he took out six patents for the regeneration of manganese dioxide by treating the manganese chloride with milk of lime and blowing air through it. The Weldon process was quickly adopted and had a notable economic effect: the price of bleaching powder came down by £6 per ton and production went up fourfold.

By the time of his death, nearly all chlorine works in the world used Weldon's process. The distinguished French chemist J.B.A. Dumas said of the process, when presenting Weldon with a gold medal, 'every sheet of paper and every yard of calico has been cheapened throughout the world'. Weldon played an active part in the founding of the Society of Chemical Industry.

Principal Honours and Distinctions
FRS 1882. President, Society of Chemical Industry 1883–4.

Further Reading
T.C. Barker and J.R. Harris, 1954, *A Merseyside Town in the Industrial Revolution: St Helens, 1750–1900*, Liverpool: Liverpool University Press; reprinted with corrections, 1959, London: Cass.
S. Miall, 1931, *A History of the British Chemical Industry*.

LRD

Wells, Horace
b. 1815 Connecticut, USA
d. 1848 Hartford, Connecticut, USA

American dentist, pioneer of dental extraction under nitrous oxide gas (laughing gas) anaesthesia.

Practising in Hartford, Connecticut, he was in partnership with W.T.G. **Morton** during 1842–3. Following experiences at a party in December 1844, where laughing gas (nitrous oxide) was used, Wells experimented with it as an anaesthetic during dental extractions, using himself as the first subject. By January 1845 he had employed the technique successfully in fifteen cases and made arrangements for its use as a general anaesthetic for a major operation at Massachusetts General Hospital. The experiment was a failure and he became discouraged from further enterprise in the field. He was eventually confined in an asylum, and very shortly after committed suicide.

Bibliography
1838, *An Essay on Teeth*.
1847, *A History of the Discovery of the Application of Nitrous Oxide Gas, Ether and Other Vapours to Surgical Operations*, Hartford.

Further Reading
B.M. Duncum, 1947, *Development of Inhalational Anaesthesia*.

MG

Welsbach, Baron Carl Auer von
b. 1 September 1858 Vienna, Austria
d. 4 August 1929 Treibach, Austria

Austrian inventor of the gas mantle.

Welsbach studied at Vienna Polytechnic and then at Heidelberg under the distinguished German chemist **Bunsen**. He carried out research into the rare earth elements and in 1885 succeeded in separating didymium into two earths, neodymium and praesodymium. He observed that asbestos fibres impregnated with rare earths, when strongly heated, gave off a bright light. This was the basis for his invention of the incandescent gas mantle, which he patented in 1885. He found that a mixture of 99 per cent thoria and 1 per cent ceria produced the best light. The invention was well timed, for during the 1880s gas light was being challenged by the new electric light and the Welsbach mantle gave gas light a new lease of life. It was in wide use by 1900, and in that year it was further improved by the introduction of the inverted mantle burner which had a higher light efficiency and better light distribution. For industrial and street lighting, Welsbach and Lucas achieved still higher efficiencies using the regenerative principle. Welsbach sought a use for the ceria waste from the lamps and formed an alloy of 35–40 per cent ceria with iron, known as Auer metal. This material is in wide use as the flint in cigarette and gas lighters.

Bibliography
Articles in *J. Chem. Ed.*, 1929, pp. 2,051–2, and *Chemical News*, 1902, pp. 254–6.

LRD

Welte, Edwin
b. 1876 Germany
d. after 1925

German instrument maker who developed piano-music recording methods for reproducing pianos.

He was the third generation of the Freiburg (Germany) firm of M. Welte & Soehne, music box and orchestrion manufacturers, founded in 1832, and was made a partner in 1901. He was the driving force behind the development and refinement of the reproducing piano, which had an upper-class market from 1905 to *c*.1925. With his partner and brother-in-law Karl Bockisch, he also developed recording methods that made it possible to distribute perforated paper rolls representing a reasonably accurate representation of the performance of famous soloists. This is a principle for recording and replay that is totally different from the mechanical recording principle, and at that time the quality was generally regarded as higher than that of mechanical reproduction. However, because of the possibilities of editing, the source value may be less certain. Welte's contribution was the first commercial use of a coded representation of live performances. The Welte patents were licensed to several other player-piano manufacturers.

Bibliography
German patent no. 162,708 (controlling the dynamics of reproduction).

Further Reading
Q.D. Bowers, 1972, *Encyclopedia of Automatic Musical Instruments*, New York: Vestal Press, pp. 319–38 (a good if somewhat uneven account of the Welte involvement in the reproduction of recorded sound).

GB-N

Wenham, Francis Herbert

b. 1824 London, England
d. 11 August 1908 Folkestone, England

English engineer, inventor and pioneer aerodynamicist who built the first wind tunnel.

Wenham trained as a marine engineer and later specialized in screw propellers and high-pressure engines. He had many interests. He took his steamboat to the Nile and assisted the photographer F. Frith to photograph Egyptian tombs by devising a series of mirrors to deflect sunlight into the dark recesses. He experimented with gas engines and produced a hot-air engine. Wenham was a leading, if controversial, figure in the Microscopical Society and a member of the Royal Photographic Society; he developed an enlarger.

Wenham was interested in both mechanical and lighter-than-air flight. One of his friends was James Glaisher, a well-known balloonist who made many ascents to gather scientific information. When the (Royal) Aeronautical Society of Great Britain was founded in 1866, the Rules were drawn up by Wenham, Glaisher and the Honorary Secretary, F.W. Brearey. At the first meeting of the Society, on 27 June 1866, 'On aerial locomotion and the laws by which heavy bodies impelled through the air are sustained' was read by Wenham. In his paper Wenham described his experiments with a whirling arm (used earlier by **Cayley**) to measure lift and drag on flat surfaces inclined at various angles of incidence. His studies of birds' wings and, in particular, their wing loading, showed that they derived most of their lift from the front portion, hence a long, thin wing was better than a short, wide one. He published illustrations of his glider designs covering his experiments of *c.*1858–9. One of these had five slender wings one above the other, an idea later developed by Horatio **Phillips**. Wenham had some success with a model, but no real success with his full-size gliders.

In 1871, Wenham and John Browning constructed the first wind tunnel designed for aeronautical research. It utilized a fan driven by a steam engine to propel the air and had a working section of 18 in.^{2} (116 cm^2). Wenham continued to play an important role in aeronautical matters for many years, including a lengthy exchange of ideas with Octave **Chanute** from 1892 onwards.

Principal Honours and Distinctions
Honorary Member of the (Royal) Aeronautical Society.

Bibliography
Wenham published many reports and papers. These are listed, together with a reprint of his paper 'Aerial locomotion', in the *Journal of the Royal Aeronautical Society* (August 1958).

Further Reading
Two papers by J. Laurence Pritchard, 1957, 'The dawn of aerodynamics' *Journal of the Royal Aeronautical Society* (March); 1958, 'Francis Herbert Wenham', *Journal of the Royal Aeronautical Society* (August) (both papers describe Wenham and his work).
J.E. Hodgson, 1924, *History of Aeronautics in Great Britain*, London.

JDS

Westinghouse, George

b. 6 October 1846 Central Bridge, New York, USA
d. 12 March 1914 New York, New York, USA

American inventor and entrepreneur, pioneer of air brakes for railways and alternating-current distribution of electricity.

George Westinghouse's father was an ingenious manufacturer of agricultural implements; the son, after a spell in the Union Army during the Civil War, and subsequently in the Navy as an engineer, went to work for his father. He invented a rotary steam engine, which proved impracticable; a rerailing device for railway rolling stock in 1865; and a cast-steel frog for railway points, with longer life than the cast-iron frogs then used, in 1868–9. During the same period Westinghouse, like many other inventors, was considering how best to meet the evident need for a continuous brake for trains, i.e. one by which the driver could apply the brakes on all vehicles in a train simultaneously instead of relying on brakesmen on individual vehicles. By chance he encountered a magazine article about the construction of the Mont Cenis Tunnel, with a description of the pneumatic tools invented for it, and from this it occurred to him that compressed air might be used to operate the brakes along a train.

The first prototype was ready in 1869 and the

Westinghouse Air Brake Company was set up to manufacture it. However, despite impressive demonstration of the brake's powers when it saved the test train from otherwise certain collision with a horse-drawn dray on a level crossing, railways were at first slow to adopt it. Then in 1872 Westinghouse added to it the triple valve, which enabled the train pipe to charge reservoirs beneath each vehicle, from which the compressed air would apply the brakes when pressure in the train pipe was *reduced*. This meant that the brake was now automatic: if a train became divided, the brakes on both parts would be applied. From then on, more and more American railways adopted the Westinghouse brake and the Railroad Safety Appliance Act of 1893 made air brakes compulsory in the USA. Air brakes were also adopted in most other parts of the world, although only a minority of British railway companies took them up, the remainder, with insular reluctance, preferring the less effective vacuum brake.

From 1880 Westinghouse was purchasing patents relating to means of interlocking railway signals and points; he combined them with his own inventions to produce a complete signalling system. The first really practical power signalling scheme, installed in the USA by Westinghouse in 1884, was operated pneumatically, but the development of railway signalling required an awareness of the powers of electricity, and it was probably this that first led Westinghouse to become interested in electrical processes and inventions. The Westinghouse Electric Company was formed in 1886: it pioneered the use of electricity distribution systems using high-voltage single-phase alternating current, which it developed from European practice. Initially this was violently opposed by established operators of direct-current distribution systems, but eventually the use of alternating current became widespread.

Principal Honours and Distinctions
Légion d'honneur. Order of the Crown of Italy. Order of Leopold.

Bibliography
Westinghouse took out some 400 patents over forty-eight years.

Further Reading
H.G. Prout, 1922, *A Life of George Westinghouse*, London (biography inclined towards technicalities).
F.E. Leupp, 1918, *George Westinghouse: His Life and Achievements*, Boston (London 1919) (biography inclined towards Westinghouse and his career).
J.F. Stover, 1961, *American Railroads*, Chicago: University of Chicago Press, pp. 152–4.

PJGR

Weston, Edward
b. 9 May 1850 Oswestry, England
d. 20 August 1936 Montclair, New Jersey, USA

English (naturalized American) inventor noted for his contribution to the technology of electrical measurements.

Although he developed dynamos for electroplating and lighting, Weston's major contribution to technology was his invention of a moving-coil voltmeter and the standard cell which bears his name. After some years as a medical student, during which he gained a knowledge of chemistry, he abandoned his studies. Emigrating to New York in 1870, he was employed by a manufacturer of photographic chemicals. There followed a period with an electroplating company during which he built his first dynamo. In 1877 some business associates financed a company to build these machines and, later, arc-lighting equipment. By 1882 the Weston Company had been absorbed into the United States Electric Lighting Company, which had a counterpart in Britain, the Maxim Weston Company. By the time Weston resigned from the company, in 1886, he had been granted 186 patents. He then began the work in which he made his greatest contribution, the science of electrical measurement.

The Weston meter, the first successful portable measuring instrument with a pivoted coil, was made in 1886. By careful arrangement of the magnet, coil and control springs, he achieved a design with a well-damped movement, which retained its calibration. These instruments were produced commercially on a large scale and the moving-coil principle was soon adopted by many manufacturers. In 1892 he invented manganin, an alloy with a small negative temperature coefficient, for use as resistances in his voltmeters.

The Weston standard cell was invented in 1892. Using his chemical knowledge he produced a cell, based on mercury and cadmium, which replaced the Clark cell as a voltage reference source. The Weston cell became the recognized standard at the International Conference on Electrical Units and Standards held in London in 1908.

Principal Honours and Distinctions
President, AIEE 1888–9. Franklin Institute Elliott Cresson Medal 1910, Franklin medal 1924.

Bibliography
29 April 1890, British patent no. 6,569 (the Weston moving-coil instrument).
6 February 1892, British patent no. 22,482 (the Weston standard cell).

Further Reading
D.O. Woodbury, 1949, *A Measure of Greatness. A Short Biography of Edward Weston*, New York (a detailed account).
C.N. Brown, 1988, in *Proceedings of the Meeting on the History of Electrical Engineering*, IEE, 17–21 (describes Weston's meter).
H.C. Passer, 1953, *The Electrical Manufacturers: 1875–1900*, Cambridge, Mass.

GW

Whatman, James
baptized 4 October 1702 Loose, near Maidstone, Kent, England
d. 29 June 1759 Loose, near Maidstone, Kent, England

English papermaker, inventor of wove paper.

The Whatman family had been established in Kent in the fifteenth century. At the time of his marriage in 1740, Whatman was described as a tanner. His wife was the widow of Richard Harris, papermaker, and, by the marriage settlement, he with his wife became joint tenants of Turkey Mill, near Maidstone. The mill had been used for fulling since the Middle Ages, but towards the end of the seventeenth century it had been converted to papermaking. Remarkably quickly, Whatman became one of the leading papermakers in England, doubtless helped by the shortage of imported paper that resulted from the Spanish Succession War of the 1740s. By the time of his death, his mill had the largest output

in England, with a reputation for good-quality writing paper.

According to his son's account much later, Whatman introduced wove paper, made in a wove wire gauze mould, in 1756. It gave a smoother paper with a more even surface, and was probably made at the suggestion of the celebrated printer and type founder John Baskerville. Whatman printed a book in 1757 on paper with an even texture but with laid lines still discernible, indicating that at first the wire gauze was placed in a conventional wire mould. In a book printed by Baskerville two years later, these lines are no longer visible, so a wire gauze mould was in use by then.

After Whatman's death, Turkey Mill was managed by his widow for three years, until his son James (1741–98) was old enough to take charge. Under the management of the son, the mill maintained the scale and quality of its output, and in 1769 it was described as the largest paper mill in England where the best writing paper was made.

Further Reading
T. Balston, 1957, *James Whatman, Father and Son*, London: Methuen.

LRD

Wheatstone, Sir Charles
b. 1802 near Gloucester, England
d. 19 October 1875 Paris, France

English physicist, pioneer of electric telegraphy.

Wheatstone's family moved to London when he was 4 years old. He was educated at various schools in London and excelled in physics and mathematics. He qualified for a French prize but forfeited it because he was too shy to recite a speech in French at the prize-giving.

An uncle, also called Charles Wheatstone, has a musical instrument manufacturing business where young Charles went to work. He was fascinated by the science of music, but did not enjoy business life. After the uncle's death, Charles and his brother William took over the business. Charles developed and patented the concertina, which the firm assembled from parts made by 'outworkers'. He devoted much of his time to studying the physics of sound and mechanism of sound transmission through solids. He sent speech and music over considerable distances through solid rods and stretched wires, and envisaged communication at a distance. He concluded, however, that electrical methods were more promising.

In 1834 Wheatstone was appointed Professor of Experimental Philosophy – a part-time position – in the new King's College, London, which gave him some research facilities. He conducted experiments with a telegraph system using several miles of wire in the college corridors. Jointly with William Fothergill **Cooke**, in 1837 he obtained the first patent for a practical electric telegraph, and much of the remainder of his life was devoted to its improvement. In 1843 he gave a paper to the Royal Society surveying the state of electrical measurements and drew attention to a bridge circuit known ever since as the 'Wheatstone bridge', although he clearly attributed it to S.H. Christie. Wheatstone devised the 'ABC' telegraph, for use on private lines by anyone who could read, and a high-speed automatic telegraph which was adopted by the Post Office and used for many years. He also worked on the French and Belgian telegraph systems; he died when taken ill on a business visit to Paris.

Further Reading
B. Bowers, 1975, *Sir Charles Wheatstone FRS*, London: HMSO.

BB

Whinfield, John Rex
b. 16 February 1901 Sutton, Surrey, England
d. 6 July 1955 Dorking, Surrey, England

English inventor of Terylene.

Whinfield was educated at Merchant Taylors' School and Caius College, Cambridge, where he studied chemistry. Before embarking on his career as a research chemist, he worked as an unpaid assistant to the chemist C.F. **Cross**, who had taken part in the discovery of rayon. Whinfield then joined the Calico Printers' Association. There his interest was aroused by the discovery of nylon by W.H. **Carothers** to seek other polymers which could be produced in fibre form, usable by the textile industries. With his colleague J.T. **Dickson**, he discovered in 1941 that a polymerized condensate of terephthalic acid and ethylene glycol, polyethylene terephthgallate, could be drawn into strong fibres. Whinfield and Dickson filed a patent application in the

same year, but due to war conditions it was not published until 1946. The Ministry of Supply considered that the new material might have military applications and undertook further research and development. Its industrial and textile possibilities were evaluated by Imperial Chemical Industries (ICI) in 1943 and 'Terylene', as it came to be called, was soon recognized as being as important as nylon.

In 1946, Dupont acquired rights to work the Calico Printers' Association patent in the USA and began large-scale manufacture in 1954, marketing the product under the name 'Dacron'. Meanwhile ICI purchased world rights except for the USA and reached the large-scale manufacture stage in 1955. A new branch of the textile industry has grown up from Whinfield's discovery: he lived to see most people in the western world wearing something made of Terylene. It was one of the major inventions of the twentieth century, yet Whinfield, perhaps because he published little, received scant recognition, apart from the CBE in 1954.

Principal Honours and Distinctions
CBE 1954.

Further Reading
Obituary, 1966, *The Times* (7 July).
Obituary, 1967, *Chemistry in Britain* 3: 26.
J. Jewkes, D. Sawers and R. Stillerman, 1969, *The Sources of Invention*, 2nd edn, London: Macmillan.

LRD

Whipple, Squire
b. 1804 Hardwick, Massachusetts, USA
d. 15 March 1888 Albany, New York, USA

American civil engineer, author and inventor.

The son of James and Electa Whipple, his father was a farmer and later the owner of a small cotton mil at Hardwick, Massachusetts. In 1817 Squire Whipple moved with his family to Otego County, New York. He helped on the farm and attended the academy at Fairfield, Herkimer County. For a time he taught school pupils, and in 1829 he entered Union College, Schenectady, where he received the degree of AB in 1830; his interest in engineering was probably aroused by the construction of the Erie Canal near his home during his boyhood. He was first employed in a minor capacity in surveys for the Baltimore and Ohio Railroad and for the Erie Canal. In 1836–7 he was resident engineer for a division of the New York and Erie Railroad and was also employed in a number of other railroad and canal surveys, making surveying instruments in the intervals between these appointments; in 1840, he completed a lock for weighing canal boats.

Whipple received his first bridge patent on 24 April 1841; this was for a truss of arched upper chord made of cast and wrought iron. Five years later, he devised a trapezoidal truss which was used in the building of many bridges over the succeeding generation. In 1852–3 Whipple used his truss in an iron railroad bridge of 44.5 m (146 ft) span on the Rensselaer and Saratoga Railroad. He also built a number of bridges with lifting spans.

Whipple's main contribution to bridge engineering was the publication in 1847 of *A Work on Bridge Building*. In 1869 he issued a continuation of this treatise, and a fourth edition of both was published in 1883.

Principal Honours and Distinctions
Honorary Member, American Society of Civil Engineers.

IMcN

White, Canvass
b. 1790 Whitesboro, New York, USA
d. 1834 St Augustine, Florida, USA

American civil engineer.

Between 1807 and 1816 White worked for his father. He fought in the War of 1812, and worked his way to Russia and back in a merchantman; in 1817–18 he went to England and walked over 2,000 miles (3,220 km) over canal sites. After 1818 he was Principal Assistant to Benjamin Wright on the construction of the Erie Canal until its completion in 1825; he was the only one involved in this project who had any knowledge of European canal construction. He was particularly noted for the design of canal locks and their equipment; one of his main contributions was the discovery of the lime rock in New York State which could be converted into concrete, and in 1820 he obtained a patent for a waterproof cement. He supervised the Glen Falls feeder construction, and he was Chief Engineer for the Delaware and Raritan Canal in New Jer-

sey and the Lehigh and Union canals in Pennsylvania.

IMcN

White, Sir William Henry
b. 2 February 1845 Devonport, England
d. 27 February 1913 London, England

English naval architect distinguished as the foremost nineteenth-century Director of Naval Construction, and latterly as a consultant and author.

Following early education at Devonport, White passed the Royal Dockyard entry examination in 1859 to commence a seven-year shipwright apprenticeship. However, he was destined for greater achievements and in 1863 passed the Admiralty Scholarship examinations, which enabled him to study at the Royal School of Naval Architecture at South Kensington, London. He graduated in 1867 with high honours and was posted to the Admiralty Constructive Department. Promotion came swiftly, with appointment to Assistant Constructor in 1875 and Chief Constructor in 1881.

In 1883 he left the Admiralty and joined the Tyneside shipyard of Sir W.G. **Armstrong**, Mitchell & Co. at a salary of about treble that of a Chief Constructor, with, in addition, a production bonus based on tonnage produced! At the Elswick Shipyard he became responsible for the organization and direction of shipbuilding activities, and during his relatively short period there enhanced the name of the shipyard in the warship export market. It is assumed that White did not settle easily in the North East of England, and in 1885, following negotiations with the Admiralty, he was released from his five-year exclusive contract and returned to public service as Director of Naval Construction and Assistant Controller of the Royal Navy. (As part of the settlement the Admiralty released Philip **Watts** to replace White, and in later years Watts was also to move from that same shipyard and become White's successor as Director of Naval Construction.)

For seventeen momentous years White had technical control of ship production for the Royal Navy. The rapid building of warships commenced after the passing of the Naval Defence Act of 1889, which authorized directly and indirectly the construction of around seventy vessels. The total number of ships built during the White era amounted to 43 battleships, 128 cruisers of varying size and type, and 74 smaller vessels. While White did not have the stimulation of building a revolutionary capital ship as did his successor, he did have the satisfaction of ensuring that the Royal Navy was equipped with a fleet of all-round capability, and he saw the size, displacement and speed of the ships increase dramatically.

In 1902 he resigned from the Navy because of ill health and assumed several less onerous tasks. During the construction of the Cunard Liner *Mauretania* on the Tyne, he held directorships with the shipbuilders Swan, Hunter and Wigham Richardson, and also the Parsons Marine Turbine Company. He acted as a consultant to many organizations and had an office in Westminster. It was there that he died in February 1913.

White left a great literary legacy in the form of his esteemed *Manual of Naval Architecture*, first published in 1877 and reprinted several times since in English, German and other languages. This volume is important not only as a text dealing with first principles but also as an illustration of the problems facing warship designers of the late nineteenth century.

Principal Honours and Distinctions
KCB 1895. Knight Commander of the Order of the Danneborg (Denmark). FRS. FRSE. President, Institution of Civil Engineers; Mechanical Engineers; Marine Engineers. Vice-President, Institution of Naval Architects.

Bibliography
1877, *A Manual of Naval Architecture*, London.

Further Reading
D.K. Brown, 1983, *A Century of Naval Construction*, London.

FMW

Whitehead, Robert

b. 3 January 1823 Bolton-le-Moors, Lancashire, England
d. 19 November 1903 Shrivenham, Wiltshire, England

English inventor of the torpedo.

At the age of 14 Whitehead was apprenticed by his father, who ran a cotton-bleaching business, to an engineering firm in Manchester. He moved in 1847 to join his uncle, who was the Manager of another engineering firm, and three years later Whitehead set up on his own in Milan, where he made mechanical improvements to the silk-weaving industry and designed drainage machines for the Lombardy marshes.

In 1848 he was forced to move from Italy because of the revolution and settled in Fiume, which was then part of Austria. There he concentrated on designing and building engines for warships, and in 1864 the Austrians invited him to participate in a project to develop a 'floating torpedo'. In those days the torpedo was synonymous with the underwater mine, and Whitehead believed that he could do better than this proposal and produce an explosive weapon that could propel itself through the water. He set to work with his son John and a mechanic, producing the first version of his torpedo in 1866. It had a range of only 700 yd (640 m) and a speed of just 7 knots (13 km/h), as well as depth-keeping problems, but even so, especially after he had reduced the last problem by the use of a 'balance chamber', the Austrian authorities were sufficiently impressed to buy construction rights and to decorate him. Other navies quickly followed suit and within twenty years almost every navy in the world was equipped with the Whitehead torpedo, its main attraction being that no warship, however large, was safe from it. During this time Whitehead continued to improve on his design, introducing a servo-motor and gyroscope, thereby radically improving range, speed and accuracy.

Principal Honours and Distinctions
Order of Max Joseph (Austria) 1868. Légion d'honneur 1884. Whitehead also received decorations from Prussia, Denmark, Portugal, Italy and Greece.

Further Reading
Dictionary of National Biography, 1912, Vol. 3, Suppl. 2, London: Smith, Elder.

CM

Whitney, Amos

b. 8 October 1832 Biddeford, Maine, USA
d. 5 August 1920 Poland Springs, Maine, USA

American mechanical engineer and machine-tool manufacturer.

Amos Whitney was a member of the same distinguished family as Eli **Whitney**. His father was a locksmith and machinist and he was apprenticed at the age of 14 to the Essex Machine Company of Lawrence, Massachusetts. In 1850 both he and his father were working at the **Colt** Armory in Hartford, Connecticut, where he first met his future partner, F.A. **Pratt**. They both subsequently moved to the Phoenix Iron Works, also at Hartford, and in 1860 they started in a small way doing machine work on their own account. In 1862 they took a third partner, Monroe Stannard, and enlarged their workshop. The business continued to expand, but Pratt and Whitney remained at the Phoenix Iron Works until 1864 and in the following year they built their first new factory. The Pratt & Whitney Company was incorporated in 1869 with a capital of $350,000, Amos Whitney being appointed General Superintendent. The firm specialized in making machine tools and tools particularly for the armament industry. Pratt & Whitney was one of the leading firms developing the system of interchangeable manufacture which led to the need to establish national standards of measurement. The Rogers–Bond Comparator, developed with the backing of Pratt & Whitney, played an important part in the establishment of these standards, which formed the basis of the gauges of many various types made by the firm.

Amos Whitney was made Vice-President of Pratt & Whitney Company in 1893 and was President from 1898 until 1901, when the company was acquired by the Niles–Bement–Pond Company: he then remained as one of the directors. He was elected a Member of the American Society of Mechanical Engineers in 1913.

Further Reading

J.W. Roe, 1916, *English and American Tool Builders*, New Haven; reprinted 1926, New York, and 1987, Bradley, Ill. (describes the origin and development of the Pratt & Whitney Company).

RTS

Whitney, Eli

b. 8 December 1765 Westborough, Massachusetts, USA
d. 8 January 1825 New Haven, Connecticut, USA

American inventor of the cotton gin and manufacturer of firearms.

The son of a prosperous farmer, Eli Whitney as a teenager showed more interest in mechanics than school work. At the age of 15 he began an enterprise business manufacturing nails in his father's workshop, even having to hire help to fulfil his orders. He later determined to acquire a university education and, his father having declined to provide funds, he taught at local schools to obtain the means to attend Leicester Academy, Massachusetts, in preparation for his entry to Yale in 1789. He graduated in 1792 and then decided to study law. He accepted a position in Georgia as a tutor that would have given him time for study; this post did not materialize, but on his journey south he met General Nathanael Greene's widow and the manager of her plantations, Phineas Miller (1764–1803). A feature of agriculture in the southern states was that the land was unsuitable for long-staple cotton but could yield large crops of green-seed cotton. Green-seed cotton was difficult to separate from its seed, and when Whitney learned of the problem in 1793 he quickly devised a machine known as the cotton gin, which provided an effective solution. He formed a partnership with Miller to manufacture the gin and in 1794 obtained a patent. This invention made possible the extraordinary growth of the cotton industry in the United States, but the patent was widely infringed and it was not until 1807, after amendment of the patent laws, that Whitney was able to obtain a favourable decision in the courts and some financial return.

In 1798 Whitney was in financial difficulties following the failure of the initial legal action against infringement of the cotton gin patent, but in that year he obtained a government contract to supply 10,000 muskets within two years with generous advance payments. He built a factory at New Haven, Connecticut, and proposed to use a new method of manufacture, perhaps the first application of the system of interchangeable parts. He failed to supply the firearms in the specified time, and in fact the first 500 guns were not delivered until 1801 and the full contract was not completed until 1809.

In 1812 Whitney made application for a renewal of his cotton gin patent, but this was refused. In the same year, however, he obtained a second contract from the Government for 15,000 firearms and a similar one from New York State which ensured the success of his business.

Further Reading
J. Mirsky and A. Nevins, 1952, *The World of Eli Whitney*, New York (a good biography).
P.J. Federico, 1960, 'Records of Eli Whitney's cotton gin patent', *Technology and Culture* 1: 168–76 (for details of the cotton gin patent).
R.S. Woodbury, 1960, 'The legend of Eli Whitney and interchangeable parts', *Technology and Culture* 1: 235–53 (challenges the traditional view of Eli Whitney as the sole originator of the 'American' system of manufacture).
See also *Technology and Culture* 14 (1973): 592–8; 18 (1977): 146–8; 19 (1978): 609–11.

RTS

Whittle, Sir Frank
b. 1 June 1907 Coventry, England

English engineer who developed the first British jet engine.

Frank Whittle enlisted in the Royal Air Force (RAF) as an apprentice, and after qualifying as a pilot he developed an interest in the technical aspects of aircraft propulsion. He was convinced that the gas-turbine engine could be adapted for use in aircraft, but he could not convince the Air Ministry, who turned down the proposal. Nevertheless, Whittle applied for a patent for his turbojet engine the following year, 1930. While still in the RAF, he was allowed time to study for a degree at Cambridge University and carry out postgraduate research (1934–7). By 1936 the official attitude had changed, and a company called Power Jets Ltd was set up to develop Whittle's jet engine. On 12 April 1937 the experimental engine was bench-tested. After further development, an official order was placed in March 1938. Whittle's engine had a centrifugal compressor, ten combustion chambers and a turbine to drive the compressor; all the power output came from the jet of hot gases.

In 1939 an experimental aircraft was ordered from the Gloster Aircraft Company, the *E 28/39*, to house the Whittle *W 1* engine, and this made its first flight on 15 May 1941. A development of the *W 1* by Rolls-Royce, the *Welland*, was used to power the twin-engined Gloster *Meteor* fighter, which saw service with the RAF in 1944.

Whittle retired from the RAF in 1948 and became a consultant. From 1977 he lived in the United States. Comparisons between the work of Whittle and Hans von **Ohain** show that each of the two engineers developed his engine without knowledge of the other's work. Whittle was the first to take out a patent, Ohain achieved the first flight; the Whittle engine and its derivatives, however, played a much greater role in the history of the jet engine.

Principal Honours and Distinctions
Knighted 1948. Commander of the Order of the Bath 1947. Order of Merit 1986. FRS 1947. Honorary Fellow of the Royal Aeronautical Society.

Bibliography
1953, *Jet*, London (an account not only of his technical problems, but also of the difficulties with civil servants, politicians and commercial organizations).

Further Reading
J. Golley, 1987, *Whittle: The True Story*, Shrewsbury (this author based his work on *Jet*, but carried out research, aided by Whittle, to give a fuller account with the benefit of hindsight).

JDS

Whitworth, Sir Joseph
b. 21 December 1803 Stockport, Cheshire, England
d. 22 January 1887 Monte Carlo, Monaco

English mechanical engineer and pioneer of precision measurement.

Joseph Whitworth received his early education in a school kept by his father, but from the age of 12 he attended a school near Leeds. At 14 he joined his uncle's mill near Ambergate, Derbyshire, to learn the business of cotton spinning. In the four years he spent there he realized that he was more interested in the machinery than in managing a cotton mill. In 1821 he obtained employment as a mechanic with Crighton & Co., Manchester. In 1825 he moved to London and worked for Henry **Maudslay** and later for the **Holtzapffels** and Joseph **Clement**. After these years spent gaining experience, he returned to Manchester in 1833 and set up in a small workshop under a sign 'Joseph Whitworth, Tool

Maker, from London'.

The business expanded steadily and the firm made machine tools of all types and other engineering products including steam engines. From 1834 Whitworth obtained many patents in the fields of machine tools, textile and knitting machinery and road-sweeping machines. By 1851 the company was generally regarded as the leading manufacturer of machine tools in the country. Whitworth was a pioneer of precise measurement and demonstrated the fundamental mode of producing a true plane by making surface plates in sets of three. He advocated the use of the decimal system and made use of limit gauges, and he established a standard screw thread which was adopted as the national standard. In 1853 Whitworth visited America as a member of a Royal Commission and reported on American industry. At the time of the Crimean War in 1854 he was asked to provide machinery for manufacturing rifles and this led him to design an improved rifle of his own. Although tests in 1857 showed this to be much superior to all others, it was not adopted by the War Office. Whitworth's experiments with small arms led on to the construction of big guns and projectiles. To improve the quality of the steel used for these guns, he subjected the molten metal to pressure during its solidification, this fluid-compressed steel being then known as 'Whitworth steel'.

In 1868 Whitworth established thirty annual scholarships for engineering students. After his death his executors permanently endowed the Whitworth Scholarships and distributed his estate of nearly half a million pounds to various educational and charitable institutions. Whitworth was elected an Associate of the Institution of Civil Engineers in 1841 and a Member in 1848 and served on its Council for many years. He was elected a Member of the Institution of Mechanical Engineers in 1847, the year of its foundation.

Principal Honours and Distinctions

Baronet 1869. FRS 1857. President, Institution of Mechanical Engineers 1856, 1857 and 1866. Hon. LLD Trinity College, Dublin, 1863. Hon. DCL Oxford University 1868. Member of the Smeatonian Society of Civil Engineers 1864. Légion d'honneur 1868. Society of Arts Albert Medal 1868.

Bibliography

1858, *Miscellaneous Papers on Mechanical Subjects*, London; 1873, *Miscellaneous Papers on Practical Subjects: Guns and Steel*, London (both are collections of his papers to technical societies).

1854, with G. Wallis, *The Industry of the United States in Machinery, Manufactures, and Useful and Ornamental Arts*, London.

Further Reading

F.C. Lea, 1946, *A Pioneer of Mechanical Engineering: Sir Joseph Whitworth*, London (a short biographical account).

A.E. Musson, 1963, 'Joseph Whitworth: toolmaker and manufacturer', *Engineering Heritage*, Vol. 1, London, 124–9 (a short biography).

D.J. Jeremy (ed.), 1984–6, *Dictionary of Business Biography*, Vol. 5, London, 797–802 (a short biography).

W. Steeds, 1969, *A History of Machine Tools 1700–1910*, Oxford (describes Whitworth's machine tools).

RTS

Wicks, Frederick

fl. mid-nineteenth century

Scottish inventor of a typecasting machine.

During the nineteenth century, the mechanical printing press achieved great success in speeding up the output of printing matter, but it proved much more difficult to mechanize the making and setting of type. Before the advent of Monotype and Linotype machines towards the end of the century, the fastest typecasting machine was the rotary caster invented by Wicks in 1878. The machine was said to be capable of delivering 60,000 finished types an hour and was intended to meet the demands of newspaper publishers. The types were formed by forcing a stream of molten metal into moulds mounted on a chain, and the moulds were presented in turn before the nozzle of a metal pot. *The Times* newspaper installed a battery of Wicks typecasters in the 1880s that remained in use until they were replaced in 1908 with Monotype machines. Wicks also invented a typesetting machine in 1883 in which types stored in upright inclined channels were released by depressing a key. It was used for a time by some London newspapers in conjunction with type produced at the Wicks foundry in Blackfriars Road, again until overtaken by the two finally successful hot-metal machines.

Further Reading
J. Moran, 1965, *The Composition of Reading Matter*, London: Wace (provides some details about the Wicks caster).

LRD

Wilde, Henry

b. 1833 Manchester, England
d. 28 March 1919 Alderley Edge, Cheshire, England

English inventor and pioneer manufacturer of electrical generators.

After completing a mechanical engineering apprenticeship Wilde commenced in business as a telegraph and lightning conductor specialist in Lancashire. Several years spent on the design of an alphabetic telegraph resulted in a number of patents. In 1864 he secured a patent for an electromagnetic generator which gave alternating current from a shuttle-wound armature, the field being excited by a small direct-current magneto. Wilde's invention was described to the Royal Society by **Faraday** in March 1866. When demonstrated at the Paris Exhibition of 1867, Wilde's machine produced sufficient power to maintain an arc light. The small size of the generator provided a contrast to the large and heavy magneto-electric machines also exhibited. He discovered, by experiment, that alternators in synchronism could be connected in parallel. At about the same time John **Hopkinson** arrived at the same conclusions on theoretical grounds.

Between 1866 and 1877 he sold ninety-four machines with commutators for electroplating purposes, a number being purchased by Elkingtons of Birmingham. He also supplied generators for the first use of electric searchlights on battleships. In his early experiments Wilde was extremely close to the discovery of true self-excitation from remnant magnetism, a principle which he was to discover in 1867 on machines intended for electroplating. His patents proved to be financially successful and he retired from business in 1884. During the remaining thirty-five years of his life he published many scientific papers, turning from experimental work to philosophical and, finally, theological

matters. His record as an inventor established him as a pioneer of electrical engineering, but his lack of scientific training was to restrict his later contributions.

Principal Honours and Distinctions
FRS 1886.

Bibliography
1 December 1863, British patent no. 3,006 (alternator with a magneto-exciter).
1866, *Proceedings of the Royal Society* 14: 107–11 (first report on Wilde's experiments).
1900, autobiographical note, *Journal of the Institution of Electrical Engineers* 29: 3–17.

Further Reading
W.W. Haldane Gee. 1920, biography, *Memoirs, Manchester Literary and Philosophical Society* 63: 1–16 (a comprehensive account).
P. Dunsheath, 1962, *A History of Electrical Engineering*, London: Faber & Faber, pp. 110–12 (a short account).

GW

Wiles, Philip

b. 18 August 1899 London, England
d. 17 May 1967 Kingston, Jamaica

English orthopaedic surgeon involved in the development of hip-replacement surgery.

From 1917, Wiles served during the First World War in the artillery, air force and army service corps. After a short postwar period in the City, he qualified in medicine at the Middlesex Hospital in 1928. His distinguished student career led to posts at the Middlesex and the Royal National Orthopaedic Hospital. He served as a brigadier orthopaedic surgeon in the Army during the Second World War and in 1946 returned as Consultant Orthopaedic Surgeon to the Middlesex.

He made outstanding contributions to postwar developments in orthopaedics and, as well as practising, wrote extensively on a variety of subjects including joint replacement. Taking early retirement in 1959 he moved to Jamaica, where he was involved in the affairs of the University of the West Indies.

Principal Honours and Distinctions
President, British Orthopaedic Association 1955. Honorary Member of the American

Orthopedic Association. Middlesex Hospital Lyell Gold Medal 1927.

Bibliography
1965, *Essentials of Orthopaedics.*
1960, *Fractures, Dislocations and Sprains.*

MG

Wilkes, Maurice Vincent
b. 26 June 1913 Stourbridge, Worcestershire, England

English physicist who was jointly responsible for the construction of the EDSAC computer.

Educated at King Edward VI Grammar School, Stourbridge, where he began to make radio sets and read *Wireless World*, Wilkes went to St John's College, Cambridge, in 1931, graduating as a Wrangler in the Mathematical Tripos in 1934. He then carried out research at the Cavendish Laboratory, becoming a demonstrator in 1937. During the Second World War he worked on radar, differential analysers and operational research at the Bawdsey Research Station and other air-defence establishments. In 1945 he returned to Cambridge as a lecturer and as Acting Director of the Mathematical (later Computer) Laboratory, serving as Director from 1946 to 1970.

During the late 1940s, following visits to the USA for computer courses and to see the ENIAC computer, with the collaboration of colleagues he constructed the Cambridge University digital computer EDSAC (for Electronic Delay Storage Automatic Computer), using ultrasonic delay lines for data storage. In the mid-1950s a second machine, EDSAC2, was constructed using a magnetic-core memory. In 1965 he became Professor of Computer Technology. After retirement he worked for the Digital Electronic Corporation (DEC) from 1981 to 1986, serving also as Adjunct Professor of Computer Science and Electrical Engineering at the Massachusetts Institute of Technology from 1981 to 1985. In 1990 he became a research strategy consultant to the Olivetti Research Directorate.

Principal Honours and Distinctions
FRS 1956. First President, British Computer Society 1957–60. Honorary DSc Munich 1978, Bath 1987. Honorary DTech Linkoping 1975. FEng 1976. Institution of Electrical Engineers Faraday Medal 1981.

Bibliography
1948, 'The design of a practical high-speed computing machine', *Proceedings of the Royal Society* A195: 274 (describes EDSAC).
1949, *Oscillation of the Earth's Atmosphere.*
1951, *Preparation of Programs for an Electronic Digital Computer*, New York: Addison-Wesley.
1956, *Automatic Digital Computers*, London: Methuen.
1966, *A Short Introduction to Numerical Analysis.*
1968, *Time-Sharing Computer Systems*: McDonald & Jane's.
1979, *The Cambridge CAP Computer and its Operating System*: H. Holland.
1985, *Memoirs of a Computer Pioneer*, Cambridge, Mass.: MIT Press (autobiography).

Further Reading
B. Randell (ed.), 1973, *The Origins of Digital Computers*, Berlin: Springer-Verlag.

See also: **Forrester, Jay Wright**; **Goldstine, Herman H.**; **Strachey, Christopher**.

KF

Wilkinson, David
b. 5 January 1771 Smithfield (now Slatersville), Rhode Island, USA
d. 3 February 1852 Caledonia Springs, Ontario, Canada

American mechanical engineer and inventor of a screw-cutting lathe.

David Wilkinson was the third son of Oziel Wilkinson (1744–1815), a blacksmith who *c.*1783 established at Pawtucket, Rhode Island, a plant for making farm tools and domestic utensils. This enterprise he steadily expanded with the aid of his sons, until by 1800 it was regarded as the leading iron and machinery manufacturing business in New England. At the age of 13, David Wilkinson entered his father's workshops. Their products included iron screws, and the problem of cutting the threads was one that engaged his attention. After working on it for some years he devised a screw-cutting lathe, for which he obtained a patent in 1798. In about 1800 David and his brother Daniel established their own factory at Pawtucket, known as David Wilkinson & Co., where they specialized in the manufacture of textile machinery. Later they began to make cast cannon and installed a special boring machine for machining them. The firm prospered until 1829, when a financial crisis caused its collapse. David Wilkinson set up a new business in Cohoes, New York, but this was not a success and from 1836 he travelled around finding work chiefly in canal and bridge construction in New Jersey, Ohio and Canada. In 1848 he petitioned Congress for some reward for his invention of the screw-cutting lathe of 1798; he was awarded $10,000.

Further Reading

J.W. Roe, 1916, *English and American Tool Builders*, New Haven; reprinted 1926, New York, and 1987, Bradley, Ill. (provides a short account of David Wilkinson and his work).

R.S. Woodbury, 1961, *History of the Lathe to 1850*, Cleveland, Ohio (includes a description of Wilkinson's screw-cutting lathe).

RTS

Wilkinson, John

b. 1728 Clifton, Cumberland, England
d. 14 July 1808 Bradley, Staffordshire, England

English ironmaster, inventor of a cannon-boring machine.

Wilkinson's father Isaac was a farmer turned ironmaster. Soon after 1750, the family acquired Bersham furnace, near Wrexham. This was later in the hands of John and his brother William. By 1763, John had risen to take sole charge of Broseley furnace near Coalbrookdale, Shropshire, and in 1770 he set up a third furnace at Bradley, Staffordshire. By this time he had become one of the country's leading ironmasters, known for the wide range of ware made of cast iron, doubtless the reason for his nickname 'Ironmad Wilkinson'. He made a cast-iron boat which, to the surprise of many, floated. For his own eventual use, he also made a cast-iron coffin, but did not make sufficient allowance for increasing girth with age!

Wilkinson's most notable invention was his cannon-boring machine, patented in 1774. The gun barrel was held rigidly while the cutter head moved forward on a rod inside a hollow boring bar. The machine was easily adapted to bore the cylinders for **Boulton** & **Watt**'s steam engines and he became a regular supplier, as only he could bore them with the required accuracy. On the other hand, their second engine was supplied to Wilkinson to power a blowing engine to provide air blast for his Broseley furnace: this was the first use of a Boulton & Watt engine for a purpose other than pumping. By 1780 he had three further steam engines at work. Wilkinson installed the first Boulton & Watt engine in France at the Paris waterworks, for which he supplied the iron pipes. Another patent was obtained in 1794 for the invention of the cupola or furnace for melting metal for small castings, although it is now thought that the real inventor was his brother William. Apart from domestic and engineering ironware, Wilkinson was supplier of arms to the American and, illicitly, to the French.

Further Reading

H.W. Dickinson, 1914, *John Wilkinson, Ironmaster*.

LRD

Williams, Sir Edward Leader

b. 28 April 1828 Worcester, England
d. 1 June 1910 Altrincham, Cheshire, England

English civil engineer, designer and first Chief Engineer of the Manchester Ship Canal.

After an apprenticeship with the Severn Navigation, of which his father was Chief Engineer, Williams was engaged as Assistant Engineer on the Great Northern Railway, Resident Engineer at Shoreham Harbour and Engineer to the contractors for the Admiralty Pier at Dover. In 1856 he was appointed Engineer to the River Weaver Trust, and among the improvements he made was the introduction of the Anderton barge lift linking the Weaver and the Trent and Mersey Canal. After rejecting the proposal of a flight of locks he considered that barges might be lifted and lowered by hydraulic means. Various designs were submitted and the final choice fell on one by Edwin **Clark** that had two troughs counterbalancing each other through pistons. Movement of the troughs was initiated by introducing excess water into the upper trough to lift the lower. The work was carried out by Clark.

In 1872 Williams became Engineer to the Bridgewater Navigation, enlarging the locks at Runcorn and introducing steam propulsion on the canal. He later examined the possibility of upgrading the Mersey & Irwell Navigation to a

Ship Canal. In 1882 his proposals to the Provisional Committee of the proposed Manchester Ship Canal were accepted. His scheme was to use the Mersey Channel as far as Eastham and then construct a lock canal from there to Manchester. He was appointed Chief Engineer of the undertaking.

The canal's construction was a major engineering work during which Williams overcame many difficulties. He used the principle of the troughs on the Anderton lift as a guide for the construction of the Barton swing aqueduct, which replaced **Brindley**'s original masonry aqueduct on the Bridgewater Canal. The first sod was cut at Eastham on 11 November 1887 and the lower portion of the canal was used for traffic in September 1891. The canal was opened to sea-borne traffic on 1 January 1894 and was formally opened by Queen Victoria on 21 May 1894. In acknowledgement of his work, a knighthood was conferred on him. He continued as Consulting Engineer until ill health forced his retirement.

Principal Honours and Distinctions
Knighted. Vice-President, Institution of Civil Engineers 1905–7.

JHB

Williams, Sir Frederic Calland

b. 26 June 1911 Stockport, Cheshire, England
d. 11 August 1977 Prestbury, Cheshire, England

English electrical engineer who invented the Williams storage cathode ray tube, which was extensively used worldwide as a data memory in the first digital computers.

Following education at Stockport Grammar School, Williams entered Manchester University in 1929, gaining his BSc in 1932 and MSc in 1933. After a short time as a college apprentice with Metropolitan Vickers, he went to Magdalen College, Oxford, to study for a DPhil, which he was awarded in 1936. He returned to Manchester University that year as an assistant lecturer, gaining his DSc in 1939. Following the outbreak of the Second World War he worked for the Scientific Civil Service, initially at the Bawdsey Research Station and then at the Telecommunications Research Establishment at Malvern, Worcestershire. There he was involved in research on non-incandescent amplifiers and diode rectifiers and the development of the first practical radar system capable of identifying friendly aircraft. Later in the war, he devised an automatic radar system suitable for use by fighter aircraft.

After the war he resumed his academic career at Manchester, becoming Professor of Electrical Engineering and Director of the University Electrotechnical Laboratory in 1946. In the same year he succeeded in developing a data-memory device based on the cathode ray tube, in which the information was stored and read by electron-beam scanning of a charge-retaining target. The Williams storage tube, as it became known, not only found obvious later use as a means of storing single-frame, still television images but proved to be a vital component of the pioneering Manchester University *MkI* digital computer. Because it enabled both data and program instructions to be stored in the computer, it was soon used worldwide in the development of the early stored-program computers.

Principal Honours and Distinctions
Knighted 1976. OBE 1945. CBE 1961. FRS 1950. Hon. DSc Durham 1964, Sussex 1971, Wales 1971. First Royal Society of Arts Benjamin Franklin Medal 1957. City of Philadelphia John Scott Award 1960. Royal Society Hughes Medal 1963. Institution of Electrical Engineers Faraday Medal 1972. Institute of Electrical and Electronics Engineers Pioneer Award 1973.

Bibliography
Williams contributed papers to many scientific journals, including *Proceedings of the Royal Society, Proceedings of the Cambridge Philosophical Society, Journal of the Institution of Electrical Engineers, Proceedings of the Institution of Mechanical Engineers, Wireless Engineer, Post Office Electrical Engineers' Journal.* Note especially:
1948, with J. Kilburn, 'Electronic digital computers', *Nature* 162: 487;
1949, with J. Kilburn, 'A storage system for use with binary digital computing machines', *Proceedings of the Institution of Electrical Engineers* 96: 81;
1975, 'Early computers at Manchester University', *Radio & Electronic Engineer* 45: 327.
Williams also collaborated in the writing of vols 19 and 20 of the *MIT Radiation Laboratory Series.*

Further Reading
B. Randell, 1973, *The Origins of Digital Computers*, Berlin: Springer-Verlag.
M.R. Williams, 1985, *A History of Computing Technology*, London: Prentice-Hall.

See also: **Stibitz, George R.**; **Strachey, Christopher**.

KF

Williams, Thomas
b. 13 May 1737 Cefn Coch, Anglesey, Wales
d. 29 November 1802 Bath, England

Welsh lawyer, mine-owner and industrialist.

Williams was articled by his father, Owen Williams of Treffos in Anglesey, to the prominent Flintshire lawyer John Lloyd, whose daughter Catherine he is believed to have married. By 1769 Williams, lessee of the mansion and estate of Llanidan, was an able lawyer with excellent connections in Anglesey. His life changed dramatically when he agreed to act on behalf of the Lewis and Hughes families of Llysdulas, who had begun a lawsuit against Sir Nicholas Bayly of Plas Newydd concerning the ownership and mineral rights of copper mines on the western side of Parys mountain. During a prolonged period of litigation, Williams managed these mines for Margaret Lewis on behalf of Edward Hughes, who was established after a judgement in Chancery in 1776 as one of two legal proprietors, the other being Nicholas Bayly. The latter then decided to lease his portion to the London banker John Dawes, who in 1778 joined Hughes and Thomas Williams when they founded the Parys Mine Company.

As the active partner in this enterprise, Williams began to establish his own smelting and fabricating works in South Wales, Lancashire and Flintshire, where coal was cheap. He soon broke the power of Associated Smelters, a combine holding the Anglesey mine owners to ransom. The low production cost of Anglesey ore gave him a great advantage over the Cornish mines and he secured very profitable contracts for the copper sheathing of naval and other vessels. After several British and French copper-bottomed ships were lost because of corrosion failure of the iron nails and bolts used to secure the sheathing, Williams introduced a process for manufacturing heavily work-hardened copper bolts and spikes which could be substituted directly for iron fixings, avoiding the corrosion difficulty. His new product was adopted by the Admiralty in 1784 and was soon used extensively in British and European dockyards.

In 1785 Williams entered into partnership with Lord Uxbridge, son and heir of Nicholas Bayly, to run the Mona Mine Company at the Eastern end of Parys Mountain. This move ended much enmity and litigation and put Williams in effective control of all Anglesey copper. In the same year, Williams, with Matthew **Boulton** and John **Wilkinson**, persuaded the Cornish miners to establish a trade cooperative, the Cornish Metal Company, to market their ores. When this began to fall in 1787, Williams took over its administration, assets and stocks and until 1792 controlled the output and sale of all British copper. He became known as the 'Copper King' and the output of his many producers was sold by the Copper Offices he established in London, Liverpool and Birmingham. In 1790 he became Member of Parliament for the borough of Great Marlow, and in 1792 he and Edward Hughes established the Chester and North Wales Bank, which in 1900 was absorbed by the Lloyds group.

After 1792 the output of the Anglesey mines started to decline and Williams began to buy copper from all available sources. The price of copper rose and he was accused of abusing his monopoly. By this time, however, his health had begun to deteriorate and he retreated to Bath.

Further Reading
J.R. Harris, 1964, *The 'Copper King'*, Liverpool University Press.

ASD

Williamson, David Theodore Nelson
b. 15 February 1923 Edinburgh, Scotland
d. 1992 Italy

Scottish engineer, inventor of the Williamson Amplifier and computer-controlled machine tools.

D.T.N. Williamson was educated at George Heriot's School, Edinburgh, and studied mechanical engineering at the University of Edinburgh and electrical engineering at Heriot-Watt College (now Heriot-Watt University), Edinburgh. He joined the MO Valve Company in London in

1943 and worked in his spare time on improving the sound reproduction for gramophones, and in 1946 invented the 'Williamson Amplifier'.

That same year Williamson returned to Edinburgh as a development engineer with **Ferranti** Ltd, where he was employed in developing computer-controlled machining systems. In 1961 he was appointed Director of Research and Development at Molins Ltd, where he continued work on computer-controlled machine tools. He invented the Molins System 24, which employed a number of machine tools, all under computer control, and is generally acknowledged as a significant step in the development of manufacturing systems. In 1974 he joined Rank Xerox and became Director of Research before taking early retirement to live in Italy. Between 1954 and 1979 he served on numerous committees relating to computer-aided design, manufacturing technology and mechanical engineering in general.

Principal Honours and Distinctions
FRS 1968.

Bibliography
Williamson was author of several papers and articles, and contributed to the *Electronic Engineers' Reference Book* (1959), *Progress in Automation* (1960) and the *Numerical Control Handbook* (1968).

RTS

Wilson, Percy
b. 8 March 1893 Halifax, Yorkshire, England
d. May 1977

English engineer and technical writer who developed geometries for pick-arms and reproducing horns.

He graduated from The Queen's College with a BA in 1915 and an MA in 1918. He was an instructor and lecturer in the Royal Navy in 1915–19. He became an administrative officer with the Board of Education until 1938, and continued his work in the British Civil Service in the Ministry of Transport until 1949. From 1924 to 1938 he was Technical Adviser, and from 1953 Technical Editor, with *Gramophone*, a publication catering for the record- and equipment-buying public. He brought a mathematical mind to the problems of gramophone reproduction and

solved the geometrical problem of obtaining a reasonable approximation to tangential tracking across the surface of a record even though the soundbox (or pick-up) is carried by a pivoted arm. Later he tackled the problem of horns, determining that a modified exponential horn, even with a bent axis, would give optimal reproduction by a purely acoustic system. This development was used commercially during the 1930s. Wilson was for a time a member of the School Broadcasting Council and developed methods for improving subjective listening tests for evaluation of audio equipment. He was also deeply involved in the long-playing record system used for Talking Books for the Blind. He had a life-long interest in spiritualist matters and was President of the Spiritualist National Union from 1950 to 1953 and Chairman of the Psychic Press from 1951.

Bibliography
1929, with G.W. Webb, *Modern Gramophones and Electrical Reproducers*, London: Cassell (the first book to draw the consequences of the recent development of electronic filter theory for the interpretation of record wear).

Further Reading
G.A. Briggs (ed.), 1961, *Audio Biographies*, Wharfedale Wireless Works, pp. 326–34.

GB-N

Wilson, Robert
b. September 1803 Dunbar, Haddingtonshire, East Lothian, Scotland
d. 28 July 1882 Matlock, Derbyshire, England

Scottish mechanical engineer and inventor who developed the self-acting control gear applied to the steam-hammer.

Robert Wilson was the son of a fisherman who was drowned in a lifeboat rescue attempt in December 1810. He received only a meagre education and was apprenticed to a joiner. From a very early age he was much concerned with the idea of applying screw propellers to ships, and his invention was approved by the Highland Society and by the Scottish Society of Arts, who in 1832 awarded him a silver medal. He must have gained some experience as a mechanic and while working on his invention he made the acquaintance of James **Nasmyth**. In 1838 he became Works

Manager at Nasmyth's Bridgewater Foundry and made an important contribution to the success of the steam-hammer by developing the self-acting control gear. From 1845 he was with the Low Moor Ironworks near Bradford, Yorkshire, but in July 1856 he returned to the Bridgewater Foundry so that he was able to take over as Managing Partner after Nasmyth's early retirement at the end of 1856. In 1867 the name of the firm was changed to Nasmyth, Wilson & Co., and Wilson remained a partner until May 1882, when the firm became a limited company. Wilson often returned to his first invention, and two of his many patents related to improvements in screw propellers. In 1880 he received £500 from the War Department for the use of his double-action screw propeller as applied to the torpedo.

Principal Honours and Distinctions
Member, Institution of Mechanical Engineers 1857. FRSE 1873. Member, Royal Scottish Society of Arts.

Bibliography
1860, *The Screw Propeller: Who Invented It?*, Glasgow.

Further Reading
J.A. Cantrell, 1984, *James Nasmyth and the Bridgewater Foundry*, Manchester, Appendix F, pp. 262–3 (a short biographical account and a list of his patents).

RTS

Wilson, Thomas
b. 1781 Dunbar, Scotland
d. 1 December 1873 Grangemouth, Scotland

Scottish shipwright and canal engineer, builder of the barge Vulcan, the world's first properly constructed iron ship.

Wilson, the son of a sailor, spent his early years on the Forth. Later his father moved home to the west and Wilson served his apprenticeship as a shipwright on the Clyde at the small shipyards of Bowling, fifteen miles (24 km) west of Glasgow and on the river's north bank. In his late thirties Wilson was to take the leading role in what is arguably the most important development in Scotland's distinguished shipbuilding history: the building of the world's first properly constructed iron ship. This ship, the *Vulcan*, was the

culmination of several years' effort by a group of people well connected within the academic establishment of Scotland. The Forth and Clyde Canal Company had passed instructions for investigations to be made into reducing running expenses and a distinguished committee looked into this matter. They included John Robison (Secretary of the Royal Society of Edinburgh), Professor Joseph Black of Glasgow University, James **Watt** and John **Schanck**. After a period of consideration it was decided to build a new, fast-passage barge of iron, and tenders were invited from several appropriate contractors. Wilson, with the assistance of two blacksmiths, John and Thomas Smellie, was awarded the work, and the *Vulcan* was constructed and ultimately launched at Faskine near Glasgow in 1819. The work involved was far beyond the comprehension of engineers of the twentieth century, as Wilson had to arrange puddled-iron plates for the shell and hand-crafted angle irons for the frames. His genius is now apparent as every steel ship worldwide uses a form of construction literally 'hammered out on the anvil' between 1818 and 1819. The *Vulcan* was almost 64 ft (19.5 m) in length and 11 ft (3.4 m) broad. In 1822 Wilson was appointed an inspector of works for the Canal Company, and ultimately he superintended the building of the docks at Grangemouth, where he died in 1873, the same year that the *Vulcan* was broken up.

Further Reading
R. Harvey, 1919, *Early Days of Engineering in Glasgow*, Glasgow: Aird and Coghill.
F.M. Walker, 1989–90, 'Early iron shipbuilding. A reappraisal of the *Vulcan* and other pioneer vessels', *Transactions of the Institution of Engineers and Shipbuilders in Scotland* 133: 21–34.

FMW

Winans, Ross
b. 17 October 1796 Sussex County, New Jersey, USA
d. 11 April 1877 Baltimore, Maryland, USA

American inventor and locomotive builder.

Winans arrived in Baltimore in 1828 to sell horses to the Baltimore & Ohio Railroad (B & O), which was then under construction. To reduce friction in rail vehicles, he devised a system of axles which ran in oil-baths, with outside bearings. He demonstrated a hand-driven wagon with this system at the Rainhill Trials; the Liverpool & Manchester Railway bought some wagons fitted with the system, but found them on test to be inferior to wagons with grease axle boxes. Back in Baltimore, Winans assisted Peter **Cooper** in building *Tom Thumb*. He took charge of the B & O shops *c.*1834; he is said to have built the first eight-wheeled passenger coach and to have been the first to mount such a coach on two four-wheeled trucks or bogies. The arrangement soon became standard American practice, and, with partners, he built over 100 locomotives for the B & O. In 1847 he pioneered the use of anthracite as locomotive fuel, and from 1848 he built his 'Camel' locomotives with the driver's cab above the boiler.

Further Reading

J.H. White Jr, 1979, *A History of the American Locomotive – Its Development: 1830–1880*, New York: Dover Publications Inc.

P. Ransome-Wallis (ed.), 1959, *The Concise Encyclopaedia of World Railway Locomotives*, London: Hutchinson, p. 503 (biography).

Dictionary of American Biography.

H. Booth, 1980, *Henry Booth*, Ilfracombe: Arthur H. Stockwell, pp. 75 and 91–2 (for the Liverpool & Manchester wagons).

See also **Stephenson, George**.

PJGR

Winsor, Frederick Albert

b. 1763 Brunswick, Germany
d. 11 May 1830 Paris, France

German pioneer of gas lighting.

He was born Frederic Albrecht Winzer but anglicized his name after settling in England. His interest in gas lighting was aroused by the experiments of Philippe **Lebon** in Paris in 1802. Winsor had little scientific knowledge or engineering ability, but was well endowed with confidence and enterprise. He alone among the early practitioners of gas-making envisaged a central plant supplying a number of users through gas mains. He managed to discover the essentials of Lebon's process and tried without success to exploit it on the European continent. So he moved to England in 1803 and settled first in Grosvenor Square and then in Pall Mall. He gave public

demonstrations of gas lighting at the Lyceum Theatre in London and in 1804 took out his first patent. In December he lit Pall Mall, the first street to be illuminated by gas. Winsor then began to promote a grandiose scheme for the formation of a National Light and Heat Company. He struggled against bitter opposition both in and out of Parliament to obtain sanction for his company, and it was only after the third attempt that the Gas Light & Coke Company received its charter in 1812. However, Winsor lacked the knowledge to devise successful gas-producing plant, even with the help of the German immigrant chemist F.C. Accum. Winsor was dismissed in 1812 and returned to Paris the following year, while the company recovered with the appointment of an able engineer, Samuel **Clegg**. Winsor formed a company in Paris to install gas lighting, but that failed in 1819.

Further Reading

W. Matthew, 1827, *An Historical Sketch of the Origin, Progress and Present State of Gaslighting*, London.

E.G. Stewart, 1958, *Town Gas, Its Manufacture and Distribution*, London: Science Museum.

LRD

Wirth, Niklaus

fl. late 1960s Zurich, Switzerland

Swiss computer engineer noted for his development of the high-level computer language PASCAL.

For many years Wirth was Professor of Computing Science at Zurich Federal Polytechnic School. In 1969, seeking a high-level computer language suitable for teaching programming as a systematic activity, he invented PASCAL, which is now widely used with personal computers (PCs). Unlike BASIC, which is checked and run a line at a time, PASCAL programs are compiled (i.e. they are fully checked for consistency) before they are actually run.

Principal Honours and Distinctions

Institute of Electrical and Electronics Engineers Emanuel R. Piore Award 1983.

Bibliography

1971, 'The programming language PASCAL', *Acta Informatica* 1: 35.

Further Reading
R.L. Wexelblat (ed.), 1981, *History of Programming Languages*, London: Academic Press.

See also **Kemeny, John G.**; **Kurtz, Thomas E.**

KF

Wöhler, August

b. 22 June 1819 Soltau, Germany
d. 21 June 1914 Hannover, Germany

German railway engineer who first established the fatigue fracture of metals.

Wöhler, the son of a schoolteacher, was born at Soltau on the Luneburg Heath and received his early education at his father's school, where his mathematical abilities soon became apparent. He completed his studies at the Technical High School, Hannover.

In 1840 he obtained a position at the Borsig Engineering Works in Berlin and acquired there much valuable experience in railway technology. He trained as an engine driver in Belgium and in 1843 was appointed as an engineer to the first Hannoverian Railway, then being constructed between Hannover and Lehrte. In 1847 he became Chief Superintendent of rolling stock on the Lower Silesian–Brandenburg Railway, where his technical abilities influenced the Prussian Minister of Commerce to appoint him to a commission set up to investigate the reasons for the unusually high incidence of axle failures then being encountered on the railways. This was in 1852, and by 1854, when the Brandenburg line had been nationalized, Wöhler had already embarked on the long, systematic programme of mechanical testing which eventually provided him with a clear insight into the process of what is now referred to as 'fatigue failure'. He concentrated initially on the behaviour of machined iron and steel specimens subjected to fluctuating direct, bending and torsional stresses that were imposed by testing machines of his own design.

Although Wöhler was not the first investigator in this area, he was the first to recognize the state of 'fatigue' induced in metals by the repeated application of cycles of stress at levels well below those that would cause immediate failure. His method of plotting the fatigue stress amplitude 'S' against the number of stress cycles necessary to cause failure 'N' yielded the well-known S–N curve which described very precisely the susceptibility to fatigue failure of the material concerned. Engineers were thus provided with an invaluable testing technique that is still widely used in the 1990s.

Between 1851 and 1898 Wöhler published forty-two papers in German technical journals, although the importance of his work was not initially fully appreciated in other countries. A display of some of his fracture fatigue specimens at the Paris Exposition in 1867, however, stimulated a short review of his work in *Engineering* in London. Four years later, in 1871, *Engineering* published a series of nine articles which described Wöhler's findings in considerable detail and brought them to the attention of engineers. Wöhler became a member of the newly created management board of the Imperial German Railways in 1874, an appointment that he retained until 1889. He is also remembered for his derivation in 1855 of a formula for calculating the deflections under load of lattice girders, plate girders, and other continuous beams resting on more than two supports. This 'Three Moments' theorem appeared two years before Clapeyron independently advanced the same expression. Wöhler's other major contribution to bridge design was to use rollers at one end to allow for thermal expansion and contraction.

Bibliography
1855, 'Theorie rechteckiger eiserner Brückenbalken', *Zeitschrift für Bauwesen* 5: 122–66.
1870, 'Über die Festigkeitsversuche mit Eisen und Stahl', *Zeitschrift für Bauwesen* 20: 73–106.
Wöhler's experiments on the fatigue of metals were reported in *Engineering* (1867) 2: 160; (1871) 11: 199–200, 222, 243–4, 261, 299–300, 326–7, 349–50, 397, 439–41.

Further Reading
R. Blaum, 1918, 'August Wöhler', *Beiträge zur Geschichte der Technik und Industrie* 8: 35–55.
—— 1925, 'August Wöhler', *Deutsches biographisches Jahrbuch*, Vol. I, Stuttgart, pp. 103–7.
K. Pearson, 1890, 'On Wöhler's experiments on alternating stress', *Messeng. Math.* 20: 21–37.
J. Gilchrist, 1900, 'On Wöhler's Laws', *Engineer* 90: 203–4.

ASD

Wolf, Carl

b. 23 December 1838 Zwickau, Saxony, Germany
d. 30 January 1915 Zwickau, Saxony, Germany

German inventor of the most popular petroleum spirit safety lamp for use in mines.

From an old mining family in the Saxon coalfields, Wolf was aware from his youth of the urgent demand for a miner's lamp which would provide adequate light but not provoke firedamp explosions. While working as an engineer in Zwickau, Wolf spent his spare time conducting experiments for such a lamp. The basic concept of his invention was the principle that dangerous concentrations of methane and air would not explode within a small pipe; this had been established almost seventy years earlier by the English chemist Humphrey **Davy**. By combining and developing certain devices designed by earlier inventors, in 1883 Wolf produced a prototype with a glass cylinder, a primer fixed inside the lamp and a magnetic lock. Until the successful application of electric light, Wolf's invention was the safest and most popular mining safety lamp. Many earlier inventions had failed to address all the problems of lighting for mines; Davy's lamp, for example, would too quickly become sooty and hot. As Wolf's lamp burned petroleum spirit, at first it was mistrusted outside Saxony, but it successfully passed the safety tests in all the leading coal-producing countries at that time. As well as casting a safe, constant light, the appearance of the cap flame could indicate the concentration of fire-damp in the air, thus providing an additional safety measure. Wolf's first patent was soon followed by many others in several countries, and underwent many developments. In 1884 Heinrich Friemann, a merchant from Eisleben, invested capital in the new company of Friemann and Wolf, which became the leading producer of miners' safety lamps. By 1914 they had manufactured over one million lamps, and the company had branches in major mining districts worldwide.

Further Reading

F. Schwarz, 1914, *Entwickelung und gegenwärtiger Stand der Grubenbeleuchtung beim Steinkohlen-Bergbau*, Gelsenkirchen (a systematic historical outline of safety lamp designs).

WK

Wollaston, William Hyde

b. 6 August 1766 East Dereham, Norfolk, England
d. 22 December 1828 London, England

English chemist and metallurgist who discovered palladium and rhodium, pioneer in the fabrication of platinum.

Wollaston qualified in medicine at Cambridge University but gave up his practice in 1800 to devote himself to chemistry and metallurgy, funded from the profits from making malleable platinum. In partnership with Smithson Tennant, a friend from his Cambridge days, he worked on the extraction of platinum by dissolving it in aqua regia. In 1802 he found that in addition to platinum the solution contained a new metal, which he named palladium. Two years later he identified another new metal, rhodium.

Wollaston developed a method of forming platinum by means of powder metallurgy and was the first to produce malleable and ductile platinum on a commercial scale. He produced platinum vessels for sulphuric acid manufacture and scientific apparatus such as crucibles. He devised an elegant method for forming fine platinum wire. He also applied his inventive talents to improving scientific apparatus, including the sextant and microscope and a reflecting goniometer for measuring crystal angles. In 1807 he was appointed Joint Secretary of the Royal Society with Sir Humphry **Davy**, which entailed a heavy workload and required them to referee all the papers submitted to the Society for publication.

Wollaston's output of platinum began to decline after 1822. Due to ill health he ceased business operations in 1828 and at last made public the details of his secret platinum fabrication process. It was fully described in the Bakerian Lecture he delivered to the Royal Society on 28 November 1828, shortly before his death.

Principal Honours and Distinctions

FRS 1793.

Bibliography

His scientific papers were published in various journals, nearly all listed in the *Royal Society Catalogue of Scientific Papers*.

Further Reading
There is no good general biography, the best
   general account being the entry in *Dictionary
   of Scientific Biography*.
D. McDonald, 1960, *A History of Platinum from
   the Earliest Times to the Eighteen-Eighties*, London (provides a good discussion of his work on
   platinum).
M.E. Weeks, 1939, 'The discovery of the elements',
   Journal of Chemical Education: 184–5.

ASD

Wolseley, Frederick York

b. 1837 Co. Dublin, Ireland
d. 1899 England

*Irish inventor who developed the first practical
sheep shears and was also involved in the
development of the car which bore his name.*

The credit for the first design of sheep shears lies
with James Higham, who patented the idea in
1868. However, its practical and commercial
success lay in the work of a number of people, to
each of whom Frederick Wolseley provides the
connecting link.

   One of three brothers, he emigrated to Australia in 1854 and worked in New South Wales
for five years. In 1867 he produced a working
model of mechanical sheep shears, but it took a
further five years before he actually produced a
machine, whilst working as Manager of a sheep
station in Victoria. In the intervening period it is
possible that he visited America and Britain. On
returning to Australia in 1872 he and Robert
Savage produced another working model in a
workshop in Melbourne. Four years later, by
which time Wolseley had acquired the 'Euroka'
sheep station at Walgett, they tested the model
and in 1877 acquired joint patent rights. The
machine was not successful, and in 1884 another
joint patent, this time with Robert Pickup, was
taken out on a cog-gear universal joint. Development was to take several more years, during
which a highly skilled blacksmith by the name of
George Gray joined the team. It is likely that he
was the first person to remove a fleece from a
sheep mechanically. Finally, the last to be involved in the development of the shears was another Englishman, John Howard, who
emigrated to Australia in 1883 with the intention of developing a shearing machine based on
his knowledge of existing horse clippers. Wolse-

ley purchased Howard's patent rights and gave
him a job. The first public demonstration of the
shears was held at the wool stores of Goldsbo-
rough & Co. of Melbourne. Although the hand
shearers were faster, when the three sheep that
had been clipped by them were re-shorn using
the mechanical machine, a further 2 lb (900 g)
of wool was removed.

   Wolseley placed the first manufacturing order
with A.P. Parks, who employed a young Englishman by the name of Herbert **Austin**. A number
of improvements to the design were suggested
by Austin, who acquired patents and assigned
them to Wolseley in 1895 in return for shares in
the company. Austin returned to England to run
the Wolseley factory in Birmingham. He also
built there the first car to carry the Wolseley
name, and subsequently opened a car factory
carrying his own name.

   Wolseley resigned as Managing Director of
the company in 1894 and died five years later.

Further Reading
F. Wheelhouse, 1966, *Digging Stock to Rotary
   Hoe: Men and Machines in Rural Australia*
   (provides a detailed account of Wolseley's developments).

AP

Wood, Henry Alexander Wise

b. 1 March 1866 New York, USA
d. 9 April 1939 USA

*American manufacturer and inventor of
printing machinery, including a stereotype
casting machine.*

The son of a Congressman and mayor of New
York, Wood was educated at Media Academy in
Pennsylvania, specializing in scientific subjects.
The death of his father in 1881 prevented his
going on to college and he went to work at the
Campbell Printing and Manufacturing Com-
pany, of which he became President in 1896. In
the meantime, he had married the daughter of
J.L. Brower, the previous head of the company.
Later business consolidations brought into being
the Wood Newspaper Machine Corporation.

   Wood was responsible for a series of inventions
that brought great benefit to the newspaper-
printing processes. Most notable was the Auto-
plate, patented first in 1900 and finally in 1903.
This enabled a whole page of newspaper type to

767

be cast in metal at once, saving much time and effort in the forming of stereotypes; this invention earned him the Elliott Cresson gold medal of the Franklin Institute in 1909. Other inventions were the Autoreel, a high-speed press-feeder device, and the Autopaster, which automatically replaced a spent paper roll with a new one in a newspaper press, without the need to stop the press. Wood's improved presses and inventions increased the speed of newspaper production from 24,000 to 60,000 copies per hour, printed and folded.

He was also much interested in aviation and was an early member of the Aero Club of America, becoming its Vice-President for six years. He helped to found the magazine *Flying* and was its Editor from 1911 to 1919. He had predicted the part played by aircraft and submarines during the Second World War and was invited to join a panel of consulting inventors and engineers to assist the development of the US Navy. He was soon at odds with the authorities, however, and he resigned in 1915. After the war, he spent time in vigorous campaigning against immigration, America's entry into the League of Nations and on many other issues, in all of which he was highly controversial. Nevertheless, he retained his interest in the newspaper-machinery business, remaining President of his company until 1935 and Chairman of the Board thereafter. In 1934 he became Chairman of the NRA Code Authority of the newspaper-machine industry.

Further Reading
Obituary, 1939, *New York Times* (10 April).
Obituary, 1939, *New York Herald Tribune* (10 April).

LRD

Woodbury, Walter Bentley
b. 1834 Manchester, England
d. 1885 Margate, Kent, England

English photographer, inventor of the Woodburytype process.

Having been apprenticed to be an engineer, Woodbury left England in 1851 to seek his fortune in the Australian gold-fields. Like many others, he failed, and after a series of transient jobs found a post as Draughtsman at the Melbourne Waterworks. He then went on to Java,

where he practised wet-collodion photography before returning to England finally in 1863. Woodbury settled in Birmingham, where like most contemporary photographers he was concerned to find a solution to the troublesome problem of fading prints. He began working the carbon process, and in 1866 and 1867 took out a series of patents which were to lead to the development of the process that took his name. Woodburytypes were continuous-tone prints of high quality that could be mass produced more cheaply than the traditional silver print. This was an important innovation and Woodburytypes were extensively used for quality book illustrations until the introduction of more versatile photomechanical processes in the 1890s. In all, Woodbury took out twenty patents between 1864 and 1884, some relating to a wide range of photographic devices. He was still working to simplify the Woodburytype process when he died from an overdose of laudanum.

Bibliography
Woodbury took out a series of patents on his process, the most significant being:
23 September 1864, British patent no. 2,338;
12 January 1866, British patent no. 105;
11 February 1866, British patent no. 505;
8 May 1866, British patent no. 1,315;
24 July 1866, British patent no. 1,918.

Further Reading
G. Tissandier, 1876, *A History and Handbook of Photography*, trans. J. Thomson.
B.E. Jones (ed.), 1911, *Cassell's Cyclopaedia of Photography*, London (a brief biography).
J.M. Eder, 1945, *History of Photography*, trans. E. Epstean, New York.

JW

Woods, Granville
b. 1856 Columbus, Ohio, USA
d. 1919 New York (?), USA

African-American inventor of electrical equipment.

He was first apprenticed in Columbus as a machinist and blacksmith. In 1872 he moved to Missouri, where he was engaged as a fireman and then engine-driver on the Iron Mountain Railroad. In his spare time he devoted much time to the study of electrical engineering. In 1878 he went to sea for two years as engineer on a British vessel. He returned to Ohio, taking up his previous occupation as engine-driver, and in 1884 he achieved his first patent, for a locomotive firebox. However, the drive towards things electrical was too strong and he set up the Woods Electric Company in Cincinnati, Ohio, to develop and market electrical inventions. Woods gained some fame as an inventor and became known as the 'black **Edison**'. His first device, a telephone transmitter, was patented in December 1884 but faced stiff competition from similar inventions by Alexander Graham **Bell** and others. The following year he patented a device for transmitting messages in **Morse** code or by voice that was valuable enough to be bought up by the Bell Telephone Company. A stream of inventions followed, particularly for railway telegraph and electrical systems. This brought him into conflict with Edison, who was working in the same field. The US Patent Office ruled in Woods's favour; as a result of the ensuing publicity, one newspaper hailed Woods as the 'greatest electrician in the world'. In 1890 Woods moved to New York, where the opportunities for an electrical engineer seemed more favourable. He turned his attention to inventions that would improve the tramcar. One device enabled electric current to be transferred to the car with less friction than previously, incorporating a grooved wheel known as a 'troller', whence came the popular term 'trolley car'.

Further Reading

P.P. James, 1989, *The Real McCoy: African-American Invention and Innovation 1619–1930*, Washington, DC: Smithsonian Institution, pp. 94–5.

LRD

Woolrich, John Stephen

b. 1821 Birmingham, England
d. 27 February 1850 King's Norton, England

English chemist who found in the electroplating process one of the earliest commercial applications of the magneto-electric generator.

The son of a Birmingham chemist, Woolrich was educated at King Edward's Grammar School, Birmingham, and later became a lecturer in chemistry. As an alternative to primary cells for the supply of current for electroplating, he de-

vised a magneto generator. His original machine had a single compound permanent magnet; the distance between the revolving armature and the magnet could be varied to adjust the rate of deposition of metal. A more ambitious machine designed by Woolrich was constructed by Thomas Prime & Sons in 1844 and for many years was used at their Birmingham electroplating works. **Faraday**, on a visit to see the machine at work, is said to have expressed delight at his discovery of electromagnetic induction being put to practical use so soon. Similar machines were in use by Elkington's, Fern and others in Birmingham and Sheffield. One of Woolrich's machines is preserved in the Birmingham Science Museum.

Bibliography

1 August 1842, British patent no. 9,431 (the electroplating process; describes the magnetic apparatus and the electroplating chemicals).

Further Reading

1843, *Mechanics Magazine* 38: 145–9 (fully describes the Woolrich machine).
1889, *The Electrician* 23: 548 (a short account of a surviving Woolrich machine constructed in 1844 and its subsequent history).
S. Timmins, 1866, *Birmingham and the Midland Hardware District*, London, pp. 488–94.

GW

Worcester, 2nd Marquis of
See **Somerset, Edward**.

Worsdell, Nathaniel

b. 10 October 1809 London, England
d. 24 July 1886 Birkenhead, England

English coachbuilder and inventor.

Worsdell & Son, Coachbuilders, was set up in Liverpool by Thomas Clarke Worsdell and his son Nathaniel in 1827. They were introduced to George **Stephenson** and built the tender for *Rocket*. More importantly, they designed and built for the Liverpool & Manchester Railway coaches of a type comprising three coach bodies, of contemporary road-coach pattern, mounted together on a rail-wagon underframe. This became the prototype for the conventional, compartment railway coach. Nathaniel Worsdell subsequently became Carriage Superintendent of the Grand Junction Railway and patented the first mail-bag-exchange apparatus early in 1838. The terms he required for its use by the Post Office were too steep, however, and the first bag-exchange apparatus of the type subsequently used extensively on British railways was designed later the same year by John Ramsey, a senior Post Office clerk.

Further Reading

J. Marshall, 1978, *A Biographical Dictionary of Railway Engineers*, Newton Abbot: David & Charles (the article on Worsdell is derived from family records).

C. Hamilton Ellis, 1958, *Twenty Locomotive Men*, Shepperton: Ian Allan.

P.J.G. Ransom, 1990, *The Victorian Railway and How It Evolved*, London: Heinemann.

PJGR

Worsdell, Thomas William

b. 14 January 1838 Liverpool, England
d. 28 June 1916 Arnside, Westmorland, England

English locomotive engineer, pioneer of the use of two-cylinder compound locomotives in Britain.

T.W. Worsdell was the son of Nathaniel **Worsdell**. After varied training, which included some time in the drawing office of the London & North Western Railway's Crewe Works, he moved to the Pennsylvania Railroad, USA, in 1865 and shortly became Master Mechanic in charge of its locomotive workshops in Altoona. In 1871, however, he accepted an invitation from F.W. **Webb** to return to Crewe as Works Manager: it was while he was there that Webb produced his first compound locomotive by re-building an earlier simple.

In 1881 T.W. Worsdell was appointed Locomotive Superintendent of the Great Eastern Railway. Working with August von Borries, who was Chief Mechanical Engineer of the Hannover Division of the Prussian State Railways, he developed a two-cylinder compound derived from the work of J.T.A. **Mallet**. Von Borries produced his compound 2–4–0 in 1880, Worsdell followed with a 4–4–0 in 1884; the restricted British loading gauge necessitated substitution of inside cylinders for the outside cylinders used by von Borries, particularly the large low-pressure one. T.W. Worsdell's compounds were on the whole successful and many were built, particularly on

the North Eastern Railway, to which he moved as Locomotive Superintendent in 1885. There, in 1888, he started to build, uniquely, two-cylinder compound 'single driver' 4–2–2s: one of them was recorded as reaching 86 mph (138 km/h). He also equipped his locomotives with a large side-window cab, which gave enginemen more protection from the elements than was usual in Britain at that time and was no doubt appreciated in the harsh winter climate of northeast England. The idea for the cab probably originated from his American experience. When T.W. Worsdell retired from the North Eastern Railway in 1890 he was succeeded by his younger brother, Wilson Worsdell, who in 1899 introduced the first 4–6–0s intended for passenger trains in England.

Further Reading

C. Hamilton Ellis, 1958, *Twenty Locomotive Men*, Shepperton: Ian Allan, Ch. 15 (biography).

E.L. Ahrons, 1927, *The British Steam Railway Locomotive 1825–1925*, London: The Locomotive Publishing Co., pp. 253–5 (describes his locomotives).

C. Fryer, 1990, *Experiments with Steam*, Patrick Stephens, Ch. 7.

PJGR

Wozniak, Stephen G.

b. 1950 Sunnyvale, California, USA

American computer engineer who with Steven Jobs built the first home computer.

Bored by school at Sunnyvale, the young Wozniak became interested in computers and at the age of only 13 years he constructed a transistorized calculator that won a prize at the Bay Area Science Fair. After high school, he went to the University of Colorado, but he left the following year to study at the De Anza College in Cupertino, California, finally dropping out of formal education altogether and working as a programmer for a small computer company. In 1971 he made another attempt at studying for a degree in engineering, this time at the University of California at Berkeley, but he again dropped out and went to work for Hewlett–Packard, where he met 16-year-old Steve Jobs. Joining the Homebrew Computer Club, and with Jobs's help, he built a home computer based on the MOS Technology 8-bit, 6502 microprocessor chip. With 4 K of random access memory (RAM) and the first BASIC interpreter written by Wozniak himself, he demonstrated the computer to Hewlett–Packard management, but they showed little interest in taking it up. With Jobs he therefore founded Apple Company, and with assembly in Jobs's home they found an interested buyer in the shape of Paul Terrill, owner of the newly established Byte Shop chain store, who ordered 100 boards at US$500 each. As a result, with the support of a backer, Mike Markkula, Wozniak in 1976 designed a second computer, the Apple II, which had 16 K of RAM and was offered for sale (without a monitor) at $1195. This was an immediate success and sales rose from $775,000 in 1977 to $335 million in 1981 and $983 million in 1983. In the meantime, however, Wozniak was seriously injured in a plane crash in 1980. He recovered slowly from his injuries and in 1982 returned to college to complete his degree course, after which he spent much of his time with his family. Eventually he became increasingly unhappy with the chaotic management at Apple, and he left the company in 1985, subsequently forming his own computer company, Cloud 9.

Principal Honours and Distinctions
First National Technology Medal (with Jobs) 1985.

Further Reading
M. Moritz, 1984, *The Little Kingdom. The Private Story of Apple Computers*.
J.S. Young, 1988, *Steve Jobs: The Journey is the Reward*: Scott Foreman & Co.

KF

Wratten, Frederick Charles Luther

b. 1840 England
d. 8 April 1926 London, England

English inventor and manufacturer, founder of one of the first successful gelatine dry-plate companies.

He started his working life as a schoolteacher, but in his early twenties he moved to London to become a clerk with a photographic wholesaler, Soloman. There Wratten became interested in photography, and on the announcement of the new gelatine dry-plate processes he began to conduct his own experiments. In 1876 he de-

vised a means of drying gelatine emulsions and removing excess silver with alcohol, and published details in 1877 and 1878. It was during this period that he formed a partnership with Henry Wainwright to manufacture and sell photographic materials. The mass production of gelatine dry plates was a British invention and monopoly, and the new firm of Wratten & Wainwright was one of the first in the field and soon proved to be amongst the most successful. The business exported extensively to Europe, introducing a succession of plates of increasing sensitivity. Wratten continued to trade under the same name when his partner Wainwright died in 1882. His success continued, and in 1890 he moved the company to a newly equipped factory in Croydon, near London. Six years later Wratten incorporated as co-owners of the business his son, S.H. Wainwright and a young graduate from London University, C.E. Kenneth **Mees**. The newly constituted company soon introduced the first British panchromatic plates and filters. The introduction of **Lumière**'s Autochrome plates in 1907 prompted Wratten and Mees to take out a patent on a colour screen plate process of their own. The company also found work coating plates for other similar innovations. In 1912 the business was finally sold to George **Eastman** and Wratten and Mees joined Kodak Ltd at Harrow.

Bibliography
Wratten's early work on the action of alcohol on gelatine emulsions was described in a series of articles:
1877, *Photographic News*: 390, 49.
1878, *Photographic News*: 121–3.
1878, *British Journal of Photography*: 124–5.

Further Reading
E.J. Wall, 1925, *Three Colour Photography*.
C.E.K. Mees, 1961, *From Dry Plates to Ektachrome Film*, New York.

JW

Wren, Sir Christopher

b. 20 October 1632 East Knoyle, Wiltshire, England
d. 25 February 1723 London, England

English architect whose background in scientific research and achievement enhanced his handling of many near-intractable architectural problems.

Born into a High Church and Royalist family, the young Wren early showed outstanding intellectual ability and at Oxford in 1654 was described as 'that miracle of a youth'. Educated at Westminster School, he went up to Oxford, where he graduated at the age of 19 and obtained his master's degree two years later. From this time onwards his interests were in science, primarily astronomy but also physics, engineering and meteorology. While still at college he developed theories about and experimentally solved some fifty varied problems. At the age of 25 Wren was appointed to the Chair of Astronomy at Gresham College in London, but he soon returned to Oxford as Savilian Professor of Astronomy there. At the same time he became one of the founder members of the Society of Experimental Philosophy at Oxford, which was awarded its Royal Charter soon after the Restoration of 1660; Wren, together with such men as Isaac Newton, Robert Hooke, John Evelyn and Robert Boyle, then found himself a member of the Royal Society.

Wren's architectural career began with the classical chapel that he built, at the request of his uncle, the Bishop of Ely, for Pembroke College, Cambridge (1663). From this time onwards, until he died at the age of 91, he was fully occupied with a wide and taxing variety of architectural problems which he faced in the execution of all the great building schemes of the day. His scientific background and inventive mind stood him in good stead in solving such difficulties with an often unusual approach and concept. Nowhere was this more apparent than in his rebuilding of fifty-one churches in the City of London after the Great Fire, in the construction of the new St Paul's Cathedral and in the grand layout of the Royal Hospital at Greenwich.

The first instance of Wren's approach to constructional problems was in his building of the Sheldonian Theatre in Oxford (1664–9). He based his design upon that of the Roman Theatre of Marcellus (13–11 BC), which he had studied from drawings in Serlio's book of architecture. Wren's reputation as an architect was greatly enhanced by his solution to the roofing problem here. The original theatre in Rome, like all

Roman theatres, was a circular building open to the sky; this would be unsuitable in the climate of Oxford and Wren wished to cover the English counterpart without using supporting columns, which would have obscured the view of the stage. He solved this difficulty mathematically, with the aid of his colleague Dr Wallis, the Professor of Geometry, by means of a timber-trussed roof supporting a painted ceiling which represented the open sky.

The City of London's churches were rebuilt over a period of nearly fifty years; the first to be completed and reopened was St Mary-at-Hill in 1676, and the last St Michael Cornhill in 1722, when Wren was 89. They had to be rebuilt upon the original medieval sites and they illustrate, perhaps more clearly than any other examples of Wren's work, the fertility of his imagination and his ability to solve the most intractable problems of site, limitation of space and variation in style and material. None of the churches is like any other. Of the varied sites, few are level or possess right-angled corners or parallel sides of equal length, and nearly all were hedged in by other, often larger, buildings. Nowhere is his versatility and inventiveness shown more clearly than in his designs for the steeples. There was no English precedent for a classical steeple, though he did draw upon the Dutch examples of the 1630s, because the London examples had been medieval, therefore Roman Catholic and Gothic, churches. Many of Wren's steeples are, therefore, Gothic steeples in classical dress, but many were of the greatest originality and delicate beauty: for example, St Mary-le-Bow in Cheapside; the 'wedding cake' St Bride in Fleet Street; and the temple diminuendo concept of Christ Church in Newgate Street.

In St Paul's Cathedral Wren showed his ingenuity in adapting the incongruous Royal Warrant Design of 1675. Among his gradual and successful amendments were the intriguing upper lighting of his two-storey choir and the supporting of the lantern by a brick cone inserted between the inner and outer dome shells. The layout of the Royal Hospital at Greenwich illustrates Wren's qualities as an overall large-scale planner and designer. His terms of reference insisted upon the incorporation of the earlier existing Queen's House, erected by Inigo Jones, and of John Webb's King Charles II block. The Queen's House, in particular, created a difficult problem as its smaller size rendered it out of scale with the newer structures. Wren's solution was to make it the focal centre of a great vista between the main flanking larger buildings; this was a masterstroke.

Principal Honours and Distinctions
Knighted 1673. President, Royal Society 1681–3. Member of Parliament 1685–7 and 1701–2. Surveyor, Greenwich Hospital 1696. Surveyor, Westminster Abbey 1699. Surveyor-General 1669–1712.

Further Reading
R. Dutton, 1951, *The Age of Wren*, Batsford.
M. Briggs, 1953, *Wren the Incomparable*, Allen & Unwin.
M. Whinney, 1971, *Wren*, Thames & Hudson.
K. Downes, 1971, *Christopher Wren*, Allen Lane.
G. Beard, 1982, *The Work of Sir Christopher Wren*, Bartholomew.

DY

Wright, Arthur
b. 1858 London, England
d. 26 July 1931 Paignton, Devon, England

English engineer and electricity supply industry pioneer.

Arthur Wright, educated at Marlborough College, attended a course of training at the School of Submarine Telegraphy, Telephony and Electric Light in London. In 1882 he joined the Hammond Company in Brighton, the first company to afford a regular electricity supply in Britain on a commercial basis for street and private lighting. He invented a recording ammeter and also a thermal-demand indicator used in conjunction with a tariff based on maximum demand in addition to energy consumption. This indicator was to remain in use for almost half a century.

Resigning his position in Brighton in 1889, he joined the staff of S.Z. de **Ferranti** and served with him during developments at the Grosvenor Gallery and Deptford stations in London. In 1891 he returned to Brighton as its first Borough Electrical Engineer. From 1900 onwards he had an extensive consulting practice designing early power stations, and was approached by many municipalities and companies in Britain, the United States, South America and Australia, primarily on finance and tariffs. Associated with the founding of the Municipal Electrical Association

in 1905, the following year he became its first President.

Bibliography
1901, British patent no. 23,153 (thermal maximum demand indicator).
1922, 'Early days of the Brighton electricity supply', *Journal of the Institution of Electrical Engineers* 60: 497–9.

Further Reading
Obituary, 1931, *Journal of the Institution of Electrical Engineers* 69: 1,327–8.
R.H. Parsons, 1939, *Early Days of the Power Station Industry*, Cambridge, pp. 13–17 (describes Wright's pioneering inventions).

GW

Wright, Basil Martin
b. 20 December 1912 Dulwich, London, England

English physician and research physiologist, inventor of the Wright Respirometer peak-flow meter for measurement of respiratory ventilatory capacity and of 'fluid lens' spectacles.

He qualified at St Bartholomew's Hospital in 1938 and after early hospital posts served in the Army as a specialist in pathology in West Africa and Singapore. In 1947 he joined the Medical Research Council (MRC) and until 1957 he was involved with the Pneumoconiosis Research Unit in investigation of dust inhalation. In 1957 he transferred to the National Institute for Medical Research, to concentrate on instrument development, and in 1969 to the Bioengineering Division of the MRC Clinical Research Centre at Northwick Park Hospital. He was responsible for a number of instrumental developments and inventions in the fields, amongst others, of respiration measurement, blood alcohol levels and variable adjustable spectacle lenses (achieved by altering the curvature of the surface of a thin-walled transparent fluid cell).

Principal Honours and Distinctions
Fellow of the Royal College of Physicians 1989. Doctor of Medicine, Cambridge, 1969. International Inventors Fair Design Awards and Gold Medal.

Bibliography

1955, 'A respiratory anemometer', *Journal of Physiology*.

1959, with McKerrow, 'Maximum forced expiatory flow rate as a measure of respiratory capacity', *British Medical Journal*.

1978, 'Variable focus spectacles', *Transactions of the Ophthalmological Society of the UK*.

1986, 'Patient-triggered ventilation in the newborn', *Lancet*.

MG

Wright, Frank Lloyd

b. 8 June 1869 Richland Center, Wisconsin, USA

d. 9 April 1959 Phoenix, Arizona, USA

American architect who, in an unparalleled career spanning almost seventy years, became the most important figure on the modern architectural scene both in his own country and far further afield.

Wright began his career in 1887 working in the Chicago offices of Adler & **Sullivan**. He conceived a great admiration for Sullivan, who was then concentrating upon large commercial projects in modern mode, producing functional yet decorative buildings which took all possible advantage of new structural methods. Wright was responsible for many of the domestic commissions.

In 1893 Wright left the firm in order to set up practice on his own, thus initiating a career which was to develop into three distinct phases. In the first of these, up until the First World War, he was chiefly designing houses in a concept in which he envisaged 'the house as a shelter'. These buildings displayed his deeply held opinion that detached houses in country areas should be designed as an integral part of the landscape, a view later to be evidenced strongly in the work of modern Finnish architects. Wright's designs were called 'prairie houses' because so many of them were built in the Mid-West of America, which Wright described as a 'prairie'. These were low and spreading, with gently sloping rooflines, very plain and clean lined, built of traditional materials in warm rural colours, blending softly into their settings. Typical was W.W. Willit's house of 1902 in Highland Park, Illinois.

In the second phase of his career Wright began to build more extensively in modern materials, utilizing advanced means of construction. A notable example was his remarkable Imperial Hotel in Tokyo, carefully designed and built in 1916–22 (now demolished), with special foundations and structure to withstand (successfully) strong earthquake tremors. He also became interested in the possibilities of reinforced concrete; in 1906 he built his church at Oak Park, Illinois, entirely of this material. In the 1920s, in California, he abandoned his use of traditional materials for house building in favour of precast concrete blocks, which were intended to provide an 'organic' continuity between structure and decorative surfacing. In his continued exploration of the possibilities of concrete as a building material, he created the dramatic concept of 'Falling Water', a house built in 1935–7 at Bear Run in Pennsylvania in which he projected massive reinforced-concrete terraces cantilevered from a cliff over a waterfall in the woodlands. In the later 1930s an extraordinary run of original concepts came from Wright, then nearing 70 years of age, ranging from his own winter residence and studio, Taliesin West in Arizona, to the administration block for Johnson Wax (1936–9) in Racine, Wisconsin, where the main interior ceiling was supported by Minoan-style, inversely tapered concrete columns rising to spreading circular capitals which contained lighting tubes of Pyrex glass.

Frank Lloyd Wright continued to work until four days before his death at the age of 91. One of his most important and certainly controversial commissions was the Solomon R. Guggenheim Museum in New York. This had been proposed in 1943 but was not finally built until 1956–9; in this striking design the museum's exhibition areas are ranged along a gradually mounting spiral ramp lit effectively from above. Controversy stemmed from the unusual and original design of exterior banding and interior descending spiral for wall-display of paintings: some critics strongly approved, while others, equally strongly, did not.

Principal Honours and Distinctions
RIBA Royal Gold Medal 1941.

Bibliography
1945, *An Autobiography*, Faber & Faber.

Further Reading
E. Kaufmann (ed.), 1957, *Frank Lloyd Wright: an American Architect*, New York: Horizon Press.
H. Russell Hitchcock, 1973, *In the Nature of Materials*, New York: Da Capo.
T.A. Heinz, 1982, *Frank Lloyd Wright*, New York: St Martin's.

DY

Wright, Wilbur

b. 16 April 1867 Millville, Indiana, USA
d. 30 May 1912 Dayton, Ohio, USA

American co-inventor, with his brother Orville Wright (b. 19 August 1871 Dayton, Ohio, USA; d. 30 January 1948 Dayton, Ohio, USA), of the first powered aeroplane capable of sustained, controlled flight.

Wilbur and Orville designed and built bicycles in Dayton, Ohio. In the 1890s they developed an interest in flying which led them to study the experiments of gliding pioneers such as Otto Lilienthal in Germany, and their fellow American Octave Chanute. The Wrights were very methodical and tackled the many problems stage by stage. First, they developed a method of controlling a glider using movable control surfaces, instead of weight-shifting as used in the early hand-gliders. They built a wind tunnel to test their wing sections and by 1902 they had produced a controllable glider. Next they needed a petrol engine, and when they could not find one to suit their needs they designed and built one themselves.

On 17 December 1903 their *Flyer* was ready and Orville made the first short flight of 12 seconds; Wilbur followed with a 59-second flight covering 853 ft (260 m). An improved design, *Flyer II*, followed in 1904 and made about eighty flights, including circuits and simple manoeuvres. In 1905 *Flyer III* made several long flights, including one of 38 minutes covering 24½ miles (39 km). Most of the Wrights' flying was carried out in secret to protect their patents, so their achievements received little publicity. For a period of two and a half years they did not fly, but they worked to improve their *Flyer* and to negotiate terms for the sale of their invention to various governments and commercial syndicates.

In 1908 the Wright *Model A* appeared, and when Wilbur demonstrated it in France he astounded the European aviators by making several flights lasting more than one hour and one of 2 hours 20 minutes. Considerable numbers of the *Model A* were built, but the European designers rapidly caught up and overtook the Wrights. The Wright brothers became involved in several legal battles to protect their patents: one of these, with Glenn **Curtiss**, went on for many years. Wilbur died of typhoid fever in 1912. Orville sold his interest in the Wright Company in 1915, but retained an interest in aeronautical research and lived on to see an aeroplane fly faster than the speed of sound.

Principal Honours and Distinctions
Royal Aeronautical Society (London) Gold Medal (awarded to both Wilbur and Orville) May 1909. Medals from the Aero Club of America, Congress, Ohio State and the City of Dayton.

Bibliography
1951, *Miracle at Kitty Hawk. The Letters of Wilbur & Orville Wright*, ed. F.C. Kelly, New York.
1953, *The Papers of Wilbur and Orville Wright*, ed. Marvin W. McFarland, 2 vols, New York.
Orville Wright, 1953, *How We Invented the Aeroplane*, ed. F.C. Kelly, New York.

Further Reading
A.G. Renstrom, 1968, *Wilbur & Orville Wright. A Bibliography*, Washington, DC (with 2,055 entries).
C.H. Gibbs-Smith, 1963, *The Wright Brothers*, London (reprint) (a concise account).
J.L. Pritchard, 1953, 'The Wright Brothers', *Journal of the Royal Aeronautical Society* (December) (includes much documentary material).
F.C. Kelly, 1943, *The Wright Brothers*, New York (reprint) (authorized by Orville Wright).
H.B. Combs with M. Caidin, 1980, *Kill Devil Hill*, London (contains more technical information).
T.D. Crouch, 1989, *The Bishop's Boys: A Life of Wilbur & Orville Wright*, New York (perhaps the best of various subsequent biographies).

JDS

Wunderlich, Karl August Reinhold

b. 4 August 1815 Sulz am Neckar, Baden-Württemberg, Germany
d. 25 September 1877 Leipzig, Saxony, Germany

German physician who developed the clinical thermometer and studied variations of body temperature in health and disease.

Although **Sanctorius** had taken measurements of body temperature and indeed advocated detailed quantitative bio-measurement, the concept of fever as a disease *sui generis* still held sway during the early eighteenth century. Wunderlich, in his practice at Leipzig, demonstrated that fever was merely a symptom, however variable its presentation. It has been said that 'he found fever a disease and left it a symptom'.

Bibliography

1848, *Das Verhalten des Eigenwarme in Krankheiten*, Leipzig; translated and expanded as *On the Temperature in Disease: A Manual of Medical Thermometry*, London, 1871.

MG

Wyatt, John

b. April 1700 Thickbroom, Weeford, near Lichfield, England
d. 29 November 1766 Birmingham, England

English inventor of machines for making files and rolling lead, and co-constructor of a cotton-spinning machine.

John Wyatt was the eldest son of John and Jane Wyatt, who lived in the small village of Thickbroom in the parish of Weeford, near Lichfield. John the younger was educated at Lichfield school and then worked as a carpenter at Thickbroom till 1730. In 1732 he was in Birmingham, engaged by a man named Heely, a gun-barrel forger, who became bankrupt in 1734. Wyatt had invented a machine for making files and sought the help of Lewis **Paul** to manufacture this commercially.

The surviving papers of Paul and Wyatt in Birmingham are mostly undated and show a variety of machines with which they were involved. There was a machine for 'making lead hard' which had rollers, and 'a Gymcrak of some consequence' probably refers to a machine for boring barrels or the file-making machine. Wyatt is said to have been one of the unsuccessful competitors for the erection of London Bridge in 1736. He invented and perfected the compound-lever weighing machine. He had more success with this: after 1744, machines for weighing up to five tons were set up at Birmingham, Chester, Gloucester, Hereford, Lichfield and Liverpool. Road construction, bridge building, hydrostatics, canals, water-powered engines and many other schemes received his attention and it is said that he was employed for a time after 1744 by Matthew **Boulton**.

It is certain that in April 1735 Paul and Wyatt were working on their spinning machine and Wyatt was making a model of it in London in 1736, giving up his work in Birmingham. The first patent, in 1738, was taken out in the name of Lewis Paul. It is impossible to know which of these two invented what. This first patent covers a wide variety of descriptions of the vital roller drafting to draw out the fibres, and it is unknown which system was actually used. Paul's carding patent of 1748 and his second spinning patent of 1758 show that he moved away from the system and principles upon which **Arkwright** built his success. Wyatt and Paul's spinning machines were sufficiently promising for a mill to be set up in 1741 at the Upper Priory, Birmingham, that was powered by two asses. Wyatt was the person responsible for constructing the machinery. Edward Cave established another at Northampton powered by water while later Daniel **Bourn** built yet another at Leominster. Many others were interested too. The Birmingham mill did not work for long and seems to have been given up in 1743. Wyatt was imprisoned for debt in The Fleet in 1742, and when released in 1743 he tried for a time to run the Birmingham mill and possibly the Northampton one. The one at Leominster burned down in 1754, while the Northampton mill was advertised for sale in 1756. This last mill may have been used again in conjunction with the 1758 patent. It was Wyatt whom Daniel Bourn contacted about a grant for spindles for his Leominster mill in 1748, but this seems to have been Wyatt's last association with the spinning venture.

Further Reading

G.J. French, 1859, *The Life and Times of Samuel Crompton*, London (French collected many of the Paul and Wyatt papers; these should be read in conjunction with Hills 1970).

R.L. Hills, 1970, *Power in the Industrial Revolution*, Manchester (Hills shows that the roller-drafting system on this spinning machine worked on the wrong principles).

A.P. Wadsworth and J. de L. Mann, 1931, *The Cotton Trade and Industrial Lancashire, 1600–1780*, Manchester (provides good coverage of the partnership of Paul and Wyatt and of the early mills).

E. Baines, 1835, *History of the Cotton Manufacture in Great Britain*, London (this publication must be mentioned, although it is now out of date).

W. English, 1969, *The Textile Industry*, London (a more recent account).

W.A. Benton, 'John Wyatt and the weighing of heavy loads', *Transactions of the Newcomen Society* 9 (for a description of Wyatt's weighing machine).

RLH

X

Xu Guangqi (Hsu Kuang-Chhi)
b. 1562 China
d. 1633 China

Chinese writer and reporter on agricultural practice.

Living during the troubled Ming Dynasty, Xu Guangqi combined his energy and interest in scientific improvement to develop and strengthen the State: his interest in military technology was used in the formation of the defence of the State, whilst his interest in irrigation and crop husbandry was put to use in programmes of famine relief. He was a friend and protector of the Jesuit community in China, and between 1607 and 1610, when he was forced to absent himself from the political scene, he devoted his time to the study of the irrigation systems practised by the Jesuits, and also the cultivation of new crops.

Stimulated by these studies he continued to collect information on agricultural technology even after he returned to political life. In addition he prepared a number of draft texts of an agricultural treatise, which he intended to provide a practical guide to agricultural practice, but which would also give an indication of the solutions to China's economic problems at the time. Despite the fact that he had amassed a huge amount of material, it was left to the Chinese scholar Chen Ziling (Chhen Tzu-Ling) to edit the draft, which was finally published six years after the death of Xu Guangqi in 1633.

The treatise, called the *Nong Zheng Quan Shu* (Wade-Giles transliteration: *Nung Cheng Chhuan Shu*), is a massive work quoting from some 299 sources, sometimes verbatim. In addition to parts dealing with husbandry, there are also large sections devoted to rural administration and to the development of rural light industry, as well as to the introduction of cash crops such as cotton. The Ming dynasty fell in 1644, and the policies set out by Xu Guangqi within this treatise were never implemented.

Further Reading
F. Bray, Vol. VI.2 in J. Needham (ed.), *Science and Civilisation in China*, Cambridge (devotes an early chapter to her sources in a comprehensive account of Chinese agriculture).

AP

Y

Yagi, Hidetsugu

b. 28 January 1886 Osaka, Japan
d. January 1976 Osaka, Japan

Japanese engineer who, with his student Shintaro Uda, developed the directional ultra-high frequency (UHF) aerial array that bears his name.

Yagi studied engineering at Tokyo Imperial University (now Tokyo University), graduating in 1910. For the next four years he taught at Engineering High School in Sendai, Honshu, then in 1914 he was sent to study resonance phenomena under Barkhausen at Dresden University. When the First World War broke out he was touring Europe, so he travelled to London to study under Ambrose **Fleming** at University College, London. Continuing his travels, he then visited the USA, studying at Harvard under G.W. **Pierce**, before returning to his teaching post at Sendai Engineering High School, which in 1919 was absorbed into Tohoku University. There, in 1921, he obtained his doctorate, and some years later he was appointed Professor of Electrical Engineering. Having heard of the invention of the magnetron, he worked with a student, Kinjiro Okabe; in 1927 they produced microwave energy at a wavelength of a few tens of centimetres. However, he is best known for his development with another student, Shintaro Uda, of a directional, multi-element ultra-high frequency aerial, which he demonstrated during a tour of the USA in 1928. During the Second World War Yagi worked on radar systems. After his retirement he became Professor Emeritus at Tohoku and Osaka universities and formed the Yagi Antenna Company.

Principal Honours and Distinctions
Yagi received various honours, including the Japanese Cultural Order of Merit 1976, and the Valdemar **Poulsen** Gold Medal.

Bibliography
1928, 'Beam transmission of ultra-short waves', *Proceedings of the Institute of Radio Engineers* 6: 715 (describes the Yagi–Uda aerial).

Further Reading
F.E. Terman, 1943, *Radio Engineers' Handbook*, New York: McGraw-Hill (provides a review of aerials, including the Yagi system).

KF

Yale, Linus Jr

b. 4 April 1821 Salisbury, New York, USA
d. 25 December 1868 New York City, USA

American locksmith, inventor of the Yale pin-tumbler cylinder lock.

The son of a locksmith, Linus Yale Jr set out to become a portrait painter but gave this up in the 1840s to embark on the same profession as his father. He opened a shop of his own at Shelburne Falls, Massachusetts; his first products were key-operated bank locks. The Great Exhibition of 1851 in London convinced him that any lock could be picked by someone with the necessary skill; he then turned his attention to the design of combination locks, designing the first double-dial bank lock in 1863. In 1868 he formed a partnership with John Henry Towne and his son Henry Robinson Towne to form the Yale Lock Manufacturing Company in Stamford, Connecticut, to make a patented key lock which incorporated a series of pin tumblers inside a cylinder. The principle of the pin-tumbler mechanism could be traced back to ancient Egypt; in Yale's cylinder lock, the serrations of the correct key raised the pin tumblers to the height at which the cylinder could turn, withdrawing the bolt. These cylinder locks made possible the use of smaller keys and became the foundation of the modern lock industry. Yale died soon after forming his partnership with the Townes.

Further Reading
J.J. Fucini and S. Fucini, 1985, *Entrepreneurs*, Boston: C.K. Hall & Co.

IMcN

Yarrow, Sir Alfred Fernandez

b. 13 January 1842 London, England
d. 24 January 1932 London, England

English shipbuilder, naval architect, engineer and philanthropist.

At the conclusion of his schooling in the South of England, Yarrow became an indentured apprentice to the Thames engine-builder Ravenhill. During this five-year period various incidents and meetings sharpened his interest in scientific matters and he showed the skills that in later years were to be so beneficial to shipbuilding. For two years he acted as London representative for Ravenhill before joining up with a Mr Hedley to form a shipyard on the Isle of Dogs. The company lasted from 1868 until 1875 and in that period produced 350 small launches and other craft. This massive output enabled Yarrow to gain confidence in many aspects of ship design. Within two years of setting out on his own he built his first ship for the Royal Navy: a torpedo boat, then at the cutting edge of technology.

In the early 1890s the company was building watertube boilers and producing destroyers with speeds in excess of 27 knots (50 km/h); it built the Russian destroyer *Sokol*, did pioneering work with aluminium and with high-tensile steels and worked on shipboard equipment to nullify vibrational effects. With the closure of most of the Thames shipyards and the run-down in skilled labour, Yarrow decided that the shipyard must move to some other part of the United Kingdom. After careful deliberation a green field site to the west of Glasgow was chosen, and in 1908 their first Clyde-built destroyer was launched. The company expanded, more building berths were arranged, boiler construction was developed and over the years they became recognized as specialists in smaller high-speed craft and in 'knock down' ships for other parts of the world.

Yarrow retired in 1913, but at the commencement of the First World War he returned to help the yard produce, in four years, twenty-nine destroyers with speeds of up to 40 knots (74 km/h). At the end of hostilities he gave of his time and money to many charities, including those for ex-servicemen. He left a remarkable industrial organization which remains to this day the most prolific builder of surface craft for the Royal Navy.

Principal Honours and Distinctions
Created Baronet 1916. FRS 1922. Vice-President, Institution of Naval Architects 1896.

Further Reading
Lady Yarrow, 1924, *Alfred Yarrow, His Life and Work*, London: Edward Arnold.
A. Borthwick, 1965, *Yarrow and Company Limited, The First Hundred Years 1865-1965*, Glasgow.
B. Baxter, 1986, 'Alfred Fernandez Yarrow', *Dictionary of Scottish Business Biography*, Vol. I, pp. 245-7, Slaven & Checkland and Aberdeen University Press.

FMW

Yeoman, Thomas
b. *c.*1700 probably near Northampton, England
d. 24 January 1781 London, England

English surveyor and civil engineer.

Very little is known of his early life, but he was clearly a skilful and gifted engineer who had received comprehensive practical training, for in 1743 he erected the machinery in the world's first water-powered cotton mill at Northampton on the river Nene. In 1748 he invented a weighing machine for use by turnpike trusts for weighing wagons. Until 1757 he remained in Northampton, mainly surveying enclosures and turnpike roads and making agricultural machinery. He also gained a national reputation for building and installing very successful ventilating equipment (invented by Dr Stephen **Hales**) in hospitals, prisons and ships, including some ventilators of Yeoman's own design in the Houses of Parliament.

Meanwhile he developed an interest in river improvements, and in 1744 he made his first survey of the River Nene between Thrapston and Northampton; he repeated the survey in 1753 and subsequently gave evidence in parliamentary proceedings in 1756. The following year he was in Gloucestershire surveying the line of the Stroudwater Canal, an operation that he repeated in 1776. Also in 1757, he was appointed Surveyor to the River Ivel Navigation in Bedfordshire. In 1761 he was back on the Nene. During 1762-5 he carried out surveys for the Chelmer & Blackwater Navigation, although the work was not undertaken for another thirty years. In 1765 he reported on land-drainage improvements for the Kentish Sour. It was at this time that he became associated with John **Smeaton** in a major survey in 1766 of the river Lea for the Lee Navigation Trustees, having already made some surveys with Joseph Nickalls near Waltham Abbey in 1762. Yeoman modified some of Smeaton's proposals and on 1 July 1767 was officially appointed Surveyor to the Lee Navigation Trustees, a post he retained until 1771. He also advised on the work to create the Stort Navigation, and at the official opening on 24 October 1769 he made a formal speech announcing: 'Now is Bishops Stortford open to all the ports of the world.'

Among his other works were: advice on Ferriby Sluice on the River Ancholme (1766); reports on the Forth & Clyde Canal, the North Level and Wisbech outfall on the Nene, the Coventry Canal, and estimates for the Leeds and Selby Canal (1768-71); estimates for the extension of the Medway Navigation from Tonbridge to Edenbridge (1771); and between 1767 and 1777 he was consulted, with other engineers, by the City of London on problems regarding the Thames.

He joined the Northampton Philosophical Society shortly after its formation in 1743 and was President several times before he moved to London. In 1760 he became a member of the Society for the Encouragement of Arts, Manufactures and Commerce, and in 1763 he was chosen as joint Chairman of the Committee on Mechanics – a position he held until 1778. He was elected a Fellow of the Royal Society on 12 January 1764. On the formation of the Smeatonian Society of Civil Engineers, the forerunner of the present Institution of Civil Engineers, he was elected first President in 1771, remaining as such until his illness in 1780.

Principal Honours and Distinctions
FRS 1764. President, Smeatonian Society of Civil Engineers 1771–80; Treasurer 1771–7.

JHB

Yi-Xing (I-Hsing)
b. *c.*672/683 China
d. 727 China

Chinese astronomer and mathematician.

A Tantric Buddhist monk, Yi-Xing was one of the greatest astronomers and mathematicians in Chinese history. He was much influenced by Indian and therefore Hellenic astronomy. Around 725, he constructed armillary spheres with eclip-

tically mounted sighting tubes for taking measurements in ecliptic co-ordinates. With these instruments he took many readings of star positions and may even have discovered the proper motion of the stars. Yi-Xing's *Da Yan Li Shu* calendar was the result of an imperial commission to reform the calendar. It was edited the year after his death, in 728, and was officially adopted the following year. This calendar gave a nearly correct value for the irregularity of the movement of the Sun and came closer than previous attempts to calculate the day of true syzygy. Yi-Xing's method of interpolation was identical to that used by Gauss in the eighteenth century. He was also the inventor of the 'water wheel link work escapement' mechanism as used later in the clock of **Su Song**.

Further Reading
J. Needham, *Science and Civilisation in China*, Cambridge: Cambridge University Press, 1959–65, vols III, pp. 37–8; IV.2, pp. 471ff., 532–3.
—— 1960, *Heavenly Clockwork*, pp. 17–8, 20–1, 23–5, 62, 72, 74ff., 85, 89, 94, 98, 104–5, 107, 112, 122–3, 132, 139, 151, 153, 154, 166, 175, 177, 180, 182, 187.

LRD

Yost, Paul Edward
b. 30 June 1919 Bristow, Iowa, USA

American designer of balloons who reintroduced the hot-air balloon.

After the early hot-air balloons of the **Montgolfier** brothers in the 1780s, this branch of ballooning was superseded by hydrogen, coal gas and helium balloons. Following the research by Auguste **Piccard** into cosmic radiation during the 1930s, a renewed interest in this branch of research arose in the United States from 1947 onwards, using helium-filled balloons. Modern plastics were available by this time, and polythene was used for the envelopes.

Paul E. Yost developed an improved form of envelope using nylon fabric laminated with mylar plastic film. This provided a strong impermeable material that was ideal for balloons. Using this material for the envelope, Yost produced the *Vulcoon* in 1960. He also reintroduced the use of hot air to inflate his balloon and developed an easily controlled gas burner fuelled by propane gas, which was readily available in cylinders for portable cooking stoves. Yost's company, Raven Industries, developed these very basic balloons as a military project. The pilot was suspended in a sling, but they improved the design by fitting wicker or aluminium baskets and turned to a market in the field of sport. After a slow start, hot-air ballooning became popular as a sport. In 1963 Yost made the first crossing of the English Channel in a hot-air balloon, accompanied by Donald Piccard, nephew of the balloonist Auguste **Piccard**, and Charles Dollfus, the eminent French aviation historian. Yost's attempt to cross the Atlantic in his balloon *Silver Fox* during 1976 failed and he was rescued from the sea near the Azores. The popularity of hot-air ballooning increased during the 1970s, and evolved into a very original form of advertising with unusual shapes for the envelopes, including a house, a bottle and an elephant.

JDS

Young, Arthur
b. 11 September 1741 London, England
d. 20 April 1820 Bradford, England

English writer and commentator on agricultural affairs; founder and Secretary of the Board of Agriculture (later the Ministry of Agriculture, Fisheries and Food).

He was the youngest of the three children of Dr Arthur Young, who was at one time Chaplain to the Speaker of the House of Commons. He learned Latin and Greek at Lavenham School, and at the age of 17 was apprenticed to a mercantile house, an occupation he disliked. He first published *The Theatre of the Present War in North America* in 1758. He then wrote four novels and began to produce the literary magazine *The Universal Museum*. After his father's death he returned home to manage his father's farm, and in 1765 he married Martha Allen.

Young learned farming by experiment, and three years after his return he took over the rent of a 300 acre farm, Samford Hall in Essex. He was not a practical farmer, and was soon forced to give it up in favour of one of 100 acres (40.5 hectares) in Hertfordshire. He subsidized his farming with his writing, and in 1768 published *The Farmer's Letters to the People of England*. The first of his books on agricultural tours, *Six Weeks Tours through the Counties of England and Wales*,

was published in 1771. Between 1784 and 1809 he published the *Annals of Agriculture*, one of whose contributors was George III, who wrote under the pseudonym of Ralph Robinson.

By this time he was corresponding with all of influence in agricultural matters, both at home and abroad. George Washington wrote frequently to Young, and George III was reputed to travel always with a copy of his book. The Empress of Russia sent students to him and had his *Tours* published in Russian. Young made three trips to France in 1787, 1788 and 1789–90 respectively, prior to and during the French Revolution, and his *Travels in France* (1792) is a remarkable account of that period, made all the more fascinating by his personal contact with people differing as widely as Mirabeau, the French revolutionary leader, and King Louis XVI.

Unfortunately, in 1811 an unsuccessful cataract operation left him blind, and he moved from London to his native Bradford, where he remained until his death.

Principal Honours and Distinctions
Chairman, Agricultural Committee of the Society of Arts 1773: awarded three Gold Medals during his career for his achievements in practical agriculture. FRS. Honorary Member of the Dublin, York and Manchester learned societies, as well as the Economic Society of Berne, the Palatine Academy of Agriculture at Mannheim, and the Physical Society of Zurich. Honourary member, French Royal Society of Agriculture. Secretary, Board of Agriculture 1793.

Bibliography
His first novels were *The Fair Americans, Sir Charles Beaufort, Lucy Watson* and *Julia Benson.*
His earliest writings on agriculture appeared as collected letters in a periodical with the title *Museum Rusticum* in 1767.
In 1770 he published a two-volume work entitled *A Course of Experimental Agriculture,* and between 1766 and 1775 he published *The Farmer's Letters, Political Arithmetic, Political Essays Concerning the Present State of the British Empire* and *Southern, Northern and Eastern Tours,* and in 1779 he published *The Tour of Ireland.*
In addition he was author of the Board of

Agriculture reports on the counties of *Suffolk, Lincoln, Norfolk, Hertford, Essex* and *Oxford*.

Further Reading
J. Thirsk (ed.), 1989, *The Agrarian History of England and Wales*, Vol. VI (deals with the years 1750 to 1850, the period associated with Young).
T.G. Gazeley, 1973, 'The life of Arthur Young, 1741–1820', *Memoirs, American Philosophical Society* 97.

AP

Young, James
b. 13 July 1811 Glasgow, Scotland
d. 13 May 1883 Wemyss Bay, Scotland

Scottish chemist and pioneer petroleum technologist.

Young's early education took place in the evenings, after the day's work in his father's joinery. From 1830 he studied chemistry at the evening classes in Glasgow given by the distinguished Scottish chemist Thomas Graham (1805-69) and soon afterwards became Graham's assistant. When Graham moved to University College London in 1837, Young accompanied him.

From 1839 he was employed in the chemical industry, first with James **Muspratt** at St Helens, Lancashire, and from 1843 with **Tennant & Company** in Manchester. In 1848 his attention was drawn to an oil seepage in a mine at Alfreton, Derbyshire, of some 300 gallons per day; he set up his own works there to extract an oil that could be used for lighting and lubrication. When this source of oil was exhausted, three years later, Young moved to Lothian in Scotland. By distillation, he extracted oil from the oil-shale deposits there and thus founded the Scottish oil-shale industry: he obtained a high yield of paraffin oil for lighting and heating, and was a pioneer in the use of chemical methods in extracting and treating oil. In 1866 he disposed of his company for no less than £400,000.

Young's other activities included measuring the speed of light by **Fizeau**'s method and giving financial support to the expeditions of David Livingstone, who had been a fellow student in Glasgow.

Principal Honours and Distinctions
FRS 1873.

Further Reading
Obituary, 1884, *Journal of the Chemical Society* 45: 630.

LRD

Yourkevitch, Vladimir Ivanovitch
b. 17 June 1885 Moscow, Russia
d. 14 December 1964 USA

Russian (naturalized American) naval architect who worked in Russia, Western Europe and the United States and who profoundly influenced the hull design of large ships.

Yourkevitch came from an academic family, but one without any experience or tradition of sea service. Despite this he decided to become a naval architect, and after secondary education at Moscow and engineering training at the St Petersburg Polytechnic, he graduated in 1909. For the following ten years he worked designing battleships and later submarines, mostly at the Baltic Shipyard in St Petersburg. Around 1910 he became a full member of the Russian Naval Constructors Corps, and in 1915 he was a founder member and first Scientific Secretary of the Society of Naval Engineers.

Using the published data of the American Admiral D.W. **Taylor** and taking advantage of access to the Norddeutscher Lloyd Testing Tank at Bremerhaven, Yourkevitch proposed a new hull form with bulbous bow and long entrances and runs. This was the basis for the revolutionary battleships then laid down at St Petersburg, the 'Borodino' class. Owing to the war these ships were launched but never completed. At the conclusion of the war Yourkevitch found himself in Constantinople, where he experienced the life of a refugee, and then he moved to Paris where he accepted almost any work on offer. Fortunately in 1928, through an introduction, he was appointed a draughtsman at the St Nazaire shipyard. Despite his relatively lowly position, he used all his personality to persuade the French company to alter the hull form of the future record breaker *Normandie*. The gamble paid off and Yourkevitch was able to set up his own naval architecture company, BECNY, which designed many well-known liners, including the French *Pasteur*.

In 1939 he settled in North America, becoming a US citizen in 1945. On the night of the fire on the *Normandie*, he was in New York but was prevented from going close to the ship by the police, and the possibility of saving the ship was thrown away. He was involved in many projects as well as lecturing at Ann Arbor, Michigan, and at the Massachusetts Institute of Technology. He maintained connections with his technical colleagues in St Petersburg in the later years of his life. His unfulfilled dream was the creation of a superliner to carry 5,000 passengers and thus able to make dramatic cuts in the cost of transatlantic travel. Yourkevitch was a fine example of a man whose vision enabled him to serve science and engineering without consideration of international boundaries.

Principal Honours and Distinctions
Order of St Stanislav and Order of St Anna *c.*1910.

AK/FMW

Z

Zeiss, Carl
b. 11 September 1816 Weimar, Thuringia,
Germany
d. 3 December 1888 Jena, Saxony, Germany

*German lens manufacturer who introduced
scientific method to the production of compound
microscopes and made possible the production of
the first anastigmatic photographic objectives.*

After completing his early education in Weimar,
Zeiss became an apprentice to the engineer Dr
Frederick Koerner. As part of his training, Zeiss
was required to travel widely and he visited
Vienna, Berlin, Stuttgart and Darmstadt to study
his trade. In 1846 he set up a business of his own,
an optical workshop in Jena, where he began
manufacturing magnifying glasses and microscopes. Much of his work was naturally for the
university there and he had the co-operation of
some of the University staff in the development
of precision instruments. By 1858 he was seeking
to make more expensive compound microscopes, but he found the current techniques
primitive and laborious. He decided that it was
necessary to introduce scientific method to the
design of the optics, and in 1866 he sought the
advice of a professor of physics at the University
of Jena, Ernst Abbe (1840–1905). It took Zeiss
until 1869 to persuade Abbe to join his company, and two difficult years were spent working
on the calculations before success was achieved.
Within a few more years the Zeiss microscope
had earned a worldwide reputation for quality.
Abbe became a full partner in the Zeiss business
in 1875. In 1880 Abbe began an association with
Friedrich Otte Schott that was to lead to the establishment of the famous Jena glass works in
1884. With the support of the German government, Jena was to become the centre of world
production of new optical glasses for photographic objectives.

In 1886 the distinguished mathematician and
optician Paul Rudolph joined Zeiss at Jena. After
Zeiss's death, Rudolph went on to use the characteristics of the new glass to calculate the first
anastigmatic lenses. Immediately successful and
widely imitated, the anastigmats were also the
first of a long series of Zeiss photographic objectives that were to be at the forefront of lens design for years to come. Abbe took over the
management of the company and developed it
into an internationally famous organization.

Further Reading
L.W. Sipley, 1965, *Photography's Great Inven-
tors*, Philadelphia (a brief biography).
J.M. Eder, 1945, *History of Photography*, trans.
E. Epstean, New York.
K.J. Hume, 1980, *A History of Engineering Me-
trology*, London, 122–32 (includes a short ac-
count of Carl Zeiss and his company).
JW/RTS

Zeng Gonglian (Tseng Kung-Liang)
fl. 11th century China

Chinese writer on chemical subjects.

In his treatise *Wu Jing Zong Yao*, compiled with
an assistant *c.*1040, he wrote down the first formula for gunpowder to be printed and published
in any civilization, although the essentials of the
mixture had been known in China for just over a
century. The text describes several military applications of gunpowder, with an incendiary or, in
one case, a toxic chemical rather than an explosive effect; the saltpetre content was too low for
the latter, but it was steadily increased over the
years.

Bibliography
*c.*1040, *Wu Jing Zong Yao.*

Further Reading
J. Needham, *Science and Civilisation in China*,
Cambridge: Cambridge University Press,
1986, Vol. V.7, pp. 117ff.
LRD

Zeppelin, Count Ferdinand von
b. 8 July 1838 Konstanz, Germany
d. 8 March 1917 Berlin, Germany

German designer of rigid airships, which became known as Zeppelins.

Zeppelin served in the German Army and retired with the rank of General in 1890. While in the army, he was impressed by the use of balloons in the American Civil War and during the Siege of Paris. By the time he retired, non-rigid airships were just beginning to make their mark. Zeppelin decided to build an airship with a rigid framework to support the gas bags. Plans were drawn up in 1893 with the assistance of Theodore Kober, an engineer, but the idea was rejected by the authorities. A company was founded in 1898 and construction began. The *Luftschiff Zeppelin No. 1* (*LZ 1*) made its first flight on 2 July 1900. Modifications were needed and the second flight took place in October. A reporter called Hugo Eckener covered this and later flights: his comments and suggestions so impressed Zeppelin that Eckener eventually became his partner, publicist, fund-raiser and pilot.

The performance of the subsequent Zeppelins gradually improved, but there was limited military interest. In November 1909 a company with the abbreviated name DELAG was founded to operate passenger-carrying Zeppelins. The service was opened by *LZ 7 Deutschland* in mid-June 1910, and the initial network of Frankfurt, Baden-Baden and Düsseldorf was expanded. Eckener became a very efficient Director of Flight Operations, and by the outbreak of war in 1914 some 35,000 passengers had been carried without any fatalities. During the First World War many Zeppelins were built and they carried out air-raids on Britain. Despite their menacing reputation, they were very vulnerable to attack by fighters. Zeppelin, now in his seventies, turned his attention to large bombers, following the success of **Sikorsky**'s *Grand*, but he died in 1917. Eckener continued to instruct crews and improve the Zeppelin designs. When the war ended Eckener arranged to supply the Americans with an airship as part of German reparations: this became the *Los Angeles*. In 1928 a huge new airship, the *Graf Zeppelin*, was completed and Eckener took command. He took the *Graf Zeppelin* on many successful flights, including a voyage around the world in 1929.

Bibliography
1908, *Erfahrungen beim Bau von Luftschiffen*, Berlin.
1908, *Die Eroberung der Luft*, Stuttgart.

Further Reading
There are many books on the history of airships, and on Graf von Zeppelin in particular. Of note are:
H. Eckener, 1938, *Count Zeppelin: The Man and His Work*, London.
—— 1958, *My Zeppelins*, London.
P.W. Brooks, 1992, *Zeppelin: Rigid Airships 1893–1940*, London.
T. Nielson, 1955, *The Zeppelin Story: The Life of Hugo Eckener*, English edn, London (written as a novel in direct speech).
M. Goldsmith, 1931, *Zeppelin: A Biography*, New York.
W.R. Nitshe, 1977, *The Zeppelin Story*, New York.
F. Gütschow, 1985, *Das Luftschiff*, Stuttgart (a record of all the airships).

JDS

Zhang Sixun (Chang Ssu-Hsun)
b. fl. late 10th century

Chinese astronomer and clockmaker who built the earliest recorded astronomical clock tower with a hydromechanical escapement.

Most clepsydra clocks, such as that of **al-Jarazi**, measured time continuously by the constant flow of a liquid and most mechanical clocks measure time discontinuously by means of an escapement. The clepsydra clock devised by Zhang Sixun in 976 and completed in 979 was unusual as it incorporated an escapement. It consisted of a large wheel with buckets around its periphery. A constant stream of water was directed into one of the buckets until it reached a predetermined weight, this released the wheel, allowing it to rotate to a new position where the process was repeated (this mechanism may have been introduced by the Chinese astronomer and mathematician Zhang Heng in the second century). The water was later replaced by mercury to prevent freezing in winter. With suitable gearing the movement of the wheel was used to drive a celestial globe, a carousel for written time announcements and jacks for audible time signals. This clock has not survived and is known only from the work *Hsin I Hsiang Fa Yao* (New Armillary Sphere and Celestial Globe System Essentials), which was printed in 1172 and is ascribed to **Su Song**. This work also describes two similar but later astronomical clock towers with water-wheel escapements. Several models of the water-wheel escapement have been constructed from the description in this work.

Further Reading
J. Needham (ed.), 1965, *Science and Civilisation in China* Vol. IV.2, Cambridge: Cambridge University Press: 38, 111, 165, 463, 469–71, 490, 524, 527–8, 533, 540.
J.H. Combridge, 1975, 'The astronomical clocktowers of Chang Ssu-Hsun and his successors, A.D. 976 to 1126', *Antiquarian Horology* 9: 288–301.
J. Needham, Wang Ling and J. de Solla Price, 1986, *Heavenly Clockwork. The Great Astronomical Clocks of Medieval China* (2nd edn with supplement by J.H. Combridge), London (for a broader view of Chinese horology).
J.H. Combridge, 1979, 'Clockmaking in China', in *The Country Life International Dictionary of Clocks*, ed. Alan Smith, London.

DV

Ziolkowski, Konstantin Eduardovich
See **Tsiolkovsky, Konstantin Eduardovich**.

Zizka, Count Jan
b. *c.*1376
d. 11 October 1424 Pibyslav, Bohemia (now Czech Republic)

Bohemian soldier and armoured fighting vehicle pioneer.

Brought up in the court of King Wencelas IV of Bohemia, Zizka became a mercenary, fighting for the Poles and losing an eye in the process. In 1410 he returned to Bohemia and became a follower of the religious reformer Jan Hus, who was martyred five years later, although his Hussite movement continued after his death. In 1419 Wencelas died, and his half-brother, Sigismund, an anti-Hussite, attempted to secure the throne. The result was war. Zizka organized a peasant force, the Taborites, who quickly made their mark with their discipline and tactical originality. Not only was Zizka the first to handle his infantry, cavalry and artillery as one, but through the mounting of guns on armoured carts he also pioneered the concept of the armoured fighting vehicle as it is known today. In 1420 he overthrew Sigismund, but lost his remaining eye, and

continued to fight against the forces of the Pope and other Hussite bands until his death from plague.

CM

Zoll, Paul Maurice
b. 15 July 1911 Boston, Massachusetts, USA

American physician and cardiologist, inventor of the electric cardiac 'pacemaker'.

Zoll graduated MD from Harvard in 1936 and spent the next three years in practice, specializing in cardiology, in Boston. He served in the armed forces during 1939–45 and continued in cardiac research at Harvard Medical School and as a consultant in cardiology to various Boston hospitals. In 1952 he carried out the first successful human defibrillation using electric shock. In 1955 he followed this with the cardiac monitor and in 1956 with external countershock defibrillation.

Principal Honours and Distinctions
Legion of Merit.

Bibliography
1952, 'Resuscitation of the heart in ventricular standstill by external electrical stimulation', *New England Journal of Medicine.*

MG

Zonca, Vittorio
b. *c.*1568 Italy
d. 1603 Italy

Italian architect who wrote a book on machines.

All that is known of Zonca is included on the frontispiece of the book that is his only claim to fame. He is there described as architect to the 'Magnificent Community of Padua'. He compiled a book on machines entitled *Novo teatro de machine ed edificii* (New Display of Machines and Edifices), illustrated with numerous fine engravings. It was printed in Padua in 1607, four years after his death, by Francesco Bertelli, who said of the book that it 'came into my hands', as though he knew nothing of the author.

During the sixteenth and early seventeenth centuries, a number of illustrated books on technical subjects appeared, compiled by knowledgeable and educated authors. These books greatly helped the spread of information about the technical arts throughout Europe. There were several books on mechanical devices, notably those by Ramelli, Besson and Zonca. In some ways, Zonca's is the most interesting, for it seems closest to the mechanical practice of the time. Several of the machines he describes are referred to as being in use in Padua or Venice and he suggests ways of improving them. The range of machines is wider than in other similar works and includes pumps, cranes, powder mills, printing and bookbinding presses and textile machines. Perhaps the most interesting of these is the water-driven silk-threading machine, since some of its components resemble those in use in the twentieth century. Spinning mills were widely used in the silk industry in sixteenth-century Italy, and Zonca offers a full description of one. He also shows the first example of an oblique treadwheel, driven by oxen for the grinding of grain. Even so, despite all the practical detail, the book ends, like others of its kind, with fantasy, in a description of a perpetual-motion machine.

Further Reading
A.G. Keller, 1964, *A Theatre of Machines*, London: Chapman & Hall (provides brief details and illustrations from the books by Ramelli, Besson and Zonca).

LRD

Zum Gutenberg, Johann Gensfleisch
See **Gutenberg, Johann**.

Zuse, Konrad
b. 22 June 1910 Berlin, Germany

German civil engineer who developed a series of computers before, during and after the Second World War.

Zuse grew up in Braunsberg, then in East Prussia, and attended the Technische Hochschule at Berlin-Charlottenburg to study civil engineering. In 1934 he became interested in calculating-machines and the pursuit of a career in aeronautical engineering. Two years later, having taken a post as a statistician, in his spare time he built a mechanical computer, which he called *Z1*; for this he used two-state mechanical switches and punched-tape for the program input. This was followed by the design for *Z2*, which used electromechanical relays.

Called to military service in 1939, he was soon sent to the Henschel aircraft factory, where he completed *Z2*. Between 1939 and 1941 the German Aeronautical Research Institute supported his development of *Z3*, which used 2,600 relays and a keyboard input. Taken into immediate use by the aircraft industry, both it and its predecessors were destroyed in air raids. *Z4*, completed towards the end of the war and using mechanical memory, survived, and with improvements was used in Switzerland until 1960. Other achievements by Zuse included a machine to perform logical calculations (*L1*) and his *Plankalkul*, one of the first computer languages. In 1950, with two friends, he formed the Zuse KG company near Bad Hersfeld, Essen, and his first *Z5* relay computer was sold to Leitz in 1952. A series of machines followed, a milestone in 1958 being the first transistorized machine, *Z22*, of which over 200 were made. Finally, in 1969, the company was absorbed by Siemens AG and Zuse returned to scientific research.

Principal Honours and Distinctions
Honorary Doctorate Berlin Technical University 1960. Honorary Professor Göttingen University 1960.

Bibliography
11 April 1936, German patent no. Z23 1391X/42M.
16 June 1941, German patent no. Z391.
1 August 1949, German patent no. 50,746.
1993, *The Computer: My Life*, Berlin: Springer-Verlag (autobiography).

Further Reading
P.E. Ceruzzi, 1981, 'The early computers of Konrad Zuse 1935–45', *Annals of the History of Computing* 3: 241.
M.R. Williams, 1985, *A History of Computing Technology*, London: Prentice-Hall.

See also **Stibitz, George R.**

KF

Zworykin, Vladimir Kosma
b. 30 July 1889 Mourum (near Moscow), Russia
d. 29 July 1982 New York City, New York, USA

788

Russian (naturalized American 1924) television pioneer who invented the iconoscope and kinescope television camera and display tubes.

Zworykin studied engineering at the Institute of Technology in St Petersburg under Boris **Rosing**, assisting the latter with his early experiments with television. After graduating in 1912, he spent a time doing X-ray research at the Collège de France in Paris before returning to join the Russian Marconi Company, initially in St Petersburg and then in Moscow. On the outbreak of war in 1917, he joined the Russian Army Signal Corps, but when the war ended in the chaos of the Revolution he set off on his travels, ending up in the USA, where he joined the Westinghouse Corporation. There, in 1923, he filed the first of many patents for a complete system of electronic television, including one for an all-electronic scanning pick-up tube that he called the iconoscope. In 1924 he became a US citizen and invented the kinescope, a hard-vacuum cathode ray tube (CRT) for the display of television pictures, and the following year he patented a camera tube with a mosaic of photoelectric elements and gave a demonstration of still-picture TV. In 1926 he was awarded a PhD by the University of Pittsburgh and in 1928 he was granted a patent for a colour TV system.

In 1929 he embarked on a tour of Europe to study TV developments; on his return he joined the Radio Corporation of America (RCA) as Director of the Electronics Research Group, first at Camden and then Princeton, New Jersey. Securing a budget to develop an improved CRT picture tube, he soon produced a kinescope with a hard vacuum, an indirectly heated cathode, a signal-modulation grid and electrostatic focusing. In 1933 an improved iconoscope camera tube was produced, and under his direction RCA went on to produce other improved types of camera tube, including the image iconoscope, the orthicon and image orthicon and the vidicon. The secondary-emission effect used in many of these tubes was also used in a scintillation radiation counter. In 1941 he was responsible for the development of the first industrial electron microscope, but for most of the Second World War he directed work concerned with radar, aircraft fire-control and TV-guided missiles.

After the war he worked for a time on high speed memories and medical electronics, becoming Vice-President and Technical Consultant in 1947. He 'retired' from RCA and was made an honorary vice-president in 1954, but he retained an office and continued to work there almost up until his death; he also served as Director of the Rockefeller Institute for Medical Research from 1954 until 1962.

Principal Honours and Distinctions
Zworykin received some twenty-seven awards and honours for his contributions to television engineering and medical electronics, including the Institution of Electrical Engineers Faraday Medal 1965; US Medal of Science 1966; and the US National Hall of Fame 1977.

Bibliography
29 December 1923, US patent no. 2,141,059 (the original iconoscope patent; finally granted in December 1938!).
13 July 1925, US patent no. 1,691,324 (colour television system).
1930, with D.E. Wilson, *Photocells and Their Applications*, New York: Wiley.
1934, 'The iconoscope. A modern version of the electric eye'. *Proceedings of the Institute of Radio Engineers* 22: 16.
1946, *Electron Optics and the Electron Microscope*.
1940, with G.A. Morton, *Television*; revised 1954.
1949, with E.G. Ramberg, *Photoelectricity and Its Applications*.
1958, *Television in Science and Industry*.

Further Reading
J.H. Udelson, 1982, *The Great Television Race: History of the Television Industry 1925–41*: University of Alabama Press.

See also: **Baird, John Logie**; **Farnsworth, Philo Taylor**; **Jenkins, Charles Francis**.

KF

Index by Subject Area

Mechanical, pneumatic and hydraulic engineering

Mining and extraction technology

Paper and printing

Gibson, R.O.
Hyatt, John Wesley
Parkes, Alexander
Perkin, Sir William Henry
Staudinger, Hermann
Whinfield, John Rex

Telecommunications
Alexanderson, Ernst Frederik Werner
Appleton, Sir Edward Victor
Armstrong, Edwin Howard
Ayrton, William Edward
Bain, Alexander
Bakewell, Frederick C.
Baudot, Jean-Maurice-Emile
Bell, Alexander Graham
Black, Harold Stephen
Blumlein, Alan Dower
Bourseul, Charles
Branly, Edouard Eugène
Braun, Karl Ferdinand
Bright, Sir Charles Tilston
Cady, Walter Guyton
Chappe, Claude
Clarke, Arthur Charles
Colpitts, Edwin Henry
Cooke, William Fothergill
Crampton, Thomas Russell
Cros, Hortensius Emile Charles
De Forest, Lee
Dunwoody, General Henry H.C.
Eccles, William Henry
Edison, Thomas Alva
Farnsworth, Philo Taylor
Fessenden, Reginald Aubrey
Field, Cyrus West
Gooch, Sir Daniel
Gray, Elisha
Halske, Johann Georg
Hartley, Ralph V.L.
Heaviside, Oliver
Henry, Joseph
Hertz, Heinrich Rudolph
Jansky, Karl Guthe
Kao, Charles Kuen
Keller, Arthur
Kennelly, Arthur Edwin
Kompfner, Rudolf
Lenoir, Jean Joseph Etienne
Lodge, Sir Oliver Joseph
Marconi, Marchese Guglielmo
Morse, Samuel Finley Breeze
Palmer, John
Pierce, John Robinson
Popov, Aleksandr Stepanovich
Poulsen, Valdemar
Preece, Sir William

Reis, Johann Philipp
Sarnoff, David
Shannon, Claude Elwood
Shockley, William Bradford
Siemens, Sir Charles William
Smith, Willoughby
Soemmering, Samuel Thomas von
Steinheil, Carl August von
Strowger, Almon Brown
Taylor, Albert Hoyt
Thomson, Sir William
Tuve, Merle Antony
Vail, Alfred Louis
Varian, Russell Harrison
Varian, Sigurd Fergus
Wheatstone, Sir Charles
Woods, Granville
Yagi, Hidetsugu

Textiles
Anthelm, Ludwig
Arkwright, Sir Richard
Arnold, Aza
Austin, John
Bauer, H.
Berthollet, Claude-Louis
Bevan, Edward John
Bigelow, Erastus Brigham
Blanchard, Helen Augusta
Bloch, Jacob
Bodmer, Johann Georg
Bouchon, Basile
Bourn, Daniel
Caro, Heinrich
Carothers, Wallace Hume
Cartwright, Revd Edmund
Casablancas, Fernando
Cockerill, William
Cosnier, Hugues
Cotchett, Thomas
Cotton, William
Crompton, Samuel
Crosby, Caresse
Cross, Charles Frederick
Crossley, Sir Francis
Crossley, Joseph
Dale, David
Dawson, William
Deacon, Henry
Deverill, Hooton
Dickson, J.T.
Diggle, Squire
Donisthorpe, George Edmond
Dore, Samuel Griswold
Dyer, John
Dyer, Joseph Chessborough
Ewart, Peter

INDEX OF TOPICS

Index of Names